P9-CEA-096

Commentary on the Old Testament

Commentary on the OLD TESTAMENT

IN TEN VOLUMES

by

C. F. KEIL and F. DELITZSCH

VOLUME IX

Ezekiel, Daniel

by C. F. KEIL

Three Volumes in One

WILLIAM B. EERDMANS PUBLISHING COMPANY
Grand Rapids, Michigan

COMMENTARY ON THE OLD TESTAMENT
by C. F. Keil and F. Delitzsch
Translated from the German

Volumes translated by James Martin
THE PENTATEUCH
JOSHUA, JUDGES, RUTH
THE BOOKS OF SAMUEL
THE BOOKS OF THE KINGS
THE PROPHECIES OF ISAIAH
THE PROPHECIES OF EZEKIEL
THE TWELVE MINOR PROPHETS

Volumes translated by Andrew Harper
THE BOOKS OF THE CHRONICLES

Volumes translated by Sophia Taylor
THE BOOKS OF EZRA, NEHEMIAH, ESTHER

Volumes translated by Francis Bolton
THE BOOK OF JOB
THE PSALMS

Volumes translated by M. G. Easton
PROVERBS OF SOLOMON
THE SONG OF SONG AND ECCLESIASTES
THE BOOK OF DANIEL

Volumes translated by David Patrick
THE PROPHECIES OF JEREMIAH, VOL. I

Volumes translated by James Kennedy
THE PROPHECIES OF JEREMIAH, VOL. II

ISBN 0-8028-8043-6
Reprinted, January 1980

CONTENTS

INTRODUCTION.

EXPOSITION.

FIRST HALF.—THE PROPHECIES OF JUDGMENT. CHAP. I.–XXXII.

THE PROPHECIES OF EZEKIEL

INTRODUCTION.

I. THE PERSON OF THE PROPHET.

ZEKIEL, יְחֶזְקֵאל (i. 3, xxiv. 24), *i.e.* יְחַזֵּק אֵל, *God strengthens*, Ἰεζεκιήλ (LXX. and Book of Sirach, ch. xlix. 8), in the Vulgate *Ezechiel*, while Luther, after the example of the LXX., writes the name *Hesekiel*, was the son of Busi, of priestly descent, and was carried away captive into exile to Babylon in the year 599 B.C.,—*i.e.* in the eleventh year before the destruction of Jerusalem,—along with King Jehoiachin, the nobles of the kingdom, many priests, and the better class of the population of Jerusalem and of Judah (i. 2, xl. 1; cf. 2 Kings xxiv. 14 ff.; Jer. xxix. 1). He lived there in the northern part of Mesopotamia, on the banks of the Chaboras, married, and in his own house, amidst a colony of banished Jews, in a place called Tel-Abib (i. 1, iii. 15, 24, viii. 1, xxiv. 18). In the fifth year of his banishment, *i.e.* 595 B.C., he was called to be a prophet of the Lord, and laboured in this official position, as may be shown, twenty-two years; for the latest of his prophecies is dated in the twenty-seventh year of his exile, *i.e.* 572 B.C. (xxix. 17). Regarding the other circumstances and events of his life, as also of his death, nothing is known. The apocryphal legends found in the Fathers and in the Rabbinical writings, to the effect that he was put to death by a prince of his own nation for rebuking his idolatry, and was buried in the tomb of Shem and Arphaxad, etc. (cf. Carpzov, Introd. ii. p. 203 ff.), are without any historical value. So much alone is certain, that he ended his life among the exiles, where God had assigned him his sphere of labour, and did not, like his contemporary Daniel (comp. Dan. i. 21, x. 1), outlive the termination of the Captivity and the commencement of the redemption of Israel from Babylon, as his prophecies do not contain the slightest allusion to that effect.

II. THE TIMES OF THE PROPHET.

Ezekiel, like Daniel, is a prophet of the exile, but in a different fashion from the latter, who had been already carried away prisoner before him to Babylon on the first capture of Jerusalem by Nebuchadnezzar in the reign of Jehoiakim, and who lived there upwards of seventy years at the Babylonian and Medo-Persian court, and who held from time to time very important offices of State. Daniel was placed by God in this high position, which afforded him a view of the formation and evolution of the world-kingdom, in order that from this standpoint he might be enabled to see the development of the world-kingdoms in the struggle against the kingdom of God, and to predict the indestructible power and glory of the latter kingdom, which overcomes all the powers of the world. Ezekiel, on the other hand, was appointed a watcher over the exiled nation of Israel, and was in this capacity to *continue* the work of the earlier prophets, especially that of Jeremiah, with whom he in several ways associates himself in his prophecies; to preach to his contemporaries the judgment and salvation of God, in order to convert them to the Lord their God.—Rightly to understand his work as a prophet, the ripe fruit of which lies before us in his prophetic writings, we must not only keep in view the importance of the exile for the development of the kingdom of God, but also form a clear conception of the relations amidst which Ezekiel carried on his labours.

What the Lord had caused to be announced by Moses to the tribes of Israel while they were yet standing on the borders of the Promised Land, and preparing to take possession of it, viz. that if they should persistently transgress His commands, He would not only chastise them with heavy punishments, but would finally drive them out of the land which they were about to occupy, and disperse them among all nations (Lev. xxvi. 14–45; Deut. xxviii. 15–68),—this threatening, repeated by all the prophets after Moses, had been already executed by the Assyrians upon the ten tribes, who had revolted from the house of David, and was now in process of fulfilment by the Chaldeans upon the kingdom of Judah also. In the reign of Jehoiakim, Nebuchadnezzar, king of Babylon, for the first time invaded Judah, captured Jerusalem, made Jehoiakim tributary, and carried away to Babylon a number of Israelitish youths of noble birth and of the blood-royal, amongst whom was Daniel, along with a portion of the vessels of the temple, in order that these youths might be trained up for the service of his court (Dan. i. 1–7). With this invasion of the Chaldeans begin the seventy years of Chaldean servitude and exile in Babylon, predicted by Jeremiah. As Jehoiakim, so early as three years afterwards, revolted against Nebuchadnezzar, the latter, after a lengthened siege, took Jerusalem a second time, in the third month of the reign of Jehoiachin, and carried away into captivity to Babylon, along with the captive monarch and the members of his court, the nobles of Judah and Jerusalem, a great number of priests, warriors, carpenters, and smiths, leaving behind in the land only the meaner portion of the people, over whom he appointed as his vassal King Mattaniah, the uncle of the banished monarch, whose name he changed to Zedekiah (2 Kings xxiv. 10–17; Jer. xxix. 2). By this removal of the heart and strength of the nation the power of the kingdom of Judah was broken; and although Nebuchadnezzar did not at that time *destroy* it, but still allowed it to remain as a subject kingdom under his sway, yet its existence could not be of any long duration. Judah had fallen too deeply to recognise in the calamities which she had suffered the chastening hand of her God, and to bow herself repentantly under His mighty arm. Instead of listening to the voice of the prophet Jeremiah, and bearing the Chaldean yoke in patience (2 Chron. xxxvi. 12), both monarch and people placed their trust in the assistance of Egypt, and Zedekiah broke the oath of fealty which he had sworn to the king of Babylon. To punish this perfidy, Nebuchadnezzar again marched against Jerusalem, and by the capture and burning of the city and temple in the eleventh year of Zedekiah's reign put an end to the kingdom of Judah. Zedekiah, who had fled from the beleaguered city, was taken by the Chaldeans, and brought with his sons to Riblah into the presence of King Nebuchadnezzar, who first caused the sons of Zedekiah to be put to death before the eyes of their father; next, Zedekiah himself to be deprived of sight, and then commanded the blind monarch to be conducted in chains to Babylon (2 Kings xxv. 1–21; Jer. lii. 1–30). Many military officers and priests of rank were also put to death at Riblah; while those who had been taken prisoners at Jerusalem, along with the deserters and a great portion of the rest of the people, were led away into exile to Babylon (2 Kings xxv. 1–21; Jer. lii. 1–30). By this catastrophe the Old Testament theocracy lost its political existence; the covenant people were now driven out of their own land amongst the heathen, to bear the punishment of their obstinate apostasy from the Lord their God. Nevertheless this dispersion among the heathen was no entire rejection of Israel; it was merely a *suspension*, and not an *annihilation*, of the covenant of grace. Man's unfaithfulness cannot destroy the faithfulness of God. "In spite of this terrible judgment, brought down upon them by the heaviest transgressions, Israel was, and remained,"—as Auberlen (*The Prophet Daniel*, p. 27, 2d ed.) well remarks,—"the chosen people, through whom God was still to carry out His intentions towards humanity. His gifts and calling may not be repented of" (Rom. xi. 29). Even *after* the Babylonian exile the theocracy was not again restored; the covenant people did not after their return again recover their independence, but remained, with the exception of the short period when under the Maccabees they won for themselves their freedom, in constant dependence upon the heathen world-rulers, until, after the destruction of Jerusalem by the Romans, they were completely dispersed among all the nations of the earth. The kingdom of God, however, was not *really* to perish along with the external theocracy; it was only to pass into a new phase of development, which was intended to be the medium of transition towards its renewal and perfection in that kingdom of God which was to be founded by Christ. To pave the way to this end, and at the same time to serve as a witness to the exiles, that Israel, notwithstanding its dispersion among the heathen, still remained God's people, the Lord raised up in Ezekiel, the son of a priest, a prophet of uncommon power and energy in the midst of the captives, "one who raised his voice aloud, like a trumpet, and showed to Israel its misdeeds,—whose whole manifestation furnished the most powerful testimony that the Lord was still amongst His people; who was himself a temple of the Lord, before whom the visible temple, which yet remained standing for a short time at Jerusalem, sank back into its nothingness; a spiritual Samson, who seized with mighty arm the pillars of the idol temple, and dashed it to the ground; a powerful, gigantic nature, which was fitted by that very qualification to effectually subdue the Babylonian spirit of the time, which delighted in powerful, gigantic, and grotesque forms; standing alone, but equal to a hundred of the sons of the prophets" (Hengstenberg's *Christol.* II. p. 531).

The call of Ezekiel to the prophetic office took place in the fifth year of the reign of Zedekiah, in the fourth month of the year (i. 1, 2), at a point of time when, amongst those who had remained behind in the land, as well as amongst those who had been carried to Babylon, the hope of the speedy downfall of the Babylonian monarchy, and of the return of the exiles to their native country, which was then to follow, was very strong, and was powerfully encouraged by the lying statements of false prophets; cf. Jer. xxix. In the same year and month prophesied Hananiah, a prophet from Gibeon, in the temple at Jerusalem, before the eyes of the priests and the whole people, saying that Jehovah would break the yoke of the king of Babylon, and within two years bring back to Jerusalem all the temple-vessels carried away by Nebuchadnezzar, as well as King Jechoniah and all the captives who had been brought to Babylon, Jer. xxviii. 1–4. And the prophet Jeremiah, who with the word of the Lord rebuked and opposed those lying predictions and empty hopes, and foretold that the Babylonian servitude would be of long duration, was violently assailed and persecuted by the lying prophets, even by those of them who were to be found in Babylon; cf. Jer. xxviii. 5–17, xxix. 21–32. This delusion regarding the political condition of affairs, this spirit of resistance to the decree of the Lord, had seized not only upon the people, but also upon the nobles and the king, so that they formed and eagerly carried on conspiracies against the king of Babylon. The meeting of the kings of Edom, Moab, Ammon, Tyre, and Sidon, with Zedekiah in Jerusalem, had no other object than this (Jer. xxvii. 3). The embassy, moreover, sent by Zedekiah to Babylon (Jer. xxiv. 3), as well as his own journey thither in the fourth year of his reign (Jer. li. 59), were intended merely to deceive the king of Babylon, by assurances of devotion and fidelity, in order that the intended revolt might be carried out. But this baseless hope of a speedy liberation from the Babylonian yoke was ignominiously disappointed: in consequence of the treacherous rebellion of Zedekiah, Nebuchadnezzar, after a blockade and siege of a year and a half, captured Jerusalem, burnt the city and temple to the ground, and destroyed the kingdom of Judah. By this blow all the supports upon which the God-alienated nation had vainly relied were broken. The delusive statements of the false prophets had proved to be lies; the predictions of the Lord's prophets, on the contrary, had been strikingly justified as divine truth. The destruction of Jerusalem, the burning of the temple, and the downfall of the kingdom, form accordingly a turning-point for the prophetic labours of Ezekiel. Hitherto, prior to the calamity, he had to announce to the people (animated with the hope of speedy liberation from exile) the judgment of the downfall of Jerusalem and Judah, although such preaching found little acceptance. The time, however, had now arrived when, in order to preserve from despair the nation languishing in exile, and given over to the scorn, contempt, and tyranny of the heathen, he was able to open up the sources of comfort by announcing that the Lord, in requital of the ignominy heaped upon His people, would overwhelm all the heathen nations with destruction, but that, if His people whom they had oppressed would repent and return to Him, He would again gather them out of their dispersion; would make of them a holy nation, walking in His commands and yielding Him a willing service; would conduct them back to their own land; would give them His servant David for a prince, and once more gloriously establish His kingdom.

III. THE BOOK OF EZEKIEL.

The collection of the prophecies placed together in this book, as forming a complete unity, falls into two main divisions:—I. Announcements of judgment upon Israel and the heathen nations, ch. i.–xxxii.; II. Announcements of salvation for Israel, ch. xxxiii.–xlviii. Each of these main divisions is subdivided into two sections. The first, namely, contains the prophecies of judgment (*a*) upon Jerusalem and Israel, ch. iii. 22–xxiv.; (*b*) upon the heathen nations, ch. xxv.–xxxii. The second main division contains (*c*) the predictions of the redemption and restoration of Israel, and the downfall of the heathen world-power, ch. xxxiii.–xxxix.; (*d*) the prophetic picture of the re-formation and exaltation of the kingdom of God, ch. xl.–xlviii.; and the entire collection opens with the solemn dedication of Ezekiel to the prophetic office, ch. i. 1–iii. 21. The prophecies of the first, third, and fourth parts are throughout arranged in chronological order; those of the second part—the threatenings predicted against the heathen nations—are disposed according to their actual subject-matter. This is attested by the chronological data in the superscriptions, and confirmed by the contents of the whole of the groups of prophecies in the first three parts. The first part contains the following chronological notices: the fifth year of the captivity of Jehoiachin (i. 2) as the time of Ezekiel's call to the office of prophet, and of the first predictions regarding Jerusalem and Israel; then the sixth (viii. 1), seventh (xx. 1), and ninth years of the captivity of that monarch (xxiv. 1). The second part contains the predictions against seven foreign nations, of which those against Tyre fall in the eleventh (xxvi. 1), those against Egypt in the tenth (xxix. 1), twenty-seventh (xxix. 17), eleventh (xxx. 20 and xxxi. 1), and twelfth years of the exile. Of the two last parts, each contains only one chronological notice, namely, ch. xxxiii. 21, the twelfth year of the captivity, *i.e.* one year after the destruction of Jerusalem; and ch. xl. 1, the twenty-fifth year of the captivity, or the fourteenth after the destruction of Jerusalem. The remaining prophecies, which bear at their head no note of time, connect themselves closely as to their contents with those which are furnished with chronological data, so that they belong to the same period with those. From this it appears that the prophecies of the first part wholly, those of the second part to a great extent, date before the destruction of Jerusalem; those of the third and fourth parts proceed from the time after this catastrophe. This chronological relationship is in favour of the view that the prophecies against foreign nations, ch. xxv.–xxxii., are not —as the majority of expositors suppose—to be assigned to the second, but rather to the first half of the book. This view is confirmed, on the one hand, by the contents of the prophecies, inasmuch as these, without an exception, announce only the downfall of the heathen nations and kingdoms, making no reference to the future forgiveness and conversion of the residue of these nations, and through this very peculiarity connect themselves closely with the prophecies of threatening against Israel in the first part; on the other hand, by the resemblance which exists between ch. xxx. 1–20 and ch. iii. 16–21, compared with ch. xviii. 19–32, and which leaves no doubt upon the point that ch. xxxiii. 1–20 marks out to the prophet the task which was to occupy his attention after the destruction of Jerusalem, and consequently forms the introduction to the second half of his prophecies.—For further remarks upon the contents and subdivisions of the book, see the expositions in the introductory observations to the individual sections and chapters.

Ezekiel's *style of prophetic representation* has many peculiarities. In the first place, the clothing of symbol and allegory prevails in him to a greater degree than in all the other prophets; and his symbolism and allegory are not confined to general outlines and pictures, but elaborated in the minutest details, so as to present figures of a boldness surpassing reality, and ideal representations, which produce an impression of imposing grandeur and exuberant fulness. Even the simplest prophetic discourse is rich in imagery, and in bold, partly even strange, comparisons, and branches out into a copiousness which strives to exhaust the subject on all sides, in consequence of which many peculiar expressions and forms are repeated, rendering his language diffuse, and occasionally even clumsy. These peculiarities of his style of representation it has been attempted, on the one hand, to explain by the influence of the Babylonian spirit and taste upon the form of his prophecy; while others, again, would regard them as the result of a literary art, striving to supply the defect of prophetic spirit, and the failing power of the living word, by the aid of learning and an elaborate imitation of actual life. The supposed Babylonian spirit, however, in the forms of our prophet's symbolism, has no existence. The assertion of Hävernick, that "the whole of these symbols has a colossal character, which points in many ways to those powerful impressions experienced by the prophet in a foreign land,—Chaldea,—and which here are grasped and given out again with a mighty and independent spirit," remains yet to be proved. For the observation that these symbols, in reference to form and contents, resemble in many respects the symbols of his contemporary Daniel, is not sufficient for the purpose, and cannot in itself be accepted as the truth, by reference to the picture of the eagle, and the comparison of rich men to trees, cedars, in ch. xvii., because these pictures already occur in the older prophets, and lions as as well as cedars are native in Palestine. Just as little are Babylonian impressions to be recognised in the visions of the field with the dead men's bones, ch. xxxvii., and of the new temple, ch. xl., so that there only remains the representation of the cherubim with four faces, in ch. i. and x., which is peculiar to Ezekiel, as presumptive evidence of Chaldean influence. But if we leave out of account that the throne, upon which the Lord appears in human form, indisputably forms the central point of this vision, and this central point has no specific Babylonian impress, then the representation of the cherubim with faces of men, lions, oxen, and eagles, cannot be derived from the contemplation of the Assyrian or Chaldean sculptures of human figures with eagle heads and wings, or winged oxen with human heads, or sphinxes with bodies of animals and female heads, such as are found in the ruins of ancient Nineveh, inasmuch as the cherubim of Ezekiel were not pictures of oxen with lions' manes, eagles' wings, and human countenances furnished with horns,—as W. Neumann has still portrayed them in his treatise upon the tabernacle,—but had, according to Ezekiel, ch. i. 5, the *human* form. There are indeed also found, among the Assyrian sculptures, winged human figures; but these Ezekiel had no reason to copy, because the cherubic images in human form, belonging to Solomon's temple, lay much nearer to his hand. The whole of Ezekiel's symbolism is derived from the Israelitish sanctuary, and is an outcome of Old Testament ideas and views. As the picture of the ideal temple in ch. xl. ff. is sketched according to the relations of Solomon's temple, which was burnt by the Chaldeans, so the elements for the description of the majestic theophany, in ch. i. and x., are contained in the throne of Jehovah, which was above the cherubim, who were over the covering of the ark of the covenant; and in the phenomena amid which was manifested the revelation of the divine glory at the establishment of the covenant on Sinai. On the basis of these facts, Isaiah had already represented to himself the appearance of the Lord, as a vision, in which he beholds Jehovah in the temple, sitting on a high and lofty throne, and, standing around the throne, seraphim with six wings, who began to sing, "Holy, holy" (Isa. vi.). This symbolism we find modified in Ezekiel, so as to correspond with the aim of his vocation, and elaborated to a greater extent. The manner in which he works out this vision and other symbols certainly gives evidence of his capacity to describe, distinctly and attractively in words, what he had beheld in spirit; although the symbolism itself is, just as little as the vision, a mere product of poetic art, or the subjective framework of a lively fancy, without any real objective foundation; for it rests, in harmony with its contents and form, upon views which are *spiritually* real, *i.e.* produced by the Spirit of God in the soul of the prophet, in which the art of the author is reduced to a faithful and distinct reproduction of what had been seen in the spirit.—It is only the abundance of pictures and metaphors, which is in this respect *characteristic* of Ezekiel, and which betrays a lively imagination, and the many-sidedness of his knowledge. These qualities appear not merely in the sketch of the new temple (ch. xl. ff.), but also in the description of the wide-spread commerce of Tyre (ch. xxvii.), and of the relations of

Egypt (ch. xxix. and xxxi.), as well as in the endeavours manifest in *all* his representations,—not merely in the symbolical descriptions and allegorical portraits (ch. xvi. and xxiii.), but also in the simple discourses, in the rebukes of the current vices and sins, and in the threatenings of punishment and judgment,—to follow out the subject treated of into the most special details, to throw light upon it from all sides, to penetrate through it, and not to rest until he has exhausted it, and that without any effort, in so doing, to avoid repetitions. This style of representation, however, has its foundation not merely in the individuality of our prophet, but still more in the relations of his time, and in his attitude towards that generation to whom he had to announce the counsel and will of the Lord. As symbolism and the employment of parables, pictures, and proverbs is, in general, only a means for the purpose of presenting in an attractive light the truths to be delivered, and to strengthen by this attractiveness the impression made by speech and discourse, so also the copiousness and circumstantiality of the picture, and even the repetition of thoughts and expressions under new points of view, serve the same end. The people to whom Ezekiel was now to preach repentance, by announcing the divine judgment and salvation, was "a rebellious race, impudent and hard-hearted" (ch. iii. 7-9, 26, xii. 2, etc.). If he was faithfully and conscientiously to discharge the office, laid upon him by the Lord, of a watcher over the house of Israel, he must not only punish with stern words, and in drastic fashion, the sins of the people, and distinctly paint before their eyes the horrors of the judgment, but he must also set forth, in a style palpable to the senses, that salvation which was to bloom forth for the repentant nation when the judgment was fulfilled.

Closely connected with this is the other peculiarity of Ezekiel's style of prophecy, namely, the marked prominence assigned to the divine origin and contents of his announcements, which distinctly appears in the standing form of address

—"Son of man"—with which God summons the prophet to speech and action; in the continual use of אֲדֹנָי יהוה; in the formulae כֹּה אָמַר יי׳ or נְאֻם יי׳; in the introduction to almost every discourse of God's requirement to him to prophesy or to do this and that; and in the formula which recurs frequently in all the discourses,—"Ye shall know that I am Jehovah." The standing address, "Son of man," and the frequent call to speech and action, are likewise regarded by modern critics as a token of the failure of the prophetic spirit-power. Both phrases, however, could only be held to convey so much, if—in conformity with the view of Ewald, who, agreeably to the *naturalistic* representation of prophecy, assumes it to be a result of high poetic inspiration—they had been selected by Ezekiel of his own free choice, and employed with the intention of expressing the feeling of his own profound distance from God, and of imparting to himself courage to prophesy. If, on the contrary, according to the *Scriptural* conception of prophecy, God the Lord addressed Ezekiel as "son of man," and called him, moreover, on each occasion to utter predictions, then the use of the God-given name, as well as the mention of the summons, as proceeding from God only, furnishes an evidence that Ezekiel does not, like the false prophets, utter the thoughts and inspirations of his own heart, but, in all that he says and does, acts under a *divine* commission and under *divine* inspiration, and serves to impress the rebellious nation more and more with the conviction that a prophet of the Lord is in their midst (ii. 5, xxxiii. 33), and that God had not departed with His Spirit from Israel, notwithstanding their banishment among the heathen. In favour of the correctness of this view of the expressions and phrases in question, there speak decisively the manner and fashion in which Ezekiel was called and consecrated to the prophetic office; not only the instruction which God communicates to him for the performance of his calling (ii. 1–3, 21),—and which, immediately upon the first act of his prophetic activity, He supplements to the effect of enjoining upon him dumbness or entire silence, only then permitting him to open his mouth to speak when He wishes to inspire him with a word to be addressed to the rebellious people (iii. 26, 27; cf. xxiv. 27 and xxxiii. 22),—but also the theophany which inaugurated his call to the prophetic office (ch. i.), which, as will appear to us in the course of the exposition, has unmistakeably the significance of an explanation of a reality, which will not be dissolved and annihilated with the dissolution of the kingdom of Judah, and the destruction of Jerusalem, and of the temple of that covenant of grace which Jehovah had concluded with Israel.

It is usual, moreover, to quote, as a peculiarity of Ezekiel's prophecies, the prominence given to his priestly descent and disposition, especially in the visions, ch. i., cf. ch. x., ch. viii.–xi. and xl.–xlviii., and in individual traits, as iv. 13 ff., xx. 12 ff., xxii. 8, xxvi. 24, 16 ff., etc., etc., which Ewald explains as "a result of the one-sided literary conception of antiquity according to mere books and traditions, as well as of the extreme prostration of spirit intensified by the long duration of the exile and bondage of the people;" while de Wette, Gesenius, and others would see in it an intellectual narrowness on the part of the prophet. The one view is as groundless and perverse as the other, because resting upon the superficial opinion that the copious descriptions of the sacred articles in the temple were sketched by Ezekiel only for the purpose of preserving for the future the elevating recollection of the better times of the past (Ewald). When we recognise, on the contrary, the symbolical character of these descriptions, we may always say that for the portrayal of the conception of the theophany in ch. i. and x., and of the picture of the temple in ch. xl., no individual was so well fitted as a priest, familiar with the institutions of worship. In this symbolism, however, we may not venture to seek for the products of intellectual narrowness, or of sacerdotal ideas, but must rise to the conviction that God the Lord selected a priest, and no other, to be His prophet, and permitted him to behold the future of His kingdom on earth in the significant forms of the sanctuary at Jerusalem, because this form was the symbolical covering which presented the closest correspondence to the same.—Still less do the passages iv. 13 ff., xx. 12 ff., and others, in which stress is laid upon the ceremonial commands of the law, and where their violation is mentioned as a cause of the judgment that was breaking over Israel, furnish evidence of priestly one-sidedness or narrowness of spirit. Ezekiel takes up towards the Mosaic Law no other position than that which is taken by the older prophets. He finds impressed on the precepts, not only of the Moral, but also of the Ceremonial Law, divine thoughts, essential elements of the divine holiness, attesting itself in and to Israel; and penetrated by a sense of the everlasting importance of the whole law, he urges obedience to its commands. Even the close adherence to the Pentateuch is not at all peculiar to him, but is common to all the prophets, inasmuch as all, without exception, criticize and judge the life of the nation by the standard of the prescriptions in the Mosaic Law. Ezekiel, with his nearest predecessor Jeremiah, is in this respect only distinguished from the earlier prophets, that the verbal references to the Pentateuch in both occur with greater frequency, and receive a greater emphasis. But this has its ground not so much in the descent of both from a priestly family, as rather in the relations of their time, especially in the circumstance that the falling away of the nation from the law had become so great, in consequence of which the penal judgments already threatened in the Pentateuch upon transgressors had fallen upon them, so that the prophets of the Lord were obliged, with all their energy, to hold up before the rebellious race not merely the commandments, but also the threatenings of the law, if they were faithfully to discharge the office to which they had been called.

The *language* of Ezekiel is distinguished by a great number of words and forms, which do not occur elsewhere, and which, probably, were for the greater part coined by himself (see an enumeration of these in the *Manual of Historico-Critical Introduction*, § 77, Rem. 6), and shows a strong leaning towards the diction of the Pentateuch. It has, however, been unable to resist the influences of the inaccurate popular dialect, and of the Aramaic idiom, so that it betrays, in its many anomalies and corruptions, the decline and commencement of the dying out of the Hebrew tongue (cf. § 17 of the *Historico-Critical Manual*), and reminds us that the prophet's residence was in a foreign country.

The *genuineness* of Ezekiel's prophecies is, at the present day, unanimously recognised by all critics. There is, moreover, no longer any doubt that the writing down and redaction of them in the volume which has been transmitted to us were the work of the prophet himself. Only Ewald and Hitzig, for the purpose of setting aside the predictions which so much offend them, have proposed very artificial hypotheses regarding the manner and way in which the book originated; but it appears unnecessary to enter into a closer examination of these, as their probability and trustworthiness depend only upon the dogmatic views of their authors.

For the exegetical literature, see the *Historico-Critical Manual*, vol. i. p. 353 (new ed. p. 254), where is also to be added, as of very recent date, *Das Buch Ezechiels*. Uebersetzt und erklärt von Dr. Th. Kliefoth. Zwei Abtheilungen. Rostock, 1864 and 1865.

EXPOSITION

FIRST HALF.—THE PROPHECIES OF JUDGMENT.

CHAP. I.-XXXII.

CHAP. I.-III. 21.—THE CONSECRATION AND CALLING OF EZEKIEL TO THE OFFICE OF PROPHET.

IN a vision of God, Ezekiel beholds in a great cloud, through which shone the splendour of fire, and which a tempestuous wind drives from the north, the glory of the Lord above the cherubim upon a majestic throne in human form (ch. i.), and hears a voice, which sends him as a prophet to Israel, and inspires him with the subject-matter of his announcements (ii. 1–iii. 3). He is thereafter transported in spirit to Tel-abib on the Chebar, into the midst of the exiles, and the duties and responsibilities of his calling laid before him (iii. 4–21). By this divine appearance and the commission therewith connected is he consecrated, called, and ordained to the prophetic office. The whole occurrences in the vision are subdivided into the copious description of the theophany, ch. i., by which he is consecrated for his calling; and into the revelation of the word, ch. ii. 1–3, 21, which prepares him for the discharge of the same. From these contents it clearly appears that these chapters do not constitute the *first section* of the book, but the *introduction* to the whole, to which the circumstantial notices of the time and place of this revelation of God at the commencement, i. 1–3, also point.

Chap. i. The Appearance of the Glory of the Lord.—Vers. 1–3. Time and place of the same.—Ver. 1. *Now it came to pass in the thirtieth year, in the fourth (month), on the fifth (day) of the month, as I was among the captives by the river of Chebar, that the heavens were opened, and I saw visions of God.* Ver. 2. *On the fifth day of the month, it was the fifth year of King Jehoiachin's captivity,* Ver. 3. *The word of the Lord came to Ezekiel the priest, the son of Busi, in the land of the Chaldeans by the river Chebar; and the hand of the Lord was there upon him.*

Regarding וַיְהִי at the beginning of a book, as *e.g.* in Jonah i. 1, cf. the note on Josh. i. 1. The two notices of the year in vers. 1 and 2 are closely connected with the twofold introduction of the theophany. This is described in verse first, according to its form or phenomenal nature, and then in verses second and third, according to its intended purpose, and its effect upon the prophet. The phenomenon consisted in this, that the heavens were opened, and Ezekiel saw visions of God. The heaven opens not merely when to our eye a glimpse is disclosed of the heavenly glory of God (Calvin), but also when God manifests His glory in a manner perceptible to human sight. The latter was the case here. מַרְאוֹת אֱלֹהִים, "visions of God," are not "*visiones præstantissimæ,*" but visions which have divine or heavenly things for their object; cf. Isa. vi. 1; 1 Kings xxii. 19; 2 Kings vi. 17. Here it is the manifestation of Jehovah's glory described in the following verses. This was beheld by Ezekiel in the thirtieth year, which, according to verse second, was in the fifth year of the captivity of Jehoiachin. The real identity of these two dates is placed beyond doubt by the mention of the same day of the month, "on the fifth day of the month" (ver. 2 compared with ver. 1). The fifth year from the commencement of Jehoiachin's captivity is the year 595 B.C.; the thirtieth year, consequently, is the year 625 B.C. But the era, in accordance with which this date is reckoned, is matter of dispute, and can no longer be ascertained with certainty. To suppose, with Hengstenberg, that the reference is to the year of the prophet's own life, is forbidden by the addition "in the fourth month, on the fifth day of the month," which points to an era generally recognised. In the year 625 B.C., Nabopolassar became king of Babylon, and therefore many of the older expositors have supposed that Ezekiel means the thirtieth year of the era of Nabopolassar. Nothing, however, is known of any such era. Others, as the Chaldee paraphrast and Jerome, and in modern times also Ideler, are of opinion that the thirtieth year is reckoned from the eighteenth year of the reign of Josiah, because in that year the book of the law was discovered, and the regeneration of public worship completed by a solemn celebration of the Passover. No trace, however, can elsewhere be pointed out of the existence of a chronology dating from these events. The Rabbins in *Seder Olam* assume a chronology according to the periods of the years of jubilee, and so also Hitzig; but for this supposition too all reliable proofs are wanting. At the time mentioned, Ezekiel found himself בְּתוֹךְ הַגּוֹלָה, "in the midst of the exiles," *i.e. within the circuit of their settlements*, not, *in their society;* for it is evident from ch. iii. 15 that he was alone when the theophany was imparted to him, and did not repair till afterwards to the residences of the settlers. Ver. 3. By the river *Chebar*, in the land of the Chaldees, *i.e.* in Babylon or Mesopotamia. The river כְּבָר, to be distinguished from חָבוֹר, the river of Gosan, which flows into the Tigris, see on 2 Kings xvii. 6, is the Mesopotamian *Chaboras*, Ἀβόῤῥας (Strabo, xvi. 748), or *Χαβώρας* (Ptolem. v. 18, 3), خابور (Edrisi Clim. iv. p. 6, ii. p. 150, ed. Jaubert and Abulf. Mesopot. in the *N. Repertor.* III. p. xxiv.), which according to Edrisi takes its rise from "nearly three hundred springs," near the city *Ras-el-'Ain*, at the foot of the mountain range of Masius, flows through Upper Mesopotamia in a direction parallel with its two principal streams, and then, turning westward, discharges itself into the Euphrates near Kirkesion. There the hand of Jehovah came upon Ezekiel. The expression יַד יי' הָיְתָה עַל (אֶל) always signifies a miraculous working of the power or omnipotence of God upon a man,—the hand being the organ of power in action,—by which he is placed in a condition to exert superhuman power, 1 Kings xviii. 46, and is the regular expression for the supernatural transportation into the state of ecstasy for the purpose of beholding and announcing (cf. 2 Kings iii. 15), or undertaking, heavenly things; and so throughout Ezekiel, cf. iii. 22, viii. 1, xxxiii. 22, xxxvii. 1, xl. 1.

Vers. 4–28. Description of the theophany seen by the spirit of the prophet.—Ver. 4. *And I saw, and, lo, a tempestuous wind came from the north, a great cloud, and a fire rolled together like a ball, and the brightness of light round about it, and out of its midst, as the appearance of glowing metal from the midst of the fire.*—The description begins with a general outline of the phenomenon, as the same presented itself to the spiritual eye of the prophet on its approach from the north. A tempestuous wind brings hither from the north a great cloud, the centre of which appears as a lump of fire, which throws around the cloud the brightness of light, and presents in its midst the appearance of glowing metal. The coming of the phenomenon from the north is, as a matter of course, not connected with the Babylonian representation of the mountain of the gods situated in the extreme north, Isa. xiv. 13. According to the invariable usage of speech followed by the prophets, especially by Jeremiah (cf. *e.g.* i. 14, iv. 6, vi. 1, etc.), the north is the quarter from which the enemies who were to execute judgment upon Jerusalem and Judah break in. According to this usage, the coming of this divine appearance from the north signifies that it is from the north that God will bring to pass the judgment upon Judah. אֵשׁ מִתְלַקַּחַת, "fire rolled together like a ball," is an expression borrowed from Ex. ix. 10. לוֹ refers to עָנָן, and מִתּוֹכָהּ to אֵשׁ, as we see from the words in apposition, מִתּוֹךְ הָאֵשׁ. The fire, which formed the centre of the cloud, had the appearance of חַשְׁמַל. The meaning of this word, which occurs again in ver. 27 and ch. viii. ver. 2, is disputed. The Septuagint and Vulgate translate it by ἤλεκτρον, *electrum*, *i.e.* a metal having a bright lustre, and consisting of a mixture of gold and silver. Cf. Strabo, III. 146; Plin. *Hist. Nat.* xxxiii. 4. To the explanation of Bochart, that it is a compound of נְחשֶׁת, "brass," and the Talmudic word מלל or מללא, "*aurum rude*," and signifies "rough gold ore," is opposed the fact that the reading מללא in the Talmud is not certain, but purports to be ממלא (cf. Gesen. *Thesaur.* p. 535, and Buxtorf, *Lexic. Talmud*, p. 1214), as well as the circumstance that raw gold ore has not a lustre which could shine forth out of the fire. Still less probability has the supposition that it is a compound of חשל, in Syriac "*conflavit, fabricavit*," and חשם, "*fricuit*," on which Hävernick and Maurer base the meaning of "a piece of metal wrought in the fire." The word appears simply to be formed from חשם, probably "to glow," with ל appended, as כַּרְמֶל from כרם, and to denote "glowing ore." This meaning is appropriate both in ver. 27, where עֵין חַשְׁמַל is explained by מַרְאֵה־אֵשׁ, as well as in ch. viii. 2, where זֹהַר, "brilliancy," stands as parallel to it. חַשְׁמַל, however, is different from נְחשֶׁת קָלָל in ver. 7 and in Dan. x. 6, for חַשְׁמַל refers in all the three places to the person of Him who is enthroned above the cherubim; while נְחשֶׁת קָלָל in ver. 7 is spoken of the feet of the cherubim, and in Dan. x. 6 of the arms and feet of the personage who there manifests Himself. In verse fifth the appearance is described more minutely. There first present themselves to the eye of the seer four beings, whom he describes according to their figure and style.

Vers. 5–14. The four cherubim.—Ver. 5. *And out of its midst there prominently appeared a figure, consisting of four creatures, and this was their appearance: they had the figure of a man.* Ver. 6. *And each had four faces, and each of them had four wings.* Ver. 7. *And their feet were upright-standing feet; and the soles of their feet like the soles of a calf, and sparkling like the appearance of shining brass.* Ver. 8. *And the hands of a man were under their wings on their four sides; and all four had faces and wings.* Ver. 9. *Their wings were joined one to another; they turned not as they went; they went each one in the direction of his face.* Ver. 10. *And the form of their faces was that of a man; and on the right all four had a lion's face; and on the left all four had the face of an ox; and all four had an eagle's face.* Ver. 11. *And their faces and their wings were divided above, two of each uniting with one another, and two covering their bodies* Ver. 12. *And they went each in the direction of his face; whithersoever the spirit was to go, they went; they turned not as they went.* Ver. 13. *And the likeness of the creatures resembled burning coals of fire, like the appearance of torches: it (the fire) went hither and thither amongst the beings; and the fire was brilliant, and from the fire came forth lightning.* Ver. 14. *And the beings ran hither and thither in a zig-zag manner.*

From out of the fiery centre of the cloud there shows itself the form (דְּמוּת, properly "resemblance," "picture") of four חַיּוֹת, *animantia*, "living creatures;" *ζῶα*, Apoc. iv. 6; not *θηρία*, "wild beasts," as Luther has incorrectly rendered it, after the *animalia* of the Vulgate. These four creatures had דְּמוּת אָדָם, "the figure of a man." Agreeably to this notice, placed at the head of the description, these creatures are to be conceived as presenting the appearance of a human body in all points not otherwise specified in the following narrative. Each of them had four faces and four wings (אַחַת without the article stands as a distributive, and כְּנָפַיִם are "pinions," as in Isa. vi. 2, not "pairs of wings"). Their feet were רֶגֶל יְשָׁרָה, "a straight foot;" the singular stands generically, stating only the nature of the feet, without reference to their number. We have accordingly to assume in each of the four creatures two legs, as in a man. יָשָׁר, "straight," *i.e.* standing upright, not bent, as when sitting or kneeling. רֶגֶל is the whole leg, including the knee and thigh, and כַּף רֶגֶל, "sole of the foot," or the under part of the leg, with which we tread on the ground. This part, not the whole leg, resembled the calf's foot, which is firmly planted on the ground. The legs sparkled like the appearance of נְחֹשֶׁת קָלָל. The subject of נֹצְצִים is not "the כְּרוּבִים, which are understood to be intended under the חיות in verse fifth" (Hitzig), for this subject is too far distant, but רַגְלֵיהֶם, which is here construed as masculine, as in Jer. xiii. 16. In this sense are these words apprehended in the Apocalypse, i. 15, and נְחֹשֶׁת קָלָל there translated by χαλκολίβανος. On this word see Hengstenberg and Düsterdieck on the Apoc. i. 15. נח׳ קלל probably signifies "light," *i.e.* "bright, shining brass," as the old translators have rendered it. The Septuagint has ἐξαστράπτων; the Vulgate, *aes candens;* and the Chaldee paraphrast, *aes flammans.* The signification "smoothed, polished brass" (Bochart), rests upon uncertain combinations; cf. Gesen. *Thes.* p. 1217, and is appropriate neither here nor in Dan. x. 6, where these words precede, "His face had the appearance of lightning, and his eyes were as a flame of fire." Under the four wings were four hands on the four sides of each cherub, formed like the hands of a man. The wings accordingly rested upon the shoulders, from which the hands came forth. The *Chetib* וידו may certainly be defended if with Kimchi and others we punctuate וְיָדוֹ, and take the suffix distributively and אָדָם elliptically, "his (*i.e.* each of the four creatures) hands were (the hands of) a man;" cf. for such an ellipsis as this, passages like that in Ps. xviii. 34, רַגְלַי כָּאַיָּלוֹת, "my feet as the (feet) of hinds;" Job xxxv. 2, מֵאֵל, "before the righteousness of God." It is extremely probable, however, that ו is only the error of an old copyist for י, and that the *Keri* וִידֵי is the correct reading, as the taking of אדם elliptically is not in keeping with the broad style of Ezekiel, which in its verbosity verges on tautology. The second half of ver. 8 is neither, with Hävernick, to be referred to the following ninth verse, where the faces are no more spoken of, nor, with Hitzig, to be arbitrarily mutilated; but is to be taken as it stands, comprising all that has hitherto been said regarding the faces and wings, in order to append thereto in ver. 9 sqq. the description of the use and nature of these members. The definite statement, that "the wings were joined one to another," is in ver. 11 limited to the two upper wings, according to which we have so to conceive the matter, that the top or the upper right wing of each cherub came in contact with the top of the left wing of the neighbouring cherub. This junction presented to the eye of the seer the unity and coherence of all the four creatures as a complete whole—a חַיָּה, and implied, as a consequence, the harmonious action in common of the four creatures. They did not turn as they went along, but proceeded each in the direction of his face. אֶל־עֵבֶר פָּנָיו, "over against his face." The meaning is thus rightly given by Kliefoth: "As they had four faces, they needed not to turn as they went, but went on as (*i.e.* in the direction in which) they were going, always after the face." In the closer description of the faces in ver. 10, the face of the man is first mentioned as that which was turned towards the seer, that of the lion to the right side, the ox to the left, and that of the eagle (behind). In naming these three, it is remarked that all the four creatures had these faces: in naming the man's face, this remark is omitted, because the word פְּנֵיהֶם (referring to all the four) immediately precedes. In ver. 11, it is next remarked of the faces and wings, that they were divided above (מִלְמַעְלָה, "from above," "upward"); then the direction of the wings is more precisely stated. The word וּפְנֵיהֶם is neither to be referred to the preceding, "and it was their faces," nor, with Hitzig, to be expunged as a gloss; but is quite in order as a statement that not only the wings but also the faces were divided above, consequently were not like *Janus*' faces upon one head, but the four faces were planted upon four heads and necks. In the description that follows, חוֹבְרוֹת אִישׁ is not quite distinct, and אִישׁ is manifestly to be taken as an abbreviation of אִשָּׁה אֶל־אֲחוֹתָהּ in ver. 9: on each were two wings joining one another, *i.e.* touching with their tops the tips of the wings of the cherub beside them, in accordance with which we have to conceive the wings as expanded. Two were covering their bodies, *i.e.* each cherub covered his body with the pair of wings that folded downwards; not, as Kliefoth supposes, that the lower wings of the one cherub covered the body of the other cherub beside him, which also is not the meaning in ver. 23; see note on that verse. In ver. 12, what is to be said about their movements is brought to a conclusion, while both statements are repeated in ver. 9*b*, and completed by the addition of the *principium movens.* In whatever direction the רוּחַ "was to go, in that direction they went;" *i.e.* not according to the action of their own will, but wherever the רוּחַ impelled them. רוּחַ, however, signifies not "impulse," nor, in this place, even "the wind," as the vehicle of the power of the spiritual life palpable to the senses, which produced and guided their movements, (Kliefoth), but spirit. For, according to ver. 20, the movement of the wheels, which was in harmony with the movements of the cherubim, was not caused by the wind, but proceeded from the רוּחַ הַחַיָּה, *i.e.* from the spirit dwelling in the creature. On the contrary, there is not in the whole description, with the exception of the general statement that a tempestuous wind drove from the north the great cloud in which the theophany was enwrapped, any allusion to a means of motion palpable to the senses. In the 13th and 14th verses is described the entire impression produced by the movement of the whole appearance. וּדְמוּת הַחַיּוֹת precedes, and is taken absolutely "as regards the form of the creatures," and corresponds to the דְּמוּת אַרְבַּע חַיּוֹת in ver. 5, with which the description of the individual figures which appeared in the brightness of the fire was introduced. Their appearance was like burning coals of fire, like the appearance of torches. הִיא refers to אֵשׁ as the principal conception. Fire, like the fire of burning coals and torches, went, moved hither and thither amongst the four creatures. This fire presented a bright appearance, and out of it came forth lightnings. The creatures, moreover, were in constant motion. רָצוֹא, from רָצָא, an Aramaising form for the Hebrew רוּץ, to run. The *infin. absol.* stands instead of the *finite verb.* The conjecture of יָצוֹא, after Gen. viii. 7 (Hitzig), is inappropriate, because here we have not to think of "coming out," and no reason exists for the striking out of the words, as Hitzig proposes. The continued motion of the creatures is not in contradiction with their perpetually moving on straight before them. "They went hither and thither, and yet always in the direction of their countenances; because they had a countenance looking in the direction of every side" (Kliefoth). בָּזָק signifies not "lightning" (=בָּרָק), but comes from בָּזַק; in Syriac, "to be split," and denotes "the splitting," *i.e.* the zigzag course of the lightning (Kliefoth).

Vers. 15–21. The four wheels beside the cherubim.—Ver. 15. *And I saw the creatures, and, lo, there was a wheel upon the earth beside the creatures, towards their four fronts.* Ver. 16. *The appearance of the wheels and their work was like the appearance of the chrysolite; and all four had one kind of figure: and their appearance and their work was as if one wheel were within the other.* Ver. 17. *Towards their four sides they went when they moved: they turned not as they went.* Ver. 18. *And their felloes, they were high and terrible; and their felloes were full of eyes round about in all the four.* Ver. 19. *And when the creatures moved, the wheels moved beside them; and when the creatures raised themselves up from the earth, the wheels also raised themselves.* Ver. 20. *Whithersoever the spirit was to go, they went in the direction in which the spirit was to go; and the wheels raised themselves beside them: for the spirit of the creatures was in the wheels.* Ver. 21. *When the former moved, the latter moved also; when the former stood, the latter stood; and when the former raised themselves from the ground, the wheels raised themselves beside them: for the spirit of the creatures was in the wheels.*—The words, "and I saw the creatures," prepare the way for the transition to the new object which presented itself in these creatures to the eye of the seer. By the side of these creatures upon the ground he sees a wheel, and that at the four fronts, or front faces of the creatures. The singular suffix in לְאַרְבַּעַת פָּנָיו can neither be referred, with Rosenmüller, to the chariot, which is not mentioned at all, nor, with Hitzig, to the preposition אֵצֶל, nor, with Hävernick, Maurer, and Kliefoth, to אוֹפָן, and so be understood as if every wheel looked towards four sides, because a second wheel was inserted in it at right angles. This meaning is not to be found in the words. The suffix refers *ad sensum* to חַיּוֹת (Ewald), or, to express it more correctly, to the figure of the cherubim with its four faces turned to the front, conceived as a unity—as *one* creature (הַחַיָּה, ver. 22). Accordingly, we have so to represent the matter, that by the side of the four cherubim, namely, beside his front face, a wheel was to be seen upon the earth. Ezekiel then saw four wheels, one on each front of a cherub, and therefore immediately speaks in ver. 16 of wheels (in the plural). In this verse מַרְאֶה is *adspectus*, and מַעֲשֶׂה "work;" *i.e.* both statements employing the term "construction," although in the first hemistich only the appearance, in the second only the construction, of the wheels is described. תַּרְשִׁישׁ is the chrysolite of the ancients, the topaz of the moderns,—a stone having the lustre of gold. The construction of the wheels was as if one wheel were within a wheel, *i.e.* as if in the wheel a second were inserted at right angles, so that without being turned it could go towards all the four sides. גַּבֵּיהֶן, in ver. 18, stands absolutely. "As regards their felloes," they possessed height and terribleness,—the latter because they were full of eyes all round. Hitzig arbitrarily understands גֹּבַהּ of the upper sides; and יִרְאָה, after the Arabic, of the under side, or that which lies towards the back. The movement of the wheels completely followed the movement of the creatures (vers. 19–21), because the spirit of the creature was in the wheels. הַחַיָּה, in vers. 20 and 21, is not the "principle of life" (Hävernick), but the cherubic creatures conceived as a unity, as in ver. 22, where the meaning is undoubted. The sense is: the wheels were, in their motion and rest, completely bound by the movements and rest of the creatures, because the spirit which ruled in them was also in the wheels, and regulated their going, standing, and rising upwards. By the רוּחַ הַחַיָּה the wheels are bound in one with the cherub-figures, but not by means of a chariot, to or upon which the cherubim were attached.

Vers. 22–28. The throne of Jehovah.—Ver. 22. *And over the heads of the creature there appeared an expanse like the appearance of the terrible crystal, stretched out over their heads above.* Ver. 23. *And under the expanse were their wings, extended straight one towards another: each had two wings, covering to these, and each two (wings), covering to those, their bodies.* Ver. 24. *And I heard the sound of their wings, as the sound of many waters, like the voice of the Almighty, as they went: a loud rushing like the clamour of a camp: when they stood, they let down their wings.* Ver. 25. *And there came a voice from above the expanse which was above their heads; when they stood, they let their wings sink down.* Ver. 26. *Over the expanse above their heads was to be seen, like a sapphire stone, the figure of a throne: and over the figure of the throne was a figure resembling a man above it.* Ver. 27. *And I saw like the appearance of glowing brass, like the appearance of fire within the same round about; from the appearance of his loins upwards, and from the appearance of his loins downwards, I saw as of the appearance of fire, and a shining light was round about it.* Ver. 28. *Like the appearance of the bow, which is in the clouds in the day of rain, was the appearance of the shining light round about. This was the appearance of the likeness of the glory of Jehovah. And I saw it, and fell upon my face, and I heard the voice of one that spake.*—Above, over the heads of the figures of the cherubim, Ezekiel sees something like the firmament of heaven (ver.

22 sq.), and hears from above this canopy a voice, which re-echoes in the rushing of the wings of the cherubim, and determines the movement as well as the standing still of these creatures. The first sentence of ver. 22 literally signifies: "And a likeness was over the heads of the creature,—a canopy, as it were, stretched out." רָקִיעַ is not the genitive after דְּמוּת, but an explanatory apposition to it, and before רָקִיעַ; neither has כְּ fallen out (as Hitzig supposes), nor is it to be supplied. For דְּמוּת denotes not any definite likeness, with which another could be compared, but, properly, *similitudo*, and is employed by Ezekiel in the sense of "something like." רָקִיעַ, without the article, does not mean the firmament of heaven, but any expanse, the appearance of which is first described as resembling the firmament by the words כְּעֵין הַקֶּרַח. It is not the firmament of heaven which Ezekiel sees above the heads of the cherubim, but an expanse resembling it, which has the shining appearance of a fear-inspiring crystal. נוֹרָא, used of crystal, in so far as the appearance of this glittering mass dazzles the eyes, and assures terror, as in Judg. xiii. 6, of the look of the angel; and in Job xxxvii. 22, of the divine majesty. The description is based upon Ex. xxiv. 10, and the similitude of the crystal has passed over to the Apocalypse, iv. 6. Under the canopy were the wings of the cherubim, יְשָׁרוֹת, standing straight, *i.e.* spread out in a horizontal direction, so that they appeared to support the canopy. אִשָּׁה אֶל־אֲחוֹתָהּ is not, with Jerome and others, to be referred to the cherubim (הַחַיָּה), but to כַּנְפֵיהֶם, as in ver. 9. The לְאִישׁ which follows does refer, on the contrary, to the cherub, and literally signifies, "To each were two wings, covering, namely, to these and those, their bodies." לְהֵנָּה corresponds to לְאִישׁ, in a manner analogous to לְאַחַת לָהֶם in ver. 6. By the repetition of the לְהֵנָּה, "to these and those," the four cherubim are divided into two pairs, standing opposite to one another. That this statement contradicts, as Hitzig asserts, the first half of the verse, is by no means evident. If the two creatures on each side covered their bodies with the two wings, then two

other wings could very easily be so extended under the canopy that the tops of the one should touch those of the other. As the creatures moved, Ezekiel hears the sound, *i.e.* the rustling of their wings, like the roaring of mighty billows. This is strengthened by the second comparison, "like the voice of the Almighty," *i.e.* resembling thunder, cf. x. 5. The קוֹל הֲמֻלָּה that follows still depends on אֶשְׁמַע. הֲמֻלָּה, which occurs only here and in Jer. xi. 6, is probably synonymous with הָמוֹן, "roaring," "noise," "tumult." This rushing sound, however, was heard only when the creatures were in motion; for when they stood, they allowed their wings to fall down. This, of course, applies only to the upper wings, as the under ones, which covered the body, hung downwards, or were let down. From this it clearly appears that the upper wings neither supported nor bore up the canopy over their heads, but only were so extended, when the cherubim were in motion, that they *touched* the canopy. In ver. 25 is also mentioned whence the loud sound came, which was heard, during the moving of the wings, from above the canopy, consequently from him who was placed above it, so that the creatures, always after this voice resounded, went on or stood still, *i.e.* put themselves in motion, or remained without moving, according to its command. With the repetition of the last clause of ver. 24 this subject is concluded in ver. 25. Over or above upon the firmament was to be seen, like a sapphire stone, the likeness of a throne, on which sat one in the form of a man—*i.e.* Jehovah appeared in human form, as in Dan. vii. 9 sq. Upon this was poured out a fiery, shining light, like glowing brass (עֵין חַשְׁמַל, as in ver. 4) and like fire, בֵּית־לָהּ סָבִיב, "within it round about" (בֵּית = מִבֵּית, "within," and לָהּ, pointing back to דְּמוּת כִּסֵּא). This appears to be the simplest explanation of these obscure words. They are rendered differently by Hitzig, who translates them: "like fire which has a covering round about it, *i.e.* like fire which is enclosed, whose shining contrasts so much the more brightly on account of the dark surroundings." But, to say nothing of the change which would then be necessary of בֵּית into בַּיִת, this meaning seems very far-fetched, and cannot be accepted for this reason alone, that מַרְאֵה אֵשׁ, neither in the following hemistich (ver. 27*b*) nor in viii. 2, has any such or similar strengthening addition. The appearance above shows, as the centre of the cloud (ver. 4), a fiery gleam of light, only there is to be perceived upon the throne a figure resembling a man, fiery-looking from the loins upwards and downwards, and round about the figure, or rather round the throne, a shining light (נֹגַהּ, cf. ver. 4), like the rainbow in the clouds, cf. Apoc. iv. 3. This [הוּא, ver. 28, does not refer to הַנֹּגַהּ, but to the whole appearance of him who was enthroned,—the covering of light included, but throne and cherubim (x. 4, 19) excluded (Hitzig)] was the appearance of the likeness of Jehovah's glory. With these words closes the description of the vision. The following clause, "And I saw, etc.," forms the transition to the word of Jehovah, which follows on the second chapter, and which summoned Ezekiel to become a prophet to Israel. Before we pass, however, to an explanation of this word, we must endeavour to form to ourselves a clear conception of the significance of this theophany.

For its full understanding we have first of all to keep in view that it was imparted to Ezekiel not merely on his being called to the office of prophet, but was again repeated three times,—namely, in ch. iii. 22 sqq., where he was commissioned to predict symbolically the impending siege of Jerusalem; ch. viii. 4 sqq., when he is transported in spirit to the temple-court at Jerusalem for the purpose of beholding the abominations of the idol-worship practised by the people, and to announce the judgment which, in consequence of these abominations, was to burst upon the city and the temple, in which it is shown to him how the glory of the Lord abandons, first the temple and thereafter the city also; and in ch. xliii. 1 sqq., in which is shown to him the filling of the new temple with the glory of the Lord, to dwell for ever among the children of Israel. In all three passages it is expressly testified that the divine appearance was like the first which he witnessed on the occasion of his call. From this Kliefoth has drawn the right conclusion, that the theophany in ch. i. 4 sqq. bears a relation not to the call only, but to the whole prophetic work of Ezekiel: "We may not say that God so appears to Ezekiel at a later time, because He so appeared to him at his call; but we must say, conversely, that because God wills and must so appear to Ezekiel at a later time while engaged in his prophetic vocation, therefore He also appears to him in this form already at his call." The intention, however, with which God so appears to him is distinctly contained in the two last passages, ch. viii.–xi. and ch. xliii: "God withdraws in a visible manner from the temple and Jerusalem, which are devoted to destruction on account of the sin of the people: in a visible manner God enters into the new temple of the future; and because the whole of what Ezekiel was inspired to foretell was comprehended in these two things,—the destruction of the existing temple and city, and the raising up of a new and a better;—because the whole of his prophetic vocation had its fulfilment in these, therefore God appears to Ezekiel on his call to be a prophet in the same form as that in which He departs from the ancient temple and Jerusalem, in order to their destruction, and in which He enters into the new edifice in order to make it a temple. The form of the theophany, therefore, is what it is in i. 4 sqq., because its purpose was to show and announce to the prophet, on the one side the destruction of the temple, and on the other its restoration and glorification." These remarks are quite correct, only the significance of the theophany itself is not thereby made clear. If it is clear from the purpose indicated why God here has the cherubim with Him, while on the occasion of other appearances (*e.g.* Dan. vii. 9; Isa. vi. 1) He is without cherubim; as the cherubim here have no other significancy than what their figures have in the tabernacle, viz. that God has there His dwelling-place, the seat of

His gracious presence; yet this does not satisfactorily explain either the special marks by which the cherubim of Ezekiel are distinguished from those in the tabernacle and in Solomon's temple, or the other attributes of the theophany. Kliefoth, moreover, does not misapprehend those diversities in the figures of the cherubim, and finds indicated therein the intention of causing it distinctly to appear that it is the one and same Jehovah, enthroned amid the cherubim, who destroys the temple, and who again uprears it. Because Ezekiel was called to predict both events, he therefore thinks there must be excluded, on the one hand, such attributes in the form of the manifestation as would be out of harmony with the different aims of the theophany; while, on the other, those which are important for the different aims must be combined and comprehended in one form, that this one form may be appropriate to all the manifestations of the theophany. It could not therefore have in it the ark of the covenant and the mercy-seat; because, although these would probably have been appropriate to the manifestation for the destruction of the old temple (viii. 1 sqq.), they would not have been in keeping with that for entering into the new temple. Instead of this, it must show the living God Himself upon the throne among "the living creatures;" because it belongs to the new and glorious existence of the temple of the future, that it should have Jehovah Himself dwelling within it in a visible form. From this, too, may be explained the great fulness of the attributes, which are divisible into three classes: 1. Those which relate to the manifestation of God for the destruction of Jerusalem; 2. Those which relate to the manifestation of God for entering into the new temple; and, 3. Those which serve both objects in common. To the last class belongs everything which is essential to the manifestation of God in itself, *e.g.* the visibility of God in general, the presence of the cherubim in itself, and so on: to the first class all the signs that indicate wrath and judgment, consequently, first, the coming from the north, especially the fire, the lightnings, in which God appears as He who is coming to judgment; but to the second, besides the rainbow and the appearance of God in human form, especially the wheels and the fourfold manifestation in the cherubim and wheels. For the new temple does not represent the rebuilding of the temple by Zerubbabel, but the economy of salvation founded by Christ at His appearing, to which they belong as essential tokens; to be founded, on the one hand, by God's own coming and dwelling upon the earth; on the other, to be of an œcumenic character, in opposition to the particularities and local nature of the previous ancient dispensation of salvation. God appears bodily, in human form; lowers down to earth the canopy on which His throne is seated; the cherubim, which indicate God's gracious presence with His people, appear not merely in symbol, but in living reality, plant their feet upon the ground, while each cherub has at his side a wheel, which moves, not in the air, but only upon the earth. By this it is shown that God Himself is to descend to the earth, to walk and to dwell visibly among His people; while the œcumenic character of the new economy of salvation, for the establishment of which God is to visit the earth, is represented in the fourfold form of the cherubim and wheels.[1] The number four—the sign of the œcumenicity which is to come, and the symbol of its being spread abroad into all the world—is assigned to the cherubim and wheels, to portray the spreading abroad of the new kingdom of God over the whole earth. But how much soever that is true and striking this attempt at explanation may contain in details, it does not touch the heart of the subject, and is not free from bold combinations. The correctness of the assumption, that in the theophany attributes of an opposite kind are united, namely, such as should refer only to the destruction of Jerusalem and of the temple, and such as relate only to the foundation and nature of the new economy of salvation, is beset with well-founded doubts. Why, on such a hypothesis, should the form of the theophany remain the same throughout in all three or four cases? This question, which lies on the surface, is not satisfactorily answered by the remark that Ezekiel had to predict not only the destruction of the old, but also the foundation of a new and much more glorious kingdom of God. For not only would this end, but also the object of showing that it is the same God who is to accomplish both, have been fully attained if the theophany had remained the same only in those attributes which emblemize in a general way God's gracious presence in His temple; while the special attributes, which typify only the one and the other purpose of the divine appearance, would only then have been added, or brought prominently out, where this or that element of the theophany had to be announced. Moreover, the necessity in general of a theophany for the purpose alleged is not evident, much less the necessity of a theophany so peculiar in form. Other prophets also, *e.g.* Micah, without having seen a theophany, have predicted in the clearest and distinctest manner both the destruction of Jerusalem and the temple, and the raising up of a new and more glorious kingdom of God. The reason, then, why Ezekiel witnessed such a theophany, not only at his call, but had it repeated to him at every new turn in his prophetic ministry, must be deeper than that assigned; and the theophany must have another meaning than that of merely consecrating the prophet for the purpose of announcing both the judgment upon Jerusalem and the temple, and the raising up of a new and more glorious economy of salvation, and strengthening the word of the prophet by a symbolical representation of its contents.

To recognise this meaning, we must endeavour to form a distinct conception, not merely of the principal elements of our theophany, but to take into consideration at the same time their relation to other theophanies. In our theophany three elements are unmistakeably prominent,—1st, The peculiarly formed cherubim; 2d, The wheels are seen beside the cherubim; and, 3d, The firmament above, both with the throne and the form of

God in human shape seated upon the throne. The order of these three elements in the description is perhaps hardly of any importance, but is simply explicable from this, that to the seer who is on earth it is the under part of the figure which, appearing visibly in the clouds, first presents itself, and that his look next turns to the upper part of the theophany. Especially significant above all, however, is the appearance of the cherubim under or at the throne of God; and by this it is indisputably pointed out that He who appears upon the throne is the same God that is enthroned in the temple between the cherubim of the mercy-seat upon their outspread wings. Whatever opinion may be formed regarding the nature and significance of the cherubim, this much is undoubtedly established, that they belong essentially to the symbolical representation of Jehovah's gracious presence in Israel, and that this portion of our vision has its real foundation in the plastic representation of this gracious relation in the Holy of Holies of the tabernacle or temple. As, however, opinions are divided on the subject of the meaning of these symbols, and the cherubim of Ezekiel, moreover, present no inconsiderable differences in their four faces and four wings from the figures of the cherubim upon the mercy-seat and in the temple, which had only one face and two wings, we must, for the full understanding of our vision, look a little more closely to the nature and significance of the cherubim.

While, according to the older view, the cherubim are angelic beings of a higher order, the opinion at the present day is widely prevalent, that they are only symbolical figures, to which nothing real corresponds, — merely ideal representations of creature life in its highest fulness.[1] This modern view, how-

[1] Compare the investigation of the cherubim in my *Handbuch der Biblischen Archæologie*, I. pp. 86 sqq. and 113 sqq.; also Kliefoth's *Abhandlung über die Zahlensymbolik der heiligen Schrift in der Theolog. Zeitschrift von Dieckhoff und Kliefoth*, III. p. 381 sqq., where especially the older view—that the cherubim are angelic beings of a higher rank—is defended in a thorough manner, and the daring hypothesis of Hofmann signally refuted;

ever, finds in the circumstance that the cherubim in the Israelitish sanctuary, as well as in Ezekiel and in the Apocalypse, are symbolical figures of varying shape, only an apparent but no real support. The cherubim occur for the first time in the history of Paradise, where, in Gen. iii. 22–24, it is related that God, after expelling the first human pair from Paradise, placed at the east side of the garden the cherubim and the flame of a sword, which turned hither and thither, to guard the way to the tree of life. If this narrative contains historical truth, and is not merely a myth or philosopheme; if Paradise and the Fall, with their consequences, extending over all humanity, are to remain real things and occurrences,—then must the cherubim also be taken as real beings. "For God will not have placed symbols — pure creations of Hebrew fancy — at the gate of Paradise," Kliefoth. Upon the basis of this narrative, Ezekiel also held the cherubim to be spiritual beings of a higher rank. This appears from ch. xxviii. 14–16, where he compares the prince of Tyre, in reference to the high and glorious position which God had assigned him, to a cherub, and to Elohim. It does not at all conflict with the recognition of the cherubim as real beings, and, indeed, as spiritual or angelic beings, that they are employed in visions to represent super-sensible relations, or are represented in a plastic form in the sanctuary of Israel. "When angels," as Kliefoth correctly remarks in reference to this, "sing the song of praise in the holy night, this is an historical occurrence, and these angels are real angels, who testify by their appearance that there are such beings as angels; but when, in the Apocalypse, angels pour forth sounds of wrath, these angels are figures in vision, as elsewhere, also, men and objects are seen in vision." But even this employment of the angels as "figures" in vision, rests upon the belief that

lastly, Ed. C. Aug. Riehm, *De naturâ et notione symbolicâ Cheruborum*, *Commentat. Basil.* 1864, who, proceeding from the view—adopted by Bähr, Hengstenberg, and others—that the cherubim were only symbolical figures, has sought to determine more minutely the meaning of these symbols.

there are actually beings of this kind. Biblical symbolism furnishes not a single undoubted instance of abstract ideas, or ideal creations of the imagination, being represented by the prophets as living beings. Under the plastic representation of the cherubim upon the mercy-seat, and in the most holy and holy place of the tabernacle and the temple, lies the idea, that these are heavenly, spiritual beings; for in the tabernacle and temple (which was built after its pattern) essential relations of the kingdom of God are embodied, and all the symbols derived from things having a real existence. When, however, on the other hand, Hengstenberg objects, on Apoc. iv. 6, "that what Vitringa remarks is sufficient to refute those who, under the cherubim, would understand angels of rank,—viz. that these four creatures are throughout the whole of this vision connected with the assembly of the elders, and are distinguished not only from the angels, but from *all* the angels, as is done in ch. vii. 11,"—we must regard this refutation as altogether futile. From the division of the heavenly assembly before the throne into two choirs or classes (Apoc. v. and vii.),—in which the *ζῶα* (cherubim) and the elders form the one (v. 8), the *ἄγγελοι* the other choir (ver. 11),—an argument can be as little derived against the angelic nature of the cherubim, as it could be shown, from the distinction between the *στρατιὰ οὐράνιος* and *ἄγγελος*, in Luke ii. 13, that the "multitude of the heavenly host" were no angels at all. And the passage in Apoc. vii. 11 would only then furnish the supposed proof against the relationship of the cherubim to the angels, if *πάντες ἄγγελοι* in general—all angels, how numerous soever they may be—were spoken of. But the very tenor of the words, *πάντες οἱ ἄγγελοι*, "all the angels," points back to the choir of angels already mentioned in ch. v. 11, which was formed by *πολλοὶ ἄγγελοι*, whose number was ten thousand times ten thousand, and thousands of thousands.[1] From the distinction between

[1] See on this distinction Winer's *Grammar of New Testament Greek* (Moulton's translation), p. 137, where, among other remarks, it is observed

the ζῶα and the ἄγγελοι in the Apocalypse, no further inference can be deduced than that the cherubim are not common angels, "ministering spirits, sent forth to minister" (Heb. i. 14), but constitute a special class of angels of higher rank. More exact information regarding the relationship of the cherubim to the other angels, or their nature, cannot indeed be obtained, either from the name *cherubim* or from the circumstance that, with the exception of Gen. iii., they occur always only in connection with the throne of God. The etymology of the word כְּרוּב is obscure: all the derivations that have been proposed from the Hebrew or any other Semitic dialect cannot make the slightest pretensions to probability. The word appears to have come down from antiquity along with the tradition of Paradise. See my *Biblical Archæology*, p. 88 sqq. If we take into consideration, however, that Ezekiel calls them חַיּוֹת, and first in ch. x. employs the name כְּרוּבִים, known from the tabernacle, or rather from the history of Paradise; since, as may be inferred from x. 20, he first recognised, from the repetition of the theophany related in ch. x., that the living creatures seen in the vision *were* cherubim,—we may, from the designation חַיּוֹת, form a supposition, if not as to their nature, at least as to the significance of their position towards the throne of God. They are termed חַיּוֹת, "living," not as being "ideal representatives of all living things upon the earth" (Hengstenberg), but as beings which, among all the creatures in heaven and earth, possess and manifest life in the fullest sense of the word, and on that very account, of all spiritual beings, stand nearest to the God of the spirits of all flesh (who lives from eternity to eternity), and encircle His throne. With this representation harmonises not only the fact, that after the expulsion of the first human beings from Paradise, God commanded them to guard the way to the tree of life, but also the form in which

that "πᾶσαι γενεαί are all generations, whatever their number; πᾶσαι αἱ γενεαί (Matt. i. 17), *all the* generations,—those which, either from the context or in some other way, are familiar as a definite number."

they were represented in the sanctuary and in the visions. The cherubim in the sanctuary had the form of a man, and were only marked out by their wings as super-terrestrial beings, not bound by the earthly limits of space. The cherubim in Ezekiel and the Apocalypse also preserve the appearance of a man. Angels also assume the human form when they appear visibly to men on earth, because of all earthly creatures man, created in the image of God, takes the first and highest place. For although the divine image principally consists in the spiritual nature of man,—in the soul breathed into him by the Spirit of God,—yet his bodily form, as the vessel of this soul, is the most perfect corporeity of which we have any knowledge, and as such forms the most appropriate garment for rendering visible the heavenly spiritual being within. But the cherubim in our vision exhibit, besides the figure of the human body with the face of a man, also the face of the lion, of the ox, and of the eagle, and four wings, and appear as four-sided, square-formed beings, with a face on each of their four sides, so that they go in any direction without turning, and yet, while so doing, they can always proceed in the direction of one face; while in the vision in the Apocalypse, the four faces of the creatures named are divided among the four cherubim, so that each has only one of them. In the countenance of man is portrayed his soul and spirit, and in each one also of the higher order of animals, its nature. The union of the lion, ox, and eagle-faces with that of man in the cherubim, is intended, doubtless, to represent them as beings which possess the fulness and the power of life, which in the earthly creation is divided among the four creatures named. The Rabbinical dictum (*Schemoth Rabba*, Schöttgen, *Horæ Hebraicæ*, p. 1168): *Quatuor sunt qui principatum in hoc mundo tenent. Inter creaturas homo, inter aves aquila, inter pecora bos, inter bestias leo*, contains a truth, even if there lies at the foundation of it the idea that these four creatures represent the entire earthly creation. For in the cherub, the living powers of these four creatures are actually united. That the eagle, namely, comes into consideration only in reference to his power of flight, in which he excels all other birds, may be concluded from the circumstance that in Apoc. iv. 7 the fourth ζῶον is described as resembling an eagle flying. According to this principle, the ox and the lion are only to be considered in reference to their physical strength, in virtue of which the ox amongst tame animals, the lion amongst wild beasts, take the first place, while man, through the power of his mind, asserts his supremacy over all earthly creatures.[1] The number four, lastly, both of the cherubim and of the four faces of each cherub in our vision, is connected with their capacity to go in all directions without turning, and can contribute nothing in favour of the assumption that these four indicate the whole living creation, upon the simple ground that the number four is not essential to them, for on the mercy-seat only two cherubim are found. That they are also represented in the vision as higher spiritual beings, appears not only from Ezek. x. 7, where a cherub stretches forth his hand and fetches out fire from between the cherubim, and places it in the hands of the angel clothed in white linen, who was to accomplish the burning of Jerusalem; but, still more distinctly, from what is said in the Apocalypse regarding their working. Here we observe them, as Kliefoth has already pointed out, "in manifold activity: they utter day and night the Tersanctus; they offer worship, iv. 8, 9, v. 8, xix. 4; they repeat the Amen to the song of praise from all creation, v. 14; they invite John to see what the four first seals are accomplishing, vi. 1, 3, 5, 7; one of them gives to the seven angels the seven phials of wrath, xv. 7."

[1] This has been already rightly recognised by Riehm, *l.c.* p. 21 ff., who has drawn from it the inference: *quaternis igitur faciebus eximiae vires atque facultates significantur cherubis a deo ad munus suum sustinendum impertitae*, which is connected with the erroneous representation that the cherubim are intended to bear the throne of God, and to carry the Lord of the world.

Besides this activity of theirs in the carrying out of the divine counsel of salvation, we must, in order to gain as clear a view as possible of the significance of the cherubim in our vision, as well as in Biblical symbolism generally, keep also in view the position which, in the Apocalypse, they occupy around the throne of God. Those who are assembled about the throne form these three concentric circles: the four ζῶα (cherubim) form the innermost circle; the twenty-four elders, seated upon thrones, clothed in white garments, and wearing golden crowns upon their heads, compose the wider circle that follows; while the third, and widest of all, is formed by the many angels, whose number was many thousands of thousands (Apoc. iv. 4, 6, v. 6, 8, vii. 11). To these are added the great, innumerable host, standing before the throne, of the just made perfect from among all heathens, peoples, and languages, in white raiment, and with palms in their hands, who have come out of great tribulation, and have washed their robes, and made them white in the blood of the Lamb, and now, before the throne of God, serve Him day and night in His temple (vii. 9, 14, 15). Accordingly the twenty-four elders, as the patriarchs of the Old and New Testament congregation of God, have their place beside God's throne, between the cherubim and the myriads of the other angels; and in the same manner as they are exalted above the angels, are the cherubim exalted even above them. This position of the cherubim justifies the conclusion that they have the name of ζῶα from the indwelling fulness of the everlasting blessed life which is within them, and which streams out from the Creator of spirits—the King of all kings, and Lord of all lords—upon the spiritual beings of heaven, and that the cherubim immediately surround the throne of God, as being representatives and bearers of the everlasting life of blessedness, which men, created in the image of God, have forfeited by the Fall, but which they are again, from the infinitude of the divine compassion, to recover in the divine kingdom founded for the redemption of fallen humanity.

It is easier to recognise the meaning of the wheels which in our vision appear beside the cherubim. The wheel serves to put the chariot in motion. Although the throne of God is not now expressly represented and designated as a chariot-throne, yet there can be no doubt that the wheels which Ezekiel sees under the throne beside the cherubim are intended to indicate the possibility and ease with which the throne can be moved in the direction of the four quarters of the heavens. The meaning of the eyes, however, is matter of controversy, with which, according to i. 18, the felloes of the wheels, and, as is expressly mentioned in ch. x. 12, and also noted in Apoc. iv. 6, the cherubim themselves are furnished all round. According to Kliefoth, the eyes serve the purpose of motion; and as the movement of the cherubim and wheels indicates the spreading abroad over the whole earth of the new economy of salvation, this mass of eyes in the cherubim and wheels must indicate that this spreading abroad is to take place, not through blind accident, but with conscious clearness. The meaning is not appropriate to Apoc. iv. 6, where the cherubim have no wheels beside them, and where a going forth into all countries is not to be thought of. Here therefore, according to Kliefoth, the eyes only serve to bring into view the moral and physical powers which have created and supported the kingdom of God upon earth, and which are also to bring it now to its consummation. This is manifestly arbitrary, as any support from passages of the Bible in favour of the one view or the other is entirely wanting. The remark of Rosenmüller is nearer the truth, that by the multitude of the eyes is denoted *Coelestium naturarum perspicacia et* ὀξυωπία, and leads to the correct explanation of Apoc. v. 6, where the seven eyes of the Lamb are declared to be τὰ ἑπτὰ πνεύματα τοῦ Θεοῦ, τὰ ἀπεσταλμένα εἰς πᾶσαν τὴν γῆν; the eyes consequently indicate the spiritual effects which proceed from the Lamb over the entire earth in a manner analogous to His seven horns, which are the symbols of the completeness of His power. The eye, then, is the picture and mirror of the Spirit; and the ornamentation of the cherubim and wheels with eyes, shows that the power of the divine Spirit dwells within them, and determines and guides their movements.

The remaining objects of the vision are not difficult to explain. The appearance of the expanse over above the cherubim and wheels, upon which a throne is to be seen, represents the firmament or heaven as the place of God's throne. God appears upon the throne in human form, in the terrible glory of His holy majesty. The whole appearance draws nigh to the prophet in the covering of a great fiery cloud (ver. 4). This cloud points back to the "thick cloud" in which Jehovah, in the ancient time, descended upon Mount Sinai amid thunders and lightnings (Ex. xix. 16) to establish His covenant of grace, promised to the patriarchs with their seed,—the people of Israel brought forth from Egypt,—and to found His kingdom of grace upon the earth. If we observe the connection of our theophany with that manifestation of God on Sinai for the founding of the Old Testament dispensation of salvation, we shall neither confine the fire and the lightnings in our vision to the manifestation of God for the destruction of Jerusalem and the temple, nor refer the splendour which appears above the throne in the form of a rainbow to the grace which returns after the execution of judgment, or to the new dispensation of salvation which is to be established. Nor may we regard these differing attributes, by referring them specially to individual historical elements of the revelation of God in His kingdom, as in opposition; but must conceive of them, more generally and from the point of view of unity, as symbols of the righteousness, holiness, and grace which God reveals in the preservation, government, and consummation of His kingdom. It holds true also of our theophany what Düsterdieck remarks on Apoc. iv. 3 (cf. p. 219 of the second edition of his Commentary) regarding the importance of the divine appearance described in that passage: "We may not hastily apply in a general way the description before us by special reference to the judgments of God (which are seen at a later time) in their relation to the divine grace; it is enough that here, where the everlasting and personal ground of all that follows is described, the sacred glory and righteousness of God appear in the closest connection with His unchanging, friendly grace, so that the entire future development of the kingdom of God, and of the world down to the final termination, as that is determined by the marvellous unity of being which is in the holy, righteous, and gracious God, must not only according to its course, but also according to its object, correspond to this threefold glory of the living God." As this fundamental vision (of the Apocalypse) contains all that serves to alarm the enemies and to comfort the friends of Him who sits on the throne, so the vision of Ezekiel also has its fundamental significance not only for the whole of the prophet's ministry, but, generally, for the continuation and development of the kingdom of God in Israel, until its aim has been reached in its consummation in glory This, its fundamental significance, unmistakeably appears from the twofold circumstance,—firstly, that the theophany was imparted to the prophet at his call, and was then repeated at the principal points in his prophetic ministry, at the announcement both of the dissolution of the old kingdom of God by the destruction of Jerusalem and the temple, ch. ix.–xi., and also at the erection of the new temple and a new arrangement of the kingdom (ch. xl.–xlviii.). Since, as was formerly already remarked (p. 35), a theophany was not required either for the calling of Ezekiel to the office of a prophet, or for the announcement which was entrusted to him of the annihilation of the old and the foundation of the new kingdom of God, so the revelation of God, which pointed in its phenomenal shape to the dwelling of the Lord among His people in the Holy of Holies in the temple (and which was imparted in this place to Ezekiel, living among the exiles in the land of Chaldea by the banks of the Chebar), could only be intended, in view of the dissolution of the theocracy, which had already begun, and was shortly to be completed, to give to the prophet and those of his contemporaries who were living with him in exile, a real pledge that the essential element of the theocracy was not to be removed by the penal judgment which was passing over the sinful people and kingdom; but that God the Lord would still continue to attest Himself to His people as the living God, and preserve His kingdom, and one day bring it again to a glorious consummation.—In correspondence with this aim, God appears in the temple in the symbolical forms of His gracious presence as He who is throned above the cherubim; but cherubim and throne are furnished with attributes, which represent the movement of the throne in all directions, not merely to indicate the spreading of the kingdom of God over all the earth, but to reveal Himself as Lord and King, whose might extends over the whole world, and who possesses the power to judge all the heathen, and to liberate from their bondage His people, who have been given into their hands, if they repent and turn unto Him; and who will again gather them together, and raise them in the place of their inheritance to the glory which had been promised.

Such is the significance of the theophany at the inauguration of Ezekiel to the prophetic office. The significance, however, which its repetition possesses is clearly contained in the facts which the prophet was herewith permitted by God to behold. From the temple and city, polluted by sinful abominations, the gracious presence of God departs, in order that temple and city may be given over to the judgment of destruction; into the new and glorious temple there enters again the glory of God, to dwell for ever among the children of Israel.

Chap. ii. 1–iii. 3. Call of Ezekiel to the Prophetic Office.—Vers. 1 and 2. Upon the manifestation of the Lord follows the word of vocation. Having, in the feeling of his weakness and sinfulness, fallen to the ground before the terrible revelation of Jehovah's glory, Ezekiel is first of all raised up again by the voice of God, to hear the word which calls him to the prophetic function.—Ver. 1. *And He said to me, Son of man, stand upon thy feet, I will speak with thee.* Ver. 2. *Then came spirit unto me as He spake unto me, and it placed me on my feet, and I heard Him speaking unto me.*—The address בֶּן־אָדָם occurs so frequently in Ezekiel, that it must be regarded as one of the peculiarities of his prophecies. Elsewhere it occurs only once, Dan. viii. 17. That it is significant, is generally recognised, although its meaning is variously given. Most expositors take it as a reminder of the weakness and frailness of human nature; Coccejus and Kliefoth, on the contrary, connect it with the circumstance that God appears to Ezekiel in human form, and find in it a τεκμήριον *amicitiæ*, that God speaks in him as man to man, converses with him as a man with his friend. This last interpretation, however, has against it the *usus loquendi*. As בֶּן־אָדָם denotes man according to his natural condition, it is used throughout as a synonym with אֱנוֹשׁ, denoting the weakness and fragility of man in opposition to God; cf. Ps. viii. 5; Job xxv. 6; Isa. li. 12, lvi. 2; and Num. xxiii. 19. This is the meaning also of בֶּן־אָדָם in the address, as may be distinctly seen from the various addresses in Daniel. Daniel is addressed, where comfort is to be imparted to him, as אִישׁ חֲמֻדוֹת, "man greatly beloved," Dan. x. 11, 19, cf. ix. 23; but, on the contrary, in ch. viii. 17, where he has fallen on his face in terror before the appearance of Gabriel, with the words, "Understand, O son of man," in order to remind him of his human weakness. This is also the case in our verse, where Ezekiel, too, had fallen upon his face, and by God's word spoken to him, is again raised to his feet. It is only in Ezekiel that this address is constantly employed to mark the distance between the human weakness of his nature and the divine power which gives him the capacity and the impulse to speak. Not, however, with the design, mentioned by Jerome on Dan. viii. 17, "that he may not be elated on account of his high calling," because, as Hävernick subjoins, Ezekiel's extremely powerful and forcible nature may have needed to be perpetually reminded of what it is in reality before God. If this were the meaning and object of this address, it would also probably occur in the writings of several of the other prophets, as the supposition that the nature of Ezekiel was more powerful and forcible than that of the other prophets is altogether without foundation. The constant use of this form of address in Ezekiel is connected rather with the manner and fashion in which most of the revelations were imparted to him, that is, with the prevalence of "vision," in which the distinction between God and man comes out more prominently than in ordinary inspiration or revelation, effected by means of an impression upon the inner faculties of man. The bringing prominently forward, however, of the distance between God and men is to remind the prophet, as well as the people to whom he communicated his revelations, not merely of the weakness of humanity, but to show them, at the same time, how powerfully the word of God operates in feeble man, and also that God, who has selected the prophet as the organ of His will, possesses also the power to redeem the people, that were lying powerless under the oppression of the heathen, from their misery, and to raise them up again.—At the word of the Lord, "*Stand upon thy feet*," came רוּחַ into the prophet, which raised him to his feet. רוּחַ here is not "life, consciousness" (Hitzig), but the spirit-power which proceeds from God, and which is conveyed through the word which imparted to him the strength to stand before the face of God, and to undertake His command. מִדַּבֵּר, *partic. Hithpa.*, properly "*collocutor*," occurs here and in ch. xliii. 6, and in Num. vii. 89; elsewhere, only in 2 Sam. xiv. 13.

Vers. 3–7. The calling of the prophet begins with the Lord describing to Ezekiel the people to whom He is sending him, in order to make him acquainted with the difficulties of his vocation, and to encourage him for the discharge of the same.

Ver. 3. *And He said to me, Son of man, I send thee to the children of Israel, to the rebels who have rebelled against me: they and their fathers have fallen away from me, even until this very day.* Ver. 4. *And the children are of hard face, and hardened heart. To them I send thee; and to them shalt thou speak: Thus says the Lord Jehovah.* Ver. 5. *And they,—they may hear thee or fail* (*to do so*); *for they are a stiff-necked race,—they shall experience that a prophet has been in their midst.* Ver. 6. *But thou, son of man, fear not before them, and be not afraid of their words, if thistles and thorns are round about thee, and thou sittest upon scorpions; fear not before their words, and tremble not before their faces; for they are a stiff-necked race.* Ver. 7. *And speak my words to them, whether they may hear or fail* (*to do so*); *for they are stiff-necked.*

The children of Israel have become heathen, no longer a people of God, not even a heathen nation (גּוֹי, Isa. i. 4), but גּוֹיִם, "heathens," that is, as being rebels against God. הַמּוֹרְדִים (with the article) is not to be joined as an adjective to גּוֹיִם, which is without the article, but is employed substantively in the form of an apposition. They have rebelled against God in this, that they, like their fathers, have separated themselves from Jehovah down to this day (as regards פָּשַׁע בְּ, see on Isa. i. 2; and עֶצֶם הַיּוֹם הַזֶּה, as in the Pentateuch; cf. Lev. xxiii. 14; Gen. vii. 13, xvii. 23, etc.). Like their fathers, the sons are rebellious, and, in addition, they are קְשֵׁי פָנִים, of hard countenance" = חִזְקֵי מֵצַח, "of hard brow" (iii. 7), *i.e.* impudent, without hiding the face, or lowering the look for shame. This shamelessness springs from hardness of heart. To these hardened sinners Ezekiel is to announce the word of the Lord. Whether they hear it or not (אִם—וְאִם, *sive—sive*, as in Josh. xxiv. 15; Eccles. xi. 3, xii. 14), they shall in any case experience that a prophet has been amongst them. That they will neglect to hear is very probable, because they are a stiff-necked race (בַּיִת, "house" = family). The *Vau* before יָדְעוּ (ver. 5) introduces the *apodosis*. הָיָה is perfect, not present. This is demanded by the *usus loquendi* and the connection of the thought. The meaning is not: they shall know from his testimony that a prophet is there; but they shall experience from the result, viz. when the word announced by him will have been fulfilled, that a prophet has been amongst them. Ezekiel, therefore, is not to be prevented by fear of them and their words from delivering a testimony against their sins. The *ἁπαξ λεγομενα*, סָרָבִים and סַלּוֹנִים, are not, with the older expositors, to be explained adjectively: "*rebelles et renuentes*," but are substantives. As regards סַלּוֹן, the signification "thorn" is placed beyond doubt by סִלּוֹן in xxviii. 24, and סָרָב in Aramaic does indeed denote "*refractarius*;" but this signification is a derived one, and inappropriate here. סָרָב is related to צָרַב, "to burn, to singe," and means "*urtica*," "stinging-nettle, thistle," as Donasch in *Raschi* has already explained it. אוֹתָךְ is, according to the later usage, for אִתָּךְ, expressing the "by and with of association," and occurs frequently in Ezekiel. Thistles and thorns are emblems of dangerous, hostile men. The thought is strengthened by the words "to sit on (אֶל for עַל) scorpions," as these animals inflict a painful and dangerous wound. For the similitude of dangerous men to scorpions, cf. Sir. xxvi. 10, and other proof passages in Bochart, *Hierozoic.* III. p. 551 sq., ed. Rosenmüll.

Ver. 8 *ad fin.* and ch. iii. 3.—After the Lord had pointed out to the prophet the difficulties of the call laid upon him, He prepares him for the performance of his office, by inspiring him with the divine word which he is to announce.—Ver. 8. *And thou, son of man, hear what I say to thee, Be not stiff-necked like the stiff-necked race; open thy mouth, and eat what I give unto thee.* Ver. 9. *Then I saw, and, lo, a hand outstretched towards me; and, lo, in the same a roll of a book.* Ver. 10. *And He spread it out before me; the same was written upon the front and back: and there were written upon it lamentations, and sighing, and woe.* Ch. iii. 1. *And He said to me: Son of man, what thou findest eat; eat the roll, and go and speak to the house of Israel.* Ver. 2. *Then opened I my mouth, and He gave me this roll to eat.* Ver. 3. *And said to me: Son of man, feed thy belly, and fill thy body with this roll which I give thee. And I ate it, and it was in my mouth as honey and sweetness.*—The prophet is to announce to the people of Israel only that which the Lord inspires him to announce. This thought is embodied in symbol, in such a way that an outstretched hand reaches to him a book, which he is to swallow, and which also, at God's command, he does swallow; cf. Apoc. x. 9 sqq. This roll was inscribed on both sides with lamentations, sighing, and woe (הִי is either abbreviated from נְהִי, not = אִי, or as Ewald, § 101*c*, thinks, is only a more distinct form of הוֹי or הוֹ). The meaning is not, that upon the roll was inscribed a multitude of mournful expressions of every kind, but that there was written upon it all that the prophet was to announce, and what we now read in his book. These contents were of a mournful nature, for they related to the destruction of the kingdom, the destruction of Jerusalem and of the temple. That Ezekiel may look over the contents, the roll is spread out before his eyes, and then handed to him to be eaten, with the words, "Go and speak to the children of Israel," *i.e.* announce to the children of Israel what you have received into yourself, or as it is termed in ver. 5, דְּבָרַי, "my words." The words in iii. 3*a* were spoken by God while handing to the prophet the roll to be eaten. He is not merely to eat, *i.e.* take it into his mouth, but he is to fill his body and belly therewith, *i.e.* he is to receive into his innermost being the word of God presented to him, to change it, as it were, into sap and blood. Whilst eating it, it was sweet in his mouth. The sweet taste must not, with Kliefoth, be explained away into a sweet "after-taste," and made to bear this reference, that the destruction of Jerusalem would be followed by a more glorious restoration. The roll, inscribed with lamentation, sorrow, and woe, tasted to him sweetly, because its contents was God's word, which sufficed for the joy and gladness of his heart (Jer. xv. 16); for it is "infinitely sweet and lovely to be the organ and spokesman of the Omnipotent," and even the most painful of divine truths possess to a spiritually-minded man a joyful and quickening side (Hengstenberg on the Apoc. x. 9). To this it is added, that the divine penal judgments reveal not only the holiness and righteousness of God, but also prepare the way for the revelation of salvation, and minister to the saving of the soul.

Chap. iii. 4–21. THE SENDING OF THE PROPHET.—This consists in God's promise to give him power to overcome the difficulties of his vocation (vers. 4–9); in next transporting him to the place where he is to labour (vers. 10–15); and lastly, in laying upon him the responsibility of the souls entrusted to his charge (vers. 16–21). After Ezekiel had testified, by eating the roll which had been given him, his willingness to announce the word of the Lord, the Lord acquaints him with the peculiar difficulties of his vocation, and promises to bestow upon him strength to overcome them.—Ver. 4. *And He said to me, Son of man, go away to the house of Israel, and speak with my words to them.* Ver. 5. *For not to a people of hollow lips and heavy tongue art thou sent, (but) to the house of Israel.* Ver. 6. *Not to many nations of hollow lips and heavy tongue, whose words thou dost not understand; but to them have I sent thee, they can understand thee.* Ver. 7. *But the house of Israel will not hear thee, because they will not hear me; for the whole house of Israel, of hard brow and hardened heart are they.* Ver. 8. *Lo, I make thy countenance hard like their countenances, and thy brow hard like their brow.* Ver. 9. *Like to adamant, harder than rock, do I make thy brow: fear not, and tremble not before them, for they are a stiff-necked race.*—The contents of this section present a great similarity to those in ch. ii. 3–7, inasmuch as here as well as there the obduracy and stiff-neckedness of Israel is stated as a hindrance which opposes the success of Ezekiel's work. This is done here, however, in a different relation than there, so that there is no tautology.

Here, where the Lord is sending the prophet, He first brings prominently forward what lightens the performance of his mission; and next, the obduracy of Israel, which surrounds it with difficulty for him, in order at the same time to promise him strength for the vanquishing of these difficulties. Ezekiel is to speak, in the words communicated to him by God, to the house (people) of Israel. This he can do, because Israel is not a foreign nation with an unintelligible language, but possesses the capacity of understanding the words of the prophet (vers. 5–7), עַם עִמְקֵי שָׂפָה, "a people of deep lips," *i.e.* of a style of speech hollow, and hard to be understood; cf. Isa. xxxiii. 19. עִמְקֵי שׁ׳ is not genitive, and עַם is not the *status constructus*, but an adjective belonging to עַם, and used in the plural, because עַם contains a collective conception. "And of heavy tongue," *i.e.* with a language the understanding of which is attended with great difficulty. Both epithets denote a barbarously sounding, unintelligible, foreign tongue. The unintelligibility of a language, however, does not alone consist in unacquaintance with the meaning of its words and sounds, but also in the peculiarities of each nation's style of thought, of which language is only the expression in sounds. In this respect we may, with Coccejus and Kliefoth, refer the prophet's inability to understand the language of the heathen to this, that their manner of thinking and speaking was not formed according to the word of God, but was developed out of purely earthly, and even God-resisting factors. Only the exclusive prominence given by Kliefoth to this side of the subject is incorrect, because irreconcilable with the words, "many nations, whose words (discourse) thou dost not understand" (ver. 6). These words show that the unintelligibility of the language lies in not understanding the sounds of its words. Before אֶל־בֵּית יִשׁ׳, in ver. 5, the adversative particle *sed* is omitted (cf. Ewald, § 354*a*); the omission here is perhaps caused by this, that אַתָּה שָׁלוּחַ, in consequence of its position between both sentences, can be referred to both. In ver. 6 the thought of ver. 5 is expanded by the addition of עַמִּים רַבִּים, "*many nations*" with different languages, in order to show that it is not in the ability, but in the willingness, to hear the word of the Lord that the Israelites are wanting. It is not to many nations with unintelligible languages that God is sending the prophet, but to such men as are able to hear him, *i.e.* can understand his language. The second hemistich of ver. 6 is rendered by the old translators as if they had not read לֹא after אִם, "*if I sent thee to them* (the heathen), *they would hear thee.*" Modern expositors have endeavoured to extract this meaning, either by taking אִם לֹא as a particle of adjuration, *profecto*, "verily" (Rosenmüller, Hävernick, and others), or reading אִם לֻא, as Ewald does, after Gen. xxiii. 13. But the one is as untenable as the other: against אִם לֻא stands the fact that לֹו is written with ו, not with א; against the view that it is a particle of adjuration, stands partly the position of the words before אֲלֵיהֶם של׳, which, according to the sense, must belong to הֵמָּה ישמ׳, partly the impossibility of taking שְׁלַחְתִּיךָ conditionally after the preceding אִם לֹא. "If such were the case, Ezekiel would have really done all he could to conceal his meaning" (Hitzig), for אִם לֹא, after a negative sentence preceding, signifies "but;" cf. Gen. xxiv. 38. Consequently neither the one view nor the other yields an appropriate sense. "If I had sent thee to the heathen," involves a repenting of the act, which is not beseeming in God. Against the meaning "*profecto*" is the consideration that the idea, "Had I sent thee to the heathen, verily they would hear thee," is in contradiction with the designation of the heathen as those whose language the prophet does not understand. If the heathen spoke a language unintelligible to the prophet, they consequently did not understand his speech, and could not therefore comprehend his preaching. It only remains, then, to apply the sentence simply to the Israelites, "not to heathen nations, but to the Israelites have I sent thee," and to take יִשְׁמְעוּ as potential, "they are able ,to fear thee," "they can understand thy words." This in ver. 7 is closed by the *antithesis*,

"But the house of Israel will not hear thee, because they will not hear me (Jehovah), as they are morally hardened." With 7*b*, cf. ii. 4. The Lord, however, will provide His prophet with power to resist this obduracy; will lend him unbending courage and unshaken firmness, ver. 8; cf. Jer. xv. 20. He will make his brow hard as adamant (cf. Zech. vii. 12), which is harder than rock; therefore he shall not fear before the obduracy of Israel. צר, as in Ex. iv. 25, = צוּר. As parallel passages in regard of the subject-matter, cf. Isa. l. 7 and Jer. i. 18.

Vers. 10–15. Prepared then for his vocation, Ezekiel is now transported to the sphere of his activity.—Ver. 10. *And He said to me, Son of man, all my words which I shall speak to thee, take into thy heart, and hear with thine ears.* Ver. 11. *And go to the exiles, to the children of thy people, and speak to them, and say to them, "Thus saith the Lord Jehovah," whether they may hear thee or fail (to hear thee).* Ver. 12. *And a wind raised me up, and I heard behind me the voice of a great tumult, "Praised be the glory of Jehovah," from their place hitherward.* Ver. 13. *And the noise of the wings of the creatures touching each other, and the noise of the wheels beside them, the noise of a great tumult.* Ver. 14. *And a wind raised me up, and took me, and I went thither embittered in the warmth of my spirit; and the hand of Jehovah was strong upon me.* Ver. 15. *And I came to Tel-Abib to the exiles, who dwelled by the river Chebar, and where they sat there sat I down seven days, motionless and dumb, in their midst.*—The apparent *hysteron proteron*, "take into thy heart, and hear with thine ears" (ver. 10), disappears so soon as it is observed that the clause "hear with thine ears" is connected with the following "go to the exiles," etc. The meaning is not, "*postquam auribus tuis percèpisses mea mandata, ea ne oblivioni tradas, sed corde suscipe et animo infige*" (Rosenmüller), but this, "All my words which I shall speak to thee lay to heart, that thou mayest obey them. When thou hast heard my words with thine ears, then go to the exiles and announce them to them." With ver. 11 cf. ii. 4, 5. Observe that it is still בְּנֵי עַמֶּךָ, "the children of thy" (not "my") "people." Stiff-necked Israel is no longer Jehovah's people. The command "to go to the people" is, in ver. 12 sqq., immediately executed by the prophet, the wind raising him up and transporting him to Tel-Abib, among the exiles. רוּחַ, phenomenally considered, is a wind of which God makes use to conduct the prophet to the scene of his labour; but the wind is only the sensible substratum of the spirit which transports him thither. The representation is, that "he was borne thither through the air by the wind" (Kliefoth); but not as Jerome and Kliefoth suppose, *in ipso corpore*, *i.e.* so that an actual bodily removal through the air took place, but the raising up and taking away by the wind was effected in spirit in the condition of ecstasy. Not a syllable indicates that the theophany was at an end before this removal; the contrary rather is clearly indicated by the remark that Ezekiel heard behind him the noise of the wings of the cherubim and of the wheels. And that the words תִּשָּׂאֵנִי רוּחַ do not necessitate us to suppose a bodily removal is shown by the comparison with viii. 3, xi. 1, 24, where Kliefoth also understands the same words in a spiritual sense of a merely internal—*i.e.* experienced in a state of ecstasy—removal of the prophet to Jerusalem and back again to Chaldea. The great noise which Ezekiel hears behind him proceeds, at least in part, from the appearance of the כְּבוֹד יה' being set in motion, but (according to ver. 13) not in order to remove itself from the raptured prophet, but by changing its present position, to attend the prophet to the sphere of his labour. It tells decidedly in favour of this supposition, that the prophet, according to ver. 23, again sees around him the same theophany in the valley where he begins his work. This reappearance, indeed, presupposes that it had previously disappeared from his sight, but the disappearance is to be supposed as taking place only after his call has been completed, *i.e.* after ver. 21. While being removed in a condition of ecstasy, Ezekiel heard the rushing sound, "Praised be the glory of Jehovah." מִמְּקוֹמוֹ

belongs not to בָּרוּךְ וגו׳, which would yield no appropriate sense, but to אֶשְׁמַע, where it makes no difference of importance in the meaning whether the suffix is referred to יהוה or to כבוד. Ezekiel heard the voice of the praise of God's glory issuing forth from the place where Jehovah or His glory were to be found, *i.e.* where they had appeared to the prophet, not at all from the temple. Who sounded this song of praise is not mentioned. Close by Ezekiel heard the sound, the rustling of the wings of the cherubim setting themselves in motion, and how the wings came into contact with the tips of each other, touched each other (מַשִּׁיקוֹת, from נָשַׁק, "to join," "to touch one another"). Ver. 14 describes the prophet's mood of mind as he is carried away. Raised by the wind, and carried on, he went, *i.e.* drove thither, מַר בַּחֲמַת רוּחִי, "bitter in the heat of his spirit." Although מַר is used as well of grief and mourning as of wrath and displeasure, yet mourning and sorrow are not appropriate to חֵמָה, "warmth of spirit," "anger." The supposition, however, that sorrow as well as anger were in him, or that he was melancholy while displeased (Kliefoth), is incompatible with the fundamental idea of מַר as "sharp," "bitter." Ezekiel feels himself deeply roused, even to the bitterness of anger, partly by the obduracy of Israel, partly by the commission to announce to this obdurate people, without any prospect of success, the word of the Lord. To so heavy a task he feels himself unequal, therefore his natural man rebels against the Spirit of God, which, seizing him with a strong and powerful grasp, tears him away to the place of his work; and he would seek to withdraw himself from the divine call, as Moses and Jonah once did. The hand of the Lord, however, was strong upon him, *i.e.* "held him up in this inner struggle with unyielding power" (Kliefoth); cf. Isa. viii. 11. חָזָק, "firm," "strong," differs from כָּבֵד, "heavy," Ps. xxxii. 4. תֵּל אָבִיב, *i.e.* "the hill of ears," is the name of the place where resided a colony of the exiles. The place was situated on the river Chebar (see on ch. i. 3), and derived its name, no doubt, from the fertility of the valley, rich in grain (הַבִּקְעָה, ver. 23), by which it was surrounded; nothing further, however, is known of it; cf. Gesen. *Thesaur.* p. 1505. The *Chetib* ואשר, at which the Masoretes and many expositors have unnecessarily taken offence, is to be read וָאֲשֶׁר, and to be joined with the following שָׁם, "where they sat" (so rightly the Chaldee, Syriac, and Vulgate). That this signification would be expressed differently, as Hitzig thinks, cannot be established by means of Job xxxix. 30. The *Keri* וָאֵשֵׁב is not only unnecessary, but also inappropriate, which holds true also of other conjectures of modern expositors. Ezekiel sat there seven days, מַשְׁמִים, *i.e.* neither "deprived of sensation," nor "being silent," but as the *partic. Hiphil* from שָׁמֵם, as מְשׁוֹמֵם in Ezra ix. 3, 4, "rigidly without moving," therefore "motionless and dumb." The seven days are not regarded as a period of mourning, in support of which Job ii. 13 is referred to; but as both the purification and the dedication and preparation for a holy service is measured by the number seven, as being the number of God's works (cf. Ex. xxix. 29 sqq.; Lev. viii. 33 sqq.; 2 Chron. xxix. 17), so Ezekiel sits for a week "motionless and dumb," to master the impression which the word of God, conveyed to him in ecstatic vision, had made upon his mind, and to prepare and sanctify himself for his vocation (Kliefoth).

Vers. 16–21. When these seven days are completed, there comes to him the final word, which appoints him watchman over Israel, and places before him the task and responsibility of his vocation.—Ver. 16. *And it came to pass after the lapse of seven days, that the word of Jehovah came to me as follows:* Ver. 17. *Son of man, I have set thee to be a watchman over the house of Israel; thou shalt hear the word from my mouth, and thou shalt warn them from me* Ver. 18. *If I say to the sinner, Thou shalt surely die, and thou warnest him not, and speakest not to warn the sinner from his evil way that he may live, then shall he, the sinner, die because of his evil deeds, but his blood will I require at thy hand.* Ver. 19. *But if thou warnest the sinner, and he turn not from his wickedness and his evil way, then shall he die because of his evil deeds, but thou hast saved thy soul.* Ver. 20. *And if a righteous man turn from his righteousness, and do unrighteousness, and I lay a stumblingblock before him, then shall he die; if thou hast not warned him, he shall die because of his sin, and his righteousness which he has done shall not be remembered, but his blood will I require at thy hand.* Ver. 21. *But if thou warnest him—the righteous man—so that the righteous man sin not, and he do not sin, then will he live, because he has been warned, and thou hast saved thy soul.*—As a prophet for Israel, Ezekiel is like one standing upon a watch-tower (Hab. ii. 1), to watch over the condition of the people, and warn them of the dangers that threaten them (Jer. vi. 17; Isa. lvi. 10). As such, he is responsible for the souls entrusted to his charge. From the mouth of Jehovah, *i.e.* according to God's word, he is to admonish the wicked to turn from their evil ways, that they die not in their sins. מִמֶּנִּי, "from me," *i.e.* in my name, and with my commission. "If I say to the sinner," *i.e.* if I commission thee to say to him (Kimchi). As מוֹת תָּמוּת reminds us of Gen. ii. 17, so is the threatening, "his blood will I require at thy hand," an allusion to Gen. ix. 5. If the prophet does not warn the wicked man, as God has commanded him, he renders himself guilty of a deadly sin, for which God will take vengeance on him as on the murderer for the shedding of blood. An awfully solemn statement for all ministers of the word. הָרְשָׁעָה, in vers. 18 and 19, at which the LXX. have stumbled, so that they have twice omitted it, is not a substantive, and to be changed, with Hitzig, into רִשְׁעָה, but is an adjective, *foemin. gen.*, and belongs to דַּרְכּוֹ, which is construed as feminine. The righteous man who backslides is, before God, regarded as equal with the sinner who persists in his sin, if the former, notwithstanding the warning, perseveres in his backsliding (ver. 20 sqq.). שׁוּב מִצִּדְקוֹ, "to turn oneself from his righteousness," denotes the formal falling away from the path of righteousness, not mere "stumbling or sinning from weakness." עָשָׂה עָוֶל, "to do unrighteousness," "to act perversely," is "*se prorsus dedere impietati*" (Calvin). וְנָתַתִּי מִכְשׁוֹל belongs still to the *protasis*, הוּא יָמוּת forming the *apodosis*, not a relative sentence, — as Ewald and Hitzig suppose,—"so that he, or, in consequence of which, he die." מִכְשׁוֹל, "object of offence," by which any one comes to fall, is not destruction, considered as punishment deserved (Calvin, Hävernick), but everything that God puts in the way of the sinner, in order that the sin, which is germinating in his soul, may come forth to the light, and ripen to maturity. God, indeed, neither causes sin, nor desires the death of the sinner; and in this sense He does not tempt to evil (Jas. i. 13), but He guides and places the sinner in relations in life in which he must come to a decision for or against what is good and divine, and either suppress the sinful lusts of his heart, or burst the barriers which are opposed to their satisfaction. If he does not do the former, but the latter, evil gains within him more and more strength, so that he becomes the servant of sin, and finally reaches a point where conversion is impossible. In this consists the מִכְשׁוֹל, which God places before him, who turns away from righteousness to unrighteousness or evil, but not in this, that God lets man run on in order that he may die or perish. For יָמוּת does not stand for וָמֵת, and there is therefore no ground for a change of punctuation to carry forward *Athnach* to הִזְהַרְתּוֹ (Hitzig). For the subject spoken of is not that the backsliding righteous man "in general only dies if he is not warned" (Hitzig),—that meaning is not in ver. 21, "that he, in contrast to the רָשָׁע, gives sure obedience to the warning," —but only the possibility is supposed that a צַדִּיק, who has transgressed upon the way of evil, will yield obedience to the warning, but not that he will of a certainty do this. As with the רָשָׁע in ver. 19, only the case of his resisting the warning is expressly mentioned; while the opposite case—that he may, in consequence of the warning, be converted—is not excluded; so in ver. 21, with the צַדִּיק, who has entered upon the path of unrighteousness, only the case of conversion in consequence of the warning is expressly mentioned, without the possibility of his hardening himself against the prophet's word being thereby excluded. For the instruction of the prophet it was sufficient to bring forward the two cases mentioned, as it appears from them that in the one case as well as in the other he has done his duty, and saved his soul.

CHAP. III. 22–V. 17. THE DESTINY OF JERUSALEM AND ITS INHABITANTS.

Vers. 22–27 in ch. iii. no longer belong to the prophet's inauguration and introduction into office, nor do they form the conclusion of his call, but the introduction to his first prophetic act and prediction, as has been rightly recognised by Ewald and Kliefoth. This appears already from the introductory formula, "The hand of Jehovah came upon me" (ver. 22), and, more distinctly still, from the glory of Jehovah appearing anew to the prophet (when, in obedience to a divine impulse, he had gone down into the valley), in the form in which he had seen it by the river Chebar, and giving him a commission to announce by word and symbol the siege of Jerusalem, and the fate of its inhabitants. For, that the divine commission did not consist merely in the general directions, ch. iii. 25–27, but is first given in its principal parts in ch. iv. and v., is indisputably evident from the repetition of the words וְאַתָּה בֶן־אָדָם in ch. iii. 25, iv. 1, and v. 1. With וְאַתָּה neither can the first nor, in general, a new prophecy begin. This has been recognised by Hitzig himself in ch. iv. 1, where he remarks that the first of the three oracles which follow down to viii. 1, and which he makes begin with iv. 1, "attaches itself to ch. iii. 25–27 as a continuation of the same." But what holds true of iv. 1 must hold true also of iii. 25, viz. that no new oracle can begin with this verse, but that it is connected with iii. 22–24. The commencement, then, we have to seek in the formula, "and the hand of Jehovah came upon me" (iii. 22), with which also viii. 1 (where only וַתִּפֹּל stands instead of וַתְּהִי) and xl. 1—new oracles—are introduced. No doubt these passages are preceded by chronological notices, while in iii. 22 every note of time is wanting. But nothing further can be inferred from this, than that the divine word contained in iii. 25–v. 17 was imparted to the prophet immediately after his consecration and call, so that it still falls under the date of ch. i. 2; which may also be discovered from this, that the שָׁם in ver. 22 points to the locality named in ver. 15.

Immediately after his call, then, and still in the same place where the last word of calling (iii. 16–21) was addressed to him, namely, at Tel-Abib, in the midst of the exiles, Ezekiel received the first divine revelation which, as prophet, he was to announce to the people. This revelation is introduced by the words in ch. iii. 22–24; and divided into three sections by the thrice-occurring, similar address, "And thou, son of man" (iii. 25, iv. 1, v. 1). In the first section, ch. iii. 25–27, God gives him general injunctions as to his conduct while carrying out the divine commission; in the second, ch. iv., He commands him to represent symbolically the siege of Jerusalem with its miseries; and in the third, ch. v., the destiny of the inhabitants after the capture of the city.

Chap. iii. 22–27. Introduction to the first prophetic announcement.—Ver. 22. *And there came upon me there the hand of Jehovah, and He said to me, Up! go into the valley, there will I speak to thee.* Ver. 23. *And I arose, and went into the valley: and, lo, there stood the glory of Jehovah, like the glory which I had seen at the river Chebar: and I fell upon my face.* Ver. 24. *And spirit came into me, and placed me on my feet, and He spake with me, and said to me, Go, and shut thyself in thy house.*—הַבִּקְעָה is, without doubt, the valley situated near Tel-Abib. Ezekiel is to go out from the midst of the exiles—where, according to ver. 15, he had found himself—into the valley, because God will reveal Himself to him only in solitude.

When he had complied with this command, there appears to him there the glory of Jehovah, in the same form in which it had appeared to him at the Chaboras (i. 4–28); before it he falls, a second time, on his face; but is also, as on the first occasion, again raised to his feet, cf. i. 28–ii. 2. Hereupon the Lord commands him to shut himself up in his house,—which doubtless he inhabited in Tel-Abib,—not probably "as a sign of his future destiny," as a realistic explanation of the words, "Thou canst not walk in their midst (ver. 25); they will prevent thee by force from freely exercising thy vocation in the midst of the people." For in that case the "shutting of himself up in the house" would be an arbitrary identification with the "binding with fetters" (ver. 25); and besides, the significance of the address וְאַתָּה בֶן אָדָם, and its repetition in iv. 1 and v. 1, would be misconceived. For as in iv. 1 and v. 1 there are introduced with this address the principal parts of the duty which Ezekiel was to perform, so the proper divine instruction may also first begin with the same in iii. 25; consequently the command "to shut himself up in his house" can only have the significance of a preliminary divine injunction, without possessing any significancy in itself; but only "serve as a means for carrying out what the prophet is commissioned to do in the following chapters" (Kliefoth), *i.e.* can only mean that he is to perform in his own house what is commanded him in ch. iv. and v., or that he is not to leave his house during their performance. More can hardly be sought in this injunction, nor can it at all be taken to mean that, having shut himself up from others in his house, he is to allow no one to approach him; but only that he is not to leave his dwelling. For, according to iv. 3, the symbolical representation of the siege of Jerusalem is to be a sign for the house of Israel; and according to iv. 12, Ezekiel is, during this symbolical action, to bake his bread before their eyes. From this it is seen that his contemporaries might come to him and observe his proceedings.

Vers. 25–27. The general divine instructions.—Ver. 25. *And thou, son of man, lo, they will lay cords upon thee, and bind thee therewith, so that thou canst not go out into their midst.* Ver. 26. *And I shall make thy tongue cleave to thy palate, that thou mayest be dumb, and mayest not serve them as a reprover: for they are a stiff-necked generation.* Ver. 27. *But when I speak to thee, I will open thy mouth, that thou mayest say to them, Thus sayeth the Lord Jehovah, Let him who wishes to hear, hear, and let him who neglects, neglect (to hear): for they are a stiff necked generation.*—The meaning of this general injunction depends upon the determination of the subject in נָתְנוּ, ver. 25. Most expositors think of the prophet's countrymen, who are to bind him with cords so that he shall not be able to leave his house. The words וְלֹא תֵצֵא בְּתוֹכָם appear to support this, as the suffix in בְּתוֹכָם indisputably refers to his countrymen. But this circumstance is by no means decisive; while against this view is the twofold difficulty,—firstly, that a binding of the prophet with cords by his countrymen is scarcely reconcilable with what he performs in ch. iv. and v.; secondly, of hostile attacks by the exiles upon the prophet there is not a trace to be discovered in the entire remainder of the book. The house of Israel is indeed repeatedly described as a stiff-necked race, as hardened and obdurate towards God's word; but any embitterment of feeling against the prophet, which should have risen so far as to bind him, or even to make direct attempts to prevent him from exercising his prophetic calling, can, after what is related in xxxiii. 30–33 regarding the position of the people towards him, hardly be imagined. Further, the binding and fettering of the prophet is to be regarded as of the same kind with the cleaving of his tongue to his jaws, so that he should be silent and not speak (ver. 26). It is God, however, who suspends this dumbness over him; and according to iv. 8, it is also God who binds him with cords, so that he cannot stir from one side to the other. The demonstrative power of the latter passage is not to be weakened by the objection that it is a passage of an altogether different kind, and the connection altogether different (Hävernick). For the complete difference between the two passages would first have to be proved. The object, indeed, of the binding of the prophet in iv. 8 is different from that in our verse. Here it is to render it impossible for the prophet to go out of the house; in iv. 8, it is to prevent him from moving from one side to the other. But the one object does not exclude the other; both statements coincide, rather, in the general thought that the prophet must adapt himself entirely to the divine will,—not only not leave the house, but lie also for 390 days upon one side without turning.—We might rather, with Kliefoth, understand iv. 8 to mean that God accomplished the binding of the prophet by human instruments—viz. that He caused him to be bound by foreigners (iii. 25). But this supposition also would only be justified, if either the sense of the words in iii. 25, or other good reasons, pronounced in favour of the view that it was the exiles who had bound the prophet. But as this is not the case, so we are not at liberty to explain the definite נָתַתִּי, "I lay on" (iv. 8), according to the indefinite נָתְנוּ, "they lay on," or "one lays on" (iii. 25); but must, on the contrary, understand our verse in accordance with iv. 8, and (with Hitzig) think of heavenly powers as the subject to נָתְנוּ,—as in Job vii. 3; Dan. iv. 28; Luke xii. 20,—without, in so doing, completely identifying the declaration in our verse with that in iv. 8, as if in the latter passage only that was brought to completion which had been here (iii. 25) predicted. If, however, the binding of the prophet proceeds from invisible powers, the expression is not to be understood literally,—of a binding with material cords;—but God binds him by a spiritual power, so that he can neither leave his house nor go forth to his countrymen, nor, at a later time (iv. 8), change the position prescribed to him. This is done, however, not to prevent the exercise of his vocation, but, on the contrary, to make him fitted for the successful performance of the work commanded him. He is not to quit his house, nor enter into fellowship and intercourse with his exiled countrymen, that he may show himself, by separation from them, to be a prophet and organ of the Lord. On the same grounds he is also (vers. 26, 27) to keep silence, and not even correct them with words, but only to speak when God opens his mouth for that purpose; to remain, moreover, unconcerned whether they listen to his words or not (cf. ii. 4, 7). He is to do both of these things, because his contemporaries are a stiff-necked race; cf. ver. 9 and ii. 5, 7. That he may not speak from any impulse of his own, God will cause his tongue to cleave to his jaws, so that he cannot speak; cf. Ps. cxxxvii. 6. "That the prophet is to refrain from all speech—even from the utterance of the words given him by God—will, on the one hand, make the divine words which he utters appear the more distinctly as such; while, on the other, be an evidence to his hearers of the silent sorrow with which he is filled by the contents of the divine word, and with which they also ought justly to be filled" (Kliefoth).

This state of silence, according to which he is only then to speak when God opened his mouth for the utterance of words which were to be given him, is, indeed, at first imposed upon the prophet—as follows from the relation of vers. 25–27 to ch. iv. and v.—only for the duration of the period ch. iii. 25 to v. 17, or rather vii. 27. But the divine injunction extends, as Kliefoth has rightly recognised, still further on—over the whole period up to the fulfilment of his prophecies of threatening by the destruction of Jerusalem. This appears especially from this, that in xxiv. 27 and xxxiii. 22 there is an undeniable reference to the silence imposed upon him in our verse, and with reference to which it is said, that when the messenger should bring back the news of the fall of Jerusalem, his mouth should be opened and he should be no longer dumb. The reference in xxiv. 27 and in xxxiii. 22 to the verse before us has been observed by most expositors; but several of them would limit the silence of the prophet merely to the time which lies between ch. xxiv. and xxxiii. 21 sqq. This is quite arbitrary, as neither in ch. xxiv. nor in ch. xxxiii. is silence imposed upon him; but in both chapters it is only stated that he should no longer be dumb after the receipt of the intelligence that Jerusalem had been destroyed by the Chaldeans. The supposition of Schmieder, moreover, is untenable, that the injunction of ver. 25 refers to the turning-point in the prophet's office, which commenced on the day when the siege of Jerusalem actually began. For although this day forms a turning-point in the prophetic activity of Ezekiel, in so far as he on it announced to the people for the last time the destruction of Jerusalem, and then spake no more to Israel until the occurrence of this event, yet it is not said in xxiv. 27 that he was then to be dumb from that day onwards. The hypothesis then only remains, that what was imposed and enjoined on the prophet, in vers. 26 and 27, should remain in force for the whole period from the commencement of his prophetic activity to the receipt of the news of the fall of Jerusalem, by the arrival of a messenger on the banks of the Chaboras. Therewith is also connected the position of this injunction at the head of the first prophecy delivered to him (not at his call), if only the contents and importance of this oracle be understood and recognised, that it embraces not merely the siege of Jerusalem, but also the capture and destruction of the city, and the dispersion of the people among the heathen,—consequently contains *in nuce* all that Ezekiel had to announce to the people down to the occurrence of this calamity, and which, in all the divine words from ch. vi. to ch. xxiv., he had again and again, though only in different ways, actually announced. If all the discourses down to ch. xxiv. are only further expositions and attestations of the revelation of God in ch. iv. and v., then the behaviour which was enjoined on him at the time of this announcement was to be maintained during all following discourses of similar contents. Besides, for a correct appreciation of the divine precept in vers. 26 and 27, it is also to be noticed that the prophet is not to keep entire silence, except when God inspires him to speak; but that his keeping silence is explained to mean, that he is to be to his contemporaries no אִישׁ מוֹכִיחַ, "no reprover," and consequently will place their sins before them to no greater extent, and in no other way, than God expressly directs him. Understood in this way, the silence is in contradiction neither with the words of God communicated in ch. vi. to xxiv., nor with the predictions directed against foreign nations in ch. xxv.–xxxiii., several of which fall within the time of the siege of Jerusalem. Cf. with this the remark upon xxiv. 27 and xxxiii. 22.

Chap. iv. THE SIGN OF THE SIEGE OF JERUSALEM.—This sign, which Ezekiel is to perform in his own house before the eyes of the exiles who visit him, consists in three interconnected and mutually-supplementary symbolical acts, the first of which is described in vers. 1–3, the second in vers. 4–8, and the third in vers. 9–17. In the first place, he is symbolically to represent the impending siege of Jerusalem (vers. 1–3); in the second place, by lying upon one side, he is to announce the punishment of Israel's sin (vers. 4–8); in the third place, by the nature of his food, he is, while lying upon one side, to hold forth to view the terrible consequences of the siege to Israel. The close connection as to their subject-matter of these three actions appears clearly from this, that the prophet, accord-to ver. 7, while lying upon one side, is to direct his look and his arm upon the picture of the besieged city before him; and, according to ver. 8, is to lie upon his side as long as the siege lasts, and during that time is to nourish himself in the manner prescribed in ver. 9 sqq. In harmony with this is the formal division of the chapter, inasmuch as the three acts, which the prophet is to perform for the purpose of portraying the impending siege of Jerusalem, are co-ordinated to each other by the repetition of the address וְאַתָּה in vers. 3, 4, and 8, and subordinated to the general injunction—to portray Jerusalem as a besieged city—introduced in ver. 1 with the words וְאַתָּה בֶן אָדָם.

Vers. 1–3. The first symbolical action.—Ver. 1. *And thou, son of man, take to thyself a brick, and lay it before thee, and draw thereon a city, Jerusalem:* Ver. 2. *And direct a siege against it; build against it siege-towers, raise up a mound against it, erect camps against it, and place battering-rams against it round about.* Ver. 3. *And thou, take to thyself an iron pan, and place it as an iron wall between thee and the city, and direct thy face towards it; thus let it be in a state of siege, and besiege it. Let it be a sign to the house of Israel.*

The directions in vers. 1 and 2 contain the general basis for the symbolical siege of Jerusalem, which the prophet is to lay before Israel as a sign. Upon a brick he is to sketch a city (חָקַק, to engrave with a writing instrument) which is to represent Jerusalem: around the city he is to erect siege-works—towers, walls, camps, and battering-rams; *i.e.* he is to inscribe the representation of them, and place before himself the picture of the besieged city. The selection of a brick, *i.e.* of a tile-stone, not burnt in a kiln, but merely dried in the sun, is not, as Hävernick supposes, a reminiscence of Babylon and monumental inscriptions; in Palestine, also, such bricks were a common building material (Isa. ix. 9), in consequence of which the selection of such a soft mass of clay, on which a picture might be easily inscribed, was readily suggested. נָתַן מָצוֹר = שׂוּם מָצוֹר, Mic. iv. 14, "to make a siege," *i.e.* "to bring forward siege-works." מָצוֹר is therefore the general expression which is specialized in the following clauses by דָּיֵק, "siege-towers" (see on 2 Kings xxv. 1); by סֹלְלָה, "mound" (see on 2 Sam. xx. 15); מַחֲנוֹת, "camps" in the plural, because the hostile army raises several camps around the city; כָּרִים, "battering-rams," "wall-breakers," *arietes;* according to Joseph Kimchi, "iron rams," to break in the walls (and gates, xxi. 27). They consisted of strong beams of hard wood, furnished at the end with a ram's head made of iron, which were suspended by a chain, and driven forcibly against the wall by the soldiers. Compare the description of them by Josephus, *de bello Judaico* iii. 7. 19. The suffix in עָלֶיהָ, in ver. 2, refers to עִיר. The siege-works which are named were not probably to be placed by Ezekiel as little figures around the brick, so that the latter would represent the city, but to be engraved upon the brick around the city thereon portrayed. The expressions, "to *make* a siege," "to *build* towers," "to erect a mound," etc., are selected because the drawing was to represent what is done when a city is besieged. In ver. 3, in reference to this, the inscribed picture of the city is at once termed "city," and in ver. 7 the picture of the besieged Jerusalem, "the siege of Jerusalem." The meaning of the picture is clear. Every one who saw it was to recognise that Jerusalem will be besieged. But the prophet is to do still more; he is to take in hand the siege itself, and to carry it out. To that end, he is to place an iron pan as an iron wall between himself and the city sketched on the brick, and direct his countenance stedfastly towards the city (הֵכִין), and so besiege it. The iron pan, erected as a wall, is to represent neither the wall of the city (Ewald) nor the enemies' rampart, for this was already depicted on the brick; while to represent it, *i.e.* the city wall, as "iron," *i.e.* immoveably fast, would be contrary to the meaning of the prophecy. The iron wall represents, as Rosenmüller, after the hints of Theodoret, Cornelius a Lapide, and others, has already observed, a firm, impregnable wall of partition, which the prophet as messenger and representative of God is to raise between himself and the beleaguered city, *ut significaret, quasi ferreum murum interjectum esse cives inter et se*, i.e. *Deum Deique decretum et sententiam contra illos latam esse irrevocabilem, nec Deum civium preces et querimonias auditurum aut iis ad misericordiam flectendum.* Cf. Isa lix. 2; Lam. iii. 44. מַחֲבַת, "pan," *i.e.* an iron plate for baking their loaves and slices of cakes; see on Lev. ii. 5. The selection of such an iron plate for the purpose mentioned is not to be explained, as Kliefoth thinks, from the circumstance that the pan is primarily to serve the prophet for preparing his food while he is occupied in completing his sketch. The text says nothing of that. If he were to have employed the pan for such a purpose, he could not, at the same time, have placed it as a wall between himself and the city. The choice is to be explained simply from this, that such a plate was to be found in every household, and was quite fitted for the object intended. If any other symbolical element is contained in it, the hard ignoble metal might, perhaps, with Grotius, be taken to typify the hard, wicked heart of the inhabitants of Jerusalem; cf. xxii. 18; Jer. xv. 12. The symbolical siege of Jerusalem is to be a sign for the house of Israel, *i.e.* a pre-announcement of its impending destiny. The house of Israel is the whole covenant people, not merely the ten tribes as in ver. 5, in contradistinction to the house of Judah (ver. 6).

Vers. 4–8. The second symbolical act.—Ver. 4. *And do thou lay thyself upon thy left side, and lay upon it the evil deeds of the house of Israel; for the number of the days during which thou liest thereon shalt thou bear their evil deeds.* Ver. 5. *And I reckon to thee the years of their evil deeds as a number of days; three hundred and ninety days shalt thou bear the evil deeds of the house of Israel.* Ver. 6. *And (when) thou hast completed these, thou shalt then lay thyself a second time upon thy right side, and bear the evil deeds of the house of Judah forty days; each day I reckon to thee as a year.* Ver. 7. *And upon the siege of Jerusalem shalt thou stedfastly direct thy countenance, and thy naked arm, and shalt prophesy against it.* Ver. 8. *And, lo, I lay cords upon thee, that thou stir not from one side to the other until thou hast ended the days of thy siege.*—Whilst Ezekiel, as as God's representative, carries out in a symbolical manner the siege of Jerusalem, he is in this situation to portray at the same time the destiny of the people of Israel beleaguered in their metropolis. Lying upon his left side for 390 days without turning, he is to bear the guilt of Israel's sin; then, lying 40 days more upon his right side, he is to bear the guilt of Judah's sin. In so doing, the number of the *days* during which he reclines upon his sides shall be accounted as exactly equal to the same number of *years* of their sinning. נָשָׂא עָוֹן, "to bear the evil deeds," *i.e.* to take upon himself the consequence of sin, and to atone for them, to suffer the punishment of sin; cf. Num. xiv. 34, etc. Sin, which produces guilt and punishment, is regarded as a burden or weight, which Ezekiel is to lay upon the side upon which he reclines, and in this way bear it. This bearing, however, of the guilt of sin is not to be viewed as vicarious and mediatorial, as in the sacrifice of atonement, but is intended as purely epideictic and symbolical; that is to say, Ezekiel, by his lying so long bound under the burden of Israel and Judah which was laid upon his side, is to show to the people how they are to be cast down by the siege of Jerusalem, and how, while lying on the ground, without the possibility of turning or rising, they are to bear the punishment of their sins. The full understanding of this symbolical act, however, depends upon the explanation of the specified periods of time, with regard to which the various views exhibit great discrepancy.

In the first place, the separation of the guilt into that of the house of Israel and that of the house of Judah is closely connected with the division of the covenant people into the two kingdoms of Israel and Judah. That Ezekiel now is to bear the sin of Israel upon the left, that of Judah on the right side, is not fully explained by the circumstance that the kingdom of the ten tribes lay to the left, *i.e.* to the north, the kingdom of Judah to the right, *i.e.* to the south of Jerusalem, but must undoubtedly point at the same time to the pre-eminence of Judah over Israel; cf. Eccles. x. 2. This pre-eminence of Judah is manifestly exhibited in its period of punishment extending only to 40 days = 40 years; that of Israel, on the contrary, 390 days = 390 years. These numbers, however, cannot be satisfactorily explained from a chronological point of view, whether they be referred to the time during which Israel and Judah sinned, and heaped upon themselves guilt which was to be punished, or to the time during which they were to atone, or suffer punishment for their sins. Of themselves, both references are possible; the first, viz. in so far as the days in which Ezekiel is to bear the guilt of Israel, might be proportioned to the number of the years of their guilt, as many Rabbins, Vatablus, Calvin, Lightfoot, Vitringa, J. D. Michaelis, and others suppose, while in so doing the years are calculated very differently; cf. des Vignoles, *Chronol.* I. p. 479 sqq., and Rosenmüller, *Scholia, Excurs.* to ch. iv. All these hypotheses, however, are shattered by the impossibility of pointing out the specified periods of time, so as to harmonize with the chronology. If the days, reckoned as years, correspond to the duration of their sinning, then, in the case of the house of Israel, only the duration of this kingdom could come into consideration, as the period of punishment began with the captivity of the ten tribes. But this kingdom lasted only 253 years. The remaining 137 years the Rabbins have attempted to supply from the period of the Judges; others, from the time of the destruction of the ten tribes down to that of Ezekiel, or even to that of the destruction of Jerusalem. Both are altogether arbitrary. Still less can the 40 years of Judah be calculated, as all the determinations of the beginning and the end are mere phantoms of the air. The fortieth year before our prophecy would nearly coincide with the eighteenth year of Josiah's reign, and therefore with the year in which this pious king effected the reformation of religion. Ezekiel, however, could not represent this year as marking the commencement of Judah's sin. We must therefore, as the literal meaning of the words primarily indicates, regard the specified periods of time as periods of punishment for Israel and Judah. Since Ezekiel, then, had to maintain during the symbolical siege of Jerusalem this attitude of reclining for Israel and Judah, and after the completion of the 390 days for Israel must lie a second time (שֵׁנִית, ver. 6) 40 days for Judah, he had to recline in all 430 (390 + 40) days. To include the *forty* days in the *three hundred and ninety* is contrary to the statements in the text. But to reckon the two periods *together* has not only no argument against it, but is even suggested by the circumstance that the prophet, while reclining on his left and right sides, is to represent the siege of Jerusalem. Regarded, however, as periods of punishment, both the numbers cannot be explained consistently with the chronology, but must be understood as having a symbolical signification. The space of 430 years, which is announced to both kingdoms together as the duration of their chastisement, recalls the 430 years which in the far past Israel had spent in Egypt in bondage (Ex. xii. 40). It had been already intimated to Abraham (Gen. xv. 13) that the sojourn in Egypt would be a period of servitude and humiliation for his seed; and at a later time, in consequence of the oppression which the Israelites then experienced on account of the rapid increase of their number, it was—upon the basis of the threat in Deut. xxviii. 68, that God would punish Israel for their persistent declension, by bringing them back into ignominious bondage in Egypt—taken by the prophet as a type of the banishment of rebellious Israel among the *heathen*. In this sense Hosea already threatens (viii. 13, ix. 3, 6) the ten tribes with being carried back to Egypt; see on Hos. ix. 3. Still more frequently, upon the basis of this conception, is the redemption from Assyrian and Babylonian exile announced as a new and miraculous exodus of Israel from the bondage of Egypt, *e.g.* Hos. ii. 2; Isa. xi. 15, 16.—This typical meaning lies also at the foundation of the passage before us, as, in accordance with the statement of Jerome,[1] it was already accepted by the Jews of his time, and has been again recognised in

[1] *Alii vero et maxime Judaei a secundo anno Vespasiani, quando Hierusalem a Romanis capta templumque subversum est, supputari volunt in tribulatione et angustia et captivitatis jugo populi constitui annos quadringentos*

modern times by Hävernick and Hitzig. That Ezekiel looked upon the period during which Israel had been subject to the heathen in the past as "typical of the future, is to be assumed, because only then does the number of 430 cease to be arbitrary and meaningless, and at the same time its division into 390 + 40 become explicable."—Hitzig. This latter view is not, of course, to be understood as Hitzig and Hävernick take it, *i.e.* as if the 40 years of Judah's chastisement were to be viewed apart from the 40 years' sojourn of the Israelites in the wilderness, upon which the look of the prophet would have been turned by the sojourn in Egypt. For the 40 years in the wilderness are not included in the 430 years of the Egyptian sojourn, so that Ezekiel could have reduced these 430 years to 390, and yet have added to them the 40 years of the desert wanderings. For the coming period of punishment, which is to commence for Israel with the siege of Jerusalem, is fixed at 430 years with reference to the Egyptian bondage of the Israelites, and this period is divided into 390 and 40; and this division therefore must also have, if not its point of commencement, at least a point of connection, in the 430 years of the Egyptian sojourn. The division of the period of chastisement into two parts is to be explained probably from the sending of the covenant people into the kingdom of Israel and Judah, and the appointment of a longer period of chastisement for Israel than for Judah, from the greater guilt of the ten tribes in comparison with Judah, but not the incommensurable relation of the divisions into 390 and 40 years. The foundation of this division can, first of all, only lie in this, that the number *forty* already possessed the symbolical significance of a measured period of divine visitation. This significance it had already received, not through the 40 years of the desert wandering, but through the 40 days of rain at the time of the deluge (Gen. vii. 17), so that, in conformity

triginta, et sic redire populum ad pristinum statum ut quomodo filii Israel 430 annis fuerunt in Aegypto, sic in eodem numero finiatur: scriptumque esse in Ex. xii. 40.—HIERONYMUS.

with this, the punishment of dying in the wilderness, suspended over the rebellious race of Israel at Kadesh, is already stated at 40 years, although it included in reality only 38 years; see on Num. xiv. 32 sqq. If now, however, it should be supposed that this penal sentence had contributed to the fixing of the number 40 as a symbolical number to denote a longer period of punishment, the 40 years of punishment for Judah could not yet have been viewed apart from this event. The fixing of the chastisement for Israel and Judah at 390 + 40 years could only in that case be measured by the sojourn of the Israelites in Egypt, if the relations of this sojourn presented a point of connection for a division of the 430 years into 390 and 40, *i.e.* if the 40 last years of the Egyptian servitude could somehow be distinguished from the preceding 390. A point of contact for this is offered by an event in the life of Moses which falls within that period, and was fertile in results for him as well as for the whole of Israel, viz. his flight from Egypt in consequence of the slaughter of an Egyptian who had ill-treated an Israelite. As the Israelites, his brethren, did not recognise the meaning of this act, and did not perceive that God would save them by his hand, Moses was necessitated to flee into the land of Midian, and to tarry there 40 years as a stranger, until the Lord called him to be the saviour of his nation, and sent him as His messenger to Pharaoh (Ex. ii. 11–iii. 10; Acts vii. 23–30). These 40 years were for Moses not only a time of trial and purification for his future vocation, but undoubtedly also the period of severest Egyptian oppression for the Israelites, and in this respect quite fitted to be a type of the coming time of punishment for Judah, in which was to be repeated what Israel had experienced in Egypt, that, as Israel had lost their helper and protector with the flight of Moses, so now Judah was to lose her king, and be given over to the tyranny of the heathen world-power.[1]

[1] Another ingenious explanation of the numbers in question has been attempted by Kliefoth, *Comment.* p. 123. Proceeding from the symbolical

While Ezekiel thus reclines upon one side, he is to direct his look unchangingly upon the siege of Jerusalem, *i.e.* upon the picture of the besieged city, and keep his arm bare, *i.e.* ready for action (Isa. lii. 10), and outstretched, and prophesy against the city, especially through the menacing attitude which he had taken up against it. To be able to carry this out, God will bind him with cords, *i.e.* fetter him to his couch (see on iii. 25), so that he cannot stir from one side to another until he has completed the time enjoined upon him for the siege. In this is contained the thought that the siege of Jeru-

signification of the number 40 as a measure of time for divine visitation and trial, he supposes that the prescription in Deut. xxv. 3—that if an Israelite were to be subjected to corporal punishment, he was not to receive more than 40 stripes—is founded upon this symbolical signification,—a prescription which, according to 2 Cor. xi. 24, was in practice so carried out that only 39 were actually inflicted. From the application and bearing thus given to the number 40, the symbolical numbers in the passage before us are to be explained. Every year of punishment is equivalent to a stripe of chastisement. To the house of Israel 10×39 years = stripes, were adjudged, *i.e.* to each of the ten tribes 39 years = stripes; the individual tribes are treated as so many single individuals, and each receives the amount of chastisement usual in the case of one individual. Judah, on the contrary, is regarded as the one complete historical national tribe, because in the two faithful tribes of Judah and Benjamin the people collectively were represented. Judah, then, may receive, not the number of stripes falling to individuals, but that only which fell upon one, although, as a fair compensation, not the usual number of 40, but the higher number—compatible with the Torah—of 40 stripes = years. To this explanation we would give our assent, if only the transformation into stripes or blows of the days of the prophet's reclining, or of the years of Israel's punishment, could be shown to be probable through any analogous *Biblical* example, and were not merely a deduction from the modern law of punishment, in which corporal punishment and imprisonment hold the same importance. The assumption, then, is altogether arbitrary irrespective of this, that in the case of the house of Israel the measure of punishment is fixed differently from that of Judah; in the former case, according to the number of the tribes; in the latter, according to the unity of the kingdom: in the former at 39, in the latter at 40 stripes. Finally, the presupposition that the later Jewish practice of inflicting only 39 instead of 40 stripes—in order not to transgress the letter of the law in the enumeration which probably was made at the infliction of the punishment—goes back to the time of the exile, is extremely improbable, as it altogether breathes the spirit of Pharisaic micrology.

salem is to be mentally carried on until its capture; but no new symbol of the state of prostration of the besieged Jerusalem is implied. For such a purpose the food of the prophet (ver. 9 sqq.) during this time is employed.

Vers. 9–17. The third symbolical act.—Ver. 9. *And do thou take to thyself wheat, and barley, and beans, and lentiles, and millet, and spelt, and put them in a vessel, and prepare them as bread for thyself, according to the number of the days on which thou liest on thy side; three hundred and ninety days shalt thou eat it.* Ver. 10. *And thy food, which thou eatest, shall be according to weight, twenty shekels for a day; from time to time shalt thou eat it.* Ver. 11. *And water shalt thou drink according to measure, a sixth part of the hin, from time to time shalt thou drink it.* Ver. 12. *And as barley cakes shalt thou eat it, and shalt bake it before their eyes with human excrement.* Ver. 13. *And Jehovah spake; then shall the children of Israel eat their bread polluted amongst the heathen, whither I shall drive them.* Ver. 14. *Then said I: Ah! Lord, Jehovah, my soul has never been polluted; and of a carcase, and of that which is torn, have I never eaten from my youth up until now, and abominable flesh has not come into my mouth.* Ver. 15. *Then said He unto me: Lo, I allow thee the dung of animals instead of that of man; therewith mayest thou prepare thy bread.* Ver. 16. *And He said to me, Son of man, lo, I will break the staff of bread in Jerusalem, so that they will eat bread according to weight, and in affliction, and drink water by measure, and in amazement.* Ver. 17. *Because bread and water shall fail, and they shall pine away one with another, and disappear in their guilt.*—For the whole duration of the symbolical siege of Jerusalem, Ezekiel is to furnish himself with a store of grain corn and leguminous fruits, to place this store in a vessel beside him, and daily to prepare in the form of bread a measured portion of the same, 20 shekels in weight (about 9 ounces), and to bake this as barley cakes upon a fire, prepared with dried dung, and then to partake of it at the different hours for meals throughout the day. In addition to this, he is, at the hours appointed for eating, to drink water, in like manner according to measure, a sixth part of the hin daily, *i.e.* a quantity less than a pint (cf. *Biblisch. Archäol.* II. p. 141). The Israelites, probably, *generally* prepared the עֻגוֹת from wheat flour, and not merely when they had guests (Gen. xviii. 6). Ezekiel, however, is to take, in addition, other kinds of grain with leguminous fruits, which were employed in the preparation of bread when wheat was deficient; barley—baked into bread by the poor (Judg. vii. 13; 2 Kings iv. 42; John vi. 9; see on 1 Kings v. 8); פּוֹל, "beans," a common food of the Hebrews (2 Sam. xvii. 28), which appears to have been mixed with other kinds of grain for the purpose of being baked into bread.[1] This especially holds true of the lentiles, a favourite food of the Hebrews (Gen. xxv. 29 sq.), from which, in Egypt at the present day, the poor still bake bread in times of severe famine (Sonnini, *R.* II. 390; ἄρτος φάκινος, *Athenaeus*, IV. 158). דֹּחַן, "millet," termed by the Arabs "*Dochn*" (دخن), *panicum*, a fruit cultivated in Egypt, and still more frequently in Arabia (see Wellsted, *Arab.* I. 295), consisting of longish round brown grain, resembling rice, from which, in the absence of better fruits, a sort of bad bread is baked. Cf. Celsius, *Hierobotan*, i. 453 sqq.; and Gesen. *Thesaur.* p. 333. כֻּסְּמִים, "spelt or German corn" (cf. Ex. ix. 32), a kind of grain which produces a finer and whiter flour than wheat flour; the bread, however, which is baked from it is somewhat dry, and is said to be less nutritive than wheat bread; cf. Celsius, *Hierobotan*, ii. 98 sq. Of all these fruits Ezekiel is to place certain quantities in a vessel—to indicate that all kinds of grain and leguminous fruits capable of being converted into bread will be collected, in order to bake bread for the appeasing of hunger. In the intermixture of various kinds of flour we are not, with Hitzig, to seek a transgression of the

[1] Cf. Plinii *Histor. Natur.* xviii. 30: "*Inter legumina maximus honos fabae, quippe ex qua tentatus sit etiam panis . . . Frumento etiam miscetur apud plerasque gentes et maxime panico solida ac delicatius fracta.*"

law in Lev. xix. 19; Deut. xxii. 9. מִסְפַּר is the accusative of measure or duration. The quantity is to be fixed according to the number of the days. In ver. 9 only the 390 days of the house of Israel's period of punishment are mentioned—*quod plures essent et fere universa summa* (Prado); and because this was sufficient to make prominent the hardship and oppression of the situation, the 40 days of Judah were omitted for the sake of brevity.[1] מַאֲכָלְךָ וגו׳, "thy food which thou shalt eat," *i.e.* the definite portion which thou shalt have to eat, shall be according to weight (between subject and predicate the substantive verb is to be supplied). Twenty shekels = 8 or 9 ounces of flour, yield 11 or 12 ounces of bread, *i.e.* at most the half of what a man needs in southern countries for his daily support.[2] The same is the case with the water. A sixth part of a hin, *i.e.* a quantity less than a pint, is a very niggardly allowance for a day. Both, however,—eating the

[1] Kliefoth's supposition is untenable, that what is required in vers. 9–17 refers in reality only to the 390 days of Israel, and not also to the 40 days of Judah, so that so long as Ezekiel lay and bore the sins of Israel, he was to eat his food by measure, and unclean. For this is in contradiction with the distinct announcement that during the whole time that he lay upon the one side and the other, he was besieging Jerusalem; and by the scanty and unclean food, was to portray both the deficiency of bread and water which occurred in the besieged city (ver. 17), as well as the eating of unclean bread, which impended over the Israelites when among the heathen nations. The famine which took place in Jerusalem during the siege did not affect the ten tribes, but that of Judah; while unclean bread had to be eaten among the heathen not only by the Israelites, but also by the Jews transported to Babylon. By the limitation of what is prescribed to the prophet in vers. 9–15 to the time during which the sin of Israel was to be borne, the significance of this symbolical act for Jerusalem and Judah is taken away.

[2] In our climate (Germany) we count 2 lbs. of bread for the daily supply of a man; but in warm countries the demand for food is less, so that scarcely 1½ lbs. are required. Wellsted (*Travels in Arabia*, II. p. 200) relates that "the Bedoweens will undertake a journey of 10 to 12 days without carrying with them any nutriment, save a bottle full of small cakes, baked of white flour and camel or goat's milk, and a leather bag of water. Such a cake weighs about 5 ounces. Two of them, and a mouthful of water, the latter twice within 24 hours, is all which they then partake of."

bread and drinking the water,—he shall do from time to time, *i.e.* "not throughout the entire fixed period of 390 days" (Hävernick); but he shall not eat the daily ration at once, but divided into portions according to the daily hours of meals, so that he will never be completely satisfied. In addition to this is the pollution (ver. 12 sqq.) of the scanty allowance of food by the manner in which it is prepared. עֻגַת שְׂעֹרִים is predicate: "as barley cakes," "prepared in the form of barley cakes," shalt thou eat them. The suffix in תֹּאכְלֶנָּה is neuter, and refers to לֶחֶם in ver. 9, or rather to the kinds of grain there enumerated, which are ground and baked before them: לֶחֶם, *i.e.* "food." The addition שְׂעֹרִים is not to be explained from this, that the principal part of these consisted of barley, nor does it prove that in general no other than barley cakes were known (Hitzig), but only that the cakes of barley meal, baked in the ashes, were an extremely frugal kind of bread, which that prepared by Ezekiel was to resemble. The עֻגָה was probably always baked on hot ashes, or on hot stones (1 Kings xix. 6), not on pans, as Kliefoth here supposes. The prophet, however, is to bake them in (with) human ordure. This is by no means to be understood as if he were to mix the ordure with the food, for which view Isa. xxxvi. 12 has been erroneously appealed to; but —as עֲלֵיהֶם in ver. 15 clearly shows—he is to bake it *over* the dung, *i.e.* so that dung forms the material of the fire. That the bread must be polluted by this is conceivable, although it cannot be proved from the passages in Lev. v. 3, vii. 21, and Deut. xxiii. 13 that the use of fire composed of dung made the food prepared thereon levitically unclean. The use of fire with human ordure must have communicated to the bread a loathsome smell and taste, by which it was rendered unclean, even if it had not been immediately baked in the hot ashes. That the pollution of the bread is the object of this injunction, we see from the explanation which God gives in ver. 13: "Thus shall the children of Israel eat their defiled bread among the heathen." The heart of the prophet, however, rebels against such food.

He says he has never in his life polluted himself by eating food forbidden in the law; from his youth up he has eaten no unclean flesh, neither of a carcase, nor of that which was torn by wild beasts (cf. Ex. xxii. 30; Deut. xiv. 21), nor flesh of sacrifices decayed or putrefying (פִּגּוּל, see on Lev. vii. 18; Isa. lxv. 4). On this God omits the requirement in ver. 12, and permits him to take for firing the dung of oxen instead of that of men.[1] In ver. 16 sq., finally, is given the explanation of the scanty allowance of food meted out to the prophet, namely, that the Lord, at the impending siege of Jerusalem, is to take away from the people the staff of bread, and leave them to languish in hunger and distress. The explanation is in literal adherence to the threatenings of the law (Lev. xxvi. 26 and 39), which are now to pass into fulfilment. Bread is called "staff of bread" as being indispensable for the preservation of life. To בְּמִשְׁקָל, Lev. xxvi. 26, בִּדְאָגָה, "in sorrow," is added; and to the water, בְּשִׁמָּמוֹן, "in astonishment," *i.e.* in fixed, silent pain at the miserable death, by hunger and thirst, which they see before them. נָמַקּוּ בַּעֲוֹנָם as Lev. xxvi. 39. If we, finally, cast a look over the contents of this first sign, it says that Jerusalem is soon to be besieged, and during the siege is to suffer hunger and terror as a punishment for the sins of Israel

[1] The use of dung as a material for burning is so common in the East, that it cannot be supposed that Ezekiel first became acquainted with it in a foreign country, and therefore regarded it with peculiar loathing. Human ordure, of course, so far as our knowledge goes, is never so employed, although the objection raised by Hitzig, on the other hand, that it would not yield so much heat as would be necessary for roasting without immediate contact, *i.e.* through the medium of a brick, rests upon an erroneous representation of the matter. But the employment of cattle-dung for firing could not be unknown to the Israelites, as it forms in the Hauran (the ancient Bashan) the customary firing material; cf. Wetzstein's remarks on Delitzsch's *Job*, vol. I. pp. 377, 8 (Eng. tran.), where the preparation of the *ǵelle*—this prevalent material for burning in the Hauran—from cow-dung mixed with chopped straw is minutely described; and this remark is made among others, that the flame of the *ǵelle*, prepared and dried from the dung of oxen that feed at large, is entirely without smoke, and that the ashes, which retain their heat for a lengthened time, are as clean as those of wood.

and Judah; that upon the capture of the city of Israel (Judah) they are to be dispersed among the heathen, and will there be obliged to eat unclean bread. To this in ch. v. is joined a second sign, which shows further how it shall fare with the people at and after the capture of Jerusalem (vers. 1–4); and after that a longer oracle, which developes the significance of these signs, and establishes the necessity of the penal judgment (vers. 5–17).

Chap. v. 1–4.—The Sign which is to portray Israel's impending Destiny.—Ver. 1. *And thou, son of man, take to thyself a sharp sword, as a razor shalt thou take it to thyself, and go with it over thy head, and over thy chin, and take to thee scales, and divide it (the hair).* Ver. 2. *A third part burn with fire in the midst of the city, when the days of the siege are accomplished: and take the (other) third, smite with the sword round about it: and the (remaining) third scatter to the winds; and the sword will I draw out after them.* Ver. 3. *Yet take a few of them by number, and bind them in the skirt of thy garment.* Ver. 4. *And of these again take a few, and cast them into the fire, and burn them with fire; from thence a fire shall go forth over the whole house of Israel.*—The description of this sign is easily understood. תַּעַר הַגַּלָּבִים, "razor of the barbers," is the predicate, which is to be understood to the suffix in תִּקָּחֶנָּה; and the clause states the purpose for which Ezekiel is to use the sharp sword—viz. as a razor, in order to cut off therewith the hair of his head and beard. The hair, when cut off, he is to divide into three parts with a pair of scales (the suffix in חִלַּקְתָּם refers *ad sensum* to the hair). The one third he is to burn in the city, *i.e.* not in the actual Jerusalem, but in the city, sketched on the brick, which he is symbolically besieging (iv. 3). To the city also is to be referred the suffix in סְבִיבוֹתֶיהָ, ver. 2, as is placed beyond doubt by ver. 12. In the last clause of ver. 2, which is taken from Lev. xxvi. 33, the description of the sign passes over into its exposition, for אַחֲרֵיהֶם does not refer to the hair, but to the inhabitants of Jerusalem. The significance also of this symbolical act is easily recognised, and is, moreover, stated in ver. 12. Ezekiel, in this act, represents the besieged Jerusalem. What he does to his hair, that will God do to the inhabitants of Jerusalem. As the hair of the prophet falls under the sword, used as a razor, so will the inhabitants of Jerusalem fall, when the city is captured, into destruction, and that verily an ignominious destruction. This idea is contained in the picture of the hair-cutting, which was a dishonour done to what forms the ornament of a man. See on 2 Sam. x. 4 sqq. A third of the same is to perish in the city. As the fire destroys the hair, so will pestilence and hunger consume the inhabitants of the beleaguered city (ver. 12). The second third will, on the capture of the city, fall by the sword in the environs (ver. 12); the last third will God scatter to the winds, and—as Moses has already threatened the people—will draw forth the sword after them, still to persecute and smite them (ver. 12). This sign is continued (vers. 3 and 4) in a second symbolical act, which shadows forth what is further to happen to the people when dispersed among the heathen. Of the third scattered to the winds, Ezekiel is to bind a small portion in the skirt of his garment. מִשָּׁם, "from thence," refers not to הַשְּׁלִישִׁית, but, *ad sensum*, to תִּזְרֶה לָרוּחַ: "from the place where the third that is scattered to the winds is found"—*i.e.*, as regards the subject-matter, of those who are to be found among the dispersion. The binding up into the כְּנָפַיִם, "the corners or ends of the garment" (cf. Jer. ii. 34), denotes the preservation of the few, who are gathered together out of the whole of those who are dispersed among the heathen; cf. 1 Sam. xxv. 29; Ezek. xvi. 8. But even of these few He shall still cast some into the fire, and consume them. Consequently those who are gathered together out of exile are not all to be preserved, but are still to be sifted by fire, in which process a part is consumed. This image does not refer to those who remain behind in the land, when the nation is led away captive to Babylon (Theodoret, Grotius, and others), but, as Ephrem the Syrian and Jerome saw, to those who were saved from Babylon, and to their further destiny, as is already clear from the מִשָּׁם, rightly understood. The meaning of the last clause of ver. 4 is disputed; in it, as in the final clause of ver. 2, the symbolical representation passes over into the announcement of the thing itself. מִמֶּנּוּ, which Ewald would arbitrarily alter into מִמֶּנִּי, cannot, with Hävernick, be referred to אֶל־תּוֹךְ הָאֵשׁ, because this yields a very forced sense, but relates to the whole act described in vers. 3 and 4: that a portion thereof is rescued and preserved, and yet of this portion many are consumed by fire,—from that a fire shall go forth over the whole house of Israel. This fire is explained by almost all expositors, from Theodoret and Jerome onwards, of the penal judgments which were inflicted after the exile upon the Jews, which reached their culminating point in the siege and destruction of Jerusalem by the Romans, and which still continue in their dispersion throughout the whole world. But this view, as Kliefoth has already remarked, is not only in decided antagonism to the intention of the text, but it is, moreover, altogether impossible to see how a judgment of extermination for all Israel can be deduced from the fact that a small number of the Israelites, who are scattered to the winds, is saved, and that of those who are saved a part is still consumed with fire. From thence there can only come forth a fire of purification for the whole of Israel, through which the remnant, as Isaiah had already predicted (vi. 12 sqq.), is converted into a holy seed. In the last clause, consuming by fire is not referred to. The fire, however, has not merely a destructive, but also a cleansing, purifying, and quickening power. To kindle such a fire on earth did Christ come (Luke xii. 49), and from Him the same goes out over the whole house of Israel. This view, for which Kliefoth has already rightly decided, receives a confirmation through ch. vi. 8–10, where is announced the conversion of the remnant of those Israelites who had been dispersed among the nations.

So far the symbolical acts. Before, however, we pass on to the explanation of the following oracle, we must still briefly touch the question, whether these acts were undertaken and performed by the prophet in the world of external reality, or whether they were occurrences only *internally* real, which Ezekiel experienced in spirit—*i.e.* in an ecstatic condition—and afterwards communicated to the people. Amongst modern expositors, Kliefoth has defended the former view, and has adduced the following considerations in support: A significant act, and yet also a silent, leisurely one, must be performed, that it may show something to those who behold it. Nor is the case such, as Hitzig supposes, that it would have been impossible to carry out what had been required of the prophet in ch. iv. 1–17. It had, indeed, its difficulty; but God sometimes requires from His servants what is difficult, although He also helps them to the performance of it. So here He will make it easy for the prophet to recline, by binding him (iv. 8). "In the sign, this certainly was kept in view, that it should be performed; and it, moreover, *was* performed, although the text, in a manner quite intelligible with reference to an act commanded by God, does not expressly state it." For these latter assertions, however, there is anything but convincing proof. The matter is not so simple as Kliefoth supposes, although we are at one with him in this, that neither the difficulty of carrying out what was commanded in the world of external reality, nor the non-mention of the actual performance, furnishes sufficient grounds for the supposition of merely internal, spiritual occurrences. We also are of opinion that very many of the symbolical acts of the prophets were undertaken and performed in the external world, and that this supposition, as that which corresponds most fully with the literal meaning of the words, is on each occasion the most obvious, and is to be firmly adhered to, unless there can be good grounds for the opposite view. In the case now before us, we have first to take into consideration that the oracle which enjoins these symbolical acts on Ezekiel stands in close connection, both as to time and place, with the inauguration of Ezekiel to the prophetic office. The hand of the Lord comes upon him at the same place, where the concluding word at his call was addressed to him (the שָׁם, iii. 22, points back to שָׁם in iii. 15); and the circumstance that Ezekiel found himself still on the same spot to which he had been transported by the Spirit of God (iii. 14), shows that the new revelation, which he here still received, followed very *soon*, if not *immediately*, after his consecration to the office of prophet. Then, upon the occasion of this divine revelation, he is again, as at his consecration, transported into an ecstatic condition, as is clear not only from the formula, "the hand of the Lord came upon me," which in our book always has this signification, but also most undoubtedly from this, that he again sees the glory of Jehovah in the same manner as he had seen it in ch. i. —viz. when in an ecstatic condition. But if this were an ecstatic vision, it is obvious that the acts also which the divine appearance imposed upon him must be regarded as ecstatic occurrences; since the assertion that every significant act must be *performed*, in order that something may be *shown* to those who witness it, is fundamentally insufficient for the proof that this act must fall within the domain of the earthly world of sense, because the occurrences related in ch. viii.–xi. are viewed even by Kliefoth himself as purely *internal* events. As decisive, however, for the purely internal character of the symbolical acts under consideration (ch. iv. and v.), is the circumstance that the supposition of Ezekiel having, in his own house, actually lain 390 days upon his left, and then, again, 40 days upon his right side without turning, stands in irreconcilable contradiction with the fact that he, according to ch. viii. 1 sqq., was carried away in ecstasy to Jerusalem, there to behold in the temple the monstrosities of Israel's idolatry and the destruction of Jerusalem. For the proof of this, see the introduction to ch. viii.

Vers. 5–17. THE DIVINE WORD WHICH EXPLAINS THE SYMBOLICAL SIGNS, in which the judgment that is announced is laid down as to its cause (5–9) and as to its nature (10–17). —Ver. 5. *Thus says the Lord Jehovah : This Jerusalem have I placed in the midst of the nations, and raised about her the countries.* Ver. 6. *But in wickedness she resisted my laws more than the nations, and my statutes more than the countries which are round about her; for they rejected my laws, and did not walk in my statutes.* Ver. 7. *Therefore thus says the Lord Jehovah : Because ye have raged more than the nations round about you, and have not walked in my statutes, and have not obeyed my laws, and have not done even according to the laws of the nations which are round about you ;* Ver. 8. *Therefore thus saith the Lord Jehovah : Lo, I, even I, shall be against thee, and will perform judgments in thy midst before the eyes of the nations.* Ver. 9. *And I will do unto thee what I have never done, nor will again do in like manner, on account of all thine abominations.*

זאת יְרוּשׁ׳, not "this is Jerusalem," *i.e.* this is the *destiny* of Jerusalem (Hävernick), but "this Jerusalem" (Hitzig); זאת is placed before the noun in the sense of *iste*, as in Ex. xxxii. 1; cf. Ewald, § 293*b*. To place the culpability of Jerusalem in its proper prominence, the censure of her sinful conduct opens with the mention of the exalted position which God had assigned her upon earth. Jerusalem is described in ver. 5 as forming the central point of the earth : this is done, however, neither in an external, geographical (Hitzig), nor in a purely typical sense, as the city that is blessed more than any other (Calvin, Hävernick), but in a historical sense, in so far as "God's people and city actually stand in the central point of the God-directed world-development and its movements" (Kliefoth); or, in relation to the history of salvation, as the city in which God hath set up His throne of grace, from which shall go forth the law and the statutes for all nations, in order that the salvation of the whole world may be accomplished (Isa. ii. 2 sqq.; Mic. iv. 1 sqq.). But instead of keeping the laws and statutes of the Lord, Jerusalem has, on the contrary, turned to do wickedness more than the heathen nations in all the lands round about (הִמְרָה, *cum accusat. object.*, "to act rebelliously towards"). Here we may not quote Rom. ii. 12, 14 against this, as if the heathen, who did not know the law of God, did not also transgress the same, but sinned ἀνόμως; for the sinning ἀνόμως, of which the apostle speaks, is really a transgression of the law written on the heart of the heathen. With לָכֵן, in ver. 7, the penal threatening is introduced; but before the punishment is laid down, the correspondence between guilt and punishment is brought forward more prominently by repeatedly placing in juxtaposition the godless conduct of the rebellious city. הֲמָנְכֶם is infinitive, from הָמַן, a secondary form הָמוֹן, in the sense of הָמָה, "to rage," *i.e.* to rebel against God; cf. Ps. ii. 1. The last clause of ver. 7 contains a climax: "And ye have not even acted according to the laws of the heathen." This is not in any real contradiction to ch. xi. 12 (where it is made a subject of reproach to the Israelites that they have acted according to the laws of the heathen), so that we would be obliged, with Ewald and Hitzig, to expunge the לֹא in the verse before us, because wanting in the Peshito and several Hebrew manuscripts. Even in these latter, it has only been omitted to avoid the supposed contradiction with xi. 12. The solution of the apparent contradiction lies in the double meaning of the מִשְׁפְּטֵי הַגּוֹיִם. The heathen had laws which were opposed to those of God, but also such as were rooted in the law of God written upon their hearts. Obedience to the latter was good and praiseworthy; to the former, wicked and objectionable. Israel, which hated the law of God, followed the wicked and sinful laws of the heathen, and neglected to observe their *good* laws. The passage before us is to be judged by Jer. ii. 10, 11, to which Raschi had already made reference.[1] In ver. 8 the announcement of

[1] Coccejus had already well remarked on ch. xi. 12: "*Haec probe concordant. Imitabantur Judaei gentiles vel fovendo opiniones gentiles, vel etiam assumendo ritus et sacra gentilium. Sed non faciebant ut gentes, quae integre*

the punishment, interrupted by the repeated mention of the cause, is again resumed with the words לָכֵן כֹּה וגו׳. Since Jerusalem has acted worse than the heathen, God will execute His judgments upon her before the eyes of the heathen. עָשָׂה שְׁפָטִים or עָשָׂה מִשְׁפָּטִים (vers. 10, 15, ch. xi. 9, xvi. 41, etc.), "to accomplish or execute judgments," is used in Ex. xii. 12 and Num. xxxiii. 4 of the judgments which God suspended over Egypt. The punishment to be suspended shall be so great and heavy, that the like has never happened before, nor will ever happen again. These words do not require us either to refer the threatening, with Coccejus, to the last destruction of Jerusalem, which was marked by greater severity than the earlier one, or to suppose, with Hävernick, that the prophet's look is directed to both the periods of Israel's punishment—the times of the Babylonian and Roman calamity together. Both suppositions are irreconcilable with the words, as these can only be referred to the first impending penal judgment of the destruction of Jerusalem. This was, so far, more severe than any previous or subsequent one, inasmuch as by it the existence of the people of God was for a time suspended, while that Jerusalem and Israel, which were destroyed and annihilated by the Romans, were no longer the people of God, inasmuch as the latter consisted at that time of the Christian community, which was not affected by that catastrophe (Kliefoth).

Vers. 10–17. Further execution of this threat.—Ver. 10. *Therefore shall fathers devour their children in thy midst, and children shall devour their fathers: and I will exercise judgments upon thee, and disperse all thy remnant to the winds.* Ver. 11. *Therefore, as I live, is the declaration of the Lord Jehovah, Verily, because thou hast polluted my sanctuary with all thine abominations and all thy crimes, so shall I take away mine eye without mercy, and will not spare.* Ver. 12. *A third of thee shall die by the pestilence, and perish by hunger in thy*

diis suis serviebant. Nam Israelitae nomine Dei abutebantur et ipsius populus videri volebant."

midst; and the third part shall fall by the sword about thee; and the third part will I scatter to all the winds; and will draw out the sword after them. Ver. 13. *And my anger shall be fulfilled, and I will cool my wrath against them, and will take vengeance. And they shall experience that I, Jehovah, have spoken in my zeal, when I accomplish my wrath upon them.* Ver. 14. *And I will make thee a desolation and a mockery among the nations which are round about thee, before the eyes of every passer-by.* Ver. 15. *And it shall be a mockery and a scorn, a warning and a terror for the nations round about thee, when I exercise my judgments upon thee in anger and wrath and in grievous visitations. I, Jehovah, have said it.* Ver. 16. *When I send against thee the evil arrows of hunger, which minister to destruction, which I shall send to destroy you; for hunger shall I heap upon you, and shall break to you the staff of bread:* Ver. 17. *And I shall send hunger upon you, and evil beasts, which shall make thee childless; and pestilence and blood shall pass over thee; and the sword will I bring upon thee. I, Jehovah, have spoken it.*— As a proof of the unheard-of severity of the judgment, there is immediately mentioned in ver. 10 a most horrible circumstance, which had been already predicted by Moses (Lev. xxvi. 29; Deut. xxviii. 53) as that which should happen to the people when hard pressed by the enemy, viz. a famine so dreadful, during the siege of Jerusalem, that parents would eat their children, and children their parents; and after the capture of the city, the dispersion of those who remained "to all the winds, *i.e.* to all quarters of the world." This is described more minutely, as an appendix to the symbolical act in vers. 1 and 2, in vers. 11 and 12, with a solemn oath, and with repeated and prominent mention of the sins which have drawn down such chastisements. As sin, is mentioned the pollution of the temple by idolatrous abominations, which are described in detail in ch. viii. The אֶגְרַע, which is variously understood by the old translators (for which some *Codices* offer the explanatory correction אגדע), is to be explained, after Job xxxvi. 7, of the "turning away of the eye," and the עֵינִי following as the object; while וְלֹא־תָחוֹס, "that it feel no compassion," is interjected between the verb and its object with the adverbial signification of "mercilessly." For that the words ולא תחוס are adverbially subordinate to אֶגְרַע, distinctly appears from the correspondence—indicated by וְגַם אֲנִי—between אֶגְרַע and לֹא אֶחְמוֹל. Moreover, the thought, "Jehovah will mercilessly withdraw His care for the people," is not to be termed "feeble" in connection with what follows; nor is the contrast, which is indicated in the clause וְגַם־אֲנִי, lost, as Hävernick supposes. וְגַם־אֲנִי does not require גָּרַע to be understood of a positive act, which would correspond to the desecration of the sanctuary. This is shown by the last clause of the verse. The withdrawal without mercy of the divine providence is, besides, in reality, equivalent to complete devotion to destruction, as it is particularized in ver. 12. For ver. 12 see on vers. 1 and 2. By carrying out the threatened division of the people into three parts, the wrath of God is to be fulfilled, *i.e.* the full measure of the divine wrath upon the people is to be exhausted (cf. 7, 8), and God is to appear and "cool" His anger. הֵנִיחַ חֵמָה, "*sedavit iram*," occurs again in xvi. 42, xxi. 22, xxiv. 13. הִנֶּחָמְתִּי, *Hithpael*, pausal form for הִנַּחַמְתִּי, "*se consolari*," "to procure satisfaction by revenge;" cf. Isa. i. 24, and for the thing, Deut. xxviii. 63. In ver. 14 sqq. the discourse turns again from the people to the city of Jerusalem. It is to become a wilderness, as was already threatened in Lev. xxvi. 31 and 33 to the cities of Israel, and thereby a "mockery" to all nations, in the manner described in Deut. xxix. 23 sq. וְהָיְתָה, in ver. 15, is not to be changed, after the LXX., Vulgate, and some MSS., into the second person; but Jerusalem is to be regarded as the subject which is to become the object of scorn and hatred, etc., when God accomplishes His judgments. מוּסָר is a warning-example. Among the judgments which are to overtake it, in ver. 16, hunger is again made specially prominent (cf. iv. 16); and first in ver. 17 are wild beasts, pestilence, blood, and sword added, and a quartette of judgments announced as in

xiv. 21. For pestilence and blood are comprehended together as a unity by means of the predicate. Their connection is to be understood according to xiv. 19, and the number four is significant, as in xiv. 21; Jer. xv. 3 sqq. For more minute details as to the meaning, see on xiv. 21. The evil arrows point back to Deut. xxxii. 23; the evil beasts, to Lev. xxiv. 22 and Deut. xxxii. 24 sqq. To produce an impression, the prophet heaps his words together. *Unum ejus consilium fuit penetrare in animos populi quasi lapideos et ferreos. Hæc igitur est ratio, cur hic tanta varietate utatur et exornet suam doctrînam variis figuris* (Calvin).

CHAP. VI. THE JUDGMENT UPON THE IDOLATROUS PLACES, AND ON THE IDOL-WORSHIPPERS.

To God's address in vers. 5–17, explaining the signs in ch. iv. 1–5, are appended in ch. vi. and vii. two additional oracles, which present a further development of the contents of these signs, the judgment portrayed by them in its extent and greatness. In ch. vi. there is announced, in the first section, to the idolatrous places, and on their account to the land, desolation, and to the idolaters, destruction (vers. 3–7); and to this is added the prospect of a remnant of the people, who are dispersed among the heathen, coming to be converted to the Lord (vers. 8–10). In the second section the necessity and terrible character of the impending judgment is repeatedly described at length as an appendix to vers. 12, 14 (vers. 11–14).

Vers. 1–7. The desolation of the land, and destruction of the idolaters.—Ver. 1. *And the word of the Lord came to me, saying:* Ver. 2. *Son of man, turn thy face towards the mountains of Israel, and prophesy against them.* Ver. 3. *And say, Ye mountains of Israel, hear the word of the Lord Jehovah: Thus saith the Lord Jehovah to the mountains, and to the hills, to the valleys, and to the low grounds, Behold, I bring the sword upon you, and destroy your high places.* Ver. 4. *Your altars shall be made desolate, and your sun-pillars shall be broken; and I shall make your slain fall in the presence of your idols.* Ver. 5. *And I will lay the corpses of the children of Israel before their idols, and will scatter your bones round about your altars.* Ver. 6. *In all your dwellings shall the cities be made desolate, and the high places waste; that your altars may be desolate and waste, and your idols broken and destroyed, and your sun-pillars hewn down, and the works of your hands exterminated.* Ver. 7. *And the slain will fall in your midst; that you may know that I am Jehovah.*—With ver. 1 cf. iii. 16. The prophet is to prophesy against the mountains of Israel. That the mountains are mentioned (ver. 2) as *pars pro toto*, is seen from ver. 3, when to the mountains and hills are added also the valleys and low grounds, as the places where idolatry was specially practised; cf. Hos. iv. 13; Jer. ii. 20, iii. 6; see on Hos. *l.c.* and Deut. xii. 2. אֲפִיקִים, in the older writings, denotes the "river channels," "the beds of the stream;" but Ezekiel uses the word as equivalent to valley, *i.e.* נַחַל, a valley with a brook or stream, like the Arabic wady. גַּיְא, properly "deepening," "the deep ground," "the deep valley;" on the form גֵּאָיוֹת, cf. Ewald, § 186*da*. The juxtaposition of mountains and hills, of valleys and low grounds, occurs again in xxxvi. 4, 6, and xxxv. 8; the opposition between mountains and valleys also, in xxxii. 5, 6, and xxxiv. 13. The valleys are to be conceived of as furnished with trees and groves, under the shadow of which the worship of Astarte especially was practised; see on ver. 15. On the mountains and in the valleys were sanctuaries erected to Baal and Astarte. The announcement of their destruction is appended to the threatening in Lev. xxvi. 30, which Ezekiel takes up and describes at greater length. Beside the בָּמוֹת, the places of sacrifice and worship, and the חַמָּנִים, pillars or statues of Baal, dedicated to him as the sun-god, he names also the altars, which, in Lev. *l.c.* and other places, are comprehended along with the בָּמוֹת; see on Lev. xxvi. 30 and 1 Kings iii. 3. With the destruction of the idol temples, altars, and statues, the idol-worshippers are also to be smitten, so as to fall down in the presence of their idols. The fundamental meaning of the word גִּלּוּלִים, "idols," borrowed from Lev. *l.c.*, and frequently employed by Ezekiel, is uncertain; signifying either "logs of wood," from גָּלַל, "to roll" (Gesen.), or *stercorei*, from גֵּל, "dung;" not "monuments of stone" (Hävernick). Ver. 5*a* is taken quite literally from Lev. xxvi. 30*b*. The ignominy of the destruction is heightened by the bones of the slain idolaters being scattered round about the idol altars. In order that the idolatry may be entirely rooted out, the cities throughout the whole land, and all the high places, are to be devastated, ver. 6. The forms תִּישַׁמְנָה and יֶאְשְׁמוּ are probably not to be derived from שָׁמֵם (Ewald, § 138*b*), but to be referred back to a stem-form יָשֵׁם, with the signification of שָׁמֵם, the existence of which appears certain from the old name יְשִׁימוֹן in Ps. lxviii. and elsewhere. The א in יאשמו is certainly only *mater lectionis*. In ver. 7, the singular חָלָל stands as indefinitely general. The thought, "slain will fall *in your midst*," involves the idea that not all the people will fall, but that there will survive some who are saved, and prepares for what follows. The falling of the slain—the idolaters with their idols—leads to the recognition of Jehovah as the omnipotent God, and to conversion to Him.

Vers. 8-10. The survivors shall go away into banishment amongst the heathen, and shall remember the word of the Lord that will have been fulfilled.—Ver. 8. *But I shall preserve a remnant, in that there shall be to you some who have escaped the sword among the nations, when ye shall be dispersed among the lands.* Ver. 9. *And those of you who have escaped, will make mention of me among the nations whither they are led captive, when I have broken to me their whorish heart, which had departed from me, and their eyes, which went a whoring after their idols: and they shall loathe themselves because of the evil which they have done in reference to all their abominations.* Ver. 10. *And ye shall know that I am Jehovah. Not in vain have I spoken this evil to you.*—הוֹתִיר, *superstites facere*, "to make or preserve survivors." The connection with בִּהְיוֹת וגו׳ is analogous to the construction of

הוֹתִיר, in the sense of "giving a superabundance," with בְּ *rei*, Deut. xxviii. 11 and xxx. 9, and is not to be rejected, with Ewald and Hitzig, as inadmissible. For בִּהְיוֹת is supported by the old versions, and the change of וְהוֹתַרְתִּי into וְדִבַּרְתִּי, which would have to be referred to ver. 7, is in opposition to the two-fold repetition of the וִידַעְתֶּם כִּי אֲנִי יהוה (וְיָדְעוּ), vers. 10 and 14, as this repetition shows that the thought in ver. 7 is different from that in 17, 21, not "they shall know that Jehovah has spoken," but "they shall know that He who has done this is Jehovah, the God of Israel." The preservation of a remnant will be shown in this, that they shall have some who have escaped the sword. הִזָּרוֹתֵיכֶם is *infin. Niph.* with a plural form of the suffix, as occurs elsewhere only with the plural ending וֹת of nouns, while Ezekiel has extended it to the וֹת of the infinitive of ל״ה verbs; cf. xvi. 31, and Ewald, § 259*b*. The remembrance of Jehovah (ver. 9) is the commencement of conversion to Him. אֲשֶׁר before נִשְׁבַּרְתִּי is not to be connected as relative pronoun with לִבָּם, but is a conjunction, though not used conditionally, "if," as in Lev. iv. 22, Deut. xi. 27, and elsewhere, but of time, ὅτε, "when," as Deut. xi. 6 and 2 Chron. xxxv. 20, and נִשְׁבַּרְתִּי in the signification of the *futur. exact.* The *Niphal* נִשְׁבַּר here is not to be taken as passive, but middle, *sibi frangere, i.e.* לִבָּם, *poenitentiâ conterere animum eorum ut ad ipsum* (*Deum*) *redeant* (Maurer, Hävernick). Besides the heart, the eyes also are mentioned, which God is to smite, as the external senses which allure the heart to whoredom. וְנָקֹטּוּ corresponds to וְזָכְרוּ at the beginning of the verse. קוּט, the later form for קוּץ, "to feel a loathing," *Hiphil*, "to be filled with loathing;" cf. Job x. 1 with ב *object.*, "in (on) their פָּנִים, faces," *i.e.* their persons or themselves: so also in xx. 43, xxxvi. 31. אֶל הָרָעוֹת, in allusion to the evil things; לְכָל־תוֹעב', in reference to all their abominations. This fruit, which is produced by chastisement, namely, that the idolaters are inspired with loathing for themselves, and led to the knowledge of Jehovah, will furnish the proof that God has not spoken in vain.

Vers. 11–14. The punishment is just and well deserved.—Ver. 11. *Thus saith the Lord Jehovah, Smite with thy hand, and stamp with thy foot, and say, Woe on all the wicked abominations of the house of Israel! that they must perish by sword, hunger, and pestilence.* Ver. 12. *He that is afar off will die by the pestilence; and he that is near at hand shall fall by the sword; and he who survives and is preserved will die of hunger: and I shall accomplish my wrath upon them.* Ver. 13. *And ye shall know that I am Jehovah, when your slain lie in the midst of your idols round about your altars, on every high hill, upon all the summits of the mountains, and under every green tree, and under every thick-leaved terebinth, on the places where they brought their pleasant incense to all their idols.* Ver. 14. *And I will stretch out my hand against them, and make the land waste and desolate more than the wilderness of Diblath, in all their dwellings: so shall ye know that I am Jehovah.*—Through clapping of the hands and stamping of the feet—the gestures which indicate violent excitement—the prophet is to make known the displeasure of Jehovah at the horrible idolatry of the people, and thereby make manifest that the penal judgment is well deserved. הַכֵּה בְכַפְּךָ is in xxi. 19 expressed more distinctly by הַךְ כַּף אֶל כַּף, "to strike one hand against the other," *i.e.* "to clap the hands;" cf. Num. xxiv. 10. אָח, an exclamation of lamentation, occurring only here and in xxi. 20. אֲשֶׁר, ver. 11, is a conjunction, "*at.*" Their abominations are so wicked, that they must be exterminated on account of them. This is specially mentioned in ver. 12. No one will escape the judgment: he who is far removed from its scene as little as he who is close at hand; while he who escapes the pestilence and the sword is to perish of hunger. נָצוּר, *servatus*, preserved, as in Isa. xlix. 6. The signification "besieged" (LXX., Vulgate, Targum, etc.), Hitzig can only maintain by arbitrarily expunging הַנִּשְׁאָר as a gloss. On ver. 12*b*, cf. v. 13; on 13*a*, cf. ver. 5; and on 13*b*, cf. ver. 3, and Hos. iv. 13; Jer. ii. 20, iii. 6; Deut. xii. 2. אֶל כָּל־גב׳, according to later usage, for עַל כָּל־גב׳. רֵיחַ נִיחֹחַ, used in the Pentateuch of sacrifices pleasing to God, is here transferred to idol sacrifices; see on Lev. i. 9 and Gen. viii. 21. On account of the prevalence of idolatry in all parts, God will make the land entirely desolate. The union of שְׁמָמָה וּמְשַׁמָּה serves to strengthen the idea; cf. xxxiii. 8 sqq., xxxv. 3. The words מִמִּדְבַּר דִּבְלָתָה are obscure, either "in the wilderness towards Diblath" (even to Diblath), or "more than the wilderness of Diblath" (מִן of comparison). There is no doubt that דִּבְלָתָה is a *nom. prop.;* cf. the name of the city דִּבְלָתַיִם in Jer. xlviii. 22; Num. xxxiii. 46. The second acceptation of the words is more probable than the first. For, if מִמִּדְבַּר is the *terminus a quo*, and דִּבְלָתָה the *terminus ad quem* of the extent of the land, then must מִמִּדְבָּר be punctuated not only as *status absolut.*, but it must also have the article; because a definite wilderness—that, namely, of Arabia—is meant. The omission of the article cannot be justified by reference to xxi. 3 or to Ps. lxxv. 7 (Hitzig, Ewald), because both passages contain general designations of the quarters of the world, with which the article is always omitted. In the next place, no *Dibla* can be pointed out in the north; and the change of *Diblatha* into *Ribla*, already proposed by Jerome, and more recently brought forward again by J. D. Michaelis, has not only against it the authority of all the old versions, but also the circumstance that the *Ribla* mentioned in 2 Kings xxiii. 33 did not form the northern boundary of Palestine, but lay on the other side of it, in the land of *Hamath;* while the הָרִבְלָה, named in Num. xxxiv. 11, is a place on the eastern boundary to the north of the Sea of Gennesareth, which would, moreover, be inappropriate as a designation of the northern boundary. Finally, the extent of the land from the south to the north is constantly expressed in a different way; cf. Num. xiii. 21 (xxxiv. 8); Josh. xiii. 5; 1 Kings viii. 65; 2 Kings xiv. 65; Amos vi. 14; 1 Chron. xiii. 5; 2 Chron. vii. 8; and even by Ezekiel himself (xlviii. 1) לְבוֹא חֲמָת is named as the boundary on the north. The form דִּבְלָתָה is similar to תִּמְנָתָה for תִּמְנָה, although the name is hardly to be explained, with Hävernick, as an appellation, after the Arabic دَبْل, *calamitas, exitium.* The wilderness of *Diblah* is unknown. With וְיָדְעוּ כִּי וגו׳ the discourse is rounded of in returning to the beginning of ver. 13, while the thoughts in vers. 13 and 14 are only a variation of vers. 4–7.

CHAP. VII. THE OVERTHROW OF ISRAEL.

The second "word of God," contained in this chapter, completes the announcement of judgment upon Jerusalem and Judah, by expanding the thought, that the end will come both quickly and inevitably upon the land and people. This word is divided into two unequal sections, by the repetition of the phrase, "Thus saith Adonai Jehovah" (vers. 2 and 5). In the first of these sections the theme is given in short, expressive, and monotonous clauses; namely, the end is drawing nigh, for God will judge Israel without mercy according to its abominations. The second section (vers. 5–27) is arranged in four strophes, and contains, in a form resembling the lamentation in chap. xix., a more minute description of the end predicted.

Vers. 1–4. The end cometh.—Ver. 1. *And the word of Jehovah came to me thus:* Ver. 2. *And thou, son of man, thus saith the Lord Jehovah: An end to the land of Israel! the end cometh upon the four borders of the land.* Ver. 3. *Now (cometh) the end upon thee, and I shall send my wrath upon thee, and judge thee according to thy ways, and bring upon thee all thine abominations.* Ver. 4. *And my eye shall not look with pity upon thee, and I shall not spare, but bring thy ways upon thee; and thy abominations shall be in the midst of thee, that ye may know that I am Jehovah.*—וְאַתָּה, with the copula, connects this word of God with the preceding one, and shows it to be a continuation. It commences with an emphatic utterance of the thought, that the end is coming to the land of Israel, *i.e.* to the kingdom of Judah, with its capital Jerusalem. Desecrated as it has been by the abominations of its inhabitants, it will cease to be the land of God's people Israel. לְאַדְמַת יִשׂ׳ (to the land of Israel) is not to be taken with כֹּה אָמַר (thus saith the Lord) in opposition to the accents, but is connected with קֵץ (an end), as in the Targ. and Vulgate, and is placed first for the sake of greater emphasis. In the construction, compare Job vi. 14. אַרְבַּעַת כַּנְפוֹת הָאָרֶץ is limited by the parallelism to the four extremities of the land of Israel. It is used elsewhere for the whole earth (Isa. xi. 12). The *Chetib* אַרְבַּעַת is placed, in opposition to the ordinary rule, before a noun in the feminine gender. The *Keri* gives the regular construction (*vid.* Ewald, § 267*c*). In ver. 3 the end is explained to be a wrathful judgment. "Give (נָתַן) thine abominations upon thee;" *i.e.* send the consequences, inflict punishment for them. The same thought is expressed in the phrase, "thine abominations shall be in the midst of thee;" in other words, they would discern them in the punishments which the abominations would bring in their train. For ver. 4*a* compare ch. v. 11.

Vers. 5-27. The execution of the judgment announced in vers. 2-4, arranged in four strophes: vers. 5-9, 10-14, 15-22, 23-27.—The *first* strophe depicts the end as a terrible calamity, and as near at hand. Vers. 3 and 4 are repeated as a refrain in vers. 8 and 9, with slight modifications. Ver. 5. *Thus saith the Lord Jehovah: Misfortune, a singular misfortune, behold, it cometh.* Ver. 6. *End cometh: there cometh the end; it waketh upon thee; behold, it cometh.* Ver. 7. *The fate cometh upon thee, inhabitants of the land: the time cometh, the day is near; tumult and not joy upon the mountains.* Ver. 8. *Now speedily will I pour out my fury upon thee, and accomplish mine anger on thee; and judge thee according to thy ways, and bring upon thee all thine abominations.* Ver. 9. *My eye shall not look with pity upon thee, and I shall not spare; according to thy ways will I bring it upon thee, and thy abominations shall be in the midst of thee, that ye may know that I, Jehovah, am smiting.*—Misfortune of a singular kind shall come. רָעָה is made more emphatic by אַחַת רָעָה, in which אַחַת is placed first for the sake of emphasis, in the sense of *unicus, singularis;* a calamity singular (unique) of its kind, such as never had occurred before (cf. ch. v. 9). In ver. 6 the poetical הֵקִיץ, it (the end) waketh upon thee, is suggested by the paronomasia with הַקֵּץ. The force of the words is weakened by supplying Jehovah as the subject to הֵקִיץ, in opposition to the context. And it will not do to supply רָעָה (evil) from ver. 5 as the subject to הִנֵּה בָאָה (behold, it cometh). בָאָה is construed impersonally: It cometh, namely, every dreadful thing which the end brings with it. The meaning of *tz^ephirâh* is doubtful. The only other passage in which it occurs is Isa. xxviii. 5, where it is used in the sense of diadem or crown, which is altogether unsuitable here. Raschi has therefore had recourse to the Syriac and Chaldee צַפְרָא, *aurora, tempus matutinum,* and Hävernick has explained it accordingly, "the dawn of an evil day." But the dawn is never used as a symbol or omen of misfortune, not even in Joel ii. 2, but solely as the sign of the bursting forth of light or of salvation. Abarbanel was on the right track when he started from the radical meaning of צָפַר, to twist, and taking *tz^ephirâh* in the sense of *orbis, ordo,* or periodical return, understood it as probably denoting *rerum fatique vicissitudinem in orbem redeuntem* (Ges. *Thes.* p. 1188). But it has been justly observed, that the rendering succession, or periodical return, can only give a forced sense in ver. 10. Winer has given a better rendering, viz. *fatum, malum fatale,* fate or destiny, for which he refers to the Arabic صَبَرَم, *intortum,* then *fatum haud mutandum inevitabile.* Different explanations have also been given of הֵד הָרִים. But the opinion that it is synonymous with הֵידָד, the joyous vintage cry (Jer. xxv. 30; Isa. xvi. 10), is a more probable one than that it is an unusual form of הוֹד, *splendor, gloria.* So much at any rate is obvious from the context, that the *hapax legomenon* הֵד is the antithesis of מְהוּמָה, tumult, or the noise of war. The shouting of the mountains, is shouting, a rejoicing upon the mountains. מִקָּרוֹב, from the immediate vicinity, in a temporal not a local sense, as in Deut. xxxii. 17 (=immediately). For כִּלָּה אַף, see ch. vi. 12. The remainder of the strophe (vers. 8*b* and 9) is a repetition of vers. 3 and 4; but מַכֶּה is added in the last clause. They shall learn that it is Jehovah who smites. This thought is expanded in the following strophe.

Vers. 10–14. *Second* strophe.—Ver. 10. *Behold the day, behold, it cometh; the fate springeth up; the rod sprouteth; the pride blossometh.* Ver. 11. *The violence riseth up as the rod of evil: nothing of them, nothing of their multitude, nothing of their crowd, and nothing glorious upon them.* Ver. 12. *The time cometh, the day approacheth: let not the buyer rejoice, and let not the seller trouble himself; for wrath cometh upon the whole multitude thereof.* Ver. 13. *For the seller will not return to that which was sold, even though his life were still among the living: for the prophecy against its whole multitude will not turn back; and no one will strengthen himself as to his life through his iniquity.* Ver. 14. *They blow the trumpet and make everything ready; but no one goeth into the battle: for my wrath cometh upon all their multitude.*—The rod is already prepared; nothing will be left of the ungodly. This is the leading thought of the strophe. The three clauses of ver. 10*b* are synonymous; but there is a gradation in the thought. The approaching fate springs up out of the earth (יָצָא, applied to the springing up of plants, as in 1 Kings v. 13; Isa. xi. 1, etc.); it sprouts as a rod, and flowers as pride. *Matteh*, the rod as an instrument of chastisement (Isa. x. 5). This rod is then called *zâdhōn*, pride, inasmuch as God makes use of a proud and violent people, namely the Chaldeans (Hab. i. 6 sqq.; Jer. l. 31 *seq.*), to inflict the punishment. Sprouting and blossoming, which are generally used as figurative representations of fresh and joyous prosperity, denote here the vigorous growth of that power which is destined to inflict the punishment. Both *châmâs* (violence) and *zâdhōn* (pride) refer to the enemy who is to chastise Israel. The violence which he employs rises up into the chastening rod of "evil," *i.e.* of ungodly Israel. In ver. 11*b* the effect of the blow is described in short, broken sentences. The emotion apparent in the frequent repetition of לֹא is intensified by the omission of the verb, which gives to the several clauses the character of exclamations. So far as the meaning is concerned, we have to insert יִהְיֶה in thought, and to take מִן in a partitive sense: there will not be anything of them, *i.e.* nothing will be left of them (the Israelites, or the inhabitants of the land). מֵהֶם (of them) is explained by the nouns which follow. הָמוֹן and the ἁπ. λεγ. הֶמְהֶם, plural of הָם or הֶמֶה, both derivatives of הָמָה, are so combined that הָמוֹן signifies the tumultuous multitude of people, הֶמֶה the multitude of possessions (like הָמוֹן, Isa. lx. 2; Ps. xxxvii. 16, etc.). The meaning which Hävernick assigns to *hâmeh*, viz. anxiety or trouble, is unsupported and inappropriate. The ἁπ. λεγ. נֹהַּ is not to be derived from נָהָה, to lament, as the Rabbins affirm; or interpreted, as Kimchi—who adopts this derivation—maintains, on the ground of Jer. xvi. 4 sqq., as signifying that, on account of the multitude of the dying, there will be no more lamentation for the dead. This leaves the *Mappik* in ה unexplained. נֹהַּ is a derivative of a root נָוָה; in Arabic, نَاهَ, *elata fuit res, eminuit, magnificus fuit*; hence נֹהַּ, *res magnifica.* When everything disappears in such a way as this, the joy occasioned by the acquisition of property, and the sorrow caused by its loss, will also pass away (ver. 12). The buyer will not rejoice in the property he has bought, for he will not be able to enjoy it; and the seller will not mourn that he has been obliged to part with his possession, for he would have lost it in any case.[1] The wrath of God is kindled against their whole multitude; that is to say, the judgment falls equally upon them all. The suffix in הֲמוֹנָהּ refers, as

[1] "It is a natural thing to rejoice in the purchase of property, and to mourn over its sale. But when slavery and captivity stare you in the face, rejoicing and mourning are equally absurd."—JEROME.

Jerome has correctly shown, to the "land of Israel" (*admath*, Yisrâēl) in ver. 2, *i.e.* to the inhabitants of the land. The words, "the seller will not return to what he has sold," are to be explained from the legal regulations concerning the year of jubilee in Lev. xxv., according to which all landed property that had been sold was to revert to its original owner (or his heir), without compensation, in the year of jubilee; so that he would then return to his *mimkâr* (Lev. xxv. 14, 27, 28). Henceforth, however, this will take place no more, even if חַיָּתָם, their (the sellers') life, should be still alive (*sc.* at the time when the return to his property would take place, according to the regulations of the year of jubilee), because Israel will be banished from the land. The clause וְעוֹד בַּחַיִּים ה' is a conditional circumstantial clause. The seller will not return (לֹא יָשׁוּב) to his possession, because the prophecy concerning the whole multitude of the people will not return (לֹא יָשׁוּב), *i.e.* will not turn back (for this meaning of שׁוּב, compare Isa. xlv. 23, lv. 11). As לֹא יָשׁוּב corresponds to the previous לֹא יָשׁוּב, so does חָזוֹן אֶת־כֹּל הֲמוֹנָהּ to חָרוֹן אֶל־כָּל־הֲמוֹנָהּ in ver. 12. In the last clause of ver. 13, חַיָּתוֹ is not to be taken with בַּעֲוֹנוֹ in the sense of "in the iniquity of his life," which makes the suffix in בַּעֲוֹנוֹ superfluous, but with יִתְחַזָּקוּ, the *Hithpael* being construed with the accusative, "strengthen himself in his life." Whether these words also refer to the year of jubilee, as Hävernick supposes, inasmuch as the regulation that every one was to recover his property was founded upon the idea of the restitution and re-creation of the theocracy, we may leave undecided; since the thought is evidently simply this: ungodly Israel shall be deprived of its possession, because the wicked shall not obtain the strengthening of his life through his sin. This thought leads on to ver. 14, in which we have a description of the utter inability to offer any successful resistance to the enemy employed in executing the judgment. There is some difficulty connected with the word בַּתָּקוֹעַ, since the *infin. absolute*, which the form תָּקוֹעַ seems to indicate, cannot be construed with either a preposition or the article. Even if the expression בִּתְקוֹעַ תִּקְעוּ in Jer. vi. 1 was floating before the mind of Ezekiel, and led to his employing the bold phrase בַּתָּקוֹעַ, this would not justify the use of the infinitive absolute with a preposition and the article. תָּקוֹעַ must be a substantive form, and denote not *clangour*, but the instrument used to sound an alarm, viz. the *shōphâr* (ch. xxxiii. 3). הָכִין, an unusual form of the *inf. abs.* (see Josh. vii. 7), used in the place of the finite tense, and signifying to equip for war, as in Nah. ii. 4. הַכֹּל, everything requisite for waging war. And no one goes into the battle, because the wrath of God turns against them (Lev. xxvi. 17), and smites them with despair (Deut. xxxii. 30).

Vers. 15–22. *Third* strophe. Thus will they fall into irresistible destruction; even their silver and gold they will not rescue, but will cast it away as useless, and leave it for the enemy.—Ver. 15. *The sword without, and pestilence and famine within: he who is in the field will die by the sword; and famine and pestilence will devour him that is in the city.* Ver. 16. *And if their escaped ones escape, they will be upon the mountains like the doves of the valleys, all moaning, every one for his iniquity.* Ver. 17. *All hands will become feeble, and all knees flow with water.* Ver. 18. *They will gird themselves with sackcloth, and terrors will cover them; on all faces there will be shame, and baldness on all their heads.* Ver. 19. *They will throw their silver into the streets, and their gold will be as filth to them. Their silver and their gold will not be able to rescue them in the day of Jehovah's wrath; they will not satisfy their souls therewith, nor fill their stomachs thereby, for it was to them a stumbling-block to guilt.* Ver. 20. *And His beautiful ornament, they used it for pride; and their abominable images, their abominations they made thereof: therefore I make it filth to them.* Ver. 21. *And I shall give it into the hand of foreigners for prey, and to the wicked of the earth for spoil, that they may defile it.* Ver. 22. *I shall turn my face from them, that they defile my treasure;*

and oppressors shall come upon it and defile it.—The chastisement of God penetrates everywhere (ver. 15 compare with ch. v. 12); even flight to the mountains, that are inaccessible to the foe (compare 1 Macc. ii. 28; Matt. xxiv. 16), will only bring misery. Those who have fled to the mountains will coo —*i.e.* mourn, moan—like the doves of the valleys, which (as Bochart has correctly interpreted the simile in his *Hieroz.* II. p. 546, ed. Ros.), "when alarmed by the bird-catcher or the hawk, are obliged to forsake their natural abode, and fly elsewhere to save their lives. The mountain doves are contrasted with those of the valleys, as wild with tame." In כֻּלָּם הֹמוֹת the figure and the fact are fused together. The words actually relate to the men who have fled; whereas the gender of הֹמוֹת is made to agree with that of כְּיוֹנֵי. The cooing of doves was regarded by the ancients as a moan (*hâgâh*), a mournful note (for proofs, see Gesen. on Isa. xxxviii. 14); for which Ezekiel uses the still stronger expression *hâmâh fremere*, to howl or growl (cf. Isa. lix. 11). The low moaning has reference to their iniquity, the punishment of which they are enduring. When the judgment bursts upon them, they will all (not merely those who have escaped, but the whole nation) be overwhelmed with terror, shame, and suffering. The words, "all knees flow with water" (for *hâlak* in this sense, compare Joel iv. 18), are a hyperbolical expression used to denote the entire loss of the strength of the knees (here, ver. 17 and ch. xxi. 12), like the heart melting and turning to water in Josh. vii. 5. With this utter despair there are associated grief and horror at the calamity that has fallen upon them, and shame and pain at the thought of the sins that have plunged them into such distress. For כִּסְּתָה פַלָּצוּת, compare Ps. lv. 6; for אֶל־כָּל־פָּנִים בּוּשָׁה, Mic. vii. 10, Jer. li. 51; and for בְּכָל־רָאשֵׁ' קָרְחָה, Isa. xv. 2, Amos viii. 10. On the custom of shaving the head bald on account of great suffering or deep sorrow, see the comm. on Mic. i. 16.—In this state of anguish they will throw all their treasures away as sinful trash (ver. 19 sqq.). By the silver and gold which they will throw away (ver. 19), we are not to understand idolatrous images particularly, — these are first spoken of in ver. 20,—but the treasures of precious metals on which they had hitherto set their hearts. They will not merely throw these away as worthless, but look upon them as *niddâh*, filth, an object of disgust, inasmuch as they have been the servants of their evil lust. The next clause, "silver and gold cannot rescue them," are a reminiscence from Zeph. i. 18. But Ezekiel gives greater force to the thought by adding, "they will not appease their hunger therewith,"—that is to say, they will not be able to protect their lives thereby, either from the sword of the enemy (see the comm. on Zeph. i. 18) or from death by starvation, because there will be no more food to purchase within the besieged city. The clause כִּי מִכְשׁוֹל וגו׳ assigns the reason for that which forms the leading thought of the verse, namely, the throwing away of the silver and gold as filth; מִכְשׁוֹל עֲוֹנָם, a stumbling-block through which one falls into guilt and punishment; צְבִי עֶדְיוֹ, the beauty of his ornament, *i.e.* his beautiful ornament. The allusion is to the silver and gold; and the singular suffix is to be explained from the fact that the prophet fixed his mind upon the people as a whole, and used the singular in a general and indefinite sense. The words are written absolutely at the commencement of the sentence; hence the suffix attached to שָׂמָהוּ. Jerome has given the true meaning of the words: "what I (God) gave for an ornament of the possessors and for their wealth, they turned into pride." And not merely to ostentatious show (in the manner depicted in Isa. iii. 16 sqq.), but to abominable images, *i.e.* idols, did they apply the costly gifts of God (cf. Hos. viii. 4, xiii. 2). עָשָׂה בְּ, to make of (gold and silver); בְּ denoting the material with which one works and of which anything is made (as in Ex. xxxi. 4, xxxviii. 8). God punishes this abuse by making it (gold and silver) into *niddâh* to them, *i.e.*, according to ver. 19, by placing them in such circumstances that they cast it away as filth, and (ver. 21) by giving it as booty to the foe. The enemy is described as "the wicked of the earth" (cf. Ps. lxxv. 9), *i.e.* godless men, who not only seize upon the possession of Israel, but in the most wicked manner lay hands upon all that is holy, and defile it. The *Chetib* חִלְּלוּהָ is to be retained, notwithstanding the fact that it was preceded by a masculine suffix. What is threatened will take place, because the Lord will turn away His face from His people (מֵהֶם, from the Israelites), *i.e.* will withdraw His gracious protection from them, so that the enemy will be able to defile His treasure. *Tsâphūn*, that which is hidden, the treasure (Job xx. 26; Obad. ver. 6). *Tsᵉphūnī* is generally supposed to refer to the temple, or the Most Holy Place in the temple. Jerome renders it *arcanum meum*, and gives this explanation: "signifying the Holy of Holies, which no one except the priests and the high priest dared to enter." This interpretation was so commonly adopted by the Fathers, that even Theodoret explains the rendering given in the Septuagint, *τὴν ἐπισκοπήν μου*, as signifying the Most Holy Place in the temple. On the other hand, the Chaldee has אַרְעָא בֵית שְׁכִינְתִּי, "the land of the house of my majesty;" and Calvin understands it as signifying "the land which was safe under His (*i.e.* God's) protection." But it is difficult to reconcile either explanation with the use of the word *tsâphūn*. The verb *tsâphan* signifies to hide, shelter, lay up in safety. These meanings do not befit either the Holy of Holies in the temple or the land of Israel. It is true that the Holy of Holies was unapproachable by the laity, and even by the ordinary priests, but it was not a secret, a hidden place; and still less was this the case with the land of Canaan. We therefore adhere to the meaning, which is so thoroughly sustained by Job xx. 26 and Obad. ver. 6,—namely, "treasure," by which, no doubt, the temple-treasure is primarily intended. This rendering suits the context, as only treasures have been referred to before; and it may be made to harmonize with בָאוּ בָהּ which follows. בּוֹא בְּ signifies not merely *intrare in locum*, but also *venire in* (*e.g.* 2 Kings vi. 23; possibly Ezek.

xxx. 4), and may therefore be very properly rendered, "to get possession of," since it is only possible to obtain possession of a treasure by penetrating into the place where it is laid up or concealed. There is nothing at variance with this in the word חִלֵּל, *profanare*, since it has already occurred in ver. 21 in connection with the defiling of treasures and jewels. Moreover, as Calvin has correctly observed, the word is employed here to denote "an indiscriminate abuse, when, instead of considering to what purpose things have been entrusted to us, we squander them rashly and without selection, in contempt and even in scorn."

Vers. 23–27. *Fourth* strophe. Still worse is coming, namely, the captivity of the people, and overthrow of the kingdom.—Ver. 23. *Make the chain, for the land is full of capital crime, and the city full of outrage.* Ver. 24. *I shall bring evil ones of the nations, that they may take possession of their houses; and I shall put an end to the pride of the strong, that their sanctuaries may be defiled.* Ver. 25. *Ruin has come; they seek salvation, but there is none.* Ver. 26. *Destruction upon destruction cometh, and report upon report ariseth; they seek visions from prophets, but the law will vanish away from the priest, and counsel from the elders.* Ver. 27. *The king will mourn, and the prince will clothe himself in horror, and the hands of the common people will tremble. I will deal with them according to their way, and according to their judgments will I judge them, that they may learn that I am Jehovah.*—Those who have escaped death by sword or famine at the conquest of Jerusalem have captivity and exile awaiting them. This is the meaning of the command to make the chain, *i.e.* the fetters needed to lead the people into exile. This punishment is necessary, because the land is full of *mishpat dâmim*, judgment of blood. This cannot mean, there is a judgment upon the shedding of blood, *i.e.* upon murder, which is conducted by Jehovah, as Hävernick supposes. Such a thought is irreconcilable with מָלְאָה, and with the parallel מָלְאָה חָמָס. מִשְׁפַּט דָּמִים is to be explained after the same manner as מִשְׁפַּט מָוֶת (a matter for sentence of death, a capital crime) in Deut. xix. 6, 21, 22, as signifying a matter for sentence of bloodshed, *i.e.* a crime of blood, or capital crime, as the Chaldee has already rendered it. Because the land is filled with capital crime, and the city (Jerusalem) with violence, the Lord will bring רָעֵי גוֹיִם, evil ones of the heathen, *i.e.* the worst of the heathen, to put an end to the pride of the Israelites. גְּאוֹן עַזִּים is not "pride of the insolents;" for עַזִּים does not stand for עַזֵּי פָנִים (Deut. xxviii. 50, etc.). The expression is rather to be explained from גְּאוֹן עֹז, pride of strength, in ch. xxiv. 21, xxx. 6, 18 (cf. Lev. xxvi. 19), and embraces everything on which a man (or a nation) bases his power and rests his confidence. The Israelites are called עַזִּים, because they thought themselves strong, or, according to ch. xxiv. 21, based their strength upon the possession of the temple and the holy land. This is indicated by וְנִחֲלוּ מְקַדְשֵׁיהֶם which follows. נִחַל, *Niphal* of חָלַל and מְקַדְשֵׁיהֶם, not a participle *Piel*, from מְקַדֵּשׁ, with the Dagesh dropped, but an unusual form, from מִקְדָּשׁ for מִקְדְּשֵׁיהֶם (*vid.* Ew. § 215*a*).—The ἀπ. λεγ. קְפָדָה, with the tone drawn back on account of the tone-syllable which follows (cf. Ges. § 29. 3. 6), signifies *excidium*, destruction (according to the Rabbins), from קָפַד, to shrink or roll up (Isa. xxxviii. 12). בָּא is a prophetic perfect. In ver. 25 the ruin of the kingdom is declared to be certain, and in vers. 26 and 27 the occurrence of it is more minutely depicted. Stroke upon stroke does the ruin come; and it is intensified by reports, alarming accounts, which crowd together and increase the terror, and also by the desperation of the spiritual and temporal leaders of the nation,—the prophets, priests, and elders,—whom God deprives of revelation, knowledge, and counsel; so that all ranks (king and princes and the common people) sink into mourning, alarm, and horror. That it is to no purpose that visions or prophecies are sought from the prophets (ver. 26), is evident from the antithetical statement concerning the priests and elders which immediately follows. The three statements serve as complements of one another. They seek for predictions from prophets, but the prophets receive no vision, no revelation. They seek instruction from priests, but instruction is withdrawn from the priests; and so forth. *Tōrâh* signifies instruction out of the law, which the priests were to give to the people (Mal. ii. 7). In ver. 27, the three classes into which the people were divided are mentioned—viz. king, prince (*i.e.* tribe-princes and heads of families), and, in contradistinction to both, עַם הָאָרֶץ, the common people, the people of the land, in distinction from the civil rulers, as in 2 Kings xxi. 24, xxiii. 30. מִדַּרְכָּם, literally from their way, their mode of action, will I do to them: *i.e.* my action will be derived from theirs, and regulated accordingly. אוֹתָם for אִתָּם, as in ch. iii. 22, etc. (See the comm. on ch. xvi. 59.)

CHAP. VIII.–XI. VISION OF THE DESTRUCTION OF JERUSALEM.

A year and two months after his call, the glory of the Lord appeared to the prophet a second time, as he had seen it by the Chebar. He is transported in spirit to Jerusalem into the court of the temple (ch. viii. 1–4), where the Lord causes him to see, first the idolatry of Israel (ch. viii. 5–18), and secondly, the judgment why, on account of this idolatry, all the inhabitants of Jerusalem are smitten (chap. ix.), the city is burned with fire, and the sanctuary forsaken by God (ch. x.). Lastly, after he has been charged to foretell to the representatives of the people more especially the coming judgment, and to those who are sent into exile a future salvation (ch. xi. 1–21), he describes how the gracious presence of God forsakes the city before his own eyes (ch. xi. 22, 23). After this has taken place, Ezekiel is carried back in the vision to Chaldea once more; and there, after the vision has come to an end, he announces to the exiles what he has seen and heard (ch. xi. 24, 25).

Chap. viii. ABOMINATIONS OF THE IDOLATRY OF THE HOUSE OF ISRAEL.—Vers. 1-4. Time and place of the divine revelation.—Ver. 1. *And it came to pass in the sixth year, in the sixth (month), on the fifth (day) of the month, I was sitting in my house, and the elders of Judah were sitting before me; there fell upon me the hand of the Lord Jehovah there.* Ver. 2. *And I saw, and behold a figure like the look of fire, from the look of its loins downwards fire, and from its loins upwards like a look of brilliance, like the sight of red-hot brass.* Ver. 3. *And he stretched out the form of a hand, and took me by the locks of my head, and wind carried me away between earth and heaven, and brought me to Jerusalem in visions of God, to the entrance of the gate of the inner court, which faces towards the north, where the image of jealousy exciting jealousy had its stand.* Ver. 4. *And, behold, the glory of the God of Israel was there, like the vision which I have seen in the valley.*—The place where Ezekiel received this new theophany agrees with the statements in ch. iii. 24 and iv. 4, 6, that he was to shut himself up in his house, and lie 390 days upon the left side, and 40 days upon the right side—in all, 430 days. The use of the word יֹשֵׁב, "I sat," is not at variance with this, as יָשַׁב does not of necessity signify sitting as contrasted with lying, but may also be used in the more general sense of staying, or living, in the house. Nor is the presence of the elders of Judah opposed to the command, in ch. iii. 24, to shut himself up in the house, as we have already observed in the notes on that passage. The new revelation is made to him in the presence of these elders, because it is of the greatest importance to them. They are to be witnesses of his ecstasy; and after this has left the prophet, are to hear from his lips the substance of the divine revelation (ch. xi. 25). It is otherwise with the time of the revelation. If we compare the date given in ch. viii. 1 with those mentioned before, this new vision apparently falls within the period required for carrying out the symbolical actions of the previous vision. Between ch. i. 1, 2 (the fifth day of the fourth month in the fifth year) and ch. viii. 1 (the fifth day of the sixth month in the sixth year) we have one year and two months, that is to say (reckoning the year as a lunar year at 354 days, and the two months at 59 days), 413 days; whereas the two events recorded in ch. i. 1–vii. 27 require at least 437 days, namely 7 days for ch. iii. 15, and 390+40=430 days for ch. iv. 5, 6. Consequently the new theophany would fall within the 40 days, during which Ezekiel was to lie upon the right side for Judah. To get rid of this difficulty, Hitzig conjectures that the fifth year of Jehoiachin (ch. i. 2) was a leap year of 13 months or 385 days, by which he obtains an interval of 444 days after adding 59 for the two months,—a period sufficient not only to include the 7 days (ch. iii. 15) and 390+40 days (ch. iv. 5, 6), but to leave 7 days for the time that elapsed between ch. vii. and viii. But however attractive this reckoning may appear, the assumption that the fifth year of the captivity of Jehoiachin was a leap year is purely conjectural; and there is nothing whatever to give it probability. Consequently the only thing that could lead us to adopt such a solution, would be the impossibility of reconciling the conclusion to be drawn from the chronological data, as to the time of the two theophanies, with the substance of these divine revelations. If we assume that Ezekiel carried out the symbolical acts mentioned in ch. iv. and v. in all their entirety, we can hardly imagine that the vision described in the chapters before us, by which he was transported in spirit to Jerusalem, occurred within the period of forty days, during which he was to typify the siege of Jerusalem by lying upon his right side. Nevertheless, Kliefoth has decided in favour of this view, and argues in support of it, that the vision described in ch. viii. 1 sqq. took place in the prophet's own house, that it is identical in substance with what is contained in ch. iii. 22–vii. 27, and that there is no discrepancy, because all that occurred here was purely internal, and the prophet himself was to address the words contained in ch. xi. 4–12 and xi. 14–21 to the inhabitants of Jerusalem in his state of ecstasy.

Moreover, when it is stated in ch. xi. 25 that Ezekiel related to the exiles all that he had seen in the vision, it is perfectly open to us to assume that this took place at the same time as his report to them of the words of God in ch. vi. and vii., and those which follow in ch. xii. But, on the other hand, it may be replied that the impression produced by ch. xi. 25 is not that the prophet waited several weeks after his visionary transport to Jerusalem before communicating to the elders what he saw in the vision. And even if the possibility of this cannot be disputed, we cannot imagine any reason why the vision should be shown to the prophet four weeks before it was to be related to the exiles. Again, there is not sufficient identity between the substance of the vision in ch. viii.–xi. and the revelation in ch. iv.–vii., to suggest any motive for the two to coincide. It is true that the burning of Jerusalem, which Ezekiel sees in ch. viii.–xi., is consequent upon the siege and conquest of that city, which he has already predicted in ch. iv.–vii. both in figure and word; but they are not so closely connected, that it was necessary on account of this connection for it to be shown to him before the completion of the symbolical siege of Jerusalem. And, lastly, although the ecstasy as a purely internal process is so far reconcilable with the prophet's lying upon his right side, that this posture did not preclude a state of ecstasy or render it impossible, yet this collision would ensue, that while the prophet was engaged in carrying out the former word of God, a new theophany would be received by him, which must necessarily abstract his mind from the execution of the previous command of God, and place him in a condition in which it would be impossible for him to set his face firmly upon the siege of Jerusalem, as he had been commanded to do in ch. iv. 7. On account of this collision, we cannot subscribe to the assumption, that it was during the time that Ezekiel was lying bound by God upon his right side to bear the sin of Jerusalem, that he was transported in spirit to the temple at Jerusalem. On the contrary, the fact that this transport occurred, according to ch. viii. 1, at a time when he could not have ended the symbolical acts of ch. iv., if he had been required to carry them out in all their external reality, furnishes us with conclusive evidence of the correctness of the view we have already expressed, that the symbolical acts of ch. iv. and v. did not lie within the sphere of outward reality (see comm. on ch. v. 4).—And if Ezekiel did not really lie for 430 days, there was nothing to hinder his having a fresh vision 14 months after the theophany in ch. i. and ch. iii. 22 sqq. For תִּפֹּל עָלַי יַד יי׳, see at ch. iii. 22 and i. 3.

The figure which Ezekiel sees in the vision is described in ver. 2 in precisely the same terms as the appearance of God in ch. i. 27. The sameness of the two passages is a sufficient defence of the reading כְּמַרְאֵה־אֵשׁ against the arbitrary emendation כמ׳ אִישׁ, after the Sept. rendering ὁμοίωμα ἀνδρός, in support of which Ewald and Hitzig appeal to ch. i. 26, though without any reason, as the reading there is not אִישׁ, but אָדָם. It is not expressly stated here that the apparition was in human form—the fiery appearance is all that is mentioned; but this is taken for granted in the allusion to the מָתְנַיִם (the loins), either as self-evident, or as well known from ch. i. זֹהַר is synonymous with נֹגַהּ in ch. i. 4, 27. What is new in the present theophany is the stretching out of the hand, which grasps the prophet by the front hair of his head, whereupon he is carried by wind between heaven and earth, *i.e.* through the air, to Jerusalem, not in the body, but in visions of God (cf. ch. i. 1), that is to say, in spiritual ecstasy, and deposited at the entrance of the inner northern door of the temple. הַפְּנִימִית is not an adjective belonging to שַׁעַר, for this is not a feminine noun, but is used as a substantive, as in ch. xliii. 5 (=הֶחָצֵר הַפְּנִימִית: cf. ch. xl. 40): gate of the inner court, *i.e.* the gate on the north side of the inner court which led into the outer court. We are not informed whether Ezekiel was placed on the inner or outer side of this gate, *i.e.* in the inner or outer court; but it is evident from ver. 5 that he was placed in the inner court, as his position commanded a view of the image which stood at the entrance of the gate towards the north. The further statement, "where the standing place of the image of jealousy was," anticipates what follows, and points out the reason why the prophet was placed just there. The expression "image of jealousy" is explained by הַמַּקְנֶה, which excites the jealousy of Jehovah (see the comm. on Ex. xx. 5). Consequently, we have not to think of any image of Jehovah, but of an image of a heathen idol (cf. Deut. xxxii. 21); probably of Baal or Asherah, whose image had already been placed in the temple by Manasseh (2 Kings xxi. 7); certainly not the image of the corpse of Adonis moulded in wax or clay. This opinion, which Hävernick advances, is connected with the erroneous assumption that all the idolatrous abominations mentioned in this chapter relate to the celebration of an Adonis-festival in the temple. There (ver. 4) in the court of the temple Ezekiel saw once more the glory of the God of Israel, as he had seen it in the valley (ch. iii. 22) by the Chaboras, *i.e.* the appearance of God upon the throne with the cherubim and wheels; whereas the divine figure, whose hand grasped him in his house, and transported him to the temple (ver. 2), showed neither throne nor cherubim. The expression "God of Israel," instead of Jehovah (ch. iii. 23), is chosen as an antithesis to the strange god, the heathen idol, whose image stood in the temple. As the God of Israel, Jehovah cannot tolerate the image and worship of another god in *His* temple. To set up such an image in the temple of Jehovah was a practical renunciation of the covenant, a rejection of Jehovah on the part of Israel as its covenant God.

Here, in the temple, Jehovah shows to the prophet the various kinds of idolatry which Israel is practising both publicly and privately, not merely in the temple, but throughout the whole land. The arrangement of these different forms of idolatry in four groups or abomination scenes (vers. 5, 6, 7–12, 13–15, and 16–18), which the prophet sees both in and from the court of the temple, belong to the visionary drapery of this divine revelation. It is altogether erroneous to interpret the vision as signifying that all these forms of idolatry were practised in the temple itself; an assumption which cannot be carried out without doing violence to the description, more especially of the second abomination in vers. 7–12. Still more untenable is Hävernick's view, that the four pictures of idolatrous practices shown to the prophet are only intended to represent different scenes of a festival of Adonis held in the temple. The selection of the courts of the temple for depicting the idolatrous worship, arises from the fact that the temple was the place where Israel was called to worship the Lord its God. Consequently the apostasy of Israel from the Lord could not be depicted more clearly and strikingly than by the following series of pictures of idolatrous abominations practised in the temple under the eyes of God.

Vers. 5 and 6. *First* abomination-picture.—Ver. 5. *And He said to me, Son of man, lift up thine eyes now towards the north. And I lifted up my eyes towards the north, and, behold, to the north of the gate of the altar was this image of jealousy at the entrance.* Ver. 6. *And He said to me, Son of man, seest thou what they do? great abominations, which the house of Israel doeth here, that I may go far away from my sanctuary; and thou shalt yet again see greater abominations still.*—As Ezekiel had taken his stand in the inner court at the entrance of the north gate, and when looking thence towards the north saw the image of jealousy to the north of the altar gate, the image must have stood on the outer side of the entrance, so that the prophet saw it as he looked through the open doorway. The altar gate is the same as the northern gate of the inner court mentioned in ver. 3. But it is impossible to state with certainty how it came to be called the altar gate. Possibly from the circumstance that the sacrificial animals were taken through this gate to the altar, to be slaughtered on the northern side of the altar, according to Lev. i. 4, v. 11, etc. מָהֵם, contracted from מָה־הֵם, like

מַזֶּה from מָה זֶּה in Ex. iv. 2. The words "what they are doing here" do not force us to assume that at that very time they were worshipping the idol. They simply describe what was generally practised there. The setting up of the image involved the worship of it. The subject to לְרָחֳקָה is not the house of Israel, but Jehovah. They perform great abominations, so that Jehovah is compelled to go to a distance from His sanctuary, *i.e.* to forsake it (cf. ch. xi. 23), because they make it an idol-temple.

Vers. 7–12. *Second* abomination: Worship of beasts.—Ver. 7. *And He brought me to the entrance of the court, and I saw, and behold there was a hole in the wall.* Ver. 8. *And He said to me, Son of man, break through the wall: and I broke through the wall, and behold there was a door.* Ver. 9. *And He said to me, Come and see the wicked abominations which they are doing here.* Ver. 10. *And I came and saw, and behold there were all kinds of figures of reptiles, and beasts, abominations, and all kinds of idols of the house of Israel, drawn on the wall round about.* Ver. 11. *And seventy men of the elders of the house of Israel, with Jaazaniah the son of Shaphan standing among them, stood in front, every man with his censer in his hand; and the smell of a cloud of incense arose.* Ver. 12. *And He said to me, Seest thou, son of man, what the elders of the house of Israel do in the dark, every one in his image-chambers? For they say: Jehovah doth not see us; Jehovah hath forsaken the land.*—The entrance of the court to which Ezekiel was now transported cannot be the principal entrance to the outer court towards the east (Ewald). This would be at variance with the context, as we not only find the prophet at the northern entrance in vers. 3 and 5, but at ver. 14 we find him there still. If he had been taken to the eastern gate in the meantime, this would certainly have been mentioned. As that is not the case, the reference must be to that entrance to the court which lay between the entrance-gate of the inner court (ver. 3) and the northern entrance-gate to the house of Jehovah (ver. 14), or northern gate of the outer court, in other words, the northern entrance into the outer court. Thus the prophet was conducted out of the inner court through its northern gate into the outer court, and placed in front of the northern gate, which led out into the open air. There he saw a hole in the wall, and on breaking through the wall, by the command of God, he saw a door, and having entered it, he saw all kinds of figures of animals engraved on the wall round about, in front of which seventy of the elders of Israel were standing and paying reverence to the images of beasts with burning incense. According to ver. 12, the prophet was thereby shown what the elders of Israel did in the dark, every one in his image-chamber. From this explanation on the part of God concerning the picture shown to the prophet, it is very evident that it had no reference to any idolatrous worship practised by the elders in one or more of the cells of the outer court of the temple. For even though the objection raised by Kliefoth to this view, namely, that it cannot be proved that there were halls with recesses in the outer court, is neither valid nor correct, since the existence of such halls is placed beyond the reach of doubt by Jer. xxxv. 4, 2 Kings xxiii. 11, and 1 Chron. xxviii. 12; such a supposition is decidedly precluded by the fact, that the cells and recesses at the gates cannot have been large enough to allow of seventy-one men taking part in a festive idolatrous service. The supposition that the seventy-one men were distributed in different chambers is at variance with the distinct words of the text. The prophet not only sees the seventy elders standing along with Jaazaniah, but he could not look through one door into a number of chambers at once, and see the pictures drawn all round upon their walls. The assembling of the seventy elders in a secret cell by the northern gate of the outer temple to worship the idolatrous images engraved on the walls of the cell, is one feature in the visionary form given to the revelation of what the elders of the people were doing secretly throughout the whole land. To bring out more strikingly the secrecy of this idolatrous worship, the cell is so completely hidden in the wall, that the prophet is obliged to enlarge the hole by breaking through the wall before he can see the door which leads to the cell and gain a view of them and of the things it contains, and the things that are done therein.[1] And the number of the persons assembled there suggests the idea of a symbolical representation, as well as the secrecy of the cell. The seventy elders represent the whole nation; and the number is taken from Ex. xxiv. 1 sqq. and Num. xi. 16, xxiv. 25, where Moses, by the command of God, chooses seventy of the elders to represent the whole congregation at the making of the covenant, and afterwards to support his authority. This representation of the congregation was not a permanent institution, as we may see from the fact that in Num. xi. seventy other men are said to have been chosen for the purpose named. The high council, consisting of seventy members, the so-called Sanhedrim, was formed after the captivity on the basis of these Mosaic types. In the midst of the seventy was Jaazaniah the son of Shaphan, a different man therefore from the Jaazaniah mentioned in ch. xi. 1. Shaphan is probably the person mentioned as a man of distinction in 2 Kings xxii. 3 sqq.; Jer. xxix. 3, xxxvi. 10, xxxix. 14. It is impossible to decide on what ground Jaazaniah is specially mentioned by name; but it can hardly be on account of the meaning of the name he bore, "Jehovah hears," as Hävernick supposes. It is probable that he held a prominent position among the elders of the nation, so that he is mentioned here by name as the leader of this national representation. —On the wall of the chamber round about there were drawn all kinds of figures of רֶמֶשׂ וּבְהֵמָה, reptiles and quadrupeds (see Gen. i. 24). שֶׁקֶץ is in apposition not only to בְּהֵמָה, but also to רֶמֶשׂ, and therefore, as belonging to both, is not to be connected with בְּהֵמָה in the construct state. The drawing of

[1] "Because the whole is exhibited pictorially and figuratively, he says that he saw one hole in a wall, and was directed to dig through and make it larger, that he might enter as if through an open door, and see the things which he could not possiby have seen while stationed outside."—Jerome.

reptiles and quadrupeds became a *sheqetz*, or abomination, from the fact that the pictures had been drawn for the purpose of religious worship. The following clause, "and all the idols of the house of Israel," is co-ordinate with כָּל־תַּבְנִית וגו'. Besides the animals drawn on the walls, there were idols of other kinds in the chamber. The drawing of reptiles and quadrupeds naturally suggests the thought of the animal-worship of Egypt. We must not limit the words to this, however, since the worship of animals is met with in the nature-worship of other heathen nations, and the expression כָּל־תַּבְנִית, "all kinds of figures," as well as the clause, "all kinds of idols of the house of Israel," points to every possible form of idol-worship as spread abroad in Israel. עָתָר, according to the Aramaean usage, signifies *suffimentum*, perfume, בַּחֹשֶׁךְ, in the dark, *i.e.* in secret, like בַּסֵּתֶר in 2 Sam. xii. 12; not in the sacred darkness of the cloud of incense (Hävernick). חַדְרֵי מַשְׂכִּית, image-chambers, is the term applied to the rooms or closets in the dwelling-houses of the people in which idolatrous images were set up and secretly worshipped. מַשְׂכִּית signifies idolatrous figures, as in Lev. xxvi. 1 and Num. xxxiii. 52. This idolatry was justified by the elders, under the delusion that "Jehovah seeth us not;" that is to say, not: "He does not trouble Himself about us," but He does not see what we do, because He is not omniscient (cf. Isa. xxix. 15); and He has forsaken the land, withdrawn His presence and His help. Thus they deny both the omniscience and omnipresence of God (cf. ch. ix. 9).

Vers. 13–15. *Third* abomination: Worship of Thammuz.—Ver. 13. *And He said to me, Thou shalt yet again see still greater abominations which they do.* Ver. 14. *And He brought me to the entrance of the gate of the house of Jehovah, which is towards the north, and behold there sat the women, weeping for Thammuz.* Ver. 15. *And He said to me, Dost thou see it, O son of man? Thou shalt yet again see still greater abominations than these.*—The prophet is taken from the entrance into the court to the entrance of the gate of the temple, to see the women sitting there weeping for Thammuz. The article in הַנָּשִׁים is used generically. Whilst the men of the nation, represented by the seventy elders, were secretly carrying on their idolatrous worship, the women were sitting at the temple gate, and indulging in public lamentation for Thammuz. Under the weeping for Thammuz, Jerome (with Melito of Sardis and all the Greek Fathers) has correctly recognised the worship of Adonis. "תַּמּוּז, Θαμμούζ or Θαμμούς," says Jerome, "whom we have interpreted as Adonis, is called *Thamuz* both in Hebrew and Syriac; and because, according to the heathen legend, this lover of Venus and most beautiful youth is said to have been slain in the month of June and then restored to life again, they call this month of June by the same name, and keep an annual festival in his honour, at which he is lamented by women as though he were dead, and then afterwards celebrated in songs as having come to life again." This view has not been shaken even by the objections raised by Chwolson in his *Ssaabins* (II. 27. 202 sqq.), his relics of early Babylonian literature (p. 101), and his Tammuz and human-worship among the ancient Babylonians. For the myth of Thammuz, mentioned in the Nabataean writings as a man who was put to death by the king of Babylon, whom he had commanded to introduce the worship of the seven planets and the twelve signs of the zodiac, and who was exalted to a god after his death, and honoured with a mourning festival, is nothing more than a refined interpretation of the very ancient nature-worship which spread over the whole of Hither Asia, and in which the power of the sun over the vegetation of the year was celebrated. The etymology of the word *Tammuz* is doubtful. It is probably a contraction of תַּמְזוּז, from מָזַז = מָסַס, so that it denotes the decay of the force of nature, and corresponds to the Greek ἀφανισμὸς 'Αδώνιδος (see Hävernick *in loc.*).

Vers. 16–18. *Fourth* abomination: Worship of the sun by the priests.—Ver. 16. *And He took me into the inner court of the house of Jehovah, and behold, at the entrance into the temple of*

Jehovah, between the porch and the altar, as it were five and twenty men, with their backs towards the temple of Jehovah and their faces towards the east; they were worshipping the sun towards the east. Ver. 17. *And He said to me, Seest thou this, son of man? Is it too little for the house of Judah to perform the abominations which they are performing here, that they also fill the land with violence, and provoke me to anger again and again? For behold they stretch out the vine-branch to their nose.* Ver. 18. *But I also will act in fury; my eye shall not look compassionately, and I will not spare; and if they cry with a loud voice in my ears, I will not hear them.*—After Ezekiel has seen the idolatrous abominations in the outer court, or place for the people, he is taken back into the inner court, or court of the priests, to see still greater abominations there. Between the porch of the temple and the altar of burnt-offering, the most sacred spot therefore in the inner court, which the priests alone were permitted to tread (Joel ii. 17), he sees as if twenty-five men, with their backs toward the temple, were worshipping the sun in the east. כְּ before עֶשְׂרִים is not a preposition, *circa*, about, but a particle of comparison (an appearance): as if twenty-five men; after the analogy of כְּ before an accusative (*vid.* Ewald, § 282*e*). For the number here is not an approximative one; but twenty-five is the exact number, namely, the twenty-four leaders of the classes of priests (1 Chron. xxiv. 5 sqq.; 2 Chron. xxxvi. 14; Ezra x. 5), with the high priest at the head (see Lightfoot's *Chronol. of O. T.*, Opp. I. 124). As the whole nation was seen in the seventy elders, so is the entire priesthood represented here in the twenty-five leaders as deeply sunk in disgraceful idolatry. Their apostasy from the Lord is shown in the fact that they turn their back upon the temple, and therefore upon Jehovah, who was enthroned in the temple, and worship the sun, with their faces turned towards the east. The worship of the sun does not refer to the worship of Adonis, as Hävernick supposes, although Adonis was a sun-god; but generally to the worship of the heavenly bodies, against which

Moses had warned the people (Deut. iv. 19, xvii. 3), and which found its way in the time of Manasseh into the courts of the temple, whence it was afterwards expelled by Josiah (2 Kings xxiii. 5, 11). The form מִשְׁתַּחֲוִיתֶם must be a copyist's error for מִשְׁתַּחֲוִים; as the supposition that it is an unusual form, with a play upon הִשְׁחִית,[1] is precluded by the fact that it would in that case be a 2d per. plur. perf., and such a construction is rendered impossible by the הֵמָּה which immediately precedes it (cf. Ewald, § 118*a*).—To these idolatrous abominations Judah has added other sins, as if these abominations were not bad enough in themselves. This is the meaning of the question in ver. 17, הֲנָקֵל וגו': is it too little for the house of Judah, etc.? נָקֵל with מִן, as in Isa. xlix. 6. To indicate the fulness of the measure of guilt, reference is again briefly made to the moral corruption of Judah. חָמָס embraces all the injuries inflicted upon men; תּוֹעֵבוֹת, impiety towards God, *i.e.* idolatry. By violent deeds they provoke God repeatedly to anger (שׁוּב, followed by an infinitive, expresses the repetition of an action). The last clause of ver. 17 (וְהִנָּם שֹׁלְחִים וגו') is very obscure. The usual explanation, which has been adopted by J. D. Michaelis and Gesenius: "they hold the twig to their nose," namely, the sacred twig Barsom, which the Parsees held in their hands when praying (*vid.* Hyde, *de relig. vet. Pars.* p. 350, ed. 2; and Kleuker, *Zend-Avesta*, III. p. 204), suits neither the context nor the words. According to the position of the clause in the context, we do not expect an allusion to a new idolatrous rite, but an explanation of the way in which Judah had excited the wrath of God by its violent deeds. Moreover, זְמוֹרָה is not a suitable word to apply to the Barsom,—*Z'mōrâh* is a shoot or tendril of the vine (cf. ch. xv. 2; Isa. xvii. 10; Num. xiii. 23). The Barsom, on the other hand, consisted of bunches of twigs of the tree *Gez* or *Hom*, or of branches of the pomegranate, the tamarisk, or the date (cf. Kleuker *l.c.*, and Strabo, XV. 733),

[1] "An extraordinary form, invented for the purpose of more effectually expressing their extraordinary abomination."—LIGHTFOOT.

and was not held to the nose, but kept in front of the mouth as a magical mode of driving demons away (*vid.* Hyde, *l.c.*). Lastly, שָׁלַח אֶל does not mean to hold anything, but to stretch out towards, to prepare to strike, to use violence. Of the other explanations given, only two deserve any consideration,—namely, first, the supposition that it is a proverbial expression, "to apply the twig to anger," in the sense of adding fuel to the fire, which Doederlein (*ad Grotii adnott.*) applies in this way, "by these things they supply food, as it were, to my wrath, which burns against themselves," *i.e.* they bring fuel to the fire of my wrath. Lightfoot gives a similar explanation in his *Hor. hebr. ad* John xv. 6. The second is that of Hitzig: "they apply the sickle to their nose," *i.e.* by seeking to injure me, they injure themselves. In this case זְמוֹרָה must be taken in the sense of מְזַמֵּרָה, a sickle or pruning-knife, and pointed זַמּוֹרָה. The saying does appear to be a proverbial one, but the origin and meaning of the proverb have not yet been satisfactorily explained.—Ver. 18. Therefore will the Lord punish unsparingly (cf. ch. vii. 4, 9, v. 11). This judgment he shows to the prophet in the two following chapters.

Chap. ix. THE ANGELS WHICH SMITE JERUSALEM.—Vers. 1–3. At the call of Jehovah, His servants appear to execute the judgment.—Ver. 1. *And He called in my ears with a loud voice, saying, Come hither, ye watchmen of the city, and every one his instrument of destruction in his hand.* Ver. 2. *And behold six men came by the way of the upper gate, which is directed toward the north, every one with his smashing-tool in his hand; and a man in the midst of them, clothed in white linen, and writing materials by his hip; and they came and stood near the brazen altar.* Ver. 3. *And the glory of the God of Israel rose up from the cherub, upon which it was, to the threshold of the house, and called to the man clothed in white linen, by whose hip the writing materials were.*—פְּקֻדּוֹת הָעִיר does not mean the punishments of the city. This rendering does not suit the context, since it is not the punishments that are introduced, but the men who execute them; and it is not established by the usage of the language. פְּקֻדָּה is frequently used, no doubt, in the sense of visitation or chastisement (*e.g.* Isa. x. 3; Hos. ix. 7); but it is not met with in the plural in this sense. In the plural it only occurs in the sense of supervision or protectorate, in which sense it occurs not only in Jer. lii. 11 and Ezek. xliv. 11, but also (in the singular) in Isa. lx. 17, and as early as Num. iii. 38, where it relates to the presidency of the priests, and very frequently in the Chronicles. Consequently פְּקֻדּוֹת are those whom God has appointed to watch over the city, the city-guard (2 Kings xi. 18),—not earthly, but heavenly watchmen,—who are now to inflict punishment upon the ungodly, as the authorities appointed by God. קָרְבוּ is an imperative *Piel*, as in Isa. xli. 21, and must not be altered into קִרְבוּ (*Kal*), as Hitzig proposes. The *Piel* is used in an intransitive sense, *festinanter appropinquavit*, as in ch. xxxvi. 8. The persons called come by the way of the upper northern gate of the temple, to take their stand before Jehovah, whose glory had appeared in the inner court. The upper gate is the gate leading from the outer court to the inner, or upper court, which stood on higher ground,—the gate mentioned in ch. viii. 3 and 5. In the midst of the six men furnished with smashing-tools there was one clothed in white byssus, with writing materials at his side. The dress and equipment, as well as the instructions which he afterwards receives and executes, show him to be the prince or leader of the others. Kliefoth calls in question the opinion that these seven men are angels; but without any reason. Angels appearing in human form are frequently called אֲנָשִׁים or אִישׁ, according to their external *habitus*. But the number seven neither presupposes the dogma of the seven archangels, nor is copied from the seven Parsic *amschaspands*. The dress worn by the high priest, when presenting the sin-offering on the great day of atonement (Lev. xvi. 4, 23), was made of בַּד, *i.e.* of white material woven from byssus thread (see the comm. on Ex. xxviii. 42). It has been inferred from this, that the figure clothed in white linen was the angel of Jehovah, who appears as the heavenly high priest, to protect and care for his own. In support of this, the circumstance may be also adduced, that the man whom Daniel saw above the water of the Tigris, and whose appearance is described, in Dan. x. 5, 6, in the same manner as that of Jehovah in Ezek. i. 4, 26, 27, and that of the risen Christ in Rev. i. 13–15, appears clothed in בַּדִּים (Dan. x. 5, xii. 6, 7).[1] Nevertheless, we cannot regard this view as established. The shining white talar, which is evidently meant by the plural בַּדִּים, occurring only here and in Daniel (*ut. sup.*), is not a dress peculiar to the angel of Jehovah or to Christ. The seven angels, with the vials of wrath, also appear in garments of shining white linen (ἐνδεδυμένοι λίνον καθαρὸν λαμπρόν, Rev. xv. 6); and the shining white colour, as a symbolical representation of divine holiness and glory (see comm. on Lev. xvi. 4 and Rev. xix. 8), is the colour generally chosen for the clothing both of the heavenly spirits and of "just men made perfect" (Rev. xix. 8). Moveover, the angel with the writing materials here is described in a totally different manner from the appearance of Jehovah in Ezek. i. and Dan. x., or that of Christ in Rev. i.; and there is nothing whatever to indicate a being equal with God. Again, the distinction between him and the other six men leads to no other conclusion, than that he stood in the same relation to them as the high priest to the Levites, or the chancellor to the other officials. This position is indicated by the writing materials on his hips, *i.e.* in the girdle on

[1] לָבוּשׁ בַּדִּים is rendered by the LXX., in the passage before us, ἐνδεδυκὼς ποδήρη. It is in accordance with this that Christ is described in Rev. i. 13 as clothed with a ποδήρης, and not after Dan. x. 5, as Hengstenberg supposes. In Dan. x. 5, the Septuagint has ἐνδεδυμένος βαδδίν or τὰ βαδδίν. In other places, the Sept. rendering of בַּד is λίνον (thus Lev. xvi. 4, 23, vi. 3; Ex. xxviii. 42, etc.); and hence the λίνον λαμπρόν of Rev. xv. 6 answers to the בַּד made of שֵׁשׁ, βύσσος, and is really the same as the βύσσινον λαμπρόν of Rev. xix. 8.

his hips, in which scribes in the East are accustomed to carry their writing materials (*vid.* Rosenmüller, *A. u. N. Morgenland*, IV. p. 323). He is provided with these for the execution of the commission given to him in ver. 4. In this way the description can be very simply explained, without the slightest necessity for our resorting to Babylonian representations of the god Nebo, *i.e.* Mercury, as the scribe of heaven. The seven men take their station by the altar of burnt-offering, because the glory of God, whose commands they were about to receive, had taken up its position there for the moment (Kliefoth); not because the apostate priesthood was stationed there (Hävernick). The glory of Jehovah, however, rose up from the cherub to the threshold of the house. The meaning of this is not that it removed from the interior of the sanctuary to the outer threshold of the temple-building (Hävernick), for it was already stationed, according to ch. viii. 16, above the cherub, between the porch and the altar. It went back from thence to the threshold of the temple-porch, through which one entered the Holy Place, to give its orders there. The reason for leaving its place above the cherubim (the singular כְּרוּב is used collectively) to do this, was not that "God would have had to turn round in order to address the seven from the throne, since, according to ch. viii. 4 and 16, He had gone from the north gate of the outer court into the inner court, and His servants had followed Him" (Hitzig); for the cherubim moved in all four directions, and therefore God, even from the throne, could turn without difficulty to every side. God left His throne, that He might issue His command for the judgment upon Israel from the threshold of the temple, and show Himself to be the judge who would forsake the throne which He had assumed in Israel. This command He issues from the temple court, because the temple was the place whence God attested Himself to His people, both by mercy and judgment.

Vers. 4–7. The divine command.—Ver. 4. *And Jehovah said to him, Go through the midst of the city, through the midst of*

Jerusalem, and mark a cross upon the foreheads of the men who sigh and groan over all the abominations which take place in their midst. Ver. 5. *And to those he said in my ears: Go through the city behind him, and smite. Let not your eye look compassionately, and do not spare.* Ver. 6. *Old men, young men, and maidens, and children, and women, slay to destruction: but ye shall not touch any one who has the cross upon him; and begin at my sanctuary. And they began with the old men, who were before the house.* Ver. 7. *And He said to them, Defile the house, and fill the courts with slain; go ye out. And they went out, and smote in the city.*—God commands the man provided with the writing materials to mark on the forehead with a cross all the persons in Jerusalem who mourn over the abominations of the nation, in order that they may be spared in the time of the judgment. תָּו, the last letter of the Hebrew alphabet, had the form of a cross in the earlier writing. הִתְוָה תָו, to mark a ת, is therefore the same as to make a mark in the form of a cross; although there was at first no other purpose in this sign than to enable the servants employed in inflicting the judgment of God to distinguish those who were so marked, so that they might do them no harm. Ver. 6. And this was the reason why the תָּו was to be marked upon the forehead, the most visible portion of the body; the early Christians, according to a statement in Origen, looked upon the sign itself as significant, and saw therein a prophetic allusion to the sign of the cross as the distinctive mark of Christians. A direct prophecy of the cross of Christ is certainly not to be found here, since the form of the letter *Tâv* was the one generally adopted as a sign, and, according to Job xxxi. 35, might supply the place of a signature. Nevertheless, as Schmieder has correctly observed, there is something remarkable in this coincidence to the thoughtful observer of the ways of God, whose counsel has carefully considered all beforehand, especially when we bear in mind that in the counterpart to this passage (Rev. vii. 3) the seal of the living God is stamped upon the foreheads of the servants of

God, who are to be exempted from the judgment, and that according to Rev. xiv. 1 they had the name of God written upon their foreheads. So much, at any rate, is perfectly obvious from this, namely, that the sign was not arbitrarily chosen, but was inwardly connected with the fact which it indicated; just as in the event upon which our vision is based (Ex. xii. 13, 22 sqq.) the distinctive mark placed upon the houses of the Israelites in Egypt, in order that the destroying angel might pass them by, namely, the smearing of the door-posts with the blood of the paschal lamb that had been slain, was selected on account of its significance and its corresponding to the thing signified. The execution of this command is passed over as being self-evident; and it is not till ver. 11 that it is even indirectly referred to again.—In vers. 5, 6 there follows, first of all, the command given to the other six men. They are to go through the city, behind the man clothed in white linen, and to smite without mercy all the inhabitants of whatever age or sex, with this exception, that they are not to touch those who are marked with the cross. The עַל for אַל before תָּחוֹס is either a slip of the pen, or, as the continued transmission of so striking an error is very improbable, is to be accounted for from the change of א into ע, which is so common in Aramaean. The *Chetib* עֵינֵיכֶם is the unusual form grammatically considered, and the singular, which is more correct, has been substituted as *Keri*. תַּהַרְגוּ is followed by לְמַשְׁחִית, to increase the force of the words and show the impossibility of any life being saved. They are to make a commencement at the sanctuary, because it has been desecrated by the worship of idols, and therefore has ceased to be the house of the Lord. To this command the execution is immediately appended; they began with the old men who were before the house, *i.e.* they began to slay them. הָאֲנָשִׁים הַזְּקֵנִים are neither the twenty-five priests (ch. viii. 16) nor the seventy elders (ch. viii. 11). The latter were not לִפְנֵי הַבָּיִת, but in a chamber by the outer temple gate; whereas לִפְנֵי הַבָּיִת, in front of the temple house, points to the inner court. This locality makes it natural to think of priests, and consequently the LXX. rendered מִמִּקְדָּשִׁי by ἀπὸ τῶν ἁγίων μου. But the expression אֲנָשִׁים זְקֵנִים is an unsuitable one for the priests. We have therefore no doubt to think of men advanced in years, who had come into the court possibly to offer sacrifice, and thereby had become liable to the judgment. In ver. 7 the command, which was interrupted in ver. 6*b*, is once more resumed. They are to defile the house, *i.e.* the temple, namely, by filling the courts with slain. It is in this way that we are to connect together, so far as the sense is concerned, the two clauses, "defile . . . and fill." This is required by the facts of the case. For those slain "before the house" could only have been slain in the courts, as there was no space between the temple house and the courts in which men could have been found and slain. But לִפְנֵי הַבָּיִת cannot be understood as signifying "in the neighbourhood of the temple," as Kliefoth supposes, for the simple reason that the progressive order of events would thereby be completely destroyed. The angels who were standing before the altar of burnt-offering could not begin their work by going out of the court to smite the sinners who happened to be in the neighbourhood of the temple, and then returning to the court to do the same there, and then again going out into the city to finish their work there. They could only begin by slaying the sinners who happened to be in the courts, and after having defiled the temple by their corpses, by going out into the city to slay all the ungodly there, as is related in the second clause of the verse (ver. 7*b*).

Vers. 8–11. Intercession of the prophet, and the answer of the Lord.—Ver. 8. *And it came to pass when they smote and I remained, I fell upon my face, and cried, and said: Alas! Lord Jehovah, wilt Thou destroy all the remnant of Israel, by pouring out Thy wrath upon Jerusalem?* Ver. 9. *And He said to me: The iniquity of the house of Israel and Judah is immeasurably great, and the land is full of blood-guiltiness, and the city full of perversion; for they say Jehovah hath forsaken the land, and Jehovah seeth not.* Ver. 10. *So also shall my eye not look with pity, and I will not spare; I will give their way upon their head.* Ver. 11. *And, behold, the man clothed in white linen, who had the writing materials on his hip, brought answer, and said: I have done as thou hast commanded me.*—The *Chetib* נאשאר is an incongruous form, composed of participle and imperfect fused into one, and is evidently a copyist's error. It is not to be altered into אֶשָּׁאֵר, however (the 1st pers. imperf. *Niph.*), but to be read as a participle נִשְׁאָר, and taken with כְּהַכּוֹתָם as a continuation of the circumstantial clause. For the words do not mean that Ezekiel alone was left, but that when the angels smote and he was left, *i.e.* was spared, was not smitten with the rest, he fell on his face, to entreat the Lord for mercy. These words and the prophet's intercession both apparently presuppose that among the inhabitants of Jerusalem there was no one found who was marked with the sign of the cross, and therefore could be spared. But this is by no means to be regarded as established. For, in the first place, it is not stated that *all* had been smitten by the angels; and, secondly, the intercession of the prophet simply assumes that, in comparison with the multitude of the slain, the number of those who were marked with the sign of the cross and spared was so small that it escaped the prophet's eye, and he was afraid that they might all be slain without exception, and the whole of the remnant of the covenant nation be destroyed. The שְׁאֵרִית of Israel and Judah is the covenant nation in its existing state, when it had been so reduced by the previous judgments of God, that out of the whole of what was once so numerous a people, only a small portion remained in the land. Although God has previously promised that a remnant shall be preserved (ch. v. 3, 4), He does not renew this promise to the prophet, but begins by holding up the greatness of the iniquity of Israel, which admits of no sparing, but calls for the most merciless punishment, to show him that, according to the strict demand of justice, the whole nation has deserved destruction. מֻטֶּה (ver. 9) is not equivalent to מוּטָה, oppression (Isa. lviii. 9), but signifies perversion of justice; although מִשְׁפָּט is not mentioned, since this is also omitted in Ex. xxiii. 2, where הַטָּה occurs in the same sense. For ver. 9*b*, *vid.* ch. viii. 12. For דַּרְכָּם בר׳ נָתַתִּי (ver. 10 and ch. xi. 21, 22, 31), *vid.* 1 Kings viii. 32. While God is conversing with the prophet, the seven angels have performed their work; and in ver. 11 their leader returns to Jehovah with the announcement that His orders have been executed. He does this, not in his own name only, but in that of all the rest. The first act of the judgment is thus shown to the prophet in a figurative representation. The second act follows in the next chapter.

Chap. x. Burning of Jerusalem, and Withdrawal of the Glory of Jehovah from the Sanctuary.—This chapter divides itself into two sections. In vers. 1–8 the prophet is shown how Jerusalem is to be burned with fire. In vers. 9–22 he is shown how Jehovah will forsake His temple.

Vers. 1–8. The angel scatters coals of fire over Jerusalem.—Ver. 1. *And I saw, and behold upon the firmament, which was above the cherubim, it was like sapphire-stone, to look at as the likeness of a throne; He appeared above them.* Ver. 2. *And He spake to the man clothed in white linen, and said: Come between the wheels below the cherubim, and fill thy hollow hands with fire-coals from between the cherubim, and scatter them over the city: and he came before my eyes.* Ver. 3. *And the cherubim stood to the right of the house when the man came, and the cloud filled the inner court.* Ver. 4. *And the glory of Jehovah had lifted itself up from the cherubim to the threshold of the house; and the house was filled with the cloud, and the court was full of the splendour of the glory of Jehovah.* Ver. 5. *And the noise of the wings of the cherubim was heard to the outer court, as the voice of the Almighty God when He speaketh.* Ver. 6. *And it came to pass, when He commanded the man clothed in white linen, and said, Take fire from between the wheels, from between the cherubim, and he came and stood by the side of the wheel,* Ver. 7. *That the cherub stretched out his hand between the cherubim to the fire, which was between the cherubim, and lifted (some) off and gave it into the hands of the man clothed in white linen. And he took it, and went out.* Ver. 8. *And there appeared by the cherubim the likeness of a man's hand under their wings.*— Ver. 1 introduces the description of the second act of the judgment. According to ch. ix. 3, Jehovah had come down from His throne above the cherubim to the threshold of the temple to issue His orders thence for the judgment upon the inhabitants of Jerusalem, and according to ch. x. 4 He goes thither once more. Consequently He had resumed His seat above the cherubim in the meantime. This is expressed in ver. 1, not indeed in so many words, but indirectly or by implication. Ezekiel sees the theophany; and on the firmament above the cherubim, like sapphire-stone to look at, he beholds the likeness of a throne on which Jehovah appeared. To avoid giving too great prominence in this appearance of Jehovah to the bodily or human form, Ezekiel does not speak even here of the form of Jehovah, but simply of His throne, which he describes in the same manner as in ch. i. 26. אֶל stands for עַל according to the later usage of the language. It will never do to take אֶל in its literal sense, as Kliefoth does, and render the words: "Ezekiel saw it move away to the firmament;" for the object to וָאֶרְאֶה וְהִנֵּה is not יְהוָֹה or כְּבוֹד יְהוָֹה, but the form of the throne sparkling in sapphire-stone; and this throne had not separated itself from the firmament above the cherubim, but Jehovah, or the glory of Jehovah, according to ch. ix. 3, had risen up from the cherubim, and moved away to the temple threshold. The כְּ before מַרְאֵה is not to be erased, as Hitzig proposes after the LXX., on the ground that it is not found in ch. i. 26; it is quite appropriate here. For the words do not affirm that Ezekiel saw the likeness of a throne like sapphire-stone; but that he saw something like sapphire-stone, like the appearance of the form of a throne. Ezekiel does not see Jehovah, or the glory of Jehovah, move away to the firmament, and then return to the throne. He simply sees once more the resemblance of a throne upon the firmament, and the Lord appearing thereon. The latter is indicated in נִרְאָה עֲלֵיהֶם. These words are not to be taken in connection with כְּמַרְאֵה וגו', so as to form one sentence; but have been very properly separated by the *athnach* under כִּסֵּא, and treated as an independent assertion. The subject to נִרְאָה might, indeed, be דְמוּת כִּסֵּא, "the likeness of a throne appeared above the cherubim;" but in that case the words would form a pure tautology, as the fact of the throne becoming visible has already been mentioned in the preceding clause. The subject must therefore be Jehovah, as in the case of וַיֹּאמֶר in ver. 2, where there can be no doubt on the matter. Jehovah has resumed His throne, not "for the purpose of removing to a distance, because the courts of the temple have been defiled by dead bodies" (Hitzig), but because the object for which He left it has been attained. He now commands the man clothed in white linen to go in between the wheels under the cherubim, and fill his hands with fire-coals from thence, and scatter them over the city (Jerusalem). This he did, so that Ezekiel could see it. According to this, it appears as if Jehovah had issued the command from His throne; but if we compare what follows, it is evident from ver. 4 that the glory of Jehovah had risen up again from the throne, and removed to the threshold of the temple, and that it was not till after the man in white linen had scattered the coals over the city that it left the threshold of the temple, and ascended once more up to the throne above the cherubim, so as to forsake the temple (ver. 18 sqq.). Consequently we can only understand vers. 2–7 as implying that Jehovah issued the command in ver. 2, not from His throne, but from the threshold of the temple, and that He had therefore returned to the threshold of the temple for this purpose, and for the very same reason as in ch. ix. 3. The possibility of interpreting the verses in this way is apparent from the fact that ver. 2 contains a summary of the whole of the contents of this section, and that vers. 3–7 simply furnish more minute explanations, or contain circumstantial clauses, which throw light upon the whole affair. This is obvious in the case of ver. 3, from the form of the clause; and in vers. 4 and 5, from the fact that in vers. 6 and 7 the command (ver. 2) is resumed, and the execution of it, which was already indicated in וַיָּבֹא לְעֵינַי (ver. 2), more minutely described and carried forward in the closing words of the seventh verse, וַיִּקַּח וַיֵּצֵא. הַגַּלְגַּל in ver. 2 signifies the whirl or rotatory motion, *i.e.* the wheel-work, or the four *ōphannim* under the cherubim regarded as moving. The angel was to go in between these, and take coals out of the fire there, and scatter them over the city. "In the fire of God, the fire of His wrath, will kindle the fire for consuming the city" (Kliefoth). To depict the scene more clearly, Ezekiel observes in ver. 3, that at this moment the cherubim were standing to the right of the house, *i.e.* on the south or rather south-east of the temple house, on the south of the altar of burnt-offering. According to the Hebrew usage the right side was the southern side, and the prophet was in the inner court, whither, according to ch. viii. 16, the divine glory had taken him; and, according to ch. ix. 2, the seven angels had gone to the front of the altar, to receive the commands of the Lord. Consequently we have to picture to ourselves the cherubim as appearing in the neighbourhood of the altar, and then taking up their position to the south thereof, when the Lord returned to the threshold of the temple. The reason for stating this is not to be sought, as Calvin supposes, in the desire to show "that the way was opened for the angel to go straight to God, and that the cherubim were standing there ready, as it were, to contribute their labour." The position in which the cherubim appeared is more probably given with prospective reference to the account which follows in vers. 9–22 of the departure of the glory of the Lord from the temple. As an indication of the significance of this act to Israel, the glory which issued from this manifestation of the divine *doxa* is described in vers. 3*b*–5. The cloud, as the earthly vehicle of the divine *doxa*, filled the inner court; and when the glory of the Lord stood upon the threshold, it filled the temple also, while the court became full of the splendour of the divine glory. That is to say, the brilliancy of the divine nature shone through the cloud, so that the court and the temple were lighted by the shining of the light-cloud. The brilliant splendour is a symbol of the light of the divine grace. The wings of the cherubim rustled, and at the movement of God (i. 24) were audible even in the outer court.

After this picture of the glorious manifestation of the divine *doxa*, the fetching of the fire-coals from the space between the wheels under the cherubim is more closely described in vers. 6 and 7. One of the cherub's hands took the coals out of the fire, and put them into the hands of the man clothed in white linen. To this a supplementary remark is added in ver. 8, to the effect that the figure of a hand was visible by the side of the cherubim under their wings. The word וַיֵּצֵא, "and he went out," indicates that the man clothed in white linen scattered the coals over the city, to set it on fire and consume it.

Vers. 9–22. The glory of the Lord forsakes the temple.—Ver. 9. *And I saw, and behold four wheels by the side of the cherubim, one wheel by the side of every cherub, and the appearance of the wheels was like the look of a chrysolith stone.* Ver. 10. *And as for their appearance, they had all four one form, as if one wheel were in the midst of the other.* Ver. 11. *When they went, they went to their four sides; they did not turn in going; for to the place to which the head was directed, to that they went; they did not turn in their going.* Ver. 12. *And their whole body, and their back, and their hands, and their wings, and the wheels, were full of eyes round about: by all four their wheels.* Ver. 13. *To the wheels, to them was called, "whirl!" in my hearing.* Ver. 14. *And every one had four faces; the face of the first was the face of the cherub, the face of the second a man's face, and the third a lion's face, and the fourth an eagle's face.*

Ver. 15. *And the cherubim ascended. This was the being which I saw by the river Chebar.* Ver. 16. *And when the cherubim went, the wheels went by them; and when the cherubim raised their wings to ascend from the earth, the wheels also did not turn from their side.* Ver. 17. *When those stood, they stood; and when those ascended, they ascended with them; for the spirit of the being was in them.* Ver. 18. *And the glory of Jehovah went out from the threshold of the house, and stood above the cherubim.* Ver. 19. *And the cherubim raised their wings, and ascended from the earth before my eyes on their going out, and the wheels beside them; and they stopped at the entrance of the eastern gate of the house of Jehovah; and the glory of the God of Israel was above them.* Ver. 20. *This was the being which I saw under the God of Israel by the river Chebar, and I perceived that they were cherubim.* Ver. 21. *Every one had four faces, each and every one four wings, and something like a man's hands under their wings.* Ver. 22. *And as for the likeness of their faces, they were the faces which I had seen by the river Chebar, their appearance and they themselves. They went every one according to its face.*— With the words "I saw, and behold," a new feature in the vision is introduced. The description of the appearance of the cherubim in these verses coincides for the most part *verbatim* with the account of the theophany in ch. i. It differs from this, however, not only in the altered arrangement of the several features, and in the introduction of certain points which serve to complete the former account; but still more in the insertion of a number of narrative sentences, which show that we have not merely a repetition of the first chapter here. On the contrary, Ezekiel is now describing the moving of the appearance of the glory of Jehovah from the inner court or porch of the temple to the outer entrance of the eastern gate of the outer court; in other words, the departure of the gracious presence of the Lord from the temple: and in order to point out more distinctly the importance and meaning of this event, he depicts once more the leading features of the theophany itself. The narrative sentences are found in vers. 13, 15, 18, and 19. In ver. 13 we have the exclamation addressed to the wheels by the side of the cherubim to set themselves in motion; in ver. 15, the statement that the cherubim ascended; and in vers. 18 and 19, the account of the departure of the glory of the Lord from the inner portion of the temple. To this we may add the repeated remark, that the appearance was the same as that which the prophet had seen by the river Chebar (vers. 15, 20, 22). To bring clearly out to view both the independence of these divine manifestations and their significance to Israel, Ezekiel repeats the leading features of the former description; but while doing this, he either makes them subordinate to the thoughts expressed in the narrative sentences, or places them first as introductory to these, or lets them follow as explanatory. Thus, for example, the description of the wheels, and of the manner in which they moved (vers. 9–12), serves both to introduce and explain the call to the wheels to set themselves in motion. The description of the wheels in vers. 9–11 harmonizes with ch. i. 16 and 17, with this exception, however, that certain points are given with greater exactness here; such, for example, as the statement that the movements of the wheels were so regulated, that in whichever direction the front one turned, the others did the same. הָרֹאשׁ, the head, is not the head-wheel, or the wheel which was always the first to move, but the front one, which originated the motion, drawing the others after it and determining their direction. For ver. 12*b* and the fact that the wheels were covered with eyes, see ch. i. 18. In ver. 12*a* we have the important addition, that the whole of the body and back, as well as the hands and wings, of the cherubim were full of eyes. There is all the less reason to question this addition, or remove it (as Hitzig does) by an arbitrary erasure, inasmuch as the statement itself is apparently in perfect harmony with the whole procedure; and the significance possessed by the eyes in relation to the wheels was not only appropriate in the case of the cherubim, but necessarily to be assumed in such a connection. The fact that the suffixes in בְּשָׂרָם, גַּבֵּהֶם, etc., refer to the cherubim, is obvious enough, if we consider that the wheels to which immediate reference is made were by the side of the cherubim (ver. 9), and that the cherubim formed the principal feature in the whole of the vision.—Ver. 13 does not point back to ver. 2, and bring the description of the wheelwork to a close, as Hitzig supposes. This assumption, by which the meaning of the whole description has been obscured, is based upon the untenable rendering, "and the wheels they named before my ears whirl" (J. D. Mich., Ros., etc.). Hävernick has already pointed out the objection to this, namely, that with such a rendering בְּאָזְנָי forms an unmeaning addition; whereas it is precisely this addition which shows that קָרָא is used here in the sense of addressing, calling, and not of naming. One called to the wheels הַגַּלְגַּל, whirl; *i.e.* they were to verify their name *galgal*, viz. to revolve or whirl, to set themselves in motion by revolving. This is the explanation given by Theodoret: ἀνακυκλεῖσθαι καὶ ἀνακινεῖσθαι προσετάχθησαν. These words therefore gave the signal for their departure, and accordingly the rising up of the cherubim is related in ver. 15. Ver. 14 prepares the way for their ascent by mentioning the four faces of each cherub; and this is still further expanded in vers. 16 and 17, by the statement that the wheels moved according to the movements of the cherubim. לְאֶחָד without an article is used distributively (every one), as in ch. i. 6 and 10. The fact that in the description which follows only one face of each of the four cherubs is given, is not at variance with ch. i. 10, according to which every one of the cherubs had the four faces named. It was not Ezekiel's intention to mention all the faces of each cherub here, as he had done before; but he regarded it as sufficient in the case of each cherub to mention simply the one face, which was turned toward him. The only striking feature which still remains is the statement that the face of the one, *i.e.* of the first, was the face of the cherub instead of the face of an ox (cf. ch. i. 10), since the faces of the man, the lion, and the eagle were also cherubs' faces. We may, no doubt, get rid of the difficulty by altering the text, but this will not solve it; for it would still remain inexplicable how הַכְּרוּב could have grown out of שׁוֹר by a copyist's error; and still more, how such an error, which might have been so easily seen and corrected, could have been not only perpetuated, but generally adopted. Moreover, we have the article in הַכְּרוּב, which would also be inexplicable if the word had originated in an oversight, and which gives us precisely the index required to the correct solution of the difficulty, showing as it does that it was not merely *a* cherub's face, but the face of *the* cherub, so that the allusion is to one particular cherub, who was either well known from what had gone before, or occupied a more prominent position than the rest. Such a cherub is the one mentioned in ver. 7, who had taken the coals from the fire between the wheels, and stood nearest to Ezekiel. There did not appear to be any necessity to describe his face more exactly, as it could be easily seen from a comparison with ch. i. 10.—In ver. 15, the fact that the cherubim arose to depart from their place is followed by the remark that the cherubic figure was the being (הַחַיָּה, singular, as in ch. i. 22) which Ezekiel saw by the Chaboras, because it was a matter of importance that the identity of the two theophanies should be established as a help to the correct understanding of their real signification. But before the departure of the theophany from the temple is related, there follows in vers. 16 and 17 a repetition of the circumstantial description of the harmonious movements of the wheels and the cherubim (cf. ch. i. 19–21); and then, in ver. 18, the statement which had such practical significance, that the glory of the Lord departed from the threshold of the temple, and resumed the throne above the cherubim; and lastly, the account in ver. 19, that the glory of the God of Israel, seated upon this throne, took up its position at the entrance of the eastern gate of the temple. The entrance of this gate is not the gate of the temple, but the outer side of the eastern gate of the outer court, which formed the principal entrance to the whole of the temple-space. The expression "God of Israel" instead of "Jehovah" is significant, and is used to intimate that God, as the covenant God, withdrew His gracious presence from the people of Israel by this departure from the temple; not, indeed, from the whole of the covenant nation, but from the rebellious Israel which dwelt in Jerusalem and Judah; for the same glory of God which left the temple in the vision before the eyes of Ezekiel had appeared to the prophet by the river Chebar, and by calling him to be the prophet for Israel, had shown Himself to be the God who kept His covenant, and proved that, by the judgment upon the corrupt generation, He simply desired to exterminate its ungodly nature, and create for Himself a new and holy people. This is the meaning of the remark which is repeated in vers. 20–22, that the apparition which left the temple was the same being as Ezekiel had seen by the Chaboras, and that he recognised the beings under the throne as cherubim.

Chap. xi. THREATENING OF JUDGMENT AND PROMISE OF MERCY. CONCLUSION OF THE VISION.—This chapter contains the concluding portion of the vision; namely, *first*, the prediction of the destruction of the ungodly rulers (vers. 1–13); *secondly*, the consolatory and closing promise, that the Lord would gather to Himself a people out of those who had been carried away into exile, and would sanctify them by His Holy Spirit (vers. 14–21); and, *thirdly*, the withdrawal of the gracious presence of God from the city of Jerusalem, and the transportation of the prophet back to Chaldea with the termination of his ecstasy (vers. 22–25).

Vers. 1–13. Judgment upon the rulers of the nation.—Ver. 1. *And a wind lifted me up, and took me to the eastern gate of the house of Jehovah, which faces towards the east; and behold, at the entrance of the gate were five and twenty men, and I saw among them Jaazaniah the son of Azzur, and Pelatiah the son of*

Benaiah, the chiefs of the nation. Ver. 2. *And he said to me: Son of man, these are the men who devise iniquity, and counsel evil counsel in this city;* Ver. 3. *Who say, It is not near to build houses; it is the pot, and we are the flesh.* Ver. 4. *Therefore prophesy against them; prophesy, son of man.*—Ezekiel is once more transported from the inner court (ch. viii. 16) to the outer entrance of the eastern gate of the temple (תִּשָּׂא רוּחַ, as in ch. viii. 3), to which, according to ch. x. 19, the vision of God had removed. There he sees twenty-five men, and among them two of the princes of the nation, whose names are given. These twenty-five men are not identical with the twenty-five priests mentioned in ch. viii. 16, as Hävernick supposes. This is evident, not only from the difference in the locality, the priests standing between the porch and the altar, whereas the men referred to here stood at the outer eastern entrance to the court of the temple, but from the fact that the two who are mentioned by name are called שָׂרֵי הָעָם (princes of the people), so that we may probably infer from this that all the twenty-five were secular chiefs. Hävernick's opinion, that שָׂרֵי הָעָם is a term that may also be applied to princes among the priests, is as erroneous as his assertion that the priest-princes are called "princes" in Ezra viii. 20, Neh. x. 1, and Jer. xxxv. 4, whereas it is only to national princes that these passages refer. Hävernick is equally incorrect in supposing that these twenty-five men take the place of the seventy mentioned in ch. viii. 11; for those seventy represented the whole of the nation, whereas these twenty-five (according to ver. 2) were simply the counsellors of the city—not, however, the twenty-four *duces* of twenty-four divisions of the city, with a prince of the house of Judah, as Prado maintains, on the strength of certain Rabbinical assertions; or twenty-four members of a Sanhedrim, with their president (Rosenmüller); but the twelve tribe-princes (princes of the nation) and the twelve royal officers, or military commanders (1 Chron. xxvii.), with the king himself, or possibly with the commander-in-chief of the army; so that these twenty-five men represent the civil government of Israel, just as the twenty-four priest-princes, together with the high priest, represent the spiritual authorities of the covenant nation. The reason why two are specially mentioned by name is involved in obscurity, as nothing further is known of either of these persons. The words of God to the prophet in ver. 2 concerning them are perfectly applicable to representatives of the civil authorities or temporal rulers, namely, that they devise and give unwholesome and evil counsel. This counsel is described in ver. 3 by the words placed in their mouths: "house-building is not near; it (the city) is the caldron, we are the flesh." These words are difficult, and different interpretations have consequently been given. The rendering, "it (the judgment) is not near, let us build houses," is incorrect; for the infinitive construct בְּנוֹת cannot stand for the imperative or the infinitive absolute, but must be the subject of the sentence. It is inadmissible also to take the sentence as a question, "Is not house-building near?" in the sense of "it is certainly near," as Ewald does, after some of the ancient versions. For even if an interrogation is sometimes indicated simply by the tone in an energetic address, as, for example, in 2 Sam. xxiii. 5, this cannot be extended to cases in which the words of another are quoted. Still less can לֹא בְקָרוֹב mean *non est tempus*, it is not yet time, as Maurer supposes. The only way in which the words can be made to yield a sense in harmony with the context, is by taking them as a tacit allusion to Jer. xxix. 5. Jeremiah had called upon those in exile to build themselves houses in their banishment, and prepare for a lengthened stay in Babylon, and not to allow themselves to be deceived by the words of false prophets, who predicted a speedy return; for severe judgments had yet to fall upon those who had remained behind in the land. This word of Jeremiah the authorities in Jerusalem ridiculed, saying "house-building is not near," *i.e.* the house-building in exile is still a long way off; it will not come to this, that Jerusalem should fall either permanently or entirely into the hands of the king of Babylon. On the contrary, Jerusalem is the pot, and we, its inhabitants, are the flesh. The point of comparison is this: as the pot protects the flesh from burning, so does the city of Jerusalem protect us from destruction.[1] On the other hand, there is no foundation for the assumption that the words also contain an allusion to other sayings of Jeremiah, namely, to Jer. i. 13, where the judgment about to burst in from the north is represented under the figure of a smoking pot; or to Jer. xix., where Jerusalem is depicted as a pot about to be broken in pieces by God; for the reference in Jer. xix. is simply to an earthen pitcher, not to a meat-caldron; and the words in the verse before us have nothing at all in common with the figure in Jer. i. 13. The correctness of our explanation is evident both from ch. xxiv. 3, 6, where the figure of pot and flesh is met with again, though differently applied, and from the reply which Ezekiel makes to the saying of these men in the verses that follow (vers. 7–11). This saying expresses not only false confidence in the strength of Jerusalem, but also contempt and scorn of the predictions of the prophets sent by God. Ezekiel is therefore to prophesy, as he does in vers. 5–12, against this pernicious counsel, which is confirming the people in their sins.

Ver. 5. *And the Spirit of Jehovah fell upon me, and said to me: Say, Thus saith Jehovah, So ye say, O house of Israel, and what riseth up in your spirit, that I know.* Ver. 6. *Ye have increased your slain in this city, and filled its streets with slain.* Ver. 7. *Therefore, thus saith the Lord Jehovah, Your slain, whom ye have laid in the midst of it, they are the flesh, and it is the pot; but men will lead you out of it.* Ver. 8. *The sword you fear; but the sword shall I bring upon you, is the saying of the Lord Jehovah.* Ver. 9. *I shall lead you out of it and give you into*

[1] "This city is a pot, our receptacle and defence, and we are the flesh enclosed therein; as flesh is preserved in its caldron till it is perfectly boiled, so shall we continue here till an extreme old age."—Hülsemann in *Calov. Bibl. Illustr.*

the hand of foreigners, and shall execute judgments upon you. Ver. 10. *By the sword shall ye fall: on the frontier of Israel shall I judge you; and ye shall learn that I am Jehovah.* Ver. 11. *It shall not be as a pot to you, so that you should be flesh therein: on the frontier of Israel shall I judge.* Ver. 12. *And ye shall learn that I am Jehovah, in whose statutes ye have not walked, and my judgments ye have not done, but have acted according to the judgments of the heathen who are round about you.*—For תִּפֹּל עָלַי רוּחַ יי, compare ch. viii. 1. Instead of the "hand" (ch. viii. 1), the Spirit of Jehovah is mentioned here; because what follows is simply a divine inspiration, and there is no action connected with it. The words of God are directed against the "house of Israel," whose words and thoughts are discerned by God, because the twenty-five men are the leaders and counsellors of the nation. מַעֲלוֹת רוּחַ, thoughts, suggestions of the mind, may be explained from the phrase עָלָה עַל לֵב, to come into the mind. Their actions furnish the proof of the evil suggestions of their heart. They have filled the city with slain; not "turned the streets of the city into a battle-field," however, by bringing about the capture of Jerusalem in the time of Jeconiah, as Hitzig would explain it. The words are to be understood in a much more general sense, as signifying murder, in both the coarser and the more refined signification of the word.[1] מִלֵּאתֶים is a copyist's error for מִלֵּאתֶם. Those who have been murdered by you are the flesh in the caldron (ver. 7). Ezekiel gives them back their own words, as words which contain an undoubted truth, but in a different sense from that in which they have used them. By their bloodshed they have made the city into a pot in which the flesh of the slain is pickled. Only in this sense is Jerusalem a pot for them; not a pot to protect the flesh from burning while cooking, but a

[1] Calvin has given the correct explanation, thus: "He does not mean that men had been openly assassinated in the streets of Jerusalem; but under this form of speech he embraces all kinds of injustice. For we know that all who oppressed the poor, deprived men of their possessions, or shed innocent blood, were regarded as murderers in the sight of God."

pot into which the flesh of the slaughtered is thrown. Yet even in this sense will Jerusalem not serve as a pot to these worthless counsellors (ver. 11). They will lead you out of the city (הוֹצִיא, in ver. 7, is the 3d pers. sing. with an indefinite subject). The sword which ye fear, and from which this city is to protect you, will come upon you, and cut you down—not in Jerusalem, but on the frontier of Israel. עַל־גְּבוּל, in ver. 10, cannot be taken in the sense of "away over the frontier," as Kliefoth proposes; if only because of the synonym אֶל־גְּבוּל in ver. 11. This threat was literally fulfilled in the bloody scenes at Riblah (Jer. lii. 24–27). It is not therefore a *vaticinium ex eventu,* but contains the general thought, that the wicked who boasted of security in Jerusalem would not find protection either in Jerusalem or in the land of Israel as a whole, but were to be led out of the land, and judged outside. This threat intensifies the punishment, as Calvin has already shown.[1] In ver. 11 the negation (לֹא) of the first clause is to be supplied in the second, as, for example, in Deut. xxxiii. 6. For ver. 12, compare the remarks on ch. v. 7. The truth and the power of this word are demonstrated at once by what is related in the following verse.

Ver. 13. *And it came to pass, as I was prophesying, that Pelatiah the son of Benaiah died: then I fell upon my face, and cried with a loud voice, and said: Alas! Lord Jehovah, dost Thou make an end of the remnant of Israel?*—The sudden death of one of the princes of the nation, while Ezekiel was prophesying, was intended to assure the house of Israel of the certain fulfilment of this word of God. So far, however, as

[1] "He threatens a double punishment; *first,* that God will cast them out of Jerusalem, in which they delight, and where they say that they will still make their abode for a long time to come, so that exile may be the first punishment. He then adds, *secondly,* that He will not be content with exile, but will send a severer punishment, after they have been cast out, and both home and land have spued them out as a stench which they could not bear. *I will judge you at the frontier of Israel, i.e.* outside the holy land, so that when one curse shall have become manifest in exile, a severer and more formidable punishment shall still await you."

the fact itself is concerned, we must bear in mind, that as it was only in spirit that Ezekiel was at Jerusalem, and prophesied to the men whom he saw in spirit there, so the death of Pelatiah was simply a part of the vision, and in all probability was actually realized by the sudden death of this prince during or immediately after the publication of the vision. But the occurrence, even when the prophet saw it in spirit, made such an impression upon his mind, that with trembling and despair he once more made an importunate appeal to God, as in ch. ix. 8, and inquired whether He meant to destroy the whole of the remnant of Israel. עָשָׂה כָלָה, to put an end to a thing, with אֵת before the object, as in Zeph. i. 18 (see the comm. on Nah. i. 8). The Lord then gives him the comforting assurance in vers. 14–21, that He will preserve a remnant among the exiles, and make them His people once more.

Vers. 14–21. Promise of the gathering of Israel out of the nations.—Ver. 14. *And the word of Jehovah came to me, saying,* Ver. 15. *Son of man, thy brethren, thy brethren are the people of thy proxy, and the whole house of Israel, the whole of it, to whom the inhabitants of Jerusalem say, Remain far away from Jehovah; to us the land is given for a possession.* Ver. 16. *Therefore say, Thus saith the Lord Jehovah, Yea, I have sent them far away, and have scattered them in the lands, but I have become to them a sanctuary for a little while in the lands whither they have come.* Ver. 17. *Therefore say, Thus saith the Lord Jehovah, And I will gather you from the nations, and will collect you together from the lands in which ye are scattered, and will give you the land of Israel.* Ver. 18. *And they will come thither, and remove from it all its detestable things, and all its abominations.* Ver. 19. *And I will give them one heart, and give a new spirit within you; and will take the heart of stone out of their flesh, and give them a heart of flesh;* Ver. 20. *That they may walk in my statutes, and preserve my rights, and do them: and they will be my people, and I will be their God.* Ver. 21. *But those whose heart goeth to the heart of their detestable things and their abominations, I will give their way upon their head, is the saying of the Lord Jehovah.*—The prophet had interceded, first of all for the inhabitants of Jerusalem (ch. ix. 8), and then for the rulers of the nation, and had asked God whether He would entirely destroy the remnant of Israel. To this God replies that his brethren, in whom he is to interest himself, are not these inhabitants of Jerusalem and these rulers of the nation, but the Israelites carried into exile, who are regarded by these inhabitants at Jerusalem as cut off from the people of God. The nouns in ver. 15*a* are not "accusatives, which are resumed in the suffix to הִרְחַקְתִּים in ver. 16," as Hitzig imagines, but form an independent clause, in which אַחֶיךָ is the subject, and אַנְשֵׁי גְאֻלָּתֶךָ as well as כָּל־בֵּית יִשְׂרָאֵל the predicates. The repetition of "thy brethren" serves to increase the force of the expression: thy true, real brethren; not in contrast to the priests, who were lineal relations (Hävernick), but in contrast to the Israelites, who had only the name of Israel, and denied its nature. These brethren are to be the people of his proxy; and toward these he is to exercise גְּאֻלָּה. גְּאֻלָּה is the business, or the duty and right, of the *Goël*. According to the law, the *Goël* was the brother, or the nearest relation, whose duty it was to come to the help of his impoverished brother, not only by redeeming (buying back) his possession, which poverty had compelled him to sell, but to redeem the man himself, if he had been sold to pay his debts (*vid.* Lev. xxv. 25, 48). The *Goël* therefore became the possessor of the property of which his brother had been unjustly deprived, if it were not restored till after his death (Num. v. 8). Consequently he was not only the avenger of blood, but the natural supporter and agent of his brother; and גְּאֻלָּה signifies not merely redemption or kindred, but *proxy*, *i.e.* both the right and obligation to act as the legal representative, the avenger of blood, the heir, etc., of the brother. The words "and the whole of the house of Israel" are a second predicate to "thy brethren," and affirm that the brethren, for whom Ezekiel can and is to intercede, form the whole of the house of Israel, the term "whole" being rendered more emphatic by the repetition of כֹּל in כֻּלֹּה. A contrast is drawn between this "whole house of Israel" and the inhabitants of Jerusalem, who say to those brethren, "Remain far away from Jehovah, to us is the land given for a possession." It follows from this, first of all, that the brethren of Ezekiel, towards whom he was to act as *Goël*, were those who had been taken away from the land, his companions in exile; and, secondly, that the exiles formed the whole of the house of Israel, that is to say, that they alone would be regarded by God as His people, and not the inhabitants of Jerusalem or those left in the land, who regarded the exiles as no longer a portion of the nation: simply because, in their estrangement from God, they looked upon the mere possession of Jerusalem as a pledge of participation in the grace of God. This shows the prophet where the remnant of the people of God is to be found. To this there is appended in ver. 16 sqq. a promise of the way in which the Lord will make this remnant His true people. לָכֵן, therefore, viz. because the inhabitants of Jerusalem regard the exiles as rejected by the Lord, Ezekiel is to declare to them that Jehovah is their sanctuary even in their dispersion (ver. 16); and because the others deny that they have any share in the possession of the land, the Lord will gather them together again, and give them the land of Israel (ver. 17). The two לָכֵן are co-ordinate, and introduce the antithesis to the disparaging sentence pronounced by the inhabitants of Jerusalem upon those who have been carried into exile. The כִּי before the two leading clauses in ver. 16 does not mean "because," serving to introduce a protasis, to which ver. 17 would form the apodosis, as Ewald affirms; but it stands before the direct address in the sense of an assurance, which indicates that there is some truth at the bottom of the judgment pronounced by their opponents, the inhabitants of Jerusalem. The thought is this: the present position of affairs is unquestionably that Jehovah has scattered them (the house of Israel) among the Gentiles; but He has not therefore cast them off. He has become a sanctuary to them in the lands of their dispersion. *Migdâsh* does not mean either asylum or an object kept sacred (Hitzig), but a sanctuary, more especially the temple. They had, indeed, lost the outward temple (at Jerusalem); but the Lord Himself had become their temple. What made the temple into a sanctuary was the presence of Jehovah, the covenant God, therein. This even the exiles were to enjoy in their banishment, and in this they would possess a substitute for the outward temple. This thought is rendered still more precise by the word מְעַט, which may refer either to time or measure, and signify "for a short time," or "in some measure." It is difficult to decide between these two renderings. In support of the latter, which Kliefoth prefers (after the LXX. and Vulgate), it may be argued that the manifestation of the Lord, both by the mission of prophets and by the outward deliverances and inward consolations which He bestowed upon the faithful, was but a partial substitute to the exile for His gracious presence in the temple and in the holy land. Nevertheless, the context, especially the promise in ver. 17, that He will gather them again and lead them back into the land of Israel, appears to favour the former signification, namely, that this substitution was only a provisional one, and was only to last for a short time, although it also implies that this could not and was not meant to be a perfect substitute for the gracious presence of the Lord. For Israel, as the people of God, could not remain scattered abroad; it must possess the inheritance bestowed upon it by the Lord, and have its God in the midst of it in its own land, and that in a manner more real than could possibly be the case in captivity among the Gentiles. This will be fully realized in the heavenly Jerusalem, where the Lord God Almighty and the Lamb will be a temple to the redeemed (Rev. xxi. 22). Therefore will Jehovah gather together the dispersed once more, and lead them back into the land of Israel, *i.e.* into the land which He designed for Israel; whereas the inhabitants of

Jerusalem, who boast of their possession of Canaan (ver. 15), will lose what they now possess. Those who are restored will then remove all idolatrous abominations (ver. 17), and receive from God a new and feeling heart (ver. 19), so that they will walk in the ways of God, and be in truth the people of God (ver. 20).

The fulfilment of this promise did, indeed, begin with the return of a portion of the exiles under Zerubbabel; but it was not completed under either Zerubbabel or Ezra, or even in the Maccabean times. Although Israel may have entirely relinquished the practice of gross idolatry after the captivity, it did not then attain to that newness of heart which is predicted in vers. 19, 20. This only commenced with the Baptist's preaching of repentance, and with the coming of Christ; and it was realized in the children of Israel, who accepted Jesus in faith, and suffered Him to make them children of God. Yet even by Christ this prophecy has not yet been perfectly fulfilled in Israel, but only in part, since the greater portion of Israel has still in its hardness that stony heart which must be removed out of its flesh before it can attain to salvation. The promise in ver. 19 has for its basis the prediction in Deut. xxx. 6. "What the circumcision of the heart is there, viz. the removal of all uncleanliness, of which outward circumcision was both the type and pledge, is represented here as the giving of a heart of flesh instead of one of stone" (Hengstenberg). I give them *one* heart. לֵב אֶחָד, which Hitzig is wrong in proposing to alter into לֵב אַחֵר, *another* heart, after the LXX., is supported and explained by Jer. xxxii. 39, "I give them *one* heart and *one* way to fear me continually" (cf. Zeph. iii. 9 and Acts iv. 32). *One* heart is not an upright, undivided heart (לֵב שָׁלֵם), but a harmonious, united heart, in contrast to the division or plurality of hearts which prevails in the natural state, in which every one follows his own heart and his own mind, turning "every one to his own way" (Isa. liii. 6). God gives *one* heart, when He causes all hearts and minds to become one. This can only be effected by His giving a "new spirit," taking away the stone-heart, and giving a heart of flesh instead. For the old spirit fosters nothing but egotism and discord. The heart of stone has no susceptibility to the impressions of the word of God and the drawing of divine grace. In the natural condition, the heart of man is as hard as stone. "The word of God, the external leadings of God, pass by and leave no trace behind. The latter may crush it, and yet not break it. Even the fragments continue hard; yea, the hardness goes on increasing" (Hengstenberg). The heart of flesh is a tender heart, susceptible to the drawing of divine grace (compare ch. xxxvi. 26, where these figures, which are peculiar to Ezekiel, recur; and for the substance of the prophecy, Jer. xxxi. 33). The fruit of this renewal of heart is walking in the commandments of the Lord; and the consequence of the latter is the perfect realization of the covenant relation, true fellowship with the Lord God. But judgment goes side by side with this renewal. Those who will not forsake their idols become victims to the judgment (ver. 21). The first hemistich of ver. 21 is a relative clause, in which אֲשֶׁר is to be supplied and connected with לִבָּם: "Whose heart walketh after the heart of their abominations." The heart, which is attributed to the abominations and detestations, *i.e.* to the idols, is the inclination to idolatry, the disposition and spirit which manifest themselves in the worship of idols. Walking after the heart of the idols forms the antithesis to walking after the heart of God (1 Sam. xiii. 14). For דַּרְכָּם וגו׳, "I will give their way," see ch. ix. 10.

Vers. 22–25. The promise that the Lord would preserve to Himself a holy seed among those who had been carried away captive, brought to a close the announcement of the judgment that would fall upon the ancient Israel and apostate Jerusalem. All that is now wanting, as a conclusion to the whole vision, is the practical confirmation of the announcement of judgment. This is given in the two following verses.—Ver. 22. *And the cherubim raised their wings, and the wheels beside them; and the glory of the God of Israel was up above them.* Ver. 23. *And the glory of Jehovah ascended from the midst of the city, and took its stand upon the mountain which is to the east of the city.* Ver. 24. *And wind lifted me up, and brought me to Chaldea to the exiles, in the vision, in the Spirit of God; and the vision ascended away from me, which I had seen.* Ver. 25. *And I spoke to the exiles all the words of Jehovah, which He had shown to me.*—The manifestation of the glory of the Lord had already left the temple, after the announcement of the burning of Jerusalem, and had taken its stand before the entrance of the eastern gate of the outer court, that is to say, in the city itself (ch. x. 19, xi. 1). But now, after the announcement had been made to the representatives of the authorities of their removal from the city, the glory of the God of Israel forsook the devoted city also, as a sign that both temple and city had ceased to be the seats of the gracious presence of the Lord. The mountain on the east of the city is the Mount of Olives, which affords a lofty outlook over the city. There the glory of God remained, to execute the judgment upon Jerusalem. Thus, according to Zech. xiv. 4, will Jehovah also appear at the last judgment on the Mount of Olives above Jerusalem, to fight thence against His foes, and prepare a way of escape for those who are to be saved. It was from the Mount of Olives also that the Son of God proclaimed to the degenerate city the second destruction (Luke xix. 21; Matt. xxiv. 3); and from the same mountain He made His visible ascension to heaven after His resurrection (Luke xxiv. 50; cf. Acts i. 12); and, as Grotius has observed, "thus did Christ ascend from this mountain into His kingdom, to execute judgment upon the Jews."

After this vision of the judgments of God upon the ancient people of the covenant and the kingdom of God, Ezekiel was carried back in the spirit into Chaldea, to the river Chaboras. The vision then vanished; and he related to the exiles all that he had seen.

CHAP. XII. DEPARTURE OF THE KING AND PEOPLE; AND BREAD OF TEARS.

The words of God which follow in ch. xii.–xix. do not contain any chronological data defining the exact period at which they were communicated to the prophet and reported by him. But so far as their contents are concerned, they are closely connected with the foregoing announcements of judgment; and this renders the assumption a very probable one, that they were not far removed from them in time, but fell within the space of eleven months intervening between ch. viii. 1 and xx. 1, and were designed to carry out still further the announcement of judgment in ch. viii.–xi. This is done more especially in the light thrown upon all the circumstances, on which the impenitent people rested their hope of the preservation of the kingdom and Jerusalem, and of their speedy liberation from the Babylonian yoke. The purpose of the whole is to show the worthlessness of this false confidence, and to affirm the certainty and irresistibility of the predicted destruction of Judah and Jerusalem, in the hope of awakening the rebellious and hardened generation to that thorough repentance, without which it was impossible that peace and prosperity could ever be enjoyed. This definite purpose in the prophecies which follow is clearly indicated in the introductory remarks in ch. xii. 2, xiv. 1, and xx. 1. In the first of these passages the hardness of Israel is mentioned as the motive for the ensuing prophecy; whilst in the other two, the visit of certain elders of Israel to the prophet, to seek the Lord and to inquire through him, is given as the circumstance which occasioned the further prophetic declarations. It is evident from this that the previous words of God had already made some impression upon the hearers, but that their hard heart had not yet been broken by them.

In ch. xii., Ezekiel receives instructions to depict, by means of a symbolical action, the departure of the king and people from Jerusalem (vers. 3–7), and to explain the action to the refractory generation (vers. 8–16). After this he is to exhibit, by another symbolical sign, the want and distress to which the people will be reduced (vers. 17–20). And lastly, he is to rebut the frivolous sayings of the people, to the effect that what is predicted will either never take place at all, or not till a very distant time (vers. 21–28).

Vers. 1–7. SYMBOL OF THE EMIGRATION.—Ver. 1. *And the word of Jehovah came to me, saying,* Ver. 2. *Son of man, thou dwellest amidst the refractory generation, who have eyes to see, and see not; and have ears to hear, and hear not; for they are a refractory generation.* Ver. 3. *And thou, son of man, make thyself an outfit for exile, and depart by day before their eyes; and depart from thy place to another place before their eyes: perhaps they might see, for they are a refractory generation.* Ver. 4. *And carry out thy things like an outfit for exile by day before their eyes; but do thou go out in the evening before their eyes, as when going out to exile.* Ver. 5. *Before their eyes break through the wall, and carry it out there.* Ver. 6. *Before their eyes take it upon thy shoulder, carry it out in the darkness: cover thy face, and look not upon the land; for I have set thee as a sign to the house of Israel.* Ver. 7. *And I did so as I was commanded: I carried out my things like an outfit for exile by day, and in the evening I broke through the wall with my hand; I carried it out in the darkness; I took it upon my shoulder before their eyes.*— In ver. 2 the reason is assigned for the command to perform the symbolical action, namely, the hard-heartedness of the people. Because the generation in the midst of which Ezekiel dwelt was blind, with seeing eyes, and deaf, with hearing ears, the prophet was to depict before its eyes, by means of the sign that followed, the judgment which was approaching; in the hope, as is added in ver. 3, that they might possibly observe and lay the sign to heart. The refractoriness (בֵּית מְרִי, as in ch. ii. 5, 6, iii. 26, etc.) is described as obduracy, viz. having eyes, and not seeing; having ears, and not hearing, after Deut. xxix. 3 (cf. Jer. v. 21; Isa. vi. 9; Matt. xiii. 14, 15). The root of this mental blindness and deafness was to be found in obstinacy, *i.e.* in not willing; "in that presumptuous insolence," as Michaelis says, "through which divine light can obtain no admission." כְּלֵי גוֹלָה, the goods (or outfit) of exile, were a pilgrim's staff and traveller's wallet, with the provisions and utensils necessary for a journey. Ezekiel was to carry these out of the house into the street in the day-time, that the people might see them and have their attention called to them. Then in the evening, after dark, he was to go out himself, not by the door of the house, but through a hole which he had broken in the wall. He was also to take the travelling outfit upon his shoulder and carry it through the hole and out of the place, covering his face all the while, that he might not see the land to which he was going. "Thy place" is thy dwelling-place. כְּמוֹצָאֵי גוֹלָה: as the departures of exiles generally take place, *i.e.* as exiles are accustomed to depart, not "at the usual time of departure into exile," as Hävernick proposes. For מוֹצָא, see the comm. on Mic. v. 1. בָּעֲלָטָה differs from בָּעֶרֶב, and signifies the darkness of the depth of night (cf. Gen. xv. 17); not, however, "darkness artificially produced, equivalent to, with the eyes shut, or the face covered; so that the words which follow are simply explanatory of בָּעֲלָטָה," as Schmieder imagines. Such an assumption would be at variance not only with ver. 7, but also with ver. 12, where the covering or concealing of the face is expressly distinguished from the carrying out "in the dark." The order was to be as follows: In the day-time Ezekiel was to take the travelling outfit and carry it out into the road; then in the evening he was to go out himself, having first of all broken a hole through the wall as evening was coming on; and in the darkness of night he was to place upon his shoulders whatever he was about to carry with him, and take his departure. This he was to do, because God had made him a *mōphēth* for Israel: in other words, by doing this he was to show himself to be a marvellous sign to Israel. For *mōphēth*, see the comm. on Ex. iv. 21. In ver. 7, the execution of the command, which evidently took place in the strictness of the letter, is fully described. There was nothing impracticable in the action, for breaking through the wall did not preclude the use of a hammer or some other tool.

Vers. 8–16. Explanation of the symbolical action.—Ver. 8. *And the word of Jehovah came to me in the morning, saying,* Ver. 9. *Son of man, have they not said to thee, the house of Israel, the refractory generation, What art thou doing?* Ver. 10. *Say to them, Thus saith the Lord Jehovah, This burden applies to the prince in Jerusalem, and to all the house of Israel to whom they belong.* Ver. 11. *Say, I am your sign: as I have done, so shall it happen to them; into exile, into captivity, will they go.* Ver. 12. *And the prince who is in the midst of them he will lift it upon his shoulder in the dark, and will go out: they will break through the wall, and carry it out thereby: he will cover his face, that he may not see the land with eyes.* Ver. 13. *And I will spread my net over him, so that he will be caught in my snare: and I will take him to Babel, into the land of the Chaldeans; but he will not see it, and will die there.* Ver. 14. *And all that is about him, his help and all his troops, I will scatter into all winds, and draw out the sword behind them.* Ver. 15. *And they shall learn that I am Jehovah, when I scatter them among the nations, and winnow them in the lands.* Ver. 16. *Yet I will leave of them a small number of men from the sword, from the famine, and from the pestilence; that they may relate all their abominations among the nations whither they have come; and learn that I am Jehovah.*—As queries introduced with הֲלֹא have, as a rule, an affirmative sense, the words "have they not asked," etc., imply that the Israelites had asked the prophet what he was doing, though not in a proper state of mind, not in a penitential manner, as the epithet בֵּית הַמְּרִי plainly shows. The prophet is therefore to interpret the action which he had just been performing, and all its different stages. The words הַנָּשִׂיא הַמַּשָּׂא הַזֶּה, to which very different renderings have been given, are to be translated simply "the prince is this burden," *i.e.* the object of this burden. *Hammassâ* does not mean the carrying, but the burden, *i.e.* the threatening prophecy, the prophetic action of the prophet, as in the headings to the oracles (see the comm. on Nah. i. 1). The "prince" is the king, as in ch. xxi. 30, though not Jehoiachin, who had been carried into exile, but Zedekiah. This is stated in the apposition "in Jerusalem," which belongs to "the prince," though it is not introduced till after the predicate, as in Gen. xxiv. 24. To this there is appended the further definition, "the whole house of Israel," which, being co-ordinated with הַנָּשִׂיא, affirms that all Israel (the covenant nation) will share the fate of the prince. In the last clause of ver. 10 בְּתוֹכָם does not stand for בְּתוֹכָהּ, so that the suffix would refer to Jerusalem, "in the midst of which they (the house of Israel) are." אֲשֶׁר cannot be a nominative, because in that case הֵמָּה would be superfluous; it is rather to be taken with בְּתוֹכָם, and הֵמָּה to be understood as referring to the persons addressed, *i.e.* to the Israelites in exile (Hitzig, Kliefoth): in the midst of whom they are, *i.e.* to whom they belong. The sentence explains the reason why the prophet was to announce to those in exile the fate of the prince and people in Jerusalem; namely, because the exiles formed a portion of the nation, and would be affected by the judgment which was about to burst upon the king and people in Jerusalem. In this sense Ezekiel was also able to say to the exiles (in ver. 11), "I am *your* sign;" inasmuch as his sign was also of importance for them, as those who were already banished would be so far affected by the departure of the king and people which Ezekiel depicted, that it would deprive them of all hope of a speedy return to their native land. לָהֶם, in ver. 11, refers to the king and the house of Israel in Jerusalem. בַּגּוֹלָה is rendered more forcible by the addition of בַּשְּׁבִי. The announcement that both king and people must go into exile, is carried out still further in vers. 12 and 13 with reference to the king, and in ver. 14 with regard to the people. The king will experience all that Ezekiel has described. The literal occurrence of what is predicted here is related in Jer. xxxix. 1 sqq., lii. 4 sqq.; 2 Kings xxv. 4 sqq. When the Chaldeans forced their way into the city after a two years' siege, Zedekiah and his men of war fled by night out of the city through the gate between the two walls. It is not expressly stated, indeed, in the historical accounts that a breach was made in the wall; but the expression "through the gate between the two walls" (Jer. xxxix. 4, lii. 7; 2 Kings xxv. 4) renders this very probable, whether the gate had been walled up during the siege, or it was necessary to break through the wall at one particular spot in order to reach the gate. The king's attendants would naturally take care that a breach was made in the wall, to secure for him a way of escape; hence the expression, "*they* will break through." The covering of the face, also, is not mentioned in the historical accounts; but in itself it is by no means improbable, as a sign of the shame and grief with which Zedekiah left the city. The words, "that he may not see the land with eyes," do not appear to indicate anything more than the necessary consequence of covering the face, and refer primarily to the simple fact that the king fled in the deepest sorrow, and did not want to see the land; but, as ver. 13 clearly intimates, they were fulfilled in another way, namely, by the fact that Zedekiah did not see with his eyes the land of the Chaldeans into which he was led, because he had been blinded at Riblah (Jer. xxxix. 5, lii. 11; 2 Kings xxv. 7). לְעַיִן, by eye = with his eyes, is added to give prominence to the idea of seeing. For the same purpose, the subject, which is already implied in the verb, is rendered more emphatic by הוּא; and this הוּא is placed after the verb, so that it stands in contrast with הָאָרֶץ. The capture of the king was not depicted by Ezekiel; so that in this respect the announcement (ver. 13) goes further than the symbolical action, and removes all doubt as to the credibility of the prophet's word, by a distinct prediction of the fate awaiting him. At the same time, his not seeing the land of Babylon is left so indefinite, that it cannot be regarded as a *vaticinium post eventum.* Zedekiah died in prison at Babylon (Jer. lii. 11). Along with the king, the whole of his military force will be scattered in all directions (ver. 14). עֶזְרֹה, his help, *i.e.* the troops that break through with him. כָּל־אֲגַפָּיו, all his wings (the wings of his army), *i.e.* all the rest of his forces. The word is peculiar to Ezekiel, and is rendered "wings" by Jos. Kimchi, like *k^enâphaim* in Isa. viii. 8. For the rest of the verse compare ch. v. 2; and for the fulfilment, Jer. lii. 8, xl. 7, 12. The greater part of the people will perish, and only a small number remain, that they may relate among the heathen, wherever they are led, all the abominations of Israel, in order that the heathen may learn that it is not from weakness, but simply to punish idolatry, that God has given up His people to them (cf. Jer. xxii. 8).

Vers. 17–20. SIGN DEPICTING THE TERRORS AND CONSEQUENCES OF THE CONQUEST OF JERUSALEM.—Ver. 17. *And the word of Jehovah came to me, saying,* Ver. 18. *Son of man, thou shalt eat thy bread with quaking, and drink thy water with trembling and trouble;* Ver. 19. *And say to the people of the land, Thus saith the Lord Jehovah to the inhabitants of Jerusalem, in the land of Israel, They will eat their bread in trouble, and drink their water in amazement, because her land is laid waste of all its fulness for the wickedness of all who dwell therein.* Ver. 20. *And the inhabited cities become desolate, and the land will be laid waste; that ye may learn that I am Jehovah.*—The carrying out of this sign is not mentioned; not that there is any doubt as to its having been done, but that it is simply taken for granted. The trouble and trembling could only be expressed by means of gesture. רַעַשׁ, generally an earthquake or violent convulsion; here, simply shaking, synonymous with רָגְזָה, trembling. "Bread and water" is the standing expression for food; so that even here the idea of scanty provisions is not to be sought therein. This idea is found merely in the signs of anxiety and trouble with which Ezekiel was to eat his food. אֶל־אַדְמַת = עַל־אד׳, "upon the land," equivalent to "in the land." This is appended to show that the prophecy does not refer to those who had already been carried into exile, but to the inhabitants of Jerusalem who were still in the land. For the subject-matter, compare ch. iv. 16, 17. לְמַעַן indicates not the intention, "in order that," but the motive, "because."

Vers. 21–28. Declarations to remove all Doubt as to the Truth of the Threat.—The scepticism of the people as to the fulfilment of these threatening prophecies, which had been made still more emphatic by signs, manifested itself in two different ways. Some altogether denied that the prophecies would ever be fulfilled (ver. 22); others, who did not go so far as this, thought that it would be a long time before they came to pass (ver. 27). These doubts were fed by the lying statements of false prophets. For this reason the refutation of these sceptical opinions (vers. 21–28) is followed in the next chapter by a stern reproof of the false prophets and prophetesses who led the people astray.—Ver. 21. *And the word of Jehovah came to me, saying,* Ver. 22. *Son of man, what kind of proverb have ye in the land of Israel, that ye say, The days become long, and every prophecy comes to nothing?* Ver. 23. *Therefore say to them, Thus saith the Lord Jehovah, I will put an end to this saying, and they shall say it no more in Israel; but say to them, The days are near, and the word of every prophecy.* Ver. 24. *For henceforth there shall be no vain prophecy and flattering soothsaying in the midst of the house of Israel.* Ver. 25. *For I am Jehovah; I speak; the word which I speak will come to pass, and no longer be postponed; for in your days, O refractory generation, I speak a word and do it, is the saying of the Lord Jehovah.—Mâshâl,* a proverb, a saying current among the people, and constantly repeated as a truth. "The days become long," etc., *i.e.* the time is lengthening out, and yet the prophecy is not being fulfilled. אָבַד, *perire,* to come to nothing, to fail of fulfilment, is the opposite of בּוֹא, to come, to be fulfilled. God will put an end to these sayings, by causing a very speedy fulfilment of the prophecy. The days are near, and every word of the prophecy, *i.e.* the days in which every word predicted shall come to pass. The reason for this is given in vers. 24 and 25, in two co-ordinate sentences, both of which are introduced with כִּי. First, every false prophecy shall henceforth cease in Israel (ver. 24); secondly, God will bring about the fulfilment of His own word, and that without delay (ver. 25). Different explanations have been given of the meaning of ver. 24. Kliefoth proposes to take שָׁוְא and מִקְסַם חָלָק as the predicate to חָזוֹן: no prophecy in Israel shall be vain and flattering soothsaying, but all prophecy shall become true, *i.e.* be fulfilled. Such an explanation, however, is not only artificial and unnatural, since מִקְסַם would be inserted as a predicate in a most unsuitable manner, but it contains this incongruity, that God would apply the term מִקְסַם, soothsaying, to the predictions of prophets inspired by Himself. On the other hand, there is no force in the objection raised by Kliefoth to the ordinary rendering of the words, namely, that the statement that God was about to put an end to false prophecy in Israel would anticipate the substance of the sixth word of God (*i.e.* ch. xiii.). It is impossible to see why a thought should not be expressed here, and then still further expanded in ch. xiii. חָלָק, smooth, *i.e.* flattering (compare Hos. x. 2; and for the prediction, Zech. xiii. 4, 5). The same reply serves also to overthrow the sceptical objection raised by the frivolous despisers of the prophet's words. Hence there is only a brief allusion made to them in vers. 26–28.—Ver. 26. *And the word of Jehovah came to me, saying,* Ver. 27. *Son of man, behold, the house of Israel saith, The vision that he seeth is for many days off, and he prophesies for distant times.* Ver. 28. *Therefore say to them, Thus saith the Lord Jehovah, All my words shall be no longer postponed: the word which I shall speak shall come to pass, saith the Lord Jehovah.*—The words are plain; and after what has already been said, they need no special explanation. Ver. 20 compare with ver. 25.

CHAP. XIII. AGAINST THE FALSE PROPHETS AND PROPHETESSES.

The way was already prepared for the address in this chapter by the announcement in ch. xii. 24. It divides itself into two parts, viz. vers. 1–16, directed against the false prophets; and vers. 17–23, against the false prophetesses. In both parts their conduct is first described, and then the punishment foretold. Jeremiah, like Ezekiel, and sometimes still more strongly, denounces the conduct of the false prophets, who are therefore to be sought for not merely among the exiles, but principally among those who were left behind in the land (*vid.* Jer. xxiii. 9 sqq.). A lively intercourse was kept up between the two, so that the false prophets extended their operations from Canaan to the Chaboras, and *vice versa.*

Vers. 1–16. AGAINST THE FALSE PROPHETS.—Vers. 1–7. Their conduct.—Ver. 1. *And the word of Jehovah came to me, saying,* Ver. 2. *Son of man, prophesy against the prophets of Israel who prophesy, and say to the prophets out of their heart, Hear ye the word of Jehovah.* Ver. 3. *Thus saith the Lord Jehovah, Woe upon the foolish prophets, who go after their spirit, and that which they have not seen!* Ver. 4. *Like foxes in ruins have thy prophets become, O Israel.* Ver. 5. *Ye do not stand before the breaches, nor wall up the wall around the house of Israel to stand firm in the battle on the day of Jehovah.* Ver. 6. *They see vanity and lying soothsaying, who say, "Oracle of Jehovah;" and Jehovah hath not sent them; so that they might hope for the fulfilment of the word.* Ver. 7. *Do ye not see vain visions, and speak lying soothsaying, and say, Oracle of Jehovah; and I have not spoken?*—The addition הַנִּבָּאִים, "who prophesy," is not superfluous. Ezekiel is not to direct his words against the prophets as a body, but against those who follow the vocation of prophet in Israel without being called to it by God on receiving a divine revelation, but simply prophesying out of their own heart, or according to their own subjective imagination. In the name of the Lord he is to threaten them with woes, as fools who follow their own spirit; in connection with which we must bear in mind that folly, according to the Hebrew idea, was not merely a moral failing, but actual godlessness (cf. Ps. xiv. 1). The phrase "going after their spirit" is interpreted and rendered more emphatic by לְבִלְתִּי רָאוּ, which is to be taken as a relative clause, "that which they have not seen," *i.e.* whose prophesying does not rest upon intuition inspired by God. Consequently they cannot promote the welfare of the nation, but (ver. 4) are like foxes in ruins or desolate places. The point of comparison is to be found in the undermining of the ground by foxes, *qui per cuniculos subjectam terram excavant et suffodiunt* (Bochart). For the thought is not exhausted by the circumstance that they withdraw to their holes instead of standing in front of the breach (Hitzig); and there is no force in the objection that, with this explanation, בֶּחֳרָבוֹת is passed over and becomes in fact tautological (Hävernick). The expression "in ruins" points to the fall of the theocracy, which the false prophets cannot prevent, but, on the contrary, accelerate by undermining the moral foundations of the state. For (ver. 5) they do not stand in the breaches, and do not build up the wall around the house of Israel (לֹא belongs to both clauses). He who desires to keep off the enemy, and prevent his entering the fortress, will stand in the breach. For the same purpose are gaps and breaches in the fortifications carefully built up. The sins of the people had made gaps and breaches in the walls of Jerusalem; in other words, had caused the moral decay of the city. But they had not stood in the way of this decay and its causes, as the calling and duty of prophets demanded, by reproving the sins of the people, that they might rescue the people and kingdom from destruction by restoring its moral and religious life. לַעֲמֹד בַּמִּלְחָמָה, to stand, or keep ground, *i.e.* so that ye might have kept your ground in the war. The subject is the false prophets, not Israel, as Hävernick supposes. "In the day of Jehovah," *i.e.* in the judgment which Jehovah has decreed. Not to stand, does not mean merely to avert the threatening judgment, but not to survive the judgment itself, to be overthrown by it. This arises from the fact that their prophesying is a lie; because Jehovah, whose name they have in their mouths, has not sent them (ver. 6). וְיִחֲלוּ is dependent upon שְׁלָחָם: God has not sent them, so that they could hope for the fulfilment of the word which they speak. The rendering adopted by others, "and they cause to hope," is untenable; for יִחַל with לְ does not mean "to cause to hope," or give hope, but simply to hope for anything. This was really the case; and it is affirmed in the declaration, which is repeated in the form of a direct appeal in ver. 7, to the effect that their visions were vain and lying soothsaying. For this they are threatened with the judgment described in the verses which follow.

Vers. 8–16. Punishment of the false prophets.—Ver. 8. *Therefore thus saith the Lord Jehovah, Because ye speak vanity and prophesy lying, therefore, behold, I will deal with you, is the saying of the Lord Jehovah.* Ver. 9. *And my hand shall be against the prophets who see vanity and divine lies: in the council of my people they shall not be, and in the register of the house of Israel they shall not be registered, and into the land of Israel shall they not come; and ye shall learn that I am the Lord Jehovah.* Ver. 10. *Because, yea because they lead my people astray, and say, "Peace," though there is no peace; and when it (my people) build a wall, behold, they plaster it with cement:* Ver. 11. *Say to the plasterers, that it will fall: there cometh a pouring rain; and ye hailstones fall, and thou stormy wind break loose!* Ver. 12. *And, behold, the wall falleth; will men not say to you, Where is the plaster with which ye have plastered it?* Ver. 13. *Therefore thus saith the Lord Jehovah, I cause a stormy wind to break forth in my wrath, and a pouring rain will come in my anger, and hailstones in wrath, for destruction.* Ver. 14. *And I demolish the wall which ye have plastered, and cast it to the ground, that its foundation may be exposed, and it shall fall, and ye shall perish in the midst of it; and shall learn that I am Jehovah.* Ver. 15. *And I will exhaust my wrath upon the wall, and upon those who plaster it; and will say to you, It is all over with the wall, and all over with those who plastered it;* Ver. 16. *With the prophets of Israel who prophesied to Jerusalem, and saw visions of peace for her, though there is no peace, is the saying of the Lord Jehovah.*—In ver. 8 the punishment which is to fall upon the false prophets is threatened in general terms; and in ver. 9 it is more specifically described in the form of a climax, rising higher and higher in the severity of its announcements. (1) They are no longer to form part of the council of the people of God; that is to say, they will lose their influential position among the people. (סוֹד is the sphere of counsellors, not the social sphere.) (2) Their names shall not be registered in the book of the house of Israel. The book of the house of Israel is the register in which the citizens of the kingdom of God are entered. Any one whose name was not admitted into this book, or was struck out of it, was separated thereby from the citizenship of Israel, and lost all the privileges which citizenship conferred. The figure of the book of life is a similar one (cf. Ex. xxxii. 32). For Israel is not referred to here with regard to its outward nationality, but as the people of God; so that exclusion from Israel was also exclusion from fellowship with God. The circumstance that it is not the erasure of their names from the book that is mentioned here, but their not being entered in the book at all, may be accounted for from the reference contained in the words to the founding of the new kingdom of God. The old theocracy was abolished, although Jerusalem was not yet destroyed. The covenant nation had fallen under the judgment; but out of that portion of Israel which was dispersed among the heathen, a remnant would be gathered together again, and having been brought back to its own land, would be made anew into a holy people of God (cf. ch. xi. 17 sqq.). But the false prophets are not to be received into the citizenship of the new kingdom. (3) They are not even to come into the land of Israel; *i.e.* they are not merely to remain in exile, but to lose all share in the privileges and blessings of the kingdom of God. This judgment will come upon them because they lead astray the people of God, by proclaiming peace where there is no peace; *i.e.* by raising and cherishing false hopes of prosperity and peace, by which they encourage the people in their sinful lives, and lead them to imagine that all is well, and there is no judgment to be feared (cf. Jer. xxiii. 17 and Mic. iii. 5). The exposure of this offence is introduced by the solemn יַעַן וּבְיַעַן, because and because (cf. Lev. xxvi. 43); and the offence itself is exhibited by means of a figure. When the people build a wall, the false prophets plaster the wall with lime. וְהוּא (ver. 10) refers to עַמִּי, and the clause is a circumstantial one. תָּפֵל signifies the plaster coating or cement of a wall, probably from the primary meaning of תָּפַל, to stick or plaster over (=טָפַל, *conglutinare*, to glue, or fasten together), from which the secondary meaning of weak, insipid, has sprung. The proper word for plaster or cement is טִיחַ (ver. 12), and תָּפֵל is probably chosen with an allusion to the tropical signification of that which is silly or absurd (Jer. xxiii. 13; Lam. ii. 14). The meaning of the figure is intelligible enough. The people build up foolish hopes, and the prophets not only paint these hopes for them in splendid colours, but even predict their fulfilment, instead of denouncing their folly, pointing out to the people the perversity of their ways, and showing them that such sinful conduct must inevitably be followed by punishment and ruin. The plastering is therefore a figurative description of deceitful flattery or hypocrisy, *i.e.* the covering up of inward corruption by means of outward appearance (as in Matt. xxiii. 27 and Acts xxiii. 3). This figure leads the prophet to describe the judgment which they are bringing upon the nation and themselves, as a tempest accompanied with hail and pouring rain, which throws down the wall that has been erected and plastered over; and in connection with this figure he opens out this double thought: (1) the conduct of the people, which is encouraged by the false prophets, cannot last (vers. 11 and 12); and (2) when this work of theirs is overthrown, the false prophets themselves will also meet with the fate they deserve (vers. 13–16). The threat of judgment commences with the short, energetic וְיִפֹּל, let it (the wall) fall, or it shall fall, with *Vav* to indicate the train of thought (Ewald, § 347*a*). The subject is תָּפֵל, to which יִפֹּל suggests a resemblance in sound. In ver. 12 this is predicted as the fate awaiting the plastered wall. In the description of the bursting storm the account passes with וְאַתֵּנָה (and ye) into a direct address; in other words, the description assumes the form of an appeal to the destructive forces of nature to burst forth with all their violence against the work plastered over by the prophets, and to destroy it. גֶּשֶׁם שׁוֹטֵף, pouring rain; cf. ch. xxxviii. 22. אַבְנֵי אֶלְגָּבִישׁ here and ch. xxxviii. 22 are hail-stones. The word אֶלְגָּבִישׁ, which is peculiar to Ezekiel, is probably גָּבִישׁ (Job xxviii. 18), with the Arabic article אל; ice, then crystal. רוּחַ סְעָרוֹת, wind of storms, a hurricane or tempest. תְּבַקַּע (ver. 11) is used intransitively, to break loose; but in ver. 13 it is transitive, to cause to break loose. The active rendering adopted by Kliefoth, "the storm will rend," *sc.* the plaster of the wall, is inappropriate in ver. 11; for a tempest does not rend either the plaster or the wall, but throws the wall down. The translation which Kliefoth gives in ver. 13, "I will rend by tempest," is at variance with both the language and the sense. Jehovah will cause this tempest to burst forth in His wrath and destroy the wall, and lay it level with the ground. The suffix in בְּתוֹכָהּ refers (*ad sensum*) to Jerusalem, not to קִיר (the wall), which is masculine, and has no תָּוֶךְ (midst). The words pass from the figure to the reality here; for the plastered wall is a symbol of Jerusalem, as the centre of the theocracy, which is to be destroyed, and to bury the lying prophets in its ruins. וְכִלֵּיתִי (ver. 15) contains a play upon the word לְכָלָה in ver. 13. By a new turn given to כלה, Ezekiel repeats the thought that the wrath of God is to destroy the wall and its plasterers; and through this repetition he rounds off the threat with the express declaration, that the false prophets who are ever preaching peace are the plasterers to whom he refers.

Vers. 17–23. AGAINST THE FALSE PROPHETESSES. — As the Lord had not endowed men only with the gifts of prophecy, but sometimes women also, *e.g.* Miriam, Deborah, and Huldah; so women also rose up along with the false prophets, and prophesied out of their own hearts without being impelled by the Spirit of God. Vers. 17–19. Their conduct.—Ver. 17. *And thou, son of man, direct thy face towards the daughters of thy people, who prophesy out of their heart and prophesy against them,* Ver. 18. *And say, Thus saith the Lord Jehovah, Woe to those who sew coverings together over all the joints of my hands, and make caps for the head of every size, to catch souls! Ye catch the souls of my people, and keep your souls alive.* Ver. 19. *And ye profane me with my people for handfuls of barley and for pieces of bread, to slay souls which should not die, and to keep alive which should not live, by your lying to my people who hearken to lying.*—Like the prophets in ver. 2, the prophetesses are here described as prophesying out of their own heart (ver. 17); and in vers. 18 and 19 their offences are more particularly described. The meaning of these verses is entirely dependent upon the view to be taken of יָדַי, which the majority of expositors, following the lead of the LXX., the Syriac, and the Vulgate, have regarded as identical with יָדַיִם or יָדָיו, and understood as referring to the hands of the women or prophetesses. But there is nothing to justify the assumption that יָדַי is an unusual form for יָדַיִם, which even Ewald takes it to be (*Lehrbuch*, § 177*a*). Still less can it stand for the singular יָד. And we have not sufficient ground for altering the text, as the expression זְרוֹעֹתֵיכֶם in ver. 20 (I will tear the כְּסָתוֹת from your arms) does not require the assumption that the prophetesses had hidden their arms in כסתות; and such a supposition is by no means obviously in harmony with the facts. The word כְּסָתוֹת, from כֶּסֶת, with ת fem. treated as a radical letter (cf. Ewald, § 186*e*), means a covering or concealment = כְּסוּת. The meaning "cushion" or "pillow" (LXX. *προσκεφάλαια*, Vulg. *pulvilli*) is merely an inference drawn from this passage, and is decidedly erroneous; for the word תָּפַר (to sew together) is inapplicable to cushions, as well as the phrase עַל כָּל־אַצִּילֵי יָדַי, inasmuch as cushions are not placed upon the joints of the hands, and still less are they sewed together upon them. The latter is also a decisive reason for rejecting the explanation given by Hävernick, namely, that the *kesâthōth* were carpets, which were used as couches, and upon which these voluptuous women are represented as reclining. For cushions or couches are not placed upon, but under, the arm-joints (or elbows) and the shoulders, which Hävernick understands by אַצִּילֵי יָד. This also overthrows another explanation given of the words, namely, that they refer to carpets, which the prophetesses had sewed together for all their arm-joints, so as to form comfortable beds upon splendid carpets, that they may indulge in licentiousness thereon. The explanation given by Ephraem Syrus, and adopted by Hitzig, namely, that the *kesâthōth* were amulets or straps, which they wound round their arm-joints when they received or delivered their oracles, is equally untenable. For, as Kliefoth has observed, "it is evident that there is not a word in the text about adultery, or amulets, or straps used in prayer." And again, when we proceed to the next clause, the traditional rendering of מִסְפָּחוֹת, as signifying either pillows (*ὑπαυχένια*, Symm.; *cervicalia*, Vulg.) or broad cloaks = מִטְפָּחוֹת (Hitzig, Hävernick, etc.), is neither supported by the usage of the language, nor in harmony with עַל ראשׁ. *Mispâchōth*, from *sâphach*, to join, cannot have any other meaning in the present context than a cap fitting close to the head; and עַל must denote the pattern which was followed, as in Ps. cx. 4, Esth. ix. 26: they make the caps after (answering to) the head of every stature. The words of both clauses are figurative, and have been correctly explained by Kliefoth as follows: "A double charge is brought against the prophetesses. In the first place, they sew coverings together to wrap round all the joints of the hand of God, so that He cannot touch them; *i.e.* they cover up and conceal the word of God by their prophesying, more especially its rebuking and threatening force, so that the threatening and judicial arm of God, which ought above all to become both manifest and effective through His prophetic word, does not become either one or the other. In the second place, they make coverings upon the heads of men, and construct them in such a form that they exactly fit the stature or size of every individual, so that the men neither hear nor see; *i.e.*, by means of their flattering lies, which adapt themselves to the subjective inclinations of their hearers at the time, they cover up the senses of the men, so that they retain neither ear nor eye for the truth." They do both of these to catch souls. The inevitable consequence of their act is represented as having been intended by them; and this intention is then still further defined as being to catch the souls of the people of God; *i.e.* to allure them to destruction, and take care of their own souls. The clause הַנְּפָשׁוֹת תְּצוֹדֵדְנָה is not to be taken as a question, "Will ye catch the souls?" implying a doubt whether they really thought that they could carry on such conduct as theirs with perfect impunity (Hävernick). It contains a simple statement of what really took place in their catching of souls, namely, "they catch the souls of the people of God, and preserve their own souls;" *i.e.* they rob the people of God of their lives, and take care of their own (Kliefoth). לְעַמִּי is used instead of the genitive (*stat. constr.*) to show that the accent rests upon עַמִּי. And in the same way we have לָכֵנָה instead of the suffix. The construction is the same as in 1 Sam xiv. 16. Ver. 19 shows how great their sin had been. They profane God among His people; namely, by delivering the suggestions of their own heart to the people as divine revelations, for the purpose of getting their daily bread thereby (cf. Mic. iii. 5); by hurling into destruction, through their lies, those who are only too glad to listen to lying; by slaying the souls of the people which ought to live, and by preserving those which ought not to live, *i.e.* their own souls (Deut. xviii. 20). The punishment for this will not fail to come.

Vers. 20–23. Punishment of the false prophetesses.—Ver. 20. *Therefore thus saith the Lord Jehovah, Behold, I will deal with your coverings with which ye catch, I will let the souls fly; and I will tear them away from your arms, and set the souls free, which ye catch, the souls to fly.* Ver. 21. *And I will tear your caps in pieces, and deliver my people out of your hand, and they shall no more become a prey in your hand; and ye shall learn that I am Jehovah.* Ver. 22. *Because ye grieve the heart of the righteous with lying, when I have not pained him; and strengthen the hands of the wicked, so that he does not turn from his evil way, to preserve his life.* Ver. 23. *Therefore ye shall no more see vanity, and no longer practise soothsaying: and I will deliver my people out of your hand; and ye shall learn that I am Jehovah.*—The threat of judgment is closely connected with the reproof of their sins. Vers. 20 and 21 correspond to the reproof in ver. 18, and vers. 22 and 23 to that in ver. 19. In the first place, the Lord will tear in pieces the coverings and caps, *i.e.* the tissue of lies woven by the false prophetesses, and rescue the people from their snares (vers. 20 and 21); and, secondly, He will entirely put an end to the pernicious conduct of the persons addressed (vers. 22 and 23). The words from אֲשֶׁר אַתֵּנָה to לְפֹרְחוֹת (ver. 20*a*), when taken as one clause, as they generally are, offer insuperable difficulties, since it is impossible to get any satisfactory meaning from שָׁם, and לְפֹרְחוֹת will not fit in. Whether we understand by *k*[e]*sâthōth* coverings or cushions, the connection of שָׁם with אֲשֶׁר (*where* ye catch the souls), which the majority of commentators prefer, is untenable; for coverings and cushions were not the places where the souls were caught, but could only be the means employed for catching them. Instead of שָׁם we should expect בָּם or בָּהֶם; and Hitzig proposes to amend it in this way. Still less admissible is the proposal to take שָׁם as referring to Jerusalem ("wherewith ye catch souls *there*"); as שָׁם would not only contain a perfectly superfluous definition of locality, but would introduce a limitation altogether at variance with the context. It is not affirmed either of the prophets or of the prophetesses that they lived and prophesied in Jerusalem alone. In vers. 2 and 17 reference is made in the most general terms to the prophets of Israel and the daughters of thy people; and in ver. 16 it is simply stated that the false prophets prophesied peace to Jerusalem when there was no peace at all. Consequently we must regard the attempt to find in שָׁם an allusion to Jerusalem (cf. ver. 16) as a mere loophole, which betrays an utter inability to get any satisfactory sense from the word. Moreover, if we construe the words in this manner, לְפֹרְחוֹת is also incomprehensible. Commentators have for the most part admitted that פָּרַח is used here in the Aramaean sense of *volare*, to fly. In the second half of the verse there is no doubt about its having this meaning. For שִׁלַּח is used in Deut. xxii. 7 for liberating a bird, or letting it fly; and the combination שִׁלַּח אֶת־הנפ' לְפֹרְחוֹת is supported by the expression שִׁלַּח לַחָפְשִׁי in Ex. xxi. 26, while the comparison of souls to birds is sustained by Ps. xi. 1 and cxxiv. 7. Hence the true meaning of the whole passage שִׁלַּחְתִּי אֶת־הַנְּפָשׁוֹת . . . לְפֹרְחוֹת is, I send away (set free) the souls, which ye have caught, as flying ones, *i.e.* so that they shall be able to fly away at liberty. And in the first half also we must not adopt a different rendering for לְפֹרְחוֹת, since אֶת־הַנְּפָשׁוֹת is also connected with it there. But if the words in question are combined into one clause in the first hemistich, they will give us a sense which is obviously wrong, viz. "wherewith ye catch the souls to let them fly." As the impossibility of adopting this rendering has been clearly seen, the attempt has been made to cloak over the difficulty by means of paraphrases. Ewald, for example, renders לְפֹרְחוֹת in both cases "as if they were birds of passage;" but in the first instance he applies it to birds of passage, for which nets are spread for the purpose of catching them; and in the second, to birds of passage which are set at liberty. Thus, strictly speaking, he understands the first לְפֹרְחוֹת as signifying the catching of birds; and the second, letting them fly: an explanation which refutes itself, as *pârach*, to fly, cannot mean "to catch" as well. The rendering adopted by Kimchi, Rosenmüller, and others, who translate לְפֹרְחוֹת *ut advolent ad vos* in the first hemistich, and *ut avolent* in the second, is no better. And the difficulty is not removed by resorting to the dialects, as Hävernick, for the purpose of forcing upon פֹּרְחוֹת the meaning dissoluteness or licentiousness, for which there is no authority in the Hebrew language itself. If, therefore, it is impossible to obtain any satisfactory meaning from the existing text, it cannot be correct; and no other course is open to us than to alter the unsuitable שָׁם into שָׂם, and divide the words from אֲשֶׁר אַתֵּנָה to לְפֹרְחוֹת into two clauses, as we have done in our translation above. There is no necessity to supply anything to the relative אֲשֶׁר, as צוּד is construed with a double accusative (*e.g.* Mic. vii. 2, צוּד חֵרֶם, to catch with a net), and the object to מְצֹדְדוֹת, viz. the souls, can easily be supplied from the next clause. שָׂם, as a participle, can either be connected with הִנְנִי, "behold, I make," or taken as introducing an explanatory clause: "making the souls into flying ones," *i.e.* so that they are able to fly (שׂוּם לְ, Gen. xii. 2, etc.). The two clauses of the first hemistich would then exactly correspond to the two clauses of the second half of the verse. וְקָרַעְתִּי אֹתָם is explanatory of הִנְנִי אֶל כסת', I will tear off the coverings from their arms. These words do not require the assumption that the prophetesses wore the כסתות on their arms, but may be fully explained from the supposition that the persons in question prepared them with their own hands. וְשִׁלַּחְתִּי וגו׳ corresponds to שָׁם אֶת־הַנְּפָשׁוֹת וגו׳; and לְפֹרְחוֹת is governed by שִׁלַּחְתִּי. The insertion of אֶת־הַנְּפָשִׁים is to be accounted for from the copious nature of Ezekiel's style; at the same time, it is not merely a repetition of אֶת־הַנְּפָשׁוֹת, which is separated from לְפֹרְחוֹת by the relative clause אֲשֶׁר אַתֶּם מצ׳, but as the unusual plural form נְפָשִׁים shows, is intended as a practical explanation of the fact, that the souls, while compared to birds, are regarded as living beings, which is the meaning borne by נֶפֶשׁ in other passages. The omission of the article after אֶת may be explained, however, from the fact that the souls had been more precisely defined just before; just as, for example, in 1 Sam. xxiv. 6, 2 Sam. xviii. 18, where the more precise definition follows immediately afterwards (cf. Ewald, § 277*a*, p. 683).—The same thing is said in ver. 21, with regard to the caps, as has already been said of the coverings in ver. 20. God will tear these in pieces also, to deliver His people from the power of the lying prophetesses. In what way God will do this is explained in vers. 22 and 23, namely, not only by putting their lying prophecies to shame through His judgments, but by putting an end to soothsaying altogether, and exterminating the false prophetesses by making them an object of ridicule and shame. The reason for this threat is given in ver. 22, where a further description is given of the disgraceful conduct of these persons; and here the disgracefulness of their conduct is exhibited in literal terms and without any figure. They do harm to the righteous and good, and strengthen the hands of the wicked. הַכְאוֹת, *Hiphil* of כָּאָה, in Syriac, to use harshly or depress; so here in the *Hiphil*, connected with לֵב, to afflict the heart. שֶׁקֶר is used adverbially: with lying, or in a lying manner; namely, by predicting misfortune and divine punishments, with which they threatened the godly, who would not acquiesce in their conduct; whereas, on the contrary, they predicted prosperity and peace to the ungodly, who were willing to be ensnared by them, and thus strengthened them in their evil ways. For this God would put them to shame through His judgments, which would make their deceptions manifest, and their soothsaying loathsome.

CHAP. XIV. ATTITUDE OF GOD TOWARDS THE WORSHIPPERS OF IDOLS, AND CERTAINTY OF THE JUDGMENTS.

This chapter contains two words of God, which have obviously an internal connection with each other. The first (vers. 1–11) announces to the elders, who have come to the prophet to inquire of God, that the Lord will not allow idolaters to inquire of Him, but will answer all who do not turn from idolatry with severe judgments, and will even destroy the prophets who venture to give an answer to such inquirers. The second (vers. 12–23) denounces the false hope that God will avert the judgment and spare Jerusalem because of the righteousness of the godly men therein.

Vers. 1–11. THE LORD GIVES NO ANSWER TO THE IDOLATERS.—Ver. 1 narrates the occasion for this and the following words of God: *There came to me men of the elders of Israel, and sat down before me.* These men were not deputies from the Israelites in Palestine, as Grotius and others suppose, but elders of the exiles among whom Ezekiel had been labouring. They came to visit the prophet (ver. 3), evidently with the intention of obtaining, through him, a word of God concerning the future of Jerusalem, or the fate of the kingdom of Judah. But Hävernick is wrong in supposing that we may infer, from either the first or second word of God in this chapter, that they had addressed to the prophet a distinct inquiry of this nature, to which the answer is given in vers. 12–23. For although their coming to the prophet showed that his prophecies had made an impression upon them, it is not stated in ver. 1 that they had come to inquire of God, like the elders in ch. xx. 1, and there is no allusion to any definite questions in the words of

God themselves. The first (vers. 2–11) simply assumes that they have come with the intention of asking, and discloses the state of heart which keeps them from coming to inquire; and the second (vers. 12–23) points out the worthlessness of their false confidence in the righteousness of certain godly men.

Ver. 2. *And the word of Jehovah came to me, saying,* Ver. 3. *Son of man, these men have let their idols rise up in their heart, and have set the stumbling-block to guilt before their face: shall I allow myself to be inquired of by them?* Ver. 4. *Therefore speak to them, and say to them, Thus saith the Lord Jehovah, Every man of the house of Israel who lifteth up his idols in his heart, and setteth the stumbling-block to his sin before his face, and cometh to the prophet, to him do I, Jehovah, show myself, answering according thereto, according to the multitude of his idols;* Ver. 5. *To grasp the house of Israel by their heart, because they have turned away from me, all of them through their idols.*—We have not to picture these elders to ourselves as given up to gross idolatry. הֶעֱלָה עַל לֵב means, to allow anything to come into the mind, to permit it to rise up in the heart, to be mentally busy therewith. "To set before one's face" is also to be understood, in a spiritual sense, as relating to a thing which a man will not put out of his mind. מִכְשׁוֹל עֲוֹנָם, stumbling-block to sin and guilt (cf. ch. vii. 19), *i.e.* the idols. Thus the two phrases simply denote the leaning of the heart and spirit towards false gods. God does not suffer those whose heart is attached to idols to seek and find Him. The interrogative clause הַאִדָּרֹשׁ וגו' contains a strong negation. The emphasis lies in the infinitive absolute אִדָּרֹשׁ placed before the verb, in which the ה is softened into א, to avoid writing ה twice. נִדְרַשׁ, to allow oneself to be sought, involves the finding of God; hence in Isa. lxv. 1 we have נִדְרַשׁ as parallel to נִמְצָא. In vers. 4, 5, there follows a positive declaration of the attitude of God towards those who are devoted to idolatry in their heart. Every such Israelite will be answered by God according to the measure of the multitude of his idols. The *Niphal* נַעֲנָה has not the signification of the *Kal*, and does not mean "to be answerable," as Ewald supposes, or to converse; but is generally used in a passive sense, "to be answered," *i.e.* to find or obtain a hearing (Job xi. 2, xix. 7). It is employed here in a reflective sense, to hold or show oneself answering. בה, according to the *Chetib* בָּה, for which the *Keri* suggests the softer gloss בא, refers to בְּרֹב גִל' which follows; the nominative being anticipated, according to an idiom very common in Aramaean, by a previous pronoun. It is written here for the sake of emphasis, to bring the following object into more striking prominence. ב is used here in the sense of *secundum*, according to, not because, since this meaning is quite unsuitable for the ב in ver. 7, where it occurs in the same connection (בִּי). The manner in which God will show Himself answering the idolatry according to their idols, is reserved till ver. 8. Here, in ver. 5, the design of this procedure on the part of God is given: viz. to grasp Israel by the heart; *i.e.* not merely to touch and to improve them, but to bring down their heart by judgments (cf. Lev. xxvi. 41), and thus move them to give up idolatry and return to the living God. נָזֹרוּ, as in Isa. i. 4, to recede, to draw away from God. כֻּלָּם is an emphatic repetition of the subject belonging to נָזֹרוּ.

Vers. 6–8. In these verses the divine threat, and the summons to repent, are repeated, expanded, and uttered in the clearest words.—Ver. 6. *Therefore say to the house of Israel, Thus saith the Lord Jehovah, Repent, and turn away from your idols; and turn away your face from all your abominations.* Ver. 7. *For every one of the house of Israel, and of the foreigners who sojourn in Israel, if he estrange himself from me, and let his idols rise up in his heart, and set the stumbling-block to his sin before his face, and come to the prophet to seek me for himself; I will show myself to him, answering in my own way.* Ver. 8. *I will direct my face against that man, and will destroy him, for a sign and for proverbs, and will cut him off out of my people; and ye shall learn that I am Jehovah.*—לָכֵן in ver. 6 is co-ordinate with the

לָכֵן in ver. 4, so far as the thought is concerned, but it is directly attached to ver. 5*b*: because they have estranged themselves from God, therefore God requires them to repent and turn. For God will answer with severe judgments every one who would seek God with idols in his heart, whether he be an Israelite, or a foreigner living in the midst of Israel. שׁוּבוּ, turn, be converted, is rendered still more emphatic by the addition of הָשִׁיבוּ . . . פְּנֵיכֶם. This double call to repentance corresponds to the double reproof of their idolatry in ver. 3, viz. שׁוּבוּ, to הֶעֱלָה גל' עַל לֵב; and הָשִׁיבוּ פְּנֵיכֶם, to their setting the idols נֹכַח פְּנֵיהֶם. הָשִׁיבוּ is not used intransitively, as it apparently is in ch. xviii. 30, but is to be taken in connection with the object פְּנֵיכֶם, which follows at the end of the verse; and it is simply repeated before פניכם for the sake of clearness and emphasis. The reason for the summons to repent and give up idolatry is explained in ver. 7, in the threat that God will destroy every Israelite, and every foreigner in Israel, who draws away from God and attaches himself to idols. The phraseology of ver. 7*a* is adopted almost *verbatim* from Lev. xvii. 8, 10, 13. On the obligation of foreigners to avoid idolatry and all moral abominations, *vid.* Lev. xx. 2, xviii. 26, xvii. 10; Ex. xii. 19, etc. The ו before יִנָּזֵר and יַעַל does not stand for the *Vav relat.*, but simply supposes a case: "should he separate himself from my followers, and let his idols rise up, etc." לִדְרָשׁ־לוֹ בִי does not mean, "to seek counsel of him (the prophet) from me," for לוֹ cannot be taken as referring to the prophet, although דָּרַשׁ with לְ does sometimes mean to seek any one, and לְ may therefore indicate the person to whom one goes to make inquiry (cf. 2 Chron. xv. 13, xvii. 4, xxxi. 21), because it is Jehovah who is sought in this case; and Hävernick's remark, that "דָּרַשׁ with לְ merely indicates the external object sought by a man, and therefore in this instance the medium or organ through whom God speaks," is proved to be erroneous by the passages just cited. לוֹ is reflective, or to be taken as a *dat. commodi*, denoting the inquirer or seeker. The person approached for the purpose of inquiring or seeking, *i.e.* God, is indicated by the preposition בְּ, as in 1 Chron. x. 14 (דָּרַשׁ בַּיהוָה); and also frequently, in the case of idols, when either an oracle or help is sought from them (1 Sam. xxviii. 7; 2 Kings i. 2 sqq.). It is only in this way that לוֹ and בִּי can be made to correspond to the same words in the apodosis: Whosoever seeks counsel of God, to him will God show Himself answering בִּי, in Him, *i.e.* in accordance with His nature, in His own way,—namely, in the manner described in ver. 8. The threat is composed of passages in the law: נָתַתִּי פָּנַי וגו' and הִכְרַתִּי וגו', after Lev. xx. 3, 5, 6; and וַהֲשִׁמוֹתִיהוּ וגו', though somewhat freely, after Deut. xxviii. 37 (הָיָה לְשַׁמָּה לְמָשָׁל וגו'). There is no doubt, therefore, that הֲשִׁמוֹתִי is to be derived from שָׁמֵם, and stands for הֲשִׁמּוֹתִי, in accordance with the custom in later writings of resolving the *Dagesh forte* into a long vowel. The allusion to Deut. xxviii. 37, compared with הָיָה לְאוֹת in ver. 46 of the same chapter, is sufficient to set aside the assumption that השמותי is to be derived from שִׂים, and pointed accordingly; although the LXX., Targ., Syr., and Vulg. have all renderings of שִׂים (cf. Ps. xliv. 16). Moreover, שִׂים in the perfect never takes the *Hiphil* form; and in ch. xx. 26 we have אֲשִׁמֵּם in a similar connection. The expression is a pregnant one: I make him desolate, so that he becomes a sign and proverbs.

Vers. 9-11. No prophet is to give any other answer.—Ver. 9. *But if a prophet allow himself to be persuaded, and give a word, I have persuaded this prophet, and will stretch out my hand against him, and cut him off out of my people Israel.* Ver. 10. *They shall bear their guilt: as the guilt of the inquirer, so shall the guilt of the prophet be;* Ver. 11. *In order that the house of Israel may no more stray from me, and may no more defile itself with all its transgressions; but they may be my people, and I their God, is the saying of the Lord Jehovah.*—The prophet who allows himself to be persuaded is not a prophet מִלִּבּוֹ (ch. xiii. 2), but one who really thinks that he has a word of God. פִּתָּה, to persuade, to entice by friendly words (in a good sense,

Hos. ii. 16); but generally *sensu malo*, to lead astray, or seduce to that which is unallowable or evil. "If he allow himself to be persuaded:" not necessarily "with the hope of payment from the hypocrites who consult him" (Michaelis). This weakens the thought. It might sometimes be done from unselfish good-nature. And "the word" itself need not have been a divine oracle of his own invention, or a false prophecy. The allusion is simply to a word of a different character from that contained in vers. 6–8, which either demands repentance or denounces judgment upon the impenitent: every word, therefore, which could by any possibility confirm the sinner in his security.—By אֲנִי יְהוָה (ver. 9) the apodosis is introduced in an emphatic manner, as in vers. 4 and 7; but פִּתֵּיתִי cannot be taken in a future sense ("I will persuade"). It must be a perfect; since the persuading of the prophet would necessarily precede his allowing himself to be persuaded. The Fathers and earlier Lutheran theologians are wrong in their interpretation of פִּתֵּיתִי, which they understand in a permissive sense, meaning simply that God allowed it, and did not prevent their being seduced. Still more wrong are Storr and Schmieder, the former of whom regards it as simply declaratory, "I will declare him to have gone astray from the worship of Jehovah;" the latter, "I will show him to be a fool, by punishing him for his disobedience." The words are rather to be understood in accordance with 1 Kings xxii. 20 sqq., where the persuading (*pittâh*) is done by a lying spirit, which inspires the prophets of Ahab to predict success to the king, in order that he may fall. As Jehovah sent the spirit in that case, and put it into the mouth of the prophets, so is the persuasion in this instance also effected by God: not merely divine permission, but divine ordination and arrangement; though this does not destroy human freedom, but, like all "persuading," presupposes the possibility of not allowing himself to be persuaded. See the discussion of this question in the commentary on 1 Kings xxii. 20 sqq. The remark of Calvin on the verse before us is correct: "it teaches that neither impostures nor frauds take place apart from the will of God" (*nisi Deo volente*). But this willing on the part of God, or the persuading of the prophets to the utterance of self-willed words, which have not been inspired by God, only takes place in persons who admit evil into themselves, and is designed to tempt them and lead them to decide whether they will endeavour to resist and conquer the sinful inclinations of their hearts, or will allow them to shape themselves into outward deeds, in which case they will become ripe for judgment. It is in this sense that God persuades such a prophet, in order that He may then cut him off out of His people. But this punishment will not fall upon the prophet only. It will reach the seeker or inquirer also, in order if possible to bring Israel back from its wandering astray, and make it into a people of God purified from sin (vers. 10 and 11). It was to this end that, in the last times of the kingdom of Judah, God allowed false prophecy to prevail so mightily,—namely, that it might accelerate the process of distinguishing between the righteous and the wicked; and then, by means of the judgment which destroyed the wicked, purify His nation and lead it on to the great end of its calling.

Vers. 12–23. The Righteousness of the Godly will not avert the Judgment.—The threat contained in the preceding word of God, that if the idolaters did not repent, God would not answer them in any other way than with an exterminating judgment, left the possibility still open, that He would avert the destruction of Judah and Jerusalem for the sake of the righteous therein, as He had promised the patriarch Abraham that He would do in the case of Sodom and Gomorrah (Gen. xviii. 23 sqq.). This hope, which might be cherished by the people and by the elders who had come to the prophet, is now to be taken from the people by the word of God which follows, containing as it does the announcement, that if any land should sin so grievously against God by its apostasy, He would be driven to inflict upon it the punishments threatened by Moses against apostate Israel (Lev. xxvi. 22, 25, 26, and elsewhere), namely, to destroy both man and beast, and make the land a desert; it would be of no advantage to such a land to have certain righteous men, such as Noah, Daniel, and Job, living therein. For although these righteous men would be saved themselves, their righteousness could not possibly secure salvation for the sinners. The manner in which this thought is carried out in vers. 13–20 is, that four exterminating punishments are successively supposed to come upon the land and lay it waste; and in the case of every one, the words are repeated, that even righteous men, such as Noah, Daniel, and Job, would only save their own souls, and not one of the sinners. And thus, according to vers. 21–23, will the Lord act when He sends His judgments against Jerusalem; and He will execute them in such a manner that the necessity and righteousness of His acts shall be made manifest therein.—This word of God forms a supplementary side-piece to Jer. xv. 1–4, where the Lord replies to the intercession of the prophet, that even the intercession of a Moses and a Samuel on behalf of the people would not avert the judgments which were suspended over them.

Ver. 12. *And the word of Jehovah came to me, saying,* Ver. 13. *Son of man, if a land sin against me to act treacherously, and I stretch out my hand against it, and break in pieces for it the support of bread, and send famine into it, and cut off from it man and beast:* Ver. 14. *And there should be these three men therein, Noah, Daniel, and Job, they would through their righteousness deliver their soul, is the saying of the Lord Jehovah.* Ver. 15. *If I bring evil beasts into the land, so that they make it childless, and it become a desert, so that no one passeth through it because of the beasts:* Ver. 16. *These three men therein, as I live, is the saying of the Lord Jehovah, would not deliver sons and daughters; they only would be delivered, but the land would become a desert.* Ver. 17. *Or I bring the sword into that land, and say, Let the sword go through the land; and I cut off from it man and beast:* Ver. 18. *These three men therein, as I live, is the saying of the Lord Jehovah, would not deliver sons and daughters, but they only would be delivered.* Ver. 19. *Or I send pestilence into that land, and pour out my fury upon it in blood, to cut off from it man and beast:* Ver. 20. *Verily, Noah, Daniel, and Job, in the midst of it, as I live, is the saying of the Lord Jehovah, would deliver neither son nor daughter; they would only deliver their own soul through their righteousness.*— אֶרֶץ in ver. 13 is intentionally left indefinite, that the thought may be expressed in the most general manner. On the other hand, the sin is very plainly defined as לִמְעָל־מַעַל. מָעַל, literally, to cover, signifies to act in a secret or treacherous manner, especially towards Jehovah, either by apostasy from Him, in other words, by idolatry, or by withholding what is due to Him (see comm. on Lev. v. 15). In the passage before us it is the treachery of apostasy from Him by idolatry that is intended. As the epithet used to denote the sin is taken from Lev. xxvi. 40 and Deut. xxxii. 51, so the four punishments mentioned in the following verses, as well as in ch. v. 17, are also taken from Lev. xxvi.,—viz. the breaking up of the staff of bread, from ver. 26; the evil beasts, from ver. 22; and the sword and pestilence, from ver. 25. The three men, Noah, Daniel, and Job, are named as examples of true righteousness of life, or צְדָקָה (vers. 14, 20); *i.e.*, according to Calvin's correct explanation, *quicquid pertinet ad regulam sancte et juste vivendi.* Noah is so described in Gen. vi. 9; and Job, in the Book of Job i. 1, xii. 4, etc.; and Daniel, in like manner, is mentioned in Dan. i. 8 sqq., vi. 11 sqq., as faithfully confessing his faith in his life. The fact that Daniel is named before Job does not warrant the conjecture that some other older Daniel is meant, of whom nothing is said in the history, and whose existence is merely postulated. For the enumeration is not intended to be chronological, but is arranged according to the subject-matter; the order being determined by the nature of the deliverance experienced by these men for their righteousness in the midst of great judgments. Consequently, as Hävernick and Kliefoth have shown, we have a climax here: Noah saved his family along with himself; Daniel was able to save his friends (Dan. ii. 17, 18); but Job, with his righteousness, was not even able to save his children.—The second judgment (ver. 15) is introduced with לוּ, which, as a rule, supposes a case that is not expected to occur, or even regarded as possible; here, however, לוּ is used as perfectly synonymous with אִם. שִׁכְּלַתָּה has no *Mappik*, because the tone is drawn back upon the penultima (see comm. on Amos i. 11). In ver. 19, the expression "to pour out my wrath in blood" is a pregnant one, for to pour out my wrath in such a manner that it is manifested in the shedding of blood or the destruction of life, for the life is in the blood. In this sense pestilence and blood were also associated in ch. v. 17.—If we look closely at the four cases enumerated, we find the following difference in the statements concerning the deliverance of the righteous: that, in the first instance, it is simply stated that Noah, Daniel, and Job would save their soul, *i.e.* their life, by their righteousness; whereas, in the three others, it is declared that as truly as the Lord liveth they would not save either sons or daughters, but they alone would be delivered. The difference is not merely a rhetorical climax or progress in the address by means of asseveration and antithesis, but indicates a distinction in the thought. The first case is only intended to teach that in the approaching judgment the righteous would save their lives, *i.e.* that God would not sweep away the righteous with the ungodly. The three cases which follow are intended, on the other hand, to exemplify the truth that the righteousness of the righteous will be of no avail to the idolaters and apostates; since even such patterns of righteousness as Noah, Daniel, and Job would only save their own lives, and would not be able to save the lives of others also. This tallies with the omission of the asseveration in ver. 14. The first declaration, that God would deliver the righteous in the coming judgments, needed no asseveration, inasmuch as this truth was not called in question; but it was required in the case of the declaration that the righteousness of the righteous would bring no deliverance to the sinful nation, since this was the hope which the ungodly cherished, and it was this hope which was to be taken from them. The other differences which we find in the description given of the several cases are merely formal in their nature, and do not in any way affect the sense; *e.g.* the use of לֹא, in ver. 18, instead of the particle אִם, which is commonly employed in oaths, and which we find in vers. 16 and 20; the choice of the singular בֵּן and בַּת, in ver. 20, in the place of the plural בָּנִים וּבָנוֹת, used in vers. 16 and 18; and the variation in the expressións, יְנַצְּלוּ נַפְשָׁם (ver. 14), יַצִּילוּ נַפְשָׁם (ver. 20), and הֵמָּה לְבַדָּם יִנָּצֵלוּ (vers. 16 and 18), which Hitzig proposes to remove by altering the first two forms into the third, though without the slightest reason. For although the *Piel* occurs in Ex. xii. 36 in the sense of taking away or spoiling, and is not met with anywhere else in the sense of delivering, it may just as well be used in this sense, as the *Hiphil* has both significations.

Vers. 21–23. The rule expounded in vers. 13–20 is here applied to Jerusalem. — Ver. 21. *For thus saith the Lord Jehovah, How much more when I send my four evil judgments, sword, and famine, and evil beasts, and pestilence, against Jerusalem, to cut off from it man and beast?* Ver. 22. *And, behold, there remain escaped ones in her who will be brought out, sons and daughters; behold, they will go out to you, that ye may see their walk and their works; and console yourselves concerning the evil which I have brought upon Jerusalem.* Ver. 23. *And they will console you, when ye see their walk and their works: and ye will see that I have not done without cause all that I have done to her, is the saying of the Lord Jehovah.* — By כִּי in ver. 21 the application of the general rule to Jerusalem is made in the form of a reason. The meaning, however, is not, that the reason why Jehovah was obliged to act in this unsparing manner was to be found in the corrupt condition of the nation, as Hävernick supposes,—a thought quite foreign to the context; but כִּי indicates that the judgments upon Jerusalem will furnish a practical proof of the general truth expressed in vers. 13–20, and so confirm it. This כִּי is no more an emphatic yea than the following "אַף is a forcible introduction to the antithesis formed by the coming fact, to the merely imaginary cases mentioned above" (Hitzig). אַף has undoubtedly the force of a climax, but not of an asseveration, "verily" (Häv.); a meaning which this particle never has. It is used here, as in Job iv. 19, in the sense of אַף כִּי; and the כִּי which follows אַף in this case is a conditional particle of time, "when." Consequently כי ought properly to be written twice; but it is only used once, as in ch. xv. 5; Job ix. 14, etc. The thought is this: how much more will this be the case, namely, that even a Noah, Daniel, and Job will not deliver either sons or daughters when I send my judgments upon Jerusalem. The perfect שִׁלַּחְתִּי is used, and not the imperfect, as in ver. 13, because God has actually resolved upon sending it, and does not merely mention it as a possible case. The number four is significant, symbolizing the universality of the judgment, or the thought that it will fall on all sides, or upon the whole of Jerusalem; whereby it must also be borne in mind that Jerusalem as the capital represents the kingdom of Judah, or the whole of Israel, so far as it was still in Canaan. At the same time, by the fact that the Lord allows sons and daughters to escape death, and to be led away to Babylon, He forces the acknowledgment of the necessity and righteousness of His judgments among those who are in exile. This is in general terms the thought contained in vers. 22 and 23, to which very different meanings have been assigned by the latest expositors. Hävernick, for example, imagines that, in addition to the four ordinary judgments laid down in the law, ver. 22 announces a new and extraordinary one; whereas Hitzig and Kliefoth have found in these two verses the consolatory assurance, that in the time of the judgments a few of the younger generation will be rescued and taken to those already in exile in Babylon, there to excite pity as well as to express it, and to give a visible proof of the magnitude of the judgment which has fallen upon Israel. They differ so far from each other, however, that Hitzig regards those of the younger generation who are saved as צַדִּיקִים, who have saved themselves through their innocence, but not their guilty parents, and who will excite the commiseration of those already in exile through their blameless conduct; whilst Kliefoth imagines that those who are rescued are simply less criminal than the rest, and when they come to Babylon will be pitied by those who have been longer in exile, and will pity them in return.—Neither of these views does justice to the words themselves or to the context. The meaning of ver. 22*a* is clear enough; and in the main there has been no difference of opinion concerning it. When man and beast are cut off out of Jerusalem by the four judgments, all will not perish; but פְּלֵטָה, *i.e.* persons who have escaped destruction, will be left, and will be led out of the city. These are called sons and daughters, with an allusion to vers. 16, 18, and 20; and consequently we must not take these words as referring to the younger generation in contrast to the older. They will be led out of Jerusalem, not to remain in the land, but to come to "you," *i.e.* those already in exile, that is to say, to go into exile to Babylon. This does not imply either a modification or a sharpening of the punishment; for the cutting off of man and beast from a town may be effected not only by slaying, but by leading away. The design of God in leaving some to escape, and carrying them to Babylon, is explained in the clauses which follow from וּרְאִיתֶם onwards, the meaning of which depends partly upon the more precise definition of דַּרְכָּם and עֲלִילוֹתָם, and partly upon the explanation to be given of נִחַמְתֶּם עַל־הָרָעָה and וְנִחֲמוּ אֶתְכֶם. The ways and works are not to be taken without reserve as good and righteous works, as Kliefoth has correctly shown in his reply to Hitzig. Still less can ways and works denote their experience or fate, which is the explanation given by Kliefoth of the words, when expounding the meaning and connection of vers. 21–23. The context certainly points to wicked ways and evil works. And it is only the sight of such works that could lead to the conviction that it was not חִנָּם, in vain, *i.e.* without cause, that God had inflicted such severe judgments upon Jerusalem. And in addition to this effect, which is mentioned in ver. 23 as produced upon those who were already in exile, by the sight of the conduct of the פְּלֵיטָה that came to Babylon, the immediate design of God is described in ver. 22*b* as וְנִחַמְתֶּם עַל־הָרָעָה וגו'. The verb נִחַם with עַל cannot be used here in the sense of to repent of anything, or to grieve over it (Hitzig); still less can it mean to pity any one (Kliefoth). For a man cannot repent of, or be sorry for, a judgment which God has inflicted upon him, but only of evil which he himself has done; and נִחַם does not mean to pity a person, either when construed in the *Piel* with an accusative of the person, or in the *Niphal* *c.* עַל, *rei.* נִחַמְתֶּם is *Niphal*, and signifies here to console oneself, as in Gen. xxxviii. 12 with עַל, concerning anything, as in 2 Sam. xiii. 39, Jer. xxxi. 15, etc.; and נִחֲמוּ (ver. 23), with the accusative of the person, to comfort any one, as in Gen. li. 21; Job ii. 11, etc. But the works and doings of those who came to Babylon could only produce this effect upon those who were already there, from the fact that they were of such a character as to demonstrate the necessity for the judgments which had fallen upon Jerusalem. A conviction of the necessity for the divine judgments would cause them to comfort themselves with regard to the evil inflicted by God; inasmuch as they would see, not only that the punishment endured was a chastisement well deserved, but that God in His righteousness would stay the punishment when it had fulfilled His purpose, and restore the penitent sinner to favour once more. But the consolation which those who were in exile would derive from a sight of the works of the sons and daughters who had escaped from death and come to Babylon, is attributed in ver. 23 (נִחֲמוּ אֶתְכֶם) to the persons themselves. It is in this sense that it is stated that "they will comfort you;" not by expressions of pity, but by the sight of their conduct. This is directly affirmed in the words, "when ye shall see their conduct and their works." Consequently ver. 23*a* does not contain a new thought, but simply the thought already expressed in ver. 22*b*, which is repeated in a new form to make it the more emphatic. And the expression אֵת כָּל־אֲשֶׁר הֵבֵאתִי עָלֶיהָ, in ver. 22, serves to increase the force; whilst אֵת, in the sense of *quoad*, serves to place the thought to be repeated in subordination to the whole clause (cf. Ewald, § 277*a*, p. 683).

CHAP. XV. JERUSALEM, THE USELESS WOOD OF A WILD VINE.

As certainly as God will not spare Jerusalem for the sake of the righteousness of the few righteous men therein, so certain is it that Israel has no superiority over other nations, which could secure Jerusalem against destruction. As the previous word of God overthrows false confidence in the righteousness of the godly, what follows in this chapter is directed against the fancy that Israel cannot be rejected and punished by the overthrow of the kingdom, because of its election to be the people of God.

Ver. 1. *And the word of Jehovah came to me, saying,* Ver. 2. *Son of man, what advantage has the wood of the vine over every wood, the vine-branch, which was among the trees of the forest?* Ver. 3. *Is wood taken from it to use for any work? or do men take a peg from it to hang all kinds of vessels upon?* Ver. 4. *Behold, it is given to the fire to consume. If the fire has consumed its two ends, and the middle of it is scorched, will it then be fit for any work?* Ver. 5. *Behold, when it is uninjured, it is not used for any work: how much less when the fire has consumed it and scorched it can it be still used for work!* Ver. 6. *Therefore thus saith the Lord Jehovah, As the wood of the vine among the wood of the forest, which I give to the fire to consume, so do I give up the inhabitants of Jerusalem,* Ver. 7. *And direct my face against them. They have gone out of the fire, and the fire will consume them; that ye may learn that I am Jehovah, when I set my face against them.* Ver. 8. *And I make the land a desert, because they committed treachery, is the saying of the Lord Jehovah.*—Israel is like the wood of the wild vine, which is put into the fire to burn, because it is good for nothing. From Deut. xxxii. 32, 33 onwards, Israel is frequently compared to a vine or a vineyard (cf. Ps. lxxx. 9 sqq.; Isa. v.; Hos. x. 1; Jer. ii. 21), and always, with the exception of Ps. lxxx., to point out its degeneracy. This comparison lies at the foundation of the figure employed, in vers. 2–5, of the wood of the wild vine. This wood has no superiority over any other kind of wood. It cannot be used, like other timber, for any useful purposes; but is only fit to be burned, so that it is really inferior to all other wood (vers. 2 and 3*a*). And if, in its perfect state, it cannot be used for anything, how much less when it is partially scorched and consumed (vers. 4 and 5)! מַה־יִּהְיֶה, followed by מִן, means, what is it above (מִן, comparative)?—*i.e.* what superiority has it to כָּל־עֵץ, all kinds of wood? *i.e.* any other wood. הַזְּמוֹרָה אֲשֶׁר וגו׳ is in apposition to עֵץ הַגֶּפֶן, and is not to be connected with מִכָּל־עֵץ, as it has been by the LXX. and Vulgate,—notwithstanding the Masoretic accentuation,—so as to mean every kind of fagot; for זְמוֹרָה does not mean a fagot, but the tendril or branch of the vine (cf. ch. viii. 17), which is still further defined by the following relative clause: to be a wood-vine, *i.e.* a wild vine, which bears only sour, uneatable grapes. The preterite הָיָה (which *was;* not, "*is*") may be explained from the idea that the vine had been fetched from the forest in order that its wood might be used. The answer given in ver. 3 is, that this vine-wood cannot be used for any purpose whatever, not even as a peg for hanging any kind of domestic utensils upon (see comm. on Zech. x. 4). It is too weak even for this. The object has to be supplied to לַעֲשׂוֹת לִמְלָאכָה: to make, or apply *it,* for any work. Because it cannot be used as timber, it is burned. A fresh thought is introduced in ver. 4*b* by the words אֵת שְׁנֵי ק'. The two clauses in ver. 4*b* are to be connected together. The first supposes a case, from which the second is deduced as a conclusion. The question, "Is it fit for any work?" is determined in ver. 5 in the negative. אַף כִּי: as in ch. xiv. 21. נָחָר: perfect; and יֵחָר: imperfect, *Niphal*, of חָרַר, in the sense of, to be burned or scorched. The subject to וַיֵּחָר is no doubt the wood, to which the suffix in אֲכָלַתְהוּ refers. At the same time, the two clauses are to be understood, in accordance with ver. 4*b*, as relating to the burning of the ends and the scorching of the middle.—Vers. 6–8. In the application of the parable, the only thing to which prominence is given, is the fact that God will deal with the inhabitants of Jerusalem in the same manner as with the vine-wood, which cannot be used for any kind of work. This implies that Israel resembles the wood of a forest-vine. As this possesses no superiority to other wood, but, on the contrary, is utterly useless, so Israel has no superiority to other nations, but is even worse than they, and therefore is given up to the fire. This is accounted for in ver. 7: "They have come out of the fire, and the fire will consume them" (the inhabitants of Jerusalem). These words are not to be interpreted proverbially, as meaning, "he who escapes one judgment falls into another" (Hävernick), but show the application of vers. 4*b* and 5 to the inhabitants of Jerusalem. Out of a fire one must come either burned or scorched. Israel has been in the fire already. It resembles a wild vine which has been consumed at both ends by the fire, while the middle has been scorched, and which is now about to be given up altogether to the fire. We must not restrict the fire, however, out of which it has come half consumed, to the capture of Jerusalem in the time of Jehoiachin, as Hitzig does, but must extend it to all the judgments which fell upon the covenant nation, from the destruction of the kingdom of the ten tribes to the catastrophe in the reign of Jehoiachin, and in consequence of which Israel now resembled a vine burned at both ends and scorched in the middle. The threat closes in the same manner as the previous one. Compare ver. 7*b* with ch. xiv. 8*b*, and ver. 8 with ch. xiv. 15 and 13.

CHAP. XVI. INGRATITUDE AND UNFAITHFULNESS OF JERUSALEM. ITS PUNISHMENT AND SHAME.

The previous word of God represented Israel as a wild and useless vine, which had to be consumed. But as God had planted this vine in His vineyard, as He had adopted Israel as His own people, the rebellious nation, though met by these threatenings of divine judgment, might still plead that God would not reject Israel, on account of its election as the covenant nation. This proof of false confidence in the divine covenant of grace is removed by the word of God in the present chapter, which shows that by nature Israel is no better than other nations; and that, in consequence of its shameful ingratitude towards the Lord, who saved it from destruction in the days of its youth, it has sinned so grievously against Him, and has sunk so low among the heathen through its excessive idolatry, that God is obliged to punish and judge it in the same manner as the others. At the same time, the Lord will continue mindful of His covenant; and on the restoration of Sodom and Samaria, He will also turn the captivity of Jerusalem,—to the deep humiliation and shame of Israel,—and will establish an everlasting covenant with it.—The contents of this word of God divide themselves, therefore, into three parts. In the *first*, we have the description of the nation's sin, through its falling away from its God into idolatry (vers. 2–34); in the *second*, the announcement of the punishment (vers. 35–52); and in the *third*, the restoration of Israel to favour (vers. 53–63). The past, present, and future of Israel are all embraced, from its first commencement to its ultimate consummation.—These copious contents are draped in an allegory, which is carried out on a magnificent scale. Starting from the representation of the covenant relation existing between the Lord and His people, under the figure of a marriage covenant,—which runs through the whole of the Scriptures,—Jerusalem, the capital of the kingdom of God, as the representative of Israel, the covenant nation, is addressed as a wife; and the attitude of God to Israel, as well of that of Israel to its God, is depicted under this figure.

Vers. 1–14. Israel, by nature unclean, miserable, and near to destruction (vers. 3–5), is adopted by the Lord and clothed in splendour (vers. 6–14). Vers. 1 and 2 form the introduction.—Ver. 1. *And the word of Jehovah came to me, saying,* Ver. 2. *Son of man, show Jerusalem her abominations.*—The "abominations" of Jerusalem are the sins of the covenant nation, which were worse than the sinful abominations of Canaan and Sodom. The theme of this word of God is the declaration of these abominations. To this end the nation is first of all shown what it was by nature.—Ver. 3. *And say, Thus saith the Lord Jehovah to Jerusalem, Thine origin and thy birth are from the land of the Canaanites; thy father was the Amorite, and thy mother a Hittite.* Ver. 4. *And as for thy birth, in the day of thy birth thy navel was not cut, and thou wast not bathed in water for cleansing; and not rubbed with salt, and not wrapped in bandages.* Ver. 5. *No eye looked upon thee with pity, to do one of these to thee in compassion; but thou wast cast into the field, in disgust at thy life, on the day of thy birth.*—According to the allegory, which runs through the whole chapter, the figure adopted to depict the origin of the Israelitish nation is that Jerusalem, the existing representative of the nation, is described as a child, born of Canaanitish parents, mercilessly exposed after its birth, and on the point of perishing. Hitzig and Kliefoth show that they have completely misunderstood the allegory, when they not only explain the statement concerning the descent of Jerusalem, in ver. 3, as relating to the city of that name, but restrict it to the city alone, on the ground that "Israel as a whole was not of

Canaanitish origin, whereas the city of Jerusalem was radically a Canaanitish, Amoritish, and Hittite city." But were not all the cities of Israel radically Canaanaean? Or was Israel not altogether, but only half, of Aramaean descent? Regarded merely as a city, Jerusalem was neither of Amoritish nor Hittite origin, but simply a Jebusite city. And it is too obvious to need any proof, that the prophetic word does not refer to the city as a city, or to the mass of houses; but that Jerusalem, as the capital of the kingdom of Judah at that time, so far as its inhabitants were concerned, represents the people of Israel, or the covenant nation. It was not the mass of houses, but the population,—which was the foundling,—that excited Jehovah's compassion, and which He multiplied into myriads (ver. 7), clothed in splendour, and chose as the bride with whom He concluded a marriage covenant. The descent and birth referred to are not physical, but spiritual descent. Spiritually, Israel sprang from the land of the Canaanites; and its father was the Amorite and its mother a Hittite, in the same sense in which Jesus said to the Jews, "Ye are of your father the devil" (John viii. 44). The land of the Canaanites is mentioned as the land of the worst heathen abominations; and from among the Canaanitish tribes, the Amorites and Hittites are mentioned as father and mother, not because the Jebusites are placed between the two, in Num. xiii. 29, as Hitzig supposes, but because they were recognised as the leaders in Canaanitish ungodliness. The iniquity of the Amorites (הָאֱמֹרִי) was great even in Abraham's time, though not yet full or ripe for destruction (Gen. xv. 16); and the daughters of Heth, whom Esau married, caused Rebekah great bitterness of spirit (Gen. xxvii. 46). These facts furnish the substratum for our description. And they also help to explain the occurrence of הָאֱמֹרִי with the article, and חִתִּית without it. The plurals מְכֹרֹתַיִךְ and מֹלְדֹתַיִךְ also point to spiritual descent; for physical generation and birth are both acts that take place once for all. מְכֹרָה or מְכוּרָה (ch. xxi. 35, xxix. 14) is not the place of begetting, but generation itself, from כָּרָה=כּוּר, to dig = to beget (cf. Isa. li. 1). It is not equivalent to מָקוֹר, or a plural corresponding to the Latin *natales, origines.* מוֹלֶדֶת: birth. Vers. 4 and 5 describe the circumstances connected with the birth. וּמוֹלְדוֹתַיִךְ (ver. 4) stands at the head as an absolute noun. At the birth of the child it did not receive the cleansing and care which were necessary for the preservation and strengthening of its life, but was exposed without pity. The construction הוּלֶּדֶת אוֹתָךְ (the passive, with an accusative of the object) is the same as in Gen. xl. 20, and many other passages of the earlier writings. כָּרַּת: for כֹּרַת (Judg. vi. 28), *Pual* of כָּרַת; and שָׁרֵּךְ: from שֹׁר, with the reduplication of the ר, which is very rare in Hebrew (*vid.* Ewald, § 71). By cutting the navel-string, the child is liberated after birth from the blood of the mother, with which it was nourished in the womb. If the cutting be neglected, as well as the tying of the navel-string, which takes place at the same time, the child must perish when the decomposition of the *placenta* begins. The new-born child is then bathed, to cleanse it from the impurities attaching to it. מִשְׁעִי cannot be derived from שָׁעָה = שָׁעַע; because neither the meaning to see, to look (שׁעה), nor the other meaning to smear (שׁעע), yields a suitable sense. Jos. Kimchi is evidently right in deriving it from מָשַׁע, in Arabic مسّع, ii. and iv., to wipe off, cleanse. The termination י is the Aramaean form of the absolute state, for the Hebrew מִשְׁעִית, cleansing (cf. Ewald, § 165*a*). After the washing, the body was rubbed with salt, according to a custom very widely spread in ancient times, and still met with here and there in the East (*vid. Hieron. ad h. l. Galen, de Sanit.* i. 7; *Troilo Reisebeschr.* p. 721); and that not merely for the purpose of making the skin drier and firmer, or of cleansing it more thoroughly, but probably from a regard to the virtue of salt as a protection from putrefaction, "to express in a symbolical manner a hope and desire for the vigorous health of the child" (Hitzig and Hävernick). And, finally, it was bound round with swaddling-clothes. Not one of these things, so indispensable to the preservation and strengthening of the child, was performed in the case of Israel at the time of its birth from any feeling of compassionate love (לְהֶמְלָה, infinitive, to show pity or compassion towards it); but it was cast into the field, *i.e.* exposed, in order that it might perish בְּגוֹעַל נַפְשֵׁךְ. in disgust at thy life (compare גָּעַל, to thrust away, reject, despise, Lev. xxvi. 11, xv. 30). The day of the birth of Jerusalem, *i.e.* of Israel, was the period of its sojourn in Egypt, where Israel as a nation was born,—the sons of Jacob who went down to Egypt having multiplied into a nation. The different traits in this picture are not to be interpreted as referring to historical peculiarities, but have their explanation in the totality of the figure. At the same time, they express much more than "that Israel not only stood upon a level with all other nations, so far as its origin and its nature were concerned, but was more helpless and neglected as to both its nature and its natural advantages, possessing a less gifted nature than other nations, and therefore inferior to the rest" (Kliefoth). The smaller gifts, or humbler natural advantages, are thoughts quite foreign to the words of the figure as well as to the context. Both the Canaanitish descent and the merciless exposure of the child point to a totally different point of view, as indicated by the allegory. The Canaanitish descent points to the moral depravity of the nature of Israel; and the neglected condition of the child is intended to show how little there was in the heathen surroundings of the youthful Israel in Canaan and Egypt that was adapted to foster its life and health, or to educate Israel and fit it for its future destination. To the Egyptians the Israelites were an abomination, as a race of shepherds; and not long after the death of Joseph, the Pharaohs began to oppress the growing nation.

Vers. 6–14. Israel therefore owes its preservation and exaltation to honour and glory to the Lord its God alone.—Ver. 6. *Then I passed by thee, and saw thee stamping in thy blood, and said to thee, In thy blood live! and said to thee, In thy blood live!* Ver. 7. *I made thee into myriads as the growth of the field, and thou grewest and becamest tall, and camest to ornament of cheeks. The breasts expanded, and thy hair grew, whereas thou wast naked and bare.* Ver. 8. *And I passed by thee, and saw thee, and, behold, it was thy time, the time of love; and I spread my wing over thee, and covered thy nakedness; and I swore to thee, and entered into covenant with thee, is the saying of the Lord Jehovah, and thou becamest mine.* Ver. 9. *And I bathed thee in water, and rinsed thy blood from thee, and anointed thee with oil.* Ver. 10. *And I clothed thee with embroidered work, and shod thee with morocco, and wrapped thee round with byssus, and covered thee with silk.* Ver. 11. *I adorned thee with ornaments, and put bracelets upon thy hands, and a chain around thy neck.* Ver. 12. *And I gave thee a ring in thy nose, and earrings in thine ears, and a splendid crown upon thy head.* Ver. 13. *And thou didst adorn thyself with gold and silver; and thy clothing was byssus, and silk, and embroidery. Wheaten-flour, and honey, and oil thou didst eat; and thou wast very beautiful; and didst thrive to regal dignity.* Ver. 14. *Thy name went forth among the nations on account of thy beauty; for it was perfect through my glory, which I put upon thee, is the saying of the Lord Jehovah.*—The description of what the Lord did for Israel in His compassionate love is divided into two sections by the repetition of the phrase "I passed by thee" (vers. 6 and 8). The first embraces what God had done for the preservation and increase of the nation; the second, what He had done for the glorification of Israel, by adopting it as the people of His possession. When Israel was lying in the field as a neglected new-born child, the Lord passed by and adopted it, promising it life, and giving it strength to live. To bring out the magnitude of the compassion of God, the fact that the child was lying in its blood is mentioned again and again. The explanation to be given of מִתְבּוֹסֶסֶת (the *Hithpolel* of בּוּס, to trample upon, tread under foot) is doubtful, arising from the difficulty of deciding whether the *Hithpolel* is to be taken in a passive or a reflective sense. The passive rendering, "trampled upon" (Umbreit), or *ad conculcandum projectus*, thrown down, to be trodden under foot (Gesenius, etc.), is open to the objection that the *Hophal* is used for this. We therefore prefer the reflective meaning, treading oneself, or stamping; as the objection offered to this, namely, that a new-born child thrown into a field would not be found stamping with the feet, has no force in an allegorical description. In the clause ver. 6*b*, which is written twice, the question arises whether בְּדָמַיִךְ is to be taken with חֲיִי or with וָאֹמַר לָךְ: I said to thee, "In thy blood live;" or, "I said to thee in thy blood, 'Live.'" We prefer the former, because it gives a more emphatic sense. בְּדָמַיִךְ is a concise expression; for although lying in thy blood, in which thou wouldst inevitably bleed to death, yet thou shalt live. Hitzig's proposal to connect בְּדָמַיִךְ in the first clause with חיי, and in the second with אמר, can hardly be entertained. A double construction of this kind is not required either by the repetition of אֹמַר לָךְ, or by the uniform position of בדמיך before חיי in both clauses, as compared with 1 Kings xx. 18 and Isa. xxvii. 5.—In ver. 7*a* the description of the real fact breaks through the allegory. The word of God חֲיִי, live, was visibly fulfilled in the innumerable multiplication of Israel. But the allegory is resumed immediately. The child grew (רָבָה, as in Gen. xxi. 20; Deut. xxx. 16), and came into ornament of cheeks (בּוֹא with בְּ, to enter into a thing, as in ver. 8; not to proceed in, as Hitzig supposes). עֲדִי עדיים, not most beautiful ornament, or highest charms, for עדיים is not the plural of עֲדִי; but according to the *Chetib* and most of the editions, with the tone upon the penultima, is equivalent to עֲדָיַיִם, a dual form; so that עֲדִי cannot mean ornament in this case, but, as in Ps. xxxix. 9 and ciii. 5, "the cheek," which is the traditional meaning (cf. Ges. *Thes.* p. 993). Ornament of cheeks is youthful freshness and beauty of face. The clauses which follow describe the arrival of puberty. נָכוֹן, when applied to the breasts, means to expand, lit. to raise oneself up. שֵׂעָר = שֵׂעַר רַגְלַיִם, *pubes*. The description given in these verses refers to the preservation and marvellous multiplication of Israel in Egypt, where the sons of Israel grew into a nation under the divine blessing. Still it was quite naked and bare (עֵרֹם and עֶרְיָה are substantives in the abstract sense of nakedness and bareness, used in the place of adjectives to give greater emphasis). Naked and bare are figurative expressions for still destitute of either clothing or ornaments. This implies something more than "the poverty of the people in the wilderness attached to Egypt" (Hitzig). Nakedness represents deprivation of all the blessings of salvation with which the Lord endowed Israel and made it glorious, after He had adopted it as the people of His possession. In Egypt, Israel was living in a state of nature, destitute of the gracious revelations of God.—Ver. 8. The Lord then went past again, and chose for His bride the virgin, who had already grown up to womanhood, and with whom He contracted marriage by the conclusion of the covenant at Sinai. עִתֵּךְ, thy time, is more precisely defined as עֵת דֹּדִים, the time of conjugal love. I spread my wing over thee, *i.e.* the lappet of my garment, which also served as a counterpane; in other words, I married thee (cf. Ruth iii. 9), and thereby covered thy nakedness. "I swore to thee," *sc.* love and fidelity (cf. Hos. ii. 21, 22), and entered into a covenant with thee, *i.e.* into that gracious connection formed by the adoption of Israel as the possession of Jehovah, which is represented as a marriage covenant (compare Ex. xxiv. 8 with xix. 5, 6, and Deut. v. 2:—אִתָּךְ for אִתָּךְ). Vers. 9 sqq. describe how Jehovah provided for the purification, clothing, adorning, and maintenance of His wife. As the bride prepares herself for the wedding by washing and anointing, so did the Lord cleanse Israel from the blemishes and impurities which adhered to it from its birth. The rinsing from the blood must not be understood as specially referring either to the laws of purification given to the nation (Hitzig), or as relating solely to the purification effected by the covenant sacrifice (Hävernick). It embraces all that the Lord did for the purifying of the people from the pollution of sin, *i.e.* for its sanctification. The anointing with oil indicates the powers of the Spirit of God, which flowed to Israel from the divine covenant of grace. The clothing with costly garments, and adorning with all the jewellery of a wealthy lady or princess, points to the equipment of Israel with all the gifts that promote the beauty and glory of life. The clothing is described as made of the costliest materials with which queens were accustomed to clothe themselves. רִקְמָה, embroidered cloth (Ps. xlv. 15). תַּחַשׁ, probably the sea-cow, *Manati* (see the comm. on Ex. xxv. 5). The word is used here for a fine description of leather of which ornamental sandals were made; a kind of morocco. "I bound thee round with byssus:" this refers to the headband; for חָבַשׁ is the technical expression for the binding or winding round of the turban-like headdress (cf. ch. xxiv. 17; Ex. xxix. 9; Lev. viii. 13), and is applied by the Targum to the headdress of the priests. Consequently covering with מֶשִׁי, as distinguished from clothing, can only refer to covering with the veil, one of the principal articles of a woman's toilet. The ἁπ. λεγ. מֶשִׁי (vers. 10 and 13) is explained by the Rabbins as signifying silk. The LXX. render it τρίχαπτον. According to Jerome, this is a word formed by the LXX.: *quod tantae subtilitatis fuerit vestimentum, ut pilorum et capillorum tenuitatem habere credatur.* The jewellery included not only armlets, nose-rings, and ear-rings, which the daughters of Israel were generally accustomed to wear, but also necklaces and a crown, as ornaments worn by princesses and queens. For רָבִיד, see comm. on Gen. xli. 42. Ver. 13 sums up the contents of vers. 9–12. שֵׁשִׁי is made to conform to מֶשִׁי; the food is referred to once more; and the result of the whole is said to have been, that Jerusalem became exceedingly beautiful, and flourished even to royal dignity. The latter cannot be taken as referring simply to the establishment of the monarchy under David, any more than merely to the spiritual sovereignty for which Israel was chosen from the very beginning (Ex. xix. 5, 6). The expression includes both, viz. the call of Israel to be a kingdom of priests, and the historical realization of this call through the Davidic sovereignty. The beauty, *i.e.* glory, of Israel became so great, that the name or fame of Israel sounded abroad in consequence among the nations. It was perfect, because the Lord had put His glory upon His Church. This, too, we must not restrict (as Hävernick does) to the far-sounding fame of Israel on its departure from Egypt (Ex. xv. 14 sqq.); it refers pre-eminently to the glory of the theocracy under David and Solomon, the fame of which spread into all lands.—Thus had Israel been glorified by its God above all the nations, but it did not continue in fellowship with its God.

Vers. 15–34. The apostasy of Israel. Its origin and nature, vers. 15–22; its magnitude and extent, vers. 23–34. In close connection with what precedes, this apostasy is described as whoredom and adultery.—Ver. 15. *But thou didst trust in thy beauty, and didst commit fornication upon thy name, and didst pour out thy fornication over every one who passed by: his it became.* Ver. 16. *Thou didst take of thy clothes, and didst make to thyself spotted heights, and didst commit fornication upon them: things which should not come, and that which should not take place.* Ver. 17. *And thou didst take jewellery of thine ornament of my gold and of my silver, which I had given thee, and didst make thyself male images, and didst commit fornication with them;* Ver. 18. *And thou didst take thy embroidered clothes, and didst cover them therewith: and my oil and my incense thou didst set before them.* Ver. 19. *And my bread, which I gave to thee, fine flour, and oil, and honey, wherewith I fed thee, thou didst set before them for a pleasant odour: this came to pass, is the saying of the Lord Jehovah.* Ver. 20. *And thou didst take thy sons and thy daughters, whom thou barest to me, and didst sacrifice them to them to devour. Was thy fornication too little?* Ver. 21. *Thou didst slay my sons, and didst give them up, devoting them to them.* Ver. 22. *And in all thine abominations and thy fornications thou didst not remember the days of thy youth, when thou wast naked and bare, and layest stamping in thy blood.*—The beauty, *i.e.* the glory, of Israel led to its fall, because it made it the ground of its confidence; that is to say, it looked upon the gifts and possessions conferred upon it as its desert; and forgetting the giver, began to traffic with the heathen nations, and allowed itself to be seduced to heathen ways. For the fact, compare Deut. xxxii. 15 and Hos. xiii. 6. "We are inflamed with pride and arrogance, and consequently profane the gifts of God, in which His glory ought to be resplendent" (Calvin). תִּזְנִי עַל שְׁמֵךְ does not mean either "thou didst commit fornication notwithstanding thy name" (Winer and Ges. *Thes.* p. 422), or "against thy name" (Hävernick); for עַל connected with זָנָה has neither of these meanings, even in Judg. xix. 2. It means, "thou didst commit fornication upon thy name, *i.e.* in reliance upon thy name" (Hitzig and Maurer); only we must not understand שֵׁם as referring to the name of the city of God, but must explain it, in accordance with ver. 14, as denoting the name, *i.e.* the renown, which Israel had acquired among the heathen on account of its beauty. In the closing words, לוֹ יֶהִי, לוֹ refers to כָּל־עוֹבֵר, and יֶהִי stands for וַיְהִי, the copula having been dropped from וַיְהִי because לוֹ ought to stand first, and only יְהִי remaining (compare יַךְ, Hos. vi. 1). The subject to יְהִי is יָפִי; the beauty became his (cf. Ps. xlv. 12). This fornication is depicted in concrete terms in vers. 16–22; and with the marriage relation described in vers. 8–13 still in view, Israel is represented as giving up to idolatry all that it had received from its God.—Ver. 16. With the clothes it made spotted heights for itself. בָּמוֹת stands for בָּתֵּי בָמוֹת, temples of heights, small temples erected upon heights by the side of the altars (1 Kings xiii. 32; 2 Kings xvii. 29; for the fact, see the comm. on 1 Kings iii. 2), which may probably have consisted simply of tents furnished with carpets. Compare 2 Kings xxiii. 7, where the women are described as weaving tents for Astarte, also the tent-like temples of the Slavonian tribes in Germany, which consisted of variegated carpets and curtains (see Mohne on Creuzer's *Symbolik*, V. p. 176). These *bamoth* Ezekiel calls טְלֻאוֹת, not variegated, but spotted or speckled (cf. Gen. xxx. 32), possibly with the subordinate idea of patched (מְטֻלָּא, Josh. ix. 5), because they used for the carpets not merely whole garments, but pieces of cloth as well; the word being introduced here for the purpose of indicating contemptuously the worthlessness of such conduct. "Thou didst commit whoredom upon them," *i.e.* upon the carpets in the tent-temples. The words לֹא בָאוֹת וגו' are no doubt relative clauses; but the usual explanation, "which has not occurred, and will not be," after Ex. x. 14, cannot be vindicated, as it is impossible to prove either the use of בּוֹא in the sense of occurring or happening (= הָיָה), or the use of the participle instead of the preterite in connection with the future. The participle בָּאוֹת in this connection can only supply one of the many senses of the imperfect (Ewald, § 168*c*), and, like יִהְיֶה, express that which ought to be. The participial form בָּאוֹת is evidently chosen for the sake of obtaining a *paronomasia* with בָּמוֹת: the heights which should not come (*i.e.* should not be erected); while לֹא יִהְיֶה points back to וַתִּזְנִי עֲלֵיהֶם: "what should not happen."—Ver. 17. The jewellery of gold and silver was used by Israel for צַלְמֵי זָכָר, idols of the male sex, to commit fornication with them. Ewald thinks that the allusion is to Penates (*teraphim*), which were set up in the house, with ornaments suspended upon them, and worshipped with *lectisternia*. But there is no more allusion to *lectisternia* here than in ch. xxiii. 41. And there is still less ground for thinking, as Vatke, Movers, and Hävernick do, of Lingam- or Phallus-worship, of which it is impossible to find the slightest trace among the Israelites. The arguments used by Hävernick have been already proved by Hitzig to have no force whatever. The context does not point to idols of any particular kind, but to the many varieties of Baal-worship; whilst the worship of Moloch is specially mentioned in vers. 20 sqq. as being the greatest abomination of the whole. The fact that נָתַן לִפְנֵיהֶם, to set before them (the idols), does not refer to *lectisternia*, but to sacrifices offered as food for the gods, is indisputably evident from the words לְרֵיחַ נִיחֹחַ, the technical expression for the sacrificial odour ascending to God (cf. Lev. i. 9, 13, etc.). וַיֶּהִי (ver. 19), and it came to pass (*sc.* this abomination), merely serves to give emphatic expression to the disgust which it occasioned (Hitzig).—Vers. 20, 21. And not even content with this, the adulteress sacrificed the children which God had given her to idols. The revulsion of feeling produced by the abominations of the Moloch-worship is shown in the expression לֶאֱכוֹל, thou didst sacrifice thy children to idols, that they might devour them; and still more in the reproachful question הַמְעַט מת', "was there too little in thy whoredom?" מִן before תַּזְנוּתַיִךְ is used in a comparative sense, though not to signify "was this a smaller thing than thy whoredom?" which would mean far too little in this connection. The מִן is rather used, as in ch. viii. 17 and Isa. xlix. 6, in the sense of *too:* was thy whoredom, already described in vers. 16–19, too little, that thou didst also slaughter thy children to idols? The *Chetib* תזנותךְ (vers. 20 and 25) is a singular, as in vers. 25 and 29; whereas the *Keri* has treated it as a plural, as in vers. 15, 22, and 33, but without any satisfactory ground. The indignation comes out still more strongly in the description given of these abominations in ver. 21: "thou didst slay *my* sons" (whereas in ver. 20 we have simply "thy sons, whom thou hast born to me"), "and didst give them up to them, בְּהַעֲבִיר, by making them pass through," *sc.* the fire. הַעֲבִיר is used here not merely for lustration or februation by fire, but for the actual burning of the children slain as sacrifices, so that it is equivalent to הַעֲבִיר בָּאֵשׁ לַמֹּלֶךְ (2 Kings xxiii. 10). By the process of burning, the sacrifices were given to Moloch to devour. Ezekiel has the Moloch-worship in his eye in the form which it had assumed from the times of Ahaz downwards, when the people began to burn their children to Moloch (cf. 2 Kings xvi. 3, xxi. 6, xxiii. 10), whereas all that can be proved to have been practised in earlier times by the Israelites was the passing of children through fire without either slaying or burning; a februation by fire (compare the remarks on this subject in the comm. on Lev. xviii. 21).—Amidst all these abominations Israel did not remember its youth, or how the Lord had adopted it out of the deepest wretchedness to be His people, and had made it glorious through the abundance of His gifts. This base ingratitude shows the depth of its fall, and magnifies its guilt. For ver. 22*b* compare vers. 7 and 6.

Vers. 23–34. Extent and magnitude of the idolatry.—Ver. 23. *And it came to pass after all thy wickedness—Woe, woe to thee! is the saying of the Lord Jehovah*—Ver. 24. *Thou didst build thyself arches, and didst make thyself high places in all the streets.* Ver. 25. *Thou didst build thy high places at every cross road, and didst disgrace thy beauty, and stretch open thy feet for every one that passed by, and didst increase thy whoredom.* Ver. 26. *Thou didst commit fornication with the sons of Egypt thy neighbours, great in flesh, and didst increase thy whoredom to provoke me.* Ver. 27. *And, behold, I stretched out my hand against thee, and diminished thine allowance, and gave thee up to the desire of those who hate thee, the daughters of the Philistines, who are ashamed of thy lewd way.* Ver. 28. *And thou didst commit fornication with the sons of Asshur, because thou art never satisfied; and didst commit fornication with them, and wast also not satisfied.* Ver. 29. *And thou didst increase thy whoredom to Canaan's land, Chaldaea, and even thereby wast not satisfied.* Ver. 30. *How languishing is thy heart! is the saying of the Lord Jehovah, that thou doest all this, the doings of a dissolute prostitute.* Ver. 31. *When thou buildest thy arches at every cross road, and madest thy high places in every road, thou wast not like the harlot, since thou despisedst payment.* Ver. 32. *The adulterous wife taketh strangers instead of her husband.* Ver. 33. *Men give presents to all prostitutes; but thou gavest thy presents to all thy suitors, and didst reward them for coming to thee from all sides, for fornication with thee.* Ver. 34. *And there was in thee the very opposite of the women in thy whoredom, that men did not go whoring after thee. In that thou givest payment, and payment was not given to thee, thou wast the very opposite.*— By אַחֲרֵי כָּל־רָעָתֵךְ, the picture of the wide spread of idolatry, commenced in ver. 22, is placed in the relation of chronological sequence to the description already given of the idolatry itself. For all sin, all evil, must first exist before it can spread. The spreading of idolatry was at the same time an increase of apostasy from God. This is not to be sought, however, in the fact that Israel forsook the sanctuary, which God had appointed for it as the scene of His gracious presence, and built itself idol-temples (Kliefoth). It consisted rather in this, that it erected idolatrous altars and little temples at all street-corners and cross-roads (vers. 24, 25), and committed adultery with all heathen nations (vers. 26, 28, 29), and could not be induced to relinquish idolatry either by the chastisements of God (ver. 27), or by the uselessness of such conduct (vers. 32–34). כָּל־רָעָתֵךְ is the whole of the apostasy from the Lord depicted in vers. 15–22, which prevailed more and more as idolatry spread. The picture of this extension of idolatry is introduced with woe! woe! to indicate at the outset the fearful judgment which Jerusalem was bringing upon itself thereby. The exclamation of woe is inserted parenthetically; for וַתִּבְנִי (ver. 24) forms the apodosis to וַיְהִי in ver. 23. גַּב and רָמָה are to be taken as general terms; but, as the singular גַּבֵּךְ with the plural רָמֹתַיִךְ in ver. 39 plainly shows, גַּב is a collective word. Hävernick has very properly called attention to the analogy between גַּב and קֻבָּה in Num. xxv. 8, which is used there to denote an apartment furnished or used for the service of Baal-Peor. As קֻבָּה, from קָבַב, signifies literally that which is arched, a vault; so גַּב, from גָּבַב, is literally that which is curved or arched, a hump or back, and hence is used here for buildings erected for idolatrous purposes, small temples built on heights, which were probably so called to distinguish them as chapels for fornication. The ancient translations suggest this, viz.:

LXX. οἴκημα πορνικόν and ἔκθεμα, which Polychron. explains thus: προαγώγιον, ἔνθα τὰς πόρνας τρέφειν εἰώθασι; Vulg.: *lupanar* and *prostibulum*. רָמָה signifies artificial heights, *i.e.* altars built upon eminences, commonly called *bâmōth*. The word *râmâh* is probably chosen here with an allusion to the primary signification, height, as Jerome has said: *quod excelsus sit ut volentibus fornicari procul appareat fornicationis locus et non necesse sit quaeri*. The increase of the whoredom, *i.e.* of the idolatry and illicit intercourse with heathenish ways, is individualized in vers. 26–29 by a specification of historical facts. We cannot agree with Hitzig in restricting the illicit intercourse with Egypt (ver. 26), Asshur (ver. 28), and Chaldaea (ver. 29) to political apostasy, as distinguished from the religious apostasy already depicted. There is nothing to indicate any such distinction. Under the figure of whoredom, both in what precedes and what follows, the inclination of Israel to heathen ways in all its extent, both religious and political, is embraced. Egypt stands first; for the apostasy of Israel from the Lord commenced with the worship of the golden calf, and the longing in the wilderness for the fleshpots of Egypt. From time immemorial Egypt was most deeply sunken in the heathenish worship of nature. The sons of Egypt are therefore described, in accordance with the allegory, as גִּדְלֵי בָשָׂר, *magni carne* (*bâzâr*, a euphemism; cf. ch. xxiii. 20), *i.e.* according to the correct explanation of Theodoret: μεθ' ὑπερβολῆς τῇ τῶν εἰδώλων θεραπείᾳ προστετηκότας, οὗτοι γὰρ καὶ τράγους καὶ βόας καὶ πρόβατα, κύνας τε καὶ πιθήκους καὶ κροκοδείλους καὶ ἴβεις καὶ ἱέρακας προσεκύνησαν. The way in which God punished this erring conduct was, that, like a husband who endeavours by means of chastisement to induce his faithless wife to return, He diminished the supply of food, clothing, etc. (*chōg*, as in Prov. xxx. 8), intended for the wife (for the fact compare Hos. ii. 9, 10); this He did by "not allowing Israel to attain to the glory and power which would otherwise have been conferred upon it; that is to say, by not permitting it to acquire the undisturbed and undivided possession of Canaan, but giving it up to the power and scorn of the princes of the Philistines" (Kliefoth). נָתַן בְּנֶפֶשׁ, to give any one up to the desire of another. The daughters of the Philistines are the Philistian states, corresponding to the representation of Israel as an adulterous wife. The Philistines are mentioned as the principal foes, because Israel fell completely into their power at the end of the period of the Judges (cf. Judg. xiii.–xvi.; 1 Sam. iv.); and they are referred to here, for the deeper humiliation of Israel, as having been ashamed of the licentious conduct of the Israelites, because they adhered to their gods, and did not exchange them for others as Israel had done (compare Jer. ii. 10, 11). זִמָּה (ver. 27) is in apposition to דַּרְכֵּךְ: thy way, which is *zimmâh*. *Zimmâh* is applied to the sin of profligacy, as in Lev. xviii. 17.—But Israel was not improved by this chastisement. It committed adultery with Asshur also from the times of Ahaz, who sought help from the Assyrians (2 Kings xvi. 7 sqq.); and even with this it was not satisfied; that is to say, the serious consequences brought upon the kingdom of Judah by seeking the friendship of Assyria did not sober it, so as to lead it to give up seeking for help from the heathen and their gods. In ver. 28, תִּזְנִי אֶל is distinguished from תִּזְנִים (זָנָה, with accus.). The former denotes the immoral pursuit of a person for the purpose of procuring his favour; the latter, adulterous intercourse with him, when his favour has been secured. The thought of the verse is this: Israel sought the favour of Assyria, because it was not satisfied with illicit intercourse with Egypt, and continued to cultivate it; yet it did not find satisfaction or sufficiency even in this, but increased its adultery אֶל־אֶרֶץ כְּנַעַן כַּשְׂדִּימָה, to the Canaan's-land Chaldaea. אֶרֶץ כְּנַעַן is not the proper name of the land of Canaan here, but an appellative designation applied to Chaldaea (*Kasdim*) or Babylonia, as in ch. xvii. 4 (Raschi). The explanation of the words, as signifying the land of Canaan, is precluded by the fact that an allusion to Canaanitish idolatry and intercourse after the mention of Asshur would be out of place, and would not coincide with the historical order of things; since it cannot be shown that "a more general diffusion of the religious customs of Canaan took place after the Assyrian era." And it is still more decidedly precluded by the introduction of the word כַּשְׂדִּימָה, which cannot possibly mean as far as, or unto, Chaldaea, and can only be a more precise definition of ארץ כנען. The only thing about which a question can be raised, is the reason why the epithet כנען should have been applied to Chaldaea; whether it merely related to the commercial spirit, in which Babylon was by no means behind the Canaanitish Tyre and Sidon, or whether allusion was also made to the idolatry and immorality of Canaan. The former is by no means to be excluded, as we find that in ch. xvii. 4 "the land of Canaan" is designated "a city of merchants" (*rōkh^elim*). But we must not exclude the latter either, inasmuch as in the Belus- and Mylitta-worship of Babylon the voluptuous character of the Baal- and Astarte-worship of Canaan had degenerated into shameless unchastity (cf. Herodotus, i. 199).

In ver. 30, the contents of vers. 16–29 are summed up in the verdict which the Lord pronounces upon the harlot and adulteress: "yet how languishing is thy heart!" אֲמֻלָה (as a participle *Kal* ἁπ. λεγ.; since the verb only occurs elsewhere in the *Pual*, and that in the sense of faded or pining away) can only signify a morbid pining or languishing, or the craving of immodest desire, which has grown into a disease. The form לִבָּה is also ἁπ. λεγ.; but it is analogous to the plural לִבּוֹת.[1] שַׁלֶּטֶת, powerful, commanding; as an epithet applied to *zōnâh*, one who knows no limit to her actions, unrestrained;

[1] Hitzig objects to the two forms, which do not occur elsewhere; and with the help of the Sept. rendering τὶ διαθῶ τὴν θυγατέρα σου, which is a mere guess founded upon the false reading מה אמלה לבתך, he adopts the conjectural reading מָה אמְלָה לְבִתֵּךְ, "what hope is there for thy daughter?" by which he enriches the Hebrew language with a new word (אמְלָה), and the prophecy contained in this chapter with a thought which is completely foreign to it, and altogether unsuitable.

hence in Arabic, insolent, shameless. Ver. 31 contains an independent sentence, which facilitates the transition to the thought expanded in vers. 32–34, namely, that Jerusalem had surpassed all other harlots in her whoredoms. If we take ver. 31 as dependent upon the protasis in ver. 30, we not only get a very draggling style of expression, but the new thought expressed in ver. 31*b* is reduced to a merely secondary idea; whereas the expansion of it in vers. 32 sqq. shows that it introduces a new feature into the address. And if this is the case, וְלֹא־הָיִיתִי cannot be taken as co-ordinate with עָשִׂיתִי, but must be construed as the apodosis: "in thy building of rooms . . . thou wast not like the (ordinary) harlot, since thou disdainest payment." For the plural suffix attached to בִּבְנוֹתַיִךְ, see the commentary on ch. vi. 8. The infinitive לְקַלֵּס answers to the Latin gerund in *ndo* (*vid.* Ewald, § 237*c* and 280*d*), indicating wherein, or in what respect, the harlot Jerusalem differed from an ordinary prostitute; namely, in the fact that she disdained to receive payment for her prostitution. That this is the meaning of the words, is rendered indisputable by vers. 32–34. But the majority of expositors have taken לְקַלֵּס אֶתְנָן as indicating the point of comparison between Israel and other harlots, *i.e.* as defining in what respect Israel resembled other prostitutes; and then, as this thought is at variance with what follows, have attempted to remove the discrepancy by various untenable explanations. Most of them resort to the explanation: thou wast not like the other prostitutes, who disdain to receive the payment offered for their prostitution, in the hope of thereby obtaining still more,[1]—an explanation which imports into the

[1] Jerome adopts this rendering: *non facta es quasi meretrix fastidio augens pretium*, and gives the following explanation: "thou hast not imitated the cunning prostitutes, who are accustomed to raise the price of lust by increasing the difficulties, and in this way to excite their lovers to greater frenzy." Rosenmüller and Maurer have adopted a similar explanation: "thou differest greatly from other harlots, who despise the payment offered them by their lovers, that they may get still more; for thou acceptest any reward, being content with the lowest payment; yea, thou dost even offer a price to thine own lovers."

words a thought that has no existence in them at all. Hävernick seeks to fix upon קלס, by means of the Aramaean, the meaning to cry out (crying out payment), in opposition to the ordinary meaning of קלס, to disdain, or ridicule, in which sense Ezekiel also uses the noun קַלָּסָה in ch. xxii. 4. Hitzig falls back upon the handy method of altering the text; and finally, Kliefoth gives to לְ the imaginary meaning "so far as," *i.e.* "to such a degree that," which cannot be defended either through Ex. xxxix. 19 or from Deut. xxiv. 5.—With the loose way in which the infinitive construct with לְ is used, we grant that the words are ambiguous, and might have the meaning which the majority of the commentators have discovered in them; but this view is by no means necessary, inasmuch as the subordinate idea introduced by לְקַלֵּס אֶתְנָן may refer quite as well to the subject of the sentence, "*thou,*" as to the *zōnâh* with whom the subject is compared. Only in the latter case the קַלֵּס אֶתְנָן would apply to other harlots as well as to Israel; whereas in the former it applies to Israel alone, and shows in what it was that Israel did not resemble ordinary prostitutes. But the explanation which followed was a sufficient safeguard against mistake. In this explanation adulteresses are mentioned first (ver. 32), and then common prostitutes (vers. 33, 34). Ver. 32 must not be taken, as it has been by the majority of commentators, as an exclamation, or a reproof addressed to the adulteress Jerusalem: O thou adulterous wife, that taketh strangers instead of her husband! Such an exclamation as this does not suit the connection at all. But the verse is not to be struck out on that account, as Hitzig proposes. It has simply to be construed in another way, and taken as a statement of what adulteresses do (Kliefoth). They take strangers instead of their husband, and seek their recompense in the simple change, and the pleasure of being with other men. תַּחַת אִישָׁהּ, lit. under her husband, *i.e.* as a wife subject to her husband, as in the connection with זָנָה in ch. xxiii. 5 and Hos. iv. 12 (see the comm. on Num. v. 19).—Vers. 33, 34. Common prostitutes give themselves up for presents; but Israel, on the contrary, gave presents to its lovers, so that it did the very opposite to all other harlots, and the practice of ordinary prostitutes was left far behind by that of Israel. The change of forms נֵדֶא and נָדָן (a present) is probably to be explained simply on the ground that the form נדא was lengthened into נדן with a consonant as the termination, because the suffix could be attached more easily to the other. הֶפֶךְ, the reverse, the opposite, *i.e.* with the present context, something unheard of, which never occurred in the case of any other harlot.—Ezekiel has thus fulfilled the task appointed him in ver. 2, to charge Jerusalem with her abominations. The address now turns to an announcement of the punishment.

Vers. 35–52. As Israel has been worse than all the heathen, Jehovah will punish it notwithstanding its election, so that its shame shall be uncovered before all the nations (vers. 36–42), and the justice of the judgment to be inflicted upon it shall be made manifest (vers. 43–52). According to these points of view, the threat of punishment divides itself into two parts in the following manner:—In the first (vers. 35–42) we have, first of all (in ver. 36), a recapitulation of the guilty conduct described in vers. 16–34; and secondly, an announcement of the punishment corresponding to the guilt, as the punishment of adultery and murder (vers. 37 and 48), and a picture of its infliction, as retribution for the enormities committed (vers. 39–42). In the second part (vers. 43–52) there follows a proof of the justice of this judgment.

Vers. 35–42. The punishment will correspond to the sin. —Ver. 35. *Therefore, O harlot, hear the word of Jehovah!* Ver. 36. *Thus saith the Lord Jehovah, Because thy brass has been lavished, and thy shame exposed in thy whoredom with thy lovers, and because of all the idols of thine abominations, and according to the blood of thy sons, which thou hast given them;* Ver. 37. *Therefore, behold, I will gather together all thy lovers, whom thou hast pleased, and all whom thou hast loved, together with all whom thou hast hated, and will gather them against thee from round about, and will expose thy shame to them, that they may see all thy shame.* Ver. 38. *I will judge thee according to the judgment of adulteresses and murderesses, and make thee into blood of wrath and jealousy.* Ver. 39. *And I will give thee into their hand, that they may destroy thy arches, and pull down thy heights; that they may strip thy clothes off thee, and take thy splendid jewellery, and leave thee naked and bare.* Ver. 40. *And they shall bring up a company against thee, and stone thee, and cut thee in pieces with their swords.* Ver. 41. *And they shall burn thy houses with fire, and execute judgment upon thee before the eyes of many women. Thus do I put an end to thy whoredom; and thou wilt also give payment no more.* Ver. 42. *And I quiet my fury toward thee, and will turn away my jealousy from thee, that I may repose and vex myself no more.*—In the brief summary of the guilt of the whore, the following objects are singled out, as those for which she is to be punished: (1) the pouring out of her brass and the exposure of her shame; (2) the idols of her abominations (with עַל before the noun, corresponding to יַעַן before the infinitive); (3) the blood of her sons, with the preposition כְּ, according to, to indicate the measure of her punishment. Two things are mentioned as constituting the first ground of punishment. The first is, "because thy brass has been poured out." Most of the commentators have explained this correctly, as referring to the fact that Israel had squandered the possessions received from the Lord, viz. gold, silver, jewellery, clothing, and food (vers. 10–13 and 16–19), upon idolatry. The only difficulty connected with this is the use of the word *nᵉchōsheth*, brass or copper, in the general sense of money or metal, as there are no other passages to support this use of the word. At the same time, the objection raised to this, namely, that *nᵉchōsheth* cannot signify money, because the Hebrews had no copper coin, is an assertion without proof, since all that can be affirmed with certainty is, that the use of copper or brass as money is not mentioned anywhere in the Old Testament, with the exception of the passage before us. But we cannot infer with certainty from this that it was not then in use. As soon as the Hebrews began to stamp coins, bronze or copper coins were stamped as well as the silver shekels, and specimens of these are still in existence from the time of the Maccabees, with the inscription "Simon, prince of Israel" (cf. Cavedoni, *Bibl. Numismatik*, transl. by Werlhof, p. 20 sqq.). Judging from their size, these coins were in all probability worth a whole, a half, and a quarter gerah (Caved. pp. 50, 51). If, then, the silver shekel of the value of 21 grains contained twenty gerahs in Moses' time, and they had already silver pieces of the weight of a shekel and half shekel, whilst quarter shekels are also mentioned in the time of Samuel, there would certainly be metal coins in use of the value of a gerah for the purposes of trade and commerce, and these would in all probability be made of brass, copper, or bronze, as silver coins of the value of a penny would have been found too small. Consequently it cannot be positively denied that brass or copper may have been used as coin for the payment of a gerah, and therefore that the word *n^e^chōsheth* may have been applied to money. We therefore adhere to the explanation that brass stands for money, which has been already adopted by the LXX. and Jerome; and we do so all the more, because every attempt that has been made to fasten another meaning upon *n^e^chōsheth*, whether by allegorical interpretation (Rabb.), or from the Arabic, or by altering the text, is not only arbitrary, but does not even yield a meaning that suits the context. הִשָּׁפֵךְ, to be poured out = squandered or lavished. To the squandering of the possessions bestowed by the Lord upon His congregation, there was added the exposure of its shame, *i.e.* the disgraceful sacrifice of the honour and dignity of the people of God, of which Israel had made itself guilty by its whoredom with idols, *i.e.* by falling into idolatry, and adopting heathen ways. עַל־מְאַהֲבַיִךְ, to (towards), *i.e.* with thy lovers (עַל standing for אֶל, according to later usage: *vid.* Ewald, § 217*i*, p. 561), is to be explained after the analogy of

זָנָה אֶל, as signifying to commit adultery towards a person, *i.e.* with him. But it was not enough to sacrifice the gifts of the Lord, *i.e.* His possessions and His glory, to the heathen and their idols; Israel also made for itself כָּל־גִּלּוּלֵי תוֹעֲבוֹת, all kinds of logs of abominations, *i.e.* of idols, upon which it hung its ornaments, and before which it set oil and incense, meal and honey (vers. 18 and 19). And it was not even satisfied with this, but gave to its idols the blood of its sons, by slaying its children to Moloch (ver. 20). Therefore (vers. 37 sqq.) the Lord will uncover the shame of His people before all the nations. He will gather them together, both friend and foe, against Jerusalem, and let them execute the judgment. The punishment will correspond to the sin. Because Israel has cultivated friendship with the heathen, it shall now be given up altogether into their power. On the uncovering of the nakedness as a punishment, compare Hos. ii. 12. The explanation of the figure follows in ver. 38. The heathen nations shall inflict upon Jerusalem the punishment due to adultery and bloodshed. Jerusalem (*i.e.* Israel) had committed this twofold crime. It had committed adultery, by falling away from Jehovah into idolatry; and bloodshed, by the sacrifices offered to Moloch. The punishment for adultery was death by stoning (see the comm. on ver. 40); and blood demanded blood (Gen. ix. 6; Ex. xxi. 12). וּנְתַתִּיךְ דַּם וגו׳ does not mean, "I will put blood in thee" (Ros.), or "I will cause thy blood to be shed in anger" (De Wette, Maurer, etc.); but I make thee into blood; which we must not soften down, as Hitzig proposes, into cause thee to bleed. The thought is rather the following: thou shalt be turned into blood, so that nothing but blood may be left of thee, and that the blood of fury and jealousy, as the working of the wrath and jealousy of God (compare ver. 42). To this end the heathen will destroy all the objects of idolatry (גַּב and רָמוֹת, ver. 39, as in vers. 24, 25), then take from the harlot both clothes and jewellery, and leave her naked, *i.e.* plunder Jerusalem and lay it waste, and, lastly, execute upon her the punishment of death by stoning and by sword; in other words, destroy both city and kingdom. The words הֶעֱלוּ וגו׳, they bring (up) against thee an assembly, may be explained from the ancient mode of administering justice, according to which the popular assembly (*qâhâl*, cf. Prov. v. 14) sat in judgment on cases of adultery and capital crimes, and executed the sentence, as the law for stoning expressly enjoins (Lev. xx. 2; Num. xv. 36; Deut. xxii. 21; compare my *Bibl. Archäol.* II. p. 257). But they are also applicable to the foes, who would march against Jerusalem (for *qâhâl* in this sense, compare ch. xvii. 17). The punishment of adultery (according to Lev. xx. 10) was death by stoning, as we may see from Lev. xx. 2–27 and Deut. xx. 24 compared with John viii. 5. This was the usual mode of capital punishment under the Mosaic law, when judicial sentence of death was pronounced upon individuals (see my *Archäol.* II. p. 264). The other form of punishment, slaying by the sword, was adopted when there were many criminals to be put to death, and was not decapitation, but cutting down or stabbing (*bâthaq*, to hew in pieces) with the sword (see my *Archäol. l.c.*). The punishment of death was rendered more severe by the burning of the corpse (Lev. xx. 14, xxi. 9). Consequently the burning of the houses in ver. 41 is also to be regarded as intensifying the punishment; and it is in the same light that the threat is to be regarded, that the judgment would be executed "before the eyes of many women.' The many women are the many heathen nations, according to the description of Jerusalem or Israel as an unfaithful wife. "As it is the greatest punishment to an adulterous woman to be exposed in her sin before the eyes of other women; so will the severest portion of Israel's punishment be, that it will stand exposed in its sin before the eyes of all other nations" (Kliefoth). This is the way in which God will put an end to the fornication, and appease His wrath and jealousy upon the harlot (vers. 41*b* and 42). הִשְׁבִּית, with מִן, to cause a person to cease to be or do anything. For ver. 42, compare ch. v. 13.

By the execution of the judgment the jealousy (קִנְאָה) of the injured husband is appeased.

Vers. 43–52. This judgment is perfectly just; for Israel has not only forgotten the grace of its God manifested towards it in its election, but has even surpassed both Samaria and Sodom in its abominations.—Ver. 43. *Because thou hast not remembered the days of thy youth, and hast raged against me in all this; behold, I also give thy way upon thy head, is the saying of the Lord Jehovah, that I may not do that which is wrong above all thine abominations.* Ver. 44. *Behold, every one that useth proverbs will use this proverb concerning thee: as the mother, so the daughter.* Ver. 45. *Thou art the daughter of thy mother, who casteth off her husband and her children; and thou art the sister of thy sisters, who cast off their husbands and their children. Your mother is a Hittite, and your father an Amorite.* Ver. 46. *And thy great sister is Samaria with her daughters, who dwelleth at thy left; and thy sister, who is smaller than thou, who dwelleth at thy right, is Sodom with her daughters.* Ver. 47. *But thou hast not walked in their ways and done according to their abominations a little only; thou didst act more corruptly than they in all thy ways.* Ver. 48. *As I live, is the saying of the Lord Jehovah, Sodom thy sister, she with her daughters hath not done as thou hast done with thy daughters.* Ver. 49. *Behold, this was the sin of Sodom, thy sister: pride, superabundance of food, and rest undisturbed had she with her daughters, and the hand of the poor and needy she did not hold.* Ver. 50. *They were haughty, and did abominations before me; and I swept them away when I saw it.* Ver. 51. *And Samaria, she hath not sinned to the half of thy sins; thou hast increased thine abominations more than they, and hast made thy sisters righteous by all thine abominations which thou hast done.* Ver. 52. *Bear, then, also thy shame, which thou hast adjudged to thy sisters. Through thy sins, which thou hast committed more abominably than they, they become more righteous than thou. Be thou, then, also put to shame, and bear thy disgrace, as thou hast justified thy sisters.*—יַעַן אֲשֶׁר, which corresponds to יַעַן in ver. 36, introduces a new train of thought. Most of the commentators take ver. 43 in connection with what precedes, and place the pause at ver. 44. But the perfect נָתַתִּי shows that this is wrong. If ver. 43 simply contained a recapitulation, or a concluding summary, of the threat of judgment in vers. 35–42, the punishment would be announced in the future tense, as it is in ver. 37. By the perfect נָתַתִּי, on the contrary, the punishment is exhibited as a completed fact, and further reasons are then assigned in vindication of the justice of the divine procedure, which we find in vers. 44 sqq. To this end the guilt of Jerusalem is mentioned once more: "thou didst not remember the days of thy youth," *i.e.* what thou didst experience in thy youth; the misery in which thou didst find thyself, and out of which I rescued thee and exalted thee to glory (vers. 4–14). To this there was added rage against Jehovah, which manifested itself in idolatrous acts. רָגַז לְ, to be excited upon or against any person, to rage; thus in *Hithpael* with אֶל in 2 Kings xix. 27, 28. For נָתַן דֶּרֶךְ בְּרֹאשׁ, compare ch. ix. 10. The last clause of ver. 43, וְלֹא עָשִׂיתִי וגו׳, has been misinterpreted in many ways. According to the Masoretic pointing, עשׂיתי is the second person; but this does not yield a suitable meaning. For עָשָׂה זִמָּה is not used in the sense adopted by the Targum, upon which the Masoretic pointing is undoubtedly based, and which Raschi, Kimchi, and Rosenmüller retain, viz. *cogitationem facere:* "thou hast not taken any thought concerning all thy abominations," *i.e.* hast not felt any remorse. The true meaning is to commit a crime, a wrong, and is used for the most part of unnatural offences (cf. Judg. xx. 6; Hos. vi. 9). There is all the more reason for retaining this meaning, that זִמָּה (apart from the plural מְזִמּוֹת=זִמּוֹת) only occurs *sensu malo,* and for the most part in the sense of an immoral action (*vid.* Job xxxi. 11). Consequently we should have to adopt the rendering: and thou no longer committest this immorality above all thine abominations.

But in that case not only would עוֹר have to be supplied, but a distinction would be drawn between the abominations committed by Israel and the sin of lewdness, *i.e.* adultery, which is quite foreign to the connection and to the contents of the entire chapter; for, according to these, the abominations of Israel consisted in adultery or the sin of lewdness. We must therefore take עָשִׂיתִי as the first person, as Symm. and Jerome have done, and explain the words from Lev. xix. 29, where the toleration by a father of the whoredom of a daughter is designated as *zimmâh*. If we adopt this interpretation, Jehovah says that He has punished the spiritual whoredom of Israel, in order that He may not add another act of wrong to the abominations of Israel by allowing such immorality to go on unpunished. If He did not punish, He would commit a *zimmâh* Himself,—in other words, would make Himself accessory to the sins of Israel. The concluding characteristic of the moral degradation of Israel fits in very appropriately here in vers. 44 sqq., in which Jerusalem is compared to Samaria and Sodom, both of which had been punished long ago with destruction on account of their sins. This characteristic is expressed in the form of proverbial sayings. Every one who speaks in proverbs (*mōshēl*, as in Num. xxi. 27) will then say over thee: as the mother, so her daughter. Her abominable life is so conspicuous, that it strikes every one, and furnishes occasion for proverbial sayings. אִמָּה may be a feminine form of אֵם, as לִבָּה is of לֵב (ver. 30); or it may also be a *Raphe* form for אִמָּהּ: as her (the daughter's) mother, so her (the mother's) daughter (cf. Ewald, § 174*e*, note, with § 21, 22[3]). The daughter is of course Jerusalem, as the representative of Israel. The mother is the Canaanitish race of Hittites and Amorites, whose immoral nature had been adopted by Israel (cf. vers. 3 and 45*b*). In ver. 45 the sisterly relation is added to the maternal, to carry out the thought still further. Some difficulty arises here from the statement, that the mothers and the sisters despise their husbands and their children, or put them away. For it is unquestionable that the participle נֹּעֶלֶת belongs to אִמֵּךְ, and not to בַּת, from the parallel relative clause אֲשֶׁר גָּעֲלוּ, which applies to the sisters. The husband of the wife Jerusalem is Jehovah, as the matrimonial head of the covenant nation or congregation of Israel. The children of the wives, viz. the mother, her daughter, and her sisters, are the children offered in sacrifice to Moloch. The worship of Moloch was found among the early Canaanites, and is here attributed to Samaria and Sodom also, though we have no other proofs of its existence there than the references made to it in the Old Testament. The husband, whom the mother and sisters have put away, cannot therefore be any other than Jehovah; from which it is evident that Ezekiel regarded idolatry generally as apostasy from Jehovah, and Jehovah as the God not only of the Israelites, but of the heathen also.[1] אֲחוֹתֵךְ (ver. 45) is a plural noun, as the relative clause which follows and ver. 46 clearly show, and therefore is a contracted form of אֲחוֹתַיִךְ (ver. 51) or אֲחְיוֹתֵךְ (ver. 52; *vid.* Ewald, § 212*b*, p. 538). Samaria and Sodom are called sisters of Jerusalem, not because both cities belonged to the same mother-land of Canaan, for the origin of the cities does not come into consideration here at all, and the cities represent the kingdoms, as the additional words "her daughters," that is to say, the cities of a land or kingdom dependent upon the capital, clearly prove. Samaria and Sodom, with the daughter cities belonging to them, are sisters of Jerusalem in a spiritual sense, as animated by the same spirit of idolatry. Samaria is called the great (greater) sister of Jerusalem, and Sodom the smaller sister. This is not equivalent to the older and the younger, for Samaria was not more deeply sunk in idolatry than Sodom, nor was her idolatry more ancient than that of Sodom (Theodoret and Grotius); and Hävernick's explanation, that "the finer form

[1] Theodoret has explained it correctly in this way: "He shows by this, that He is not the God of Jews only, but of Gentiles also; for God once gave oracles to them, before they chose the abomination of idolatry. Therefore he says that they also put away both the husband aud the children by denying God, and slaying the children to demons."

of idolatry, the mixture of the worship of Jehovah with that of nature, as represented by Samaria, was the first to find an entrance into Judah, and this was afterwards followed by the coarser abominations of heathenism," is unsatisfactory, for the simple reason that, according to the historical books of the Old Testament, the coarser forms of idolatry forced their way into Judah at quite as early a period as the more refined. The idolatry of the time of Rehoboam and Abijam was not merely a mixture of Jehovah-worship with the worship of nature, but the introduction of heathen idols into Judah, along with which there is no doubt that the syncretistic worship of the high places was also practised. גָּדוֹל and קָטָן do not generally mean old and young, but great and small. The transferred meaning old and young can only apply to men and animals, when greatness and littleness are really signs of a difference in age; but it is altogether inapplicable to kingdoms or cities, the size of which is by no means dependent upon their age. Consequently the expressions great and small simply refer to the extent of the kingdoms or states here named, and correspond to the description given of their situation: "at the left hand," *i.e.* to the north, and "at the right hand," *i.e.* to the south of Jerusalem and Judah.

Jerusalem had not only equalled these sisters in sins and abominations, but had acted more corruptly than they (ver. 47). The first hemistich of this verse, "thou walkest not in their ways," etc., is more precisely defined by וַתַּשְׁחִתִי מֵהֵן in the second half. The link of connection between the two statements is formed by כִּמְעַט קָט. This is generally rendered, "soon was there disgust," *i.e.* thou didst soon feel disgust at walking in their ways, and didst act still worse. But apart from the fact that while disgust at the way of the sisters might very well constitute a motive for forsaking those ways, *i.e.* relinquishing their abominations, it could not furnish a motive for surpassing those abominations. This explanation is exposed to the philological difficulty, that קָט by itself cannot signify *taeduit te*, and the impersonal use of קוּם would at all events require לָךְ, which could not be omitted, even if קַט were intended for a substantive. These difficulties fall away if we interpret קַט from the Arabic قَطْ, *omnino, tantum*, as Alb. Schultens has done, and connect the definition "a little only" with the preceding clause. We then obtain this very appropriate thought: thou didst walk in the ways of thy sisters; and that not a little only, but thou didst act still more corruptly than they. This is proved in vers. 48 sqq. by an enumeration of the sins of Sodom. They were pride, satiety,—*i.e.* superabundance of bread (*vid.* Prov. xxx. 9),—and careless rest or security, which produce haughtiness and harshness, or uncharitableness, towards the poor and wretched. In this way Sodom and her daughters (Gomorrah, Admah, and Zeboim) became proud and haughty, and committed abominations לְפָנַי, *i.e.* before Jehovah (alluding to Gen. xviii. 21); and God destroyed them when He saw this. The sins of Samaria (ver. 51) are not specially mentioned, because the principal sin of this kingdom, namely, image-worship, was well known. It is simply stated, therefore, that she did not sin half so much as Jerusalem; and in fact, if we except the times of Ahab and his dynasty, pure heathenish idolatry did not exist in the kingdom of the ten tribes, so that Samaria seemed really a righteous city in comparison with the idolatry of Jerusalem and Judah, more especially from the time of Ahaz onward (*vid.* Jer. iii. 11). The punishment of Samaria by the destruction of the kingdom of the ten tribes is also passed over as being well known to every Israelite; and in ver. 52 the application is directly made to Jerusalem, *i.e.* to Judah: "Thou also, bear thy shame, thou who hast adjudged to thy sisters,"—*sc.* by pronouncing an uncharitable judgment upon them, thinking thyself better than they, whereas thou hast sinned more abominably, so that they appear more righteous than thou. צָדַק, to be righteous, and צִדֵּק, to justify, are used in a comparative sense. In comparison with the abominations of Jerusalem, the sins of Sodom and Samaria appeared perfectly trivial. After וְגַם אַתְּ, the announcement of punishment is repeated for the sake of emphasis, and that in the form of a consequence resulting from the sentence with regard to the nature of the sin: therefore be thou also put to shame, and bear thy disgrace.

Vers. 53–63. But this disgrace will not be the conclusion. Because of the covenant which the Lord concluded with Israel, Jerusalem will not continue in misery, but will attain to the glory promised to the people of God;—and that in such a way that all boasting will be excluded, and Judah, with the deepest shame, will attain to a knowledge of the true compassion of God.—Yet, in order that all false confidence in the gracious promises of God may be prevented, and the sinful nation be thoroughly humbled, this last section of our word of God announces the restoration of Sodom and Samaria as well as that of Jerusalem, so that all boasting on the part of Israel is precluded.—Ver. 53. *And I will turn their captivity, the captivity of Sodom and her daughters, and the captivity of Samaria and her daughters, and the captivity of thy captivity in the midst of them:* Ver. 54. *That thou mayest bear thy shame, and be ashamed of all that thou hast done, in comforting them.* Ver. 55. *And thy sisters, Sodom and her daughters, will return to their first estate; and Samaria and her daughters will return to their first estate; and thou and thy daughters will return to your first estate.* Ver. 56. *And Sodom thy sister was not a discourse in thy mouth in the day of thy haughtinesses,* Ver. 57. *Before thy wickedness was disclosed, as at the time of the disgrace of the daughters of Aram and all its surroundings, the daughters of the Philistines, who despised thee round about.* Ver. 58. *Thy wrongdoing and all thy abominations, thou bearest them, is the saying of Jehovah.* Ver. 59. *For thus saith the Lord Jehovah, And I do with thee as thou hast done, who hast despised oath to break covenant.* Ver. 60. *And I shall remember my covenant with thee in the days of thy youth, and shall establish an everlasting covenant with thee.* Ver. 61. *And thou wilt remember thy ways, and be ashamed, when thou receivest thy sisters, those greater than thou to those smaller than thou; and I give them to thee for daughters, although they are not of thy covenant.* Ver. 62. *And I will establish my covenant with thee; and thou wilt perceive that I am Jehovah;* Ver. 63. *That thou mayest remember, and be ashamed, and there may no longer remain to thee an opening of the mouth because of thy disgrace, when I forgive thee all that thou hast done, is the saying of the Lord Jehovah.*—The promise commences with an announcement of the restoration, not of Jerusalem, but of Sodom and Samaria. The two kingdoms, or peoples, upon which judgment first fell, shall also be the first to receive mercy; and it will not be till after then that Jerusalem, with the other cities of Judah, will also be restored to favour, in order that she may bear her disgrace, and be ashamed of her sins (ver. 54); that is to say, not because Sodom and Samaria have borne their punishment for a longer time, but to the deeper shaming, the more complete humiliation of Jerusalem. שׁוּב שְׁבוּת, to turn the captivity, not "to bring back the captives" (see the comm. on Deut. xxx. 3), is here used in a figurative sense for *restitutio in statum integritatis*, according to the explanation given of the expression in ver. 55. No carrying away, or captivity, took place in the case of Sodom. The form שְׁבִית, which the *Chetib* has adopted several times here, has just the same meaning as שְׁבוּת. שְׁבִית שְׁבִיתַיִךְ does not mean the captives of thy captivity, since the same word cannot be used first as a concrete and then as an abstract noun; nor does the combination serve to give greater emphasis, in the sense of a superlative,—viz. "the captivity of thy captivities, equivalent to thy severest or most fearful captivity,"—as Stark and Hävernick suppose. The genitive must be taken as explanatory, as already proposed by Hengstenberg and Kliefoth: "captivity, which is thy captivity;" and the pleonastic mode of expression is chosen to give greater prominence to the thought, "thine own captivity," than would have been given to it by a suffix attached to the simple noun. בְּתוֹכְהֵנָה, in their midst, does not imply, that just as Judah was situated now in the very midst between Sodom and Samaria, so its captives would return home occupying the centre between those two (Hitzig); the reference is rather to fellowship in captivity, to the fact that Jerusalem would share the same fate, and endure the same punishment, as Samaria and Sodom (Hengst., Klief.). The concluding words of ver. 54, "in that thou comfortest them," do not refer to the sins already committed by Israel (as Kliefoth, who adopts the rendering, "didst comfort them," imagines), but to the bearing of such disgrace as makes Jerusalem ashamed of its sins. By bearing disgrace, *i.e.* by its endurance of well-merited and disgraceful punishment, Jerusalem consoles her sisters Samaria and Sodom; and that not merely by fellowship in misfortune,—*solamen miseris, etc.* (Calvin, Hitzig, etc.),—but by the fact that from the punishment endured by Jerusalem, both Samaria and Sodom can discern the righteousness of the ways of God, and find therein a foundation for their hope, that the righteous God will bring to an end the merited punishment as soon as its object has been attained (see the comm. on ch. xiv. 22, 23). The turning of the captivity, according to ver. 55, will consist in the fact that Sodom, Samaria, and Jerusalem return לְקַדְמָתָן, to their original state. קַדְמָה does not mean the former or earlier state, but the original state (ὡς ἦσαν ἀπ' ἀρχῆς, LXX.), as in Isa. xxiii. 7. Kliefoth is wrong, however, in explaining this as meaning: "as they were, when they came in Adam from the creative hand of God." The original state is the *status integritatis*, not as a state of sinlessness or original righteousness and holiness,—for neither Jerusalem on the one hand, nor Samaria and Sodom on the other, had ever been in such a state as this,—but as an original state of glory, in which they were before they had fallen and sunk into ungodly ways.

But how could a restoration of Sodom and her daughters (Gomorrah, etc.) be predicted, when the destruction of these cities was accompanied by the sweeping away of all their inhabitants from off the face of the earth? Many of the commentators have attempted to remove the difficulty by assuming that Sodom here stands for the Moabites and Ammonites, who were descendants of Lot, who escaped from Sodom. But the untenableness of such an explanation is obvious, from the simple fact that the Ammonites and Moabites were no more Sodomites than Lot himself. And the view expressed by Origen and Jerome, and lately revived by Hävernick, that Sodom is a typical name denoting heathenism generally, is also unsatisfactory. The way in which Sodom is classed with Samaria and Jerusalem, and the special reference to the judgment that fell upon Sodom (vers. 49, 50), point undeniably to the real Sodom. The heathen world comes into consideration only so far as this, that the pardon of a heathen city, so deeply degraded as Sodom, carries with it the assurance that mercy will be extended to all heathen nations. We must therefore take the words as referring to the literal Sodom. Yet we certainly cannot for a moment think of any earthly restoration of Sodom. For even if we could conceive of a restoration of the cities that were destroyed by fire, and sunk into the depths of the Dead Sea, it is impossible to form any conception of an earthly and corporeal restoration of the inhabitants of those cities, who were destroyed at the same time; and in this connection it is chiefly to them that the words refer. This does not by any means prove that the thing itself is impossible, but simply that the realization of the prophecy must be sought for beyond the present order of things, in one that extends into the life everlasting.

As ver. 55 elucidates the contents of ver. 53, so the thought of ver. 54 is explained and still further expanded in vers. 56 and 57 The meaning of ver. 56*a* is a subject of dispute; but so much is indisputable, that the attempt of Kliefoth to explain vers. 56 and 57 as referring to the future, and signifying that in the coming day of its glory Israel will no longer carry

Sodom as a legend in its mouth as it does now, does violence to the grammar, and is quite a mistake. It is no more allowable to take וְלֹא הָיְתָה as a future, in the sense of "and will not be," than to render כְּמוֹ עֵת חֶרְפַּת (ver. 57), "it will be like the time of scorn." Moreover, the application of בְּיוֹם גְּאוֹנָיִךְ to the day of future glory is precluded by the fact that in ver. 49 the word גָּאוֹן is used to denote the pride which was the chief sin of Sodom; and the reference to this verse very naturally suggests itself. The meaning of ver. 56 depends upon the rendering to be given to לִשְׁמוּעָה. The explanation given by Rosenmüller and Maurer, after Jerome,—viz. *non erat in auditione*, i.e. *non audiebatur*, thou didst not think at all of Sodom, didst not take its name into thy mouth,—is by no means satisfactory. שְׁמוּעָה means proclamation, discourse, and also report. If we adopt the last, we must take the sentence as interrogatory (לוֹא for הֲלוֹא), as Hengstenberg and Hitzig have done. Although this is certainly admissible, there are no clear indexes here to warrant our assumption of an interrogation, which is only hinted at by the tone. We therefore prefer the meaning "discourse:" thy sister Sodom was not a discourse in thy mouth in the day of thy haughtinesses, that thou didst talk of the fate of Sodom and lay it to heart when thou wast in prosperity. The plural גְּאוֹנָיִךְ is more emphatic than the singular. The day of the haughtinesses is defined in ver. 57 as the period before the wickedness of Judah had been disclosed. This was effected by means of the judgment, which burst upon Jerusalem on the part of Babylon. Through this judgment Jerusalem is said to have been covered with disgrace, as at the time when the daughters of Aram, *i.e.* the cities of Syria, and those of the Philistines (Aram on the east, and the Philistines on the west, Isa. ix. 11), scorned and maltreated it round about. This refers primarily to the times of Ahaz, when the Syrians and Philistines pressed hard upon Judah (2 Kings xv. 37, xvi. 6; and 2 Chron. xxviii. 18, 19). It must not be restricted to this, however; but was repeated in the reign of

Jehoiachin, when Jehovah sent troops of the Chaldaeans, *Aramaeans*, Ammonites, and Moabites against him, to destroy Judah (2 Kings xxiv. 2). It is true, the Philistines are not mentioned here; but from the threat in Ezek. xxv. 15, we may infer that they also attempted at the same time to bring disgrace upon Judah. שָׁאַט = שׁוּט, according to Aramaean usage, to treat contemptuously, or with repudiation (cf. ch. xxviii. 24, 26). Jerusalem will have to atone for this pride, and to bear its wrong-doing and its abominations (ver. 58). For *zimmâh*, see the comm. on ver. 43. The perfect נְשָׂאתִים indicates that the certainty of the punishment is just as great as if it had already commenced. The reason assigned for this thought in ver. 59 forms a transition to the further expansion of the promise in vers. 60 sqq. ועשׂית (ver. 59) has been correctly pointed by the Masoretes as the 1st person. The ו is copulative, and shows that what follows forms the concluding summary of all that precedes. אוֹתָךְ for אִתָּךְ, as in vers. 60, etc., to deal with any one. The construction of עָשָׂה, with an accusative of the person, to treat any one, cannot be sustained either from ch. xvii. 17 and xxiii. 25, or from Jer. xxxiii. 9; and Gesenius is wrong in assuming that we meet with it in Isa. xlii. 16.—Despising the oath (אָלָה) points back to Deut. xxix. 11, 12, where the renewal of the covenant concluded at Sinai is described as an entrance into the covenant and oath which the Lord then made with His people.—But even if Israel has faithlessly broken the covenant, and must bear the consequent punishment, the unfaithfulness of man can never alter the faithfulness of God. This is the link of connection between the resumption and further expansion of the promise in ver. 60 and the closing words of ver. 59. The remembrance of His covenant is mentioned in Lev. xxvi. 42 and 45 as the only motive that will induce God to restore Israel to favour again, when the humiliation effected by the endurance of punishment has brought it to a confession of its sins. The covenant which God concluded with Israel in the day of its youth, *i.e.* when He led it out of Egypt, He will establish as an everlasting covenant. Consequently it is not an entirely new covenant, but simply the perfecting of the old one for everlasting duration. For the fact itself, compare Isa. lv. 3, where the making of the everlasting covenant is described as granting the stedfast mercies of David, *i.e.* as the fulfilment of the promise given to David (2 Sam. vii.). This promise is called by David himself an everlasting covenant which God had made with him (2 Sam. xxiii. 5). And the assurance of its everlasting duration was to be found in the fact that this covenant did not rest upon the fulfilment of the law, but simply upon the forgiving grace of God (compare ver. 63 with Jer. xxxi. 31–34).—The bestowal of this grace will put Israel in remembrance of its ways, and fill it with shame. In this sense וְזָכַרְתְּ (and thou shalt remember), in ver. 61, is placed side by side with זָכַרְתִּי (I will remember) in ver. 60. This shame will seize upon Israel when the establishment of an everlasting covenant is followed by the greater and smaller nations being associated with it in glory, and incorporated into it as children, though they are not of its covenant. The greater and smaller sisters are the greater and smaller nations, as members of the universal family of man, who are to be exalted to the glory of one large family of God. The restoration, which is promised in vers. 53 and 55 to Sodom and Samaria alone, is expanded here into a prophecy of the reception of all the greater and smaller nations into fellowship in the glory of the people of God. We may see from this that Sodom and Samaria represent the heathen nations generally, as standing outside the Old Testament dispensation: Sodom representing those that were sunk in the deepest moral degradation, and Samaria those that had fallen from the state of grace. The attitude in which these nations stand towards Israel in the everlasting covenant of grace, is defined as the relation of daughters to a mother. If, therefore, Israel, which has been thrust out among the heathen on account of its deep fall, is not to return to its first estate till after the return of Sodom, which has been destroyed, and Samaria, which has been condemned, the election of Israel before all the nations of the earth to be the first-born son of Jehovah will continue unchanged, and Israel will form the stem of the new kingdom of God, into which the heathen nations will be incorporated. The words, "and not of thy covenant," have been taken by most of the commentators in the sense of, "not because thou hast kept the covenant;" but this is certainly incorrect. For even if "thy covenant" really formed an antithesis to "my covenant" (vers. 60 and 62), "thy covenant" could not possibly signify the fulfilment of thy covenant obligations. The words belong to *bânōth* (daughters), who are thereby designated as extra-testamental,—*i.e.* as not included in the covenant which God made with Israel, and consequently as having no claim by virtue of that covenant to participate in the glory of the everlasting covenant which is hereafter to be established.—When this covenant has been established, Israel will know that God is Jehovah, the unchangeably true (for the meaning of the name *Jehovah*, see the commentary on Gen. ii. 4); that it may call to mind, *sc.* both its sinful abominations and the compassionate grace of God, and be so filled with shame and penitence that it will no more venture to open its mouth, either for the purpose of finding excuses for its previous fall, or to murmur against God and His judgments,—namely, when the Lord forgives all its sins by establishing the everlasting covenant, the kernel and essence of which consists in the forgiveness of sins (cf. Jer. xxxi. 34). Thus will the experience of forgiving grace complete what judgment has already begun, viz. the transformation of proud and haughty sinners into meek and humble children of God, for whom the kingdom has been prepared from the beginning.

This thought brings the entire prophecy to a close,—a prophecy which embraces the whole of the world's history and the New Testament, the parallel to which is contained in the apostle's words, "God hath concluded them all in unbelief, that He might have mercy upon all" (Rom. xi. 32).—As the punishment threatened to the adulteress, *i.e.* to the nation of Israel that had despised its God and King, had been fulfilled upon Jerusalem and the Jews, and is in process of fulfilment still, so has the promise also been already fulfilled, so far as its commencement is concerned, though the complete and ultimate fulfilment is only to be expected in time to come. The turning of the captivity, both of Jerusalem and her daughters, and of Samaria and her daughters, commenced with the establishment of the everlasting covenant, *i.e.* of the covenant made through Christ, and with the reception of the believing portion of Israel in Judaea, Samaria, and Galilee (Acts viii. 5 sqq., 25, ix. 31). And the turning of the captivity of Sodom commenced with the spread of the gospel among the heathen, and their entrance into the kingdom of Christ, inasmuch as Sodom with her daughters represents the morally degraded heathen world. Their reception into the kingdom of heaven, founded by Christ on earth, forms the commencement of the return of the forgiven to their first estate on the "restitution of all things," *i.e.* the restoration of all moral relations to their original normal constitution (compare Acts iii. 21 and Meyer's comm. thereon with Matt. xvii. 11), which will attain its perfection in the *παλιγγενεσία*, the general restoration of the world to its original glory (compare Matt. xix. 28 with Rom. viii. 18 sqq. and 2 Pet. iii. 13). The prophecy before us in ver. 55 clearly points to this final goal. It is true that one might understand the return of Jerusalem and Samaria to their original state, which is predicted here as simply relating to the pardon of the covenant nation, whose apostasy had led to the rejection of both its parts; and this pardon might be sought in its reception into the kingdom of Christ and its restoration as the people of God. In that case the complete fulfilment of our prophecy would take place during the present aeon in the spread of the gospel among all nations, and the conversion of that portion of Israel which still remained hardened after the entrance of the full number of the Gentiles into the kingdom of God. But this limitation would be out of harmony with the equality of position assigned to Sodom and her daughters on the one hand, and Samaria and Jerusalem on the other. Though Sodom is not merely a type of the heathen world, the restoration of Sodom and her daughters cannot consist in the reception of the descendants of the cities on which the judgment fell into the kingdom of God or the Christian Church, since the peculiar manner in which those cities were destroyed prevented the possibility of any of the inhabitants remaining alive whose descendants could be converted to Christ and blessed in Him during the present period of the world. On the other hand, the opinion expressed by C. a Lapide, that the restoration of Sodom is to be referred and restricted to the conversion of the descendants of the inhabitants of Zoar, which was spared for Lot's sake, when the other cities of the plain were destroyed, is too much at variance with the words of the passage to allow of our accepting such a solution as this. The turning of the captivity of Sodom and her daughters, *i.e.* the forgiveness of the inhabitants of Sodom and the other cities of the plain, points beyond the present aeon, and the realization can only take place on the great day of the resurrection of the dead in the persons of the former inhabitants of Sodom and the neighbouring cities. And in the same way the restoration of Samaria and Jerusalem will not be completely fulfilled till after the perfecting of the kingdom of Christ in glory at the last day.

Consequently the prophecy before us goes beyond Rom. xi. 25 sqq., inasmuch as it presents, not to the covenant nation only, but, in Samaria and Sodom, to all the larger and smaller heathen nations also, the prospect of being eventually received into the everlasting kingdom of God; although, in accordance with the main purpose of this prophetic word, namely, to bring the pride of Israel completely down, this is simply hinted at, and no precise intimation is given of the manner in which the predicted *apokatastasis* will occur. But notwithstanding this indefiniteness, we must not explain away the fact itself by arbitrary expositions, since it is placed beyond all possible doubt by other passages of the Scriptures. The words of our Lord in Matt. x. 15 and xi. 24, to the effect that it will be more tolerable in the day of judgment for Sodom than for Capernaum and every other city that shall have rejected the preaching of the gospel, teach most indisputably that the way of mercy stands open still even for Sodom itself, and that the judgment which has fallen upon it does not carry with it the final decision with regard to its inhabitants. For Sodom did not put away the perfect revelation of mercy and salvation. If the mighty works which were done in Capernaum had been done in Sodom, it would have stood to the present day (Matt. xi. 23). And from this it clearly follows that all the judgments which fell before the time of Christ, instead of carrying with them the final decision, and involving eternal damnation, leave the possibility of eventual pardon open still. The last judgment, which is decisive for eternity, does not take place till after the full revelation of grace and truth in Christ. Not only will the gospel be preached to all nations before the end comes (Matt. xxiv. 14), but even to the dead; to the spirits in prison, who did not believe at the time of Noah, it has been already preached, at the time when Christ went to them in spirit, in order that, although judged according to man's way in the flesh, they might live according to God's way in the spirit (1 Pet. iii. 19, iv. 6). What the apostle teaches in the first of these passages concerning the unbelievers before the flood, and affirms in the second concerning the dead in general, is equally applicable according to our prophecy to the Sodomites who were judged after man's way in the flesh, and indeed generally to all heathen nations who either lived before Christ or departed from this earthly life without having heard the gospel preached.—It is according to these distinct utterances of the New Testament that the prophecy before us respecting the *apokatastasis* of Sodom, Samaria, and Jerusalem is to be interpreted; and this is not to be confounded with the heretical doctrine of the restoration, *i.e.* the ultimate salvation of all the ungodly, and even of the devil himself. If the preaching of the gospel precedes the last judgment, the final sentence in the judgment will be regulated by the attitude assumed towards the gospel by both the living and the dead. All souls that obstinately reject it and harden themselves in unbelief, will be given up to everlasting damnation. The reason why the conversion of Sodom and Samaria is not expressly mentioned, is to be found in the general tendency of the promise, in which the simple fact is announced without the intermediate circumstances, for the purpose of humbling Jerusalem. The conversion of Jerusalem also is not definitely stated to be the condition of pardon, but this is assumed as well known from the words of Lev. xxvi., and is simply implied in the repeated assertion that Jerusalem will be seized with the deepest shame on account of the pardon which she receives.

CHAP. XVII. HUMILIATION AND EXALTATION OF THE DAVIDIC FAMILY.

The contents of this chapter are introduced as a riddle and a parable, and are divided into three sections. Vers. 1–10 contain the parable; vers. 11–21, the interpretation and application of it to King Zedekiah; and vers. 22–24, the promise of the Messianic kingdom.

Vers. 1–10. The Parable.—Ver. 1. *And the word of Jehovah came to me, saying,* Ver. 2. *Son of man, give a riddle, and relate a parable to the house of Israel;* Ver. 3. *And say, Thus saith the Lord Jehovah, A great eagle, with great wings and long pinions, full of feathers of variegated colours, came to Lebanon and took the top of the cedar:* Ver. 4. *He plucked off the topmost of its shoots, and brought it into Canaan's land; in a merchant-city he set it.* Ver. 5. *And he took of the seed of the land, and put it into seed-land; took it away to many waters, set it as a willow.*

Ver. 6. *And it grew, and became an overhanging vine of low stature, that its branches might turn towards him, and its roots might be under him; and it became a vine, and produced shoots, and sent out foliage.* Ver. 7. *There was another great eagle with great wings and many feathers; and, behold, this vine stretched its roots languishingly towards him, and extended its branches towards him, that he might water it from the beds of its planting.* Ver. 8. *It was planted in a good field by many waters, to send out roots and bear fruit, to become a glorious vine.* Ver. 9. *Say, Thus saith the Lord Jehovah, Will it thrive? will they not pull up its roots, and cut off its fruit, so that it withereth? all the fresh leaves of its sprouting will wither, and not with strong arm and with much people will it be possible to raise it up from its roots.* Ver. 10. *And, behold, although it is planted, will it thrive? will it not wither when the east wind touches it? upon the beds in which it grew it will wither.*

The parable (*mâshâl*, corresponding exactly to the New Testament παραβολή) is called *chīdhâh*, a riddle, because of the deeper meaning lying beneath the parabolic shell. The symbolism of this parable has been traced by many commentators to Babylonian influences working upon the prophet's mind; but without any tenable ground. The figure of the eagle, or bird of prey, applied to a conqueror making a rapid descent upon a country, has as little in it of a specifically Babylonian character as the comparison of the royal family to a cedar or a vine. Not only is Nebuchadnezzar compared to an eagle in Jer. xlviii. 40, xlix. 22, as Cyrus is to a bird of prey in Isa. xlvi. 11; but even Moses has described the paternal watchfulness of God over His own people as bearing them upon eagle's wings (Ex. xix. 4; Deut. xxxii. 11). The cedar of Lebanon and the vine are genuine Israelitish figures. The great eagle in ver. 3 is the great King Nebuchadnezzar (compare ver. 12) The article is simply used to indicate the species, for which *we* should use the indefinite article. In ver. 7, instead of the article, we have אֶחָד in the sense of "another." This first eagle has large wings and long pinions; he has already flown victoriously over wide-spread countries. אֲשֶׁר־לוֹ הָרִקְמָה, literally, which is to him the variegated ornament, *i.e.* which he has as such an ornament. The feathers of variegated ornamental colours point to the many peoples, differing in language, manners, and customs, which were united under the sceptre of Nebuchadnezzar (Hitzig, etc.); not to the wealth and splendour of the conqueror, as such an allusion is altogether remote from the tendency of the parable. He came to Lebanon. This is not a symbol of the Israelitish land, or of the kingdom of Judah; but, as in Jer. xxii. 23, of Jerusalem, or Mount Zion, with its royal palace so rich in cedar wood (see the comm. on Hab. ii. 17 and Zech. xi. 1), as being the place where the cedar was planted (compare the remarks on ver. 12). The cedar is the royal house of David, and the top of it is King Jehoiachin. The word *tzammereth* is only met with in Ezekiel, and there only for the top of a cedar (compare ch. xxxi. 3 sqq.). The primary meaning is doubtful. Some derive it from the curly, or, as it were, woolly top of the older cedars, in which the small twigs that constitute their foliage are only found at the top of the tree. Others suppose it to be connected with the Arabic ضمر, to conceal, and understand it as an epithet applied to the foliage, as the veil or covering of the tree. In ver. 4, *tzammereth* is explained to be רֹאשׁ יְנִיקוֹתָיו, the topmost of its shoots. This the eagle plucked off and carried אֶל־אֶרֶץ כְּנַעַן, an epithet applied to Babylonia here and in ch. xvi. 29, as being a land whose trading spirit had turned it into a Canaan. This is evident from the parallel עִיר רֹכְלִים, city of traders, *i.e.* Babylon (compare ver. 12). The seed of the land, according to ver. 13, is King Zedekiah, because he was of the land, the native king, in contrast to a foreign, Babylonian governor. קָח, for לָקַח, after the analogy of קָחָם in Hos. xi. 3, and pointed with Kametz to distinguish it from the imperative. לָקַח אֶל is used as in Num. xxiii. 27. The ἁπ. λεγ. צַפְצָפָה signifies, in Arabic and the Talmud, the willow, probably so called because it grows in well-watered places; according to Gesenius, it is derived from צוּף, to overflow, literally, the inundated tree. This meaning is perfectly appropriate here. "He set it as a willow" means he treated it as one, inasmuch as he took it to many waters, set it in a well-watered soil, *i.e.* in a suitable place. The cutting grew into an overhanging vine, *i.e.* to a vine spreading out its branches in all directions, though not growing very high, as the following expression שִׁפְלַת קוֹמָה more clearly shows. The object of this growth was, that its branches might turn to him (the eagle), and its roots might be under him (the eagle). The suffixes attached to אֵלָיו and תַּחְתָּיו refer to נֶשֶׁר. This allusion is required not only by the explanation in ver. 14 (? vers. 14, 15), but also by ver. 7, where the roots and branches of the vine stretch to the (other) eagle. In ver. 6*b*, what has already been affirmed concerning the growth is briefly summed up again. The form פֹּארָה is peculiar to Ezekiel. Isaiah has פֻּארָה = פֹּארָה in ch. x. 33. The word signifies branch and foliage, or a branch covered with foliage, as the ornament of a tree.—The other eagle mentioned in ver. 7 is the king of Egypt, according to ver. 15. He had also large wings and many feathers, *i.e.* a widely spread and powerful kingdom; but there is nothing said about pinions and variegated colours, for Pharaoh had not spread out his kingdom over many countries and peoples, or subjugated a variegated medley of peoples and tribes. כָּפַן, as a verb ἁπ. λεγ., signifies to yearn or pine after a thing; in Chaldee, to hunger. לְהַשְׁקוֹת, that he (the eagle-Pharaoh) might give it to drink, or water it. The words מֵעֲרֻגוֹת מַטָּעָהּ are not connected with לְהַשְׁקוֹת, but with שִׁלְחָה and כָּנְפָה, from the beds of its planting, *i.e.* in which it was planted; it stretched out roots and branches to the other eagle, that he might give it to drink. The interpretation is given in ver. 15. The words לְהַשְׁקוֹת אוֹתָהּ, which are added by way of explanation, do not interrupt the train of thought; nor are they superfluous, as Hitzig supposes, because the vine had water enough already (vers. 5 and 8). For this is precisely what the passage is intended to show, namely, that there was no occasion for this pining and stretching out of the branches towards the other eagle, inasmuch as it could thrive very well in the place where it was planted. The latter is expressly stated once more in ver. 8, the meaning of which is perfectly clear,—namely, that if Zedekiah had remained quiet under Nebuchadnezzar, as a hanging vine, his government might have continued and prospered. But, asks Ezekiel in the name of the Lord, will it prosper? תִּצְלָח is a question, and the third person, neuter gender. This question is answered in the negative by the following question, which is introduced with an affirmative הֲלוֹא. The subject to יְנַתֵּק and יְקוֹסֵס is not the first eagle (Nebuchadnezzar), but the indefinite "one" (*man*, they). In the last clause of ver. 9 מַשְׂאוֹת is a substantive formation, used instead of the simple form of the infinitive, after the form מַשָּׂא in 2 Chron. xix. 7, with the termination וֹת, borrowed from the verb ל״ה (compare Ewald, § 160*b* and 239*a*), and the construction is the same as in Amos vi. 10: it will not be to raise up = it will not be possible to raise it up (compare Ges. § 132, 3, Anm. 1). To raise it up from its root does not mean to tear it up by the root (Hävernick), but to rear the withered vine from its roots again, to cause it to sprout again. This rendering of the words corresponds to the interpretation given in ver. 17. —In ver. 10 the leading thought is repeated with emphasis, and rounded off. The east wind is peculiarly dangerous to plants on account of its dryness (compare Gen. xli. 6, and Wetstein on Job xxvii. 21 in Delitzsch's *Commentary*); and it is used very appropriately here, as the Chaldeans came from the east.

Vers. 11–21. Interpretation of the riddle.—Ver. 11. *And the word of Jehovah came to me, saying,* Ver. 12. *Say to the refractory race: Do ye not know what this is? Say, Behold, the king of Babel came to Jerusalem, and took its king and its princes, and brought them to himself to Babel.* Ver. 13. *And he took of the royal seed, and made a covenant with him, and caused him to enter into an oath; and he took the strong ones of the land:* Ver. 14. *That it might be a lowly kingdom, not to lift itself up, that he might keep his covenant, that it might stand.* Ver. 15. *But he rebelled against him by sending his messengers to Egypt, that it might give him horses and much people. Will he prosper? will he that hath done this escape? He has broken the covenant, and should he escape?* Ver. 16. *As I live, is the saying of the Lord Jehovah, surely in the place of the king, who made him king, whose oath he despised, and whose covenant he broke with him, in Babel he will die.* Ver. 17. *And not with great army and much people will Pharaoh act with him in the war, when they cast up a rampart and build siege-towers, to cut off many souls.* Ver. 18. *He has despised an oath to break the covenant, and, behold, he has given his hand and done all this; he will not escape.* Ver. 19. *Therefore thus saith the Lord Jehovah, As I live, surely my oath which he has despised, and my covenant which he has broken, I will give upon his head.* Ver. 20. *I will spread out my net over him, so that he will be taken in my snare, and will bring him to Babel, and contend with him there on account of his treachery which he has been guilty of towards me.* Ver. 21. *And all his fugitives in all his regiments, by the sword will they fall, and those who remain will be scattered to all winds; and ye shall see that I Jehovah have spoken it.*

In vers. 12–17 the parable in vers. 2–10 is interpreted; and in vers. 19–21 the threat contained in the parable is confirmed and still further expanded. We have an account of the carrying away of the king, *i.e.* Jehoiachin, and his princes to Babel in 2 Kings xxiv. 11 sqq., Jer. xxiv. 1, and xxix. 2. The king's seed (זֶרַע הַמְּלוּכָה, ver. 13, as in Jer. xli. 1 = זֶרַע הַמֶּלֶךְ, 1 Kings xi. 14) is Jehoiachin's uncle Mattaniah, whom Nebuchadnezzar made king under the name of Zedekiah (2 Kings xxiv. 17), and from whom he took an oath of fealty (2 Chron. xxxvi. 13). The strong of the land (אֵילֵי = אוּלֵי, 2 Kings xxiv. 15), whom Nebuchadnezzar took (לקח), *i.e.* took away to Babel, are not the heads of tribes and families (2 Kings xxiv. 15); but the expression is used in a wide sense for the several classes of men of wealth, who are grouped together in 2 Kings xxiv. 14 under the one term כָּל־גִּבּוֹרֵי חַיִל (אַנְשֵׁי חַיִל, 2 Kings xxiv. 16), including masons, smiths, and carpenters (2 Kings xxiv. 14 and 16), whereas the heads of tribes and families are classed with the court officials (סָרִיסִים, 2 Kings xxiv. 15) under the title שָׂרֶיהָ (princes) in ver. 12. The design of these measures was to make a lowly kingdom, which could not raise itself, *i.e.* could not revolt, and to deprive the vassal king of the means of breaking the covenant. The suffix attached to לְעָמְדָהּ is probably to be taken as referring to מַמְלָכָה rather than בְּרִיתִי, although both are admissible, and would yield precisely the same sense, inasmuch as the stability of the kingdom was dependent upon the stability of the covenant. But Zedekiah rebelled (2 Kings xxiv. 20). The Egyptian king who was to give Zedekiah horses and much people, in other words, to come to his assistance with a powerful army of cavalry and fighting men, was Hophrah, the Apries of the Greeks, according to Jer. xliv. 30 (see the comm. on 2 Kings xxiv. 19, 20). הֲיִצְלָח points back to תִּצְלָח in ver. 9; but here it is applied to the rebellious king, and is explained in the clause הֲיִמָּלֵט וגו'. The answer is given in ver. 16 as a word of God confirmed by a solemn oath: he shall die in Babel, the capital of the king, who placed him on the throne, and Pharaoh will not render him any effectual help (ver. 17). עָשָׂה אותו, as in ch. xv. 59, to act with him, that is to say, assist him, come to his help. אותו refers to Zedekiah, not to Pharaoh, as Ewald assumes in an inexplicable manner. For שְׁפֹךְ סֹלְלָה וגו', compare ch. iv. 2; and for the fact itself, Jer. xxxiv. 21, 22, and xxxvii. 5, according to which, although an Egyptian army came to the rescue of Jerusalem at the time when it was besieged by the Chaldeans, it was repulsed by the Chaldeans who marched to meet it, without having rendered any permanent assistance to the besieged.—In ver. 18, the main thought that breach of faith can bring no deliverance is repeated for the sake of appending the further expansion contained in vers. 19–21. נָתַן יָדוֹ, he gave his hand, *i.e.* as a pledge of fidelity. The oath which Zedekiah swore to the king of Babel is designated in ver. 19 as Jehovah's oath (אָלָתִי), and the covenant made with him as Jehovah's covenant, because the oath had been sworn by Jehovah, and the covenant of fidelity towards Nebuchadnezzar had thereby been made *implicite* with Jehovah Himself; so that the breaking of the oath and covenant became a breach of faith towards Jehovah. Consequently the very same expressions are used in vers. 16, 18, and 19, to designate this breach of oath, which are applied in ch. xvi. 59 to the treacherous apostasy of Jerusalem (Israel) from Jehovah, the covenant God. And the same expressions are used to describe the punishment as in ch. xii. 13, 14. נִשְׁפַּט אִתּוֹ is construed with the accusative of the thing respecting which he was to be judged, as in 1 Sam. xii. 7. Jehovah regards the treacherous revolt from Nebuchadnezzar as treachery against Himself (מָעַל בִּי); not only because Zedekiah had sworn the oath of fidelity by Jehovah, but also from the fact that Jehovah had delivered up His people and kingdom into the power of Nebuchadnezzar, so that revolt from him really became rebellion against God. אֵת before כָּל־מִבְרָחָו is *nota accus.*, and is used in the sense of *quod adtinet ad*, as, for example, in 2 Kings vi. 5. מִבְרָחָו, his fugitives, is rendered both by the Chaldee and Syriac "his brave men," or "heroes," and is therefore identified with מִבְחָרָו (his chosen ones), which is the reading in some manuscripts. But neither these renderings nor the parallel passage in ch. xii. 14, where סְבִיבֹתָיו apparently corresponds to it, will warrant our adopting this explanation, or making any alteration in the text. The Greek versions have πάσας φυγαδείας αὐτοῦ; Theodoret: ἐν πάσαις ταῖς φυγαδείαις αὐτοῦ; the Vulgate: *omnes profugi ejus;* and therefore they all had the reading מברחו, which also yields a very suitable meaning. The mention of some who remain, and who are to be scattered toward all the winds, is not at variance with the statement that all the fugitives in the wings of the army are to fall by the sword.

The latter threat simply declares that no one will escape death by flight. But there is no necessity to take those who remain as being simply fighting men; and the word "all" must not be taken too literally.

Vers. 22–24. The planting of the true twig of the stem of David.—Ver. 22. *Thus saith the Lord Jehovah, And I will take from the top of the high cedar, and will set it; from the topmost of its shoots will I pluck off a tender one, and will plant it upon a high and exalted mountain.* Ver. 23. *On the high mountain of Israel will I plant it, and it will put forth branches, and bear fruit, and become a splendid cedar, so that all the birds of every plumage will dwell under it. In the shade of its branches will they dwell.* Ver. 24. *And all the trees of the field will learn that I Jehovah have lowered the lofty tree, lifted up the low tree, made the green tree wither, and the withered tree become green. I Jehovah have said it, and have done it.*—Although the sprout of David, whom Nebuchadnezzar had made king, would lose the sovereignty because of his breach of faith, and bring about the destruction of the kingdom of Judah, the Lord would not let His kingdom be destroyed, but would fulfil the promise which He had given to the seed of David. The announcement of this fulfilment takes its form from the preceding parable. As Nebuchadnezzar broke off a twig from the top of the cedar and brought it to Babel (ver. 13), so will Jehovah Himself also pluck off a shoot from the top of the high cedar, and plant it upon a high mountain. The *Vav* before לָקַחְתִּי is the *Vav consec.*, and אָנִי is appended to the verb for the sake of emphasis; but in antithesis to the acting of the eagle, as described in ver. 3, it is placed after it. The cedar, which it designated by the epithet *râmâh*, as rising above the other trees, is the royal house of David, and the tender shoot which Jehovah breaks off and plants is not the Messianic kingdom or sovereignty, so that Zerubbabel could be included, but the Messiah Himself as "a distinct historical personage" (Hävernick). The predicate רַךְ, tender, refers to

Him; also the word יוֹנֵק, a sprout (Isa. liii. 2), which indicates not so much the youthful age of the Messiah (Hitzig) as the lowliness of His origin (compare Isa. xi. 1, liii. 2); and even when applied to David and Solomon, in 2 Sam. iii. 39, 1 Chron. xxii. 5, xxix. 1, expresses not their youthfulness, but their want of strength for the proper administration of such a government. The high mountain, described in ver. 23 as the high mountain of Israel, is Zion, regarded as the seat and centre of the kingdom of God, which is to be exalted by the Messiah above all the mountains of the earth (Isa. ii. 2, etc.). The twig planted by the Lord will grow there into a glorious cedar, under which all birds will dwell. The Messiah grows into a cedar in the kingdom founded by Him, in which all the inhabitants of the earth will find both food (from the fruits of the tree) and protection (under its shadow). For this figure, compare Dan. iv. 8, 9. צִפּוֹר כָּל־כָּנָף, birds of every kind of plumage (cf. ch. xxxix. 4, 17), is derived from Gen. vii. 14, where birds of every kind find shelter in Noah's ark. The allusion is to men from every kind of people and tribe. By this will all the trees of the field learn that God lowers the lofty and lifts up the lowly. As the cedar represents the royal house of David, the trees of the field can only be the other kings or royal families of the earth, not the nations outside the limits of the covenant. At the same time, the nations are not to be entirely excluded because the figure of the cedars embraces the idea of the kingdom, so that the trees of the field denote the kingdoms of the earth together with their kings. The clauses, "I bring down the high tree," contain a purely general thought, as in 1 Sam. ii. 7, 8, and the perfects are not to be taken as preterites, but as statements of practical truths. It is true that the thought of the royal house of David in its previous greatness naturally suggests itself in connection with the high and green tree, and that of Jehoiachin in connection with the dry tree (compare Jer. xxii. 30); and these are not to be absolutely set aside. At the same time, the omission of the article from עֵץ גָּבֹהַּ and the objects which follow, is sufficient to show that the words are not to be restricted to these particular persons, but are applicable to every high and green, or withered and lowly tree; *i.e.* not merely to kings alone, but to all men in common, and furnish a parallel to 1 Sam. ii. 4–9, "The bows of the mighty men are broken; and they that stumbled are girded with strength," etc.

CHAP. XVIII. THE RETRIBUTIVE JUSTICE OF GOD.

In the word of God contained in this chapter, the delusion that God visits the sins of fathers upon innocent children is overthrown, and the truth is clearly set forth that every man bears the guilt and punishment of his own sins (vers. 1–4). The righteous lives through his righteousness (vers. 5–9), but cannot save his wicked son thereby (vers. 10–13); whilst the son who avoids the sins and wickedness of his father, will live through his own righteousness (vers. 14–20). The man who repents and avoids sin is not even charged with his own sin; and, on the other hand, the man who forsakes the way of righteousness, and gives himself up to unrighteousness, will not be protected from death even by his own former righteousness (vers. 21–29). Thus will God judge every man according to his way; and it is only by repentance that Israel itself can live (vers. 30–32). The exposition of these truths is closely connected with the substance and design of the preceding and following prophecies. In the earlier words of God, Ezekiel had taken from rebellious Israel every support of false confidence in the preservation of the kingdom from destruction. But as an impenitent sinner, even when he can no longer evade the punishment of his sins, endeavours as much as possible to transfer the guilt from himself to others, and comforts himself with the thought that he has to suffer for sins that others have committed, and hardens himself against the chastisement of God through such false consolation as this; so even among the people of Israel, when the divine judgments burst upon them, the delusion arose that the existing generation had to suffer for the fathers' sins. If, then, the judgment were ever to bear the fruit of Israel's conversion and renovation, which God designed, the impenitent generation must be deprived even of this pretext for covering over its sins and quieting its conscience, by the demonstration of the justice which characterized the government of God in His kingdom.

Vers. 1–4. The proverb and the word of God.—Ver. 1. *And the word of Jehovah came to me, saying,* Ver. 2. *Why do you use this proverb in the land of Israel, saying, Fathers eat sour grapes, and the sons' teeth are set on edge.* Ver. 3. *As I live, is the saying of the Lord Jehovah, this proverb shall not be used any more in Israel.* Ver. 4. *Behold, all souls are mine; as the father's soul, so also the soul of the son,—they are mine; the soul which sinneth, it shall die.*—On ver. 2*a* compare ch. xii. 22. מַה־לָּכֶם, what is to you, what are you thinking of, that . . .? is a question of amazement. עַל־אַדְמַת, in the land of Israel (ch. xii. 22), not "concerning the land of Israel," as Hävernick assumes. The proverb was not, "The fathers have eaten sour grapes," for we have not אָכְלוּ, as in Jer. xxxi. 29, but יֹאכְלוּ, they eat, are accustomed to eat, and אָבוֹת has no article, because it applies to all who eat sour grapes. *Bōsĕr*, unripe, sour grapes, like *bēsĕr* in Job xvi. 33 (see the comm. *in loc.*). The meaning of the proverb is self-evident. The sour grapes which the fathers eat are the sins which they commit; the setting of the children's teeth on edge is the consequence thereof, *i.e.* the suffering which the children have to endure. The same proverb is quoted in Jer. xxxi. 29, 30, and there also it is condemned as an error. The origin of such a proverb is easily to be accounted for from the inclination of the natural man to transfer to others the guilt which has brought suffering upon himself, more especially as the law teaches that the sins of the fathers are visited upon the children (Ex. xx. 5), and the prophets announce that the Lord would put away

Judah from before His face on account of the sins of Manasseh (2 Kings xxiv. 3; Jer. xv. 4), while Jeremiah complains in Lam. v. 7 that the people are bearing the fathers' sins. Nevertheless the proverb contained a most dangerous and fatal error, for which the teaching of the law concerning the visitation of the sins of the fathers, etc., was not accountable, and which Jeremiah, who expressly mentions the doctrine of the law (Jer. xxxii. 18), condemns as strongly as Ezekiel. God will visit the sins of the fathers upon the children who hate Him, and who also walk in the footsteps of their fathers' sins; but to those who love Him, and keep His commandments, He will show mercy to the thousandth generation. The proverb, on the other hand, teaches that the children would have to atone for their fathers' sins without any culpability of their own. How remote such a perversion of the truth as to the transmission of sins and their consequences, viz. their punishment, was from the law of Moses, is evident from the express command in Deut. xxiv. 16, that the children were not to be put to death with the fathers for the sins which the latter had committed, but that every one was to die for his own sin. What God here enjoins upon the judicial authorities must apply to the infliction of His own judgments. Consequently what Ezekiel says in the following verses in opposition to the delusion, which this proverb helped to spread abroad, is simply a commentary upon the words, "every one shall die for his own sin," and not a correction of the law, which is the interpretation that many have put upon these prophetic utterances of Jeremiah and Ezekiel. In ver. 3, the Lord declares with an oath that this proverb shall not be used any more. The apodosis to אִם יִהְיֶה וגו׳, which is not expressed, would be an imprecation, so that the oath contains a solemn prohibition. God will take care that this proverb shall not be used any more in Israel, not so much by the fact that He will not give them any further occasion to make use of it, as by the way in which He will convince them, through the judgments which He sends, of the justice of His ways. The following is Calvin's admirable paraphrase: "I will soon deprive you of this boasting of yours; for your iniquity shall be made manifest, so that all the world may see that you are but enduring just punishment, which you yourselves have deserved, and that you cannot cast it upon your fathers, as you have hitherto attempted to do." At the same time, this only gives one side; we must also add the other, which is brought out so prominently in Jer. xxxi. 29 sqq., namely, that after the judgment God will manifest His grace so gloriously in the forgiveness of sins, that those who are forgiven will fully recognise the justice of the judgments inflicted. Experience of the love and compassion of the Lord, manifesting itself in the forgiveness of sin, bows down the heart so deeply that the pardoned sinner has no longer any doubt of the justice of the judgments of God. "*In Israel*" is added, to show that such a proverb is opposed to the dignity of Israel. In ver. 4, the reason assigned for the declaration thus solemnly confirmed by an oath commences with a general thought which contains the thesis for further discussion. All souls are mine, the soul of the father as well as that of the son, saith the Lord. In these words, as Calvin has well said, "God does not merely vindicate His government or His authority, but shows that He is moved with paternal affection toward the whole of the human race which He created and formed." There is no necessity for God to punish the one for the other, the son for the father, say because of the possibility that the guilty person might evade Him; and as the Father of all, He cannot treat the one in a different manner from the other, but can only punish the one by whom punishment has been deserved. The soul that sinneth shall die. הַנֶּפֶשׁ is used here, as in many other passages, for "man," and מוּת is equivalent to suffering death as a punishment. "Death" is used to denote the complete destruction with which transgressors are threatened by the law, as in Deut. xxx. 15 (compare Jer. xxi. 8; Prov. xi. 10). This sentence is explained in the verses which follow (vers. 5–20).

Vers. 5–9. The righteous man shall not die.—Ver. 5. *If a man is righteous, and doeth right and righteousness*, Ver. 6. *And doth not eat upon the mountains, and doth not lift up his eyes to the idols of the house of Israel, and doth not defile his neighbour's wife, and doth not approach his wife in her uncleanness*, Ver. 7. *Oppresseth no one, restoreth his security* (lit. debt-pledge), *committeth no robbery, giveth his bread to the hungry, and covereth the naked with clothes*, Ver. 8. *Doth not give upon usury, and taketh not interest, withholdeth his hand from wrong, executeth judgment of truth between one and another*, Ver. 9. *Walketh in my statutes, and keepeth my rights to execute truth; he is righteous, he shall live, is the saying of the Lord "Jehovah."*—The exposition of the assertion, that God only punishes the sinner, not the innocent, commences with a picture of the righteousness which has the promise of life. The righteousness consists in the fulfilment of the commandments of the law: viz. (1) those relating to religious duties, such as the avoidance of idolatry, whether of the grosser kind, such as eating upon the mountains, *i.e.* observing sacrificial festivals, and therefore sacrificing to idols (cf. Deut. xii. 2 sqq.), or of a more refined description, *e.g.* lifting up the eyes to idols, to look to them, or make them the object of trust, and offer supplication to them (cf. Ps. cxxi. 1; Deut. iv. 19), as Israel had done, and was doing still (cf. ch. vi. 13); and (2) those relating to moral obligations, such as the avoidance of adultery (compare Ex. xx. 14; Lev. xx. 10; Deut. xxii. 22; and for טִמֵּא, Gen. xxxiv. 5), and of conjugal intercourse with a wife during menstruation, which was a defilement of the marriage relation (cf. Lev. xviii. 19, xx. 18). All these sins were forbidden in the law on pain of death. To these there are appended duties to a neighbour (vers. 7 sqq.), viz. to abstain from oppressing any one (Ex. xxii. 28; Lev. xxv. 14, 17), to restore the pledge to a debtor (Ex. xxii. 25; Deut. xxiv. 6, 10 sqq.). חוֹב is hardly to be taken in any other sense than as in apposition to חֲבֹלָתוֹ, "his pledge, which is debt," equivalent to his debt-pledge or security, like דִּרְכֵּךְ זִמָּה in ch. xvi. 27. The supposition of Hitzig, that חוֹב is a participle, like קוֹם in 2 Kings xvi. 7, in the sense of debtor, is a far less natural one, and has no valid support in the free rendering of the LXX., ἐνεχυρασμὸν ὀφείλοντος. The further duties are to avoid taking unlawful possession of the property of another (cf. Lev. v. 23); to feed the hungry, clothe the naked (cf. Isa. lviii. 5; Matt. xxv. 26; Jas. ii. 15, 16); to abstain from practising usury (Deut. xxiii. 20; cf. Ex. xxii. 24) and taking interest (Lev. xxv. 36, 37); in judicial sentences, to draw back the hand from wrong, and promote judgment of truth,—a sentence in accordance with the true nature of the case (see the comm. on Zech. vii. 9); and, lastly, to walk in the statutes and rights of the Lord,—an expression which embraces, in conclusion, all that is essential to the righteousness required by the law.—This definition of the idea of true righteousness, which preserves from death and destruction, and ensures life to the possessor, is followed in vers. 10 sqq. by a discussion of the attitude which God sustains towards the sons.

Vers. 10–13. The righteousness of the father does not protect the wicked, unrighteous son from death.—Ver. 10. *If, however, he begetteth a violent son, who sheddeth blood, and doeth only one of these things,* Ver. 11. *But he himself hath not done all this,—if he even eateth upon the mountains, and defileth his neighbour's wife,* Ver. 12. *Oppresseth the suffering and poor, committeth robbery, doth not restore a pledge, lifteth up his eyes to idols, committeth abomination,* Ver. 13. *Giveth upon usury, and taketh interest: should he live? He shall not live! He hath done all these abominations; he shall be put to death; his blood shall be upon him.*—The subject to וְהוֹלִיד, in ver. 10, is the righteous man described in the preceding verses. פָּרִיץ, violent, literally, breaking in or through, is rendered more emphatic by the words "shedding blood" (cf. Hos. iv. 2). We regard אַח in the next clause as simply a dialectically different form of writing and pronouncing, for אַךְ, "only," and he doeth only one of these, the sins previously mentioned (vers. 6 sqq.). מֵאַחַד, with a partitive מִן, as in Lev. iv. 2, where it is used in a similar connection; the form מֵאַחַד is also met with in Deut. xv. 7. The explanation given by the Targum, "and doeth one of these to his brother," is neither warranted by the language nor commended by the sense. עָשָׂה is never construed with the accusative of the person to whom anything is done; and the limitation of the words to sins against a brother is unsuitable in this connection. The next clause, וְהוּא . . . לֹא עָשָׂה, which has also been variously rendered, we regard as an adversative circumstantial clause, and agree with Kliefoth in referring it to the begetter (father): "and he (the father) has not committed any of these sins." For it yields no intelligible sense to refer this clause also to the son, since כָּל־אֵלֶּה cannot possibly refer to different things from the preceding מֵאֵלֶּה, and a man cannot at the same time both do and not do the same thing. The כִּי which follows signifies "if," as is frequently the case in the enumeration of particular precepts or cases; compare, for example, Ex. xxi. 1, 7, 17, etc., where it is construed with the imperfect, because the allusion is to things that may occur. Here, on the contrary, it is followed by the perfect, because the sins enumerated are regarded as committed. The emphatic גַּם (even) forms an antithesis to אַח מֵאַחַד (אַךְ), or rather an *epanorthosis* of it, inasmuch as כִּי גַּם resumes and carries out still further the description of the conduct of the wicked son, which was interrupted by the circumstantial clause; and that not only in a different form, but with a gradation in the thought. The thought, for instance, is as follows: the violent son of a righteous father, even if he has committed only one of the sins which the father has not committed, shall die. And if he has committed even the gross sins named, viz. idolatry, adultery, violent oppression of the poor, robbery, etc., should he then continue to live? The ו in וָחָי introduces the apodosis, which contains a question, that is simply indicated by the tone, and is immediately denied. The antique form חָי for חָיָה, 3d pers.

perf., is taken from the Pentateuch (cf. Gen. iii. 22 and Num. xxi. 8). The formulae מוֹת יוּמָת and דָּמָיו בּוֹ are also derived from the language of the law (cf. Lev. xx. 9, 11, 13, etc.).

Vers. 14–20. The son who avoids his father's sin will live; but the father will die for his own sins.—Ver. 14. *And behold, he begetteth a son, who seeth all his father's sins which he doeth; he seeth them, and doeth not such things.* Ver. 15. *He eateth not upon the mountains, and lifteth not up his eyes to the idols of the house of Israel; he defileth not his neighbour's wife,* Ver. 16. *And oppresseth no one; he doth not withhold a pledge, and committeth not robbery; giveth his bread to the hungry, and covereth the naked with clothes.* Ver. 17. *He holdeth back his hand from the distressed one, taketh not usury and interest, doeth my rights, walketh in my statutes; he will not die for the sin of his father; he shall live.* Ver. 18. *His father, because he hath practised oppression, committed robbery upon his brother, and hath done that which is not good in the midst of his people; behold, he shall die for his sin.* Ver. 19. *And do ye say, Why doth the son not help to bear the father's sin? But the son hath done right and righteousness, hath kept all my statutes, and done them; he shall live.* Ver. 20. *The soul that sinneth, it shall die. A son shall not help to bear the father's sin, and a father shall not help to bear the sin of the son. The righteousness of the righteous shall be upon him, and the wickedness of the wicked shall be upon him.*—The case supposed in these verses forms the antithesis to the preceding one; the father is the transgressor in this instance, and the son a keeper of the law. The subject to הוֹלִיד in ver. 14 is not the righteous man described in ver. 15, but a man who is described immediately afterwards as a transgressor of the commandments of God. The *Chetib* וירא in the last clause of ver. 14 is not to be read וַיִּרָא, *καὶ φοβηθῇ, et timuerit,* as it has been by the translators of the Septuagint and Vulgate; nor is it to be altered into וַיִּרְאֶה, as it has been by the Masoretes, to make it accord with ver. 28; but it is the apocopated form וַיֵּרֶא, as in the preceding clause, and the object is to be repeated from what precedes, as in the similar case which we find in Ex. xx. 15 (18). Ewald and Hitzig propose to alter מֵעָנִי in ver. 17 into מֵעָוֶל after ver. 8, but without the slightest necessity. The LXX. are not to be taken as an authority for this, since the Chaldee and Syriac have both read and rendered עָנִי; and Ezekiel, when repeating the same sentences, is accustomed to make variations in particular words. Holding back the hand from the distressed, is equivalent to abstaining from seizing upon him for the purpose of crushing him (compare ver. 12); בְּתוֹךְ עַמָּיו, in the midst of his countrymen = בְּתוֹךְ עַמּוֹ, is adopted from the language of the Pentateuch. מֵת after הִנֵּה is a participle. The question, "Why does the son not help to bear?" is not a direct objection on the part of the people, but is to be taken as a pretext, which the people might offer on the ground of the law, that God would visit the sin of the fathers upon the sons in justification of their proverb. Ezekiel cites this pretext for the purpose of meeting it by stating the reason why this does not occur. נָשָׂא בְּ, to carry, near or with, to join in carrying, or help to carry (cf. Num. xi. 17). This proved the proverb to be false, and confirmed the assertion made in ver. 4*b*, to which the address therefore returns (ver. 20). The righteousness of the righteous man will come upon him, *i.e.* upon the righteous man, namely, in its consequences. The righteous man will receive the blessing of righteousness, but the unrighteous man the curse of his wickedness. There is no necessity for the article, which the *Keri* proposes to insert before רָשָׁע.

Vers. 21–26. Turning to good leads to life; turning to evil is followed by death.—Ver. 21. *But if the wicked man turneth from all his sins which he hath committed, and keepeth all my statutes, and doeth right and righteousness, he shall live, and not die.* Ver. 22. *All his transgressions which he hath committed, shall not be remembered to him: for the sake of the righteousness which he hath done he will live.* Ver. 23. *Have I then pleasure in the death of the wicked? is the saying of Jehovah: and not rather that he turn from his ways, and live?* Ver. 24. *But if the righteous man turn from his righteousness, and doeth wickedness, and acteth according to all the abominations which the ungodly man hath done, should he live? All the righteousness that he hath done shall not be remembered: for his unfaithfulness that he hath committed, and for his sin that he hath sinned, for these he shall die.* Ver. 25. *And ye say, "The way of the Lord is not right." Hear now, O house of Israel: Is my way not right? Is it not your ways that are not right?* Ver. 26. *If a righteous man turneth from his righteousness, and doeth wickedness, and dieth in consequence, he dieth for his wickedness that he hath done.*—The proof that every one must bear his sin did not contain an exhaustive reply to the question, in what relation the righteousness of God stood to the sin of men? For the cases supposed in vers. 5–20 took for granted that there was a constant persistence in the course once taken, and overlooked the instances, which are by no means rare, when a man's course of life is entirely changed. It still remained, therefore, to take notice of such cases as these, and they are handled in vers. 21–26. The ungodly man, who repents and turns, shall live; and the righteous man, who turns to the way of sin, shall die. "As the righteous man, who was formerly a sinner, is not crushed down by his past sins; so the sinner, who was once a righteous man, is not supported by his early righteousness. Every one will be judged in that state in which he is found" (Jerome). The motive for the pardon of the repenting sinner is given in ver. 23, in the declaration that God has no pleasure in the death of the wicked man, but desires his conversion, that he may live. God is therefore not only just, but merciful and gracious, and punishes none with death but those who either will not desist from evil, or will not persevere in the way of His commandments. Consequently the complaint, that the way of the Lord, *i.e.* His conduct toward men, is not weighed (יִתָּכֵן, see comm. on 1 Sam. ii. 3), *i.e.* not just and right, is altogether unfounded, and recoils upon those who make it. It is not God's ways, but the sinner's, that are wrong (ver. 25). The proof of this, which Hitzig overlooks, is contained in the declarations made in vers. 23 and 26,—viz. in the fact that God does not desire the death of the sinner, and in His mercy forgives the penitent all his former sins, and does not lay them to his charge; and also in the fact that He punishes the man who turns from the way of righteousness and gives himself up to wickedness, on account of the sin which he commits; so that He simply judges him according to his deeds.—In ver. 24, וְעָשָׂה is the continuation of the infinitive שׁוּב, and וָחָי is interrogatory, as in ver. 13.

Vers. 27–32. The vindication of the ways of God might have formed a fitting close to this divine oracle. But as the prophet was not merely concerned with the correction of the error contained in the proverb which was current among the people, but still more with the rescue of the people themselves from destruction, he follows up the refutation with another earnest call to repentance.—Ver. 27. *If a wicked man turneth from his wickedness which he hath done, and doeth right and righteousness, he will keep his soul alive.* Ver. 28. *If he seeth and turneth from all his transgressions which he hath committed, he shall live and not die.* Ver. 29. *And the house of Israel saith, The way of the Lord is not right. Are my ways not right, O house of Israel? Is it not rather your ways that are not right?* Ver. 30. *Therefore, every one according to his ways, will I judge you, O house of Israel, is the saying of the Lord Jehovah. Turn and repent of all your transgressions, that it may not become to you a stumbling-block to guilt.* Ver. 31. *Cast from you all your transgressions which ye have committed, and make yourselves a new heart and a new spirit! And why will ye die, O house of Israel?* Ver. 32. *For I have no pleasure in the death of the dying, is the saying of the Lord Jehovah. Therefore repent, that ye may live.*—For the purpose of securing an entrance into their hearts for the call to repentance, the prophet not only repeats, in vers. 27

and 28, the truth declared in vers. 21 and 22, that he who turns from his sin finds life, but refutes once more in ver. 29, as he has already done in ver. 25, the charge that God's ways are not right. The fact that the singular יִתָּכֵן is connected with the plural דַּרְכֵיכֶם, does not warrant our altering the plural into דַּרְכְּכֶם, but may be explained in a very simple manner, by assuming that the ways of the people are all summed up in one, and that the meaning is this: what you say of my way applies to your own ways,—namely, "it is not right; there is just measure therein." לָכֵן, "therefore, etc.;" because my way, and not yours, is right, I will judge you, every one according to his way. Repent, therefore, if ye would escape from death and destruction. שׁוּבוּ is rendered more emphatic by הָשִׁיבוּ, *sc.* פְּנֵיכֶם, as in ch. xiv. 6. In the last clause of ver. 30, עָוֹן is not to be taken as the subject of the sentence according to the accents, but is a genitive dependent upon מִכְשׁוֹל, as in ch. vii. 19 and xiv. 3; and the subject is to be found in the preceding clause: that it (the sinning) may not become to you a stumbling-block of iniquity, *i.e.* a stumbling-block through which ye fall into guilt and punishment.—The appeal in ver. 31 points back to the promise in ch. xi. 18, 19. הִשְׁלִיךְ, to cast away. The application of this word to transgressions may be explained from the fact that they consisted for the most part of idols and idolatrous images, which they had made.—"*Make yourselves* a new heart and a new spirit:" a man cannot, indeed, create either of these by his own power; God alone can give them (ch. xi. 19). But a man both can and should come to God to receive them: in other words, he can turn to God, and let both heart and spirit be renewed by the Spirit of God. And this God is willing to do; for He has no pleasure בְּמוֹת הַמֵּת, in the death of the dying one. In the repetition of the assurance given in ver. 23, הַמֵּת is very appropriately substituted for רָשָׁע, to indicate to the people that while in sin they are lying in death, and that it is only by conversion and renewal that they can recover life again.

CHAP. XIX. LAMENTATION FOR THE PRINCES OF ISRAEL.

Israel, the lioness, brought up young lions in the midst of lions. But when they showed their leonine nature, they were taken captive by the nations and led away, one to Egypt, the other to Babylon (vers. 1–9). The mother herself, once a vine planted by the water with vigorous branches, is torn from the soil, so that her strong tendrils wither, and is transplanted into a dry land. Fire, emanating from a rod of the branches, has devoured the fruit of the vine, so that not a cane is left to form a ruler's sceptre (vers. 10–14).—This lamentation, which bewails the overthrow of the royal house and the banishment of Israel into exile, forms a finale to the preceding prophecies of the overthrow of Judah, and was well adapted to annihilate every hope that things might not come to the worst after all.

Vers. 1–9. Capture and Exile of the Princes.—Ver. 1. *And do thou raise a lamentation for the princes of Israel,* Ver. 2. *And say, Why did thy mother, a lioness, lie down among lionesses; bring up her whelps among young lions?* Ver. 3. *And she brought up one of her whelps: it became a young lion, and he learned to take prey; he devoured man.* Ver. 4. *And nations heard of him; he was caught in their pit, and they brought him with nose-rings into the land of Egypt.* Ver. 5. *And when she saw that her hope was exhausted, overthrown, she took one of her whelps, made it a young lion.* Ver. 6. *And he walked among lionesses, he became a young lion, and learned to take prey. He devoured man.* Ver. 7. *He knew its widows, and laid waste their cities; and the land and its fulness became waste, at the voice of his roaring.* Ver. 8. *Then nations round about from the provinces set up against him, and spread over him their net: he was caught in their pit.* Ver. 9. *And they put him in the cage with nose-rings, and brought him to the king of Babylon: brought him into a fortress, that his voice might not be heard any more on the mountains of Israel.*

The princes of Israel, to whom the lamentation applies, are the kings (נָשִׂיא, as in ch. xii. 10), two of whom are so clearly pointed out in vers. 4 and 9, that there is no mistaking Jehoahaz and Jehoiachin. This fact alone is sufficient to protect the plural נְשִׂיאֵי against the arbitrary alteration into the singular נְשִׂיא, proposed by Houbigant and Hitzig, after the reading of the LXX. The lamentation is not addressed to one particular prince, either Zedekiah (Hitzig) or Jehoiachin (Ros., Maurer), but to Israel as a nation; and the mother (ver. 2) is the national community, the theocracy, out of which the kings were born, as is indisputably evident from ver. 10. The words from מָה אִמְּךָ to רָבָצָה form one sentence. It yields no good sense to separate מָה אִמְּךָ from רָבָצָה, whether we adopt the rendering, "what is thy mother?" or take מָה with לְבִיָּא and render it, "how is thy mother a lioness?" unless, indeed, we supply the arbitrary clause "now, in comparison with what she was before," or change the interrogative into a preterite: "how has thy mother become a lioness?" The lionesses, among which Israel lay down, are the other kingdoms, the Gentile nations. The words have no connection with Gen. xlix. 9, where Judah is depicted as a warlike lion. The figure is a different one here. It is not so much the strength and courage of the lion as its wildness and ferocity that are the points of resemblance in the passage before us. The mother brings up her young ones among young lions, so that they learn to take prey and devour men. גּוּר is the lion's whelp, *catulus;* כְּפִיר, the young lion, which is old enough to go out in search of prey. וַתַּעַל is a *Hiphil,* in the tropical sense, to cause to spring up, or grow up, *i.e.* to bring up. The thought is the following: Why has Israel entered into fellowship with the heathen nations? Why, then, has it put itself upon a level with the heathen nations, and adopted the rapacious and tyrannical nature of the powers of the world? The question "why then?" when taken with what follows, involves the reproof that Israel has struck out a course opposed to its divine calling, and will now have to taste the bitter fruits of this assumption of heathen ways. The heathen nations have taken captive its king, and led him away into heathen lands. יִשְׁמְעוּ אֵלָיו, they heard of him (אֵלָיו for עָלָיו). The fate of Jehoahaz, to which ver. 4 refers, is related in 2 Kings xxiii. 31 sqq.—Vers. 5–7 refer to Jehoiachin, the son of Jehoiakim, and not to Zedekiah, as Hitzig imagines. For the fact that Jehoiachin went out of his own accord to the king of Babylon (2 Kings xxiv. 12), is not at variance with the figure contained in ver. 8, according to which he was taken (as a lion) in a net. He simply gave himself up to the king of Babylon because he was unable to escape from the besieged city. Moreover, Jehoahaz and Jehoiachin are simply mentioned as examples, because they both fell into the hands of the world-powers, and their fate showed clearly enough "what the end must inevitably be, when Israelitish kings became ambitious of being lions, like the kings of the nations of the world" (Kliefoth). Jehoiakim was not so suitable an example as the others, because he died in Jerusalem. נוֹחֲלָה, which has been explained in different ways, we agree with Ewald in regarding as the *Niphal* of יחל = חול, in the sense of feeling vexed, being exhausted or deceived, like the Syriac ܐܘܚܠ, *viribus defecit, desperavit.* For even in Gen. viii. 12, נוֹחַל simply means to wait; and this is inapplicable here, as waiting is not equivalent to waiting in vain. The change from חול to יָחַל is established by Judg. iii. 25, where חול or חִיל occurs in the sense of יָחַל. In ver. 7, the figurative language passes into a literal description of the ungodly course pursued by the king. He knew, *i.e.* dishonoured, its (Israel's, the nation's) widows. The Targum reads וירע here instead of וידע, and renders it accordingly, "he destroyed its palaces;" and Ewald has adopted the same rendering. But רעע, to break, or smash in pieces, *e.g.* a vessel (Ps. ii. 9), is never used for the destruction of buildings; and אַלְמְנוֹת does not mean palaces (אַרְמְנוֹת), but windows. There is nothing in the use of the word in Isa. xiii. 22 to support the meaning "palaces," because the palaces are simply called *'almânōth* (widows) there, with a sarcastic side glance at their desolate and widowed condition. Other conjectures are still more inadmissible. The thought is as follows: Jehoiachin went much further than Jehoahaz. He not only devoured men, but laid hands on defenceless widows, and laid the cities waste to such an extent that the land with its inhabitants became perfectly desolate through his rapacity. The description is no doubt equally applicable to his father Jehoiakim, in whose footsteps Jehoiachin walked, since Jehoiakim is described in Jer. xxii. 13 sqq. as a grievous despot and tyrant. In ver. 8 the object רִשְׁתָּם also belongs to יִתְּנוּ: they set up and spread out their net. The plural מְצֹדוֹת is used in a general and indefinite manner: in lofty castles, mountain-fortresses, *i.e.* in one of them (cf. Judg. xii. 7).

Vers. 10–14. Destruction of the Kingdom, and Banishment of the People.—Ver. 10. *Thy mother was like a vine, planted by the water in thy repose; it became fruitful and rich in tendrils from many waters.* Ver. 11. *And it had strong shoots for rulers' sceptres; and its growth ascended among the clouds, and was visible in its height in the multitude of its branches.* Ver. 12. *Then it was torn up in fury, cast to the ground, and the east wind dried up its fruit; its strong shoots were broken off, and withered; fire devoured them.* Ver. 13. *And now it is planted in the desert, in a dry and thirsty land.* Ver. 14. *There goeth out fire from the shoot of its branches, devoureth its fruit, so that there is no more a strong shoot upon it, a sceptre for ruling.—A lamentation it is, and it will be for lamentation.*—From the lamentable fate of the princes transported to Egypt and Babylon, the ode passes to a description of the fate, which the lion-like rapacity of the princes is preparing for the kingdom and people. Israel resembled a vine planted by the water. The difficult word בְּדָמְךָ we agree with Hävernick and Kliefoth in tracing to the verb דָּמָה, to rest (Jer. xiv. 17), and regard it as synonymous with בִּדְמִי in Isa. xxxviii. 10: "in thy repose," *i.e.* in the time of peaceful, undisturbed prosperity. For neither of the other renderings, "in thy blood" and "in thy likeness," yields a suitable meaning. The latter explanation, which originated with Raschi and Kimchi, is precluded by the fact that Ezekiel always uses the word דְּמוּת to express the idea of resemblance. —For the figure of the vine, compare Ps. lxxx. 9 sqq. This vine sent out strong shoots for rulers' sceptres; that is to say, it brought forth powerful kings, and grew up to a great height, even into the clouds. עֲבֹתִים signifies "clouds," lit. thicket of clouds, not only here, but in ch. xxxi. 3, 10, 14. The rendering "branches" or "thicket of foliage" is not suitable in any of these passages. The form of the word is not to be taken as that of a new plural of עָבוֹת, the plural of עָב, which occurs in 2 Sam. xxiii. 4 and Ps. lxxvii. 18; but is the plural of עֲבֹת, an interlacing or thicket of foliage, and is simply transferred to the interlacing or piling up of the clouds. The clause וַיֵּרָא וגו׳, and it appeared, was seen, or became visible, simply serves to depict still further the glorious and vigorous growth, and needs no such alteration as Hitzig proposes. This picture is followed in ver. 12 sqq., without any particle of transition, by a description of the destruction of this vine. It was torn up in fury by the wrath of God, cast down to the ground, so that its fruit withered (compare the similar figures in ch. xvii. 10). מַטֵּה עֻזָּהּ is used collectively, as equivalent to מַטּוֹת עֹז (ver. 11); and the suffix in אֲכָלָתְהוּ is written in the singular on account of this collective use of מַטֵּה. The uprooting ends in the transplanting of the vine into a waste, dry, unwatered land,—in other words, in the transplanting of the people, Israel, into exile. The dry land is Babylon, so described as being a barren soil in which the kingdom of God could not flourish. According to ver. 14, this catastrophe is occasioned by the princes. The fire, which devours the fruit of the vine so that it cannot send out any more branches, emanates מִמַּטֵּה בַדֶּיהָ, from the shoot of its branches, *i.e.* from its branches, which are so prolific in shoots. מַטֶּה is the shoot which grew into rulers' sceptres, *i.e.* the royal family of the nation. The reference is to Zedekiah, whose treacherous breach of covenant (ch. xvii. 15) led to the overthrow of the kingdom and of the earthly monarchy. The picture from ver. 12 onwards is prophetic. The tearing up of the vine, and its transplantation into a dry land, had already commenced with the carrying away of Jeconiah; but it was not completed till the destruction of Jerusalem and the carrying away of Zedekiah, which were still in the future at the time when these words were uttered.—The clause קִינָה הִיא וגו' does not contain a concluding historical notice, as Hävernick supposes, but simply the *finale* of the lamentation, indicating the credibility of the prediction which it contains. וַתְּהִי is prophetic, like the perfects from וַתֻּתַּשׁ in ver. 12 onwards; and the meaning is this: A lamentation forms the substance of the whole chapter; and it will lead to lamentation, when it is fulfilled.

CHAP. XX. THE PAST, PRESENT, AND FUTURE OF ISRAEL.

The date given in ch. xx. 1 applies not only to ch. xx., but also to ch. xx.–xxiii. (compare ch. xxiv. 1); the prophetic utterances in these four chapters being bound together into a group of connected words of God, both by their contents and by the threefold repetition of the expression, "wilt thou judge?" (*vid.* ch. xx. 4, xxii. 2, and xxiii. 36). The formula הֲתִשְׁפֹּט, which is only omitted from the threat of punishment contained in ch. xxi., indicates at the same time both the nature and design of these words of God. The prophet is to judge, *i.e.* to hold up before the people once more their sinful abominations, and to predict the consequent punishment. The circumstance which occasioned this is narrated in ch. xx. 1–3. Men of the elders of Israel came to the prophet to inquire of the Lord. The occasion is therefore a similar one to that described in the previous group; for we have already been informed, in ch. xiv. 1, that elders had come to the prophet to hear God's word from him; but they had not gone so far as to inquire. Here, however (ch. xx.), they evidently address a question to the prophet, and through him to the Lord; though the nature of their inquiry is not given, and can only be gathered from the answer, which was given to them by the Lord through the prophet. The ground for the following words of God is therefore essentially the same as for those contained in ch. xiv.–xix.; and this serves to explain the relation in which the two groups stand to each other, namely, that ch. xx.–xxiv. simply contain a further expansion of the reproachful and threatening addresses of ch. xiv.–xix.

In ch. xx. the prophet points out to the elders, in the form of a historical survey, how rebellious Israel had been towards the Lord from the very first, even in Egypt (vers. 5–9) and the desert (vers. 10–17 and 18–26), both the older and later generations, how they had sinned against the Lord their God through their idolatry, and how it was only for His own name's sake that the Lord had not destroyed them in His anger (vers. 27–31). And as Israel hath not given up idolatry even in Canaan, the Lord would not suffer Himself to be inquired of by the idolatrous generation, but would refine it by severe judgments among the nations (vers. 32–38), and sanctify it thereby into a people well-pleasing to Him, and would then gather it again out of the dispersion, and bring it into the land promised to the fathers, where it would serve Him with sacrifices and gifts upon His holy mountain (vers. 39–44). This word of God is therefore a more literal repetition of the allegorical description contained in ch. xvi.

Vers. 1–4. Date, occasion, and theme of the discourse which follows.—Ver. 1. *And it came to pass in the seventh year, in the fifth (moon), on the tenth of the moon, there came men of the elders of Israel, to inquire of Jehovah, and sat down before me.* Ver. 2. *Then the word of Jehovah came to me, saying*, Ver. 3. *Son of man, speak to the elders of Israel, and say to them, Thus saith the Lord Jehovah, Have ye come to inquire of me? As I live, if I suffer myself to be inquired of by you, is the saying of the Lord Jehovah.* Ver. 4. *Wilt thou judge them? Wilt thou judge, O son of man? Make known the abominations of their fathers to them.*—If we compare the date given in ver. 1 with ch. viii. 1, we shall find that this word of God was uttered only eleven months and five days after the one in chap. viii.; two years, one month, and five days after the call of Ezekiel to be a prophet (ch. i. 2); and two years and five months before the blockading of Jerusalem by the Chaldeans (ch. xxiv. 1). Consequently it falls almost in the middle of the first section of Ezekiel's prophetic work. דָּרַשׁ אֶת יְהוָֹה, to seek Jehovah, *i.e.* to ask a revelation from Him. The Lord's answer in ver. 3 is similar to that in ch. xiv. 3. Instead of giving a revelation concerning the future, especially with regard to the speedy termination of the penal sufferings, which the elders had, no doubt, come to solicit, the prophet is to judge them, *i.e.* as the following clause explains, not only in the passage before us, but also in ch. xxii. 3 and xxiii. 36, to hold up before them the sins and abominations of Israel. It is in anticipation of the following picture of the apostasy of the nation from time immemorial that the sins of the fathers are mentioned here. "No reply is given to the sinners, but chiding for their sins; and He adds the oath, 'as I live,' that the sentence of refusal may be all the stronger" (Jerome). The question הֲתִשְׁפּוֹט, which is repeated with emotion, "gives expression to an impatient wish, that the thing could have been done already" (Hitzig). The interrogative form of address is therefore adopted simply as a more earnest mode of giving expression to the command to go and do the thing. Hence the literal explanation of the word הֲתִשְׁפּוֹט is also appended in the form of an imperative (הוֹדִיעֵם).—The prophet is to revert to the sins of the fathers, not merely for the purpose of exhibiting the magnitude of the people's guilt, but also to hold up before the sinners themselves, the patience and long-suffering which have hitherto been displayed by the Lord.

Vers. 5–9. Election of Israel in Egypt. Its resistance to the commandments of God.—Ver. 5. *And say to them, Thus saith the Lord Jehovah, In the day that I chose Israel, and lifted my hand to the seed of Jacob, and made myself known to them in the land of Egypt, and lifted my hand to them, saying, I am Jehovah, your God:* Ver. 6. *In that day I lifted my hand to them, to bring them out of the land of Egypt into the land which I sought out for them, which floweth with milk and honey—it is an ornament of all lands:* Ver. 7. *And said to them, Cast away every man the abominations of his eyes, and do not defile yourselves with the idols of Egypt. I am Jehovah, your God.* Ver. 8. *But they were rebellious against me, and would not hearken to me. Not one of them threw away the abominations of his eyes, and they did not forsake the idols of Egypt. Then I thought to pour out my wrath upon them, to accomplish my anger upon them in the midst of the land of Egypt.* Ver. 9. *But I did it for my name's sake, that it might not be profaned before the eyes of the nations, in the midst of which they were, before whose eyes I had made myself known to them, to bring them out of the land of Egypt.*—Vers. 5 and 6 form one period. בְּיוֹם בָּחֳרִי (ver. 5) is resumed in בַּיּוֹם הַהוּא (ver. 6), and the sentence continued. With וָאֶשָּׂא the construction with the infinitive passes over into the finite verb. Lifting the hand, *sc.* to heaven, is a gesture employed in taking an oath (see the comm. on Ex. vi. 8). The substance of the oath is introduced by the word לֵאמֹר at the close of ver. 5; but the clause וָאִוָּדַע וגו׳ (and made myself known) is previously inserted, and then the lifting of the hand mentioned again to indicate the importance of this act of divine grace. The contents of vers. 5 and 6 rest upon Ex. vi. 2 sqq., where the Lord makes Himself known to Moses, and through him to the children of Israel, according to the nature involved in the name Jehovah, in which He had not yet revealed Himself to the patriarchs (Ex. vi. 3). Both נָשָׂאתִי יָדִי (I lifted my hand) and אֲנִי יְהוָֹה are taken from Ex. vi. 8. The word תַּרְתִּי, from תּוּר, to seek out, explore, also belongs to the Pentateuch (compare Deut. i. 33); and the same may be said of the description given of Canaan as "a land flowing with milk and honey" (*vid.* Ex. iii. 8, etc.). But צְבִי, ornament, as an epithet applied to the land of Israel, is first employed by the prophets of the time of the captivity—namely, in vers. 6 and 15 of this chapter, in Jer. iii. 19, and in Dan. viii. 9, xi. 16, 41. The election of the Israelites to be the people of Jehovah, contained *eo ipso* the command to give up the idols of Egypt, although it was at Sinai that the worship of other gods was for the first time expressly prohibited (Ex. xx. 3), and Egyptian idolatry is only mentioned in Lev. xvii. 7 (cf. Josh. xxiv. 14). Ezekiel calls the idols "abominations of their eyes," because, "although they were abominable and execrable things, they were looked upon with delight by them" (Rosenmüller). It is true that there is nothing expressly stated in the Pentateuch as to the refusal of the Israelites to obey the command of God, or their unwillingness to give up idolatry in Egypt; but it may be inferred from the statements contained in Ex. vi. 9 and 12, to the effect that the Israelites did not hearken to Moses when he communicated to them the determination of God to lead them out of Egypt, and still more plainly from their relapse into Egyptian idolatry, from the worship of the golden calf at Sinai (Ex. xxxii.), and from their repeated desire to return to Egypt while wandering in the desert.[1] Nor is there anything said in the Pentateuch concerning the determination of God to pour out His wrath

[1] The remarks of Calvin upon this point are very good. "We do not learn directly from Moses," he says, "that they had been rebels against God, because they would not throw away their idols and superstitions; but the conjecture is a very probable one, that they had always been so firmly fixed in their abominations as to prevent in a certain way the hand of God from bringing them relief. And assuredly, if they had embraced what Moses promised them in the name of God with promptness of mind, the

upon the idolatrous people in Egypt. We need not indeed assume on this account that Ezekiel derived his information from some special traditional source, as Vitringa has done *Observv. ss.* I. 263), or regard the statement as a revelation made by God to Ezekiel, and through him to us. The words do not disclose to us either a particular fact or a definite decree of God; they simply contain a description of the attitude which God, from His inmost nature, assumes towards sinners who rebel against His holy commandments, and which He displayed both in the declaration made concerning Himself as a zealous, or jealous God, who visits iniquities (Ex. xx. 5), and also in the words addressed to Moses when the people fell into idolatry at Sinai, "Let me alone, that my wrath may wax hot against them, and that I may consume them" (Ex. xxxii. 10). All that God expresses here, His heart must have felt in Egypt towards the people who would not desist from idolatry. For the words themselves, compare ch. vii. 8, vi. 12, v. 13. וָאַעַשׂ (ver. 9), "but I did it for my name's sake." The missing object explaining what He did, namely, abstain from pouring out His wrath, is to be gathered from what follows: "that I might not profane my name." This would have taken place if God had destroyed Israel by pouring out His wrath; in other words, have allowed them to be destroyed by the Egyptians. The heathen might then have said that Jehovah had been unable to liberate His people from their hand and power (cf. Num. xiv. 16 and Ex. xxxii. 12). הֵחֵל is an *infin. Niphal* of חָלַל for הֵחַל (cf. Lev. xxi. 4).

Vers. 10–17. Behaviour of Israel in the desert.—Ver. 10. *And I led them out of the land of Egypt, and brought them*

execution of the promise would have been more prompt and swift. But we may learn that it was their own obtuseness which hindered God from stretching out His hand forthwith and actually fulfilling all that He had promised It was necessary, indeed, that God should contend with Pharaoh, that His power might be more conspicuously displayed; but the people would not have been so tyrannically afflicted if they had not closed the door of divine mercy."

into the desert; Ver. 11. *And gave them my statutes, and my rights I made known to them, which man is to do that he may live through them.* Ver. 12. *I also gave them my Sabbaths, that they might be for a sign between me and them, that they might know that I Jehovah sanctify them.* Ver. 13. *But the house of Israel was rebellious against me in the desert: they did not walk in my statutes, and my rights they rejected, which man is to do, that he may live through them, and my Sabbaths they greatly profaned: Then I thought to pour out my wrath upon them in the desert to destroy them.* Ver. 14. *But I did it for my name's sake, that it might not be profaned before the eyes of the nations, before whose eyes I had led them out.* Ver. 15. *I also lifted my hand to them in the desert, not to bring them into the land which I had given (them), which floweth with milk and honey; it is an ornament of all lands,* Ver. 16. *Because they rejected my rights, did not walk in my statutes, and profaned my Sabbaths, for their heart went after their idols.* Ver. 17. *But my eye looked with pity upon them, so that I did not destroy them, and make an end of them in the desert.*—God gave laws at Sinai to the people whom He had brought out of Egypt, through which they were to be sanctified as His own people, that they might live before God. On ver. 11 compare Deut. xxx. 16 and 19. Ver. 12 is taken almost word for word from Ex. xxxi. 13, where God concludes the directions for His worship by urging upon the people in the most solemn manner the observance of His Sabbaths, and thereby pronounces the keeping of the Sabbath the kernel of all divine worship. And as in that passage we are to understand by the Sabbaths the actual weekly Sabbaths, and not the institutions of worship as a whole, so here we must retain the literal signification of the word. It is only of the Sabbath recurring every week, and not of all the fasts, that it could be said it was a sign between Jehovah and Israel. It was a sign, not as a token, that they who observed it were Israelites, as Hitzig supposes, but to know (that they might know) that Jehovah was sanctifying them, namely, by the

Sabbath rest—as a refreshing and elevation of the mind, in which Israel was to have a foretaste of that blessed resting from all works to which the people of God was ultimately to attain (see the comm. on Ex. xx. 11). It is from this deeper signification of the Sabbath that the prominence given to the Sabbaths here is to be explained, and not from the outward circumstance that in exile, when the sacrificial worship was necessarily suspended, the keeping of the Sabbath was the only bond which united the Israelites, so far as the worship of God was concerned (Hitzig). Historical examples of the rebellion of Israel against the commandments of God in the desert are given in Ex. xxxii. 1–6 and Num. xxv. 1–3; and of the desecration of the Sabbath, in Ex. xvi. 27 and Num. xv. 32. For the threat referred to in ver. 13*b*, compare Ex. xxxii. 10; Num. xiv. 11, 12.—Vers. 15 and 16 are not a repetition of ver. 13 (Hitzig); nor do they introduce a limitation of ver. 14 (Kliefoth). They simply relate what else God did to put bounds to the rebellion after He had revoked the decree to cut Israel off, at the intercession of Moses (Num. xiv. 11–19). He lifted His hand to the oath (Num. xiv. 21 sqq.), that the generation which had come out of Egypt should not come into the land of Canaan, but should die in the wilderness. Therewith He looked with pity upon the people, so that He did not make an end of them by following up the threat with a promise that the children should enter the land. עָשָׂה כָלָה, as in ch. xi. 13.

Vers. 18–26. The generation that grew up in the desert.—Ver. 18. *And I spake to their sons in the desert, Walk not in the statutes of your fathers, and keep not their rights, and do not defile yourselves with their idols.* Ver. 19. *I am Jehovah your God; walk in my statutes, and keep my rights, and do them,* Ver. 20. *And sanctify my Sabbaths, that they may be for a sign between me and you, that ye may know that I am Jehovah your God.* Ver. 21. *But the sons were rebellious against me; they walked not in my statutes, and did not keep my rights, to do them, which man should do that he may live through them; they pro-*

faned my Sabbaths. Then I thought to pour out my wrath upon them, to accomplish my anger upon them in the desert. Ver. 22. *But I turned back my hand and did it for my name's sake, that it might not be profaned before the eyes of the nations, before whose eyes I had them out.* Ver. 23. *I also lifted my hand to them in the desert, to scatter them among the nations, and to disperse them in the lands;* Ver. 24. *Because they did not my rights, and despised my statutes, profaned my Sabbaths, and their eyes were after the idols of their fathers.* Ver. 25. *And I also gave them statutes, which were not good, and rights, through which they did not live;* Ver. 26. *And defiled them in their sacrificial gifts, in that they caused all that openeth the womb to pass through, that I might fill them with horror, that they might know that I am Jehovah.*— The sons acted like their fathers in the wilderness. Historical proofs of this are furnished by the accounts of the Sabbath-breaker (Num xv. 32 sqq.), of the rebellion of the company of Korah, and of the murmuring of the whole congregation against Moses and Aaron after the destruction of Korah's company (Num. xvi. and xvii.). In the last two cases God threatened that He would destroy the whole congregation (cf. Num. xvi. 21 and xvii. 9, 10); and on both occasions the Lord drew back His hand at the intercession of Moses, and his actual intervention (Num. xvi. 22 and xvii. 11 sqq.), and did not destroy the whole nation for His name's sake. The statements in vers. 21*b* and 22 rest upon these facts. The words of ver. 23 concerning the oath of God, that He would scatter the transgressors among the heathen, are also founded upon the Pentateuch, and not upon an independent tradition, or any special revelation from God. Dispersion among the heathen is threatened in Lev. xxvi. 33 and Deut. xxviii. 64, and there is no force in Kliefoth's argument that "these threats do not refer to the generation in the wilderness, but to a later age." For in both chapters the blessings and curses of the law are set before the people who were then in the desert; and there is not a single word to intimate that either blessing or curse would only be fulfilled upon the generations of later times. On the contrary, when Moses addressed to the people assembled before him his last discourse concerning the renewal of the covenant (Deut. xxix. and xxx.), he called upon them to enter into the covenant, "which Jehovah maketh with thee *this day*" (Deut. xxix. 12), and to keep all the words of this covenant and do them. It is upon this same discourse, in which Moses calls the threatenings of the law אָלָה, an oath (Deut. xxix. 13), that "the lifting of the hand of God to swear," mentioned in ver. 23 of this chapter, is also founded. Moreover, it is not stated in this verse that God lifted His hand to scatter among the heathen the generation which had grown up in the wilderness, and to disperse them in the lands before their entrance into the land promised to the fathers; but simply that He had lifted His hand in the wilderness to threaten the people with dispersion among the heathen, without in any way defining the period of dispersion. In the blessings and threatenings of the law contained in Lev. xxvi. and Deut. xxviii.–xxx., the nation is regarded as a united whole; so that no distinction is made between the successive generations, for the purpose of announcing this particular blessing or punishment to either one or the other. And Ezekiel acts in precisely the same way. It is true that he distinguishes the generation which came out of Egypt and was sentenced by God to die in the wilderness from the sons, *i.e.* the generation which grew up in the wilderness; but the latter, or the sons of those who had fallen, the generation which was brought into the land of Canaan, he regards as one with all the successive generations, and embraces the whole under the common name of "fathers" to the generation living in his day ("your fathers" ver. 27), as we may clearly see from the turn given to the sentence which describes the apostasy of those who came into the land of Canaan (עוֹד זאת וגו׳). In thus embracing the generation which grew up in the wilderness and was led into Canaan, along with the generations which followed and lived in

Canaan, Ezekiel adheres very closely to the view prevailing in the Pentateuch, where the nation in all its successive generations is regarded as one united whole. The threat of dispersion among the heathen, which the Lord uttered in the wilderness to the sons of those who were not to see the land, is also not mentioned by Ezekiel as one which God designed to execute upon the people who were wandering in the desert at the time. For if he had understood it in this sense, he would have mentioned its non-fulfilment also, and would have added a וָאַעַשׂ לְמַעַן שְׁמִי וגו׳, as he has done in the case of the previous threats (cf. vers. 22, 14, and 9). But we do not find this either in ver. 24 or ver. 26. The omission of this turn clearly shows that ver. 23 does not refer to a punishment which God designed to inflict, but did not execute for His name's sake; but that the dispersion among the heathen, with which the transgressors of His commandments were threatened by God when in the wilderness, is simply mentioned as a proof that even in the wilderness the people, whom God had determined to lead into Canaan, were threatened with that very punishment which had now actually commenced, because rebellious Israel had obstinately resisted the commandments and rights of its God.

These remarks are equally applicable to vers. 25 and 26. These verses are not to be restricted to the generation which was born in the wilderness and gathered to its fathers not long after its entrance into Canaan, but refer to their descendants also, that is to say, to the fathers of our prophet's contemporaries, who were born and had died in Canaan. God gave them statutes which were not good, and rights which did not bring them life. It is perfectly self-evident that we are not to understand by these statutes and rights, which were not good, either the Mosaic commandments of the ceremonial law, as some of the Fathers and earlier Protestant commentators supposed, or the threatenings contained in the law; so that this needs no elaborate proof. The ceremonial commandments given by God were good, and had the promise attached to them, that obedience to them would give life; whilst the threats of punishment contained in the law are never called חֻקִּים and מִשְׁפָּטִים. Those statutes only are called "not good" the fulfilment of which did not bring life or blessing and salvation. The second clause serves as an explanation of the first. The examples quoted in ver. 26 show what the words really mean. The defiling in their sacrificial gifts (ver. 26), for example, consisted in their causing that which opened the womb to pass through, *i.e.* in the sacrifice of the first-born. הַעֲבִיר כָּל־פֶּטֶר רַחַם points back to Ex. xiii. 12; only לַיהוָה, which occurs in that passage, is omitted, because the allusion is not to the commandment given there, but to its perversion into idolatry. This formula is used in the book of Exodus (*l.c.*) to denote the dedication of the first-born to Jehovah; but in ver. 13 this limitation is introduced, that the first-born of man is to be redeemed. הַעֲבִיר signifies a dedication through fire (=הַעֲבִיר בָּאֵשׁ, ver. 31), and is adopted in the book of Exodus, where it is joined to לַיהוָה, in marked opposition to the Canaanitish custom of dedicating children to Moloch by februation in fire (see the comm. on Ex. xiii. 12). The prophet refers to this Canaanitish custom, and cites it as a striking example of the defilement of the Israelites in their sacrificial gifts (טִמֵּא, to make unclean, not to declare unclean, or treat as unclean). That this custom also made its way among the Israelites, is evident from the repeated prohibition against offering children through the fire to Moloch (Lev. xviii. 21 and Deut. xviii. 10). When, therefore, it is affirmed with regard to a statute so sternly prohibited in the law of God, that Jehovah gave it to the Israelites in the wilderness, the word נָתַן (give) can only be used in the sense of a judicial sentence, and must not be taken merely as indicating divine permission; in other words, it is to be understood, like 2 Thess. ii. 11 ("God sends them strong delusion") and Acts vii. 42 ("God turned, and gave them up to worship the host of heaven"), in the sense of hardening, whereby whoever will not renounce idolatry is so given up to its power, that it draws him deeper and deeper in. This is in perfect keeping with the statement in ver. 26 as the design of God in doing this: "that I might fill them with horror;" *i.e.* might excite such horror and amazement in their minds, that if possible they might be brought to reflect and to return to Jehovah their God.

Vers. 27–31. Israel committed these sins in Canaan also, and to this day has not given them up; therefore God will not allow the idolatrous generation to inquire of Him.—Ver. 27. *Therefore speak to the house of Israel, O son of man, and say to them, Thus saith the Lord Jehovah, Still further have your fathers blasphemed me in this, with the faithlessness which they have shown toward me.* Ver. 28. *When I had brought them into the land, which I had lifted my hand to give them, then they looked out every high hill and every thickly covered tree, and offered their sacrifices there, and gave their irritating gifts there, and presented the fragrance of their pleasant odour there, and poured out their drink-offerings there.* Ver. 29. *And I said to them, What height is that to which ye go? And its name is called Height to this day.* Ver. 30. *Therefore say to the house of Israel, Thus saith the Lord Jehovah, What? Do ye defile yourselves in the way of your fathers; and go whoring after their abominations;* Ver. 31. *And defile yourselves in all your idols to this day, by lifting up your gifts, and causing your sons to pass through the fire; and should I let myself be inquired of by you? As I live, is the saying of the Lord Jehovah, I will not let myself be inquired of by you.*—The לָכֵן in ver. 27 is resumed in ver. 30; and there the answer given by God to the elders, who had come to inquire of Him, is first communicated, after an express declaration of the fact that Israel had continued its idolatry in the most daring manner, even after its entrance into Canaan. But the form in which this is done—עוֹד זֹאת, "still further in this"—is to be understood as intimating that the conduct of the fathers of the existing generation, and therefore not merely of those who grew up in the wilderness, but also of those who had lived in Canaan, has already been described in general terms in the preceding verses, and that what follows simply adds another novel feature. But this can only be the case if vers. 23–26 are taken in the sense given above. זאת is an accusative; and גִּדֵּף is construed with the accusative both of the person and thing. The more precise definition of זאת is not given in בְּמַעֲלָם בִּי at the end of the verse, but in the idolatry depicted in ver. 28. מַעַל refers to the faithlessness involved in the breach of the covenant and in idolatry. This is the general description; whilst the idolatry mentioned in ver. 28*b* constituted one particular feature, in which the faithlessness appeared in the form of blasphemy. For the fact itself, namely, the worship on high places, which was practised on every hand, see ch. vi. 13, xvi. 24, 25; 1 Kings xiv. 23; 2 Kings xvii. 10. In the enumeration of the offerings, there is something striking in the position in which כַּעַס קָרְבָּנָם stands, namely, between the slaughtered sacrifices (זְבָחִים) and the increase- and drink-offerings; and this is no doubt the reason why the clause וַיִּתְּנוּ שָׁם וגו' is omitted from the *Cod. Vat.* and *Alex.* of the LXX.; and even Hitzig proposes to strike it out. But Theodoret found this reading in the Alex. Version; and Hitzig is wrong in affirming that קָרְבָּן is used in connection with sacrifices, meat-offerings, and drink-offerings. The meat-offerings are not expressly named, for רֵיחַ נִיחוֹחַ does not signify meat-offerings, but is used in the law for the odour of all the offerings, both slaughtered sacrifices and meat-offerings, even though in Ezek. xvi. 19 it is applied to the odour of the bloodless offerings alone. And in the same way does קָרְבָּן embrace all the offerings, even the slain offerings, in Ezek. xl. 43, in harmony with Lev. i. 2, ii. 1, and other passages. That it is used in this general signification here, is evident from the introduction of the word כַּעַס, irritation or provocation of their gifts, *i.e.* their gifts which provoked irritation on the part of God, because they were offered to idols. As this sentence applies to all the sacrifices (bloody and bloodless), so also does the clause which follows, וַיָּשִׂימוּ שָׁם וגו', refer to all the offerings which were burned upon the altar, without regard to the material employed. Consequently Ezekiel mentions only slain offerings and drink-offerings, and, by the two clauses inserted between, describes the offering of the slaughtered sacrifices as a gift of irritation to God, and of pleasant fragrance to the idolatrous worshippers who presented them. He does not mention the meat-offerings separately, because they generally formed an accompaniment to the slain offerings, and therefore were included in these. But although God had called the people to account for this worship on high places, they had not relinquished it even "to this day." This is no doubt the meaning of ver. 29, which has been interpreted in very different ways. The context shows, in the most conclusive manner, that הַבָּמָה is to be taken collectively, and that the use of the singular is to be explained from the antithesis to the one divinely appointed Holy Place in the temple, and not, as Kimchi and Hävernick suppose, from any allusion to one particular *bâmâh* of peculiar distinction, viz. "the great high place at Gibeon." The question מָה הַבָּמָה is not expressive of contempt (Hitzig), but "is founded upon the assumption that they would have to give an account of their doings; and merely asks, What kind of heights are those to which you are going? Who has directed you to go thither with your worship?" (Kliefoth). There is no need to refute the trivial fancy of J. D. Michaelis, which has been repeated by Hitzig, namely, that Ezekiel has taken בָּמָה as a derivative from בא and מה. Again, the question does not presuppose a word addressed by God to Israel, which Ezekiel only has handed down to us; but is simply a rhetorical mode of presenting the condemnation by God of the worship of the high places, to which both the law and the earlier prophets had given utterance. The next clause, "and their name was called Height" (high place), is not to be regarded as containing merely a historical notice of the name given to these idolatrous places of worship; but the giving of the name is a proof of the continued existence of the thing; so that the words affirm, that notwithstanding the condemnation on the part of God, Israel had retained these high places,—had not abolished them to this day.—Vers. 30 and 31 facilitate the transition from the first part of this word of God to the second. What has already been said in vers. 5–29 concerning the idolatry of the people, from the time of its election onwards, is here expressly applied to the existing generation, and carries with it the declaration to them, that inasmuch as they are defiling themselves by idolatry, as their fathers did, Jehovah cannot permit Himself to be inquired of by them. The thought is couched in the form of a question, to express astonishment that those who denied the Lord, and dishonoured Him by their idolatry, should nevertheless imagine that they could obtain revelations from Him. The lifting up (שְׂאֵת, from נָשָׂא) of gifts signifies the offering of sacrifices upon the altars of the high places. For ver. 31*b*, compare ver. 3.—With this declaration God assigns the reason for the refusal to listen to idolaters, which had already been given in ver. 3. But it does not rest with this refusal. God now proceeds to disclose to them the thoughts of their own hearts, and announces to them that He will refine them by severe judgments, and bring them thereby to repentance of their sins, that He may then gather them out of the dispersion, and make them partakers of the promised salvation as a people willingly serving Him.—In this way do vers. 32–44 cast a prophetic glance over the whole of the future history of Israel.

Vers. 32–38. The judgment awaiting Israel of purification among the heathen.—Ver. 32. *And that which riseth up in your mind shall not come to pass, in that ye say, We will be like the heathen, like the families of the lands, to serve wood and stone.* Ver. 33. *As I live, is the saying of the Lord Jehovah, with strong hand and with outstretched arm, and with wrath poured out, will I rule over you.* Ver. 34. *And I will bring you out of the nations, and gather you out of the lands in which ye have been scattered, with strong hand and with outstretched arm, and with wrath poured out,* Ver. 35. *And will bring you into the desert of the nations, and contend with you there face to face.* Ver. 36. *As I contended with your fathers in the desert of the land of Egypt, so will I contend with you, is the saying of the Lord Jehovah.* Ver. 37. *And I will cause you to pass through under the rod, and bring you into the bond of the covenant.* Ver. 38. *And I will separate from you the rebellious, and those who are apostates from me; out of the land of their sojourning will I lead them out, but into the land of Israel shall they not come; that ye may know that I am Jehovah.*—הָעֹלָה עַל רוּחַ, that which rises up in the spirit, is the thought that springs up in the mind. What this thought was is shown in ver. 32*b*, viz. we will be like the heathen in the lands of the earth, to serve wood and stone; that is to say, we will become idolaters like the heathen, pass into heathenism. This shall not take place; on the contrary, God will rule over them as King with strong arm and fury. The words, "with strong hand and stretched-out arm," are a standing expression in the Pentateuch for the mighty acts by which Jehovah liberated His people from the power of the Egyptians, and led them out of Egypt (cf. Ex. vi. 1, 6; Deut. iv. 34, v. 15, vii. 19, etc.), and are connected in Ex. vi. 6 with וּבִשְׁפָטִים גְּדֹלִים. Here, on the contrary, they are connected with בְּחֵמָה שְׁפוּכָה, and are used in ver. 33 with reference to the government of God over Israel, whilst in ver. 34 they are applied to the bringing out of Israel from the midst of the heathen. By the introduction of the clause "with fury poured out," the manifestation of the omnipotence of God which Israel experienced in its dispersion, and which it was still to experience among the heathen, is described as an emanation of the divine wrath, a severe and wrathful judgment. The leading and gathering of Israel out of the nations (ver. 34) is neither their restoration from the existing captivity in Babylon, nor their future restoration to Canaan on the conversion of the people who were still hardened, and therefore rejected by God. The former assumption would be decidedly at variance with both מִן הָעַמִּים and מִן הָאֲרָצוֹת, since Israel was dispersed only throughout one land and among one people at the time of the Babylonian captivity. Moreover, neither of the assumptions is reconcilable with the context, more especially with ver. 35. According to the context, this leading out is an act of divine anger, which Israel is to feel in connection therewith; and this cannot be affirmed of either the redemption of the people out of the captivity in Babylon, or the future gathering of Israel from its dispersion. According to ver. 35, God will conduct those who are brought out from the nations and gathered together out of the lands into the desert of the nations, and contend with them there. The "desert of the nations" is not the desert lying between Babylonia and Palestine, on the coast-lands of the Mediterranean, through which the Israelites would have to pass on their way home from Babylon (Rosenmüller, Hitzig, and others). For there is no imaginable reason why this should be called the desert of the nations in distinction from the desert of Arabia, which also touched the borders of several nations. The expression is doubtless a typical one, the future guidance of Israel being depicted as a repetition of the earlier guidance of the people from Egypt to Canaan; as it also is in Hos. ii. 16. All the separate features in the description indicate this, more especially vers. 36 and 37, where it is impossible to overlook the allusion to the guidance of Israel in the time of Moses. The more precise explanation of the words must depend, however, upon the sense in which we are to understand the expression, "desert of the land of Egypt." Here also the supposition that the Arabian desert is referred to, because it touched the border of Egypt, does not furnish a sufficient explanation. It touched the border of Canaan as well. Why then did not Ezekiel name it after the land of Canaan? Evidently for no other reason than that the time spent by the Israelites in the Arabian desert resembled their sojourn in Egypt much more closely than their settlement in Canaan, because, while there, they were still receiving their training for their entrance into Canaan, and their possession and enjoyment of its benefits, just as much as in the land of Egypt. And in a manner corresponding to this, the "desert of the nations" is a figurative expression applied to the world of nations, from whom they were indeed spiritually distinct, whilst outwardly they were still in the midst of them, and had to suffer from their oppression. Consequently the leading of Israel out of the nations (ver. 34) is not a local and corporeal deliverance out of heathen lands, but a spiritual severance from the heathen world, in order that they might not be absorbed into it or become inseparably blended with the heathen. God will accomplish this by means of severe chastisements, by contending with them as He formerly contended with their fathers in the Arabian desert. God contends with His people when He charges them with their sin and guilt, not merely in words, but also with deeds, *i.e.* through chastening and punishments. The words "face to face" point back to Deut. v. 4: "Jehovah talked with you face to face in the mount, out of the midst of the fire." Just as at Sinai the Lord talked directly with Israel, and made known to it the devouring fire of His own holy nature, in so terrible a manner that all the people trembled and entreated Moses to act the part of a mediator between them, promising at the same time obedience to him (Ex. xx. 19); so will the Lord make Himself known to Israel in the desert of the world of nations with the burning zeal of His anger, that it may learn to fear Him. This contending is more precisely defined in vers. 37 and 38. I will cause you to pass through under the (shepherd's) rod. A shepherd lets his sheep pass through under his rod for the purpose of counting them, and seeing whether they are in good condition or not (*vid.* Jer. xxxiii. 13). The figure is here applied to God. Like a shepherd, He will cause His flock, the Israelites, to pass through under His rod, *i.e.* take them into His special care, and bring them "into the bond of the covenant" (מָסֹרֶת, not from מסר [Raschi], but from אָסַר, for מַאֲסֹרֶת, a fetter); that is to say, not "I will bind myself to you and you to me by a new covenant" (Bochart, *Hieroz.* I. p. 508), for this is opposed to the context, but, as the Syriac version has rendered it, ܒܡܪܕܘܬܐ (*in disciplina*), "the discipline of the covenant." By this we are not merely to understand the covenant punishments, with which transgressors of the law are threatened, as Hävernick does, but the covenant promises must also be included. For not only the threats of the covenant, but the promises of the covenant, are *bonds* by which God trains His people; and אָסַר is not only applied to burdensome and crushing fetters, but to the bonds of love as well (*vid.* Song of Sol. vii. 6). Kliefoth understands by the fetter of the covenant the Mosaic law, as being the means employed by God to preserve the Israelites from mixing with the nations while placed in the midst of them, and to keep them to Himself, and adds the following explanation,—"this law, through which they should have been able to live, they have now to wear as a fetter, and to feel the chastisement thereof." But however correct the latter thought may be in itself, it is hardly contained in the words, "lead them into the fetter (band) of the law." Moreover, although the law did indeed preserve Israel from becoming absorbed into the world of nations, the fact that the Jews were bound to the law did not bring them to the knowledge of the truth, or bring to pass the purging of the rebellious from among the people, to which ver. 38 refers. All that the law accomplished in this respect in the case of those who lived among the heathen was effected by its threatenings and its promises, and not by its statutes and their faithful observance. This discipline will secure the purification of the people, by severing from the nation the rebellious and apostate. God will bring them forth out of the land of their pilgrimage, but will not bring them into the land of Israel. אֶרֶץ מְגוּרִים is the standing epithet applied in the Pentateuch to the land of

Canaan, in which the patriarchs lived as pilgrims, without coming into actual possession of the land (cf. Gen. xvii. 8, xxviii. 4, xxxvi. 7; Ex. vi. 4). This epithet Ezekiel has transferred to the lands of Israel's exile, in which it was to lead a pilgrim-life until it was ripe for entering Canaan. הוֹצִיא, to lead out, is used here for clearing out by extermination, as the following clause, "into the land of Israel shall they not come," plainly shows. The singular יָבוֹא is used distributively: not one of the rebels will enter.

Vers. 39–44. The ultimate gathering of Israel, and its conversion to the Lord.—Ver. 39. *Ye then, O house of Israel, thus saith the Lord Jehovah, Go ye, serve every one his idols! but afterwards—truly ye will hearken to me, and no longer desecrate my holy name with your sacrificial gifts and your idols,* Ver. 40. *But upon my holy mountain, upon the high mountain of Israel, is the saying of the Lord Jehovah, there will all the house of Israel serve me, the whole of it in the land; there will I accept them gladly; there will I ask for your heave-offerings and the first-fruits of your gifts in all that ye make holy.* Ver. 41. *As a pleasant odour will I accept you gladly, when I bring you out from the nations, and gather you out of the lands, in which you have been scattered, and sanctify myself in you before the eyes of the heathen nations.* Ver. 42. *And ye shall know that I am Jehovah, when I bring you into the land of Israel, into the land which I lifted up my hand to give to your fathers;* Ver. 43. *And there ye will think of your ways and your deeds, with which ye have defiled yourselves, and will loathe yourselves* (lit. experience loathing before yourselves) *on account of all your evil deeds which ye have performed;* Ver. 44. *And ye will know that I am Jehovah, when I deal with you for my name's sake, not according to your evil ways and according to your corrupt deeds, O house of Israel, is the saying of Jehovah.*—After the Lord has declared to the people that He will prevent its being absorbed into the heathen world, and will exterminate the ungodly by severe judgments, the address passes on, with the direction henceforth to serve idols only, to a prediction of the eventual conversion, and the restoration to Canaan of the purified nation. The direction, "Go ye, serve every one his idols," contains, after what precedes it, a powerful appeal to repent. God thereby gives up the impenitent to do whatever they will, having first of all told them that not one of them will come into the land of Canaan. Their opposition will not frustrate His plan of salvation. The words which follow from וְאַחַר onwards have been interpreted in different ways. It is opposed to the usage of the language to connect וְאַחַר with עֲבֹדוּ, serve ye hereafter also (De Wette, etc.), for ו has not the force of the Latin *et = etiam*, and still less does it signify "afterwards just as before." Nor is it allowable to connect וְאַחַר closely with what follows, in the sense of "and hereafter also, if ye will hearken to me, profane ye my name no more" (Rosenmüller, Maurer). For if תְּחַלְּלוּ were used as an imperative, either it would have to stand at the beginning of the sentence, or it would be preceded by אַל instead of לֹא. Moreover, the antithesis between not being willing to hear and not profaning the name of God, is imported arbitrarily into the text. The name of the Lord is profaned not only by sacrifices offered in external form to Jehovah and in the heart to idols, but also by disobedience to the word and commandments of God. It is much better to take וְאַחַר by itself, and to render the following particle, אִם, as the ordinary sign of an oath: "but afterwards (*i.e.* in the future) . . . verily, ye will hearken to me;" that is to say, ye will have been converted from your idolatry through the severe judgments that have fallen upon you. The ground for this thought is introduced in ver. 40 by a reference to the fact that all Israel will then serve the Lord upon His holy mountain. כִּי is not "used emphatically before a direct address" (Hitzig), but has a causal signification. For הַר מְרוֹם יִשׂ׳, see the comm. on ch. xvii. 23. In the expression "all Israel," which is rendered more emphatic by the addition of כֻּלֹּה, there is an allusion to the eventual termination of the severance of the people of God (compare ch. xxxvii. 22). Then will the Lord accept with delight both them and their sacrificial gifts. תְּרוּמוֹת, heave-offerings (see the comm. on Ex. xxv. 2 and Lev. ii. 9), used here in the broader sense of all the sacrificial gifts, along with which the gifts of first-fruits are specially named. מַשְׂאוֹת, as applied to holy offerings in the sense of ἀναθήματα, belongs to the later usage of the language. בְּכָל־קָדְשֵׁיכֶם, consisting of all your consecrated gifts. קָדָשִׁים, as in Lev. xxii. 15. This promise includes *implicite* the bringing back of Israel from its banishment. This is expressly mentioned in ver. 41; but even there it is only introduced as self-evident in the subordinate clause, whereas the cheerful acceptance of Israel on the part of God constitutes the leading thought. בְּרֵיחַ נִיחֹחַ, as an odour of delight (בְּ, the so-called *Beth essentiae*), will God accept His people. רֵיחַ נִיחֹחַ, odour of satisfaction, is the technical expression for the cheerful (well-pleased) acceptance of the sacrifice, or rather of the feelings of the worshipper presenting the sacrifice, which ascend to God in the sacrificial odour (see the comm. on Gen. viii. 21). The thought therefore is the following: When God shall eventually gather His people out of their dispersion, He will accept them as a sacrifice well-pleasing to Him, and direct all His good pleasure towards them. וְנִקְדַּשְׁתִּי בָכֶם does not mean, I shall be sanctified through you, and is not to be explained in the same sense as Lev. xxii. 32 (Rosenmüller), for בְּ is not equivalent to בְּתוֹךְ; but it signifies "I will sanctify myself on you," as in Num. xx. 13, Lev. x. 3, and other passages, where נִקְדַּשׁ is construed with בְּ *pers.* (cf. Ezek. xxviii. 25, xxxvi. 23, xxxviii. 16, xxxix. 27), in the sense of proving oneself holy, mostly by judgment, but here through having made Israel into a holy nation by the refining judgment, and one to which He can therefore grant the promised inheritance.—Vers. 42 sqq. Then will Israel also recognise its God in His grace, and be ashamed of its former sins. For ver. 43, compare ch. vi. 9 and xvi. 61.—With regard to the fulfilment, as Kliefoth has correctly observed, "in the prediction contained in vers. 32–38, the whole of the searching judgments, by which God would lead Israel to conversion, are summed up in one, which includes not only the Babylonian captivity, the nearest and the first, but the still more remote judgment, namely, the present dispersion; for it is only in the present dispersion of Israel that God has really taken it into the wilderness of the nations, just as it was only in the rejection of Christ that its rebellious attitude was fully manifested. And as the prophecy of the state of punishment combines in this way both the nearer and more remote; so are both the nearer and more distant combined in what vers. 40 to 44 affirm with regard to the ultimate fate of Israel." The gathering of Israel from among the heathen will be fulfilled in its conversion to Christ, and hitherto it has only taken place in very small beginnings. The principal fulfilment is still to come, when Israel, as a nation, shall be converted to Christ. With regard to the bringing back of the people into "the land of Israel," see the comm. on ch. xxxvii., where this promise is more fully expanded.

CHAP. XX. 45 TO CHAP. XXI. 32 (HEB. CHAP. XXI.[1]). PROPHECY OF THE BURNING FOREST AND THE SWORD OF THE LORD.

A fire kindled by the Lord will burn the forest of the south (ch. xx. 45–48). This figurative announcement is explained in what follows, in order that the divine threat may make an impression upon the people (ver. 49). The Lord will draw His sword from its scabbard, and cut off from Jerusalem and the land of Israel both righteous and wicked (ch. xxi. 1–17); that is to say, the king of Babylon will draw his sword against

[1] In the Hebrew Bible the previous chapter closes at ver. 44, and ch. xxi. commences there. Keil has adhered to this division of chapters; but for the sake of convenience we have followed the arrangement adopted in the English authorized version.—Tr.

Jerusalem and the sons of Ammon, and will, first of all, put an end to the kingdom of Judah, and then destroy the Ammonites (vers. 18–32). The prophecy divides itself accordingly into three parts: viz. (1) the prediction of the destruction of the kingdom of Judah; (2) the explanation of this prediction by the threat that the sword of the Lord will smite all the inhabitants of Judah, which threat is divisible into three sections, ch. xxi. 1–7, 8–13, and 14–17; (3) the application of what is said with regard to the sword to Nebuchadnezzar's expedition against Jerusalem and the Ammonites, which may also be divided into three sections,—viz. (*a*) the general announcement of Nebuchadnezzar's design (vers. 18–23) and its execution; (*b*) by his expedition against Jerusalem, to destroy the kingdom of Judah (vers. 24–27); and (*c*) by his expedition against the Ammonites (vers. 28–32).—The first four or five verses are taken by many in connection with chap. xx.; and Kliefoth still maintains that they should be separated from what follows, and attached to that chapter as a second word of God. But neither ch. xx. 49 nor the formula in ch. xxi. 1, "the word of Jehovah came to me," warrants our separating the parabolic prediction in ch. xx. 45–48 from the interpretation in vers. 1–17. And the third part is also connected with what precedes, so as to form one single discourse, by the allusion to the sword in vers. 19 and 28, and by the fact that the figure of the fire is resumed in vers. 31 and 32. And there is all the less ground for taking the formula, "and the word of Jehovah came to me," as determining the division of the several portions in this particular instance, from the circumstance that the section (vers. 1–17) in which it occurs both at the commencement and in the middle (vers. 1 and 8), is obviously divided into the minor sections or turns by the threefold occurrence of the verb וְהִנָּבֵא ("and prophesy: vers. 2, 9, and 14).

Chap. xx. 45–49. The burning forest.—Ver. 45. *And the word of Jehovah came to me, saying,* Ver. 46. *Son of man, direct thy face toward the south, and trickle down towards the south, and prophesy concerning the forest of the field in the south land;* Ver. 47. *And say to the forest of the south land, Hear the word of Jehovah; Thus saith the Lord Jehovah, Behold, I kindle a fire in thee, which will consume in thee every green tree, and every dry tree: the blazing flame will not be extinguished, and all faces from the south to the north will be burned thereby.* Ver. 48. *And all flesh shall see that I, Jehovah, have kindled it: it shall not be extinguished.* Ver. 49. *And I said, Ah, Lord Jehovah! they say of me, Does he not speak in parables?*—The prophet is to turn his face toward the south, and prophesy concerning the forest of the field there. הִטִּיף is used for prophesying, as in Amos vii. 16 and Mic. ii. 6, 11. The distinction between the three epithets applied to the south is the following: תֵּימָן is literally that which lies on the right hand, hence the south is a particular quarter of the heavens; דָּרוֹם, which only occurs in Ezekiel and Ecclesiastes, with the exception of Deut. xxxiii. 23 and Job xxxvii. 17, is derived from דָּרַר, to shine or emit streams of light, and probably signifies the brilliant quarter; נֶגֶב, the dry, parched land, is a standing epithet for the southern district of Palestine and the land of Judah (see the comm. on Josh. xv. 21).—The forest of the field in the south is a figure denoting the kingdom of Judah (נֶגֶב is in apposition to הַשָּׂדֶה, and is appended to it as a more precise definition). שָׂדֶה is not used here for a field, as distinguished from a city or a garden; but for the fields in the sense of country or territory, as in Gen. xiv. 7 and xxxii. 3. In ver. 47, יַעַר הַנֶּגֶב, forest of the south land, is the expression applied to the same object (הַנֶּגֶב, with the article, is a geographical term for the southern portion of Palestine). The forest is a figure signifying the population, or the mass of people. Individual men are trees. The green tree is a figurative representation of the righteous man, and the dry tree of the ungodly (ver. 3, compare Luke xxiii. 31). The fire which Jehovah kindles is the fire of war. The combination of the synonyms לַהֶבֶת שַׁלְהֶבֶת, flame of the flaming brightness, serves to strengthen the expression, and is equivalent to the strongest possible flame, the blazing fire. כָּל־פָּנִים, all faces are not human faces or persons, in which case the prophet would have dropped the figure; but *pânim* denotes generally the outside of things, which is the first to feel the force of the flame. "All the faces" of the forest are every single thing in the forest, which is caught at once by the flame. In ver. 4, *kŏl-pânim* (all faces) is interpreted by *kŏl-bâsar* (all flesh). From south to north, *i.e.* through the whole length of the land. From the terrible fierceness of the fire, which cannot be extinguished, every one will know that God has kindled it, that it has been sent in judgment. The words of the prophet himself, in ch. xx. 49, presuppose that he has uttered these parabolic words in the hearing of the people, and that they have ridiculed them as obscure (*mâshâl* is used here in the sense of obscure language, words difficult to understand, as παραβολή also is in Matt. xiii. 10). At the same time, it contains within itself a request that they may be explained. This request is granted; and the simile is first of all interpreted in ch. xxi. 1–7, and then still further expanded in vers. 8 sqq.

Chap. xxi. 1–7. The sword of the Lord and its disastrous effects.—Ver. 1. *And the word of Jehovah came to me, saying,* Ver. 2. *Son of man, set thy face toward Jerusalem, and trickle over the holy places, and prophesy over the land of Israel,* Ver. 3. *And say to the land of Israel, Thus saith Jehovah, Behold, I will deal with thee, and will draw my sword out of its scabbard, and cut off from thee the righteous and the wicked.* Ver. 4. *Because I will cut off from thee the righteous and the wicked, therefore shall my sword go forth from its scabbard against all flesh from south to north.* Ver. 5. *And all flesh shall know that I, Jehovah, have drawn my sword out of its scabbard: it shall not return again.* Ver. 6. *And thou, son of man, sigh! so that the hips break; and with bitter pain sigh before their eyes!* Ver. 7. *And when they say to thee, Wherefore dost thou sigh? say, Because of a report that it is coming; and every heart will sink, and all hands become powerless, and every spirit will become dull, and all knees turn into water: Behold, it cometh, and will happen, is the saying of the Lord Jehovah.*—In the preceding parable, the expression "forest of the field in the south," or "forest of the south-land," was enigmatical. This is explained to signify Jerusalem with its holy places (מִקְדָּשִׁים, see comm. on ch. vii. 24), and the land of Israel, *i.e.* the kingdom of Judah. In accordance with this, the fire kindled by the Lord is interpreted as being the sword of the Lord. It is true that this is a figurative expression; but it is commonly used for war, which brings with it devastation and death, and would be generally intelligible. The sword will cut off both righteous and wicked. This applies to the outer side of the judgment, inasmuch as both good and bad fall in war. This is the only aspect brought into prominence here, since the great purpose was to alarm the sinners, who were boasting of their security; but the distinction between the two, as described in ch. ix. 4 sqq., is not therefore to be regarded as no longer existing. This sword will not return, *sc.* into the scabbard, till it has accomplished the result predicted in ver. 3 (cf. 2 Sam. i. 22; Isa. lv. 11). As Tremellius has aptly observed upon this passage, "the last slaughter is contrasted with the former ones, in which, after the people had been chastened for a time, the sword was returned to its scabbard again." In order to depict the terrors of this judgment before the eyes of the people, the prophet is commanded to groan before their eyes in the most painful way possible (vers. 6 sqq.). בְּשִׁבְרוֹן מָתְנַיִם, with breaking of the hips, *i.e.* with pain sufficient to break the hips, the seat of strength in man (compare Nah. ii. 11; Isa. xxi. 3). מְרִירוּת, bitterness, *i.e.* bitter anguish. The reason which he is to assign to the questioners for this sighing is "on account of the report that is coming,"—an *antiptosis* for "on account of the coming report" (cf. Gen. i. 4, etc.). The report comes when the substance of it is realized. The reference is to the report of the sword of the Lord,—that is to say, of the approach of the Chaldeans to destroy Jerusalem and the kingdom of

Judah. The impression which this disclosure will make upon the hearers will be perfectly paralyzing (ver. 7*b*). All courage and strength for offering resistance will be crippled and broken. נָמֵס כָּל־לֵב (cf. Nah. ii. 11) is strengthened by כִּהֲתָה כָל־רוּחַ, every spirit will become dull, so that no one will know what counsel to give. כָּל־בִּרְכַּיִם תֵּלַכְנָה וגו' corresponds to רָפוּ כָל־יָדַיִם (cf. ch. vii. 17). The threat is strengthened by the words, "behold, it cometh, and will take place." The subject is שְׁמוּעָה, the report, *i.e.* the substance of the report.—This threat is more fully expanded in vers. 8–17; vers. 8–13 corresponding to vers. 1–5, and vers. 14–17 to vers. 6, 7.

Vers. 8–17. The sword is sharpened for slaying.—Ver. 8. *And the word of Jehovah came to me, saying,* Ver. 9. *Son of man, prophesy, and say, Thus saith Jehovah, A sword, a sword sharpened and also polished:* Ver. 10. *That it may effect a slaughter is it sharpened; that it may flash is it polished: or shall we rejoice (saying), the sceptre of my son despiseth all wood?* Ver. 11. *But it has been given to be polished, to take it in the hand; it is sharpened, the sword, and it is polished, to give it into the hand of the slayer.* Ver. 12. *Cry and howl, son of man, for it goeth over my people, it goeth over all the princes of Israel: they have fallen by the sword along with my people: therefore smite upon the thigh.* Ver. 13. *For the trial is made, and what if the despising sceptre shall not come? is the saying of the Lord Jehovah.* Ver. 14. *And thou, son of man, prophesy and smite the hands together, and the sword shall double itself into threefold, the sword of the pierced: it is the sword of a pierced one, of the great one, which encircles them.* Ver. 15. *That the heart may be dissolved, and stumbling-blocks may be multiplied, I have set the drawing of the sword against all their gates: Alas! it is made into flashing, drawn for slaying.* Ver. 16. *Gather thyself up to the right hand, turn to the left, whithersoever thine edge is intended.* Ver. 17. *And I also will smite my hands together, and quiet my wrath: I, Jehovah, have spoken it.*—The description of the sword is thrown into a lyrical form (vers. 8–13),—a kind of sword-song, commemorating the terrible devastation to be effected by the sword of the Lord. The repetition of חֶרֶב in ver. 9 is emphatic. הוּחַדָּה is the perfect *Hophal* of חָדַד, to sharpen. מְרוּטָּה is the passive participle of מָרַט, to polish; מֹרָטָּה (ver. 10), the participle *Pual*, with מ dropped, and *Dagesh euphon.* הֱיֹה, a rare form of the infinitive for הֱיוֹת. The polishing gives to the sword a flashing brilliancy, which renders the sharpness of its edge still more terrible. The very obscure words, אוֹ נָשִׂישׂ וגו׳, I agree with Schmieder and Kliefoth in regarding as a protest, interposed by the prophet in the name of the people against the divine threat of the sword of vengeance, on the ground of the promises which had been given to the tribe of Judah. אוֹ, or perhaps; introducing an opposite case, or an exception to what has been said. The words שֵׁבֶט בְּנִי וגו׳ are to be taken as an objection, so that לֵאמֹר is to be supplied in thought. The objection is taken from the promise given in Jacob's blessing to the tribe of Judah: "the sceptre will not depart from Judah" (Gen. xlix. 10). שֵׁבֶט בְּנִי points unquestionably to this. בְּנִי is taken from ver. 9, where the patriarch addresses Judah, whom he compares to a young lion, as בְּנִי. Consequently the sceptre of my son is the command which the patriarch holds out to view before the tribe of Judah. This sceptre despises all wood, *i.e.* every other ruler's staff, as bad wood. This view is not rendered a doubtful one by the fact that שֵׁבֶט is construed as a feminine here, whereas it is construed as a masculine in every other case; for this construction is unquestionable in ver. 7 (12), and has many analogies in its favour. All the other explanations that have been proposed are hardly worth mentioning, to say nothing of refuting, as they amount to nothing more than arbitrary conjectures; whereas the assumption that the words are to be explained from Gen. xlix. 10 is naturally suggested by the unquestionable allusion to the prophecy in that passage, which we find in ver. 27 of the present chapter. וַיִּתֵּן in ver. 11 is to be taken adversatively, "but he gave it (the sword) to be sharpened." The subject to וַיִּתֵּן is not Jehovah, but is indefinite, "one" (*man*, Angl. they), although it is actually God who has prepared the sword for the slaughter of Israel. The train of thought is the following: Do not think we have no reason to fear the sharply-ground sword of Jehovah, because Judah has received the promise that the sceptre shall not depart from it; and this promise will certainly be fulfilled, and Judah be victorious over every hostile power. The promise will not help you in this instance. The sword is given to be ground, not that it may be put into the scabbard, but that it may be taken in the hand by a slayer, and smite all the people and all its princes. In the phrase הִיא הוּחַדָּה חֶרֶב, חֶרֶב is in apposition to the subject הִיא, and is introduced to give emphasis to the words. It is not till ver. 19 that it is stated who the slayer is; but the hearers of the prophecy could be in no doubt. Consequently—this is the connection with ver. 12—there is no ground for rejoicing from a feeling of security and pride, but rather an occasion for painful lamentation. This is the meaning contained in the command to the prophet to cry and howl. For the sword will come upon the nation and its princes. It is the simplest rendering to take הִיא as referring to חֶרֶב, הָיָה בְּ, to be at a person, to fasten to him, to come upon him, as in 1 Sam. xxiv. 14; 2 Sam. xxiv. 17. מְגוּרֵי, not from גּוּר, but the passive participle of מָגַר in the *Pual*, to overthrow, cast down (Ps. lxxxix. 45): "fallen by the sword have they (the princes) become, along with my people." The perfects are prophetic, representing that which will speedily take place as having already occurred.—Smiting upon the thigh is a sign of alarm and horror (Jer. xxxi. 19). בֹּחַן, perfect *Pual*, is used impersonally: the trial is made. The words allude to the victories gained already by Nebuchadnezzar, which have furnished tests of the sharpness of his sword. The question which follows וּמָה contains an *aposiopesis:* and what? Even if the despising sceptre shall not come, what will be the case then? שֵׁבֶט מֹאֶסֶת, according to ver. 10, is the sceptre of

Judah, which despises all other sceptres as bad wood. יִהְיֶה, in this instance, is not "to be," in the sense of to remain, but to become, to happen, to come (come to pass), to enter. The meaning is, if the sceptre of Judah shall not display, or prove itself to possess, the strength expected of it.—With ver. 14 the address takes a new start, for the purpose of depicting still further the operations of the sword. Smiting the hands together (smiting hand in hand) is a gesture expressive of violent emotion (cf. ch. vi. 11; Num. xxiv. 10). The sword is to double, *i.e.* multiply itself, into threefold (שְׁלִישִׁתָה, adverbial), namely, in its strength, or its edge. Of course this is not to be taken arithmetically, as it has been by Hitzig, but is a bold paradoxical statement concerning the terrible effect produced by the sword. It is not even to be understood as referring to three attacks made at different times by the Chaldeans upon Jerusalem, as many of the commentators suppose. The sword is called חֶרֶב חֲלָלִים, sword of pierced ones, because it produces the pierced or slain. The following words are rendered by Hitzig and Kliefoth: the great sword of the slain. But apart from the tautology which this occasions, the rendering can hardly be defended on grammatical grounds. For, in the first place, we cannot see why the singular חָלָל should have been chosen, when the expression was repeated, instead of the plural חֲלָלִים; and secondly, הַגָּדוֹל cannot be an adjective agreeing with חֶרֶב, for חרב is a noun of the feminine gender, and is construed here as a feminine, as הַחֹדֶרֶת clearly shows. הַגָּדוֹל is in apposition to חָלָל, "sword of a pierced man, the great one;" and the great man pierced is the king, as Ewald admits, in agreement with Hengstenberg and Hävernick. The words therefore affirm that the sword will not only slay the mass of the people, but pierce the king himself. (See also the comm. on ver. 25.)—Ver. 15*a* is not dependent upon what precedes, but introduces a new thought, viz. for what purpose the sword is sharpened. God has placed the flashing sword before all the gates of the Israelites, in order that (לְמַעַן לְ, pleonastic for לְמַעַן) the heart may dissolve, the inhabitants may lose all their courage for defence, and to multiply *offendicula*, *i.e.* occasions to fall by the sword. The ἀπ. λεγ. אִבְחַת signifies the rapid motion or turning about of the sword (cf. Gen. iii. 24); אבח, related to הפך, in the *Mishna* אפך. The ἀπ. λεγ. מְעֻטָּה, fem. of מָעֹט, does not mean smooth, *i.e.* sharpened, synonymous with מֹרָט, but, according to the Arabic مغط, *eduxit e vagina gladium*, drawn (from the scabbard). In ver. 16 the sword is addressed, and commanded to smite right and left. הִתְאַחֲדִי, gather thyself up, *i.e.* turn with all thy might toward the right (Tanchum). To the verb הָשִׂימִי it is easy to supply פָּנַיִךְ, from the context, "direct thine edge toward the left." אָנָה, whither, without an interrogative, as in Josh. ii. 5 and Neh. ii. 16. מֻעָדוֹת, from יָעַד, intended, ordered; not, directed, turned. The feminine form may be accounted for from a construction *ad sensum*, the gender regulating itself according to the חֶרֶב addressed in פָּנַיִךְ. The command to the sword is strengthened by the explanation given by Jehovah in ver. 17, that He also (like the prophet, ver. 14) will smite His hands together and cool His wrath upon them (cf. ch. v. 13).

Vers. 18–22. The sword of the king of Babylon will smite Jerusalem, and then the Ammonites also.—Ver. 18. *And the word of Jehovah came to me, saying,* Ver. 19. *And thou, son of man, make to thyself two ways, that the sword of the king of Babylon may come by them; out of one land shall they both come forth, and draw a hand, at the cross road of the city do thou draw it.* Ver. 20. *Make a way that the sword may come to Rabbah of the sons of Ammon, and to Judah into fortified Jerusalem.* Ver. 21. *For the king of Babylon is stopping at the cross road, at the parting of the two ways, to practise divination. He is shaking the arrows, inquiring of the teraphim, looking at the liver.* Ver. 22. *The divination falls to his right: Jerusalem, to set battering-rams, to open the mouth with a death-cry, to lift up the voice with a war-cry, to set battering-rams at the gates, to heap up a rampart, to build siege towers.*—After the picture of the terrible devastation which the sword of the Lord will produce, the last word of God in this prophecy answers the questions, in whose hand Jehovah will place His sword, and whom it will smite. The slayer into whose hand the sharpened sword is given (ver. 11) is the king of Babylon, and it will smite not only Judah, but the Ammonites also. Jerusalem and Judah will be the first to fall, and then the arch-enemy of the covenant nation, namely Ammon, will succumb to the strokes of the sword of Jehovah, in order that the embittered enemies of the Lord and His people may learn that the fall of Jerusalem is not, as they fancy, a proof of the impotence, but rather of the omnipotence, of its God. In this way does our prophecy expand into a prediction of the judgment which will fall upon the whole of the world in hostility to God. For it is only as the arch-enemies of the kingdom of God that the Ammonites come into consideration here. The parallel between Israel and the sons of Ammon is carried out in such a way as to give constant prominence to the distinction between them. Jerusalem will fall, the ancient theocracy will be destroyed till he shall come who will restore the right (vers. 26 and 27). Ammon, on the other hand, will perish, and not a trace be left (vers. 31, 32).—This prediction is exhibited to the eye by means of a sign. The prophet is to make two ways, *i.e.* to prepare a sketch representing a road leading from a country, viz. Babylon, and dividing at a certain spot into two roads, one of which leads to Rabbath-Ammon, the capital of the kingdom of the Ammonites, the other to Judah, into Jerusalem. He is to draw the ways for the coming (לָבוֹא) of the sword of the king of Babylon. At the fork of the road he is to engrave a hand, יָד, *i.e.* an index. בָּרֵא signifies in the *Piel* to cut away (Josh. xvii. 15, 18), to dig or hew (Ezek. xxiii. 47), here to engrave written characters in hard material. The selection of this word shows that Ezekiel was to sketch the ways upon some hard material, probably a brick or tile (cf. ch. iv. 1). יָד does not mean *locus spatium*, but a hand, *i.e.* an index. רֹאשׁ דֶּרֶךְ, the beginning of the road, *i.e.*

the fork of the road (ch. xvi. 25), is explained in ver. 21, where it is called אֵם הַדֶּרֶךְ, mother of the road, inasmuch as the roads start from the point of separation, and רֹאשׁ שְׁנֵי הַדְּרָכִים, beginning of the two roads. דֶּרֶךְ עִיר, the road to a city. For *Rabbath-Ammon*, which is preserved in the ruins of *Ammân*, on the Upper Jabbok (*Nahr Ammân*), see the comm. on Deut. iii. 11. The road to Judah is still more precisely defined by בִּירוּשָׁלַםִ בְּצוּרָה, into fortified Jerusalem, because the conquest of Jerusalem was the purpose of Nebuchadnezzar's expedition. The omission of the article before בְּצוּרָה may be explained from the nature of the participle, in which, even in prose, the article may be left out after a definite noun (cf. Ewald, § 335*a*). The drawing is explained in vers. 21 and 22. The king of Babylon is halting (עָמַד, to stand still, stop) to consult his oracles, and inquire which of the two roads he is to take. קְסֹם קֶסֶם, to take in hand, or practise divination. In order that he may proceed safely, he avails himself of all the means of divination at his command. He shakes the arrows (more strictly, the quiver with the arrows). On the practice itself Jerome writes as follows: "He consults the oracle according to the custom of his nation, putting his arrows into a quiver, and mixing them together, with the names of individuals inscribed or stamped upon them, to see whose arrow will come out, and which state shall be first attacked."[1] He consults the *Teraphim*, or Penates, worshipped as oracular deities and gods of good fortune (see the comm. on Gen. xxxi. 19 and my *Biblical Archaeology*, § 90). Nothing is known concerning the way in which these deities were consulted and gave their oracles. He examines the liver. The practice of ἡπατο-

[1] The arrow-lot (*Belomantie*) of the ancient Greeks (Homer, *Il.* iii. 324, vii. 182, 183) was similar to this; also that of the ancient Arabs (*vid.* Pococke, *Specim. hist. Arab.* pp. 327 sqq., and the passages from Nuweiri quoted by Reiske, *Samml. einiger Arab. Sprichwörter von den Stecken oder Stäben*, p. 21). Another kind, in which the lot was obtained by shooting off the arrows, was common according to the *Fihrist el Ulum* of En-Nedîm among the Hananian Ssabians (see Chwolsohn, *Ssabier*, ii. pp. 26 and 119, 200.

σκοπία, *extispicium*, in which signs of good or bad luck, of the success or failure of any enterprise, were obtained from the peculiar condition of the liver of the sacrificial animals, was a species of divination to which great importance was attached by both the Babylonians (*vid.* Diod. Sic. ii. 29) and the Romans (Cicero, *de divin.* vi. 13), and of which traces were found, according to *Barhebr. Chron.* p. 125, as late as the eighth century of the Christian era among the Ssabians of Haran.—The divination resulted in a decision for Jerusalem. בִּימִינוֹ הָיָה is not to be translated "in his right hand was," but "into his right hand there came." הָיָה: ἐγένετο (LXX.), נְפַל (Chald.), קֶסֶם does not mean lot (Ges.), but soothsaying, divination. יְרוּשָׁלַיִם is connected with this in the form of a noun in apposition: the divination which indicated Jerusalem. The right hand is the more important of the two. The meaning of the words cannot be more precisely defined, because we are not acquainted with the kind of divination referred to; even if we were to take the words as simply relating to the arrow in this sense, that an arrow with the inscription "Jerusalem" came into his right hand, and thus furnished the decision, which was afterwards confirmed by consulting the Teraphim and examining the liver. But the circumstance itself, that is to say, the fact that the divination coincided with the purpose of God, must not be taken, as Hävernick supposes, as suggesting a point of contact between Hebraism and the soothsaying of heathenism, which was peculiar to Ezekiel or to the time of the captivity. All that is proved by this fact is, that even heathenism is subject to the rule and guidance of Almighty God, and is made subservient to the accomplishment of the plans of both His kingdom and His salvation. In the words, to set battering rams, etc., the substance of the oracle obtained by Nebuchadnezzar is more minutely given. It is a double one, showing what he is to do: viz. (1) to set battering rams, *i.e.* to proceed to the siege of Jerusalem, as still further described in the last portion of the verse (ch. iv. 2); and (2) to raise the war-cry for storming the city, that is to say, to take it by storm. The two clauses לִפְתֹּחַ וגו' and לְהָרִים וגו' are synonymous; they are not "pure tautology," however, as Hitzig affirms, but are chosen for the purpose of giving greater emphasis to the thought. The expression בְּרֶצַח creates some difficulty, inasmuch as the phrase "*ut aperiat os in caede*" (Vulg.), to open the mouth in murder or ruin, *i.e.* to put to death or lay in ruins, is a very striking one, and could hardly be justified as an "energetic expression for the battle-cry" (Hävernick). ב does not mean "to," and cannot indicate the intention, all the less because בְּרֶצַח is parallel to בִּתְרוּעָה, where תרועה is that in which the raising of the voice expresses itself. There is nothing left then but to take רֶצַח in the sense of field- or war-cry, and to derive this meaning either from רָצַח or, *per metathesin*, from צָרַח.

Vers. 23–27. This announcement will appear to the Judaeans, indeed, to be a deceptive divination, but nevertheless it will be verified.—Ver. 23. *And it is like deceptive divination in their eyes; sacred oaths are theirs* (lit. to them); *but he brings the iniquity to remembrance, that they may be taken.* Ver. 24. *Therefore thus saith the Lord Jehovah, Because ye bring your iniquity to remembrance, in that your offences are made manifest, so that your sins appear in all your deeds, because ye are remembered ye shall be taken with the hand.* Ver. 25. *And thou pierced one, sinner, prince of Israel, whose day is come at the time of the final transgression,* Ver. 26. *Thus saith the Lord Jehovah, The turban will be removed, the crown taken off. This is not this; the low will be lifted up, and the lofty lowered.* Ver. 27. *Overthrown, overthrown, overthrown will I make it; even this shall not be, till He cometh, to whom is the right, to Him do I give it.*—In ver. 23 (28), לָהֶם, which is more precisely defined by בְּעֵינֵיהֶם, refers to the Israelites, *i.e.* the Judaeans. This also applies to the following לָהֶם, which cannot possibly be taken as referring to a different subject, say, for example, the Chaldeans. It is evident, therefore, that it is impossible to sustain the rendering given in Gesenius' *Thesaurus* (*s.v.*) to the obscure words שְׁבֻעֵי שְׁבֻעוֹת, viz. *qui juramenta jurarunt eis* (*sc.* Chaldaeis), which Maurer has modified and expounded thus: "they will not fear these auguries; they will swear oaths to them (the Chaldeans), that is to say, according to their usual custom, these truce-breakers will take fresh oaths, hoping that the Chaldeans will be conciliated thereby." Moreover, the thought itself is an unsuitable one, inasmuch as "the defiant attitude of confidence with which they looked such awfully threatening danger in the face must have had some other ground than a reliance upon false oaths and Chaldean credulity" (Hävernick). The common explanation, which Rosenmüller and Kliefoth uphold, is, "because the Chaldeans are sworn allies, sworn confederates of theirs;" or as Kliefoth explains it, "on account of the oath of fealty or vassalage sworn by Zedekiah to Nebuchadnezzar, they have sworn confederates in the Chaldeans, and relying upon this, they are confident that they have no hostile attack to fear from them." But this is altogether untenable, not only because it is perfectly arbitrary to supply "the Chaldeans," but still more for the reason adduced by Maurer. "How," he justly asks, "could the Judaeans despise these auguries *because* the Chaldeans were bound to them by an oath when they themselves had broken faith? When a treaty has been violated by one party, is not the other released from his oath?" We therefore adopt the same explanation as Hävernick: "oaths of oaths are theirs (to them), *i.e.* the most sacred oaths are (made) to them, namely, by God." They rely upon that which God has solemnly sworn to them, without considering upon what this promise was conditional, namely, upon a faithful observance on their part of the commandments of God. For the fact itself, compare ch. xx. 42, and such passages as Ps. cv. 9 sqq., etc. The form שְׁבֻעֵי by the side of שְׁבֻעוֹת may be explained in a very simple way from the relation of the construct state, *i.e.* from the endeavour to secure an obvious form for the construct state, and cannot in any case furnish a well-founded argument against the correctness of our explanation. As Ezekiel uses נְפָשִׁים for נְפָשׁוֹת in ch.

xiii. 20, he may also have formed שְׁבֻעִים (שְׁבֻעֵי) by the side of שְׁבֻעוֹת.—As they rely upon the promises of God without reflecting upon their own breach of covenant, God will bring their sin to remembrance through His judgment. וְהוּא is Jehovah, upon whose oaths they rely. עָוֹן must not be restricted to Zedekiah's breach of covenant, since ver. 24 clearly shows that it is the wrong-doing of Judah generally. לְהִתָּפֵשׂ in ver. 24 (29) is also to be understood of the whole nation, which is to be taken and punished by the king of Babylon. For ver. 24 (29) introduces the reason for the statement made in the last clause of ver. 23 (28). God must put the people in remembrance of their iniquity by inflicting punishment, because they have called it to remembrance by sins committed without any shame, and thereby have, so to speak, compelled God to remember them, and to cause the sinners to be grasped by the hand of the slayer. הַזְכִּיר עָוֹן is used in ver. 24 (29) in a different sense from ver. 23 (28), and is therefore explained by בְּהִגָּלוֹת וגו׳. בַּכַּף, which is indefinite in itself, points back to יַד הוֹרֵג in ver. 11 (16), and receives from that its more exact definition.

With ver. 25 the address turns to the chief sinner, the godless King Zedekiah, who was bringing the judgment of destruction upon the kingdom by his faithless breach of oath. The words חָלָל, רָשָׁע, and נְשִׂיא יִשׂ׳ are *asyndeta*, co-ordinate to one another. חָלָל does not mean profane or infamous (βέβηλε, LXX.), but simply pierced, slain. This meaning is to be retained here. This is demanded not only by the fixed usage of the language, but also by the relation in which חָלָל stands both to ver. 14 and to חַלְלֵי רְשָׁעִים in ver. 29 (34). It is true that Zedekiah was not pierced by the sword either at that time or afterwards, but was simply blinded and led in captivity to Babylon, where he died. But all that follows from this is, that חָלָל is used here in a figurative sense, given up to the sword, *i.e.* to death; and Zedekiah is so designated for the purpose of announcing in a more energetic manner the certainty of his fate. The selection of the term חָלָל is the more natural, because throughout the whole prophecy the description of the judgment takes its character from the figure of the sword of Jehovah. As God does not literally wield a sword, so חָלָל is no proof of actual slaying with the sword. יוֹמוֹ, his day, is the day of his destruction (cf. 1 Sam. xxvi. 10), or of the judgment upon him. The time of the final transgression is not the time when the transgression reaches its end, *i.e.* its completion, but the time when the wickedness brings the end, *i.e.* destruction (cf. ch. xxxv. 5, and for קֵץ in this sense, ch. vii. 2, 3). The fact that the end, the destruction, is come, *i.e.* is close at hand, is announced in ver. 26 to the prince, and in his person to the whole nation. If we understand the connection in this way, which is naturally suggested by ver. 25*b*, we get rid of the objection, which led Kliefoth to question the fact that it is the king who is addressed in ver. 25*a*, and to take the words as collective, "ye slaughtered sinners, princes of Israel," and to understand them as referring to the entire body of rulers, including the priests,—an explanation that is completely upset by the words אַתָּה . . . נָשִׂיא (thou . . . prince), which are so entirely opposed to the collective view. Again, the remark that "what follows in ver. 26, viz. the statement to be made to the נָשִׂיא, has really nothing to do with him, since the sweeping away of the priesthood did not affect Zedekiah personally" (Kliefoth), is neither correct nor conclusive. For ver. 26 contains an announcement not only of the abrogation of the priesthood, but also of the destruction of the kingdom, which did affect Zedekiah both directly and personally. Moreover, we must not isolate the king addressed, even as an individual, from the position which he occupied, or, at any rate, which he ought to have occupied as a theocratic monarch, so as to be able to say that the abrogation of the priesthood did not affect him. The priesthood was one of the fundamental pillars of the theocracy, the removal of which would necessarily be followed by the collapse of the divine state, and therefore by the destruction of the monarchy. Hence it is that the abolition of the priesthood is mentioned first. The infinitives absolute (not imperatives) הָסִיר and הָרִים are selected for the purpose of expressing the truth in the most emphatic manner; and the verbs are synonymous. הָרִים, to lift up, *i.e.* not to elevate, but to take away, to abolish, as in Isa. lvii. 14; Dan. viii. 11. מִצְנֶפֶת does not mean the royal diadem, like צָנִיף in Isa. lxii. 3, but the tiara of the high priest, as it does in every instance in the Pentateuch, from which Ezekiel has taken the word. הָעֲטָרָה, the king's crown. The diadem of the priest and the regal crown are the insignia of the offices of high priest and king; and consequently their removal is the abolition of both high-priesthood and monarchy. These words contain the sentence of death upon the theocracy, of which the Aaronic priesthood and the Davidic monarchy constituted the foundations.—They predict not merely a temporary, but a complete abolition of both offices and dignities; and their fulfilment took place when the kingdom of Judah was destroyed by the king of Babylon. The earthly sovereignty of the house of David was not restored again after the captivity; and the high-priesthood of the restoration, like the second temple, was only a shadowy outline of the glory and essential features of the high-priesthood of Aaron. As the ark with the Shechinah, or the gracious presence of God, was wanting in the temple of Zerubbabel; so were the Urim and Thummim wanting to the high-priesthood, and these were the only means by which the high priest could really carry out the mediation between the Lord and the people. זאת לא זאת (this is not this) does not refer to the tiara (mitre) and crown. זאת is neuter, and therefore construed with the masculine הָיָה. This (mitre and crown) will not be this (הָיָה is prophetic), *i.e.* it will not continue, it will be all over with it (Hävernick, Maurer, and Kliefoth). To this there is appended the further thought, that a general inversion of things will take place. This is the meaning of the words—the low will be lifted up, and the lofty lowered. הַגְבֵּהַ and הַשְׁפִּיל are infinitives, and are chosen in the same sense as in the first hemistich. The form הַשָּׁפָלָה, with ה

without the tone, is masculine; the ָה probably serving merely to give greater fulness to the form, and to make it correspond more nearly to הַגְּבֹהַּ.[1]—This general thought is expressed still more definitely in ver. 27*a*. עַוָּה, which is repeated twice to give greater emphasis to the thought, is a noun derived from עִוָּה, inversion, overthrow; and the suffix in אֲשִׂימֶנָּה points back to זאת in ver. 26 (31). This, the existing state, the high-priesthood and the monarchy, will I make into destruction, or utterly overthrow. But the following זאת cannot also refer to the tiara and crown, as Kliefoth supposes, on account of the גַּם which precedes it. This shows that זאת relates to the thing last mentioned. Even this, the overthrow, shall have no durability; or, as Tanch. has correctly expressed it, *neque haec conditio erit durabilis.* The following עַד־בֹּא attaches itself not so much to this last clause as to the main thought: overthrow upon overthrow will ensue. The thought is this: "nowhere is there rest, nowhere security; all things are in a state of flux till the coming of the great Restorer and Prince of peace" (Hengstenberg). It is generally acknowledged that the words עַד־בֹּא אֲשֶׁר־לוֹ הַמִּשְׁפָּט contain an allusion to Gen. xlix. 10, עַד כִּי יָבוֹא שִׁילֹה; and it is only by a false interpretation of the preceding clauses, wrung from the words by an arbitrary alteration of the text, that Hitzig is able to set this connection aside. At

[1] Hitzig has given a most preposterous exposition of this verse. Taking the words הָסִיר and הָרִים as antithetical, in the sense of removing and exalting or sustaining in an exalted position, and regarding the clauses as questions signifying, "Shall the high-priesthood be abolished, and the real dignity, on the contrary, remain untouched?" he finds the answer to these questions in the words זאת לֹא זאת (this, not this). They contain, in his opinion, an affirmation of the former and a negation of the latter. But he does not tell us how זאת לֹא זאת without a verb can possibly mean, "the former (the abrogation of the high-priesthood) will take place, but the latter (the exaltation of the monarchy) will not occur." And, finally, the last clause, "the low shall be lifted up," etc., is said to contain simply a watchword, which is not for the time being to be followed by any result. Such trifling needs no refutation. We simply observe, therefore, that there is no ground for the assertion, that הָרִים without מִן cannot possibly signify to abolish.

the same time, אֲשֶׁר־לוֹ הַמִּשְׁפָּט is of course not to be taken as a philological explanation of the word שִׁילֹה, but is simply a theological interpretation of the patriarchal prophecy, with direct reference to the predicted destruction of the existing relations in consequence of the ungodliness and unrighteousness of the leaders of the theocracy up to that time. הַמִּשְׁפָּט is not the rightful claim to the mitre and crown, but right in an objective sense, as belonging to God (Deut. i. 17), and entrusted by God to the earthly government as His representative. He then, to whom this right belongs, and to whom God will give it, is the Messiah, of whom the prophets from the times of David onwards have prophesied as the founder and restorer of perfect right on earth (cf. Ps. lxxii.; Isa. ix. 6, xlii. 1; Jer. xxiii. 5, xxxiii. 17). The suffix attached to נְתַתִּיו is not a dative, but an accusative, referring to מִשְׁפָּט (cf. Ps. lxxii. 1). There was no necessity to mention the person again to whom God would give the right, as He had already been designated in the previous expression אֲשֶׁר לוֹ.

Vers. 28–32. Overthrow of the Ammonites.—Ver. 28. *And thou, son of man, prophesy and say, Thus saith the Lord Jehovah, concerning the sons of Ammon, and concerning their scorn, sword, sword, drawn to slay, polished, that it may devour, that it may flash!* Ver. 29. *While they prophesy deceit to thee, while they divine lying to thee, it shall lay thee by the necks of the sinners slain, whose day cometh at the time of the final transgression.* Ver. 30. *Put it in its scabbard again. At the place where thou wast created, in the land of thy birth will I judge thee,* Ver. 31. *And pour out my anger upon thee, kindle the fire of my wrath against thee, and give thee into the hand of foolish men, of smiths of destruction.* Ver. 32. *Thou shalt be for the fire to devour; thy blood shall remain in the midst of the land; thou shalt be remembered no more; for I Jehovah have spoken it.*—As Judah in Jerusalem will fall by the sword of the king of Babylon, contrary to all expectation; so will the Ammonites be punished for their scorn with utter extermination. חֶרְפָּה is scorn at the overthrow of Israel (cf. ch. xxv. 3, 6, and Zeph. ii. 8). The sword is already drawn against them. פְּתוּחָה, taken out of the scabbard, as in Ps. xxxvii. 14. לְטֶבַח is to be connected with פְּתוּחָה, notwithstanding the accents, and לְהָכִיל with מְרוּטָה. This is required by the correspondence of the clauses. הָכִיל is regarded as a derivative of כּוּל by Ewald and others, in the sense of *ad sustinendum*, according to capacity, *i.e.* as much as possible. But the adverbial rendering is opposed to the context, and cannot be sustained from ch. xxiii. 32. Moreover, כּוּל, to contain, is applicable enough to goblets and other vessels, but not to a sword. Hitzig therefore explains it from the Arabic كلّ, to blunt (*sc.* the eyes), *i.e.* to blind. But this is open to the objection that the form הָכִיל points to the verb כּוּל rather than כָּלַל; and also to a still greater one,—namely, that there is nothing in the Hebrew usage to suggest the use of כלל in such a sense as this, and even if it were used in the sense of blunting, it would be perfectly arbitrary to supply עֵינַיִם; and lastly, that even the flashing of the sword does not suggest the idea of blinding, but is intended to heighten the terror occasioned by the sharpness of the sword. We therefore adhere to the derivation of הָכִיל from אָכַל, and regard it as a defective form for הַאֲכִיל, like תֹּמְרוּ for תֹּאמְרוּ in 2 Sam. xix. 14, יַהֵל as syncopated form for יַאֲהֵל (Isa. xiii. 20), and וַתֹּחֶז for וַתֹּאחֶז in 2 Sam. xx. 9; literally, to cause it to eat or devour, *i.e.* to make it fit for the work of devouring. לְמַעַן בָּרָק, literally, for the sake of the lightning (flash) that shall issue therefrom (cf. ver. 10).—In ver. 29 (34), לָתֵת (to lay, or place) is also dependent upon חֶרֶב פְּתוּחָה, drawn to lay thee; so that the first half of the verse is inserted as a parenthesis, either to indicate the occasion for bringing the sword into the land (Hitzig), or to introduce an attendant circumstance, according to the sense in which the ב in בַּחֲזוֹת is taken. The parenthetical clause is understood by most of the commentators as referring to deceptive oracles of Ammonitish soothsayers, which either determined the policy of Ammon, as Hitzig supposes (cf. Jer. xxvii. 9, 10), or inspired the Ammonites with confidence, that they had nothing to fear from the Chaldeans. Kliefoth, on the other hand, refers the words to the oracles consulted by Nebuchadnezzar, according to ver. 23. "These oracles, which directed the king not to march against the Ammonites, but against Jerusalem, proved themselves, according to ver. 29, to be deceptive prophesying to the Ammonites, inasmuch as they also afterwards fell by the sword; just as, according to ver. 23, they proved themselves to be genuine so far as the Israelites were concerned, inasmuch as they were really the first to be smitten." This view is a very plausible one, if it only answered in any degree to the words. But it is hard to believe that the words, "while it (one) prophesies falsehood to thee," are meant to be equivalent to "while its prophecy proves itself to be false to thee." Moreover, Nebuchadnezzar did not give the Ammonites any oracle, either false or true, by the circumstance that his divination at the cross-road led him to decide in favour of the march to Jerusalem; for all that he did in consequence was to postpone his designs upon the Ammonites, but not to relinquish them. We cannot understand the words in any other sense, therefore, than as relating to oracles, which the Ammonites received from soothsayers of their own.—Hitzig takes offence at the expression, "that it (the sword) may lay thee by (to) the necks of the sinners slain," because *colla* cannot stand for *corpora decollata*, and consequently proposes to alter אוֹתָךְ into אוֹתָהּ, to put it (the sword) to the necks. But by this conjecture he gets the not less striking thought, that the sword was to be put to the necks of those already slain; a thing which would be perfectly unmeaning, and is therefore not generally done. The sinners slain are the Judaeans who have fallen. The words point back to ver. 25, the second half of which is repeated here, and predict the same fate to the Ammonites. It is easy to supply חֶרֶב to הָשֵׁב אֶל־תַּעְרָהּ: put the sword into its scabbard again. These words can only be addressed to the Ammonites; not to the Chaldeans, as Kliefoth imagines, for the latter does not harmonize in any way with what follows, viz. in the place of thy birth will I judge thee. God does not execute the judgment independently of the Chaldeans, but through the medium of their sword. The difficulties occasioned by taking the words as referring to the Ammonites are not so great as to necessitate an alteration of the text (Hitzig), or to call for the arbitrary explanation: put it now or for the present into the scabbard (Kliefoth). The use of the masculine הָשַׁב (with *Patach* for הָשֵׁב, as in Isa. xlii. 22), if Ammon is addressed by the side of the feminine אוֹתָךְ, may be explained in a very simple way, from the fact that the sword is carried by men, so that here the thought of the people, the warriors, is predominant, and the representation of the kingdom of the Ammonites as a woman falls into the background. The objection that the suffix in תַּעְרָהּ can only refer to the sword (of the Chaldean) mentioned in ver. 28, is more plausible than conclusive. For inasmuch as the scabbard presupposes a sword, and every sword has a scabbard, the suffix may be fully accounted for from the thing itself, as the words, "put the sword into its scabbard," would lead any hearer to think at once of the sword of the person addressed, without considering whether that particular sword had been mentioned before or not. The meaning of the words is this: every attempt to defend thyself with the sword and avert destruction will be in vain. In thine own land will God judge thee. For מְכֻרוֹתַיִךְ, see the comm. on ch. xvi. 3. This judgment is still further explained in ver. 31, where the figure of the sword is dropped, and that of the fire of the wrath of God introduced in its place. בְּאֵשׁ . . . אָפִיחַ, we render: "the fire of my wrath I blow (kindle) against thee," after Isa. liv. 16, and not "with the fire . . . do I blow, or snort, against thee," as others have done; because blowing with the fire is an unnatural figure, and the interpretation of the words in accordance with Isa. *l.c.* is all the more natural, that in the closing words of the verse, חָרָשֵׁי מַשְׁחִית, the allusion to that passage is indisputable, and it is only from this that the combination of the two words can be accounted for.—Different explanations have been given of בֹּעֲרִים. Some render it *ardentes*, and in accordance with Isa. xxx. 27 : burning with wrath. But בָּעַר is never used in this sense. Nor can the rendering "scorching men" (Kliefoth) be sustained, for בָּעַר, to burn, only occurs in connection with things which are combustible, *e.g.* fire, pitch, coals, etc. The word must be explained from Ps. xcii. 7, "brutish," foolish, always bearing in mind that the Hebrew associated the idea of godlessness with folly, and that cruelty naturally follows in its train.—Ver. 32. Thus will Ammon perish through fire and sword, and even the memory of it be obliterated. For ver. 32*a* compare ch. xv. 4. The words, "thy blood will be בְּתוֹךְ הָאָרֶץ in the midst of the land," can hardly be understood in any other sense than "thy blood will flow over all the land." For the rendering proposed by Ewald, "remain in the midst of the earth, without thy being mentioned," like that given by Kliefoth, "thy blood will the earth drink," does not harmonize with ch. xxiv. 7, where דָּמָהּ בְּתוֹכָהּ הָיָה is affirmed of blood, which cannot penetrate into the earth, or be covered with dust. For תִּזָּכֵרִי, see ch. xxv. 10. Ammon as the enemy of the kingdom of God will utterly perish, leaving no trace behind, and without any such hope of restoration as that held out in ver. 27 to the kingdom of Judah or the people of Israel.

CHAP. XXII. THE SINS OF JERUSALEM AND ISRAEL.

To the prediction of the judgment in ch. xxi. there is appended another description of the sins of Jerusalem and Israel, by which this judgment is occasioned. The chapter contains three words of God, which are connected together both in substance and design, viz. (1) The blood-guiltiness and idolatry of Jerusalem accelerate the coming of the days when the city will be an object of scorn to all the world (vers. 1–16);

(2) The house of Israel has become dross, and is to be melted in the fire of tribulation (vers. 17–22); (3) All ranks of the kingdom—prophets, priests, princes, and people—are thoroughly corrupt, therefore has the judgment burst upon them (vers. 23–31).

Vers. 1–16. Blood-guiltiness of Jerusalem and the burden of its sins. Vers. 1–5 contain the principal accusation relating to bloodshed and idolatry; and vers. 6–16 a further account of the sins of the people and their rulers, with a brief threatening of punishment.—Ver. 1. *And the word of Jehovah came to me, saying,* Ver. 2. *And thou, son of man, wilt thou judge? wilt thou judge the city of blood-guiltiness? then show it all its abominations,* Ver. 3. *And say, Thus saith the Lord Jehovah, City, which sheddeth blood in the midst of it, that her time may come, and maketh idols within itself for defilement.* Ver. 4. *Through thy blood which thou hast shed hast thou made thyself guilty, and through thine idols which thou hast made hast thou defiled thyself, and hast drawn thy days near, and hast come to thy years; therefore I make thee a scorn to the nations, and ridicule to all lands.* Ver. 5. *Those near and those far off from thee shall ridicule thee as defiled in name, rich in confusion.*—The expression הֲתִשְׁפֹּט וגו' proves this address to be a continuation of the reproof of Israel's sins, which commenced in ch. xx. 4. The epithet city of blood-guiltiness, as in ch. xxiv. 6, 9 (compare Nah. iii. 1), is explained in ver. 3. The apodosis commences with וְהוֹדַעְתָּהּ, and is continued in ver. 3 (וְאָמַרְתָּ). לָבוֹא עִתָּהּ, that her time, *i.e.* her time of punishment, may come: עִתָּהּ, like יוֹמוֹ in ch. xxi. 30. וְעָשְׂתָה is not a continuation of the infinitive לָבוֹא, but of the participle שֹׁפֶכֶת. עָלֶיהָ, of which different renderings have been given, does not mean "over itself," *i.e.* as a burden with which it has laden itself (Hävernick); still less "for itself" (Hitzig), a meaning which עַל never has, but literally "upon," *i.e.* in itself, covering the city with it, as it were. וַתַּקְרִיבִי, thou hast brought near, brought on thy days, that is to say, the days of judgment, and hast come to, arrived at thy years, *sc.* the years of visitation and punishment (cf. Jer. xi. 23). This meaning is readily supplied by the context. טְמֵאַת הַשֵּׁם, defiled, unclean with regard to the name, *i.e.* having forfeited the name of a holy city through capital crimes and other sinful abominations. מְהוּמָה is internal confusion, both moral and religious, as in Amos iii. 9 (cf. Ps. lv. 10–12).

In vers. 6–12 there follows an enumeration of a multitude of sins which had been committed in Jerusalem.—Ver. 6. *Behold, the princes of Israel are every one, according to his arm, in thee to shed blood.* Ver. 7. *Father and mother they despise in thee; toward the foreigner they act violently in the midst of thee; orphans and widows they oppress in thee.* Ver. 8. *Thou despisest my holy things, and desecratest my Sabbaths.* Ver. 9. *Slanderers are in thee to shed blood, and they eat upon the mountains in thee; they practise lewdness in thee.* Ver. 10. *They uncover the father's nakedness in thee; they ravish the defiled in her uncleanness in thee.* Ver. 11. *And one committeth abomination with his neighbour's wife, and another defileth his daughter-in-law by incest, and the third ravisheth his sister, his father's daughter in thee.* Ver. 12. *They take gifts in thee to shed blood; interest and usury thou takest, and overreachest thy neighbours with violence, and thou forgettest me, is the saying of the Lord Jehovah.*—By the repetition of the refrain, to shed blood (vers. 6, 9, and 12), the enumeration is divided into three groups of sins, which are placed in the category of blood-guiltiness by the fact that they are preceded by this sentence and the repetition of it after the form of a refrain. The first group (vers. 6–8) embraces sins which are committed in daring opposition to all the laws of morality. By the princes of Israel we are to understand primarily the profligate kings, who caused innocent persons to be put to death, such, for example, as Jehoiakim (2 Kings xxiv. 4), Manasseh (2 Kings xxi. 16), and others. The words אִישׁ לִזְרֹעוֹ הָיוּ are rendered by Hitzig and Kliefoth, they were ready to help one another; and in support of the rendering they appeal to Ps. lxxxiii. 9. But in that case אִישׁ לִזְרֹעוֹ

would stand for לְזְרֹעַ אִישׁ, or rather for אִישׁ זְרוֹעַ לְאִישׁ,—a substitution which cannot be sustained. Nor can they be taken in the sense proposed by Hävernick, every one relying upon his arm, *i.e.* looking to physical force alone, but simply every one according to his arm, *i.e.* according to his strength or violence, are they in thee. In this case הָיוּ does not require anything to be supplied, any more than in the similar combination in ver. 9. Followed by לְמַעַן with an infinitive, it means to be there with the intention of doing anything, or making an attempt, *i.e.* to direct his efforts to a certain end. In ver. 7 it is not the princes who are the subject, but the ungodly in general. הֵקַלּוּ is the opposite of כַּבֵּד (Ex. xx. 12). In the reproofs which follow, compare Ex. xxii. 20 sqq.; Lev. xix. 13; Deut. xxiv. 14 sqq. With insolence and violence toward men there is associated contempt of all that is holy. For ver. 8*b*, see ch. xx. 13.—In the second group, vers. 9–11, in addition to slander and idolatry, the crimes of lewdness and incest are the principal sins for which the people are reproved; and here the allusion to Lev. xviii. and xix. is very obvious. The reproof of slander also points back to the prohibition in Lev. xix. 16. Slander to shed blood, refers to malicious charges and false testimony in a court of justice (*vid.* 1 Kings xxi. 10, 11). For eating upon the mountains, see ch. xviii. 6. The practice of *zimmâh* is more specifically described in vers. 10 and 11. For the thing itself, compare Lev. xviii. 7, 8, xix. 15 and 9. The threefold אִישׁ in ver. 11 does not mean every one, but one, another, and the third, as the correlative רֵעֵהוּ shows.—The third group, ver. 12, is composed of sins of covetousness. For the first clause, compare the prohibition in Ex. xxiii. 2; for the second, ch. xviii. 8, 13. The reproof finishes with forgetfulness of God, which is closely allied to covetousness.

Vers. 13–16. The Lord is enraged at such abominable doings. He will interfere, and put an end to them by scattering Judah among the heathen.—Ver. 13. *And, behold, I smite my hand because of thy gain which thou hast made, and over thy blood-*

guiltiness which is in the midst of thee. Ver. 14. *Will thy heart indeed stand firm, or will thy hands be strong for the day when I shall deal with thee? I Jehovah have spoken it, and also do it.* Ver. 15. *I will scatter thee among the nations, and disperse thee in the lands, and will utterly remove thine uncleanness from thee.* Ver. 16. *And thou wilt be desecrated through thyself before the eyes of the nations, and know that I am Jehovah.*—Ver. 13 is closely connected with the preceding verse. This serves to explain the fact that the only sins mentioned as exciting the wrath of God are covetousness and blood-guiltiness. הִכָּה כַף, as 2 Kings xi. 12 clearly shows, is a contracted expression for הִכָּה כַף אֶל כַּף (ch. xxi. 19), and the smiting of the hands together is a gesture indicative of wrathful indignation. For the form דָּמֵךְ, contracted from דָּמַיִךְ, see the comm. on ch. xvi. 45.—As ver. 13 leads on to the threatening of judgment, so does ver. 14 point in anticipation to the terrible nature of the judgment itself. The question, "will thy heart stand firm?" involves a warning against security. עָמַד is the opposite of נָמֵס (cf. ch. xxi. 12), as standing forms the antithesis to passing away (cf. Ps. cii. 27). עָשָׂה אוֹתָךְ, as in ch. xvi. 59 and vii. 27. The Lord will scatter them (cf. ch. xii. 15, xx. 23), and remove the uncleanness of sin, namely, by purifying the people in exile (cf. Isa. iv. 4). הֵתֵם, from תָּמַם, to cause to cease, with מִן, to take completely away. נִחַלְתְּ, *Niphal* of חָלַל, connected with לְעֵינֵי גוֹיִם, as in ch. xx. 9, not from נָחַל, as many of the commentators who follow the Septuagint and Vulgate suppose. בָּךְ, not *in te*, in thyself, but through thee, *i.e.* through thy sinful conduct and its consequences.

Vers. 17–22. Refining of Israel in the furnace of besieged Jerusalem.—Ver. 17. *And the word of Jehovah came to me, saying,* Ver. 18. *Son of man, the house of Israel has become to me as dross; they are all brass, and tin, and iron, and lead in the furnace; dross of silver have they become.* Ver. 19. *Therefore thus saith the Lord Jehovah, Because ye have all become dross, therefore, behold, I gather you together in Jerusalem.* Ver. 20. *As men gather together silver, and brass, and iron, and lead, and tin into the furnace, to blow the fire upon it for melting, so will I gather (you) together in my anger and my wrath, and put you in and melt you.* Ver. 21. *And I will collect you together, and blow the fire of my wrath upon you, that ye may be melted therein.* Ver. 22. *As silver is melted in the furnace, so shall ye be melted therein* (viz. in Jerusalem), *and shall learn that I Jehovah have poured out my wrath upon you.*—This second word of God rests no doubt upon the figure in ver. 15*b*, of the uncleanness or dirt of sin; but it is not an exposition of the removal of the dirt, as predicted there. For that was to be effected through the dispersion of Israel among the nations, whereas the word of God, from ver. 17 onwards, represents the siege awaiting Jerusalem as a melting process, through which God will separate the silver ore contained in Israel from the baser metals mingled with it. In ver. 18 it commences with a description of the existing condition of Israel. It has turned to dross. הָיוּ is clearly a perfect, and is not to be taken as a prophetical future, as Kliefoth proposes. Such a rendering is not only precluded by the clause יַעַן הֱיוֹת וגו' in ver. 19, but could only be made to yield an admissible sense by taking the middle clause of the verse, "all of them brass and tin," etc., as a statement of what Israel had become, or as a preterite in opposition to all the rules of Hebrew syntax, inasmuch as this clause merely furnishes an explanation of הָיוּ־לְסוּג. סוּג, which only occurs here, for סִיג signifies dross, not smelting-ore (Kliefoth), literally, *recedanea*, the baser ingredients which are mixed with the silver, and separated from it by smelting. This is the meaning here, where it is directly afterwards interpreted as consisting of brass, tin, iron, and lead, and then still further defined as סִגִים כֶּסֶף, dross of silver, *i.e.* brass, tin, iron, and lead, with a mixture of silver. Because Israel had turned into silver-dross of this kind, the Lord would gather it together in Jerusalem, to smelt it there as in a smelting furnace; just as men gather together brass, iron, lead, and tin in a furnace to smelt them, or rather to separate the silver contained therein. קְבֻצַת כֶּסֶף, literally, a collection of silver, etc., for "like a collection." The כ *simil.* is probably omitted for the sake of euphony, to avoid the discord occasioned by prefixing it to קְבֻצַת. Ezekiel mentions the silver as well, because there is some silver contained in the brass, iron, etc., or the dross is silver-dross. הִתּוּךְ, *nomen verbale*, from נָתַךְ in the *Hiphil*, smelting; literally, as the smelting of silver takes place in the furnace. The smelting is treated here simply as a figurative representation of punishment, and consequently the result of the smelting, namely, the refining of the silver by the removal of the baser ingredients, is not referred to any further, as is the case in Isa. i. 22, 25; Jer. vi. 27–30; Mal. iii. 2, 3. This smelting process was experienced by Israel in the last siege of Jerusalem by the Chaldeans.

Vers. 23–31. The corrupt state of all classes in the kingdom is the immediate cause of its destruction.—Ver. 23. *And the word of Jehovah came to me, saying,* Ver. 24. *Son of man, say to it, Thou art a land which is not shined upon, nor rained upon in the day of anger.* Ver. 25. *Conspiracy of its prophets is within it; like a roaring lion, which rends in pieces the prey, they devour souls, take possessions and money; they multiply its widows within it.* Ver. 26. *Its priests violate my law and profane my holy things; they make no distinction between holy and unholy, and do not teach the difference between clean and unclean, and they hide their eyes from my Sabbaths, and I am profaned among them.* Ver. 27. *Its princes in the midst of it are like wolves, which rend prey in pieces, that they may shed blood, destroy souls, to acquire gain.* Ver. 28. *And its prophets plaster it with cement, seeing what is worthless, and divining lies for them, saying, "Thus saith the Lord Jehovah," when Jehovah hath not spoken.* Ver. 29. *The common people offer violence and commit theft; they crush the wretched and the poor, and oppress the foreigner against right.* Ver. 30. *I seek among them for a man who might build a wall and step into the breach before me on behalf of the land, that I might not destroy it, but I find none.* Ver. 31. *Therefore I pour out my anger upon them; I destroy them in the fire of my wrath, I give their way upon their head, is the saying of the Lord Jehovah.*—To show the necessity for the predicted judgment still more clearly, in the third word of God contained in this chapter a description is given of the spread of deep corruption among all classes of the people, and the impossibility of saving the kingdom is plainly shown. The words אֱמָר־לָהּ, "say unto her," are taken by most of the commentators as referring to Jerusalem, the abominations of which the prophet is commanded to declare. But although the clause, "thou art a land," etc. (ver. 24), could unquestionably be made to harmonize with this, yet the words of ver. 30, "I sought for a man who might stand in the gap before Jehovah for the land," indicate most unquestionably that this word of God is directed against the land of Judah, and consequently לָהּ must be taken as referring to אֶרֶץ which follows, the pronoun in this case being placed before the noun to which it refers, as in Num. xxiv. 17. Any allusion to the city of Jerusalem would therefore be somewhat out of place, inasmuch as in the preceding word of God the object referred to was not the city, but the house of Israel, or the nation generally, from which a transition is here made to the land, or the kingdom of Judah. The meaning of ver. 24 is a disputed question. לֹא מְטֹהָרָה הִיא, which is rendered ἡ οὐ βρεχομένη in the Sept., is taken by most of the expositors to mean, "it is not cleansed," the form מְטֹהָרָה being correctly rendered as a participle *Pual* of טָהֵר. But this rendering does not furnish any appropriate sense, unless the following words לֹא גֻשְּׁמָהּ are taken as a threat: there shall not be rain, or it shall not be rained upon in the day of wrath. But this view is hardly reconcilable with the form of the word. גֻשְּׁמָהּ, according to the Masoretic pointing with *Mappik* in the ה, is evidently meant to be taken as a noun גֶּשֶׁם = גֹּשֶׁם. In that case, if the words were intended to contain a threat, יִהְיֶה ought not to be omitted. But without a verb the words contain a statement in harmony with what precedes. We regard the *Chetib* גשמה as the perfect *Pual*

גֻּשְּׁמָה. And let it not be objected to this that the *Pual* of this verb is not met with elsewhere, for the form of the noun גֹּשֶׁם with the *u* sound does not occur anywhere else. As a perfect *Pual*, לֹא גֻשְּׁמָה is a simple continuation of the participial clause לֹא מְטֹהָרָה הִיא, containing like this an affirmation, and cannot possibly be taken as a threat or prediction. But "not cleansed" and "not rained upon" do not agree together, as rain is not a means of purification according to the Hebrew idea. It is true that in the law the withdrawal or suspension of rain is threatened as a punishment from God, and the pouring out of rain is promised as a theocratical blessing. But even if the words are taken in a tropical sense, as denoting a withdrawal of the blessings of divine grace, they will not harmonize with the other clause, "not cleansed." We therefore take מְטֹהָרָה in the sense of "shined upon by the light," or provided with brightness; a meaning which is sustained by Ex. xxiv. 10, where *tohar* occurs in the sense of splendour, and by the kindred word *tzohar*, light. In this way we obtain the suitable thought, land which has neither sunlight nor rain in the day of wrath, *i.e.* does not enjoy a single trace of the divine blessing, but is given up to the curse of barrenness. The reason for this threat is given in vers. 25 sqq., where a picture is drawn of the moral corruption of all ranks; viz. of the prophets (ver. 25), the priests (ver. 26), the princes (ver. 27), and the common people (ver. 29). There is something very striking in the allusion to the prophets in ver. 25, not so much because they are mentioned again in ver. 28,—for this may be accounted for on the ground that in the latter passage they are simply introduced as false advisers of the princes,—as on account of the statement made concerning them in ver. 25, namely, that, like lions tearing their prey, they devour souls, etc.; a description which is not given either in chap. xiii. or elsewhere. Hitzig therefore proposes to alter נְבִיאֶיהָ into נְשִׂיאֶיהָ, after the rendering ἀφηγούμενοι given by the LXX. This alteration of the text, which confines itself to a single letter, is rendered very plausible by the fact that almost the same is affirmed of the persons mentioned in ver. 25 as of the princes in ver. 27, and that in the passage in Zephaniah (iii. 3, 4), which is so similar to the one before us, that Ezekiel appears to have had it in his mind, the princes (שָׂרֶיהָ) and the judges (שֹׁפְטֶיהָ) are called the prophets and the priests. The נְשִׂיאִים here would correspond to the שָׂרִים of Zephaniah, and the שָׂרִים to the שֹׁפְטִים. According to ver. 6, the נְשִׂיאִים would indicate primarily the members of the royal family, possibly including the chief officers of the crown; and the שָׂרִים (ver. 27) would be the heads of tribes, of families, and of fathers' houses, in whose hands the national administration of justice principally lay (cf. Ex. xviii. 19 sqq.; Deut. i. 13–18; and my *Bibl. Archäol.* ii. § 149). I therefore prefer this conjecture, or correction, to the Masoretic reading, although the latter is supported by ancient witnesses, such as the Chaldee with its rendering סַפְרַיָּא, scribes, and the version of Jerome. For the statement which the verse contains is not applicable to prophets, and the best explanation given of the Masoretic text—namely, that by Michaelis, "they have made a compact with one another as to what kind of teaching they would or would not give; and in order that their authority may continue undisturbed, they persecute even to blood those who do not act with them, or obey them, but rather contradict"—does not do justice to the words, but weakens their sense. קֶשֶׁר is not a predicate to 'נב, "they are (*i.e.* form) a conspiracy;" but 'נב is a genitive. At the same time, there is no necessity to take קֶשֶׁר in the sense of "company," a rendering which cannot be sustained. The fact that in what follows, where the comparison to lions is introduced, the נביאים (נשיאים) are the subject, simply proves that in the first clause also these men actually form the prominent idea. There is no ground for supplying הֵמָּה to כַּאֲרִי וגו' (they are like, etc.); but the simile is to be linked on to the following clause. נֶפֶשׁ אָכָלוּ is to be explained from the comparison to a lion, which devours the prey that it has captured in its blood, in which is the soul, or *nephesh* (Gen.

ix. 4; Lev. xvii. 11 sqq.). The thought is this: in their insatiable greed for riches they sacrifice men and put them to death, and thereby multiply the number of victims (for the fact, see chap. xix. 5, 7). What is stated in ver. 26 concerning the priests is simply a further expansion of Zeph. iii. 4, where the first two clauses occur word for word; for קֹדֶשׁ in Zephaniah is really equivalent to קָדָשִׁי, holy things and deeds. The desecration of the holy things consisted in the fact that they made no distinction between sacred and profane, clean and unclean. For the fact, compare Lev. x. 10, 11. Their covering their eyes from the Sabbaths showed itself in their permitting the Sabbaths to be desecrated by the people, without offering any opposition (cf. Jer. xvii. 27).—The comparison of the rulers (*sārim*) to ravening wolves is taken from Zeph. iii. 3. For the following clause, compare ver. 12 and ch. xiii. 10. Destroying souls to acquire gain is perfectly applicable to unjust judges, inasmuch as, according to Ex. xviii. 21, the judges were to hate בֶּצַע. All that is affirmed in ver. 28 of the conduct of the false prophets is repeated for the most part *verbatim* from ch. xiii. 10, 9, and 7. By לָהֶם, which points back to the three classes of men already mentioned, and not merely to the *sārim*, the prophets are represented as helpers of those who support the ungodly in their wicked ways, by oracles which assured them of prosperity. עַם הָאָרֶץ (ver. 29), as distinguished from the spiritual and secular rulers of the nation, signifies the common people. With reference to their sins and wickedness, see ch. xviii. 7, 12, 18; and for the command against oppressing the poor and foreigners, compare Ex. xxii. 20, 21; Deut. xxiv. 17.—The corruption is so universal, that not a man is to be found who could enter into the gap as a righteous man, or avert the judgment of destruction by his intercession. מֵהֶם refers not merely to the prophets, who did not enter into the gap according to ch. xiii. 5, but to all the classes previously mentioned. At the same time, it does not follow from this, that entering into the gap by means of intercession cannot be the thing intended, as Hitzig supposes. The expression לִפְנֵי בְעַד הָאָרֶץ clearly refers to intercession. This is apparent from the simple fact that, as Hitzig himself observes, the intercession of Abraham for Sodom (Gen. xviii. 13 sqq.) was floating before the mind of Ezekiel, since the concluding words of the verse contain an obvious allusion to Gen. xviii. 28. Because the Lord does not find a single righteous man, who might intercede for the land, He pours out His anger upon it, to destroy the inhabitants thereof. With reference to the fact and the separate words employed, compare ch. xxi. 36, vii. 4, ix. 10, xi. 21, and xvi. 43. It does not follow from the word וָאֶשְׁפֹּךְ, that Ezekiel "is speaking after the catastrophe" (Hitzig). For although וָאֶשְׁפֹּךְ expresses the consequence of Jehovah's seeking a righteous man and not finding one, it by no means follows from the occurrence of the preterite וְלֹא מָצָאתִי that וָאֶשְׁפֹּךְ is also a preterite. וָאֶשְׁפֹּךְ is simply connected with וָאֲבַקֵּשׁ as a consequence; and in both verbs the *Vav consec.* expresses the sequence of thought, and not of time. The seeking, therefore, with the result of not having found, cannot be understood in a chronological sense, *i.e.* as an event belonging to the past, for the simple reason that the preceding words do not record the chronological order of events. It merely depicts the existing moral condition of the people, and ver. 30 sums up the result of the description in the thought that there was no one to be found who could enter in the gap before God. Consequently we cannot determine from the imperfect with *Vav consec.* either the time of the seeking and not finding, or that of the pouring out of the wrath.

CHAP. XXIII. OHOLAH AND OHOLIBAH, THE HARLOTS SAMARIA AND JERUSALEM.

Samaria and Jerusalem, as the capitals and representatives of the two kingdoms Israel and Judah, are two sisters, who have practised whoredom from the days of Egypt onwards (vers. 2–4). Samaria has carried on this whoredom with Assyria and Egypt, and has been given up by God into the power of the Assyrians as a consequent punishment (vers. 5–10). But Jerusalem, instead of allowing this to serve as a warning, committed fornication still more grievously with Assyria and the Chaldeans, and, last of all, with Egypt again (vers. 11–21). In consequence of this, the Lord will permit the Chaldeans to make war upon them, and to plunder and put them to shame, so that, as a punishment for their whoredom and their forgetfulness of God, they may, in the fullest measure, experience Samaria's fate (vers. 22–35). In conclusion, both kingdoms are shown once more, and in still severer terms, the guilt of their idolatry (vers. 36–44), whilst the infliction of the punishment for both adultery and murder is foretold (vers. 45–49).

In its general character, therefore, this word of God is coordinate with the two preceding ones in ch. xxi. and xxii., setting forth once more in a comprehensive way the sins and the punishment of Israel. But this is done in the form of an allegory, which closely resembles in its general features the allegorical description in ch. xvi.; though, in the particular details, it possesses a character peculiarly its own, not only in certain original turns and figures, but still more in the arrangement and execution of the whole. The allegory in ch. xvi. depicts the attitude of Israel towards the Lord in the past, the present, and the future; but in the chapter before us, the guilt and punishment of Israel stand in the foreground of the picture throughout, so that a parallel is drawn between Jerusalem and Samaria, to show that the punishment of destruction, which Samaria has brought upon itself through its adulterous intercourse with the heathen, will inevitably fall upon Jerusalem and Judah also.

Vers. 1–4. The sisters Oholah and Oholibah.—Ver. 1. *And the word of Jehovah came to me, saying,* Ver. 2. *Son of man, two women, daughters of one mother were they,* Ver. 3. *They committed whoredom in Egypt, in their youth they committed whoredom; there were their breasts pressed, and there men handled their virgin bosom.* Ver. 4. *Their names are Oholah, the greater, and Oholibah her sister; and they became mine, and bare sons and daughters. But their names are: Samaria is Oholah, and Jerusalem is Oholibah.*—The name אָהֳלִיבָה is formed from אָהֳלִי בָהּ, "my tent in her;" and, accordingly, אָהֳלָה is to be derived from אָהֳלָהּ, "her tent," and not to be regarded as an abbreviation of אָהֳלָהּ בָּהּ, "her tent in her," as Hitzig and Kliefoth maintain. There is no ground for this assumption, as "her tent," in contrast with "my tent in her," expresses the thought with sufficient clearness, that she had a tent of her own, and the place where her tent was does not come into consideration. The "tent" is the sanctuary: both tabernacle and temple. These names characterize the two kingdoms according to their attitude toward the Lord. Jerusalem had the sanctuary of Jehovah; Samaria, on the other hand, had her own sanctuary, *i.e.* one invented by herself. Samaria and Jerusalem, as the historical names of the two kingdoms, represent Israel of the ten tribes and Judah. Oholah and Oholibah are daughters of one mother, because they were the two halves of the one Israel; and they are called women, because Jehovah had married them (ver. 4). Oholah is called הַגְּדוֹלָה, the great, *i.e.* greater sister (not the elder, see the comm. on ch. xvi. 46); because ten tribes, the greater portion of Israel, belonged to Samaria, whereas Judah had only two tribes. They committed whoredom even in Egypt in their youth, for even in Egypt the Israelites defiled themselves with Egyptian idolatry (see the comm. on ch. xx. 7). מִיעֵךְ, to press, to crush: the *Pual* is used here to denote lewd handling. In a similar manner the *Piel* עִשָּׂה is used to signify *tractare, contrectare mammas*, in an obscene sense.

Vers. 5–10. Samaria's whoredom and punishment.—Ver. 5. *And Oholibah played the harlot under me, and burned towards her lovers, even as far as Assyria, standing near;* Ver. 6. *Clothed in purple, governors and officers, all of them choice men of good deportment, horsemen riding upon horses.* Ver. 7. *And she directed her whoredom toward them, to the choice of the sons of Assyria all of them, and with all towards whom she burned, with all their idols she defiled herself.* Ver. 8. *Also her whoredom from Egypt she did not give up; for they had lain with her in her youth, and they had handled her virgin bosom, and had poured out their lust upon her.* Ver. 9. *Therefore I have given her into the hand of her lovers, into the hand of the sons of Assyria, towards whom she was inflamed.* Ver. 10. *They uncovered her nakedness, took away her sons and her daughters, and slew her with the sword, so that she became a legend among the women, and executed judgments upon her.*—Coquetting and whoring with Assyria and Egypt denote religious and political leaning towards and connection with these nations and kingdoms, including idolatry and the formation of alliances with them, as in chap. xvi. תַּחְתַּי is to be interpreted in accordance with תַּחַת אִישָׁהּ (ch. xvi. 32). עָגַב, which only occurs in Ezekiel and once in Jeremiah, denotes the eager desire kindled by passionate love towards any one. By the words אֶל־אַשּׁוּר the lovers are more precisely defined. קְרוֹבִים without an article is not an adjective, belonging to מְאַהֲבֶיהָ, but in apposition, which is continued in the next verse. In these appositions the particular features, which excited the ardent passion towards the lovers, are pointed out. קָרוֹב is not to be taken in an outward or local sense, but as signifying inward or spiritual nearness: standing near, equivalent to inwardly related, as in Ps. xxxviii. 12; Job xix. 14. The description given of the Assyrians in ver. 6 contains the thought that Israel, dazzled by Assyria's splendour, and overpowered by the might of that kingdom, had been drawn into intercourse with the Assyrians, which led her astray into idolatry. The predicate, clothed in purple, points to the splendour and glory of this imperial power; the other predicates, to the magnitude of its military force. פַּחוֹת וּסְגָנִים are rulers of higher and lower grades (cf. Jer. li. 57). "Here the expression is a general one, signifying the different classes of office-bearers in the kingdom" (Hävernick). With regard to פֶּחָה, see my comm. on Hag. i. 1; and for סָגָן, see Delitzsch on Isa. xli. 25. "Riding upon horses" is added to פָּרָשִׁים to denote the noblest horsemen, in contrast to riders upon asses and camels (cf. Isa. xxi. 7). In ver. 7*b* בְּכָל־גִּלּוּלֵיהֶם is in apposition to בְּכֹל אֲשֶׁר־עָגְבָה, and defines more precisely the instigation to pollution: with all towards whom she burned in love, namely, with all their (the lovers') idols. The thought is as follows: it was not merely through her intercourse with the Assyrians that Israel defiled herself, but also through their idols. At the same time, Samaria did not give up the idolatry which it had derived from Egypt. It was from Egypt that the worship of God under the image of the golden calves had been imported. The words are much too strong for us to understand them as relating simply to political intercourse, as Hitzig has done. We have already observed at ch. xx. 7, that even in Egypt itself the Israelites had defiled themselves with Egyptian idolatry, as is also stated in ver. 8*b*.—Vers. 9, 10. As a punishment for this, God gave Samaria into the power of the Assyrians, so that they executed judgment upon the harlot. In ver. 10*b* the prophecy passes from the figure to the fact. The uncovering of the nakedness consisted in the transportation of the sons and daughters, *i.e.* the population of Samaria, into exile by the Assyrians, who slew the woman herself with the sword; in other words, destroyed the kingdom of Samaria. Thus did Samaria become a name for women; that is to say, her name was circulated among the nations, her fate became an object of conversation and ridicule to the nations, not "a nickname for the nations," as Hävernick supposes (*vid.* ch. xxxvi. 3). שְׁפוּטִים, a later form for שְׁפָטִים (cf. ch. xvi. 41).

Vers. 11–21. Whoredom of Judah.—Ver. 11. *And her sister Oholibah saw it, and carried on her coquetry still more wantonly than she had done, and her whoredom more than the whoredom of her sister.* Ver. 12. *She was inflamed with lust towards the sons of Asshur, governors and officers, standing near, clothed in perfect beauty, horsemen riding upon horses, choice men of good deportment.* Ver. 13. *And I saw that she had defiled herself; they both went one way.* Ver. 14. *And she carried her whoredom still further; she saw men engraved upon the wall, figures of Chaldeans engraved with red ochre,* Ver. 15. *Girded about the hips with girdles, with overhanging caps upon their heads, all of them knights in appearance, resembling the sons of Babel, the land of whose birth is Chaldea:* Ver. 16. *And she was inflamed with lust toward them, when her eyes saw them, and sent messengers to them to Chaldea.* Ver. 17. *Then the sons of Babylon came to her to the bed of love, and defiled her with their whoredom; and when she had defiled herself with them, her soul tore itself away from them.* Ver. 18. *And when she uncovered her whoredom, and uncovered her nakedness, my soul tore itself away from her, as my soul had torn itself away from her sister.* Ver. 19. *And she increased her whoredom, so that she remembered the days of her youth, when she played the harlot in the land of Egypt.* Ver. 20. *And she burned toward their paramours, who have members like asses and heat like horses.* Ver. 21. *Thou lookest after the lewdness of thy youth, when they of Egypt handled thy bosom because of thy virgin breasts.*—The train of thought in these verses is the following:—Judah went much further than Samaria. It not only indulged in sinful intercourse with Assyria, which led on to idolatry as the latter had done, but it also allowed itself to be led astray by the splendour of Chaldea, to form alliances with that imperial power, and to defile itself with her idolatry. And when it became tired of the Chaldeans, it formed impure connections with the Egyptians, as it had done once before during its sojourn in Egypt. The description of the Assyrians in ver. 12 coincides with that in vers. 5 and 6, except that some of the predicates are placed in a different order, and לְבֻשֵׁי מִכְלוֹל is substituted for לְבֻשֵׁי תְכֵלֶת. The former expression, which occurs again in ch. xxxviii. 4, must really mean the same as לב׳ תְכֵלֶת. But it does not follow from this that מִכְלוֹל signifies purple, as

Hitzig maintains. The true meaning is perfection; and when used of the clothing, it signifies perfect beauty. The Septuagint rendering, εὐπάρυφα, with a beautiful border,—more especially a variegated one,—merely expresses the sense, but not the actual meaning of מִכְלוֹל. The Chaldee rendering is לבשׁי גמר, *perfecte induti.*—There is great obscurity in the statement in ver. 14 as to the way in which Judah was seduced to cultivate intercourse with the Chaldeans. She saw men engraved or drawn upon the wall (מְחֻקֶּה, a participle *Pual* of חָקַק, engraved work, or sculpture). These figures were pictures of Chaldeans, engraved (drawn) with שָׁשַׁר, red ochre, a bright-red colour. חֲגוֹרֵי, an adjective form חָגוֹר, wearing a girdle. טְבוּלִים, coloured cloth, from טָבַל, to colour; here, according to the context, variegated head-bands or turbans. סְרוּחַ, the overhanging, used here of the cap. The reference is to the *tiarae tinctae* (Vulgate), the lofty turbans or caps, as they are to be seen upon the monuments of ancient Nineveh. שָׁלִישִׁים, not chariot-warriors, but knights: "*tristatae*, the name of the second grade after the regal dignity" (Jerome. See the comm. on Ex. xiv. 7 and 2 Sam. xxiii. 8). The description of these engravings answers perfectly to the sculptures upon the inner walls of the Assyrian palaces in the monuments of Nimrud, Khorsabad, and Kouyunjik (see Layard's *Nineveh and its Remains*, and Vaux, *Nineveh and Persepolis*). The pictures of the Chaldeans are not mythological figures (Hävernick), but sculptures depicting war-scenes, triumphal processions of Chaldean rulers and warriors, with which the Assyrian palaces were adorned. We have not to look for these sculptures in Jerusalem or Palestine. This cannot be inferred from ch. viii. 10, as Hävernick supposes; nor established by Hitzig's argument, that the woman must have been in circumstances to see such pictures. The intercourse between Palestine and Nineveh, which was carried on even in Jonah's time, was quite sufficient to render it possible for the pictures to be seen. When Israelites travelled to Nineveh, and saw the palaces there, they could easily make the people acquainted with the glory of Nineveh by the accounts they would give on their return. It is no reply to this, to state that the woman does not send ambassadors till afterwards (ver. 16), as Hitzig argues; for Judah sent ambassadors to Chaldea not to view the glories of Assyria, but to form alliances with the Chaldeans, or to sue for their favour. Such an embassy, for example, was sent to Babylon by Zedekiah (Jer. xxix. 3); and there is no doubt that in ver. 16*b* Ezekiel has this in his mind. Others may have preceded this, concerning which the books of Kings and Chronicles are just as silent as they are concerning that of Zedekiah. The thought in these verses is therefore the following:—The acquaintance made by Israel (Judah) with the imperial splendour of the Chaldeans, as exhibited in the sculptures of their palaces, incited Judah to cultivate political and mercantile intercourse with this imperial power, which led to its becoming entangled in the heathen ways and idolatry of the Chaldeans. The Chaldeans themselves came and laid the foundation for an intercourse which led to the pollution of Judah with heathenism, and afterwards filled it with disgust, because it was brought thereby into dependence upon the Chaldeans. The consequence of all this was, that the Lord became tired of Judah (vers. 17, 18). For instead of returning to the Lord, Judah turned to the other power of the world, namely, to Egypt; and in the time of Zedekiah renewed its ancient coquetry with that nation (vers. 19–21 compared with ver. 8). The form וַתַּעְגְּבָה in ver. 20, which the *Keri* also gives in ver. 18, has taken *ah* as a feminine termination (not the cohortative *ah*), like תָּרֹנָּה in Prov. i. 20, viii. 1 (*vid.* Delitzsch, *On Job*, pp. 117 and 268). פִּלַגְשִׁים are *scorta mascula* here (Kimchi),—a drastically sarcastic epithet applied to the *sârisim*, the eunuchs, or courtiers. The figurative epithet answers to the licentious character of the Egyptian idolatry. The sexual heat both of horses and asses is referred to by Aristotle, *Hist. anim.* vi. 22, and Columella, *de re rust.* vi. 27; and that of the horse has already been applied to the idolatry of the people by Jeremiah (*vid.* Jer. v. 8). בְּשַׂר, as in ch. xvi. 26. פָּקַד (ver. 21), to look about for anything, *i.e.* to search for it; not to miss it, as Hävernick imagines.

Vers. 22–35. Punishment of the harlot Jerusalem.—Ver. 22. *Therefore, Oholibah, thus saith the Lord Jehovah, Behold, I raise up thy lovers against thee, from whom thy soul has torn itself away, and cause them to come upon thee from every side;* Ver. 23. *The sons of Babel, and all the Chaldeans, rulers, lords, and nobles, all the sons of Assyria with them: chosen men of graceful deportment, governors and officers together, knights and counsellors, all riding upon horses.* Ver. 24. *And they will come upon thee with weapons, chariots, and wheels, and with a host of peoples; target and shield and helmet will they direct against thee round about: and I commit to them the judgment, that they may judge thee according to their rights.* Ver. 25. *And I direct my jealousy against thee, so that they shall deal with thee in wrath: nose and ears will they cut off from thee; and thy last one shall fall by the sword: they will take thy sons and thy daughters; and thy last one will be consumed by fire.* Ver. 26. *They will strip off thy clothes from thee, and take thy splendid jewellery.* Ver. 27. *I will abolish thy lewdness from thee, and thy whoredom from the land of Egypt: that thou mayest no more lift thine eyes to them, and no longer remember Egypt.* Ver. 28. *For thus saith the Lord Jehovah, Behold, I give thee into the hand of those whom thou hatest, into the hand of those from whom thy soul has torn itself away:* Ver. 29. *And they shall deal with thee in hatred, and take all thy gain, and leave thee naked and bare; that thy whorish shame may be uncovered, and thy lewdness and thy whoredom.* Ver. 30. *This shall happen to thee, because thou goest whoring after the nations, and on account of thy defiling thyself with their idols.* Ver. 31. *In the way of thy sister hast thou walked; therefore I give her cup into thy hand.* Ver. 32. *Thus saith the Lord Jehovah, The cup of thy sister thou shalt drink, the deep and broad one; it will be for laughter and for derision, because it contains so much.* Ver. 33. *Thou wilt become full of drunkenness and misery: a cup of desolation and devastation is the cup of thy sister Samaria.* Ver. 34. *Thou wilt drink it up and drain it, and gnaw its fragments, and tear thy breasts (therewith); for I have spoken it, is the saying of the Lord Jehovah.* Ver. 35. *Therefore thus saith the Lord Jehovah, Because thou hast forgotten me, and hast cast me behind thy back, thou shalt also bear thy lewdness and thy whoredom.*—As Jerusalem has given herself up to whoredom, like her sister Samaria, she shall also share her sister's fate. The paramours, of whom she has become tired, God will bring against her as enemies. The Chaldeans will come with all their might, and execute the judgment of destruction upon her.—For the purpose of depicting their great and powerful forces, Ezekiel enumerates in vers. 23 and 24 the peoples and their military equipment: viz. the sons of Babel, *i.e.* the inhabitants of Babylonia, the Chaldeans,—the ruling people of the empire at that time,—and all the sons of Asshur, *i.e.* the inhabitants of the eastern portions of the empire, the former rulers of the world. There is some obscurity in the words פְּקוֹד וְשׁוֹעַ וְקוֹעַ, which the older theologians have almost unanimously taken to be the names of different tribes in the Chaldean empire. Ewald also adopts this view, but it is certainly incorrect; for the words are in apposition to וְכָל־כַּשְׂדִּים, as the omission of the copula ו before פְּקוֹד is sufficient to show. This is confirmed by the fact that שׁוֹעַ is used, in Isa. xxxii. 5 and Job xxxiv. 19, in the sense of the man of high rank, distinguished for his prosperity, which is quite in harmony with the passage before us. Consequently פְּקוֹד is not to be taken in the sense of visitation or punishment, after Jer. l. 21; but the meaning is to be sought in the verb פָּקַד, to exercise supervision, or lead; and the abstract oversight is used for overseer, or ruler, as an equivalent to פָּקִיד. Lastly, according to Rabbins, the Vulgate, and others, קוֹעַ signifies princes, or nobles. The predicates in ver. 23*b* are repeated from vers. 6

and 12, and קְרוּאִים alone is added. This is a word taken from the Pentateuch, where the heads of the tribes and families, as being members of the council of the whole congregation of Israel, are called קְרוּאֵי הָעֵדָה or קְרוּאֵי מוֹעֵד, persons called or summoned to the meeting (Num. i. 16, xvi. 2). As Michaelis has aptly observed, "he describes them sarcastically in the very same way in which he had previously described those upon whom she doted."—There is a difficulty in explaining the ἀπ. λεγ. הֹצֶן,—for which many MSS. read חֹצֶן,—as regards not only its meaning, but its position in the sentence. The fact that it is associated with רֶכֶב וְגַלְגַּל would seem to indicate that הֹצֶן is also either an implement of war or some kind of weapon. At the same time, the words cannot be the subject to וּבָאוּ; but as the expression וּבִקְהַל עַמִּים, which follows, clearly shows, they simply contain a subordinate definition of the manner in which, or the things with which, the peoples mentioned in vers. 23, 24 will come, while they are governed by the verb in the freest way. The attempts which Ewald and Hitzig have made to remove the difficulty, by means of conjectures, are forced and extremely improbable. נָתַתִּי לִפְנֵיהֶם, I give up to them (not, I place before them); נָתַן לִפְנֵי, as in 1 Kings viii. 46, to deliver up, or give a thing into a person's hand or power. לִפְנֵי is used in this sense in Gen. xiii. 9 and xxiv. 51.—In vers. 25, 26, the execution of the judgment is depicted in detail. The words, "they take away thy nose and ears," are not to be interpreted, as the earlier expositors suppose, from the custom prevalent among the Egyptians and other nations of cutting off the nose of an adulteress; but depict, by one particular example, the mutilation of prisoners captured by their enemies. אַחֲרִית: not posterity, which by no means suits the last clause of the verse, and cannot be defended from the usage of the language (see the comm. on Amos iv. 2); but the last, according to the figure employed in the first clause, the trunk; or, following the second clause, the last thing remaining in Jerusalem, after the taking away of the sons and daughters, *i.e.* after the slaying and the deportation of the inhabitants,—viz. the empty houses. For ver. 26, compare ch. xvi. 39.—In ver. 27, "from the land of Egypt" is not equivalent to "dating from Egypt;" for according to the parallel מִמֵּךְ, from thee, this definition does not belong to זְנוּתֵךְ, "thy whoredom," but to הִשְׁבַּתִּי, "I cause thy whoredom to cease from Egypt" (Hitzig).—For ver. 28*a*, compare ch. xvi. 37; for ver. 28*b*, *vid.* ver. 17 above; and for ver. 29, see vers. 25 and 26, and ch. xvi. 39.—Ver. 31 looks back to ver. 13; and ver. 31*b* is still further expanded in vers. 32–34. Judah shall drink the cup of the wrathful judgment of God, as Samaria has done. For the figure of the cup, compare Isa. li. 17 and Jer. xxv. 15. This cup is described in ver. 32 as deep and wide, *i.e.* very capacious, so that whoever exhausts all its contents must be thoroughly intoxicated. תִּהְיֶה is the third person; but the subject is מִרְבָּה, and not כּוֹס. The greatness or breadth of the cup will be a subject of laughter and ridicule. It is very arbitrary to supply "*to thee*," so as to read: will be for laughter and ridicule to thee, which does not even yield a suitable meaning, since it is not Judah but the nations who laugh at the cup. Others regard תִּהְיֶה as the second person, thou wilt become; but apart from the anomaly in the gender, as the masculine would stand for the feminine, Hitzig has adduced the forcible objection, that according to this view the words would not only anticipate the explanation given of the figure in the next verse, but would announce the consequences of the שִׁכָּרוֹן וְיָגוֹן mentioned there. Hitzig therefore proposes to erase the words from תִּהְיֶה to וּלְלַעַג as a gloss, and to alter מִרְבָּה into מַרְבָּה: which contains much, is very capacious. But there is not sufficient reason to warrant such critical violence as this. Although the form מִרְבָּה is ἁπ. λεγ., it is not to be rejected as a *nomen subst.*; and if we take מִרְבָּה לְהָכִיל, the magnitude to hold, as the subject of the sentence, it contains a still further description of the cup, which does not anticipate what follows, even though the cup will be an object of laughter and ridicule, not so much for its size, as because of its being destined to be drunk completely empty. In ver. 33 the figure and the fact are combined,—יָגוֹן, lamentation, misery, being added to שִׁכָּרוֹן, drunkenness, and the cup being designated a cup of devastation. The figure of drinking is expanded in the boldest manner in ver. 34 into the gnawing of the fragments of the cup, and the tearing of the breasts with the fragments.—In ver. 35 the picture of the judgment is closed with a repetition of the description of the nation's guilt. For ver. 35*b*, compare ch. xvi. 52 and 58.

Vers. 36–49. Another summary of the sins and punishment of the two women.—Ver. 36. *And Jehovah said to me, Son of man, wilt thou judge Oholah and Oholibah, then show them their abominations;* Ver. 37. *For they have committed adultery, and blood is in their hands; and they have committed adultery with their idols; and their sons also whom they bare to me they have caused to pass through to them to be devoured.* Ver. 38. *Yea more, they have done this to me; they have defiled my sanctuary the same day, and have desecrated my Sabbaths.* Ver. 39. *When they slaughtered their sons to their idols, they came into my sanctuary the same day to desecrate it; and, behold, they have acted thus in the midst of my house.* Ver. 40. *Yea, they have even sent to men coming from afar; to them was a message sent, and, behold, they came, for whom thou didst bathe thyself, paint thine eyes, and put on ornaments,* Ver. 41. *And didst seat thyself upon a splendid cushion, and a table was spread before them, thou didst lay thereon my incense and my oil.* Ver. 42. *And the loud noise became still thereat, and to the men out of the multitude there were brought topers out of the desert, and they put armlets upon their hands, and glorious crowns upon their heads.* Ver. 43. *Then I said to her who was debilitated for adultery, Now will her whoredom itself go whoring,* Ver. 44. *And they will go in to her as they go in to a whore; so did they go in to Oholah and Oholibah, the lewd women.* Ver. 45. *But righteous men, these shall judge them according to the judgment of adulteresses and according to the judgment of murderesses; for they are adulter-*

esses, and there is blood in their hands. Ver. 46. *For thus saith the Lord Jehovah, I will bring up against them an assembly, and deliver them up for maltreating and for booty.* Ver. 47. *And the assembly shall stone them, and cut them in pieces with their swords; their sons and their daughters shall they kill, and burn their houses with fire.* Ver. 48. *Thus will I eradicate lewdness from the land, that all women may take warning and not practise lewdness like you.* Ver. 49. *And they shall bring your lewdness upon you, and ye shall bear the sins of your idols, and shall learn that I am the Lord Jehovah.*—The introductory words הֲתִשְׁפּוֹט וגו׳ point back not only to ch. xxii. 2, but also to ch. xx. 4, and show that this section is really a summary of the contents of the whole group (ch. xx. 23). The actual subject-matter of these verses is closely connected with ver. 16, more especially in the designation of the sins as adultery and bloodshed (compare vers. 37 and 45 with ch. xvi. 38). נִאֵף אֶת־גל׳, to commit adultery with the idols, whereby the idols are placed on a par with Jehovah as the husband of Israel (compare Jer. iii. 8 and ii. 27). For the Moloch-worship in ver. 37*b*, compare ch. xvi. 20, 21, and ch. xx. 31. The desecration of the sanctuary (ver. 38*a*) is more minutely defined in ver. 39. בַּיּוֹם הַהוּא in ver. 38, which has so offended the LXX. and Hitzig that it is omitted by the former, while the latter proposes to strike it out as a gloss, is added for the purpose of designating the profanation of the sanctuary as contemporaneous with the Moloch-worship of ver. 37*b*, as is evident from ver. 39. For the fact itself, compare 2 Kings xxi. 4, 5, 7. The desecration of the Sabbaths, as in ch. xx. 13, 16. For ver. 39*a*, compare ch. xvi. 21. The words are not to be understood as signifying that they sacrificed children to Moloch in the temple, but simply that immediately after they had sacrificed children to Moloch, they went into the temple of Jehovah, that there they might worship Jehovah also, and thus placed Jehovah upon a par with Moloch. This was a profanation (חִלֵּל) of His sanctuary.

In vers. 40–44 the allusion is not to actual idolatry, but to the ungodly alliance into which Judah had entered with Chaldea. Judah sent ambassadors to Chaldea, and for the purpose of receiving the Chaldeans, adorned herself as a woman would do for the reception of her paramours. She seated herself upon a splendid divan, and in front of this there was a table spread, upon which stood the incense and the oil that she ought to have offered to Jehovah. This is the explanation which Kliefoth has correctly given of vers. 40 and 41. The emphatic וְאַף כִּי in ver. 40 is sufficient to show that the reference is to a new crime deserving of punishment. This cannot be idolatry, because the worship of Moloch has already been mentioned in vers. 38 and 39 as the worst of all the idolatrous abominations. Moreover, sending for (or to) men who come from afar does not apply to idolatry in the literal sense of the word; for men to whom the harlot sent messengers to invite them to come to her could not be idols for which she sent to a distant land. The allusion is rather to Assyrians or Chaldeans, and, according to ver. 42, it is the former who are referred to here (compare Isa. xxxix. 3). There is no force in Hitzig's objection, namely, that the one woman sent to these, and that their being sent for and coming have already been disposed of in ver. 16. For the singulars in the last clause of ver. 40 show that even here only one woman is said to have sent for the men. Again, תִּשְׁלַחְנָה might even be the third person singular, as this form does sometimes take the termination נָה (*vid.* Ewald, § 191*c*, and Ges. § 47, Anm. 3). At the same time, there is nothing in the fact that the sending to Chaldea has already been mentioned in ver. 16 to preclude another allusion to the same circumstance from a different point of view. The woman adorned herself that she might secure the favour of the men for whom she had sent. כָּחַל is the Arabic كحل, to paint the eyes with stibium (*kohol*). For the fact itself, see the remarks on 2 Kings ix. 30. She then seated herself upon a cushion (not lay down upon a bed; for יָשַׁב does not mean to lie down), and in front of this there was a table, spread with different kinds of food, upon which she placed incense and oil. The suffix to עָלֶיהָ refers to שֻׁלְחָן, and is to be taken as a neuter, which suits the table as a thing, whilst שֻׁלְחָן generally takes the termination וֹת in the plural. In ver. 41, Ewald and Hävernick detect a description of the *lectisternia* and of the licentious worship of the Babylonian Mylitta. But neither the sitting (יָשַׁב) upon a cushion (divan), nor the position taken by the woman behind the table, harmonizes with this. As Hitzig has correctly observed, "if she has taken her seat upon a cushion, and has a table spread before her, she evidently intends to dine, and that with the men for whom she has adorned herself. The oil is meant for anointing at meal-time (Amos vi. 6; Prov. xxi. 17; cf. Ps. xxiii. 5), and the incense for burning." "My incense and my oil" are the incense and oil given to her by God, which she ought to have devoted to His service, but had squandered upon herself and her foreign friends (cf. ch. xvi. 18; Hos. ii. 10). The oil, as the produce of the land of Palestine, was the gift of Jehovah; and although incense was not a production of Palestine, yet as the money with which Judah purchased it, or the goods bartered for it, were the gifts of God, Jehovah could also call it His incense. Ver. 42 is very obscure. Such renderings of the first clause as *et vox multitudinis exultantis in ea* (Vulg.), and "the voice of a careless multitude within her" (Hävernick), can hardly be sustained. In every other passage in which קוֹל הָמוֹן occurs, it does not signify the voice of a multitude, but a loud tumult; compare Isa. xiii. 4, xxxiii. 3, Dan. x. 6, and 1 Sam. iv. 14, where קוֹל הֶהָמוֹן is used as synonymous with קוֹל הַצְּעָקָה. Even in cases where הָמוֹן is used for a multitude, it denotes a noisy, boisterous, tumultuous crowd. Consequently שָׁלֵו cannot be taken as an adjective connected with הָמוֹן, because a quiet tumult is a contradiction, and שָׁלֵו does not mean either *exultans* or recklessly breaking loose (Hävernick), but simply living in quiet, peaceful and contented. שָׁלֵו must therefore be the predicate to קוֹל הָמוֹן; the sound of the tumult or the loud noise was (or became) quiet, still. בָּהּ, thereat (neuter, like בָּהּ, thereby, Gen. xxiv. 14). The words which follow, וְאֶל אֲנָשִׁים וגו׳, are not to be taken with the preceding clause, as the connection would yield no sense. They belong to what follows. אֲנָשִׁים מֵרֹב אָדָם can only be the men who came from afar (ver. 40). In addition to these, there were brought, *i.e.* induced to come, topers from the desert. The *Chetib* סובְאִים is no doubt a participle of סָבָא, drinkers, topers; and the *Hophal* מוּבָאִים is chosen instead of the *Kal* בָּאִים, for the sake of the paronomasia, with סוֹבָאִים. The former, therefore, can only be the Assyrians (בְּנֵי אַשּׁוּר, vers. 5 and 7), the latter (the topers) the Chaldeans (בְּנֵי בָבֶל, ver. 15). The epithet drinkers is a very appropriate one for the sons of Babylon; as Curtius (ver. 1) describes the Babylonians as *maxime in vinum et quae ebrietatem sequuntur effusi.* The phrase "from the desert" cannot indicate the home of these men, although מִמִּדְבָּר corresponds to מִמֶּרְחָק in ver. 40, but simply the place from which they came to Judah, namely, from the desert of Syria and Arabia, which separated Palestine from Babylon. These peoples decorated the arms of the harlots with clasps, and their heads with splendid wreaths (crowns). The plural suffixes indicate that the words apply to both women, and this is confirmed by the fact that they are both named in ver. 44. The subject to וַיִּתְּנוּ is not merely the סוֹבְאִים, but also the אֲנָשִׁים מִמֶּרְחָק in ver. 40. The thought is simply that Samaria and Judah had attained to wealth and earthly glory through their intercourse with these nations; the very gifts with which, according to ch. xvi. 11 sqq., Jehovah Himself had adorned His people. The meaning of the verse, therefore, when taken in its connection, appears to be the following:—When the Assyrians began to form alliances with Israel, quiet was the immediate result. The Chaldeans were afterwards added to these, so that through their adulterous intercourse with both these nations Israel and Judah acquired both wealth and glory. The sentence which God pronounced upon this conduct was, that Judah had sunk so deeply into adultery that it would be impossible for it ever to desist from the sin. This is the way in which we understand ver. 43, connecting לַבָּלָה נִאֻפִים with וָאֹמַר: "I said concerning her who was debilitated with whoredom." בָּלָה, feminine of בָּלֶה, used up, worn out; see, for example, Josh. ix. 4, 5, where it is applied to clothes; here it is transferred to persons decayed, debilitated, in which sense the verb occurs in Gen. xviii. 12. נִאֻפִים, which is co-ordinated with בָּלָה, does not indicate the means by which the strength has been exhausted, but is an accusative of direction or reference, debilitated with regard to adultery, so as no longer to be capable of practising it.[1] In the next clause 'עַתָּ יִזְנֶה וגו, תַּזְנוּתֶיהָ is the subject to יִזְנֶה, and the *Chetib* is correct, the *Keri* being erroneous, and the result of false exposition. If תזנותיה were the object to יִזְנֶה, so that the woman would be the subject, we should have the feminine תִּזְנֶה. But if, on the other hand, תזנותיה is the subject, there is no necessity for this, whether we regard the word as a plural, from תַּזְנוּתִים, or take it as a singular, as Ewald (§ 259*a*) has done, inasmuch as in either case it is still an abstract, which might easily be preceded by the verb in the masculine form. וָהִיא gives greater force, not only to the suffix, but also to the noun—and that even she (her whoredom). The sin of whoredom is personified, or regarded as רוּחַ זְנוּנִים (Hos. iv. 12), as a propensity to whoredom, which continues in all its force after the capacity of the woman herself is gone.—Ver. 44 contains the result of the foregoing description of the adulterous conduct of the two women, and this is followed in vers. 45 sqq. by an account of the attitude assumed by God, and the punishment of the sinful women. וַיָּבוֹא, with an indefinite subject, they (*man*, one) went to her. אֵלֶיהָ, the one woman,

[1] The proposal of Ewald to take לַבָּלָה נִאֻפִים as an independent clause, "adultery to the devil," cannot be defended by the usage of the language; and that of Hitzig, "the withered hag practises adultery," is an unnatural invention, inasmuch as לְ, if taken as *nota dativi*, would give this meaning: the hag has (possesses) adultery as her property—and there is nothing to indicate that it should be taken as a question.

Oholibah. It is only in the apodosis that what has to be said is extended to both women. This is the only interpretation of ver. 44 which does justice both to the verb וַיָּבוֹא (imperfect with *Vav consec.* as the historical tense) and the perfect בָּאוּ. The plural אִשֹּׁת does not occur anywhere else. Hitzig would therefore alter it into the singular, as "unheard of," and confine the attribute to Oholibah, who is the only one mentioned in the first clause of the verse, and also in vers. 43, 40, and 41. The judgment upon the two sisters is to be executed by righteous men (ver. 45). The Chaldeans are not designated as righteous in contrast to the Israelites, but as the instruments of the punitive righteousness of God in this particular instance, executing just judgment upon the sinners for adultery and bloodshed (*vid.* ch. xvi. 38). The infinitives הַעֲלֵה and נָתוֹן in ver. 46 stand for the third person future. For other points, compare the commentary on ch. xvi. 40 and 41. The formula נָתַן לְזַעֲוָה is derived from Deut. xxviii. 25, and has been explained in the exposition of that passage. וּבָרֵא is the *inf. abs. Piel.* For the meaning of the word, see the comm. on ch. xxi. 24. From this judgment all women, *i.e.* all nations, are to take warning to desist from idolatry. נִוַּסְּרוּ is a mixed form, compounded of the *Niphal* and *Hithpael,* for הִתְוַסְּרוּ, like נִכַּפֵּר in Deut. xxi. 8 (see the comm. *in loc.*).—For ver. 49, *vid.* ch. xvi. 58.—The punishment is announced to both the women, Israel and Judah, as still in the future, although Oholah (Samaria) had been overtaken by the judgment a considerable time before. The explanation of this is to be found in the allegory itself, in which both kingdoms are represented as being sisters of one mother; and it may also be defended on the ground that the approaching destruction of Jerusalem and the kingdom of Judah affected the remnants of the kingdom of the ten tribes, which were still to be found in Palestine; whilst, on the other hand, the judgment was not restricted to the destruction of the two kingdoms, but also embraced the later judgments which fell upon the entire nation.

CHAP. XXIV. PREDICTION OF THE DESTRUCTION OF JERUSALEM BOTH IN PARABLE AND BY SIGN.

On the day on which the king of Babylon commenced the siege and blockade of Jerusalem, this event was revealed by God to Ezekiel on the Chaboras (vers. 1 and 2); and he was commanded to predict to the people through the medium of a parable the fate of the city and its inhabitants (vers. 3–14). God then foretold to him the death of his own wife, and commanded him to show no sign of mourning on account of it. His wife died the following evening, and he did as he was commanded. When he was asked by the people the reason of this, he explained to them, that what he was doing was symbolical of the way in which they were to act when Jerusalem fell (vers. 15–24). The fall would be announced to the prophet by a fugitive, and then he would no longer remain mute, but would speak to the people again (vers. 25–27).—Apart, therefore, from the last three verses, this chapter contains two words of God, the first of which unfolds in a parable the approaching calamities, and the result of the siege of Jerusalem by the Chaldeans (vers. 1–14); whilst the second typifies by means of a sign the pain and mourning of Israel, namely, of the exiles at the destruction of the city with its sanctuary and its inhabitants. These two words of God, being connected together by their contents, were addressed to the prophet on the same day, and that, as the introduction (vers. 1 and 2) expressly observes, the day on which the siege of Jerusalem by the king of Babylon began.

Ver. 1. *And the word of Jehovah came to me in the ninth year, in the tenth month, on the tenth of the month, saying,* Ver. 2. *Son of man, write for thyself the name of the day, this same day! The king of Babylon has fallen upon Jerusalem this same day.*—The date given, namely, the tenth day of the tenth month of the ninth year after the carrying away of Jehoiachin (ch. i. 2), or what is the same thing, of the reign of Zedekiah, who was appointed king in his stead, is mentioned in Jer. lii. 4, xxxix. 1, and 2 Kings xxv. 1, as the day on which Nebuchadnezzar blockaded the city of Jerusalem by throwing up a rampart; and after the captivity this day was still kept as a fast-day in consequence (Zech. viii. 19). What was thus taking place at Jerusalem was revealed to Ezekiel on the Chaboras the very same day; and he was instructed to announce it to the exiles, "that they and the besieged might learn both from the time and the result, that the destruction of the city was not to be ascribed to chance or to the power of the Babylonians, but to the will of Him who had long ago foretold that, on account of the wickedness of the inhabitants, the city would be burned with fire; and that Ezekiel was a true prophet, because even when in Babylon, which was at so great a distance, he had known and had publicly announced the state of Jerusalem." The definite character of this prediction cannot be changed into a *vaticinium post eventum*, either by arbitrary explanations of the words, or by the unfounded hypothesis proposed by Hitzig, that the day was not set down in this definite form till after the event.—Writing the name of the day is equivalent to making a note of the day. The reason for this is given in ver. 2*b*, namely, because Nebuchadnezzar had fallen upon Jerusalem on that very day. סָמַךְ signifies to support, hold up (his hand); and hence both here and in Ps. lxxxviii. 8 the meaning to press violently upon anything. The rendering "to draw near," which has been forced upon the word from the Syriac (Ges., Winer, and others), cannot be sustained.

Vers. 3–14. Parable of the Pot with the Boiling Pieces.—Ver. 3. *And relate a parable to the rebellious house, and say to them, Thus saith the Lord Jehovah, Set on the pot, set on and also pour water into it.* Ver. 4. *Gather its pieces of flesh into it, all the good pieces, haunch and shoulder, fill it with choice bones.* Ver. 5. *Take the choice of the flock, and also a pile of wood underneath for the bones; make it boil well, also cook its bones therein.* Ver. 6. *Therefore, thus saith the Lord Jehovah, Woe! O city of murders! O pot in which is rust, and whose rust doth not depart from it; piece by piece fetch it out, the lot hath not fallen upon it.* Ver. 7. *For her blood is in the midst of her; she hath placed it upon the naked rock; she hath not poured it upon the ground, that they might cover it with dust.* Ver. 8. *To bring up fury, to take vengeance, I have made her blood come upon the naked rock, that it might not be covered.* Ver. 9. *Therefore thus saith the Lord Jehovah, Woe to the city of murders! I also will make the pile of wood great.* Ver. 10. *Heap up the wood, stir the fire, do the flesh thoroughly, make the broth boil, that the bones may also be cooked away.* Ver. 11. *And set it empty upon the coals thereof, that its brass may become hot and glowing, that the uncleanness thereof may melt within it, its rust pass away.* Ver. 12. *He hath exhausted the pains, and her great rust doth not go from her; into the fire with her rust!* Ver. 13. *In thine uncleanness is abomination; because I have cleansed thee, and thou hast not become clean, thou wilt no more become clean from thy uncleanness, till I quiet my fury upon thee.* Ver. 14. *I Jehovah have spoken it; it cometh, and I will do it; I will not cease, nor spare, nor let it repent me. According to thy ways, and according to thy deeds, shall they judge thee, is the saying of the Lord Jehovah.*

The contents of these verses are called מָשָׁל, a proverb or parable; and Ezekiel is to communicate them to the refractory generation. It follows from this that the ensuing act, which the prophet is commanded to perform, is not to be regarded as a symbolical act which he really carried out, but that the act forms the substance of the *mâshâl*, in other words, belongs to the parable itself. Consequently the interpretation of the parable in vers. 10 sqq. is clothed in the form of a thing actually done. The pot with the pieces of flesh and the bones, which are to be boiled in it and boiled away, represents Jerusalem with its inhabitants. The fire, with which they are boiled, is the fire of war, and the setting of the pot upon the fire is the commencement of the siege, by which the population of the city is to be boiled away like the flesh and bones in a pot. שְׁפֹת is used, as in 2 Kings iv. 38, to signify the setting of a pot by or upon the fire. אֱסֹף וגו׳: put in its pieces all together. נְתָחֶיהָ, its pieces of flesh, *i.e.* the pieces belonging to the cooking-pot. These are defined still more minutely as the best of the pieces of flesh, and of these the thigh (haunch) and shoulder are mentioned as the most important pieces, to which the choicest of the bones are to be added. This is rendered still more emphatic by the further instruction to take the choice of the flock in addition to these. The choicest pieces of flesh and the pieces of bone denote the strongest and ablest portion of the population of the city. To boil these pieces away, more especially the bones, a large fire is requisite. This is indicated by the words, "and also a pile of wood underneath for the bones." דּוּר in ver. 5, for which מְדוּרָה is substituted in ver. 9, signifies a pile of wood, and occurs in this sense in Isa. xxx. 33, from דּוּר, to lay round, to arrange, pile up. דּוּר הָעֲצָמִים cannot mean a heap of bones, on account of the article, but simply a pile of wood for the (previously mentioned) bones, namely, for the purpose of boiling them away. If we pay attention to the article, we shall see that the supposition that Ezekiel was to place a heap of bones under the pot, and the alteration proposed by Böttcher, Ewald, and Hitzig of הָעֲצָמִים into עֵצִים, are alike untenable. Even if דּוּר in itself does not mean a pile of wood, but simply *strues*, an irregular heap, the fact that it is wood which is piled up is apparent enough from the context. If הָעֲצָמִים had grown out of עֵצִים through a corruption of the text, under the influence of the preceding עצמים, it would not have had an article prefixed. Hitzig also proposes to alter רְתָחֶיהָ into נְתָחֶיהָ, though without any necessity. The fact that רְתָחִים does not occur again proves nothing at all. The noun is added to the verb to intensify its force, and is *plurale tant.* in the sense of boiling. גַּם־בָּשְׁלוּ וגו׳ is dependent upon the previous clause גַּם taking the place of the copulative י. On בָּשַׁל, to be cooked, thoroughly done, see the comm. on Ex. xii. 9.

In vers. 6–8 the interpretation of the parable is given, and that in two trains of thought introduced by לָכֵן (vers. 6 and 9). The reason for commencing with לָכֵן, therefore, may be found in the fact that in the parable contained in vers. 3 sqq., or more correctly in the blockade of Jerusalem, which furnished the occasion for the parable, the judgment about to burst upon Jerusalem is plainly indicated. The train of thought is the following:—Because the judgment upon Jerusalem is now about to commence, therefore woe to her, for her blood-guiltiness is so great that she must be destroyed. But the punishment answering to the magnitude of the guilt is so distributed in the two strophes, vers. 6–8 and vers. 9–13, that the first strophe treats of the punishment of the inhabitants of Jerusalem; the second, of the punishment of the city itself. To account for the latter feature, there is a circumstance introduced which is not mentioned in the parable itself, namely, the rust upon the pot, and the figure of the pot is thereby appropriately extended. Moreover, in the explanation of the parable the figure and the fact pass repeatedly the one into the other. Because Jerusalem is a city of murders, it resembles a pot on which there are spots of rust that cannot be removed. Ver. 6*b* is difficult, and has been expounded in various ways. The ל before the twofold נְתָחֶיהָ is, no doubt, to be taken distributively: according to its several pieces, *i.e.* piece by piece, bring it out. But the suffix attached to הוֹצִיאָהּ cannot be taken as referring to סִיר, as Kliefoth proposes, for this does not yield a suitable meaning. One would not say: bring out the pot by its pieces of flesh, when nothing more is meant than the bringing of the pieces of flesh out of the pot. And this difficulty is not removed by giving to הוֹצִיא the meaning to reach hither. For, apart from the fact that there is nothing in the usage of the language to sustain the meaning, reach it hither for the purpose of setting it upon the fire, one would not say: reach hither the pot according to its several pieces of flesh, piece by piece, when all that was meant was, bring hither the pot filled with pieces of flesh. The suffix to הוֹצִיאָהּ refers to the city (עִיר), *i.e.* to its population, "to which the blood-guiltiness really adhered, and not to its collection of houses" (Hitzig). It is only in appearance also that the suffix to נְתָחֶיהָ refers to the pot; actually it refers to the city, *i.e.* to the whole of its population, the different individuals in which are the separate pieces of flesh. The meaning of the instructions therefore is by no means doubtful: the whole of the population to be found in Jerusalem is to be brought out, and that without any exception, inasmuch as the lot, which would fall upon one and not upon another, will not be cast upon her. There is no necessity to seek for any causal connection between the reference to the rust upon the pot and the bringing out of the pieces of flesh that are cooking within it, and to take the words as signifying that all the pieces, which had been rendered useless by the rust upon the pot, were to be taken out and thrown away (Hävernick); but through the allusion to the rust the interpretation already passes beyond the limits of the figure. The pieces of flesh are to be brought out, after they have been thoroughly boiled, to empty the pot, that it may then be set upon the fire again, to burn out the rust adhering to it (ver. 11). There is no force in Kliefoth's objection, that this exposition does not agree with the context, inasmuch as, "according to the last clause of ver. 5 and vers. 10 and 11, the pieces of flesh and even the bones are not to be taken out, but to be boiled away by a strong fire; and the pot is to become empty not by the fact that the pieces of flesh are taken out and thrown away, but by the pieces being thoroughly boiled away, first to broth and then to nothing." For "boiling away to nothing" is not found in the text, but simply that even the bones are to be thoroughly done, so as to turn into the softness of jelly.—So far as the fact is concerned, we cannot follow the majority of commentators, who suppose that the reference is simply to the carrying away of the inhabitants into exile. Bringing the pieces of flesh out of the pot, denotes the sweeping away of the inhabitants from the city, whether by death (*vid.* ch. xi. 7) or by their being carried away captive. The city is to be emptied of men in consequence of its being blockaded by the king of Babylon. The reason of this is given in vers. 7 and 8, where the guilt of Jerusalem is depicted. The city has shed blood, which is not covered with earth, but has been left uncovered, like blood poured out upon a hard rock, which the stone cannot absorb, and which cries to God for vengeance, because it is uncovered (cf. Gen. iv. 10; Job xvi. 18; and Isa. xxvi. 21). The thought is this: she has sinned in an insolent and shameless manner, and has done nothing to cover her sin, has shown no sign of repentance or atonement, by which she might have got rid of her sin. This has all been ordered by God. He has caused the blood that was shed to fall upon a bare rock, that it might lie uncovered, and He might be able to execute vengeance for the crime.

The second turn in the address (ver. 9) commences in just the same manner as the first in ver. 6, and proceeds with a further picture of the execution of punishment. To avenge the guilt, God will make the pile of wood large, and stir up a fierce fire. The development of this thought is given in ver. 10 in the form of a command addressed to the prophet, to put much wood underneath, and to kindle a fire, so that both flesh and bones may boil away. הָתֵם, from תָּמַם, to finish, complete; with בָּשָׁר, to cook thoroughly. There are differences of opinion as to the true meaning of הָרְקַח הַמֶּרְקָחָה; but the rendering sometimes given to רָקַח, namely, to spice, is at all events unsuitable, and cannot be sustained by the usage of the language. It is true that in Ex. xxx. 25 sqq. the verb רָקַח is used for the preparation of the anointing oil, but it is not the mixing of the different ingredients that is referred to, but in all probability the thorough boiling of the spices, for the purpose of extracting their essence, so that "thorough boiling" is no doubt the true meaning of the word. In Job xli. 23 (31), מֶרְקָחָה is the boiling unguent-pot. יֵחָרוּ is a cohortative *Hiphil*, from חָרַר, to become red-hot, to be consumed.—Ver. 11. When the flesh and bones have thus been thoroughly boiled, the pot is to be placed upon the coals empty, that the rust upon it may be burned away by the heat. The emptying of the pot or kettle by pouring out the flesh, which has been boiled to broth, is passed over as self-evident. The uncleanness of the pot is the rust upon it. תִּתֻּם is an Aramaean form for תִּתֹּם = תִּתַּם. Michaelis has given the true explanation of the words: "*civibus caesis etiam urbs consumetur*" (when the inhabitants are slain, the city itself will be destroyed).[1]—In vers. 12 sqq. the reason is given, which rendered it necessary to inflict this exterminating judgment. In ver. 12 the address still keeps to the figure, but in ver. 13 it passes over to the actual fact. It (the pot) has exhausted the pains (תְּאֻנִים, ἀπ. λεγ.), namely, as ver. 13 clearly shows, the pains, or wearisome exertions, to make it clean by milder means, and not (as Hitzig erroneously infers from the following clause) to eat away the rust by such extreme heat. הֶלְאָת, third pers. *Hiphil* of לָאָה, is the earlier form, which fell into almost entire disuse in later times (*vid.*

[1] Hitzig discovers a *Hysteronproteron* in this description, because the cleaning of the pot ought to have preceded the cooking of the flesh in it, and not to have come afterwards, and also because, so far as the actual fact is concerned, the rust of sin adhered to the people of the city, and not to the city itself as a collection of houses. But neither of these objections is sufficient to prove what Hitzig wants to establish, namely, that the untenable character of the description shows that it is not really a prophecy; nor is there any force in them. It is true that if one intended to boil flesh in a pot for the purpose of eating, the first thing to be done would be to clean the pot itself. But this is not the object in the present instance. The flesh was simply to be thoroughly boiled, that it might be destroyed and thrown away, and there was no necessity to clean the pot for this purpose. And so far as the second objection is concerned, the defilement of sin does no doubt adhere to man, though not, as Hitzig assumes, to man alone. According to the Old Testament view, it extends to things as well (*vid.* Lev. xviii. 25, xxvii. 28). Thus leprosy, for example, did not pollute men only, but clothes and houses also. And for the same reason judgments were not restricted to men, but also fell upon cities and lands.

Ges. § 75, Anm. 1). The last words of ver. 11, I agree with Hitzig, Hävernick, and others, in taking as an exclamation. Because the pot has exhausted all the efforts made to cleanse it, its rust is to go into the fire. In ver. 13 Jerusalem is addressed, and זִמָּה is not a genitive belonging to בְּטֻמְאָתֵךְ, "on account of thy licentious uncleanness" (Ewald and Hitzig), but a predicate, "in thine uncleanness is (there lies) זִמָּה, *i.e.* an abomination deserving of death" (see Lev. xviii. 17 and xx. 14, where the fleshly sins, which are designated as *zimmâh*, are ordered to be punished with death). The cleansings which God had attempted, but without Jerusalem becoming clean, consisted in the endeavour, which preceded the Chaldean judgment of destruction, to convert the people from their sinful ways, partly by threats and promises communicated through the prophets (*vid.* 2 Chron. xxxvi. 15), and partly by means of chastisements. For הֵנִיחַ חֵמָה, see ch. v. 13. In ver. 14 there is a summary of the whole, which brings the threat to a close.

Vers. 15–24. THE SIGN OF SILENT SORROW CONCERNING THE DESTRUCTION OF JERUSALEM.—Ver. 15. *And the word of Jehovah came to me, saying,* Ver. 16. *Son of man, behold, I take from thee thine eyes' delight by a stroke, and thou shalt not mourn nor weep, and no tear shall come from thee.* Ver. 17. *Sigh in silence; lamentation for the dead thou shalt not make; bind thy head-attire upon thee, and put thy shoes upon thy feet, and do not cover thy beard, and eat not the bread of men.* Ver. 18. *And I spake to the people in the morning, and in the evening my wife died, and I did in the morning as I was commanded.* Ver. 19. *Then the people said to me, Wilt thou not show us what this signifies to us that thou doest so?* Ver. 20. *And I said to them, The word of Jehovah has come to me, saying,* Ver. 21. *Say to the house of Israel, Thus saith the Lord Jehovah, Behold, I will profane my sanctuary, the pride of your strength, the delight of your eyes, and the desire of your soul; and your sons and your daughters, whom ye have left, will fall by the sword.* Ver. 22. *Then will ye do as I have done, ye will not cover the beard, nor eat the bread of men;* Ver. 23. *And ye will have your head-attire upon your heads, and your shoes upon your feet; ye will not mourn nor weep, but will pine away in your iniquity, and sigh one toward another.* Ver. 24. *Thus will Ezekiel be a sign to you; as he hath done will ye do; when it cometh, ye will know that I the Lord am Jehovah.*—From the statements in ver. 18, to the effect that the prophet spoke to the people in the morning, and then in the evening his wife died, and then again in the (following) morning, according to the command of God, he manifested no grief, and in answer to the inquiry of the people explained to them the meaning of what he did, it is evident that the word of God contained in this section came to him on the same day as the preceding one, namely, on the day of the blockade of Jerusalem; for what he said to the people on the morning of this day (ver. 18) is the prophecy contained in vers. 3–14. Immediately after He had made this revelation to him, God also announced to him the approaching death of his wife, together with the significance which this event would have to the people generally. The delight of the eyes (ver. 16) is his wife (ver. 18) בְּמַגֵּפָה by a stroke, *i.e.* by a sudden death inflicted by God (*vid.* Num. xiv. 37, xvii. 13). On the occurrence of her death, he is neither to allow of any loud lamentings, nor to manifest any sign of grief, but simply to sigh in silence. מֵתִים אֵבֶל does not stand for אֵבֶל מֵתִים, but the words are both accusatives. The literal rendering would be: the dead shalt thou not make an object of mourning, *i.e.* thou shalt not have any mourning for the dead, as Storr (*Observv.* p. 19) has correctly explained the words. On occasions of mourning it was customary to uncover the head and strew ashes upon it (Isa. lxi. 3), to go barefoot (2 Sam. xv. 30; Isa. xx. 2), and to cover the beard, that is to say, the lower part of the face as far as the nose (Mic. iii. 7). Ezekiel is not to do any of these things, but to arrange his head-attire (פְּאֵר, the head-attire generally, or turban, *vid.* ver. 23 and Isa. lxi. 3, and not specially that of the priests, which is called פַּאֲרֵי הַמִּגְבָּעֹת in Ex. xxxix. 28), and to put on his shoes, and also to eat no mourning bread. לֶחֶם אֲנָשִׁים does not mean *panis miserorum, cibus lugentium*, in which case אֲנָשִׁים would be equivalent to אֲנֻשִׁים, but bread of men, *i.e.* of the people, that is to say, according to the context, bread which the people were accustomed to send to the house of mourning in cases of death, to manifest their sympathy and to console and refresh the mourners,—a custom which gave rise in the course of time to that of formal funeral meals. These are not mentioned in the Old Testament; but the sending of bread or food to the house of mourning is clearly referred to in Deut. xxvi. 14, Hos. ix. 4, and Jer. xvi. 7 (see also 2 Sam. iii. 35).—When Ezekiel thus abstained from all lamentation and outward sign of mourning on the death of his dearest one, the people conjectured that such striking conduct must have some significance, and asked him what it was that he intended to show thereby. He then announced to them the word of God (vers. 20–24). As his dearest one, his wife, had been taken from him, so should its dearest object, the holy temple, be taken from the nation by destruction, and their children by the sword. When this occurred, then would they act as he was doing now; they would not mourn and weep, but simply in their gloomy sorrow sigh in silence on account of their sins, and groan one toward another. The profanation (חִלֵּל) of the sanctuary is effected through its destruction (cf. ch. vii. 24). To show the magnitude of the loss, the worth of the temple in the eyes of the nation is dwelt upon in the following clauses. גְּאוֹן עֻזְּכֶם is taken from Lev. xxvi. 19. The temple is called the pride of your strength, because Israel based its might and strength upon it as the scene of the gracious presence of God, living in the hope that the Lord would not give up His sanctuary to the heathen to be destroyed, but would defend the temple, and therewith Jerusalem and its inhabitants also (cf. Jer. vii. 4). מַחְמַל נַפְשְׁכֶם,

the desire or longing of the soul (from חָמַל, in Arabic, *desiderio ferri ad aliquam rem*). The sons and daughters of the people are the relatives and countrymen whom the exiles had been obliged to leave behind in Canaan.—The explanation of this lamentation and mourning on account of the destruction of the sanctuary and death of their relations, is to be found in the antithesis: וּנְמַקֹּתֶם בַּעֲו׳, ye will pine or languish away in your iniquities (compare ch. iv. 17 and Lev. xxvi. 39). Consequently we have not to imagine either "stolid indifference" (Eichhorn and Hitzig), or "stolid impenitence" (Ewald), but overwhelming grief, for which there were no tears, no lamentation, but only deep inward sighing on account of the sins which had occasioned so terrible a calamity. נָהַם, lit. to utter a deep growl, like the bears (Isa. lix. 11); here to sigh or utter a deep groan. "One toward another," *i.e.* manifesting the grief to one another by deep sighs; not "full of murmuring and seeking the sin which occasioned the calamity in others rather than in themselves," as Hitzig supposes. The latter exposition is entirely at variance with the context. This grief, which consumes the bodily strength, leads to a clear perception of the sin, and also to true repentance, and through penitence and atonement to regeneration and newness of life. And thus will they attain to a knowledge of the Lord through the catastrophe which bursts upon them (cf. Lev. xxvi. 40 sqq.). For מוֹפֵת, a sign, see the comm. on Ex. iv. 21.

Vers. 25–27. SEQUEL OF THE DESTRUCTION OF JERUSALEM TO THE PROPHET HIMSELF.—Ver. 25. *And thou, son of man, behold, in the day when I take from them their might, their glorious joy, the delight of their eyes and the desire of their soul, their sons and their daughters,* Ver. 26. *In that day will a fugitive come to thee, to tell it to thine ears.* Ver. 27. *In that day will thy mouth be opened with the fugitive, and thou wilt speak, and no longer be mute; and thus shalt thou be a sign to them that they may know that I am Jehovah.*—As the destruction of Jerusalem would exert a powerful influence upon the future history of the exiles on the Chaboras, and be followed by most important results, so was it also to be a turning-point for the prophet himself in the execution of his calling. Hävernick has thus correctly explained the connection between these closing verses and what precedes, as indicated by וְאַתָּה in ver. 25. As Ezekiel up to this time was to speak to the people only when the Lord gave him a word for them, and at other times was to remain silent and dumb (ch. iii. 26 and 27); from the day on which a messenger should come to bring him the tidings of the destruction of Jerusalem and the temple, he was to open his mouth, and not continue dumb any longer. The execution of this word of God is related in ch. xxxiii. 21, 22. The words, "when I take from them their strength," etc., are to be understood in accordance with ver. 21. Consequently מָעֻזָּם is the sanctuary, which was taken from the Israelites through the destruction of Jerusalem. The predicates which follow down to מַשָּׂא נַפְשָׁם refer to the temple (cf. ver. 21). מַשָּׂא נֶפֶשׁ, an object toward which the soul lifts itself up (נָשָׂא), *i.e.* for which it cherishes a desire or longing; hence synonymous with מַחְמַל נֶפֶשׁ in ver. 21. The sons and daughters are attached *ἀσυνδέτως*. בַּיּוֹם הַהוּא (in that day), in ver. 26, which resumes the words בְּיוֹם קַחְתִּי וגו׳ (in the day when I take, etc.) in ver. 25, is not the day of the destruction of the temple, but generally the time of this event, or more precisely, the day on which the tidings would reach the prophet. הַפָּלִיט, with the generic article, a fugitive (*vid.* Gen. xiv. 13). לְהַשְׁמָעוּת אָזְנָיִם, to cause the ears to hear (it), *i.e.* to relate it, namely to the bodily ears of the prophet, whereas he had already heard it in spirit from God. הַשְׁמָעוּת, a verbal noun, used instead of the infinitive *Hiphil*. אֶת־הַפָּלִיט, with the escaped one, *i.e.* at the same time "with the mouth of the fugitive" (Hitzig). אֵת expresses association, or so far as the fact is concerned, simultaneousness. The words, "then wilt thou speak, and no longer be dumb," do not imply that it was only from that time forward that Ezekiel was to keep silence, but point back to ch. iii. 26 and 27, where silence is imposed upon him, with the exceptions mentioned there, from the very commencement of his ministry; and in comparison with that passage, simply involve *implicite* the thought that the silence imposed upon him then was to be observed in the strictest manner from the present time until the receipt of the intelligence of the fall of Jerusalem, when his mouth would be opened once more. Through the "words of God" that were given to His prophet (ch. iv.–xxiv.), the Lord had now said to the people of Israel all that He had to say concerning the approaching catastrophe for them to consider and lay to heart, that they might be brought to acknowledge their sin, and turn with sorrow and repentance to their God. Therefore was Ezekiel from this time forward to keep perfect silence toward Israel, and to let God the Lord speak by His acts and the execution of His threatening words. It was not till after the judgment had commenced that his mouth was to be opened again for still further announcements (*vid.* ch. xxxiii. 22).—Ezekiel was thereby to become a sign to the Israelites. These words have a somewhat different meaning in ver. 27 from that which they have in ver. 24. There, Ezekiel, by the way in which he behaved at the death of his wife, was to be a sign to the people of the manner in which they were to act when the judgment should fall upon Jerusalem; whereas here (ver. 27), לְמוֹפֵת refers to the whole of the ministry of the prophet, his silence hitherto, and that which he was still to observe, as well as his future words. Through both of these he was to exhibit himself to his countrymen as a man whose silence, speech, and action were alike marvellous and full of meaning to them, and all designed to lead them to the knowledge of the Lord, the God of their salvation.

Chap. XXV.-XXXII.—PREDICTIONS OF JUDGMENT UPON THE HEATHEN NATIONS.

While the prophet's mouth was to be mute to Israel, the Lord directed him to speak against the heathen nations, and to foretell to them the judgment of destruction, that they might not be lifted up by the fall of the people and kingdom of God, but might recognise in the judgment upon Israel a work of the omnipotence and righteousness of the Lord, the Judge of the whole earth. There are seven heathen nations whose destruction Ezekiel foretells in this section of his book, viz. (1) Ammon; (2) Moab; (3) Edom; (4) the Philistines (ch. xxv.); (5) Tyre, (6) Sidon (ch. xxvi.–xxviii.); and (7) Egypt (ch. xxix.–xxxii.). These prophecies are divided into thirteen words of God by the introductory formula, "The word of Jehovah came to me," the utterances against Ammon, Moab, Edom, and the Philistines, being all comprehended in one word of God; whereas there are four separate words of God directed against Tyre, one against Sidon, and seven against Egypt. In the seven nations and the seven words of God directed against Egypt we cannot fail to discover an allusion to the symbolical significance of the number. Sidon, which had lost its commanding position and become dependent upon Tyre long before the time of Ezekiel, is evidently selected for a special word of God only for the purpose of making up the number seven. And in order to make it the more apparent that the number has been chosen on account of its significance, Ezekiel divides his announcement of the judgment upon the seventh people into seven words of God. On the basis of Gen. i., seven is the number denoting the completion of the works of God. When, therefore, Ezekiel selects seven nations and utters seven words of God concerning the principal nation, namely Egypt, he evidently intends to indicate thereby that the judgment predicted will be executed and completed upon the heathen world and its peoples through the word and acts of God.—The predictions of judgment upon these seven heathen nations are divisible, accordingly, into two groups. Ammon, Moab, Edom, Philistia, Tyre, and Sidon form one group, while the second treats of Egypt alone. This is certainly the way in which the cycle of these prophecies is to be divided rather than the plan ordinarily adopted, according to which the nations included in ch. xxv., as representatives of the one phase of the world-power, are placed in contrast with the other phase of heathenism represented by Tyre, Sidon, and Egypt. The latter is the opinion entertained by Hävernick, for example, with regard to the "beautiful and symmetrical arrangement" of these prophecies. "First of all," says he, "the prophet shows in one series of nations how the idea of the judgment of God was realized in the case of those nations which rose up in direct and open hostility to the theocracy, and thereby represented the might of heathenism as turned away from God and engaged in downright rebellion against Him (ch. xxv.). The prophecies concerning Tyre and Sidon contemplate heathenism in a second aspect (ch. xxvi.–xxviii.). In Tyre we have an exhibition of pride or carnal security, which looks away from God, and plunges deeper and deeper into the sin and worthlessness of the natural life. Both aspects are then finally combined in Egypt, that ancient foe of the covenant nation, which had grown into a world-power, and while displaying in this capacity unbending arrogance and pride, was now, like all the rest, about to be hurled down from the summit of its ancient glory into a bottomless deep." But this interpretation is, in more than one respect, manifestly at variance with the substance of the prophecies. This applies, in the first place, to the antithesis which is said to exist between the nations threatened in ch. xxv. on the one hand, and Tyre and Sidon on the other. In the case of Ammon, Moab, Edom, and the Philistines, for example, the sins mentioned as those for which they would be overthrown by the judgment are their malicious delight at the fall of Israel, and their revengeful, hostile behaviour towards the covenant nation (ch. xxv. 3, 8, 12, 15). And in the same way, according to ch. xxvi. 2, Tyre had involved itself in guilt by giving utterance to its delight at the destruction of Jerusalem, which inspired the hope that everything would now flow into its own store. On the other hand, nothing is said in the case of Pharaoh and Egypt about malicious pleasure, or hostility, or enmity towards Israel or the kingdom of God; but Pharaoh has rendered himself guilty by saying: the Nile is mine, I have made it for myself; and by the fact that Egypt had become a staff of reed to the house of Israel, which broke when they sought to lean upon it (ch. xxix. 3, 6, 7). According to these obvious explanations, Ezekiel reckoned Tyre and Sidon among the nations that were inimically disposed towards Israel, even though the hostile attitude of the Phoenicians was dictated by different motives from those of Edom and the other nations mentioned in ch. xxv.; and the heathen nations are arranged in two groups, and not in three. This is established beyond all doubt, when we observe that each of these two groups terminates with a promise for Israel. To the threat of judgment uttered against Sidon there is appended the promise: and there shall be no more for Israel a malicious briar and smarting thorn from all that are round about them who despise them; and when the Lord shall gather Israel from its dispersion, then will He cause it to dwell safely and prosperously in His land, inasmuch as He will execute judgment upon all round about them who despise them (ch. xxviii. 24–26). And the prediction of judgment upon Egypt in the last prophecy uttered concerning this land, in the twenty-seventh year of the captivity (ch. xxix. 17), closes in a similar manner, with the promise that at the time when the Lord gives Egypt as spoil to the king of Babylon, He will cause a horn to grow to the house of Israel (ch. xxix. 21). The fact that these two prophecies correspond to each other would not have been overlooked by the commentators if the prophecy concerning Egypt, which was really the last in order of time, had been placed in its proper chronological position in the book of Ezekiel, namely, at the close of the words of God directed against that land.

The date of the great mass of these prophecies falls within the period of the last siege of Jerusalem by the Chaldeans, that is to say, in the interval between ch. xxiv. and ch. xxxiii., as the chronological data in the headings plainly affirm. The first word concerning Tyre is from the eleventh year of the captivity of Jehoiachin (ch. xxvi. 1). Of the prophecies against Egypt, the one in ch. xxix. 1–16 dates from the tenth month of the tenth year; that in ch. xxx. 20–26, from the first month of the eleventh year; that in ch. xxxi., from the third month of the same year; the two in ch. xxxii. 1 sqq. and 17 sqq., from the twelfth month of the twelfth year; and lastly, the brief utterance in ch. xxix. 17–21, from the twenty-seventh year of the captivity. There are no chronological data attached to the others. But the short, threatening words against the Ammonites, Moabites, Edomites, and Philistines in ch. xxv. belong to the time immediately succeeding the fall of Jerusalem, since they presuppose its having occurred. The second and third utterances concerning Tyre in ch. xxvii. and ch. xxviii. 1–19 as well as that concerning Sidon in ch. xxviii. 20 sqq., are closely connected, so far as their contents are concerned, with the first word of God against Tyre belonging to the eleventh year of the captivity. And lastly, the threatening word concerning Egypt in ch. xxx. 1–19, to which no definite chronological data are attached, appears to stand nearer in point of time to ch. xxix. 1–16 than to ch. xxix. 17–21.—Consequently the arrangement is based upon the subject-matter of the prophecies, and the chronological sequence is kept subordinate to this, or rather to the comparative importance of the several nations in relation to the theocracy.

These prophecies evidently rest upon the predictions of the earlier prophets against the same nations, so far as their contents are concerned; and in the threats directed against Tyre and Egypt, more especially, many of the thoughts contained in the prophecies of Isaiah (Isa. xxiii. and xix.) are reproduced and expanded. But notwithstanding this resting upon the utterances of earlier prophets, Ezekiel's prophecy against the heathen nations is distinguished in a characteristic manner from that of the other prophets, by the fact that he does not say a word about the prospect of these nations being ultimately pardoned, or of the remnant of them being converted to the Lord, but stops with the announcement of the utter destruction of the earthly and temporal condition of all these kingdoms and nations. The prophecy concerning Egypt in ch. xxix. 13–16, to the effect that after forty years of chastisement God will turn its captivity, and gather it together again, is only an apparent and not a real exception to this; for this turning of the judgment is not to bring about a restoration of Egypt to its former might and greatness or its glorification in the future; but, according to vers. 14 sqq., is simply to restore a lowly and impotent kingdom, which will offer no inducement to Israel to rely upon its strength. Through this promise, therefore, the threat of complete destruction is only somewhat modified, but by no means withdrawn. The only thing which Ezekiel positively holds out to view before the seven heathen nations is, that in consequence of the judgment falling upon them, they will learn that God is Jehovah, or the Lord. This formula regularly returns in the case of all the nations (*vid.* ch. xxv. 5, 7, 11, 17, xxvi. 6, xxviii. 22, 23, xxix. 6, 9, xxx. 8, 19, 25, 26, xxxii. 15); and we might take it to mean, that through the judgment of their destruction in a temporal respect, these nations will come to the knowledge of the God of salvation. And with this interpretation it would contain a slight allusion to the salvation, which will flourish in consequence of and after the judgment, in the case of those who have escaped destruction. If, however, we consider, on the one hand, that in the case of Edom (ch. xxv. 14) the formula takes a harsher form, namely, not that they shall know Jehovah, but that they shall experience His vengeance; and, on the other hand, that the mighty Tyre is repeatedly threatened with destruction, even eternal extinction (ch. xxvi. 20, 21, xxvii. 36, xxviii. 19), and that the whole cycle of these prophecies closes with a funeral-dirge on the descent of all the heathen nations into Sheol (ch. xxxii. 17–32),—we shall see that the formula in question cannot be taken in the sense indicated above, as Kliefoth maintains, but must be understood as signifying that these nations will discern in their destruction the punitive righteousness of God, so that it presents no prospect of future salvation, but simply increases the force of the threat. There is nothing in this distinction, however, to establish a discrepancy between Ezekiel and the earlier prophets; for Ezekiel simply fixes his eye upon the judgment, which will fall upon the heathen nations, partly on account of their hostile attitude towards the kingdom of God, and partly on account of their deification of their own might, and is silent as to the salvation which will accrue even to them out of the judgment itself, but without in the least degree denying it. The reason for his doing this is not that the contemplation of the particular features, which form the details of the immediate fulfilment, has led him to avert his eye from the more comprehensive survey of the entire future;[1] but that the proclamation of the spread of salvation among the heathen lay outside the limits of the calling which he had received from the Spirit of God. The prophetic mission of Ezekiel was restricted to the remnant of the covenant nation, which was carried into exile, and scattered among the heathen. To this remnant he was to foretell the destruction

[1] Drechsler (in his commentary on Isa. xxiii.) has given the following explanation of the distinction to be observed between the prophecies of Isaiah and those of Ezekiel concerning Tyre,—namely, that in the case of Isaiah the spirit of prophecy invests its utterances with the character of totality, in accordance with the position assigned to this prophet at the entrance upon a new era of the world, embracing the entire future even to the remotest times, and sketching with grand simplicity the ground-plan and outline of the whole; whereas in the case of the later prophets, such as Jeremiah and Ezekiel, who were living in the midst of the historical execution, the survey of the whole gives place to the contemplation of

of the kingdom of Judah, and after the occurrence of that catastrophe the preservation and eventual restoration of the kingdom of God in a renewed and glorified form. With this commission, which he had received from the Lord, there was associated, it is true, the announcement of judgment upon the heathen, inasmuch as such an announcement was well fitted to preserve from despair the Israelites, who were pining under the oppression of the heathen, and to revive the hope of the fulfilment of the promise held out before the penitent of their future redemption from their state of misery and restoration to the position of the people of God. But this would not apply to the prophecies of the reception of the heathen into the renovated kingdom of God, as they contained no special element of consolation to the covenant people in their depression.

In connection with this we have the equally striking circumstance, that Ezekiel does not mention Babylon among the heathen nations. This may also be explained, not merely from the predominance of the idea of the judgment upon Israel and Jerusalem, which the Chaldeans were to execute as "righteous men" (ch. xxiii. 45), so that they only came before him as such righteous men, and not as a world-power also (Kliefoth), but chiefly from the fact that, for the reason described above, Ezekiel's prophecy of the judgment upon the heathen is restricted to those nations which had hitherto cherished and displayed either enmity or false friendship toward Israel, and the Chaldeans were not then reckoned among the number.—For the further development of the prophecy concerning the future of the whole heathen world, the Lord had called the

particular features belonging to the details of the immediate fulfilment. But this explanation is not satisfactory, inasmuch as Jeremiah, notwithstanding the fact that he lived in the midst of the execution of the judgment, foretold the turning of judgment into salvation at least in the case of some of the heathen nations. For example, in ch. xlviii. 47 he prophesies to the Moabites, and in ch. xlix. 6 to the Ammonites, that in the future time Jehovah will turn their captivity; and in ch. xlvi. 26 he says, concerning Egypt, that after the judgment it will be inhabited as in the days of old.

prophet Daniel at the same time as Ezekiel, and assigned him his post at the seat of the existing heathen imperial power.

CHAP. XXV. AGAINST AMMON, MOAB, EDOM, AND THE PHILISTINES.

The prophecies, comprehended in the heading (ver. 1) in one "word of the Lord," against Ammon (vers. 1–7), Moab (vers. 8–11), Edom (vers. 12–14), and the Philistines (vers. 15–17), those four border-nations of Israel, are very concise, the judgment of destruction being foretold to them, in a few forcible lines, partly on account of their scorn at the fall of the people and kingdom of God, and partly because of actual hostility manifested toward them. The date of these utterances is not given in the heading; but in vers. 3, 6, and 8 the destruction of Jerusalem is presupposed as having already occurred, so that they cannot have been delivered till after this catastrophe.

Vers. 1–7. Against the Ammonites.—Ver. 1. *And the word of Jehovah came to me, saying,* Ver. 2. *Son of man, direct thy face towards the sons of Ammon, and prophesy against them,* Ver. 3. *And say to the sons of Ammon, Hear ye the word of the Lord Jehovah! Thus saith the Lord Jehovah, Because thou sayest, Aha! concerning my sanctuary, that it is profaned; and concerning the land of Israel, that it is laid waste; and concerning the house of Judah, that they have gone into captivity;* Ver. 4. *Therefore, behold, I will give thee to the sons of the east for a possession, that they may pitch their tent-villages in thee, and erect their dwellings in thee; they shall eat thy fruits, and they shall drink thy milk.* Ver. 5. *And Rabbah will I make a camel-ground, and the sons of Ammon a resting-place for flocks; and ye shall know that I am Jehovah.* Ver. 6. *For thus saith the Lord Jehovah, Because thou hast clapped thy hand, and stamped with thy foot, and hast rejoiced in soul with all thy contempt concerning the house of Israel,* Ver. 7. *Therefore, behold, I will stretch out my hand against thee, and give thee to the nations for booty, and cut thee off from the peoples, and exterminate thee from the lands; I will destroy thee, that thou mayst learn that I am Jehovah.*—In ch. xxi. 28 sqq., when predicting the expedition of Nebuchadnezzar against Jerusalem, Ezekiel had already foretold the destruction of the Ammonites, so that these verses are simply a resumption and confirmation of the earlier prophecy. In the passage referred to, Ezekiel, like Zephaniah before him (Zeph. ii. 8, 10), mentions their reviling of the people of God as the sin for which they are to be punished with destruction. This reviling, in which their hatred of the divine calling of Israel found vent, was the radical sin of Ammon. On the occasion of Judah's fall, it rose even to contemptuous and malicious joy at the profanation of the sanctuary of Jehovah by the destruction of the temple (a comparison with ch. xxiv. 21 will show that this is the sense in which נִחַל is to be understood), at the devastation of the land of Israel, and at the captivity of Judah, —in other words, at the destruction of the religious and political existence of Israel as the people of God. The profanation of the sanctuary is mentioned first, to intimate that the hostility to Israel, manifested by the Ammonites on every occasion that presented itself (for proofs, see the comm. on Zeph. ii. 8), had its roots not so much in national antipathies, as in antagonism to the sacred calling of Israel. As a punishment for this, they are not only to lose their land (vers. 4 and 5), but to be cut off from the number of the nations (vers. 6 and 7). The Lord will give up their land, with its productions, for a possession to the sons of the east, *i.e.*, according to Gen. xxv. 13–18, to the Arabs, the Bedouins (for בְּנֵי קֶדֶם, see the comm. on Judg. vi. 3 and Job i. 3). The *Piel* יִשְּׁבוּ, although only occurring here, is not to be rejected as critically suspicious, and to be changed into *Kal*, as Hitzig proposes. The *Kal* would be unsuitable, because the subject of the sentence can only be בְּנֵי קֶדֶם, and not טִירוֹתֵיהֶם; and יָשַׁב in the *Kal* has an intransitive sense. For טִירוֹת, tent-villages of nomads, see the comm. on Gen.

xxv. 16. מִשְׁכָּנִים, dwellings, are the separate tents of the shepherds. In the last clauses of ver. 4, הֵמָּה is repeated for the sake of emphasis; and Hitzig's opinion, that the first הֵמָּה corresponds to the subject in the clause וְיָשְׁבוּ וגו׳, the second to that in וְנָתְנוּ, is to be rejected as a marvellous flight of imagination, which approaches absurdity in the assertion that פְּרִי הָאָרֶץ signifies the folds, *i.e.* the animals, of the land. Along with the fruit of the land, *i.e.* the produce of the soil, milk is also mentioned as a production of pastoral life, and the principal food of nomads. On the wealth of the Ammonites in flocks and herds, see Judg. vi. 5. The words are addressed to Ammon, as a land or kingdom, and hence the feminine suffix. The capital will also share the fate of the land. *Rabbah* (see the comm. on Deut. iii. 11) will become a camel-ground, a waste spot where camels lie down and feed. This has been almost literally fulfilled. The ruins of *Ammân* are deserted by men, and Seetzen found Arabs with their camels not far off (*vid.* von Raumer, *Palestine*, p. 268). In the parallel clause, the sons of Ammon, *i.e.* the Ammonites, are mentioned instead of their land.—In vers. 6 and 7, the Lord announces to the nation of the Ammonites the destruction that awaits them, and reiterates with still stronger emphasis the sin which occasioned it, namely, the malicious delight they had manifested at Israel's fall. בְּכָל־שָׁאטֵךְ is strengthened by בְּנֶפֶשׁ: with all thy contempt in the soul, *i.e.* with all the contempt which thy soul could cherish. In ver. 7 the ἀπ. λεγ. לְבַג occasions some difficulty. The *Keri* has substituted לְבַז, for booty to the nations (cf. ch. xxvi. 5); and all the ancient versions have adopted this. Consequently בַּג might be a copyist's error for בַּז; and in support of this the circumstance might be adduced, that in ch. xlvii. 13, where גֵּה stands for זֶה, we have unquestionably a substitution of ג for ז. But if the *Chetib* בג be correct, the word is to be explained—as it has been by Benfey (*Die Montasnamen*, p. 194) and Gildemeister (in Lassen's *Zeitschrift für die Kunde des Morgenlandes*, iv. 1, p. 213 sqq.)—from the Sanscrit *bhâga*, *pars, portio*, and has passed into the Semitic languages from the Aryan, like the Syriac ܦܬܓܡܐ, *esca*, which P. Boetticher (*Horae aram.* p. 21) has correctly traced to the Sanscrit *bhaj*, *coquere*.—The executors of the judgment are not named; for the threat that God will give up the land of the Ammonites to the Bedouins for their possession, does not imply that they are to exterminate the Ammonites. On the contrary, a comparison of this passage with Amos i. 13–15 and Jer. xlix. 1–5, where the Ammonites are threatened not only with the devastation of their land, but also with transportation into exile, will show that the Chaldeans are to be thought of as executing the judgment. (See the comm. on ver. 11.)

Vers. 8–11. AGAINST THE MOABITES.—Ver. 8. *Thus saith the Lord Jehovah, Because Moab, like Seir, saith, Behold, like all other nations is the house of Judah:* Ver. 9. *Therefore, behold, I will open the shoulder of Moab from the cities, from its cities even to the last, the ornament of the land, Beth-hayeshimoth, Baal-meon, and as far as Kiryathaim,* Ver. 10. *To the sons of the east, together with the sons of Ammon, and will give it for a possession, that the sons of Ammon may no more be remembered among the nations.* Ver. 11. *Upon Moab will I execute judgments; and they shall learn that I am Jehovah.*—Moab has become guilty of the same sin against Judah, the people of God, as Ammon, namely, of misunderstanding and despising the divine election of Israel. Ammon gave expression to this, when Judah was overthrown, in the malicious assertion that the house of Judah was like all the heathen nations,—that is to say, had no pre-eminence over them, and shared the same fate as they. There is something remarkable in the allusion to Seir, *i.e.* Edom, in connection with Moab, inasmuch as no reference is made to it in the threat contained in vers. 9–11; and in vers. 12, 13, there follows a separate prediction concerning Edom. Hitzig therefore proposes to follow the example of the LXX., and erase it from the text as a gloss, but without being able in the smallest degree to show in what way it is probable that such a gloss could have found admission into an obviously unsuitable place. Seir is mentioned along with Moab to mark the feeling expressed in the words of Moab as springing, like the enmity of Edom towards Israel, from hatred and envy of the spiritual birthright of Israel, *i.e.* of its peculiar prerogatives in sacred history. As a punishment for this, Moab was to be given up, like Ammon, to the Bedouins for their possession, and the people of the Moabites were to disappear from the number of the nations. Vers. 9 and 10 form one period, לִבְנֵי קֶדֶם in ver. 10 being governed by פֹּתֵחַ in ver. 9. The shoulder of Moab is the side of the Moabitish land. In the application of the word כָּתֵף to lands or provinces, regard is had to the position of the shoulder in relation to the whole body, but without reference to the elevation of the district We find an analogy to this in the use of כָּתֵף in connection with the sides of a building. In מֵהֶעָרִים וגו׳, the מִן cannot be taken, in a privative sense, for מִהְיוֹת; for neither the article הֶעָרִים, nor the more emphatic מֵעָרָיו מִקָּצֵהוּ, allows this; but מִן indicates the direction, "from the cities onwards," "from its cities onwards, reckoning to the very last,"—that is to say, in its whole extent. מִקָּצֵהוּ, as in Isa. lvi. 11, Gen. xix. 4, etc. This tract of land is first of all designated as a glorious land, with reference to its worth as a possession on account of the excellence of its soil for the rearing of cattle (see the comm. on Num. xxxii. 4), and then defined with geographical minuteness by the introduction of the names of some of its cities. *Beth-Hayeshimoth*, *i.e.* house of wastes (see the comm. on Num. xxii. 1), has probably been preserved in the ruins of *Suaime*, which F. de Saulcy discovered on the north-eastern border of the Dead Sea, a little farther inland (*vid. Voyage en terre sainte*, Paris 1865, t. i. p. 315). *Baal-Meon*,—when written fully, *Beth-Baal-Meon* (Josh. xiii. 17),—contracted into *Beth-Meon* in Jer. xlviii. 23, is to be sought for to the south-east of this, in the ruins of

Myun, three-quarters of an hour's journey to the south of Heshbon (see the comm. on Num. xxxii. 38). *Kiryathaim* was still farther south, probably on the site of the ruins of *El Teym* (see the comm. on Gen. xiv. 5 and Num. xxxii. 37). The *Chetib* קריתמה is based upon the form קִרְיָתָם, a secondary form of קִרְיָתַיִם, like דֹּתָן, a secondary form of דֹּתַיִן, in 2 Kings vi. 13. The cities named were situated to the north of the Arnon, in that portion of the Moabitish land which had been taken from the Moabites by the Amorites before the entrance of the Israelites into Canaan (Num. xxi. 13, 26), and was given to the tribe of Reuben for its inheritance after the defeat of the Amoritish kings by the Israelites; and then, still later, when the tribes beyond the Jordan were carried into captivity by the Assyrians, came into the possession of the Moabites again, as is evident from Isa. xv. and xvi., and Jer. xlviii. 1, 23, where these cities are mentioned once more among the cities of the Moabites. This will explain not only the naming of this particular district of the Moabitish country, but the definition, "from its cities." For the fact upon which the stress is laid in the passage before us is, that the land in question rightfully belonged to the Israelites, according to Num. xxxii. 37, 38, xxxiii. 49, Josh. xii. 2, 3, xiii. 20, 21, and that it was therefore unlawfully usurped by the Moabites after the deportation of the trans-Jordanic tribes; and the thought is this, that the judgment would burst upon Moab from this land and these cities, and they would thereby be destroyed (Hävernick and Kliefoth). עַל בְּנֵי־עַמּוֹן, not "over the sons of Ammon," but "in addition to the sons of Ammon." They, that is to say, their land, had already been promised to the sons of the east (ver. 4). In addition to this, they are now to receive Moab for their possession (Hitzig and Kliefoth). Thus will the Lord execute judgments upon Moab. Ver. 11 sums up what is affirmed concerning Moab in vers. 9 and 10, in the one idea of the judgments of God upon this people.—The execution of these judgments commenced with the subjugation of the Ammonites and Moabites by Nebuchadnezzar, five years after the destruction of Jerusalem (*vid.* Josephus, *Antt.* x. 9. 7, and M. von Niebuhr, *Gesch. Assurs*, etc., p. 215). Nevertheless the Ammonites continued to exist as a nation for a long time after the captivity, so that Judas the Maccabaean waged war against them (1 Macc. v. 6, 30–43); and even Justin Martyr speaks of *'Αμμανιτῶν νῦν πολὺ πλῆθος* (*Dial. Tryph.* p. 272).—But Origen includes their land in the general name of Arabia (lib. i. *in Job*). The name of the Moabites appears to have become extinct at a much earlier period. After the captivity, it is only in Ezra ix. 1, Neh. xiii. 1, and Dan. xi. 41, that we find any notice of them as a people. Their land is mentioned by Josephus in the *Antiq.* xiii. 14. 2, and xv. 4, and in the *Bell. Jud.* iii. 3. 3.—A further fulfilment by the Messianic judgment, which is referred to in Zeph. ii. 10, is not indicated in these words of Ezekiel; but judging from the prophecy concerning the Edomites (see the comm. on ver. 14), it is not to be excluded.

Vers. 12–14. Against the Edomites.—Ver. 12. *Thus saith the Lord Jehovah, Because Edom acteth revengefully towards the house of Judah, and hath been very guilty in avenging itself upon them,* Ver. 13. *Therefore, thus saith the Lord Jehovah, I will stretch out my hand over Edom, and cut off man and beast from it, and make it a desert from Teman, and unto Dedan they shall fall by the sword.* Ver. 14. *And I will inflict my vengeance upon Edom by the hand of my people Israel, that they may do to Edom according to my anger and my wrath; and they shall experience my vengeance, is the saying of the Lord Jehovah.*—Whilst the Ammonites and the Moabites are charged with nothing more than malicious pleasure at the fall of Israel, and disregard of its divine calling, the Edomites are reproached with revengeful acts of hostility towards the house of Judah, and threatened with extermination in consequence. The עֲשׂוֹת, doing or acting of Edom, is more precisely defined as בִּנְקוֹם וגו׳, *i.e.* as consisting in the taking of vengeance, and designated as very guilty, אָשׁוֹם יֶאְשְׁמוּ. עָשָׂה, followed by בְּ with an infinitive, as in ch. xvii. 17. Edom had sought every opportunity of acting thus revengefully towards Israel (*vid.* Obad. vers. 11 sqq.; Amos i. 11), so that in ch. xxxv. 5 Ezekiel speaks of the "eternal enmity" of Edom against Israel. For this reason we must not restrict the reproach in ver. 12 to particular outbreaks of this revenge at the time of the devastation and destruction of Judah by the Chaldeans, of which the Psalmist complains in Ps. cxxxvii., and for which he invokes the vengeance of God upon Edom. Man and beast are to be cut off from Edom in consequence, and the land to become a desert from Teman to Dedan. These names denote not cities, but districts. *Teman* is the southern portion of Idumaea (see the comm. on Amos i. 12); and *Dedan* is therefore the northern district. *Dedan* is probably not the Cushite tribe mentioned in Gen. x. 7, but the tribe of the same name which sprang from the sons of Abraham by Keturah (Gen. xxv. 3), and which is also mentioned in Jer. xlix. 8 in connection with Edom. דְּדָנֶה has ה local with *Seghol* instead of *Kametz*, probably on account of the preceding *a* (*vid.* Ewald, § 216*c*). There is no necessity to connect מִתֵּימָן with the following clause, as Hitzig and Kliefoth have done, in opposition to the accents. The two geographical names, which are used as a periphrasis for Idumaea as a whole, are distributed equally through the *parallelismus membrorum* between the two clauses of the sentence, so that they belong to both clauses, so far as the sense is concerned. Edom is to become a desert from Teman to Dedan, and its inhabitants from Teman to Dedan are to fall by the sword. This judgment of vengeance will be executed by God through His people Israel. The fulfilment of this threat, no doubt, commenced with the subjugation of the Edomites by the Maccabees; but it is not to be limited to that event, as Rosenmüller, Kliefoth, and others suppose, although the foundation was thereby laid for the disappearance of the national existence of Edom. For it is impossible with this limitation to do justice to the emphatic expression, "*my people* Israel." On the ground, therefore, of the prophecies in Amos ix. 12 and Obad. vers. 17 sqq., that the people of God are to take possession of Edom, when the fallen tabernacle of David is raised up again, *i.e.* in the Messianic times, which prophecies point back to that of Balaam in Num. xxiv. 18, and have their roots, as this also has, in the promise of God concerning the twin sons of Isaac, "the elder shall serve the younger" (Gen. xxv. 23), we must seek for the complete fulfilment in the victories of the people of God over all their foes, among whom Edom from time immemorial had taken the leading place, at the time when the kingdom of God is perfected. For even here Edom is not introduced merely as a single nation that was peculiarly hostile to Judah, but also as a type of the implacable enmity of the heathen world towards the people and kingdom of God, as in ch. xxxv., Isa. xxxiv. 63, etc. The vengeance, answering to the anger and wrath of Jehovah, which Israel, as the people of God, is to execute upon Edom, consists not merely in the annihilation of the national existence of Edom, which John Hyrcanus carried into effect by compelling the subjugated Edomites to adopt circumcision (see the comm. on Num. xxiv. 18), but chiefly in the wrathful judgment which Israel will execute in the person of Christ upon the arch-enemy of the kingdom of God by its complete extinction.

Vers. 15–17. Against the Philistines.—Ver. 15. *Thus saith the Lord Jehovah, Because the Philistines act with revenge, and avenge themselves with contempt in the soul to destroy in everlasting enmity,* Ver. 16. *Therefore thus saith the Lord Jehovah, Behold, I will stretch out my hand over the Philistines, and cut off the Cretans, and destroy the remnant by the sea-shore.* Ver. 17. *And I will execute great vengeance upon them through chastisements of wrath, and they shall know that*

I am Jehovah, when I bring my vengeance upon them.—The Philistines resembled the Edomites and Ammonites in their disposition towards the covenant nation, the former in their thirst for revenge, the latter in their malicious rejoicing at Israel's fall. For this reason they had already been classed by Isaiah (xi. 14) with Edom, Moab, and Ammon as enemies, who would be successfully attacked and overcome by Israel, when the Lord had gathered it again from its dispersion. In the description of its sin towards Israel we have a combination of elements taken from the conduct of Edom and Ammon (vers. 12 and 6). They execute revenge with contempt in the soul (שְׁאָט בְּנֶפֶשׁ, as in ver. 6), with the intention to destroy (לְמַשְׁחִית) Israel; and this revenge springs from eternal, never-ending hostility. The Lord will cut off the whole of the people of the Philistines for this. כְּרֵתִים, Cretans, originally a branch of the Philistian people, settled in the south-west of Canaan. The name is used by Ezekiel for the people, as it had already been by Zephaniah (ii. 5), for the sake of the *paronomasia* with הִכְרַתִּי. The origin of the name is involved in obscurity, as the current derivation from *Creta* rests upon a very doubtful combination (cf. Stark, *Gaza*, pp. 66 and 99 sqq.). By the "remnant of the sea-coast," *i.e.* the remnant of the inhabitants of the coast of the Mediterranean, in other words, of the Philistines, the destruction of which had already been predicted by Amos (i. 8), Isaiah (xiv. 30), and Jeremiah (xlvii. 4), we are to understand the whole nation to the very last man, all that was still left of the Philistines (see the comm. on Amos i. 8).—The execution of the vengeance threatened by God began in the Chaldean period, in which Gaza was attacked by Pharaoh, and, judging from Jer. xlvii., the whole of Philistia was laid waste by the Chaldeans (see the fuller comments on this in the exposition of Jer. xlvii.). But the ultimate fulfilment will take place in the case of Philistia also, through the Messianic judgment, in the manner described in the commentary on Zeph. ii. 10.

CHAP. XXVI.-XXVIII.—AGAINST TYRE AND SIDON.

The greater portion of these three chapters is occupied with the prophecy concerning Tyre, which extends from ch. xxvi. 1 to ch. xxviii. 19. The prophecy against Sidon is limited to ch. xxviii. 20-26. The reason for this is, that the grandeur and importance of Phoenicia were concentrated at that time in the power and rule of Tyre, to which Sidon had been obliged to relinquish the hegemony, which it had formerly possessed over Phoenicia. The prophecy against Tyre consists of four words of God, of which the first (ch. xxvi.) contains the threat of destruction to the city and state of Tyre; the second (ch. xxvii.), a lamentation over this destruction; the third (ch. xxviii. 1–10), the threat against the king of Tyre; the fourth (ch. xxviii. 11–19), a lamentation over his fall.

CHAP. XXVI. THE FALL OF TYRE.

In four sections, commencing with the formula, "thus saith the Lord," Tyre, the mistress of the sea, is threatened with destruction. In the first strophe (vers. 2–6) there is a general threat of its destruction by a host of nations. In the second (vers. 7–14), the enemy is mentioned by name, and designated as a powerful one; and the conquest and destruction emanating from him are circumstantially described. In the third (vers. 15–18), the impression which this event would produce upon the inhabitants of the islands and coast-lands is depicted. And in the fourth (vers. 19–21), the threat is repeated in an energetic manner, and the prophecy is thereby rounded off.

This word of God bears in the introduction the date of its delivery to the prophet and enunciation by him.—Ver. 1. *It came to pass in the eleventh year, on the first of the month, that the word of Jehovah came to me, saying.*—The eleventh year of the exile of Jehoiachin was the year of the conquest and destruction of Jerusalem (Jer. lii. 6, 12), the occurrence of which is presupposed in ver. 2 also. There is something striking in the omission of the number of the month both here and in ch. xxxii. 17, as the day of the month is given. The attempt to discover in the words בְּאֶחָד לַחֹדֶשׁ an indication of the number of the month, by understanding לַחֹדֶשׁ as signifying the first month of the year: "on the first as regards the month," equivalent to, "in the first month, on the first day of it" (LXX., Luther, Kliefoth, and others), is as forced and untenable as the notion that that particular month is intended which had peculiar significance for Ezekiel, namely, the month in which Jerusalem was conquered and destroyed. The first explanation is proved to be erroneous by ver. 2, where the destruction of Jerusalem, which occurred in the fifth month of the year named, is assumed to have already happened. The second view is open to the objection that the conquest of Jerusalem happened in the fourth month, and the destruction in the fifth (Jer. lii. 6 and 12); and it cannot be affirmed that the conquest was of less importance to Ezekiel than the destruction. We cannot escape the conclusion, therefore, that the number of the month has been dropped through a corruption of the text, which has occurred in copying; but in that case we must give up all hope of being able to determine what the month really was. The conjecture offered by Ewald and Hitzig, that one of the last months of the year is intended, because Ezekiel could not have known before then what impression the conquest of Jerusalem had made upon Tyre, stands or falls with the naturalistic view entertained by these writers with regard to prophecy.

Vers. 2–6. Tyre shall be broken and utterly destroyed.—Ver. 2. *Son of man, because Tyre saith concerning Jerusalem, "Aha, the door of the nations is broken; it turneth to me; I shall become full; she is laid waste;"* Ver. 3. *Therefore thus saith the Lord Jehovah, Behold, I will come upon thee, O Tyre, and will bring up against thee many nations, as the sea bringing up its waves.* Ver. 4. *They will destroy the walls of Tyre, and throw down her towers; and I will sweep away her dust from her, and make her a bare rock.* Ver. 5. *She shall become a place for the spreading of nets in the midst of the sea, for I have spoken it, is the saying of the Lord Jehovah; and she shall become booty for the nations.* Ver. 6. *And her daughters which are in the land shall be slain with the sword; and they shall learn that I am Jehovah.*—TYRE, as in the prophecy of Isaiah (ch. xxiii.), is not the city of that name upon the mainland, *ἡ πάλαι Τύρος* or *Παλαίτυρος*, Old Tyre, which was taken by Shalmaneser and destroyed by Alexander (as Perizon., Marsh, Vitringa, J. D. Michaelis, and Eichhorn supposed), but Insular Tyre, which was three-quarters of a mile farther north, and only 1200 paces from the land, being built upon a small island, and separated from the mainland by a strait of no great depth (*vid.* Movers, *Phoenizier*, II. p. 288 sqq.). This Insular Tyre had successfully resisted the Assyrians (Josephus, *Antt.* ix. 14. 2), and was at that time the market of the nations; and in Ezekiel's day it had reached the summit of its greatness as mistress of the sea and the centre of the commerce of the world. That it is against this Tyre that our prophecy is chiefly directed, is evident from vers. 5 and 14, according to which Tyre is to become a bare rock in the midst of the sea, and from the allusion to the daughter cities, בַּשָּׂדֶה, in the field, *i.e.* on the mainland (in ver. 6), as contrasted with the position occupied by Tyre upon a rocky island in the sea; and, lastly, from the description given in ch. xxvii. of the maritime trade of Tyre with all nations, to which Old Tyre never attained, inasmuch as it possessed no harbour (*vid.* Movers, *l.c.* p. 176). This may easily be reconciled with such passages as vers. 6, 8, and ch. xxvii., xxviii., in which reference is also made to the continental Tyre, and the conquest of Tyre is depicted as the conquest of a land-city (see the exposition of these verses).—The threat against Tyre commences, as in the case of the nations threatened in ch. xxv., with a brief description of its sin. Tyre gave expression to its joy at the fall of Jerusalem, because it hoped to derive profit therefrom through the extension of its commerce and increase of its wealth. Different explanations have been given of the meaning of the words put into the mouth of Tyre. "The door of the nations is broken in pieces." The plural דַּלְתוֹת indicates the folding doors which formed the gate, and are mentioned in its stead. Jerusalem is the door of the nations, and is so called according to the current opinion of expositors, because it was the centre of the commerce of the nations, *i.e.* as a place of trade. But nothing is known to warrant the idea that Jerusalem was ever able to enter into rivalry with Tyre as a commercial city. The importance of Jerusalem with regard to other nations was to be found, not in its commerce, nor in the favourable situation which it occupied for trade, in support of which Hävernick refers to Herodotus, iii. 5, and Hitzig to Ezekiel xxiii. 40, 41, but in its sanctuary, or the sacred calling which it had received for the whole world of nations. Kliefoth has therefore decided in favour of the following view: That Jerusalem is called a gate of the nations, not because it had hitherto been open to the nations for free and manifold intercourse, but for the very opposite reason, namely, because the gate of Jerusalem had hitherto been closed and barred against the nations, but was now broken in pieces through the destruction of the city, and thereby opened to the nations. Consequently the nations, and notably Tyre, would be able to enter now; and from this fact the Tyrians hoped to derive advantage, so far as their commercial interests were concerned. But this view is not in harmony with the text. Although a gate is opened by being broken in pieces, and one may force an entrance into a house by breaking the door (Gen. xix. 9), yet the expression "door of the nations" cannot signify a door which bars all entrance on the part of the nations, inasmuch as doors and gates are not made to secure houses and cities against the forcible entrance of men and nations, but to render it possible for them to go out and in. Moreover, the supposition that "door of the nations" is equivalent to shutting against the nations, is not in harmony with the words נָסֵבָּה אֵלַי which follow. The expression "it has turned to me," or it is turned to me, has no meaning unless it signifies that through the breaking of the door the stream of the nations would turn away from Jerusalem to Tyre, and therefore that hitherto the nations had turned to Jerusalem. נָסֵבָּה is the 3d pers. perf. *Niphal* of סָבַב, for נָסַבָּה, formed after the analogy of נָמַס, etc. The missing subject to נָסֵבָּה is to be found *ad sensum* in דַּלְתוֹת הָעַמִּים. It is not the door itself, but the entrance and streaming in of the nations, which had previously been directed towards Jerusalem, and would now turn to Tyre. There is no necessity, therefore, for Hitzig's conjecture, that אִמָּלְאָה should be altered into מְלֵאָה, and the latter taken as the subject. Consequently we must understand the words of the Tyrians as signifying that they had regarded the drawing of the nations to Jerusalem, *i.e.* the force of attraction which Jerusalem had hitherto exerted upon the nations, as the seat of the divine revelation of mercy, or of the law and judgment of the Lord, as interfering with their endeavour to draw all nations to themselves and gain them over to their purposes, and that they rejoiced at the destruction of Jerusalem, because they hoped that henceforth they would be able to attract the nations to themselves and enrich themselves with their possessions. This does not require that we should accredit the Tyrians with any such insight into the spiritual calling of Jerusalem as would lie beyond their heathen point of view. The simple circumstance, that the position occupied by Jerusalem in relation to the world apparently interfered with the mercantile interests of the Tyrians, would be quite sufficient to excite a malignant pleasure at the fall of the city of God, as the worship of God and the worship of Mammon are irreconcilably opposed. The source from which the envy and the enmity manifesting itself in this malicious pleasure took their rise, is indicated in the last words: "I shall fill myself, she (Jerusalem) is laid waste," which Jerome has correctly linked together thus: *quia illa deserta est, idcirco ego implebor.* הִמָּלֵא, to be filled with merchandise and wealth, as in ch. xxvii. 25. On account of this disposition toward the kingdom of God, which led Tyre to expect an increase of power and wealth from its destruction, the Lord God would smite it with ruin and annihilation. הִנְנִי עָלַיִךְ, behold, I will come upon thee, as in ch. xiii. 8; Jer. l. 31, Nah. iii. 5. God will lead a powerful army against Tyre, which shall destroy its walls and towers. Instead of the army, "many nations" are mentioned, because Tyre is hoping to attract more nations to itself in consequence of the destruction of Jerusalem. This hope is to be fulfilled, though in a different sense from that which Tyre intended. The comparison of the advancing army to the advancing waves of the sea is very significant when the situation of Tyre is considered. הַיָּם is the subject to כְּהַעֲלוֹת, and the *Hiphil* is construed with לְ instead of the accusative (compare Ewald, § 292*c* with § 277*e*). Accord-to Arrian, ii. 18. 3, and Curtius, iv. 2. 9, 12, and 3. 13, Insular Tyre was fortified all round with lofty walls and towers, which were certainly in existence as early as Nebuchadnezzar's time. Even the dust of the demolished buildings (עֲפָרָהּ) God would sweep away (סְחֵיתִי, ἁπ. λεγ., with a play upon שִׁחֲתוּ), so that the city, *i.e.* the site on which it had stood, would become a bare and barren rock (צְחִיחַ סֶלַע, as in ch. xxiv. 7), a place where fishermen would spread out their nets to dry. "Her daughters" also, that is to say, the towns dependent upon Tyre, "on the field," *i.e.* the open country,—in other words, their inhabitants,—would be slain with the sword.

In vers. 7–14 the threat is carried still further.—Ver. 7. *For thus saith the Lord Jehovah, Behold, I will bring against Tyre Nebuchadnezzar, the king of Babylon, from the north, the king of kings, with horses, and chariots, and horsemen, and a multitude of much people.* Ver. 8. *Thy daughters in the field he will slay with the sword, and he will erect siege-towers against thee, and throw up a rampart against thee, and set up shields against thee,* Ver. 9. *And direct his battering-rams against thy walls, and throw down thy towers with his swords.* Ver. 10. *From the multitude of his horses their dust will cover thee; from the noise of the horsemen, wheels, and chariots, thy walls will shake when he shall enter into thy gates, as they enter a city broken open.* Ver. 11. *With the hoofs of his horses he will tread down all thy streets; thy people he will slay with the sword, and thy glorious pillars will fall to the ground.* Ver. 12. *They will make booty of thy possessions, and plunder thy merchandise, destroy thy walls, and throw down thy splendid mansions, and sink thy stones, thy wood, and thy dust in the water.* Ver. 13. *I will put an end to the sound of thy songs, and the music of thy harps shall be heard no more.* Ver. 14. *I will make thee a bare rock; thou shalt be a place for the spreading of nets, and be built no more; for I Jehovah have spoken it, is the saying of the Lord Jehovah.*—Nebuchadnezzar, the great king of Babylon,—this is the meaning of the rhetorical description in these verses,—will come with a powerful army (ver. 7), smite with the sword the inland cities dependent upon Tyre (ver. 8, compare ver. 6), then commence the siege of Tyre, destroy its walls and towers (vers. 8*b* and 9), enter with his army the city in which breaches have been made, put the inhabitants to death (vers. 10 and 11), plunder the treasures, destroy walls and buildings, and cast the ruins into the sea (ver. 12). *Nebuchadrezzar*, or *Nebuchadnezzar* (for the name see the comm. on 2 Kings xxiv. 1), is called king of kings, as the supreme ruler of the Babylonian empire, because the kings of conquered provinces and lands were subject to him as vassals (see the comm. on Isa. x. 8). His army consists of war-chariots, and cavalry, and a great multitude of infantry. קָהָל וְעַם־רָב are co-ordinate, so far as the rhetorical style is concerned; but in reality עַם־רָב is subordinate to קָהָל, as in ch. xxiii. 24, inasmuch as the קָהָל consisted of עַם־רָב. On the siege-works mentioned in ver. 8*b*, see the comm. on ch. iv. 2. הֵקִים צִנָּה signifies the construction of a roof with shields, by which the besiegers were accustomed to defend themselves from the missiles of the defenders of the city wall while pursuing their labours. Herodotus repeatedly mentions such shield-roofs as used by the Persians (ix. 61. 99, 102), though, according to Layard, they are not to be found upon the Assyrian monuments (see the comm. on Nah. ii. 6). There is no doubt that מְחִי קָבָלוֹ signifies the battering-ram, called כַּר in ch. xxi. 27, though the meaning of the words is disputed. מְחִי, literally, thrusting or smiting. קבלו, from קֳבֵל, to be pointed either קָבְלוֹ or קָבָלוֹ (the form קֳבָלוֹ adopted by v. d. Hooght and J. H. Michaelis is opposed to the grammatical rules), has been explained by Gesenius and others as signifying *res opposita*, that which is opposite; hence מחי קבלו, the thrusting or demolishing of that which stands opposite. In the opinion of others, קֳבֵל is an instrument employed in besieging; but there is nothing in the usage of the language to sustain either this explanation or that adopted by Hävernick, "destruction of his defence." חַרְבוֹתָיו, his swords, used figuratively for his weapons or instruments of war, "his irons," as Ewald has very aptly rendered it. The description in ver. 10 is hyperbolical. The number of horses is so great, that on their entering the city they cover it with dust, and the walls shake with the noise of the horsemen and chariots. כִּמְבוֹאֵי עִיר מב׳, literally, as the marchings into a broken city, *i.e.* a city taken by storm, generally are. The simile may be explained from the peculiar situation of Insular Tyre. It means that the enemy will enter it as they march into a land-fortress into which a breach has been made by force. The words presuppose that the besieger has made a road to the city by throwing up an embankment or dam. מַצְּבוֹת עֻזֵּךְ, the memorial pillars of thy might, and the pillars dedicated to Baal, two of which are mentioned by Herodotus (ii. 44) as standing in the temple of Hercules at Tyre, one of gold, the other of emerald; not images of gods, but pillars, as symbols of Baal. These sink or fall to the ground before the overwhelming might of the foe (compare Isa. xlvi. 1, xxi. 9, and 1 Sam. v. 3). After the slaughter of the inhabitants and the fall of the gods, the plundering of the treasures begins, and then follows the destruction of the city.

בָּתֵּי חֶמְדָּה are not pleasure-houses ("pleasure-towers, or garden-houses of the wealthy merchants," as Ewald supposes), for there was not space enough upon the island for gardens (Strabo, xvi. 2. 23), but the lofty, magnificent houses of the city, the palaces mentioned in Isa. xxiii. 13. Yea, the whole city shall be destroyed, and that so completely that they will sweep stones, wood, and rubbish into the sea.—Thus will the Lord put an end to the exultation and rejoicing in Tyre (ver. 13; compare Isa. xiv. 11 and Amos v. 23).—The picture of the destruction of this powerful city closes with the repetition of the thought from ver. 5, that Tyre shall be turned into a bare rock, and shall never be built again.

Vers. 15–18. The tidings of the destruction of Tyre will produce great commotion in all her colonies and the islands connected with her.—Ver. 15. *Thus saith the Lord Jehovah to Tyre, Will not the islands tremble at the noise of thy fall, at the groaning of the wounded, at the slaughter in the midst of thee?* Ver. 16. *And all the princes of the sea will come down from their thrones, and will lay aside their robes and take off their embroidered clothes, and dress themselves in terrors, sit upon the earth, and they will tremble every moment, and be astonished at thee.* Ver. 17. *They will raise a lamentation for thee, and say to thee: How hast thou perished, thou who wast inhabited from out of the sea, thou renowned city, she who was mighty upon the sea, she and her inhabitants, who inspired all her inhabitants with fear of her!* Ver. 18. *Now do the islands tremble on the day of thy fall, and the islands in the sea are confounded at thy departure.*—הֲלֹא, *nonne*, has the force of a direct affirmation. קוֹל מַפֵּלָה, the noise of the fall, stands for the tidings of the noise, since the noise itself could not be heard upon the islands. The fall takes place, as is added for the purpose of depicting the terrible nature of the event, at or amidst the groaning of the wounded, and the slaughter in the midst of thee. בֵּהָרֶג is the infinitive *Niphal*, with the accent drawn back on account of the following *Milel*, and should be pointed בֵּהָרֵג. The word

אִיִּים, islands, is frequently used so as to embrace the coast lands of the Mediterranean Sea; we have therefore to understand it here as applied to the Phoenician colonies on the islands and coasts of that sea. The "princes of the sea" are not kings of the islands, but, according to Isa. xxiii. 8, the merchants presiding over the colonies of Tyre, who resembled princes. כִּסְאוֹת, not royal thrones, but chairs, as in 1 Sam. iv. 13, etc. The picture of their mourning recalls the description in Jonah iii. 6; it is not derived from that passage, however, but is an independent description of the mourning customs which commonly prevailed among princes. The antithesis introduced is a very striking one: clothing themselves in terrors, putting on terrors in the place of the robes of state which they have laid aside (see the similar trope in ch. vii. 27). The thought is rendered still more forcible by the closing sentences of the verse: they tremble לִרְגָעִים, by moments, *i.e.* as the moments return,—actually, therefore, "every moment" (*vid.* Isa. xxvii. 3).—In the lamentation which they raise (ver. 17), they give prominence to the alarming revolution of all things, occasioned by the fact that the mistress of the seas, once so renowned, has now become an object of horror and alarm. נוֹשֶׁבֶת מִיַּמִּים, inhabited from the seas. This is not to be taken as equivalent to "as far as the seas," in the sense of, whose inhabitants spread over the seas and settle there, as Gesenius (*Thes.*) and Hävernick suppose; for being inhabited is the very opposite of sending the inhabitants abroad. If מִן were to be taken in the geographical sense of direction or locality, the meaning of the expression could only be, whose inhabitants spring from the seas, or have migrated thither from all seas; but this would not apply to the population of Tyre, which did not consist of men of all nations under heaven. Hitzig has given the correct interpretation, namely, from the sea, or out of the seas, which had as it were ascended as an inhabited city out of the bosom of the sea. It is not easy to explain the last clause of ver. 17: who inspired all her inhabitants with their terror, or with terror of them (of themselves); for if the relative אֲשֶׁר is taken in connection with the preceding יֹשְׁבֶיהָ, the thought arises that the inhabitants of Tyre inspired her inhabitants, *i.e.* themselves, with their terror, or terror of themselves. Kimchi, Rosenmüller, Ewald, Kliefoth, and others, have therefore proposed to take the suffix in the second יוֹשְׁבֶיהָ as referring to הַיָּם, all the inhabitants of the sea, *i.e.* all her colonies. But this is open to the objection, that not only is יָם of the masculine gender, but it is extremely harsh to take the same suffix attached to the two יֹשְׁבֶיהָ as referring to different subjects. We must therefore take the relative אֲשֶׁר and the suffix in חִתִּיתָם as both referring to הִיא וְיֹשְׁבֶיהָ: the city with its population inspired all its several inhabitants with fear of itself. This is not to be understood, however, as signifying that the inhabitants of Tyre kept one another in a state of terror and alarm; but that the city with its population, through its power upon the sea, inspired all the several inhabitants with fear of this its might, inasmuch as the distinction of the city and its population was reflected upon every individual citizen. This explanation of the words is confirmed by the parallel passages in ch. xxxii. 24 and 26.—This city had come to so appalling an end, that all the islands trembled thereat. The two hemistichs in ver. 18 are synonymous, and the thought returns by way of conclusion to ver. 15. אִיִּן has the Aramaean form of the plural, which is sometimes met with even in the earlier poetry (*vid.* Ewald, § 177*a*). צֵאת, departure, *i.e.* destruction.

Vers. 19–21. Thus will Tyre, covered by the waves of the sea, sink into the region of the dead, and vanish for ever from the earth.—Ver. 19. *For thus saith the Lord Jehovah, When I make thee a desolate city, like the cities which are no longer inhabited, when I cause the deep to rise over thee, so that the many waters cover thee,* Ver. 20. *I cast thee down to those who have gone into the grave, to the people of olden time, and cause thee to dwell in the land of the lower regions, in the ruins from the olden time, with those who have gone into the grave, that thou mayest be no longer inhabited, and I create that which is glorious in the land of the living.* Ver. 21. *I make thee a terror, and thou art no more; they will seek thee, and find thee no more for ever, is the saying of the Lord Jehovah.*—Not only will ruin and desolation come upon Tyre, but it will sink for ever into the region of the dead. In this concluding thought the whole threat is summed up. The infinitive clauses of ver. 19 recapitulate the leading thoughts of the previous strophes, for the purpose of appending the closing thought of banishment to the under-world. By the rising of the deep we are to understand, according to ver. 12, that the city in its ruins will be sunk into the depths of the sea. יוֹרְדֵי בוֹר, those who go down into the pit or grave, are the dead. They are described still further as עַם עוֹלָם, not "those who are sleeping the long sleep of death," or the generation of old whom all must join; but the people of the "old world" before the flood (2 Pet. ii. 5), who were buried by the waters of the flood, in accordance with Job xxii. 15, where עוֹלָם denotes the generations of the primeval world, and after the analogy of the use of עַם עוֹלָם in Isa. xliv. 7, to describe the human race as existing from time immemorial. In harmony with this, חֳרָבוֹת מֵעוֹלָם are the ruins of the primeval world which perished in the flood. As עַם עוֹלָם adds emphasis to the idea of יוֹרְדֵי בוֹר, so also does בֶּחֳרָבוֹת מֵעוֹלָם to that of אֶרֶץ תַּחְתִּיּוֹת. Tyre shall not only descend to the dead in Sheol, but be thrust down to the people of the dead, who were sunk into the depths of the earth by the waters of the flood, and shall there receive its everlasting dwelling-place among the ruins of the primeval world which was destroyed by the flood, beside that godless race of the olden time. אֶרֶץ תַּחְתִּיּוֹת, land of the lowest places (cf. ch. xxxii. 18, 24), is a periphrasis for Sheol, the region of the dead (compare Eph. iv. 9, "the lower parts of the earth"). On וְנָתַתִּי צְבִי וגו' Hitzig has observed with perfect correctness: "If we retain the pointing as the first person, with which the place assigned to the *Athnach* (֑) coincides, we must at any rate not regard the clause as still dependent upon לְמַעַן, and the force of the לֹא as continued. We should then have to take the clause as independent and affirmative, as the accentuators and the Targum have done." But as this would give rise to a discrepancy between the two halves of the verse, Hitzig proposes to alter נָתַתִּי into the second person וְנָתַתְּ, so that the clause would still be governed by לְמַעַן לֹא. But the want of agreement between the two halves of the verse does not warrant an alteration of the text, especially if it lead to nothing better than the forced rendering adopted by Hitzig, "and thou no longer shinest with glory in the land of the living," which there is nothing in the language to justify. And even the explanation proposed by Hävernick and Kliefoth, "that I no longer produce anything glorious from thee (Tyre) in the land of the living," is open to this objection, that "from thee" is arbitrarily interpolated into the text; and if this were what Ezekiel meant, he would either have added לָךְ or written נְתַתִּיךְ. Moreover, the change of person is a sufficient objection to our taking נָתַתִּי as dependent upon לְמַעַן, and supplying לֹא. וְנָתַתִּי is evidently a simple continuation of וְהוֹשַׁבְתִּיךְ. And nothing but the weightiest objections should lead us to give up a view which so naturally suggests itself. But no such objections exist. Neither the want of harmony between the two halves of the verse, nor the context,—according to which Tyre and its destruction are referred to both before and immediately after,—forces us to the adoption of explanations at variance with the simple meaning of the words. We therefore adhere to the natural interpretation of the words, "and I set (establish) glory in the land of the living;" and understand by the land of the living, not the theocracy especially, but the earth, in contrast to the region of the dead. The words contain the general thought, that on and after the overthrow of the glory of the ungodly power of the world, He will create that which is glorious on the earth to endure for ever; and this He really does by the establishing of His kingdom.—Tyre, on the contrary, shall become, through its fate, an object of terror, or an example of sudden destruction, and pass away with all its glory, not leaving a trace behind. For ver. 21*b*, compare Isa. xli. 12 and Ps. xxxvii. 36. וּתְבֻקְשִׁי, imperf. *Pual*, has *Chateph-patach* between the two *u*, to indicate emphatically that the syllable is only a very loosely closed one (*vid.* Ewald, § 31*b*, p. 95).

CHAP. XXVII. LAMENTATION OVER THE FALL OF TYRE.

The lamentation commences with a picture of the glory of the city of Tyre, its situation, its architectural beauty, its military strength and defences (vers. 3–11), and its wide-spread commercial relations (vers. 12–25); and then passes into mournful lamentation over the ruin of all this glory (vers. 26–36).

Vers. 1–11. Introduction and description of the glory and might of Tyre.—Ver. 1. *And the word of Jehovah came to me, saying,* Ver. 2. *And do thou, O son of man, raise a lamentation over Tyre,* Ver. 3. *And say to Tyre, Thou who dwellest at the approaches of the sea, merchant of the nations to many islands, thus saith the Lord Jehovah, Tyre, thou sayest, I am perfect in beauty.* Ver. 4. *In the heart of the seas is thy territory; thy builders have made thy beauty perfect.* Ver. 5. *Out of cypresses of Senir they built all double-plank-work for thee; they took cedars of Lebanon to make a mast upon thee.* Ver. 6. *They made thine oars of oaks of Bashan, thy benches they made of ivory set in box from the islands of the Chittaeans.* Ver. 7. *Byssus in embroidery from Egypt was thy sail, to serve thee for a banner; blue and red purple from the islands of Elishah was thine awning.* Ver. 8. *The inhabitants of Sidon and Arvad were thy rowers; thy skilful men, O Tyre, were in thee, they were thy sailors.* Ver. 9. *The elders of Gebal and its skilful men were with thee to repair thy leaks; all the ships of the sea and their mariners were in thee to barter thy goods.* Ver. 10. *Persian and Lydian and Libyan were in thine army, thy men of war; shield and helmet they hung up in thee; they gave brilliancy to thee.* Ver. 11. *The sons of Arvad and thine army were upon thy walls round about, and brave men were upon thy towers; they hung up their shields upon thy walls round about; they have made thy beauty perfect.*—The lamentation commences with an address to Tyre, in which its favourable situation for purposes of trade, and the perfect beauty of which she was conscious, are placed in the foreground (ver. 3). Tyre is sitting, or dwelling, at the approaches of the sea. מְבוֹאֹת יָם, approaches or entrances of the sea, are harbours into which ships sail and from which they depart, just as מְבוֹא הָעִיר, the gate of the city, is both entrance and exit. This description does not point to the city on the mainland, or Old Tyre, but answers exactly to Insular Tyre with its two harbours.[1] יֹשֶׁבְתִי, with the connecting *i*, which is apparently confounded here after the Aramaean fashion with the *i* of the feminine pronoun, and has therefore been marked by the Masora as superfluous (*vid.* Ewald, § 211*b*). The combination of רֹכֶלֶת with אֶל אִיִּים ר׳ may be accounted for from the primary meaning of רָכַל, to travel about as a merchant: thou who didst go to the nations on many shores to carry on thy trade. Tyre itself considers that she is perfect in her beauty, partly on account of her strong position in the sea, and partly because of her splendid edifices.[2] In the description which follows of this

[1] Insular Tyre possessed two harbours, a northern one called the Sidonian, because it was on the Sidonian side, and one on the opposite or south-eastern side, which was called the Egyptian harbour from the direction in which it pointed. The Sidonian was the more celebrated of the two, and consisted of an inner harbour, situated within the wall of the city, and an outer one, formed by a row of rocks, which lay at a distance of about three hundred paces to the north-west of the island, and ran parallel to the opposite coast of the mainland, so as to form a roadstead in which ships could anchor (*vid.* Arrian, ii. 20; Strabo, xvi. 2. 23). This northern harbour is still held by the city of *Sur*, whereas the Egyptian harbour with the south-eastern portion of the island has been buried by the sand driven against the coasts by the south winds, so that even the writers of the Middle Ages make no allusion to it. (See Movers, *Phönizier*, II. 1, pp. 214 sqq.)

[2] Curtius, iv. 2: *Tyrus et claritate et magnitudine ante omnes urbes Syriae Phoenicesque memorabilis.* (Cf. Strabo, xvi. 2. 22.)

beauty and glory, from ver. 4 onwards, Tyre is depicted allegorically as a beautiful ship, splendidly built and equipped throughout, and its destruction is afterwards represented as a shipwreck occasioned by the east wind (vers. 26 sqq.).[1] The words, "in the heart of the seas is thy territory" (ver. 4*a*), are equally applicable to the city of Tyre and to a ship, the building of which is described in what follows. The comparison of Tyre to a ship was very naturally suggested by the situation of the city in the midst of the sea, completely surrounded by water. As a ship, it must of necessity be built of wood. The shipbuilders selected the finest kinds of wood for the purpose; cypresses of Antilibanus for double planks, which formed the sides of the vessel, and cedar of Lebanon for the mast. *S^e^nir*, according to Deut. iii. 9, was the Amoritish name of *Hermon* or *Antilibanus*, whereas the Sidonians called it *Sirion*. On the other hand, *S^e^nir* occurs in 1 Chron. v. 23, and *Sh^e^nir* in Song of Sol. iv. 8, in connection with *Hermon*, where they are used to denote separate portions of Antilibanus. Ezekiel evidently uses *Senir* as a foreign name, which had been retained to his own time, whereas *Sirion* had possibly become obsolete, as the names had both the same meaning (see the comm. on Deut. iii. 9). The naming of the places from which the several materials were obtained for the fitting out of the ship, serve to heighten the glory of its construction and give an ideal character to the picture. All lands have contributed their productions to complete the glory and might of Tyre. Cypress-wood was frequently used by the ancients for buildings and (according to Virgil, *Georg*. ii. 443) also for ships, because it was

[1] Jerome recognised this allegory, and has explained it correctly as follows: "He (the prophet) speaks τροπικῶς, as though addressing a ship, and points out its beauty and the abundance of everything. Then, after having depicted all its supplies, he announces that a storm will rise, and the south wind (*auster*) will blow, by which great waves will be gathered up, and the vessel will be wrecked. In all this he is referring to the overthrow of the city by King Nabuchodonosor," etc. Raschi and others give the same explanation.

exempt from the attacks of worms, and was almost imperishable, and yet very light (Theophr. *Hist. plant.* v. 8; Plinii *Hist. nat.* xvi. 79). לֻחֹתַיִם, a dual form, like חֹמֹתַיִם in 2 Kings xxv. 4, Isa. xxii. 11, double-planks, used for the two side-walls of the ship. For oars they chose oaks of Bashan (מִשּׁוֹט as well as מָשׁוֹט in ver. 29 from שׁוּט, to row), and the rowing benches (or deck) were of ivory inlaid in box. קֶרֶשׁ is used in Ex. xxvi. 15 sqq. for the boards or planks of the wooden walls of the tabernacle; here it is employed in a collective sense, either for the rowing benches, of which there were at least two, and sometimes three rows in a vessel, one above another, or more properly, for the deck of the vessel (Hitzig). This was made of *shēn*, or ivory, inlaid in wood. The ivory is mentioned first as the most valuable material of the קֶרֶשׁ, the object being to picture the ship as possessing all possible splendour. The expression בַּת־אֲשֻׁרִים occasions some difficulty, partly on account of the use of the word בַּת, and partly in connection with the meaning of אֲשֻׁרִים, although so much may be inferred from the context, that the allusion is to some kind of wood inlaid with ivory, and the custom of inlaying wood with ivory for the purpose of decoration is attested by Virgil, *Aen.* x. 137:

> "*Vel quale per artem*
> *Inclusum buxo, aut Oricia terebintho*
> *Lucet ebur.*"

But the use of בַּת does not harmonize with the relation of the wood to the ivory inserted in wood; nor can it be defended by the fact that in Lam. iii. 3 an arrow is designated "the son of the quiver." According to this analogy, the ivory ought to have been called the son of the Ashurim, because the ivory is inserted in the wood, and not the wood in the ivory.[1] We must therefore adopt the solution proposed by R. Salomo and others, —namely, that the Masoretic division of בת־אשרים into two words is founded upon a mistake, and that it should be read as

[1] The Targum has paraphrased it in this way: דַּפִּין דאשכרעין מכבשין בְּשֵׁן דְּפִיל, *i.e.* planks of box or pine inlaid with ivory.

one word בְּתְאַשֻּׁרִים, ivory in תְּאַשֻּׁרִים, *i.e.* either sherbin-cedar (according to more recent expositors), or box-wood, for which Bochart (*Phal.* III. 5) has decided. The fact that in Isa. lx. 13 the תְּאַשּׁוּר is mentioned among the trees growing upon Lebanon, whereas here the תְּאַשֻּׁרִים are described as coming from the islands of the כִּתִּים, does not furnish a decisive argument to the contrary. We cannot determine with certainty what species of tree is referred to, and therefore it cannot be affirmed that the tree grew upon Lebanon alone, and not upon the islands of the Mediterranean. כִּתִּים are the *Κιτιεῖς*, the inhabitants of the port of *Κίτιον* in Cyprus; then the Cyprians generally; and here, as in Jer. ii. 10, where אִיִּים of the כִּתִּים are mentioned, in a still broader sense, inhabitants of Cyprus and other islands and coast-lands of the Mediterranean. In 1 Macc. i. 1 and viii. 5, even Macedonia is reckoned as belonging to the *γῆ Χεττειεῖμ* or *Κιτίεων*. Consequently the place from which the תְּאַשֻּׁרִים were brought does not furnish any conclusive proof that the Cyprian pine is referred to, although this was frequently used for ship-building. There is just as much ground for thinking of the box, as Bochart does, and we may appeal in support of this to the fact that, according to Theophrastus, there is no place in which it grows more vigorously than on the island of Corsica. In any case, Ezekiel mentions it as a very valuable kind of wood; though we cannot determine with certainty to what wood he refers, either from the place where it grew or from the accounts of the ancients concerning the kinds of wood that ship-builders used. The reason for this, however, is a very simple one,—namely, that the whole description has an ideal character, and, as Hitzig has correctly observed, "the application of the several kinds of wood to the different parts of the ship is evidently only poetical."

The same may be said of the materials of which, according to ver. 7, the sails and awning of the ship were made. *Byssus* in party-coloured work (רִקְמָה, see comm. on Ex. xxvi. 36), *i.e.*

woven in mixed colours, probably not merely in stripes, but woven with figures and flowers.[1] "From Egypt;" the byssus-weaving of Egypt was celebrated in antiquity, so that byssus-linen formed one of the principal articles of export (*vid.* Movers, *ut supra*, pp. 317 sqq.). מִפְרָשׂ, literally, spreading out, evidently signifies the sail, which we expect to find mentioned here, and with which the following clause, "to serve thee for a banner," can be reconciled, inasmuch as it may be assumed either that the sails also served for a banner, because the ships had no actual flag, like those in Wilkinson's engraving, or that the flag (נֵס) being also extended is included under the term מִפְרָשׂ (Hitzig). The covering of the ship, *i.e.* the awning which was put up above the deck for protection from the heat of the sun, consisted of purple (תְּכֵלֶת and אַרְגָּמָן, see the comm. on Ex. xxv. 4) from the islands of *Elishah*, *i.e.* of the Grecian Peloponnesus, which naturally suggests the Laconian purple so highly valued in antiquity on account of its splendid colour (Plin. *Hist. nat.* ix. 36, xxi. 8). The account of the building of the ship is followed by the manning, and the attention paid to its condition. The words of ver. 8*a* may be taken as referring quite as much to the ship as to the city, which was in possession of ships, and is mentioned by name in ver. 8*b*. The reference to the *Sidonians* and *Arvad*, *i.e.* to the inhabitants of *Aradus*, a rocky island to the north of Tripolis, as rowers, is not at variance with the latter; since there is no need to understand by the rowers either slaves or servants employed to row, and the Tyrians certainly drew their rowers from the whole of the Phoenician population, whereas the chief men in command of

[1] See Wilkinson, *Manners and Customs*, III. Pl. xvi., where engravings are given of Egyptian state-ships with embroidered sails. On one ship a large square sail is displayed in purple-red and purple-blue checks, surrounded by a gold border. The vessel of Antony and Cleopatra in the battle of Actium had also purple sails; and in this case the purple sails were the sign of the admiral's ship, just as in Ezekiel they serve as a mark of distinction (נֵס). See Movers, II. 3, p. 165, where the accounts of ancient writers concerning such state-ships are collected together.

the ships, the captain and pilot (חֹבְלִים), were no doubt as a rule citizens of Tyre. The introduction of the inhabitants of *Gebal*, *i.e.* the *Byblos* of the Greeks, the present *Jebail*, between Tripolis and Berytus (see the comm. on Josh. xiii. 5), who were noted even in Solomon's time as skilful architects (1 Kings v. 32), as repairers of the leak, decidedly favours the supposition that the idea of the ship is still kept in the foreground; and by the naming of those who took charge of the piloting and condition of the vessel, the thought is expressed that all the cities of Phoenicia assisted to maintain the might and glory of Tyre, since Tyre was supreme in Phoenicia. It is not till ver. 9*b* that the allegory falls into the background. Tyre now appears no longer as a ship, but as a maritime city, into which all the ships of the sea sail, to carry on and improve her commerce.—**Vers. 10, 11.** Tyre had also made the best provision for its defence. It maintained an army of mercenary troops from foreign countries to protect its colonies and extend its settlements, and entrusted the guarding of the walls of the city to fighting men of Phoenicia. The hired troops specially named in ver. 10 are *Pharas*, *Lud*, and *Phut*. פּוּט is no doubt an African tribe, in Coptic *Phaiat*, the Libyans of the ancients, who had spread themselves over the whole of North Africa as far as Mauretania (see the comm. on Gen. x. 6). לוּד is not the Semitic people of that name, the Lydians (Gen. x. 22), but here, as in ch. xxx. 5, Isa. lxvi. 19, and Jer. xlvi. 9, the Hamitic people of לוּדִים (Gen. x. 13), probably a general name for the whole of the Moorish tribes, since לוּד (ch. xxx. 5) and לוּדִים (Jer. xliv. 9) are mentioned in connection with פּוּט as auxiliaries in the Egyptian army. There is something striking in the reference to פָּרַס, the Persians. Hävernick points to the early intercourse carried on by the Phoenicians with Persia through the Persian Gulf, through which the former would no doubt be able to obtain mercenary soldiers, for which it was a general rule to select tribes as remote as possible. Hitzig objects to this, on the ground that there is no proof that this intercourse with Persia through the Persian Gulf was carried on in Ezekiel's time, and that even if it were, it does not follow that there were any Persian mercenaries. He therefore proposes to understand by פרס, Persians who had settled in Africa in the olden time. But this settlement cannot be inferred with sufficient certainty either from Sallust, *Jug.* c. 18, or from the occurrence of the African *Μάκαι* of Herodotus, iv. 175, along with the Asiatic (Ptol. vi. 7. 14), to take it as an explanation of פָּרַס. If we compare ch. xxxviii. 5, where *Pâras* is mentioned in connection with *Cush* and *Phut*, *Gomer* and *Togarmah*, as auxiliaries in the army of *Gog*, there can be no doubt that Asiatic Persians are intended there. And we have to take the word in the same sense here; for Hitzig's objections consist of pure conjectures which have no conclusive force. Ezekiel evidently intends to give the names of tribes from the far-off east, west, and south, who were enlisted as mercenaries in the military service of Tyre. Hanging the shields and helmets in the city, to ornament its walls, appears to have been a Phoenician custom, which Solomon also introduced into Judah (1 Kings x. 16, 17; Song of Sol. iv. 4), and which is mentioned again in the times of the Maccabees (1 Macc. iv. 57).—A distinction is drawn in ver. 11 between the mercenary troops on the one hand, and the Aradians, and חֵילֵךְ, thine army, the military corps consisting of Tyrians, on the other. The latter appear upon the walls of Tyre, because native troops were employed to watch and defend the city, whilst the mercenaries had to march into the field. The ἁπ. λεγ. גַּמָּדִים (*Gammâdim*) signifies brave men, as Roediger has conclusively shown from the Syrian usage, in his *Addenda* to Gesenius' *Thes.* p. 70 seq. It is therefore an *epitheton* of the native troops of Tyre.—With the words, "they (the troops) completed thy beauty," the picture of the glory of Tyre is rounded off, returning to its starting-point in vers. 4 and 5.

Vers. 12–25. This is followed by a description of the commerce of Tyre with all nations, who delivered their productions in the market of this metropolis of the commerce of the world, and received the wares and manufactures of this city in return. —Ver. 12. *Tarshish traded with thee for the multitude of goods of all kinds; with silver, iron, tin, and lead they paid for thy sales.* Ver. 13. *Javan, Tubal, and Meshech, they were thy merchants; with souls of men and brazen vessels they made thy barter.* Ver. 14. *From the house of Togarmah they paid horses, riding-horses, and mules for thy sales.* Ver. 15. *The sons of Dedan were thy merchants; many islands were at thy hand for commerce; ivory horns and ebony they brought thee in payment.* Ver. 16. *Aram traded with thee for the multitude of thy productions; with carbuncle, red purple, and embroidery, and byssus, and corals, and rubies they paid for thy sales.* Ver. 17. *Judah and the land of Israel, they were thy merchants; with wheat of Minnith and confectionery, and honey and oil, and balsam they made thy barter.* Ver. 18. *Damascus traded with thee in the multitude of thy productions, for the multitude of goods of all kinds, with wine of Chelbon and white wool.* Ver. 19. *Vedan and Javan from Uzal gave wrought iron for thy sales; cassia and calamus were for thy barter.* Ver. 20. *Vedan was thy merchant in cloths spread for riding.* Ver. 21. *Arabia and all the princes of Kedar, they were at thy hand for commerce; lambs and rams and he-goats, in these they traded with thee.* Ver. 22. *The merchants of Sheba and Ragmah, they were thy merchants; with all kinds of costly spices and with all kinds of precious stones and gold they paid for thy sales.* Ver. 23. *Haran, and Canneh, and Eden, the merchants of Sheba, Asshur, Chilmad, were thy merchants;* Ver. 24. *They were thy merchants in splendid clothes, in purple and embroidered robes, and in treasures of twisted yarn, in wound and strong cords for thy wares.* Ver. 25. *The ships of Tarshish were thy caravans, thy trade, and thou wast filled and glorious in the heart of the seas.*—The enumeration of the different peoples, lands, and cities, which carried on trade with Tyre, commences with Tarshish (Tartessus) in the extreme west, then turns to the north, passes through the different lands of Anterior Asia and the Mediterranean to the remotest north-east, and ends by mentioning Tarshish again, to round off the list. But the lands and peoples, which are mentioned in vers. 5–11 as furnishing produce and manufactures for the building of Tyre, viz. Egypt and the tribes of Northern Africa, are left out.—To avoid wearisome uniformity in the enumeration, Ezekiel has used interchangeably the synonymous words which the language possessed for trade, besides endeavouring to give life to the description by a variety of turns of expression. Thus סֹחַרְתֵּךְ (vers. 12, 16, 18), סֹחֲרַיִךְ (ver. 21), and סְחֹרַת יָדֵךְ (ver. 15), or סֹחֲרֵי יָדֵךְ (ver. 21), are interchanged with רֹכְלַיִךְ (vers. 13, 15, 17, 22, 24), רֹכַלְתֵּךְ (vers. 20, 23), and מַרְכֻּלְתֵּךְ (ver. 24); and, again, נָתַן עִזְבוֹנַיִךְ (vers. 12, 14, 22) or נָתַן בְּעִזְבוֹנַיִךְ (vers. 16, 19) with נָתַן מַעֲרָבֵךְ (vers. 13, 17), and בְּמַעֲרָבֵךְ הָיָה (ver. 19), and הֵשִׁיב אֶשְׁכָּרֵךְ (ver. 15). The words סֹחֵר, participle of סָחַר, and רֹכֵל, from רָכַל, signify merchants, traders, who travel through different lands for purposes of trade. סֹחֶרֶת, literally, the female trader; and סְחֹרָה, literally, trade; then used as abstract for concrete, the tradesman or merchant. רֹכֵל, the travelling merchant.—רֹכֶלֶת, the female trader, a city carrying on trade. מַרְכֹּלֶת, trade or a place of trade, a commercial town. עִזְבוֹנִים (*pluralet.*) does not mean a place of trade, market, and profits (Gesenius and others); but according to its derivation from עָזַב, to leave, relinquish, literally, leaving or giving up, and as Gusset. has correctly explained it, "that which you leave with another in the place of something else which he has given up to you." Ewald, in accordance with this explanation, has adopted the very appropriate rendering *Absatz*, or sale. נָתַן עִזְבוֹנַיִךְ, with בְּ, or with a double accusative, literally, to make thy sale with something, *i.e.* to pay or to give, *i.e.* pay, something as an equivalent for the sale; נָתַן בְּעִזּ׳, to give something for the sale, or the goods to be sold. מַעֲרָב, barter, goods bartered with נָתַן, to give bartered goods, or carry on trade by barter.

The following are the countries and peoples enumerated:—
תַּרְשִׁישׁ, the Tyrian colony of *Tarshish* or *Tartessus*, in *Hispania Baetica*, which was celebrated for its wealth in silver (Jer. x. 9), and, according to the passage before us, also supplied iron, tin, and lead (*vid.* Plin. *Hist. nat.* iii. 3 (4), xxxiii. 6 (31), xxxiv. 14 (41); Diod. Sic. v. 38). Further particulars concerning Tarshish are to be found in Movers, *Phoeniz.* II. 2, pp. 588 sqq., and II. 3, p. 36.—*Javan*, *i.e.* Jania, Greece or Greeks.—*Tubal* and *Meshech* are the *Tibareni* and *Moschi* of the ancients between the Black and Caspian Seas (see the comm. on Gen. x. 2). They supplied souls of men, *i.e.* slaves, and things in brass. The slave trade was carried on most vigorously by the Ionians and Greeks (see Joel iv. 6, from which we learn that the Phoenicians sold prisoners of war to them); and both Greeks and Romans drew their largest supplies and the best slaves from the Pontus (for proofs of this, see Movers, II. 3, pp. 81 seq.). It is probable that the principal supplies of brazen articles were furnished by the Tibareni and Moschi, as the Colchian mountains still contain an inexhaustible quantity of copper. In Greece, copper was found and wrought in *Euboea* alone; and the only other rich mines were in Cyprus (*vid.* Movers, II. 3, pp. 66, 67).—Ver. 14. "From the house of *Togarmah* they paid," *i.e.* they of the house of Togarmah paid. *Togarmah* is one of the names of the *Armenians* (see the comm. on Gen. x. 3); and Strabo (XI. 14. 9) mentions the wealth of Armenia in horses, whilst that in asses is attested by Herodotus (i. 194), so that we may safely infer that mules were also bred there.—Ver. 15. The sons of *Dedan*, or the Dedanites, are, no doubt, the Dedanites mentioned in Gen. x. 7 as descendants of Cush, who conducted the carrying trade between the Persian Gulf and Tyre, and whose caravans are mentioned in Isa. xxi. 13. Their relation to the Semitic Dedanites, who are evidently intended in ver. 20, and by the inhabitants of *Dedan* mentioned in connection with Edom in ch. xxv. 13 and Jer. xlix. 8, is involved in obscurity (see the

comm. on Gen. x. 7). The combination with אִיִּים רַבִּים and the articles of commerce which they brought to Tyre, point to a people of southern Arabia settled in the neighbourhood of the Persian Gulf. The many אִיִּים are the islands and coasts of Arabia on the Persian Gulf and Erythraean Sea.[1] סְחֹרַת יָדֵךְ, the commerce of thy hand, *i.e.* as *abstr. pro concr.*, those who were ready to thy hand as merchants. קַרְנוֹת שֵׁן, ivory horns. This is the term applied to the elephants' tusks (*shēn*) on account of their shape and resemblance to horns, just as Pliny (*Hist. nat.* xviii. 1) also speaks of *cornua elephanti*, although he says, in viii. 3 (4), that an elephant's weapons, which Juba calls *cornua*, are more correctly to be called *dentes.*[2] The ἁπ. λεγ. הוֹבְנִים, *Keri* הָבְנִים, signifies ἔβενος, *hebenum*, ebony. The ancients obtained both productions partly from India, partly from Ethiopia (Plin. xii. 4 (8)). According to Dioscor. i. 130, the Ethiopian ebony was preferred to the Indian. הֵשִׁיב אֶשְׁכָּר, to return payment (see the comm. on Ps. lxxii. 10).—In ver. 16, J. D. Michaelis, Ewald, Hitzig, and others read אֱדֹם for אֲרָם, after the LXX. and Pesh., because Aram did not lie in the road from Dedan and the אִיִּים to Israel (ver. 17), and it is not till ver. 18 that Ezekiel reaches Aram. Moreover, the corruption ארם for אדום could arise all the more readily from the simple fact that the defective form אֱדֹם only occurs in Ezekiel (xxv. 14), and is altogether an extraordinary one. These reasons are undoubtedly worthy of consideration; still they are not conclusive, since the enumeration does not follow a strictly geographical

[1] Movers (II. 3, pp. 303 sqq.) adduces still further evidence in addition to that given above, namely, that "unquestionable traces of the ancient name have been preserved in the region in which the ancient Dedanites are represented as living, partly on the coast in the names *Attana*, *Attene*, which have been modified according to well-known laws,—the former, a commercial town on the Persian Gulf, visited by Roman merchants (Plin. vi. 32, § 147); the latter, a tract of country opposite to the island of Tylos (Plin. *l.c.* § 49),—and partly in the islands of the Persian Gulf" (p. 304).

[2] The Ethiopians also call ivory *Karna nage*, i.e. *cornu elephanti*; and suppose that it is from horns, and not from tusks, that ivory comes (*vid.* Hiob Ludolph, *Hist. Aeth.* I. c. 10)

order, inasmuch as Damascus is followed in vers. 19 sqq. by many of the tribes of Southern Arabia, so that *Aram* might stand, as Hävernick supposes, for Mesopotamian Aram, for which the articles mentioned in ver. 16 would be quite as suitable as for Edom, whose chief city *Petra* was an important place of commerce and emporium for goods. רֹב מַעֲשָׂיִךְ, the multitude of thy works, thy manufactures. Of the articles of commerce delivered by אֲרָם, the red purple, embroidery, and בּוּץ (the Aramaean name for byssus, which appears, according to Movers, to have originally denoted a species of cotton), favour Aram, particularly Babylonia, rather than Edom. For the woven fabrics of Babylonia were celebrated from the earliest times (*vid.* Movers, II. 3, pp. 260 sqq.); and Babylon was also the oldest and most important market for precious stones (*vid.* Movers, p. 266). נֹפֶךְ is the carbuncle (see the comm. on Ex. xxviii. 18). כַּדְכֹּד, probably the ruby; in any case, a precious stone of brilliant splendour (*vid.* Isa. liv. 12). רָאמוֹת, corals or pearls (*vid.* Delitzsch on Job xxviii. 18).—*Judah* (ver. 17) delivered to Tyre wheat of *Minnith, i.e.* according to Judg. xi. 33, an Ammonitish place, situated, according to the *Onomast.*, four Roman miles from Heshbon in the direction of Philadelphia. That Ammonitis abounded in wheat, is evident from 2 Chron. xxvii. 5, although the land of Israel also supplied the Tyrians with wheat (1 Kings v. 25). The meaning of the ἀπ. λεγ. פַּנַּג cannot be definitely ascertained. The rendering confectionery is founded upon the Aramaean פַּנֵּק, *deliciari*, and the Chaldee translation, קוֹלְיָא, *i.e.* κολία, according to Hesychius, τὰ ἐκ μέλιτος τρωγάλια, or sweetmeats made from honey. Jerome renders it *balsamum*, after the μύρων of the LXX.; and in Hitzig's opinion, *Pannaga* (literally, a snake) is a name used in Sanscrit for a sweet-scented wood, which was employed in medicine as a cooling and strengthening drug (?). Honey (from bees) and oil are well-known productions of Palestine. צֳרִי is balsam; whether *resina* or the true balsam grown in gardens about Jericho (*opobalsamum*), it is impossible to decide (see my *Bibl. Archäol.* I. p. 38, and Movers, II. 3, pp. 220 sqq.). *Damascus* supplied Tyre with wine of *Chelbon.* חֶלְבּוֹן still exists in the village of *Helbôn,* a place with many ruins, three hours and a half to the north of Damascus, in the midst of a valley of the same name, which is planted with vines wherever it is practicable, from whose grapes the best and most costly wine of the country is made (*vid.* Robinson, *Biblical Researches*). Even in ancient times this wine was so celebrated, that, according to Posidonius (in *Athen. Deipnos.* i. 22), the kings of Persia drank only Chalybonian wine from Damascus (*vid.* Strabo, XV. 3. 22). צֶמֶר צַחַר, wool of dazzling whiteness; or, according to others, wool of *Zachar,* for which the Septuagint has ἔρια ἐκ Μιλήτου, Milesian wool.[1]—Ver. 19. Various explanations have been given of the first three words. וְדָן is not to be altered into וּדְדָן, as it has been by Ewald, both arbitrarily and unsuitably with ver. 20 immediately following; nor is it to be rendered "*and Dan.*" It is a decisive objection to this, that throughout the whole enumeration not a single land or people is introduced with the copula ו. *Vedan,* which may be compared with the *Vaheb* of Num. xxi. 14, a place also mentioned only once, is the name of a tribe and tract of land not mentioned elsewhere in the Old Testament. Movers (p. 302) conjectures that it is the celebrated city of *Aden* (عدن). *Javan* is also the name of an Arabian place or tribe; and, according to a notice in the *Kamus,* it is a place in *Yemen.* Tuch (*Genesis,* p. 210) supposes it to be a Greek (Ionian) settlement, the founders of which had been led by their enterprising spirit to cross the land of Egypt into Southern Arabia. For the purpose of distinguishing this Arabian *Javan* from Greece itself, or in order to define it more precisely, מְאוּזָּל is

[1] According to Movers (II. 3, p. 269), צַחַר is the *Sicharia of Aethicus* (Cosm. § 108): SICHARIA *regio, quae postea Nabathaea, nuncupatur, silvestris valde, ubi Ismaelitae eminus,*—an earlier name for the land of the Nabathaeans, who dwelt in olden time between Palestine and the Euphrates, and were celebrated for their wealth in flocks of sheep.

appended, which all the older translators have taken to be a proper name. According to the Masoretic pointing מְאוּזָּל, the word is, no doubt, to be regarded as a participle *Pual* of אֱזַל, in the sense of spun, from אָזַל, to spin. But apart from the fact that it would be a surprising thing to find spun goods mentioned in connection with the trade of the Arabian tribes, the explanation itself could not be sustained from the usage of the language; for there is nothing in the dialects to confirm the idea that אזל is a softened form of עזל, inasmuch as they have all עזל (Aram.) and غزل (Arab.), and the Talmudic אזל, *texere*, occurs first of all in the Gemara, and may possibly have been derived in the first instance from the Rabbinical rendering of our מאזל by "spun." Even the fact that the word is written with *Shurek* is against this explanation rather than in its favour; and in all probability its origin is to be traced to the simple circumstance, that in vers. 12, 14, 16 the articles of commerce are always mentioned before נָתְנוּ עִזְבוֹנָיִךְ, and in this verse they would appear to be omitted altogether, unless they are covered by the word מאזל. But we can very properly take the following words בַּרְזֶל עָשׁוֹת as the object of the first hemistich, since the Masoretic accentuation is founded upon the idea that מאזל is to be taken as the object here. We therefore regard מֵאוּזָל as the only admissible pointing, and take אוּזָל as a proper name, as in Gen. x. 27: "from *Uzal*," the ancient name of *Sanaa*, the subsequent capital of *Yemen*. The productions mentioned bear this out. Forged or wrought iron, by which Tuch (*l.c.* p. 260) supposes that sword-blades from Yemen are chiefly intended, which were celebrated among the Arabs as much as the Indian. Cassia and calamus (see the comm. on Ex. xxx. 23 and 24), two Indian productions, as Yemen traded with India from the very earliest times.—*Dedan* (ver. 20) is the inland people of that name, living in the neighbourhood of Edom (cf. ch. xxv. 13; see the comm. on ver. 15). They furnished בִּגְדֵי חֹפֶשׁ, *tapetes straguli*, cloths for spreading out, most likely costly riding-cloths, like the *middim* of Judg. v. 10.

עֲרַב and קֵדָר represent the nomad tribes of Central Arabia, the Bedouins. For עֲרַב is never used in the Old Testament for the whole of Arabia; but, according to its derivation from עֲרָבָה, a steppe or desert, simply for the tribes living as nomads in the desert (as in Isa. xiii. 20; Jer. iii. 2; cf. Ewald, *Grammat. Arab.* I. p. 5). *Kedar*, descended from Ishmael, an Arabian nomad tribe, living in the desert between Arabia Petraea and Babylonia, the *Cedrei* of Pliny (see the comm. on Gen. xxv. 13). They supplied lambs, rams, and he-goats, from the abundance of their flocks, in return for the goods obtained from Tyre.—Ver. 22. Next to these the merchants of *Sheba* and *Ragmah* (רַעְמָה) are mentioned. They were Arabs of Cushite descent (Gen. x. 7) in south-eastern Arabia (*Oman*); for רַעְמָה, Ῥέγμα, was in the modern province of Oman in the bay of the same name in the Persian Gulf. Their goods were all kinds of spices, precious stones, and gold, in which southern Arabia abounded. רֹאשׁ כָּל־בֹּשֶׂם, the chief or best of all perfumes (on this use of רֹאשׁ, see the comm. on Ex. xxx. 23; Song of Sol. iv. 14), is most likely the genuine balsam, which grew in *Yemen* (*Arabia felix*), according to Diod. Sic. iii. 45, along with other costly spices, and grows there still; for Forskal found a shrub between Mecca and Medina, called *Abu sham*, which he believed to be the true balsam, and of which he has given a botanical account in his *Flora Aeg.* pp. 79, 80 (as *Amyris opobalsamum*), as well as of two other kinds. Precious stones, viz. onyx-stones, rubies, agates, and cornelians, are still found in the mountains of Hadramaut; and in Yemen also jaspers, crystals, and many good rubies (*vid.* Niebuhr, *Descript.* p. 125, and Seetzen in Zach's *Monatl. Corresp.* xix. p. 339). And, lastly, the wealth of Yemen in gold is too strongly attested by ancient writers to be called in question (cf. Bochart, *Phal.* II. 28), although this precious metal is not found there now.—In vers. 23, 24 the trade with Mesopotamia is mentioned. חָרָן, the *Carrhae* of the Romans in north-western Mesopotamia (see the comm. on Gen. xi. 31), was situated at the crossing of the caravan-roads which intersect Mesopotamia; for it was at this point that the two caravan routes from Babylonia and the Delta of the Persian Gulf joined the old military and commercial road to Canaan (Movers, p. 247). The eastern route ran along the Tigris, where *Calneh*, the later *Ktesiphon*, was the most important commercial city. It is here called כַּנֵּה (Canneh), contracted from כַּלְנֵה (see the comm. on Gen. x. 10; Amos vi. 2). The western route ran along the Euphrates, past the cities mentioned in ver. 23*b*. עֶדֶן is not the Syrian, but the Mesopotamian *Eden* (2 Kings xix. 12; Isa. xxxvii. 12), the situation of which has not yet been determined, though Movers (p. 257) has sought for it in the Delta of the Euphrates and Tigris. The singular circumstance that the merchants of Sheba should be mentioned in connection with localities in Mesopotamia, which has given rise both to arbitrary alterations of the text and to various forced explanations, has been explained by Movers (p. 247 compared with p. 139) from a notice of Juba in Pliny's *Hist. nat.* xii. 17 (40), namely, that the Sabaeans, the inhabitants of the spice country, came with their goods from the Persian Gulf to Carrhae, where they held their yearly markets, and from which they were accustomed to proceed to Gabba (Gabala in Phoenicia) and Palestinian Syria. Consequently the merchants of Sabaea are mentioned as those who carried on the trade between Mesopotamia and Tyre, and are not unsuitably placed in the centre of those localities which formed the most important seats of trade on the two great commercial roads of Mesopotamia. *Asshur* and *Chilmad*, as we have already observed, were on the western road which ran along the Euphrates. כִּלְמַד has already been discovered by Bochart (*Phal.* I. 18) in the *Charmande* of Xenophon (*Anab.* i. 5. 10), and Sophaenetus (see Steph. Byz. *s.v.* *Χαρμάνδη*), a large and wealthy city in a desert region "beyond the river Euphrates." The *Asshur* mentioned along with *Chilmad*, in the midst of purely commercial cities, cannot be the land of Assyria, but must be the emporium *Sura* (Movers, p. 252), the present

Essurieh, which stands upon the bank on this side of the Euphrates above Thapsacus and on the caravan route, which runs from Palmyra past Rusapha (*Rezeph*, Isa. xxxvii. 12; 2 Kings xix. 12) to Nicephorium or Rakka, then in a northerly direction to Haran, and bending southwards, runs along the bank of the river in the direction of Chilmad or Charmande (Ritter, *Erdk.* XI. pp. 1081 sqq.). The articles of commerce from these emporia, which were brought to Tyre by Sabaean caravans, consisted of מַכְלֻלִים, literally, articles of perfect beauty, either state-dresses (cf. מִכְלֹל, ch. xxiii. 12 and xxxiv. 4), or more generally, costly works of art (Hävernick). The omission of the copula ו before בִּגְלוֹמֵי is decisive in favour of the former, as we may infer from this that בגל' is intended as an explanatory apposition to מַכְלֻלִים. גְּלוֹמֵי תְּכֵלֶת וְרִקְמָה, cloaks (גְּלוֹם connected with χλαμύς) of hyacinth-purple and embroidery, for which Babylonia was celebrated (for proofs of this, see Movers, pp. 258 sqq.). The words which follow cannot be explained with certainty. All that is evident is, that בַּחֲבָלִים חב' ואר' is appended to בְּגִנְזֵי בְּרֹמִים without a copula, as בגלומי וגו' is to בְּמַכְלֻלִים in the first hemistich, and therefore, like the latter, is intended as an explanatory apposition. חֲבָלִים does not mean either cloths or threads, but lines or cords. חֲבֻשִׁים signifies literally bound or wound up; probably twisted, *i.e.* formed of several threads wound together or spun; and אֲרֻזִים, firm, compact, from أَرَزَ, to be drawn together. Consequently גִּנְזֵי בְּרֹמִים וגו' can hardly have any other meaning than treasures of spun yarns, *i.e.* the most valuable yarns formed of different threads. For "treasures" is the only meaning which can be assigned to גְּנָזִים with any certainty on philological grounds, and בְּרֹמִים, from בָּרַם, برم, *contorsit*, is either yarn spun from several or various threads, or cloth woven from such threads. But the latter would not harmonize with חֲבָלִים. Movers (II. 3, pp. 263 sqq.) adopts a similar conclusion, and adduces evidence that silk yarn, bombyx, and cotton came to Tyre through the Mesopotamian trade, and were there dyed in the splendid Tyrian purples, and woven into cloths, or brought for sale with the dyeing complete. All the other explanations which have been given of these difficult words are arbitrary and untenable; not only the Rabbinical rendering of גִּנְזֵי בְּרֹמִים, viz. chests of damask, but that of Ewald, "pockets of damask," and that proposed by Hartmann, Hävernick, and others, viz. girdles of various colours, *ζῶναι σκιωταί*. In ver. 25 the description is rounded off with a notice of the lever of this world-wide trade. שָׁרוֹת cannot mean "walls" in this instance, as in Jer. v. 10, and like שׁוּרוֹת in Job xxiv. 11, because the ships, through which Tyre became so rich, could not be called walls. The word signifies "caravans," after שׁוּר = سار (Isa. lvii. 9), corresponding to the Aramaean שְׁיָרָא. מַעֲרָבֵךְ might be regarded as an accusative of more precise definition: caravans, with regard to (for) thy bartering trade. At the same time it is more rhetorical to take מַעֲרָבֵךְ as a second predicate: they were thy trade, *i.e.* the carriers of thy trade. What the caravans were for the emporia of trade on the mainland, the ships of Tarshish were for Tyre, and these on the largest sea-going ships are mentioned *instar omnium*. By means of these vessels Tyre was filled with goods, and rendered weighty (נִכְבַּד), *i.e.* rich and glorious.—But a tempest from the east would destroy Tyre with all its glory.

Vers. 26–36. Destruction of Tyre.—Ver. 26. *Thy rowers brought thee into great waters: the east wind broke thee up in the heart of the seas.* Ver. 27. *Thy riches and thy sales, thy bartering wares, thy seamen and thy sailors, the repairers of thy leaks and the traders in thy wares, and all thy fighting men in thee, together with all the multitude of people in thee, fell into the heart of the seas in the day of thy fall.* Ver. 28. *At the noise of the cry of thy sailors the places tremble.* Ver. 29. *And out of their ships come all the oarsmen, seamen, all the sailors of the sea; they come upon the land,* Ver. 30. *And make their voice heard over thee, and cry bitterly, and put dust upon their heads, and cover themselves with ashes;* Ver. 31. *And shave themselves bald on thy account, and gird on sackcloth, and weep for thee in anguish of soul a bitter wailing.* Ver. 32. *They raise over thee in their grief a lamentation, and lament over thee: Who is like Tyre! like the destroyed one in the midst of the sea!* Ver. 33. *When thy sales came forth out of the seas, thou didst satisfy many nations; with the abundance of thy goods and thy wares thou didst enrich kings of the earth.* Ver. 34. *Now that thou art wrecked away from the seas in the depths of the water, thy wares and all thy company are fallen in thee.* Ver. 35. *All the inhabitants of the islands are amazed at thee, and their kings shudder greatly; their faces quiver.* Ver. 36. *The traders among the nations hiss over thee; thou hast become a terror, and art gone for ever.*—The allusion to the ships of Tarshish, to which Tyre was indebted for its glory, serves as an introduction to a renewal in ver. 26 of the allegory of vers. 5–9*a;* Tyre is a ship, which is wrecked by the east wind (cf. Ps. xlviii. 8). In Palestine (Arabia and Syria) the east wind is characterized by continued gusts; and if it rises into a tempest, it generally causes great damage on account of the violence of the gusts (see Wetzstein in Delitzsch's commentary on Job xxvii. 1). Like a ship broken in pieces by the storm, Tyre with all its glory sinks into the depths of the sea. The repetition of בְּלֵב יַמִּים in vers. 26 and 27 forms an effective contrast to ver. 25; just as the enumeration of all the possessions of Tyre, which fall with the ship into the heart of the sea, does to the wealth and glory in ver. 25*b*. They who manned the ship also perish with the cargo,—"the seamen," *i.e.* sailors, rowers, repairers of leaks (calkers), also the merchants on board, and the fighting men who defended the ship and its goods against pirates,—the whole *qâhâl*, or gathering of people, in the ship. The difficult expression בְּכָל־קְהָלֵךְ can only be taken as an explanatory apposition to אֲשֶׁר בָּךְ: all the men who are in thee, namely, in the multitude of people in thee. Ver. 28. When the vessel is wrecked, the managers of the ship raise such a cry that the *migreshōth* tremble. מִגְרָשׁ is used in Num. xxxv. 2 for the precincts around the Levitical cities, which were set apart as pasture ground for the flocks; and in Ezek. xlv. 2, xlviii. 17, for the ground surrounding the holy city. Consequently מִגְרְשׁוֹת cannot mean the suburbs of Tyre in the passage before us, but must signify the open places on the mainland belonging to Tyre, *i.e.* the whole of its territory, with the fields and villages contained therein. The rendering "fleet," which Ewald follows the Vulgate in adopting, has nothing to support it.—Vers. 29 sqq. The ruin of this wealthy and powerful metropolis of the commerce of the world produces the greatest consternation among all who sail upon the sea, so that they forsake their ships, as if they were no longer safe in them, and leaving them for the land, bewail the fall of Tyre with deepest lamentation. הִשְׁמִיעַ with בְּקוֹל, as in Ps. xxvi. 7; 1 Chron. xv. 19, etc. For the purpose of depicting the lamentation as great and bitter in the extreme, Ezekiel groups together all the things that were generally done under such circumstances, viz. covering the head with dust (cf. Josh. vii. 6; 1 Sam. iv. 12; and Job ii. 12) and ashes (הִתְפַּלֵּשׁ, to strew, or cover oneself, not to roll oneself: see the comm. on Mic. i. 10); shaving a bald place (see ch. vii. 18 and the comm. on Mic. i. 16); putting on sackcloth; loud, bitter weeping (בְּמַר נֶפֶשׁ, as in Job vii. 11 and x. 1); and singing a mournful dirge (vers. 32 sqq.). בְּנִיהֶם, *in lamento eorum;* נִי contracted from נְהִי (Jer. ix. 17, 18; cf. הִי, ch. ii. 10). The reading adopted by the LXX., Theodot., Syr., and eleven Codd. (בְּנֵיהֶם) is unsuitable, as there is no allusion to sons, but the seamen themselves raise the lamentation. The correction proposed by Hitzig, בְּפִיהֶם, is altogether inappropriate. The exclamation, Who is like Tyre! is more precisely defined by כְּדֻמָּה, like the destroyed one in the midst of the sea. דֻּמָּה, participle *Pual*, with the מ dropt, as in 2 Kings ii. 10, etc. (*vid.* Ges. § 52. 2, Anm. 6). It is quite superfluous to assume that there was a noun דֻּמָּה signifying destruction. בצֵאת עזב' has been aptly explained by Hitzig: "inasmuch as thy wares sprang out of the sea, like the plants and field-fruits out of the soil" (the selection of the word הִשְׂבַּעְתְּ also suggested this simile); "not as being manufactured at Tyre, and therefore in the sea, but because the sea floated the goods to land for the people in the ships, and they satisfied the desire of the purchasers." Tyre satisfied peoples and enriched kings with its wares, not only by purchasing from them and paying for their productions with money or barter, but also by the fact that the Tyrians gave a still higher value to the raw material by the labour which they bestowed upon them. הוֹנַיִךְ in the plural is only met with here.—Ver. 34. But now Tyre with its treasures and its inhabitants has sunk in the depths of the sea. The antithesis in which ver. 34 really stands to ver. 33 does not warrant our altering עֵת נִשְׁבֶּרֶת into עַתְּ נִשְׁבַּרְתְּ, as Ewald and Hitzig propose, or adopting a different division of the second hemistich. עֵת is an adverbial accusative, as in ch. xvi. 57: "at the time of the broken one away from the seas into the depth of the waters, thy wares and thy people have fallen, *i.e.* perished." עֵת נִשְׁבֶּרֶת, *tempore quo fracta es.* נִשְׁבֶּרֶת מִיַּמִּים is intentionally selected as an antithesis to נוֹשֶׁבֶת מִיַּמִּים in ch. xxvi. 17.—Ver. 35. All the inhabitants of the islands and their kings, *i.e.* the inhabitants of the (coast of the) Mediterranean and its islands, will be thrown into consternation at the fall of Tyre; and (ver. 36) the merchants among the nations, *i.e.* the foreign nations, the rivals of Tyre in trade, will hiss thereat; in other words, give utterance to malicious joy. שָׁמֵם, to be laid waste, or thrown into perturbation with terror and amazement. רָעַם פָּנִים, to tremble or quiver in the face, *i.e.* to tremble so much that the terror shows itself in the countenance.—In ver. 36*b* Ezekiel brings the lamentation to a close in a similar manner to the threat contained in ch. xxvi. (*vid.* ch. xxvi. 21).

CHAP. XXVIII. 1–19. AGAINST THE PRINCE OF TYRE.

As the city of Tyre was first of all threatened with destruction (ch. xxvi.), and then her fall was confirmed by a lamentation (ch. xxvii.), so here the prince of Tyre is first of all forewarned of his approaching death (vers. 1–10), and then a lamentation is composed thereon (vers. 11–19).

Vers. 1–10. Fall of the Prince of Tyre.—Ver. 1. *And the word of Jehovah came to me, saying,* Ver. 2. *Son of man, say to the prince of Tyre, Thus saith the Lord Jehovah, Because thy heart has lifted itself up, and thou sayest, "I am a God, I sit upon a seat of Gods, in the heart of the seas," when thou art a man and not God, and cherishest a mind like a God's mind,* Ver. 3. *Behold, thou art wiser than Daniel; nothing secret is obscure to thee;* Ver. 4. *Through thy wisdom and thy understanding hast thou acquired might, and put gold and silver in thy treasuries;* Ver. 5. *Through the greatness of thy wisdom hast thou increased thy might by thy trade, and thy heart has lifted itself up on account of thy might,* Ver. 6. *Therefore thus saith the Lord Jehovah, Because thou cherishest a mind like a God's mind,* Ver. 7. *Therefore, behold, I will bring foreigners upon thee, violent men of the nations; they will draw their swords against the beauty of thy wisdom, and pollute thy splendour.* Ver. 8. *They will cast thee down into the pit, that thou mayest die the death of the slain in the heart of the seas.* Ver. 9. *Wilt thou indeed say, I am a God, in the face of him that slayeth thee, when thou art a man and not God in the hand of him that killeth thee?* Ver. 10. *Thou wilt die the death of the uncircumcised at the hand of foreigners; for I have spoken it, is the saying of the Lord Jehovah.*—This threat of judgment follows in general the same course as those addressed to other nations (compare especially ch. xxv.), namely, that the sin is mentioned first (vers. 2–5), and then the punishment consequent upon the sin (vers. 6–10). In ver. 12 מֶלֶךְ is used instead of נָגִיד, *dux*. In the use of the term נָגִיד to designate the king,

Kliefoth detects an indication of the peculiar position occupied by the prince in the commercial state of Tyre, which had been reared upon municipal foundations; inasmuch as he was not so much a monarch, comparable to the rulers of Babylon or to the Pharaohs, as the head of the great mercantile aristocracy. This is in harmony with the use of the word נָגִיד for the prince of Israel, David for example, whom God chose and anointed to be the *nâgîd* over His people; in other words, to be the leader of thè tribes, who also formed an independent commonwealth (*vid.* 1 Sam. xiii. 14; 2 Sam. vii. 8, etc.). The pride of the prince of Tyre is described in ver. 2 as consisting in the fact that he regarded himself as a God, and his seat in the island of Tyre as a God's seat. He calls his seat מוֹשַׁב אֱלֹהִים, not "because his capital stood out from the sea, like the palace of God from the ocean of heaven" (Ps. civ. 3), as Hitzig supposes; for, apart from any other ground, this does not suit the subsequent description of his seat as God's mountain (ver. 16), and God's holy mountain (ver. 14). The God's seat and God's mountain are not the palace of the king of Tyre, but Tyre as a state, and that not because of its firm position upon a rocky island, but as a holy island (*ἁγία νῆσος*, as Tyre is called in Sanchun. ed. Orelli, p. 36), the founding of which has been glorified by myths (*vid.* Movers, *Phoenizier*, I. pp. 637 sqq.). The words which Ezekiel puts into the mouth of the king of Tyre may be explained, as Kliefoth has well expressed it, "from the notion lying at the foundation of all natural religions, according to which every state, as the production of its physical factors and bases personified as the native deities of house and state, is regarded as a work and sanctuary of the gods." In Tyre especially the national and political development went hand in hand with the spread and propagation of its religion. "The Tyrian state was the production and seat of its gods. He, the prince of Tyre, presided over this divine creation and divine seat; therefore he, the prince, was himself a god, a manifestation of the deity, having its work and home in the state of Tyre." All heathen rulers looked upon themselves in this light; so that the king of Babylon is addressed in a similar manner in Isa. xiv. 13, 14. This self-deification is shown to be a delusion in ver. 2*b;* He who is only a man makes his heart like a God's heart, *i.e.* cherishes the same thought as the Gods. לֵב, the heart, as the seat of the thoughts and imaginations, is named instead of the disposition. This is carried out still further in vers. 3–5 by a description of the various sources from which this imagination sprang. He cherishes a God's mind, because he attributes to himself superhuman wisdom, through which he has created the greatness, and might, and wealth of Tyre. The words, "behold, thou art wiser," etc. (ver. 3), are not to be taken as a question, "art thou indeed wiser?" as they have been by the LXX., Syriac, and others; nor are they ironical, as Hävernick supposes; but they are to be taken literally, namely, inasmuch as the prince of Tyre was serious in attributing to himself supernatural and divine wisdom. Thou art, *i.e.* thou regardest thyself as being, wiser than Daniel. No hidden thing is obscure to thee (עָמַם, a later word akin to the Aramaean, "to be obscure"). The comparison with Daniel refers to the fact that Daniel surpassed all the magi and wise men of Babylon in wisdom through his ability to interpret dreams, since God gave him an insight into the nature and development of the power of the world, such as no human sagacity could have secured. The wisdom of the prince of Tyre, on the other hand, consisted in the cleverness of the children of this world, which knows how to get possession of all the good things of the earth. Through such wisdom as this had the Tyrian prince acquired power and riches. חַיִל, might, possessions in the broader sense; not merely riches, but the whole of the might of the commercial state of Tyre, which was founded upon riches and treasures got by trade. In ver. 5 בִּרְכֻלָּתְךָ is in apposition to בְּרֹב חָכְמָתְךָ, and is introduced as explanatory. The fulness of its wisdom showed itself in its commerce and the manner in which it conducted it, whereby Tyre had become rich and powerful. It is not till we reach ver. 6 that we meet with the apodosis answering to יַעַן גָּבַהּ וגו' in ver. 2, which has been pushed so far back by the intervening parenthetical sentences in vers. 2*b*–5. For this reason the sin of the prince of Tyre in deifying himself is briefly reiterated in the clause יַעַן תִּתְּךָ וגו' (ver. 6*b*, compare ver. 2*b*), after which the announcement of the punishment is introduced with a repetition of לָכֵן in ver. 7. Wild foes approaching with barbarous violence will destroy all the king's resplendent glory, slay the king himself with the sword, and hurl him down into the pit as a godless man. The enemies are called עָרִיצֵי גוֹיִם, violent ones of the peoples,—that is to say, the wild hordes composing the Chaldean army (cf. ch. xxx. 11, xxxi. 12). They drew the sword "against the beauty (יְפִי, the construct state of יֳפִי) of thy wisdom," *i.e.* the beauty produced by thy wisdom, the beautiful Tyre itself, with all that it contains (ch. xxvi. 3, 4). יִפְעָה, splendour; it is only here and in ver. 17 that we meet with it as a noun. The king himself they hurl down into the pit, *i.e.* the grave, or the nether world. מְמוֹתֵי חָלָל, the death of a pierced one, substantially the same as מוֹתֵי עֲרֵלִים. The plural מְמוֹתֵי and מוֹתֵי here and Jer. xvi. 4 (*mortes*) is a *pluralis exaggerativus*, a death so painful as to be equivalent to dying many times (see the comm. on Isa. liii. 9). In ver. 9 Ezekiel uses the *Piel* מְחַלֵּל in the place of the *Poel* מְחוֹלֵל, as חִלֵּל in the *Piel* occurs elsewhere only in the sense of *profanare*, and in Isa. li. 9 the *Poel* is used for piercing. But there is no necessity to alter the pointing in consequence, as we also find the *Pual* used by Ezekiel in ch. xxxii. 26 in the place of the *Poal* of Isa. liii. 5. The death of the uncircumcised is such a death as godless men die—a violent death. The king of Tyre, who looks upon himself as a god, shall perish by the sword like a godless man. At the same time, the whole of this threat applies, not to the one king, *Ithobal*, who was reigning at the time of the siege of Tyre by the Chaldeans, but to the king as the founder and creator of the might of Tyre (vers. 3–5), *i.e.* to the supporter of that royalty which was to perish along with Tyre itself.—It is to the king, as the representative of the might and glory of Tyre, and not merely to the existing possessor of the regal dignity, that the following lamentation over his fall refers.

Vers. 11–19. Lamentation over the King of Tyre.—Ver. 11. *And the word of Jehovah came to me, saying,* Ver. 12. *Son of man, raise a lamentation over the king of Tyre, and say to him, Thus saith the Lord Jehovah, Thou seal of a well-measured building, full of wisdom and perfect in beauty.* Ver. 13. *In Eden, the garden of God, wast thou; all kinds of precious stones were thy covering, cornelian, topaz, and diamond, chrysolite, beryl, and jasper, sapphire, carbuncle, and emerald, and gold: the service of thy timbrels and of thy women was with thee; on the day that thou wast created, they were prepared.* Ver. 14. *Thou wast a cherub of anointing, which covered, and I made thee for it; thou wast on a holy mountain of God; thou didst walk in the midst of fiery stones.* Ver. 15. *Thou wast innocent in thy ways from the day on which thou wast created, until iniquity was found in thee.* Ver. 16. *On account of the multitude of thy commerce, thine inside was filled with wrong, and thou didst sin: I will therefore profane thee away from the mountain of God; and destroy thee, O covering cherub, away from the fiery stones!* Ver. 17. *Thy heart has lifted itself up because of thy beauty, thou hast corrupted thy wisdom together with thy splendour: I cast thee to the ground, I give thee up for a spectacle before kings.* Ver. 18. *Through the multitude of thy sins in thine unrighteous trade thou hast profaned thy holy places; I therefore cause fire to proceed from the midst of thee, which shall devour thee, and make thee into ashes upon the earth before the eyes of all who see thee.* Ver. 19. *All who know thee among the peoples are amazed at thee: thou hast become a terror, and art gone for ever.*—The lamentation over the fall of the king of Tyre commences with a picture of the super-terrestrial glory of his position, so as to correspond to his self-deification as depicted in the foregoing word of God. In ver. 12 he is addressed as חֹתֵם תָּכְנִית. This does not mean, "artistically wrought signet-ring;" for חֹתֵם does not stand for חוֹתָם, but is a participle of חָתַם, to seal. There is all the more reason for adhering firmly to this meaning, that the following predicate, מָלֵא חָכְמָה, is altogether inapplicable to a signet-ring, though Hitzig once more scents a corruption of the text in consequence. תָּכְנִית, from תָּכַן, to weigh, or measure off, does not mean perfection (Ewald), beauty (Ges.), *façon* (Hitzig), or symmetry (Hävernick); but just as in ch. xliii. 10, the only other passage in which it occurs, it denotes the measured and well-arranged building of the temple, so here it signifies a well-measured and artistically arranged building, namely, the Tyrian state in its artistic combination of well-measured institutions (Kliefoth). This building is sealed by the prince, inasmuch as he imparts to the state firmness, stability, and long duration, when he possesses the qualities requisite for a ruler. These are mentioned afterwards, namely, "full of wisdom, perfect in beauty." If the prince answers to his position, the wisdom and beauty manifest in the institutions of the state are simply the impress received from the wisdom and beauty of his own mind. The prince of Tyre possessed such a mind, and therefore regarded himself as a God (ver. 2). His place of abode, which is described in vers. 13 and 14, corresponded to his position. Ezekiel here compares the situation of the prince of Tyre with that of the first man in Paradise; and then, in vers. 15 and 16, draws a comparison between his fall and the fall of Adam. As the first man was placed in the garden of God, in Eden, so also was the prince of Tyre placed in the midst of paradisaical glory. עֵדֶן is shown, by the apposition גַּן אֱלֹהִים, to be used as the proper name of Paradise; and this view is not to be upset by the captious objection of Hitzig, that Eden was not the garden of God, but that this was situated in Eden (Gen. ii. 8). The fact that Ezekiel calls Paradise גַּן־עֵדֶן in ch. xxxvi. 35, proves nothing more than that the terms *Eden* and *Garden of*

God do not cover precisely the same ground, inasmuch as the garden of God only occupied one portion of Eden. But notwithstanding this difference, Ezekiel could use the two expressions as synonymous, just as well as Isaiah (Isa. li. 3). And even if any one should persist in pressing the difference, it would not follow that בְּעֵדֶן was corrupt in this passage, as Hitzig fancies, but simply that גן אלהים defined the idea of עֵדֶן more precisely—in other words, restricted it to the garden of Paradise. There is, however, another point to be observed in connection with this expression, namely, that the epithet גן אלהים is used here and in ch. xxxi. 8, 9; whereas, in other places, Paradise is called גן יהוה (*vid.* Isa. li. 3; Gen. xiii. 10). Ezekiel has chosen Elohim instead of Jehovah, because Paradise is brought into comparison, not on account of the historical significance which it bears to the human race in relation to the plan of salvation, but simply as the most glorious land in all the earthly creation. The prince of Tyre, placed in the pleasant land, was also adorned with the greatest earthly glory. Costly jewels were his coverings, that is to say, they formed the ornaments of his attire. This feature in the pictorial description is taken from the splendour with which Oriental rulers are accustomed to appear, namely, in robes covered with precious stones, pearls, and gold. מְסֻכָּה, as a noun *ἁπ. λεγ.*, signifies a covering. In the enumeration of the precious stones, there is no reference to the breastplate of the high priest. For, in the first place, the order of the stones is a different one here; secondly, there are only nine stones named instead of twelve; and lastly, there would be no intelligible sense in such a reference, so far as we can perceive. Both precious stones and gold are included in the glories of Eden (*vid.* Gen. ii. 11, 12). For the names of the several stones, see the commentary on Ex. xxviii. 17–20. The words מְלֶאכֶת תֻּפֶּיךָ וגו׳—which even the early translators have entirely misunderstood, and which the commentators down to Hitzig and Ewald have made marvellous attempts to explain—present no peculiar difficulty, apart from the plural נקביך, which is only met with here. As the meaning timbrels, tambourins (*aduffa*), is well established for תֻּפִּים, and in 1 Sam. x. 5 and Isa. v. 12 flutes are mentioned along with the timbrels, it has been supposed by some that נְקָבִים must signify flutes here. But there is nothing to support such a rendering either in the Hebrew or in the other Semitic dialects. On the other hand, the meaning *pala gemmarum* (Vulgate), or ring-casket, has been quite arbitrarily forced upon the word by Jerome, Rosenmüller, Gesenius, and many others. We agree with Hävernick in regarding נְקָבִים as a plural of נְקֵבָה (*foeminae*), formed, like a masculine, after the analogy of נָשִׁים, פִּלַגְשִׁים, etc., and account for the choice of this expression from the allusion to the history of the creation (Gen. i. 27). The service (מְלֶאכֶת, performance, as in Gen. xxxix. 11, etc.) of the women is the leading of the circular dances by the odalisks who beat the timbrels: "the harem-pomp of Oriental kings." This was made ready for the king on the day of his creation, *i.e.* not his birthday, but the day on which he became king, or commenced his reign, when the harem of his predecessor came into his possession with all its accompaniments. Ezekiel calls this the day of his creation, with special reference to the fact that it was God who appointed him king, and with an allusion to the parallel, underlying the whole description, between the position of the prince of Tyre and that of Adam in Paradise.[1] The next verse (ver. 14) is a more difficult one. אַתְּ is an abbreviation of אַתָּה, אַתְּ, as in Num. xi. 15; Deut. v. 24 (see Ewald, § 184*a*). The ἁπ. λεγ. מִמְשַׁח has been explained in very different ways, but mostly according to the Vulgate rendering,

[1] In explanation of the fact alluded to, Hävernick has very appropriately called attention to a passage of Athen. (xii. 8, p. 531), in which the following statement occurs with reference to Strato, the Sidonian king: "Strato, with flute-girls, and female harpers and players on the cithara, made preparations for the festivities, and sent for a large number of *hetaerae* from the Peloponnesus, and many singing-girls from Ionia, and young *hetaerae* from the whole of Greece, both singers and dancers." See also other passages in Brissonius, *de regio Pers. princ.* pp. 142–3.

tu Cherub extentus et protegens, as signifying spreading out or extension, in the sense of "with outspread wings" (Gesenius and many others). But מָשַׁח does not mean either to spread out or to extend. The general meaning of the word is simply to anoint; and judging from מִשְׁחָה and מָשְׁחָה, *portio*, Lev. vii. 35 and Num. xviii. 8, also to measure off, from which the idea of extension cannot possibly be derived. Consequently the meaning "anointing" is the only one that can be established with certainty in the case of the word מִמְשַׁח. So far as the form is concerned, מִמְשַׁח might be in the construct state; but the connection with הַסּוֹכֵךְ, anointing, or anointed one, of the covering one, does not yield any admissible sense. A comparison with ver. 16, where כְּרוּב הַסּוֹכֵךְ occurs again, will show that the מִמְשַׁח, which stands between these two words in the verse before us, must contain a more precise definition of כְּרוּב, and therefore is to be connected with כְּרוּב in the construct state: cherub of anointing, *i.e.* anointed cherub. This is the rendering adopted by Kliefoth, the only commentator who has given the true explanation of the verse. מִמְשַׁח is the older form, which has only been retained in a few words, such as מִרְמָס in Isa. x. 6, together with the tone-lengthened *a* (*vid.* Ewald, § 160*a*). The prince of Tyre is called an anointed cherub, as Ephraem Syrus has observed, because he was a king even though he had not been anointed. הַסּוֹכֵךְ is not an abstract noun, either here or in Nah. ii. 6, but a participle; and this predicate points back to Ex. xxv. 20, "the cherubim covered (סוֹכְכִים) the capporeth with their wings," and is to be explained accordingly. Consequently the king of Tyre is called a cherub, because, as an anointed king, he covered or overshadowed a sanctuary, like the cherubim upon the ark of the covenant. What this sanctuary was is evident from the remarks already made at ver. 2 concerning the divine seat of the king. If the "seat of God," upon which the king of Tyre sat, is to be understood as signifying the state of Tyre, then the sanctuary which he covered or overshadowed as a cherub will also be the Tyrian state, with its holy places and sacred things. In the next clause, וּנְתַתִּיךָ is to be taken by itself according to the accents, "and I have made thee (so)," and not to be connected with בְּהַר קֹדֶשׁ. We are precluded from adopting the combination which some propose—viz. "I set thee upon a holy mountain; thou wast a God"—by the incongruity of first of all describing the prince of Tyre as a cherub, and then immediately afterwards as a God, inasmuch as, according to the Biblical view, the cherub, as an angelic being, is simply a creature and not a God; and the fanciful delusion of the prince of Tyre, that he was an *El* (ver. 2), could not furnish the least ground for his being addressed as *Elohim* by Ezekiel. And still more are we precluded from taking the words in this manner by the declaration contained in ver. 16, that Jehovah will cast him out "from the mountain of Elohim," from which we may see that in the present verse also *Elohim* belongs to *har*, and that in ver. 16, where the mountain of God is mentioned again, the predicate קֹדֶשׁ is simply omitted for the sake of brevity, just as מִמְשַׁח is afterwards omitted on the repetition of כְּרוּב הַסּוֹכֵךְ. The missing but actual object to נְתַתִּיךָ can easily be supplied from the preceding clause,—namely, this, *i.e.* an overshadowing cherub, had God made him, by placing him as king in paradisaical glory. The words, "thou wast upon a holy mountain of God," are not to be interpreted in the sense suggested by Isa. xiv. 13, namely, that Ezekiel was thinking of the mountain of the gods (Alborj) met with in Asiatic mythology, because it was there that the cherub had its home, as Hitzig and others suppose; for the Biblical idea of the cherub is entirely different from the heathen notion of the griffin keeping guard over gold. It is true that God placed the cherub as guardian of Paradise, but Paradise was not a mountain of God, nor even a mountainous land. The idea of a holy mountain of God, as being the seat of the king of Tyre, was founded partly upon the natural situation of Tyre itself, built as it was upon one or two rocky islands of the Mediterranean, and partly upon the heathen notion of the sacredness of this island as the seat of the Deity, to which the Tyrians attributed the grandeur of their state. To this we may probably add a reference to Mount Zion, upon which was the sanctuary, where the cherub covered the seat of the presence of God. For although the comparison of the prince of Tyre to a cherub was primarily suggested by the description of his abode as Paradise, the epithet הַסּוֹכֵךְ shows that the place of the cherub in the sanctuary was also present to the prophet's mind. At the same time, we must not understand by הַר קֹדֶשׁ Mount Zion itself. The last clause, "thou didst walk in the midst of (among) fiery stones," is very difficult to explain. It is admitted by nearly all the more recent commentators, that "stones of fire" cannot be taken as equivalent to "every precious stone" (ver. 13), both because the precious stones could hardly be called stones of fire on account of their brilliant splendour, and also being covered with precious stones is not walking in the midst of them. Nor can we explain the words, as Hävernick has done, from the account given by Herodotus (II. 44) of the two emerald pillars in the temple of Hercules at Tyre, which shone resplendently by night; for pillars shining by night are not stones of fire, and the king of Tyre did not walk in the temple between these pillars. The explanation given by Hofmann and Kliefoth appears to be the correct one, namely, that the stones of fire are to be regarded as a wall of fire (Zech. ii. 9), which rendered the cherubic king of Tyre unapproachable upon his holy mountain.

In ver. 15, the comparison of the prince of Tyre to Adam in Paradise is brought out still more prominently. As Adam was created sinless, so was the prince of Tyre innocent in his conduct in the day of his creation, but only until perverseness was found in him. As Adam forfeited and lost the happiness conferred upon him through his fall, so did the king of Tyre forfeit his glorious position through unrighteousness and sin, and cause God to cast him from his eminence down to the ground.

He fell into perverseness in consequence of the abundance of his trade (ver. 16*a*). Because his trade lifted him up to wealth and power, his heart was filled with iniquity. מָלוּ for מָלְאוּ, like מִלּוֹ for מִלוֹא in ch. xli. 8, and נָשׂוּ for נָשְׂאוּ in ch. xxxix. 26. תּוֹכְךָ is not the subject, but the object to מָלוּ; and the plural מָלוּ, with an indefinite subject, "they filled," is chosen in the place of the passive construction, because in the Hebrew, as in the Aramaean, active combinations are preferred to passive whenever it is possible to adopt them (*vid.* Ewald, § 294*b* and 128*b*). מָלֵא is used by Ezekiel in the transitive sense "to fill" (ch. viii. 17 and xxx. 11). תָּוֶךְ, the midst, is used for the interior in a physical sense, and not in a spiritual one; and the expression is chosen with an evident allusion to the history of the fall. As Adam sinned by eating the forbidden fruit of the tree, so did the king of Tyre sin by filling himself with wickedness in connection with trade (Hävernick and Kliefoth). God would therefore put him away from the mountain of God, and destroy him. חִלֵּל with מִן is a pregnant expression: to desecrate away from, *i.e.* to divest of his glory and thrust away from. וָאַבֶּדְךָ is a contracted form for וָאֲאַבֶּדְךָ (*vid.* Ewald, § 232*h* and § 72*c*).—Vers. 17 and 18 contain a comprehensive description of the guilt of the prince of Tyre, and the approaching judgment is still further depicted. עַל יִפְעָתֶךָ cannot mean, "on account of thy splendour," for this yields no appropriate thought, inasmuch as it was not the splendour itself which occasioned his overthrow, but the pride which corrupted the wisdom requisite to exalt the might of Tyre,—in other words, tempted the prince to commit iniquity in order to preserve and increase his glory. We therefore follow the LXX., Syr., Ros., and others, in taking עַל in the sense of *una cum*, together with. רַאֲוָה is an infinitive form, like אַהֲבָה for רְאוֹת, though Ewald (§ 238*e*) regards it as so extraordinary that he proposes to alter the text. רָאָה with ב is used for looking upon a person with malicious pleasure. בְּעֶוֶל רְכֻלָּתְךָ shows in what the guilt (עָוֹן) consisted (עֶוֶל is the construct state of עָוֶל). The sanctuaries (*miqdâshim*) which the king of Tyre desecrated by the unrighteousness of his commerce, are not the city or the state of Tyre, but the temples which made Tyre a holy island. These the king desecrated by bringing about their destruction through his own sin. Several of the codices and editions read מִקְדָּשְׁךָ in the singular, and this is the reading adopted by the Chaldee, Syriac, and Vulgate versions. If this were the true reading, the sanctuary referred to would be the holy mountain of God (vers. 14 and 16). But the reading itself apparently owes its origin simply to this interpretation of the words. In the clause, "I cause fire to issue from the midst of thee," מִתּוֹכְךָ is to be understood in the same sense as תּוֹכְךָ in ver. 16. The iniquity which the king has taken into himself becomes a fire issuing from him, by which he is consumed and burned to ashes. All who know him among the peoples will be astonished at his terrible fall (ver. 19, compare ch. xxvii. 36).

If we proceed, in conclusion, to inquire into the fulfilment of these prophecies concerning Tyre and its king, we find the opinions of modern commentators divided. Some, for example Hengstenberg, Hävernick, Drechsler (on Isa. xxiii.), and others, assuming that, after a thirteen years' siege, Nebuchadnezzar conquered the strong Island Tyre, and destroyed it; while others—viz. Gesenius, Winer, Hitzig, etc.—deny the conquest by Nebuchadnezzar, or at any rate call it in question; and many of the earlier commentators suppose the prophecy to refer to Old Tyre, which stood upon the mainland. For the history of this dispute, see Hengstenberg, *De rebus Tyriorum comment.* (Berol. 1832); Hävernick, *On Ezekiel*, pp. 420 sqq.; and Movers, *Phoenizier*, II. 1, pp. 427 sqq.—The denial of the conquest of Insular Tyre by the king of Babylon rests partly on the silence which ancient historians, who mention the siege itself, have maintained as to its result; and partly on the statement contained in Ezek. xxix. 17–20.—All that Josephus (*Antt.* x. 11. 1) is able to quote from the ancient historians on this point is the following:—In the first place, he states, on the authority of the third book of the Chaldean history of Berosus, that when the father of Nebuchadnezzar, on account of his own age and consequent infirmity, had transferred to his son the conduct of the war against the rebellious satrap in Egypt, Coelesyria, and Phoenicia, Nebuchadnezzar defeated him, and brought the whole country once more under his sway. But as the tidings reached him of the death of his father just at the same time, after arranging affairs in Egypt, and giving orders to some of his friends to lead into Babylon the captives taken from among the Judaeans, the Phoenicians, the Syrians, and the Egyptians, together with the heavy armed portion of the army, he himself hastened through the desert to Babylon, with a small number of attendants, to assume the government of the empire. Secondly, he states, on the authority of the Indian and Phoenician histories of Philostratus, that when Ithobal was on the throne, Nebuchadnezzar besieged Tyre for thirteen years. The accounts taken from Berosus are repeated by Josephus in his *c. Apion* (i. § 19), where he also adds (§ 20), in confirmation of their credibility, that there were writings found in the archives of the Phoenicians which tallied with the statement made by Berosus concerning the king of Chaldea (Nebuchadnezzar), viz. "that he conquered all Syria and Phoenicia;" and that Philostratus also agrees with this, since he mentions the siege of Tyre in his histories (*μεμνημένος τῆς Τύρου πολιορκίας*). In addition to this, for synchronistic purposes, Josephus (*c. Ap.* i. 21) also communicates a fragment from the Phoenician history, containing not only the account of the thirteen years' siege of Tyre by Nebuchadnezzar in the reign of Ithobal, but also a list of the kings of Tyre who followed Ithobal, down to the time of Cyrus of Persia.[1] The siege of Tyre is

[1] The passage reads as follows: "In the reign of Ithobal the king, Nebuchadnezzar besieged Tyre for thirteen years. After him judges were appointed. Ecnibalus, the son of Baslachus, judged for two months; Chelbes, the son of Abdaeus, for ten months; Abbarus, the high priest, for three months; Myttonus and Gerastartus, the sons of Abdelemus, for

therefore mentioned three times by Josephus, on the authority of Phoenician histories; but he never says anything of the conquest and destruction of that city by Nebuchadnezzar. From this circumstance the conclusion has been drawn, that this was all he found there. For if, it is said, the siege had terminated with the conquest of the city, this glorious result of the thirteen years' exertions could hardly have been passed over in silence, inasmuch as in *Antt.* x. 11. 1 the testimony of foreign historians is quoted to the effect that Nebuchadnezzar was "an active man, and more fortunate than the kings that were before him." But the argument is more plausible than conclusive. If we bear in mind that Berosus simply relates the account of a subjugation and devastation of the whole of Phoenicia, without even mentioning the siege of Tyre, and that it is only in Phoenician writings therefore that the latter is referred to, we cannot by any means conclude, from their silence as to the result or termination of the siege, that it ended gloriously for the Tyrians and with humiliation to Nebuchadnezzar, or that he was obliged to relinquish the attempt without success after the strenuous exertions of thirteen years. On the contrary, considering how all the historians of antiquity show the same anxiety, if not to pass over in silence such events as were unfavourable to their country, at all events to put them in as favourable a light as possible, the fact that the Tyrian historians observe the deepest silence as to the result of the thirteen years' siege of Tyre would rather force us to the conclusion that it was very humiliating to Tyre. And this could only be the case if Nebuchadnezzar really conquered Tyre at the end of thirteen years. If he had been obliged to relinquish the siege because he found himself unable to conquer so strong a city, the Tyrian historians would most assuredly have related

six years; after whom Balatorus reigned for one year. When he died, they sent for and fetched Merbalus from Babylon, and he reigned four years. At his death they sent for his brother Eiramus, who reigned twenty years. During his reign, Cyrus ruled over the Persians."

this termination of the thirteen years' strenuous exertions of the great and mighty king of Babylon.

The silence of the Tyrian historians concerning the conquest of Tyre is no proof, therefore, that it did not really take place. But Ezek. xxix. 17–20 has also been quoted as containing positive evidence of the failure of the thirteen years' siege; in other words, of the fact that the city was not taken. We read in this passage, that Nebuchadnezzar caused his army to perform hard service against Tyre, and that neither he nor his army received any recompense for it. Jehovah would therefore give him Egypt to spoil and plunder as wages for this work of theirs in the service of Jehovah. Gesenius and Hitzig (on Isa. xxiii.) infer from this, that Nebuchadnezzar obtained no recompense for the severe labour of the siege, because he did not succeed in entering the city. But Movers (*l.c.* p. 448) has already urged in reply to this, that "the passage before us does not imply that the city was not conquered any more than it does the opposite, but simply lays stress upon the fact that it *was not plundered.* For nothing can be clearer in this connection than that what we are to understand by the wages, which Nebuchadnezzar did not receive, notwithstanding the exertions connected with his many years' siege, is simply the treasures of Tyre;" though Movers is of opinion that the passage contains an intimation that the siege was brought to an end with a certain compromise which satisfied the Tyrians, and infers, from the fact of stress being laid exclusively upon the neglected plundering, that the termination was of such a kind that plundering might easily have taken place, and therefore that Tyre was either actually conquered, but treated mildly from wise considerations, or else submitted to the Chaldeans upon certain terms. But neither of these alternatives can make the least pretension to probability. In Ezek. xxix. 20 it is expressly stated that "as wages, for which he (Nebuchadnezzar) has worked, I give him the land of Egypt, because they (Nebuchadnezzar and his army) have done it for me;" in other words, have done the work for me. When, therefore, Jehovah promises to give Egypt to Nebuchadnezzar as a reward or wages for the hard work which has been done for Him at Tyre, the words presuppose that Nebuchadnezzar had really accomplished against Tyre the task entrusted to him by God. But God had committed to him not merely the siege, but also the conquest and destruction of Tyre. Nebuchadnezzar must therefore have executed the commission, though without receiving the expected reward for the labour which he had bestowed; and on that account God would compensate him for his trouble with the treasures of Egypt. This precludes not only the supposition that the siege was terminated, or the city surrendered, on the condition that it should not be plundered, but also the idea that for wise reasons Nebuchadnezzar treated the city leniently after he had taken possession. In either case Nebuchadnezzar would not have executed the will of Jehovah upon Tyre in such a manner as to be able to put in any claim for compensation for the hard work performed. The only thing that could warrant such a claim would be the circumstance, that after conquering Tyre he found no treasures to plunder. And this is the explanation which Jerome has given of the passage *ad litteram.* "Nebuchadnezzar," he says, "being unable, when besieging Tyre, to bring up his battering-rams, besieging towers, and *vineae* close to the walls, on account of the city being surrounded by the sea, employed a very large number of men from his army in collecting rocks and piling up mounds of earth, so as to fill up the intervening sea, and make a continuous road to the island at the narrowest part of the strait. And when the Tyrians saw that the task was actually accomplished, and the foundations of the walls were being disturbed by the shocks from the battering-rams, they placed in ships whatever articles of value the nobility possessed in gold, silver, clothing, and household furniture, and transported them to the islands; so that when the city was taken, Nebuchadnezzar found nothing to compensate him for all his labour. And because he had done the will of God in all this, some years after the conquest of Tyre, Egypt was given to him by God."[1] It is true that we have no historical testimony from any other quarter to support this interpretation. But we could not expect it in any of the writings which have come down to us, inasmuch as the Phoenician accounts extracted by Josephus simply contain the fact of the thirteen years' siege, and nothing at all concerning its progress and result. At the same time, there is the greatest probability that this was the case. If Nebuchadnezzar really besieged the city, which was situated upon an island in the sea, he could not have contented himself with cutting off the supply of drinking water from the city simply on the land side, as Shalmanezer, the king of Assyria, is said to have done (*vid.* Josephus, *Antt.* ix. 14. 2), but must have taken steps to fill up the strait between the city and the mainland with a mound, that he might construct a road for besieging and assaulting the walls, as Alexander of Macedonia afterwards did. And the words of Ezek. xxix. 18, according to which every head was bald, and the skin rubbed off every shoulder with the severity of the toil, point indisputably to the undertaking of some such works as these. And if the Chaldeans really carried out their operations upon the city in this way, as the siege-works advanced, the Tyrians would not neglect any precaution to defend themselves as far as possible, in the event of the capture of the city. They would certainly send the possessions and treasures of the city by ship into the colonies, and thereby place them in security; just as, according to Curtius, iv. 3, they sent off their families to Carthage, when the city was besieged by Alexander.

This view of the termination of the Chaldean siege of Tyre receives a confirmation of no little weight from the fragment of Menander already given, relating to the succession of rulers in Tyre after the thirteen years' siege by Nebuchadnezzar. It is there stated that after Ithobal, Baal reigned for ten years,

[1] Cyrill. Alex. gives the same explanation in his commentary on Isa. xxiii.

that judges (*suffetes*) were then appointed, nearly all of whom held office for a few months only; that among the last judges there was also a king *Balatorus*, who reigned for a year; that after this, however, the Tyrians sent to Babylon, and brought thence *Merbal*, and on his death *Hiram*, as kings, whose genuine Tyrian names undoubtedly show that they were descendants of the old native royal family. This circumstance proves not only that Tyre became a Chaldean dependency in consequence of the thirteen years' siege by Nebuchadnezzar, but also that the Chaldeans had led away the royal family to Babylonia, which would hardly have been the case if Tyre had submitted to the Chaldeans by a treaty of peace.

If, however, after what has been said, no well-founded doubt can remain as to the conquest of Tyre by Nebuchadnezzar, our prophecy was not so completely fulfilled thereby, that Tyre became a bare rock on which fishermen spread their nets, as is threatened in ch. xxvi. 4, 5, 14. Even if Nebuchadnezzar destroyed its walls, and laid the city itself in ruins to a considerable extent, he did not totally destroy it, so that it was not restored. On the contrary, two hundred and fifty years afterwards, we find Tyre once more a splendid and powerful royal city, so strongly fortified, that Alexander the Great was not able to take it till after a siege of seven months, carried on with extraordinary exertions on the part of both the fleet and army, the latter attacking from the mainland by means of a mound of earth, which had been thrown up with considerable difficulty (Diod. Sic. xvii. 40 sqq.; Arrian, *Alex.* ii. 17 sqq.; Curtius, iv. 2–4). Even after this catastrophe it rose once more into a distinguished commercial city under the rule of the Seleucidae and afterwards of the Romans, who made it the capital of Phoenicia. It is mentioned as such a city in the New Testament (Matt. xv. 21; Acts xxi. 3, 7); and Strabo (xvi. 2. 23) describes it as a busy city with two harbours and very lofty houses. But Tyre never recovered its ancient grandeur. In the first centuries of the Christian era, it is frequently mentioned as an archbishop's see. From A.D. 636 to A.D. 1125 it was under the rule of the Saracens, and was so strongly fortified, that it was not till after a siege of several months' duration that they succeeded in taking it. Benjamin of Tudela, who visited Tyre in the year 1060, describes it as a city of distinguished beauty, with a strongly fortified harbour, and surrounded by walls, and with the best glass and earthenware in the East. "Saladin, the conqueror of Palestine, broke his head against Tyre in the year 1189. But after Acre had been taken by storm in the year 1291 by the Sultan El-Ashraf, on the day following this conquest the city passed without resistance into the hands of the same Egyptian king; the inhabitants having forsaken Tyre by night, and fled by sea, that they might not fall into the power of such bloodthirsty soldiers" (Van de Velde). When it came into the hands of the Saracens once more, its fortifications were demolished; and from that time forward Tyre has never risen from its ruins again. Moreover, it had long ceased to be an insular city. The mound which Alexander piled up, grew into a broader and firmer tongue of land in consequence of the sand washed up by the sea, so that the island was joined to the mainland, and turned into a peninsula. The present *Sûr* is situated upon it, a market town of three or four thousand inhabitants, which does not deserve the name of a city or town. The houses are for the most part nothing but huts; and the streets are narrow, crooked, and dirty lanes. The ruins of the old Phoenician capital cover the surrounding country to the distance of more than half an hour's journey from the present town gate. The harbour is so thoroughly choked up with sand, and filled with the ruins of innumerable pillars and building stones, that only small boats can enter. The sea has swallowed up a considerable part of the greatness of Tyre; and quite as large a portion of its splendid temples and fortifications lie buried in the earth. To a depth of many feet the soil trodden at the present day is one solid mass of building stones, shafts of pillars, and rubbish composed of marble, porphyry, and granite. Fragments of pillars of the costly *verde antiquo* (green marble) also lie strewn about in large quantities. The crust, which forms the soil that is trodden to-day, is merely the surface of this general heap of ruins. Thus has Tyre actually become "a bare rock, and a place for the spreading of nets in the midst of sea;" and "the dwelling-places, which are now erected upon a portion of its former site, are not at variance with the terrible decree, 'thou shalt be built no more'" (compare Robinson's *Palestine*, and Van de Velde's *Travels*).—Thus has the prophecy of Ezekiel been completely fulfilled, though not directly by Nebuchadnezzar; for the prophecy is not a bare prediction of historical details, but is pervaded by the idea of the judgment of God. To the prophet, Nebuchadnezzar is the instrument of the punitive righteousness of God, and Tyre the representative of the ungodly commerce of the world. Hence, as Hävernick has already observed, Nebuchadnezzar's action is more than an isolated deed in the prophet's esteem. "In his conquest of the city he sees the whole of the ruin concentrated, which history places before us as a closely connected chain. The breaking of the power of Tyre by Nebuchadnezzar stands out before his view as inseparably connected with its utter destruction. This was required by the internal theocratic signification of the fact in its relation to the destruction of Jerusalem." Jerusalem will rise again to new glory out of its destruction through the covenant faithfulness of God (ch. xxviii. 25, 26). But Tyre, the city of the world's commerce, which is rejoicing over the fall of Jerusalem, will pass away for ever (ch. xxvi. 14, xxvii. 36).

CHAP. XXVIII. 20–26. PROPHECY AGAINST SIDON AND PROMISE FOR ISRAEL.

The threatening word against Sidon is very brief, and couched in general terms, because as a matter of fact the prophecy against Tyre involved the announcement of the fall of Sidon, which was dependent upon it; and, as we have already observed, Sidon received a special word of God simply for the purpose of making up the number of the heathen nations mentioned to the significant number seven. The word of God against Sidon brings to a close the cycle of predictions of judgment directed against those heathen nations which had given expression to malicious pleasure at the overthrow of the kingdom of Judah. There is therefore appended a promise for Israel (vers. 25, 26), which is really closely connected with the threatening words directed against the heathen nations, and for which the way is prepared by ver. 24. The correspondence of נִקְדַּשְׁתִּי בָהּ (I shall be sanctified in her) in ver. 22 to נִקְדַּשְׁתִּי בָם (I shall be sanctified in them) in ver. 25, serves to place the future fate of Israel in antithesis not merely to the future fate of Sidon, but, as vers. 24 and 26 clearly show, to that of all the heathen nations against which the previous threats have been directed.

Ver. 20. *And the word of Jehovah came to me, saying,* Ver. 21. *Son of man, direct thy face towards Sidon, and prophesy against it,* Ver. 22. *And say, Thus saith the Lord Jehovah, Behold, I will be against thee, O Sidon, and will glorify myself in the midst of thee; and they shall know that I am Jehovah, when I execute judgments upon it, and sanctify myself upon it.* Ver. 23. *I will send pestilence into it, and blood into its streets; slain will fall in the midst of it by the sword, which cometh upon it from every side; and they shall learn that I am Jehovah.* Ver. 24. *And there shall be no more to the house of Israel a malignant thorn and smarting sting from all round about them, who despise them; but they shall learn that I am the Lord Jehovah.*—Jehovah will glorify Himself as the Lord upon Sidon, as He did before upon Pharaoh (compare Ex. xiv. 4, 16, 17, to which the word נִכְבַּדְתִּי in ver. 22, an unusual expression for Ezekiel, evidently points). The glorification is effected by judgments, through which He proves Himself to be holy upon the enemies of His people. He executes the judgments through pestilence and blood (*vid.* ch. v. 17, xxxviii. 22), *i.e.* through disease and bloodshed occasioned by war, so that men fall, slain by the sword (cf. ch. vi. 7). Instead of נָפַל we have the intensive form נִפְלַל, which is regarded by Ewald and Hitzig as a copyist's error, because it is only met with here. Through these judgments the Lord will liberate His people Israel from all round about, who increase its suffering by their contempt. These thoughts sum up in ver. 24 the design of God's judgments upon all the neighbouring nations which are threatened in ch. xxv.–xxviii., and thus prepare the way for the concluding promise in vers. 25 and 26. The figure of the sting and thorn points back to Num. xxxiii. 55, where it is said that the Canaanites whom Israel failed to exterminate would become thorns in its eyes and stings in its sides. As Israel did not keep itself free from the Canaanitish nature of the heathen nations, God caused it to feel these stings of heathenism. Having been deeply hurt by them, it was now lying utterly prostrate with its wounds. The sins of Canaan, to which Israel had given itself up, had occasioned the destruction of Jerusalem (chap. xvi.). But Israel is not to succumb to its wounds. On the contrary, by destroying the heathen powers, the Lord will heal His people of the wounds which its heathen neighbours have inflicted upon it. סִלּוֹן, synonymous with סַלּוֹן in ch. ii. 6, a word only found in Ezekiel. מַמְאִיר, on the contrary, is taken from Lev. xiii. 51 and xiv. 44, where it is applied to malignant leprosy (see the comm. on the former passage).—For הַשָּׁאטִים אוֹתָם, see ch. xvi. 57 and xxv. 6.

Ver. 25. *Thus saith the Lord Jehovah, When I shall gather the house of Israel out of the peoples among whom they have been scattered, I shall sanctify myself upon them before the eyes of the heathen nations, and they will dwell in their land which I have given to my servant Jacob.* Ver. 26. *They will dwell there securely, and build houses and plant vineyards, and will dwell securely when I execute judgments upon all who despise them of those round about them; and they shall learn that I Jehovah am their God.*—Whilst the heathen nations succumb to the judgments of God, Israel passes on to a time of blessed peace. The Lord will gather His people from their dispersion among the heathen, bring them into the land which He gave to the patriarch Jacob, His servant, and give them in that land rest, security, and true prosperity. (For the fact itself, compare ch. xi. 17, xx. 41, xxxvi. 22 sqq.)

BIBLICAL COMMENTARY

ON THE

PROPHECIES OF EZEKIEL

BY

CARL FRIEDRICH KEIL, D.D.,

DOCTOR AND PROFESSOR OF THEOLOGY.

Translated from the German

BY

REV. JAMES MARTIN, B.A.

VOLUME II

CONTENTS

EXPOSITION—*continued.*

PREDICTIONS OF JUDGMENT UPON THE HEATHEN NATIONS—*continued* (CHAP. XXIX.-XXXII.).

SECOND HALF.—THE ANNOUNCEMENT OF SALVATION. CHAP. XXXIII.-XLVIII.

THE PROPHECIES OF EZEKIEL

Chap. XXIX.–XXXII.—AGAINST EGYPT.

THE announcement of the judgment upon Egypt is proclaimed in seven "words of God." The first five are threats. The first (ch. xxix. 1–16) contains a threat of the judgment upon Pharaoh and his people and land, expressed in grand and general traits. The second (ch. xxix. 17–21) gives a special prediction of the conquest and plundering of Egypt by Nebuchadnezzar. The third (ch. xxx. 1–19) depicts the day of judgment which will break upon Egypt and its allies. The fourth (ch. xxx. 20–26) foretells the annihilation of the might of Pharaoh by the king of Babylon; and the fifth (ch. xxxi.) holds up as a warning to the king and people of Egypt the glory and the overthrow of Assyria. The last two words of God in ch. xxxii. contain lamentations over the destruction of Pharaoh and his might, viz. ch. xxxii. 1–16, a lamentation over the king of Egypt; and ch. xxxii. 17–32, a second lamentation over the destruction of his imperial power.—Ezekiel's prophecy concerning Egypt assumes this elaborate form, because he regards the power of Pharaoh and Egypt as the embodiment of that phase of the imperial power which imagines in its ungodly self-deification that it is able to uphold the kingdom of God, and thus seduces the people of God to rely with false confidence upon the imperial power of this world.

CHAP. XXIX. 1–16. THE JUDGMENT UPON PHARAOH AND HIS PEOPLE AND LAND.

Because Pharaoh looks upon himself as the creator of his kingdom and of his might, he is to be destroyed with his men of war (vers. 2–5*a*). In order that Israel may no longer put its trust in the fragile power of Egypt, the sword shall cut off from Egypt both man and beast, the land shall be turned into a barren wilderness, and the people shall be scattered over the lands (vers. 5*b*–12). But after the expiration of the time appointed for its punishment, both people and land shall be restored, though only to remain an insignificant kingdom (vers. 13–16).—According to ver. 1, this prophecy belongs to the tenth year of the captivity of Jehoiachin; and as we may see by comparing it with the other oracles against Egypt of which the dates are given, it was the first word of God uttered by Ezekiel concerning this imperial kingdom. The contents also harmonize with this, inasmuch as the threat which it contains merely announces in general terms the overthrow of the might of Egypt and its king, without naming the instrument employed to execute the judgment, and at the same time the future condition of Egypt is also disclosed.

Vers. 1–12. Destruction of the might of Pharaoh, and devastation of Egypt.—Ver. 1. *In the tenth year, in the tenth (month), on the twelfth of the month, the word of Jehovah came to me, saying,* Ver. 2. *Son of man, direct thy face against Pharaoh the king of Egypt, and prophesy against him and against all Egypt.* Ver. 3. *Speak and say, Thus saith the Lord Jehovah, Behold, I will deal with thee, Pharaoh, king of Egypt, thou great dragon which lieth in its rivers, which saith, "Mine is the river, and I have made it for myself."* Ver. 4. *I will put a ring into thy jaws, and cause the fishes of thy rivers to hang upon thy scales, and draw thee out of thy rivers, and all the fishes of thy rivers which hang upon thy scales;* Ver. 5. *And will cast thee into the desert, thee and all the fishes of thy rivers; upon the surface of the field wilt thou fall, thou wilt not be lifted up nor gathered together; I give thee for food to the beasts of the earth and the birds of the heaven.* Ver. 6. *And all the inhabitants of Egypt shall learn that I am Jehovah. Because it is a reed-staff to the house of Israel,*—Ver. 7. *When they grasp thee by thy branches, thou crackest and tearest open all their shoulder; and when they lean upon thee, thou breakest and causest all their loins to shake,*—Ver. 8. *Therefore thus saith the Lord Jehovah, Behold, I bring upon thee the sword, and will cut off from thee man and beast;* Ver. 9. *And the land of Egypt will become a waste and desolation, and they shall learn that I am Jehovah. Because he saith: "The river is mine, and I have made it,"* Ver. 10. *Therefore, behold, I will deal with thee and thy rivers, and will make the land of Egypt into barren waste desolations from Migdol to Syene, even to the border of Cush.* Ver. 11. *The foot of man will not pass through it, and the foot of beast will not pass through it, and it will not be inhabited for forty years.* Ver. 12. *I make the land of Egypt a waste in the midst of devastated lands, and its cities shall be waste among desolate cities forty years; and I scatter the Egyptians among the nations, and disperse them in the lands.*—The date given, viz. "in the tenth year," is defended even by Hitzig as more correct than the reading of the LXX., ἐν τῷ ἔτει τῷ δωδεκάτῳ; and he supposes the Alexandrian reading to have originated in the fact that the last date mentioned in ch. xxvi. 1 had already brought down the account to the eleventh year.—Pharaoh, the king of Egypt, against whom the threat is first directed, is called "the great dragon" in ver. 3. תַּנִּים (here and ch. xxxii. 2) is equivalent to תַּנִּין, literally, the lengthened animal, the snake; here, the water-snake, the crocodile, the standing symbol of Egypt in the prophets (cf. Isa. li. 9, xxvii. 1; Ps. lxxiv. 13), which is here transferred to Pharaoh, as the ruler of Egypt and representative of its power. By יְאֹרִים we are to understand the arms and canals of the Nile (*vid.* Isa. vii. 18). The predicate, "lying in the midst of his rivers," points at once to the proud security in his own power to which Pharaoh gave himself up. As the crocodile lies quietly in the waters of the Nile, as though he were lord of the river; so did Pharaoh regard himself as the omnipotent lord of Egypt. His words affirm this: "the river is mine, I have made it for myself." The suffix attached to עֲשִׂיתִנִי stands in the place of לִי, as ver. 9, where the suffix is wanting, clearly shows. There is an incorrectness in this use of the suffix, which evidently passed into the language of literature from the popular phraseology (cf. Ewald, § 315*b*). The rendering of the Vulgate, *ego feci memetipsum*, is false. יְאֹרִי is the expression used by him as a king who regards the land and its rivers as his own property; in connection with which we must bear in mind that Egypt is indebted to the Nile not only for its greatness, but for its actual existence. In this respect Pharaoh says emphatically לִי, it is mine, it belongs to me, because he regards himself as the creator. The words, "I have made it for myself," simply explain the reason for the expression לִי, and affirm more than "I have put myself in possession of this through my own power, or have acquired its blessings for myself" (Hävernick); or, "I have put it into its present condition by constructing canals, dams, sluices, and buildings by the river-side" (Hitzig). Pharaoh calls himself the creator of the Nile, because he regards himself as the creator of the greatness of Egypt. This pride, in which he forgets God and attributes divine power to himself, is the cause of his sin, for which he will be overthrown by God. God will draw the crocodile Pharaoh out of his Nile with hooks, and cast him upon the dry land, where he and the fishes that have been drawn out along with him upon his scales will not be gathered up, but devoured by the wild beasts and birds of prey. The figure is derived from the manner in which even in ancient times the crocodile was caught with large hooks of a peculiar construction (compare Herod. ii. 70, and the testimonies of travellers in Oedmann's *Vermischten Sammlungen*, III. pp. 6 sqq., and Jomard in the *Déscription de l'Egypte*, I. p. 27). The form חחיים with a double *Yod* is a copyist's error, probably occasioned by the double *Yod* occurring after ח in בִּלְחָיֶיךָ, which follows. A dual form for חַיִּים is unsuitable, and is not used anywhere else even by Ezekiel (cf. ch. xix. 4, 9, and more especially ch. xxxviii. 4).—The fishes which hang upon the scales of the monster, and are drawn along with it out of the Nile, are the inhabitants of Egypt, for the Nile represents the land. The casting of the beast into the wilderness, where it putrefies and is devoured by the beasts and birds of prey, must not be interpreted in the insipid manner proposed by Hitzig, namely, that Pharaoh would advance with his army into the desert of Arabia and be defeated there. The wilderness is the dry and barren land, in which animals that inhabit the water must perish; and the thought is simply that the monster will be cast upon the desert land, where it will finally become the food of the beasts of prey.—In ver. 6 the construction is a subject of dispute, inasmuch as many of the commentators follow the Hebrew division of the verse, taking the second hemistich יַעַן הֱיוֹתָם וגו' as dependent upon the first half of the verse, for which it assigns the reason, and then interpreting ver. 7 as a further development of ver. 6*b*, and commencing a new period with ver. 8 (Hitzig, Kliefoth, and others). But it is decidedly wrong to connect together the two halves of the sixth verse, if only for the simple reason that the formula וְיָדְעוּ כִּי אֲנִי יְהוָֹה, which occurs so frequently elsewhere in Ezekiel, invariably closes a train of thought, and is never followed by the addition of a further reason. Moreover, a sentence commencing with יַעַן is just as invariably followed by an apodosis introduced by לָכֵן, of which we have an example just below in vers. 9*b* and 10*a*. For both these reasons it is absolutely necessary that we should regard יַעַן הֱיוֹתָם וגו' as the beginning of a protasis, the apodosis to which commences with לָכֵן in ver. 8. The correctness of this construction is established beyond all doubt by the fact that from ver. 6*b* onwards it is no longer Pharaoh who is spoken of, as in vers. 3–5, but Egypt; so that יַעַן introduces a new train of thought. But ver. 7 is clearly shown, both by the contents and the form, to be an explanatory intermediate clause inserted as a parenthesis. And inasmuch as the protasis is removed in consequence to some distance from its apodosis, Ezekiel has introduced the formula "thus saith the Lord Jehovah" at the commencement of the apodosis, for the purpose of giving additional emphasis to the announcement of the punishment. Ver. 7 cannot in any case be regarded as the protasis, the apodosis to which commences with the לָכֵן in ver. 8, as Hävernick maintains. The suffix attached to הֱיוֹתָם, to which Hitzig takes exception, because he has misunderstood the construction, and which he would conjecture away, refers to מִצְרַיִם as a land or kingdom. Because the kingdom of Egypt was a reed-staff to the house of Israel (a figure drawn from the physical character of the banks of the Nile, with its thick growth of tall, thick rushes, and recalling to mind Isa. xxxvi. 6), the Lord would bring the sword upon it and cut off from it both man and beast. But before this apodosis the figure of the reed-staff is more clearly defined: "when they (the Israelites) take thee by thy branches, thou breakest," etc. This explanation is not to be taken as referring to any particular facts either of the past or future, but indicates the deceptive nature of Egypt as the standing characteristic of that kingdom. At the same time, to give greater vivacity to the description, the words concerning Egypt are changed into a direct address to the Egyptians, *i.e.* not to Pharaoh, but to the Egyptian people regarded as a single individual. The expression בכפך causes some difficulty, since the ordinary meaning of כַּף (hand) is apparently unsuitable, inasmuch as the verb תֵּרוֹץ, from רָצַץ, to break or crack (not to break in pieces, *i.e.* to break quite through), clearly shows that the figure of the reed is still continued. The *Keri* בַּכַּף is a bad emendation, based upon the rendering "to grasp with the hand," which is grammatically inadmissible. תָּפַשׂ with ב does not mean to grasp with something, but to seize upon something, to take hold of a person

(Isa. iii. 6; Deut. ix. 17), so that בכפך can only be an explanatory apposition to בְּךָ. The meaning grip, or grasp of the hand, is also unsuitable and cannot be sustained, as the plural כַּפּוֹת alone is used in this sense in Song of Sol. v. 5. The only meaning appropriate to the figure is that of branches, which is sustained, so far as the language is concerned, by the use of the plural כַּפּוֹת for palm-branches in Lev. xxiii. 40, and of the singular כִּפָּה for the collection of branches in Job xv. 32, and Isa. ix. 13, xix. 15; and this is apparently in perfect harmony with natural facts, since the tall reed of the Nile, more especially the papyrus, is furnished with hollow, sword-shaped leaves at the lower part of the stalk. When it cracks, the reed-staff pierces the shoulder of the man who has grasped it, and tears it; and if a man lean upon it, it breaks in pieces and causes all the loins to tremble. הֶעֱמִיד cannot mean to cause to stand, or to set upright, still less to render stiff and rigid. The latter meaning cannot be established from the usage of the language, and would be unsuitable here. For if a stick on which a man leans should break and penetrate his loins, it would inflict such injury upon them as to cause him to fall, and not to remain stiff and rigid. העמד cannot have any other meaning than that of הַמְעֵד, to cause to tremble or relax, as in Ps. lxix. 24, to shake the firmness of the loins, so that the power to stand is impaired.—In the apodosis the thought of the land gives place to that of the people; hence the use of the feminine suffixes עָלַיִךְ and מִמֵּךְ in the place of the masculine suffixes בְּךָ and עָלֶיךָ in ver. 7. Man and beast shall be cut off, and the land made into a desert waste by the sword, *i.e.* by war. This is carried out still further in vers. 9*b*–12; and once again in the protasis 9*b* (cf. ver. 3*b*) the inordinate pride of the king is placed in the foreground as the reason for the devastation of his land and kingdom. The Lord will make of Egypt the most desolate wilderness. חֳרָבוֹת is intensified into a superlative by the double genitive חֹרֶב שְׁמָמָה, desolation of the wilderness. Throughout its whole extent from *Migdol, i.e.*

Magdolo, according to the *Itiner. Anton.* p. 171 (ed. Wessel), twelve Roman miles from Pelusium; in the Coptic *Meshtol*, Egyptian *Ma'ktr* (Brugsch, *Geogr. Inschr.* I. pp. 261 seq.), the most northerly place in Egypt. סְוֵנֵה, to Syene (for the construction see ch. xxx. 6 and xxi. 3), Συήνη, *Sun* in the inscriptions, according to Brugsch (*Geogr. Inschr.* I. p. 155), probably the profane designation of the place (Coptic *Souan*), the most southerly border town of Egypt in the direction of Cush, *i.e.* Ethiopia, on the eastern bank of the Nile, some ruins of which are still to be seen in the modern *Assvan* (*Assuan*, اسوان) which is situated to the north-east of them (*vid.* Brugsch, *Reiseber. aus Aegypten*, p. 247, and Leyrer in Herzog's *Encyclopaedia*). The additional clause, "and to the border of Cush," does not give a fresh terminal point, still further advanced, but simply defines with still greater clearness the boundary toward the south, viz. to Syene, where Egypt terminates and Ethiopia begins. In ver. 11*a* the desolation is more fully depicted. לֹא תֵשֵׁב, it will not dwell, poetical for "be inhabited," as in Joel iv. (iii.) 20, Isa. xiii. 20, etc. This devastation shall last for forty years, and so long shall the people of Egypt be scattered among the nations. But after the expiration of that time they shall be gathered together again (ver. 13). The number forty is neither a round number (Hitzig) nor a very long time (Ewald), but is a symbolical term denoting a period appointed by God for punishment and penitence (see the comm. on ch. iv. 6), which is not to be understood in a chronological sense, or capable of being calculated.

Vers. 13–16. Restoration of Egypt.—Ver. 13. *For thus saith the Lord Jehovah, At the end of forty years I will gather the Egyptians out of the nations, whither they were scattered.* Ver. 14. *And I will turn the captivity of Egypt, and will bring them back into the land of Pathros, into the land of their origin, and they shall be a lowly kingdom there.* Ver. 15. *Lowlier than the kingdoms shall it be, and exalt itself no more over the nations; and I will make them small, so that they shall rule no more over the nations.* Ver. 16. *And it shall be no more the confidence of the house of Israel, bringing iniquity to remembrance when they incline towards it; and they shall learn that I am the Lord Jehovah.*—The turning of the period of Egypt's punishment is connected by כִּי, which refers to the time indicated, viz. "forty years." For forty years shall Egypt be utterly laid waste; for after the expiration of that period the Lord will gather the Egyptians again from their dispersion among the nations, turn their captivity, *i.e.* put an end to their suffering (see the comm. on ch. xvi. 53), and lead them back into the land of their birth, *i.e.* of their origin (for מְכוּרָה, see ch. xvi. 3), namely, to Pathros. פַּתְרוֹס, the Egyptian *Petorēs* (Παθούρης, LXX. Jer. xliv. 1), or south land, *i.e.* Upper Egypt, the Thebais of the Greeks and Romans. The designation of Upper Egypt as the mother country of the Egyptians, or the land of their nativity, is confirmed not only by the accounts given by Herodotus (ii. 4 and 15) and Diodorus Sic. (i. 50), but also by the Egyptian mythology, according to which the first king who reigned after the gods, viz. *Menes* or *Mena*, sprang from the city of *Thinis* (*Thynis*), Egypt. *Tenj*, in the neighbourhood of Abydos in Upper Egypt, and founded the city of *Memphis* in Lower Egypt, which became so celebrated in later times (*vid.* Brugsch, *Histoire d'Egypte*, I. p. 16). But Egypt shall not attain to its former power any more. It will be and continue a lowly kingdom, that it may not again become a ground of confidence to Israel, a power upon which Israel can rely, so as to fall into guilt and punishment. The subject to וְלֹא יִהְיֶה is Egypt as a nation, notwithstanding the fact that it has previously been construed in the feminine as a land or kingdom, and in אַחֲרֵיהֶם the Egyptians are spoken of in the plural number. For it is out of the question to take מַזְכִּיר עָוֹן as the subject to לֹא יִהְיֶה in the sense of "no more shall one who calls guilt to remembrance inspire the house of Israel with confidence," as Kliefoth proposes, not only because of the arrangement of the words, but because the more precise definition of מַזְכִּיר עָוֹן

as בְּפְנוֹתָם אח׳ clearly shows that Egypt is the subject of the sentence; whereas, in order to connect this definition in any way, Kliefoth is compelled to resort to the interpolation of the words, "which it committed." מַזְכִּיר עָוֹן is in apposition to מִבְטָח; making Egypt the ground of confidence, brings into remembrance before God the guilt of Israel, which consists in the fact that the Israelites turn to the Egyptians and seek salvation from them, so that He is obliged to punish them (*vid.* ch. xxi. 28, 29).—The truth of the prediction in vers. 13–16 has been confirmed by history, inasmuch as Egypt never recovered its former power after the Chaldean period.—Moreover, if we compare the Messianic promise for Egypt in Isa. xix. 18–25 with the prediction in vers. 13–15, we are struck at once with the peculiarity of Ezekiel, already referred to in the introductory remarks on ch. xxv.–xxxii., namely, that he leaves entirely out of sight the Messianic future of the heathen nations.

CHAP. XXIX. 17–21. CONQUEST AND PLUNDERING OF EGYPT BY NEBUCHADNEZZAR.

Ver. 17. *In the seven and twentieth year, in the first (moon), on the first of the moon, the word of Jehovah came to me, saying,* Ver. 18. *Son of man, Nebuchadnezzar, the king of Babylon, has made his army perform hard work at Tyre: every head is bald, and every shoulder grazed, and no wages have been given to him and to his army from Tyre for the work which he performed against it.* Ver. 19. *Therefore thus saith the Lord Jehovah, Behold, I give Nebuchadnezzar, the king of Babylon, the land of Egypt, that he may carry away its possessions, and plunder its plunder, and make booty of its booty, and this may be the wages of his army.* Ver. 20. *As the pay for which he worked, I give him the land of Egypt, because they did it for me, is the saying of the Lord Jehovah.* Ver. 21. *In that day will I cause a horn to sprout to the house of Israel, and I will open the mouth for thee in the midst of them; and they shall know that I am Jehovah.*—

This brief prophecy concerning Egypt was uttered about seventeen years after the preceding word of God, and was the latest of all the predictions of Ezekiel that are supplied with dates. But notwithstanding its brevity, it is not to be taken in connection with the utterance which follows in ch. xxx. 1–19 so as to form one prophecy, as Hitzig supposes. This is at variance not only with the formula in ch. xxx. 1, which is the usual introduction to a new word of God, but also with ver. 21 of the present chapter, which is obviously intended to bring the previous word of God to a close. This termination, which is analogous to the closing words of the prophecies against Tyre and Sidon in ch. xxviii. 25, 26, also shows that the present word of God contains the last of Ezekiel's prophecies against the Egyptian world-power, and that the only reason why the prophet did not place it at the end when collecting his prophecies—that is to say, after ch. xxxii.—was, that the promise in ver. 30, that the Lord would cause a horn to bud to the house of Israel, contained the correlate to the declaration that Egypt was henceforth to be but a lowly kingdom. Moreover, this threat of judgment, which is as brief as it is definite, was well fitted to prepare the way and to serve as an introduction for the more elaborate threats which follow. The contents of the prophecy, namely, the assurance that God would give Egypt to Nebuchadnezzar as spoil in return for the hard labour which he and his army had performed at Tyre, point to the time immediately following the termination of the thirteen years' siege of Tyre by Nebuchadnezzar. If we compare with this the date given in ver. 17, the siege was brought to a close in the twenty-seventh year of the captivity of Jehoiachin, *i.e.* B.C. 572, and must therefore have commenced in the year B.C. 586, or about two years after the destruction of Jerusalem, and with this the extract given by Josephus (*c. Ap.* i. 21) from the Tyrian annals agrees.[1] הֶעֱבִיד עֲבֹדָה, to cause a work to be

[1] For the purpose of furnishing the proof that the temple at Jerusalem lay in ruins for fifty years, from the time of its destruction till the com-

executed, or service to be rendered. This labour was so severe, that every head was bald and every shoulder grazed. These words have been correctly interpreted by the commentators, even by Ewald, as referring to the heavy burdens that had to be carried in order to fill up the strait which separated Insular Tyre from the mainland. They confirm what we have said above, in the remarks on ch. xxvi. 10 and elsewhere, concerning the capture of Tyre. But neither he nor his army had received any recompense for their severe toil. This does not imply that Nebuchadnezzar had been unable to accomplish the work which he had undertaken, *i.e.* to execute his design and conquer the city, but simply that he had not received the recompense which he expected after this severe labour; in other words, had not found the booty he hoped for when the city was taken (see the introductory remarks on ch. xxvi.–xxviii.). To compensate him for this, the Lord will give him the land of Egypt with its possessions as booty, וְנָשָׂא הֲמֹנָהּ, that he may carry off the abundance of its possessions, its wealth; not that he may lead away the multitude of its people (De Wette, Kliefoth, etc.), for "נשׂא is not the appropriate expression for this" (Hitzig). הָמוֹן, abundance of possessions, as in Isa. lx. 5, Ps. xxxvii. 16, etc. פְּעֻלָּה, the doing of a thing; then that which is gained by working, the recompense for labour, as in Lev. xix. 13 and other passages. אֲשֶׁר עָשׂוּ לִי is taken by Hitzig as referring to the Egyptians, and rendered, "in consequence of that which they have done to me." But although אֲשֶׁר may be taken in this sense (*vid.* Isa. lxv. 18), the arguments employed by Hitzig in

mencement of its rebuilding, Josephus gives in the passage referred to above the years of the several reigns of the kings and judges of Tyre from Ithobal to *Hirom*, in whose reign *Cyrus* took the kingdom; from which it is apparent that fifty years elapsed from the commencement of the siege of Tyre to the fourteenth year of *Hirom*, in which Cyrus began to reign. At the same time, the seventh year of Nebuchadnezzar is given by mistake instead of the seventeenth or nineteenth as the date of the beginning of the siege. (Compare on this point Movers, *Phönizier*, II. 1, pp. 437 sqq.; M. v. Niebuhr, *Gesch. Assurs u. Bab.* pp. 106 sqq.; and M. Duncker, *Gesch. des Altert.* I. p. 841.)

opposition to the ordinary rendering—"for they (Nebuchadnezzar and his army) have done it for me," *i.e.* have performed their hard work at Tyre for me and by my commission—have no force whatever. This use of עָשָׂה לִי is thoroughly established by Gen. xxx. 30; and the objection which he raises, namely, that "the assertion that Nebuchadnezzar besieged Tyre in the service of Jehovah could only have been properly made by Ezekiel in the event of the city having been really conquered," is out of place, for this simple reason, that the assumption that the city was not taken is a mere conjecture; and even if the conjecture could be sustained, the siege itself might still be a work undertaken in the service of Jehovah. And the principal argument, namely, "that we should necessarily expect עָשָׂה (instead of עָשׂוּ), inasmuch as with עָשׂוּ every Hebrew reader would inevitably take אֲשֶׁר as referring to מִצְרַיִם," is altogether wide of the mark; for מִצְרַיִם does not signify the Egyptians in this passage, but the land of Egypt alone is spoken of both in the verse before us and throughout the oracle, and for this עָשׂוּ is quite unsuitable, whereas the context suggests in the most natural way the allusion to Nebuchadnezzar and his army. But what is absolutely decisive is the circumstance that the thought itself, "in consequence of what the Egyptians have done to me," *i.e.* what evil they have done, is foreign to, if not at variance with, all the prophecies of Ezekiel concerning Egypt. For the guilt of Egypt and its Pharaoh mentioned by Ezekiel is not any crime against Jehovah, but simply Pharaoh's deification of himself, and the treacherous nature of the help which Egypt afforded to Israel. עָשָׂה לִי = לַיהוָה is not the appropriate expression for this, in support of which assertion we might point to עָשׂוּ לִי in ch. xxiii. 38.—Ver. 21. On that day, namely, when the judgment upon Egypt is executed by Nebuchadnezzar, the Lord will cause a horn to sprout or grow to the house (people) of Israel. The horn is a symbol of might and strength, by which the attacks of foreigners are warded off. By the overthrow of Judah the horn of Israel was cut off (Lam. ii. 3;

compare also Jer. xlviii. 25). In אַצְמִיחַ קֶרֶן the promise coincides, so far as the words are concerned, with Ps. cxxxii. 17; but it also points back to the prophetic words of the godly Hannah in 1 Sam. ii. 1, "My horn is exalted in Jehovah, my mouth hath opened itself wide over my enemies," and is Messianic in the broader sense of the word. The horn which the Lord will cause to sprout to the people of Israel is neither Zerubbabel nor the Messiah, but the Messianic salvation. The reason for connecting this promise of salvation for Israel with the overthrow of the power of Egypt, as Hävernick has observed, is that "Egypt presented itself to the prophet as the power in which the idea of heathenism was embodied and circumscribed." In the might of Egypt the world-power is shattered, and the overthrow of the world-power is the dawn of the unfolding of the might of the kingdom of God. Then also will the Lord give to His prophet an opening of the mouth in the midst of Israel. These words are unquestionably connected with the promise of God in ch. xxiv. 26, 27, that after the fall of Jerusalem the mouth of Ezekiel should be opened, and also with the fulfilment of that promise in ch. xxxiii. 22; but they have a much more comprehensive meaning, namely, that with the dawn of salvation in Israel, *i.e.* in the church of the Lord, the word of prophecy would sound forth in the richest measure, inasmuch as, according to Joel (ch. ii.), a universal outpouring of the Spirit of God would then take place. In this light Theodoret is correct in his remark, that "through Ezekiel He signified the whole band of prophets." But Kliefoth has quite mistaken the meaning of the words when he discovers in them the thought that "God would then give the prophet a new word of God concerning both Egypt and Israel, and that this is contained in the oracle in ch. xxx. 1–19." Such a view as this is proved at once to be false, apart from other grounds, by the expression בְּתוֹכָם (in the midst of them), which cannot be taken as applying to Egypt and Israel, but can only refer to בֵּית יִשְׂרָאֵל, the house of Israel.

CHAP. XXX. 1–19. THE DAY OF JUDGMENT UPON EGYPT.

Commencing with a call to lamentation, the prophet announces that the Lord's day of judgment upon the nations is near at hand, and will burst upon Egypt, and the nations in alliance with it (vers. 2–5). He then depicts in three strophes, with the introductory words כֹּה אָמַר יי׳, the execution of this judgment, namely: (*a*) the destruction of the might of Egypt and the devastation of the land (vers. 6–9); (*b*) the enemy by whom the judgment will be accomplished (vers. 10–12); and (*c*) the extermination of the idols of Egypt, the conquest and demolition of its fortresses, the slaughter of its male population, and the captivity of the daughters of the land (vers. 13–19).

The heading does not contain any chronological information; and the contents furnish no definite *criteria* for determining with precision the date of the prophecy. Jerome assigns this oracle to the same period as the prophecy in ch. xxix. 1–16, whilst others connect it more closely with ch. xxix. 17–21, and regard it as the latest of all Ezekiel's prophecies. The latter is the conclusion adopted by Rosenmüller, Hävernick, Hitzig, Kliefoth, and some others. The principal argument adduced for linking it on to ch. xxix. 17 sqq. is, that in ver. 3 the day of judgment upon Egypt is threatened as near at hand, and this did not apply to the tenth year (ch. xxix. 1), though it was perfectly applicable to the twenty-seventh (ch. xxix. 17), when the siege of Tyre was ended, and Nebuchadnezzar was on the point of attacking Egypt. But the expression, "the day of the Lord is near at hand," is so relative a chronological phrase, that nothing definite can be gathered from it as to the date at which an oracle was composed. Nor does the fact that our prophecy stands after the prophecy in ch. xxix. 17–21, which is furnished with a date, prove anything; for the other prophecies which follow, and are furnished with dates, all belong to a much earlier period. It is very evident from this that ch. xxix. 17–21 is inserted without regard to chronological sequence, and consequently ch. xxx. 1–19 may just as well belong to the period between the tenth month of the tenth year (ch. xxix. 1) and the first month of the eleventh year (ch. xxx. 20), as to the twenty-seventh year (ch. xxix. 17), since all the reasons assigned for the closer connection of our prophecy with the one immediately preceding (ch. xxix. 17–21), which is supposed to indicate similarity of date, are invalid; whilst, on the other hand, the resemblance of vers. 6 and 17 to ch. xxix. 10 and 12 is not sufficient to warrant the assumption of a contemporaneous origin.

Vers. 1–5. Announcement of the judgment upon Egypt and its allies.—Ver. 1. *And the word of Jehovah came to me, saying,* Ver. 2. *Son of man, prophesy, and say, Thus saith the Lord Jehovah, Howl ye! Woe to the day!* Ver. 3. *For the day is near, the day of Jehovah near, a day of cloud, the time of the heathen will it be.* Ver. 4. *And the sword will come upon Egypt, and there will be pangs in Ethiopia, when the slain fall in Egypt, and they take her possessions, and her foundations are destroyed.* Ver. 5. *Ethiopians and Libyans and Lydians, and all the rabble, and Chub, and the sons of the covenant land, will fall by the sword with them.*—In the announcement of the judgment in vers. 2*b* and 3, Ezekiel rests upon Joel i. 13, 15, and ii. 2, where the designation already applied to the judgment upon the heathen world by Obadiah, viz. "the day of Jehovah" (Obad. ver. 15), is followed by such a picture of the nearness and terrible nature of that day, that even Isaiah (Isa. xiii. 6, 9) and Zephaniah (Zeph. i. 7, 14) appropriate the words of Joel. Ezekiel also does the same, with this exception, that he uses הָהּ instead of אֲהָהּ, and adds to the force of the expression by the repetition of קָרוֹב יוֹם. In ver. 3*b*, the words from יוֹם עָנָן to יִהְיֶה are not to be taken together as forming one sentence, "a day of cloud will the time of the nations be" (De Wette), because the idea of a "time of the nations" has not been mentioned before, so as to prepare the way for a description of its real nature here. יוֹם עָנָן and עֵת גּוֹיִם contain two co-ordinate affirmations concerning the day of Jehovah. It will be a day of cloud, *i.e.* of great calamity (as in Joel ii. 2), and a time of the heathen, *i.e.* when heathen (גּוֹיִם without the article) are judged, when their might is to be shattered (cf. Isa. xiii. 22). This day is coming upon Egypt, which is to succumb to the sword. Ethiopia will be so terrified at this, that it will writhe convulsively with anguish (חַלְחָלָה, as in Nah. ii. 11 and Isa. xxi. 3). לָקַח הֲמוֹנָהּ signifies the plundering and removal of the possessions of the land, like נָשָׂא הֲמוֹנָהּ in ch. xxix. 19. The subject to לָקְחוּ is indefinite, "they," *i.e.* the enemy. The foundations of Egypt, which are to be destroyed, are not the foundations of its buildings, but may be understood in a figurative sense as relating to persons, after the analogy of Isa. xix. 10; but the notion that Cush, Phut, etc. (ver. 9), *i.e.* the mercenary troops obtained from those places, which are called the props of Egypt in ver. 6, are intended, as Hitzig assumes, is not only extremely improbable, but decidedly erroneous. The announcement in ver. 6, that Cush, Phut, etc., are to fall by the sword along with the Egyptians (אִתָּם), is sufficient of itself to show that these tribes, even if they were auxiliaries or mercenaries of Egypt, did not constitute the foundations of the Egyptian state and kingdom; but that, on the contrary, Egypt possessed a military force composed of native troops, which was simply strengthened by auxiliaries and allies. We there interpret יְסוֹדֹתֶיהָ, after the analogy of Ps. xi. 3 and lxxxii. 5, as referring to the real foundations of the state, the regulations and institutions on which the stability and prosperity of the kingdom rest. The neighbouring, friendly, and allied peoples will also be smitten by the judgment together with the Egyptians. *Cush*, *i.e.* the Ethiopians, *Phut* and *Lud*, *i.e.* the Libyans and African Lydians (see the comm. on ch. xxvii. 10), are mentioned here primarily as auxiliaries of Egypt, because, according to Jer. xlvi. 9, they served in Necho's army. By כָּל־הָעֶרֶב, the whole of the mixed crowd (see the comm. on 1 Kings x. 15,—πάντες οἱ ἐπίμικτοι,

LXX.), we are then to understand the mercenary soldiers in the Egyptian army, which were obtained from different nations (chiefly Greeks, Ionians, and Carians, οἱ ἐπίκουροι, as they are called by Herodotus, iii. 4, etc.). In addition to these, כּוּב (ἀπ. λεγ.) is also mentioned. Hävernick connects this name with the people of *Kufa*, so frequently met with on the Egyptian monuments. But, according to Wilkinson (*Manners*, etc., I. 1, pp. 361 sqq.), they inhabited a portion of Asia farther north even than Palestine; and he ranks them (p. 379) among the enemies of Egypt. Hitzig therefore imagines that *Kufa* is probably to be found in *Kohistan*, a district of Media, from which, however, the Egyptians can hardly have obtained mercenary troops. And so long as nothing certain can be gathered from the advancing Egyptological researches with regard to the name *Cub*, the conjecture that כּוּב is a mis-spelling for לוּב is not to be absolutely set aside, the more especially as this conjecture is naturally suggested by the לוּבִים of Nah. iii. 9 and 2 Chron. xvi. 8, and the form לוּב by the side of לוּבִים is analogous to לוּד by the side of לוּדִים in Jer. xlvi. 9, whilst the *Liby-Aegyptii* of the ancients, who are to be understood by the term לוּבִים (see the comm. on Gen. x. 13), would be quite in keeping here. On the other hand, the conjecture offered by Gesenius (*Thes.* p. 664), viz. נוּב, *Nubia*, has but a very weak support in the Arabic translator; and the supposition that לוּב may have been the earlier Hebrew form for Nubia (Hitzig), is destitute of any solid foundation. Maurer suggests *Cob*, a city (*municipium*) of Mauretania, in the *Itiner. Anton.* p. 17, ed. Wessel.—The following expression, "sons of the covenant land," is also obscure. Hitzig has correctly observed, that it cannot be synonymous with בַּעֲלֵי בְרִיתָם, their allies. But we certainly cannot admit that the covenant land (made definite by the article) is Canaan, the Holy Land (Hitzig and Kliefoth); although Jerome writes without reserve, *de filiis terrae foederis, i.e. de populo Judaeorum*; and the LXX. in their translation, καὶ τῶν υἱῶν τῆς διαθήκης μου, undoubtedly thought of the

Jews, who fled to Egypt, according to Theodoret's exposition, along with Jeremiah after the destruction of Jerusalem and the murder of the governor Gedaliah, for fear of the vengeance of the Chaldeans (Jer. xlii., xliii., and xliv.). For the application of the expression "land of the covenant" to the Holy Land is never met with either in the Old or New Testament, and cannot be inferred, as Hitzig supposes, from Ps. lxxiv. 20 and Dan. xi. 28, or supported in any way from either the epithet "the land of promise" in Heb. xi. 9, or from Acts iii. 25, where Peter calls the Jews "the children of the prophets and of the covenant." We therefore agree with Schmieder in regarding אֶרֶץ הַבְּרִית as signifying a definite region, though one unknown to us, in the vicinity of Egypt, which was inhabited by a tribe that was independent of the Egyptians, yet bound to render help in time of war.

Vers. 6–9. All the supports and helpers of Egypt will fall, and the whole land with its cities will be laid waste.—Ver. 6. *Thus saith the Lord Jehovah, Those who support Egypt will fall, and its proud might will sink; from Migdol to Syene will they fall by the sword therein, is the saying of the Lord Jehovah.* Ver. 7. *And they will lie waste in the midst of waste lands, and its cities be in the midst of desolate cities.* Ver. 8. *They shall learn that I am Jehovah, when I bring fire into Egypt, and all its helpers are shattered.* Ver. 9. *In that day will messengers go forth from me in ships to terrify the confident Ethiopia, and there will be writhing among them as in the day of Egypt; for, behold, it cometh.*—"Those who support Egypt" are not the auxiliary tribes and allies, for they are included in the term עֹזְרֶיהָ in ver. 8, but the idols and princes (ver. 13), the fortified cities (ver. 15), and the warriors (ver. 17), who formed the foundation of the might of the kingdom. גְּאוֹן עֻזָּהּ, "the pride of its might," which is an expression applied in ch. xxiv. 21 to the temple at Jerusalem, is to be taken here in a general sense, and understood not merely of the temples and idols of Egypt, but as the sum total of all the things on which the Egyptians rested the might of their kingdom, and on the ground of which they regarded it as indestructible. For מִמִּגְדֹּל וגו׳, see the comm. on ch. xxix. 10. The subject to יִפְּלוּ בָהּ is the סֹמְכֵי מצר׳. Ver. 7 is almost a literal repetition of ch. xxix. 12; and the subject to נָשַׁמּוּ is מִצְרַיִם regarded as a country, though the number and gender of the verb have both been regulated by the form of the noun. The fire which God will bring into Egypt (ver. 8) is the fire of war. Ver. 9. The tidings of this judgment of God will be carried by messengers to Ethiopia, and there awaken the most terrible dread of a similar fate. In the first hemistich, the prophet has Isa. xviii. 2 floating before his mind. The messengers, who carry the tidings thither, are not the warlike forces of Chaldea, who are sent thither by God; for they would not be content with performing the service of messengers alone. We have rather to think of Egyptians, who flee by ship to Ethiopia. The messengers go, מִלְּפָנַי, from before Jehovah, who is regarded as being present in Egypt, while executing judgment there (cf. Isa. xix. 1). צִים, as in Num. xxiv. 24 = צִיִּים (Dan. xi. 30), ships, *trieres*, according to the Rabbins, in Hieron. *Symm.* on Isa. xxxiii. 21, and the Targum on Num. (cf. Ges. *Thes.* p. 1156). בֶּטַח is attached to כּוּשׁ, Cush secure or confident, equivalent to the confident Cush (Ewald, § 287*c*). וְהָיְתָה חלח׳, repeated from ver. 4. בָּהֶם, among the Ethiopians. כְּיוֹם מצר׳, as in the day of Egypt, *i.e.* not the present day of Egypt's punishment, for the Ethiopians have only just heard of this from the messengers; but the ancient, well-known day of judgment upon Egypt (Ex. xv. 12 sqq.). Ewald and Hitzig follow the LXX. in taking כְּיוֹם for בְּיוֹם; but this is both incorrect and unsuitable, and reduces בְּיוֹם מצר׳ into a tame repetition of בַּיּוֹם הַהוּא. The subject to הִנֵּה בָאָה is to be taken from the context, viz. that which is predicted in the preceding verses (vers. 6–8).

Vers. 10–12. The executors of the judgment.—Ver. 10. *Thus saith the Lord Jehovah, And I will put an end to the tumult of Egypt through Nebuchadnezzar king of Babylon.*

Ver. 11. *He and his people with him, violent of the nations, will be brought to destroy the land; they will draw their swords against Egypt, and fill the land with slain.* Ver. 12. *And I will make the rivers dry, and sell the land into the hand of wicked men, and lay waste the land and its fulness by the hand of foreigners; I Jehovah have spoken it.*—הָמוֹן cannot be understood as signifying either the multitude of people only, or the abundance of possessions alone; for הִשְׁבִּית is not really applicable to either of these meanings. They are evidently both included in the הָמוֹן, which signifies the tumult of the people in the possession and enjoyment of their property (cf. ch. xxvi. 13). The expression is thus specifically explained in vers. 11 and 12. Nebuchadnezzar will destroy the land with his men of war, slaying the people with its possessions. עָרִיצֵי גוֹיִם, as in ch. xxviii. 7. מוּבָאִים, as in ch. xxiii. 42. הֵרִיק וגו׳, cf. ch. xii. 14, xxviii. 7. מָלְאוּ . . . חָלָל, as in ch. xi. 6. יְאֹרִים, the arms and canals of the Nile, by which the land was watered, and on which the fertility and prosperity of Egypt depended. The drying up of the arms of the Nile must not be restricted, therefore, to the fact that God would clear away the hindrances to the entrance of the Chaldeans into the land, but embraces also the removal of the natural resources on which the country depended. מָכַר, to sell a land or people into the hand of any one, *i.e.* to deliver it into his power (cf. Deut. xxxii. 30; Judg. ii. 14, etc.). For the fact itself, see Isa. xix. 4–6. For הֲשִׁמֹּתִי וגו׳, see ch. xix. 7.

Vers. 13–19. Further description of the judgment.—Ver. 13. *Thus saith the Lord Jehovah, I will exterminate the idols and cut off the deities from Noph, and there shall be no more a prince from the land of Egypt; and I put terror upon the land of Egypt.* Ver. 14. *And I lay Pathros waste, and bring fire into Zoan, and execute judgments upon No;* Ver. 15. *And I pour out my fury upon Sin, the stronghold of Egypt, and cut off the multitude of No;* Ver. 16. *And I put fire in Egypt; Sin will writhe in pain, and No will be broken open, and Noph—enemies by day.* Ver. 17. *The men of On and Bubastus will fall by the sword, and they themselves will go into captivity.* Ver. 18. *At Tachpanches the day will be darkened when I shatter the yokes of Egypt there, and an end will be put to its proud haughtiness; cloud will cover it, and its daughters will go into captivity.* Ver. 19. *And thus I execute judgments upon Egypt, that they may know that I am Jehovah.*—Egypt will lose its idols and its princes (cf. Jer. xlvi. 25). גִּלּוּלִים and אֱלִילִים are synonymous, signifying not the images, but the deities; the former being the ordinary epithet applied to false deities by Ezekiel (see the comm. on ch. vi. 4), the latter traceable to the reading of Isa. xix. 1. נֹף, contracted from מְנֹף, *Manoph* or *Menoph* = מֹף in Hos. ix. 6, is *Memphis*, the ancient capital of Lower Egypt, with the celebrated temple of *Ptah*, one of the principal seats of Egyptian idolatry (see the comm. on Hos. ix. 6 and Isa. xix. 13). In ver. 13*b* מֵאֶרֶץ מצר׳ belongs to נָשִׂיא, there shall be no more a prince from the land of Egypt, *i.e.* a native prince. נָתַן יִרְאָה, to put fear upon (cf. ch. xxvi. 17*b*). From Lower Egypt Ezekiel passes in ver. 14 to Upper Egypt (*Pathros*, see the comm. on ch. xxix. 14), which is also to be laid waste, and then names several more of the principal cities of Lower Egypt along with the chief city of Upper Egypt. צֹעַן, Egypt. *Zane*, Copt. *Jane*, is the *Τανίς*, *Tanis*, of the Greeks and Romans, on the Tanitic arm of the Nile, an ancient city of Lower Egypt; see the comm. on Num. xiii. 22 and Isa. xix. 11. נֹא = נֹא אָמוֹן in Nah. iii. 8, probably "abode of Amon," Egypt. *P-amen*, *i.e.* house of Amon, the sacred name of *Thebes*, the celebrated royal city of Upper Egypt, the *Διὸς πόλις ἡ μεγάλη* of the Greeks (see the comm. on Nah. iii. 8). סִין (literally, mire; compare the Aram. סְיָן) is *Πηλούσιον*, *Pelusium*, which derives its name from *πηλός* (*ὠνόμασται ἀπὸ τοῦ πηλοῦ πηλός*, Strab. xvii. p. 802), because there were swamps all round. It was situated on the eastern arm of the Nile, to which it gave its name, at a distance of twenty stadia from the sea. The Egyptian name *Pheromi* also signifies dirty, or muddy. From this the Arabs have made

Elfarama; and in the vicinity of the few ruins of the ancient Pelusium there is still a castle called طينة, Tineh (compare the Chaldee טִינָא, clay, in Dan. ii. 41). Ezekiel calls it the "fortress or bulwark of Egypt," because, as Strabo (*l.c.*) observes, "Egypt is difficult of access here from places in the East;" for which reason Hirtius (*de bell. Al.* c. 27) calls it "the key of Egypt," and Suidas (*s.v.*) "the key both of the entrance and exit of Egypt." On the history of this city, see Leyrer in Herzog's *Encyclopaedia*. In הֲמוֹן נֹא many of the commentators find a play upon the name of the god אָמוֹן (Jer. xlvi. 25), the chief deity of Thebes, which is possible, but not very probable, as we should not expect to find a god mentioned again here after ver. 13; and הִכְרַתִּי would be inappropriate.—In ver. 16 *Sin* (= *Pelusium*) is mentioned again as the border fortress, *No* (= *Thebes*) as the chief city of Upper Egypt, and *Noph* (= *Memphis*) as the capital of Upper Egypt, as all falling within the range of the judgment. The expression נֹף צָרֵי יוֹמָם has caused some difficulty and given occasion to various conjectures, none of which, however, commend themselves as either simple or natural explanations.[1] As Hitzig has correctly observed, צָרֵי יוֹמָם is the same as שֹׁדֵד בַּצָּהֳרַיִם in Jer. xv. 8, and is the opposite of שֹׁדְדֵי לַיְלָה in Obad. ver. 5. The enemy who comes by day, not in the night, is the enemy who does not shun open attack. The connection with נֹף is to be explained by the same rule as Jer. xxiv. 2, "the one basket—very good figs." Memphis will have enemies in broad daylight,

[1] Ewald proposes to alter צָרֵי into צְדָי (after the Aramaean), "rust," and renders it: "Memphis will be eternal rust." But to this Hitzig has very properly objected that in ch. xxiv. 6, 11, rust is called חֶלְאָה; and that even in Ps. vi. 3 יוֹמָם does not mean perpetual or eternal. Hävernick proposes to explain צָרִים, from the Aramaean ܨܪܐ, to rend or tear in pieces, "Memphis shall become perpetual rents." To this also it may be objected, that צָרִים in Hebrew has the standing meaning of oppressors; and that יוֹמָם, *interdiu*, is not equivalent to perpetual; and still further, that the preposition לְ could not be omitted before צָרֵי.

i.e. will be filled with them. אָוֶן = אוֹן, אֹן, in Gen. xli. 45, 50 (Egyptian *An*, or *Anu*), is the popular name of *Heliopolis* in Lower Egypt (see the comm. on Gen. xli. 45); and the form אָוֶן (a vain thing, or idol) is probably selected intentionally in the sense of an idol-city (see the comm. on Hos. iv. 15), because *On-Heliopolis* (בֵּית־שֶׁמֶשׁ in Jer. xliii. 13) was from time immemorial one of the principal seats of the Egyptian worship of the sun, and possessed a celebrated temple of the sun, with a numerous and learned priesthood (see the comm. on Gen. xli. 45, ed. 2). פִּי־בֶסֶת, *i.e.* *Βουβαστός* (LXX.) or *Βουβαστίς* (Herod. ii. 59), Egyptian *Pi-Pasht*, *i.e.* the place of *Pasht*, so called from the cat-headed *Bubastis* or *Pasht*, the Egyptian *Diana*, which was worshipped there in a splendid temple. It was situated on the royal canal leading to Suez, which was begun by Necho and finished under Ptolemy II., not far from its junction with the Pelusiac arm of the Nile. It was the chief seat of the *Nomos Bubastites*, was destroyed by the Persians, who demolished its walls (Diod. Sic. xvi. 51), and has entirely disappeared, with the exception of some heaps of ruins which still bear the name of *Tel Bastah*, about seven hours' journey from the Nile (compare Ges. *Thes.* pp. 1101 sqq., and Leyrer in Herzog's *Encyclopaedia*, *s.v.*). The Nomos of Bubastis, according to Herod. ii. 166, was assigned to the warrior-caste of Calasirians. The בַּחוּרִים, the young military men, will fall by the sword; and הֵנָּה, not *αἱ γυναῖκες* (LXX. and others), but the cities themselves, *i.e.* their civil population as distinguished from the military garrison, shall go into exile. This explanation of הֵנָּה is commended by בְּנוֹתֶיהָ in ver. 18. תְּחַפְנְחֵס or תַּחְפַּנְחֵס (Jer. xliii. 7 sqq., xliv. 1, xlvi. 14), and תַּחְפְּנֵס in Jer. ii. 16 (*Chetib*), is *Τάφναι*, *Τάφνη* (LXX.), or *Δάφναι* (Herod. ii. 30. 107), a frontier city of Egypt in the vicinity of Pelusium, after the time of Psammetichus a fortification with a strong garrison, where a palace of Pharaoh was also to be found, according to Jer. xliii. 9. After the destruction of Jerusalem, a portion of the Jews took refuge there, and to them Jeremiah predicted the punishment of God on the conquest of Egypt by Nebuchadnezzar (Jer. xliii. 7 sqq., xliv. 1 sqq.). In the case of חשך the reading varies; the printed *Masora* at Gen. xxxix. 3 giving חָשַׂךְ as the reading to be found in all the codices examined by the author of the *Masora;* whereas many of the codices and printed editions have חָשַׁךְ, and this is adopted in all the ancient versions. This is evidently the correct reading, as חשׂךְ does not furnish an appropriate meaning, and the parallel passages, ch. xxxii. 8, Isa. xiii. 10, Joel iii. 4, Amos viii. 9, all favour חשׁךְ. The darkening of the day is the phenomenal prognostic of the dawning of the great day of judgment upon the nations (cf. Joel ii. 10, iii. 4, iv. 15; Isa. xiii. 10, etc.). This day is to dawn upon Egypt at Tachpanches, the border fortress of the land towards Syria and Palestine, when the Lord will break the yokes of Egypt. These words point back to Lev. xxvi. 13, where the deliverance of Israel from the bondage of Egypt is called the breaking in pieces of its yokes (see also Ezek. xxxiv. 27). That which took place then is to be repeated here. The yokes which Egypt put upon the nations are to be broken; and all the proud might of that kingdom is to be brought to an end (גְּאוֹן עֻזָּהּ, as in ver. 6). In ver. 18*b*, הִיא, which stands at the head in an absolute form, points back to בִּתְחַפְנְחֵס. The city (*Daphne*) will be covered with cloud, *i.e.* will be overthrown by the judgment; and her daughters, *i.e.* the smaller cities and hamlets dependent upon her (cf. ch. xvi. 46 and xxvi. 6), will go into captivity in the persons of their inhabitants. It follows from this that *Daphne* was the chief city of a *Nomos* in Lower Egypt; and this is confirmed by the circumstance that there was a royal palace there. If we compare the threat in this verse, that in Tachpanches an end is to be put to the proud might of Pharaoh, with the threatening words of Jer. xliii. 9 sqq., to the effect that Nebuchadnezzar would set up his throne at Tachpanches and smite Egypt, it is evident that the situation of Daphne must at that time have been such that the war between Egypt and Babylonia would necessarily be decided in or near this city. These prophetic utterances cannot be explained, as Kliefoth supposes, from the fact that many Jews had settled in Daphne; nor do the contents of this verse furnish any proof that Ezekiel did not utter this prophecy of his till after the Jews had settled there (Jer. xliii. and xliv.). Ver. 19 serves to round off the prophecy.

CHAP. XXX. 20–26. DESTRUCTION OF THE MIGHT OF PHARAOH BY NEBUCHADNEZZAR.

According to the heading in ver. 20, "*In the eleventh year, in the first (month), on the seventh of the month, the word of Jehovah came to me, saying,*" this short word of threatening against Egypt falls in the second year of the siege of Jerusalem by the Chaldeans, and, as ver. 21 clearly shows, after the army of Pharaoh Hophra, which marched to the relief of Jerusalem, had been defeated by the Chaldeans who turned to meet it (Jer. xxxvii. 5, 7). If we compare with this the date of the first prophecy against Egypt in ch. xxix. 1, the prophecy before us was separated from the former by an interval of three months. But as there is no allusion whatever in ch. xxix. to Pharaoh's attempt to come to the relief of the besieged city of Jerusalem, or to his repulse, the arrival of the Egyptian army in Palestine, its defeat, and its repulse by the Chaldeans, seems to have occurred in the interval between these two prophecies, towards the close of the tenth year.

Ver. 21. *Son of man, the arm of Pharaoh the king of Egypt have I broken; and, behold, it will no more be bound up, to apply remedies, to put on a bandage to bind it up, that it may grow strong to grasp the sword.* Ver. 22. *Therefore thus saith the Lord Jehovah, Behold, I will deal with Pharaoh the king of Egypt, and will break both his arms, the strong one and the broken one, and will cause the sword to fall out of his hand.* Ver. 23. *And I will scatter the Egyptians among the nations and disperse them in the lands*, Ver. 24. *And will strengthen the arms of the king of Babylon, and give my sword into his hand, and will break the arms of Pharaoh, so that he shall groan the groanings of a pierced one before him.* Ver. 25. *I will strengthen the arms of the king of Babylon, and the arms of Pharaoh will fall; and they shall know that I am Jehovah, when I give my sword into the hand of the king of Babylon, that he may stretch it against the land of Egypt.* Ver. 26. *I will scatter the Egyptians among the nations, and disperse them in the lands; and they shall know that I am Jehovah.*—The perfect שָׁבַרְתִּי in ver. 21 is not a prophetic utterance of the certainty of the future, but a pure preterite. This may be seen "both from the allusion in ver. 21*b* to the condition resulting from the שֶׁבֶר, and also to the obviously antithetical relation of ver. 22, in which future events are predicted" (Hitzig). The arm is a figurative expression for power, here for military power, as it wields the sword. God broke the arm of Pharaoh by the defeat which the Chaldeans inflicted upon Pharaoh Hophra, when he was marching to the relief of besieged Jerusalem. חֻבְּשָׁה is a present, as is apparent from the infinitive clauses (לָתֵת וגו׳) which follow, altogether apart from הִנֵּה; and חבשׁ signifies to bind up, for the purpose of healing a broken limb, that remedies may be applied and a bandage put on. לְחָזְקָהּ, that it may become strong or sound, is subordinate to the preceding clause, and governs the infinitive which follows. The fact that the further judgment which is to fall upon Pharaoh is introduced with לָכֵן (therefore) here (ver. 22), notwithstanding the fact that it has not been preceded by any enumeration of the guilt which occasioned it, may be accounted for on the ground that the causal לָכֵן forms a link with the concluding clause of ver. 21: the arm shall not be healed, so as to be able to grasp or hold the sword. Because Pharaoh is not to attain any more to victorious power, therefore God will shatter both of his arms, the strong, *i.e.* the sound one and the broken one, that is to say, will smite it so completely, that the sword will fall from his hand. The

Egyptians are to be scattered among the nations, as is repeated in ver. 23 *verbatim* from ch. xxix. 12. God will give the sword into the hand of the king of Babylon, and equip and strengthen him to destroy the might of Pharaoh, that the latter may groan before him like one who is pierced with the sword. This thought is repeated in vers. 25 and 26 with an intimation of the purpose of this divine procedure. That purpose is: that men may come to recognise Jehovah as God the Lord. The subject to וְיָדְעוּ is indefinite; and the rendering of the LXX. is a very good one, καὶ γνώσονται πάντες.

CHAP. XXXI. THE GLORY AND FALL OF ASSHUR A TYPE OF EGYPT.

In two months *minus* six days from the time when the preceding word of God was uttered, Ezekiel received another threatening word against the king and the people of Egypt, in which the former announcement of the destruction of the might of Egypt was confirmed by a comparison drawn between the power of Egypt and that of Asshur. Ezekiel having opened his prophecy with the question, whom does Pharaoh with his might resemble (ver. 2), proceeds to depict Asshur as a mighty towering cedar (vers. 3–9) which has been felled and cast down by the prince of the nations on account of its height and pride (vers. 10–14), so that everything mourned over its fall, because many nations went down with it to hell (vers. 15-17). The question, whom Pharaoh resembles, is then repeated in ver. 18; and from the preceding comparison the conclusion is drawn, that he will perish like that lofty cedar.—The reminiscence of the greatness of the Assyrian empire and of its destruction was well adapted to overthrow all reliance upon the might and greatness of Egypt. The fall of that great empire was still so fresh in the mind at the time, that the reminiscence could not fail to make a deep impression upon the prophet's hearers.

Vers. 1–9. The might of Pharaoh resembles the greatness and glory of Asshur.—Ver. 1. *In the eleventh year, in the third (month), on the first of the month, the word of Jehovah came to me, saying,* Ver. 2. *Son of man, say to Pharaoh the king of Egypt, and to his tumult, Whom art thou like in thy greatness?* Ver. 3. *Behold, Asshur was a cedar-tree upon Lebanon, beautiful in branches, a shadowing thicket, and its top was high in growth, and among the clouds.* Ver. 4. *Water brought him up, the flood made him high, its streams went round about its plantation, and it sent its channels to all the trees of the field.* Ver. 5. *Therefore its growth became higher than all the trees of the field, and its branches became great, and its boughs long from many waters in its shooting out.* Ver. 6. *In its branches all the birds of the heaven made their nests, and under its boughs all the beasts of the field brought forth, and in its shadow sat great nations of all kinds.* Ver. 7. *And he was beautiful in his greatness, in the length of his shoots; for his root was by many waters.* Ver. 8. *Cedars did not obscure him in the garden of God, cypresses did not resemble his branches, and plane-trees were not like his boughs; no tree in the garden of God resembled him in his beauty.* Ver. 9. *I had made him beautiful in the multitude of his shoots, and all the trees of Eden which were in the garden of God envied him.*—The word of God is addressed to King Pharaoh and to הֲמוֹנוֹ, his tumult, *i.e.* whoever and whatever occasions noise and tumult in the land. We must not interpret this, however, as Hitzig has done, as signifying the ruling classes and estates in contrast with the quiet in the land, for no such use of הָמוֹן is anywhere to be found. Nor must we regard the word as applying to the multitude of people only, but to the people with their possessions, their riches, which gave rise to luxury and tumult, as in ch. xxx. 10. The inquiry, whom does Pharaoh with his tumult resemble in his greatness, is followed in the place of a reply by a description of Asshur as a glorious cedar (vers. 3–9). It is true that Ewald has followed the example of Meibom (*vanarum in Cod. Hebr. interprett. spec.* III. p. 70) and J. D. Michaelis, and endeavours to set aside the allusion to Asshur, by taking the word אַשּׁוּר in an appellative sense, and understanding אַשּׁוּר אֶרֶז as signifying a particular kind of cedar, namely, the tallest species of all. But apart altogether from there being no foundation whatever for such an explanation in the usage of the language, there is nothing in the fact to justify it. For it is not anywhere affirmed that Pharaoh resembled this cedar; on the contrary, the question, whom does he resemble? is asked again in ver. 18 (Hitzig). Moreover, Michaelis is wrong in the supposition that "from ver. 10 onwards it becomes perfectly obvious that it is not Assyria but Egypt itself which is meant by the cedar-tree previously described." Under the figure of the felling of a cedar there is depicted the overthrow of a king or monarchy, which has already taken place. Compare vers. 12 and 16, where the past is indicated quite as certainly as the future in ver. 18. And as ver. 18 plainly designates the overthrow of Pharaoh and his power as still in the future, the cedar, whose destruction is not only threatened in vers. 10–17, but declared to have already taken place, can only be Asshur, and not Egypt at all.

The picture of the glory of this cedar recalls in several respects the similar figurative description in ch. xvii. Asshur is called a cedar upon Lebanon, because it was there that the most stately cedars grew. חֹרֶשׁ מֵצַל, a shade-giving thicket (מֵצַל is a *Hiphil* participle of צָלַל), belongs to יְפֵה עָנָף as a further expansion of עָנָף, corresponding to the further expansion of גְּבַהּ קֹמָה by "its top was among the clouds." If we bear this in mind, the reasons assigned by Hitzig for altering חֹרֶשׁ into an adjective חֲרֵשׁ, and taking מֵצַל as a substantive formation after the analogy of מֵסַב, lose all their force. Analogy would only require an adjective in the construct state in the event of the three statements יְפֵה ע׳, חֹרֶשׁ מ׳, and גְּבַהּ ק׳ being co-ordinate with one another. But what is decisive against the proposed conjecture is the fact that neither the noun מֵצַל nor the adjective חֲרֹשׁ is ever met with, and that, in any case, מֵצַל cannot signify foliage. The rendering of the Vulgate, "*frondibus nemorosus*," is merely guessed at, whilst the Seventy have omitted the word as unintelligible to them. For עֲבֹתִים, thicket of clouds, see the comm. on ch. xix. 11; and for צַמֶּרֶת, that on ch. xvii. 3. The cedar grew to so large a size because it was richly watered (ver. 4). A flood poured its streams round about the place where the cedar was planted, and sent out brooks to all the trees of the field. The difficult words אֶת־נַהֲרֹתֶיהָ וגו' are to be taken literally thus: as for its (the flood's) streams, it (the flood) was going round about its plantation, *i.e.* round about the plantation belonging to the flood or the place situated near it, where the cedar was planted. אֵת is not to be taken as a preposition, but as a sign of the accusative, and אֶת־נַהֲרֹתֶיהָ as an accusative used for the more precise definition of the manner in which the flood surrounded the plantation. It is true that there still remains something striking in the masculine הֹלֵךְ, since תְּהוֹם, although of common gender, is construed throughout as a feminine, even in this very verse. But the difficulty remains even if we follow Ewald, and take הֹלֵךְ to be a defectively written or irregular form of the *Hiphil* הוֹלִיךְ; a conjecture which is precluded by the use of הוֹלִיךְ, to cause to run = to cause to flow away, in ch. xxxii. 14. מַטָּעָהּ, its (the flood's) plantation, *i.e.* the plantation for which the flood existed. תְּהוֹם is used here to signify the source or starting-point of a flood, as in Deut. viii. 7, where תְּהֹמֹת are co-ordinate with עֲיָנֹת.—While the place where the cedar was planted was surrounded by the streams of the flood, only the brooks and channels of this flood reached to the trees of the field. The cedar therefore surpassed all the trees of the field in height and luxuriance of growth (ver. 5). גָּבְהָא, an Aramean mode of spelling for גָּבְהָה; and סַרְעַפֹּת, ἅπ. λεγ., an Aramean formation with ר inserted, for סְעַפֹּת, branches. For פֹּארֹת, see the comm. on ch. xvii. 6. בְּשַׁלְּחוֹ cannot mean "since it (the stream) sent out the water" (Ewald); for although תְּהוֹם in ver. 4 is also construed as a masculine, the suffix cannot be taken as referring to תְּהוֹם, for this is much too far off. And the explanation proposed by Rosenmüller, Hävernick, Kliefoth, and others, "as it (the tree) sent them (the branches) out," is open to this objection, that בְּשַׁלְּחוֹ would then contain a spiritless tautology; since the stretching out of the branches is already contained in the fact of their becoming numerous and long. The tautology has no existence if the object is left indefinite, "in its spreading out," *i.e.* the spreading not only of the branches, but also of the roots, to which שִׁלַּח is sometimes applied (cf. Jer. xvii. 8). By the many waters which made the cedar great, we must not understand, either solely or especially, the numerous peoples which rendered Assyria great and mighty, as the Chaldee and many of the older commentators have done. It must rather be taken as embracing everything which contributed to the growth and greatness of Assyria. It is questionable whether the prophet, when describing the flood which watered the cedar plantation, had the description of the rivers of Paradise in Gen. ii. 10 sqq. floating before his mind. Ewald and Hävernick think that he had; but Hitzig and Kliefoth take a decidedly opposite view. There is certainly no distinct indication of any such allusion. We meet with this for the first time from ver. 8 onwards. In vers. 6–9 the greatness and glory of Asshur are still further depicted. Upon and under the branches of the stately tree, all creatures, birds, beasts, and men, found shelter and protection for life and increase (ver. 6; cf. ch. xvii. 23 and Dan. iv. 9). In כֹּל־גּוֹיִם רַבִּים, all kinds of great nations, the fact glimmers through the figure. The tree was so beautiful (וַיִּיף from יָפָה) in its greatness, that of all the trees in the garden of God not one was to be compared with it, and all envied it on that account; that is to say, all the other nations and kingdoms in God's creation were far inferior to Asshur in greatness and glory. גַּן אֱלֹהִים is the garden of Paradise; and consequently עֵדֶן in vers. 9, 16, and 18 is also Paradise, as in ch. xxviii. 13. There is no ground for Kliefoth's objection, that if עֵדֶן be taken in this sense, the words "which are in the garden of God" will contain a superfluous pleonasm, a mere tautology. In Gen. ii. 8 a distinction is also made between עֵדֶן and the garden in *Eden*. It was not all Eden, but the garden planted by Jehovah in Eden, which formed the real paradisaical creation; so that the words "which are in the garden of God" give intensity to the idea of the "trees of Eden." Moreover, as Hävernick has correctly pointed out, there is a peculiar emphasis in the separation of בְּגַן אֱלֹהִים from אֲרָזִים in ver. 8: "cedars . . . even such as were found in the garden of God." Not one even of the other and most glorious trees, viz. cypresses and planes, resembled the cedar Asshur, planted by God by many waters, in its boughs and branches. It is not stated in so many words in vers. 8 and 9 that the cedar Asshur stood in the garden of God; but it by no means follows from this, that by the garden of God we are to understand simply the world and the earth as the creation of God, as Kliefoth imagines, and in support of which he argues that "as all the nations and kingdoms of the world are regarded as trees planted by God, the world itself is quite consistently called a garden or plantation of God." The very fact that a distinction is made between trees of the field (vers. 4 and 5) and trees of Eden in the garden of God (vers. 8 and 9), shows that the trees are not all regarded here as being in the same sense planted by God. If the garden of God stood for the world, where should we then have to look for the field (הַשָּׂדֶה)? The thought of vers. 8 and 9 is not that "not a single tree in all God's broad earth was to be compared to the cedar Asshur," but that even of the trees of Paradise, the garden in Eden, there was not one so beautiful and glorious as the cedar Asshur, planted by God by many waters.

Vers. 10–14. The felling of this cedar, or the overthrow of Asshur on account of its pride.—Ver. 10. *Therefore thus said the Lord Jehovah, Because thou didst exalt thyself in height, and he stretched his top to the midst of the clouds, and his heart exalted itself in its height,* Ver. 11. *I will give him into the hand of the prince of the nations; he shall deal with him: for his wickedness I rejected him.* Ver. 12. *And strangers cut him down, violent ones of the nations, and cast him away: upon the mountains and in all the valleys his shoots fell, and his boughs were broken in pieces into all the deep places of the earth; and all the nations of the earth withdrew from his shadow, and let him lie.* Ver. 13. *Upon his fallen trunk all the birds of the heaven settle, and all the beasts of the field are over his branches:* Ver. 14. *That no trees by the water may exalt themselves on account of their height, or stretch their top to the midst of the clouds, and no water-drinkers stand upon themselves in their exaltation: for they are all given up to death into hell, in the midst of the children of men, to those that go into the grave.*—In the description of the cause of the overthrow of Asshur which commences with יַעַן אֲשֶׁר, the figurative language changes in the third clause into the literal fact, the towering of the cedar being interpreted as signifying the lifting up of the heart in his height,—that is to say, in his pride. In the first clause the tree itself is addressed; but in the clauses which follow, it is spoken of in the third person. The direct address in the first clause is to be explained from the vivid manner in which the fact presented itself. The divine sentence in vers. 10 and 11 is not directed against Pharaoh, but against the Assyrian, who is depicted as a stately cedar; whilst the address in ver. 10*a*, and the imperfect (future) in ver. 11*a*, are both to be accounted for from the fact that the fall of Asshur is related in the form in which it was denounced on the part of Jehovah upon that imperial kingdom. The perfect אָמַר is therefore a preterite here: the Lord said . . . for His part: because Asshur has exalted itself in the pride of its greatness, I give it up. The form וְאֶתְּנֵהוּ is not to be changed into וָאֶתְּנֵהוּ, but is defended against critical caprice by the imperfect יַעֲשֶׂה which follows. That the penal sentence of God is not to be regarded as being first uttered in the time then present, but belongs to the past,—and therefore the words merely communicate what God had already spoken,—is clearly shown by the preterites commencing with גֵּרַשְׁתִּיהוּ, the historical tenses וַיִּכְרְתֻהוּ and וַיִּטְּשֻׁהוּ, and the preterite נָפְלוּ, which must not be turned into futures in violation of grammar. גָּבַהּ בְּקוֹמָה does not mean, to be high in its height, which would be a tautology; but to exalt itself (be proud) in, or on account of, its height. And in the same way is רוּם also affirmed of the heart, in the sense of exultation from pride. For the fact itself, compare Isa. x. 5 sqq. אֵל גּוֹיִם does not mean God, but a powerful one of the nations, *i.e.* Nebuchadnezzar. אֵל is a simple appellative from אוּל, the strong one; and is neither a name of God nor a defective form for אֵיל, the construct state of אַיִל, a ram. For this defective form is only met with once in the case of אַיִל, a ram, namely, in Job xlii. 8, where we have the plural אֵלִים, and nowhere else; whereas, in the case of אֵל, אֵלִים, in the sense of a strong one, the *scriptio plena* very frequently alternates with the *defectiva*. Compare, for example, Job xlii. 8, where both readings occur just as in this instance, where many MSS. have אֵיל (*vid.* de Rossi, *variae lectt. ad h. l.*); also Ex. xv. 15 and Ezek. xvii. 13, אֵילֵי, compared with אֵלֵי in Ezek. xxxii. 21, after the analogy of נֵירִי, 2 Sam. xxii. 29, and נֵרִים, 2 Chron. ii. 16. עָשׂוֹ יַעֲשֶׂה לוֹ is not a relative clause, "who should treat him ill," nor is the ו *relat.* omitted on account of the preceding עָשׂוֹ, as Hitzig imagines; but it is an independent sentence, and יַעֲשֶׂה is a forcible expression for the imperative: he will deal with him, equivalent to, "let him deal with him." עָשָׂה לְ, to do anything to a person, used here as it frequently is in an evil sense; compare Ps. lvi. 5. בְּרִשְׁעוֹ—or כְּרִשְׁעוֹ, which Norzi and Abarbanel (in de Rossi, *variae lectt. ad h. l.*) uphold as the reading of many of the more exact manuscripts and editions—belongs to גֵּרַשְׁתִּיהוּ: for, or according to, his wickedness, I rejected him. In ver. 12 the figure of the tree is resumed; and the extinction of the Assyrian empire is described as the cutting down of the proud cedar. זָרִים עָרִיצֵי גוֹיִם as in ch. xxviii. 7 and xxx. 11, 12. וַיִּטְּשֻׁהוּ: they cast him away and let him lie, as in ch. xxix. 5,

xxxii. 4; so that in the first sentence the idea of casting away predominates, and in the second that of letting lie. By the casting away, the tree became so shattered to atoms that its boughs and branches fell upon the mountains and on the low ground and valleys of the earth, and the nations which had sat under its shadow withdrew. וַיֵּרְדוּ (they descended) is to be explained from the idea that the tree had grown upon a high mountain (namely Lebanon); and Hitzig is mistaken in his conjecture that וַיִּדְּדוּ was the original reading, as נָדַד, to fly, is not an appropriate expression for עַמִּים. On the falling of the tree, the birds which had made their nests in its branches naturally flew away. If, then, in ver. 13, birds and beasts are said to settle upon the fallen trunk, as several of the commentators have correctly observed, the description is based upon the idea of a corpse, a מַפֶּלֶת (Judg. xiv. 8), around which both birds and beasts of prey gather together to tear it in pieces (cf. ch. xxxii. 4 and Isa. xviii. 6). הָיָה אֶל, to come towards or over any one, to be above it. The thought expressed is, that many nations took advantage of the fall of Asshur and rose into new life upon its ruins.—Ver. 14. This fate was prepared for Asshur in order that henceforth no tree should grow up to the sky any more, *i.e.* that no powerful one of this earth (no king or prince) should strive after superhuman greatness and might. לְמַעַן אֲשֶׁר is dependent upon גֵּרַשְׁתִּיהוּ in ver. 11; for vers. 12 and 13 are simply a further expansion of the thought expressed in that word. עֲצֵי מַיִם are trees growing near the water, and therefore nourished by water. For לֹא יִגְבְּהוּ וגו', see ver. 10. The words וְלֹא יַעַמְדוּ אֵלֵיהֶם וגו' are difficult. As אֵלֵיהֶם, with *Tzere* under א, to which the *Masora* calls attention, cannot be the preposition אֶל with the suffix, many have taken אליהם to be a noun, in the sense of *fortes*, *principes*, or *terebinthi* (*vid.* Isa. lxi. 3), and have rendered the clause either *ut non perstent terebinthi eorum in altitudine sua, omnes* (*ceterae arbores*) *bibentes aquam* (Vatabl., Starck, Maurer, and Kliefoth), or, that their princes may not lift themselves up in their pride, all the drinkers of water (Hävernick). But both renderings founder on the simple fact that they leave the suffix הֶם in אליהם either unnoticed or unexplained. As only the trees of the water have been spoken of previously, the suffix must be taken as referring to them. But the water-trees have neither terebinths nor princes; on the contrary, these are what they must either be, or signify. Terebinths, or princes of the water-trees, would be senseless ideas. Ewald has therefore taken אֵלֵיהֶם as the object, and rendered it thus: "and (that) no water-drinkers may contend with their gods in their pride." He has not proved, however, but has simply asserted, that עָמַד is to endure = to contend (!). The only remaining course is to follow the LXX., Targum, and many commentators, and to take אליהם as a pronoun, and point it אֲלֵיהֶם. עָמַד אֶל: to station oneself against, or upon = עָמַד עַל (ch. xxxiii. 26), in the sense of resting, or relying upon anything. The suffix is to be taken in a reflective sense, as in ch. xxxiv. 2, etc. (*vid.* Ewald, § 314*c*), and precedes the noun to which it refers, as in Prov. xiv. 20 for example. בְּגָבְהָם, as in ver. 10, referring to pride. כָּל־שֹׁתֵי מַיִם, the subject of the sentence, is really synonymous with כָּל־עֲצֵי מַיִם, except that the figure of the tree falls into the background behind the fact portrayed. The rendering of the Berleburg Bible is very good: "and no trees abounding in water stand upon themselves (rely upon themselves) on account of their height." The water-drinkers are princes of this earth who have attained to great power through rich resources. "As a tree grows through the moisture of water, so men are accustomed to become proud through their abundance, not reflecting that these waters have been supplied to them by God" (Starck). The reason for this warning against proud self-exaltation is given in ver. 14*b* in the general statement, that all the proud great ones of this earth are delivered up to death. כֻּלָּם, all of them, the water-drinkers or water-trees already named, by whom kings, earthly potentates, are intended. אֶרֶץ תַּחְתִּית = אֶרֶץ תַּחְתִּיּוֹת (ch. xxvi. 20). בְּתוֹךְ בְּנֵי אָדָם: in the midst of the children of men, *i.e.* like all other men. "Thus the prophet teaches that princes must die as well as the people, that death and decomposition are common to both. Hence he takes all ground of proud boasting away" (Starck).

Vers. 15–18. Impression made upon the nations by the fall of Asshur; and its application to Pharaoh.—Ver. 15. *Thus saith the Lord Jehovah, In the day that he went down to hell I caused a mourning: covered the flood for his sake, and stopped its streams, and the great waters were held back: I caused Lebanon to blacken itself for him, and all the trees of the field pined for him.* Ver. 16. *I made the nations tremble at the noise of his fall, when I cast him down to hell to those who go into the grave: and they comforted themselves in the nether world, even all the trees of Eden, the choice and most beautiful of Lebanon, all the water-drinkers.* Ver. 17. *They also went with him into hell, to those pierced with the sword, who sat as his helpers in his shade among the nations.* Ver. 18. *Whom dost thou thus resemble in glory and greatness among the trees of Eden? So shalt thou be thrust down to the trees of Eden into the nether world, and lie among uncircumcised ones with those pierced with the sword. This is Pharaoh and all his tumult, is the saying of the Lord Jehovah.*—In order that the overthrow of the Assyrian, *i.e.* the destruction of the Assyrian empire, may be placed in the clearest light, a picture is drawn of the impression which it made upon the whole creation. There is no necessity to understand כֹּה אָמַר in a past sense, as in ver. 10. What God did on the overthrow of Asshur He may even now, for the first time, make known through the prophet, for a warning to Pharaoh and the people of Israel. That this is the way in which the words are to be interpreted, is evident from the use of the perfect הֶאֱבַלְתִּי, followed by the historical imperfects, which cannot be taken in a prophetical sense, as Kliefoth supposes, or turned into futures. It is contrary to Hebrew usage to connect הֶאֱבַלְתִּי and כִּסֵּתִי together as *asyndeton*, so as to form one idea, viz. "to veil in mourning," as Ewald and Hävernick propose. The circumstances under which two verbs are joined together to form one idea are of a totally different kind. In this instance הֶאֱבַלְתִּי is placed first as an absolute; and in the sentences which follow, it is more specifically defined by a detail of the objects which were turned into mourning. כִּסֵּה עָלָיו אֶת־תְּהוֹם cannot mean here, "to cover the flood upon (over) him" (after ch. xxiv. 7 and xxvi. 19); for this is altogether unsuitable to either the more remote or the more immediate context. The tree Asshur was not destroyed by a flood, but cut down by strangers. The following clauses, "I stopped its streams," etc., show very plainly that the connection between the flood (תְּהוֹם) and the tree which had been felled is to be understood in accordance with ver. 4. A flood, which poured its נַהֲרוֹת round about its plantation, made the cedar-tree great; and now that the tree has been felled, God covers the flood on its account. כִּסָּה is to be explained from כִּסָּה שַׂק, to veil or wrap in mourning, as Raschi, Kimchi, Vatablus, and many others have shown. The word שַׂק is omitted, because it appeared inappropriate to תְּהוֹם. The mourning of the flood is to be taken as equivalent to drying up, so that the streams which issued from it were deprived of their water. Lebanon, *i.e.* the cedar-forest (Isa. x. 34), and all the other trees, mourned over the fall of the cedar Asshur. הִקְדִּיר, to clothe in black, *i.e.* to turn into mourning. עֻלְפֶּה is regarded by Ewald as a *Pual* formed after the Aramean mode, that is to say, by attaching the syllable *ae* instead of doubling the middle radical; whilst Hitzig proposes to change the form into עֻלָּפָה. In any case the word must be a perfect *Pual*, as a *nomen verbale* appears unsuitable; and it must also be a third person feminine, the termination ־ָה being softened into ־ֶה, as in זוּרֶה (Isa. lix. 5), and the doubling of the לְ being dropped on account of the *Sheva;* so that the plural is construed with the singular feminine (Ewald, § 317*a*). עָלַף, to faint with grief (cf. Isa. li. 20). The thought is the following: all nature was so painfully affected by the fall of Asshur, that the whole of the resources from which its prosperity and might had been derived were dried up. To interpret the different figures as specially relating to princes and nations appears a doubtful procedure, for the simple reason that in ver. 16 the trembling of the nations is expressly named. —Whilst all the nations on the surface of the earth tremble at the fall of Assyria, because they are thereby warned of the perishable nature of all earthly greatness and of their own destruction, the inhabitants of the nether world console themselves with the thought that the Assyrian is now sharing their fate (for this thought, compare ch. xxxii. 31 and Isa. xiv. 9, 10). "All the trees of Eden" are all the powerful and noble princes. The idea itself, "trees of Eden," is explained by the apposition, "the choice and beautiful ones of Lebanon," *i.e.* the picked and finest cedars, and still further strengthened by the expression כָּל־שֹׁתֵי מָיִם (cf. ver. 14). מִבְחַר וְטוֹב are connected, as in 1 Sam. ix. 2; and both words are placed side by side in the construct state, as in Dan. i. 4 (cf. Ewald, § 339*b*). They comfort themselves because they have gone down with him into Sheol, so that he has no advantage over them. They come thither to those pierced with the sword, *i.e.* to the princes and peoples whom Asshur slew in wars to establish his imperial power. וּזְרֹעוֹ might also belong to יָרְדוּ as a second subject. In that case יָשְׁבוּ בְצִלּוֹ should be taken in a relative sense: "and his arm," *i.e.* his resources, "which sat in his shadow among the nations." With this explanation זְרֹעוֹ would be different from הֵם, and could only denote the army of the Assyrian. But this does not harmonize with the sitting in his shadow among the nations, for these words obviously point back to ver. 6; so that זְרֹעוֹ is evidently meant to correspond to כָּל־גּוֹיִם רַבִּים (ver. 6), and is actually identical with הֵם, *i.e.* with all the trees of Eden. We therefore agree with Osiander, Grotius, and others, in regarding the whole of the second hemistich as more precisely determining the subject,—in other words, as a declaration of the reason for their descending into hell along with the Assyrians,—and render the passage thus: "for as his arm (as his might) they sat in his shadow among the nations;" so that the cop. ו is used in place of a causal particle. In any case, the conjecture which Ewald has adopted from the LXX. and the Syriac, viz. וְזַרְעוֹ, and his seed, in support of which appeal might be made to Isa. xiv. 21, is unsuitable, for the simple reason that the statement, that it sat in his shadow among the nations, does not apply.—After this description of the greatness and the destruction of the imperial power of Assyria, Ezekiel repeats in ver. 18 the question already asked in ver. 3: to whom is Pharaoh like? כָּכָה, so, *i.e.* under such circumstances, when the glorious cedar Asshur has been smitten by such a fate (Hitzig). The reply to this question is really contained in the description given already; so that it is immediately followed by the announcement, "and thou wilt be thrust down," etc. עֲרֵלִים, uncircumcised, equivalent to ungodly heathen הוּא פ׳, not "he is," as that would require פַּרְעֹה הוּא; but הוּא is the predicate: this is (*i.e.* so does it happen to) Pharaoh. הֲמוֹנוֹ, as in ver. 2.

CHAP. XXXII. LAMENTATIONS OVER THE RUIN OF PHARAOH AND HIS PEOPLE.

The chapter contains two lamentations composed at different times: the first, in vers. 1–16, relating to the fall of Pharaoh, which rests upon the prophecy contained in ch. xxix. 1–16 and ch. xxx. 20–26; the second, in vers. 17–32, in which the prophecy concerning the casting down of this imperial power into hell (ch. xxxi. 14–17) is worked out in elegiac form.

Vers. 1–16. LAMENTATION OVER THE KING OF EGYPT.—Pharaoh, a sea-monster, is drawn by the nations out of his waters with the net of God, and cast out upon the earth. His flesh is given to the birds and beasts of prey to devour, and the earth is saturated with his blood (vers. 2–6). At his destruction the lights of heaven lose their brightness, and all the nations will be amazed thereat (vers. 7–10). The king of Babel will come upon Egypt, will destroy both man and beast, and will make the land a desert (vers. 11–16).—The date given in ver. 1—"*In the twelfth year, in the twelfth month, on the first of the month, the word of Jehovah came to me, saying*"—agrees entirely with the relation in which the substance of the ode itself stands to the prophecies belonging to the tenth and eleventh years in ch. xxix. 1–16 and ch. xxx. 20–26; whereas the different date found in the Septuagint cannot come into consideration for a moment.

Vers. 2–6. The destruction of Pharaoh.—Ver. 2. *Son of man, raise a lamentation over Pharaoh the king of Egypt, and say to him, Thou wast compared to a young lion among the nations, and yet wast like a dragon in the sea; thou didst break forth in thy streams, and didst trouble the waters with thy feet, and didst tread their streams.* Ver. 3. *Thus saith the Lord Jehovah, Therefore will I spread out my net over thee in the midst of many nations, that they may draw thee up in my yarn;* Ver. 4. *And will cast thee upon the land, hurl thee upon the surface of the field, and will cause all the birds of the heaven to settle upon thee, and the beasts of the whole earth to satisfy themselves with thee.* Ver. 5. *Thy flesh will I put upon the mountains, and fill the valleys with thy funeral heap.* Ver. 6. *I will saturate the earth with thine outflow of thy blood even to the mountains, and the low places shall become full of thee.*—This lamentation begins, like others, with a picture of the glory of the fallen king. Hitzig objects to the ordinary explanation of the words כְּפִיר גּוֹיִם נִדְמֵיתָ, λέοντι ἐθνῶν ὡμοιώθης (LXX.), *leoni gentium assimilatus es* (Vulg.), on the ground that the frequently recurring נִדְמָה would only have this meaning in the present passage, and that נִמְשָׁל, which would then be synonymous, is construed in three other ways, but not with the nominative. For these reasons he adopts the rendering, "lion of the nations, thou belongest to death." But it would be contrary to the analogy of all the קִינוֹת to commence the lamentation with such a threat; and Hitzig's objections to the ordinary rendering of the words will not bear examination. The circumstance that the *Niphal* נִדְמָה is only met with here in the sense of ὁμοιοῦσθαι, proves nothing; for דָּמָה has this meaning in the *Kal*, *Piel*, and *Hithpael*, and the construction of the *Niphal* with the accusative (not nominative; as Hitzig says) may be derived without difficulty from the construction of the synonymous נִמְשַׁל with כ. But what is decisive in favour of this rendering is the fact that the following clause is connected by means of the adversative וְאַתָּה (but thou), which shows that the comparison of Pharaoh to a תַּנִּים forms an antithesis to the clause in which he is compared to a young lion. If כְּפִיר ג' נִדְמֵיתָ contained a declaration of destruction, not only would this antithesis be lost, but the words addressed to it as a lion of the nations would float in the air and be used without any intelligible meaning. The lion is a figurative representation of a powerful and victorious ruler; and כְּפִיר גּוֹיִם is really equivalent to אֵל גּוֹיִם in ch. xxxi. 11. Pharaoh was regarded as a mighty conqueror of the nations, "though he was rather to be compared to the crocodile, which stirs up the streams, the fresh waters, and life-giving springs of the nations most perniciously with mouth and feet, and renders turbid all that is pure" (Ewald). תַּנִּים, as in ch. xxix. 3. Ewald and Hitzig have taken offence at the words תָּגַח בְּנַהֲרוֹתֶיךָ, "thou didst break forth in thy streams," and alter בְּנַהֲרוֹתֶיךָ into בְּנַחֲרֹתֶיךָ, with thy nostrils (Job xli. 12); but they have not considered that תָּגַח would be quite out of place with such an alteration, as גִּיחַ in both the *Kal* and *Hiphil* (Judg. xx. 33) has only the intransitive meaning to break out. The thought is simply this: the crocodile lies in the sea, then breaks occasionally forth in its streams, and makes the waters and their streams turbid with its feet. Therefore shall Pharaoh also end like such a monster (vers. 3–6). The guilt of Pharaoh did not consist in the fact that he had assumed the position of a ruler among the nations (Kliefoth); but in his polluting the water-streams, stirring up and disturbing the life-giving streams of the nations. God will take him in His net by a gathering of nations, and cause him to be drawn out of his element upon the dry land, where he shall become food to the birds and beasts of prey (cf. ch. xxix. 4, 5, xxxi. 12, 13). The words בִּקְהַל עַמִּים ר' are not to be understood as referring to the nations, as spectators of the event (Hävernick); but ב denotes the instrument, or medium employed, here the persons by whom God causes the net to be thrown, as is evident from the וְהֶעֱלוּךָ which follows. According to the *parallelismus membrorum*, the ἀπ. λεγ. רָמוּת can only refer to the carcase of the beast, although the source from which this meaning of the word is derived has not yet been traced. There is no worth to be attached to the reading רִמּוֹת in some of the codices, as רִמָּה does not yield a suitable meaning either in the sense of reptile, or in that of putrefaction or decomposed bodies, which has been attributed to it from the Arabic. Under these circumstances we adhere to the derivation from רוּם, to be high, according to which רָמוּת may signify a height or a heap, which the context defines as a funeral-pile. צָפָה, strictly speaking, a participle from צוּף, to flow, that which flows out, the outflow (Hitzig), is not to be taken in connection with אֶרֶץ, but is a second object to הִשְׁקֵיתִי; and the appended word מִדָּמְךָ indicates the source whence the flowing takes place, and of what the outflow consists. אֶל הֶהָרִים, to the mountains, *i.e.* up to the top of the mountains. The thought in these verses is probably simply this, that the fall of Pharaoh would bring destruction upon the whole of the land of Egypt, and that many nations would derive advantage from his fall.

Vers. 7–10. His overthrow fills the whole world with mourning and terror.—Ver. 7. *When I extinguish thee, I will cover the sky and darken its stars; I will cover the sun with cloud, and the moon will not cause its light to shine.* Ver. 8. *All the shining lights in the sky do I darken because of thee, and I bring darkness over thy land, is the saying of the Lord Jehovah.* Ver. 9. *And I will trouble the heart of many nations when I bring out thine overthrow among the nations into lands which thou knowest not,* Ver. 10. *And I will make many nations amazed at thee, and their kings shall shudder at thee when I brandish my sword before their face; and they shall tremble every moment, every one for his life on the day of his fall.*—The thought of vers. 7 and 8 is not exhausted by the paraphrase, "when thou art extinguished, all light will be extinguished, so far as Egypt is concerned," accompanied with the remark, that the darkness consequent thereupon is a figurative representation of utterly hopeless circumstances (Schmieder). The thought on which the figure rests is that of the day of the Lord, the day of God's judgment, on which the lights of heaven lose their brightness (cf. ch. xxx. 3 and Joel ii. 10, etc.). This day bursts upon Egypt with the fall of Pharaoh, and on it the shining stars of heaven are darkened, so that the land of Pharaoh becomes dark. Egypt is a world-power represented by Pharaoh, which collapses with his fall. But the overthrow of this world-power is an omen and prelude of the overthrow of every ungodly world-power on the day of the last judgment, when the present heaven and the present earth will perish in the judgment-fire. Compare the remarks to be found in the commentary on Joel iii. 4 upon the connection between the phenomena of the heavens and great catastrophes on earth. The contents of both verses may be fully explained from the biblical idea of the day of the Lord and the accompanying phenomena; and for the explanation of בְּכַבּוֹתְךָ, there is no necessity to assume, as Dereser and Hitzig have done, that the sea-dragon of Egypt is presented here under the constellation of a dragon; for there is no connection between the comparison of Egypt to a *tannim* or sea-dragon, in ver. 2 and ch. xxix. 3 (=רַהַב, Isa. li. 9), and the constellation of the dragon (see the comm. on Isa. li. 9 and xxx. 7). In בְּכַבּוֹתְךָ Pharaoh is no doubt regarded as a star of the first magnitude in the sky; but in this conception Ezekiel rests upon Isa. xiv. 12, where the king of Babylon is designated as a bright morning-star. That this passage was in the prophet's mind, is evident at once from the fact that ver. 7 coincides almost *verbatim* with Isa. xiii. 10.—The extinction and obscuration of the stars are not merely a figurative representation of the mourning occasioned by the fall of Pharaoh; still less can vers. 9 and 10 be taken as an interpretation in literal phraseology of the figurative words in vers. 7 and 8. For vers. 9 and 10 do not relate to the mourning of the nations, but to anxiety and terror into which they are plunged by God through the fall of Pharaoh and his might. הִכְעִים לֵב, to afflict the heart, does not mean to make it sorrowful, but to fill it with anxiety, to deprive it of its peace and cheerfulness. "When I bring thy fall among the nations" is equivalent to "spread the report of thy fall." Consequently there is no need for either the arbitrary alteration of שִׁבְרְךָ into שִׁבְרְךָ, which Ewald proposes, with the imaginary rendering announcement or report; nor for the marvellous assumption of Hävernick, that שִׁבְרְךָ describes the prisoners scattered among the heathen as the ruins of the ancient glory of Egypt, in support of which he adduces the rendering of the LXX. *αἰχμαλωσίαν σου*, which is founded upon the change of שברך into שִׁבְיֵךְ. For ver. 10*a* compare ch. xxvii. 35. עוֹפֵף, to cause to fly, to brandish. The sword is brandished before their face when it falls time after time upon their brother the king of Egypt, whereby they are thrown into alarm for their own lives. לִרְגָעִים, by moments = every moment (see the comm. on Isa. xxvii. 3).

Vers. 11–16. The judgment upon Egypt will be executed by the king of Babylon.—Ver. 11. *For thus saith the Lord Jehovah, The sword of the king of Babylon will come upon thee.* Ver. 12. *By swords of heroes will I cause thy tumult to fall, violent ones of the nations are they all, and will lay waste the pride of Egypt, and all its tumult will be destroyed.* Ver. 13. *And I will cut off all its cattle from the great waters, that no foot of man may disturb them any more, nor any hoof of cattle disturb them.* Ver. 14. *Then will I cause their waters to settle and their streams to flow like oil, is the saying of the Lord Jehovah,* Ver. 15. *When I make the land of Egypt a desert, and the land is made desolate of its fulness, because I smite all the inhabitants therein, and they shall know that I am Jehovah.* Ver. 16. *A lamentation* (mournful ode) *is this, and they will sing it mournfully; the daughters of the nations will sing it mournfully, over Egypt and over all its tumult will they sing it mournfully, is the saying of the Lord Jehovah.*—In this concluding strophe the figurative announcement of the preceding one is summed up briefly in literal terms; and toward the close (ver. 14) there is a slight intimation of a better future. The destruction of the proud might of Egypt will be effected through the king of Babylon and his brave and violent hosts. עָרִיצֵי גוֹיִם, as in ch. xxxi. 12 (see the comm. on ch. xxviii. 7). הָמוֹן in vers. 12 and 13 must not be restricted to the multitude of people. It signifies tumult, and embraces everything in Egypt by which noise and confusion were made (as in ch. xxxi. 2 and 18); although the idea of a multitude of people undoubtedly predominates in the use of הָמוֹן in ver. 12*a*. גְּאוֹן מִצְרַיִם, the pride of Egypt, is not that of which Egypt is proud, but whatever is proud or exalts itself in Egypt. The utter devastation of Egypt includes the destruction of the cattle, *i.e.* of the numerous herds which fed on the grassy banks of the Nile and were driven to the Nile to drink (cf. Gen. xlvii. 6, xli. 2 sqq.; Ex. ix. 3); and this is therefore specially mentioned in ver. 13, with an allusion to the consequence thereof, namely, that the waters of the Nile would not be disturbed any more either by the foot of man or hoof of beast (compare ver. 13*b* with ch. xxix. 11). The disturbing of the water is mentioned with evident reference to ver. 2, where Pharaoh is depicted as a sea-monster, which disturbs the streams of water. The disturbance of the water is therefore a figurative representation of the wild driving of the imperial power of Egypt, by which the life-giving streams of the nations were stirred up.—Ver. 14. Then will God cause the waters of Egypt to sink. Hitzig and Kliefoth understand this as signifying the diminution of the abundance of water in the Nile, which had previously overflowed the land and rendered it fertile, but for which there was no further purpose now. According to this explanation, the words would contain a continued picture of the devastation of the land. But this is evidently a mistake, for the simple reason that it is irreconcilable with the אָז, by which the thought is introduced. אָז, *tunc*, is more precisely defined by בְּתִתִּי וגו' in ver. 15 as the time when the devastation has taken place; whereas Kliefoth takes the 15th verse, in opposition both to the words and the usage of the language, as the sequel to ver. 14, or in other words, regards בְּתִתִּי as synonymous with וְנָתַתִּי. The verse contains a promise, as most of the commentators, led by the Chaldee and Jerome, have correctly assumed.[1] הִשְׁקִיעַ, to make the water sink, might no doubt signify in itself a diminution of the abundance of water. But if we consider the context, in which reference is made to the disturbance of the water through its being trodden with the feet (ver. 13), השקיע can only signify to settle, *i.e.* to become clear through the sinking to the bottom of the slime which had been stirred up (cf. ch. xxxiv. 18). The correctness of this explanation is confirmed by the parallel clause, to make their streams flow with oil. To understand this as signifying the slow and gentle flow of the diminished water, would introduce a figure of which there is no trace in Hebrew. Oil is used throughout the Scriptures as a figurative representation of the divine blessing, or the power of the divine Spirit. כַּשֶּׁמֶן, like oil, according to Hebrew phraseology, is equivalent to "like rivers of oil." And oil-rivers are not rivers which flow quietly like oil, but rivers which contain oil instead of water (cf. Job xxix. 6), and are symbolical of the rich blessing of God (cf. Deut. xxxii. 13). The figure is a very appropriate one for Egypt, as the land is indebted to the Nile for all its fertility. Whereas its water had been stirred up and rendered turbid by Pharaoh; after the fall of Pharaoh the Lord will cause the waters of the stream,

[1] The explanation of Jerome is the following: "Then will purest waters, which had been disturbed by the sway of the dragon, be restored not by another, but by the Lord Himself; so that their streams flow like oil, and are the nutriment of true light."

which pours its blessing upon the land, to purify themselves, and will make its streams flow with oil. The clarified water and flowing oil are figures of the life-giving power of the word and Spirit of God. But this blessing will not flow to Egypt till its natural power is destroyed. Ewald has therefore given the following as the precise meaning of ver. 14: "The Messianic times will then for the first time dawn on Egypt, when the waters no more become devastating and turbid, that is to say, through the true knowledge to which the chastisement leads." Ver. 16 "rounds off the passage by turning back to ver. 2" (Hitzig). The daughters of the nations are mentioned as the singers, because mourning for the dead was for the most part the business of women (cf. Jer. ix. 16). The words do not contain a summons to the daughters of the nations to sing the lamentation, but the declaration that they will do it, in which the thought is implied that the predicted devastation of Egypt will certainly occur.

Vers. 17–32. FUNERAL-DIRGE FOR THE DESTRUCTION OF THE MIGHT OF EGYPT.—This second lamentation or mourning ode, according to the heading in ver. 17, belongs to the same year as the preceding, and to the 15th of the month, no doubt the 12th month; in which case it was composed only fourteen days after the first. The statement of the month is omitted here, as in ch. xxvi. 1; and the omission is, no doubt, to be attributed to a copyist in this instance also. In the ode, which Ewald aptly describes as a "dull, heavy lamentation," we have six regular strophes, preserving the uniform and monotonous character of the lamentations for the dead, in which the thought is worked out, that Egypt, like other great nations, is cast down to the nether world. The whole of it is simply an elegiac expansion of the closing thought of the previous chapter (ch. xxxi.).

Vers. 18–21. Introduction and first strophe.—Ver. 18. *Son of man, lament over the tumult of Egypt, and hurl it down, her, like the daughters of glorious nations, into the nether world, to those who go into the pit!* Ver. 19. *Whom dost thou surpass in loveliness? Go down and lay thyself with the uncircumcised.* Ver. 20. *Among those slain with the sword will they fall; the sword is handed, draw her down and all her tumult.* Ver. 21. *The strong ones of the heroes say of it out of the midst of hell with its helpers: they are gone down, they lie there, the uncircumcised, slain with the sword.*—נְהֵה, utter a lamentation, and וְהוֹרִדֵהוּ, thrust it (the tumult of Egypt) down, are co-ordinate. With the lamentation, or by means thereof, is Ezekiel to thrust down the tumult of Egypt into hell. The lamentation is God's word; and as such it has the power to accomplish what it utters. אוֹתָהּ is not intended as a repetition of the suffix ־ֵהוּ, but resumes the principal idea contained in the object already named, viz. מִצְרַיִם, Egypt, *i.e.* its population. אוֹתָהּ and the daughters of glorious nations are co-ordinate. בְּנוֹת, as in the expression, daughter Tyre, daughter Babel, denotes the population of powerful heathen nations. The גּוֹיִם אַדִּרִם can only be the nations enumerated in vers. 22, 24 sqq., which, according to these verses, are already in Sheol, not about to be thrust down, but thrust down already. Consequently the copula ו before בְּנוֹת is to be taken in the sense of a comparison, as in 1 Sam. xii. 15 (cf. Ewald, § 340*b*). All these glorious nations have also been hurled down by the word of God; and Egypt is to be associated with them. By thus placing Egypt on a level with all the fallen nations, the enumeration of which fills the middle strophes of the ode, the lamentation over Egypt is extended into a funeral-dirge on the fall of all the heathen powers of the world. For אֶרֶץ תַּחְתִּיּוֹת and יוֹרְדֵי בוֹר, compare ch. xxvi. 20. The ode itself commences in ver. 19, by giving prominence to the glory of the falling kingdom. But this prominence consists in the brief inquiry מִמִּי נָעָמְתְּ, before whom art thou lovely? *i.e.* art thou more lovely than any one else? The words are addressed either to הֲמוֹן מִצְרַיִם (ver. 18), or what is more probable, to Pharaoh with all his tumult (cf. ver. 32), *i.e.* to the world-power, Egypt, as embodied in the person of Pharaoh; and the meaning of the question is the following:—Thou, Egypt, art indeed lovely; but thou art not better or more lovely than other mighty heathen nations; therefore thou canst not expect any better fate than to go down into Sheol, and there lie with the uncircumcised. עֲרֵלִים, as in ch. xxxi. 18. This is carried out still further in ver. 20, and the ground thereof assigned. The subject to יִפֹּלוּ is the Egyptians, or Pharaoh and his tumult. They fall in the midst of those pierced with the sword. The sword is already handed to the executor of the judgment, the king of Babel (ch. xxxi. 11). Their destruction is so certain, that the words are addressed to the bearers of the sword: "Draw Egypt and all its tumult down into Sheol" (מָשְׁכוּ is imperative for מִשְׁכוּ in Ex. xii. 21), and, according to ver. 21, the heathen already in Sheol are speaking of his destruction. יְדַבְּרוּ לוֹ is rendered by many, "there speak to him, address him, greet him," with an allusion to Isa. xiv. 9 sqq., where the king of Babel, when descending into Sheol, is greeted with malicious pleasure by the kings already there. But however obvious the fact may be that Ezekiel has this passage in mind, there is no address in the verse before us as in Isa. xiv. 10, but simply a statement concerning the Egyptians, made in the third person. Moreover, אֶת־עֹזְרָיו could hardly be made to harmonize with יְדַבְּרוּ לוֹ, if לוֹ signified *ad eum*. For it is not allowable to connect אֶת־עֹזְרָיו (taken in the sense of along with their helpers) with אֵלֵי גִבּוֹרִים as a noun in apposition, for the simple reason that the two are separated by מִתּוֹךְ שְׁאוֹל. Consequently אֶת־עֹזְרָיו can only belong to יְדַבְּרוּ: they talk (of him) with his helpers. עֹזְרָיו, his (Pharaoh's) helpers are his allies, who have already gone down before him into hell (cf. ch. xxx. 8). The singular suffix, which has offended Hitzig, is quite in order as corresponding to לוֹ. The words, "they have gone down, lie there," etc., point once more to the fact that the same fate has happened to the Egyptians as to all the rest of the rulers and nations of the world whom God has judged. For אֵלֵי גִבּוֹרִים, strong ones of the heroes, compare the comm. on ch. xxxi. 11. שְׁאוֹל, hell = the nether world, the gathering-place of the dead; not the place of punishment for the damned. חַלְלֵי חֶרֶב without the article is a predicate, and not in apposition to הָעֲרֵלִים. On the application of this epithet to the Egyptians, Kliefoth has correctly observed that "the question whether the Egyptians received circumcision is one that has no bearing upon this passage; for in the sense in which Ezekiel understands circumcision, the Egyptians were uncircumcised, even if they were accustomed to circumcise their flesh."

In the four following strophes (vers. 22–30) a series of heathen nations is enumerated, whom the Egyptian finds already in hell, and with whom he will share the same fate. There are six of these—namely, Asshur, Elam, Meshech-Tubal, Edom, the princes of the north, and Sidon. The six are divisible into two classes—three great and remote world-powers, and three smaller neighbouring nations. In this no regard is paid to the time of destruction. With the empire of Asshur, which had already fallen, there are associated Elam and Meshech-Tubal, two nations, which only rose to the rank of world-powers in the more immediate and more remote future; and among the neighbouring nations, the Sidonians and princes of the north, *i.e.* the Syrian kings, are grouped with Edom, although the Sidonians had long ago given up their supremacy to Tyre, and the Aramean kings, who had once so grievously oppressed the kingdom of Israel, had already been swallowed up in the Assyrian and Chaldean empire. It may, indeed, be said that "in any case, at the time when Ezekiel prophesied, princes enough had already descended into Sheol both of the Assyrians and Elamites, etc., to welcome the Egyptians as soon as they came" (Kliefoth); but with the same justice may it also be said that many of the rulers and countrymen of Egypt had also descended into Sheol already, at the time when Pharaoh, reigning in Ezekiel's day, was to share the same fate. It is evident, therefore, that "any such reflection upon chronological relations is out of place in connection with our text, the intention of which is merely to furnish an exemplification" (Kliefoth), and that Ezekiel looks upon Egypt more in the light of a world-power, discerning in its fall the overthrow of all the heathen power of the world, and predicting it under the prophetic picture, that Pharaoh and his tumult are expected and welcomed by the princes and nations that have already descended into Sheol, as coming to share their fate with them.

Vers. 22, 23. Second strophe.—Ver. 22. *There is Asshur and all its multitude, round about it their graves, all of them slain, fallen by the sword.* Ver. 23. *Whose graves are made in the deepest pit, and its multitude is round about its grave; all slain, fallen by the sword, who spread terror in the land of the living.*—The enumeration commences with Asshur, the world-power, which had already been overthrown by the Chaldeans. It is important to notice here, that אַשּׁוּר, like עֵילָם in ver. 24, and מֶשֶׁךְ תֻּבַל in ver. 26, is construed as a feminine, as הֲמוֹנָהּ which follows in every case plainly shows. It is obvious, therefore, that the predominant idea is not that of the king or people, but that of the kingdom or world-power. It is true that in the suffixes attached to סְבִיבוֹתָיו קִבְרֹתָיו in ver. 22, and סְבִיבוֹתָיו in vers. 25 and 26, the masculine alternates with the feminine, and Hitzig therefore proposes to erase these words; but the alternation may be very simply explained, on the ground that the ideas of the kingdom and its king are not kept strictly separate, but that the words oscillate from one idea to the other. It is affirmed of Asshur, that as a world-power it lies in Sheol, and the graves of its countrymen are round about the graves of its ruler. They all lie there as those who have fallen by the sword, *i.e.* who have been swept away by a judgment of God. To this is added in ver. 23 the declaration that the graves of Asshur lie in the utmost sides, *i.e.* the utmost or deepest extremity of Sheol; whereas so long as this power together with its people was in the land of the living, *i.e.* so long as they ruled on earth, they spread terror all around them by their violent deeds. From the loftiest height of earthly might and greatness, they are hurled down to the lowest hell. The higher on earth, the deeper in the nether world. Hävernick has entirely misunderstood the words "round about Asshur are its graves" (ver. 22), and "its multitude is round about its grave" (the grave of this world-power), when he finds therein the thought that the graves and corpses are to be regarded as separated, so that the dead are waiting near their graves in deepest sorrow, looking for the honour of burial, but looking in vain. There is not a word of this in the text, but simply that the graves of the people lie round about the grave of their ruler.

Vers. 24 and 25. Third strophe.—Ver. 24. *There is Elam, and all its multitude round about its grave; all of them slain, fallen by the sword, who went down uncircumcised into the nether world, who spread terror before them in the land of the living, and bear their shame with those who went into the pit.* Ver. 25. *In the midst of the slain have they made it a bed with all its multitude, round about it are their graves; all of them uncircumcised, pierced with the sword; because terror was spread before them in the land of the living, they bear their shame with those who have gone into the pit. In the midst of slain ones is he laid.*—Asshur is followed by עֵילָם, Elam, the warlike people of Elymais, *i.e.* Susiana, the modern Chusistan, whose archers served in the Assyrian army (Isa. xxii. 6), and which is mentioned along with the Medes as one of the conquerors of Babylon (Isa. xxi. 2), whereas Jeremiah prophesied its destruction at the commencement of Zedekiah's reign (Jer. xlix. 34 sqq.). Ezekiel says just the same of Elam as he has already said of Asshur, and almost in the same words. The only difference is, that his description is more copious, and that he expresses more distinctly the thought of shameful destruction which is implied in the fact of lying in Sheol among the slain, and repeats it a second time, and that he also sets the bearing of shame into Sheol in contrast with the terror which Elam had spread around it during its life on earth. נָשָׂא כְלִמָּה, as in ch. xvi. 52. The ב in בְּכָל־הֲמוֹנָהּ is either the "with of association," or the fact of being in the midst of a crowd. לָהּ refers to עֵילָם; and נִתְּנוּ has an indefinite subject, "they gave" = there was given. מִשְׁכָּב, the resting-place of the dead, as in 2 Chron. xvi. 14. The last clause in ver. 25 is an emphatic repetition of the leading thought: he (Elam) is brought or laid in the midst of the slain.

Vers. 26–28. Fourth strophe.—Ver. 26. *There is Meshech-Tubal and all its multitude, its graves round about it; all of them uncircumcised, slain with the sword, because they spread terror before them in the land of the living.* Ver. 27. *They lie not with the fallen heroes of uncircumcised men, who went down into hell with their weapons of war, whose swords they laid under their heads; their iniquities have come upon their bones, because they were a terror of the heroes in the land of the living.* Ver. 28. *Thou also wilt be dashed to pieces among uncircumcised men, and lie with those slain with the sword.*—מֶשֶׁךְ and תֻּבַל, the Moschi and Tibareni of the Greeks (see the comm. on ch. xxvii. 13), are joined together ἀσυνδετῶς here as one people or heathen power; and Ewald, Hitzig, and others suppose that the reference is to the Scythians, who invaded the land in the time of Josiah, and the majority of whom had miserably perished not very long before (Herod. i. 106). But apart from the fact that the prophets of the Old Testament make no allusion to any invasion of Palestine by the Scythians (see *Minor Prophets*, vol. ii. p. 124, Eng. transl.), this view is founded entirely upon the erroneous supposition that in this funeral-dirge Ezekiel mentions only such peoples as had sustained great defeats a longer or shorter time before. Meshech-Tubal comes into consideration here, as in ch. xxxviii., as a northern power, which is overcome in its conflict with the kingdom of God, and is prophetically exhibited by the prophet as having already fallen under the judgment of death. In ver. 26 Ezekiel makes the same announcement as he has already made concerning Asshur in vers. 22, 23, and with regard to Elam in vers. 24, 25. But the announcement in ver. 27 is obscure. Rosenmüller, Ewald, Hävernick, and others, regard this verse as a question (וְלֹא in the sense of הֲלֹא): "and should they not lie with (rest with) other fallen heroes of the uncircumcised, who . . . ?" *i.e.* they do lie with them, and could not possibly expect a better fate. But although the interrogation is merely indicated by the tone where the language is excited, and therefore וְלֹא might stand for הֲלֹא, as in Ex. viii. 22, there is not the slightest indication of such excitement in the description given here as could render this assumption a probable one. On the contrary, וְלֹא at the commencement of the sentence suggests the supposition that an antithesis is intended to the preceding verse. And the probability of this conjecture is heightened by the allusion made to heroes, who have descended into the nether world with their weapons of war; inasmuch as, at all events, something is therein affirmed which does not apply to all the heroes who have gone down into hell. The custom of placing the weapons of fallen heroes along with them in the grave is attested by Diod. Sic. xviii. 26; Arrian, i. 5; Virgil, *Aen.* vi. 233 (cf. Dougtaei *Analectt.* ss. i. pp. 281, 282); and, according to the ideas prevailing in ancient times, it was a mark of great respect to the dead. But the last place in which we should expect to meet with any allusion to the payment of such honour to the dead would be in connection with Meshech and Tubal, those wild hordes of the north, who were only known to Israel by hearsay. We therefore follow the Vulgate, the Rabbins, and many of the earlier commentators, and regard the verse before us as containing a declaration that the slain of Meshech-Tubal would not receive the honour of resting in the nether world along with those fallen heroes whose weapons were buried with them in the grave, because they fell with honour.[1] כְּלֵי

[1] C. a Lapide has already given the true meaning: "He compares them, therefore, not with the righteous, but with the heathen, who, although

מִלְחָמָה, instruments of war, weapons, as in Deut. i. 41. The text leaves it uncertain who they were who had been buried with such honours. The Seventy have confounded מֵעֲרֵלִים with מֵעוֹלָם, and rendered נֹפְלִים מֵעֲרֵלִים, τῶν πεπτωκότων ἀπ' αἰῶνος, possibly thinking of the *gibborim* of Gen. vi. 4. Dathe and Hitzig propose to alter the text to this; and even Hävernick imagines that the prophet may possibly have had such passages as Gen. vi. 4 and x. 9 sqq. floating before his mind. But there is not sufficient ground to warrant an alteration of the text; and if Ezekiel had had Gen. vi. 4 in his mind, he would no doubt have written הַגִּבּוֹרִים. The clause וַתְּהִי עֲוֹנוֹתָם is regarded by the more recent commentators as a continuation of the preceding וַיִּתְּנוּ וגו', which is a very natural conclusion, if we simply take notice of the construction. But if we consider the sense of the words, this combination can hardly be sustained. The words, "and so were their iniquities upon their bones" (or they came upon them), can well be understood as an explanation of the reason for their descending into Sheol with their weapons, and lying upon their swords. We must therefore regard וַתְּהִי עֲוֹנוֹתָם as a continuation of יִשְׁכְּבוּ, so that their not resting with those who were buried with their weapons of war furnishes the proof that their guilt lay upon their bones. The words, therefore, have no other meaning than the phrase יִשְׂאוּ כְלִמָּתָם in vers. 24 and 30. Sin comes upon the bones when the punishment consequent upon it falls upon the bones of the sinner. In the last clause we connect גִּבּוֹרִים with חִתִּית, terror of the heroes, *i.e.* terrible even to heroes on account of their savage and cruel nature. In ver. 28 we cannot take אַתָּה as referring to Meshech-Tubal, as many of the commentators propose. A direct address to that people would be at variance with the whole plan of the ode. Moreover, the declaration contained in the verse would contradict what pre-

uncircumcised, had met with a glorious death, *i.e.* they will be more wretched than these; for the latter went down to the shades with glory, but they with ignominy, as if conquered and slain."

cedes. As Meshech-Tubal is already lying in Sheol among the slain, according to ver. 26, the announcement cannot be made to it for the first time here, that it is to be dashed in pieces and laid with those who are slain with the sword. It is the Egyptian who is addressed, and he is told that this fate will also fall upon him. And through this announcement, occurring in the midst of the list of peoples that have already gone down to Sheol, the design of that list is once more called to mind.

Vers. 29 and 30. Fifth strophe.—Ver. 29. *There are Edom, its kings and all its princes, who in spite of their bravery are associated with those that are pierced with the sword; they lie with the uncircumcised and with those that have gone down into the pit.* Ver. 30. *There are the princes of the north, all of them, and all the Sidonians who have gone down to the slain, been put to shame in spite of the dread of them because of their bravery; they lie there as uncircumcised, and bear their shame with those who have gone into the pit.*—In this strophe Ezekiel groups together the rest of the heathen nations in the neighbourhood of Israel; and in doing so, he changes the שָׁם of the preceding list for שָׁמָּה, thither. This might be taken prophetically: thither will they come, "to these do they also belong" (Hävernick), only such nations being mentioned here as are still awaiting their destruction. But, in the first place, the perfects אֲשֶׁר נִתְּנוּ, אֲשֶׁר יָרְדוּ, in vers. 29, 30, do not favour this explanation, inasmuch as they are used as preterites in vers. 22, 24, 25, 26, 27; and, secondly, even in the previous strophes, not only are such peoples mentioned as have already perished, but some, like Elam and Meshech-Tubal, which did not rise into historical importance, or exert any influence upon the development of the kingdom of God till after Ezekiel's time, whereas the Edomites and Sidonians were already approaching destruction. We therefore regard שָׁמָּה as simply a variation of expression in the sense of "thither have they come," without discovering any allusion to the future.—In the case of Edom, kings and נְשִׂיאִים, *i.e.* tribe-princes, are mentioned. The allusion is to the *'allu-*

phim or phylarchs, literally chiliarchs, the heads of the leading families (Gen. xxxvi. 15 sqq.), in whose hands the government of the people lay, inasmuch as the kings were elective, and were probably chosen by the phylarchs (see the comm. on Gen. xxxvi. 31 sqq.). בִּגְבוּרָתָם, in, or with their bravery, *i.e.* in spite of it. There is something remarkable in the allusion to princes of the north (נְסִיכֵי, lit. persons enfeoffed, vassal-princes; see the comm. on Josh. xiii. 21 and Mic. v. 4) in connection with the Sidonians, and after Meshech-Tubal the representative of the northern nations. The association with the Sidonians renders the conjecture a very natural one, that allusion is made to the north of Palestine, and more especially to the Aram of Scripture, with its many separate states and princes (Hävernick); although Jer. xxv. 26, "the kings of the north, both far and near," does not furnish a conclusive proof of this. So much, at any rate, is certain, that the princes of the north are not to be identified with the Sidonians. For, as Kliefoth has correctly observed, "there are six heathen nations mentioned, viz. Asshur, Elam, Meshech-Tubal, Edom, the princes of the north, and Sidon; and if we add Egypt to the list, we shall have seven, which would be thoroughly adapted, as it was eminently intended, to depict the fate of universal heathenism." A principle is also clearly discernible in the mode in which they are grouped. Asshur, Elam, and Meshech-Tubal represent the greater and more distant world-powers; Edom the princes of the north, and Sidon the neighbouring nations of Israel on both south and north. בְּחִתִּיתָם מִגְּבוּרָתָם, literally, in dread of them, (which proceeded) from their bravery, *i.e.* which their bravery inspired. וַיִּשְׂאוּ וגו׳, as in ver. 24.

Vers. 31 and 32. Sixth and last strophe.—Ver. 31. *Pharaoh will see them, and comfort himself over all his multitude. Pharaoh and all his army are slain with the sword, is the saying of the Lord Jehovah.* Ver. 32. *For I caused him to spread terror in the land of the living, therefore is he laid in the midst of uncircumcised, those slain with the sword, Pharaoh and all his multi-*

tude, is the saying of the Lord Jehovah.—In these verses the application to Egypt follows. Pharaoh will see in the nether world all the greater and smaller heathen nations with their rulers; and when he sees them all given up to the judgment of death, he will comfort himself over the fate which has fallen upon himself and his army, as he will perceive that he could not expect any better lot than that of the other rulers of the world. נִחַם עַל, to comfort oneself, as in ch. xxxi. 16 and xiv. 22. Hitzig's assertion, that נִחַם עַל never signifies *to comfort oneself*, is incorrect (see the comm. on ch. xiv. 22). נָתַתִּי אֶת־חִתִּיתוֹ, I have given terror of him, *i.e.* I have made him an instrument of terror. The *Keri* חִתִּיתִי arose from a misunderstanding. The *Chetib* is confirmed by vers. 24 and 26. In ver. 32*b* the ode is brought to a close by returning even in expression to vers. 19 and 20*a*.

If, now, we close with a review of the whole of the contents of the words of God directed against Egypt, in all of them is the destruction of the might of Pharaoh and Egypt as a world-power foretold. And this prophecy has been completely fulfilled. As Kliefoth has most truly observed, "one only needs to enter the pyramids of Egypt and its catacombs to see that the glory of the Pharaohs has gone down into Sheol. And it is equally certain that this destruction of the glory of ancient Egypt dates from the times of the Babylonio-Persian empire. Moreover, this destruction was so thorough, that even to the New Egypt of the Ptolemies the character of the Old Egypt was a perfect enigma, a thing forgotten and incomprehensible." But if Ezekiel repeatedly speaks of Nebuchadnezzar the king of Babylon as executing this judgment upon Egypt, we must bear in mind that here, as in the case of Tyre (see the comm. on ch. xxviii. 1–19), Ezekiel regards Nebuchadnezzar as the instrument of the righteous punishment of God in general, and discerns in what he accomplishes the sum of all that in the course of ages has been gradually fulfilling itself in history. At the same time, it is equally certain that this view of the prophet would have no foundation in truth unless Nebuchadnezzar really did conquer Egypt and lay it waste, and the might and glory of this ancient empire were so shattered thereby, that it never could recover its former greatness, but even after the turning of its captivity, *i.e.* after its recovery from the deadly wounds which the imperial monarchy of Babylonia and afterwards of Persia inflicted upon it, still remained a lowly kingdom, which could "no more rule over the nations" (ch. xxix. 13-16). Volney, however, in his *Recherch. nouv. sur l'hist. anc.* (III. pp. 151 sqq.), and Hitzig (*Ezek.* p. 231), dispute the conquest and devastation of Egypt by Nebuchadnezzar, because the Greek historians, with Herodotus (ii. 161 sqq.) at their head, make no allusion whatever to an invasion of Egypt; and their statements are even opposed to such an occurrence. But the silence of Greek historians, especially of Herodotus, is a most "miserable" argument. The same historians do not say a word about the defeat of Necho by Nebuchadnezzar at Carchemish; and yet even Hitzig accepts this as an indisputable fact. Herodotus and his successors derived their accounts of Egypt from the communications of Egyptian priests, who suppressed everything that was humiliating to the pride of Egypt, and endeavoured to cover it up with their accounts of glorious deeds which the Pharaohs had performed. But Hitzig has by no means proved that the statements of the Greeks are at variance with the assumption of a Chaldean invasion of Egypt, whilst he has simply rejected but not refuted the attempts of Perizonius, Vitringa, Hävernick, and others, to reconcile the biblical narrative of the conquest of Egypt by Nebuchadnezzar with the accounts given by Herodotus, Diodorus Siculus, and other Greeks, concerning the mighty feats of Necho, and his being slain by Amasis. The remark that, in the description given by Herodotus, Amasis appears as an independent king by the side of Cambyses, only less powerful than the Persian monarch, proves nothing more, even assuming the correctness of the fact, than that Amasis had made Egypt once more independent of Babylonia on the sudden overthrow of the Chaldean monarchy.

The conquest of Egypt by Nebuchadnezzar, after the attitude which Pharaoh Necho assumed towards the Babylonian empire, and even attempted to maintain in the time of Zedekiah by sending an army to the relief of Jerusalem when besieged by the Chaldeans, is not only extremely probable in itself, but confirmed by testimony outside the Bible. Even if no great importance can be attached to the notice of Megasthenes, handed down by Strabo (xv. 1. 6) and Josephus (*c. Ap.* i. 20): "he says that he (Nebuchadnezzar) conquered the greater part of Libya and Iberia;" Josephus not only quotes from Berosus (*l.c.* i. 19) to the effect that "the Babylonian got possession of *Egypt*, Syria, Phoenicia, Arabia," but, on the ground of such statements, relates the complete fulfilment of the prophecies of Scripture, saying, in *Antt.* x. 9. 7, with reference to Nebuchadnezzar, "he fell upon Egypt to conquer it. And the reigning king he slew; and having appointed another in his place, made those Jews prisoners who had hitherto resided there, and led them into Babylon." And even if Josephus does not give his authority in this case, the assertion that he gathered this from the prophecies of Jeremiah is untrue; because, immediately before the words we have quoted, he says that what Jeremiah had prophesied (Jer. xliii. and xliv.) had thus come to pass; making a distinction, therefore, between prophecy and history. And suspicion is not to be cast upon this testimony by such objections as that Josephus does not mention the name of the Egyptian king, or state precisely the time when Egypt was conquered, but merely affirms in general terms that it was after the war with the Ammonites and Moabites.

SECOND HALF

THE ANNOUNCEMENT OF SALVATION

CHAP. XXXIII.-XLVIII.

IN the first half of his book, Ezekiel has predicted severe judgments, both to the covenant nation and to the heathen nations. But to the people of Israel he has also promised the turning of its captivity, after the judgment of the destruction of the kingdom and the dispersion of the refractory generation in the heathen lands; not merely their restoration to their own land, but the setting up of the covenant made with the fathers, and the renewing of the restored nation by the Spirit of God, so that it will serve the Lord upon His holy mountain with offerings acceptable to Him (compare ch. xi. 16–21, xvi. 60, and xx. 40 sqq.). On the other hand, he has threatened the heathenish peoples and kingdoms of the world with devastation and everlasting destruction, so that they will be remembered no more (compare ch. xxi. 36, 37, xxv. 7, 10, 16, xxvi. 21, xxvii. 36, and xxviii. 19), or rather with the lasting humiliation and overthrow of their glory in the nether world (compare ch. xxix. 13 sqq., xxxi. 15 sqq., and xxxii. 17 sqq.); whilst God will create a glorious thing in the land of the living, gather Israel from its dispersion, cause it to dwell safely and happily in the land given to His servant Jacob, and a horn to grow thereto (ch. xxvi. 20, xxviii. 25 sqq., and xxix. 21).—This announcement is carried out still further in the second half of the book, where first of all the pardon, blessing, and glorification promised to the covenant nation, after its sifting by the judgment of exile, are unfolded according to their leading features, and the destruction of its foes is foretold (ch. xxxiv.–xxxix.); and then, secondly, there is depicted the establishment of the renovated kingdom of God for everlasting continuance (ch. xl.–xlviii.). The prophet's mouth was opened to make the announcement when a fugitive brought the tidings of the destruction both of Jerusalem and of the kingdom to the captives by the Chaboras; and this constitutes the second half of the prophetic ministry of Ezekiel. The introduction to this is contained in ch. xxxiii., whilst the announcement itself is divisible into two parts, according to its contents, as just indicated,—namely, first, the promise of the restoration and glorification of Israel (ch. xxxiv.–xxxix.); and secondly, the apocalyptic picture of the new constitution of the kingdom of God (ch. xl.–xlviii.).

CHAP. XXXIII. THE CALLING OF THE PROPHET, AND HIS FUTURE ATTITUDE TOWARDS THE PEOPLE.

This chapter is divided into two words of God of an introductory character, which are separated by the historical statement in vers. 21 and 22, though substantially they are one. The first (vers. 1–20) exhibits the calling of the prophet for the time to come; the second (vers. 23–33) sets before him his own attitude towards the people, and the attitude of the people towards his further announcement. The first precedes the arrival of the messenger, who brought to the prophet and the exiles the tidings of the conquest and destruction of Jerusalem by the Chaldeans (ver. 21). The second was uttered afterwards. The fall of the holy city formed a turning-point in the prophetic work of Ezekiel. Previous to this catastrophe, God had appointed him to be a watchman over Israel: to show the people their sins, and to proclaim the consequent punishment, namely, the destruction of Jerusalem and Judah, together with the dispersion of the people among the heathen. But after the city had fallen, and the judgment predicted by him had taken place, the object to be aimed at was to inspire those who were desponding and despairing of salvation with confidence and consolation, by predicting the restoration of the fallen kingdom of God in a new and glorious form, to show them the way to new life, and to open the door for their entrance into the new kingdom of God. The two divisions of our chapter correspond to this, which was to be henceforth the task imposed upon the prophet. In the first (vers. 1–20), his calling to be the spiritual watchman over the house of Israel is renewed (vers. 2–9), with special instructions to announce to the people, who are inclined to despair under the burden of their sins, that the Lord has no pleasure in the death of the sinner, but will give life to him who turns from his iniquity (vers. 10–20). The kernel and central point of this word of God are found in the lamentation of the people: "Our transgressions and sins lie upon us, and we are pining away through them; how then can we live?" (ver. 10), together with the reply given by the Lord: "By my life, I have no pleasure in the death of the wicked . . . turn ye, turn yourselves; why do ye wish to die?" (ver. 11). The way is prepared for this by vers. 2–9, whilst vers. 12–20 carry out this promise of God still further, and assign the reason for it.—The thoughts with which the promise of the Lord, thus presented as an antidote to despair, is introduced and explained are not new, however, but repetitions of earlier words of God. The preparatory introduction in vers. 2–9 is essentially a return to the word in ch. iii. 17–21, with which the Lord closes the prophet's call by pointing out to him the duty and responsibility connected with his vocation. And the reason assigned in vers. 12–20, together with the divine promise in ver. 11, is taken from ch. xviii., where the prophet unfolds the working of the righteousness of God; and more precisely from vers. 20–32 of that chapter, where the thought is more fully expanded, that the judgments of God can be averted by repentance and conversion. From all this it is indisputably evident that the first section of this chapter contains an introduction to the second half of the prophecies of Ezekiel; and this also explains the absence of any date at the head of the section, or the "remarkable" fact that the date (vers. 21 and 22) is not given till the middle of the chapter, where it stands between the first and second of the words of God contained therein.—The word of God in vers. 23 sqq. was no doubt addressed to the prophet after the fugitive had arrived with the tidings of the fall of Jerusalem; whereas the word by which the prophet was prepared for his further labours (vers. 1–20) preceded that event, and coincided in point of time with the working of God upon the prophet on the evening preceding the arrival of the fugitive, through which his mouth was opened for further *speaking* (ver. 22); and it is placed before this historical statement because it was a renewal of his call.[1]

Vers. 1–20. *Calling of the Prophet for the Future.*

Vers. 1–9. The prophet's office of watchman.—Ver. 1. *And the word of Jehovah came to me, saying,* Ver. 2. *Son of man, speak to the sons of thy people, and say to them, When I bring the sword upon a land, and the people of the land take a man from their company and set him for a watchman,* Ver. 3. *And he seeth the sword come upon the land, and bloweth the trumpet, and warneth the people;* Ver. 4. *If, then, one should hear the blast of the trumpet and not take warning, so that the sword*

[1] It is incomprehensible how Kliefoth could find "no sign of introductory thoughts" in this section, or could connect it with the preceding oracles against the foreign nations, for no other reason than to secure fourteen words of God for that portion of the book which contains the prophecies against the foreign nations. For there is no force in the other arguments which he adduces in support of this combination; and the assertion that "the section, ch. xxxiii. 1–20, speaks of threatenings and warnings, and of the faithfulness with which Ezekiel is to utter them, and of the manner in which Israel is to receive them," simply shows that he has neither correctly nor perfectly understood the contents of this section and its train of thought.

should come and take him away, his blood would come upon his own head. Ver. 5. *He heard the blast of the trumpet, and took not warning; his blood will come upon him: whereas, if he had taken warning, he would have delivered his soul.* Ver. 6. *But if the watchman seeth the sword come, and bloweth not the trumpet, and the people is not warned; and the sword should come and take away a soul from them, he is taken away through his guilt; but his blood will I demand from the watchman's hand.* Ver. 7. *Thou, then, son of man, I have set thee for the watchman to the house of Israel; thou shalt hear the word from my mouth, and warn them for me.* Ver. 8. *If I say to the sinner, Sinner, thou wilt die the death; and thou speakest not to warn the sinner from his way, he, the sinner, will die for his iniquity, and his blood I will demand from thy hand.* Ver. 9. *But if thou hast warned the sinner from his way, to turn from it, and he does not turn from his way, he will die for his iniquity; but thou hast delivered thy soul.*—Vers. 7–9, with the exception of slight deviations which have little influence upon the sense, are repeated *verbatim* from ch. iii. 17–19. The repetition of the duty binding upon the prophet, and of the responsibility connected therewith, is introduced, however, in vers. 2–6, by an example taken from life, and made so plain that every one who heard the words must see that Ezekiel was obliged to call the attention of the people to the judgment awaiting them, and to warn them of the threatening danger, and that this obligation rested upon him still. In this respect the expansion, which is wanting in ch. iii., serves to connect the following prophecies of Ezekiel with the threats of judgment contained in the first part. The meaning of it is the following: As it is the duty of the appointed watchman of a land to announce to the people the approach of the enemy, and if he fail to do this he is deserving of death; so Ezekiel also, as the watchman of Israel appointed by God, not only is bound to warn the people of the approaching judgment, in order to fulfil his duty, but has already warned them of it, so that whoever has not taken warning has been overtaken by the sword because of his sin. As, then, Ezekiel has only discharged his duty and obligation by so doing, so has he the same duty still further to perform.—In ver. 2 אֶרֶץ is placed at the head in an absolute form; and כִּי אָבִיא וגו׳, "if I bring the sword upon a land," is to be understood with this restriction: "so that the enemy is on the way and an attack may be expected" (Hitzig). מִקְצֵיהֶם, from the end of the people of the land, *i.e.* one taken from the whole body of the people, as in Gen. xlvii. 2 (see the comm. on Gen. xix. 4). Blowing the trumpet is a signal of alarm on the approach of an enemy (compare Amos iii. 6; Jer. iv. 5). נִזְהָר in ver. 5*b* is a participle; on the other hand, both before and afterwards it is a perfect, pointed with *Kametz* on account of the tone. For vers. 7–9, see the exposition of ch. iii. 17–19.

Vers. 10–20. As watchman over Israel, Ezekiel is to announce to those who are despairing of the mercy of God, that the Lord will preserve from destruction those who turn from their sin, and lead them into life.—Ver. 10. *Thou then, son of man, say to the house of Israel, Ye rightly say, Our transgressions and our sins lie upon us, and in them we vanish away; how, then, can we live?* Ver. 11. *Say to them, As truly as I live, is the saying of the Lord Jehovah, I have no pleasure in the death of the sinner; but when the sinner turneth from his way, he shall live. Turn ye, turn ye from your evil ways! for why will ye die, O house of Israel?* Ver. 12. *And thou, son of man, say to the sons of thy people, The righteousness of the righteous man will not deliver him in the day of his transgression, and the sinner will not fall through his sin in the day that he turneth from his sin, and the righteous man will not be able to live thereby in the day that he sinneth.* Ver. 13. *If I say to the righteous man that he shall live, and he relies upon his righteousness and does wrong, all his righteousnesses will not be remembered; and for his wrong that he has done, he will die.* Ver. 14. *If I say to the sinner, Thou shalt die, and he turns from his sin, and does justice and righteous-*

ness, Ver. 15. *So that the wicked returns the pledge, restores what has been robbed, walks in the statutes of life without doing wrong, he will live, not die.* Ver. 16. *All his sins which he has committed shall not be remembered against him; he has done justice and righteousness, he will live.* Ver. 17. *And the sons of thy people say, The way of the Lord is not right; but they—their way is not right.* Ver. 18. *If the righteous man turneth from his righteousness and doeth wrong, he shall die thereby;* Ver. 19. *But if the wicked man turneth from his wickedness and doeth right and righteousness, he will live thereby.* Ver. 20. *And yet ye say, The way of the Lord is not right. I will judge you every one according to his ways, O house of Israel.*—In vers. 10 and 11 the prophet's calling for the future is set before him, inasmuch as God instructs him to announce to those who are in despair on account of their sins the gracious will of the Lord. The threat contained in the law (Lev. xxvi. 39), יִמַּקּוּ בַּעֲוֹנָם, of which Ezekiel had repeatedly reminded the people with warning, and, last of all, when predicting the conquest and destruction of Jerusalem by the Chaldeans (compare ch. iv. 17 and xxiv. 23), had pressed heavily upon their heart, when the threatened judgment took place, so that they quote the words, not "in self-defence," as Hävernick erroneously supposes, but in despair of any deliverance. Ezekiel is to meet this despair of little faith by the announcement that the Lord has no pleasure in the death of the sinner, but desires his conversion and his life. Ezekiel had already set this word of grace before the people in ch. xviii. 23, 32, accompanied with the summons to salvation for them to lay to heart: there, it was done to overthrow the delusion that the present generation had to atone for the sins of the fathers; but here, to lift up the hearts of those who were despairing of salvation; and for this reason it is accompanied with the asseveration (wanting in ch. xviii. 23 and 32): "as truly as I live, saith the Lord," and with the urgent appeal to repent and turn. But in order to preclude the abuse of this word of consolation by making it a ground of false confidence in their own righteousness, Ezekiel repeats in vers. 12–20 the principal thoughts contained in that announcement (ch. xviii. 20–32)—namely, first of all, in vers. 12–16, the thought that the righteousness of the righteous is of no avail to him if he gives himself up to the unrighteousness, and that the sinner will not perish on account of his sin if he turns from his wickedness and strives after righteousness (יִכָּשֵׁל בָּהּ, ver. 12, as in Hos. v. 5, Jer. vi. 15; compare ch. xviii. 24, 25, and xxi., xxii.; and for vers. 14 and 15, more especially ch. xviii. 5 and 7); and then, secondly, in vers. 17–20, the reproof of those who find fault with the way of the Lord (compare ch. xviii. 25, 27, 29, 30).

Vers. 21 and 22. Tidings of the fall of Jerusalem, and the consequences with regard to the prophet.—Ver. 21. *And it came to pass in the twelfth year, in the tenth (month), on the fifth of the month after our being taken captive, there came to me a fugitive from Jerusalem, and said, The city is smitten.* Ver. 22. *And the hand of Jehovah had come upon me in the evening before the arrival of the fugitive, and He opened my mouth, till he came to me in the morning; and so was my mouth opened, and I was silent no more.*—In these verses the fulfilment of the promise made by God to the prophet in ch. xxiv. 25–27, after the prediction of the destruction of Jerusalem, is recorded. The chronological datum, as to the precise time at which the messenger arrived with the account of the destruction of Jerusalem, serves to mark with precision the point of time at which the obstacle was removed, and the prophet was able to speak and prophesy without restraint.—The fact that the tidings of the destruction of Jerusalem, which took place in the fifth month of the eleventh year, are said to have only reached the exiles in the tenth month of the twelfth year, that is to say, nearly a year and a half after it occurred, does not warrant our following the Syriac, as Doederlein and Hitzig have done, calling in question the correctness of the text and substituting the eleventh year for the twelfth. With the distance at which Ezekiel was living, namely, in northern Mesopotamia, and with the fearful confusion which followed the catastrophe, a year and a half might very easily pass by before a fugitive arrived with the information. But Hitzig's assertion, that Ezekiel would contradict himself, inasmuch as, according to ch. xxvi. 1, 2, he received intelligence of the affair in the eleventh year, is founded upon a misinterpretation of the passage quoted. It is not stated there that Ezekiel received this information through a fugitive or any man whatever, but simply that God had revealed to him the fall of Jerusalem even before it occurred. לְגָלוּתֵנוּ, after our being led away (ver. 21 and ch. xl. 1), coincides with לְגָלוּת הַמֶּלֶךְ יוֹיָכִין in ch. i. 2. הֻכְּתָה, smitten, *i.e.* conquered and destroyed, exterminated. In the clause וְיַד יְהוָֹה וגו׳, the verb הָיְתָה is a pluperfect, and אֵלַי stands for עָלַי, according to the later usage. The formula indicates the translation of the prophet into an ecstatic state (see the comm. on ch. i. 3), in which his mouth was opened to speak, that is to say, the silence imposed upon him was taken away. The words, "till he came to me in the morning," etc., are not to be understood as signifying that the prophet's mouth had only been opened for the time from evening till morning; for this would be opposed to the following sentence. They simply affirm that the opening of the mouth took place before the arrival of the fugitive, the night before the morning of his arrival. וַיִּפָּתַח פִּי, which follows, is an emphatic repetition, introduced as a link with which to connect the practically important statement that from that time forward he was not speechless any more.—It was in all probability shortly afterwards that Ezekiel was inspired with the word of God which follows in vers. 23–33, as we may infer from the contents of the word itself, which laid the foundation for the prophet's further prophesying. But nothing can be gathered from ver. 22 with regard to the time when this and the following words of God (as far as ch. xxxix.), of which no chronological data are given, were communicated to the prophet and uttered by him. His being "silent no more" by no means involves immediate or continuous speaking, but simply recalls the command to be speechless. There is no ground for the assumption that all these words of God were communicated to him in one night (Hävernick, Hengstenberg, and others), either in ver. 22 or in the contents of these divine revelations.

Vers. 23–33. *Preaching of Repentance after the Fall of Jerusalem.*

The first word of God, which Ezekiel received after the arrival of the fugitive with the intelligence of the destruction of Jerusalem, was not of a consolatory, but of a rebuking nature, and directed against those who, while boasting in an impenitent state of mind of the promise given to the patriarchs of the everlasting possession of the Holy Land, fancied that they could still remain in possession of the promised land even after the destruction of Jerusalem and of the kingdom of Judah. This delusion the prophet overthrows by the announcement that the unrighteous are to have no share in the possession of the land of Israel, but are to perish miserably, and that the land is to be utterly waste and without inhabitants (vers. 23–29). The Lord then shows him that his countrymen will indeed come to him and listen to his words, but will only do that which is pleasant to themselves; that they will still seek after gain, and not do his words; and that it will not be till after his words have been fulfilled that they will come to the knowledge of the fact that he really was a prophet (vers. 30–33). We perceive from these last verses that the threat uttered in vers. 24–29 was to form the basis for Ezekiel's further prophecies, so that the whole of this word of God has only the force of an introduction to his further labours. But however the two halves of this word of God may appear to differ, so far as their contents are concerned, they are nevertheless closely connected. The state of heart disclosed in the first half, with reference to the judgment that has already fallen upon the land and kingdom, is to preclude the illusion, that the fact of the people's coming to the prophet to hear his words is a sign of penitential humiliation under the punishing hand of God, and to bring out the truth, that the salvation which he is about to foretell to the people is only to be enjoyed by those who turn with sincerity to the Lord.

Vers. 23–29. False reliance upon God's promises.—Ver. 23. *And the word of Jehovah came to me, saying,* Ver. 24. *Son of man, the inhabitants of these ruins in the land of Israel speak thus: Abraham was one, and received the land for a possession; but we are many, the land is given to us for a possession.* Ver. 25. *Therefore say to them, Thus saith the Lord Jehovah, Ye eat upon the blood, and lift up your eyes to your idols, and shed blood, and would ye possess the land?* Ver. 26. *Ye rely upon your sword, do abomination, and one defileth another's wife, and would ye possess the land?* Ver. 27. *Speak thus to them, Thus saith the Lord Jehovah, By my life, those who are in the ruins shall fall by the sword, and whoever is in the open field him do I give to the beasts to devour, and those who are in the fortresses and caves shall die of the pestilence.* Ver. 28. *And I make the land devastation and waste, and its proud might shall have an end, and the mountains of Israel shall be waste, so that no one passeth through.* Ver. 29. *And they shall know that I am Jehovah, when I make the land devastation and waste because of all the abominations which they have done.*—This threat is directed against the people who remained behind in the land of Judah after the destruction of Jerusalem. יֹשְׁבֵי הֶחֳרָבוֹת are the Israelites who dwelt amidst the ruins of the Holy Land, the remnant of the people left behind in the land. For it is so evident as to need no proof that Kliefoth is wrong in asserting that by הֶחֳרָבוֹת we are to understand the district bordering on the Chaboras, which was not properly cultivated; and by the inhabitants thereof, the exiles who surrounded Ezekiel. It is only by confounding אָמַר and דִּבֵּר that Kliefoth is able to set aside the more precise definition of the inhabitants of these ruins contained in the words עַל אַדְמַת יִשְׂרָאֵל, and to connect עַל אד׳ יש׳ with אֹמְרִים, "they speak concerning the land of Israel;" and in ver. 27 it is only in a forced manner that he can generalize הֶחֳרָבוֹת, and take it as referring to the waste places both in the Holy Land and on the Chaboras. The fact, moreover, that vers. 30–33 treat of the Israelites by the Chaboras, is no proof whatever that they must also be referred to in vers. 24–29. For the relation in which the two halves of this word of God stand to one another is not that "vers. 30–33 depict the impression made upon the hearers by the words contained in vers. 24–29," so that "the persons alluded to in vers. 30–33 must necessarily be the hearers of vers. 24–29." Vers. 30–33 treat in quite a general manner of the attitude which the prophet's countrymen would assume towards his words—that is to say, not merely to his threats, but also to his predictions of salvation; they would only attend to that which had a pleasant sound to them, but they would not do his words (vers. 31, 32). It is quite in harmony with this, that in vers. 23–29 these people should be told of the state of heart of those who had remained behind on the ruins of the Holy Land, and that it should be announced to them that the fixed belief in the permanent possession of the Holy Land, on which those who remained behind in the land relied, was a delusion, and that those who were victims of this delusion should be destroyed by sword and pestilence. Just as in the first part of this book Ezekiel uttered the threatened prophecies concerning the destruction of Jerusalem and Judah in the presence of his countrymen by the Chaboras, and addressed them to these, because they stood in the same internal relation to the Lord as their brethren in Jerusalem and Judah; so here does he hold up this delusion before them as a warning, in order that he may disclose to them the worthlessness of such vain hope, and preach repentance and conversion as the only way to life. The meaning of the words spoken by these people, "Abraham was one," etc., is, that if Abraham, as one solitary individual, received the land of Canaan for a possession by the promise of God, the same God could not take this possession away from them, the many sons of Abraham. The antithesis of the "one" and the "many" derived its significance, in relation to their argument, from the descent of the many from the one, which is taken for granted, and also from the fact, which is assumed to be well known from the book of Genesis, that the land was not promised and given to the patriarch for his own possession, but for his seed or descendants to possess. They relied, like the Jews of the time of Christ (John viii. 33, 39), upon their corporeal descent from Abraham (compare the similar words in ch. xi. 15). Ezekiel, on the other hand, simply reminds them of their own sinful conduct (vers. 25, 26), for the purpose of showing them that they have thereby incurred the loss of this possession. Eating upon the blood, is eating flesh in which the blood is still lying, which has not been cleansed from blood, as in Lev. xix. 26 and 1 Sam. xiv. 32, 33; an act the prohibition of which was first addressed to Noah (Gen. ix. 4), and is repeatedly urged in the law (cf. Lev. vii. 26, 27). This is also the case with the prohibition of idolatry, lifting up the eyes to idols (cf. ch. xviii. 6), and the shedding of blood (cf. ch. xviii. 10, xxii. 3, etc.). עָמַד עַל חַרְבּוֹ, to support oneself, or rely (עָמַד, used as in ch. xxxi. 14) upon the sword, *i.e.* to put confidence in violence and bloodshed. In this connection we are not to think of the use of the sword in war. To work abomination, as in ch. xviii. 12. עֲשִׂיתֶן is not a feminine, "ye women," but ן is written in the place of ם on account of the ת which follows, after the analogy of פִּדְיוֹן for פִּדְיוֹם (Hitzig). On the defiling of a neighbour's wife, see the comm. on ch. xviii. 6. Such daring sinners the Lord would destroy wherever they might be. In ver. 37 the punishment is individualized (cf. ch. xiv. 21). Those in the חֳרָבוֹת shall fall by the חֶרֶב (the play upon the word is very obvious); those in the open country shall perish by wild beasts (compare 2 Kings xvii. 25; Ex. xxiii. 19; Lev. xxvi. 22); those who are in mountain fastnesses and caves, where they are safe from the sword and ravenous beasts, shall perish by plague and pestilence. This threat is not to be restricted to the acts of the Chaldeans in the land after the destruction of Jerusalem, but applies to all succeeding times. Even the devastation and utter depopulation of the land, threatened in ver. 28, are not to be taken as referring merely to the time of the Babylonian captivity, but embrace the devastation which accompanied and followed the destruction of Jerusalem by the Romans. For גְּאוֹן עֻזָּהּ, see the comm. on ch. vii. 24. For ver. 29, compare ch. vi. 14.

Vers. 30–33. Behaviour of the people towards the prophet.—Ver. 30. *And thou, son of man, the sons of thy people converse about thee by the walls and in the house-doors; one talketh to another, every one to his brother, saying, Come and let us hear what kind of word goeth out from Jehovah.* Ver. 31. *And they will come to thee, like an assembly of the people, and sit before thee as my people, and will hear thy words, but not do them; but that which is pleasant in their mouth they do; their heart goeth after their gain.* Ver. 32. *And, behold, thou art unto them like a pleasant singer, beautiful in voice and playing well; they will hear thy words, but they will not do them.* Ver. 33. *But when it cometh—behold, it cometh—they will know that a prophet was in the midst of them.*—This addition to the preceding word of God, which is addressed to Ezekiel personally, applies to the whole of the second half of his ministry, and stands in obvious connection with the instructions given to the prophet on the occasion of his first call (ch. iii. 16 sqq.), and repeated, so far as their substance is concerned, in vers. 7–9, as Kliefoth himself acknowledges, in opposition to his assumption that vers. 1–20 of this chapter belong to the prophecies directed against the foreign nations. As God had directed the prophet's attention, on the occasion of his call, to the difficulties connected with the discharge of the duties of a watchman with which he was entrusted, by setting before him the object and the responsibility of his vocation, and had warned him not to allow himself to be turned aside by the opposition of the people; so here in vers. 30–33, at the commencement of the second section of his ministry, another word is addressed to him personally, in order that he may not be influenced in the further prosecution of his calling by either the pleasure or displeasure of men.—His former utterances had already induced the elders of the people to come to him to hear the word of God (cf. ch. xiv. 1 and xx. 1). But now that his prophecies concerning Jerusalem had been fulfilled, the exiles could not fail to be still more attentive to his words, so that they talked of him both secretly and openly, and encouraged one another to come and listen to his discourses. God foretells this to him, but announces to him at the same time that this disposition on the part of his countrymen to listen to him is even now no sign of genuine conversion to the word of God, in order that he may not be mistaken in his expectations concerning the people. Kliefoth has thus correctly explained the contents, design, and connection of these verses as a whole. In ver. 30 the article before the participle נִדְבָּרִים takes the place of the relative אֲשֶׁר, and the words are in apposition to בְּנֵי עַמְּךָ, the sons of thy people who converse about thee. נִדְבַּר is reciprocal, as in Mal. iii. 13, 16, and Ps. cxix. 23. But ב is to be understood, not in a hostile sense, as in the passage cited from the Psalms, but in the sense of concerning, like דִּבֶּר ב in 1 Sam. xix. 3 as contrasted with דִּבֶּר ב in Num. xxi. 7, to speak against a person. The participle is continued by the finite וְדִבֶּר, and the verb belonging to בְּנֵי עַמְּךָ follows, in the וְיָבֹאוּ of ver. 31, in the form of an apodosis. There is something monstrous in Hitzig's assumption, that the whole passage from ver. 30 to ver. 33 forms but one clause, and that the predicate to בְּנֵי עַמְּךָ does not occur till the וְיָדְעוּ of ver. 33.—אֵצֶל הַקִּירוֹת, by the side of the walls, *i.e.* sitting against the walls, equivalent to secretly; and in the doors of the houses, in other words publicly, one neighbour conversing with another. חַד, Aramean for אֶחָד, and אִישׁ by the side of אֶחָד, every one; not merely one here or there, but every man to his neighbour.

כְּמְבוֹא־עָם, lit. as the coming of a people, *i.e.* as when a crowd of men flock together in crowds or troops. עַמִּי is a predicate, as my people, *i.e.* as if they wished, like my people, to hear my word from thee. But they do not think of doing thy words, *i.e.* what thou dost announce to them as my word. עֲגָבִים are things for which one cherishes an eager desire, pleasant things in their mouth, *i.e.* according to their taste (cf. Gen. xxv. 28). Hävernick is wrong in taking עֲגָבִים to mean illicit love. The word בְּפִיהֶם is quite inapplicable to such a meaning. The rendering, they do it with their mouth, is opposed both to the construction and the sense. בִּצְעָם, their gain, the source from which they promise themselves advantage or gain. In ver. 32 a clearer explanation is given of the reason why they come to the prophet, notwithstanding the fact that they do not wish to do his words. "Thou art to them כְּשִׁיר עֲגָבִים;" this cannot mean like a pleasant song, but, as מֵטִב נַגֵּן (one who can play well) clearly shows, like a singer of pleasant songs. The abstract שִׁיר stands for the concrete שָׁר, a singer, a man of song (Hitzig). In ver. 32*b*, "they hear thy words, but do them not," is repeated with emphasis, for the purpose of attaching the threat in ver. 33. But when it cometh,—namely, what thou sayest, or prophesiest,—behold, it cometh, *i.e.* it will come as surely as thy prophecies concerning the destruction of Jerusalem; then will they know that a prophet was among them (cf. ch. ii. 5), that is to say, that he proclaimed God's word to them. Therefore Ezekiel is not to be prevented, by the misuse which will be made of his words, from preaching the truth.—This conclusion of the word of God, which points back to ch. ii. 5, also shows that it forms the introduction to the prophecies which follow.

CHAP. XXXIV.–XXXIX.—THE RESTORATION OF ISRAEL, AND DESTRUCTION OF GOG AND MAGOG.

The promise of the salvation, which is to blossom for the covenant nation after the judgment, commences with the announcement that the Lord will deliver Israel out of the hand of its evil shepherds, who only feed themselves and destroy the flock, and will take care of His own flock, gather them together, feed and tend them on a good meadow, protect the weak sheep against the strong, and through His servant David bring security and blessing to the whole of the flock (ch. xxxiv.). This comprehensive promise is carried out still further in the following chapters in various phases. Because Edom cherishes perpetual enmity against the sons of Israel, and has sought to take possession of their land, in which Jehovah was, the mountains of Seir shall become a perpetual desert (ch. xxxv.); whereas the devastated land of Israel shall be rebuilt, and sown once more, bear fruit, and be filled with man and beast (ch. xxxvi. 1–15). The Lord will do this for His holy name's sake, will cleanse His people from their sins, when gathered out of the nations, by sprinkling them with pure water, and renew them by His Spirit in heart and mind, that they may walk in His commandments, and multiply greatly in their land, when it has been glorified into a garden of God (ch. xxxvi. 16–38). The house of Israel, which has been slain with the sword, and has become like a field full of dry bones of the dead, the Lord will awaken to new life, and bring in peace into the land of Israel (ch. xxxvii. 1–14); the two divided peoples and kingdoms of Israel He will unite into one people and kingdom, will liberate them from their sins, cause them to dwell in the land given to His servant Jacob under the sovereignty of His servant David, will make with them a covenant of peace for ever, and dwell above them as their God for ever in the sanctuary, which He will establish in the midst of them (ch. xxxvii. 15–28). And, finally, in the last time, when Israel is dwelling in its own land in security and peace, the Lord will bring Gog from the land of Magog, the prince of Rosh, Meshech, and Tubal, with a powerful army of numerous peoples, into the land that has been restored from the sword; but when he has come to plunder and prey, the Lord will destroy him with all his army, and by this judgment display His glory among the nations, and so have compassion upon the whole house of Israel, and because He has poured out His Spirit upon it, will hide His face from it no more (ch. xxxviii. and xxxix.).—From this general survey it is evident that the words of God contained in ch. xxxiv.-xxxvii. announce the restoration and exaltation of Israel to be the sanctified people of God, and ch. xxxviii. and xxxix. the lasting establishment of this salvation, through the extermination of those enemies who rise up against the restored people of God.

CHAP. XXXIV. DEPOSITION OF THE BAD SHEPHERDS; COLLECTING AND TENDING OF THE FLOCK; AND APPOINTMENT OF THE ONE GOOD SHEPHERD.

The shepherds, who have fed themselves and neglected the flock, so that it has been scattered and has become a prey to wild beasts, will be deprived by the Lord of their office of shepherd (vers. 1–10). And He will take charge of His own flock, gather it together from its dispersion in the lands, feed and tend it on good pasture in the land of Israel, and sift it by the extermination of the fat and violent ones (vers. 11–22). He will appoint His servant David shepherd over His flock, make a covenant of peace with His people, and bless the land with fruitfulness, so that Israel may dwell there in security, and no more be carried off either as booty for the nations or by famine, and may acknowledge Jehovah as its God (vers. 23–31).

This word of God is a repetition and further expansion of the short prophecy of Jeremiah in Jer. xxiii. 1–8. The threat against the bad shepherds simply forms the foil for the promise, that the flock, which has been plunged into misery by bad shepherds, shall be gathered and tended by the Lord and His servant David, whom Jehovah will appoint prince over His people, so that it is essentially a prophecy of salvation for Israel.—The question in dispute among the commentators, whether we are to understand by the shepherds, out of whose hand and tyranny the Lord will rescue Israel His flock, the priests and kings (Ephr., Syr., and Theodoret), or the false prophets and false teachers of the people (Glass and others), or simply the kings (Hengst., Häv., and others), or all those who, by reason of their office, were leaders of the people, rulers, priests, and prophets, "the whole body of official persons charged with the direction of the nation" (Kliefoth), may be settled by the simple conclusion, that only the rulers of the nation are intended. This is proved not only by the biblical idea of the shepherd generally, which (probably in distinction from the idea of the bell-wether) is everywhere employed to denote rulers alone, but more particularly by the primary passage already referred to (Jer. xxiii. 1–8), where we are to understand by the shepherds, kings and princes, to the exclusion of priests and prophets, against whom Jeremiah first prophesies from ver. 9 onwards; and, lastly, by the antithesis to the good shepherd, David, who is to feed the flock of Jehovah as prince (נָשִׂיא), and not as priest or prophet (vers. 23, 24). Only we must not take the term rulers as applying to the kings alone, but must understand thereby all the persons entrusted with the government of the nation, or the whole body of the civil authorities of Israel, among whom priests and prophets come into consideration, not on account of their spiritual calling and rank, but only so far as they held magisterial offices. And apart from other grounds, we are not warranted in restricting the idea of shepherds to the kings alone; for the simple reason that our prophecy, which dates from the time succeeding the destruction of Jerusalem, does not apply to the former rulers only, *i.e.* the kings who had fallen along with the kingdom of Judah, but although treating of shepherds, who had scattered Israel among the nations, assumes that the rule of these shepherds is still continuing, and announces their removal, or the deliverance of the flock out of their hand, as something to be effected in the future (cf. vers. 8–10); so that it also refers to the civil rulers who governed Israel after the overthrow of the monarchy, and even after the captivity until the coming of the Messiah, the promised Prince of David.

Vers. 1–10. Woe to the bad shepherds.—Ver. 1. *And the word of Jehovah came to me, saying,* Ver. 2. *Son of man, prophesy concerning the shepherds of Israel; prophesy, and say to them, to the shepherds, Thus saith the Lord Jehovah, Woe to the shepherds of Israel, who fed themselves; should not the shepherds feed the flock?* Ver. 3. *Ye eat the fat, and clothe yourselves with the wool; ye slay the fattened; the flock ye do not feed.* Ver. 4. *The weak ones ye do not strengthen, and that which is sick ye do not cure, the wounded one ye bind not up, the scattered ye bring not back, and the lost one ye do not seek; and ye rule over them with violence and with severity.* Ver. 5. *Therefore they were scattered, because without shepherd, and became food to all the beasts of the field, and were scattered.* Ver. 6. *My sheep wander about on all the mountains, and on every high hill; and over all the land have my sheep been scattered, and there is no one who asks for them, and no one who seeks them.* Ver. 7. *Therefore, ye shepherds, hear ye the word of Jehovah:* Ver. 8. *As I live, is the saying of the Lord Jehovah, because my sheep become a prey, and my sheep become food to all the beasts of the field, because there is no shepherd, and my shepherds do not inquire after my sheep, and the shepherds feed themselves, but do not feed the sheep,* Ver. 9. *Therefore, ye shepherds, hear ye the word of Jehovah,* Ver. 10. *Thus saith the Lord Jehovah, Behold, I will deal with the shepherds, and will demand my sheep from their hand, and cause them to cease to feed my flock, that they may feed themselves no more; and I will deliver my sheep from their mouth, that they may be food to them no more.*—In ver. 2 לָרֹעִים is an explanatory apposition to אֲלֵיהֶם, and is not to be taken in connection with כֹּה אָמַר יי׳, in opposition to the constant use of this formula, as Kliefoth maintains. The reason for the woe pronounced is given in the apposition, who fed themselves, whereas they ought to have fed the flock; and the charge that they only care for themselves is still further explained by a description of their conduct (vers. 3 and 4), and of the dispersion of the flock occasioned thereby (vers. 5 and 6). Observe the periphrastic preterite הָיוּ רֹעִים, they were feeding, which shows that the woe had relation chiefly to the former shepherds or rulers of the nation. אוֹתָם is reflective, *se ipsos* (cf. Gesen § 124. 1*b*). The disgracefulness of their feeding themselves is brought out by the question, "Ought not the shepherds to feed the flock?" Ver. 3 shows how they fed themselves, and ver. 4 how they neglected the flock. חֵלֶב, the fat, which Bochart and Hitzig propose to alter into הֶחָלָב, the milk, after the Septuagint and Vulgate, is not open to any objection. The fat, as the best portion of the flesh, which was laid upon the altar, for example, in the case of the sacrifices, as being the flower of all the flesh, is mentioned here as *pars melior pro toto.* Hävernick has very properly pointed, in vindication of the reading in the text, to Zech. xi. 16, where the two clauses, ye eat the fat, and slay the fattened, are joined together in the one clause, "the flesh of the fattened one will he eat." There is no force in the objection raised by Hitzig, that "the slaughtering of the fat beasts, which ought to be mentioned first, is not introduced till afterwards;" for this clause contains a heightening of the thought that they use the flock to feed themselves: they do not even kill the leaner beasts, but those that are well fattened; and it follows very suitably after the general statement, that they make use of both the flesh and the wool of the sheep for their own advantage. They care nothing for the wellbeing of the flock: this is stated in the last clause of ver. 3, which is explained in detail in ver. 4. נַחְלוֹת is the *Niphal* participle of

חָלָה, and is a contracted form of נַחֲלוֹת, like נַחְלָה in Isa. xvii. 11. The distinction between נַחְלוֹת and חוֹלָה is determined by the respective predicates חִזֵּק and רִפָּא. According to these, נַחְלָה signifies that which is weak in consequence of sickness, and חֹלָה that which is weak in itself. נִשְׁבֶּרֶת, literally, that which is broken, an animal with a leg or some other member injured. נִדָּח, scattered, as in Deut. xxii. 1. In the last clause of ver. 4, the neglect of the flock is summed up in the positive expression, to rule over them with violence and severity. רָדָה בְפֶרֶךְ is taken from Lev. xxv. 43, 46; but there as well as here it points back to Ex. i. 13, 14, where בְּפָרֶךְ is applied to the tyrannical measures adopted by Pharaoh for the oppression of the Israelites. The result of this (vers. 5, 6) was, that the sheep were scattered, and became food to the beasts of prey. מִבְּלִי רֹעֶה, on account of there not being a shepherd, *i.e.* because there was no shepherd worthy of the name. This took place when Israel was carried away into exile, where it became a prey to the heathen nations. When we find this mournful fate of the people described as brought about by the bad shepherds, and attributable to faults of theirs, we must not regard the words as applying merely to the mistaken policy of the kings with regard to external affairs (Hitzig); for this was in itself simply a consequence of their neglect of their theocratic calling, and of their falling away from the Lord into idolatry. It is true that the people had also made themselves guilty of this sin, so that it was obliged to atone not only for the sins of its shepherds, but for its own sin also; but this is passed by here, in accordance with the design of this prophecy. And it could very properly be kept out of sight, inasmuch as the rulers had also occasioned the idolatry of the people, partly by their neglect of their duty, and partly by their bad example. וַתְּפוּצֶינָה is repeated with emphasis at the close of ver. 5; and the thought is still further expanded in ver. 6. The wandering upon all the mountains and hills must not be understood as signifying the straying of the people to the worship on high places, as Theodoret and

Kliefoth suppose. The fallacy of this explanation is clearly shown by the passage on which this figurative description rests (1 Kings xxii. 17), where the people are represented as scattered upon the mountains in consequence of the fall of the king in battle, like a flock that had no shepherd. The words in the next clause, corresponding to the mountains and hills, are כָּל־פְּנֵי הָאָרֶץ, the whole face of the land, not "of the earth" (Kliefoth). For although the dispersion of the flock actually consisted in the carrying away of the people into heathen lands, the actual meaning of the figure is kept in the background here, as is evident from the fact that Ezekiel constantly uses the expression הָאֲרָצוֹת (plural) when speaking of the dispersion among the heathen (cf. ver. 13). The distinction between דָּרַשׁ and בִּקֵּשׁ is, that דרשׁ signifies rather to ask, inquire for a thing, to trouble oneself about it, whereas בקשׁ means to seek for that which has strayed or is lost. In vers. 7–10, the punishment for their unfaithfulness is announced to the shepherds themselves; but at the same time, as is constantly the case with Ezekiel, their guilt is once more recapitulated as an explanation of the threatening of punishment, and the earnest appeal to listen is repeated in ver. 9. The Lord will demand His sheep of them; and because sheep have been lost through their fault, He will depose them from the office of shepherd, and so deliver the poor flock from their violence. If we compare with this Jer. xxiii. 2: "Behold, I will visit upon you the wickedness of your doings," the threat in Ezekiel has a much milder sound. There is nothing said about the punishment of the shepherd, but simply that the task of keeping the sheep shall be taken from them, so that they shall feed themselves no more. This distinction is to be explained from the design of our prophecy, which is not so much to foretell the punishment of the shepherds, as the deliverance from destruction of the sheep that have been plunged into misery. The repetition of צֹאנִי, *my* flock (vers. 8 and 10, as before in ver. 6), is also connected with this. The rescue of the sheep out of the hand of the bad shepherds had already commenced with the overthrow of the monarchy on the destruction of Jerusalem. If, then, it is here described as only to take place in the future, justice is not done to these words by explaining them, as Hitzig does, as signifying that what has already actually taken place is now to be made final, and not to be reversed. For although this is implied, the words clearly affirm that the deliverance of the sheep out of the hand of the shepherds has not yet taken place, but still remains to be effected, so that the people are regarded as being at the time in the power of bad shepherds, and their rescue is predicted as still in the future. How and when it will be accomplished, by the removal of the bad shepherds, is shown in the announcement, commencing with ver. 11, of what the Lord will do for His flock.

Vers. 11–22. Jehovah Himself will seek His flock, gather it together from the dispersion, lead it to good pasture, and sift it by the destruction of the bad sheep.—Ver. 11. *For thus saith the Lord Jehovah, Behold, I myself, I will inquire after my flock, and take charge thereof.* Ver. 12. *As a shepherd taketh charge of his flock in the day when he is in the midst of his scattered sheep, so will I take charge of my flock, and deliver them out of all the places whither they have been scattered in the day of cloud and cloudy night.* Ver. 13. *And I will bring them out from the nations, and gather them together out of the lands, and bring them into their land, and feed them upon the mountains of Israel, in the valleys, and in all the dwelling-places of the land.* Ver. 14. *I will feed them in a good pasture, and on the high mountains of Israel will their pasture-ground be: there shall they lie down in a good pasture-ground, and have fat pasture on the mountains of Israel.* Ver. 15. *I will feed my flock, and I will cause them to lie down, is the saying of the Lord Jehovah.* Ver. 16. *That which is lost will I seek, and that which is driven away will I bring back; that which is wounded will I bind up, and that which is sick will I strengthen: but that which is fat and strong will I destroy, and feed them according to justice.*

Ver. 17. *And you, my sheep, thus saith the Lord Jehovah, Behold, I will judge between sheep and sheep, and the rams and the he-goats.* Ver. 18. *Is it too little for you, that ye eat up the good pasture, and what remains of your pasture ye tread down with your feet? and the clear water ye drink, and render muddy what remains with your feet?* Ver. 19. *And are my sheep to have for food that which is trodden down by your feet, and to drink that which is made muddy by your feet?* Ver. 20. *Therefore thus saith the Lord Jehovah to them, Behold I, I will judge between fat sheep and lean.* Ver. 21. *Because ye press with side and shoulder, and thrust all the weak with your horns, till ye have driven them out;* Ver. 22. *I will help my sheep, so that they shall no more become a prey; and will judge between sheep and sheep.*—All that the Lord will do for His flock is summed up in ver. 11, in the words דָּרַשְׁתִּי אֶת־צֹאנִי וּבִקַּרְתִּים, which stand in obvious antithesis to וְאֵין דּוֹרֵשׁ וגו׳ in ver. 6,—an antithesis sharply accentuated by the emphatic הִנְנִי אָנִי, which stands at the head in an absolute form. The fuller explanation is given in the verses which follow, from ver. 12 onwards. Observe here that בִּקֵּר is substituted for בִּקֵּשׁ. בִּקֵּר, to seek and examine minutely, involves the idea of taking affectionate charge. What the Lord does for His people is compared in ver. 12*a* to the care which a shepherd who deserves the name manifests towards sheep when they are scattered (נִפְרָשׁוֹת without the article is connected with צֹאנוֹ in the form of apposition); and in ver. 12*b* it is still more particularly explained. In the first place, He will gather them from all the places to which they have been scattered. הִצִּיל implies that in their dispersion they have fallen into a state of oppression and bondage among the nations (cf. Ex. vi. 6). בְּיוֹם עָנָן וַעֲרָפֶל belongs to the relative clause: whither they have been scattered. The circumstance that these words are taken from Joel ii. 2 does not compel us to take them in connection with the principal clause, as Hitzig and Kliefoth propose, and to understand them as relating to the time when God will hold His judgment of the heathen world. The notion that the words in Joel signify "God's day of judgment upon all the heathen" (Kliefoth), is quite erroneous; and even Hitzig does not derive this meaning from Joel ii. 2, but from the combination of our verse with Ezek. xxx. 3 and xxix. 21. The deliverance of the sheep out of the places to which they have been scattered, consists in the gathering together of Israel out of the nations, and their restoration to their own land, and their feeding upon the mountains and all the dwelling-places of the land (מוֹשָׁב, a place suitable for settlement), and that in good and fat pasture (ver. 14); and lastly, in the fact that Jehovah bestows the necessary care upon the sheep, strengthens and heals the weak and sick (vers. 15 and 16),—that is to say, does just what the bad shepherds have omitted (ver. 4),—and destroys the fat and strong. In this last clause another side is shown of the pastoral fidelity of Jehovah. אַשְׁמִיד has been changed by the LXX., Syr., and Vulg. into אֶשְׁמוֹר, φυλάξω; and Luther has followed them in his rendering, "I will watch over them." But this is evidently a mistake, as it fails to harmonize with אֶרְעֶנָּה בְמִשְׁפָּט. The fat and strong sheep are characterized in vers. 18 and 19 as those which spoil the food and water of the others. The allusion, therefore, is to the rich and strong ones of the nation, who oppress the humble and poor, and treat them with severity. The destruction of these oppressors shows that the loving care of the Lord is associated with righteousness—that He feeds the flock בְּמִשְׁפָּט. This thought is carried out still further in vers. 17–21, the sheep themselves being directly addressed, and the Lord assuring them that He will judge between sheep and sheep, and put an end to the oppressive conduct of the fat sheep and the strong. בֵּין שֶׂה לָשֶׂה: between the one sheep and the other. לָשֶׂה is extended in the apposition, "the rams and he-goats," which must not be rendered, "with regard to the rams and he-goats," as it has been by Kliefoth. The thought is not that Jehovah will divide the rams and he-goats from the sheep, as some have explained it, from an inappropriate comparison with Matt.

xxv. 32; but the division is to be effected in such a manner that sheep will be separated from sheep, the fat sheep being placed on one side with the rams and he-goats, and kept apart from the lean (רָזָה, ver. 20) and the sickly sheep (נַחְלוֹת, ver. 21). It is to the last-named sheep, rams, and he-goats that vers. 18 and 19 are addressed. With regard to the charge brought against them, that they eat up the pasture and tread down the remainder with their feet, etc., Bochart has already correctly observed, that "if the words are not quite applicable to actual sheep, they are perfectly appropriate to the mystical sheep intended here, *i.e.* to the Israelites, among whom many of the rich, after enjoying an abundant harvest and vintage, grudged the poor their gleaning in either one or the other." מִשְׁקַע, a substantive formation, like מִרְמָס, literally, precipitation of the water, *i.e.* the water purified by precipitation; for שָׁקַע, to sink, is the opposite of רָפַשׂ, to stir up or render muddy by treading with the feet (compare ch. xxxii. 14 and 2). בִּרְיָה, ver. 20 = בְּרִאָה or בְּרִיָּה. Ver. 22 brings to a close the description of the manner in which God will deliver His flock, and feed it with righteousness. וְהוֹשַׁעְתִּי points back to וְהִצַּלְתִּי in ver. 12, and וְשָׁפַטְתִּי to אֶרְעֶנָּה בְמִשְׁפָּט in ver. 16.—To this there is appended in vers. 23 sqq. a new train of thought, describing how God will still further display to His people His pastoral fidelity.

Vers. 23–31. Appointment of David as shepherd, and blessing of the people.—Ver. 23. *And I will raise up one shepherd over them, who shall feed them, my servant David; he will feed them, and he will be to them a shepherd.* Ver. 24. *And I, Jehovah, will be God to them, and my servant David prince in the midst of them: I, Jehovah, have spoken it.* Ver. 25. *And I will make a covenant of peace with them, and destroy the evil beasts out of the land, so that they will dwell safely in the desert and sleep in the forests.* Ver. 26. *And I will make them and the places round my hill a blessing, and cause the rain to fall in its season: showers of blessing shall there be.* Ver. 27. *The tree of the field will give its fruit, and the land will give its produce, and they will be safe in their land, and will know that I am Jehovah, when I break their yoke-bars in pieces, and deliver them out of the hand of those who made them servants.* Ver. 28. *They will be no more a prey to the nations, and the wild beasts will not devour them; but they will dwell safely, and no one will terrify them.* Ver. 29. *And I will raise up for them a plantation for a name, so that they will no more be swept away by famine in the land, and shall no longer bear the disgrace of the heathen nations.* Ver. 30. *And they shall know that I, Jehovah, their God, am with them, and they are my people, the house of Israel, is the saying of the Lord Jehovah.* Ver. 31. *And ye are my sheep, the flock of my pasture; ye are men, I am your God, is the saying of the Lord Jehovah.*—God will cause to stand up, raise up, one single shepherd over His flock. הֵקִים, the standing expression for the rising up of a person in history through the interposition of God (cf. Deut. xviii. 15, 2 Sam. vii. 12, and other passages). רֹעֶה אֶחָד, not *unicus, singularis*, a shepherd unique in his kind, but *one* shepherd, in contrast not only with the many bad shepherds, but with the former division of the people into two kingdoms, each with its own separate king. Compare ch. xxxvii. 24 with Jer. xxiii. 6, where it is expressly said that the David to be raised up is to feed Israel and Judah, the two peoples that had been divided before. "My servant David:" Jehovah calls him עַבְדִּי, not merely with reference to the obedience rendered (Hävernick), but also with regard to his election (Isa. xlii. 1; Hengstenberg). There is no necessity to refute the assertion of Hitzig, David Strauss, and others, that Ezekiel expected the former King David to be raised from the dead. The reference is to the sprout of David (Jer. xxiii. 5), already called simply David in Hos. iii. 5 and Jer. xxx. 9. In ver. 24 the relation of Jehovah to this David is more precisely defined: Jehovah will then be God to His people, and David be prince in the midst of them. The last words point back to 2 Sam. vii. 8*b*. Through the government of David, Jehovah will become in truth God of His people Israel; for David will feed the people in perfect unity with Jehovah,—will merely carry out the will of Jehovah, and not place himself in opposition to God, like the bad shepherds, because, as is therewith presupposed, he is connected with God by unity of nature.—In vers. 25 sqq. the thought is carried out still further,—how God will become God to His people, and prove Himself to be its covenant God through the pastoral fidelity of the future David. God will fully accomplish the covenant mercies promised to Israel. The making of the covenant of peace need not be restricted, in accordance with Hos. ii. 20 (18), to a covenant which God would make with the beasts in favour of His people. The thought is a more comprehensive one here, and, according to Lev. xxvi. 4–6, the passage which Ezekiel had in his mind involves all the salvation which God had included in His promises to His people: viz. (1) the extermination of everything that could injure Israel, of all the wild beasts, so that they would be able to sleep securely in the deserts and the forests (ver. 25; compare Lev. xxvi. 6); (2) the pouring out of an abundant rain, so that the field and land would yield rich produce (vers. 26, 27; cf. Lev. xxvi. 4, 5). "I make them, the Israelites, and the surroundings of my hill, a blessing." גִּבְעָתִי, the hill of Jehovah, is, according to Isa. xxxi. 4, Mount Zion, the temple-mountain, including the city of Jerusalem. The surroundings of this hill are the land of Israel, that lay around it. But Zion, with the land around, is not mentioned in the place of the inhabitants; and still less are we to understand by the surroundings of the hill the heathen nations, as Hengstenberg does, in opposition both to the context and the usage of the language. The thought is simply that the Lord will make both the people and the land a blessing (Hävernick, Kliefoth). בְּרָכָה, a blessing, is stronger than "blessed" (cf. Gen. xii. 2) The blessing is brought by the rain in its season, which fertilizes the earth. This will take place when the Lord breaks the yokes laid upon His people. These words are from Lev.

xxvi. 13, where they refer to the deliverance of Israel from the bondage of Egypt; and they are transferred by Ezekiel to the future redemption of Israel from the bondage of the heathen. For עֹבְדִים בָּהֶם, compare Ex. i. 14. This thought is carried out still further in ver. 28; and then, in ver. 29, all that has been said is summed up in the thoughts, "I raise up for them a plantation for a name," etc. מַטָּע, a plantation, as in ch. xvii. 7; not a land for planting (Hitzig). לְשֵׁם, for a name, *i.e.* not for the glory of God (De Wette); but the plantation, which the Lord will cause to grow by pouring down showers of blessing (ver. 26), is to bring renown to the Israelites, namely, among the heathen, who will see from this that Israel is a people blessed by its God. This explanation of the words is supplied by the following clause: they shall no more be swept away by famine in the land, and no more bear the disgrace of the heathen, *i.e.* the disgrace which the heathen heaped upon Israel when in distress (compare Zeph. iii. 19; Jer. xiii. 11; and the primary passage, Deut. xxvi. 29). From this blessing they will learn that Jehovah their God is with them, and Israel is His people. The promise concludes in ver. 31 with these words, which set a seal upon the whole: "Ye are my flock, the flock of my pasture (lit. my pasture-flock; צֹאן מַרְעִית, Jer. xxiii. 1, the flock fed by God Himself); men are ye, I am your God." That these last words do not serve merely as an explanation of the figurative expression "flock," is a fact of which no proof is needed. The figure of a flock was intelligible to every one. The words "call attention to the depth and greatness of the divine condescension, and meet the objection of men of weak faith, that man, who is taken from the earth הָאֲדָמָה, and returns to it again, is incapable of so intimate a connection with God" (Hengstenberg).

If we take another survey, in conclusion, of the contents of our prophecy, the following are the three features of the salvation promised to the people of Israel:—(1) The Lord will liberate His people from the hand of the bad shepherds, and

He Himself will feed it as His flock; (2) He will gather it together from its dispersion, bring it back to the land of Israel and feed it there, will take charge of the sheep in need of help, and destroy the fat and strong sheep by which the weak ones are oppressed; (3) He will raise up the future David for a shepherd, and under his care He will bestow upon His people the promised covenant blessings in richest measure. These saving acts of God for His people, however, are not depicted according to their several details and historical peculiarities, as Kliefoth has correctly observed, nor are they narrated in the chronological order in which they would follow one another in history; but they are grouped together according to their general design and character, and their essential features. If, then, we seek for the fulfilment, the Lord raised up His servant David as a shepherd to Israel, by sending Jesus Christ, who came to seek and to save that which was lost (Luke xix. 10; Matt. xviii. 11), and who calls Himself the Good Shepherd with obvious reference to this and other prophetic declarations of a similar kind (John x. 11 sqq.). But the sending of Christ was preceded by the gathering of Israel out of the Babylonian exile, by which God had already taken charge of His flock. Yet, inasmuch as only a small portion of Israel received the Messiah, who appeared in Jesus, as its shepherd, there fell upon the unbelieving Israel a new judgment of dispersion among all nations, which continues still, so that a gathering together still awaits the people of Israel at some future time. No distinction is made in the prophecy before us between these two judgments of dispersion, which are associated with the twofold gathering of Israel; but they are grouped together as one, so that although their fulfilment commenced with the deliverance of Israel from the Babylonian captivity and the coming of Jesus Christ as the Good Shepherd of the family of David, it was only realized in that portion of Israel, numerically the smallest portion, which was willing to be gathered and fed by Jesus Christ, and the full realization will only be effected when that conversion of Israel shall take place, which the Apostle Paul foretells in Rom. xi. 25 sqq.—For further remarks on the ultimate fulfilment, we refer the reader to a later page.

CHAP. XXXV. 1–XXXVI. 15. DEVASTATION OF EDOM, AND RESTORATION OF THE LAND OF ISRAEL.

The two sections, ch. xxxv. 1–15 and ch. xxxvi. 1–15, form a connected prophecy. This is apparent not only from their formal arrangement, both of them being placed together under the introductory formula, "And the word of Jehovah came to me, saying," but also from their contents, the promise in relation to the mountains of Israel being so opposed to the threat against the mountains of Seir (ch. xxxv. 1–15) as to form the obverse and completion of the latter; whilst allusion is evidently made to it in the form of expression employed (compare ch. xxxvi. 4, 6, with ch. xxxv. 8; and ch. xxxvi. 5*a* with ch. xxxv. 15*b*). The contents are the following: The mountains of Seir shall be laid waste (ch. xxxv. 1–4), because Edom cherishes eternal enmity and bloody hatred towards Israel (vers. 5–9), and because it has coveted the land of Israel and blasphemed Jehovah (vers. 10–15). On the other hand, the mountain-land of Israel, which the heathen have despised on account of its devastation, and have appropriated to themselves as booty (ch. xxxvi. 1–7), shall be inhabited by Israel again, and shall be cultivated and no longer bear the disgrace of the heathen (vers. 8–15). This closing thought (ver. 15) points back to ch. xxxiv. 29, and shows that our prophecy is intended as a further expansion of that conclusion; and at the same time, that in the devastation of Edom the overthrow of the heathen world as a whole, with its enmity against God, is predicted, and in the restoration of the land of Israel the re-erection of the fallen kingdom of God.

Chap. xxxv. The Devastation of Edom.—Ver. 1. *And*

the word of Jehovah came to me, saying, Ver. 2. *Son of man, set thy face against Mount Seir, and prophesy against it,* Ver. 3. *And say to it, Thus saith the Lord Jehovah, Behold, I will deal with thee, Mount Seir, and will stretch out my hand against thee, and make thee waste and devastation.* Ver. 4. *Thy cities will I make into ruins, and thou wilt become a waste, and shalt know that I am Jehovah.* Ver. 5. *Because thou cherishest eternal enmity, and gavest up the sons of Israel to the sword at the time of their distress, at the time of the final transgression,* Ver. 6. *Therefore, as truly as I live, is the saying of the Lord Jehovah, I will make thee blood, and blood shall pursue thee; since thou hast not hated blood, therefore blood shall pursue thee.* Ver. 7. *I will make Mount Seir devastation and waste, and cut off therefrom him that goeth away and him that returneth,* Ver. 8. *And fill his mountains with his slain; upon thy hills, and in thy valleys, and in all thy low places, those pierced with the sword shall fall.* Ver. 9. *I will make thee eternal wastes, and thy cities shall not be inhabited; and ye shall know that I am Jehovah.* Ver. 10. *Because thou sayest, The two nations and the two lands they shall be mine, and we will take possession of it, when Jehovah was there;* Ver. 11. *Therefore, as truly as I live, is the saying of the Lord Jehovah, I will do according to thy wrath and thine envy, as thou hast done because of thy hatred, and will make myself known among them, as I shall judge thee.* Ver. 12. *And thou shalt know that I, Jehovah, have heard all thy reproaches which thou hast uttered against the mountains of Israel, saying, "they are laid waste, they are given to us for food."* Ver. 13. *Ye have magnified against me with your mouth, and heaped up your sayings against me; I have heard it.* Ver. 14. *Thus saith the Lord Jehovah, When the whole earth rejoiceth, I will prepare devastation for thee.* Ver. 15. *As thou hadst thy delight in the inheritance of the house of Israel, because it was laid waste, so will I do to thee; thou shalt become a waste, Mount Seir and all Edom together; and they shall know that I am Jehovah.*

The theme of this prophecy, viz. "Edom and its cities are

to become a desert" (vers. 2–4), is vindicated and earnestly elaborated in two strophes, commencing with יַעַן וגו׳ (vers. 5 and 10), and closing, like the announcement of the theme itself (ver. 4*b*), with וִידַעְתֶּם (וְיָדְעוּ) כִּי אֲנִי י״, by a distinct statement of the sins of Edom.—Already, in ch. xxv., Edom has been named among the hostile border nations which are threatened with destruction (vers. 12–14). The earlier prophecy applied to the Edomites, according to their historical relation to the people of Israel and the kingdom of Judah. In the present word of God, on the contrary, Edom comes into consideration, on the ground of its hostile attitude towards the covenant people, as the representative of the world and of mankind in its hostility to the people and kingdom of God, as in Isa. xxxiv. and lxiii. 1–6. This is apparent from the fact that devastation is to be prepared for Edom, when the whole earth rejoices (ver. 14), which does not apply to Edom as a small and solitary nation, and still more clearly from the circumstance that, in the promise of salvation in ch. xxxvi., not all Edom alone (ver. 5), but the remnant of the heathen nations generally (ch. xxxvi. 3–7 and 15), are mentioned as the enemies from whose disgrace and oppression Israel is to be delivered. For ver. 2, compare ch. xiii. 17. הַר שֵׂעִיר is the name given to the mountainous district inhabited by the Edomites, between the Dead Sea and the Elanitic Gulf (see the comm. on Gen. xxxvi. 9). The prophecy is directed against the land; but it also applies to the nation, which brings upon itself the desolation of its land by its hostility to Israel. For ver. 3, compare ch. vi. 14, etc. חָרְבָּה, destruction. The sin of Edom mentioned in ver. 5 is eternal enmity toward Israel, which has also been imputed to the Philistines in ch. xxv. 15, but which struck deeper root, in the case of Edom, in the hostile attitude of Esau toward Jacob (Gen. xxv. 22 sqq. and xxvii. 37), and was manifested, as Amos (i. 11) has already said, in the constant retention of its malignity toward the covenant nation, so that Edom embraced every opportunity to effect its destruction, and according to the charge brought against it by Ezekiel, gave up the sons of Israel to the sword when the kingdom of Judah fell. הִגִּיר עַל יְדֵי חָרֶב, lit. to pour upon (— into) the hands of the sword, *i.e.* to deliver up to the power of the sword (cf. Ps. lxiii. 11; Jer. xviii. 21). בְּעֵת אֵידָם recalls to mind בְּיוֹם אֵידָם in Obad. 13; but here it is more precisely defined by בְּעֵת עֲוֹן קֵץ, and limited to the time of the overthrow of the Israelites, when Jerusalem was taken and destroyed by the Chaldeans. בְּעֵת עֲוֹן קֵץ, as in ch. xxi. 30. On account of this display of its hostility, the Lord will make Edom blood (ver. 6). This expression is probably chosen for the play upon the words דָּם and אֱדֹם. Edom shall become what its name suggests. Making it blood does not mean merely filling it with bloodshed, or reddening the soil with blood (Hitzig); but, as in ch. xvi. 38, turning it as it were into blood, or causing it to vanish therein. Blood shall pursue thee, "as blood-guiltiness invariably pursues a murderer, cries for vengeance, and so delivers him up to punishment" (Hävernick). אִם לֹא cannot be the particle employed in swearing, and dependent upon חַי־אָנִי, since this particle introduces an affirmative declaration, which would be unsuitable here, inasmuch as דָּם in this connection cannot possibly signify blood-relationship. אִם לֹא means "if not," in which the conditional meaning of אִם coincides with the causal, "if" being equivalent to "since." The unusual separation of the לֹא from the verb is occasioned by the fact that דָּם is placed before the verb to avoid collision with וְדָם. To hate blood is the same as to have a horror of bloodshed or murder. This threat is carried out still further in vers. 7 and 8. The land of Edom is to become a complete and perpetual devastation; its inhabitants are to be exterminated by war. The form שִׁמֲמָה stands for שְׁמָמָה, and is not to be changed into מְשַׁמָּה. Considering the frequency with which מְשַׁמָּה occurs, the supposition that we have here a copyist's error is by no means a probable one, and still less probable is the perpetuation of such an error. עֹבֵר וָשָׁב, as in Zech. vii. 14. For ver. 8 compare ch. xxxii. 5, 6 and ch.

xxxi. 12. The *Chetib* תֵּישַׁבְנָה is *scriptio plena* for תֵּשַׁבְנָה, the imperfect *Kal* of יָשַׁב in the intransitive sense to be inhabited. The *Keri* תָּשֹׁבְנָה, from שׁוּב, is a needless and unsuitable correction, since שׁוּב does not mean *restitui.*

In the second strophe, vers. 10–15, the additional reason assigned for the desolation of Edom is its longing for the possession of Israel and its land, of which it desired to take forcible possession, although it knew that they belonged to Jehovah, whereby the hatred of Edom toward Israel became contempt of Jehovah. The two peoples and the two lands are Israel and Judah with their lands, and therefore the whole of the holy people and land. אֵת is the sign of the accusative: as for the two peoples, they are mine. The suffix appended to יְרַשְׁנוּהָ is neuter, and is to be taken as referring generally to what has gone before. וַיהוָה שָׁם הָיָה is a circumstantial clause, through which the desire of Edom is placed in the right light, and characterized as an attack upon Jehovah Himself. Jehovah was there—namely, in the land of which Edom wished to take possession. Kliefoth's rendering, "and yet Jehovah *is* there," is opposed to Hebrew usage, by changing the preterite הָיָה into a present; and the objection which he offers to the only rendering that is grammatically admissible, viz. "when Jehovah was there," to the effect "that it attributes to Ezekiel the thought that the Holy Land had once been the land and dwelling-place of God, but was so no longer," calls in question the actual historical condition of things without the slightest reason. For Jehovah had really forsaken His dwelling-place in Canaan before the destruction of the temple, but without thereby renouncing His right to the land; since it was only for the sins of Israel that He had given up the temple, city, and land to be laid waste by the heathen. "But Edom had acted as if Israel existed among the nations without God, and Jehovah had departed from it for ever" (Hävernick); or rather as if Jehovah were a powerless and useless Deity, who had not been able to defend His people against the might of the heathen nations.

The Lord will requite Edom for this, in a manner answering to its anger and envy, which had both sprung from hatred. נוֹדַעְתִּי בָם, "I will make myself known among them (the Israelites) when I judge thee;" *i.e.*, by the fact that He punishes Edom for its sin, He will prove to Israel that He is a God who does not suffer His people and His possession to be attacked with impunity. From this shall Edom learn that He is Jehovah, the omniscient God, who has heard the revilings of His enemies (vers. 12, 13), and the almighty God, who rewards those who utter such proud sayings according to their deeds (vers. 14 and 15). נָאָצוֹת has retained the *Kametz* on account of the guttural in the first tone, in contrast with נֶאָצוֹת in Neh. ix. 18, 26 (cf. Ewald, § 69*b*).—The expression "mountains of Israel," for the land of Israel, in ver. 12 and ch. xxxvi. 1, is occasioned by the antithesis "mountain (mountain-range) of Seir." The *Chetib* שממה is to be pronounced שְׁמֵמָה, and to be retained in spite of the *Keri*. The singular of the neuter gender is used with emphasis in a broken and emotional address, and is to be taken as referring *ad sensum* to the land. הִגְדִּיל בְּפֶה, to magnify or boast with the mouth, *i.e.* to utter proud sayings against God, in other words, actually to deride God (compare הִגְדִּיל פֶּה in Obad. 12, which has a kindred meaning). הֶעְתִּיר, used here according to Aramean usage for הֶעֱשִׁיר, to multiply, or heap up. In כִּשְׂמֹחַ, in ver. 14, כְּ is a particle of time, as it frequently is before infinitives (*e.g.* Josh. vi. 20), when all the earth rejoices, not "over thy desolation" (Hitzig), which does not yield any rational thought, but when joy is prepared for all the world, I will prepare devastation for thee. Through this antithesis כָּל־הָאָרֶץ is limited to the world, with the exception of Edom, *i.e.* to that portion of the human race which stood in a different relation to God and His people from that of Edom; in other words, which acknowledged the Lord as the true God. It follows from this, that Edom represents the world at enmity against God. In כְּשִׂמְחָתְךָ (ver. 15) כ is a particle of comparison; and the meaning of ver. 15 is: as thou didst rejoice over the desolation of the inheritance of the house of Israel, so will I cause others to rejoice over thy desolation. In ver. 15*b* we agree with the LXX., Vulgate, Syriac, and others, in taking תִּהְיֶה as the second person, not as the third. כָּל־אֱדוֹם כֻּלָּהּ serves to strengthen הַר־שֵׂעִיר (compare ch. xi. 15 and xxxvi. 10).

Chap. xxxvi. 1–15. THE RESTORATION AND BLESSING OF ISRAEL.—Ver. 1. *And thou, son of man, prophesy to the mountains of Israel, and say, Mountains of Israel, hear the word of Jehovah:* Ver. 2. *Thus saith the Lord Jehovah, Because the enemy saith concerning you, Aha! the everlasting heights have become ours for a possession:* Ver. 3. *Therefore prophesy, and say, Thus saith the Lord Jehovah, Because, even because they lay you waste, and pant for you round about, so that ye have become a possession to the remnant of the nations, and have come to the talk of the tongue and gossip of the people:* Ver. 4. *Therefore, ye mountains of Israel, hear the word of the Lord Jehovah: Thus saith the Lord Jehovah to the mountains and hills, to the low places and valleys, and to the waste ruins and the forsaken cities, which have become a prey and derision to the remnant of the nations round about;* Ver. 5. *Therefore thus saith the Lord Jehovah, Truly in the fire of my jealousy I have spoken against the remnant of the nations, and against Edom altogether, which have made my land a possession for themselves in all joy of heart, in contempt of soul, to empty it out for booty.* Ver. 6. *Therefore prophesy concerning the land of Israel, and say to the mountains and hills, to the low places and valleys, Thus saith the Lord Jehovah, Behold, in my jealousy and fury have I spoken, because ye have borne the disgrace of the nations.* Ver. 7. *Therefore thus saith the Lord Jehovah, I, I have lifted up my hand; truly the nations round about you, they shall bear their disgrace.* Ver. 8. *But ye, ye mountains of Israel, shall put forth your branches, and bear your fruit to my people Israel; for they will soon come.* Ver. 9. *For, behold, I will deal with you, and turn toward you, and ye shall be tilled and sown.* Ver. 10.

I will multiply men upon you, all the house of Israel at once; and the cities shall be inhabited, and the ruins built. Ver. 11. *And I will multiply upon you man and beast; they shall multiply and be fruitful: and I will make you inhabited as in your former time, and do more good to you than in your earlier days; and ye shall know that I am Jehovah.* Ver. 12. *I will cause men, my people Israel, to walk upon you; and they shall possess thee, and thou shalt be an inheritance to them, and make them childless no more.* Ver. 13. *Thus saith the Lord Jehovah, Because they say to you, "Thou art a devourer of men, and hast made thy people childless;"* Ver. 14. *Therefore thou shalt no more devour men, and no more cause thy people to stumble, is the saying of the Lord Jehovah.* Ver. 15. *And I will no more cause thee to hear the scoffing of the nations, and the disgrace of the nations thou shalt bear no more, and shalt no more cause thy people to stumble, is the saying of the Lord Jehovah.*

This prophecy is uttered concerning the land of Israel, as is plainly declared in ver. 6; whereas in vers. 1 and 4 the mountains of Israel are mentioned instead of the land, in antithesis to the mountains of Seir (ch. xxxv.; see the comm. on ch. xxxv. 12). The promise takes throughout the form of antithesis to the threat against Edom in ch. xxxv. Because Edom rejoices that the Holy Land, which has been laid waste, has fallen to it for a possession, therefore shall the devastated land be cultivated and sown again, and be inhabited by Israel as in the former time. The heathen nations round about shall, on the other hand, bear their disgrace; Edom, as we have already observed, being expanded, so far as the idea is concerned, into all the heathen nations surrounding Israel (vers. 3–7). In ver. 2, הָאוֹיֵב, the enemy, is mentioned in quite a general manner; and what has already been stated concerning Edom in ch. xxxv. 5 and 10, is here predicted of the enemy. In vers. 3 and 4 this enemy is designated as a remnant of the heathen nations; and it is not till ver. 5 that it is more precisely defined by the clause, "and all Edom altogether." The

גּוֹיִם round about (אֲשֶׁר מִסָּבִיב, ver. 4, compared with ver. 3) are the heathen nations which are threatened with destruction in ch. xxv. and xxvi., on account of their malicious rejoicing at the devastation of Jerusalem and Judah. This serves to explain the fact that these nations are designated as שְׁאֵרִית הַגּוֹיִם, the rest, or remnant of the heathen nations, which presupposes that the judgment has fallen upon them, and that only a remnant of them is left, which remnant desires to take possession of the devastated land of Israel. The epithet applied to this land, בָּמוֹת עוֹלָם, everlasting, *i.e.* primeval heights, points back to the גִּבְעוֹת עוֹלָם of Gen. xlix. 26 and Deut. xxxiii. 15, and is chosen for the purpose of representing the land as a possession secured to the people of Israel by primeval promises, in consequence of which the attempt of the enemy to seize upon this land has become a sin against the Lord God. The indignation at such a sin is expressed in the emotional character of the address. As Ewald has aptly observed, "Ezekiel is seized with unusual fire, so that after the brief statement in ver. 2 'therefore' is repeated five times, the charges brought against these foes forcing themselves in again and again, before the prophecy settles calmly upon the mountains of Israel, to which it was really intended to apply." For יַעַן בְּיַעַן, see the comm. on ch. xiii. 10. שַׁמּוֹת is an infinitive *Kal*, formed after the analogy of the verbs ל״ה (cf. Ewald, § 238*e*), from שָׁמֵם, to be waste, to devastate, as in Dan. viii. 13, ix. 27, xii. 11, and is not to be taken in the sense of נָשַׁם, after Isa. xlii. 14, as Hitzig supposes. שָׁאַף, to pant for a thing; here it is equivalent to snapping at anything. This is required by a comparison with ver. 4*b*, where הָיָה לְבַז corresponds to שַׁמּוֹת וְשָׁאֹף, and לְלַעַג to תַּעֲלוּ עַל שְׂפַת וגו׳. In the connection שְׂפַת לָשׁוֹן, שָׂפָה signifies the lip as an organ of speech, or, more precisely, the words spoken; and לָשׁוֹן, the tongue, is personified, and stands for אִישׁ לָשׁוֹן (Ps. cxl. 12), a tongue-man, *i.e.* a talker. In ver. 4 the idea expressed in "the mountains of Israel" is expanded into mountains, hills, lowlands, and valleys (cf. ch.

xxxi. 12, xxxii. 5, 6); and this periphrastic description of the land is more minutely defined by the additional clause, "waste ruins and forsaken cities." אִם לֹא in ver. 5 is the particle used in oaths (cf. ch. v. 11, etc.); and the perfect דִּבַּרְתִּי is not merely prophetic, but also a preterite. God has already uttered a threatening word concerning the nations round about in ch. xxv., xxvi., and xxxv.; and here He once more declares that they shall bear their disgrace. אֵשׁ קִנְאָה is the fiery jealousy of wrath. כֻּלָּא is an Aramean form for כֻּלָּהּ (ch. xxxv. 15). For בִּשְׁאָט נֶפֶשׁ, see ch. xxv. 6. In the expression לְמַעַן מִגְרָשָׁהּ לָבַז, which has been rendered in various ways, we agree with Gesenius and others in regarding מִגְרַשׁ as an Aramean form of the infinitive of גָּרַשׁ, with the meaning to empty out, which is confirmed by the Syriac; for מִגְרָשׁ cannot be a substantive, on account of the לְמַעַן; and Hitzig's conjecture, that לבז should be pointed לָבֹז, and the clause rendered "to plunder its produce," is precluded by the fact that the separation of the preposition לְמַעַן לְ, by the insertion of a word between, is unexampled, to say nothing of the fact that מִגְרָשׁ does not mean produce at all. The thought expressed in vers. 6 and 7 is the following: because Israel has hitherto borne the contempt of the heathen, the heathen shall now bear their own contempt. The lifting of the hand is a gesture employed in taking an oath, as in ch. xx. 6, etc. But the land of Israel is to receive a blessing. This blessing is described in ver. 8 in general terms, as the bearing of fruit by the mountains, *i.e.* by the land of Israel; and its speedy commencement is predicted. It is then depicted in detail in vers. 9 sqq. In the clause כִּי קֵרְבוּ לָבוֹא, the Israelites are not to be regarded as the subject, as Kliefoth supposes, in which case their speedy return from exile would be announced. The כִּי shows that this cannot be the meaning; for it is immediately preceded by לְעַמִּי יִשׂ׳, which precludes the supposition that, when speaking of the mountains, Ezekiel had the inhabitants in his mind. The promised blessings are the subject, or the branches and fruits, which the mountains are to bear. Nearly all the commentators have agreed in adopting this explanation of the words, after the analogy of Isa. lvi. 1. With the כִּי in ver. 9 the carrying out of the blessing promised is appended in the form of a reason assigned for the general promise. The mountains shall be cultivated, the men upon them, viz. all Israel, multiplied, the desolated cities rebuilt, so that Israel shall dwell in the land as in the former time, and be fruitful and blessed. This promise was no doubt fulfilled in certain weak beginnings after the return of a portion of the people under Zerubbabel and Ezra; but the multiplying and blessing, experienced by those who returned from Babylon, did not take place till long after the salvation promised here, and more especially in vers. 12–15. According to ver. 12, the land is to become the inheritance of the people Israel, and will no more make the Israelites childless, or (according to ver. 14) cause them to stumble; and the people are no more to bear the contempt of the heathen. But that portion of the nation which returned from exile not only continued under the rule of the heathen, but had also in various ways to bear the contempt of the heathen still; and eventually, because Israel not only stumbled, but fell very low through the rejection of its Saviour, it was scattered again out of the land among the heathen, and the land was utterly wasted . . . until this day. In ver. 12 the masculine suffix attached to וִירֵשׁוּךָ refers to the land regarded as הַר, which is also the subject to הָיִיתָ and תוֹסִף. It is not till vers. 13, 14, where the idea of the land becomes so prominent, that the feminine is used. שִׁכַּלְתָּם, to make them (the Israelites) childless, or bereaved, is explained in vers. 13, 14 by אֹכֶלֶת אָדָם, devouring men. That the land devours its inhabitants, is what the spies say of the land of Canaan in Num. xiii. 32; and in 2 Kings ii. 19 it is affirmed of the district of Jericho that it causes מְשַׁכֶּלֶת, *i.e.* miscarriages, on account of its bad water. The latter passage does not come into consideration; but the former (Num. xiii. 32) probably does, and Ezekiel evidently refers to this. For there is no doubt whatever that he explains or expands שַׁכָּלָם by אֹכֶלֶת אָדָם. Although, for example, the charge that the land devours men is brought against it by the enemies or adversaries of Israel (אֹמְרִים לָכֶם, they say to you), the truth of the charge is admitted, since it is said that the land shall henceforth no more devour men, though without a repetition of the שַׁכֵּל. But the sense in which Ezekiel affirms of the land that it had been אֹכֶלֶת אָדָם, and was henceforth to be so no more, is determined by וְגוֹיֵךְ לֹא תַכְשִׁלִי עוֹד, thou wilt no more cause thy people to stumble, which is added in ver. 14*b* in the place of מְשַׁכֶּלֶת גּוֹיֵךְ הָיִית in ver. 14*a*. Hence the land became a devourer of men by the fact that it caused its people to stumble, *i.e.* entangled them in sins (the *Keri* תְּשַׁכְּלִי for תַּכְשִׁלִי is a bad conjecture, the incorrectness of which is placed beyond all doubt by the לֹא־תַכְשִׁלִי עוֹד of ver. 15). Consequently we cannot understand the "devouring of men," after Num. xiii. 32, as signifying that, on account of its situation and fruitfulness, the land is an apple of discord, for the possession of which the nations strive with one another, so that the inhabitants are destroyed, or at all events we must not restrict the meaning to this; and still less can we agree with Ewald and Hitzig in thinking of the restless hurrying and driving by which individual men were of necessity rapidly swept away. If the sweeping away of the population is connected with the stumbling, the people are devoured by the consequences of their sins, *i.e.* by penal judgments, unfruitfulness, pestilence, and war, with which God threatened Israel for its apostasy from Him. These judgments had depopulated the land; and this fact was attributed by the heathen in their own way to the land, and thrown in the teeth of the Israelites as a disgrace. The Lord will henceforth remove this charge, and take away from the heathen all occasion to despise His people, namely, by bestowing upon His land and people the blessing which He promised in the law to those who kept His commandments. But this can only be done by His removing the occasion to stumble or sin, *i.e.*, according to vers. 25 sqq. (compared with ch. xi. 18 sqq.), by His cleansing His people from all uncleannesses and idols, and giving them a new heart and a new spirit. The *Keri* גּוֹיַיִךְ in vers. 13, 14, and 15 is a needless alteration of the *Chetib* גּוֹיֵךְ.—In ver. 15 this promise is rounded off and concluded by another summing up of the principal thoughts.

CHAP. XXXVI. 16–38. THE SALVATION OF ISRAEL FOUNDED UPON ITS SANCTIFICATION.

Because Israel has defiled its land by its sins, God has scattered the people among the heathen; but because they also profaned His name among the heathen, He will exercise forbearance for the sake of His holy name (vers. 16–21), will gather Israel out of the lands, cleanse it from its sins, and sanctify it by the communication of His Spirit, so that it will walk in His ways (vers. 22–28), and will so bless and multiply it, that both the nations around and Israel itself will know that He is the Lord (vers. 29–38).—This promise is shown by the introductory formula in ver. 16 and by the contents to be an independent word of God; but it is substantially connected in the closest manner with the preceding word of God, showing, on the one hand, the motive which prompted God to restore and bless His people; and, on the other hand, the means by which He would permanently establish the salvation predicted in ch. xxxiv. and ch. xxxvi. 1–15.—The kernel of this promise is formed by vers. 25–28, for which the way is prepared in vers. 17–24, whilst the further extension is contained in vers. 29–38.

Vers. 16–21. The Lord will extend His forbearance, for the sake of His holy name, to the people who have been rejected on account of their sins.—Ver. 16. *And the word of Jehovah came to me, saying,* Ver. 17. *Son of man, the house of Israel dwelt in its land, and defiled it with its way and its doings; like the uncleanness of the unclean woman, was its way before me.* Ver. 18. *Then I poured out my fury upon them on account of the blood which they had shed in the land, and because they had defiled it through their idols,* Ver. 19. *And scattered them among the nations, and they were dispersed in the lands; according to their way and their doings I judge them.* Ver. 20. *And they came to the nations whither they came, and profaned my holy name, for men said of them, "These are Jehovah's people, and they have come out of His land."* Ver. 21. *And so I had pity upon my holy name, which the house of Israel profaned among the nations whither they came.*—The address commences with a description of the reasons why God had thrust out His people among the heathen, namely, on account of their sins and idolatrous abominations, by which the Israelites had defiled the land (cf. Lev. xviii. 28 and Num. xxxv. 34). Their conduct resembled the most offensive uncleanness, namely, the uncleanness of a woman in her menstruation (Lev. xv. 19), to which the moral depravity of the people had already been compared in Isa. lxiv. 5.—In ver. 18 the consequence of the defiling of the land by the people is introduced with the expression וָאֶשְׁפֹּךְ. In ver. 17, וַיְטַמְּאוּ is the continuation of the participle יֹשְׁבִים; and the participle is expressive of the condition in the past, as we may see from the words וָאֶשְׁפֹּךְ וגו׳. The simile in ver. 17*b* is an explanatory, circumstantial clause. For ver. 18, compare ch. vii. 8, and for עַל הַדָּם וגו׳, ch. xxii. 3, 6. The last clause, "and through their idols they have defiled it," is loosely appended; but it really contains a second reason for the pouring out of the wrath of God upon the people. For ver. 19, compare ch. xxii. 15. וַיָּבוֹא in ver. 20 refers to בֵּית־יִשְׂרָאֵל; but there is no necessity to read וַיָּבֹאוּ on that account. It is perfectly arbitrary to supply the subject proposed by Kliefoth, viz. "the report of what had happened to Israel" came to the heathen, which is quite foreign to the connection; for it was not the report concerning Israel, but Israel itself, which came to the heathen, and profaned the sacred name of God. This is not only plainly expressed in ver. 21*b*, but has been already stated in ver. 20.

The fact that the words of the heathen, by which the name of God was profaned, are quoted here, does not prove that it is the heathen nations who are to be regarded as those who profaned the name of God, as Kliefoth imagines. The words, "these are Jehovah's people, and have come out of His (Jehovah's) land," could only contain a profanation of the holy name of God, if their coming out was regarded as involuntary, *i.e.* as an exile enforced by the power of the heathen; or, on the other hand, if the Israelites themselves had denied the holiness of the people of God through their behaviour among the heathen. Most of the commentators have decided in favour of the former view. Vatablus, for example, gives this explanation: "if their God whom they preach had been omnipotent, He would not have allowed them to be expelled from His land." And we must decide in favour of this exposition, not only because of the parallel passages, such as Num. xiv. 16 and Jer. xxxiii. 24, which support this view; but chiefly on account of the verses which follow, according to which the sanctification of the name of God among the nations consists in the fact that God gathers Israel out of its dispersion among the nations, and leads them back into His own land (*vid.* vers. 23 and 24). Consequently the profanation of His name can only have consisted in the fact that Israel was carried away out of its own land, and scattered in the heathen lands. For, since the heathen acknowledged only national gods, and regarded Jehovah as nothing more than such a national god of Israel, they did not look upon the destruction of the kingdom of Judah and the carrying away of the people as a judgment of the almighty and holy God upon His people, but concluded that that catastrophe was a sign of the inability of Jehovah to defend His land and save His people. The only way in which God could destroy this delusion was by manifesting Himself to the heathen as the almighty God and Lord of the whole world through the redemption and glorification of His people. וָאֶחְמֹל עַל־שֵׁם ק׳: so I had pity, compassion upon my holy name. The preterite is prophetic, inasmuch as the compassion consists in the gathering of Israel out of the nations, which is announced in vers. 22 sqq. as still in the future. The rendering, "I spared (them) for my holy name's sake" (LXX., Hävernick), is false; for חָמַל is construed with עַל, governing the person or the thing toward which the compassion is shown (*vid.* ch. xvi. 5 and 2 Chron. xxxvi. 15, 17).

Vers. 22–28. For His holy name's sake the Lord will bring Israel back from its dispersion into His own land, purify it from its sins, and sanctify it by His Spirit to be His own people.—Ver. 22. *Therefore say to the house of Israel, Thus saith the Lord Jehovah, I do it not for your sakes, O house of Israel, but for my holy name's sake, which ye have profaned among the nations whither ye have come.* Ver. 23. *I will sanctify my great name, which is profaned among the nations, which ye have profaned in the midst of them, so that the nations shall know that I am Jehovah, is the saying of the Lord Jehovah, when I prove myself holy upon you before their eyes.* Ver. 24. *I will take you out of the nations, and gather you out of all lands, and bring you into your land,* Ver. 25. *And will sprinkle clean water upon you, that ye may become clean; from all your uncleannesses and from all your idols will I cleanse you,* Ver. 26. *And I will give you a new heart, and give a new spirit within you; I will take the heart of stone out of your flesh, and give you a heart of flesh.* Ver. 27. *I will put my Spirit within you, and cause you to walk in my statutes, and keep my rights, and do them.* Ver. 28. *And ye shall dwell in the land which I have given to your fathers, and shall become my people, and I will be your God.*—These verses show in what way the Lord will have compassion upon His holy name, and how He will put an end to the scoffing thereat, and vindicate His honour in the sight of the heathen. "Not for your sake," *i.e.* not because you have any claim to deliverance on account of your behaviour (cf. Isa. xlviii. 11 and Deut. ix. 6), but for my holy name's sake, *i.e.* to manifest as holy the name which has been profaned among the heathen, I do it, namely, what follows from ver. 23 onwards. The Lord will sanctify His name, *i.e.* show it to be holy by proving Himself to be holy upon Israel. קִדֵּשׁ is not equivalent to glorify, although the holiness of God involves the idea of glory. Sanctifying is the removing or expunging of the blots and blemishes which adhere to anything. The giving up of His people was regarded by the heathen as a sign of the weakness of Jehovah. This blot through which His omnipotence and glory were dishonoured, God would remove by gathering Israel out of the heathen, and glorifying it. Instead of לְעֵינֵיכֶם, the ancient versions have rendered לְעֵינֵיהֶם. This reading is also found in many of the *codices* and the earliest editions, and is confirmed by the great Masora, and also commended by the parallel passages, ch. xx. 41 and xxviii. 25, so that it no doubt deserves the preference, although לעיניכם can also be justified. For inasmuch as Israelites had despaired in the midst of their wretchedness through unbelief, it was necessary that Jehovah should sanctify His great name in their sight as well. The great name of Jehovah is His almighty exaltation above all gods (cf. Mal. i. 11, 12). The first thing that Jehovah does for the sanctification of His name is to bring back Israel from its dispersion into its own land (ver. 24, compare ch. xi. 17 and xx. 41, 42); and then follows the purifying of Israel from its sins. The figurative expression, "to sprinkle with clean water," is taken from the lustrations prescribed by the law, more particularly the purifying from defilement from the dead by sprinkling with the water prepared from the ashes of a red heifer (Num. xix. 17–19; compare Ps. li. 9). Cleansing from sins, which corresponds to justification, and is not to be confounded with sanctification (Schmieder), is followed by renewal with the Holy Spirit, which takes away the old heart of stone and puts within a new heart of flesh, so that the man can fulfil the commandments of God, and walk in newness of life (vers. 26–28; compare ch. xi. 18–20, where this promise has already occurred, and the necessary remarks concerning its fulfilment have been made).—With regard to the construction עָשָׂה אֵת אֲשֶׁר וגו׳, to make or effect your walking, compare Ewald, § 337*b*.

Vers. 29–38. The Lord will richly bless, multiply, and glorify His people, when thus renewed and sanctified.—Ver. 29. *And I will save you from all your uncleannesses, and will call the corn, and multiply it, and no more bring famine upon you;* Ver. 30. *But I will multiply the fruit of the tree and the produce of the field, so that ye will no more bear the reproach of famine among the nations.* Ver. 31. *But ye will remember your evil ways, and your deeds which were not good, and will loathe yourselves on account of your iniquities and your abominations.* Ver. 32. *Not for your sake do I this, is the saying of the Lord Jehovah, be this known to you; be ye ashamed and blush for your ways, O house of Israel!* Ver. 33. *Thus saith the Lord Jehovah, In the day when I shall cleanse you from all your iniquities, I will make the cities inhabited, and the ruins shall be built,* Ver. 34. *And the devastated land shall be tilled instead of being a desert before the eyes of every one who passed by.* Ver. 35. *And men will say, This land, which was laid waste, has become like the garden of Eden, and the desolate and ruined cities are fortified and inhabited.* Ver. 36. *And the nations, which have been left round about you, shall know that I Jehovah build up that which is destroyed, and plant that which is laid waste. I, Jehovah, have said it, and do it.* Ver. 37. *Thus saith the Lord Jehovah, I will still let myself be sought by the house of Israel in this, to do it for them; I will multiply them, like a flock, in men;* Ver. 38. *Like a flock of holy sacrifices, like the flock of Jerusalem on its feast-days, so shall the desolate cities be full of flocks of men; and they shall know that I am Jehovah.*—The words הוֹשַׁעְתִּי וגו׳, I help or save you from all your uncleannesses, cannot be understood as relating to their purification from the former uncleannesses; for they have already been cleansed from these, according to ver. 25. The טֻמְאוֹת can only be such defilements as are still possible even after the renewing of the people; and הוֹשַׁע, to help, means to guard them against any further recurrence of such defilements (cf. ch. xxxvii. 23), and not to deliver them from the consequences of their former pollutions. But if God preserves His people from these, there is no longer any occasion for a fresh suspension of judgments over them, and God can bestow His blessing upon the sanctified nation without reserve. It is in this way that the further promises are appended; and, first of all, in vers. 29*b* and 30, a promise that He will bless them with an abundant crop of fruits, both of the orchard and the field. "I call to the corn," *i.e.* I cause it to come or grow, so that famine will occur no more (for the fact, compare ch. xxxiv. 29). In consequence of this blessing, Israel will blush with shame at the thought of its former sins, and will loathe itself for those abominations (ver. 31); compare ch. xx. 43, where the same thought has already occurred. To this, after repeating what has been said before in ver. 22, namely, that God is not doing all this for the sake of the Israelites themselves, the prophet appends the admonition to be ashamed of their conduct, *i.e.* to repent, which is so far inserted appropriately in the promise, that the promise itself is meant to entice Israel to repent and return to God. Then, secondly, in two strophes introduced with כֹּה אָמַר יי', the promise is still further expanded. In vers. 33–36, the prophet shows how the devastated land is to be restored and rebuilt, and to become a paradise; and in vers. 37 and 38, how the people are to be blessed through a large increase in their numbers. Both of these strophes are simply a further elaboration of the promise contained in vers. 9–12. הוֹשִׁיב, causative of יָשַׁב, to cause to be inhabited, to populate, as in Isa. liv. 3. לְעֵינֵי כָּל־עוֹבֵר, as in ch. v. 14. The subject to וְאָמְרוּ in ver. 35 is, "those who pass by." For the comparison to the garden of Eden, see ch. xxxi. 9. בְּצוּרוֹת is a circumstantial word belonging to יָשָׁבוּ: they shall be inhabited as fortified cities, that is to say, shall afford to their inhabitants the security of fortresses, from which there is no fear of their being expelled. In ver. 36 the expression, "the heathen nations which shall be left round about you," presupposes that at the time of Israel's redemption the judgment will have fallen upon the heathen (compare ch. xxx. 3 with ch. xxix. 21), so that only a remnant of them will be still in existence; and this remnant will recognise the work of Jehovah in the restoration of Israel. This recognition, however, does not involve the conversion of the heathen to Jehovah, but is simply preparatory to it. For the fact itself, compare ch. xvii. 24. הִדָּרֵשׁ, to let oneself be asked or entreated, as in ch. xiv. 3. זֹאת, with regard to this, is explained by לַעֲשׂוֹת לָהֶם. What God will do follows in אַרְבֶּה וגו׳. God will multiply His people to such an extent, that they will resemble the flock of lambs, sheep, and goats brought to Jerusalem to sacrifice upon the feast days. Compare 2 Chron. xxxv. 7, where Josiah is said to have given to the people thirty thousand lambs and goats for the feast of the passover. כַּצֹּאן אָדָם does not mean, like a flock of men. אָדָם cannot be a genitive dependent upon צֹאן, on account of the article in כַּצֹּאן, but belongs to אַרְבֶּה, either as a supplementary apposition to אֹתָם, or as a second object, so that אַרְבֶּה would be construed with a double accusative, after the analogy of verbs of plenty, to multiply them in men. Kliefoth's rendering, "I will multiply them, so that they shall be the flock of men" (of mankind), is grammatically untenable. צֹאן קָדָשִׁים, a flock of holy beasts, *i.e.* of sacrificial lambs. The flock of Jerusalem is the flock brought to Jerusalem at the yearly feasts, when the male population of the land came to the sanctuary (Deut. xvi. 16): So shall the desolate cities be filled again with flocks of men (compare Mic. ii. 12).

CHAP. XXXVII. RESURRECTION OF ISRAEL AND REUNION AS ONE NATION.

This chapter contains two revelations from God (vers. 1–14 and vers. 15–28). In the first, the prophet is shown in a vision the resurrection of Israel to a new life. In the second, he is commanded to exhibit, by means of a symbolical act, the reunion of the divided kingdoms into a single nation under one king. Both of these he is to announce to the children of Israel. The substantial connection between these two prophecies will be seen from the exposition.

Vers. 1–14. *Resurrection of Israel to new Life.*

Ver. 1. *There came upon me the hand of Jehovah, and Jehovah led me out in the spirit, and set me down in the midst of the valley; this was full of bones.* Ver. 2. *And He led me past them round about; and, behold, there were very many on the surface of the valley, and, behold, they were very dry.* Ver. 3. *And He said to me, Son of man, will these bones come to life? and I said, Lord, Jehovah, thou knowest.* Ver. 4. *Then He said to me, Prophesy over these bones, and say to them, Ye dry bones, hear ye the word of Jehovah.* Ver. 5. *Thus saith the Lord Jehovah to these bones, Behold, I bring breath into you, that ye may come to life.* Ver. 6. *I will create sinews upon you, and cause flesh to grow upon you, and cover you with skin, and bring breath into you, so that ye shall live and know that I am Jehovah.* Ver. 7. *And I prophesied as I was commanded; and there was a noise as I prophesied, and behold a rumbling, and the bones came together, bone to bone.* Ver. 8. *And I saw, and behold sinews came over them, and flesh grew, and skin drew over it above; but there was no breath in them.* Ver. 9. *Then He said to me, Prophesy to the breath, prophesy, son of man, and say to the breath, Thus saith the Lord Jehovah, Come from the four winds, thou breath, and blow upon these slain, that they may come to life.* Ver. 10. *And I prophesied as I was commanded;*

then the breath came into them, and they came to life, and stood upon their feet, a very, very great army. Ver. 11. *And He said to me, Son of man, these bones are the whole house of Israel; behold, they say, our bones are dried, and our hope has perished; we are destroyed!* Ver. 12. *Therefore prophesy, and say to them, Thus saith the Lord Jehovah, Behold, I will open your graves, and cause you to come out of your graves, my people, and bring you into the land of Israel.* Ver. 13. *And ye shall know that I am Jehovah, when I open your graves, and cause you to come out of your graves, my people.* Ver. 14. *And I will put my Spirit into you, and will place you in your land, and ye shall know that I, Jehovah, have spoken and do it, is the saying of Jehovah.*—This revelation divides itself into two sections. Vers. 1–10 contain the vision, and vers. 11–14 give the interpretation. There are no particular difficulties in the description of the vision, so far as the meaning of the words is concerned. By a supernatural intervention on the part of God, Ezekiel is taken from his own home in a state of spiritual ecstasy into a valley which was full of dead men's bones. For the expression הָיְתָה עָלַי יַד יי׳, see the comm. on ch. i. 3. In the second clause of ver. 1 יְהוָֹה is the subject, and is not to be taken as a genitive in connection with בְּרוּחַ, as it has been by the Vulgate and Hitzig in opposition to the accents. בְּרוּחַ stands for בְּרוּחַ אֱלֹהִים (ch. xi. 24), and אֱלֹהִים is omitted simply because יְהוָֹה follows immediately afterwards. הֵנִיחַ, to set down, here and ch. xl. 2; whereas in other cases the form הִנִּיחַ is usually employed in this sense. The article prefixed to הַבִּקְעָה appears to point back to ch. iii. 22, to the valley where Ezekiel received the first revelation concerning the fate of Jerusalem and its inhabitants. That עֲצָמִים are dead men's bones is evident from what follows. הֶעֱבִירַנִי עֲלֵיהֶם, not "He led me over them round about," but past them, in order that Ezekiel might have a clear view of them, and see whether it were possible for them to come to life again. They were lying upon the surface of the valley, *i.e.* not under, but upon the ground, and not piled up in a heap, but scattered over the valley, and they were very dry. The question asked by God, whether these bones could live, or come to life again, prepares the way for the miracle; and Ezekiel's answer, "Lord, Thou knowest" (cf. Rev. vii. 14), implies that, according to human judgment, it was inconceivable that they could come to life any more, and nothing but the omnipotence of God could effect this.—After this introduction there follows in vers. 4 sqq. the miracle of the raising to life of these very dry bones, accomplished through the medium of the word of God, which the prophet addresses to them, to show to the people that the power to realize itself is inherent in the word of Jehovah proclaimed by Ezekiel; in other words, that Jehovah possesses the power to accomplish whatever He promises to His people. The word in ver. 5, "Behold, I bring breath into you, that ye may come to life," announces in general terms the raising of them to life, whilst the process itself is more minutely described in ver. 6. God will put on them (clothe them with) sinews, flesh, and skin, and then put רוּחַ in them. רוּחַ is the animating spirit or breath = רוּחַ חַיִּים (Gen. vi. 17, vii. 17). קָרַם, ἀπ. λεγ. in Syriac *incrustare*, *obducere*. When Ezekiel prophesied there arose or followed a sound (קוֹל), and then a shaking (רַעַשׁ), and the bones approached one another, every bone to its own bone. Different explanations have been given of the words קוֹל and רַעַשׁ. קוֹל signifies a sound or voice, and רַעַשׁ a trembling, an earthquake, and also a rumbling or a loud noise (compare ch. iii. 12 and Isa. ix. 4). The relation between the two words as they stand here is certainly not that the sound (קוֹל) passes at once into a loud noise, or is continued in that form; whilst רַעַשׁ denotes the rattling or rustling of bones in motion. The fact that the moving of the bones toward one another is represented by וַתִּקְרְבוּ (with *Vav consec.*), as the sequel to רַעַשׁ, is decisive against this. Yet we cannot agree with Kliefoth, that by קוֹל we are to understand the trumpet-blast, or voice of God, that wakes the dead from their graves, according to those passages of the New Testament which treat of the resurrection, and by רַעַשׁ the earthquake which opens the graves. This explanation is precluded, not only by the philological difficulty that קוֹל without any further definition does not signify either the blast of a trumpet or the voice of God, but also by the circumstance that the קוֹל is the result of the prophesying of Ezekiel; and we cannot suppose that God would make His almighty call dependent upon a prophet's prophesying. And even in the case of רַעַשׁ, the reference to ch. xxxviii. 19 does not prove that the word must mean earthquake in this passage also, since Ezekiel uses the word in a different sense in ch. xii. 18 and iii. 12. We therefore take קוֹל in the general sense of a loud noise, and רַעַשׁ in the sense of shaking (*sc.* of the bones), which was occasioned by the loud noise, and produced, or was followed by, the movement of the bones to approach one another. The coming together of the bones was followed by their being clothed with sinews, flesh, and skin; but there was not yet any breath in them (ver. 8). To give them this the prophet is to prophesy again, and that to the breath, that it come from the four winds or quarters of the world and breathe into these slain (ver. 9). Then, when he prophesied, the breath came into them, so that they received life, and stood upright upon their feet. In vers. 9 and 10 רוּחַ is rendered by some "wind," by others "spirit;" but neither of these is in conformity with what precedes it. רוּחַ does not mean anything else than the breath of life, which has indeed a substratum in the wind, perceptible to the senses, but is not identical with it. The wind itself brings no life into dead bodies. If, therefore, the dead bodies become living, receive life through the blowing of the רוּחַ into them, what enters into them by the blowing cannot be a symbol of the breath of life, but must be the breath of life itself—namely, that divine breath of life which pervades all nature, giving and sustaining the life of all creatures (cf. Ps. civ. 29, 30). The expression פְּחִי בַּהֲרוּגִים points back to Gen. ii. 7. The representation of the bringing of the dead bones to life in two acts may also be explained from the fact that it is based upon the history of the creation of man in Gen. ii., as Theodoret[1] has observed, and serves plainly to depict the creative revivification here, like the first creation there, as a work of the almighty God. For a correct understanding of the vision, it is also necessary to observe that in ver. 9 the dead bones, clothed with sinews, flesh, and skin, are called הֲרוּגִים, slain, killed, and not merely dead. It is apparent at once from this that our vision is not intended to symbolize the resurrection of all the dead, but simply the raising up of the nation of Israel, which has been slain. This is borne out by the explanation of the vision which God gives to the prophet in vers. 11–14, and directs him to repeat to the people. The dead bones are the "whole house of Israel" that has been given up to death; in other words, Judah and Ephraim. "These bones" in ver. 11 are the same as in vers. 3 and 5, and not the bodies brought to life in ver. 10; though Hitzig maintains that they are the latter, and then draws the erroneous conclusion that vers. 11–14 do not interpret the vision of the first ten verses, but that the bones in the valley are simply explained in these verses as signifying the dead of Israel. It is true that the further explanation in ver. 12 sqq. of what is described in vers. 5–10 as happening to the dead bones is not given in the form of an exposition of the separate details of that occurrence, but is summed up in the announcement that God will open their graves, bring them out of their graves, and transport them to their own land. But it does not follow from this that the announcement is merely an application of the vision to the restoration of Israel to new life, and therefore that something different is represented from what is announced in vers. 12–14. Such a view is at variance with the words, "these bones are the whole house of Israel." Even if these words are not to be taken so literally as that we are to under-

[1] "For as the body of our forefather Adam was first moulded, and then the soul was thus breathed into it; so here also both combined in fitting harmony."—THEODORET.

stand that the prophet was shown in the vision the bones of the slain and deceased Israelites, but simply mean: these dead bones represent the house of Israel, depict the nation of Israel in its state of death,—they express so much in the clearest terms concerning the relation in which the explanation in vers. 12–14 stands to the visionary occurrence in vers. 4–10, namely, that God has shown to Ezekiel in the vision what He commands him to announce concerning Israel in vers. 12–14; in other words, that the bringing of the dead bones to life shown to him in the vision was intended to place visibly before him the raising of the whole nation of Israel to new life out of the death into which it had fallen. This is obvious enough from the words: these bones are the whole house of Israel. כָּל־בֵּית יִשְׂרָאֵל points forward to the reunion of the tribes of Israel that are severed into two nations, as foretold in vers. 15 sqq. It is they who speak in ver. 11*b*. The subject to אֹמְרִים is neither the bones nor the dead of Israel (Hitzig), but the כָּל־בֵּית יִשְׂרָאֵל already named, which is also addressed in ver. 12. All Israel says: our bones are dried, *i.e.* our vital force is gone. The bones are the seat of the vital force, as in Ps. xxxii. 3; and יָבֵשׁ, to dry up, applied to the marrow, or vital sap of the bones, is substantially the same as בָּלָה in the psalm (*l.c.*). Our hope has perished (cf. ch. xix. 5). תִּקְוָה is here the hope of rising into a nation once more. נִגְזַרְנוּ לָנוּ: literally, we are cut off for ourselves, *sc.* from the sphere of the living (cf. Lam. iii. 54; Isa. liii. 8), equivalent to "it is all over with us."

To the people speaking thus, Ezekiel is to announce that the Lord will open their graves, bring them out of them, put His breath of life into them, and lead them into their own land. If we observe the relation in which vers. 12 and 13 stand to ver. 14, namely, that the two halves of the 14th verse are parallel to the two verses 12 and 13, the clause וִידַעְתֶּם כִּי אֲנִי יי' in ver. 14*b* to the similar clause in ver. 13, there can be no doubt that the contents of ver. 14*a* also correspond to those of ver. 12—that is to say, that the words, "I put my breath

(Spirit) into you, that ye may live, and place you in your own land" (bring you to rest therein), affirm essentially the same as the words, "I bring you out of your graves, and lead you into the land of Israel;" with this simple difference, that the bringing out of the graves is explained and rendered more emphatic by the more definite idea of causing them to live through the breath or Spirit of God put into them, and the הֵבִיא by הֵנִיחַ, the leading into the land by the transporting and bringing them to rest therein. Consequently we are not to understand by נָתַתִּי רוּחִי בָּכֶם either a divine act differing from the raising of the dead to life, or the communication of the Holy Spirit as distinguished from the imparting of the breath of life. רוּחִי, the Spirit of Jehovah, is identical with the רוּחַ, which comes, according to vers. 9 and 10, into the bones of the dead when clothed with sinews, flesh, and skin, *i.e.* is breathed into them. This spirit or breath of life is the creative principle both of the physical and of the ethical or spiritual life. Consequently there are not three things announced in these verses, but only two: (1) The raising to life from a state of death, by bringing out of the graves, and communicating the divine Spirit of life; (2) the leading back to their own land to rest quietly therein. When, therefore, Kliefoth explains these verses as signifying that for the consolation of Israel, which is mourning hopelessly in its existing state of death, "God directs the prophet to say—(1) That at some future time it will experience a resurrection in the literal sense, that its graves will be opened, and that all its dead, those deceased with those still alive, will be raised up out of their graves; (2) that God will place them in their own land; and (3) that when He has so placed them in their land, He will put His Spirit within them that they may live: in the first point the idea of the future resurrection, both of those deceased and of those still living, is interpolated into the text; and in the third point, placing them in their land before they are brought to life by the Spirit of God, would be at variance with the text, according to which the giving of the Spirit precedes the removal to their own land. The repetition of עַמִּי in vers. 12 and 13 is also worthy of notice: you who are my people, which bases the comforting promise upon the fact that Israel is the people of Jehovah.

If, therefore, our vision does not set forth the resurrection of the dead in general, but simply the raising to life of the nation of Israel which is given up to death, it is only right that, in order still further to establish this view, we should briefly examine the other explanations that have been given.—The Fathers and most of the orthodox commentators, both of ancient and modern times, have found in vers. 1–10 a *locus classicus* for the doctrine of the resurrection of the dead, and that quite correctly. But their views differ widely as to the strict meaning and design of the vision itself; inasmuch as some regard the vision as a direct and immediate prophecy of the general resurrection of the dead at the last day, whilst others take the raising of the dead to life shown to the prophet in the vision to be merely a figure or type of the waking up to new life of the Israel which is now dead in its captivity. The first view is mentioned by Jerome; but in later times it has been more especially defended by Calov, and last of all most decidedly by Kliefoth. Yet the supporters of this view acknowledge that vers. 11–14 predict the raising to life of the nation of Israel. The question arises, therefore, how this prediction is to be brought into harmony with such an explanation of the vision. The persons noticed by Jerome, who supported the view that in vers. 4–10 it is the general resurrection that is spoken of, sought to remove the difficulties to which this explanation is exposed, by taking the words, "these bones are the whole house of Israel," as referring to the resurrection of the saints, and connecting them with the first resurrection in Rev. xx. 5, and by interpreting the leading of Israel back to their own land as equivalent to the inheriting of the earth mentioned in Matt. v. 5. Calov, on the other hand, gives the following explanation of the relation in which vers. 11–14 stand to vers. 1–10: "In this striking vision there was shown by the Lord to the prophet the resurrection of the dead; but the *occasion*, the *cause*, and the *scope* of this vision were the *resurrection of the Israelitish people*, not so much into its earlier political form, as for the restoration of the ecclesiastical hierarchy and the establishment of the worship of God, both of which were indeed restored in the time of Zerubbabel, but were first brought to perfection at the coming of Jesus Christ." He also assumes that the raising of the dead is represented in the vision, "because God would have this representation exhibited for a *figure and confirmation* of the restitution of the people." And lastly, according to Kliefoth, vers. 11–14 do not furnish a literal exposition of the vision, but simply make an application of it to the bringing of Israel to life.—We cannot regard either of these views as correct, because neither of them does justice to the words of the text. The idea of the Fathers, that vers. 11–14 treat of the resurrection of the saints (believers), cannot be reconciled either with the words or with the context of our prophecy, and has evidently originated in perplexity. And the assumption of Calov and Kliefoth, that vers. 11–14 contain simply an application of the general resurrection of the dead exhibited in vers. 1–10 to the resurrection of Israel, by no means exhausts the meaning of the words, "these bones are the whole house of Israel," as we have already observed in our remarks on ver. 11. Moreover, in the vision itself there are certain features to be found which do not apply to the general resurrection of the dead. In proof of this, we will not lay any stress upon the circumstance that Ezekiel sees the resurrection of the dead within certain limits; that it is only the dead men's bones lying about in one particular valley, and not the dead of the whole earth, though a very great army, that he sees come to life again; but, on the other hand, we must press the fact that in ver. 9 those who are to be raised to life are called הֲרוּגִים, a word which does not signify the dead of all kinds, but simply those who have been slain, or have perished by the sword, by famine, or by other violent deaths, and which indisputably proves that Ezekiel was not shown the resurrection of all the dead, but simply the raising to life of Israel, which had been swept away by a violent death. Kliefoth would account for this restriction from the purpose for which the vision was shown to the prophet. Because the design of the vision was to comfort Israel concerning the wretchedness of its existing condition, and that wretchedness consisted for the most part in the fact that the greater portion of Israel had perished by sword, famine, and pestilence, he was shown the resurrection of the dead generally and universally, as it would take place not in the case of the Israelites alone, but in that of all the dead, though here confined within the limits of one particular field of dead; and stress is laid upon the circumstance that the dead which Ezekiel saw raised to life *instar omnium*, were such as had met with a violent death. This explanation would be admissible, if only it had been indicated or expressed in any way whatever, that the bones of the dead which Ezekiel saw lying about in the בִּקְעָה represented all the dead of the whole earth. But we find no such indication; and because in the whole vision there is not a single feature contained which would warrant any such generalization of the field of the dead which Ezekiel saw, we are constrained to affirm that the dead men's bones seen by Ezekiel in the valley represent the whole house of Israel alone, and not the deceased and slain of all mankind; and that the vision does not set forth the resurrection of all the dead, but only the raising to life of the nation of Israel which had been given up to death.

Consequently we can only regard the figurative view of the vision as the correct one, though this also has been adopted in very different ways. When Jerome says that Ezekiel "is prophesying of the restoration of Israel through the parable of the resurrection," and in order to defend himself from the charge of denying the dogma of the resurrection of the dead, adds that "the similitude of a resurrection would never have been employed to exhibit the restoration of the Israelitish people, if that resurrection had been a delusion, and it had not been believed that it would really take place; because no one confirms uncertain things by means of things which have no existence;"—Hävernick very justly replies, that the resurrection of the dead is not to be so absolutely regarded as a dogma already completed and defined, or as one universally known and having its roots in the national belief; though Hävernick is wrong in affirming in support of this that the despair of the people described in ver. 11 plainly shows that so general a belief cannot possibly be presupposed. For we find just the same despair at times when faith in the resurrection of the dead was a universally accepted dogma. The principal error connected with this view is the assumption that the vision was merely a parable formed by Ezekiel in accordance with the dogma of the resurrection of the dead. If, on the contrary, the vision was a spiritual intuition produced by God in the soul of the prophet, it might set forth the resurrection of the dead, even if the belief in this dogma had no existence as yet in the consciousness of the people, or at all events was not yet a living faith; and God might have shown to the prophet the raising of Israel to life under this figure, for the purpose of awakening this belief in Israel.[1] In that case, however, the vision was not merely a parable, but a symbolical representation of a real fact, which was to serve as a pledge to the nation of

[1] No conclusive evidence can be adduced that the doctrine of the resurrection of the dead was not only known to Ezekiel, but was regarded by the people as indisputably sure, as both Hengstenberg (*Christology*, vol. III. p. 51, transl.) and Pareau (*Comment. de immortal.* p. 109) assume. Such passages as Isa. xxv. 8 and xxvi. 19, even if Ezekiel referred to them, merely prove that the belief or hope of the resurrection of the dead could not be altogether unknown to the believers of Israel, because Isaiah had already declared it. But the obvious announcement of this dogma in Dan. xii. 2 belongs to a later period than our vision; and even Daniel does not speak of it as a belief that prevailed throughout the nation, but simply communicates it as a consolation offered by the angel of the Lord in anticipation of the times of severe calamity awaiting the people of God.

its restoration to life. Theodoret comes much nearer to the truth when he gives the following as his explanation of the vision: that "on account of the unbelief of the Jews in exile, who were despairing of their restoration, the almighty God makes known His might; and the resurrection of the dead bodies, which was much more difficult than their restoration, is shown to the prophet, in order that all the nation may be taught thereby that everything is easy to His will;"[1] and when, accordingly, he calls what occurs in the vision "a type not of the calling to life of the Jews only, but also of the resurrection of all men." The only defect in this is, that Theodoret regards the dead bones which are brought to life too much as a figurative representation of any dead whatever, and thereby does justice neither to the words, "these bones are the whole house of Israel," which he paraphrases by *τύπος τοῦ 'Ισραὴλ ταῦτα*, nor to the designation applied to them as הֲרוּגִים, though it may fairly be pleaded as a valid excuse so far as הרוגים is concerned, that the force of this word has been completely neutralized in the Septuagint, upon which he was commenting, by the rendering *τοὺς νεκροὺς τούτους*.—Hävernick has interpreted the vision in a much more abstract manner, and evaporated it into the general idea of a symbolizing of the creative, life-giving power of God, which can raise even the bones of the dead to life again. His exposition is the following: "There is no express prediction of the resurrection in these words, whether of a general resurrection or of the particular resurrection of Israel; but this is only thought of here, inasmuch as it rests upon the creative activity of God, to which even such a conquest of death as this is possible."[2]

[1] His words are these: *ἐπειδὴ γὰρ δι' ἣν ἐνόσουν ἀπιστίαν τὰς χρηστοτέρας ἀπηγόρευσαν ἐλπίδας οἱ ἐκ τῆς 'Ιουδαίας αἰχμάλωται γενόμενοι, τὴν οἰκείαν αὐτοῖς ὁ τῶν ὅλων Θεὸς ἐπιδείκνυσι δύναμιν, καὶ τὴν πολλῷ τῆς ἀνακλήσεως ἐκείνης δυσκολωτέραν τῶν νεκρῶν σωμάτων ἀνάστασιν ἐπιδείκνυσι τῷ προφήτῃ καὶ δι' ἐκείνου πάντα διδάσκει τὸν λαὸν, ὡς πάντα αὐτῷ ῥᾴδια βουλομένῳ.*

[2] The view expressed by Hofmann (*Schriftbeweis*, II. 2, pp. 507 sqq.) is a kindred one, namely, that it is not the future resurrection of the dead, or

The calling to life of the thoroughly dried dead bones shown to the prophet in the vision, is a figure or visible representation of that which the Lord announces to him in vers. 11–14, namely, that He will bring Israel out of its graves, give it life with His breath, and bring it into its own land; and consequently a figure of the raising of Israel to life from its existing state of death. The opening of the graves is also a figure; for those whom the Lord will bring out of their graves are they who say, "Our bones are dried," etc. (ver. 11), and therefore not those who are deceased, nor even the spiritually dead, but those who have lost all hope of life. We are not, however, to understand by this merely *mors civilis* and *vita civilis*, as Grotius has done. For Israel was destroyed, not only politically as a nation, but spiritually as a church of the Lord, through the destruction of its two kingdoms and its dispersion among the heathen; and in a very large number of its members it had also been given up to the power of physical death and sunk into the grave. Even then, if we keep out of sight those who were deceased, Israel, as the people of God, was slain (הֲרוּג), without any hope of coming to life again, or a resurrection to new life. But the Lord now shows the prophet this resurrection under the figure of the raising to life of the very dry bones that lie scattered all around. This is fulfilled through the restoration of Israel as the people of Jehovah, to which the leading of the people back into the land of Israel essentially belongs. The way was opened and prepared for this fulfilment by the return of a portion of the people from the Babylonian captivity under Zerubbabel and Ezra, which was

the resurrection of the deceased Israelites, which is indicated in the vision, and that it does not even set forth to view the unconditioned power of God over death, or an idea which is intended as a pledge of the resurrection of the dead; but that by the revelation made manifest to the prophet in the state of ecstasy, the completeness of that state of death out of which Israel is to be restored is exhibited, and thus the truth is set before his eyes that the word of prophecy has the inherent power to ensure its own fulfilment, even when Israel is in a condition which bears precisely the same resemblance to a nation as the state of death to a human being.

brought to pass by the Lord, by the rebuilding of the cities of Judah and the temple which had been destroyed, and by the restoration of political order. But all this was nothing more than a pledge of the future and complete restoration of Israel. For although the Lord still raised up prophets for those who had returned and furthered the building of His house, His glory did not enter the newly erected temple, and the people never attained to independence again,—that is to say, not to permanent independence,—but continued in subjection to the imperial power of the heathen. And even if, according to Ezra, very many more of the exiles may have returned to their native land, by whom, for example, Galilee was repopulated and brought into cultivation again, the greater portion of the nation remained dispersed among the heathen. The true restoration of Israel as the people of the Lord commenced with the founding of the new kingdom of God, the "kingdom of heaven," through the appearing of Christ upon the earth. But inasmuch as the Jewish nation as such, or in its entirety, did not acknowledge Jesus Christ as the Messiah foretold by the prophets and sent by God, but rejected its Saviour, there burst afresh upon Jerusalem and the Jewish nation the judgment of dispersion among the heathen; whereas the kingdom of God founded by Christ spread over the earth, through the entrance of believers from among the Gentiles. This judgment upon the Jewish people, which is hardened in unbelief, still continues, and will continue until the time when the full number of the Gentiles has entered into the kingdom of God, and Israel as a people shall also be converted to Christ, acknowledge the crucified One as its Saviour, and bow the knee before Him (Rom. xi. 25, 26). Then will "all Israel" be raised up out of its graves, the graves of its political and spiritual death, and brought back into its own land, which will extend as far as the Israel of God inhabits the earth. Then also will the hour come in which all the dead will hear the voice of the Son of God, and come forth out of their graves to the resurrection (Dan.

xii. 2; John v. 25–29); when the Lord shall appear in His glory, and descend from heaven with the trump of God (1 Thess. iv. 16), to call all the dead to life, and through the judgment upon all the nations to perfect His kingdom in glory, and bring the righteous into the Canaan of the new earth, into the heavenly Jerusalem, to the imperishable life of everlasting blessedness.

All these several factors in the restoration of Israel, which has been given up to the death of exile on account of its sins, though far removed from one another, so far as the time of their occurrence is concerned, are grouped together as one in the vision of the coming to life of the dead bones of the whole house of Israel. The two features which are kept distinct in the visionary description—namely, (1) the coming together of the dry bones, and their being clothed with sinews, flesh, and skin; and (2) the bringing to life of the bones, which have now the form of corpses, through the divine breath of life—are not to be distinguished in the manner proposed by Hengstenberg, namely, that the first may be taken as referring to the restoration of the civil condition—the external *restitutio in integrum;* the second, to the giving of new life through the outpouring of the Spirit of God.—Even according to our view, the vision contains a prophecy of the resurrection of the dead, only not in this sense, that the doctrine of the general resurrection of the dead is the premiss, or the design, or the direct meaning of the vision; but that the figurative meaning constitutes the foreground, and the full, literal meaning of the words the background of the prophetic vision, and that the fulfilment advances from the figurative to the literal meaning,—the raising up of the people of Israel out of the civil and spiritual death of exile being completed in the raising up of the dead out of their graves to everlasting life at the last day.

Vers. 15–28. *Reunion of Israel as one Nation under the future King David.*

This word of God directs the prophet to represent by a sign the reunion of the tribes of Israel, which have been divided into two kingdoms (vers. 15–17), and to explain this sign to the people (vers. 18–21), and predict its sanctification and blessedness under the reign of the future David (vers. 22–28). What is new in this word of God is the express prediction, embodied in a symbolical action, of the reunion of the divided tribes of Israel into one single people of God, which has been already hinted at in the promise of the raising to life of "the whole house of Israel" (ver. 11). This brief indication is here plainly expressed and more fully developed.

Ver. 15. *And the word of Jehovah came to me, saying,* Ver. 16. *And thou, son of man, take to thyself a piece of wood, and write upon it: Of Judah, and the sons of Israel, his associates; and take another piece of wood, and write upon it: Of Joseph, the wood of Ephraim, and the whole house of Israel, his associates;* Ver. 17. *And put them together, one to the other, into one piece of wood to thee, that they may be united in thy hand.* Ver. 18. *And when the sons of thy people say to thee, Wilt thou not show us what thou meanest by this?* Ver. 19. *Say to them, Thus saith the Lord Jehovah, Behold, I will take the wood of Joseph, which is in the hand of Ephraim, and the tribes of Israel, his associates, which I put thereon, with the wood of Judah, and will make them into one stick, that they may be one in my hand.* Ver. 20. *And the pieces of wood upon which thou hast written shall be in thy hand before their eyes.* Ver. 21. *And say to them, Thus saith the Lord Jehovah, Behold, I will take the sons of Israel out of the nations among whom they walk, and will gather them from round about, and lead them into their land.* Ver. 22. *I will make them into one nation in the land, upon the mountains of Israel, and one king shall be king over them all; and it shall not become two nations any more, and they shall not henceforth be divided into two kingdoms any more;* Ver. 23. *And shall not defile themselves by their idols and their abominations, and by all their transgressions; but I will help them from all their dwelling-places, in which they have sinned, and will cleanse them; so that they shall be my people, and I will be their God.* Ver. 24. *And my servant David will be king over them, and be a shepherd for them all; and they will walk in my rights, and keep my statutes and do them.* Ver. 25. *And they will dwell in the land which I gave to my servant Jacob, in which their fathers dwelt; there will they dwell, and their children's children for ever; and my servant David will be a prince to them for ever.* Ver. 26. *And I make a covenant of peace with them for ever, an everlasting covenant shall be with them; and I will place them, and multiply them, and put my sanctuary in the midst of them for ever.* Ver. 27. *And my dwelling will be over them; I will be their God, and they will be my people.* Ver. 28. *And the nation shall know that I am Jehovah, who sanctifieth Israel, when my sanctuary shall be in the midst of them for ever.*

The symbolical action commanded in vers. 16 and 17, which the prophet no doubt performed in all its external reality (cf. vers. 19 and 20), is easily understood, and expresses the thing to be represented in the clearest manner. The writing of the names of the tribes composing the two kingdoms recalls to mind the similar act on the part of Moses (Num. xvii. 17 sqq.). But the act itself is a different one here, and neither the passage referred to nor Ezek. xxi. 15 furnishes any proof that עֵץ signifies a staff or rod. Ezekiel would undoubtedly have used מַטֶּה for a staff. Nor have we even to think of flat boards, but simply of pieces of wood upon which a few words could be written, and which could be held in one hand. The לְ before the names to be written upon each piece of wood is the sign of the genitive, indicating to whom it belongs, as in the case of the heading to David's psalms (לְדָוִד). This is evident from the fact that in עֵץ אֶפְרַיִם the construct state is used instead. The name is to indicate that the piece of wood belongs to Judah or

Ephraim, and represents it. The command to Ezekiel to write upon one piece of wood, not only Judah, but "the sons of Israel, his associates," arose from the circumstance that the kingdom of Judah included, in addition to the tribe of Judah, the greater portion of Benjamin and Simeon, the tribe of Levi and those pious Israelites who emigrated at different times from the kingdom of the ten tribes into that of Judah, who either were or became associates of Judah (2 Chron. xi. 12 sqq., xv. 9, xxx. 11, 18, xxxi. 1). In the writing upon the second piece of wood, עֵץ אֶפְרַיִם is an explanatory apposition to לְיוֹסֵף, and an accusative governed by כְּתֹב. But the command is not to be understood as signifying that Ezekiel was to write the words עץ אפרים upon the piece of wood; all that he was to write was, "Joseph and the whole house of Israel, his associates." The name of Joseph is chosen, in all probability, not as the more honourable name, as Hävernick supposes, but because the house of Joseph, consisting of the two powerful tribes of Ephraim and Manasseh, formed the trunk of the kingdom of the ten tribes (Kliefoth). The "whole house of Israel, his associates," are the rest of the tribes belonging to that kingdom. The two pieces of wood, with these inscriptions upon them, Ezekiel is to put together, and hold in his hand bound together in one. מָה־אֵלֶּה לָּךְ, what these (two pieces of wood) are to thee, is equivalent to, what thou meanest to indicate by them. For the rest, compare ch. xxiv. 19. In the word of God explaining the action (ver. 19), the wood of Joseph is not the piece of wood with Joseph's name written upon it, but the kingdom represented by this piece of wood which was in Ephraim's hand, inasmuch as the hegemony was with the tribe of Ephraim. Instead of the wood, therefore, the tribes (not staffs) of Israel, *i.e.* the Israelites who constituted these tribes, are mentioned as his associates. God will put these upon the wood of Joseph (עָלָיו), *i.e.* will join them together, and then place them with the wood of Judah, *i.e.* the kingdom of Judah, and unite them into one wood (or nation).

אֶת־עֵץ יְהוּדָה, the construction of which has been misunderstood by Hitzig, is neither in apposition to עָלָיו, nor governed by נָתַתִּי: "and will put them thereupon, upon the wood of Judah" (Hitzig and Kliefoth), or, "I add them to it, (namely) with the wood of Judah" (De Wette); but it is dependent upon לֹקֵחַ, "I take the wood of Joseph . . . and the tribes of Israel, his associates, which I put thereon, along with the wood of Judah, and make them into one wood." The construction is rendered obscure simply by the fact that the relative clause, "which I put thereon," is attached to the principal clause אֲנִי לֹקֵחַ וגו׳ by *Vav consec.* In בְּיָדִי, "they shall be one *in my hand*," there is probably an antithesis to בְּיַד אֶפְרַיִם, those who have come into Ephraim's hand, the tribes severed by Ephraim from the kingdom of God, will God once more bring together with Judah, and hold in His hand as an undivided nation.—In ver. 20 the description of the sign is completed by the additional statement, that the pieces of wood on which the prophet has written are to be in his hand before their eyes, and consequently that the prophet is to perform the act in such a way that his countrymen may see it; from which it follows that he performed it in its outward reality. The fulfilment of the instructions is not specially mentioned, as being self-evident; but in vers. 21–28 the further explanation of the symbolical action is given at once; and the interpretation goes beyond the symbol, inasmuch as it not only describes the manner in which God will effect the union of the divided tribes, but also what He will do for the preservation of the unity of the reunited people, and for the promotion of their blessedness. This explanation is arranged in two strophes through the repetition of the concluding thought: "they will be my people," etc., in vers. 23 and 27. Each of these strophes contains a twofold promise. The first (vers. 21–23) promises (*a*) the gathering of the Israelites out of their dispersion, their restoration to their own land, and their union as one nation under the rule of David (vers. 21, 22); (*b*) their purification from all sins, and sanctification as the true people of the Lord (ver. 23). The second strophe (vers. 24–27) promises (*a*) their undisturbed eternal abode in the land, under David their prince (ver. 25); (*b*) the blessedness conferred upon them through the conclusion of an everlasting covenant of peace (vers. 26 and 27). This second promise, therefore, constitutes the completion of the first, securing to the nation of Israel its restoration and sanctification for all time. The whole promise, however, is merely a repetition of that contained in ch. xxxiv. 11–31 and xxxvi. 22–30. —The three factors—the gathering out of the nations, restoration to the land of Israel, and reunion as one people—form the first act of divine grace. The union of the Israelites, when brought back to their land, is accomplished by God giving them in David a king who will so rule the reunited people that they will not be divided any more into two peoples and two kingdoms. The *Chetib* יִהְיֶה is not to be altered into the plural יִהְיוּ, as in the *Keri;* but גּוֹי is to be supplied in thought, from the preceding clause, as the súbject to the verb. The division of the nation into two kingdoms had its roots, no doubt, in the ancient jealousy existing between the two tribes Ephraim and Judah; but it was primarily brought to pass through the falling away of Solomon from the Lord. Consequently it could only be completely and for ever terminated through the righteous government of the second David, and the purification of the people from their sins. This is the way in which ver. 23 is attached to ver. 22. For ver. 23*a* compare ch. xiv. 11 and xxxvi. 25. Different interpretations have been given of the words, "I help them from all their dwelling-places, in which they have sinned." They recall to mind ch. xxxvi. 29, "I help them from all their uncleannesses." As הוֹשִׁיעַ מִן signifies, in that case, "to preserve therefrom," so in the present instance the thought can only be, "God will preserve them from all the dwelling-places in which they have sinned." Hengstenberg is of opinion that the redemption from the dwelling-places does not take place locally, but spiritually, through the cleansing away of all traces of sin, first from the hearts, and then, in consequence, from all around. In this way is the land changed, through the power of the Lord, into another land, from a sinful to a holy one; just as before it had been changed from a holy to a sinful one through the guilt of the people. But if this were the only thought which the words contained, Ezekiel would certainly have placed the וְטִהַרְתִּי אוֹתָם before וְהוֹשַׁעְתִּי וגו׳. As the words read, the deliverance of the people from their sinful dwelling-places is to precede their purification, to prepare the way for it and bring it to pass, and not to follow after it. The dwelling-places, at or in which they have sinned, cannot be the settlements in foreign lands, as Hitzig supposes, but only the dwelling-places in Canaan, to which the Lord would bring them after gathering them from their dispersion. הוֹשַׁע does not signify, "leading out from these dwelling-places," which is the explanation given by Kliefoth, who consequently thinks that we must understand the words as denoting the leading over of Israel from the present Canaan, or the Canaan of this life, to which its sins adhere, to the glorified, new, and eternal Canaan. This view is utterly irreconcilable both with the words themselves and also with the context. Even if הוֹשַׁע meant to lead out, it would not be allowable to transform the "leading out" from the sinful Canaan into a "leading in" to the glorified and heavenly Canaan. Moreover, the further development of this promise in ver. 25 also shows that it is not in the glorified, eternal Canaan that Israel is to dwell, but in the earthly Canaan in which its fathers dwelt. It is obvious from this, that in all the promise here given there is no allusion to a transformation and glorification of Canaan itself. The helping or saving from all dwelling-places in which they have sinned would rather consist in the fact, therefore, that God would remove from their dwelling-places everything that could offer them an inducement to sin. For although sin has its seat, not in the things without us, but in the heart, the external circumstances of a man do offer various inducements to sin.

Before the captivity, Canaan offered such an inducement to the Israelites through the idolatry and moral corruption of the Canaanites who were left in the land. And with reference to this the Lord promises that in future, when His people are brought back to Canaan, He will preserve them from the sinful influence of their dwelling-places. But this preservation will only be effected with complete success when God purifies Israel itself, and, by means of its renovation, eradicates all sinful desire from the heart (cf. ch. xxxvi. 26, 27). In this way וְטִהַרְתִּי is appended in the most fitting way to וְהוֹשַׁעְתִּי וגו׳.—Through the removal of all sinful influences from around them, and the purifying of the heart, Israel will then become in truth the people of God, and Jehovah the God of Israel (ver. 23).—Israel, when thus renewed, will walk in the rights of the Lord and fulfil His commandments, under the protection of its one shepherd David, *i.e.* of the Messiah (ver. 24, cf. ch. xxxvi. 27, and xxxiv. 23); and its children and children's children will dwell for ever in its own land, David being its prince for ever (ver. 25, cf. ch. xxxvi. 28 and xxxiv. 24). What is new in this promise, which is repeated from ch. xxxiv. and xxxvi., is contained in לְעוֹלָם, which is to be taken in the strict sense of the word. Neither the dwelling of Israel in Canaan, nor the government of the David-Messiah, will ever have an end. לְעוֹלָם is therefore repeated in ver. 26 in the promise of the covenant which the Lord will make with His people. The thought itself has already been expressed in ch. xxxiv. 25, and בְּרִית שָׁלוֹם is to be understood, both here and there, as comprehending all the saving good which the Lord will bestow upon His sanctified people. There are only two factors of this salvation mentioned here in vers. 26*b* and 27, namely, the multiplication of the people, as the earthly side of the divine blessing, and the establishing of His eternal sanctuary in the midst of them as the spiritual side. These two points refer back to the former acts of God, and hold up to view the certain and full realization in the future of what has hitherto been neither perfectly nor permanently accomplished on account of the sins of the people. וְנָתַתִּים, in ver. 26, is not to be taken in connection with וְהִרְבֵּיתִי אוֹתָם, so as to form one idea in the sense of *dabo eos multiplicatos* (Venema and Hengstenberg), for we have no analogies of such a mode of combination; but נְתַתִּים, I make, or place them, is to be taken by itself, and completed from the context, "I make them into a nation, and I multiply them (cf. ch. xxxvi. 10, 11, 37). Ezekiel has here Lev. xxvi. 9 and 11 in his mind, as we may see from the fact that the words, "I give my sanctuary in the midst of them for ever," are obviously formed after Lev. xxvi. 11, "I give my dwelling in the midst of them;" in such a manner, however, that by the substitution of מִקְדָּשִׁי for מִשְׁכָּנִי, and the addition of לְעוֹלָם, the promise is both deepened and strengthened. In the change of מִשְׁכָּנִי into מִקְדָּשִׁי, he may indeed have had the words of Ex. xxv. 8 floating before his mind, "they shall make me a sanctuary, that I may dwell among them;" nevertheless he deliberately selected the expression "my sanctuary," to indicate that the Lord would dwell in the midst of Israel as the Holy One, and the Sanctifier of His people. Moreover, the words are not, "my dwelling will be in the midst of them, or among them" (בְּתוֹכָם), but עֲלֵיהֶם, over them. This expression is transferred from the site of the temple, towering above the city (Ps. lxviii. 30), to the dwelling of God among His people, to give prominence to the protective power and saving grace of the God who rules in Israel (cf. Hengstenberg on Ps. lxviii. 30). The sanctuary which Jehovah will give in Israel for ever, *i.e.* will found and cause to endure, that He may dwell in the midst of it to shelter and bless, is the temple, but not the temple built by Zerubbabel. As an objection to this Jewish interpretation, Jerome has justly said: "but how could it be said to stand '*for ever*,' when that temple which was built in the time of Zerubbabel, and afterwards restored by many others, was consumed by Roman fire? All these things are to be taken as referring to the church in the time of the Saviour, when His tabernacle was placed in the church." There is no reference whatever here to the rebuilding of the temple by Zerubbabel; not because that temple did not stand for ever and was destroyed by the Romans, but chiefly because God did not make it His abode, or fill this temple with His gracious presence (Shechinah). The sanctuary which God will place for ever among His people is the sanctuary seen by Ezekiel in ch. xl. sqq.; and this is merely a figurative representation of the "dwelling of God in the midst of His people through His Son and Holy Spirit" (cf. Vitringa, *Observv.* I. p. 161), which began to be realized in the incarnation of the Logos, who is set forth in John i. 14 as the true מִשְׁכָּן, in the words ἐσκήνωσεν ἐν ἡμῖν, and is continued in the spiritual dwelling of God in the heart of believers (1 Cor. iii. 16, vi. 19), and will be completed at the second coming of our Lord in the "tabernacle (σκηνή) of God with men" of the new Jerusalem, of which the Lord God Almighty and the Lamb are the temple, since Israel will then first have become in truth the people of God, and Jehovah (God with them) their God (Rev. xxi. 3, 22).—The promise concludes in ver. 28 with an allusion to the impression which these acts of God in Israel will make upon the heathen (cf. ch. xxxvi. 36). From the fact that Jehovah erects His sanctuary in the midst of Israel for ever, they will learn that it is He who sanctifieth Israel. קִדֵּשׁ, to sanctify, means, "to remove from all connection either with sin or with its consequences. Here the reference is to the latter, because these alone strike the eyes of the heathen; but the former is presupposed as the necessary foundation" (Hengstenberg). The words rest upon the promises of the Pentateuch, where God describes Himself as He who will and does sanctify Israel (compare Ex. xxxi. 13; Lev. xxii. 31–33). This promise, which has hitherto been only imperfectly fulfilled on account of Israel's guilt, will be perfectly realized in the future, when Israel will walk in the ways of the Lord, renewed by the Spirit of God.

Thus does this prophecy of Ezekiel span the whole future of

the people of God even to eternity. But the promise in which it culminates, namely, that the Lord will erect His sanctuary in the midst of His restored people, and there take up His abode above them for ever (ch. xxxvii. 26 sqq.), is of importance as helping to decide the question, how we are to understand the fulfilment of the restoration to Canaan into the land given to the fathers, which is promised to all Israel; whether, in a literal manner, by the restoration of the Israelites to Palestine; or spiritually, by the gathering together of the Israelites converted to the Lord their God and Saviour, and their introduction into the kingdom of God founded by Christ, in which case Canaan, as the site of the Old Testament kingdom of God, would be a symbolical or typical designation of the earthly soil of the heavenly kingdom, which has appeared in the Christian church. —These two different views have stood opposed to one another from time immemorial, inasmuch as the Jews expect from the Messiah, for whose advent they still hope, not only their restoration to Palestine, but the erection of the kingdom of David and the rebuilding of the temple upon Mount Zion, together with the sacrificial worship of the Levitical law; whereas in the Christian church, on the ground of the New Testament doctrine, that the old covenant has been abolished along with the Levitical temple-worship through the perfect fulfilment of the law by Christ and the perpetual efficacy of His atoning sacrifice, the view has prevailed that, with the abolition of the Old Testament form of the kingdom of God, even Palestine has ceased to be the chosen land of the revelation of the saving grace of God, and under the new covenant Canaan extends as far as the Israel of the new covenant, the church of Jesus Christ, is spread abroad over the earth, and that Zion or Jerusalem is to be sought wherever Christendom worships God in spirit and in truth, wherever Christ is with His people, and dwells in the hearts of believers through the Holy Spirit. It was by J. A. Bengel and C. F. Oetinger that the so-called "realistic" interpretation of the Messianic prophecies of the

Old Testament—according to which, after the future conversion to Christ of the Jewish people who are hardened still, the establishment of the kingdom of God in Palestine and its capital Jerusalem is to be expected—has been revived and made into one of the leading articles of Christian hope. By means of this "realistic" exposition of the prophetic word the chiliastic dogma of the establishment of a kingdom of glory before the last judgment and the end of the world is then deduced from the twentieth chapter of the Apocalypse; and many of the theologians of our day regard this as the certain resultant of a deeper study of the Scriptures. In the more precise definition of the dogma itself, the several supporters diverge very widely from one another; but they all agree in this, that they base the doctrine chiefly upon the prophetic announcement of the eventual conversion and glorification of all Israel. —As Ezekiel then stands out among all the prophets as the one who gives the most elaborate prediction of the restoration of Israel under the government of the Messiah, and he not only draws in ch. xl.–xlviii. a detailed picture of the new form of the kingdom of God, but also in ch. xxxviii. and xxxix., in the prophecy concerning Gog and Magog, foretells an attack on the part of the heathen world upon the restored kingdom of God, which appears, according to Rev. xx. 7–9, to constitute the close of the thousand years' reign; we must look somewhat more closely at this view, and by examining the arguments *pro* and *con*, endeavour to decide the question as to the fulfilment of the Old Testament prophecies concerning the future of Israel. In doing this, however, we shall fix our attention exclusively upon the exegetical arguments adduced in support of the chiliastic view by its latest supporters.[1]

[1] These are, C. A. Auberlen, "The Prophet Daniel and the Revelation of John;" also in a treatise on the Messianic Prophecies of the Mosaic times, in the *Jahrbb. f. deutsche Theologie*, IV. pp. 778 sqq.; J. C. K. Hofmann, in his *Weissagung und Erfüllung im A. u. N. Testamente*, and in the *Schriftbeweis*, vol. II. p. 2; Mich. Baumgarten, article "Ezekiel" in Herzog's

The prophetic announcement, that the Lord will one day gather together again the people of Israel, which has been thrust out among the heathen for its unfaithfulness, will bring it back into the land given to the fathers, and there bless and greatly multiply it, has its roots in the promises of the law. If the stiff-necked transgressors of the commandments of God—these are the words of Lev. xxvi. 40–45—bear the punishment of their iniquity in the land of their enemies, and confess their sins, and their uncircumcised heart is humbled, then will the Lord remember His covenant with the patriarchs, and not cast them off even in the land of their enemies, to destroy them, and to break His covenant with them; but will remember the covenant which He made with their ancestors, when He brought them out of Egypt before the eyes of the nations to be their God. He will, as this is more precisely defined in Deut. xxx. 3 sqq., gather them together again out of the heathen nations, lead them back into the land which their fathers possessed, and multiply Israel more than its fathers. On the ground of this promise, of which Moses gives a still further pledge to the people in his dying song (Deut. xxxii. 36–43), all the prophets announce the restoration and ultimate glorification of Israel. This song, which closes with the promise, "Rejoice, ye nations, over His people; for He will avenge the blood of His servants, and repay vengeance to His adversaries, and expiate His land, His people," continues to resound—to use the words of Hofmann (*Schriftbeweis*, II. 2, pp. 89, 90)—"through all the Old Testament prophecy. Not only when Obadiah (ver. 17) and Joel (ch. iii. 5) promise good to their nation do they call Mount Zion and the city of Jerusalem the place where there is protection from the judgment upon the nations of the world; but Micah also, who foretells the destruction of the temple and

Cyclopaedia, and here and there in his commentary on the Old Testament; C. E. Luthardt, *The Doctrine of the Last Things in Treatises and Expositions of Scripture* (1851); and Dr. Volck, in the *Dorpater Zeitschrift für Theologie und Kirche*, IX. pp. 142 sqq.; and others.

the carrying away of his people to Babylon, beholds Mount Zion exalted at last above all the seats of worldly power, and his people brought back to the land of their fathers (ch. iv. 1, vii. 14). The same Isaiah, who was sent to harden his people with the word of his prophecy, is nevertheless certain that at last a holy nation will dwell in Jerusalem, a remnant of Israel (Isa. iv. 3, x. 21); and the holy mountain of Jehovah, to which His scattered people return from all the ends of the world, is that abode of peace where even wild beasts do no more harm under the rule of the second David (Isa. xi. 9, 11). After all the calamities which it was the mournful lot of Jeremiah to foretell and also to witness, Jehovah showed this prophet the days when He would restore His people, and bring them back to the land which He gave to their fathers (Jer. xxx. 3). . . . And the same promise is adhered to even after the return. In every way is the assurance given by Zechariah, that Judah shall be God's holy possession in God's holy land."[1] This restoration of Israel Ezekiel describes, in harmony with Jer. xxxi.,

[1] Compare with this the words of Auberlen (*der Prophet Daniel*, p. 399, ed. 2): "The doctrine of the glorious restoration of Israel to Canaan, after severe chastisement and humiliation, is so essential and fundamental a thought of all prophecy, that the difficulty is not so much to find passages to support it, as to make a selection from them. By way of example, let us notice Isa. ii. 2–4, iv. 2–6, ix. 1–6, xi. and xii.; more especially xi. 11 sqq., xxiv. sqq., lx. sqq.; Jer. xxx.–xxxiii.; Ezek. xxxiv. 23–31, xxxvi., xxxvii.; Hos. ii. 16–25, iii. 4, 5, xi. 8–11, xiv. 2 sqq.; Joel iii. 1–5, iv. 16–21; Amos ix. 8–15; Obad. vers. 17–21; Mic. ii. 12, 13, iv., v., vii. 11–20; Zeph. iii. 14–20; Zech. ii. 4 sqq., viii. 7 sqq., ix. 9 sqq., x. 8–12, xii. 2–xiii. 6, xiv. 8 sqq." Auberlen (pp. 400 sq.) then gives the following as the substance of these prophetic descriptions: "Israel having been brought back to its own land, will be the people of God in a much higher and deeper sense than before; inasmuch as sin will be averted, the knowledge of God will fill the land, and the Lord will dwell again in the midst of His people at Jerusalem. A new period of revelation is thus commenced, the Spirit of God is richly poured out, and with this a plenitude of such gifts of grace as were possessed in a typical manner by the apostolic church. And this rich spiritual life has also its perfect external manifestation both in a priestly and a regal form. The priesthood of Israel was more especially seen by Ezekiel, the son of a priest, in his mysterious vision in ch. xl.–xlviii.; the monarchy by Daniel, the statesman; while

though in a much more detailed picture, in the following way:—"The condition of things in the future will differ from that in the past, simply in the fact that Israel will then have a heart converted to fidelity and obedience by the Spirit of God (ch. xi. 19, xxxvi. 27), and will live in good peace and prosperity under the shelter of its God, who is known and acknowledged by all the world (ch. xxxvi. 23). The land to which it is restored, a land most decidedly represented by Ezekiel as the same as that in which its fathers lived (ch. xxxvii. 25), appears throughout merely as a happy earthly dwelling-place, and the promise of its possession as an assurance given to a nation continuing to propagate itself in peace" (Hofmann, p. 576). This manner of depicting the condition of the Israel restored and glorified by the Messiah, as a peaceful settlement and a happy life in the land of the fathers, a life rich in earthly possessions, is not confined, however, to Jeremiah and Ezekiel, but stands out more or less conspicuously in the Messianic pictures of all the prophets. What follows, then, from this in

Jeremiah, for example, unites the two (ch. xxxiii. 17–22). What took place only in an outward way, *i.e.* in the letter, during the Old Testament times, and withdrew, on the other hand, into the inward and hidden spirit-life during the time of the Christian church, will then manifest itself outwardly also, and assume an external though pneumatic form. In the Old Testament the whole of the national life of Israel in its several forms of manifestation, domestic and political life, labour and art, literature and culture, was regulated by religion, though only at first in an outward and legal way. The church, on the other hand, has, above all, to urge a renewal of the heart, and must give freedom to the outward forms which life assumes, enjoining upon the conscience of individual men, in these also to glorify Christ. In the thousand years' reign all these departments of life will be truly Christianized, and that from within. Looked at in this light, there will be nothing left to give offence, if we bear in mind that the ceremonial law of Moses corresponds to the priesthood of Israel, and the civil law to the monarchy. The Gentile church has only been able to adopt the moral law, however certainly it has been directed merely to the inwardly working means of the word, or of the prophetic office. But when once the priesthood and the kingly office have been restored, then, without doing violence to the Epistle to the Hebrews, the ceremonial and civil law of Moses will unfold its spiritual depths in the worship and constitution of the thousand years' reign."

relation to the mode in which these prophecies are to be fulfilled? Is it that the form assumed by the life of the people of Israel when restored will be only a heightened repetition of the conditions of its former life in Palestine, undisturbed by sin? By no means. On the contrary, it follows from this that the prophets have depicted the glorious restoration of Israel by the Messiah by means of figures borrowed from the past and present of the national life of Israel, and therefore that their picture is not to be taken literally, but symbolically or typically, and that we are not to expect it to be literally fulfilled.

We are forced to this conclusion by the fact that, through the coming of Christ, and the kingdom of heaven which began with Him, the idea of the people of God has been so expanded, that henceforth not the lineal descendants of Abraham, or the Jewish nation merely, but the church of confessors of Jesus Christ, gathered together out of Israel and the Gentiles, has become the people of God, and the economy of the Old Testament has ceased to constitute the divinely appointed form of the church of God. If, therefore, the Jewish people, who have rejected the Saviour, who appeared in Jesus Christ, and have hardened themselves against the grace and truth revealed in Him, are not cast off for ever, but, according to the promises of the Old Testament and the teaching of the Apostle Paul (Rom. xi.), will eventually repent, and as a people turn to the crucified One, and then also realize the fulfilment of the promises of God; there is still lacking, with the typical character of the prophetic announcement, any clear and unambiguous biblical evidence that all Israel, whose salvation is to be looked for in the future, will be brought back to Palestine, when eventually converted to Christ the crucified One, and continue there as a people separated from the rest of Christendom, and form the earthly centre of the church of the Lord gathered out of all nations and tongues. For, however well founded the remark of Hofmann (*ut sup.* p. 88) may be, that "holy people and holy land are demanded by one another;" this proves nothing more than that the holy people, gathered out of all the families of the earth through the believing reception of the gospel, will also have a holy land for its dwelling-place; in other words, that, with the spread of the church of the Lord over all the quarters of the globe, the earth will become holy land or Canaan, so far as it is inhabited by the followers of Christ. The Apostle Paul teaches this in the same Epistle in which he foretells to Israel, hardened in unbelief, its eventual restoration and blessedness; when he explains in Rom. iv. 9–13 that to Abraham or his seed the promise that he was to be the heir of the world was not fulfilled through the law, but through the righteousness of the faith, which Abraham had when still uncircumcised, that he might become a father of all those who believe, though they be not circumcised, and a father of the circumcision, not merely of those who are of the circumcision, but of those also who walk in the footsteps of his faith. As the apostle, when developing this thought, interprets the promise given to the patriarch in Gen. xii. 7 and xv. 18: "to thy seed will I give this land" (*i.e.* the land of Canaan), by *κληρονομεῖν κόσμον* (inheriting the world), he regards Canaan as a type of the world or of the earth, which would be occupied by the children born of faith to the patriarch.

This typical interpretation of the promise, given in the Old Testament to the seed of Abraham, of the everlasting possession of the land of Canaan, which is thus taught by the Apostle Paul, and has been adopted by the church on his authority, corresponds also to the spirit and meaning of the Old Testament word of God. This is evident from Gen. xvii., where the Lord God, when instituting the covenant of circumcision, gives not to Abraham only, but expressly to Sarah also, the promise to make them into peoples (לְגוֹיִם), that kings of nations (מַלְכֵי עַמִּים) shall come from them through the son, whom they are to receive (vers. 6 and 16), and at the same time promises to give to the seed of Abraham, thus greatly to be multiplied, the land of his pilgrimage, the whole land of Canaan, for an everlasting possession (ver. 8). This promise the Lord, as the "almighty God," has not carried into effect by making Abraham and Sarah into nations through the lineal posterity of Isaac, but only through the spiritual seed of Abraham, believers out of all nations, who have become, and still will become, children of Abraham in Christ. It was only through these that Abraham became the father of a multitude of nations (לְאַב הֲמוֹן גּוֹיִם, ver. 5). For although two peoples sprang from Isaac, the Israelites through Jacob, and the Edomites through Esau, and Abraham also became the ancestor of several tribes through Ishmael and the sons of Keturah, the divine promise in question refers to the people of Israel alone, because Esau was separated from the seed of the promise by God Himself, and the other sons of Abraham were excluded by the fact that they were not born of Sarah. The twelve tribes, however, formed but one people; and although Ezekiel calls them two peoples (ch. xxxv. 10 and xxxvii. 22), having in view their division into two kingdoms, they are never designated or described in the Old or New Testament as הֲמוֹן גּוֹיִם. To this one people God did indeed give the land of Canaan for a possession, according to the boundaries described in Num. xxxiv., so that it dwelt therein until it was driven out and scattered among the heathen for its persistent unfaithfulness. But inasmuch as that portion of the promise which referred to the multiplication of the seed of Abraham into peoples was only to receive its complete fulfilment in Christ, according to the counsel and will of God, through the grafting of the believing Gentile nations into the family of Abraham, and has so received it, we are not at liberty to restrict the other portion of this promise, relating to the possession of the land of Canaan, to the lineal posterity of the patriarch, or the people of Israel by lineal descent, but must assume that in the promise of the land to be given to the seed of Abraham God even then spoke of Canaan as a type of the land which was to be possessed by the posterity of Abraham multiplied into nations.

This typical phraseology runs through all the prophetical writings of the Old Testament, and that both with regard to the promised seed, which Abraham received through Isaac (Gen. xxi. 12) in the people of Israel, and also with reference to the land promised to this seed for an inheritance, although, while the old covenant established at Sinai lasted, Israel according to the flesh was the people of God, and the earthly Canaan between the Euphrates and the river of Egypt was the dwelling-place of this people. For inasmuch as Abraham received the promise at the very time of his call, that in his seed all the families of the earth should be blessed, and the germs of the universal destination of the people and kingdom of God were deposited, according to Gen. xvii., in the subsequent patriarchal promises, the prophets continued to employ the names of Israel and Canaan more and more in their Messianic prophecies as symbolical terms for the two ideas of the people and kingdom of God. And from the time when the fortress of Jerusalem upon Mount Zion was exalted by David into the capital of his kingdom and the seat of his government over Israel, and was also made the site of the dwelling of Jehovah in the midst of His people, by the removal of the ark of the covenant to Zion, and the building of the temple which was planned by David, though only carried into execution by Solomon his son, they employed Zion and Jerusalem in the same typical manner as the seat and centre of the kingdom of God; so that, in the Messianic psalms and the writings of the prophets, Zion or Jerusalem is generally mentioned as the place from which the king (David-Messiah), anointed by Jehovah as prince over His people, extends His dominion over all the earth, and whither the nations pour to hear the law of the Lord, and to be instructed as to His ways and their walking in His paths.

Consequently neither the prominence expressly given to the land in the promises contained in Lev. xxvi. 42 and Deut. xxxii. 43, upon which such stress is laid by Auberlen (*die messianische Weissagungen*, pp. 827 and 833), nor the fact that Mount Zion or the city of Jerusalem is named as the place of judgment upon the world of nations and the completion of the kingdom of God, to which both Hofmann and Auberlen appeal in the passages already quoted, furnishes any valid evidence that the Jewish people, on its eventual conversion to Christ, will be brought back to Palestine, and that the Lord, at His second coming, will establish the millennial kingdom in the earthly Jerusalem, and take up His abode on the material Mount Zion, in a temple built by human hands.

Even the supporters of the literal interpretation of the Messianic prophecies cannot deny the symbolico-typical character of the Old Testament revelation. Thus Auberlen, for example, observes (*die mess. Weiss.* p. 821) that, "in their typical character, the sacrifices furnish us with an example of the true signification of *all the institutions* of the Old Testament kingdom of God, while *the latter* exhibit to us in external symbol and type the truly holy people and the Messianic kingdom in its perfection, just as the former set forth the sacrifice of the Messiah." But among these institutions the Israelitish sanctuary (tabernacle or temple) undoubtedly occupied a leading place as a symbolico-typical embodiment of the kingdom of God established in Israel, as is now acknowledged by nearly all the expositors of Scripture who have any belief in revelation. It is not merely the institutions of the old covenant, however, which have a symbolico-typical signification, but this is also the case with the history of the covenant nation of the Old Testament, and the soil in which this history developed itself. This is so obvious, that Auberlen himself (*ut sup.* p. 827) has said that "it is quite a common thing with the prophets to represent the approaching dispersion and enslaving of Israel among the heathen as a renewal of their condition in Egypt, and the eventual restoration of both the people and kingdom as a new exodus from Egypt and entrance into Canaan (Hos. ii. 1, 2 and 16, 17, ix. 3 and 6, xi. 5, 11; Mic. ii. 12, 13,

vii. 15, 16; Isa. x. 24, 26, xi. 11; Jer. xvi. 14, 15, and other passages)." And even Hofmann, who sets aside this typical phraseology of the prophets in Isa. xi. 11–15, where the restoration of Israel from its dispersion throughout all the world is depicted as a repetition of its deliverance from Egypt through the miraculous division of the Red Sea, with the simple remark, "that the names of the peoples mentioned in the 14th as well as in the 11th verse, and the obstacles described in the 15th verse, merely serve to elaborate the thought" (*Schriftbeweis*, II. 2, p. 548), cannot help admitting (at p. 561) "that in Isa. xxxiv. 5 אֱדוֹם is not to be understood as a special prophecy against the Edomitish people, but as a symbolical designation of the world of mankind in its enmity against God." But if *Edom* is a type of the human race in its hostility to God in this threatening of judgment, "the ransomed of Jehovah" mentioned in the corresponding announcement of salvation in Isa. xxxv., who are to "return to Zion with songs, and everlasting joy upon their heads," cannot be the rescued remnant of the Jewish people, or the Israel of the twelve tribes who will ultimately attain to blessedness, nor can the Zion to which they return be the capital of Palestine. If *Edom* in this eschatological prophecy denotes the world in its enmity against God, the ransomed of Jehovah who return to Zion are the people of God gathered from both Gentiles and Jews, who enter into the blessedness of the heavenly Jerusalem. By adopting this view of *Edom*, Hofmann has admitted the typical use of the ideas, both of the people of Jehovah (Israel) and of Zion, by the prophets, and has thereby withdrawn all firm foundation from his explanation of similar Messianic prophecies when the Jewish nation is concerned. The same rule which applies to Edom and Zion in Isa. xxxiv. and xxxv. must also be applicable in Isa. xl.–lxvi. The prophecy concerning Edom in Isa. xxxv. has its side-piece in Isa. lxiii. 1–6; and, as Delitzsch has said, the announcement of the return of the ransomed of Jehovah to Zion in ch. xxxvi., "as a whole and in every particular, both in thought and language, is a prelude of this book of consolation for the exiles (*i.e.* the one which follows in Isa. xl.–lxvi)." Ezekiel uses Edom in the same way, in the prediction of the everlasting devastation of Edom and the restoration of the devastated land of Israel, to be a lasting blessing for its inhabitants. As Edom in this case also represents the world in its hostility to God (see the comm. on ch. xxxv. 1–xxxvi. 15), the land of Israel also is not Palestine, but the kingdom of the Messiah, the boundaries of which extend from sea to sea, and from the river to the ends of the world (Ps. lxxii. 8 and Zech. ix. 10). It is true that in the case of our prophet there is no express mention made of the spread of the kingdom of God over the lands, inasmuch as he is watchman over the house of Israel, and therefore, for the most part, principally speaks of the restoration of Israel; but it is also obvious that this prophetic truth was not unknown to him, from the fact that, according to ch. xlvii. 22, 23, in the fresh division of the land among the tribes by lot, the foreigners as well as the natives are to be reckoned among the children of Israel, and to receive their portion of the land as well, which plainly abolishes the difference in lineal descent existing under the old covenant. Still more clearly does he announce the reception of the heathen nations into the kingdom of God in ch. xvi. 53 sqq., where he predicts the eventual turning of the captivity, not of Jerusalem only, but also of Samaria and Sodom, as the goal of the ways of God with His people. If, therefore, in His pictures of the restoration and glorification of the kingdom of God, he speaks of the land of Israel alone, the reason for this mode of description is probably also to be sought in the fact that he goes back to the fundamental prophecies of the Pentateuch more than other prophets do; and as, on the one hand, he unfolds the fulfilment of the threats in Lev. xxvi. and Deut. xxviii.–xxxii. in his threatenings of judgments, so, on the other hand, does he display the fulfilment of the promises of the law in his predictions of salvation. If we bear this in mind, we must not take his prophecy of the very numerous multiplication of Israel and of the eternal possession of Canaan and its blessings in any other sense than in that of the divine promise in Gen. xvii.; that is to say, we must not restrict the numerous multiplication of Israel to the literal multiplication of the remnant of the twelve tribes, but must also understand thereby the multiplication of the seed of Abraham into peoples in the manner explained above, and interpret in the same way the restoration of Israel to the land promised to the fathers.

This view of the Old Testament prophecy concerning the eventual restoration of Israel on its conversion to Christ is confirmed as to its correctness by the New Testament also; if, for example, we consider the plain utterances of Christ and His apostles concerning the relation of the Israel according to the flesh, *i.e.* of the Jewish nation, to Christ and His kingdom, and do not adhere in a one-sided manner to the literal interpretation of the eschatological pictures contained in the language of the Old Testament prophecy. For since, as Hofmann has correctly observed in his *Schriftbeweis* (II. 2, pp. 667, 668), "the apostolical doctrine of the end of the present condition of things, namely, of the reappearance of Christ, of the glorification of His church, and the resurrection of its dead, or even of the general resurrection of the dead, of the glorification of the material world, the destruction of the present and the creation of a new one, stands in this relation to the Old Testament prophecy of the end of things, that it is merely a repetition of it under the new point of view, which accompanied the appearing and glorification of Jesus and the establishment of His church of Jews and Gentiles;" these eschatological pictures are also clothed in the symbolico-typical form peculiar to the Old Testament prophecy, the doctrinal import of which can only be determined in accordance with the unambiguous doctrinal passages of the New Testament. Of these doctrinal passages the first which presents itself is Rom. xi., where the Apostle Paul tells the Christians at Rome as a *μυστήριον*, that hardness in part has happened to Israel, till the *pleroma* of the Gentiles has entered into the kingdom of God, and so (*i.e.* after this has taken place) all Israel will be rescued or saved (vers. 25, 26). He then supports this by a scriptural quotation formed from Isa. lix. 20 and xxvii. 9 (LXX.), with an evident allusion to Jer. xxxi. 34 (? 33) also: "there shall come out of Zion the deliverer, and shall turn away ungodliness from Jacob," etc.; whilst he has already shown how, as the fall of Israel, or its ἀποβολή, is the riches of the Gentiles and reconciliation of the world, the πρόσληψις will be nothing else than life from the dead (ζωὴ ἐκ νεκρῶν, vers. 11–15). The apostle evidently teaches here that the partial hardening of Israel, in consequence of which the people rejected the Saviour, who appeared in Jesus, and were excluded from the salvation in Christ, is not an utter rejection of the old covenant nation; but that the hardening of Israel will cease after the entrance of the pleroma of the Gentiles into the kingdom of God, and so all Israel (πᾶς Ἰσραήλ in contrast with ἐκ μέρους, *i.e.* the people of Israel as a whole) will attain to salvation, although this does not teach the salvation of every individual Jew.[1] But Auberlen (*die mess. Weissagungen*, pp. 801 sqq.) puts too much into these words of the apostle when he combines them with Ex. xix. 5, 6, and from the fact that Israel in the earlier ages of the Old Testa-

[1] "All Israel," says Philippi in the 3d ed. of his *Commentary on the Epistle to the Romans* (p. 537), "as contrasted with ἐκ μέρους (in part) in ver. 25, and also in the connection in which it stands with the train of thought in ch. ix.–xi., which, as the chapter before us more especially shows, has only to do with the bringing of the nations as a whole to the Messianic salvation, cannot be understood in any other sense than as signifying the people of Israel as a whole (see also vers. 28–32). The explanation of the words as denoting the spiritual Israel, the 'Israel of God' (Gal. vi. 16), according to which all the true children of Abraham and of God are to be saved through the entrance of the chosen Gentiles, and at the same time also of the ἐκλογή of the Israel that has not been hardened, is just as arbitrary as it is to take 'all Israel' as referring merely to the believing portion of the Jews, the portion chosen by God, who have belonged in all ages to the λεῖμμα κατ' ἐκλογὴν χάριτος." But in the appendix to the third edition he has not only given full expression to the opposite view,

ment was once a people and kingdom, but not really a holy and priestly one, and that in the first ages of the New Testament it was once holy and priestly, though not as a people and kingdom, draws the conclusion, not only that the Jewish nation must once more become holy as a people and kingdom, but also that the apostle of the Gentiles here declares "that the promise given to the people of Israel, that it is to be a holy people, will still be fulfilled in its experience, and that in connection with this, after the present period of the kingdom of God, there is a new period in prospect, when the converted and sanctified Israel, being called once for all to be a priestly kingdom, will become the channel of the blessing of fellowship with God to the nations in a totally different and far more glorious manner than before." For if the apostle had intended to teach the eventual accomplishment of this promise in the case of the Israel according to the flesh, he would certainly have quoted it, or at all events have plainly hinted at it, and not merely have spoken of the σώζεσθαι of the Israel which was hardened then. There is nothing to show, even in the remotest way, that Israel will eventually be exalted into the holy and priestly people and kingdom for the nations, either in the assurance that "all Israel shall be saved," or in the declaration that the "receiving" (πρόσληψις) of Israel will work, or be followed

which Besser in his *Bibelstunden* has supported in the most decided manner, after the example of Luther and many of the Lutheran expositors, but is inclined to give the preference, even above the view which he previously upheld, to the idea that "*all Israel* is the whole of the Israel intended by the prophetic word, and included in the divine word of promise, to which alone the name of Israel truly and justly belongs according to the correct understanding of the Old Testament word of God—that is to say, those lineal sons of Abraham who walk in the footsteps of his faith (ch. iv. 12), those Jews who are so not merely outwardly in the flesh, but also inwardly in the spirit, through circumcision of heart (ch. ii. 28, 29);" and also to the following exposition which Calovius gives of the whole passage, namely, that "it does not relate to a simultaneous or universal conversion of the Israelites, or to the conversion of a great multitude, which is to take place at the last times of the world, and is to be looked forward to still, but rather to successive conversions continuing even to the end of the world."

by, "life from the dead" (ver. 15); and the proposition from which Paul infers the future deliverance of the people of Israel—viz., "if the first-fruit be holy, the lump is also holy; and if the root be holy, so are the branches" (ver. 16)—shows plainly that it never entered the apostle's mind to predict for the branches that were broken off the olive tree for a time an exaltation to even greater holiness than that possessed by the root and beginning of Israel when they should be grafted in again.

There is also another way in which Hofmann (*Schriftbeweis*, II. 2, pp. 96 and 668) makes insertions in the words of the apostle,—namely, when he draws the conclusion from the prophetic quotation in vers. 25, 26, that the apostle takes the thought from the prophetic writings, that Zion and Israel are the place where the final revelation of salvation will be made, and then argues in support of this geographical exposition of the words, "shall come out of Zion," on the ground that in these words we have not to think of the first coming of the Saviour alone, but the apostle extends to the second coming with perfect propriety what the Old Testament prophecy generally affirms with regard to the coming of Christ, and what had already been verified at His first coming. This argument is extremely weak. Even if one would or could insist upon the fact that, when rendering the words וּבָא לְצִיּוֹן גּוֹאֵל (there will come *for* Zion a Redeemer), in Isa. lix. 20, by ἥξει ἐκ Σιὼν ὁ ῥυόμενος (the Redeemer will come *out of* Zion), the apostle designedly adopted the expression ἐκ Σιών, it would by no means follow "that he meant the material Zion or earthly Jerusalem to be regarded as the final site of the New Testament revelation." For if the apostle used the expression "come out of Zion," with reference to the second coming of the Lord, because it had been verified at the first coming of Jesus, although Jesus did not then come out of Zion, but out of Bethlehem, according to the prophecy of Mic. v. 1 (cf. Matt. i. 5, 6), he cannot have meant the material Mount Zion by ἐκ Σιών, but must have taken *Zion* in the prophetico-typical sense of the central seat of the kingdom of God; a meaning which it also has in such passages in the Psalms as Ps. xiv. 7, liii. 7, and cx. 2, which he appears to have had floating before his mind. It was only by taking this view of Zion that Paul could use ἐκ Σιών for the לְצִיּוֹן of Isaiah, without altering the meaning of the prophecy, that the promised Redeemer would come for Zion, *i.e.* for the citizens of Zion, the Israelites. The apostle, when making this quotation from the prophets, had no more intention of giving any information concerning the place where Christ would appear to the now hardened Israel, and prove Himself to be the Redeemer, than concerning the land in which the Israel scattered among the nations would be found at the second coming of our Lord. And there is nothing whatever in the New Testament to the effect that "the Lord will not appear again till He has prepared both Israel and Zion for the scene of His reappearing" (Hofmann, p. 97). All that Christ says is, that the gospel of the kingdom will be preached in the whole world for a witness concerning all nations, and then will the end come (Matt. xxiv. 14). And if, in addition to this, on His departing for ever from the temple, He exclaimed to the Jews who rejected Him, "Your house will be left unto you desolate; for I say unto you, Ye will not see me henceforth, till ye shall say, Blessed be he that cometh in the name of the Lord" (Matt. xxiii. 38, 39), all that He means is, that He will not appear to them or come to them before they receive Him with faith, "greet Him as the object of their longing expectation;" and by no means that He will not come till they have been brought back from their dispersion to Palestine and Jerusalem.

Even Matt. xxvii. 53 and Rev. xi. 2, where Jerusalem is called the holy city, do not furnish any tenable proof of this, because it is so called, not with regard to any glorification to be looked for in the future, but as the city in which the holiest events in the world's history had taken place; just as Peter (2 Pet. i. 18) designates the Mount of Transfiguration the holy mount, with reference to that event, and not with any anticipation of a future glorification of the mountain; and in 1 Kings xix. 8 Horeb is called the Mount of God, because in the olden time God revealed Himself there. "The old Jerusalem is even now the holy city still to those who have directed their hopeful eyes to the new Jerusalem alone" (Hengstenberg). This also applies to the designation of the temple as the "holy place" in Matt. xxiv. 15, by which Hofmann (p. 91) would also, though erroneously, understand Jerusalem.

And the words of Christ in Luke xxi. 24, that Jerusalem will be trodden down by the Gentiles, ἄχρι πληρωθῶσιν καιροὶ ἐθνῶν, cannot be used as furnishing a proof that the earthly Jerusalem will be occupied by the converted Jews before or at the second coming of the Lord. For if stress be laid upon the omission of the article, and the appointed period be understood in such a manner as to lead to the following rendering, viz.: "till Gentile periods shall be fulfilled," *i.e.* "till certain periods which have been appointed to Gentile nations for the accomplishment of this judgment of wrath from God shall have elapsed" (Meyer), we may assume, with Hengstenberg (*die Juden und die christl. Kirche*, 3 art.), that these times come to an end when the overthrow of the might of the Gentiles is effected through the judgment of God, and the Christian church takes their place; and we may still further say with him, that "the treading down of Jerusalem by the heathen, among whom, according to the Christian view, the Mahometans also are to be reckoned, has ceased twice already,—namely, in the reign of Constantine, and in the time of the Crusades, when a Christian kingdom existed in Jerusalem. And what then happened, though only in a transient way, will eventually take place again, and that definitively, on the ground of this declaration of the Lord. Jerusalem will become the possession of the Israel of the Christian church." If, on the other hand, we adopt Hofmann's view (pp. 642, 643), that by καιροὶ ἐθνῶν we are to understand the times of the nations, when the world belongs to them, in accordance with Dan. viii. 14, in support of which Rev. xi. 2 may also be adduced, these times "come to an end when the people of God obtain the supremacy;" and, according to this explanation, it is affirmed "that this treading down of the holy city will not come to an end till the filling up of the time, during which the world belongs to the nations, and therefore not till the end of the present course of this world." But if the treading down of Jerusalem by the Gentiles lasts till then, even the converted Jews cannot recover possession of it at that time; for at the end of the present course of this world the new creation of the heaven and earth will take place, and the perfected church of Christ, gathered out of Israel and the Gentile nations, will dwell in the heavenly Jerusalem that has come down upon the new earth.—However, therefore, we may interpret these words of the Lord, we are not taught in Luke xxi. 24 any more than in Matt. xxiv. 15 and xxvii. 53, or Rom. xi. 26, that the earthly Jerusalem will come into the possession of the converted Jews after its liberation from the power of the Gentiles, that it will hold a central position in the world, or that the temple will be erected there again.

And lastly, a decisive objection to these Jewish, millenarian hopes, and at the same time to the literal interpretation of the prophetic announcements of the restoration of Israel, is to be found in the fact that the New Testament says nothing whatever concerning a rebuilding of the Jerusalem temple and a restoration of the Levitical worship; but that, on the contrary, it teaches in the most decided manner, that, with the completion of the reconciliation of men with God through the sacrifice of Christ upon Golgotha, the sacrificial and temple service of the Levitical law was fulfilled and abolished (Heb. vii.–x.), on the ground of the declaration of Christ, that the hour cometh, and now is, when men shall worship neither upon Gerizim nor at Jerusalem; but the true worshippers shall worship the Father in spirit and in truth (John iv. 21–24), in accordance with the direction given by the apostle in Rom. xii. 1. But the prophets of the Old Testament do not merely predict the return of the Israelites to their own land, and their everlasting abode in that land under the rule of the Messiah; but this prediction of theirs culminates in the promise that Jehovah will establish His sanctuary, *i.e.* His temple, in the midst of His redeemed people, and dwell there with them and above them for ever (Ezek. xxxvii. 27, 28), and that all nations will come to this sanctuary of the Lord upon Zion year by year, to worship before the King Jehovah of hosts, and keep the Feast of tabernacles (Zech. xiv. 16; cf. Isa. lxvi. 23). If, then, the Jewish people should receive Palestine again for its possession either at or after its conversion to Christ, in accordance with the promise of God, the temple with the Levitical sacrificial worship would of necessity be also restored in Jerusalem. But if such a supposition is at variance with the teaching of Christ and the apostles, so that this essential feature in the prophetic picture of the future of the kingdom of God is not to be understood literally, but spiritually or typically, it is an unjustifiable inconsistency to adhere to the literal interpretation of the prophecy concerning the return of Israel to Canaan, and to look for the return of the Jewish people to Palestine, when it has come to believe in Jesus Christ.

CHAP. XXXVIII. AND XXXIX. DESTRUCTION OF GOG WITH HIS GREAT ARMY OF NATIONS.

Gog, in the land of Magog, prince of Rosh, Meshech, and Tubal, will invade the restored land of Israel from the far distant northern land by the appointment of God in the last times, and with a powerful army of numerous nations (ch. xxxviii. 1–9), with the intention of plundering Israel, now dwelling in security, that the Lord may sanctify Himself upon him before all the world (vers. 10–16). But when Gog, of whom earlier prophets have already prophesied, shall fall upon

Israel, he is to be destroyed by a wrathful judgment from the Lord, that the nations may know that God is the Lord (vers. 17–23). On the mountains of Israel will Gog with all his hosts and nations succumb to the judgment of God (ch. xxxix. 1–8). The inhabitants of the cities of Israel will spend seven years in burning the weapons of the fallen foe, and seven months in burying the corpses in a valley, which will receive its name from this, so as to purify the land (vers. 9–16); whilst in the meantime all the birds and wild beasts will satiate themselves with the flesh and blood of the fallen (vers. 17–20). By this judgment will all the nations as well as Israel know that it was on account of its sins that the Lord formerly gave up Israel into the power of the heathen, but that now He will no more forsake His redeemed people, because He has poured out His Spirit upon it (vers. 21–29).

Vers. 1–9. Introduction. Preparation of Gog and his army for the invasion of the restored land of Israel.—Ver. 1. *And the word of Jehovah came to me, saying,* Ver. 2. *Son of man, set thy face toward Gog in the land of Magog, the prince of Rosh, Meshech, and Tubal, and prophesy against him,* Ver. 3. *And say, Thus saith the Lord Jehovah, Behold, I will deal with thee, Gog, thou prince of Rosh, Meshech, and Tubal,* Ver. 4. *And will mislead thee, and will put rings in thy jaws, and lead thee out, and all thine army, horses, and riders, all clothed in perfect beauty, a great assembly, with buckler and shield, all wielding swords;* Ver. 5. *Persian, Ethiopian, and Libyan with them, all of them with shield and helmet;* Ver. 6. *Gomer and all his hosts, the house of Togarmah in the uttermost north with all his hosts; many peoples with thee.* Ver. 7. *Be prepared and make ready, thou and all thine assembly, who have assembled together to thee, and be thou their guard.* Ver. 8. *After many days shalt thou be visited, at the end of the years shalt thou come into the land, which is brought back from the sword, gathered out of many peoples, upon the mountains of Israel, which were constantly laid waste, but now it is brought out of the nations, and they dwell together in safety;* Ver. 9. *And thou shalt come up, come like a storm, like a cloud to cover the land, thou and all thy hosts and many peoples with thee.*—Vers. 1 and 2. Command to prophesy against Gog. גּוֹג, *Gog*, the name of the prince against whom the prophecy is directed, is probably a name which Ezekiel has arbitrarily formed from the name of the country, *Magog;* although *Gog* does occur in 1 Chron. v. 4 as the name of a Reubenite, of whom nothing further is known. The construction גּוֹג אֶרֶץ מָגוֹג, Gog of the land of Magog, is an abbreviated expression for "Gog from the land of Magog;" and אֶרֶץ מג׳ is not to be taken in connection with שִׂים פָּנֶיךָ, as the local object ("toward Gog, to the land of Magog"), as Ewald and Hävernick would render it; since it would be very difficult in that case to explain the fact that גּוֹג is afterwards resumed in the apposition נְשִׂיא וגו׳. מָגוֹג, *Magog*, is the name of a people mentioned in Gen. x. 2 as descended from Japhet, according to the early Jewish and traditional explanation, the great Scythian people; and here also it is the name of a people, and is written with the article (הַמָּגוֹג), to mark the people as one well known from the time of Genesis, and therefore properly the land of the Magog (-people). Gog is still further described as the prince of *Rosh, Meshech,* and *Tubal.* It is true that Ewald follows Aquila, the Targum, and Jerome, and connects ראשׁ with נְשִׂיא as an appellative in the sense of *princeps capitis,* chief prince. But the argument used in support of this explanation, namely, that there is no people of the name of *Rosh* mentioned either in the Old Testament or by Josephus, is a very weak one; whilst, on the other hand, the appellative rendering, though possible, no doubt, after the analogy of הַכֹּהֵן ראשׁ in 1 Chron xxvii. 5, is by no means probable, for the simple reason that the נְשִׂיא ראשׁ occurs again in ver. 3 and ch. xxxix. 1, and in such repetitions circumstantial titles are generally abbreviated. The Byzantine and Arabic writers frequently mention a people called Ῥῶς, روس, *Rûs,* dwelling in the country of the Taurus, and reckoned among the Scythian tribes (for the passages, see Ges. *Thesaurus*, p. 1253), so that there is no reason to question the existence of a people known by the name of *Rosh*; even though the attempt of Bochart to find a trace of such a people in the Ῥωξαλᾶνοι (Ptol. iii. 5) and *Roxalani* (Plin. *h. n.* iv. 12), by explaining this name as formed from a combination of *Rhos* (*Rhox*) and *Alani*, is just as doubtful as the conjecture, founded upon the investigations of Frähn (Ibn Foszlan, *u. a. Araber Berichte über die Russen älterer Zeit*, St. Petersburg 1823), that the name of the Russians is connected with this Ῥῶς, روس, and our ראשׁ. *Meshech* and *Tubal* (as in ch. xxvii. 13 and xxxii. 26), the *Moschi* and *Tibareni* of classical writers (see the comm. on Gen. x. 2), dwelt, according to the passage before us, in the neighbourhood of Magog. There were also found in the army of Gog, according to ver. 5, *Pharas* (Persians), *Cush*, and *Phut* (Ethiopians and Libyans, see the comm. on ch. xxx. 5 and xxvii. 10), and, according to ver. 6, *Gomer* and the house of *Togarmah*. From a comparison of this list with Gen. x. 2, Kliefoth draws the conclusion that Ezekiel omits all the peoples mentioned in Gen. x. 2 as belonging to the family of Japhet, who had come into historical notice in his time, or have done so since, namely, the Medes, Greeks, and Thracians; whilst, on the other hand, he mentions all the peoples enumerated, who have never yet appeared upon the stage of history. But this remark is out of place, for the simple reason that Ezekiel also omits the Japhetic tribes of Ashkenaz and Riphath (Gen. x. 3), and still more from the fact that he notices not only the פָּרַס, or Persians, who were probably related to the מָדַי, but also the Hamitic peoples *Cush* and *Phut*, two African families. Consequently the army of Gog consisted not only of wild Japhetic tribes, who had not yet attained historical importance, but of Hamitic tribes also, that is to say, of peoples living at the extreme north (יַרְכְּתֵי צָפוֹן, ver. 6) and east (Persians) and south (Ethiopians), *i.e.* on the borders of the then known world. These are all summoned by Gog, and gathered together for an attack upon the people of God. This points to a time when their former foes, Ammon, Moab, Edom, Philistines, and Syrians, and the old imperial powers, Egypt, Asshur, Babel, Javan, will all have passed away from the stage of history, and the people of God will stand in the centre of the historical life of the world, and will have spread so widely over the earth, that its foes will only be found on the borders of the civilised world (compare Rev. xx. 8).

Vers. 3-9 contain in general terms the determinate counsel of God concerning Gog.—Vers. 3-6. Jehovah is about to mislead Gog to a crusade against His people Israel, and summons him to prepare for the invasion of the restored land of Israel. The announcement of the purpose for which Jehovah will make use of Gog and his army, and the summons addressed to him to make ready, form two strophes, which are clearly marked by the similarity of the conclusion in vers. 6 and 9.—Ver. 3. God will deal with Gog, to sanctify Himself upon him by means of judgment (cf. ver. 10). He therefore misleads him to an attack upon the people of Israel. שׁוֹבֵב, an intensive form from שׁוּב, may signify, as *vox media*, to cause to return (ch. xxxix. 27), and to cause to turn away, to lead away from the right road or goal, to lead astray (Isa. xlvii. 10). Here and in ch. xxxix. 2 it means to lead or bring away from his previous attitude, *i.e.* to mislead or seduce, in the sense of enticing to a dangerous enterprise; according to which the Chaldee has rendered it correctly, so far as the actual sense is concerned, אֲשַׁדְּלִנָּךְ, *alliciam te.* In the words, "I place rings in thy jaws" (cf. ch. xxix. 4), Gog is represented as an unmanageable beast, which is compelled to follow its leader (cf. Isa. xxxvii. 29); and the thought is thereby expressed, that Gog is compelled to obey the power of God against his will. הוֹצִיא, to lead him away from his land, or natural soil. The passage in Rev. xx. 8, "to deceive the nations (πλανῆσαι τὰ ἔθνη), Gog and Magog, to gather them together to battle," corresponds to these words so far as the material sense is concerned; with this exception, that Satan is mentioned as the seducer of the nations in the Apocalypse, whereas Ezekiel gives prominence to the leading of God, which controls the manifestations even of evil, "so that these two passages stand in the same relation to one another as 2 Sam. xxiv. 1 and 1 Chron. xxi. 1" (Häv.). In vers. 4*b*–6 the army is depicted as one splendidly equipped and very numerous. For לְבֻשֵׁי מִכְלוֹל, see the comm. on ch. xxiii. 12, where the Assyrian satraps are so described. קָהָל רָב, as in ch. xvii. 17. The words buckler and shield are loosely appended in the heat of the discourse, without any logical subordination to what precedes. Besides the defensive arms, the greater and smaller shield, they carried swords as weapons of offence. In the case of the nations in ver. 5, only the shield and helmet are mentioned as their equipment, for the sake of variation, as in ch. xxvii. 10; and in ver. 6 two other nations of the extreme north with their hosts are added. *Gomer:* the Cimmerians; and *the house of Togarmah:* the Armenians (see the comm. on ch. xxvii. 14). For אֲגַפִּים, see the comm. on ch. xii. 14. The description is finally rounded off with עַמִּים רַבִּים אִתָּךְ. In ver. 7, the *infin. abs. Niphal* הִכֹּון, which occurs nowhere else except in Amos iv. 12, is used emphatically in the place of the imperative. The repetition of the same verb, though in the imperative *Hiphil*, equip, *i.e.* make ready, *sc.* everything necessary (cf. ch. vii. 14), also serves to strengthen the thought. Be thou to them לְמִשְׁמָר, for heed, or watch, *i.e.* as *abstr. pro concr.*, one who gives heed to them, keeps watch over them (cf. Job vii. 12 and Neh. iv. 3, 16), in actual fact their leader. Vers. 8 and 9 indicate for what Gog was to hold himself ready. The first clause reminds so strongly of מֵרֹוב יָמִים יִפָּקֵדוּ in Isa. xxiv. 22, that the play upon this passage cannot possibly be mistaken; so that Ezekiel uses the words in the same sense as Isaiah, though Hävernick is wrong in supposing that הִפָּקֵד is used in the sense of being missed or wanting, *i.e.* of perishing. The word never has the latter meaning; and to be missed does not suit the context either here or in Isaiah, where יִפָּקֵד means to be visited, *i.e.* brought to punishment. And here also this meaning, *visitari* (Vulg.), is to be retained, and that in the sense of a penal visitation. The objection raised, namely, that there is no reference to punishment here, but that this is first mentioned in ver. 16 or 18, loses all its force if we bear in mind that visiting is a more general idea than punishing; and the visitation consisted in the fact of God's leading Gog to invade the land of Israel, that He might sanctify Himself upon him by judgment. This might very fittingly be here announced, and it also applies to the parallel clause which follows: thou wilt come into the land, etc., with which the explanation commences of the way in which God would visit him. The only other meaning which could also answer to the parallelism of the clauses, viz. to be commanded, to receive command (Hitzig and Kliefoth), is neither sustained by the usage of the language, nor in accordance with the context. In the passages quoted in support of this, viz. Neh. vii. 1 and xii. 44, נִפְקַד merely signifies to be charged with the oversight of a thing; and it never means only to receive command to do anything. Moreover, Gog has already been appointed leader of the army in ver. 7, and therefore is not "to be placed in the supreme command" for the first time after many days. מִיָּמִים רַבִּים, after many days, *i.e.* after a long time (cf. Josh. xxiii. 1), is not indeed equivalent in itself to בְּאַחֲרִית הַשָּׁנִים, but signifies merely the lapse of a lengthened period; yet this is defined here as occurring in the אַחֲרִית הַשָּׁנִים.—אַחֲרִית הַשָּׁנִים, equivalent to אַחֲרִית הַיָּמִים (ver. 16), is the end of days, the last time, not the future generally, but the final future, the Messianic time of the completing of the kingdom of God (see the comm. on Gen. xlix. 1). This meaning is also applicable here. For Gog is to come up to the mountains of Israel, which have been laid waste תָּמִיד, continually, *i.e.* for a long time, but are now inhabited again. Although, for example, תָּמִיד signifies a period of time relatively long, it evidently indicates a longer period than the seventy or fifty years' desolation of the land during the Babylonian captivity; more especially if we take it in connection with the preceding and following statements, to the effect that Gog will come into the land, which has been brought back from the sword and gathered out of many peoples. These predicates show that in אֶרֶץ the idea of the population of the land is the predominant one; for this alone could be gathered out of many nations, and also brought back from the sword, *i.e.* not from the consequences of the calamity of war, viz. exile (Rosenmüller), but restored from being slain and exiled by the sword of the enemy. מְשׁוֹבֶבֶת, passive participle of the *Pilel* שׁוֹבֵב, to restore (cf. Isa. lviii. 12); not turned away from the sword, *i.e.* in no expectation of war (Hitzig), which does not answer to the parallel clause, and cannot be sustained by Mic. ii. 8. מֵעַמִּים רַבִּים, gathered out of *many* peoples, points also beyond the Babylonian captivity to the dispersion of Israel in all the world, which did not take place till the second destruction of Jerusalem, and shows that תָּמִיד denotes a much longer devastation of the land than the Chaldean devastation was. וְהִיא introduces a circumstantial clause; and הִיא points back to אֶרֶץ, *i.e.* to the inhabitants of the land. These are now brought out of the nations, *i.e.* at the time when Gog invades the land, and are dwelling in their own land upon the mountains of Israel in untroubled security. עָלָה signifies the advance of an enemy, as in Isa. vii. 1, etc. שׁוֹאָה, a tempest, as in Prov. i. 27, from שָׁאָה, to roar. The comparison to a cloud is limited to the covering; but this does not alter the signification of the cloud as a figurative representation of severe calamity.

Vers. 10–16. Account of the motive by which Gog was induced to undertake his warlike expedition, and incurred guilt, notwithstanding the fact that he was led by God, and in consequence of which he brought upon himself the judgment of destruction that was about to fall upon him.—Ver. 10. *Thus saith the Lord Jehovah, It shall come to pass in that day, that things will come up in thy heart, and thou wilt devise an evil design,* Ver. 11. *And say, I will go up into the open country, I will come upon the peaceful ones, who are all dwelling in safety, who dwell without walls, and have not bars and gates,* Ver. 12. *To take plunder and to gather spoil, to bring back thy hand against the ruins that are inhabited again, and against a people gathered out of the nations, carrying on trade and commerce, who dwell on the navel of the earth.* Ver. 13. *Sabaea and Dedan, and the merchants of Tarshish, and all her young lions, will say to thee, Dost thou come to take plunder? Hast thou gathered thy multitude of people to take spoil? Is it to carry away gold and silver, to take possession and gain, to plunder a great spoil?* Ver. 14. *Therefore prophesy, son of man, and say to Gog, Thus saith the Lord Jehovah, Is it not so? On that day, when my people Israel dwelleth in security, thou wilt observe it,* Ver. 15. *And come from thy place from the extreme north, thou and many peoples with thee, all riding upon horses, a great crowd and a numerous army,* Ver. 16. *And wilt march against my people Israel, to cover the land like a cloud; at the end of the days it will take place; then shall I lead thee against my land, that the nations may know me, when I sanctify myself upon thee before their eyes, O Gog.*—In ver. 10 דְּבָרִים are not words, but things which come into his mind. What things these are, we learn from vers. 11 and 12; but first of all, these things are described as evil thoughts or designs. Gog resolves to fall upon Israel, now living in peace and security, and dwelling in open unfortified places, and to rob and plunder it. אֶרֶץ פְּרָזוֹת, literally, land of plains, *i.e.* a land which has no fortified towns, but only places lying quite exposed (see the comm. on Zech. ii. 8); because its inhabitants are living in undisturbed peace and safe repose, and therefore dwell in places that have no walls with gates and bars (cf. Judg. xviii. 7; Jer. xlix. 31). This description of Israel's mode of life also points beyond the times succeeding the Babylonian captivity to the Messianic days, when the Lord will have destroyed the horses and war-chariots and fortresses (Mic. v. 9), and Jerusalem will be inhabited as an open country because of the multitude of the men and cattle, and the Lord will be a wall of fire round about her (Zech. ii. 8, 9). For ver. 12*a*, compare Isa. x. 6. לְהָשִׁיב יָדְךָ is not dependent upon אֶעֱלֶה, like the preceding infinitives, but is subordinate to אָמַרְתָּ אעלה וגו׳: "thou sayest, I will go up . . . to turn thy hand." הָשִׁיב, to bring back, is to be explained from the fact that the heathen had already at an earlier period turned their hand against the towns of Israel, and plundered their possessions and goods. חֳרָבוֹת נוֹשָׁבוֹת in this connection are desolate places which are inhabited again, and therefore have been rebuilt (cf. ch. xii. 20, xxvi. 19). מִקְנֶה and קִנְיָן are synonyms; and מִקְנֶה does not mean flocks or herds, but gain, possession (cf. Gen. xxxvi. 6, xxxi. 18, xxxiv. 23). One motive of Gog for making the attack was to be found in the possessions of Israel; a second is given in the words: who dwell upon the navel of the earth. This figurative expression is to be explained from ch. v. 5: "Jerusalem in the midst of the nations." The navel is not a figure denoting the high land, but signifies the land situated in the middle of the earth, and therefore the land most glorious and most richly blessed; so that they who dwell there occupy the most exalted position among the nations. A covetous desire for the possessions of the people of God, and envy at his exalted position in the centre of the world, are therefore the motives by which Gog is impelled to enter upon his predatory expedition against the people living in the depth of peace. This covetousness is so great, that even the rich trading populations of Sabaea, Dedan, and Tarshish (cf. ch. xxvii. 22, 20, and 12) perceive it, and declare that it is this alone which has determined Gog to undertake his expedition. The words of these peoples (ver. 13) are not to be taken as expressing their sympathies (Kliefoth), but serve to give prominence to the obvious thirst for booty which characterizes the multitude led by Gog. כְּפִירֶיהָ, their young lions, are the rapacious rulers of these trading communities, according to ch. xix. 3 and xxxii. 2.—Ver. 14 introduces the announcement of the punishment, which consists of another summary account of the daring enterprise of Gog and his hosts (cf. vers. 14, 15, and 16*a* with vers. 4–9), and a clear statement of the design of God in leading him against His people and land. תֵּדָע (ver. 14, close), of which different renderings have been given, does not mean, thou wilt experience, or be aware of, the punishment; but the object is to be taken from the context: thou wilt know, or perceive, *sc.* that Israel dwells securely, not expecting any hostile invasion. The rendering of the LXX. (ἐγερθήσῃ) does not furnish any satisfactory ground for altering תֵּדָע into תער = תֵּעוֹר (Ewald, Hitzig). With the words וַהֲבִיאוֹתִיךָ וגו׳ (ver. 16*b*) the opening thought of the whole picture (ver. 4*a*) is resumed and defined with greater precision, for the purpose of attaching to it the declaration of the design of the Lord in bringing Gog, namely, to sanctify Himself upon him before the eyes of the nations (cf. ver. 23 and ch. xxxvi. 23).

Vers. 17–23. Announcement of the wrathful judgment upon Gog, as a proof of the holiness of the Lord.—Ver. 17. *Thus saith the Lord Jehovah, Art thou he of whom I spoke in the former days through my servants the prophets of Israel, who prophesied for years in those days, that I would bring thee over them?* Ver. 18. *And it cometh to pass in that day, in the day when Gog cometh into the land of Israel, is the saying of the Lord Jehovah, that my wrath will ascend into my nose.* Ver. 19. *And in my jealousy, in the fire of my anger, have I spoken, Truly in that day will a great trembling come over the land of Israel;* Ver. 20. *The fishes of the sea, and the birds of heaven, and the beasts of the field, and every creeping thing that creepeth upon the ground, and all the men that are upon the ground, will tremble before me; and the mountains will be destroyed, and the rocky heights fall, and every wall will fall to the ground.* Ver. 21. *I will call the sword against him to all my holy mountains, is the saying of the Lord Jehovah: the sword of the one will be against the other.* Ver. 22. *And I will strive with him by pestilence and by blood, and overflowing rain-torrents and hailstones; fire and brimstone will I rain upon him and all his hosts, and upon the many peoples that are with him;* Ver. 23. *And will prove myself great and holy, and will make myself known before the eyes of many nations, that they may know that I am Jehovah.*—The announcement of the way in which the Lord will sanctify Himself upon Gog (ver. 16) commences with the statement in ver. 17, that Gog is he of whom God has already spoken by the earlier prophets. This assertion is clothed in the form of a question: הַאַתָּה, not הֲלֹא אַתָּה, which is the interrogative form used for an emphatic assurance; whereas הַאַתָּה does not set down the point in question as indisputably certain, but suggests the inquiry for the purpose of giving a definite answer. The affirmative reply to the question asked is contained in the last clause of the verse: "to bring *thee* upon them;" so that הַאַתָּה הוּא really means, thou art truly he. The statement, that Gog is he of whom God had already spoken by the earlier prophets, does not mean that those prophets had actually mentioned Gog, but simply that Gog was the enemy of whose rising up against the people of God the prophets of the former time had prophesied, as well as of his destruction by a wrathful judgment of the Lord. שָׁנִים (for years, or years long) is an accusative of measure, not asyndeton to בַּיָּמִים, as the LXX. and many of the commentators down to Hävernick have taken it to be. The design of this remark is not to accredit the prophecy by referring to the utterances of earlier prophets, but to show that the attack of the peoples gathered together by Gog, upon the land and people of the Lord, is not an unexpected event, or one at variance with the promise of the restoration of Israel as a kingdom of peace.. To what utterances of the older prophets these words refer is a question difficult to answer. Zechariah (xii. 2, 3, xiv. 2, 3) is of course not to be thought of, as Zechariah himself did not prophesy till after the captivity, and therefore not till after Ezekiel. But we may recall Joel iv. 2 and 11 sqq.; Isa. xxv. 5, 10 sqq., xxvi. 21; Jer. xxx. 23 and 25; and, in fact, all the earlier prophets who prophesied of Jehovah's day of judgment upon all the heathen.[1] —Vers. 18 and 19 do not contain words which Jehovah spoke through the ancient prophets, and which Ezekiel now transfers to Gog and the time of his appearing (Hitzig and Kliefoth). The perfect דִּבַּרְתִּי in ver. 19 by no means warrants such an assumption; for this is purely prophetic, expressing the certainty of the divine determination as a thing clearly proved. Still less can נְאֻם אד' in ver. 18 be taken as a preterite, as Kliefoth supposes; nor can vers. 18 and 19 be regarded as a thing long predicted, and so be separated from vers. 20–23 as a word of God which is now for the first time uttered. For the anthropopathetic expression, "my wrath ascends in my nose," compare Ps. xviii. 9, "smoke ascends in His nose." The outburst of wrath shows itself in the vehement breath which the wrathful man inhales and exhales through his nose (see the comm. on the Psalm, *l.c.*). The bursting out of the wrath of God is literally explained in ver. 19. In the jealousy of His wrath God has spoken, *i.e.* determined, to inflict a great trembling upon the land of Israel. בְּקִנְאָתִי (cf. ch. v. 13) is strengthened by בְּאֵשׁ עֶבְרָתִי (cf. ch. xxi. 36, xxii. 21). The trembling which will come upon the land of Israel, so that all creatures in the sea, in the air, and upon the ground, tremble before Jehovah (מִפָּנַי), who appears to judgment, will rise in nature into an actual earthquake, which overthrows mountains, hills, and walls. מַדְרֵגוֹת are steep heights, which can only be ascended by steps (Song of Sol. ii. 14). This picture of the trembling of the whole world, with all the creatures, before the Lord who is coming to judgment, both here and in Joel iv. 16,

[1] Aug. Kueper (*Jeremias librr. sacrr. interpr. atque vindex*, p. 82) has correctly observed concerning this verse, that "it is evident enough that there is no reference here to prophecies concerning Gog and Magog, which have been lost; but those general prophecies, which are met with on every hand directed against the enemies of the church, are here referred to Gog." And before him, J. F. Starck had already said: "In my opinion, we are to understand all those passages in the prophets which treat of the enemies of the church and its persecutions . . . these afflictions were preludes and shadows of the bloody persecution of Gog."

Zech. xiv. 4, 5, rests upon the fact which actually occurred in connection with the revelation of God upon Sinai, when the whole mountain was made to quake (Ex. xix. 16 sqq.). The inhabitants of the land of Israel tremble at the terrible phenomena attending the revelation of the wrath of God, although the wrathful judgment does not apply to them, but to their enemies, Gog and his hosts. The Lord calls the sword against Gog, that his hosts may wound and slay one another. This feature of the destruction of the enemy by wounds inflicted by itself, which we meet with again in Zech. xiv. 13, has its typical exemplar in the defeat of the Midianites in the time of Gideon (Judg. vii. 22), and also in that of the enemy invading Judah in the reign of Jehoshaphat (2 Chron. xx. 23). In לְכָל־הָרַי the לְ is not distributive, but indicates the direction: "to all my mountains." The overthrow of the enemy is intensified by marvellous plagues inflicted by God — pestilence and blood (cf. ch. xxviii. 23), torrents of rain and hailstones (cf. ch. xiii. 11), and the raining of fire and brimstone upon Gog, as formerly upon Sodom and Gomorrah (Gen. xix. 24). — Thus will Jehovah prove Himself to be the almighty God by judgment upon His enemies, and sanctify Himself before all the nations (ver. 23, compare ver. 16 and ch. xxxvi. 23).

Ch. xxxix. 1–20. Further description of the judgment to fall upon Gog and his hosts.—Vers. 1–8. General announcement of his destruction.—Ver. 1. *And thou, son of man, prophesy against Gog, and say, Thus saith the Lord Jehovah, Behold, I will deal with thee, Gog, thou prince of Rosh, Meshech, and Tubal.* Ver. 2. *I will mislead thee, and conduct thee, and cause thee to come up from the uttermost north, and bring thee to the mountains of Israel;* Ver. 3. *And will smite thy bow from thy left hand, and cause thine arrows to fall from thy right hand.* Ver. 4. *Upon the mountains of Israel wilt thou fall, thou and all thy hosts, and the peoples which are with thee: I give thee for food to the birds of prey of every plumage, and to the beasts of the field.* Ver. 5. *Upon the open field shalt thou fall, for I have spoken it, is the saying of the Lord Jehovah.* Ver. 6. *And I will send fire in Magog, and among those who dwell in security upon the islands, that they may know that I am Jehovah.* Ver. 7. *I will make known my holy name in the midst of my people Israel, and will not let my holy name be profaned any more, that the nations may know that I am Jehovah, holy in Israel.* Ver. 8. *Behold, it comes and happens, is the saying of the Lord Jehovah; this is the day of which I spoke.*—The further description of the judgment with which Gog and his hosts are threatened in ch. xxxviii. 21–23, commences with a repetition of the command to the prophet to prophesy against Gog (ver. 1, cf. ch. xxxviii. 2, 3). The principal contents of ch. xxxviii. 4–15 are then briefly summed up in ver. 2. שֹׁבַבְתִּיךָ, as in ch. xxxviii. 4, is strengthened by שִׁשֵּׁתִיךָ. שׁשׁא, *ἅπαξ λεγ.*, is not connected with שֵׁשׁ in the sense of "I leave a sixth part of thee remaining," or afflict thee with six punishments; but in the Ethiopic it signifies to proceed, or to climb, and here, accordingly, it is used in the sense of leading on (LXX. *καθοδηγήσω σε*, or, according to another reading, *κατάξω*; Vulg. *educam*). For ver. 2*b*, compare ch. xxxviii. 15 and 8. In the land of Israel, God will strike his weapons out of his hands, *i.e.* make him incapable of fighting (for the fact itself, compare the similar figures in Ps. xxxvii. 15, xlvi. 10), and give him up with all his army as a prey to death. עַיִט, a beast of prey, is more precisely defined by צִפּוֹר, and still further strengthened by the genitive כָּל־כָּנָף: birds of prey of every kind. The judgment will not be confined to the destruction of the army of Gog, which has invaded the land of Israel, but (ver. 6) will also extend to the land of Gog, and to all the heathen nations that are dwelling in security. אֵשׁ, fire, primarily the fire of war; then, in a further sense, a figure denoting destruction inflicted directly by God, as in ch. xxxviii. 22, which is therefore represented in Rev. xx. 9 as fire falling from heaven. *Magog* is the population of the land of Magog (ch. xxxviii. 2). With this the inhabitants of the distant coastlands of the west (the אִיִּים) are associated, as representatives of the remotest heathen nations. Vers. 7, 8. By this judgment the Lord will make known His holy name in Israel, and show the heathen that He will not let it be blasphemed by them any more. For the fact itself, compare ch xxxvi. 20 For ver. 8, compare ch. xxi. 12, and for הַיּוֹם, see ch. xxxviii. 18, 19.

Vers. 9–20 Total destruction of Gog and his hosts.—Ver. 9. *Then will the inhabitants of the cities of Israel go forth, and burn and heat with armour and shield and target, with bow and arrows and hand-staves and spears, and will burn fire with them for seven years;* Ver. 10 *And will not fetch wood from the field, nor cut wood out of the forests, but will burn fire with the armour, and will spoil those who spoiled them, and plunder those who plundered them, is the saying of the Lord Jehovah.* Ver. 11. *And it will come to pass in that day, that I will give Gog a place where his grave in Israel shall be, the valley of the travellers on the front of the sea; and it will stop the way to the travellers, and there will they bury Gog and all his multitude, and will call it the valley of Gog's multitude.* Ver 12 *They of the house of Israel will bury them, to purify the land for seven months.* Ver. 13. *And all the people of the land will bury, and it will be to them for a name on the day when I glorify myself, is the saying of the Lord Jehovah.* Ver. 14. *And they will set apart constant men, such as rove about in the land, and such as bury with them that rove about those who remain upon the surface of the ground, to cleanse it, after the lapse of seven months will they search it through.* Ver. 15. *And those who rove about will pass through the land; and if one sees a man's bone, he will set up a sign by it, till the buriers of the dead bury it in the valley of the multitude of Gog.* Ver. 16. *The name of a city shall also be called Hamonah (multitude). And thus will they cleanse the land.* Ver 17. *And thou, son of man, thus saith the Lord Jehovah, Say to the birds of every plumage, and to all the beasts of the field, Assemble yourselves, and come, gather together from round about to my sacrifice, which I slaughter for you, to a great sacrifice upon the mountains of*

Israel, and eat flesh and drink blood. Ver. 18. *Flesh of heroes shall ye eat, and drink blood of princes of the earth; rams, lambs, and he-goats, bullocks, all fattened in Bashan.* Ver. 9. *And ye shall eat fat to satiety, and drink blood to intoxication, of my sacrifice which I have slaughtered for you.* Ver. 20. *And ye shall satiate yourselves at my table with horses and riders, heroes and all kinds of men of war, is the saying of the Lord Jehovah.*—To show how terrible the judgment upon Gog will be, Ezekiel depicts in three special ways the total destruction of his powerful forces. In the *first* place, the burning of all the weapons of the fallen foe will furnish the inhabitants of the land of Israel with wood for firing for seven years, so that there will be no necessity for them to fetch fuel from the field or from the forest (vers. 9 and 10). But Hävernick is wrong in supposing that the reason for burning the weapons is that, according to Isa. ix. 5, weapons of war are irreconcilable with the character of the Messianic times of peace. This is not referred to here; but the motive is the complete annihilation of the enemy, the removal of every trace of him. The prophet therefore crowds the words together for the purpose of enumerating every kind of weapon that was combustible, even to the hand-staves which men were accustomed to carry (cf. Num. xxii. 27). The quantity of the weapons will be so great, that they will supply the Israelites with all the fuel they need for seven years. The number seven in the seven years as well as in the seven months of burying (ver. 11) is symbolical, stamping the overthrow as a punishment inflicted by God, the completion of a divine judgment.—With the gathering of the weapons for burning there is associated the plundering of the fallen foe (ver. 10*b*), by which the Israelites do to the enemy what he intended to do to them (ch. xxxviii. 12), and the people of God obtain possession of the wealth of their foes (cf. Jer. xxx. 16). In the *second* place, God will assign a large burying-place for the army of Gog in a valley of Israel, which is to be named in consequence "the multitude of Gog;" just as a city in that region will also be called *Hamonah* from this event. The Israelites will bury the fallen of Gog there for seven months long, and after the expiration of that time they will have the land explored by men specially appointed for the purpose, and bones that may still have been left unburied will be sought out, and they will have them interred by buriers of the dead, that the land may be thoroughly cleansed (vers. 11–16). מְקוֹם שָׁם קֶבֶר, a place where there was a grave in Israel, *i.e.* a spot in which he might be buried in Israel. There are different opinions as to both the designation and the situation of this place. There is no foundation for the supposition that גֵּי הָעֹבְרִים derives its name from the mountains of *Abarim* in Num. xxvii. 12 and Deut. xxxii. 49 (Michaelis, Eichhorn), or that it signifies valley of the haughty ones (Ewald), or that there is an allusion to the valley mentioned in Zech. xiv. 4 (Hitzig), or the valley of Jehoshaphat (Kliefoth). The valley cannot even have derived its name (הָעֹבְרִים) from the עֹבְרִים, who passed through the land to search out the bones of the dead that still remained unburied, and have them interred (vers. 14, 15). For הָעֹבְרִים cannot have any other meaning here than that which it has in the circumstantial clause which follows, where those who explored the land cannot possibly be intended, although even this clause is also obscure. The only other passage in which חָסַם occurs is Deut. xxv. 4, where it signifies a muzzle, and in the Arabic it means to obstruct, or cut off; and hence, in the passage before us, probably, to stop the way. הָעֹבְרִים are not the Scythians (Hitzig), for the word עָבַר is never applied to their invasion of the land, but generally the travellers who pass through the land, or more especially those who cross from Peraea to Canaan. The valley of הָעֹבְרִים is no doubt the valley of the Jordan above the Dead Sea. The definition indicates this, viz. קִדְמַת הַיָּם, on the front of the sea; not to the east of the sea, as it is generally rendered, for קִדְמַת never has this meaning (see the comm. on Gen. ii. 14). By הַיָּם we cannot understand "the Mediterranean," as the majority of the commentators have done, as there would then be no meaning in the words, since the whole of the land of Israel was situated to the east of the Mediterranean Sea. הַיָּם is the Dead Sea, generally called הַיָּם הַקַּדְמוֹנִי (ch. xlvii. 18); and קִדְמַת הַיָּם, "on the front side of the (Dead) Sea," as looked at from Jerusalem, the central point of the land, is probably the valley of the Jordan, the principal crossing place from Gilead into Canaan proper, and the broadest part of the Jordan-valley, which was therefore well adapted to be the burial-place for the multitude of slaughtered foes. But in consequence of the army of Gog having there found its grave, this valley will in future block up the way to the travellers who desire to pass to and fro. This appears to be the meaning of the circumstantial clause.—From the fact that Gog's multitude is buried there, the valley itself will receive the name of *Hamon-Gog.* The Israelites will occupy seven months in burying them, so enormously great will be the number of the dead to be buried (ver. 12), and this labour will be for a name, *i.e.* for renown, to the whole nation. This does not mean, of course, "that it will be a source of honour to them to assist in this work;" nor is the renown to be sought in the fact, that as a privileged people, protected by God, they can possess the grave of Gog in their land (Hitzig),—a thought which is altogether remote, and perfectly foreign to Israelitish views; but the burying of Gog's multitude of troops will be for a name to the people of Israel, inasmuch as they thereby cleanse the land and manifest their zeal to show themselves a holy people by sweeping all uncleanness away. יוֹם is an accusative of time: on the day when I glorify myself.—Vers. 14, 15. The effort made to cleanse the land perfectly from the uncleanness arising from the bones of the dead will be so great, that after the great mass of the slain have been buried in seven months, there will be men specially appointed to bury the bones of the dead that still lie scattered here and there about the land. אַנְשֵׁי תָמִיד are people who have a permanent duty to discharge. The participles עֹבְרִים and

מְקַבְּרִים are co-ordinate, and are written together *asyndetos*, men who go about the land, and men who bury with those who go about. That the words are to be understood in this sense is evident from ver 15, according to which those who go about do not perform the task of burying, but simply search for bones that have been left, and put up a sign for the buriers of the dead. רָאָה, with the subject indefinite; if one sees a human bone, he builds (erects) a צִיּוּן, or stone, by the side of it (cf. 2 Kings xxiii. 17).—Ver 16. A city shall also receive the name of *Hamonah*, *i.e.* multitude or tumult To שֶׁם־עִיר we may easily supply יִהְיֶה from the context, since this puts in the future the statement, "the name of the city *is*," for which no verb was required in Hebrew. In the last words, וְטִהֲרוּ הָאָרֶץ, the main thought is finally repeated and the picture brought to a close.—Vers. 17–20. In the *third* place, God will provide the birds of prey and beasts of prey with an abundant meal from this slaughter. This cannot be understood as signifying that only what remain of the corpses, and have not been cleared away in the manner depicted in vers. 11–16, will become the prey of wild beasts; but the beasts of prey will make their meal of the corpses before it is possible to bury them, since the burying cannot be effected immediately or all at once.—The several features in the picture, of the manner in which the enemies are to be destroyed till the last trace of them is gone, are not arranged in chronological order, but according to the subject-matter; and the thought that the slaughtered foes are to become the prey of wild beasts is mentioned last as being the more striking, because it is in this that their ignominious destruction culminates. To give due prominence to this thought, the birds and beasts of prey are summoned by God to gather together to the meal prepared for them. The picture given of it as a sacrificial meal is based upon Isa. xxxiv. 6 and Jer. xlvi. 10. In harmony with this picture the slaughtered foes are designated as fattened sacrificial beasts, rams, lambs, he-goats, bullocks; on which Grotius has correctly remarked, that "these names of animals, which were generally employed in the sacrifices, are to be understood as signifying different orders of men, chiefs, generals, soldiers, as the Chaldee also observes."

Vers. 21–29. The result of this judgment, and the concluding promise.—Ver. 21. *Then will I display my glory among the nations, and all nations shall see my judgment which I shall execute, and my hand which I shall lay upon them.* Ver. 22. *And the house of Israel shall know that I am Jehovah their God from this day and forward.* Ver. 23. *And the nations shall know that because of their wickedness the house of Israel went into captivity; because they have been unfaithful toward me, I hid my face from them, and gave them into the hand of their oppressors, so that they all fell by the sword.* Ver. 24. *According to their uncleanness, and according to their transgressions, I dealt with them, and hid my face from them.* Ver. 25. *Therefore thus saith the Lord Jehovah, Now will I bring back the captivity of Jacob, and have pity upon all the house of Israel, and be jealous for my holy name.* Ver. 26. *Then will they bear their reproach and all their faithlessness which they have committed toward me when they dwell in their land in security, and no one alarms them;* Ver. 27. *When I bring them back out of the nations, and gather them out of the lands of their enemies, and sanctify myself upon them before the eyes of the many nations.* Ver. 28. *And they will know that I, Jehovah, am their God, when I have driven them out to the nations, and then bring them together again into their land, and leave none of them there any more.* Ver. 29. *And I will not hide my face from them any more, because I have poured out my Spirit upon the house of Israel, is the saying of the Lord Jehovah.*—The terrible judgment upon Gog will have this twofold effect as a revelation of the glory of God—*first*, Israel will know that the Lord is, and will always continue to be, its God (ver. 22); *secondly*, the heathen will know that He gave Israel into their power, and thrust it out of its own land, not from weakness, but to punish it for its faithless apostasy (vers. 23 and 24; compare ch. xxxvi. 17 sqq.) עָשָׂה אֹתָם (ver. 24), as in ch. vii. 27, etc. But because this was the purpose of the Lord with His judgments, He will now bring back the captives of Israel, and have compassion upon all His people. This turn of the prophecy in ver. 25 serves to introduce the promise to Israel with which the prophecy concerning Gog and the whole series of prophecies, contained in ch. xxxv. 1 onwards, are brought to a close (vers. 25–29). This promise reverts in עַתָּה אָשִׁיב וגו׳ to the prophet's own time, to which Ezekiel had already gone back by mentioning the carrying away of Israel in vers. 23 and 24. The restoration of the captives of Jacob commences with the liberation of Israel from the Babylonian exile, but is not to be restricted to this. It embraces all the deliverances which Israel will experience from the termination of the Babylonian exile till its final gathering out of the nations on the conversion of the remnant which is still hardened and scattered. לָכֵן, therefore, *sc.* because God will prove Himself to be holy in the sight of the heathen nations by means of the judgment, and will make known to them that He has punished Israel solely on account of its sins, and therefore will He restore His people and renew it by His Spirit (ver. 29).—In what the jealousy of God for His holy name consists is evident from ver. 7, and still more plainly from ch. xxxvi. 22, 23, namely, in the fact that by means of the judgment He manifests Himself as the holy God. וְנָשׂוּ is not to be altered into וְנָשׁוּ, "they will forget," as Dathe and Hitzig propose, but is a defective spelling for וְנָשְׂאוּ (like מָלוּ for מָלְאוּ in ch. xxviii. 16): they will bear their reproach. The thought is the same as in ch. xvi. 54 and 61, where the bearing of reproach is explained as signifying their being ashamed of their sins and their consequences, and feeling disgust thereat. They will feel this shame when the Lord grants them lasting peace in their own land. Raschi has correctly explained it thus: "When I shall have done them good, and not rewarded them as their iniquity deserved, they will be filled with shame, so that they will not dare to lift up their face."—Ver. 27 is only a further expansion of ver. 26*b*. For the fact itself, compare ch. xxxvi. 23, 24, xx. 41, etc. And not only will Israel then be ashamed of its sins, but (vers. 28, 29) it will also know that Jehovah is its God from henceforth and for ever, as was affirmed in ver. 22, when He shall fully restore to their own land the people that was thrust into exile, and withdraw His favour from it no more, because He has poured out His Spirit upon it, and thereby perfectly sanctified it as His own people (cf. ch. xxxvi. 27).

The promise with which the prophecy concerning the destruction of Gog is brought to a close, namely, that in this judgment all nations shall see the glory of God, and all Israel shall know that henceforth Jehovah will be their God, and will no more hide His face from them, serves to confirm the substance of the threat of punishment; inasmuch as it also teaches that, in the destruction of Gog and his gathering of peoples, the last attack of the heathen world-power upon the kingdom of God will be judged and overthrown, so that from that time forth the people of God will no more have to fear a foe who can disturb its peace and its blessedness in the everlasting possession of the inheritance given to it by the Lord. Gog is not only depicted as the last foe, whom the Lord Himself entices for the purpose of destroying him by miracles of His almighty power (ch. xxxviii. 3, 4, 19–22), by the fact that his appearance is assigned to the end of the times, when all Israel is gathered out of the nations and brought back out of the lands, and dwells in secure repose in the open and unfortified towns of its own land (ch. xxxviii. 8, 11, 12); but this may also be inferred from the fact that the gathering of peoples led by Gog against Israel belongs to the heathen nations living on the borders of the known world, since this points to a time when not only will the ancient foes of the kingdom of Gog, whose destruction was predicted in ch. xxv.–xxxii., have departed from the stage of history and perished, but the boundaries of Israel will also stretch far beyond the limits of Palestine, to the vicinity of these hordes of peoples at the remotest extremities on the north, the east, and the south of the globe.—So much may be gathered from the contents of our prophecy in relation to its historical fulfilment. But in order to determine with greater precision what is the heathen power thus rising up in Gog of Magog against the kingdom of God, we must take into consideration the passage in the Apocalypse (Rev. xx. 8 and 9), where our prophecy is resumed. Into this, however, we will not further enter till after the exposition of ch. xl.–xlviii., when we shall take up the question as to the historical realization of the new temple and kingdom of God which Ezekiel saw.

Chap. XL.–XLVIII.—THE NEW KINGDOM OF GOD.

The last nine chapters of Ezekiel contain a magnificent vision, in which the prophet, being transported in an ecstatic state into the land of Israel, is shown the new temple and the new organization of the service of God, together with the new division of Canaan among the tribes of Israel, who have been brought back from among the nations. This last section of our book, which is perfectly rounded off in itself, is indeed sharply distinguished by its form from the preceding prophecies; but it is closely connected with them so far as the contents are concerned, and forms the second half of the entire book, in which the announcement of salvation for Israel is brought to its full completion, and a panoramic vision displays the realization of the salvation promised. This announcement (ch. xxxiv.–xxxvii.) commenced with the promise that the Lord would bring back all Israel from its dispersion into the land of Canaan given to the fathers, and would cause it to dwell there as a people renewed by His Spirit and walking in His commandments; and closed with the assurance that He would make an eternal covenant of peace with His restored people, place His sanctuary in the midst of them, and there dwell above them as their God for ever (ch. xxxvii. 26–28). The picture shown to the prophet in the chapters before us, of the realization of this promise, commences with the description and measuring of the new sanctuary (ch. xl.–xlii.), into which the glory of the Lord enters with the assurance, "This is the place of my throne, where I shall dwell for ever among the sons of Israel" (ch. xliii. 1–12); and concludes with the definition of the boundaries and the division of Canaan among the twelve tribes, as well as of the extent and building of the new Jerusalem (ch. xlvii. 13–xlviii. 35). The central portion of this picture is occupied by the new organization of the service of God, by observing which all Israel is to prove itself to be a holy people of the Lord (ch. xliii. 13–xlvi. 24), so as to participate in the blessing which flows like a river from the threshold of the temple and spreads itself over the land (ch. xlvii. 1–12).

From this brief sketch of these nine chapters, it is evident that this vision does not merely treat of the new temple and the new order of the temple-worship, although these points are described in the most elaborate manner; but that it presents a picture of the new form assumed by the whole of the kingdom of God, and in this picture exhibits to the eye the realization of the restoration and the blessedness of Israel. The whole of it may therefore be divided into three sections: viz. (*a*) the description of the new temple (ch. xl.–xliii. 12); (*b*) the new organization of the worship of God (ch. xliii. 13–xlvi. 24); (*c*) the blessing of the land of Canaan, and the partition of it among the tribes of Israel (ch. xlvii. 1–xlviii. 35); although this division is not strictly adhered to, inasmuch as in the central section not only are several points relating to the temple—such as the description of the altar of burnt-offering (ch. xliii. 13–17), and the kitchens for the sacrifices (ch. xlvi. 19–24)—repeated, but the *therumah* to be set apart as holy on the division of the land, and the prince's domain, are also mentioned and defined (ch. xlv. 1–8).

CHAP. XL.–XLIII. 12. THE NEW TEMPLE.

After a short introduction announcing the time, place, and design of the vision (ch. xl. 1–4), the picture of the temple shown to the prophet commences with a description of the courts, with their gates and cells (ch. xl. 5–47). It then turns to the description of the temple-house, with the porch and side-building, of the erection upon the separate place (ch. xl. 48–xli. 26), and also of the cells in the outer court set apart for the sacrificial meals of the priests, and for the custody of their official robes; and proceeds to define the extent of the outer circumference of the temple (ch. xlii.). It closes with the consecration of the temple, as the place of the throne of God, by the entrance into it of the glory of the Lord (ch. xliii. 1–12).[1]

Chap. xl. 1–4. *Introduction.*

Ver. 1. *In the five and twentieth year of our captivity, at the beginning of the year, on the tenth of the month, in the fourteenth*

[1] For the exposition of this section, compare the thorough, though critically one-sided, work of Jul. Fr. Böttcher (*Exegetisch kritischer Versuch über die ideale Beschreibung der Tempelgebäude Ezech.* ch. xl.–xlii., xlvi. 19–24) in the *Proben alttestamentlicher Schrifterklärung*, Lpz. 1833, pp. 218–365, with two plates of illustrations.—On the other hand, the earlier monographs upon these chapters: Jo. Bapt. Villalpando, *de postrema Ezechielis visione*, *Pars II.* of *Pradi et Villalpandi in Ezech. explanatt.*, Rom. 1604; Matth. Hafenreffer, *Templum Ezechielis s. in IX. postr. prophetiae capita*, Tüb. 1613; Leonh. Cph. Sturm, *Sciagraphia templi Hierosol. . . . praesertim ex visione Ezech.*, Lips. 1694; and other writings mentioned in Rosenmüller's *Scholia ad Ez. XL.*, by no means meet the scientific demands of our age. This also applies to the work of Dr. J. J. Balmer-Rinck, with its typographical beauty, *Des Propheten Ezechiel Ansicht vom Tempel, mit* 5 *Tafeln und* 1 *Karte*, Ludwigsb. 1858, and to the description and engraving of Ezekiel's temple in Gust. Unruh's *das alte Jerusalem und seine Bauwerke*, Langensalza 1861.

year after the city was smitten, on this same day the hand of Jehovah came upon me, and He brought me thither. Ver. 2. *In visions of God He brought me into the land of Israel, and set me down upon a very high mountain; and upon it there was like a city-edifice toward the south.* Ver. 3. *And He brought me thither, and behold there was a man, his appearance like the appearance of brass, and a flaxen cord in his hand, and the measuring-rod; and he stood by the gate.* Ver. 4. *And the man spake to me: Son of man, see with thine eyes, and hear with thine ears, and set thy heart upon all that I show thee; for thou art brought hither to show it thee. Tell all that thou seest to the house of Israel.*— The twofold announcement of the time when the prophet was shown the vision of the new temple and the new kingdom of God points back to ch. i. 1 and xxxiii. 21, and places this divine revelation concerning the new building of the kingdom of God in a definite relation, not only to the appearance of God by which Ezekiel was called to be a prophet (ch. i. 1, 3), but also to the vision in ch. viii.–xi., in which he was shown the destruction of the ancient, sinful Jerusalem, together with its temple. The twenty-fifth year of the captivity, and the fourteenth year after the city was smitten, *i.e.* taken and reduced to ashes, are the year 575 before Christ. There is a difference of opinion as to the correct explanation of בְּרֹאשׁ הַשָּׁנָה, at the beginning of the year; but it is certainly incorrect to take the expression as denoting the beginning of the economical or so-called civil year, the seventh month (*Tishri*). For, in the first place, the custom of beginning the year with the month *Tishri* was introduced long after the captivity, and was probably connected with the adoption of the era of the Seleucidae; and, secondly, it is hardly conceivable that Ezekiel should have deviated from the view laid down in the *Torah* in so important a point as this. The only thing that could render this at all probable would be the assumption proposed by Hitzig, that the year 575 B.C. was a year of jubilee, since the year of jubilee did commence with the day of atonement on the tenth of the seventh month. But the supposition that a jubilee year fell in the twenty-fifth year of the captivity cannot be raised into a probability. We therefore agree with Hävernick and Kliefoth in adhering to the view of the older commentators, that רֹאשׁ הַשָּׁנָה is a contracted repetition of the definition contained in Ex. xii. 2, רֹאשׁ חֳדָשִׁים רִאשׁוֹן לְחָדְשֵׁי הַשָּׁנָה, and signifies the opening month of the year, *i.e.* the month *Abib* (*Nisan*). The tenth day of this month was the day on which the preparations for the Passover, the feast of the elevation of Israel into the people of God, were to commence, and therefore was well adapted for the revelation of the new constitution of the kingdom of God. On that day was Ezekiel transported, in an ecstatic state, to the site of the smitten Jerusalem. For הָיְתָה עָלַי יַד יי׳, compare ch. xxxvii. 1 and i. 3. שָׁמָּה evidently points back to הָעִיר in ver. 2*b*: thither, where the city was smitten. מַרְאוֹת אֱלֹהִים, as in ch. i. 1. יְנִיחֵנִי אֶל הַר ג׳: he set me down upon (not by) a very high mountain (אֶל for עַל, as in many other instances; *e.g.* ch. xviii. 6 and xxxi. 12). The very high mountain is Mount Zion, which is exalted above the tops of all the mountains (Mic. iv. 1; Isa. ii. 2),—the mountain upon which, according to what follows, the new temple seen in the vision stood, and which has already been designated as the lofty mountain of Israel in ch. xvii. 22, 23.[1] Upon this mountain Ezekiel saw something like a city-edifice toward the south (lit. from the south hither). מִבְנֵה עִיר is not the building of the new Jerusalem (Hävernick, Kliefoth, etc.). For even if what was to be seen *as* a city-edifice really could be one, although no tenable proof can be adduced of this use of כ *simil.*, nothing is said about the city till ch. xlv. 6 and xlviii. 15 and 30 sqq., and even there it is only in combination with the measuring and dividing of the land; so that Hävernick's remark, that "the

[1] J. H. Michaelis has already explained it correctly, viz.: "The *highest mountain*, such as Isaiah (ii. 2) had also predicted that Mount Zion would be, not physically, but in the eminence of gospel dignity and glory; cf. Rev. xxi. 10."

revelation has reference to the sanctuary and the city; these two principal objects announce themselves at once as such in the form of vision," is neither correct nor conclusive. The revelation has reference to the temple and the whole of the holy land, including the city; and the city itself does not come at all into such prominence as to warrant us in assuming that there is already a reference made to it here in the introduction. If we look at the context, the man with the measure, whom Ezekiel saw at the place to which he was transported, was standing at the gate (ver. 3). This gate in the wall round about the building was, according to vers. 5, 6, a temple gate. Consequently what Ezekiel saw as a city-edifice can only be the building of the new temple, with its surrounding wall and its manifold court buildings. The expressions עָלָיו and מִנֶּגֶב can both be brought into harmony with this. עָלָיו refers to the very high mountain mentioned immediately before, to the summit of which the prophet had been transported, and upon which the temple-edifice is measured before his eyes. But מִנֶּגֶב does not imply, that as Ezekiel looked from the mountain he saw *in the distance*, toward the south, a magnificent building like a city-edifice; but simply that, looking from his standing-place in a southerly direction, or southwards, he saw this building upon the mountain,—that is to say, as he had been transported from Chaldea, *i.e.* from the north, into the land of Israel, he really saw it before him towards the south; so that the rendering of מִנֶּגֶב by *ἀπέναντι* in the Septuagint is substantially correct, though without furnishing any warrant to alter מִנֶּגֶב into מִנֶּגֶד. In ver. 3*a*, וַיָּבִיא אוֹתִי שָׁמָּה is repeated from the end of ver. 1, for the purpose of attaching the following description of what is seen, in the sense of, "when He brought me thither, behold, there (was) a man." His appearance was like the appearance of brass, *i.e.* of shining brass (according to the correct gloss of the LXX. χαλκοῦ στίλβοντος = נְחֹשֶׁת קָלָל, ch. i. 7). This figure suggests a heavenly being, an angel, and as he is called Jehovah in ch. xliv. 2, 5, the angel of Jehovah.

Kliefoth's opinion, that in ch. xliv. 2, 5, it is not the man who is speaking, but that the prophet is there addressed directly by the apparition of God (ch. xliii. 2 sqq.), is proved to be untenable by the simple fact that the speaker (in ch. xliv.) admonishes the prophet in ver. 5 to attend, to see, and to hear, in the same words as the man in ver. 4 of the chapter before us. This places the identity of the two beyond the reach of doubt. He had in his hand a flaxen cord for measuring, and the measuring rod,—that is to say, two measures, because he had to measure many and various things, smaller and larger spaces, for the former of which he had the measuring rod, for the latter the measuring line. The gate at which this man stood (ver. 3) is not more precisely defined, but according to ver. 5 it is to be sought for in the wall surrounding the building; and since he went to the east gate first, according to ver. 6, it was not the east gate, but probably the north gate, as it was from the north that Ezekiel had come.

Vers. 5–27. *The Outer Court, with Boundary Wall, Gate-Buildings, and Cells.*

Ver. 5.—THE SURROUNDING WALL.—*And, behold, a wall (ran) on the outside round the house; and in the man's hand was the measuring rod of six cubits, each a cubit and a handbreadth; and he measured the breadth of the building a rod, and the height a rod.*—The description of the temple (for, according to what follows, הַבַּיִת is the house of Jehovah) (cf. ch. xliii. 7) commences with the surrounding wall of the outer court, whose breadth (*i.e.* thickness) and height are measured (see the illustration, Plate I. *a a a a*), the length of the measuring rod having first been given by way of parenthesis. This was six cubits (*sc.* measured) by the cubit and handbreadth—that is to say, six cubits, each of which was of the length of a (common) cubit and a handbreadth (cf. ch. xliii. 13); in all, therefore, six cubits and six handbreadths. The ordinary or common cubit, judging from the statement in 2 Chron. iii. 3, that the measure of Solomon's temple was regulated according to the earlier measure, had become shorter in the course of time than the old Mosaic or sacred cubit. For the new temple, therefore, the measure is regulated according to a longer cubit, in all probability according to the old sacred cubit of the Mosaic law, which was a handbreadth longer than the common cubit according to the passage before us, or seven handbreadths of the ordinary cubit. הַבִּנְיָן, the masonry, is the building of the wall, which was one rod broad, *i.e.* thick, and the same in height. The length of this wall is not given, and can only be learned from the further description of the whole wall (see the comm. on ch. xl. 27).

Vers. 6–16. THE BUILDINGS OF THE EAST GATE.—(See Plate II. 1).—Ver. 6. *And he went to the gate, the direction of which was toward the east, and ascended the steps thereof, and measured the threshold of the gate one rod broad, namely, the first threshold one rod broad,* Ver. 7. *And the guard-room one rod long and one rod broad, and between the guard-rooms five cubits, and the threshold of the gate by the porch of the gate from the temple hither one rod.* Ver. 8. *And he measured the porch of the gate from the temple hither one rod.* Ver. 9. *And he measured the porch of the gate eight cubits, and its pillars two cubits; and the porch of the gate was from the temple hither.* Ver. 10. *And of the guard-rooms of the gate toward the east there were three on this side and three on that side; all three had one measure, and the pillars also one measure on this side and on that.* Ver. 11. *And he measured the breadth of the opening of the gate ten cubits, the length of the gate thirteen cubits.* Ver. 12. *And there was a boundary fence before the guard-rooms of one cubit, and a cubit was the boundary fence on that side, and the guard-rooms were six cubits on this side and six cubits on that side.* Ver. 13. *And he measured the gate from the roof of the guard-rooms to the roof of them five and twenty cubits broad, door against door.* Ver. 14. *And he fixed the pillars at sixty cubits, and the court round about the gate reached to the pillars.* Ver. 15.

And the front of the entrance gate to the front of the porch of the inner gate was fifty cubits. Ver. 16. *And there were closed windows in the guard-rooms, and in their pillars on the inner side of the gate round about, and so also in the projections of the walls; there were windows round about on the inner side, and palms on the pillars.*—וַיָּבוֹא אֶל שַׁעַר is not to be rendered, "he went in at the gate." For although this would be grammatically admissible, it is not in harmony with what follows, according to which the man first of all ascended the steps, and then commenced the measuring of the gate-buildings with the threshold of the gate. The steps (*B* in the illustration) are not to be thought of as in the surrounding wall, but as being outside in front of them; but in the description which follows they are not included in the length of the gate-buildings. The number of steps is not given here, but they have no doubt been fixed correctly by the LXX. at seven, as that is the number given in vers. 22 and 26 in connection with both the northern and southern gates. From the steps the man came to the threshold (*C*), and measured it. "The actual description of the first building, that of the eastern gate, commences in the inside; first of all, the entire length is traversed (vers. 6–9), and the principal divisions are measured on the one side; then (vers. 10–12) the inner portions on both sides are given more definitely as to their character, number, and measure; in vers. 13–15 the relations and measurement of the whole building are noticed; and finally (ver. 16), the wall-decorations observed round about the inside. The exit from the gate is first mentioned in ver. 17; consequently all that is given in vers. 6–16 must have been visible within the building, just as in the case of the other gates the measurements and descriptions are always to be regarded as given from within" (Böttcher). The threshold (*C*) was a rod in breadth,—that is to say, measuring from the outside to the inside,—and was therefore just as broad as the wall was thick (ver. 5). But this threshold was the one, or first threshold, which had to be crossed by any one who entered the gate from the outside, for the gate-building had a second threshold at the exit into the court, which is mentioned in ver. 7. Hence the more precise definition וְאֵת סַף אֶחָד, "and that the one, *i.e.* first threshold," in connection with which the breadth is given a second time. אֵת is neither *nota nominativi*, nor is it used in the sense of זֹאת; but it is *nota accus.*, and is also governed by וַיָּמָד. And אֶחָד is not to be taken in a pregnant sense, "only one, *i.e.* not broken up, or composed of several" (Böttcher, Hävernick), but is employed, as it frequently is in enumeration, for the ordinal number: *one* for the first (*vid. e.g.* Gen. i. 5, 7). The length of the threshold, *i.e.* its measure between the two door-posts (from north to south), is not given; but from the breadth of the entrance door mentioned in ver. 11, we can infer that it was ten cubits. Proceeding from the threshold, we have next the measurement of the guard-room (*G*), mentioned in ver. 7. According to 1 Kings xiv. 28, תָּא is a room constructed in the gate, for the use of the guard keeping watch at the gate. This was a rod in length, and the same in breadth. A space of five cubits is then mentioned as intervening between the guard-rooms. It is evident from this that there were several guard-rooms in succession; according to ver. 10, three on each side of the doorway, but that instead of their immediately joining one another, they were separated by intervening spaces (*H*) of five cubits each. This required two spaces on each side. These spaces between the guard-rooms, of which we have no further description, must not be thought of as open or unenclosed, for in that case there would have been so many entrances into the court, and the gateway would not be closed; but we must assume "that they were closed by side walls, which connected the guard-rooms with one another" (Kliefoth).—After the guard-rooms there follows, thirdly, the threshold of the gate on the side of, or near the porch of, the gate "in the direction from the house," *i.e.* the second threshold, which was at the western exit from the gate-buildings near the porch (*D*); in other words, which stood as you entered immediately in front of the porch leading out into the court (*C C*), and was also a cubit in breadth, like the first threshold at the eastern entrance into the gate. מֵהַבָּיִת, "in the direction from the house," or, transposing it into our mode of viewing and describing directions, "going toward the temple-house." This is added to אֻלָם הַשַּׁעַר to indicate clearly the position of this porch as being by the inner passage of the gate-buildings leading into the court, so as to guard against our thinking of a porch erected on the outside in front of the entrance gate. Böttcher, Hitzig, and others are wrong in identifying or interchanging מֵהַבָּיִת with מִבַּיִת, inwardly, *intrinsecus* (ch. vii. 15; 1 Kings vi. 15), and taking it as referring to סַף, as if the intention were to designate this threshold as the inner one lying within the gate-buildings, in contrast to the first threshold mentioned in ver. 6.

In vers. 8 and 9 two different measures of this court-porch (*D*) are given, viz. first, one rod = six cubits (ver. 8), and then eight cubits (ver. 9). The ancient translators stumbled at this difference, and still more at the fact that the definition of the measurement is repeated in the same words; so that, with the exception of the Targumists, they have all omitted the eighth verse; and in consequence of this, modern critics, such as Houbigant, Ewald, Böttcher, and Hitzig, have expunged it from the text as a gloss. But however strange the repetition of the measurement of the porch with a difference in the numbers may appear at the first glance, and however naturally it may suggest the thought of a gloss which has crept into the text through the oversight of a copyist, it is very difficult to understand how such a gloss could have been perpetuated; and this cannot be explained by the groundless assumption that there was an unwillingness to erase what had once been erroneously written. To this must be added the difference in the terms employed to describe the dimensions, viz. first, a rod, and then eight cubits, as well as the circumstance that in ver. 9, in addition to the measure of the porch, that of the pillars adjoining the porch is given immediately afterwards. The attempts of the earlier commentators to explain the two measurements of the porch have altogether failed; and Kliefoth was the first to solve the difficulty correctly, by explaining that in ver. 8 the measurement of the porch is given in the clear, *i.e.* according to the length within, or the depth (from east to west), whilst in ver. 9 the external length of the southern (or northern) wall of the porch (from east to west) is given. Both of these were necessary, the former to give a correct idea of the inner space of the porch, as in the case of the guard-rooms in ver. 7; the latter, to supply the necessary data for the entire length of the gate-buildings, and to make it possible to append to this the dimensions of the pillars adjoining the western porch-wall. As a portion of the gate-entrance or gateway, this porch was open to the east and west; and toward the west, *i.e.* toward the court, it was closed by the gate built against it. Kliefoth therefore assumes that the porch-walls on the southern and northern sides projected two cubits toward the west beyond the inner space of the porch, which lay between the threshold and the gate that could be closed, and was six cubits long, and that the two gate-pillars, with their thickness of two cubits each, were attached to this prolongation of the side walls. But by this supposition we do not gain a porch (אֻלָם), but a simple extension of the intervening wall between the third guard-room and the western gate. If the continuation of the side walls, which joined the masonry bounding the western threshold on the south and north, was to have the character of a porch, the hinder wall (to the east) could not be entirely wanting; but even if there were a large opening in it for the doorway, it must stand out in some way so as to strike the eye, whether by projections of the wall at the north-east and south-east corners, or what may be more probable, by the fact that the southern and northern side walls receded at least a cubit in the inside, if not more, so that the masonry of the walls of the porch was weaker (thinner) than that at the side of the threshold and by the pillars, and the porch in the clear from north to south was broader than the doorway. The suffix attached to אֵילָו is probably to be taken as referring to אֻלָם הַשַּׁעַר, and not merely to שַׁעַר, and the word itself to be construed as a plural (אֵילָיו): the pillars of the gate-porch (*E*) were two cubits thick, or strong. This measurement is not to be divided between the two pillars, as the earlier commentators supposed, so that each pillar would be but one cubit thick, but applies to each of them. As the pillars were sixty cubits high (according to ver. 14), they must have had the strength of at least two cubits of thickness to secure the requisite firmness. At the close of the ninth verse, the statement that the gate-porch was directed towards the temple-house is made for the third time, because it was this peculiarity in the situation which distinguished the gate-buildings of the outer court from those of the inner; inasmuch as in the case of the latter, although in other respects its construction resembled that of the gate-buildings of the outer court, the situation was reversed, and the gate-porch was at the side turned away from the temple toward the outer court, as is also emphatically stated three times in vers. 31, 34, and 37 (Kliefoth).

On reaching the gate-porch and its pillars, the measurer had gone through the entire length of the gate-buildings, and determined the measure of all its component parts, so far as the length was concerned. Having arrived at the inner extremity or exit, the describer returns, in order to supply certain important particulars with regard to the situation and character of the whole structure. He first of all observes (in ver. 10), with reference to the number and relative position of the guard-houses (*G*), that there were three of them on each side opposite to one another, that all six were of the same measure, *i.e.* one rod in length and one in breadth (ver. 7); and then, that the pillars mentioned in ver. 9, the measurement of which was determined (*E*), standing at the gate-porch on either side, were of the same size. Many of the commentators have erroneously imagined that by לָאֵילִם we are to understand the walls between the guard-rooms or pillars in the guard-rooms. The connecting walls could not be called אֵילִים; and if pillars belonging to the guard-rooms were intended, we should expect to find לְאֵילָיו.—In ver. 11 there follow the measurements of the breadth and length of the doorway. The breadth of the opening, *i.e.* the width of the doorway, was ten cubits. "By this we are naturally to understand the breadth of the whole doorway in its full extent, just as the length of the two thresholds and the seven steps, which was not given in vers. 6 and 7, is also fixed at ten cubits" (Kliefoth).—The measurement which follows, viz. "the length of the gate, thirteen cubits," is difficult to explain, and has been interpreted in very different ways. The supposition of Lyra, Kliefoth, and others, that by the *length* of the gate we are to understand the *height* of the trellised gate, which could be opened and shut, cannot possibly be correct. אֹרֶךְ, length, never stands for קוֹמָה, height; and הַשַּׁעַר in this connection cannot mean the gate that was opened and shut. הַשַּׁעַר, as distinguished from פֶּתַח הַשַּׁעַר, can only signify either the whole of the gate-building (as in ver. 6), or, in a more limited sense, that portion of the building which bore the character of a gate in a conspicuous way; primarily, therefore, the masonry enclosing the threshold on the two sides, together with its roof; and then, generally, the covered doorway, or that portion of the gate-building which was roofed over, in distinction from the uncovered portion of the building between the two gates (Böttcher, Hitzig, and Hävernick); inasmuch as it cannot be supposed that a gate-building of fifty cubits long was entirely roofed in. Now, as there are two thresholds mentioned in vers. 6 and 7, and the distinction in ver. 15 between the (outer) entrance-gate and the porch of the inner gate implies that the gate-building had two gates, like the gate-building of the city of Mahanaim (2 Sam. xviii. 24), one might be disposed to distribute the thirteen cubits' length of the gate between the two gates, because each threshold had simply a measurement of six cubits. But such a supposition as this, which is not very probable in itself, is proved to be untenable, by the fact that throughout the whole description we never find the measurements of two or more separate portions added together, so that no other course is open than to assume, as Böttcher, Hitzig, and Hävernick have done, that the length of thirteen cubits refers to one covered doorway, and that, according to the analogy of the measurements of the guard-rooms given in ver. 7, it applies to the second gateway also; in which case, out of the forty cubits which constituted the whole length of the gate-building (without the front porch), about two-thirds (twenty-six cubits) would be covered gateway (*b b*), and the fourteen cubits between would form an uncovered court-yard (*c c*) enclosed on all sides by the gate-buildings. Consequently the roofing of the gate extended from the eastern and western side over the guard-room, which immediately adjoined the threshold of the gate, and a cubit beyond that, over the wall which intervened between the guard-rooms, so that only the central guard-room on either side, together with a portion of the walls which bounded it, stood in the uncovered portion or court of the gate-building.—According to ver. 12, there was a גְּבוּל, or boundary, in front of the guard-rooms, *i.e.* a boundary fence of a cubit in breadth, along the whole of the guard-room, with its breadth of six cubits on either side. The construction of this boundary fence or barrier (*a*) is not explained; but the design of it is clear, namely, to enable the sentry to come without obstruction out of the guard-room, to observe what was going on in the gate both on the right and left, without being disturbed by those who were passing through the gate. These boundary fences in front of the guard-rooms projected into the gateway to the extent described, so that there were only eight (10 – 2) cubits open space between the guard-rooms, for those who were going out and in. In ver. 12 we must supply מִפֹּה after the first אַחַת because of the parallelism. Ver. 12*b* is a substantial repetition of ver. 7*a*.—In ver. 13 there follows the measure of the breadth of the gate-building. From the roof of the one guard-room to the roof of the other guard-room opposite (לְנֶגְדּוֹ is an abbreviated expression for לְנֶגֶד הַתָּא) the breadth was twenty-five cubits, "door against door." These last words are added for the sake of clearness, to designate the direction of the measurement as taken right across the gateway. The door of the guard-room, however, can only be the door in the outer wall, by which the sentries passed to and fro between the room and the court. The measurement given will not allow of our thinking of a door in the inner wall, *i.e.* the wall of the barrier of the gateway, without touching the question in dispute among the commentators, whether the guard-rooms had walls toward the gateway or not, *i.e.* whether they were rooms that could be closed, or sentry-boxes open in front. All that the measuring from roof to roof presupposes as indisputable is, that the guard-rooms had a roof. The measurement given agrees, moreover, with the other measurements. The breadth of the gateway with its ten cubits, added to that of each guard-room with six, and therefore of both together with twelve, makes twenty-two cubits in all; so that if we add three cubits for the thickness of the two outer walls, or a cubit and a half each, that is to say, according to ver. 42, the breadth of one hewn square stone, we obtain twenty-five cubits for the breadth of the whole gate-building, the dimension given in vers. 21, 25, and 29.

There is a further difficulty in ver. 14. The אֵילִים, whose measurement is fixed in the first clause at sixty cubits, can only be the gate-pillars (אֵילָיו) mentioned in ver. 9; and the measurement given can only refer to their height. The height of sixty cubits serves to explain the choice of the verb וַיַּעַשׂ, in the general sense of *constituit*, instead of וַיָּמָד, inasmuch as such a height could not be measured from the bottom to the top with the measuring rod, but could only be estimated and fixed at such and such a result. With regard to the offence taken by modern critics at the sixty cubits, Kliefoth has very correctly observed, that "if it had been considered that our church towers have also grown out of gate-pillars, that we may see for ourselves not only in Egyptian obelisks and Turkish minarets, but in our own hollow factory-chimneys, how pillars of sixty cubits can be erected upon a pedestal of two cubits square; and lastly, that we have here to do with a colossal building seen in a vision,—there would have been no critical difficulties discovered in this statement as to the height." Moreover, not only the number, but the whole text is verified as correct by the Targum and Vulgate, and defended by them against all critical caprice; whilst the verdict of Böttcher himself concerning the Greek and Syriac texts is, that they are senselessly mutilated and disfigured.—In the second half of the verse אַיִל stands in a collective sense: "and the court touched the pillars." הֶחָצֵר is not a court situated within the gate-building (Hitzig, Hävernick, and others), but the outer court of the temple. הַשַּׁעַר is an accusative, literally, with regard to the gate round about, *i.e.* encompassing the gate-building round about, that is to say, on three sides. These words plainly affirm what is implied in the preceding account, namely, that the gate-building stood within the outer court, and that not merely so far as the porch was concerned, but in its whole extent.—To this there is very suitably attached in ver. 15 the account of the length of the whole building. The words, "at the front of the entrance gate to the front of the porch of the inner gate," are a concise topographical expression for "from the front side of the entrance gate to the front side of the porch of the inner gate." At the starting-point of the measurement מִן (מֵעַל) was unnecessary, as the point of commencement is indicated by the position of the word; and in עַל לִפְנֵי, as distinguished from עַל פְּנֵי, the direction toward the terminal point is shown, so that there is no necessity to alter עַל into עַד, since עַל, when used of the direction in which the object aimed at lies, frequently touches the ordinary meaning of עַד (cf. עַל קְצוֹתָם, Ps. xix. 7, and עַל תַּבְלִיתָם, Isa. x. 25); whilst here the direction is rendered perfectly plain by the ל (in לִפְנֵי). The *Chetib* היאתון, a misspelling for הָאִיתוֹן, we agree with Gesenius and others in regarding as a substantive: "entrance." The entrance gate is the outer gate, at the flight of steps leading into the gate-building. Opposite to this was the "inner gate" at the end of the gate-building, by the porch leading into the court. The length from the outer to the inner gate was fifty cubits, which is the resultant obtained from the measurements of the several portions of the gate-building, as given in vers. 6–10; namely, six cubits the breadth of the first threshold, $3 \times 6 = 18$ cubits that of the three guard-rooms, $2 \times 5 = 10$ cubits that of the spaces intervening between the guard-rooms, 6 cubits that of the inner threshold, 8 cubits that of the gate-porch, and 2 cubits that of the gate-pillars ($6+18+10+6+8+2=50$).

Lastly, in ver. 16, the windows and decorations of the gate-buildings are mentioned. חַלּוֹנוֹת אֲטֻמוֹת, closed windows, is, no doubt, a contracted expression for חַלּוֹנֵי שְׁקֻפִים אֲטֻמִים (1 Kings vi. 4), windows of closed bars, *i.e.* windows, the lattice-work of which was made so fast, that they could not be opened at pleasure like the windows of dwelling-houses. But it is difficult to determine the situation of these windows. According to the words of the text, they were in the guard-rooms and in אֵלֵיהֵמָּה and also לְאֵלַמּוֹת, and that לִפְנִימָה לַשַּׁעַר into the interior of the gate-building, *i.e.* going into the inner side of the gateway סָבִיב סָבִיב, round about, *i.e.* surrounding the gateway on all sides. To understand these statements, we must endeavour, first of all, to get a clear idea of the meaning of the words אֵילִים and אֵלַמּוֹת. The first occurs in the singular אַיִל, not only in vers. 14, 16, and ch. xli. 3, but also in 1 Kings vi. 31; in the plural only in this chapter and in ch. xli. 1. The second אֵילָם or אֵלָם is met with only in this chapter, and always in the plural, in the form אֵלַמּוֹת only in vers. 16 and 30, in other cases always אֵילַמִּים, or with a suffix אֵילַמָּיו, after the analogy of תָּאוֹת in ver. 12 by the side of תָּאִים in vers. 7 and 16, תָּאֵי in ver. 10, and תָּאָיו or תָּאָו in vers. 21, 29, 33, 36, from which it is apparent that the difference in the formation of the plural (אילמות and אילמים) has no influence upon the meaning of the word. On the other hand, it is evident from our verse (ver. 16), and still more so from the expression אֵילָ֣י וְאֵלַמָּ֔ו, which is repeated in vers. 21, 24, 29, 33, and 36 (cf. vers. 26, 31, and 34), that אֵלִים and אֵלַמִּים must signify different things, and are not to be identified, as Böttcher and others suppose. The word אַיִל, as an architectural term, never occurs except in connection with doors or gates. It is used in this connection as early as 1 Kings vi. 31, in the description of the door of the most holy place in Solomon's temple, where הָאַיִל signifies the projection on the door-posts, *i.e.* the projecting portion of the wall in which the door-posts were fixed. Ezekiel uses אֵיל הַפֶּתַח in ch. xli. 3 in the same sense in relation to the door of the most holy place, and in an analogous manner applies the term אֵילִים to the pillars which rose up to a colossal height at or by the gates of the courts (vers. 9, 10, 14, 21, 24, etc.), and also of the pillars at the entrance into the holy place (ch. xli. 1). The same meaning may also be retained in ver. 16, where pillars (or posts) are attributed to the guard-rooms, since the suffix in אֵלֵיהֵמָּה can only be taken as referring to הַתָּאִים. As these guard-rooms had doors, the doors may also have had their posts. And just as in ver. 14 אֶל־אַיִל points back to the אֵלִים previously mentioned, and the singular is used in a collective sense; so may the אֶל אַיִל in ver. 16 be taken collectively, and referred to the pillars mentioned before.—There is more difficulty in determining the meaning of אֵילָם (plural אֵלַמִּים or אֵלַמּוֹת), which has been identified sometimes with אוּלָם, sometimes with אֵילִים. Although etymologically connected with these two words, it is not only clearly distinguished from אֵילִים, as we have already observed, but it is also distinguished from אוּלָם by the fact that, apart from ch. xli. 15, where the plural אוּלַמֵּי signifies the front porches in all the gate-buildings of the court, אוּלָם only occurs in the singular, because every gate-building had only one front porch, whereas the plural is always used in the case of אֵלַמִּים. So far as the form is concerned, אֵילָם is derived from אַיִל; and since אַיִל signifies the projection, more especially the pillars on both sides of the doors and gates, it has apparently the force of an abstract noun, projecting work; but as distinguished from the prominent pillars, it seems to indicate the projecting works or portions on the side walls of a building of large dimensions. If, then, we endeavour to determine the meaning of אֵילָם more precisely in our description of the gate-building, where alone the word occurs, we find from ver. 30 that there were אֵלַמּוֹת round about the gate-buildings; and again from vers. 16 and 25, that the אֵלַמִּים had windows, which entered into the gateway; and still further from vers. 22 and 26, that when one ascended the flight of steps, they were לִפְנֵי, "in front of them." And lastly, from vers. 21, 29, and 33, where guard-rooms, on this side and on that side, pillars (אֵלִים), and אֵלַמִּים are mentioned as constituent parts of the gate-building or gateway, and the length of the gateway is given as fifty cubits, we may infer that the אֵלַמִּים, with the guard-rooms and pillars, formed the side enclosures of the gateway throughout its entire length. Consequently we shall not be mistaken, if we follow Kliefoth in understanding by אֵלַמִּים those portions of the inner side walls of the gateway which projected in the same manner as the two pillars by the porch, namely, the intervening walls between the three guard-rooms, and also those portions of the side walls which enclosed the two thresholds on either side. For "there was nothing more along the gateway, with the exception of the portions mentioned," that projected in any way, inasmuch as these projecting portions of the side enclosures, together with the breadth of the guard-rooms and the porch, along with its pillars, made up the entire length of the gateway, amounting to fifty cubits. This explanation of the word is applicable to all the passages in which it occurs, even to vers. 30 and 31, as the exposition of these verses will show.—It follows from this that the windows mentioned in ver. 16 can only be sought for in the walls of the guard-rooms and the projecting side walls of the gateway; and therefore that וְאֶל אֵלֵיהֵמָּה is to be taken as a more precise definition of אֶל־הַתָּאִים: "there were windows in the guard-rooms, and, indeed (that is to say), in their pillars," *i.e.* by the side of the pillars enclosing the door. These windows entered into the interior of the gateway. It still remains questionable, however, whether these windows looked out of the guard-rooms into the court, and at the same time threw light into the interior of the gateway, because the guard-rooms were open towards the gateway, as Böttcher, Hitzig, Kliefoth, and others assume; or whether the guard-rooms had also a wall with a door opening into the gateway, and windows on both sides, to which allusion is made here. The latter is by no means probable, inasmuch as, if the guard-rooms were not open towards the gateway, the walls between them would not have projected in such a manner as to allow of their being designated as אֵלַמּוֹת. For this reason we regard the former as the correct supposition. There is some difficulty also in the further expression סָבִיב סָבִיב; for, strictly speaking, there were not windows round about, but simply on both sides of the gateway. But if we bear in mind that the windows in the hinder or outer wall of the guard-rooms receded considerably in relation to the windows in the projecting side walls, the expression סָבִיב סָבִיב can be justified in this sense: "all round, wherever the eye turned in the gateway." וְכֵן לָאֵלַמּוֹת, likewise in the projecting walls, *sc.* there were such windows. וְכֵן implies not only that there were windows in these walls, but also that they were constructed in the same manner as those in the pillars of the guard-rooms. It was only thus that the gateway came to have windows round about, which went inwards. Consequently this is repeated once more; and in the last clause of the verse it is still further observed, that אֶל אַיִל, *i.e.*, according to ver. 15, on the two lofty pillars in front of the porch, there were תִּמֹּרִים added, *i.e.* ornaments in the form of palms, not merely of palm branches or palm leaves.—This completes the description of the eastern gate of the outer court. The measuring angel now leads the prophet over the court to the other two gates, the north gate and the south gate. On the way, the outer court is described and measured.

Vers. 17–19. The Outer Court described and measured.—Ver. 17. *And he led me into the outer court, and behold there were cells and pavement made round the court; thirty cells on the pavement.* Ver. 18. *And the pavement was by the side of the gates, corresponding to the length of the gates, (namely) the lower pavement.* Ver. 19. *And he measured the breadth from the front of the lower gate to the front of the inner court, about a hundred cubits on the east side and on the north side.*—Ezekiel having been led through the eastern gate into the outer court, was able to survey it, not on the eastern side only, but also on the northern and southern sides; and there he perceived cells and רִצְפָּה, *pavimentum*, mosaic pavement, or a floor paved with stones laid in mosaic form (2 Chron. vii. 3; Esth. i. 6), made round the court; that is to say, according to the more precise description in ver. 18, on both sides of the gate-buildings, of a breadth corresponding to their length, running along the inner side of the wall of the court, and consequently not covering the floor of the court in all its extent, but simply running along the inner side of the surrounding wall as a strip of about fifty cubits broad, and that not uniformly on all four sides, but simply on the eastern, southern, and northern sides, and at the north-west and south-west corners of the western side, so far, namely, as the outer court surrounded the inner court and temple (see Plate I. *b b b*); for on the western side the intervening space from the inner court and temple-house to the surrounding wall of the outer court was filled by a special building of the separate place. It is with this limitation that we have to take סָבִיב סָבִיב. עָשׂוּי may belong either to לְשָׁכוֹת וְרִצְפָה or merely to רִצְפָה, so far as grammatical considerations are concerned; for in either case there would be an irregularity in the gender, and the participle is put in the singular as a neuter. If we look fairly at the fact itself, not one of the reasons assigned by Kliefoth, for taking עָשׂוּי as referring to רִצְפָה only, is applicable throughout. If the pavement ran round by the side of the gate-buildings on three sides of the court, and the cells were by or upon the pavement, they may have stood on three sides of the court without our being forced to assume, or even warranted in assuming, that they must of necessity have filled up the whole length on every side from the shoulder of the gate-building to the corner, or rather to the space that was set apart in every corner, according to ch. xlvi. 21–24, for the cooking of the sacrificial meals of the people. We therefore prefer to take עָשׂוּי as referring to the cells and the pavement; because this answers better than the other, both to the construction and to the fact. In ver. 18 the pavement is said to have been by the shoulder of the gates. הַשְּׁעָרִים is in the plural, because Ezekiel had probably also in his mind the two gates which are not described till afterwards. כֶּתֶף, the shoulder of the gate-buildings regarded as a body, is the space on either side of the gate-building along the wall, with the two angles formed by the longer side of the gate-buildings and the line of the surrounding wall. This is more precisely defined by לְעֻמַּת אֹרֶךְ הַשׁ׳, alongside of the length of the gates, *i.e.* running parallel with it (cf. 2 Sam. xvi. 13), or stretching out on both sides with a breadth corresponding to the length of the gate-buildings. The gates were fifty cubits long, or, deducting the thickness of the outer wall, they projected into the court to the distance of forty-four cubits. Consequently the pavement ran along the inner sides of the surrounding wall with a breadth of forty-four cubits. This pavement is called the lower pavement, in distinction from the pavement or floor of the inner court, which was on a higher elevation. All that is said concerning the לְשָׁכוֹת is, that there were thirty of them, and that they were אֶל הָרִצְפָּה (see Plate I. *C*). The dispute whether אֶל signifies *by* or *upon* the pavement has no bearing upon the fact itself. As Ezekiel frequently uses אֶל for עַל, and *vice versâ*, the rendering *upon* can be defended; but it cannot be established, as Hitzig supposes, by referring to 2 Kings xvi. 17. If we retain the literal meaning of אֶל, *at* or *against*, we cannot picture to ourselves the position of the cells as projecting from the inner edge of the pavement into the unpaved portion of the court; for in that case, to a person crossing the court, they would have stood in front of (לִפְנֵי) the pavement rather than against the pavement. The prep. אֶל, *against*, rather suggests the fact that the cells were built near the surrounding wall, so that the pavement ran along the front of them, which faced the inner court in an unbroken line. In this case it made no difference to the view whether the cells were erected upon the pavement, or the space occupied by the cells was left unpaved, and the pavement simply joined the lower edge of the walls of the cells all round. The text contains no account of the manner in which they were distributed on the three sides of the court. But it is obvious from the use of the plural לְשָׁכוֹת, that the reference is not to thirty entire buildings, but simply to thirty rooms, as לִשְׁכָּה does not signify a building consisting of several rooms, but always a single room or cell in a building. Thus in 1 Sam. ix. 22 it stands for a room appointed for holding the sacrificial meals, and that by no means a small room, but one which could accommodate about thirty persons. In Jer. xxxvi. 12 it is applied to a room in the king's palace, used as the chancery. Elsewhere לִשְׁכָּה is the term constantly employed for the rooms in the court-buildings and side-buildings of the temple, which served partly as a residence for the officiating priests and Levites, and partly for the storing of the temple dues collected in the form of tithes, fruits, and money (*vid.* 2 Kings xxiii. 11; Jer. xxxv. 4, xxxvi. 10; 1 Chron. ix. 26; Neh. x. 38–40). Consequently we must not think of thirty separate buildings, but have to distribute the thirty cells on the three sides of the court in such a manner that there would be ten on each side, and for the sake of symmetry five in every building, standing both right and left between the gate-building and the corner kitchens.—In ver. 19 the size or compass of the outer court is determined. The breadth from the front of the lower gate to the front of the inner court was 100 cubits.

הַשַּׁעַר הַתַּחְתּוֹנָה, the gate of the lower court, *i.e.* the outer gate, which was lower than the inner. הַתַּחְתּוֹנָה is not an adjective agreeing with שַׁעַר, for apart from Isa. xiv. 31 שַׁעַר is never construed as a feminine; but it is used as a substantive for חָצֵר הַתַּחְתּוֹנָה, the lower court, see the comm. on ch. viii. 3. מִלִּפְנֵי denotes the point from which the measuring started, and לִפְנֵי הֶחָצֵר the direction in which it proceeded, including also the terminus: "to before the inner court," equivalent to "up to the front of the inner court." The terminal point is more precisely defined by מִחוּץ, from without, which Hitzig proposes to erase as needless and unusual, but without any reason. For, inasmuch as the gateways of the inner court were built into the outer court, as is evident from what follows, מִחוּץ simply affirms that the measuring only extended to the point where the inner court commenced within the outer, namely, to the front of the porch of the gate, not to the boundary wall of the inner court, as this wall stood at a greater distance from the porch of the outer court-gate by the whole length of the court-gate, that is to say, as much as fifty cubits. From this more precise definition of the terminal point it follows still further, that the starting-point was not the boundary-wall, but the porch of the gate of the outer court; in other words, that the hundred cubits measured by the man did not include the fifty cubits' length of the gate-building, but this is expressly excluded. This is placed beyond all doubt by vers. 23 and 27, where the distance of the inner court-gate from the gate (of the outer court) is said to have been a hundred cubits.—The closing words הַקָּדִים וְהַצָּפוֹן have been very properly separated by the Masoretes from what precedes, by means of the *Athnach*, for they are not to be taken in close connection with וַיָּמָד; nor are they to be rendered, "he measured . . . toward the east and toward the north," for this would be at variance with the statement, "to the front of the inner court." They are rather meant to supply a further appositional definition to the whole of the preceding clause: "he measured from . . . a hundred cubits," relating to the east side and the north side of the court, and affirm that the measuring took place from gate to gate both on the eastern and on the northern side; in other words, that the measure given, a hundred cubits, applied to the eastern side as well as the northern; and thus they prepare the way for the description of the north gate, which follows from ver. 20 onwards.

Vers. 20–27. The North Gate and the South Gate of the Outer Court (1 Plate I. *A*).—The description of these two gate-buildings is very brief, only the principal portions being mentioned, coupled with the remark that they resembled those of the east gate. The following is the description of the north gate.—Ver. 20. *And the gate, whose direction was toward the north, touching the outer court, he measured its length and its breadth,* Ver. 21. *And its guard-rooms, three on this side and three on that, and its pillars and its wall-projections. It was according to the measure of the first gate, fifty cubits its length, and the breadth five and twenty cubits.* Ver. 22. *And its windows and its wall-projections and its palms were according to the measure of the gate, whose direction was toward the east; and by seven steps they went up, and its wall-projections were in front of it.* Ver. 23. *And a gate to the inner court was opposite the gate to the north and to the east; and he measured from gate to gate a hundred cubits.*—With the measuring of the breadth of the court the measuring man had reached the north gate, which he also proceeded to measure now. In ver. 20 the words וְהַשַּׁעַר to הַחִיצוֹנָה are written absolutely; and in ver. 21 the verb הָיָה does not belong to the objects previously enumerated, viz. guard-rooms, pillars, etc., but these objects are governed by וַיָּמָד, and הָיָה points back to the principal subject of the two verses, הַשַּׁעַר: it (the gate) was according to the measure . . . (cf. vers. 15 and 13). For the use of בּ in definitions of measurement, "25 בָּאַמָּה" (*by* the cubit, *sc.* measured), as in Ex. xxvii. 18, etc., see Gesenius, § 120. 4,

Anm. 2. The "first gate" is the east gate, the one first measured and described. In ver. 23*b* the number of steps is given which the flight leading into the gateway had; and this of course applies to the flight of steps of the east gate also (ver. 6). In ver. 22, כְּמִדַּת is not to be regarded as doubtful, as Hitzig supposes, or changed into כְּ; for even if the windows of the east gate were not measured, they had at all events a definite measurement, so that it might be affirmed with regard to the windows of the north gate that their dimensions were the same. This also applies to the palm-decorations. With regard to the אֵלַמִּים (ver. 21), however, it is simply stated that they were measured; but the measurement is not given. לִפְנֵיהֶם (ver. 22, end) is not to be altered in an arbitrary and ungrammatical way into לִפְנִימָה, as Böttcher proposes. The suffix הֶם refers to the steps. *Before* the steps there were the אֵילַמִּים of the gate-building. This "before," however, is not equivalent to "outside the flight of steps," as Böttcher imagines; for the measuring man did not go out of the inside of the gate, or go down the steps into the court, but came from the court and ascended the steps, and as he was going up he saw in front (*vis-à-vis*) of the steps the אֵילַמִּים of the gate, *i.e.* the wall-projections on both sides of the threshold of the gate. In ver. 23 it is observed for the first time that there was a gate to the inner court opposite to the northern and the eastern gate of the outer court already described, so that the gates of the outer and inner court stood *vis-à-vis*. The distance between these outer and inner gates is then measured, viz. 100 cubits, in harmony with ver. 19*b*.

In vers. 24–27 the south gate is described with the same brevity. Ver. 24. *And he led me toward the south, and behold there was a gate toward the south, and he measured its pillars and its wall-projections according to the same measures.* Ver. 25. *And there were windows in it and its wall-projections round about like those windows; fifty cubits was the length, and the breadth five and twenty cubits.* Ver. 26. *And seven steps were its ascent and its wall-projections in the front of them, and it had palm-work, one upon this side and one upon that on its pillars.* Ver. 27. *And there was a gate to the inner court toward the south, and he measured from gate to gate toward the south a hundred cubits.*—This gate also was built exactly like the two others. The description simply differs in form, and not in substance, from the description of the gate immediately preceding. כְּמִדּוֹת הָאֵלֶּה, "like those measures," is a concise expression for "like the measures of the pillars already described at the north and east gates." For ver. 25, compare vers. 16 and 21*b;* and for ver. 26*a*, *vid.* ver. 22*b*. Ver. 26*b* is clearly explained from ver. 16*b*, as compared with ver. 9*b*. And lastly, ver. 27 answers to the 23d verse, and completes the measuring of the breadth of the court, which was also a hundred cubits upon the south side, from the outer gate to the inner gate standing opposite, as was the case according to ver. 19 upon the eastern side. Hävernick has given a different explanation of ver. 27, and would take the measurement of a hundred cubits as referring to the distance between the gates of the inner court which stood opposite to each other, because in ver. 27 we have מִשַּׁעַר in the text, and not מִן הַשַּׁעַר; so that we should have to render the passage thus, "he measured from a gate to the gate toward the south a hundred cubits," and not "from the gate (already described) of the outer court," but from another gate, which according to the context of the verse must also be a gate of the inner court. But it is precisely the context which speaks decidedly against this explanation. For since, according to ver. 18, the measuring man did not take the prophet into the inner court, for the purpose of measuring it before his eyes, till after he had measured from (a) gate to the south gate of the inner court, the distance which he had previously measured and found to be a hundred cubits is not to be sought for within the inner court, and therefore cannot give the distance between the gates of the inner court, which stood opposite to one another, but must be that from the south gate of the outer court to the south gate of the inner. This is the case not only here, but also in ver. 23, where the north gate is mentioned. We may see how little importance is to be attached to the omission of the article in מִשַּׁעַר from the expression מִשַּׁעַר אֶל שַׁעַר in ver. 23, where neither the one gate nor the other is defined, because the context showed which gates were meant. Hävernick's explanation is therefore untenable, notwithstanding the fact that, according to ver. 47, the size of the inner court was a hundred cubits both in breadth and length.—From the distance between the gates of the outer court and the corresponding gates of the inner, as given in vers. 27, 23, and 19, we find that the outer court covered a space of two hundred cubits on every side,—namely, fifty cubits the distance which the outer court building projected into the court, and fifty cubits for the projection of the gate-building of the inner court into the outer court, and a hundred cubits from one gate-porch to the opposite one $(50 + 50 + 100 = 200)$.

Consequently the full size of the building enclosed by the wall (ch. xl. 5), *i.e.* of the temple with its two courts, may also be calculated, as it has been by many of the expositors. If we proceed, for example, from the outer north gate to the outer south gate upon the ground plan (Plate I.), we have, to quote the words of Kliefoth, "first the northern breadth of the outer court (*D*) with its two hundred cubits; then the inner court, which measured a hundred cubits square according to ch. xl. 47 (*E*), with its hundred cubits; and lastly, the south side of the outer court with two hundred cubits more (*D*); so that the sanctuary was five hundred cubits broad from north to south. And if we start from the entrance of the east gate of the court (*A*), we have first of all the eastern breadth of the outer court, viz. two hundred cubits; then the inner court (*E*) with its hundred cubits; after that the temple-buildings, which also covered a space of a hundred cubits square according to ch. xli. 13, 14, including the open space around them (*G*), with another hundred cubits; and lastly, the גִּזְרָה (*J*), which was situated to the west of the temple-buildings, and also covered a space of a hundred cubits square according to ch. xli. 13, 14, with another hundred cubits; so that the sanctuary was also five hundred cubits long from east to west, or, in other words, formed a square of five hundred cubits."

Vers. 28–47. *The Inner Court, with its Gates, Cells, and Slaughtering-Tables.*

Vers. 28–37. The Gates of the Inner Court.—(*Vid.* Plate I. *B* and Plate II. II.)—Ver. 28. *And he brought me into the inner court through the south gate, and measured the south gate according to the same measures;* Ver. 29. *And its guard-rooms, and its pillars, and its wall-projections, according to the same measures; and there were windows in it and in its wall-projections round about: fifty cubits was the length, and the breadth five and twenty cubits.* Ver. 30. *And wall-projections were round about, the length five and twenty cubits, and the breadth five cubits.* Ver. 31. *And its wall-projections were toward the outer court; and there were palms on its pillars, and eight steps its ascendings.* Ver. 32. *And he led me into the inner court toward the east, and measured the gate according to the same measures;* Ver. 33. *And its guard-rooms, and its pillars, and its wall-projections, according to the same measures; and there were windows in it and its wall-projections round about: the length was fifty cubits, and the breadth five and twenty cubits.* Ver. 34. *And its wall-projections were toward the outer court; and there were palms on its pillars on this side and on that side, and eight steps its ascent.* Ver. 35. *And he brought me to the north gate, and measured it according to the same measures;* Ver. 36. *Its guard-rooms, its pillars, and its wall-projections; and there were windows in it round about: the length was fifty cubits, and the breadth five and twenty cubits.* Ver. 37. *And its pillars stood toward the outer court; and palms were upon its pillars on this side and on that; and its ascent was eight steps.*—In ver. 27 the measuring man had measured the distance from the south gate of the outer court to the south gate of the inner court, which stood opposite to it. He then took the prophet through the latter (ver. 28) into the inner court, and measured it as he went through, and found the same measurements as he had found in the gates of the outer court. This was also the case with the measurements of the guard-rooms, pillars, and wall-projections, and with the position of the windows, and the length and breadth of the whole of the gate-building (ver. 29); from which it follows, as a matter of course, that this gate resembled the outer gate in construction, constituent parts, and dimensions. This also applied to both the east gate and north gate, the description of which in vers. 32–37 corresponds exactly to that of the south gate, with the exception of slight variations of expression. It is true that the porch is not mentioned in the case of either of these gates; but it is evident that this was not wanting, and is simply passed over in the description, as we may see from ver. 39, where the tables for the sacrifices are described as being in the porch (בְּאוּלָם). There are only two points of difference mentioned in vers. 31, 34, and 37, by which these inner gates were distinguished from the outer. In the first place, that the flights of steps to the entrances to these gates had eight steps according to the closing words of the verses just cited, whereas those of the outer gates had only seven (cf. vers. 22 and 26); whilst the expression also varies, מַעֲלָו being constantly used here instead of עֹלוֹתָו (ver. 26). עֹלוֹת, from עָלָה, the ascending, are literally ascents, *i.e.* places of mounting, for a flight of steps or staircase. מַעֲלָו, the plural of מַעֲלָה, the ascent (not a singular, as Hitzig supposes), has the same meaning. The second difference, which we find in the first clause of the verses mentioned, is of a more important character. It is contained in the words, "and its אֵלַמִּים (the projecting portions of the inner side-walls of the gateway) were directed toward the outer court" (אֶל and לְ indicating the direction). The interpretation of this somewhat obscure statement is facilitated by the fact that in ver. 37 אֵילָו stands in the place of אֵילַמּוֹ (vers. 31 and 34). אֵילוֹ are the two lofty gate-pillars by the porch of the gate, which formed the termination of the gate-building towards the inner court in the case of the outer gates. If, then, in the case of the inner gates, these pillars stood toward the outer court, the arrangement of these gates must have taken the reverse direction to that of the outer gates; so that a person entering the gate would not go from the flight of steps across the threshold to the guard-rooms, and then across the second threshold to the porch, but would first of all enter the porch by the pillars in front, and then go across the threshold to the guard-rooms, and, lastly, proceed across the second threshold, and so enter the inner court. But if this gate-building, when looked at from without, commenced with the porch-pillars and the front porch, this porch at any rate must have been situated outside the dividing wall of the two courts, that is to say, must have been within the limits of the outer court. And further, if the אֵילַמִּים, or wall-projections between the guard-rooms and by the thresholds, were also directed toward the outer court, the whole of the gate-building must have been built within the limits of that court. This is affirmed by the first clauses of vers. 31, 34, and 37, which have been so greatly misunderstood; and there is no necessity to alter וְאֵילוֹ in ver. 37 into וְאֵלַמָּו, in accordance with vers. 31 and 34. For what is stated in vers. 31 and 34 concerning the position or direction of the אֵילַמִּים, also applies to the אֵילִים; and they are probably mentioned in ver. 37 because of the intention to describe still further in ver. 38 what stood near the אֵילִים. Kliefoth very properly finds it incomprehensible, "that not a few of the commentators have been able, in spite of these definite statements in vers. 31, 34, and 37, to adopt the conclusion that the gate-buildings of the inner gates were situated within the inner court, just as the gate-buildings of the outer gates were situated within the outer court. As the inner court measured only a hundred cubits square, if the inner gates had stood within the inner court, the north and south gates of the inner court would have met in the middle, and the porch of the east gate of the inner court would have stood close against the porches of the other two gates. It was self-evident that the gate-buildings of the inner gates stood within the more spacious outer court, like those of the outer gates. Nevertheless, the reason why the situation of the inner gates is so expressly mentioned in the text is evidently, that this made the position of the inner gates the reverse of that of the outer gates. In the case of the outer gates, the first threshold was in the surrounding wall of the outer court, and the steps stood in front of the wall; and thus the gate-building stretched into the outer court. In that of the inner gates, on the contrary, the second threshold lay between the surrounding walls of the inner court, and the gate-building stretched thence into the outer court, and its steps stood in front of the porch of the gate. Moreover, in the case of the east gates, for example, the porch of the outer gate stood toward the west, and the porch of the inner gate toward the east, so that the two porches stood opposite to each other in the outer court, as described in vers. 23 and 27."

In ver. 30 further particulars respecting the אֵילַמִּים are given, which are apparently unsuitable; and for this reason the verse has been omitted by the LXX., while J. D. Michaelis, Böttcher, Ewald, Hitzig, and Maurer, regard it as an untenable gloss. Hävernick has defended its genuineness; but inasmuch as he regards אֵילַמִּים as synonymous with אוּלָם, he has explained it in a most marvellous and decidedly erroneous manner, as Kliefoth has already proved. The expression סָבִיב סָבִיב, and the length and breadth of the אֵלַמּוֹת here given, both appear strange. Neither the length of twenty-five cubits nor the breadth of five cubits seems to tally with the other measures of the gate-building. So much may be regarded as certain, that the twenty-five cubits' length and the five cubits' breadth of the אֵלַמּוֹת cannot be in addition to the total length of the gate-building, namely fifty cubits, or its total breadth of twenty-five cubits, but must be included in them. For the אֵלַמּוֹת were simply separate portions of the side-enclosure of the gateway, since this enclosure of fifty cubits long consisted of wall-projections (אֵלַמּוֹת), three open guard-rooms, and a porch with pillars. The open space of the guard-rooms was 3 × 6 = 18 cubits, and the porch was six cubits broad in the clear (vers. 7 and 8), and the pillars two cubits thick. If we deduct these 18 + 6 + 2 = 26 cubits from the fifty cubits of the entire length, there remain twenty-four cubits for the walls by the side of the thresholds and between the guard-rooms, namely, 2 × 5 = 10 cubits for the walls between the three guard-rooms, 2 × 6 = 12 cubits for the walls of the threshold, and 2 cubits for the walls of the porch; in all, therefore, twenty-four cubits for the אֵלַמּוֹת; so that only one cubit is wanting to give us the measurement stated, viz. twenty-five cubits. We obtain this missing cubit if we assume that the front of the wall-projections by the guard-rooms and thresholds was a handbreadth and a half, or six inches wider than the thickness of the walls, that is to say, that it projected three inches on each side in the form of a moulding. —The breadth of the אֵלַמּוֹת in question, namely five cubits, was the thickness of their wall-work, however, or the dimension of the intervening wall from the inside to the outside on either side of the gateway. That the intervening walls should be of such a thickness will not appear strange, if we consider that the surrounding wall of the court was six cubits thick, with a height of only six cubits (ver. 5). And even the striking expression סָבִיב סָבִיב becomes intelligible if we take into consideration the fact that the projecting walls bounded not only the entrance to the gate, and the passage through it on the two sides, but also the inner spaces of the gate-building (the guard-rooms and porch) on all sides, and, together with the gates, enclosed the gateway on every side. Consequently ver. 30 not only has a suitable meaning, but furnishes a definite measurement of no little value for the completion of the picture of the gate-buildings. The fact that this definite measure was not given in connection with the gates of the outer court, but was only supplemented in the case of the south gate of the inner court, cannot furnish any ground for suspecting its genuineness, as several particulars are supplemented in the same manner in this description. Thus, for example, the number of steps in front of the outer gates is first given in ver. 22, where the north gate is described. Still less is there to surprise us in the fact that these particulars are not repeated in the case of the following gates, in which some writers have also discovered a ground for suspecting the genuineness of the verse.

From the south gate the measuring man led the prophet (ver. 32) into the inner court toward the east, to measure for him the inner east gate, the description of which (vers. 33 and 34) corresponds exactly to that of the south gate. Lastly, he led him (ver. 35) to the inner north gate for the same purpose; and this is also found to correspond to those previously mentioned, and is described in the same manner. The difficulty which Hitzig finds in אֶל־הֶחָצֵר הַפְּנִימִי דֶּרֶךְ הַקָּדִים in ver. 32, and which drives him into various conjectures, with the assistance of the LXX., vanishes, if instead of taking דֶּרֶךְ הַקָּדִים along with הֶחָצֵר הַפְּנִימִי as a further definition of the latter, we connect it with וַיְבִיאֵנִי as an indication of the direction taken: he led me into the inner court, the way (or direction) toward the east, and measured the gate (situated there). The words, when taken in this sense, do not warrant the conclusion that he had gone out at the south gate again.—וּמָדַד in ver. 35 is an Aramaic form for וַיָּמָד in vers. 32 and 28.

Vers. 38–47. The Cells and Arrangements for the Sacrificial Worship by and in the Inner Court.—Ver. 38. *And a cell with its door was by the pillars at the gates; there they had to wash the burnt-offering.* Ver. 39. *And in the porch of the gate were two tables on this side and two tables on that, to slay thereon the burnt-offering, the sin-offering, and the trespass-offering.* Ver. 40. *And at the shoulder outside, to one going up to the opening of the gate toward the north, stood two tables; and at the other shoulder, by the porch of the gate, two tables.* Ver. 41. *Four tables on this side and four tables on that side, at the shoulder of the gate; eight tables on which they were to slaughter.* Ver. 42. *And four tables by the steps, hewn stone, a cubit and a half long, and a cubit and a half broad, and a cubit high; upon these they were to lay the instruments with which they slaughtered the burnt-offerings and other sacrifices.* Ver. 43. *And the double pegs, a span long, were fastened round about the house; but the flesh of the sacrifice was placed upon the tables.* Ver. 44. *And outside the inner gate were two cells in the inner court, one at the shoulder of the north gate, with its front side toward the south; one at the shoulder of the south gate, with the front toward the north.* Ver. 45. *And he said to me, This cell, whose front is toward the south, is for the priests who attend to the keeping of the house;* Ver. 46. *And the cell whose front is toward the north is for the priests who attend to the keeping of the altar. They are the sons of Zadok, who draw near to Jehovah of the sons of Levi, to serve Him.* Ver. 47. *And he measured the court, the length a hundred cubits, and the breadth a hundred cubits in the square, and the altar stood before the house.*—The opinions of modern commentators differ greatly as to the situation of the cells mentioned in ver. 38, since Böttcher and Hitzig have adjusted a text to suit their own liking, founded upon the Septuagint and upon decidedly erroneous suppositions. The dispute, whether בָּאֵלִים is to be rendered *in* or *by* the אֵילִם, may be easily set at rest by the simple consideration that the אֵילִם in front of the porch of the gate were pillars of two cubits long and the same broad (ver. 9), in which it was impossible that a room could be constructed. Hence the לִשְׁכָּה could only be by (near) the pillars of the gate. To בָּאֵלִים there is also added הַשְּׁעָרִים (by the gates) in loose coordination (*vid.* Ewald, § 293*e*), not for the purpose of describing the position of the pillars more minutely, which would be quite superfluous after ver. 9, but to explain the plural אֵלִים, and extend it to the pillars of all the three inner gates, so that we have to assume that there was a לִשְׁכָּה by the pillars of all these gates (Plate I. *O*). This is also demanded by the purpose of these cells, viz. "for the cleansing or washing of the burnt-offering." As the sacrifices were not taken through one gate alone, but through all the gates, the Sabbath-offering of the prince being carried, according to ch. xlvi. 1, 2, through the east gate, which was closed during the week, and only opened on the Sabbath, there must have been a cell, not by the north gate alone (Böttcher, Hävernick), or by the east gate only (Ewald, Hitzig), but by every gate, for the cleansing of the burnt-offering. Hävernick, Hitzig, and others are wrong in supposing that הָעֹלָה is a synecdochical designation applied to every kind of animal sacrifice. This is precluded not only by the express mention of the burnt-offerings, sin-offerings, and trespass-offerings (ver. 39), and by the use of the word קָרְבָּן in this sense in ver. 43, but chiefly by the circumstance that neither the Old Testament nor the Talmud makes any allusion to the washing of every kind of flesh offered in sacrifice, but that they merely speak of the washing of the entrails and legs of the animals sacrificed as burnt-offerings (Lev. i. 9), for which purpose the basins upon the *mechonoth* in Solomon's temple were used (2 Chron. iv. 6, where the term רָחַץ used in Lev. i. 9 is interpreted by the apposition אֶת־מַעֲשֵׂה הָעוֹלָה יָדִיחוּ בָם). A room at every gate (not by every pillar) was sufficient for this purpose. If there had been a לִשְׁכָּה of this kind on each side of the gate, as many have assumed on symmetrical grounds, this would have been mentioned, just as in the case of the slaughtering-tables (vers. 39–42). The text furnishes no information as to the side of the doorway on which it stood, whether by the right or the left pillar. On the ground plan we have placed the one at the east gate, on the right side, and those by the north and south gates on the western side (Plate I. *O O O*).

Moreover, according to vers. 39–41, there were twice two tables on each side, eight therefore in all, which served for slaughtering. Two pairs stood "in the porch of the gate," *i.e.*

in the inner space of the porch, one pair on this side, the other pair on that, *i.e.* on the right and left sides to a person entering the porch, probably near the wall (see Plate II. II. *ff*). The expression לִשְׁחוֹט אֲלֵיהֶם, to slaughter at the tables (vers. 39 and 40), stands for "to use when slaughtering"—that is, for the purpose of laying the slaughtered flesh upon. This is apparent from the fact itself in ver. 39. For the slaughtering was not performed within the front porch, but outside, and somewhere near it. The front porch of the gate-building was not a slaughter-house, but the place where those who entered the gate could assemble. The only purpose, therefore, for which the tables standing here could be used was to place the sacrificial flesh upon when it was prepared for the altar, that the priests might take it thence and lay it upon the altar. בְּאֻלָם הַשַּׁעַר is to be understood as signifying the inner space of the porch; this is required by the antithesis in ver. 40, where two pair of tables outside the porch are mentioned. Two of these stood "by the shoulder outside to one going up to the gate opening, the northern" (Plate II. II. *d d*). The meaning of these not very intelligible words is apparent from the second half of the verse, which adds the correlative statement as to the two opposite tables. When it is said of these tables that they stood by the other shoulder (אֶל־הַכָּתֵף הָאַחֶרֶת) which the porch of the gate had, not only is לְפֶתַח הַשַּׁעַר of the first hemistich more precisely defined hereby as the gate-porch, but הַצְּפוֹנָה is also rendered intelligible, namely, that as it corresponds to הָאַחֶרֶת, it is an adjective belonging to אֶל הַכָּתֵף, "at the northern shoulder outside to a person going up the steps to the opening of the gate" (מִחוּצָה, the outer side, in contrast to the inside of the porch, בָּאֻלָם, ver. 39). The shoulder of the gate, or rather of the porch of the gate, is the side of it, and that the outer side. Consequently these four tables stood by the outer sides of the porch, two by the right wall and two by the left. In ver. 41, what has already been stated concerning the position of the tables mentioned in vers. 39 and 40 is summed up: Four tables stood on each side of the porch, two inside, and two against the outer wall, eight tables in all, which were used for slaughtering purposes. There is nothing strange in לְכֶתֶף הַשַּׁעַר as an abbreviated expression for לְכָתֵף אֲשֶׁר לְאֻלָם הַשַּׁעַר in ver. 40, as want of clearness was not to be feared after ver. 40. In addition to these there were four other tables (וְאַרְבָּעָה, *and* four, ver. 42) of stone, from which it may be inferred that the four already mentioned were of wood. The four stone tables stood לָעוֹלָה, *i.e.* at (near) the flight of steps (cf. לְפִי קָרֶת, at the entrance to the city, Prov. viii. 3), and were of hewn square stones, as no doubt the steps also were (see Plate II. II. *e e*). It yields no sense whatever to render לָעוֹלָה "for the burnt-offering" (LXX. and others); and the expression עֹלוֹת in ver. 26 thoroughly warrants our translating עוֹלָה, a flight of steps or staircase). These stone tables served as flesh-benches, on which the slaughtering tools were laid. אֲלֵיהֶם וְיַנִּיחוּ belong together, the ו being inserted "as if at the commencement of a new sentence after a pause in the thought" (cf. Prov. xxiii. 24, xxx. 28; Gen. xl. 9, Böttcher). It is not expressly stated, indeed, that these four tables were distributed on the two sides of the steps; but this may be inferred with certainty from the position of the other tables. Moreover, the twelve tables mentioned were not merely to be found at one of the gate-porches, but by all three of the inner gates, as was the case with the washing-cells (ver. 38), for sacrificial animals were taken to the altar and slaughtered at every gate; so that what is stated in vers. 39–42 with reference to one porch, namely, the porch of the east gate, to judge from הַצָּפוֹנָה in ver. 40, is applicable to the porches of the south and north gates also.

In ver. 43 another provision for the slaughtering of the sacrificial animals is mentioned, concerning which the opinions of the older translators and commentators are greatly divided. But the only explanation that can be sustained, so far as both the usage of the language and the facts are concerned, is that adopted by the Chaldee, viz. וְעִנְקְלִין נַפְקִין פֻּשַּׁךְ חַד קְבִיעִין בְּעַמּוּדֵי

בֵּית מַטַּבַּחְיָא, *et uncini egrediebantur (longitudine) unius palmi defixi in columnis domus macelli*, to which not only Böttcher, but Roediger (Ges. *Thes.* p. 1470) and Dietrich (*Lex.*) have given their adhesion. For שְׁפַתַּיִם, from שָׁפַת, to set or stand (act.), signifies stakes or pegs (in Ps. lxviii. 14, the folds constructed of stakes), here pegs a span long on the wall, into which they were inserted, and from which they projected to the length of a span. In the *dual* it stands for double pegs, forked pegs, upon which the carcases of the beasts were hung for the purpose of flaying, as Dav. Kimchi has interpreted the words of the Chaldee. The article indicates the kind, viz. the pegs required for the process of slaughtering. This explanation is also in harmony with the verb מוּכָנִים, *Hophal* of כּוּן, fastened, which by no means suits the rendering originated by the LXX., viz. ledges round the edge or the rim of the table. The only remaining difficulty is the word בַּבַּיִת, which Böttcher interprets as signifying "in the interior of the gate-porch and pillars" (Roediger, *in interiore parte, nempe in ea atrii parte, ubi hostiae mactandae essent*), on the just ground that the interior of the front porch could not be the place for slaughtering, but that this could only be done outside, either in front of or near the porch. But even *in interiore parte atrii* is not really suitable, and at all events is too indefinite for מוּכָנִים. It would therefore be probably more correct to render it "fastened against the house," *i.e.* to the outer walls of the gate-porch buildings, so that בַּיִת would stand for buildings in the sense of בִּנְיָה, although I cannot cite any passage as a certain proof of the correctness of this rendering. But this does not render the explanation itself a doubtful one, as it would be still more difficult to interpet בַּבַּיִת if שְׁפַתַּיִם were explained in any other way. סָבִיב סָבִיב refers to the three outer sides of the porch. The description of the slaughtering apparatus closes in ver. 43*b* with the words, "and upon the tables (mentioned in vers. 39–42) came the flesh of the offering." קָרְבָּן, the general word for sacrificial offerings, as in Lev. i. 2 sqq.

In vers. 44–46 we have a description of cells for the officiating priests, and in vers. 45 and 46 two such cells are plainly mentioned according to their situation and purpose (*vid.* Plate I. *F F*). But it is impossible to bring the Masoretic text of ver. 44 into harmony with this, without explaining it in an arbitrary manner. For, in the first place, the reference there is to לִשְׁכוֹת שָׁרִים, cells of the singers; whereas these cells, according to vers. 45 and 46, were intended for the priests who performed the service in the temple-house and at the altar of burnt-offering. The attempt of both the earlier and the more recent supporters of the Masoretic text to set aside this discrepancy, by arguing that the priests who had to attend to the service in the temple and at the altar, according to vers. 45 and 46, were singers, is overturned by the fact that in the Old Testament worship a sharp distinction is made between the Levitical singers and the priests, *i.e.* the Aaronites who administered the priesthood; and Ezekiel does not abolish this distinction in the vision of the temple, but sharpens it still further by the command, that none but the sons of Zadok are to attend to the priestly service at the sanctuary, while the other descendants of Aaron, *i.e.* the Aaronites who sprang from Ithamar, are only to be employed in watching at the gate of the house, and other non-priestly occupations (ch. xliv. 10 sqq.). Consequently Ezekiel could not identify the priests with the singers, or call the cells intended for the officiating priests singers' cells. Moreover, only two cells, or cell-buildings, are mentioned in vers. 45 and 46, and their position is described in the same words as that of the cells mentioned in ver. 44, so that there can be no doubt as to the identity of the former and the altter cells. In ver. 44 the supposed singers' cells are placed at the north gate, with the front toward the south, which only applies, according to ver. 45, to the one cell intended for the priests who attended to the service in the holy place; and again, in ver. 44, another cell is mentioned at the east gate, with the front toward the north, which was set apart, according to ver. 46, for the priests who attended to the altar service. Consequently, according to our Masoretic text of the 44th verse, there would be first singers' cells (in the plural), and then one cell, at least three cells therefore; whereas, according to vers. 45 and 46, there were only two. And lastly, the אֶחָד in ver. 44*b* can only be understood by our taking it in the sense of "another," in opposition to the usage of the language. For these reasons we are compelled to alter שרים into שְׁתַּיִם, and אֲשֶׁר into אַחַת, after the LXX., and probably also הַקָּדִים into הַדָּרוֹם, and in consequence of this to adopt the pointing לְשָׁכוֹת, and to read פָּנֶיהָ instead of פְּנֵיהֶם. Further alterations are not requisite or indicated by the LXX., as the rest of the deviations in their text are to be explained from their free handling of the original. According to the text with these alterations, even in ver. 44 there are only two cells mentioned. They were situated "outside the inner gate." This definition is ambiguous, for you are outside the inner gate not only before entering the gate, *i.e.* while in the outer court, but also after having passed through it and entered the inner court. Hence there follows the more precise definition, "in the inner court." If, then, we read אַחַת for אֲשֶׁר, there follows, in perfect accordance with the fact, a more precise statement as to the situation of both the one and the other of these cells, אַחַת and אֶחָד corresponding to one another. The second אֶחָד, instead of אַחַת, which is grammatically the more correct, is to be attributed to a *constructio ad sensum*, as the לְשָׁכוֹת were not separate rooms, but buildings with several chambers. One cell stood by the shoulder (side) of the north gate, with the front (פָּנִים) toward the south; the other at the shoulder of the south gate, with the front toward the north. They stood opposite to one another, therefore, with their fronts facing each other. Instead of the *south* gate, however, the Masoretic text has שַׁעַר הַקָּדִים, the east gate; and ver. 46 contains nothing that would be expressly at variance with this, so that הַקָּדִים could be defended in case of need. But only in case of need—that is to say, if we follow Kliefoth in assuming that it stood on the left of the gateway to persons entering through the east gate, and explaining the fact that its front turned toward the north, on the ground that the priests who resided in it were charged with the duty of inspecting the sacrifices brought through the east gate, or watching the bringing in of the sacrifices, so that this cell was simply a watchman's cell after all. But this assumption is founded upon a misinterpretation of the formula שָׁמַר מִשְׁמֶרֶת הַמִּזְבֵּחַ, to keep the keeping of the altar. This formula does not mean to watch and see that nothing unlawful was taken to the altar, but refers to the altar service itself, the observance of everything devolving upon the servants of the altar in the performance of the sacrificial worship, or the offering of the sacrifices upon the altar according to the precepts of the law. If, then, this duty was binding upon the priests who resided in this cell, it would have been very unsuitable for the front of the cell to be turned toward the north, in which case it would have been absolutely impossible to see the altar from the front of the cell. This unsuitability can only be removed by the supposition that the cell was built at the south gate, with the front toward the north, *i.e.* looking directly toward the altar. For this reason we must also regard הַקָּדִים as a corruption of הַדָּרוֹם, and look for this second cell at the south gate, so that it stood opposite to the one built at the north gate.—All that remains doubtful is, whether these two cells were on the east or the west side of the south and north gates, a point concerning which we have no information given in the text. In our sketch we have placed them on the west side (*vid.* Plate I. *F*), so that they stood in front of the altar and the porch-steps. The concluding words of ver. 46, in which הֵמָּה refers to the priests mentioned in vers. 45 and 46, state that in the new sanctuary only priests of the sons of Zadok were to take charge of the service at the altar and in the holy place; and this is still further expanded in ch. xliv. 10 sqq.—Finally, in ver. 47 the description of the courts is concluded with the account of the measure of the inner court, a hundred cubits long and the same in breadth, according to which it formed a perfect square surrounded by a wall, according to ch. xlii. 10. The only other observation made is, that it was within this space that the altar of burnt-offering stood, the description of which is given afterwards in ch. xliii. 13 sqq. (see Plate I. *H*).

Chap. xl. 48–xli. 26. *The Temple-house, with the Porch, Side-storeys, and Back-building.*

Chap. xl. 48, 49. THE TEMPLE-PORCH (See Plate III. *A*). —The measuring angel conducts the prophet still farther to the porch of the temple, and measures its breadth and length. —Ver. 48. *And he led me to the porch of the house, and measured the pillar of the porch, five cubits on this side and five cubits on that side; and the breadth of the gate, three cubits on this side and three cubits on that side.* Ver. 49. *The length of the porch was twenty cubits, and the breadth eleven cubits, and that by the steps by which one went up; and columns were by the pillars, one on this side and one on that side.*— הַבַּיִת is the temple in the more restricted sense of the word, the temple-house, as in 1 Kings vi. 2, etc.; and אֻלָם, the porch before the entrance into the holy place (cf. 1 Kings vi. 3). The measurements in vers. 48 and 49, which are apparently irreconcilable with one another, led the LXX. to the adoption of arbitrary interpolations and conjectures in ver. 49,[1] in accordance with which Böttcher, Hitzig, and others have made corrections in the text, which have a plausible justification in the many artificial and for the most part mistaken interpretations that have been given of the text. The measures in ver. 49*a* are perfectly plain, namely, the length of the porch twenty cubits, and the breadth eleven cubits; and there is no question

[1] The text of the LXX. reads thus: . . . καὶ διεμέτρησε τὸ αἴλ τοῦ αἰλὰμ πηχῶν πέντε τὸ πλάτος ἔνθεν καὶ πηχῶν πέντε ἔνθεν, καὶ τὸ εὖρος τοῦ θυρώματος πηχῶν δεκατεσσάρων, καὶ ἐπωμίδες τῆς θυρᾶς τοῦ αἰλὰμ πηχῶν τριῶν ἔνθεν καὶ πηχῶν τριῶν ἔνθεν. Καὶ τὸ μῆκος τοῦ αἰλὰμ πηχῶν εἴκοσι καὶ τὸ εὖρος πηχῶν δώδεκα· καὶ ἐπὶ δέκα ἀναβαθμῶν ἀνέβαινον ἐπ᾽ αὐτό κ.τ.λ.

that these measurements are to be understood in the clear, that is to say, as referring to the internal space, excluding the side-walls, as in the case of the holy place, the most holy place, and the inner court. The only question is whether the length signifies the dimension from east to west, *i.e.* the distance which had to be traversed on entering the temple, and therefore the breadth, the extent from north to south; or whether we are to understand by the length the larger dimension, and by the breadth the smaller, in which case the measurement from north to south, which formed the breadth of the house, would be designated the length of the porch, and that from east to west the breadth. Nearly all the commentators have decided in favour of the latter view, because, in the porch of Solomon's temple, the length of twenty cubits was measured according to the breadth of the house. But the fact has been overlooked, that in 1 Kings vi. 3 the length given is more precisely defined by the clause, "in front of the breadth of the house." There is no such definition here, and the analogy of the building of Solomon's temple is not sufficient in itself to warrant our regarding the construction of the porch in the temple seen by Ezekiel as being precisely the same; since it was only in the essential portions, the form of which was of symbolical significance (the holy place and the most holy), that this picture of a temple resembled the temple of Solomon, whereas in those which were less essential it differed from that temple in various ways. At the very outset, therefore, the more probable assumption appears to be, that just as in the case of the holy place and the holy of holies, so also in that of the porch, we are to understand by the length, the distance to be traversed (from east to west), and by the breadth, the extension on either side (*i.e.* from south to north). If, then, we understand the measurements in ver. 49 in this way, the measures given in ver. 48 may also be explained without any alterations in the text. The measuring of the pillar of the porch on either side, and of the gate on this side and that (ver. 48), is sufficient of itself to lead to the conclusion that the front turned toward a person entering is the breadth from south to north. This breadth presented to the eye a pillar on this side and one on that,—two pillars, therefore, each five cubits broad (*c c*), and a breadth of gate of three cubits on this side and three on that, six cubits in all (*b*), that is to say, a total breadth (*k*—*k*) of $5 + 3 + 3 + 5 = 16$ cubits. The only thing that can surprise one here is the manner in which the breadth of the gate is defined: three cubits on this side and that, instead of simply six cubits. But the only reason in all probability is, that the pillars on either side are mentioned just before, and the gate of six cubits' breadth consisted of two halves, which had their hinges fastened to the adjoining pillars, so that each half was measured by itself from the pillar to which it was attached. The breadth of front mentioned, viz. sixteen cubits, agrees very well with the breadth of the porch inside, *i.e.* eleven cubits (*m*—*m*), for it allows a thickness of two cubits and a half for each side wall (*a*), and this was sufficient for the walls of a porch. The pillars, which were five cubits broad on the outer face, were therefore only half that breadth ($2\frac{1}{2}$ cubits) in the inner side within the porch, the other two cubits and a half forming the side wall. All the particulars given in ver. 48 may be explained in this way without any artifice, and yield a result the proportions of which are in harmony with those of the entire building. For the porch, with an external breadth of sixteen cubits, was half as broad as the house, which had a breadth of twenty cubits in the clear, and side walls of six cubits in thickness (ch. xli. 5), so that when measured on the outside it was $6 + 20 + 6 = 32$ cubits broad. The breadth of the interior also is apparently perfectly appropriate, as the porch was not intended either for the reception of vessels or for the abode of individuals, but was a simple erection in front of the entrance into the holy place, the door of which (*d*) was ten cubits broad (ch. xli. 2), that is to say, half a cubit narrower on either side than the porch-way leading to it. And lastly, the length of the porch was also in good proportion to the holy place, which followed the porch; the porch being twenty cubits long, and the holy place forty cubits. If we add to this the front wall, with a thickness of two cubits and a half, corresponding to that of the side walls, we obtain an external length of twenty-two cubits and a half for the porch. In front were the steps by which one went up to the porch (*l*). It is generally supposed that there were ten steps, the אֲשֶׁר after בַּמַּעֲלוֹת being changed into עֶשֶׂר (ten) after the example of the LXX. But however this alteration may commend itself when the facts of the case are considered, ten steps in front of the porch answering very well to the eight steps before the gateway of the inner court, and to the seven steps in front of the gateway of the outer court, it is not absolutely necessary, and in all probability is merely a conjecture of the Seventy, who did not know what to do with אֲשֶׁר, and possibly it is not even correct (see at ch. xli. 8). The words וּבַמַּעֲלוֹת אֲשֶׁר can be attached without difficulty to the preceding account of the breadth: "the breadth was eleven cubits, and that at the steps by which they went up to it," *i.e.* when measured on the side on which the flight of steps stood. If the words are taken in this way, they serve to remove all doubt as to the side which is designated as the breadth, with special reference to the fact that the porch of Solomon's temple was constructed in a different manner. The number of steps, therefore, is not given, as was also the case with the east gate of the outer court (ch. xl. 6), because it was of no essential importance in relation to the entire building. The last statement, "and there were columns by the pillars on this side and on that," is free from difficulty, although there is also a difference of opinion among the commentators as to the position of these columns. הָאֵילִים points back to אֶל אֵלָם (ver. 48). The preposition אֶל does not imply that the columns stood close to the pillars, and had the form of half-columns, but simply that they stood near the pillars (see Plate III. *K*), like the columns Jachin and Boaz in Solomon's temple, to which they correspond.

Chap. xli. 1–4. THE INNER SPACE OF THE TEMPLE (see Plate III. *B* and *C*).—Ver. 1. *And he led me into the temple, and measured the pillars, six cubits breadth on this side and six cubits breadth on that side, with regard to the breadth of the tent.* Ver. 2. *And the breadth of the door was ten cubits; and the shoulders of the door, five cubits on this side, and five cubits on that: and he measured its length, forty cubits; and the breadth, twenty cubits.* Ver. 3. *And he went within and measured the pillar of the door, two cubits; and the door, six cubits; and the breadth of the door, seven cubits.* Ver. 4. *And he measured its length, twenty cubits; and the breadth, twenty cubits, toward the temple; and said to me, This is the holy of holies.*—Vers. 1 and 2 give the measurements of the holy place. הֵיכָל is used here in the more restricted sense for the nave of the temple, the holy place (*B*), without the porch and the holy of holies (cf. 1 Kings vi. 17). The measuring commences with the front (eastern) wall, in which there was the entrance door. This wall had pillars (*e e*) of six cubits breadth on either side (on the right hand and the left), and between the pillars a door (*d*) ten cubits broad, with door-shoulders (*e e*) of five cubits on this side and that (ver. 2*a*). These measurements (6 + 6 + 10 + 5 + 5) yield for the front wall a total breadth of thirty-two cubits. This agrees with the measurements which follow: twenty cubits, the (internal) breadth of the holy place, and six cubits the thickness of the wall (*e*) on either side (ver. 5). The only remaining difficulty is in the very obscure words appended, רֹחַב הָאֹהֶל, in which Ewald and Hitzig propose to alter האהל into הָאַיִל, because the LXX. have substituted τοῦ αἰλάμ, but without making any improvement, as הָאַיִל is still more inexplicable. Kliefoth, after examining the various attempts to explain these words, comes to the conclusion that no other course is left than to take הָאֹהֶל as signifying the inner space of Ezekiel's temple, consisting of the holy place and the holy of holies, which was the same in the entire building as the tabernacle had been,—viz. the tent of God's meeting with His people, and which is designated as אֹהֶל to show the substantial identity of this space and the tabernacle. The clause רֹחַב הָאֹהֶל is thus attached to the preceding double מִפֹּה (*i.e.* to the measurement of the two pillars bounding the holy space), in an elliptical manner, in the following sense: "he measured the breadth of the pillars, on this side and that, which marked off the breadth of the tent, on the outside, that is to say, of the inner space of the holy place which resembled the tabernacle;" so that this clause formed a loose apposition, meaning, "with regard to the breath of the tent." כִּתְפוֹת הַפֶּתַח are the walls on both sides of the door (*e e*), between the door and the boundary pillars.—The internal length and breadth of the holy place are the same as in the holy place of Solomon's temple (1 Kings vi. 2, 17).—Vers. 3 and 4 refer to the holy of holies (*c*). "He went within." We have וּבָא (for וַיָּבוֹא) and not וַיְבִיאֵנִי (ver. 1), because the prophet was not allowed to tread the most holy place, and therefore the angel went in alone. פְּנִימָה is defined in ver. 4 as the holy of holies. The measurements in ver. 3 refer to the partition wall between the holy place and the most holy (*g*). אֵיל הַפֶּתַח, the pillar-work of the door, stands for the pillars on both sides of the door; and the measurement of two cubits no doubt applies to each pillar, denoting, not the thickness, but the breadth which it covered on the wall. There is a difficulty in the double measurement which follows: the door six cubits, and the breadth of the door seven cubits. As the latter is perfectly clear, and also apparently in accordance with the fact, and on measuring a door the height is the only thing which can come into consideration in addition to the breadth, we agree with Kliefoth in taking the six cubits as a statement of the height. The height of six cubits bears a fitting proportion to the breadth of seven cubits, if there were folding-doors; and the seven is significant in the case of the door to the holy of holies, the dwelling of God. The Seventy, however, did not know what to do with this text, and changed רֹחַב הַפֶּתַח שֶׁבַע אַמּוֹת into τὰς ἐπωμίδας τοῦ θυρώματος πηχῶν ἑπτὰ ἔνθεν καὶ ἔνθεν, in which they have been followed by Böttcher, Hitzig, and others. But it is obvious at once that the Seventy have simply derived these *data* from the measurements of the front of the holy place (ver. 2), and have overlooked the fact, that in the first place, beside the measure of the כִּתְפוֹת הַפֶּתַח, *i.e.* ἐπωμίδες τοῦ πυλῶνος, the רֹחַב הַפֶּתַח, or *breadth* of the door, is also expressly measured there, whereas here, on the contrary, it is preceded by הַפֶּתַח alone, without רֹחַב; and secondly, as the measurement of the אֵילִים given in ver. 1 indicates their breadth (from south to north), in the present instance also the measure ascribed to the אֵיל הַפֶּתַח can only refer to the breadth of the אַיִל, and not to its thickness (from east to west). But if we explain the first clause of ver. 3 in this manner, as both the language and the fact require, the reading of the LXX. is proved to be a false correction, by the fact that it yields a breadth of twenty-two or twenty-four cubits (2 + 2 + 6 + 7 + 7), whereas the holy of holies, like the holy place, was only twenty cubits broad. The dimensions of the holy of holies also correspond to the space covered by the holy of holies in Solomon's temple (1 Kings vi. 20). The expression אֶל־פְּנֵי הַהֵיכָל, "toward the holy place," is to be explained by the supposition that the measuring angel, after he had proceeded to the western end of the holy of holies for the purpose of measuring the length, turned round again to measure the breadth, so that this breadth lay "toward the holy place."

Vers. 5–11. THE WALL AND THE SIDE-BUILDING.—Ver. 5. *And he measured the wall of the house six cubits, and the breadth of the side storey four cubits round the house round about.* Ver. 6. *And of the side-rooms there were room upon room three, and that thirty times, and they came upon the wall, which the house had by the side-rooms round about, so that they were held, and yet they were not held in the wall of the house.* Ver. 7. *And it spread out, and was surrounded upwards more and more to the side-rooms, for the enclosure of the house went upwards more and more round about the house; therefore the house received breadth upwards; and so the lower ascended to the upper after the proportion of the central one.* Ver. 8. *And I saw in the house a height round about, with regard to the foundations of the side-rooms a full rod, six cubits to the joint.* Ver. 9. *The breadth of the wall, which the side storey had on the outside, was five cubits, and so also what was left free was by the side-chamber building of the house.* Ver. 10. *And between the cells was a breadth of twenty cubits round the house round about.* Ver. 11. *And the door of the side-chamber building led toward what was left free, one door toward the north and one door toward the south, and the breadth of the space left free was five cubits round about.*—From the interior of the sanctuary the measuring man turned to the outer work, and measured, first of all, the wall of the house (ver. 5), *i.e.* the wall commencing with the pillars in the front (ver. 1), which surrounded the holy place and the holy of holies on the north, the west, and the south (*e*). This was six cubits thick. He then measured the breadth of the צֵלָע, *i.e.* of the building consisting of three storeys of side-rooms, which was erected against the north, west, and south sides of the sanctuary (*h*). For צֵלָע signifies not only a single side-room, but collectively the whole range of these side-chambers, the entire building against the sides of the temple house, called יָצוּעַ in 1 Kings vi. 5, 6, with which הַצֵּלָע (ver. 8) is also used alternately there (see the comm. on 1 Kings vi. 5).—The breadth of the side-building was four cubits in the clear, that is to say, the space from the temple wall to the outer wall of the side-building (*f*), which was five cubits thick (ver. 9), and that uniformly all round the temple.—The further particulars concerning the side-rooms in vers. 6 and 7 are very obscure, so that they can only be made perfectly intelligible by comparing them with the description of the similar building in Solomon's temple. According to this, ver. 6*a* is to be taken thus: "and as for the side-rooms, there were room upon room (אֶל for עַל) three, and (that) thirty times," and understood as signifying that there were three side-rooms standing one above another, and that this occurred thirty times, so that the side-building had three storeys, each containing thirty rooms (chambers), so that there were thirty times three rooms standing one above another (*h h h*). There is no necessity, therefore, for the transposition of שָׁלוֹשׁ וּשְׁלֹשִׁים into שְׁלֹשִׁים וְשָׁלוֹשׁ, which Böttcher, Hitzig, and Hävernick have adopted from the LXX., because of their having taken אֶל in the sense of against, room against room thirty, and that three times, which yields the same thought, no doubt, but not so clearly, inasmuch as it remains indefinite whether the three times thirty rooms were above one another or side by side. Nothing is said about the distribution of the thirty rooms in each storey; but it is very probable that the distribution was uniform, so that on each of the longer sides, *i.e.* against the northern and southern walls of the temple, there were twelve rooms, and six against the shorter western wall. The northern and southern walls were sixty cubits, *plus* six cubits the thickness of the wall, *plus* four cubits the breadth of the side building against the western wall (60+6+4), in all therefore seventy cubits, or, deducting five cubits for the thickness of the outer wall at the front of the building, sixty-five cubits long; and the western wall was $20 + 2 \times 6$ (the thickness of the side wall), *i.e.* thirty-two cubits long. If, therefore, we fix the length of each side-room at $4\frac{1}{2}$ cubits, there remain five cubits against the western wall for the seven party walls required, or five-sevenths of a cubit for each, and against the northern and southern walls eleven cubits for party walls and staircase, and reckoning the party walls at four-sevenths of a cubit in thickness, there are left four cubits and a seventh for the space for the stairs, quite a sufficient space for a winding staircase.—The clauses which follow relate to the connection between these side-rooms and the temple house. בָּאוֹת בַּקִּיר, they were coming (going) upon the wall. בּוֹא בְּ, generally *intrare in locum*, here, on account of what follows, to tread upon the wall; that is to say, they were built against the wall in such a manner that the beams of the floors of the three storeys rested on the temple wall on the inner side, *i.e.* were held or borne by it, but not so as to be inserted in the wall and held fast thereby. The only way in which this could be effected was by so constructing the temple wall that it had a ledge at every storey on which the beams of the side storeys could rest, *i.e.* by making it recede half a cubit, or become so much thinner on the outer side, so that if the thickness of the wall at the bottom was six cubits, it would be five cubits and a half at the first storey, five cubits at the second, and four and a half at the third. In this way the side-rooms were supported by the temple wall, but not in such a manner that the beams laid hold of the walls of the sanctuary, or were dovetailed into them, which would have done violence to the sanctity of the temple house; and the side storeys appeared as, what they should be, an external building, which did not interfere with the integrity of the sanctuary. That this is the meaning of the words is rendered certain by a comparison with 1 Kings vi. 6, where the ledges on the temple wall are expressly mentioned, and the design of these is said to be לְבִלְתִּי אֲחֹז בְּקִירוֹת, that the beams might not be fastened in the walls of the house, to which the last words of our verse, וְלֹא־יִהְיוּ אֲחוּזִים בְּקִיר הַבָּיִת, refer. Kliefoth's rendering of בָּאוֹת בַּקִּיר, "they went against the wall," is grammatically untenable, as בּוֹא with ב does not mean to go against anything. אֲשֶׁר לַבַּיִת לַצְּלָעוֹת, which the (temple) house had toward the side-rooms. סָבִיב סָבִיב, round about, *i.e.* on all three sides of the temple. The peculiarity of the storeys, arising from this resting upon the temple, is described in ver. 7, of which different explanations have been given, but the general meaning of which is that it occasioned a widening of the side-rooms proceeding upwards from storey to storey, as is plainly stated in 1 Kings vi. 6. The words וְרָחֲבָה וְנָסְבָה are not to be taken together, as expressing one idea, viz. "it spread round about"

(De Wette), but contain two different assertions, which are more precisely defined in what follows by the substantives מוּסָב and רֹחַב. Neither קִיר nor הַצֵּלָע is to be taken as the subject; but the verbs are to be regarded as impersonal: "there spread out and surrounded," *i.e.* a widening and a surrounding took place. The double לְמַעְלָה has been correctly explained by Bochart, viz. "by continued ascending," *i.e.* the higher one went the more extension and compass did one find, with regard to, *i.e.* according to the measure of, the side-rooms or side-storeys. לַצְּלָעוֹת belongs to לְמַעְלָה, and is added for the purpose of defining more precisely how the widening took place, not gradually, but at each storey; for "these צְלָעוֹת are the three rooms standing one above another, spoken of in ver. 6" (Kliefoth). This statement is explained, and the reason assigned, in the clause introduced with כִּי, the meaning of which depends upon the explanation of the word מוּסָב. This word may mean a way round, and a surrounding. The Rabbins, whom Hävernick follows, understand by מוּסָב a winding staircase, the לוּלִים mentioned in 1 Kings vi. 8, which led from the lower storey to the upper ones. This is decidedly wrong; for apart from the question whether this meaning can be grammatically sustained, it is impossible to attach any rational meaning to the words, "a winding staircase of the house was upwards more and more round about the house," since a winding staircase could never run round about a building seventy cubits long and forty cubits broad, but could only ascend at one spot, which would really give it the character of a winding staircase. Böttcher's explanation is equally untenable: "for the winding round of the interior was upwards more and more round and round inwards." For, in the first place, הַבַּיִת does not mean the interior, and לַבַּיִת does not mean inwards; and secondly, "winding round" is not equivalent to an alteration of form in the shape of the rooms, through which those in the bottom storey were oblongs running lengthwise, those in the central storey squares, and those in the third oblongs running inwards, which Böttcher imagines to have been the case. It would be much easier to adopt the explanation of Kliefoth and others, who take מוּסָב in the sense of a way round, and regard it as signifying a passage running round the house in the form of a gallery, by which one could walk all round the house, and so reach the rooms in the upper storeys. This, as Kliefoth still further remarks, was the reason why the surrounding of (circuit round) the house was greater the higher one ascended, and also the reason why it became wider up above in the upper storeys, as the words, "therefore the breadth of the house increased upwards," affirm. In these words Kliefoth finds a distinct assertion "that there is no foundation for the assumption that the widening upwards was occasioned by the receding of the temple walls; but that the widening of the building, which took place above, arose from the passages round that were attached to the second and third storeys, and that these passages ran round the building, and consequently were attached to the outside in the form of galleries." But we are unable to see how this can be *distinctly* asserted in the words רֹחַב לַבַּיִת לְמַעְלָה. Even if הַבַּיִת, in connection with מוּסָב, signified the side-building, including the temple house, the only thought contained in the words would be, that the side-building became broader at each storey as you ascended, *i.e.* that the breadth of the side-building increased with each storey. But even then it would not be stated in what manner the increase in breadth arose; whether in consequence of the receding of the temple wall at each storey, or from the fact that the side-rooms were built so as to project farther out, or that the side-storeys were widened by the addition of a passage in the form of a gallery. And the decision in favour of one or other of these possibilities could only be obtained from the preceding clause, where it is stated that מוּסָב הַבַּיִת went round about the side-building, and that in favour of the last. But, in the first place, the assumption that הַבַּיִת and לַבַּיִת denote the side-building, to the exclusion of the temple house, is extremely harsh, as throughout the whole section הַבַּיִת

signifies the temple house; and in ver. 6 לַבַּיִת is used again in this sense. If we understand, however, by מוּסַב הַבַּיִת a passage or a surrounding all round the temple house, the words by no means imply that there were outer galleries running round the side-rooms. In the second place, it is extremely harsh to take מוּסָב in the sense of a passage round, if the preceding נָסְבָה is to signify surrounded. As מוּסָב takes up the word נָסְבָר again, and "precisely the same thing is signified by the two verbs רָחֲבָה וְנָסְבָה as by the substantives רֹחַב and מוּסָב afterwards," we cannot render נסבה by surrounded, and מוסב by a passage round. If, therefore, מוּסָב signified a passage, a gallery running round the building, this would necessarily be expressed in the verb נָסְבָה, which must be rendered, "there went round," *i.e.* there was a passage round, more and more upwards, according to the measure of the storeys. But this would imply that the passage round existed in the case of the bottom storey also, and merely increased in breadth in the central and upper storeys. Now a gallery round the bottom storey is shown to be out of the question by the measurements which follow. From this we may see that the supposition that there were galleries on the outside round the second and third storeys is not required by the text, and possibly is irreconcilable with it; and there is not even a necessity to adduce the further argument, that Kliefoth's idea, that the entire building of three storeys was simply upheld by the outer wall, without any support to the beams from the wall of the temple, is most improbable, as such a building would have been very insecure, and useless for the reception of any things of importance. We therefore take נָסַב and מוּסָב in the sense of surrounded and surrounding. In this case, ver. 7 simply affirms that the surrounding of the house, *i.e.* the side-building round about the temple house, became broader toward the top, increasing (more and more) according to the measure of the storeys; for it increased the more in proportion to the height against the temple house, so that the house became broader as you ascended.

To this there is appended by means of וְכֵן the last statement of the verse: "and so the lower ascended to the upper after the measure of the central one." This clause is taken by the majority of the commentators to mean: thus they ascended from the lower to the upper after the central one. But many have observed the folly of an arrangement by which they ascended a staircase on the outside from the lower storey to the upper, and went from that into the central one, and have therefore followed the LXX. in changing וְכֵן into וּמִן and לַתִּיכוֹנָה into בַּתִּיכוֹנָה, "and from the lower (they ascended) to the upper through the central one." But there is no apparent necessity for these alterations of the text, as the reading in the text yields a good sense, if we take הַתַּחְתּוֹנָה as the subject to יַעֲלֶה: and thus the lower storey ascended to the upper after the measure of the central one,—a rendering to which no decisive objection can be urged on the ground of the difference of gender (the masc. יַעֲלֶה). וְכֵן affirms that the ascent took place according to the mode of widening already mentioned.

In the 8th verse we have a further statement concerning the side-rooms, as we may see from the middle clause; but it has also been explained in various ways. Böttcher, for example, renders the first clause thus: "and I saw what the height round about was in an inwardly direction;" but this is both grammatically false and senseless, as לַבַּיִת does not mean inwardly, and "in an inwardly direction" yields no conceivable sense. Kliefoth adopts the rendering: "I fixed my eyes upon the height round about to the house;" but this is also untenable, as רָאָה does not mean to fix the eyes upon, in the sense of measuring with the eyes, and in this case also the article could hardly be omitted in the case of גֹּבַהּ. The words run simply thus: "I saw in the house a height" = an elevation round about. What this means is shown in the following words: the side-rooms had foundations a full rod, *i.e.* the foundation of the rooms was a full rod (six cubits) high. מיסדות is not a substantive מֵיסְדוֹת, but a participle *Pual* מְיֻסָּדוֹת; and the *Keri* is substantially correct, though an unnecessary correction; מְלוֹ for מְלוֹא (compare ch. xxviii. 16, מָלוֹ for מָלְאוּ). The side-building did not stand on level ground, therefore, but had a foundation six cubits high. This is in harmony with the statement in ch. xl. 49, that they ascended by steps to the temple porch, so that the temple house with its front porch was raised above the inner court. As this elevation was a full rod or six cubits, not merely for the side-building, but also for the temple porch, we may assume that there were twelve steps, and not ten after the LXX. of ch. xl. 49, as half a cubit of Ezekiel's measurement was a considerable height for steps.—The expression which follows, "six cubits אַצִּילָה," is obscure, on account of the various ways in which אצילה may be understood. So much, however, is beyond all doubt, that the words cannot contain merely an explanation of the length of the rod measure: "six cubits (measured) to the wrist," because the length of the rod has already been fixed in ch. xl. 5, and therefore a fresh definition would be superfluous, and the one given here would contradict that of ch. xl. 5. אָצִיל signifies connection or joint, and when applied to a building can hardly mean anything else than the point at which one portion of the building joins on to the other. Hävernick and Kliefoth therefore understand by אָצִיל the point at which one storey ends and another begins, the connecting line of the rooms standing one above another; and Hävernick takes the clause to be a more precise definition of מיסדות הצ׳, understanding by מיסדות the foundations of the rooms, *i.e.* the floors. Kliefoth, on the other hand, regards the clause as containing fresh information, namely, concerning the height of the storeys, so that according to the statement in this verse the side-building had a foundation of six cubits in height, and each of the storeys had also a height of six cubits, and consequently the whole building was twenty-four cubits high, reckoning from the ground. So much is clear, that מְיָסְּדוֹת does not signify the floors of the rooms, so that Hävernick's explanation falls to the ground. And Kliefoth's view is also open to this objection, that if the words gave the height of the storeys, and therefore supplied a second measurement, the copula ו could hardly fail to stand before them. The absence of this copula evidently leads to the conclusion that the "six cubits" אַצִּילָה are merely intended to furnish a further substantial explanation as to the foundation, which was a full rod high, the meaning of which has not yet been satisfactorily cleared up, as all the explanations given elsewhere are still further from the mark.

In ver. 9 there follow two further particulars with reference to the side-building. The wall of it without, *i.e.* on the outside (*f*), was five cubits thick or broad, and therefore one cubit thinner than the temple wall. The מֻנָּח in the side-building was just the same breadth. In the clause beginning with וַאֲשֶׁר the measure (five cubits) given in the first clause is to be repeated, so that we may render וַ by "*and also*," and must take the words in the sense of "just as broad." מֻנָּח, the *Hophal* participle of הִנִּיחַ, to let alone, in the case of a building, is that portion of the building space which is not built upon like the rest; and in ver. 11, where it is used as a substantive, it signifies the space left open by the sides of the building (Plate I. *i*). The Chaldee rendering is אֲתַר שְׁבִיק, *locus relictus.* בֵּית צְלָעוֹת is an adverbial or locative accusative: against the house of side-chambers, or all along it; and אֲשֶׁר לַבַּיִת is an appositional explanation: "which was to the temple," *i.e.* belonged to it, was built round about it.—Consequently there is no necessity for any alteration of the text, not even for changing בֵּית into בֵּין in order to connect together ver. 9*b* and ver. 10 as one clause, as Böttcher and Hitzig propose; though all that they gain thereby is the discrepancy that in vers. 9*b* and 10 the space left open between the side-rooms against the temple house and between the cells against the wall of the court is said to have been twenty cubits broad, whereas in ver. 12 the breadth of this *munnâch* is set down as five cubits.—There follows next in ver. 10 the account of the breadth between the temple-building and the cells against the wall of the inner court, and then in ver. 11 we have further particulars concerning the side-building and the space left open. הַלְּשָׁכוֹת (ver. 10) are the cell buildings, more fully described in ch. xlii. 1 sqq., which stood along the wall dividing the inner court from the outer on the west of the north and south gates of the inner court, and therefore opposite to the temple house (Plate I. *L L*). To the expression, "and between the cells there was a breadth," there has to be supplied the correlative term from the context, namely, the space between the מֻנָּח and the לְשָׁכוֹת had a breadth of twenty cubits round about the house, *i.e.* on the north, west, and south sides of the temple house.—The description of this space closes in ver. 11 with an account of the entrances to the side-building. It had a door toward the space left open, *i.e.* leading out into this space, one to the north and one to the south (Plate III. *i i*), and the space left open was five cubits broad round about, *i.e.* on the north, west, and south sides of the temple-building. מְקוֹם הַמֻּנָּח, the place of that which remained open, *i.e.* the space left open.

If, then, in conclusion, we gather together all the measurements of the temple house and its immediate surroundings, we obtain (as is shown in Plate I.) a square of a hundred cubits in breadth and a hundred cubits in length, exclusive of the porch. The temple (*G*) was twenty cubits broad in the inside (ver. 2); the wall surrounding the sanctuary was six cubits (ver. 5), or (for the two walls) $2 \times 6 = 12$ cubits. The side-buildings being four cubits broad in the clear on each side (ver. 5), make $2 \times 4 = 8$ cubits. The outside walls of these buildings, five cubits on each side (ver. 9), make $2 \times 5 = 10$ cubits. The מֻנָּח (*i*), five cubits round about (ver. 11), makes $2 \times 5 = 10$ cubits. And the space between this and the cells standing by the wall of the court (*e-g-h-f*), twenty cubits round about (ver. 10), makes $2 \times 20 = 40$ cubits. The sum total therefore is $20 + 12 + 8 + 10 + 10 + 40 = 100$ cubits, in perfect harmony with the breadth of the inner court given in ch. xl. 47. The length was as follows: forty cubits the holy place, and twenty cubits the holy of holies (vers. 2 and 4); the western wall, six cubits; the side-rooms on the west, four cubits; and their wall, five cubits; the מֻנָּח, on the west, five cubits; and the space to the cells, twenty cubits; in all, 40 + 20 + 6 + 4 + 5 + 5 + 20 = 100 cubits, as stated in ver. 13. The porch and the thickness both of the party-wall between the holy place and the most holy, and also of the front (eastern) wall of the holy place, are not taken into calculation here. The porch is not included, because the ground which it covered belonged to the space of the inner court into which it projected. The party-wall is not reckoned, because it was merely a thin wooden partition, and therefore occupied no space worth notice. But it is difficult to say why the front wall of the holy place is not included. As there was no room for it in the square of a hundred cubits, Kliefoth assumes that there was no wall whatever on the eastern side of the holy place, and supposes that the back wall (*i.e.* the western wall) of the porch supplied its place. But this is inadmissible, for the simple reason that the porch was certainly not of the same height as the holy place, and according to ch. xl. 48 it had only sixteen cubits of external breadth; so that there would not only have been an open space left in the upper portion of the front, but also an open space of two cubits in breadth on either side, if the holy place had had no wall of its own. Moreover, the measurement both of the pillars on both sides of the front of the הֵיכָל (ver. 1), and of the shoulders on both sides of the door (ver. 2), presupposes a wall or partition on the eastern side of the holy place, which cannot be supposed to have been thinner than the side-walls, that is to say, not less than six cubits in thickness. We are shut up, therefore, to the conjecture that the forty cubits' length of the holy place was measured from the door-line, which was ten cubits broad, and that the thickness of the door-shoulders on the two sides is included in these forty cubits, or, what is the same thing, that they were not taken into account in the measurement. The objection raised to this, namely, that the space within the holy place would thereby have lost a considerable portion of its significant length of forty cubits, cannot have much weight, as the door-shoulders, the thickness of which is not reckoned, were only five cubits broad on each side, and for the central portion of the holy place, which was occupied by the door, and was ten cubits broad, the length of forty cubits suffered no perceptible diminution. Just as the pillars of the door of the holy of holies with the party-wall are reckoned in the 40 + 20 cubits' length of the sanctuary, and are not taken into consideration; so may this also have been the case with the thickness of wall of the door-shoulders of the holy place. The measurements of the space occupied by the holy place and holy of holies, which have a symbolical significance, cannot be measured with mathematical scrupulosity.

Vers. 12-14. The Separate Place, and the External Dimensions of the Temple.—Ver. 12. *And the building at the front of the separate place was seventy cubits broad on the side turned toward the west, and the wall of the building five cubits broad round about, and its length ninety cubits.* Ver. 13. *And he measured the (temple) house: the length a hundred cubits; and the separate place, and its building, and its walls: the length a hundred cubits.* Ver. 14. *And the breadth of the face of the (temple) house, and of the separate place toward the east, a hundred cubits.*—The explanation of these verses depends upon the meaning of the word גִּזְרָה. According to its derivation from גָּזַר, to cut, to separate, גִּזְרָה means that which is cut off, or separated. Thus אֶרֶץ גְּזֵרָה is the land cut off, the desert, which is not connected by roads with the inhabited country. In the passage before us, גִּזְרָה signifies a place on the western side of the temple, *i.e.* behind the temple, which was separated from the sanctuary (Plate I. *J*), and on which a building stood, but concerning the purpose of which nothing more definite is stated than we are able to gather, partly from the name and situation of the place in question, and partly from such passages as

1 Chron. xxvi. 18 and 2 Kings xxiii. 11, according to which, even in Solomon's temple, there was a similar space at the back of the temple house with buildings upon it, which had a separate way out, the gate שַׁלֶּכֶת, namely, that "this space, with its buildings, was to be used for the reception of all refuse, sweepings, all kinds of rubbish,—in brief, of everything that was separated or rejected when the holy service was performed in the temple,—and that this was the reason why it received the name of the separate place" (Kliefoth). The building upon this space was situated אֶל־פְּנֵי־הַגִּזְרָה, in the front of the *gizrah* (that is to say, as one approached it from the temple); and that פְּאַת דֶּרֶךְ־הַיָּם, on the side of the way to the sea, *i.e.* on the western side, *sc.* of the temple, and had a breadth of seventy cubits (from north to south), with a wall round about, which was five cubits broad (thick), and a length of ninety cubits. As the thickness of the wall is specially mentioned in connection with the breadth, we must add it both to the breadth and to the length of the building as given here; so that, when looked at from the outside, the building was eighty cubits broad and a hundred cubits long. In ver. 13*b* this length is expressly attributed to the separate place, and (*i.e.* along with) its building, and the walls thereof. But the length of the temple house has also been previously stated as a hundred cubits. In ver. 14 the breadth of both is also stated to have been a hundred cubits,—namely, the breadth of the outer front, or front face of the temple, was a hundred cubits; and the breadth of the separate place לַקָּדִים toward the east, *i.e.* the breadth which it showed to the person measuring on the eastern side, was the same. If, then, the building on the separate place was only eighty cubits broad, according to ver. 12, including the walls, whilst the separate place itself was a hundred cubits broad, there remains a space of twenty cubits in breadth not covered by the building; that is to say, as we need not hesitate to put the building in the centre, open spaces of ten cubits each on the northern and southern sides were left as approaches

to the building on both sides (*K*), whereas the entire length of the separate place (from east to west) was covered by the building.—All these measurements are in perfect harmony. As the inner court formed a square of a hundred cubits in length (ch. xl. 47), the temple house, which joined it on the west, extended with its appurtenances to a similar length; and the separate place behind the temple also covered a space of equal size. These three squares, therefore, had a length from east to west of three hundred cubits. If we add to this the length of the buildings of the east gates of the inner and outer courts, namely fifty cubits for each (ch. xl. 15, 21, 25, 29, 33, 36), and the length of the outer court from gate to gate a hundred cubits (ch. xl. 19, 23, 27), we obtain for the whole of the temple building the length of five hundred cubits. If, again, we add to the breadth of the inner court or temple house, which was one hundred cubits, the breadths of the outer court, with the outer and inner gate-buildings, viz. two hundred cubits on both the north and south sides, we obtain a total breadth of 100 + 200 + 200 = 500 (say five hundred) cubits; so that the whole building covered a space of five hundred cubits square, in harmony with the calculation already made (at ch. xl. 24–27) of the size of the surrounding wall.

Vers. 15–26. SUMMARY ACCOUNT OF THE MEASUREMENT, THE CHARACTER, AND THE SIGNIFICANT ORNAMENTS OF THE PROJECTING PORTIONS OF THE TEMPLE BUILDING.—Ver. 15. *And thus he measured the length of the building in the front of the separate place which was at the back thereof, and its galleries on this side and that side, a hundred cubits, and the inner sanctuary, and the porches of the court;* Ver. 16. *The thresholds, and the closed windows, and the galleries round about all three—opposite to the thresholds was wainscoting wood round about, and the ground up to the windows; but the windows were covered—* Ver. 17. (*The space*) *above the doors, both to the inner temple and outside, and on all the wall round about, within and without, had its measures.* Ver. 18. *And cherubs and palms were made, a palm between every two cherubs; and the cherub had two faces;* Ver. 19. *A man's face toward the palm on this side, and a lion's face toward the palm on that side: thus was it made round about the whole house.* Ver. 20. *From the floor to above the doors were the cherubs and palms made, and that on the wall of the sanctuary.* Ver. 21. *The sanctuary had square door-posts, and the front of the holy of holies had the same form.* Ver. 22. *The altar was of wood, three cubits high, and its length two cubits; and it had its corner-pieces and its stand, and its walls were of wood: and he said to me, This is the table which stands before Jehovah.* Ver. 23. *And the holy place and the holy of holies had two doors.* Ver. 24. *And the doors had two wings, two turning leaves; the one door two, and the other two leaves.* Ver. 25. *And there were made upon them, upon the doors of the sanctuary, cherubs and palms, as they were made upon the walls; and a moulding of wood was on the front of the porch outside.* Ver. 26. *And there were closed windows and palms on this side and on that, on the side-walls of the porch, and the side-rooms of the house, and the beams.*—Ver. 15 is the commencement of a comprehensive enumeration of particular features in the building, the greater part of which have not been mentioned before; so that וּמָדַד (for וַיָּמָד) is to be rendered, "and thus he measured." The circumstance that another measurement follows in ver. 15*a*, whereas no further numbers are given from ver. 15*b* onwards, does not warrant us in assuming that ver. 15*a* is to be joined on to ver. 14, and ver. 15*b* to be taken in connection with ver. 16. The absence of the cop. ו before הַסִּפִּים in ver. 16*a* is sufficient to preclude the latter, showing as it does that הַסִּפִּים commences a fresh statement; and the words וְהַהֵיכָל וגו׳ in ver. 15*b* are still governed by the verb וּמָדַד in ver. 15*a*. The contents of ver. 15 are also decisive against the separation mentioned. If, for instance, we connect ver. 15*a* with ver. 14, the first clause contains a pure tautology, as the length of the building has been already measured, and the result is given in ver. 13. The tautology does not exist, if the summary statements of the measurement of different portions of the whole temple building commence with ver. 15; and in connection with these a supplementary account is given of various details not mentioned before. The contents of the second clause, namely, what is stated concerning the אַתִּיקִים, belong directly to the latter. The building in front of the separate place, which was measured by the man, is more precisely defined, so far as its situation is concerned, by the words אֲשֶׁר עַל־אַחֲרֶיהָ. The feminine suffix in אחריה points back to הַגִּזְרָה; consequently אֲשֶׁר can only refer to הַבִּנְיָן: "the building . . . which was at the back of the *gizrah*." This is not at variance with the situation indicated in אֶל־פְּנֵי הַגִּזְרָה, but serves as a more exact definition of this statement, showing that the building which stood at the front of the *gizrah* occupied the hinder part of it, *i.e.* extended in length from the front of the *gizrah* to the back.—The meaning of אַתּוּקִים or אַתִּיקִים, here (*Keri*) and in ver. 16, ch. xlii. 3 and 5, the only other passages in which it occurs, is involved in obscurity. Even Raschi confesses that he does not know what it means, and the older translators have simply resorted to vague conjectures for their renderings; the LXX. here, ἀπόλοιπα, in ch. xlii. 3 and 5 *περίστυλον* and *στοαί*; the Vulgate, here, *ethecas* (the Hebrew word Latinized), in ch. xlii. *porticus*; Targum, in the London Polyglot, ver. 15, זִיוִיתְהָא; ver. 16, אַתִּיקַיָּא; ch. xlii. 3, זָוֵי; and xlii. 5, זִיוַיָּא. There is no root אָתַק in Hebrew; and the derivation of the word from עָתַק is not only uncertain, but furnishes us with nothing that can be used for tracing the architectural signification of the word. Even the context in vers. 15 and 16 of this chapter supplies nothing, for in both verses the meaning of the clauses in which אתיקים stands is a matter of dispute. It is only in ch. xlii. 3 and 5 that we find any clue. According to ch. xlii. 3, in the three-storied cell-building there was אַתִּיק אֶל־פְּנֵי אַתִּיק on the third storey; and according to ver. 5 the cells of the upper storey in this building were shorter than those of the lower and central storey, because אַתִּיקִים took space away from them; and the reason for this, again, was, that the three-storied cells had no pillars. From this we may infer with certainty that the אַתִּיקִים were galleries or passages running along the outer walls of the building, which were not supported by pillars, and therefore necessarily rested upon ledges obtained by the receding of the rooms of the upper storey. This meaning also suits the present chapter. The suffix in אַתּוּקֶיהָא (an Aramaic form for אַתִּיקֶיהָ) points back, not to בִּנְיָן, but to הַבִּנְיָה in ver. 13; for the words, "and its galleries on this side and on that," i.e. on the north and south sides of the building, are not dependent upon אֹרֶךְ הַבִּנְיָן, in the sense of "the length of the building, with its galleries on this side and on that," as ואתוקיהא is too widely separated from אֹרֶךְ הב׳ for this. ואתוקיהא is rather a second object to מָדַד: he measured (1) the length of the building; (2) its galleries on this side and that—a hundred cubits: (3) the inner temple, etc. The hundred cubits do not refer to the length of the building, but to the galleries on both sides, which were of the same length as the building, and therefore ran along its entire length,—a fact which it was not superfluous to mention, as they might possibly have been shorter. הַהֵיכָל הַפְּנִימִי is the temple house, with the buildings against it, within the inner court. In addition to these, there are also mentioned the porches of the court, i.e. at the gate-buildings of the inner and outer courts, as the projecting portions of these buildings. These three works mentioned in ver. 15 comprise the whole of the buildings, the measurements of which have been mentioned in the previous description—viz. the building to the west of the temple, in vers. 12–14; the inner temple, in vers. 1–11; the porches of the courts, to which the temple porch in front of the holy place is to be added, as having been reckoned in the measurement as belonging to the inner court, in ch. xli.—Thus the contents of our verse (ver. 15) plainly show that it not only is an indivisible whole, but forms a conclusion in which the foregoing measurements are all summed up, and which serves as as introduction, in accordance with this, to the following summary of various additional features in the temple buildings which are also worthy of mention.

In this summary there are five points noticed: (*a*) the fact that all parts of the buildings had their measurements (vers. 16 and 17); (*b*) the significant ornamentation of the inner walls of the sanctuary (vers. 18–21); (*c*) the altar in the holy place (ver. 22); (*d*) the character and decoration of the doors of the sanctuary (vers. 23–25*a*); (*e*) the style of the porch and of the side-buildings against the temple (vers. 25, 26).—Vers. 16 and 17 form one period, enlarged by the parenthetical insertion of explanatory statements, similar to the construction in vers. 18 and 19. The predicate to the three subjects—the thresholds, the closed windows, and the galleries—is not to be sought for either in סָבִיב לִשְׁלָשְׁתָּם or in הַסַּף שְׂחִיף וגו'. The latter construction, adopted by Böttcher and Hävernick, yields the unmeaning assertion that the thresholds lay across in front of the threshold. The former gives the apparently bald thought, that thresholds, windows, and galleries were round about; in which the use of the article, *the* thresholds, *the* windows, is exceedingly strange. The predicate to הַסִּפִּים וגו' is מִדּוֹת at the end of ver. 17: the thresholds, etc., had measurements; and the construction is so far anakolouthistic, that the predicate מִדּוֹת, strictly speaking, belongs to the things mentioned in ver. 17 alone, and the subjects mentioned in ver. 16 are to be regarded as absolute nominatives. The words סָבִיב לִשְׁלָשְׁתָּם belong to the three preceding subjects, as a further definition, the thresholds, windows, and galleries (which were) against these three round about. The suffix to שְׁלָשְׁתָּם, "*their* triad," refers to the three buildings mentioned in ver. 15: the one upon the separate place, the temple building, and the porches of the court; and the appositional סָבִיב is not to be so pressed as to lead to the conclusion that all three buildings, and therefore the porches of the court also, had אַתִּיקִים round about. As the סביב לשלשתם is affirmed of the thresholds, and the windows, and the galleries, and these three objects are introduced by the article, as well known, *i.e.* as already mentioned and described in the preceding verses, the more precise definition (*resp.* limitation) of the apposition, "round about these three," is to be taken from the preceding description of these three buildings, and we are simply to assume the existence of thresholds, windows, and galleries in these buildings in those cases in which they have been mentioned in that description; so that the only place in which there were galleries was the building upon the separate place. But before the intended information is given concerning the thresholds, etc., a remark is introduced, with the words from נֶגֶד הַסַּף to סָבִיב, as to the construction of the thresholds: viz. that opposite to the threshold (הַסַּף being used in a general sense for every threshold) there was שְׂחִיף עֵץ, a thin covering of wood, or wainscoting. נֶגֶד does not mean across the front (Böttcher), but "opposite;" and the part opposite to the threshold of a door is, strictly speaking, the lintel. Here, however, the word is probably used in the broader sense for the framework of the door, above and on the two sides, as is shown by סָבִיב סָבִיב which follows. With הָאָרֶץ a fresh object is introduced. הָאָרֶץ is a nominative, like הַסִּפִּים, etc.; and the thought of supplying מִן, "from the ground," has originated in a faulty interpretation of the words. The idea is this: as the thresholds, the windows, etc., so also the ground up to the windows, *i.e.* the space between the ground and the windows, had measurements. The allusion to the windows is followed by the remark, in the form of a circumstantial clause, that "the windows were covered." מְכֻסּוֹת is apparently only a substantial explanation of אֲטֻמוֹת (see the comm. on ch. xl. 16). In ver. 17 two further objects are mentioned as having measurements; not, however, in the logical position of subjects, but with prepositions עַל and אֶל: upon that which was above the opening of the door . . . and (what was) on all the walls, *i.e.* the space above the doors and on all the walls. To this periphrasis of the subject, through עַל and אֶל, there is attached the predicate מִדּוֹת, which belongs to all the subjects of vers. 16 and 17, in the sense of, "on all the walls there were measures." The meaning is, that all the parts of the building which have been named had their definite measurements, were carefully measured off. In order to express this thought in as general and comprehensive a manner as possible, the ideas contained in the subjects in ver. 17 are expanded by means of appositions: that of the space above, over the entrance door, by וְעַד הַבַּיִת הפ׳ וְלַחוּץ, both (ו—ו = *et—et*) into the inner temple, *i.e.* both the inside of the temple throughout, and also to the outside. The idea of the whole wall is expressed by "round about, in the inside and on the outside." — Thus everything in vers. 16 and 17 is clear, and in accordance with fact; and there is no necessity either for the critical scissors of Ewald and Hitzig, who cut out all that they do not understand as glosses, or for the *mal*-emendation of Böttcher, who changes מִדּוֹת into מִקְלָעוֹת (1 Kings vi. 18), and thus finds it good to ornament the temple with sculptures, even on the outsides of all the walls.

Vers. 18–21 treat of the ornamenting of the inside of the sanctuary, *i.e.* of the holy place and the holy of holies. Vers. 18 and 19 form, like vers. 16 and 17, a period extended by parentheses. The predicate עָשׂוּי, standing at the beginning of ver. 18, is resumed in ver. 19*b*, and completed by אֶל־כָּל־הַבַּיִת ס׳ ס׳. That the cherubim and palms were executed in sculpture or carving, is evident from the resemblance to Solomon's temple. They were so distributed that a cherub was followed by a palm, and this by a cherub again, so that the palm stood between the two cherubim, and the cherub turned one of its two faces to the palm on this side, and the other to the palm upon that side. In sculpture only two faces could be shown, and consequently these cherubic figures had only two faces, and not four, like those in the vision. This sculpture was placed round about the whole house, and that, as is added in ver. 20 by way of explanation, from the ground even to up above the door, namely, on the inner wall of the sanctuary (הַהֵיכָל). כָּל־הַבַּיִת is hereby limited to the הֵיכָל, the holy place and the holy of holies. וְקִיר is a local accusative. To this there is appended the further notice in ver. 21, that the sanctuary had door-posts in a square form. The loose arrangement of the words, "the sanctuary post work of square form," is a concise form of expression after the manner of brief topographical notices. מְזוּזָה invariably signifies, wherever it occurs, the door-posts, *i.e.* the projecting framework of the entrances. רָבוּעַ, "*foured*," does not mean four-cornered merely, but really square (Ex. xxvii. 1 and xxviii. 16). Consequently the words, "the door-posts of the holy place were of a square shape," might be understood as signifying not merely that the door-posts were beams cut square, but, as Kliefoth supposes, that the post work surrounding the door was made of a square form, that is to say, was of the same height as breadth, which would be quite in keeping with the predominance of the square shape, with its symbolical significance, in this picture of a temple. But the statement in the second half of the verse can hardly be reconciled with this; for whatever diversity there may be in the interpretation of this verse in particular points, it is certain that it does contain the general assertion that the doorway of the holy of holies was also shaped in the same way. But the door of the holy of holies, instead of being square, was (according to ver. 3) six cubits high and seven cubits broad. הַקּוֹדֶשׁ, as distinguished from הַהֵיכָל, is the holy of holies, which ver. 23 places beyond all doubt (for this use of הַקֹּדֶשׁ, see Lev. xvi. 2, 3, 16). פְּנֵי־הַקֹּדֶשׁ, the face of the holy of holies, the front which met the eye of a person entering the holy place. הַמַּרְאֶה כַּמַּרְאֶה is the predicate, which is attached as loosely as in the first hemistich. The front of the holy of holies had the appearance like the appearance (just described), *i.e.* like the appearance of the הֵיכָל; in fact, it had also a doorway with four-cornered posts. J. F. Starck has already given this explanation of the words: *Eadem facies et aspectus erat utriusque portae templi et adyti, utraque quadrata et quadratis postibus conspicua erat.* The proposal of Ewald, on the other hand, to connect כַּמַּרְאֶה with the following word הַמִּזְבֵּחַ, "in front of the holy of holies there was something to be seen like the shape of the altar" (LXX., Syr.), has the article in הַמַּרְאֶה against it (Böttcher).

Ver. 22. The Altar of Burnt-Offering in the holy place (see Plate III. *n*). "The abrupt style of writing is still continued." The altar wood for the altar was of wood three cubits high; its length, *i.e.* the expanse of the wall from one corner to the other, was two cubits; the breadth (thickness), which is not expressly mentioned, was the same, because the square form is presupposed from the shape of this altar in the tabernacle and Solomon's temple. Under the term מִקְצֹעוֹתָיו, its corner-pieces, the horns projecting at the corners, or the horn-shaped points, are probably included, as the simple mention of the corners appears superfluous, and the horns, which were symbolically significant features in the altar, would certainly not have been wanting. There is something strange in the occurrence of וְאָרְכּוֹ before and along with קִירוֹת, as the length is already included in the walls, and it could not be appropriately said of the length that it was of wood. אָרְכּוֹ is therefore certainly a copyist's error for אַדְנוֹ, ἡ βάσις αὐτοῦ (LXX.), its stand or pedestal. The angel describes this altar as the "table which stands before Jehovah"—in perfect harmony with the epithet already applied to the sacrifices in the Pentateuch, the "bread (לֶחֶם) of God," though not "because the altar table was intended to combine the old table of shewbread and the altar of incense" (Böttcher). The table of shewbread is not mentioned any more than the candlestick and other portions of the temple furniture.—The altar of burnt-offering stood before Jehovah, *i.e.* before the entrance into the holy of holies. This leads in vers. 23 sqq. to the notice of the doors of the sanctuary, the character of which is also described as simply openings (פֶּתַח), since the doorway had been mentioned before. דֶּלֶת signifies a moveable door, and the plural דְּלָתוֹת, doors, whether they consist of one leaf or two, *i.e.* whether they are single or folding doors. Here the דְּלָתוֹת in vers. 23 and 24 (לדלתות) are folding doors; on the other hand, the first דְּלָתוֹת in ver. 24 and דֶּלֶת *ibid.* are used for the wings of the door, and מוּסַבּוֹת דְּלָתוֹת for the swinging portions (leaves) of the separate wings. The meaning is this: the holy place (הֵיכָל) and the holy of holies (הַקֹּדֶשׁ) had two folding doors (*i.e.* each of these rooms had one). These doors had two wings, and each of these wings, in the one door and in the other, had two reversible door-leaves, so that when going in and out there was no necessity to throw open on every occasion the whole of the wing, which was at least three or four cubits broad. There is no foundation for the objection raised by Kliefoth to the interpretation of לְהֵיכָל וְלַקֹּדֶשׁ as signifying the holy place and the holy of holies; since he cannot deny that the two words are so used, הֵיכָל in 1 Kings vi. 5, 17, 31, 33, and קֹדֶשׁ in Lev. xvi. 2, 3, etc. And the artificial explanation, "to the temple space, and indeed to the holy place," not only passes without notice the agreement between our verses and 1 Kings vi. 31–34, but gains nothing further than a side door, which does violence to the dignity of the sanctuary, a passage from the side chambers into the holy place, with which Böttcher has presented Solomon's temple.—These doors were ornamented, like the walls, with figures of cherubim and palms.—Other remarks are added in vers. 25*b* and 26 concerning the porch in front of the holy place. The first is, that on the front of the porch outside there was עָב עֵץ. The only other passage in which the word עָב occurs in a similar connection is 1 Kings vii. 6, where it refers to wood-work in front of the *Ulam* of Solomon's porch of pillars; and it cannot be determined whether it signifies threshold, or moulding, or threshold-mouldings. On the shoulders, *i.e.* on the right and left side walls of the front porch, there were closed windows and figures of palms. The cherubim were omitted here.—The last words of ver. 26 are very obscure. וְצַלְעוֹת הַבַּיִת may be taken in connection with the preceding clause, "and on the side-rooms of the temple," as there is no necessity to repeat the preposition in the case of closely continuous clauses (*vid.* Ewald, § 351*a*); and the side-rooms not only must have had windows, but might also be ornamented with figures of palms. But if the words be taken in this sense, the עֻבִּים must also signify something which presented, like the walls of the porch and of the side chambers, a considerable extent of surface capable of receiving a similar decoration; although nothing definite has hitherto been ascertained with regard to the meaning of the word, and our rendering "beams" makes no pretension to correctness.

Chap. xlii. *The Holy Cells in the Court, and the Extent of the Holy Domain around the Temple.*

Vers. 1–14. THE CELL-BUILDINGS IN THE OUTER COURT FOR HOLY USE.—Ver. 1. *And he brought me out into the outer court by the way toward the north, and brought me to the cell-building, which was opposite to the separate place, and opposite to the building toward the north,* Ver. 2. *Before the long side of a hundred cubits, with the door toward the north, and the breadth fifty cubits,* Ver. 3. *Opposite to the twenty of the inner court and opposite to the stone pavement of the outer court; gallery against gallery was in the third storey.* Ver. 4. *And before the cells a walk, ten cubits broad; to the inner a way of a hundred cubits; and their doors went to the north.* Ver. 5. *And the upper cells were shortened, because the galleries took away space from them, in comparison with the lower and the central ones in the building.* Ver. 6. *For they were three-storied, and had no columns, like the columns of the courts; therefore a deduction was made from the lower and from the central ones from the ground.* Ver. 7. *And a wall outside parallel with the cells ran toward the outer court in front of the cells; its length fifty cubits.* Ver. 8. *For the length of the cells of the outer court was fifty cubits, and, behold, against the sanctuary it was a hundred cubits.* Ver. 9. *And out from underneath it rose up these cells; the entrance was from the east, when one went to them from the outer court.* Ver. 10. *In the breadth of the court wall toward the south, before the separate place and before the building, there were cells,* Ver. 11. *With a way before them, like the cells, which stood toward the north, as according to their length so according to their breadth, and according to all their exits as according to all their arrangements. And as their doorways,* Ver. 12. *So were also the doorways of the cells, which were toward the south, an entrance at the head of the way, of the way opposite to the corresponding wall, of the way from the east when one came to them.* Ver. 13. *And he said to me, The cells in the north, the cells in the south, which stood in front of the separate place, are the holy cells where the priests, who draw near to Jehovah, shall eat the most holy thing; there they shall place the most holy thing, both the meat-offering and the sin-offering and the trespass-offering; for the place is holy.* Ver. 14. *When they go in, the priests, they shall not go out of the holy place into the outer court; but there shall they place their clothes, in which they perform the service, for they are holy; they shall put on other clothes, and so draw near to what belongs to the people.*

It is evident from vers. 13 and 14, which furnish particulars concerning the cells already described, that the description itself refers to two cell-buildings only, one on the north side and the other on the south side of the separate place (see Plate I. *L*). Of these the one situated on the north is described in a more circumstantial manner (vers. 1–9); that on the south, on the contrary, is merely stated in the briefest manner to have resembled the other in the main (vers. 10–12). That these two cell-buildings are not identical either with those mentioned in ch. xl. 44 sqq. or with those of ch. xl. 17, as Hävernick supposes, but are distinct from both, is so obvious that it is impossible to understand how they could ever have been identified. The difference in the description is sufficient to show that they are not the same as those in ch. xl. 44 sqq. The cells mentioned in ch. xl. 44 were set apart as dwelling-places for the priests during their administration of the service in the holy place and at the altar; whereas these serve as places for depositing the most holy sacrificial gifts and the official dresses of the priests. To this may be added the difference of situation, which distinguishes those mentioned here both from those of ch. xl. 44 seq., and also from those of ch. xl. 17. Those in ch. xl. 44 were in the inner court, ours in the outer. It is true that those mentioned in ch. xl. 17 were also in the latter, but in entirely different situations, as the description of the position of those noticed in the chapter before us indisputably proves. Ezekiel is led out of the inner court into the outer, by the way in the direction toward the north, to הַלִּשְׁכָּה, the cell-building (that הַלִּשְׁכָּה is used here in a collective sense is evident from the plural לְשָׁכוֹת in vers. 4, 5). This stood opposite to the *gizrah*, *i.e.* the separate space behind the temple house (ch. xli. 12 sqq.), and opposite to the בִּנְיָן, *i.e.* neither the outer court wall, which is designated as בִּנְיָן in ch. xl. 5, but cannot be intended here, where there is no further definition, nor the temple house, as Kliefoth imagines, for this is invariably called הַבַּיִת. We have rather to understand by הַבִּנְיָן the building upon the *gizrah* described in ch. xli. 12 sqq., to which no valid objection can be offered on the ground of the repetition of the relative וַאֲשֶׁר, as it is omitted in ver. 10, and in general simply serves to give greater prominence to the second definition in the sense of "and, indeed, opposite to the building (*sc.* of the separate place) toward the north." As אֶל־הַצָּפוֹן belongs to אֲשֶׁר as a more precise definition of the direction indicated by נֶגֶד, the אֶל־פְּנֵי א' which follows in ver. 2 depends upon וַיְבִיאֵנִי, and is co-ordinate with אֶל־הַלִּשְׁכָּה, defining the side of the cell-building to which Ezekiel was taken: "to the face of the length," *i.e.* to the long side of the building, which extended to a hundred cubits. The article in הַמֵּאָה requires that the words should be connected in this manner, as it could not be used if the words were intended to mean "on the surface of a length of a hundred cubits." Since, then, the separate place was also a hundred cubits, that is to say, of the same length as the cell-building opposite to it, we might be disposed to assume that as the separate place reached to the outer court wall on the west, the cell-building also extended to the latter with its western narrow side. But this would be at variance with the fact that, according to ch. xlvi. 19, 20, the sacrificial kitchens for the priests stood at the western end of this portion of the court, and therefore behind the cell-building. The size of these kitchens is not given; but judging from the size of the sacrificial kitchens for the people (ch. xlvi. 22), we must reserve a space of forty cubits in length; and consequently the cell-building, which was a hundred cubits long, if built close against the kitchens, would reach the line of the back wall of the temple house with its front (or eastern) narrow side, since, according to the calculation given in the comm. on ch. xli. 1–11, this wall was forty cubits from the front of the separate place, so that there was no prominent building standing opposite to the true sanctuary on the northern or southern side, by which any portion of it could have been concealed. And not only is there no reason for leaving a vacant space between the sacrificial kitchens and the cell-buildings, but this is precluded by the fact that if the kitchens had been separated from the cell building by an intervening space, it would have been necessary to carry the holy sacrificial flesh from the kitchen to the cell in which it was eaten, after being cooked, across a portion of the outer court. It is not stated here how far this cell-building was from the northern boundary of the *gizrah*, and the open space (מֻנָּח) surrounding the temple house; but this may be inferred from ch. xli. 10, according to which the intervening space between the *munnach* and the cells was twenty cubits. For the cells mentioned there can only be those of our cell-building, as there were no other cells opposite to the northern and southern sides of the temple house. But if the distance of the southern longer side of the cell-building, so far as it stood opposite to the temple house, was only twenty cubits, the southern wall of the cell-building coincided with the boundary wall of the inner court, so that it could be regarded as a continuation of that wall.—The further definition פֶּתַח הַצָּפוֹן, door to the north, is to be taken as subordinate to the preceding clause, in the sense of "with the door to the north," because it would otherwise come in between the accounts of the length and breadth of the building, so as to disturb the connection. The breadth of the building corresponds to the breadth of the gate-buildings of the inner court.

The meaning of the third verse is a subject of dispute. "הָעֶשְׂרִים," says Böttcher, "is difficult on account of the article as well as the number, inasmuch as, with the exception of the twenty cubits left open in the temple ground (ch. xli. 10), there are no עֶשְׂרִים mentioned as belonging to the actual חָצֵר הפנ׳, and the numeral does not stand with sufficient appropriateness by the side of the following רצפה." But there is not sufficient weight in the last objection to render the reference to the twenty cubits a doubtful one, since the "twenty cubits" is simply a contracted form of expression for "the space of twenty cubits," and this space forms a fitting antithesis to the pavement (רצפה), *i.e.* the paved portion of the court. Moreover, it is most natural to supply the missing substantive to the "twenty" from the אַמּוֹת mentioned just before,—much more natural certainly than to supply לְשָׁכוֹת, as there is no allusion either before or afterwards to any other cells than those whose situation is intended to be defined according to the twenty We therefore agree with J. H. Michaelis, Rosenmüller, Hävernick, and Hitzig, that the only admissible course is to supply אַמּוֹת; for the description of the priests' cells in ch. xl. 44, to which Kliefoth imagines that הָעֶשְׂרִים refers, is far too distant for us to be able to take the word לְשָׁכוֹת thence and supply it to העשׂרים. And again, the situation of these priests' cells to the east of the cell-building referred to here does not harmonize with the נֶגֶד, as the second definition introduced by the correlative

וְנֶגֶד points to the stone pavement on the north. East and north do not form such a *vis-à-vis* as the double נֶגֶד requires.—Our view of the העשׂרים is also in harmony with the explanatory relative clause, "which were to the inner court," *i.e.* belonged to it. For the open space of twenty cubits' breadth, which ran by the long side of the temple house between the *munnach* belonging to the temple and the wall of the inner court, formed the continuation of the inner court which surrounded the temple house on the north, west, and south.[1] If, therefore, this first definition of the נֶגֶד refers to what was opposite to the cell-building on the south, the second נֶגֶד defines what stood opposite to it on the northern side. There the portion of the outer court which was paved with stones ran along the inner side of the surrounding wall. This serves to define as clearly as possible the position of the broad side of the cell-building. For Kliefoth and Hitzig are right in connecting these definitions with ver. 2*b*, and taking the words from אַתִּיק onwards as introducing a fresh statement. Even the expression itself אֶל־פְּנֵי אַתִּיק does not properly harmonize with the combination of the two halves of the third verse as one sentence, as Böttcher proposes, thus: "against the twenty cubits of the inner court and against the pavement of the outer court there ran gallery in front of gallery threefold." For if the galleries of the building were opposite to the pavement on the north, and to the space in front of the temple on the south of the building, they must of necessity have run along the northern and southern walls of the building in a parallel direction, and אֶל־פְּנֵי is not the correct expression for this. אֶל־פְּנֵי, to the front—that is to say, one gallery to the front of the other, or up to the other. This could only be the case if the galleries surrounded the

[1] The statement of Kliefoth, that "this space of twenty cubits in breadth did not belong to the inner court at all," cannot be established from ch. xl. 47, where the size of the inner court is given as a hundred cubits in length and the same in breadth. For this measurement simply refers to the space in front of the temple.

building on all four sides, or at any rate on three; for with the latter arrangement, the gallery upon the eastern side would terminate against those on the southern and northern sides. Again, the rendering "threefold," or into the threefold, cannot be defended either from the usage of the language or from the facts. The only other passage in which the plural שְׁלִשִׁים occurs is Gen. vi. 16, where it signifies chambers, or rooms of the third storey, and the singular שְׁלִשִׁי means the third. Consequently בַּשְּׁלִשִׁים is "in the third row of chambers or rooms," *i.e.* in the third storey. And so far as the fact is concerned, it does not follow from the allusion to upper, central, and lower cells (vers. 5 and 6), that there were galleries round every one of the three storeys.

Ver. 4. "Before the cells there was a walk of ten cubits' breadth" (*m*). In what sense we are to understand לִפְנֵי, "before," whether running along the northern longer side of the building, or in front of the eastern wall, depends upon the explanation of the words which follow, and chiefly of the words דֶּרֶךְ אַמָּה אֶחָת, by which alone the sense in which אֶל־הַפְּנִימִית is to be understood can also be determined. Hävernick and Kliefoth take דֶּרֶךְ אַמָּה אֶחָת, "a way of one cubit," in the sense of "the approaches (entrances into the rooms) were a cubit broad." But the words cannot possibly have this meaning; not only because the collective use of דֶּרֶךְ after the preceding מַהֲלָךְ, which is not collective, and with the plural פִּתְחֵיהֶם following, is extremely improbable, if not impossible; but principally because דֶּרֶךְ, a way, is not synonymous with מָבוֹא, an entrance, or פֶּתַח, a doorway. Moreover, an entrance, if only a cubit in breadth, to a large building would be much too narrow, and bear no proportion whatever to the walk of ten cubits in breadth. It is impossible to get any suitable meaning from the words as they stand, "a way of one cubit;" and no other course remains than to alter אמה אחת into מֵאָה אַמּוֹת, after the ἐπὶ πήχεις ἑκατόν of the Septuagint. There is no question that we have such a change of מֵאָה into אַמָּה in ver. 16, where even the Rabbins acknowledge that it has occurred. And when once מֵאָה had been turned into אַמָּה, this change would naturally be followed by the alteration of אמת into a numeral—that is to say, into אֶחָת. The statement itself, "a way of a hundred cubits" (in length), might be taken as referring to the length of the walk in front of the cells, as the cell-building was a hundred cubits long. But אֶל־הַפְּנִימִית is hardly reconcilable with this. If, for example, we take these words in connection with the preceding clause, "a walk of ten cubits broad into the interior," the statement, "a way of a hundred cubits," does not square with this. For if the walk which ran in front of the cells was a hundred cubits long, it did not lead into the interior of the cell-building, but led past it to the outer western wall. We must therefore take אֶל־הַפְּנִימִית in connection with what follows, so that it corresponds to לִפְנֵי הַלְּשָׁכוֹת: in front of the cells there was a walk of ten cubits in breadth, and to the inner there led a way of a hundred cubits in length. הַפְּנִימִית would then signify, not the interior of the cell-building, but the inner court (הֶחָצֵר הַפְּנִימִית, ch. xliv. 17, xxi. 27, etc.). This explanation derives its principal support from the circumstance that, according to vers. 9 and 11, a way ran from the east, *i.e.* from the steps of the inner court gates, on the northern and southern sides, to the cell-buildings on the north and south of the separate place, the length of which, from the steps of the gate-buildings already mentioned to the north-eastern and south-eastern corners of our cell-buildings, was exactly a hundred cubits, *as we may see from the plan in Plate* I. This way (*l*) was continued in the walk in front of the cells (*m*), and may safely be assumed to have been of the same breadth as the walk.—The last statement of the fourth verse is perfectly clear; the doorways to the cells were turned toward the north, so that one could go from the walk in front of the cells directly into the cells themselves.—In vers. 5 and 6 there follow certain statements concerning the manner in which the cells were built. The building contained upper, lower, and middle cells; so that it was three-storied. This is expressed in the words כִּי מְשֻׁלָּשׁוֹת הֵנָּה, "for the cells were tripled;" three rows stood one above another. But they were not all built alike; the upper ones were shortened in comparison with the lower and the central ones, *i.e.* were shorter than these (מִן before הַתַּחְתֹּנוֹת and הַתִּיכוֹנוֹת is comparative); "for galleries ate away part of them"—that is to say, took away a portion of them (יוכלו for יֹאכְלוּ, in an architectural sense, to take away from). How far this took place is shown in the first two clauses of the sixth verse, the first of which explains the reference to upper, lower, and middle cells, while the second gives the reason for the shortening of the upper in comparison with the lower and the central ones. As the three rows of cells built one above another had no columns on which the galleries of the upper row could rest, it was necessary, in order to get a foundation for the gallery of the third storey, that the cells should be thrown back from the outer wall, or built as far inwards as the breadth of the gallery required. This is expressly stated in the last clause, עַל־כֵּן נֶאֱצַל וגו'. נֶאֱצַל, with an indefinite subject: there was deducted from the lower and the middle cells from the ground, *sc.* which these rooms covered. מֵהָאָרֶץ is added for the purpose of elucidation. From the allusion to the columns of the courts we may see that the courts had colonnades, like the courts in the Herodian temple, and probably also in that of Solomon, though their character is nowhere described, and no allusion is made to them in the description of the courts.

The further statements concerning this cell-building in vers. 7–9 are obscure. גָּדֵר is a wall serving to enclose courtyards, vineyards, and the like. The predicate to וְגָדֵר follows in אֶל־פְּנֵי הַלְּשָׁכוֹת: a boundary wall ran along the front of the cells (אֶל־פְּנֵי stands for עַל־פְּנֵי, as the corresponding עַל־פְּנֵי הַהֵיכָל in ver. 8 shows). The course of this wall (*n*) is more precisely defined by the relative clause, "which ran outwards parallel with the cells in the direction of the outer court," *i.e.* toward the outer court. The length of this wall was fifty cubits. It is evident from this that the wall did not run along the north side of the building,—for in that case it must have been a hundred cubits in length,—but along the narrow side, the length of which was fifty cubits. Whether it was on the western or eastern side cannot be determined with certainty from ver. 7, although אֶל פְּנֵי favours the eastern, *i.e.* the front side, rather than the western side, or back. And what follows is decisive in favour of the eastern narrow side. In explanation of the reason why this wall was fifty cubits long, it is stated in ver. 8 that "the length of the cells, which were to the outer court, was fifty cubits; but, behold, toward the temple front a hundred cubits." Consequently "the cells which the outer court had" can only be the cells whose windows were toward the outer court—that is to say, those on the eastern narrow side of the building; for the sacrificial kitchens were on the western narrow side (ch. xlvi. 19, 20). The second statement in ver. 8, which is introduced by הִנֵּה as an indication of something important, is intended to preclude any misinterpretation of אֹרֶךְ הלש׳, as though by *length* we must necessarily understand the extension of the building from east to west, as in ver. 2 and most of the other measurements. The use of אֹרֶךְ for the extension of the narrow side of the building is also suggested by the אָרְכּוֹ, "length of the wall," in ver. 7, where רֹחַב would have been inadmissible, because רֹחַב, the breadth of a wall, would have been taken to mean its thickness. פְּנֵי הַהֵיכָל is the outer side of the temple house which faced the north.—A further confirmation of the fact that the boundary wall was situated on the eastern narrow side of the building is given in the first clause of the ninth verse, in which, however, the reading fluctuates. The *Chetib* gives מִתַּחְתָּה לְשָׁכוֹת, the *Keri* מִתַּחַת הַלְּשָׁכוֹת. But as we generally find, the *Keri* is an alteration for the worse, occasioned by the objection felt by the Masoretes, partly to the unusual circumstance that the singular form of the suffix is attached to תַּחַת, whereas it usually takes the suffixes in the plural form, and partly to the omission of the article from לְשָׁכוֹת by the side of the demonstrative הָאֵלֶּה, which is defined by the article. But these two deviations from the ordinary rule do not warrant any alterations, as there are analogies in favour of both. תַּחַת has a singular suffix not only in תַּחְתֶּנָּה (Gen. ii. 21) and תַּחְתֵּנִי (2 Sam. xxii. 37, 40, and 48), instead of תַּחְתַּי (Ps. xviii. 37, 40, 48), which may undoubtedly be explained on the ground that the direction whither is thought of (Ges. § 103. 1, Anm. 3), but also in תַּחְתָּם, which occurs more frequently than תַּחְתֵּיהֶם, and that without any difference in the meaning (compare, for example, Deut. ii. 12, 21, 22, 23, Josh. v. 7, Job xxxiv. 24, and xl. 12, with 1 Kings xx. 24, 1 Chron. v. 22, 2 Chron. xii. 10). And לְשָׁכוֹת הָאֵלֶּה is analogous to הַר הַגָּדוֹל in Zech. iv. 7, and many other combinations, in which the force of the definition (by means of the article) is only placed in the middle for the sake of convenience (*vid.* Ewald, § 293*a*). If, therefore, the *Chetib* is to be taken without reserve as the original reading, the suffix in תַּחְתָּה can only refer to גָּדֵר, which is of common gender: from underneath the wall were these cells, *i.e.* the cells turned toward the outer court; and the meaning is the following: toward the bottom these cells were covered by the wall, which ran in front of them, so that, when a person coming toward them from the east fixed his eyes upon these cells, they appeared to rise out of the wall. Kliefoth, therefore, who was the first to perceive the true meaning of this clause, has given expression to the conjecture that the design of the wall was to hide the windows of the lower row of cells which looked toward the east, so that, when the priests were putting on their official clothes, they might not be seen from the outside.—הַמָּבוֹא commences a fresh statement. To connect these words with the preceding clause ("underneath these cells was the entrance from the east"), as Böttcher has done, yields no meaning with which a rational idea can possibly be associated, unless the מִן in מִתַּחְתָּה be altogether ignored. The LXX. have therefore changed וּמִתַּחְתָּה, which was unintelligible to them, into καὶ αἱ θύραι (ופתחי), and Hitzig has followed them in doing so. No such conjecture is necessary if וּמִתַּחְתָּה be rightly interpreted, for in that case

הַמָּבוֹא must be the commencement of a new sentence. הַמָּבוֹא (by the side of which the senseless reading of the *Keri* הַמֵּבִיא cannot be taken into consideration for a moment) is the approach, or the way which led to the cells. This was from the east, from the outer court, not from the inner court, against the northern boundary of which the building stood. מֵהֶחָצֵר הַחִצֹנָה is not to be taken in connection with בְּבֹאוֹ לָהֵנָּה, but is co-ordinate with מֵהַקָּדִים, of which it is an explanatory apposition.

In vers. 10–12 the cell-building on the south of the separate place is described, though very briefly; all that is said in addition to the notice of its situation being, that it resembled the northern one in its entire construction. But there are several difficulties connected with the explanation of these verses, which are occasioned, partly by an error in the text, partly by the unmeaning way in which the Masoretes have divided the text, and finally, in part by the brevity of the mode of expression. In the first clause of ver. 10, הַקָּדִים is a copyist's error for הַדָּרוֹם, which has arisen from the fact that it is preceded by מֵהַקָּדִים (ver. 9). For there is an irreconcilable discrepancy between דֶּרֶךְ הַקָּדִים and אֶל־פְּנֵי הַגִּזְרָה, which follows. The building stood against, or upon, the broad side (רֹחַב) of the wall of the court, *i.e.* the wall which separated the inner court from the outer, opposite to the separate place and the building upon it (אֶל פְּנֵי, from the outer side hither, is practically equivalent to נֶגֶד in ver. 1; and הַבִּנְיָן is to be taken in the same sense here and there). The relation in which this cell-building stands to the separate place tallies exactly with the description given of the former one in ver. 2. If, then, according to ver. 2, the other stood to the north of the separate place, this must necessarily have stood to the south of it,—that is to say, upon the broad side of the wall of the court, not in the direction toward the east (דֶּרֶךְ הַקָּדִים), but in that toward the south (דֶּרֶךְ הַדָּרוֹם), as is expressly stated in vers. 12 and 13 also. Kliefoth has affirmed, it is true, in opposition to this, that "the *breadth* of the wall enclosing the inner court must, as a matter of course, have been the eastern side of the inner court;" but on the eastern side of the wall of the inner court there was not room for a cell-building of a hundred cubits in length, as the wall was only thirty-seven cubits and a half long (broad) on each side of the gate-building. If, however, one were disposed so to dilute the meaning of בְּרֹחַב גֶּדֶר הח' as to make it affirm nothing more than that the building stood upon, or against, the breadth of the wall of the court to the extent of ten or twenty cubits, and with the other eighty or ninety cubits stood out into the outer court, as Kliefoth has drawn it upon his "ground plan;" it could not possibly be described as standing אֶל־פְּנֵי הַגִּזְרָה, because it was not opposite to (in face of) the *gizrah*, but was so far removed from it, that only the north-west corner would be slightly visible from the south-east corner of the *gizrah*. And if we consider, in addition to this, that in vers. 13 and 14, where the intention of the cell-buildings described in vers. 1–12 is given, only cells on the north and on the south are mentioned as standing אֶל־פְּנֵי הַגִּזְרָה, there can be no doubt that by רֹחב we are to understand the broad side of the wall which bounded the inner court on the south side from east to west, and that דֶּרֶךְ הַקָּדִים should be altered into דֶּרֶךְ הַדָּרוֹם.—In ver. 11 the true meaning has been obscured by the fact that the Masoretic verses are so divided as to destroy the sense. The words וְדֶרֶךְ לִפְנֵיהֶם belong to לְשָׁכוֹת in ver. 10: "cells and a way before them," *i.e.* cells with a way in front. דֶּרֶךְ corresponds to the מַהֲלָךְ in ver. 4.—כְּמַרְאֵה, like the appearance = appearing, or constructed like, does not belong to דֶּרֶךְ in the sense of made to conform to the way in front of the cells, but to לְשָׁכוֹת, cells with a way in front, conforming to the cells toward the north. The further clauses from כְּאָרְכָּן to וּכְמִשְׁפְּטֵיהֶן are connected together, and contain two statements, loosely subordinated to the preceding notices, concerning the points in which the cells upon the southern side were made to conform to those upon the northern; so that they really depend upon כְּמַרְאֵה, and to render them intelligible in German (English tr.) must be attached by means of a preposition: "with regard to," or "according to" (*secundum*). Moreover, the four words contain two co-ordinated comparisons; the first expressed by כְּ . . . כֵּן, the second simply indicated by the particle כְּ before מִשְׁפְּטֵיהֶן (cf. Ewald, § 360*a*). The suffixes of all four words refer to the cells in the north, which those in the south were seen to resemble in the points referred to. The meaning is this: the cells in the south were like the cells in the north to look at, as according to their length so according to their breadth, and according to all their exits as according to their arrangements (מִשְׁפָּטִים, lit. the design answering to their purpose, *i.e.* the manner of their arrangement and their general character: for this meaning, compare Ex. xxvi. 30; 2 Kings i. 7). The last word of the verse, וּכְפִתְחֵיהֶן, belongs to ver. 12, viz. to וּכְפִתְחֵי הלשׁ׳, the comparison being expressed by וכ—כ, as in Josh. xiv. 11; Dan. xi. 29; 1 Sam. xxx. 24 (cf. Ewald, *l.c.*). Another construction also commences with כפתחיהן. וּכְפִתְחֵיהֶן is a nominative: and like their doors (those of the northern cells), so also were the doors of the cells situated toward the south. Consequently there is no necessity either to expunge וּכְפִתְחֵי arbitrarily as a gloss, for which procedure even the LXX. could not be appealed to, or to assent to the far-fetched explanation by which Kliefoth imagines that he has discovered an allusion to a third cell-building in these words.—Light is thrown upon the further statements in ver. 12 by the description of the northern cells. "A door was at the head," *i.e.* at the beginning of the way. דֶּרֶךְ corresponds to the way of a hundred cubits in ver. 4, and ראשׁ דֶּרֶךְ is the point where this way, which ran to the southern gate-building of the inner court, commenced—that is to say, where it met the walk in front of the cells (ver. 4). The further statement concerning this way is not quite clear to us, because the meaning of the ἀπ. λεγ. הֲגִינָה is uncertain. In the Chaldee and Rabbinical writings the word signifies *decens*, *conveniens*. If we take it in this sense, הַגֶּדֶרֶת הֲגִינָה is the wall corresponding (to these cells), *i.e.* the wall which ran in front of the eastern narrow side of the building parallel to the cells, the wall of fifty cubits in length described in ver. 7 in connection with the northern building (for the omission of the article before הֲגִינָה after the substantive which it defines, compare ch. xxxix. 27; Jer. ii. 21, etc.). בִּפְנֵי, *in conspectu*, which is not perfectly synonymous with לִפְנֵי, also harmonizes with this. For the way referred to was exactly opposite to this wall at its upper end, inasmuch as the wall joined the way at right angles. The last words of ver. 12 are an abbreviated repetition of ver. 9*b*; דֶּרֶךְ הַקָּדִים is equivalent to הַמָּבוֹא מֵהַקָּדִים, the way from the east on coming to them, *i.e.* as one went to these cells.

According to vers. 13 and 14, these two[1] cell-buildings were set apart as holy cells, in which the officiating priests were to deposit the most holy sacrifices, and to eat them, and to put on and off the sacred official clothes in which they drew near to the Lord. קָדְשֵׁי הַקֳּדָשִׁים were that portion of the meat-offering which was not burned upon the altar (Lev. ii. 3, 10, vi. 9-11, x. 12; see my *Bibl. Archäologie*, I. § 52), and the flesh of all the sin- and trespass-offerings, with the exception of the sin-offerings offered for the high priest and all the congregation, the flesh of which was to be burned outside the camp (cf. Lev. vi. 19-23, vii. 6). All these portions of the sacrifices were called most holy, because the priests were to eat them as the representatives of Jehovah, to the exclusion not only of all the laity, but also of their own families (women and children; see my *Archäol.* I. §§ 45 and 47). The depositing (יַנִּיחוּ) is distinguished from the eating (יֹאכְלוּ) of the most holy portions of the sacrifices; because neither the meal of the meat-offering, which was mixed with oil, nor the flesh of the sin- and trespass-offerings, could be eaten by the priests immediately after the offering of the sacri-

[1] For no further proof is needed after what has been observed above, that the relative clause, "which were in front of the separate place," belongs to the two subjects: cells of the north and cells of the south, and does not refer to a third cell-building against the eastern wall, as Kliefoth supposes.

fice; but the former had first of all to be baked, and the latter to be boiled, and it was not allowable to deposit them wherever they liked previous to their being so prepared. The putting on and off, and also the custody of the sacred official clothes, were to be restricted to a sacred place. בְּבֹאָם, on their coming, *sc.* to the altar, or into the holy place, for the performance of service. Their not going out of the holy place into the outer court applies to their going into the court among the people assembled there; for in order to pass from the altar to the sacred cells, they were obliged to pass through the inner gate and go thither by the way which led to these cells (Plate I. *l*).

Vers. 15–20. EXTENT OF THE HOLY DOMAIN AROUND THE TEMPLE.—Ver. 15. *And when he had finished the measurements of the inner house, he brought me out by the way of the gate, which is directed toward the east, and measured there round about.* Ver. 16. *He measured the eastern side with the measuring rod five hundred rods by the measuring rod round about;* Ver. 17. *He measured the northern side five hundred rods by the measuring rod round about;* Ver. 18. *The southern side he measured five hundred rods by the measuring rod;* Ver. 19. *He turned round to the western side, measured five hundred rods by the measuring rod.* Ver. 20. *To the four winds he measured it. It had a wall round about; the length was five hundred and the breadth five hundred, to divide between the holy and the common.*—There has been a division of opinion from time immemorial concerning the area, the measuring of which is related in these verses, and the length and breadth of which are stated in ver. 20 to have been five hundred; as the Seventy, and after them J. D. Michaelis, Böttcher, Maurer, Ewald, and Hitzig, understand by this the space occupied by the temple with its two courts. But as that space was five hundred cubits long and five hundred broad, according to the sum of the measurements given in ch. xl.–xlii. 15, the LXX. have omitted the word קָנִים in vers. 16, 18, and 19, whilst they have changed it into πήχεις in ver. 17, and have also attached this word to the numbers in ver. 20. According to this, only the outer circumference of the temple area would be measured in our verses, and the wall which was five hundred cubits long and five hundred cubits broad (ver. 20) would be the surrounding wall of the outer court mentioned in ch. xl. 5. Ver. 15 could certainly be made to harmonize with this view. For even if we understood by the "inner house" not merely the temple house, which the expression primarily indicates, but the whole of the inner building, *i.e.* all the buildings found in the inner and outer court, and by the east gate the eastern gate of the outer court; the expression מְדָדוֹ סָבִיב ס׳, "he measured it round about," merely affirms that he measured something round about outside this gate. The suffix in מְדָדוֹ is indefinite, and cannot be taken as referring to any of the objects mentioned before, either to הַשַּׁעַר or to הַבַּיִת הַפְּנִימִי. The inner house he had already measured; and the measurements which follow are not applicable to the gate. Nor can the suffix be taken as referring to הַבַּיִת, *illam sc. aedem* (Ros.); or at any rate, there is nothing in ver. 20 to sustain such a reference. Nevertheless, we might think of a measuring of the outer sides of the whole building comprehended under the idea of the inner house, and regard the wall mentioned in ver. 20 as that which had been measured round about on the outer side both in length and breadth. But it is difficult to reconcile this view even with ver. 20; and with the measurements given in vers. 16–19 it is perfectly irreconcilable. Even if we were disposed to expunge קָנִים as a gloss in vers. 16, 17, 18, and 19, the words, "he measured the east side with the measuring rod, five hundred by the measuring rod," are equivalent to five hundred rods, according to the well-known Hebrew usage; just as indisputably as מֵאָה בָּאַמָּה, a hundred by the cubit, is equivalent to a hundred cubits (see the comm. on ch. xl. 21 at the close). The rejection of קָנִים as an imaginary gloss is therefore not only arbitrary, but also useless; as the appended words בִּקְנֵה הַמִּדָּה, even without קָנִים, affirm that the five hundred were not cubits, but rods.[1] The סָבִיב in vers. 16 and 17 is not to be understood as signifying that on the east and north sides he measured a square on each side of five hundred rods in length and breadth, but simply indicates that he measured on all sides, as is obvious from ver. 20. For according to this, the space which was measured toward every quarter at five hundred rods had a boundary wall, which was five hundred rods long on every side. This gives an area of 250,000 square rods; whereas the temple, with the inner and outer courts, covered only a square of five hundred cubits in length and breadth, or 250,000 square cubits. It is evident from this that the measuring related in vers. 15–20 does not refer to the space occupied by the temple and its courts, and therefore that the wall which the measured space had around it (ver. 20) cannot be the wall of the outer court mentioned in ch. xl. 5, the sides of which were not more than five hundred cubits long. The meaning is rather, that around this wall, which enclosed the temple and its courts, a further space of five hundred rods in length and breadth was measured off "to separate between the holy and profane," *i.e.* a space which was intended to form a separating domain between the sanctuary and the common land. The purpose thus assigned for the space, which was measured off on all four sides of the "inner house," leaves no doubt remaining that it was not the length of the surrounding wall of the outer court that was

[1] The חֲמֵשׁ אַמּוֹת for חֲמֵשׁ מֵאוֹת in ver. 16 is utterly useless as a proof that cubits and not rods are intended; as it is obviously a copyist's error, a fact which even the Masoretes admit. Rabbi ben-Asher's view of this writing is an interesting one. Prof. Dr. Delitzsch has sent me the following, taken from a fragment in his possession copied from a codex of the Royal Library at Copenhagen. R. ben-Asher reckons אמות among the מוקדם ומאוחר, *i.e.* words written ὕστερον πρότερον, of which there are forty-seven in the whole of the Old Testament, the following being quoted by ben-Asher (*l.c.*) by way of example: גֹּלָן, Josh. xx. 8, xxi. 27; וַיִּקְלְהוּ, 2 Sam. xx. 14; בְּעַבְרוֹת, 2 Sam. xv. 28; וְהֵימִשֵׁנִי, Judg. xvi. 26; וַתָּרֹאנָה, 1 Sam. xiv. 27.

measured, but a space outside this wall. The following clause חוֹמָה לוֹ סָבִיב, "a wall was round about it," is irreconcilable with the idea that the suffix in מְדָדוֹ (vers. 20 and 15) refers to this wall, inasmuch as the לוֹ can only refer to the object indicated by the suffix attached to מְדָדוֹ. This object, *i.e.* the space which was five hundred rods long and the same broad round about, *i.e.* on every one of the four sides, had a wall enclosing it on the outside, and forming the partition between the holy and the common. הַקֹּדֶשׁ is therefore הַבַּיִת הַפְּנִימִי, "the inner house;" but this is not the temple house with its side-building, but the sanctuary of the temple with its two courts and their buildings, which was measured in ch. xl. 5–xlii. 12.

The arguments which have been adduced in opposition to this explanation of our verses,—the only one in harmony with the words of the text,—and in vindication of the alterations made in the text by the LXX., are without any force. According to Böttcher (p. 355), Hitzig, and others, קָנִים is likely to be a false gloss, (1) "because בִּקְנֵה הַמִּדָּה stands close to it; and while this is quite needless after קנים, it may also have occasioned the gloss." But this tells rather against the suspicion that קָנִים is a gloss, since, as we have already observed, according to the Hebrew mode of expression, the "five hundred" would be defined as rods by בִּקְנֵה הַמִּדָּה, even without קָנִים. Ezekiel, however, had added בִּקְנֵה הַמִּדָּה for the purpose of expressing in the clearest manner the fact that the reference here is not to cubits, but to a new measurement of an extraordinary kind, to which nothing corresponding could be shown in the earlier temple. And the Seventy, by retaining this clause, *ἐν καλάμῳ τοῦ μέτρου*, have pronounced sentence upon their own change of the rods into cubits; and it is no answer to this that the Talmud (*Midd.* c. ii. note 5) also gives only five hundred cubits to the הַר הַבַּיִת, since this Talmudic description is treating of the historical temple and not of Ezekiel's prophetic picture of a temple, although the Rabbins have transferred various statements from the latter to the former. The second and third reasons are weaker still—viz. "because there is no other instance in which the measurement is expressed by rods in the plural; and, on the other hand, אַמָּה is frequently omitted as being the ordinary measurement, and therefore taken for granted." For the first assertion is proved to be erroneous, not only by our verses, but also by ch. xlv. 1 sqq. and xlviii. 16 sqq., whilst there is no force whatever in the second. The last argument employed is a more plausible one—namely, that "the five hundred rods are not in keeping with the sanctuary, because the edifice with the courts and gates would look but a little pile according to the previous measurements in the wide expanse of 20,000 (?) rods." But although the space measured off around the temple-building for the separation between the holy and the profane was five times as long and five times as broad, according to the Hebrew text, or twenty-five times as large as the whole extent of the temple and its courts,[1] the appearance of the temple with its courts is not diminished in consequence, because the surrounding space was not covered with buildings; on the contrary, the fact that it was separated from the common by so large a surrounding space, would rather add to the importance of the temple with its courts. This broad separation is peculiar to Ezekiel's temple, and serves, like many other arrangements in the new sanctuary and worship, to symbolize the inviolable holiness of that sanctuary.

[1]

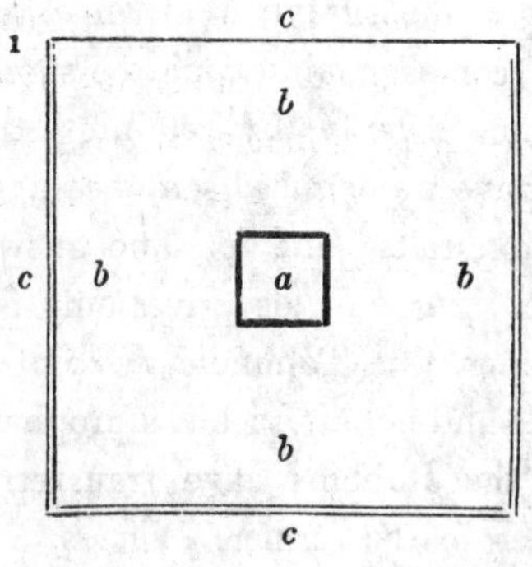

(*a*) Area of the temple with the two courts, 500 cubits square.

(*b*) Surrounding space, five hundred rods = 3000 cubits square.

(*c*) Circuit of fifty cubits in breadth around the surrounding space.—Ch. xlv. 2.

The earlier sanctuary had nothing answering to this; and Kliefoth is wrong in supposing that the outer court served the same purpose in the tabernacle and Solomon's temple, whereas in the temple of Ezekiel this had also become part of the sanctuary, and was itself holy. The tabernacle had no outer court at all, and in Solomon's temple the outer court did form a component part of the sanctuary. The people might enter it, no doubt, when they desired to draw near to the Lord with sacrifices and gifts; but this continued to be the case in Ezekiel's temple, though with certain restrictions (cf. ch. xlvi. 9 and 10). Only, in the case of Solomon's temple, the outer court bordered directly upon the common soil of the city and the land, so that the defilement of the land produced by the sin of the people could penetrate directly even into the holy space of the courts. In the sanctuary of the future, a safeguard was to be placed against this by the surrounding space which separated the holy from the common. It is true that the surface of Moriah supplied no room for this space of five hundred rods square; but the new temple was not to be built upon the real Moriah, but upon a very high mountain, which the Lord would exalt and make ready for the purpose when the temple was erected. Moreover, the circumstance that Moriah was much too small for the extent of the new temple and its surroundings, cannot furnish any argument against the correctness of our view of the verses in question, for the simple reason that in ch. xlv. and xlviii. there follow still further statements concerning the separation of the sanctuary from the rest of the land, which are in perfect harmony with this, and show most indisputably that the temple seen by Ezekiel was not to have its seat in the ancient Jerusalem.

Chap. xliii. 1–12. *Entrance of the Glory of the Lord into the New Temple.*

Ver. 1. *And he led me to the gate, the gate which looked toward the east:* Ver. 2. *And behold the glory of the God of*

Israel came from the east, and its sound was like the sound of many waters, and the earth shone with His glory. Ver. 3. *And the appearance which I saw, was to look at like the appearance which I saw when I came to destroy the city; and (there were) appearances like the appearance which I had seen by the river Chebar; and I fell down upon my face.* Ver. 4. *And the glory of Jehovah came into the house by the way of the gate, the direction of which is toward the east.* Ver. 5. *And wind lifted me up and brought me into the inner court; and, behold, the glory of Jehovah filled the house.* Ver. 6. *And I heard one speaking to me from the house, and there was a man standing by me.* Ver. 7. *And he said to me, Son of man, the place of my throne and the place of the soles of my feet, where I shall dwell in the midst of the sons of Israel for ever; and the house of Israel will no more defile my holy name, they and their kings, through their whoredom and through the corpses of their kings, their high places,* Ver. 8. *When they set their threshold by my threshold, and their door-posts by my door-posts, and there was only the wall between me and them, and they defiled my holy name by their abominations which they did, so that I destroyed them in my wrath.* Ver. 9. *Now will they remove their whoredom and the corpses of their kings from me, and I shall dwell in the midst of them for ever.* Ver. 10. *Thou, son of man, show to the house of Israel this house, that they may be ashamed of their iniquities, and may measure the well-measured building.* Ver. 11. *And when they are ashamed of all that they have done, show them the picture of the house and its arrangement, and its goings out and in, and all its forms and all its statutes, and all its forms and all its laws; and write it before their eyes, that they may keep all its form and all its statutes and do them.* Ver. 12. *This is the law of the house: Upon the top of the mountain all its territory round about is most holy. Behold, this is the law of the house.*—The angel had shown the prophet the new sanctuary as already completed, and had measured it in his presence according to its several parts. But this building only became the house of God when Jehovah as the God of Israel consecrated it, to be the dwelling-place of His divine and gracious presence in the midst of His people, by the entrance of His divine glory into the house.[1] The description of the new temple closes, therefore, with this act of consecration. That the prophet might see this act of divine grace with his own eyes, the measuring man led him from the ground surrounding the temple (ch. xlii. 15–20) back again to the east gate (ver. 1). The allusion is to the eastern gate of the outer court; for it is not till ver. 5 that Ezekiel is taken into the inner court, and, according to ch. xliv. 1, he was brought *back* to the east gate of the outer court. Standing in front of this gate, he sees the glory of the God of Israel come by the way from the east with a great noise, and lighting up the earth with its splendour. The coming of the theophany from the east points back to ch. x. 19, xi. 1 and 23, where the Shechinah, when leaving the ancient temple, went out at the east gate and ascended to the summit of the mountain, which was situated on the east of Jerusalem. It was from the east, therefore, that it returned to enter the new temple. This fact is sufficient of itself to show that the present entrance of the divine glory into the new temple did not lay the foundation for a new and more exalted bond of grace, but was simply intended to restore the relation which had existed before the removal of Israel into captivity. The tabernacle and Solomon's temple had both been consecrated by Jehovah in the same manner as the seat of His throne of grace in Israel (compare Ex. xl. 34, 35; 1 Kings viii. 10, 11; and 2 Chron. v. 13, 14, and vii. 1–3, from which the expression מָלֵא כְבוֹד־יְהוָֹה אֶת־בֵּית יְהוָֹה in ver. 5 has been borrowed). It is true that Hävernick, Kliefoth, and others find, along with this agreement, a difference in the fact that the glory of Jehovah appeared in the cloud in both the tabernacle and

1 "The Lord appears, and fills the house with His own glory; showing that the house will not only be built, but will be filled with the power of God" (Theodoret).

Solomon's temple; whereas here, on the contrary, it appeared in that peculiar form which Ezekiel had already repeatedly seen. But it does not follow that there was really a difference, because the cloud is not mentioned in the verses before us; for it is evident that the cloud was not wanting, even in the manifestation of the glory of God seen by Ezekiel, from the words found in Ezek. x. 3: "The *cloud* filled the inner court, and the glory of Jehovah had risen up from the cherubim to the threshold of the house, *and the house was filled with the cloud*, and the court was full of the splendour of the glory of Jehovah." If, therefore, it is expressly attested in ver. 3, as even Kliefoth admits, that the appearance of God which entered the temple was like the appearance which Ezekiel saw by the Chaboras and before the destruction of the temple, and in connection with the last-mentioned appearance the cloud was visible along with the brilliant splendour of the divine *doxa*, the cloud will certainly not have been wanting when it entered the new temple; and the only reason why it is not expressly mentioned must be, that it did not present a contrast to the brilliant splendour, or tend to obscure the light of the glory of God, but as a shining cloud was simply the atmospheric clothing of the theophany. If, then, the cloud did not present a contrast to the brilliancy of the divine glory, it cannot be inferred from the words, "and the earth shone with His glory," that there was any difference between this and the earlier manifestations of the divine glory at the consecration of the tabernacle and Solomon's temple; more especially as these words do not affirm that it became light on earth, but simply that the earth shone with the glory of God,—that is to say, that it threw a bright light upon the earth as it passed along, —so that this remark simply serves to indicate the intensity of the brightness of this theophany. The words קוֹלוֹ כְּקוֹל וגו׳ are not to be understood, as we may learn from ch. i. 24, as referring to a voice of the coming God, but describe the loud noise made by the moving of the theophany on account of the rustling of the wings of the cherubim. This resembled the roaring of mighty waves. In ver. 3, the expression כַּמַּרְאֶה . . . וּכַמַּרְאֵה הַמַּרְאֶה is somewhat heavy in style, but is correct Hebrew; and the remark with which Hitzig seeks to justify his alteration of וכמראה into ומראה,—namely, that כמראה "would signify 'so the appearance,' whereas Ezekiel intends to explain the present appearance from the well-known earlier one,"—is false so far as the usage of the language is concerned. When the Hebrew uses two כְּ in cases of comparison, which we are accustomed to express in German by *so . . . wie* (so . . . as), he always commences with the thing to which he compares another, and lets the thing which is to be compared follow afterwards. Thus, for example, in Gen. xviii. 25, וְהָיָה כַצַּדִּיק כָּרָשָׁע does not affirm that it happens as to the righteous so to the wicked, but *vice versâ*, that it happens to the righteous as to the wicked; and in Gen. xliv. 18, כִּי כָמוֹךָ כְּפַרְעֹה does not mean, for like thee so is Pharaoh, but "for thou art like Pharaoh." According to this genuine Hebrew expression, the present appearance of the divine glory is mentioned first in the verse before us, and then in the earlier one which the present resembled. And even the apparent pleonasm מַרְאֵה הַמַּרְאֶה vanishes if we render מַרְאֵה by "look,"—the look of the apparition which I saw was just like the apparition, etc. בְּבֹאִי לְשַׁחֵת וגו׳ refers to the ecstatic transportation of the prophet to Jerusalem (ch. viii.–xi.), to witness the destruction of the city (see more particularly ch. viii. 4, ix. 1 sqq.). "The prophet destroyed the city ideally by his prophecy, of which the fulfilment simply forms the objective reverse side" (Hitzig). וּמַרְאוֹת is appended in loose apposition,—there were appearances, visions,—and the plural is to be taken as in מַרְאוֹת אֱלֹהִים in ch. i. 1, xl. 2. For what follows, compare ch. iii. 23, x. 15. For ver. 5*a*, compare ch. iii. 14, xi. 24.

In vers. 6 and 7 the question arises, who it is who is speaking to the prophet; whether it is Jehovah, who has entered the temple, or the man who is standing by Ezekiel in the inner court?

There can be no doubt that מִדַּבֵּר אֵלָי is Jehovah here, as in ch. ii. 2; though the commentators are divided in opinion whether Jehovah spoke directly to the prophet, or through the medium of the man who stood by his side. Hävernick presses the *Hithpael* מִדַּבֵּר, and imagines that Ezekiel heard God conversing within the sanctuary, in consequence of which the angel stood by his side; so that the words of God consisted chiefly in the command to communicate to Ezekiel the divine revelation which follows in ver. 7. But this view is proved to be erroneous by the expression אֵלָי which follows מִדַּבֵּר, and which Hävernick has overlooked. Kliefoth, on the other hand, is of opinion that the words contained in ver. 7, which proceeded from the מִדַּבֵּר, were addressed to the prophet directly by God Himself; for he heard them before anything was said by the man, and neither here nor in what follows is the man said to have spoken. On the contrary, both here and in what follows, even in ch. xlvi. 20, 24, xlvii. 6, 7, it is always God Himself who appears as the speaker, and the man simply as the prophet's guide. But this is also not correct. Such passages as ch. xlvi. 20 and 24 compared with vers. 19 and 21, and ch. xlvii. 6, 8, compared with vers. 1 and 4, show undeniably that the man who conducted the prophet also talked with him. Consequently, in the case referred to in the verse before us, we must also conclude that he who spoke to the prophet from the temple addressed him through the medium of the man who stood by his side, and that אִישׁ is the subject to וַיֹּאמֶר in ver. 7; from which, however, it by no means follows that the מִדַּבֵּר was also an angel, who spoke to the prophet, not from the most holy place, but simply from within the house, as Hitzig explains the matter. The meaning is rather, that Ezekiel heard God conversing with him from the sanctuary, whilst a man, *i.e.* an angel, stood by his side and spoke to him as follows. אִישׁ is in that case not some angel merely who spoke in the name of Jehovah, but the angel of Jehovah, God's own speaker, ὁ λόγος τοῦ Θεοῦ (John i. 1 sqq.). But according to his outward *habitus*, this angel of the Lord, who is designated as אִישׁ, is identical with the angel who showed the prophet the temple, and measured it (ch. xl. 3 onwards). For according to ch. xlvii. 1 sqq. this אִישׁ had also a measuring rod, and measured. The absence of the article from אִישׁ in ver. 6, which prevents Kliefoth from admitting this identity, does not indicate decidedly that a different man from the one mentioned before is introduced here as the prophet's attendant, but simply leaves the identity of this אִישׁ with the former indefinite, so that it can only be inferred from the further course of events; because the point of importance here was neither to establish this identity by employing the article, nor to define the medium of the word of God more precisely, but simply to introduce the words which follow as the words of God Himself. The address commences with an explanation on the part of God that the temple into which the glory of the Lord had entered was the place of His throne, where He would dwell for ever among the sons of Israel. The אֶת־מְקוֹם is a concise expression, in which אֵת is *nota accus.*, and we have to supply in thought either רְאֵה or הִנֵּה: "behold the place." מְקוֹם כַּפּוֹת רַגְלַי, the place of the soles of my feet (cf. Isa. lx. 13), is equivalent to the footstool of my feet in Isa. lxvi. 1. The ark of the covenant is called the footstool of God in 1 Chron. xxviii. 2 and Ps. cxxxii. 7; compare Ps. xcix. 5 and Lam. ii. 1, where this epithet may possibly be used to designate the temple. This also applies to the throne of Jehovah, since God was enthroned above the cherubim of the ark in the holy of holies (cf. Ex. xxv. 22; 1 Sam. iv. 4, etc.). In the sanctuary which Ezekiel saw, no reference is made to the ark of the covenant, and the silence with regard to this is hardly to be regarded as a mere omission to mention it, inasmuch as none of the things contained in the temple are mentioned with the exception of the altars, not even the table of shew-bread or the candlestick. The ark of the covenant is not mentioned, because, as is stated in Jer. iii. 16, in the Messianic times the ark of the covenant will not be remembered, neither will it be missed. לְעוֹלָם, as in ch. xxxvii. 26 and 28. The promise culminates in this. לְעוֹלָם does not apply either to the tabernacle or to Solomon's temple, in which Jehovah also had His dwelling-place, though not for ever. These sanctuaries He left, and gave them up to destruction, because the Israelites had profaned His holy name by their idolatry. This will not take place any more after the erection of the new sanctuary. לֹא יְטַמְּאוּ is not imperative, but a simple future: "they will no more defile," because they come to a knowledge of their sins through the punitive judgment of exile, so that they become ashamed of them, and because the Lord will have poured out His Spirit upon them (cf. ch. xxxvii. 23 sqq., xxxix. 29).—Formerly, however (ver. 7*b*), they profaned the holy name of God by their spiritual whoredom (cf. ch. xvi.) and by dead idols, for which they erected high places in the immediate neighbourhood of the dwelling-place of Jehovah, that is to say, even in the temple courts, so that Jehovah was only separated from the idols by a wall. This is the general meaning of vers. 7*b* and 8, in which the exposition of פִּגְרֵי מַלְכֵיהֶם is difficult. Rosenmüller, Hävernick, and others understand by the "corpses of their kings," the dead idols. Ewald, Hitzig, and Kliefoth, on the other hand, take the expression in a literal sense, as referring to the corpses of kings which had been buried near to the temple, so that the temple had been defiled by the proximity of these graves. But the latter view is precluded by the fact that not a single instance can be adduced of the burial of a king in the vicinity of the temple, since Neh. iii. 15 contains no allusion to anything of the kind, and the tombs of the kings upon Zion were not so near to the temple that it could possibly be defiled in consequence. Moreover, בָּמוֹתָם cannot be reconciled with this view; and for that reason Ewald and Hitzig propose to read בְּמוֹתָם, "in their death." The attempt of Kliefoth, however, to defend the reading בָּמוֹתָם, by taking it as in apposition to בִּזְנוּתָם and not to וּבְפִגְרֵי מַלְכֵיהֶם, is a desperate remedy, which clearly shows the impossibility of connecting בָּמוֹתָם with the "corpses of the kings." We therefore understand by פִּגְרֵי the dead idols, in accordance with Lev. xxvi. 30 (cf. Jer. xvi. 18); but by מַלְכֵיהֶם we understand, not the idols, but the Israelitish kings, as in the case of the preceding מַלְכֵיהֶם; partly because it cannot be shown that the plural מְלָכִים is ever used in the sense of idols (though the singular מַלְכָּם is used of Baal in Zeph. i. 5 and Amos v. 26), and partly on account of the harshness involved in interpreting the two מלכיהם when standing so close together, in the first instance of the kings, and in the second of the idols of Israel. The corpses of the kings are therefore the dead idols, for which the kings (for example, Manasseh) had built altars or high places (בָּמוֹת) in the sanctuary, *i.e.* in the courts of the temple (2 Kings xxi. 4, 5–7). The objection that פְּגָרִים without anything further, such, for instance, as גִּלּוּלִים in Lev. xxvi. 30, cannot signify the dead idols, will not bear examination, as the more precise definition which is wanting is supplied by the context, where idolatry is the point in question. בָּמוֹתָם without the preposition ב is a loosely attached apposition to בְּפִגְרֵי מַלְכֵיהֶם and בִּזְנוּתָם, which defines more precisely in what way the whoredom of the nation and the dead idols of the kings had amounted to a defiling of the house of the Lord, namely, from the fact that the people and the kings had erected temples of high places (*bâmoth*) for dead idols by the side of the temple of the living God, and had placed them so close that the threshold and door-posts of these idol-temples touched the threshold and door-posts of the temple of Jehovah, and there was nothing but the wall of the temple (הַקִּיר) between Jehovah and the carcase-gods. בָּמוֹתָם is explained in this way in ver. 8*a*, and then the defiling of the holy name of the Lord is mentioned again for the purpose of appending, by means of וָאֲכַל (imperf. *Piel* of כָּלָה), the allusion to the penal judgment which they had thereby brought upon themselves. Ver. 9. Such profanation as this will not take place any more in time to come, and Jehovah will dwell for ever in the midst of Israel.

To lead Israel to this goal, Ezekiel is to show them the house (*i.e.* the temple). In this way are the further words of God in vers. 10–12 attached to what goes before. הַגֵּד אֶת־הַבַּיִת, show or make known the house, is equivalent to proclaim to the people the revelation concerning the new temple. In this were the Israelites to discern the magnitude of the grace of God, that they might blush at their evil deeds, and measure the well-measured building (תָּכְנִית, as in ch. xxviii. 12), *i.e.* carefully consider and ponder what the Lord had bestowed upon His people through this sanctuary, so that they might suffer themselves to be brought to repentance by means of its glory. And if they felt shame and repentance on account of their transgressions, Ezekiel was to show them the shape and arrangement of the sanctuary, with all its forms and ordinances, and write them out before their eyes, that they might have the picture of it impressed upon their minds, and keep the statutes thereof. In ver. 11 the words are crowded together, to indicate that all the several parts and arrangements of the new temple are significant and worthy of being pondered and laid to heart. צוּרָה is the shape of the temple generally, its external form; תְּכוּנָה, the internal arrangement as a whole. Both of these are noticed specifically by the allusion to the goings out and in, as well as to the forms (צוּרוֹת) of the separate parts, and their statutes and laws. חֻקּוֹת are the precepts concerning the things to be observed by Israel when appearing before the Lord in the temple, the regulations for divine worship. תּוֹרוֹת, the instructions contained in these statutes for sanctification of life. The second וְכָל־צוּרֹתָו is omitted in the LXX. and some of the Hebrew *Codd.*, and has therefore been expunged as a gloss by Dathe, Hitzig, and other critics; but it is undoubtedly genuine, and in conformity with the intentional crowding together of words.—The admonition to keep and to observe everything carefully is closed in ver. 12 with a statement of the fundamental law of the temple; that upon the lofty mountain the whole of its domain round about is to be most holy. עַל־רֹאשׁ הָהָר does not belong to הַבַּיִת in the sense of the house which is to be built upon the top of the mountain, but to the contents of the *thorâh* of this house. It is to stand upon the top of the mountain, and to be most holy in all its domain. רֹאשׁ הָהָר is to be understood in accordance with ch. xl. 2; and גְּבֻלוֹ points back to הַבַּיִת. Both by its situation upon a very high mountain, and also by the fact that not merely the inner sanctuary, and not merely the whole of the temple house, but also the whole of its surroundings (all its courts), are to be most holy, the new sanctuary is to be distinguished from the earlier one. What has been already stated—namely, that the temple shall not be profaned any more—is compressed into this clause; and by the repetition of the words, "this is the law of the house," the first section of this vision, viz. the description of the temple, is rounded off; whilst the command given to the prophet in vers. 10 and 11, to make known all the statutes and laws of this temple to the house of Israel, forms at the same time the transition to the section which follows.

CHAP. XLIII. 13–XLVI. 24. THE NEW ORDINANCES OF DIVINE WORSHIP.

With the entrance of the divine glory into the new temple, which Ezekiel saw in the spirit (ch. xliii. 1–5), the Lord God entered once more into the covenant relation of grace toward the tribes of Israel. But if the abode of Jehovah in the midst of His people was to have an eternal duration, Israel must turn in uprightness of heart to its God, and suffer itself to be renewed and sanctified in heart, mind, and spirit from within the sanctuary, through the mercy of the Lord and His Spirit. It must entirely renounce the idols to which it was formerly attached, and cherish with willingness of heart fellowship with its God in the temple, through the faithful fulfilment of all that He required of His people. The description and consecration of the new temple, as the site of the throne of Jehovah in Israel, is therefore followed by the precepts concerning the manner in which Israel was to serve its God in the sanctuary, and to sanctify His name. These precepts commence with the description and ritual of the consecration of the altar of burnt-offering, at which the people was to approach the Lord with sacrifices, to seek and obtain from Him grace, sanctification, and blessing (ch. xliii. 13–27). To these there are appended regulations,—(1) concerning the access to the sanctuary, for the prince (ch. xliv. 1–4), also for the ministers of the altar and of the holy place, the Levites and the priests, their duties and privileges (ch. xliv. 5–31); (2) concerning the attitude of all the people toward the sanctuary and its ministers, or concerning the holy portion to be set apart to the Lord for His sanctuary, and its ministers, priests, Levites, and princes on the division of the land (ch. xlv. 1–12), and also concerning the heave-offerings, which all Israel was to bring to the prince to supply the sacrifices binding upon him (ch. xlv. 13–17); (3) concerning the offerings which were to be brought on the Sabbaths, the new moons, the yearly festivals, and every day (ch. xlv. 18–xlvi. 15); and lastly, (4) by way of appendix, precepts concerning the landed property of the prince (ch. xlvi. 16–18), and the sacrificial kitchens (ch. xlvi. 19–24).

Vers. 13–27. *Description and Consecration of the Altar of Burnt-Offering.*

Vers. 13–17. Description of the Altar (see the illustration on Plate III.).—Ver. 13. *And these are the measures of the altar in cubits: The cubit a cubit and a handbreadth; a ground-framework of a cubit (in height), and a cubit in breadth, and its moulding on its border round about a span. This is the base of the altar.* Ver. 14. *And from the ground-framework of earth to the lower enclosure, two cubits (in height), and a cubit in breadth; and from the small enclosure to the greater enclosure, four cubits (in height), and one cubit in breadth.* Ver. 15. *And the mount of God, four cubits; and from the hearth of God upwards, the four horns.* Ver. 16. *And the hearth of God, twelve cubits in length by twelve cubits in breadth; squared on its four sides.* Ver. 17. *And the enclosure, fourteen cubits in length by fourteen cubits in breadth on its four sides; and the moulding round about it, half a cubit; and the ground-framework of it, a cubit round about: and its steps faced the east.*—To the heading, "these are the measures of the altar in (according to) cubits," there is once more appended, as in ch. xl. 5, in connection with the measuring of the temple, the length of the cubit measure. The description commences with the foundation of the altar, and, proceeding upwards, gives the height and breadth of the several gradations of the walls of the altar, up to the horns at the four corners (vers. 13–15). It then passes from above downwards, to supply the length and breadth, or the circumference of the different stages (vers. 16 and 17). As the first, or lowest part, the חֵיק is mentioned, literally, the bosom or lap; then by transference, the hollow formed by the sides of a chariot (1 Kings xxii. 35); here the lower hollow or base of the altar (*p*), formed by a border of a definite height, not merely "a frame running round, a stand in which the altar stood" (Hitzig), nor merely "the hollow filled with earth" (Kliefoth), but both together. This ground-framework (*p*) was a cubit (*sc.* high) and a cubit broad. That הָאַמָּה is to be taken as referring to the height, is evident from the statement of the breadth which follows. חֵיק הָאַמָּה is not to be altered into חֵיקָהּ אַמָּה, as Ewald proposes, nor is הָאַמָּה to be changed into באמה (Hitzig); but Hävernick's explanation is to be adopted: "and a bosom (was there) the cubit," *i.e.* of the height of the cubit just described. רֹחַב, breadth, is the extent to which the bosom projected beyond the next enclosure (*q*) on every side, and formed a support, the circumference of which was a cubit more than the lower cube of the altar on every side. This is shown by the measurements in vers. 16 and 17. The חֵיק had a גְּבוּל on its שָׂפָה of a span (half a cubit) in height (*o*). שָׂפָה, lip, is the rim (1 Kings vii. 26; Gen. xxii. 17); and גְּבוּל, the bordering on the rim, is a moulding. The feminine suffixes attached to גְּבוּלָהּ and שְׂפָתָהּ refer to חֵיק, which is of the masculine gender, no doubt, when used in its literal sense of bosom or lap, but is construed as a feminine in the tropical sense of an inanimate object. The ground-framework, with its moulding, formed the גַּב of the altar. גַּב, the arched, then a hump or back, signifies here the support of the altar. Upon this support the altar rose in a cubical enclosure or frame, which diminished in circumference by ledges or steps. The enclosure resting upon the support, and therefore the lowest enclosure (*q*), is mentioned in ver. 14*a;* and the one which followed (*r*) in ver. 14*b*. The word עֲזָרָה, which has probably sprung from עָצַר by the softening of צ into ז, signifies enclosure, surrounding, and is mostly used for the outer court of the temple; here it is applied to the altar, and signifies the enclosure or framework of the kernel of the altar, consisting of earth. As the altar rose in steps, a distinction is made between the lower or smaller, and the (upper or) greater עֲזָרָה. The identity of the lower עֲזָרָה and the smaller one (הַקְּטַנָּה) is so evident from the course of the description, that it is universally admitted by modern expositors. The lower one (*q*) is called the small one, in comparison with the large one which stood above it, from the fact that its height was smaller, as it was only two cubits high, whereas the upper one (*r*) was four. When, therefore, the measurement of the greater one is given in this way in ver. 14*b:* "from the small enclosure to the great enclosure, four cubits," this statement cannot be understood in any other way than as meaning, that this enclosure or frame had a height of four cubits from the lower to the upper end,—that is to say, in other words, that the lower ledge was four cubits from the upper. Consequently the statement in ver. 14*a*, "from the ground-framework of earth to the lower enclosure, two cubits," can also have no other meaning than that the lower enclosure, from the lower edge by the moulding to the upper edge, at which the second enclosure commenced, was two cubits high. This height is reckoned from the upper edge of the חֵיק, or from the first (lowest) ledge. The height of these three portions taken together, therefore, was (1 + 2 + 4) seven cubits. To this the mount of God (*s*), which was four cubits (ver. 15), has to be added, making in all eleven cubits. In ver. 14 חֵיק is followed by הָאָרֶץ: the חֵיק consisting of earth, or filled with earth. But the חֵיק, with its moulding, is designated גַּב, the back or support of the altar, and is thereby distinguished from the altar itself; so that, for the height of the altar, we have only to reckon the two enclosures, with the mount of God, which amount to ten cubits. Upon the basis of the חֵיק, with its moulding, and the two enclosures (עזרה), there rose the true altar, with its hearth, and the horns at the four corners, noticed in ver. 15. A distinction is here made between הַרְאֵל, *i.e.* mount of God, and אֲרִיאֵל; and they are not to be identified, as they have been by many of the commentators, down to Hitzig, after the example of the LXX. אֲרִיאֵל (as the word is to be written according to the *Keri*) does not mean "lion of God," but "hearth of God" (אֲרִי, from אָרָה, to burn), as in Isa. xxix. 1, 2. The hearth of God is the surface of the altar, its fire-hearth (*t*); whereas הַרְאֵל, mount of God (*s*), was the basis or foundation of the hearth. This was four cubits high, whereas no height is mentioned in connection with the hearth of God; but it is simply stated that four horns went upward from it, namely, at the four corners. With the horns of the altar, the size and height of which are not given, and which cannot be reckoned at three cubits, the description of all the parts, from the bottom to the top, is given; and all that remains to complete the measurements, is to describe the circumference of the several parts which rose one above another in the form of steps. This follows in vers. 16 and 17. The hearth of God is twelve cubits long and twelve cubits broad, and is therefore רָבוּעַ, square, of the same length and breadth on its four sides. Going downwards, there follow in ver. 17*a* the length and breadth of the עֲזָרָה, with fourteen cubits, as it was a cubit broader on every side according to ver. 14. It is very strange, however, that the length and breadth of only one עֲזָרָה are given here, as there are two of different heights mentioned in ver. 14. Many of the commentators have therefore identified the mount of God with the great עֲזָרָה, and attribute only a height of seven cubits to the altar; whereas Kliefoth regards both the עֲזָרָה of ver. 17 and the גְּבוּל and חֵיק of ver. 15 as different from the parts mentioned by the same name in vers. 13 and 14, and takes them as referring to an enclosure and a barrier of the mount of God. One is as arbitrary as the other, as the words of the text do not require either of these assumptions. The difficulty, that only one עֲזָרָה is mentioned in ver. 17, is easily solved, if we consider that in ver. 15 only the height of the mount of God is given, and no breadth is mentioned as in the case of the עֲזָרָה in ver. 14. We may see from this that the mount of God had the same breadth or the same circumference as the upper עֲזָרָה (see *r* and *s* in the illustration). In that case the length and breadth of all the parts of the altar were given, when, in addition to the length and breadth of the hearth of God (*t*), those of one עֲזָרָה, and that the lower, were given, as this alone was longer and broader than the hearth of God and the mount of God; whereas the length and breadth of the upper עֲזָרָה were identical with those of the circumference of the mount of God.

The altar, therefore, upon the upper surface, the hearth of God, was a square, of twelve cubits in length and breadth. The mount of God and the upper enclosure had the same length and breadth. The lower enclosure, on the other hand, was fourteen cubits long and broad; and the support, finally, without the moulding, was sixteen cubits in length and breadth. The height of the altar was as follows: the support, with the moulding, a cubit and a half; the lower enclosure, two cubits; the upper, four; and the mount of God, with the hearth, also four cubits in height; whereas the altar in Solomon's temple was ten cubits high, and at its lower basis twenty cubits long and broad (2 Chron. iv. 1).—The description closes in ver. 17*b* with an allusion to steps, which the altar of Ezekiel had upon the eastern side; whereas, in the case of the tabernacle, steps were not allowed to be placed by the altar (Ex. xx. 23). The form פְּנוֹת is taken by Kimchi as a noun. Others regard it as an *infin. nominasc.*; whilst Hitzig proposes to point it as a participle פֹּנוֹת.

Vers. 18–27. CONSECRATION OF THE ALTAR.—Ver. 18. *And he said to me, Son of man, Thus saith the Lord Jehovah, These are the statutes of the altar in the day when it is erected, to offer burnt-offerings upon it, and to sprinkle blood thereon.* Ver. 19. *Thou shalt give to the priests of the tribe of Levi who are of the seed of Zadok, who draw near to me, is the saying of the Lord Jehovah, a bullock, a young ox, for a sin-offering.* Ver. 20. *And thou shalt take of its blood, and put it upon its four horns, and upon the four corners of the enclosure, and upon the moulding round about; and so absolve and expiate it.* Ver. 21. *And thou shalt take the bullock of the sin-offering, and burn it at the appointed place of the house, outside the sanctuary.* Ver. 22. *And on the second day thou shalt offer a faultless he-goat for a sin-offering, that they may absolve the altar, as they absolved it with the bullock.* Ver. 23. *When thou hast completed the absolution, thou shalt offer a bullock, a young ox, without fault, and a faultless ram of the flock;* Ver. 24. *And shalt bring them before Jehovah, and the priests shall throw salt upon them, and sacrifice them as burnt-offering to Jehovah.* Ver. 25. *Seven days shalt thou offer a sin-offering goat daily and a bullock, a young ox, and a ram of the flock without fault shall they prepare.* Ver. 26. *Seven days shall they expiate the altar, and cleanse it, and fill its hand.* Ver. 27. *And when they have completed these days, it shall come to pass on the eighth day and henceforward, that the priests place your burnt-offerings and your peace-offerings upon the altar, and I will accept you with delight, is the saying of the Lord Jehovah.*

As the altar of the tabernacle and that of Solomon's temple

were consecrated before they were used (Lev. viii. 11, 15, 19, 33; 1 Kings viii. 62–66; 2 Chron. vii. 4–10), and God commanded and regulated this consecration of the altar of the tabernacle (Ex. xxix. 10 sqq.), so also is the altar of burnt-offering in the new sanctuary to be consecrated before it is used. This command is given to Ezekiel, and the consecration enjoined upon him, not as the representative of the nation, but as a prophet, upon whom, as is frequently the case in the prophetical narratives, those things are said to be enjoined, which are to be set in operation through his proclamation. This commission is given to him, however, for the day (the time) when the altar will be made or restored, from which alone we may see that the execution of the command belongs to the future, in which the temple shown him in the spirit is to be erected, and that it will take place in a manner corresponding to the realization of the temple; so that we cannot infer from this command alone that the reference is to the building of a temple and altar of stone, metal, and wood. חֻקּוֹת הַמִּזְבֵּחַ are not the regulations prescribed for the altar service generally, but simply those relating to its consecration. If we compare these with the account of the consecration of the altars of the earlier sanctuaries, we find that no detailed description is given of the consecration of the altar of Solomon's temple, but that it is simply stated that it lasted seven days (2 Chron. vii. 9). The consecration of the altar of the tabernacle lasted just the same time (Ex. xxix. 37; Lev. viii. 33). And the same period is appointed here (ver. 26). But the consecration of the altar of the tabernacle was associated with the consecration of the priests. Here, on the contrary, the existence of the priesthood is presupposed, and only the altar is consecrated. The consecration of the Mosaic altar commenced with the anointing of the altar and all its utensils, by the sprinkling of it seven times by Moses with the holy anointing oil, for the purpose of sanctifying it (Lev. viii. 11). Here, on the other hand, nothing is said about the anointing of the altar; only the absolving of it by sacrifice is mentioned, which followed the anointing in the case of the Mosaic altar. At the altar in the tabernacle Moses performed the whole act of consecration, as the mediator of the covenant, the anointing as well as the preparation of the sacrifices. Here, however, the priests already consecrated for their service are to complete the sacrificial ceremony. It is true that the expressions used in ver. 20, "take of its blood," etc., and in ver. 21, "take the bullock of the sin-offering," etc., apparently indicate that the prophet was to perform the sprinkling of the blood and the burning of the sin-offering. But it is obvious that this is only to be understood as signifying that he was to do it through the medium of the priests, *i.e.* was to enjoin the performance of it upon them, from the use of the plural חִטְּאוּ in ver. 22*b*: "they shall absolve the altar, as they have absolved it with the bullock." It is not all the priests of the tribe of Levi, however, who are to perform this service, but simply those of the family of Zadok, who alone are selected in the new temple for specifically priestly service (cf. ch. xl. 46 and xliv. 15 sqq.).—The sacred ceremony commences with the offering of a young ox as a sin-offering; vers. 19, 20, as in Lev. viii. 14, compared with Ex. xxix. 1, 10. The blood of the ox is to be put upon the four horns and the four corners of the enclosure, and upon the moulding below it round about; and the flesh is to be burned at an appointed place outside the sanctuary. For the article in הַפַּר הַחַטָּאת (ver. 21), see Ewald, § 290*b*. The pouring out of the blood —that was not used for smearing the places indicated—at the foot of the altar is not mentioned, nor the burning of the fat portions of the sacrifice upon the altar. We cannot infer, from the omission of the latter circumstance, that the fat was not consumed upon the altar, but was burned, with the flesh, skin, and bones of the animal, outside the sanctuary, as Kliefoth supposes. Without the burning of certain definite portions of the victim upon the altar, the slaughtering of the animal would not have been a complete sacrifice at all; the smearing of the blood upon the altar would not have sufficed for this. And the fact that in ver. 21 the command is given, "take the bullock and burn it," does not prove that the animal was to be burned along with those fat portions which were to be consumed upon the altar in the case of every sin-offering. In Lev. viii. 17 also, אֶת־הַפָּר stands in the place of אֶת־בְּשַׂר הַפָּר, Ex. xxix. 14. Ezekiel generally presupposes that the sacrificial ritual is well known, and therefore mentions only those points in which deviations from the ordinary ritual took place in connection with this sacrifice, such as the sprinkling of the blood, because the blood was to be smeared on particular parts of the altar, and the burning of the flesh, on account of the place where this was to be done. In the case of the burnt-offering in ver. 23, no directions are given concerning the ceremonial; because this was to be in conformity with the standing ritual, with the exception of the sprinkling with salt, which was not to be performed in the same manner as in the ordinary sacrifices. The burning is to take place בְּמִפְקַד הַבַּיִת, outside the sanctuary. מִפְקָד is a place commanded or appointed; and מִפְקַד הַבַּיִת is a place in the temple set apart for that purpose. It follows from this that the place in question, since it belonged to the house, *i.e.* to the temple, is to be sought for within the square of five hundred cubits in extent, which was covered by the temple and its courts; and at the same time that it was outside the מִקְדָּשׁ, *i.e.* upon a spot which did not form part of the sanctuary in the stricter sense of the word. Kliefoth therefore thinks of a spot within the *gizrah* (ch. xli. 12), the name of which implies that the space which it covered did not belong to the true מִקְדָּשׁ. This view is the most probable one; whereas Ewald's conjecture, that the place intended is the locality of the sacrificial kitchens of the priests described in ch. xlvi. 19, is decidedly erroneous, as these kitchens, which were set apart for the cooking of the holy sacrificial flesh to be eaten by the priests alone, were certainly reckoned as forming part of the מִקְדָּשׁ.—Ver. 22. On the second day, a he-goat was to be brought for a sin-offering, and the altar was to be cleansed from sin with this just as with the bullock on the first day; which implies that the same ceremonial was to be observed with this sacrifice as with that of the sin-offering.

After the completion of the expiation a burnt-offering was to be presented to the Lord of a bullock and a ram (vers. 23 and 24). There is a difference of opinion as to the meaning of בְּכַלּוֹתְךָ מֵחַטֵּא in these verses. Hitzig and Kliefoth suppose that the expiation was only completed on the second day, with the offering of the he-goat as a sin-offering. They both of them lay stress upon the fact that, on the one hand, in vers. 23 and 24 the offering of the burnt-offering is mentioned on the second day, and not on the first day also; and, on the other hand, in ver. 25, for the seven days of consecration, only the preparation of a he-goat for the sin-offering and the preparation of the two animals appointed for the burnt-offering are mentioned. Hitzig also adduces the fact that in ver. 26 there is no further reference to חטא, but simply to כפר and טהר, and draws the conclusion from this, that the sin attaching to the altar was removed with two sin-offerings on two days,* and then through seven days further by means of burnt-offerings the anger of God which followed the sin was appeased (כפר), and the uncleanness or profane character of the altar was expunged (טהר), so that the seven days of ver. 25 are not to be dated from ver. 19 onwards. According to this view, the consecration of the altar lasted nine days, and not seven, and the eighth day mentioned in ver. 27 would really be the tenth day, reckoning from the commencement of the consecration. To carry out this view, Hitzig is obliged to erase not only the וְכִפַּרְתָּהוּ of ver. 20, but also the first half of ver. 25 as glosses; a fact which carries its condemnation with it, as even the Septuagint furnishes no warrant for the erasure of ver. 25*a*. Moreover, the distinction which Hitzig draws between חִטֵּא on the one hand, and כִּפֶּר and טִהֵר on the other, is quite erroneous. Purification (טהר) is never mentioned in the law as the effect produced by a burnt-offering. A sin-offering followed by a burnt-offering is invariably prescribed for the removal of uncleanness; for "reconciliation and purification take place through the absolution effected by the sin-offering; and to such a sin-offering and its purifying operation the burnt-offering is then added to secure the good pleasure of God for that which has been already cleansed" (Kliefoth).—But we cannot regard even Kliefoth's view as well founded, namely, that on the first day a sin-offering alone was presented, and it was only from the second day onwards that a sin-offering and burnt-offering were presented, and this lasted for seven days, so that the consecration of the altar continued fully eight days, and on the ninth day (not the eighth, as stated in ver. 27) the regular use of the altar commenced. Kliefoth bases this conclusion principally upon the fact that vers. 19–21 attribute only the sin-offering of a bullock to the first day; and that, on the other hand, vers. 25 and 26 extend in all its details to seven days the very same ceremony as vers. 22–24 assign to the second day, whereas they do not contain a syllable to the effect that the sin-offering of the bullock was to be repeated every day, or that the sacrifices described in vers. 22–24 were also to be offered on the first day. The sinew of this demonstration consists *in silentio*, therefore; and this precarious basis of argument crumbles here, as in most other cases, as is evident from the words of ver. 26: "seven days shall ye reconcile the altar, and purify it." This perfectly general statement, which is not connected with ver. 25 by any *Vav copul.*, or placed in subordination to it, affirms in the clearest manner that the consecration of the altar was to last seven days, neither more nor less; so that if these seven days are to be reckoned from the second day, the sin-offering of the bullock upon the first day must be deprived of its reconciling and purifying worth, in direct contradiction not only to ver. 20, according to which the altar was to be absolved and reconciled through the sin-offering of the bullock to be offered on the first day, but also to ver. 22, according to which they were to absolve the altar by the sin-offering of the he-goat, in just the same manner as they had absolved it by the sin-offering of the bullock (on the first day). To take the כִּפֶּר and טִהַר in ver. 26 merely as the effect produced by the sacrifices mentioned in ver. 25, renders the שִׁבְעַת יָמִים standing at the head of ver. 26 an impossibility. Unless, therefore, we would impose upon the words of the prophet a gross contradiction, we must lay no stress either upon the fact that in ver. 23 the offering of the burnt-offering is not mentioned till after the direction concerning the sin-offering to be presented on the second day, or upon the circumstance that in ver. 25 the he-goat is mentioned as a sin-offering for all the seven days, and no allusion is made to the fact that the sin-offering of the first day was a bullock. The former (the reference to the burnt-offering after the sin-offering of the second day) may be explained very simply, on the ground that the sin-offerings of the first two days are mentioned one after the other, because different animals were prescribed for the purpose, and then, first, the burnt-offerings, which were the same for every day. And it is obvious that the explanation is to be sought for in this formal arrangement, and not in the fact that only a sin-offering without a burnt-offering was to be presented on the first day, and consequently that the expression "on the second day" refers solely to the sin-offering of that day, from the words בְּכַלּוֹתְךָ מֵחַטֵּא in ver. 23; since מֵחַטֵּא cannot be understood in a different sense from that which it bears in ver. 22*b*, the clause immediately preceding, *i.e.* must not be restricted to the sin-offering of the second day, but must be taken as referring to the sin-offerings of both the first and second days. The meaning of the words is therefore this: when the absolution by means of the sin-offering on the first and on the second day is ended, then shalt thou bring a burnt-offering. But if this is the meaning of the words, the offering of the burnt-offering prescribed in ver. 23 does not fall so exclusively under the definition of time contained in the words "on the second day," as to warrant our assigning it to the second day alone, and concluding that no such offering was presented on the first day. There was no necessity for Ezekiel to express himself more clearly on this point, as there was no fear of any misunderstanding on the part of those who were acquainted with the law; since every Israelite who had been instructed in the law knew full well that no sin-offering could ever be presented without being followed by a burnt-offering, that in fact the burnt-offering was indispensable to the accomplishment of the כַּפָּרָה, for which the sin-offering was presented. And in ver. 25 also, Ezekiel had no occasion to fear that the somewhat loose expression, "seven days shalt thou prepare a he-goat sin-offering for the day," would be misunderstood; as he had already stated that a bullock was to be taken for the sin-offering of the first day, and the period of seven days was so universally prescribed in the law for every act of consecration which lasted more than one day, that he would have indicated in a clearer manner any deviation from this rule. We therefore regard the change of the seven days devoted to the consecration of the altar into eight as being just as groundless as that into nine, and adhere to the traditional explanation of these verses, namely, that the consecration of the altar lasted only seven days, and that on every one of these days a sin-offering and a burnt-offering were to be presented, the sin-offering on the first day being a bullock, and on the other days a he-goat, whilst the burnt-offerings were to consist on all seven days of a young ox and a ram.—With regard to the burnt-offering, the direction given, that the priests are to throw or pour (הִשְׁלִיךְ), and not merely to strew or sprinkle, salt upon it, is to be regarded as significant. According to Lev. ii. 13, salt was to be added to every קָרְבָּן (bloody or bloodless) sacrifice. The express allusion to the salting of these consecrating burnt-offerings, and also the choice of the verb הִשְׁלִיךְ, point to a copious strewing with salt for the purpose of giving greater intensity to the force of these sacrifices. On the significance of salt in relation to the sacrifices, see the comm. on Lev. ii. 13. The ו attached to the *Chetib* וְכִפְּרוּ in ver. 26 is to be explained from the fact that the definition of the time שִׁבְעַת יָמִים is placed at the head absolutely. There is something bold in the application of the expression מִלֵּא יָד to the altar; since this expression arose from the ceremony peculiar to the consecrating sacrifice of the priests, namely, that the fat and fleshy portions of this sacrifice, which were intended partly for consumption upon the altar, and partly as a heave-offering for Jehovah, were to be given into the hands of the priests to be consecrated for the purpose of investing them symbolically with the gifts, which they were to offer in part to the Lord in the altar fire in the fulfilment of their official duties, and to receive in part for their service (see the comm. on Lev. viii. 25–29). Filling the hand of the altar, therefore, is equivalent to providing it with sacrificial gifts, so that it should never be without them. In this sense the symbolical act was connected with the completion of its consecration as a place of sacrifice. The *Keri* יָדָיו is incorrect, and יָדוֹ the proper reading; inasmuch as even at the consecration of the priests, when the sacrificial portions were placed in the hands of the priests, מִלֵּא יָד only is used, and not יָדַיִם (cf. Ex. xxix. 9; Lev. xxi. 10, etc.).

If we compare the directions given in the section before us concerning the consecration of the altar, with the consecration which was prescribed in Ex. xxix. for the altar of burnt-offering in the tabernacle, and was fully carried out according to Lev. viii., we find the following points of difference:—(1) the anointing of the altar is wanting here; (2) at the consecration of the Mosaic altar a bullock (young ox) was prescribed as the sin-offering for all the seven days (Ex. xxix. 36), in Ezekiel for the first day only, and a he-goat for the rest; (3) the blood of this sin-offering is smeared upon the horns of the altar in the former consecration (Ex. xxix. 12; Lev. viii. 15), in the latter upon the horns and the corners of the walls, and upon the lower moulding round about; (4) the burnt-offering there consists in a ram every day, here in a bullock and a ram daily; (5) on the other hand, the ram offered as a sacrifice of consecration in the Mosaic ceremony, which was specially connected with the institution of the priests in their office, is omitted here, as the priests were already holding their office; so that the sacrifice of consecration might be said to be here absorbed into the burnt-offering. All essential differences therefore reduce themselves to the fact that in Ezekiel the anointing of the altar is wanting, and the sin-offering of the last six days is diminished by the selection of an inferior animal, in place of which the burnt-offering is considerably intensified by the demand of a bullock and a ram for this, the same thing being also indicated by the copious pouring of salt thereon.—For the symbolical meaning of these sacrifices, compare the commentary on Lev. viii.—The consecration of the altar was completed in seven days; and from the eighth day onwards the priests were to offer the regular sacrifices upon it (ver. 27); whereas at the Mosaic consecration of the altar and priests, the constant altar service of the priests was still further inaugurated by a solemn sacrifice on the eighth day (Lev. ix.). Burnt-offerings and peace-offerings are mentioned in ver. 27 *instar omnium* as being the principal and most frequent sacrifices, whilst sin-offerings and meat-offerings are implied therein.

Chap. xliv. *Position of the different Classes of the People in relation to the New Sanctuary.*

With the consecration of the altar of burnt-offering the way is opened for the congregation of Israel to appear in the sanctuary before the Lord, to serve Him with sacrifices. If, however, the use of the new house of God was to be in harmony with the holiness of the God who dwelt therein, it was requisite that still further directions should be given concerning the entering of the people into it, and the character of the servants of both the altar and the sanctuary. These directions follow in the chapter before us,—first, as to the place which the prince was to occupy at the service in the temple (vers. 1–3); secondly, as to the admission of foreigners and the appointment of Levites and priests for the service (vers. 4–16); and lastly, as to the conditions requisite for the administration of the priest's office, and the duties and privileges of that office (vers. 17–31).

Vers. 1–3. THE PLACE OF THE PRINCE IN THE SANCTUARY. —Ver. 1. *And he brought me back by the way to the outer gate of the sanctuary, which looked toward the east; and it was shut.* Ver. 2. *And Jehovah said to me, This gate shall be shut, shall not be opened, and no one shall enter thereby; because Jehovah, the God of Israel, has entered by it, it shall be shut.* Ver. 3. *As for the prince, as prince he shall sit therein, to eat bread before Jehovah; from the way to the porch of the gate shall he go in, and from its way shall he go out.*—From the inner court where Ezekiel had received the measurements of the altar of burnt-offering and the instructions concerning its consecration (ch. xliii. 5 sqq.), he is taken back to the east gate of the outer court, and finds this gate, which formed the principal entrance to the temple, closed. Jehovah explains this fact to him through the angel (וַיֹּאמֶר יְהוָֹה is to be understood according to ch. xliii. 6 and 7) thus: "this gate is to be shut, because Jehovah, the God of Israel, has entered into the temple thereby," as we have already learned from ch. xliii. 2. Only the prince, as prince, was allowed to sit in it for the purpose of holding sacrificial meals there. So far the meaning of the words is clear and indisputable. For there can be no doubt whatever that ver. 3 introduces a more precise statement concerning the closing of the gate; in other words, that the right of sitting in the gate to eat bread before Jehovah, which is conceded to the priest, is intended as an explanation, *resp.* modification and limitation, of the statement וְהָיָה סָגוּר (ver. 2). On the other hand, the more precise definition of the prerogative granted to the prince in ver. 3 is not quite clear, and therefore open to dispute. Such a prerogative is already indicated in the prominence expressly given to the prince, consisting partly in the fact that אֶת־הַנָּשִׂיא is written first in an absolute form, and partly in the expression נָשִׂיא הוּא, which is repeated in the form of a circumstantial clause, "prince is he," equivalent to "because he is prince, he is to sit there." נָשִׂיא is neither the high priest, as many of the older commentators supposed, nor a collective term for the civil authorities of the people of Israel in the Messianic times (Hävernick), but the David who will be prince in Israel at that time, according to ch. xxxiv. 23, 24, and xxxvii. 24. "To eat bread before Jehovah" signifies to hold a sacrificial meal at the place of the divine presence, *i.e.* in the temple court, and is not to be restricted, as Kliefoth supposes, to that sacrificial meal "which was held after and along with the bloodless sacrifices, viz. the *minchoth*, and the shew-breads, and the sweet loaves of the Passover." There is no authority in the usage of the language for this literal interpretation of the expression "to eat bread," for אָכַל לֶחֶם means in general to partake of a meal, compare Gen. xxxi. 54, etc., and especially Ex. xviii. 12, where Jethro "eats bread before God" with Aaron and the elders of Israel, that is to say, joins in a sacrificial meal composed of זְבָחִים or slain-offerings. According to this view, which is the only one supported by usage, the prerogative secured to the נָשִׂיא of the future is not "that of participating in the sacrificial meals (of the priests), which were to be held daily with the *minchoth* and shew-bread, in opposition to the law which prevailed before" (Kliefoth), but simply that of holding his sacrificial meals in the gate, *i.e.* in the porch of the gate, whereas the people were only allowed to hold them in the court, namely, in the vicinity of the sacrificial kitchens.

There is also a difference of opinion concerning the meaning of the second statement in ver. 3: "from the way of the porch of the gate shall he enter in, and thence shall he go out." The suffix in מִדַּרְכּוֹ can only refer to אוּלָם, "from the way from which he came (entered), from this way shall he go out again." Hitzig follows the Rabbins, who understand the passage thus: "as the gate is to remain shut, he must go by the way to the porch which is directed inwardly, toward the court (ch. xl. 9). He must have gone into the outer court through the north or the south gate, and by the way by which he came he also went back again." But Kliefoth argues, in objection to this, that "if the prince was to eat the bread in the porch, the entrance through the south or the north gate would be of no use to him at all; as the gate which could be shut was at that door of the porch which was turned toward the outer court." Moreover, he affirms that it is not at all the meaning of the text that he was to eat the bread in the porch, but that he was to eat it in the gate-building, and he was to come thither מִדֶּרֶךְ אוּלָם הַשַּׁעַר, *i.e.* "from the place which served as a way to the gate porch, that is to say, the walk from the eastern entrance of the gate-building to the front of the porch, and from that was he to go out again." The prince, therefore, was "to go into the gate-building as far as the front of the porch through the eastern entrance, there to eat his bread before Jehovah, and to come out again from thence, so that the gate at the western side of the gate porch still remained shut." But we cannot regard either of these views as correct. There is no firm foundation in the text for Kliefoth's assertion, that he was not to eat the bread in the porch, but in the gate-building. It is true that the porch is not expressly mentioned as the place where the eating was to take place, but simply the gate (בּוֹ); yet the porch belonged to the gate as an integral part of the gate-building; and if דֶּרֶךְ אוּלָם is the way to the porch, or the way leading to the porch, the words, "by the way to the porch shall he enter in," imply clearly enough that he was to go into the porch and to eat bread there. This is also demanded by the circumstances, as the meaning of the words cannot possibly be that the prince was to hold his sacrificial meal upon the threshold of the gate, or in one of the guard-rooms, or in the middle of the gateway; and apart from the porch, there were no other places in the gate-building than those we have named. And again, the statement that the gate on the western side of the gate porch was to be shut, and not that against the eastern wall, is also destitute of proof, as דֶּרֶךְ אוּלָם, the way to the porch, is not equivalent to the way "up to the front of the porch." And if the prince was to hold the sacrificial meal behind the inner gate, which was closed, how was the food when it was prepared to be carried into the gate-building? Through a door of one of the guard-rooms? Such a supposition is hardly reconcilable with the significance of a holy sacrificial meal. In fact, it is a question whether eating in the gate-building with the inner door closed, so that it was not even possible to look toward the sanctuary, in which Jehovah was enthroned, could be called eating לִפְנֵי יְהוָֹה.—Hitzig's explanation of the words is not exposed to any of these difficulties, but it is beset by others. At the outset it is chargeable with improbability, as it is impossible to see any just ground why the prince, if he was to hold the sacrificial meal in the porch of the east gate, should not have been allowed to enter through this gate, but was obliged to take the circuitous route through the south or the north gate. Again, it is irreconcilable with the analogous statements in ch. xlvi. According to ch. xlvi. 1 sqq., the east gate of the inner court was to be shut, namely, during the six working days; but on the Sabbath and on the new moon it was to be opened. Then the prince was to come by the way of the gate porch from without, and during the preparation of his sacrifice by the priests to stand upon the threshold of the gate and worship. This same thing was to take place when the prince desired to offer a freewill offering on any of the week-days. The east gate was to be opened for him to this end; but after the conclusion of the offering of sacrifice it was to be closed again, whereas on the Sabbaths and new moons it was to stand open till the evening (ch. xlvi. 12 compared with ver. 2). It is still further enjoined, that when offering these sacrifices the prince is to enter by the way of the gate porch, and to go out again by the same way (vers. 2 and 8); whereas on the feast days, on which the people appear before Jehovah, every one who comes, the priest along with the rest, is to go in and out through the north or the south gate (vers. 9 and 10). If, therefore, on the feast days, when the people appeared before Jehovah, the prince was to go into the temple in the midst of the people through the north or the south gate to worship, whereas on the Sabbaths and new moons, on which the people were not required to appear before the Lord, so that the prince alone had to bring the offerings for himself and the people, he was to enter by the way of the porch of the east gate, and to go out again by the same, and during the ceremony of offering the sacrifice was to stand upon the threshold of the inner east gate, it is obvious that the going in and out by the way of the porch of the gate was to take place by a different way from that through the north or the south gate. This other way could only be through the east gate, as no fourth gate existed. —The conclusion to which this brings us, so far as the passage before us is concerned, is that the shutting of the east gate of the outer court was to be the rule, but that there were certain exceptions which are not fully explained till ch. xlvi., though they are hinted at in the chapter before us in the directions given there, that the prince was to hold the sacrificial meal in this gate.—The outer east gate, which was probably the one chiefly used by the people when appearing before the Lord in the earlier temple, both for going in and coming out, is to be shut in the new temple, and not to be made use of by the people for either entrance or exit, because the glory of the Lord entered into the temple thereby. This reason is of course not to be understood in the way suggested by the Rabbins, namely, that the departure of the Shechinah from the temple was to be prevented by the closing of the gate; but the thought is this:

because this gateway had been rendered holy through the entrance of the Shechinah into the temple thereby, it was not to remain open to the people, so as to be desecrated, but was to be kept perpetually holy. This keeping holy was not prejudiced in any way by the fact that the prince held the sacrificial meal in the gate, and also entered the court through this gateway for the purpose of offering his sacrifice, which was made ready by the priests before the inner gate, and then was present at the offering of the sacrifice upon the altar, standing upon the threshold of the inner gate-building. דֶּרֶךְ אוּלָם הַשַּׁעַר is therefore the way which led from the outer flight of steps across the threshold past the guard-rooms to the gate porch at the inner end of the gate-building. By this way the priest was to go into the gate opened for him, and hold the sacrificial meal therein, namely, in the porch of this gate. That the offering of the sacrifice necessarily preceded the meal is assumed as self-evident, and the law of sacrifice in ch. xlvi. first prescribes the manner in which the prince was to behave when offering the sacrifice, and how near to the altar he was to be allowed to go.

Vers. 4–16. The Position of Foreigners, Levites, and Priests in relation to the Temple and the Temple Service.—The further precepts concerning the approach to the sanctuary, and the worship to be presented there, are introduced with a fresh exhortation to observe with exactness all the statutes and laws, in order that the desecration of the sanctuary which had formerly taken place might not be repeated, and are delivered to the prophet at the north gate in front of the manifestation of the glory of God (vers. 4–8).—Ver. 4. *And he brought me by the way of the north gate to the front of the house; and I looked, and behold the glory of Jehovah filled the house of Jehovah, and I fell down upon my face.* Ver. 5. *And Jehovah said to me, Son of man, direct thy heart and see with thine eyes and hear with thine ears all that I say to thee with regard to all the statutes of the house of Jehovah and all its laws, and direct thy heart to the entering into the house through all the exits of the house,* Ver. 6. *And say to the rebellious one, to the family of Israel, Thus saith the Lord Jehovah, Let it be sufficient for you, of all your abominations, O house of Israel,* Ver. 7. *In that ye brought in foreigners, uncircumcised in heart and uncircumcised in flesh, to be in my sanctuary, to desecrate it, my house, when ye offered my food, fat and blood, and so they broke my covenant to all your abominations,* Ver. 8. *And so ye did not keep the charge of my holy things, but made them keepers of my charge for you in my sanctuary.*—From the outer gate to which Ezekiel had been taken, simply that he might be instructed concerning the entering thereby, he is once more conducted, after this has been done, by the way of the north gate to the front of the temple house, to receive the further directions there for the performance of the worship of God in the new sanctuary. The question, whether we are to understand by the north gate that of the outer or that of the inner court, cannot be answered with certainty. Hitzig has decided in favour of the latter, Kliefoth in favour of the former. The place to which he is conducted is אֶל־פְּנֵי הַבַּיִת, *ad faciem domus*, before the temple house, so that he had it before his eyes, *i.e.* was able to see it. As the gateway of the inner court was eight steps, about four cubits, higher than the outer court gate, this was hardly possible if he stood at or within the latter. הַבַּיִת, *i.e.* the temple house, could only be distinctly seen from the inner north gate. And the remark that it is more natural to think of the outer north gate, because the next thing said to the prophet has reference to the question who is to go into and out of the sanctuary, has not much force, as the instructions do not refer to the going in and out alone, but chiefly to the charge of Jehovah, *i.e.* to the maintenance of divine worship.—At the fresh standing-place the glory of the Lord, which filled the temple, met the sight of the prophet again, so that he fell down and worshipped once more (cf. ch. xliii. 3, 5). This remark is not intended "to indicate that now, after the preliminary observations in ch. xliii. 13–xliv. 3, the true *thorah* commences" (Kliefoth), but to show the unapproachable glory and holiness of the new temple. For ver. 5, see ch. xl. 4, xliii. 11, 12. In ver. 6 אֶל־מֶרִי is placed at the head in a substantive form for the sake of emphasis, and בֵּית־יִשְׂרָאֵל is appended in the form of an apposition. For the fact itself, see ch. ii. 8. רַב־לָכֶם followed by מִן, a sufficiency of anything, as in Ex. ix. 28, 1 Kings xii. 28, is equivalent to "there is enough for you to desist from it." The תּוֹעֵבוֹת, from which they are to desist, are more precisely defined in ver. 6. They consisted in the fact that the Israelites admitted foreigners, heathen, uncircumcised in heart and flesh, into the sanctuary, to desecrate it during the offering of sacrifice. It is not expressly stated, indeed, that they admitted uncircumcised heathen to the offering of sacrifice, but this is implied in what is affirmed. The offering of sacrifice in the temple of Jehovah is not only permitted in the Mosaic law to foreigners living in Israel, but to some extent prescribed (Lev. xvii. 10, 12; Num. xv. 13 sqq.). It was only in the paschal meal that no בֶּן נֵכָר' was allowed to participate (Ex. xii. 43). To do this, he must first of all be circumcised (ver. 44). Solomon accordingly prays to the Lord in his temple-prayer that He will also hearken to the prayer of the foreigner, who may come from a distant land for the Lord's name sake to worship in His house (1 Kings viii. 41 sqq.). The reproof in the verse before us is apparently at variance with this. Raschi would therefore understand by בְּנֵי־נֵכָר, Israelites who had fallen into heathen idolatry. Rosenmüller, on the other hand, is of opinion that the Israelites were blamed because they had accepted *victimas et libamina* from the heathen, and offered them in the temple, which had been prohibited in Lev. xxv. 22. Hävernick understands by the sons of the foreigner, Levites who had become apostates from Jehovah, and were therefore placed by Ezekiel on a par with the idolatrous sons of the foreigner. And lastly, Hitzig imagines that they were foreign traders, who had been admitted within the sacred precincts as sellers of sacrificial animals, incense, and so forth. All these are alike arbitrary and erroneous. The apparent discrepancy vanishes, if we consider the more precise definition of בְּנֵי נֵכָר, viz. "uncircumcised in heart and flesh." Their being uncircumcised in heart is placed first, for the purpose of characterizing the foreigners as godless heathen, who were destitute not only of the uncircumcision of their flesh, but also of that of the heart, *i.e.* of piety of heart, which Solomon mentions in his prayer as the motive for the coming of distant strangers to the temple. By the admission of such foreigners as these, who had no fear of God at all, into the temple during the sacrificial worship, Israel had defiled the sanctuary. אֶת־בֵּיתִי is in apposition to the suffix to חַלְּלוֹ. The food of Jehovah (לַחְמִי) is sacrifice, according to Lev. iii. 11, xxi. 6, etc., and is therefore explained by "fat and blood." וַיָּפֵרוּ, which the LXX. changed in an arbitrary manner into the second person, refers to the "foreigners," the heathen. By their treading the temple in their ungodliness they broke the covenant of the Lord with His people, who allowed this desecration of His sanctuary. אֶל כָּל־תּוֹעֲבוֹת', in addition to all your abominations. How grievous a sin was involved in this is stated in ver. 8. The people of Israel, by their unrighteous admission of godless heathen into the temple, not only failed to show the proper reverence for the holy things of the Lord, but even made these heathen, so to speak, servants of God for themselves in His sanctuary. These last words are not to be understood literally, but spiritually. Allowing them to tread the temple is regarded as equivalent to appointing them to take charge of the worship in the temple. For שָׁמַר מִשְׁמַרְתִּי', see Lev. xviii. 30, xxii. 9, and the commentary on Lev. viii. 35.

The Lord would guard against such desecration of His sanctuary in the future. To this end the following precepts concerning the worship in the new temple are given.—Ver. 9. *Thus saith the Lord Jehovah, No foreigner, uncircumcised in heart and uncircumcised in flesh, shall come into my sanctuary, of all the foreigners that are in the midst of the sons of Israel;* Ver. 10. *But even the Levites, who have gone away from me in the wandering of Israel, which wandered away from me after its idols, they shall bear their guilt.* Ver. 11. *They shall be servants in my sanctuary, as guards at the gates of the house and serving in the house; they shall slay the burnt-offering and the slain-offering for the people, and shall stand before it to serve them.* Ver. 12. *Because they served them before their idols, and became to the house of Israel a stumbling-block to guilt, therefore I have lifted my hand against them, is the saying of the Lord Jehovah, that they should bear their guilt.* Ver. 13. *They shall not draw near to me to serve me as priests, and to draw near to all my holy things, to the most holy, but shall bear their disgrace and all their abominations which they have done.* Ver. 14. *And so will I make them guards of the charge of the house with regard to all its service, and to all that is performed therein.* Ver. 15. *But the priests of the tribe of Levi, the sons of Zadok, who have kept the charge of my sanctuary on the wandering of the sons of Israel from me, they shall draw near to me to serve me, and stand before me, offer to me fat and blood, is the saying of the Lord Jehovah.* Ver. 16. *They shall come into my sanctuary, and they draw near to my table to serve me, and shall keep my charge.* —In order that all desecration may be kept at a distance from the new sanctuary, foreigners uncircumcised in heart and flesh are not to be admitted into it; and even of the Levites appointed for the service of the sanctuary according to the Mosaic law, all who took part in the falling away of the people into idolatry are to be excluded from investiture with the priests' office as a punishment for their departure from the Lord, and only to be allowed to perform subordinate duties in connection with the worship of God. On the other hand, the descendants of Zadok, who kept themselves free from all straying into idolatry, are to perform the specifically priestly service at the altar and in the sanctuary, and they alone. The meaning and design of the command, to shut out the foreigners uncircumcised in heart from all access to the sanctuary, are not that the intermediate position and class of foreigners living in Israel should henceforth be abolished (Kliefoth); for this would be at variance with ch. xlvii. 22 and 23, according to which the foreigners (גֵּרִים) were to receive a possession of their own in the fresh distribution of the land, which not only presupposes their continuance within the congregation of Israel, but also secures it for the time to come. The meaning is rather this: No heathen uncircumcised in heart, *i.e.* estranged in life from God, shall have access to the altar in the new sanctuary. The emphasis of the prohibition lies here, as in ver. 7, upon their being uncircumcised in heart; and the reason for the exclusion of foreigners consists not so much in the foreskin of the flesh as in the spiritual foreskin, so that not only the uncircumcised heathen, but also Israelites who were circumcised in flesh, were to keep at a distance from the sanctuary if they failed to possess circumcision of heart. The לְ before כָּל־בֶּן נ׳ serves the purpose of comprehension, as in Gen. ix. 10, Lev. xi. 42, etc. (compare *Ewald,* § 310*a*). Not only are foreigners who are estranged from God to be prevented from coming into the sanctuary, but even the Levites, who fell into idolatry at the time of the apostasy of the Israelites, are to bear their guilt, *i.e.* are to be punished for it by exclusion from the rights of the priesthood. This is the connection between the tenth verse and the ninth, indicated by כִּי אִם, which derives its meaning, *truly* (*imo*), *yea even*, from this connection, as in Isa. xxxiii. 21. הַלְוִיִּם are not the Levites here as distinguished from the priests (Aaronites), but all the descendants of Levi, including the Aaronites chosen for the priests' office, to whom what is to be said concerning the Levites chiefly applies. The division of the Levites into such as are excluded from the service and office of priests (כַּהֵן, ver. 13) on account of their former straying into idolatry, and the sons of Zadok, who kept aloof from that wandering, and therefore are to be the only persons allowed to administer the priests' office for the future, shows very clearly that the threat "they shall bear their guilt" does not apply to the common Levites, but to the Levitical priests. They are to be degraded to the performance of the inferior duties in the temple and at divine worship. The guilt with which they are charged is that they forsook Jehovah when the people strayed into idolatry. Forsaking Jehovah involves both passive and active participation in idolatry (cf. Jer. ii. 5). This wandering of the Israelites from Jehovah took place during the whole time that the tabernacle and Solomon's temple were in existence, though at different periods and with varying force and extent. Bearing the guilt is more minutely defined in vers. 11–13. The Levitical priests who have forsaken the Lord are to lose the dignity and rights of the priesthood; they are not, indeed, to be entirely deprived of the prerogative conferred upon the tribe of Levi by virtue of its election to the service of the sanctuary in the place of the first-born of the whole nation, but henceforth they are merely to be employed in the performance of the lower duties, as guards at the gates of the temple, and as servants of the people at the sacrificial worship, when they are to slaughter the animals for the people, which every one who offered sacrifice was also able to do for himself. Because they have already served the people before their idols, *i.e.* have helped them in their idolatry, they shall also serve the people in time to come in the worship of God, though not as priests, but simply in non-priestly occupations. The words הֵמָּה יַעַמְדוּ וגו' are taken from Num. xvi. 9, and the suffixes in לִפְנֵיהֶם and לְשָׁרְתָם refer to עָם. מִכְשׁוֹל עָוֹן, as in ch. vii. 19, xiv. 3, xviii. 30. נָשָׂא יָד, not to raise the arm to smite, but to lift up the hand to swear, as in ch. xx. 5, 6, etc. לָגֶשֶׁת עַל כָּל־קָדָשַׁי, to draw near to all my holy things. קֳדָשִׁים are not the rooms in the sanctuary, but those portions of the sacrifices which were sacred to the Lord. They are not to touch these, *i.e.* neither to sprinkle blood nor to burn the portions of fat upon the altar, or perform anything connected therewith. This explanation is required by the apposition אֶל־קָדְשֵׁי הַקֳּדָשִׁים, which (in the plural) does not mean the most holy place at the hinder part of the temple, but the most holy sacrificial gifts (cf. ch. xlii. 13). נָשָׂא כְלִמָּה, as in ch. xvi. 52. In ver. 14 it is once more stated in a comprehensive manner in what the bearing of the guilt and shame was to consist: God would make them keepers of the temple with regard to the inferior acts of service. The general expression שָׁמַר מִשְׁמֶרֶת הַבַּיִת, which signifies the temple service universally, receives its restriction to the inferior acts of service from לְכֹל עֲבֹדָתוֹ וגו׳, which is used in Num. iii. 26, iv. 23, 30, 32, 39, 47, for the heavy duties performed by the Merarites and Gershonites, in distinction from the עֲבֹדָה of the Kohathites, which consisted in שָׁמַר מִשְׁמֶרֶת הַקֹּדֶשׁ (Num. iii. 28) and עֲשׂוֹת מְלָאכָה בְּאֹהֶל מוֹעֵד (Num. iv. 3). The priestly service at the altar and in the sanctuary, on the other hand, was to be performed by the sons of Zadok alone, because when the people went astray they kept the charge of the sanctuary, *i.e.* performed the duties of the priestly office with fidelity. *Zadok* was the son of Ahitub, of the line of Eleazar (1 Chron. v. 34, vi. 37, 38), who remained faithful to King David at the rebellion of Absalom (2 Sam. xv. 24 sqq.), and also anointed Solomon as king in opposition to Adonijah the pretender (1 Kings i. 32 sqq.); whereas the high priest Abiathar, of the line of Ithamar, took part with Adonijah (1 Kings i. 7, 25), and was deposed from his office by Solomon in consequence, so that now the high-priesthood was in the sole possession of Zadok and his descendants (1 Kings ii. 26, 27, and 35). From this attitude of Zadok toward David, the prince given by the Lord to His people, it may be seen at once that he not only kept aloof from the wandering of the people, but offered a decided opposition thereto, and attended to his office in a manner that was well-pleasing to God. As he received the high-priesthood from Solomon in the place of Abiathar for this fidelity of his, so shall his descendants only be invested with the priestly office in the new temple. For the correct explanation of the words in these verses, however, we must pay particular regard to the clause, "who have kept the charge of my sanctuary." This implies, for example, that lineal descent from Zadok alone was not sufficient, but that fidelity in the service of the Lord must also be added as an indispensable requisite. In vers. 15*b* and 16 the priestly service is described according to its principal functions at the altar of burnt-offering, and in the holy place at the altar of incense. שֻׁלְחָנִי is the altar of incense (see ch. xli. 22).

Vers. 17–31. Requisites for the Administration of the Priests' Office, and the Obligations and Privileges of that Office.—Ver. 17. *And it shall come to pass, when they go to the gates of the inner court, they shall put on linen clothes, and no wool shall lie upon them, when they serve in the gates of the inner court and serve toward the house.* Ver. 18. *Linen turbans shall be upon their head, and linen drawers upon their hips: they shall not gird themselves in sweat.* Ver. 19. *And when they go out into the outer court, into the outer court to the people, they shall take off their clothes in which they have ministered, and put them in the holy cells, and put on other clothes, that they may not sanctify the people with their clothes.* Ver. 20. *And they shall not shave their head bald, nor let their hair grow freely; they shall cut the hair of their head.* Ver. 21. *And they shall not drink wine, no priest, when they go into the inner court.* Ver. 22. *And a widow and a divorced woman they shall not take as wives, but virgins of the seed of the house of Israel, and the widow who has become the widow of a priest they may take.* Ver. 23. *And they shall teach my people, make known to them the difference between holy and common, and between unclean and clean.* Ver. 24. *And they shall stand to judge concerning disputes; and they shall observe my laws and my statutes at all my feasts, and sanctify my Sabbaths.* Ver. 25. *And one shall not go to any corpse of a man to defile himself; only for father and mother, for son and daughter, for brother, for sister who had no husband, may they defile themselves.* Ver. 26. *And after his purification shall they reckon seven days more to him;* Ver. 27. *And on the day when he comes to the holy place, into the inner court, to serve in the holy place, he shall offer his sin-offering, is the saying of the Lord Jehovah.*—Ver. 28. *And so shall it be with their inheritance, that I am their inheritance, ye shall not give them a possession in Israel: I am their possession.* Ver. 29. *The meat-offering, and the sin-offering, and the trespass-offering, these shall they eat, and everything banned in Israel shall belong to them.* Ver. 30. *And the firstlings of all the first-fruits of everything, and every heave-offering of everything, of all your heave-offerings, shall belong to the priests; and the firstlings of all your ground meal shall ye give to the priest, that a blessing may come down upon thy house.* Ver. 31. *No carrion nor anything torn in pieces of fowl and of beast shall the priests eat.*—To the directions, who are to perform the service in the new temple, there are appended corresponding instructions concerning the bodily condition in which this service is to be performed, as the bodily condition shadows forth the state of the soul, or the spiritual constitution of the servants of God. The dress prescribed in Ex. xxviii. for the priests to wear during the holy service had this signification. The same rule is here presupposed as still in force; and it is simply renewed and partially emphasized by the enumeration of some of the leading points. At the service at the altar and in the holy place the priests are to wear linen clothes, and, after the performance of the service, they are to take them off again when they go into the outer court (vers. 17–19). In the Mosaic law, שֵׁשׁ, white byssus, or בַּד, white linen, is mentioned as the material used for the priests' clothing (Ex. xxviii. 39, 42); here the material is more distinctly designated as פִּשְׁתִּים, flax linen; and צֶמֶר, animal wool, is expressly forbidden, the motive being assigned for this regulation, namely, that the priest is not to cause himself to sweat by wearing woollen clothing. Sweat produces uncleanness; and the priest, by keeping his body clean, is to show even outwardly that he is clean and blameless. With regard to the putting on and off of the official clothes, the new *thorah* accords with the Mosaic. For we cannot agree with Kliefoth, who detects a deviation in the fact that, according to Ex. xxviii. 43, the priests were to wear the official clothes only when they entered the tabernacle and when approaching the altar, and, according to Lev. vi. 4, xvi. 23, were to take them off when the service was ended; whereas, according to ver. 17 of the chapter before us, they were to put them on as soon as they entered the inner court, and were never to come before the people in the official costume. If, according to the Mosaic law, the priests were to go before the altar of burnt-offering in the court in their holy official dress, and not otherwise, they must have put on this dress on entering the court; for they could not wait till they were in front of the altar before they changed their clothes. For the expression צֵאת אֶל הָעָם does not imply that, according to Ezekiel, they were never to appear in the presence of the people in their official costume, as it does not mean "come before the people," but "go out to the people," or "walk among the people;" nor is this involved in the words וְלֹא יְקַדְּשׁוּ וגו', they shall not sanctify the people in their clothes (by their clothes). The latter by no means affirms that they are to sanctify the people by intercourse with them, but are not to do this in official costume; the meaning is simply that they are not to move among the people in the outer court while wearing their official clothes, that they may not sanctify them by their holy clothes. This sanctification cannot be understood in any other way than as analogous to the rule laid down in the law, that touching most holy sacrificial flesh would sanctify (Lev. vi. 11, 20), which Ezekiel repeats in ch. xlvi. 20, and which does not stand in anything like an isolated position in the law, but is also affirmed in Ex. xxix. 37 and xxx. 29 of the altar of burnt-offering and the vessels of the sanctuary. The same thing which applied to these vessels —namely, that their holiness passed from them to any one who touched them—is here predicated of the holy dresses of the priests; and the moving of the priests among the people in their holy clothes is forbidden, because such holiness, acquired by contact with holy objects, imposed upon the person to whom it had passed the obligation to guard against all defilement (Lev. xxi. 1-8), which the people could not avoid in the ordinary relations of life, and thus a weakening or abolition of the distinction between things holy and common would inevitably have ensued. לִשְׁכוֹת הַקֹּדֶשׁ are the holy cell-buildings described in ch. xlii. 1–14.—To the clothing there is simply appended in ver. 20 the direction concerning the hair of the head, the natural covering of the head, in relation to which excess on either side is prohibited, either shaving the head bald or wearing the hair uncut. Both of these were forbidden to the priests in the law: shaving in Lev. xxi. 5, and letting the hair grow freely in Lev. x. 6; and the latter was simply imposed upon the Nazarites for the period of their vow (Num. vi. 5). כָּסַם only occurs here; but its meaning, to cut the hair, is obvious from the context.—Ver. 21. The prohibition of the drinking of wine when performing service agrees with Lev. x. 9; on the other hand, the instructions concerning the choice of wives are sharpened in ver. 22, as that which only applied to the high priest in the law is here extended to all the priests. In fact, Ezekiel throughout makes no distinction between the high priest and the common priests. In Lev. xxi. 14, marrying a widow is only forbidden to the high priest, who was to marry a virgin of his own people, whereas no such restriction is laid down for the ordinary priests. Here, on the other hand, marrying a widow is forbidden to all the priests, marriage with the widow of a priest being the only one allowed. מִכֹּהֵן belongs to תִּהְיֶה אַלְמָנָה, who has become the widow of a priest.[1]

[1] The Rabbins (Targ. Talm. and Masor. according to their accentuation) have endeavoured to obliterate this distinction, by applying the first hemistich to the high priest alone, and explaining the second thus: "The widow, who is really a widow, the priest may take," interpreting מִכֹּהֵן by

In vers. 23 and 24 the general official duties of the priests are mentioned, viz. to teach the people, and to instruct them concerning the difference between the holy and the unholy, the clean and the unclean, as in Lev. x. 10 (cf. Deut. xxxiii. 10 and Ezek. xxii. 26); also to administer justice in questions in dispute according to the rights of God,—a duty which had already been committed to the priests in its highest form in Deut. xvii. 8 sqq., xix. 17, and xxi. 5. עַל רִיב, concerning, in the case of, matters in dispute. עָמַד לִשְׁפֹּט, to stand to judge, *i.e.* to appear or act as judge (compare הֶעֱמִיד שֹׁפְטִים, to appoint or institute judges, in 2 Chron. xix. 5). The *Keri* לְמִשְׁפָּט is a needless emendation after 2 Chron. xix. 8. The *Chetib* וּשְׁפָטֻהוּ, on the other hand, is a copyist's error for יִשְׁפְּטֻהוּ. Lastly, at all the feasts they are to observe the laws and statutes of Jehovah, that is to say, to perform all the priestly duties binding upon them at the feasts, and to sanctify the Sabbaths, not merely by offering the Sabbath sacrifices, but also by maintaining the Sabbath rest (cf. Lev. xxiii. 3).—In vers. 25–27 there follow regulations concerning defilement from the dead, and its removal. Ver. 25 is a simple repetition of Lev. xxi. 1–3. But the instructions concerning purification from defilement from the dead are sharpened, inasmuch as not only is the purification prescribed by the law (Num. xix. 1 sqq.), and which lasted seven days, required (this is meant by טָהֳרָתוֹ), but a further period of seven days is appointed after these, at the expiration of which the presentation of a sin-offering is demanded before the service in the sanctuary can be resumed. By this demand for a heightened purification, the approach to a corpse permitted to the priests, which was prohibited to the high priest in the Mosaic law, even in the case of father and mother (Lev. xxi. 11), is tolerably equalized.

quidam sacerdotum, or *aliqui ex ordine sacerdotali*, or *ceteri sacerdotes.* But this is contrary to the usage of the language, as מִכֹּהֵן cannot possibly be understood in a partitive sense in this passage, where the priests generally are spoken of, and the plural יִקָּחוּ follows.

For these duties and obligations of service the priests are to receive corresponding emoluments. These are treated of in vers. 28–31. They are not, indeed, to receive any share of the land as their property in time to come any more than in former times; but in the place of this Jehovah will be their property and possession, and give them the necessary room for their dwellings from His own property in the land (ch. xlv. 4), and let them draw their maintenance from His altar (vers. 29 and 30). The promise that Jehovah will be the נַחֲלָה and אֲחֻזָּה of the priests is a simple repetition of the regulation in the law (Num. xviii. 20; Deut. xviii. 1, x. 9). So far as the construction in ver. 28*a* is concerned, the words אֲנִי נַחֲלָתָם are really the subject to וְהָיְתָה לָהֶם לנ׳, which we are obliged to render obliquely, "the inheritance for them shall be, I am their inheritance." For the proposal of Hitzig to take the words from אֲנִי נַחֲלָתָם to the close of the verse as a parenthesis, and to regard הַמִּנְחָה וגו׳ in ver. 29*a* as the subject to וְהָיְתָה וגו׳, is untenable, not only on account of the great harshness which such a parenthesis would involve, but principally because these portions of the sacrifices and heave-offerings which belonged to the priest were not a נַחֲלָה, and are never designated as נַחֲלָה, inheritance, *i.e.* property in land. Ver. 28 treats of the property in land, which God assigned to the Levites and priests under the Mosaic economy, by appointing them towns to dwell in, with meadows for the feeding of their cattle, within the territory of the other tribes, but would assign to them in future from the heave-offering set apart from the land for the sanctuary (ch. xlv. 4). It is not till vers. 29 and 30 that the means of support for the priests are spoken of. They are to be supported from the sacrifices and the tithes and first-fruits which Israel has to pay to Jehovah as the lord of the land, and which He transfers to His servants the priests. For the priests' share of the meat-offering, sin-offering, and trespass-offering, see Lev. ii. 3, vi. 9, 11, 19, vii. 6, 7; for that which is put under the ban, Lev. xxvii. 21; for the first-fruits, Ex. xxiii. 19, xxxiv. 26, Deut. xviii. 4, Num. xviii. 13; for the

תְּרוּמוֹת, Num. xv. 19, xviii. 19; for the רֵאשִׁית עֲרִיסוֹת, Num. xv. 20, 21. In לְהָנִיחַ וגו׳, "to cause a blessing to rest upon thy house," the individual Israelite is addressed. For the fact itself, see Mal. iii. 10.—To the enumeration of the means of support there is appended in ver. 31 an emphatic repetition of the command in Lev. xxii. 8, not to eat of any dead thing (*i.e.* anything that has died a natural death), or anything torn to pieces, either of birds or beasts, on account of its defiling (Lev. xvii. 15).

Chap. xlv. 1–17. *The Holy Heave of the Land and the Heave-offerings of the People.*

The determination of the means of support for the priesthood is followed still further by an explanation of the manner in which Jehovah will be their inheritance and possession; in other words, assign to the priests and Levites that portion of the land which was requisite for their abode. This is to be done by His causing a definite tract of land to be set apart for Himself, for the sanctuary, and for His servants, and for the capital, when the country is distributed among the tribes of Israel (vers. 1–8). On both sides of this domain the prince is also to receive a possession in land, to guard against all exaction on the part of the princes in time to come. And everywhere unrighteousness is to cease, just weight and measure are to be observed (vers. 9–12), and the people are to pay certain heave-offerings to provide for the sacrifices binding upon the prince (vers. 13–17).

Vers. 1–8. The Holy Heave from the Land.—Ver. 1. *And when ye divide the land by lot for an inheritance, ye shall lift a heave for Jehovah as a holy (portion) from the land; five and twenty thousand the length, and the breadth ten (? twenty) thousand. It shall be holy in all its circumference round about.* Ver. 2. *Of this five hundred shall belong to the Holy by five hundred square round about, and fifty cubits open space thereto round about.* Ver. 3. *And from this measured space thou shalt measure a length of five and twenty thousand, and a breadth of ten thousand, and in this shall be the sanctuary, a holy of holies.* Ver. 4. *A holy (portion) of the land shall this be; to the priests, the servants of the sanctuary, shall it belong who draw near to serve Jehovah, and it shall be to them the place for houses and a sanctuary for the sanctuary.* Ver. 5. *And five and twenty thousand in length and ten thousand in breadth shall belong to the Levites, the servants of the house, for a possession to them as gates to dwell in.* Ver. 6. *And as a possession for the city, ye shall give five thousand in breadth and five and twenty thousand in length, parallel to the holy heave; it shall belong to the whole house of Israel.* Ver. 7. *And to the prince (ye shall give) on both sides of the holy heave and of the possession of the city, along the holy heave and along the possession of the city, on the west side westwards and on the east side eastwards, and in length parallel to one of the tribe-portions, from the western border to the eastern border.* Ver. 8. *It shall belong to him as land, as a possession in Israel; and my princes shall no more oppress my people, but shall leave the land to the house of Israel according to its tribes.*—The domain to be first of all set apart from the land at the time of its distribution among the tribes is called תְּרוּמָה, *heave,* not in the general sense of the lifting or taking of a portion from the whole, but as a portion lifted or taken by a person from his property as an offering for God; for תְּרוּמָה comes from הֵרִים, which signifies in the case of the *minchah* the lifting of a portion which was burned upon the altar as אַזְכָּרָה for Jehovah (see the comm. on Lev. ii. 9). Consequently everything that was offered by the Israelites, either voluntarily or in consequence of a precept from the Lord for the erection and maintenance of the sanctuary and its servants, was called תְּרוּמָה (see Ex. xxv. 2 sqq., xxx. 15; Lev. vii. 14; Num. xv. 19, etc.). Only the principal instructions concerning the heave from the land are given here, and these are repeated in ch. xlviii. 8–22, in the section concerning the division of the land, and to some extent expanded there. The introductory words, "when ye divide the land by lot for an inheritance," point to this. (See the map on Plate IV.) הִפִּיל, *sc.* גּוֹרָל (Prov. i. 14), to cast the lot, to divide by lot, as in Josh. xiii. 6. Then shall ye lift, set apart, a heave for Jehovah as a holy (portion) from the land. מִן הָאָרֶץ is to be closely connected with קֹדֶשׁ, as shown by ver. 4. In the numbers mentioned the measure to be employed is not given. But it is obvious that cubits are not meant, as Böttcher, Hitzig, and others assume, but rods; partly from a comparison of ver. 2 with ch. xlii. 16, where the space of the sanctuary, which is given here as 500 by 500 square, is described as five hundred rods on every side; and partly also from the fact that the open space around the sanctuary is fixed at fifty cubits, and in this case אַמָּה is added, because rods are not to be understood there as in connection with the other numbers. The correctness of this view, which we meet with in Jerome and Raschi, cannot be overthrown by appealing to the excessive magnitude of a τέμενος of twenty-five thousand rods in length and ten thousand rods in breadth; for it will be seen in ch. xlviii. that the measurements given answer to the circumstances in rods, but not in cubits. The אֹרֶךְ before and after the number is pleonastic: "as for the length, twenty-five thousand rods in length." Length here is the measurement from east to west, and breadth from north to south, as we may clearly see from ch. xlviii. 10. No regard, therefore, is paid to the natural length and breadth of the land; and the greater extent of the portions to be measured is designated as length, the smaller as breadth. The expression עֲשָׂרָה אֶלֶף is a remarkable one, as עֲשֶׂרֶת אֲלָפִים is constantly used, not only in vers. 3 and 5, but also in ch. xlviii. 9, 10, 13, 18. The LXX. have εἴκοσι χιλιάδας, twenty thousand breadth. This reading appears more correct than the Masoretic, as it is demanded by vers. 3 and 5. For according to ver. 3, of the portion measured in ver. 1 twenty-five thousand rods in length and ten thousand in breadth were to be measured for the sanctuary and for the priests' land; and according to ver. 5, the Levites were also to receive twenty-five thousand rods in length and ten thousand in breadth for a possession. The first clause of ver. 3 is unintelligible if the breadth of the holy *terumah* is given in ver. 1 as only ten thousand rods, inasmuch as one cannot measure off from an area of twenty-five thousand rods in length and ten thousand rods in breadth another space of the same length and breadth. Moreover, ver. 1 requires the reading עֶשְׂרִים אֶלֶף, as the "holy *terumah*" is not only the portion set apart for the sanctuary and the priests' land, but also that which was set apart for the Levites. According to ch. xlviii. 14, this was also "holy to Jehovah;" whereas the portion measured off for the city was "common" (ch. xlviii. 15). This is borne out by the fact that in the chapter before us the domain appointed for the city is distinguished from the land of the priests and Levites by the verb תִּתְּנוּ (ver. 6), whilst the description of the size of the Levites' land in ver. 5 is closely connected with that of the land of the priests; and further, that in ver. 7, in the description of the land of the prince, reference is made only to the holy *terumah* and the possession of the city, from which it also follows that the land of the Levites is included in the holy *terumah*. Consequently ver. 1 treats of the whole of the תְּרוּמַת קֹדֶשׁ, *i.e.* the land of the priests and Levites, which was twenty-five thousand rods long and twenty thousand rods broad. This is designated in the last clause of the verse as a holy (portion) in its entire circumference, and then divided into two domains in vers. 2 and 3.—Ver. 2. Of this (מִזֶּה, of the area measured in ver. 1) there shall come, or belong, to the holy, *i.e.* to the holy temple domain, five hundred rods square, namely, the domain measured in ch. xlii. 15–20 round about the temple, for a separation between holy and common; and round this domain there is to be a מִגְרָשׁ, *i.e.* an open space of fifty cubits on every side, that the dwellings of the priests may not be built too near to the holy square of the temple building.—Ver. 3. הַמִּדָּה הַזֹּאת, this measure (*i.e.* this measured piece of land), also points back to ver. 1, and מִן cannot be taken in any other sense than in מִדָּה (ver. 2). From the whole tract of land measured in ver. 1 a portion is to be measured off twenty-five thousand rods in length and ten thousand rods in breadth, in which the sanctuary, *i.e.* the temple with its courts, is to stand as a holy of holies. This domain, in the midst of which is the temple, is to belong to the priests, as the sanctified portion of the land, as the place or space for their houses, and is to be a sanctuary for the sanctuary, *i.e.* for the temple. Ver. 5. A portion equally large is to be measured off to the Levites, as the temple servants, for their possession. The *Keri* יִהְיֶה is formed after the וְהָיָה of ver. 4, and the *Chetib* יִהְיֶה is indisputably correct. There is great difficulty in the last words of this verse, עֶשְׂרִים לְשָׁכֹת, "for a possession to them twenty cells;" for which the LXX. give *αὐτοῖς εἰς κατάσχεσιν πόλεις τοῦ κατοικεῖν*, and which they have therefore read, or for which they have substituted by conjecture, עָרִים לָשֶׁבֶת. We cannot, in fact, obtain from the עֶשְׂרִים לְשָׁכֹת of the Masoretic text any meaning that will harmonize with the context, even if we render the words, as Rosenmüller does, in opposition to the grammar, *cum viginti cubiculis*, and understand by לְשָׁכֹת capacious cell-buildings. For we neither expect to find in this connection a description of the number and character of the buildings in which the Levites lived, nor can any reason be imagined why the Levites, with a domain of twenty-five thousand rods in length and ten thousand rods in breadth assigned to them, should live together in twenty cell-buildings. Still less can we think of the "twenty cells" as having any connection with the thirty cells in the outer court near to the gate-buildings (ch. xl. 17, 18), as these temple cells, even though they were appointed for the Levites during their service in the temple, were not connected in any way with the holy *terumah* spoken of here. Hävernick's remark, that "the prophet has in his eye the priests' cells in the sanctuary,—and the dwellings of the Levites during their service, which were only on the outside of the sanctuary, were to correspond to these," is not indicated in the slightest degree by the words, but is a mere conjecture. There is no other course open, therefore, than to acknowledge a corruption of the text, and either to alter עשׂרים לשכת into לְעָרִים לָשֶׁבֶת, as Hitzig proposes (cf. Num. xxxv. 2, 3; Josh. xxi. 2), or to take עשׂרים as a mistake for שְׁעָרִים: "for a possession to them as gates to dwell in," according to the frequent use of שְׁעָרִים, gates, for עָרִים, cities, *e.g.* in what was almost a standing phrase, "the Levite who is in thy gates" (=cities; Deut. xii. 18, xiv. 27, xvi. 11; cf. Ex. xx. 10; Deut. v. 14, etc.). In that case the faulty reading would have arisen from the transposition of עש into שע, and the change of ב into כ.

Beside the holy *terumah* for sanctuary, priests, and Levites, they are also (ver. 6) to give a tract of twenty-five thousand rods in length and five thousand rods in breadth as the property of the city (*i.e.* of the capital). לְעֻמַּת: parallel to the holy heave, *i.e.* running by the longer side of it. This portion of land, which was set apart for the city, was to belong to all Israel, and not to any single tribe. The more precise directions concerning this, and concerning the situation of the whole *terumah* in the land, are not given till ch. xlviii. 8–22. Here, in the present chapter, this heave is simply mentioned in connection with the privileges which the servants of the Lord and of His sanctuary were to enjoy. These included, in a certain sense, also the property assigned to the prince in ver. 7 as the head of the nation, on whom the provision of the sacrifices for the nation devolved, and who, apart from this, also needed for his subsistence a portion of the land, which should be peculiarly his own, in accordance with his rank. They were to give him as his property (the verb תִּתְּנוּ is to be supplied to לַנָּשִׂיא from ver. 6) the land on this side and that side of the holy *terumah* and of the city-possession, and that in front (אֶל־פְּנֵי) of these two tracts of land, that is to say, adjoining them, extending to their boundaries, מִפְּאַת יָם וגו׳, "from" (*i.e.*, according to our view, "upon") the west side westward, and from (upon) the east side eastward; in other words, the land which remained on the eastern and western boundary of the holy *terumah* and of the city domain, both toward the west as far as the Mediterranean Sea, and toward the east as far as the Jordan, the two boundaries of the future Canaan. The further definition וְאֹרֶךְ לְעֻמּוֹת וגו׳ is not quite clear; but the meaning of the words is, that "the length of the portions of land to be given to the prince on the east and west side of the *terumah* shall be equal to the length of one of the tribe-portions," and not that the portions of land belonging to the prince are to be just as long from north to south as the length of one of the twelve tribe-possessions. "Length" throughout this section is the extent from east to west. It is so in the case of all the tribe-territories (cf. ch. xlviii. 8), and must be taken in this sense in connection with the portion of land belonging to the prince also. The meaning is therefore this: in length (from east to west) these portions shall be parallel to the inheritance of one of the twelve tribes from the western boundary to the eastern. Two things are stated here: first, that the prince's portion is to extend on the eastern and western sides of the *terumah* as far as the boundary of the land allotted to the tribes, *i.e.* on the east to the Jordan, and on the west to the Mediterranean (cf. ch. xlviii. 8); and secondly, that on the east and west it is to run parallel (לְעֻמּוֹת) to the length of the separate tribe-territories, *i.e.* not to reach farther toward either north or south than the *terumah* lying between, but to be bounded by the long sides of the tribe-territories which bound the *terumah* on the north and south. אֹרֶךְ is the accusative of direction; אַחַד, some one (cf. Judg. xvi. 7; Ps. lxxxii. 7).—In ver. 8, לָאָרֶץ with the article is to be retained, contrary to Hitzig's conjecture לְאָרֶץ: "to the land belonging to him as a possession shall it (the portion marked off in ver. 7) be to him." אֶרֶץ, as in 1 Kings xi. 18, of property in land. In ver. 8*b*, the motive for these instructions is given. The former kings of Israel had no land of their own, no domain; and this had driven them to acquire private property by violence and extortion. That this may not occur any more in the future, and all inducement to such oppression of the people may be taken from the princes, in the new kingdom of God the portion of land more precisely defined in ver. 7 is to be given to the prince as his own property. The plural, "my princes," does not refer to several contemporaneous princes, nor can it be understood of the king and his sons, *i.e.* of the royal family, on account of ch. xlvi. 16; but it is to be traced to the simple fact "that Ezekiel was also thinking of the past kings, and that the whole series of princes, who had ruled over Israel, and still would rule, was passing before his mind" (Kliefoth), without our being able to conclude from this that there would be a plurality of princes succeeding one another in time to come, in contradiction to ch. xxxvii. 25.—"And the land shall they (the princes) leave to the people of Israel" (נָתַן in the sense of *concedere;* and הָאָרֶץ, the land, with the exception of the portion set apart from it in vers. 1–7).—The warning against oppression and extortion, implied in the reason thus assigned, is expanded into a general exhortation in the following verses.

Vers. 9–12. General Exhortation to observe Justice and Righteousness in their Dealings.—Ver. 9. *Thus saith the Lord Jehovah, Let it suffice you, ye princes of Israel: desist from violence and oppression, and observe justice and righteousness, and cease to thrust my people out of their possession, is the saying of the Lord Jehovah.* Ver. 10. *Just scales, and a just ephah, and a just bath, shall ye have.* Ver. 11. *The ephah and the bath shall be of one measure, so that the bath holds the tenth part of the homer, and the ephah the tenth part of the homer: after the homer shall its standard be.* Ver. 12. *And the shekel shall have twenty gerahs; twenty shekels, five and twenty shekels, fifteen shekels, shall the mina be with you.*—The exhortation in ver. 9 is similar to that in ch. xliv. 6, both in form and substance. As the Levites and priests are to renounce the idolatry to which they have been previously addicted, and to serve before the Lord in purity and holiness of life, so are the princes to abstain from the acts of oppression which they have formerly practised, and to do justice and righteousness; for example, to liberate the people of the Lord from the גְּרֻשׁוֹת. גְּרוּשָׁה is unjust expulsion from one's possession, of which Ahab's conduct toward Naboth furnished a glaring example (1 Kings xxi.). These acts of violence pressed heavily upon the people, and this burden is to be removed (הֵרִים מֵעַל). In vers. 10–12 the command to practise justice and righteousness is expanded; and it is laid as a duty upon the whole nation to have just weights and measures. This forms the transition to the regulation, which follows from ver. 13 onwards, of the taxes to be paid by the people to the prince to defray the expenses attendant upon the sacrificial worship.—For ver. 10, see Lev. xix. 36 and Deut. xxv. 13 sqq. Instead of the *hin* (Lev. xix. 36), the *bath*, which contained six hins, is mentioned here as the measure for liquids. The בַּת is met with for the first time in Isa. v. 10, and appears to have been introduced as a measure for liquids after the time of Moses, having the same capacity as the *ephah* for dry goods (see my *Bibl. Archäol.* II. pp. 139 sqq.). This similarity is expressly stated in ver. 11. Both of them, the ephah as well as the bath, are to contain the tenth of a homer (לָשֵׂאת, to carry, for לְהָכִיל, to contain, to hold; compare Gen. xxxvi. 7 with Amos vii. 10), and to be regulated by the homer. Ver. 12 treats of the weights used for money. The first clause repeats the old legal provision (Ex. xxx. 13; Lev. xxvii. 25; Num. iii. 47), that the shekel, as the standard weight for money, which was afterwards stamped as a coin, is to contain twenty gerahs. The regulations which follow are very obscure: "twenty shekels, twenty-five shekels, fifteen shekels, shall the mina be to you." The *mina*, הַמָּנֶה, occurs only here and in 1 Kings x. 17; Ezra ii. 69; and Neh. vii. 71, 72,—that is to say, only in books written during the captivity or subsequent to it. If we compare 1 Kings x. 17, according to which three minas of gold were used for a shield, with 2 Chron. ix. 16, where three hundred (shekels) of gold are said to have been used for a similar shield, it is evident that a mina was equal to a hundred shekels. Now as the talent (כִּכָּר) contained three thousand (sacred or Mosaic) shekels (see the comm. on Ex. xxxviii. 25, 26), the talent would only have contained thirty minas, which does not seem to answer to the Grecian system of weights. For the Attic talent contained sixty minas, and the mina a hundred drachms; so that the talent contained six thousand drachms, or three thousand didrachms. But as the Hebrew shekel was equal to a *δίδραχμον*, the Attic talent with three thousand didrachms corresponded to the Hebrew talent with three thousand shekels; and the mina, as the sixtieth part of the talent, with a hundred drachms or fifty didrachms, ought to correspond to the Hebrew mina with fifty shekels, as the Greek name *μνᾶ* is unquestionably derived from the Semitic מָנֶה. The relation between the mina and the shekel, resulting from a comparison of 1 Kings x. 17 with 2 Chron. ix. 16, can hardly be made to square with this, by the assumption that the shekels referred to in 2 Chron. ix. 16 are not Mosaic shekels, but so-called civil shekels, the Mosaic half-shekel, the *beka*, בֶּקַע, having acquired the name of *shekel* in the course of time, as the most widely-spread silver coin of the larger size. A hundred such shekels or bekas made only fifty Mosaic shekels, which amounted to one mina; while sixty minas also formed one talent (see my *Bibl. Archäol.* II. pp. 135, 136).—But the words of the second half of the verse before us cannot be brought into harmony with this proportion, take them how we will. If, for example, we add the three numbers together, 20 + 25 + 15 shekels shall the mina be to you, Ezekiel would fix the mina at sixty shekels. But no reason whatever can be found for such an alteration of the proportion between the mina and the talent on the one hand, or the shekel on the other, if the shekel and talent were to remain unchanged. And even apart from this, the division of the sixty into twenty, twenty-five, and fifteen still remains inexplicable, and can hardly be satisfactorily accounted for in the manner proposed by the Rabbins, namely, that there were pieces of money in circulation of the respective weights of twenty, twenty-five, and fifteen shekels, for the simple reason that no historical trace of the existence of any such pieces can be found, apart from the passage before us.[1] And the other attempts that have been made to explain the difficult words are not satisfactory. The explanation given by Cocceius and J. D. Michaelis (*Supplem. ad lex.* p. 1521), that three different minas are mentioned,—a smaller one of fifteen Mosaic shekels, a medium size of twenty shekels, and a large one of twenty-five,—is open to the objection justly pointed out by Bertheau, that in an exact definition of the true weight of anything we do not expect three magnitudes, and the purely arbitrary assumption of three different minas is an obvious subterfuge. The same thing applies to Hitzig's explanation, that the triple division, twenty, twenty-five, and fifteen shekels, has reference to the three kinds of metal used for coinage, viz. gold, silver,

[1] It is true that Const. l'Empereur has observed, in the *Discursus ad Lectorem* prefixed to the *Paraphrasis Joseph. Jachiadae in Danielem*, that "as God desired that justice should be preserved in all things, He noticed the various coins, and commanded that they should have their just weight. One coin, according to Jewish testimony, was of twenty shekels, a second of twenty-five, and a third of fifteen shekels; and as these together made one mina, according to the command of God, in order that it might be manifest that each had its proper quantity, He directed that they should be weighed against the mina, so that it might be known whether each had its own weight by means of the mina, to which they ought to be equal." But the Jewish witnesses (*Judaei testes*) are no other than the Rabbins of the Middle Ages, Sal. Jarchi (Raschi), Dav. Kimchi, and Abrabanel, who attest the existence of these pieces of money, not on the ground of historical tradition, but from an inference drawn from this verse. The much earlier Targumist knows nothing whatever of them, but paraphrases the words thus: "the third part of a mina has twenty shekels; a silver mina, five and twenty shekels; the fourth part of a mina, fifteen shekels; all sixty are a mina; and a great mina (*i.e.* probably one larger than the ordinary, or civil mina) shall be holy to you;" from which all that can be clearly learned is, that he found in the words of the prophet a mina of sixty shekels. A different explanation is given by the LXX., whose rendering, according to the *Cod. Vatic.* (Tischendorf), runs as follows: πέντε σίκλοι,

and copper, so that the gold mina was worth, or weighed, twenty shekels; the silver mina, twenty-five; and the copper mina, fifteen,—which has no tenable support in the statement of Josephus, that the shekel coined by *Simon* was worth four drachms; and is overthrown by the incongruity in the relation in which it places the gold to the silver, and both these metals to the copper.—There is evidently a corruption of very old standing in the words of the text, and we are not in possession of the requisite materials for removing it by emendation.

Vers. 13–17. THE HEAVE-OFFERINGS OF THE PEOPLE.—
Ver. 13. *This is the heave-offering which ye shall heave: The sixth part of the ephah from the homer of wheat, and ye shall give the sixth part of the ephah from the homer of barley;*
Ver. 14. *And the proper measure of oil, from the bath of oil a tenth of the bath from the cor, which contains ten baths or a homer; for ten baths are a homer;*
Ver. 15. *And one head from the flock from two hundred from the watered land of Israel, for*

πέντε καὶ σίκλοι, δέκα καὶ πεντήκοντα σίκλοι ἡ μνᾶ ἔσται ὑμῖν; and according to the *Cod. Al.*: οἱ πεντε σικλοι πεντε και οἱ δεκα σικλοι δεκα και πεντηκοντα κ.τ.λ. Boeckh (*Metrol. Untersuch.* pp. 54 sqq.) and Bertheau (*Zur Gesch. der Isr.* pp. 9 sqq.) regard the latter as the original text, and punctuate it thus: οἱ πέντε σίκλοι πέντε, καὶ οἱ δέκα σίκλοι δέκα, καὶ πεντήκοντα σίκλοι ἡ μνᾶ ἔσται ὑμῖν,—interpreting the whole verse as follows: "the weight once fixed shall remain unaltered, and unadulterated in its original value: namely, a shekel shall contain ten gerahs; five shekels, or a five-shekel piece, shall contain exactly five; and so also a ten-shekel piece, exactly ten shekels; and the mina shall contain fifty shekels." But however this explanation may appear to commend itself, and although for this reason it has been adopted by Hävernick and by the author of this commentary in his *Bibl. Archäol.*, after a repeated examination of the matter I cannot any longer regard it as well-founded, but am obliged to subscribe to the view held by Hitzig and Kliefoth, "that this rendering of the LXX. carries on the face of it the probability of its resting upon nothing more than an attempt to bring the text into harmony with the ordinary value of the mina." For apart from the fact that nothing is known of the existence of five and ten shekel pieces, it is impossible to get any intelligible meaning from the words, that five shekels are to be worth five shekels, and ten shekels worth ten shekels, as it was self-evident that five shekels could not be worth either four shekels or six.

the meat-offering, and for the burnt-offering, and for the peace-offerings, to make atonement for them, is the saying of the Lord Jehovah. Ver. 16. *All the people of the land shall be held to this heave-offering for the prince in Israel.* Ver. 17. *And upon the prince shall devolve the burnt-offerings, and the meat-offering, and the drink-offering at the feasts, the new moons, and the Sabbaths, at all the festivals of the house of Israel; he shall provide the sin-offering, and the meat-offering, and the burnt-offering, and the peace-offerings, to make atonement for the house of Israel.*—The introductory precepts to employ just measures and weights are now followed by the regulations concerning the productions of nature to be paid by the Israelites to the prince for the sacrificial worship, the provision for which was to devolve on him. Fixed contributions are to be levied for this purpose, of wheat, barley, oil, and animals of the flock—namely, according to vers. 13–15, of corn the sixtieth part, of oil the hundredth part, and of the flock the two hundredth head. There is no express mention made of wine for the drink-offering, or of cattle, which were also requisite for the burnt-offering and peace-offering, in addition to animals from the flock. The enumeration therefore is not complete, but simply contains the rule according to which they were to act in levying what was required for the sacrifices. The word שִׁשִּׁיתֶם in ver. 13 must not be altered, as Hitzig proposes; for although this is the only passage in which שִׁשָּׁה occurs, it is analogous to חִמֵּשׁ in Gen. xli. 34, both in its formation and its meaning, "to raise the sixth part." A sixth of an ephah is the sixtieth part of a homer. חֹק, that which is fixed or established, *i.e.* the proper quantity. הַבַּת הַשֶּׁמֶן is in apposition to הַשֶּׁמֶן (for the article, see the comm. on ch. xliii. 21), the fixed quantity of oil, namely of the bath of oil,—*i.e.* the measure of that which is to be contributed from the oil, and that from the bath of oil,—shall be the tenth part of the bath from the cor, *i.e.* the hundredth part of the year's crop, as the cor contained ten baths. The cor is not mentioned in the preceding words (ver. 11), nor does it occur in the Mosaic law. It is another name for the homer, which is met with for the first time in the writings of the captivity (1 Kings v. 2, 25; 2 Chron. ii. 9, xxvii. 5). For this reason its capacity is explained by the words which are appended to מִכֹּר: עֲשֶׂרֶת הַבַּתִּים וגו׳, from the cor (namely) of ten baths, one homer; and the latter definition is still further explained by the clause, "for ten baths are one homer."—Ver. 15. מִמַּשְׁקֵה, from the watered soil (cf. Gen. xiii. 10), that is to say, not a lean beast, but a fat one, which has been fed upon good pasture. לְכַפֵּר עֲלֵיהֶם indicates the general purpose of the sacrifices (*vid.* Lev. i. 4).—Ver. 16. The article in הָעָם, as in הַבַּת in ver. 14. הָיָה אֶל, to be, *i.e.* to belong, to anything—in other words, to be held to it, under obligation to do it; הָיָה עַל (ver. 17), on the other hand, to be upon a person, *i.e.* to devolve upon him. In בְּכָל־מוֹעֲדֵי the feast and days of festival, which have been previously mentioned separately, are all grouped together. עָשָׂה אֶת הַחַטָּאת וגו׳, to furnish the sin-offering, etc., *i.e.* to supply the materials for them.

So far as the fact is concerned, the Mosaic law makes no mention of any contributions to the sanctuary, with the exception of the first-born, the first-fruits and the tithes, which could be redeemed with money, however. Besides these, it was only on extraordinary occasions—*e.g.* the building of the tabernacle—that the people were called upon for freewill heave-offerings. But the Mosaic law contains no regulation as to the sources from which the priests were to meet the demands for the festal sacrifices. So far, the instructions in the verses before us are new. What had formerly been given for this object as a gift of spontaneous love, is to become in the future a regular and established duty, to guard against that arbitrary and fitful feeling from which the worship of God might suffer injury.—To these instructions there are appended, from ver. 18 onwards, the regulations concerning the sacrifices to be offered at the different festivals.

Chap. xlv. 18–xlvi. 15. *Instructions concerning the Festal and Daily Sacrifices.*

The series commences with the sin-offerings in the first month (ch. xlv. 18–20). Then follow the sacrifices at the Passover and feast of tabernacles (vers. 21–25), in connection with which a way and a standing-place in the temple are assigned to the prince and the people during the offering of these sacrifices (ch. xlvi. 1–3). After these we have the burnt-offerings on the Sabbaths and new moons (ch. xlvi. 4–7), and once more a direction with regard to their entrance and exit when the prince and the people come to the temple at the yearly festivals (vers. 8–10); also the meat-offerings at the feasts (ver. 11), to which there is appended a direction with regard to the freewill-offerings of the prince (ver. 12); and, finally, the instructions concerning the daily burnt-offering and meat-offering (vers. 13–15).

Vers. 18–20. The Sin-offerings in the First Month.—Ver. 18. *Thus saith the Lord Jehovah, In the first (month), on the first of the month, thou shalt take a bullock, a young ox without blemish, and absolve the sanctuary.* Ver. 19. *And the priest shall take of the blood of the sin-offering, and put it upon the door-posts of the house, and upon the four corners of the enclosure of the altar, and upon the door-posts at the gate of the inner court.* Ver. 20. *And so shalt thou do on the seventh of the month, for the sake of erring men and of folly, that so ye may make atonement for the house.*—The Mosaic law had prescribed for the new moons generally the sin-offering of a he-goat, in addition to the burnt-offerings and meat-offerings (Num. xxviii. 15); and, besides this, had also distinguished the new-moon's day of the seventh month by a special feast-offering to be added to the regular new-moon's sacrifices, and consisting of a sin-offering of a he-goat, and burnt-offerings and meat-offerings (Num. xxix. 2–6). This distinguishing of the seventh month by a special new-moon's sacrifice is omitted in Ezekiel; but in the place of it the first month is distinguished by a sin-offering to be presented on the first and seventh days. Nothing is said in vers. 18–20 about burnt-offerings for these days; but as the burnt-offering is appointed in ch. xlvi. 6, 7 for the new-moon's day without any limitation, and the regulations as to the connection between the meat-offering and the burnt-offerings are repeated in ch. xlvi. 11 for the holy days and feast days (חַגִּים וּמוֹעֲדִים) generally, and the new-moon's day is also reckoned among the מוֹעֲדִים, there is evidently good ground for the assumption that the burnt-offering and meat-offering prescribed for the new moon in ch. xlvi. 6, 7 were also to be offered at the new moon of the first month. On the other hand, no special burnt-offering or meat-offering is mentioned for the seventh day of the first month; so that in all probability only the daily burnt-offering and meat-offering were added upon that day (ch. xlvi. 13 sqq.) to the sin-offering appointed for it. Moreover, the sin-offerings prescribed for the first and seventh days of the first month are distinguished from the sin-offerings of the Mosaic law, partly by the animal selected (a young bullock), and partly by the disposal of the blood. According to the Mosaic law, the sin-offering for the new moons, as well as for all the feast days of the year, the Passover, Pentecost, day of trumpets, day of atonement, and feast of tabernacles (all eight days), was to be a he-goat (Num. xxviii. 15, xxii. 30, xxix. 5, 11, 16, 19, 22, 25, 28, 31, 34, 38). Even the sin-offering for the congregation of Israel on the great day of atonement simply consisted in a he-goat (or two he-goats, Lev. xvi. 5); and it was only for the sin-offering for the high priest, whether on that day (Lev. xvi. 3), or when he had sinned so as to bring guilt upon the nation (Lev. iv. 3), or when the whole congregation had sinned (Lev. iv. 14), that a bullock was required. On the other hand, according to Ezekiel, the sin-offering both on the first and seventh days of the first month, and also the one to be brought by the prince on the fourteenth day of that month, *i.e.* on the day of the feast of Passover (ch. xlv. 22), for himself and for all the people, were to consist of a bullock, and only the sin-offering on the seven days of the feasts of Passover and tabernacles of a he-goat (ch. xlv. 23, 25). The Mosaic law contains no express instructions concerning the sprinkling of the blood of the sin-offering at the new moons and feasts (with the exception of the great atoning sacrifice on the day of atonement), because it was probably the same as in the case of the sin-offerings for the high priest and the whole congregation, when the blood was first of all to be sprinkled seven times against the curtain in front of the capporeth, and then to be applied to the horns of the altar of incense, and the remainder to be poured out at the foot of the altar of burnt-offering (Lev. iv. 6, 7, 17, 18); whereas, in the case of the great atoning sacrifice on the day of atonement, some of the blood was first of all to be sprinkled at or upon the front side of the capporeth and seven times upon the ground, and after that it was to be applied to the horns of the altar of incense and of the altar of burnt-offering (Lev. xvi. 15–17). But according to Ezekiel, some of the blood of the sin-offerings on the first and seventh days of the first month, and certainly also on the same days of the feasts of Passover and tabernacles, was to be smeared upon the posts of the house—that is to say, the posts mentioned in ch. xli. 21, not merely those of the הֵיכָל, the door into the holy place, but also those of the קֹדֶשׁ, the door leading into the most holy place, upon the horns and the four corners of the enclosure of the altar of burnt-offering (ch. xliii. 20), and upon the posts of the gate of the inner court. It is a point in dispute here whether שַׁעַר הֶחָצֵר is only one door, and in that case whether the east gate of the inner court is to be understood as in ch. xlvi. 2 (מְזוּזַת הַשַּׁעַר), as Hitzig and others suppose, or whether שַׁעַר is to be taken in a collective sense as signifying the three gates of the inner court (Kliefoth and others). The latter view is favoured by the collective use of the word מְזוּזָה by itself, and also by the circumstance that if only one of the three gates were intended, the statement which of the three would hardly have been omitted (cf. ch. xlvi. 1, xliv. 1, etc.).—According to ver. 18, these sin-offerings were to serve for the absolving of the sanctuary; and according to ver. 20, to make atonement for the temple on account of error or folly. Both directions mean the same thing. The reconciliation of the temple was effected by its absolution or purification from the sins that had come upon it through the error and folly of the people. Sins בִּשְׁגָגָה are sins occasioned by the weakness of flesh and blood, for which expiation could be made by sin-offerings (see the comm. on Lev. iv. 2 and Num. xv. 22 sqq.). מֵאִישׁ שֹׁגֶה, lit. away from the erring man, *i.e.* to release him from his sin. This expression is strengthened by מִפֶּתִי, away from simplicity or folly; here, as in Prov. vii. 7, as *abstractum pro concreto*, the simple man.—The great expiatory sacrifice on the day of atonement answered the same purpose, the absolution of the sanctuary from the sins of the people committed בִּשְׁגָגָה (Lev. xvi. 16 sqq.).

Vers. 21–25. Sacrifices at the Passover and Feast of Tabernacles.—Ver. 21. *In the first* (*month*), *on the fourteenth day of the month, ye shall keep the Passover, a feast of a full week; unleavened shall be eaten.* Ver. 22. *And the prince shall prepare on that day for himself and for all the people of the land a bullock as a sin-offering.* Ver. 23. *And for the seven days of the feast he shall prepare as a burnt-offering for Jehovah seven bullocks and seven rams without blemish daily, the seven days, and as a sin-offering a he-goat daily.* Ver. 24. *And as a meat-offering, he shall prepare an ephah for the bullock, and an ephah for the ram, and a hin of oil for the ephah.* Ver. 25. *In the seventh* (*month*), *on the fifteenth day of the month, at the feast he shall do the same for seven days with regard to the sin-offering, as also the burnt-offering, and the meat-offering, as also the oil.* — In the words, "shall *the*

Passover be to you," there lies the thought that the Passover is to be celebrated in the manner appointed in Ex. xii., with the paschal meal in the evening of the 14th Abib.—There is considerable difficulty connected with the following words, חַג שָׁבֻעוֹת יָמִים, which all the older translators have rendered "a feast of seven days." שָׁבֻעוֹת signifies periods of seven days or weeks. A feast of heptads of days, or weeks of days, cannot possibly mean a feast which lasted only seven days, or a week. חַג שָׁבֻעוֹת is used elsewhere for the feast of weeks (Ex. xxxiv. 22; Deut. xvi. 10), because they were to reckon seven weeks from the second day of the Passover, the day of the sheaf of first-fruits, and then to keep the feast of the loaves of first-fruits, or the feast of harvest (Deut. xvi. 9). Kliefoth retains this well-established meaning of the words in this passage also, and gives the following explanation: If the words חַג שָׁבֻעוֹת stood alone without יָמִים, it would mean that in future the Passover was to be kept like the feast of seven weeks, as the feast of the loaves of first-fruits. But the addition of יָמִים, which is to be taken in the same sense as in Dan. x. 2, 3, Gen. xxix. 14, etc., gives this turn to the thought, that in future the Passover is to be kept as a feast of seven weeks long, "a feast lasting seven weeks." According to this explanation, the meaning of the regulation is, "that in future not only the seven days of sweet loaves, but the whole of the seven weeks intervening between the feast of the wave-sheaf and the feast of the wave-loaves, was to be kept as a Passover, that the whole of the quinquagesima should be one Easter חָג, and the feast of weeks be one with the Passover." To this there is appended the further regulation, that unleavened bread is to be eaten, not merely for the seven days therefore, but for the whole of the seven weeks, till the feast of the loaves of first-fruits. This explanation is a very sagacious one, and answers to the Christian view of the Easter-tide. But it is open to objections which render it untenable. In the first place, that יָמִים, when used in the sense of lasting for days, is not usually connected with the preceding noun in the construct state, but is attached as an adverbial accusative; compare שְׁלֹשָׁה שָׁבֻעִים יָמִים in Dan. x. 2, 3, and שְׁנָתַיִם יָמִים in Gen. xli. 1, Jer. xxviii. 3, 11, etc. But a still more important objection is the circumstance that the words שִׁבְעַת יְמֵי הֶחָג in ver. 23 unquestionably point back to חַג שְׁבֻעוֹת יָמִים, as there is no other way in which the article in הֶחָג can be explained, just as בַּיּוֹם הַהוּא in ver. 22 points back to the fourteenth day mentioned in ver. 21 as the time of the *pesach* feast. It follows from this, however, that שְׁבֻעוֹת יָמִים can only signify a seven days' feast. It is true that the plural שְׁבֻעוֹת appears irreconcilable with this; for Kimchi's opinion, that שְׁבֻעוֹת is a singular, written with *Cholem* instead of *Patach*, is purely a result of perplexity, and the explanation given by Gussetius, that Ezekiel speaks in the plural of weeks, because the reference is "to the institution of the Passover as an annual festival to be celebrated many times in the series of times and ages," is no better. The plural שְׁבֻעוֹת must rather be taken as a plural of genus, as in עָרֵי, Gen. xiii. 12 and Judg. xii. 7; בְּנֵי, Gen. xix. 29; or בָּנִים, Gen. xxi. 7, Isa. xxxvii. 3; so that Ezekiel speaks indefinitely of heptads of days, because he assumes that the fact is well known that the feast only lasted one heptad of days, as he expressly states in ver. 23. If this explanation of the plural does not commend itself, we must take שְׁבֻעוֹת as a copyist's error for שִׁבְעַת, feast of a heptad of days, *i.e.* a feast lasting a full week, and attribute the origin of this copyist's error to the fact that חַג שִׁבְעַת naturally suggested the thought of חַג שָׁבֻעוֹת, feast of weeks, or Pentecost, not merely because the feast of Pentecost is always mentioned in the Pentateuch along with the feasts of Passover and tabernacles, but also because the only singular form of שָׁבֻעוֹת that we meet with elsewhere is שָׁבוּעַ (Dan. ix. 27), or in the construct state שְׁבֻעַ (Gen. xxix. 27), not שִׁבְעָה and שִׁבְעַת.—The word הַפֶּסַח is used here as in Deut. xvi. 1, 2, so that it includes the seven days' feast of unleavened bread. The *Niphal* יֵאָכֵל is construed with the accusative in the olden style: *mazzoth* shall men eat.—In vers. 22 and 23 there follow the regulations concerning the sacrifices of this festival, and first of all concerning the sin-offering to be presented on the fourteenth day, on the evening of which the paschal lamb was slaughtered and the paschal meal was held (ver. 22). The Mosaic legislation makes no allusion to this, but simply speaks of festal sacrifices for the seven days of *mazzoth*, the 15th to the 21st Abib (Lev. xxiii. 5–8; Num. xxviii. 16–25), with regard to which fresh regulations are also given here. The Mosaic law prescribes for each of these seven days as burnt-offerings two bullocks, a ram, and seven yearling lambs, as a meat-offering; three-tenths of an ephah of meal mixed with oil for each bullock, two-tenths for the ram, and one-tenth for each lamb, and a he-goat for the sin-offering (Num. xxviii. 19–22). The new law for the feasts, on the other hand, also requires, it is true, only one he-goat daily for a sin-offering on the seven feast days, but for the daily burnt-offerings seven bullocks and seven rams each; and for the meat-offering, an ephah of meal and a hin of oil for every bullock and for every ram. In the new *thorah*, therefore, the burnt-offerings and meat-offerings are much richer and more copious, and the latter in far greater measure than the former.—Ver. 25. The same number of sacrifices is to be offered throughout the feast of seven days falling upon the fifteenth day of the seventh month. This feast is the feast of tabernacles, but the name is not mentioned, doubtless because the practice of living in tabernacles (booths) would be dropped in the time to come. And even with regard to the sacrifices of this feast, the new *thorah* differs greatly from the old. According to the Mosaic law, there were to be offered, in addition to the daily sin-offering of a he-goat, seventy bullocks in all as burnt-offerings for the seven days; and these were to be so distributed that on the first day thirteen were to be offered, and the number was to be reduced by one on each of the following days, so that there would be only seven bullocks upon the seventh day; moreover, every day two rams and fourteen yearling lambs were to be offered, together with the requisite quantity of meal and oil for a meat-offering according to the number of the animals (Num. xxix. 12–34). According to Ezekiel, on the other hand, the quantity of provision made for the sacrifices remained the same as that appointed for the feast of Passover; so that the whole cost of the burnt-offerings and meat-offerings did not reach the amount required by the Mosaic law. In addition to all this, there was an eighth day observed as a closing festival in the Mosaic feast of tabernacles, with special sacrifices; and this also is wanting in Ezekiel.—But the following is still more important than the points of difference just mentioned: Ezekiel only mentions the two yearly feasts of seven days in the first and seventh months, and omits not only the Pentecost, or feast of weeks, but also the day of trumpets, on the first of the seventh month, and the day of atonement on the tenth; from which we must infer that the Israel of the future would keep only the two first named of all the yearly feasts. The correctness of this conclusion is placed beyond the reach of doubt by the fact that he practically transfers the feasts of the day of trumpets and of the day of atonement, which were preparatory to the feast of tabernacles, to the first month, by the appointment of special sin-offerings for the first and seventh days of that month (vers. 18–20), and of a sin-offering on the day of the paschal meal (ver. 22). This essentially transforms the idea which lies at the foundation of the cycle of Mosaic feasts, as we intend subsequently to show, when discussing the meaning and significance of the whole picture of the new kingdom of God, as shown in ch. xl.–xlviii.

Chap. xlvi. 1–15. *Sacrifices for the Sabbath and New Moon, Freewill-Offerings, and Daily Sacrifices.*

Vers. 1–7. SACRIFICES FOR THE SABBATH AND NEW MOON. —As, according to ch. xlv. 17, it devolved upon the prince to provide and bring the sacrifices for himself and the house of

Israel; after the appointment of the sacrifices to be offered at the yearly feasts (ch. xlv. 18–25), and before the regulation of the sacrifices for the Sabbath and new moon (ch. xlvi. 4–7), directions are given as to the conduct of the prince at the offering of these sacrifices (ch. xlvi. 1–3). For although the slaughtering and preparation of the sacrifices for the altar devolved upon the priests, the prince was to be present at the offering of the sacrifices to be provided by him, whereas the people were under no obligation to appear before the Lord in the temple except at the yearly feasts.

Ver. 1. *Thus saith the Lord Jehovah, The gate of the inner court, which looks toward the east, shall be shut the six working days, and on the Sabbath it shall be opened, and on the day of the new moon it shall be opened.* Ver. 2. *And the prince shall come by the way to the porch of the gate from without, and stand at the posts of the gate, and the priests shall prepare his burnt-offering and his peace-offerings, and he shall worship on the threshold of the gate and then go out; but the gate shall not be shut till the evening.* Ver. 3. *And the people of the land shall worship at the entrance of that gate on the Sabbaths and on the new moons before Jehovah.* Ver. 4. *And the burnt-offering which the prince shall offer to Jehovah shall consist on the Sabbath-day of six lambs without blemish and a ram without blemish;* Ver. 5. *And as a meat-offering, an ephah for the ram, and for the lambs as a meat-offering that which his hand may give, and of oil a hin to the ephah (of meal).* Ver. 6. *And on the day of the new moon there shall be a bullock, a young ox without blemish, and six lambs and a ram without blemish;* Ver. 7. *And he shall put an ephah for the bullock and an ephah for the ram for the meat-offering, and for the lambs as much as his hand affords, and of oil a hin for the ephah.*—Vers. 1–3 supply and explain the instructions given in ch. xliv. 1–3 concerning the outer eastern gate. As the east gate of the outer court (ch. xliv. 1), so also the east gate of the inner court was to remain closed during the six working days, and only to be opened on the Sabbaths and new moons, when it was to remain open till the evening. The prince was to enter this inner east gate, and to stand there and worship upon the threshold while his sacrifice was being prepared and offered. בּוֹא דֶּרֶךְ אוּלָם הַשַּׁעַר is to be taken as in ch. xliv. 3; but מִחוּץ, which is appended, is not to be referred to the entrance into the inner court, as the statement would be quite superfluous so far as this is concerned, since any one who was not already in the inner court must enter the gate-building of the inner court from without, or from the outer court. The meaning of מִחוּץ is rather that the prince was to enter, or to go to, the gate porch of the inner court through the outer east gate. There he was to stand at the posts of the gate and worship on the threshold of the gate during the sacrificial ceremony; and when this was over he was to go out again, namely, by the same way by which he entered (ch. xliv. 3). But the people who came to the temple on the Sabbaths and new moons were to worship פֶּתַח, *i.e.* at the entrance of this gate, outside the threshold of the gate. Kliefoth is wrong in taking פֶּתַח in the sense of through the doorway, as signifying that the people were to remain in front of the outer east gate, and to worship looking at the temple through this gate and through the open gate between. For הַשַּׁעַר הַהוּא, *this* gate, can only be the gate of the inner court, which has been already mentioned. There is no force in the consideration which has led Kliefoth to overlook הַהוּא, and think of the outer gate, namely, that "it would be unnatural to suppose that the people were to come into the outer court through the outer north and south gates, whilst the outer east gate remained shut (or perhaps more correctly, was opened for the prince), and so stand in front of the inner court," as it is impossible to see what there is that is unnatural in such a supposition. On the other hand, it is unnatural to assume that the people, who, according to ver. 9, were to come through the north and south gates into the outer court at all the מוֹעֲדִים to appear before Jehovah, were not allowed to enter the court upon the Sabbaths and new moons if they should wish to worship before Jehovah upon these days also, but were to stand outside before the gate of the outer court. The difference between the princes and the people, with regard to visiting the temple upon the Sabbaths and new moons, consisted chiefly in this, that the prince could enter by the outer east gate and proceed as far as the posts of the middle gate, and there worship upon the threshold of the gate, whereas the people were only allowed to come into the outer court through the outer north and south gates, and could only proceed to the front of the middle gate.—Vers. 4 sqq. The burnt-offering for the Sabbath is considerably increased when compared with that appointed in the Mosaic law. The law requires two yearling lambs with the corresponding meat-offering (Num. xxviii. 9); Ezekiel, six lambs and one ram, and in addition to these a meat-offering for the ram according to the proportion already laid down in ch. xlv. 24 for the festal sacrifices; and for the lambs, מַתַּת יָדוֹ, a gift, a present of his hand,—that is to say, not a handful of meal, but, according to the formula used in alternation with it in ver. 7, as much as his hand can afford. For כַּאֲשֶׁר תַּשִּׂיג יָדוֹ, see Lev. xiv. 30, xxv. 26.—It is different with the sacrifices of the new moon in vers. 6 and 7. The law of Moses prescribed two bullocks, one ram, and seven lambs, with the corresponding meat-offering, and a he-goat for a sin-offering (Num. xxviii. 11–15); the *thorah* of Ezekiel, on the contrary, omits the sin-offering, and reduces the burnt-offering to one bullock, one ram, and six lambs, together with a meat-offering, according to the proportion already mentioned, which is peculiar to his law. The first תְּמִימִים in ver. 6 is a copyist's error for תָּמִים.

Vers. 8–12. On the Opening of the Temple for the People, and for the Voluntary Offerings of the Prince.—Ver. 8. *And when the prince cometh, he shall go in by the way to the porch of the gate, and by its way shall he go out.* Ver. 9. *And when the people of the land come before*

Jehovah on the feast days, he who enters through the north gate to worship shall go out through the south gate; and he who enters through the south gate shall go out through the north gate: they shall not return through the gate through which they entered, but go out straight forward. Ver. 10. *And the prince shall enter in the midst of them, when they enter; and when they go out, they shall go out (together).* Ver. 11. *And at the feast days and holy days the meat-offering shall be an ephah for the bullock, an ephah for the ram, and for the lambs what his hand may give, and of oil a hin for the ephah.* Ver. 12. *And when the prince prepares a voluntary burnt-offering or voluntary peace-offerings to Jehovah, they shall open the gate that looks to the east, and he shall prepare his burnt-offerings and his peace-offering as he does on the Sabbath day; and when he has gone out they shall shut the gate after his going out.*—The coming of the people to worship before Jehovah has been already mentioned in ver. 3, but only casually, with reference to the position which they were to take behind the prince in case any individuals should come on the Sabbaths or new moons, on which they were not bound to appear. At the high festivals, on the other hand, every one was to come (Deut. xvi. 16); and for this there follow the necessary directions in vers. 9 and 10, to prevent crowding and confusion. For the purpose of linking these directions to what comes before, the rule already laid down in ver. 2 concerning the entrance and exit of the prince is repeated in ver. 8. מוֹעֲדִים is supposed by the commentators to refer to the high festivals of the first and seventh months (ch. xlv. 21 and 25); but מוֹעֲדִים does not apply to the same feasts as those which are called חַגִּים in ver. 11, as we may see from the combination of חַגִּים and מוֹעֲדִים. חַגִּים is the term applied to the greater annual feasts, as distinguished from the Sabbaths, new moons, and the day of atonement. The מוֹעֲדִים, on the contrary, are all the times and days sanctified to the Lord, including even the Sabbath (see the comm. on Lev. xxiii. 2). It is in this sense that מוֹעֲדִים is used here in ver. 9, and not חַגִּים; because what is laid down concerning the entrance and exit of the people, when visiting the temple, is not merely intended to apply to the high festivals, on which the people were bound to appear before Jehovah, but also to such feast days as the Sabbaths and new moons, whenever individuals from among the people were desirous of their own free-will to worship before the Lord. The latter cases were not to be excluded, although, as ver. 10 clearly shows, the great feasts were principally kept in mind. For the entrance and exit of the prince in the midst of the people (ver. 10) apply to the great yearly feasts alone. The *Chetib* יֵצְאוּ in ver. 9 is to be preferred to the easier *Keri* יֵצֵא, and is not merely the more difficult reading, but the more correct reading also, as two kinds of people are mentioned,—those who entered by the north gate and those who entered by the south. Both are to go out walking straight forward; and neither of them is to turn in the court for the purpose of going out by the gate through which he entered. Even in ver. 10 יֵצְאוּ is not to be altered, as Hitzig supposes, but to be taken as referring to the prince and the people.—In ver. 11, the instructions given in ch. xlv. 24, xlvi. 5, 7, concerning the quantities composing the meat-offering for the different feasts, are repeated here as rules applicable to all festal times. בַּחַגִּים וּבַמּוֹעֲדִים has been correctly explained as follows: "at the feasts, and generally at all regular (more correctly, established) seasons," cf. ch. xlv. 17. Only the daily sacrifices are excepted from this rule, other regulations being laid down for them in ver. 14.—Ver. 12. The freewill-offerings could be presented on any week-day. And the rules laid down in vers. 1 and 2 for the Sabbath-offerings of the prince are extended to cases of this kind, with one modification, namely, that the east gate, which had been opened for the occasion, should be closed again as soon as the sacrificial ceremony was over, and not left open till the evening, as on the Sabbath and new moon. נְדָבָה is a substantive: the freewill-offering, which could be either a burnt-offering or a peace-offering.

Vers. 13–15. The Daily Sacrifice.—Ver. 13. *And a yearling lamb without blemish shalt thou prepare as a burnt-offering daily for Jehovah: every morning shalt thou prepare it.* Ver. 14. *And a meat-offering shalt thou add to it every morning, a sixth of an ephah, and oil a third of a hin, to moisten the wheaten flour, as a meat-offering for Jehovah: let these be everlasting statutes, perpetually enduring.* Ver. 15. *And prepare the lamb, and the meat-offering, and the oil, every morning as a perpetual burnt-offering.*—The preparation of the daily sacrifice is not imposed upon the prince, in harmony with ch. xlv. 17; it is the duty of the congregation, which the priests have to superintend. Every morning a yearling lamb is to be brought as a burnt-offering. The Mosaic law required such a lamb both morning and evening (Num. xxviii. 3, 4). The new *thorah* omits the evening sacrifice, but increases the meat-offering to the sixth of an ephah of meal and the third of a hin of oil, against the tenth of an ephah of meal and the fourth of a hin of oil prescribed by the Mosaic law (Num. xxviii. 5). רֹס, from רָסַס, ἁπ. λεγ., to moisten (cf. רְסִיסִים, Song of Sol. v. 2). The plural חֻקּוֹת refers to the burnt-offering and meat-offering. תָּמִיד is added to give greater force, and, according to the correct remark of Hitzig, appears to be intended as a substitute for לְדוֹרֹתֵיכֶם in Lev. xxiii. 14, 21, 31. The repeated emphasizing of בַּבֹּקֶר בַּבֹּקֶר shows that the silence as to the evening sacrifice is not a mere oversight of the matter, but that in the new order of worship the evening sacrifice is to be omitted. The *Chetib* וַעֲשׂוּ is to be retained, in opposition to the *Keri* יַעֲשׂוּ.

This brings to an end the new order of worship. The verses which follow in the chapter before us introduce two supplementary notices,—namely, a regulation pointing back to ch. xlv. 7–9, concerning the right of the prince to hand down or give away his landed property (vers. 16–18); and a brief description of the sacrificial kitchens for priests and people (vers. 19–21).

Vers. 16–18. On the Right of the Prince to dispose of his Landed Property.—Ver. 16. *Thus saith the Lord Jehovah, If the prince gives a present to one of his sons, it is his inheritance, shall belong to his sons; it is their possession, in an hereditary way.* Ver. 17. *But if he gives a present from his inheritance to one of his servants, it shall belong to him till the year of liberty, and then return to the prince; to his sons alone shall his inheritance remain.* Ver. 18. *And the prince shall not take from the inheritance of the people, so as to thrust them out of their possession; from his own possession he shall transmit to his sons, that no one of my people be scattered from his possession.*—According to ch. xlv. 7, 8, at the future division of the land among the tribes, a possession was to be given to the prince on both sides of the holy heave and of the city domain, that he might not seize upon a possession by force, as the former princes had done. The prince might give away portions of this royal property, but only within such limits that the design with which a regal possession had been granted might not be frustrated. To his sons, as his heirs, he might make gifts therefrom, which would remain their own property; but if he presented to any one of his servants a portion of his hereditary property, it was to revert to the prince in the year of liberty; just as, according to the Mosaic law, the hereditary field of an Israelite, which had been alienated, was to revert to its hereditary owner (Lev. xxvii. 24, compared with xxv. 10–13). The suffix in נַחֲלָתוֹ (ver. 16) is not to be taken as referring to the prince, and connected with the preceding words in opposition to the accents, but refers to אִישׁ מִבָּנָיו. What the prince gives to one of his sons from his landed property shall be his נַחֲלָה, *i.e.* his hereditary possession. This is expressed still more generally in the next clause: to his (the prince's) sons shall it (the land presented) belong as their נַחֲלָה, *i.e.* after the manner of an hereditary possession. On the other hand, what the prince presents to one of his servants shall not become hereditary in his case, but shall revert to the prince in the year of liberty, or the year of jubilee. The second half of ver. 17 reads verbally thus: "only his inheritance is it; as for his sons, it shall belong to them."—And as the prince was not to break up his regal possession by presents made to servants, so was he (ver. 18) also not to put any one out of his possession by force, for the purpose, say, of procuring property for his own sons; but was to give his sons their inheritance from his own property alone. For הוֹנָה, compare ch. xlv. 8, and such passages as 1 Sam. viii. 14, xxii. 7. We shall return by and by to the question, how this regulation stands related to the view that the prince is the Messiah.

Vers. 19–24. THE SACRIFICIAL KITCHENS FOR THE PRIESTS AND FOR THE PEOPLE.—Ver. 19. *And he brought me up the entrance by the shoulder of the gate to the holy cells for the priests, which looked to the north; and behold there was a place on the outermost side toward the west.* Ver. 20. *And he said to me, This is the place where the priests boil the trespass-offering and the sin-offering, where they bake the meat-offering that they may not need to carry it out into the outer court, to sanctify the people.* Ver. 21. *And he led me out into the outer court, and caused me to pass by the four corners of the court; and behold, in every corner of the court there was again a court.* Ver. 22. *In the four corners of the court were closed courts of forty cubits in length and thirty cubits in breadth; all four corner spaces had one measure.* Ver. 23. *And a row of stands was round about therein in all four, and boiling hearths were under the rows made round about.* Ver. 24. *And he said to me, These are the kitchen-house, where the servants of the house boil the slain-offering of the people.*—In the list and description of the subordinate buildings of the temple, the sacrificial kitchens are passed over; and they are therefore referred to here again in a supplementary manner. Ewald has shifted vers. 19–24, and placed them after ch. xlii. 14, which would certainly have been the most suitable place for mentioning the sacrificial kitchens for the priests. But it is evident that they stood here originally, and not there; not only from the fact that in ver. 19*a* the passage to the holy cells (ch. xlii. 1 sqq.) is circumstantially described, which would have been unnecessary if the description of the kitchens had originally followed immediately after ch. xlii. 14, as Ezekiel was then standing by the cells; but also, and still more clearly, from the words that serve as an introduction to what follows, "he led me back to the door of the house" (ch. xlvii. 1), which are unintelligible unless he had changed his standing-place between ch. xlvi. 18 and xlvii. 1, as is related in ch. xlvi. 19 and 21, since Ezekiel had received the sacrificial *thorah* (ch. xliv. 5–xlvi. 18) in front of the house (ch. xliv. 4). If vers. 19–24 had originally stood elsewhere, so that ch. xlvii. 1 was immediately connected with ch. xlvi. 18, the transition-formula in ch. xlvii. 1*a* would necessarily have read very differently.—But with this section the right of the preceding one, vers. 16–18, which Ewald has arbitrarily interpolated in ch. xlv. between vers. 8 and 9, to hold its present place in the chapter before us as an appendix, is fully vindicated.—The holy cells (ver. 19) are those of the northern cell-building (ch. xlii. 1–10) described in ch. xlii. 1–14 (see Plate I. *L*). בַּמָּבוֹא is the approach or way mentioned in ch. xlii. 9, which led from the northern inner gate to these cells (see Plate I. *l*); not the place to which Ezekiel was brought (Kliefoth), but the passage along which he was led. The spot to which he was conducted follows in אֶל הַלְּשָׁכוֹת (the article before the construct state, as in ch. xliii. 21, etc.). אֶל הַכֹּהֲנִים is appended to this in the form of an apposition; and here לְשָׁכוֹת is to be repeated in thought: to those for the priests. הַפֹּנוֹת צ' belongs to הַלְּשָׁכוֹת. There, *i.e.* by the cells, was a space set apart at the outermost (hindermost) sides toward the west (Plate I. *M*), for the boiling of the flesh of the trespass-offering and sin-offering, and the baking of the *minchah*,—that is to say, of those portions of the sacrifices which the priests were to eat in their official capacity (see the comm. on ch. xlii. 13). For the motive assigned in ver. 20*b* for the provision of special kitchens for this object, see the exposition of ch. xliv. 19.—In addition to these, kitchens were required for the preparation of the sacrificial meals, which were connected with the offering of the *shelamim*, and were held by those who presented them. These sacrificial kitchens for the people are treated of in vers. 20–24. They were situated in the four corners of the outer court (Plate I. *N*). To show them to the prophet, the angel leads him into the outer court. The holy cells (ver. 19) and the sacrificial kitchens for the priests (ver. 20) were also situated by the outside wall of the inner court; and for this reason Ezekiel had already been led out of the inner court, where he had received the sacrificial *thorah*, through the northern gate of the court by the way which led to the holy cells, that he might be shown the sacrificial kitchens. When, therefore, it is stated in ver. 21 that "he led me out into the outer court," יוֹצִיאֵנִי can only be explained on the supposition that the space from the surrounding wall of the inner court to the way which led from the gate porch of that court to the holy cells, and to the passage which continued this way in front of the cells (Plate I. *l* and *m*), was regarded as an appurtenance of the inner court. In every one of the four corners of the outer court there was a (small) courtyard in the court. The repetition of חָצֵר בְּמִקְצֹעַ הח' has a distributive force. The small courtyards in the four corners of the court were קְטֻרוֹת, *i.e.* not "uncovered," as this would be unmeaning, since all courts or courtyards were uncovered; nor "contracted" (Böttcher), for קָטַר has no such meaning; nor "*fumum exhalantia*," as the Talmudists suppose; nor "bridged over" (Hitzig), which there is also nothing in the language to sustain; but in all probability *atria clausa, i. e. muris cincta et januis clausa* (Ges. *Thes.*), from קְטַר; in Aram. *ligavit*; in Ethiop. *clausit, obseravit januam*. The word מְהֻקְצָעוֹת is marked with *puncta extraordinaria* by the Masoretes as a suspicious word, and is also omitted in the Septuagint and Vulgate.

Böttcher and Hitzig have therefore expunged it as a gloss. But even Hitzig admits that this does not explain how it found its way into the text. The word is a *Hophal* participle of קָצַע, in the sense of cornered off, cut off into corners, and is in apposition to the suffix to לְאַרְבַּעְתָּם,—literally, one measure was to all four, the spaces or courtyards cut off in the corners. For this appositional use of the participle, compare 1 Kings xiv. 6. There is also a difference of opinion as to the meaning of the word טוּר, which only occurs here and in Ex. xxviii. 17 sqq. and xxxix. 10, where it signifies "row," and not "enclosure" (Kliefoth). טִירוֹת, which follows, is evidently merely the feminine plural, from טוּר, as טִירָה is also derived from טוּר, in the sense of "to encircle" (see the comm. on Ps. lxix. 26). Consequently טוּר does not mean a covering or boundary wall, but a row or shelf of brickwork which had several separate shelves, under which the cooking hearths were placed. מְבַשְּׁלוֹת, not kitchens, but cooking hearths; strictly speaking a *partic. Piel*, things which cause to boil. — בֵּית הַמְבַשְּׁלִים, kitchen house. מְשָׁרְתֵי הַבַּיִת, the temple servants, as distinguished from the servants of Jehovah (ch. xliv. 15, 16), are the Levites (ch. xliv. 11, 12). עָשׂוּי is construed as in ch. xl. 17 and xli. 18, 19.

CHAP. XLVII. AND XLVIII. BLESSING OF THE LAND OF CANAAN, AND DISTRIBUTION OF IT AMONG THE TRIBES OF ISRAEL.

After Ezekiel had seen the entrance of the glory of the Lord into the new temple, which was measured before his eyes, and had received the new *thorah* to be announced to the people concerning the service which Israel was to render to its God in the new sanctuary, a stream of living water was shown to him, proceeding from the threshold of the temple, flowing to the Arabah, and emptying itself into the Dead Sea, to fertilize the barren soil, and fill the salt water of the Dead Sea with vital power (ch. xlvii. 1-12); and finally, the command of the Lord is communicated to him concerning the boundaries of the holy land, its distribution among the twelve tribes of Israel, and the building of the holy city (ch. xlvii. 13–xlviii. 35).

Chap. xlvii. 1–12. *The River of Water of Life.*

When Jehovah shall have judged all the heathen in the valley of Jehoshaphat, and shall dwell as King of His people upon Zion His holy mountain, then will the mountains trickle with new wine, and the hills run with milk, and all the brooks of Judah flow with water; and a spring will proceed from the house of Jehovah, and water the Acacia valley. With these figures Joel (ch. iv. 18) has already described the river of salvation, which the Lord would cause to flow to His congregation in the time when the kingdom of God shall be perfected. This picture of the Messianic salvation shapes itself in the case of our prophet into the magnificent vision contained in the section before us.[1]—Ver. 1. *And he led me back to the door of the house, and, behold, water flowed out from under the threshold of the house toward the east, for the front side of the house was toward the east; and the water flowed down from below, from the right shoulder of the house on the south of the altar.* Ver. 2. *And he led me out by the way of the north gate, and caused me to go round about on the outside, to the outer gate of the way to the (gate), looking toward the east; and, behold, waters rippled for the right shoulder of the gate.* Ver. 3. *When the man went out toward the east, he had a measuring line in his hand, and he measured a thousand cubits, and caused me to go through the water—water to the ankles.* Ver. 4. *And he measured a thousand, and caused me to go through the water—water to the knees; and he measured a thousand, and caused me to go through —water to the hips.* Ver. 5. *And he measured a thousand— a river through which I could not walk, for the water was high, water to swim in, a river which could not be forded.* Ver. 6. *And he said to me, Hast thou seen it, son of man? and he led me*

[1] Compare W. Neumann, *Die Wasser des Lebens.* An exegetical study on Ezek. xlvii. 1–12. Berlin, 1848.

back again by the bank of the river. Ver. 7. *When I returned, behold, there stood on the bank of the river very many trees on this side and on that.* Ver. 8. *And he said to me, This water flows out into the eastern circle, and runs down into the plain, and reaches the sea; into the sea is it carried out, that the waters may become wholesome.* Ver. 9. *And it will come to pass, every living thing with which it swarms everywhere, whither the double river comes, will live, and there will be very many fishes; for when this water comes thither they will become wholesome, and everything will live whither the river comes.* Ver. 10. *And fishermen will stand by it, from Engedi to Eneglaim they will spread out nets; after their kind will there be fishes therein, like the fishes of the great sea, very many.* Ver. 11. *Its marshes and its swamps, they will not become wholesome, they will be given up to salt.* Ver. 12. *And by the river will all kinds of trees of edible fruit grow on its bank, on this side and on that; their leaves will not wither, and their fruits will not fail; every moon they will bear ripe fruit, for its water flows out of its sanctuary. And their fruits will serve as food, and their leaves as medicine.*

From the outer court, where Ezekiel had been shown the sacrificial kitchens for the people (ch. xlvi. 21 sqq.), he is taken back to the front of the door of the temple house, to be shown a spring of water, flowing out from under the threshold of the temple, which has swollen in the short course of four thousand cubits from its source into a deep river in which men can swim, and which flows down to the Jordan valley, to empty itself into the Dead Sea. In vers. 1 and 2, the origin and course of this water are described; in vers. 3 and 5, its marvellous increase; in ver. 6, the growth of trees on its banks; in vers. 7–12, its emptying itself into the Arabah and into the Dead Sea, with the life-giving power of its water.—Ver. 1. The door of the house is the entrance into the holy place of the temple, and מִפְתַּן הַבַּיִת the threshold of this door. קָדִימָה, not "in the east" (Hitzig), for the following sentence explaining the reason does not require this meaning; but "toward the east" of the threshold, which lay toward the east, for the front of the temple was in the east. מִתַּחַת is not to be connected with מִכֶּתֶף, but to be taken by itself, only not in the sense of downwards (Hitzig), but from beneath, namely, down from the right shoulder of the house. יָרַד, to flow down, because the temple stood on higher ground than the inner court. The right shoulder is the part of the eastern wall of the holy place between the door and the pillars, the breadth of which was five cubits (ch. xli. 1). The water therefore issued from the corner formed by the southern wall of the porch and the eastern wall of the holy place (see the sketch on Plate I.), and flowed past the altar of burnt-offering on the south side, and crossed the court in an easterly direction, passing under its surrounding wall. It then flowed across the outer court and under the pavement and the eastern wall into the open country, where the prophet, on the outside in front of the gate, saw it rippling forth from the right shoulder of that gate. That he might do this, he was led out through the north gate, because the east gate was shut (ch. xliv. 1), and round by the outside wall to the eastern outer gate. דֶּרֶךְ חוּץ is more minutely defined by אֶל־שַׁעַר הַחוּץ, and this, again, by דֶּרֶךְ הַפּוֹנֶה קָדִים, "by the way to the (gate) looking eastwards." The ἀπ. λεγ. מְפַכִּים, *Piel* of פָּכָה, related to בָּכָה, most probably signifies to ripple, not to trickle. מַיִם has no article, because it is evident from the context that the water was the same as that which Ezekiel had seen in the inner court, issuing from the threshold of the temple. The right shoulder is that portion of the eastern wall which joined the south side of the gate.—Vers. 3–5. The miraculous increase in the depth of the water. A thousand cubits from the wall, as one walked through, it reached to the ankles; a thousand cubits further, to the knees; a thousand cubits further, to the hips; and after going another thousand cubits it was impossible to wade through, one could only swim therein. The words מֵי אַפְסָיִם are a brief expression for "there was water which reached to the ankles." אֶפֶס is equivalent to

פַּס, an ankle, not the sole of the foot. In 1 Chron. xi. 13, on the other hand, we have פַּס דַּמִּים for אֶפֶס דַּמִּים. The striking expression מַיִם בִּרְכַּיִם for מֵי בִּרְכַּיִם may possibly have been chosen because מֵי בִּרְכַּיִם had the same meaning as מֵימֵי רַגְלַיִם in Isa. xxxvi. 12 (*Keri*). The measuring man directed the prophet's attention (ver. 6) to this extraordinary increase in the stream of water, because the miraculous nature of the stream was exhibited therein. A natural river could not increase to such an extent within such short distances, unless, indeed, other streams emptied themselves into it on all sides, which was not the case here. He then directed him to go back again עַל שְׂפַת, along the bank, not "to the bank," as he had never left it. The purpose for which he had been led along the bank was accomplished after he had gone four thousand cubits. From the increase in the water, as measured up to this point, he could infer what depth it would reach in its further course. He is therefore now to return along the bank to see how it is covered with trees. בְּשׁוּבֵנִי cannot be explained in any other way than as an incorrect form for בְּשׁוּבִי, though there are no corresponding analogies to be found.

In vers. 8–12 he gives him a still further explanation of the course of the river and the effect of its waters. The river flows out into הַגְּלִילָה הַקַּדְמוֹנָה, the eastern circle, which is identical with גְּלִילוֹת הַיַּרְדֵּן, the circle of the Jordan (Josh. xxii. 10, 11), the region above the Dead Sea, where the Jordan valley (Ghor) widens out into a broad, deep basin. הָעֲרָבָה is the deep valley of the Jordan, now called the *Ghor* (see the comm. on Deut. i. 1), of which Robinson says that the greater part remains a desolate wilderness. It was so described in ancient times (see Joseph. *Bell. Jud.* iii. 10. 7, iv. 8. 2), and we find it so to-day (compare v. Raumer, *Pal.* p. 58). הַיָּמָּה is the Dead Sea, called הַיָּם הַקַּדְמוֹנִי in ver. 18, and the sea of the Arabah in Deut. iii. 17, iv. 49. We agree with Hengstenberg in taking the words אֶל־הַיָּמָּה הַמּוּצָאִים as an emphatic summing up of the previous statement concerning the outflow of the water, to which the explanation concerning its effect upon the Dead Sea is attached, and supply בָּאוּ from the clause immediately preceding: "the waters of the river that have been brought out (come) to the sea, and the waters of the Dead Sea are healed." There is no need, therefore, for the emendation proposed by Hitzig, namely, אֶל הַיָּם הֵם מוּצָאִים. So much, however, is beyond all doubt, that הַיָּמָּה is no other than the Dead Sea already mentioned. The supposition that it is the Mediterranean Sea (Chald., Ros., Ewald, and others) cannot be reconciled with the words, and has only been transferred to this passage from Zech. xiv. 8. נִרְפָּא signifies, as in 2 Kings ii. 22, the healing or rendering wholesome of water that is injurious or destructive to life. The character of the Dead Sea, with which the ancients were also well acquainted, and of which Tacitus writes as follows: *Lacus immenso ambitu, specie maris sapore corruptior, gravitate odoris accolis pestifer, neque vento impellitur neque pisces aut suetas aquis volucres patitur* (*Hist.* v. c. 6),—a statement confirmed by all modern travellers (cf. v. Raumer, *Pal.* pp. 61 sqq., and Robinson, *Physical Geography of the Holy Land*),—is regarded as a disease of the water, which is healed or turned into wholesome water in which fishes can live, by the water of the river proceeding from the sanctuary. The healing and life-giving effect of this river upon the Dead Sea is described in vers. 9 and 10. Whithersoever the waters of the river come, all animated beings will come to life and flourish. In ver. 9 the dual נַחֲלַיִם occasions some difficulty. It is not likely that the dual should have been used merely for the sake of its resemblance to מַיִם, as Maurer imagines; and still less probable is it that there is any allusion to a junction of the river proceeding from the temple at some point in its course with the Kedron, which also flows into the Dead Sea (Hävernick), as the Kedron is not mentioned either before or afterwards. According to Kliefoth, the dual is intended to indicate a division which takes place in the waters of the river, that have hitherto flowed on together, as soon as they enter the sea. But this would certainly have been expressed more clearly. Hengstenberg takes the expression "double river" to mean a river with a strong current, and refers to Jer. l. 21 in support of this. This is probably the best explanation; for nothing is gained by altering the text into נַחְלָם (Ewald) or נְחָלִים (Hitzig), as נַחַל does not require definition by means of a suffix, nor does the plural answer to the context. אֶל כָּל־אֲשֶׁר וגו׳ is to be taken in connection with אֲשֶׁר יִשְׁרֹץ: "wherewith it swarms whithersoever the river comes;" though אֶל does not stand for עַל after Gen. vii. 21, as Hitzig supposes, but is to be explained from a species of attraction, as in Gen. xx. 13. יִחְיֶה is a pregnant expression, to revive, to come to life. The words are not to be understood, however, as meaning that there were living creatures in the Dead Sea before the health-giving water flowed into it; the thought is simply, that whithersoever the waters of the river come, there come into existence living creatures in the Dead Sea, so that it swarms with them. In addition to the שֶׁרֶץ, the quantity of fish is specially mentioned; and in the second hemistich the reason is assigned for the number of living creatures that come into existence by a second allusion to the health-giving power of the water of the river. The subject to וְיֵרָפְאוּ, viz. the waters of the Dead Sea, is to be supplied from the context. The great abundance of fish in the Dead Sea produced by the river is still further depicted in ver. 10. Fishermen will spread their nets along its coast from *Engedi* to *Eneglaim;* and as for their kind, there will be as many kinds of fish there as are to be found in the great or Mediterranean Sea. עֵין גֶּדִי, *i.e.* Goat's spring, now *Ain-Jidi,* a spring in the middle of the west coast of the Dead Sea, with ruins of several ancient buildings (see the comm. on Josh. xv. 62, and v. Raumer, *Pal.* p. 188). עֵין עֶגְלַיִם has not yet been discovered, though, from the statement of Jerome, "*Engallim* is at the beginning of the Dead Sea, where the Jordan enters it," it has been conjectured that it is to be found in *Ain el-Feshkhah,* a spring at the northern end of the west coast, where there are also ruins of a small square tower and other buildings to be seen (*vid.* Robinson's *Palestine*, II. pp. 491, 492), as none of the other springs on the west coast, of which there are but few, answer so well as this. לְמִינָה is pointed without *Mappik*, probably because the Masoretes did not regard the ה as a suffix, as the noun to which it alludes does not follow till afterwards.—Ver. 11 introduces an exception, namely, that notwithstanding this the Dead Sea will still retain marshes or pools and swamps, which will not be made wholesome (בִּצְּאֹת for בִּצּוֹת, pools). An allusion to the natural character of the Dead Sea underlies the words. "In the rainy season, when the sea is full, its waters overspread many low tracts of marsh land, which remain after the receding of the water in the form of moist pools or basins; and as the water in these pools evaporates rapidly, the ground becomes covered with a thick crust of salt" (Robinson's *Physical Geography*, p. 215). לְמֶלַח נִתָּנוּ, they are given up to salt, *i.e.* destined to remain salt, because the waters of the river do not reach them. The light in which the salt is regarded here is not that of its seasoning properties, but, in the words of Hengstenberg, "as the foe to all fruitfulness, all life and prosperity, as Pliny has said (*Hist. Nat.* xxxi. c. 7: *Omnis locus, in quo reperitur sal, sterilis est nihilque gignit*") (cf. Deut. xxix. 22; Jer. xvii. 6; Zeph. ii. 9; Ps. cvii. 34).—In ver. 12 the effect of the water of the river upon the vegetation of the ground, already mentioned in ver. 7, is still further described. On its coast grow all kinds of trees with edible fruits (עֵץ מַאֲכָל, as in Lev. xix. 23), whose leaves do not wither, and whose fruits do not fail, but ripen every month (בִּכֵּר, to produce first-fruits, *i.e.* fresh fruits; and לָחֳדָשִׁים distributive, as in Isa. xlvii. 13), because the waters which moisten the soil proceed from the sanctuary, *i.e.* "directly and immediately from the dwelling-place of Him who is the author of all vital power and fruitfulness" (Hitzig). The leaves and fruits of these trees therefore possess supernatural powers. The fruits serve as food, *i.e.* for the maintenance of the life produced by the river of water;

the leaves as medicine (תְּרוּפָה from רוּף = רָפָא, healing), *i.e.* for the healing of the sick and corrupt (*εἰς θεραπείαν*, Rev. xxii. 2).

In the effect of the water proceeding from the sanctuary upon the Dead Sea and the land on its shores, as described in vers. 8–12, the significance of this stream of water in relation to the new kingdom of God is implied. If, then, the question be asked, what we are to understand by this water, whether we are to take it in a literal sense as the temple spring, or in a spiritual and symbolical sense, the complete answer can only be given in connection with the interpretation of the whole of the temple vision (ch. xl.–xlviii.). Even if we assume for the moment, however, that the description of the new temple, with the worship appointed for it, and the fresh division of Canaan, is to be understood literally, and therefore that the building of an earthly temple upon a high mountain in the most holy *terumah* of the land set apart for Jehovah, and a renewal of the bleeding sacrifices in this temple by the twelve tribes of Israel, when restored to Palestine from the heathen lands, are to be taken for granted, it would be difficult to combine with this a literal interpretation of what is said concerning the effect of the temple spring. It is true that in Volck's opinion "we are to think of a glorification of nature;" but even this does not remove the difficulties which stand in the way of a literal interpretation of the temple spring. According to ver. 12, its waters possess the life-giving and healing power ascribed to them because they issue from the sanctuary. But how does the possession by the water of the power to effect the glorification of nature harmonize with its issuing from a temple in which bullocks, rams, calves, and goats are slaughtered and sacrificed? —Volck is still further of opinion that, with the spiritual interpretation of the temple spring, "nothing at all could be made of the fishermen;" because, for example, he cannot conceive of the spiritual interpretation in any other way than as an allegorical translation of all the separate features of the prophetic picture into spiritual things. But he has failed to consider that the fishermen with their nets on the shore of the sea, once dead, but now swarming with fish, are irreconcilably opposed to the assumption of a glorification of nature in the holy land, just because the inhabitants of the globe or holy land, in its paradisaically glorified state, will no more eat fish or other flesh, according to the teaching of Scripture, than the first men in Paradise. When once the wolf shall feed with the lamb, the leopard with the kid, the cow with the bear, and the lion shall eat straw like the ox, under the sceptre of the sprout from the stem of Jesse, then will men also cease their fishing, and no longer slaughter and eat either oxen or goats. To this the Israelites will form no exception in their glorified land of Canaan.—And if even these features in the vision before us decidedly favour the figurative or spiritual view of the temple spring, the necessity for this explanation is placed beyond the reach of doubt by a comparison of our picture with the parallel passages. According to Joel iv. 18, at the time when a spring issues from the house of Jehovah and the vale of Shittim is watered, the mountains trickle with new wine, and the hills run with milk. If, then, in this case we understand what is affirmed of the temple spring literally, the trickling of the mountains with new wine and the flowing of the hills with milk must be taken literally as well. But we are unable to attain to the belief that in the glorified land of Israel the mountains will be turned into springs of new wine, and the hills into fountains of milk; and in the words of the whole verse we can discern nothing but a figurative description of the abundant streams of blessing which will then pour over the entire land. And just as in Joel the context points indisputably to a non-literal or figurative explanation, so also does the free manner in which Zechariah uses this prophecy of his predecessors, speaking only of living waters which issue from Jerusalem, and flow half into the eastern (*i.e.* the Dead) sea, and half into the western (*i.e.* the Mediterranean) sea (Zech. xiv. 8), show that he was not thinking of an actual spring with earthly water. And here we are still provisionally passing by the application made of this feature in the prophetic descriptions of the glory of the new kingdom of God in the picture of the heavenly Jerusalem (Rev. xxii. 1 and 2).

The figurative interpretation, or spiritual explanation, is moreover favoured by the analogy of the Scriptures. "Water," which renders the unfruitful land fertile, and supplies refreshing drink to the thirsty, is used in Scripture as a figure denoting blessing and salvation, which had been represented even in Paradise in the form of watering (cf. Gen. xiii. 10). In Isa. xii. 3, "and with joy ye draw water from the wells of salvation," the figure is expressly interpreted. And so also in Isa. xliv. 3, "I will pour water upon the thirsty one, and streams upon the desert; I will pour my Spirit upon thy seed, and my blessing upon thine offspring:" where the *blessing* answers to the water, the *Spirit* is named as the principal form in which the blessing is manifested, "the foundation of all other salvation for the people of God" (Hengstenberg). This salvation, which Joel had already described as a spring issuing from the house of Jehovah and watering the dry acacia valley, Ezekiel saw in a visionary embodiment as water, which sprang from under the threshold of the temple into which the glory of the Lord entered, and had swollen at a short distance off into so mighty a river that it was no longer possible to wade through. In this way the thought is symbolized, that the salvation which the Lord causes to flow down to His people from His throne will pour down from small beginnings in marvellously increasing fulness. The river flows on into the barren, desolate waste of the Ghor, and finally into the Dead Sea, and makes the waters thereof sound, so that it swarms with fishes. The waste is a figure denoting spiritual drought and desolation, and the Dead Sea a symbol of the death caused by sin. The healing and quickening of the salt waters of that sea, so fatal to all life, set forth the power of that divine salvation which conquers death, and the calling to life of the world sunk in spiritual death.

From this comes life in its creative fulness and manifold variety, as shown both by the figure of the fishermen who spread their nets along the shore, and by the reference to the kinds of fish, which are as manifold in their variety as those in the great sea. But life extends no further than the water of salvation flows. Wherever it cannot reach, the world continues to lie in death. The pools and swamps of the Dead Sea are still given up to salt. And lastly, the water of salvation also possesses the power to produce trees with leaves and fruits, by which the life called forth from death can be sustained and cured of all diseases. This is the meaning, according to the express statement of the text, of the trees with their never withering leaves, upon the banks of the river, and their fruits ripening every month.

Chap. xlvii. 13–xlviii. 35. *Boundaries and Division of the Holy Land. Description of the City of God.*

Chap. xlvii. 13–23. BOUNDARIES OF THE LAND TO BE DIVIDED AMONG THE TRIBES OF ISRAEL. (See the map, Plate IV.)—Ver. 13. *Thus saith the Lord Jehovah, This is the boundary according to which ye shall divide the land among you for an inheritance, for Joseph portions.* Ver. 14. *And ye shall receive it for an inheritance, one as well as another, because I lifted up my hand to give it to your fathers; and thus shall this land fall to you for an inheritance.* Ver. 15. *And this is the boundary of the land: toward the north side, from the great sea onwards by the way to Chetlon, in the direction of Zedad;* Ver. 16. *Hamath, Berotah, Sibraim, which is between the boundary of Damascus and the boundary of Hamath, the central Hazer, which is on the boundary of Hauran.* Ver. 17. *And the boundary from the sea shall be Hazar-Enon, the boundary town of Damascus; and as for the north northwards, Hamath is the boundary. This, the north side.* Ver. 18. *And the east side between Hauran and Damascus and Gilead and the land of Israel, shall be the Jordan; from the boundary to the eastern sea ye shall measure. This, the east side.* Ver. 19. *And the south side toward the south; from Tamar to the water of strife, Kadesh, along the brook to the great sea. This, the south side toward the south.* Ver. 20. *And the west side; the great sea from the boundary to Hamath. This, the west side.* Ver. 21. *This land shall ye divide among you according to the tribes of Israel.* Ver. 22. *And it shall come to pass, ye shall divide it by lot among yourselves for an inheritance, and among the foreigners who dwell in the midst of you, who have begotten sons in the midst of you; they shall be to you like natives born among the sons of Israel; they shall cast lots with you for an inheritance among the tribes of Israel.* Ver. 23. *And it shall come to pass, in the tribe in which the foreigner dwells, there shall ye give him his inheritance, is the saying of the Lord Jehovah.*

The fixing of the boundary of the land which Israel was to divide in future according to its twelve tribes is commenced (vers. 13 and 14) and concluded (vers. 22 and 23) with certain general statements concerning the distribution. The introductory statements are attached to the heading "this is the boundary," which is therefore repeated in ver. 15. גֵּה is evidently a copyist's error for זֶה, which is adopted by all the older translators, contained in some *Codd.*, and demanded by וְזֶה in ver. 15. גְּבוּל stands here for the whole of the boundary of the land to be distributed; and אֲשֶׁר which follows is an accusative, "according to which."—"According to the *twelve* tribes,"—for all Israel is to return and dwell as *one* people of God under one prince in its own land (ch. xxxvi. 24 sqq., xxxvii. 21 sqq.). But the division among the twelve tribes is more precisely defined immediately afterwards by the clause abruptly appended, "Joseph portions," *i.e.* two portions for Joseph. There can be no doubt that this is the meaning of the words in accordance with Gen. xlviii. 22 and Josh. xvii. 14, 17. Hence the notice-like form of the expression, which should not be obliterated by pointing חבלים as a dual, חֲבָלַיִם. If the land was to be divided by lot according to twelve tribes, and the tribe of Levi was to receive its portion from the *terumah* which was set apart,

Joseph must necessarily receive two hereditary portions for his sons Ephraim and Manasseh, in accordance with the appointment of the patriarch in Gen. xlviii. 22. The commencement of ver. 14 is not at variance with this, as Hitzig imagines; for the words, "ye shall receive it for an inheritance, one as another," simply affirm, that of the twelve tribes reckoned by Israel in relation to the נַחֲלָה, all were to receive equal shares, the one as much as the other. As the reason for this command to divide the land, allusion is made to the oath with which God promised to give this land to the fathers (cf. ch. xx. 28).—The definition of the boundaries commences with ver. 15. In form it differs in many points from Num. xxxiv. 1–15, but in actual fact it is in harmony with the Mosaic definition. In Num. xxxiv. the description commences with the southern boundary, then proceeds to the western and northern boundaries, and closes with the eastern. In Ezekiel it commences with the northern boundary and proceeds to the east, the south, and the west. This difference may be explained in a very simple manner, from the fact that the Israelites in the time of Moses came from Egypt *i.e.* marching from the south, and stood by the south-eastern boundary of the land, whereas at this time they were carried away into the northern lands Assyria and Babylon, and were regarded as returning thence. Again, in Ezekiel the boundaries are described much more briefly than in Num. xxxiv., the northern boundary alone being somewhat more circumstantially described. The course which it takes is represented in a general manner in ver. 15 as running from the great sea, *i.e.* the Mediterranean, by the way to Chetlon, in the direction toward Zedad. In vers. 16 and 17 there follow the places which formed the boundary. The starting-point on the Mediterranean Sea can only be approximately determined, as the places mentioned, Chetlon and Zedad, are still unknown. Not only *Chetlon*, but *Zedad* also, has not yet been discovered. The city of *Sadad* (*Sudud*), to the east of the road leading from Damascus to Hums (Emesa), which Robinson and Wetzstein suppose to be the same, lies much too far toward the east to be used in defining the boundary either here or in Num. xxxiv. 8 (see the comm. on Num. xxxiv. 8). Among the names enumerated in ver. 16, חֲמָת is not the city of *Hamah* on the Orontes, which lay much too far to the north, but the kingdom of *Hamath*, the southern boundary of which formed the northern boundary of Canaan, though it cannot be given with exactness. *Berothah* is probably identical with *Berothai* in 2 Sam. viii. 8, a city of the king of Zobah; but the situation of it is still unknown. *Sibraim* may perhaps be identical with *Ziphron* in Num. xxxiv. 9, which has also not yet been discovered, and is not to be sought for in the ruins of *Zifran*, to the north-east of Damascus, near the road to Palmyra; for that place could not form the boundary of Damascus and Hamath. The situation of the "central *Hazer*" has also not yet been determined. *Hauran*, on the boundary of which it stood, is used here in a more comprehensive sense than Ἀυρανῖτις in Josephus and other Greek authors, and includes the later *Auranitis*, together with *Gaulanitis* (Golan) and *Batanaea* (Bashan), and probably also *Ituraea*, as only Damascus and Gilead are named in ver. 18 in addition to Hauran, on the east side of the Jordan; so that the whole tract of land between the territory of Damascus and the country of Gilead is embraced by the name Hauran. חַוְרָן, Arab. حَوْرَان, is derived from the number of caves (חוּר, חוֹר) in that district, to which Wetzstein (*Reiseber.* p. 92) indeed raises the objection that with the exception of the eastern and south-eastern Hauran, where no doubt most of the volcanic hills have been perforated by troglodytes, the dwellings in caves are by no means common in that region. But the name may have originated in this eastern district, and possibly have included even that portion of Gilead which was situated to the north of the Jabbok, namely, *Erbed* and *Suët*, the true cave-country. For further remarks concerning these districts, see the comm. on Deut. iii. 4 and 10.

The statement in ver. 17*a*, "the boundary from the sea shall be *Hazar-Enon*, the boundary of Damascus," cannot have any other meaning than that the northern boundary, which started from the Mediterranean Sea, stretched as far as *Hazar-Enon*, the frontier city of Damascus, or that *Hazar-Enon* formed the terminal point on the east, toward the boundary of Damascus, for the northern boundary proceeding from the sea. חֲצַר עֵינוֹן or חֲצַר עֵינָן (Num. xxxiv. 9), *i.e.* spring-court, we have endeavoured to identify in the comm. on Num. xxxiv. 3 with the spring *Lebweh*, which lies in the *Bekâa* at the watershed between the Orontes and the Leontes; and the designation "the boundary of Damascus" suits the situation very well. Ver. 17*b* has been aptly explained by Hitzig thus, in accordance with the literal meaning of the words, "and as for the north northwards, *Hamath* is the boundary," which he further elucidates by observing that צָפוֹנָה is intended as a supplementary note to the boundary line from west to east, which is indicated just before. וְאֵת פְּאַת צָפוֹן is a concluding formula: "this, the north side." But וְאֵת (here and vers. 18 and 19) is not to be altered into זֹאת, after ver. 20 and the Syriac version, as Hitzig supposes, but to be explained, as ver. 18 clearly shows, on the supposition that Ezekiel had תָּמֹדּוּ, "ye shall measure," floating before his mind, to which וְאֵת פ׳, "and that the northern boundary," would form a correct logical sequel.—The eastern boundary is defined in ver. 18 in the same manner as in Num. xxxiv. 10–12, except that in the latter it is more minutely described above the Lake of Gennesaret by the mention of several localities, whereas Ezekiel only names the Jordan as the boundary.—פְּאַת קָדִים, with supplementary remarks, is not to be taken as the predicate to the subject הַיַּרְדֵּן, as Hitzig has correctly observed; for the meaning of פֵּאָה does not allow of this. The explanation is rather this: as for the east side, between Hauran, etc. and the land of Israel, is the Jordan. Hauran, Damascus, and Gilead lie on the east side of the Jordan, the land of Israel on the west side. The striking circumstance that Ezekiel commences with Hauran, which lay in the middle between Damascus and Gilead,—Hauran, Damascus, and Gilead, instead of Damascus, Hauran, and Gilead,—may probably be explained from the fact that the Jordan, which he names as the boundary, for the sake of brevity, did not extend so far upwards as to the territory of Damascus, but simply formed the boundary of the land of Israel between Hauran and Gilead. מִגְּבוּל points back to the northern boundary already mentioned. From this boundary, the eastern terminal point of which was *Hazar-Enon*, they are to measure to the eastern sea, *i.e.* to the Dead Sea.—Ver. 19. The southern boundary toward the south is to proceed from Tamar to the water of strife, Kadesh, (and thence) along the brook to the great (*i.e.* Mediterranean) sea. *Tamar*, a different place from *Hazazon-Tamar*, called *Engedi* in ver. 10 (cf. 2 Chron. xx. 2), is supposed to be the *Thamara* (Θαμαρά),[1] which was a day's journey on the road from Hebron to Aelam (*Aelath*, Deut. ii. 8; 1 Kings ix. 26), according to Eusebius in the *Onomast.* ed. Lars. p. 68, and had a Roman garrison; and Robinson (*Pal.* III. pp. 178 and 186 sqq.) accordingly conjectures that it is to be found in the ruins of *Kurnub*, which lie six hours' journey to the south of *Milh*, toward the pass of *es-Sufâh*. But this conjecture is bound up with various assumptions of a very questionable character, and the situation of Kurnub hardly suits the *Tamar* of our passage, which should be sought, not to the west of the southern point of the Dead Sea, but, according to the southern boundary of Canaan as drawn in Num. xxxiv. 3–5, to the south of the Dead Sea. The waters of strife of Kadesh (Num. xx. 1–13), in the desert of Zin, were near

[1] The statement runs thus: λέγεται δέ τις Θαμαρὰ κώμη διεστῶσα Μάψις ἡμέρας ὁδόν, ἀπιόντων ἀπὸ Χεβρὼν εἰς Αἰλάμ, ἥτις νῦν φρούριόν ἐστι τῶν στρατιωτῶν. In Jerome: *est et aliud castellum, unius diei itinere a Mampsis oppido separatum, pergentibus Ailiam de Chebron, ubi nunc romanum praesidium positum est.* But on account of the Μάψις (*Mampsis*), which is evidently a corruption, the passage is obscure. Robinson's conjecture concerning *Thamara* is founded upon the assumption that the reading should be Μάλις, and that this is the *Malatha* mentioned by later writers as the station of a Roman cohort.

Kadesh-Barnea, which was in the neighbourhood of the spring *Ain Kades*, discovered by Rowland to the south of *Bir-Seba* and *Khalasa* by the fore-courts of *Jebel Helal*, *i.e.* at the north-west corner of the mountain land of the *Azazimeh* (see the comm. on Num. x. 12, xii. 16, and xx. 16). Instead of מְרִיבוֹת we have the singular מְרִיבַת in ch. xlviii. 28, as in Num. xxvii. 14 and Deut. xxxii. 51. נַחֲלָה is to be pointed נַחְלָה, from נַחַל with ה *loc.*; and the reference is to the brook of Egypt; the great wady *el-Arish* (Ῥινοκοροῦρα), along which the southern boundary of Canaan ran from Kadesh to the Mediterranean Sea (see the comm. on ch. xxxiv. 5).—Ver. 20. The Mediterranean Sea formed the western boundary. מִגְּבוּל, *i.e.* from the southern boundary mentioned in ver. 19 till opposite (עַד נֹכַח) to the coming to Hamath, *i.e.* till opposite to the point at which one enters the territory of *Hamath* (Hitzig), *i.e.* the spot mentioned in ver. 20 (? 17) as the commencement of the northern boundary in the neighbourhood of the promontory of *esh-Shûkah*, between Byblus (Gebal) and Tripolis.—Ver. 21. This land they are to divide among them according to their tribes. With this remark, which points back to ver. 13, the definition of the boundaries is brought to a close. There is simply added in vers. 22 and 23 a further regulation concerning the foreigners living in Israel. The law of Moses had already repeatedly urged upon the Israelites affectionate treatment of them, and in Lev. xix. 34 the command is given to treat them like natives in this respect, and to love them. But the full right of citizenship was not thereby conceded to them, so that they could also acquire property in land. The land was given to the Israelites alone for an hereditary possession. Foreigners could only be incorporated into the congregation of Israel under the limitations laid down in Deut. xxiii. 2–9, by the reception of circumcision. But in the future distribution of the land, on the contrary, the גֵּרִים were to receive hereditary property like native-born Israelites; and in this respect no difference was to exist between the members of the people of God born of

Abraham's seed and those born of the heathen. At the same time, this right was not to be conferred upon every foreigner who might be only temporarily living in Israel, but to those alone who should beget sons in the midst of Israel, *i.e.* settle permanently in the holy land. The *Kal* יִפְּלוּ is not to be altered into the *Hiphil* תַּפִּילוּ, as Hitzig proposes, but is used in the sense of receiving by lot, derived from the *Hiphil* signification, "to apportion by lot."

Chap. xlviii. 1–29. Division of Canaan among the Tribes, and Boundary of the Terumah.—The division of the land, like the definition of the boundaries (ch. xlvii. 15), commences in the north, and enumerates the tribes in the order in which they were to receive their inheritances from north to south: first, seven tribes from the northern boundary to the centre of the land (vers. 1–7), where the heave for the sanctuary, with the land of the priests and Levites and the city domain, together with the prince's land on the two sides, was to be set apart (vers. 8–22; and secondly, the other five tribes from this to the southern boundary (vers. 23–29). Compare the map on Plate IV.

Ver. 1. *And these are the names of the tribes: from the north end by the side of the way to Chetlon toward Hamath (and) Hazar-Enon the boundary of Damascus—toward the north by the side of Hamath there shall east side, west side belong to him: Dan one (tribe-lot).* Ver. 2. *And on the boundary of Dan from the east side to the west side: Asher one.* Ver. 3. *And on the boundary of Asher from the east side to the west side: Naphtali one.* Ver. 4. *And on the boundary of Naphtali from the east side to the west side: Manasseh one.* Ver. 5. *And on the boundary of Manasseh from the east side to the west side: Ephraim one.* Ver. 6. *And on the boundary of Ephraim from the east side to the west side: Reuben one.* Ver. 7. *And on the boundary of Reuben from the east side to the west side: Judah one.* Ver. 8. *And on the boundary of Judah from the east side to the west side shall be the heave, which ye shall lift (heave) off, five and twenty thousand (rods) in breadth, and the length like every tribe portion from the east side to the west side; and the sanctuary shall be in the midst of it.* Ver. 9. *The heave which ye shall lift (heave) for Jehovah shall be five and twenty thousand in length and ten thousand in breadth.* Ver. 10. *And to these shall the holy heave belong, to the priests, toward the north, five and twenty thousand; toward the west, breadth ten thousand; toward the east, breadth ten thousand; and toward the south, length five and twenty thousand; and the sanctuary of Jehovah shall be in the middle of it.* Ver. 11. *To the priests, whoever is sanctified of the sons of Zadok, who have kept my charge, who have not strayed with the straying of the sons of Israel, as the Levites have strayed,* Ver. 12. *To them shall a portion lifted off belong from the heave of the land; a most holy beside the territory of the Levites.* Ver. 13. *And the Levites (shall receive) parallel with the territory of the priests five and twenty thousand in length, and in breadth ten thousand; the whole length five and twenty thousand, and (the whole) breadth ten thousand.* Ver. 14. *And they shall not sell or exchange any of it, nor shall the first-fruit of the land pass to others; for it is holy to Jehovah.* Ver. 15. *And the five thousand which remain in the breadth along the five and twenty thousand are common land for the city for dwellings and for open space; and the city shall be in the centre of it.* Ver. 16. *And these are its measures: the north side four thousand five hundred, the south side four thousand five hundred, the east side four thousand five hundred, and the west side four thousand five hundred.* Ver. 17. *And the open space of the city shall be toward the north two hundred and fifty, toward the south two hundred and fifty, toward the east two hundred and fifty, and toward the west two hundred and fifty.* Ver. 18. *And the remainder in length parallel with the holy heave, ten thousand toward the east and ten thousand toward the west, this shall be beside the holy heave, and its produce shall serve the workmen of the city for food.* Ver. 19. *And as for the workmen of the city, they shall cultivate it from all the tribes.* Ver. 20. *The whole of the heave is five and twenty thousand by five and twenty thousand; a fourth of the holy heave shall ye take for the possession of the city.* Ver. 21. *And the remainder shall belong to the prince on this side and on that side of the holy heave and of the city possession; along the five and twenty thousand of the heave to the eastern boundary, and toward the west along the five and twenty thousand to the western boundary parallel with the tribe portions, it shall belong to the prince; and the holy heave and the sanctuary of the house shall be in the midst.* Ver. 22. *Thus from the possession of the Levites (as) from the possession of the city shall that which lies in the midst of what belongs to the prince between the territory of Judah and the territory of Benjamin belong to the prince.* Ver. 23. *And the rest of the tribes are from the east side to the west side: Benjamin one.* Ver. 24. *And on the boundary of Benjamin from the east side to the west side: Simeon one.* Ver. 25. *And on the boundary of Simeon from the east side to the west side: Issachar one.* Ver. 26. *And on the boundary of Issachar from the east side to the west side: Zebulon one.* Ver. 27. *And on the boundary of Zebulon from the east side to the west side: Gad one.* Ver. 28. *And on the boundary of Gad on the south side toward the south, the boundary shall be from Tamar to the water of strife from Kadesh along the brook to the great sea.* Ver. 29. *This is the land which ye shall divide by lot for inheritance to the tribes of Israel; these are their portions, is the saying of the Lord Jehovah.*

The new division of the land differs from the former one effected in the time of Joshua, in the first place, in the fact that all the tribe-portions were to extend uniformly across the entire breadth of the land from the eastern boundary to the Mediterranean Sea on the west, so that they were to form parallel tracts of country; whereas in the distribution made in the time of Joshua, several of the tribe-territories covered only half the breadth of the land. For example, Dan received his inheritance on the west of Benjamin; and the territories of half Manasseh and Asher ran up from the northern boundary of Ephraim to the northern boundary of Canaan; while Issachar, Naphtali, and Zebulon received their portions on the east of these; and lastly, Simeon received his possession within the boundaries of the tribe of Judah. And secondly, it also differs from the former, in the fact that not only are all the twelve tribes located in Canaan proper, between the Jordan and the Mediterranean Sea; whereas previously two tribes and a half had received from Moses, at their own request, the conquered land of Bashan and Gilead on the eastern side of the Jordan, so that the land of Canaan could be divided among the remaining nine tribes and a half. But besides this, the central tract of land, about the fifth part of the whole, was separated for the holy heave, the city domain, and the prince's land, so that only the northern and southern portions, about four-fifths of the whole, remained for distribution among the twelve tribes, seven tribes receiving their hereditary portions to the north of the heave and five to the south, because the heave was so selected that the city with its territory lay near the ancient Jerusalem.—In vers. 1–7 the seven tribes which were to dwell on the north of the heave are enumerated. The principal points of the northern boundary, viz. the way to Chetlon and Hazar-Enon, the boundary of Damascus, are repeated in ver. 1 from ch. xlvii. 15, 17, as the starting and terminal points of the northern boundary running from west to east. The words אֶל־יַד חֲמָת fix the northern boundary more precisely in relation to the adjoining territory; and in וְהָיוּ לוֹ פ׳ the enumeration of the tribe-lots begins with that of the tribe of Dan, which was to receive its territory against the northern boundary. לוֹ refers to the name דָּן which follows, and which Ezekiel already had in his mind. פְּאַת קָדִים הַיָּם is constructed *asyndetôs*; and פְּאַת is to be repeated in thought before הַיָּם: the east side (and) the west (side) are to belong to it, *i.e.* the tract of land toward its west and its east side. The words which follow, דָּן אֶחָד, are attached in an anacoluthistic manner: "Dan (is to receive) one portion," for " one shall belong to Dan." To אֶחָד we are to supply in thought the substantive חֶבֶל, tribe-lot, according to ch. xlvii. 13. " The assumption that one tribe was to receive as much as another (*vid.* ch. xlvii. 14), leads to the conclusion that each tribe-lot was to be taken as a *monas* " (Kliefoth). In this way the names in vers. 2–7, with the constantly repeated אֶחָד, must also be taken. The same form of description is repeated in vers. 23–28 in the case of the five tribes placed to the south of the heave.—In the order of the several tribe-territories it is impossible to discover any universal principle of arrangement. All that is clear is, that in the case of Dan, Asher, Naphtali, Manasseh, and Ephraim, regard is had to the former position of these tribe-territories as far as the altered circumstances allowed. In the time of the Judges a portion of the Danites had migrated to the north, conquered the city of Laish, and given it the name of Dan, so that from that time forward Dan is generally named as the northern boundary of the land (*e.g.* as early as 2 Sam. iii. 10, and in other passages). Accordingly Dan receives the tract of land along the northern boundary. Asher and Naphtali, which formerly occupied the most northerly portions of the land, follow next. Then comes Manasseh, as half Manasseh had formerly dwelt on the east of Naphtali; and Ephraim joins Manasseh, as it formerly joined the western half Manasseh. The reason for placing Reuben between Ephraim and Judah appears to be, that Reuben was the first-born of Jacob's sons. The position of the *terumah* between Judah and Benjamin is probably connected with the circumstance that Jerusalem formerly stood on the boundary of these two tribes, and so also in the future was to skirt Benjamin with its territory. The other tribes had then to be located on the south of Benjamin; Simeon, whose territory formerly lay to the south; Issachar and Zebulon, for which no room was left in the north; and Gad, which had to be brought over from Gilead to Canaan.

In vers. 8–22, the *terumah*, which has already been described in ch. xlv. 1–7 for a different purpose, is more precisely defined: first of all, in ver. 8, according to its whole extent—viz. twenty-five thousand rods in breadth (from north to south), and the length the same as any one (= every one) of the tribe-lots, *i.e.* reaching from the Jordan to the Mediterranean Sea (cf. ch. xlv. 7). In the centre of this separated territory the sanctuary (the temple) was to stand. בְּתוֹכוֹ, the suffix of which refers *ad sensum* to חֵלֶק instead of תְּרוּמָה, has not the indefinite meaning "therein," but signifies "in the centre;" for the priests' portion, in the middle of which the temple was to stand, occupied the central position between the portion of the Levites and the city possession, as is evident from ver. 22. The circumstance that here, as in ch. xlv. 1 sqq., in the division of the *terumah*, the priests' portion is mentioned first, then the portion of the Levites, and after this the city possession, proves nothing so far as the local order in which these three portions followed one another is concerned; but the enumeration is regulated by their spiritual significance, so that first of all the most holy land for the temple and priests is defined, then the holy portion of the Levites, and lastly, the common land for the city. The command, that the sanctuary is to occupy the centre of the whole *terumah*, leads to a more minute description in the first place (vers. 9–12) of the priests' portion, in which the sanctuary was situated, than of the heave to be lifted off for Jehovah. In ver. 10, לָאֵלֶּה, which stands at the head, is explained by לַכֹּהֲנִים which follows. The extent of this holy *terumah* on all four sides is then given; and lastly, the command is repeated, that the sanctuary of Jehovah is to be in the centre of it. In ver. 11, הַמְקֻדָּשׁ is rendered in the plural by the LXX., Chald. and Syr., and is taken in a distributive sense by Kimchi and others: to the priests whoever is sanctified of the sons of Zadok. This is required by the position of the participle between לַכֹּהֲנִים and מִבְּנֵי צָדוֹק (compare 2 Chron. xxvi. 18, and for the singular of the participle after a previous plural, Ps. viii. 9). The other rendering, "for the priests is it sanctified, those of the sons of Zadok," is at variance not only with the position of the words, but also with the fact, namely, that the assignment to the priests of a heave set apart for Jehovah is never designated as קֹדֶשׁ, and from the nature of the case could not be so designated. The apodosis to ver. 11*a* follows in ver. 12, where לַכֹּהֲנִים is resumed in לָהֶם. תְּרוּמִיָּה is an adjective formation derived from תְּרוּמָה, with the signification of an abstract: that which is lifted (the lifting) from the heave, as it were "a terumah in the second potency" (for these formations, see Ewald, §§ 164 and 165). This *terumiyah* is called most holy, in contrast with the Levites' portion of the *terumah*, which was קֹדֶשׁ (ver. 14). The priests' portion is to be beside the territory of the Levites, whether on the southern or northern side cannot be gathered from these words any more than from the definition in ver. 13: "and the Levites beside (parallel with) the territory of the priests." Both statements simply affirm that the portions of the priests and Levites were to lie side by side, and not to be separated by the town possession.—Vers. 13 and 14 treat of the Levites' portion: ver. 13, of its situation and extent; ver. 14, of its law of tenure. The seemingly tautological repetition of the measurement of the length and breadth, as "all the length and the breadth," is occasioned by the fact "that Ezekiel intends to express himself more briefly here, and not, as in ver. 10, to take all the four points of the compass singly; in 'all the length' he embraces the two long sides of the oblong, and in '(all) the breadth' the two broad sides, and affirms that 'all the length,' *i.e.* of both the north and south sides, is to be twenty-five thousand rods, and 'all the breadth,' *i.e.* of both the east and west sides, is to be ten thousand rods" (Kliefoth). Hitzig has missed the sense, and therefore proposes to alter the text. With regard to the possession of the Levites, the instructions given in Lev. xxv. 34 for the field of the Levites' cities—namely, that none of it was to be sold—are extended to the whole of the territory of the Levites: no part of it is to be alienated by sale or barter. And the character of the possession is assigned as the reason: the first-fruit of the land, *i.e.* the land lifted off (separated) as first-fruit, is not to pass into the possession of others, because as such it is holy to the Lord. The *Chetib* יַעֲבוֹר is the correct reading: to pass over, *sc.* to others, to non-Levites.

Vers. 15–18 treat of the city possession. As the *terumah* was twenty-five thousand rods in breadth (ver. 8), after measuring off ten thousand rods in breadth for the priests and ten thousand rods in breadth for the Levites from the entire breadth, there still remain five thousand rods עַל פְּנֵי, in front of, *i.e.* along, the long side, which was twenty-five thousand rods. This remnant was to be חֹל, *i.e.* common (not holy) land for the city (Jerusalem). לְמוֹשָׁב, for dwelling-places, *i.e.* for building dwelling-houses upon; and לְמִגְרָשׁ, for open space, the precinct around the city. The city was to stand in the centre of this oblong. Ver. 16 gives the size of the city: on each of the four sides, four thousand five hundred rods (the חמש, designated by the Masoretes as כתיב ולא קרי, has crept into the text through a copyist's error); and ver. 17, the extent of the open space surrounding it: on each side two hundred and fifty rods. This gives for the city, together with the open space, a square of five thousand rods on every side; so that the city with its precinct filled the entire breadth of the space left for it, and there only remained on the east and west an open space of ten thousand rods in length and five thousand rods in breadth along the holy *terumah*. This is noticed in ver. 18; its produce was to serve for bread, *i.e.* for maintenance, for the labourers of the city (the masculine suffix in תְּבוּאָתֹה refers grammatically to הַנּוֹתָר). By עֹבְדֵי הָעִיר Hitzig would understand the inhabitants of the city, because one cultivates a piece of land even by dwelling on it. But this use of עָבַד cannot be established. Nor are עֹבְדֵי הָעִיר the workmen employed in building the city, as Gesenius, Hävernick, and others suppose; for the city was not perpetually being built, so that there should be any necessity for setting apart a particular piece of land for the builders; but they are the working men of the city, the labouring class living in the city. They are not to be without possession in the future Jerusalem, but are to receive a possession in land for their maintenance. We are told in ver. 19 who these workmen are. Here הָעֹבֵד is used collectively: as for the labouring class of the city, people out of all the tribes of Israel shall work upon the land belonging to the city. The suffix in יַעַבְדוּהוּ points back to הַנּוֹתָר. The transitive explanation, to employ a person in work, has nothing in the language to confirm it. The fact itself is in harmony with the statement in ch. xlv. 6, that the city was to belong to all Israel. Lastly, in ver. 20 the dimensions of the whole *terumah*, and the relation of the city possession to the holy *terumah*, are given. כָּל־הַתְּרוּמָה is the whole heave, so far as it has hitherto been described, embracing the property of the priests, of the Levites, and of the city. In this extent it is twenty-five thousand rods long and the same broad. If, however, we add the property of the prince, which is not treated of till vers. 21–23, it is considerably longer, and reaches, as has been stated in ver. 8, to the boundaries of the land both on the east and west, the Jordan and the Mediterranean Sea, as the several tribe-territories do. But if we omit the prince's land, the space set apart for the city possession occupied the fourth part of the holy *terumah*, *i.e.* of the portion of the priests and Levites. This is the meaning of the second half of ver. 20, which literally reads thus: "to a fourth shall ye lift off the holy *terumah* for the city possession." This is not to be understood as meaning that a fourth was to be taken from the holy *terumah* for the city possession; for that would yield an incorrect proportion, as the twenty thousand rods in breadth would be reduced to fifteen thousand rods by the subtraction of the fourth part, which would be opposed to vers. 9 and 15. The meaning is rather the following: from the whole *terumah* the fourth part of the area of the holy *terumah* is to be taken off for the city possession, *i.e.* five thousand rods for twenty thousand. According to ver. 15, this was the size of the domain set apart for the city.

In vers. 21–23 the situation and extent of the prince's possession are described. For ver. 21, *vid.* ch. xlv. 7. הַנּוֹתָר, the rest of the *terumah*, as it has been defined in ver. 8, reaching in length from the Jordan to the Mediterranean. As the holy *terumah* and the city possession were only twenty-five thousand rods in length, and did not reach to the Jordan on the east, or to the sea on the west, there still remained an area on either side whose length or extent toward the east and west is not given in rods, but may be calculated from the proportion which the intervening *terumah* bore to the length of the land (from east to west). אֶל־פְּנֵי and עַל־פְּנֵי, in front of, or along, the front of the twenty-five thousand rods, refer to the eastern and western boundaries of the *terumah*, which was twenty-five thousand rods in length. In ver. 21*b* the statement is repeated, that the holy *terumah* and the sanctuary were to lie in the centre of it, *i.e.* between the portions of land appointed for the prince on either side; and lastly, in ver. 22 it is still further stated, with regard to the prince's land on both sides of the *terumah*, that it was to lie between the adjoining tribe-territories of Judah (to the north) and Benjamin (to the south), so that it was to be bounded by these two. But this is expressed in a heavy and therefore obscure manner. The words בְּתוֹךְ אֲשֶׁר לַנָּשִׂיא יִהְיֶה, "in the centre of that which belongs to the prince," belong to וּמֵאֲחֻזַּת . . . הָעִיר, and form together with the latter the subject, which is written absolutely; so that מִן is not used in a partitive, but in a local sense (from), and the whole is to be rendered thus: And as for that which lies on the side of the possession of the Levites, and of the possession of the city in the centre of what belongs to the prince, (that which lies) between the territory of Judah and the territory of Benjamin shall belong to the prince. Hitzig's explanation—what remains between Judah and Benjamin, from the city territory to the priests' domain, both inclusive, shall belong to the prince—is arbitrary, and perverts the sense. The periphrastic designation of the *terumah* bounded off between the prince's land by the two portions named together without a copula, viz. "possession of the Levites and possession of the city," is worthy of notice. This periphrasis of the whole by two portions, shows that the portions named formed the boundaries of the whole, that the third portion, which is not mentioned, was enclosed within the two, so that the priests' portion with the sanctuary lay between them.—In vers. 23–27 the rest of the tribes located to the south of the *terumah* are mentioned in order; and in vers. 28 and 29 the account of the division of the land is brought to a close with a repetition of the statement as to the southern boundary (cf. ch. xlvii. 19), and a comprehensive concluding formula.

If now we attempt, in order to form a clear idea of the relation in which this prophetic division of the land stands to the actual size of Canaan according to the boundaries described in ch. xlvii. 15 sqq., to determine the length and breadth of the *terumah* given here by their geographical dimensions, twenty-five thousand rods, according to the metrological calculations of Boeckh and Bertheau, would be 10·70 geographical miles, or, according to the estimate of the Hebrew cubit by Thenius, only 9·75 geographical miles.[1] The extent of Canaan from Beersheba, or Kadesh, up to a line running across from Râs esh-Shukah to the spring El Lebweh, is $3\frac{1}{3}$ degrees, *i.e.* fifty geographical miles, ten of which are occupied by the *terumah*, and forty remain for the twelve tribe-territories, so that each

[1] According to Boeckh, one sacred cubit was equal to $234\frac{1}{3}$ Paris lines = 528·62 millimètres; according to Thenius = $214\frac{1}{2}$ P. l. = 481·62 millim. Now as one geographical mile, the 5400th part of the circumference of the globe, which is 40,000,000 metres, is equivalent to 7407·398 metres = 22,803·290 old Paris feet, the geographical mile according to Boeckh is $14{,}012\frac{1}{10}$ cubits = $2335\frac{1}{2}$ rods (sacred measure); according to Thenius, $15{,}380\frac{1}{6}$ cubits = $2563\frac{1}{3}$ rods (s. m.), from which the numbers given in the text may easily be calculated.

tribe-lot would be $3\frac{1}{3}$ geographical miles in breadth. If, now, we reckon three geographical miles as the breadth of each of the five tribe-lots to the south of the *terumah*, and as the land becomes broader toward the south a breadth of $3\frac{4}{7}$ geographical miles for the seven tribe-lots to the north, the *terumah* set apart in the centre of the land would extend from the site of Jerusalem to Dothan or Jenin. If, however, we take into consideration the breadth of the land from east to west in the neighbourhood of Jerusalem, or where the Jordan enters the Dead Sea, Canaan is eleven geographical miles in breadth, whereas at Jenin it is hardly ten geographical miles broad. If, therefore, the length of the *terumah* (from east to west) was fully ten geographical miles, there would only remain a piece of land of half a mile in breadth on the east and west at the southern boundary, and nothing at all at the northern, for prince's land. We have therefore given to the *terumah* upon the map (Plate IV.) the length and breadth of eight geographical miles, which leaves a tract of two miles on the average for the prince's land, so that it would occupy a fifth of the area of the holy *terumah*, whereas the city possession covered a fourth. No doubt the breadth of the *terumah* from south to north is also diminished thereby, so that it cannot have reached quite down to Jerusalem or quite up to Jenin.—If, now, we consider that the distances of places, and therefore also the measurements of a land in length and breadth, are greater in reality than those given upon the map, on account partly of the mountains and valleys and partly of the windings of the roads, and, still further, that our calculations of the Hebrew cubit are not quite certain, and that even the smaller estimates of Thenius are possibly still too high, the measurements of the *terumah* given by Ezekiel correspond as exactly to the actual size of the land of Canaan as could be expected with a knowledge of its extent obtained not by trigonometrical measurement, but from a simple calculation of the length of the roads.—But this furnishes a confirmation by no means slight of our assumption, that the lengths and breadths indicated here are measured by rods and not by cubits. Reckoned by cubits, the *terumah* would be only a mile and a half or a mile and two-thirds in length and breadth, and the city possession would be only a third of a mile broad; whereas the prince's land would be more than six times as large as the whole of the *terumah*,—*i.e.* of the territory of the Levites, the priests, and the city,—thirteen times as large as the priests' land, and from thirty to thirty-two times as large as the city possession = proportions the improbability of which is at once apparent.

Vers. 30–35. Size, Gates, and Name of the City.—To complete the whole picture of the future land of Israel, what has been stated in vers. 15 and 16 concerning the size of the holy city is still further expanded here.—Ver. 30. *And these are the outgoings of the city from the north side, four thousand and five hundred (rods) measurement.* Ver. 31. *And the gates of the city according to the names of the tribes of Israel: three gates toward the north; the gate of Reuben one, the gate of Judah one, the gate of Levi one.* Ver. 32. *And on the east side four thousand five hundred (rods): and three gates; namely, the gate of Joseph one, the gate of Benjamin one, the gate of Dan one.* Ver. 33. *And to the south side, four thousand five hundred measurement: and three gates; the gate of Simeon one, the gate of Issachar one, the gate of Zebulon one.* Ver. 34. *To the west side, four thousand five hundred — their gates three; the gate of Gad one, the gate of Asher one, the gate of Naphtali one.* Ver. 35. *Round about, eighteen thousand (rods); and the name of the city: from henceforth Jehovah there.*—The situation of the city of God within the *terumah* and its external dimensions have already been generally indicated in vers. 15, 16. Here the measurement of the several sides is specified with a notice of their gates, and this is preceded by the heading, "the outlets of the city." תּוֹצָאֹת, the outgoings (not extensions, for the word never has this meaning) are the furthest extremities in which a city or a tract of land terminates; not outlets or gates, which are expressly distinguished from them, but outgoing sides; hence the definition of the extent or length of the several sides is appended immediately afterwards. The enumeration commences, as above in the case of the land, with the north side. Each side has three gates, so that the whole city has twelve, which bear the names of the twelve tribes, like the gates of the heavenly Jerusalem in Rev. xxi. 12, because it will be the city of the true people of God. Levi is included here, and consequently Ephraim and Manasseh are united in the one tribe of Joseph. The three sons of Leah commence the series with the northern gates. They also stand first in the blessing of Moses in Deut. xxxiii. 6–8: the first-born in age, the first-born by virtue of the patriarchal blessing, and the one chosen by Jehovah for His own service in the place of the first-born. Then follow, for the eastern gates, the two sons of Rachel, according to their age (thus deviating from Deut. xxxiii. 12 and 13), and, along with them, the elder son of Rachel's maid; for the southern gates, the three other sons of Leah; and lastly, for the western gates, the three other sons of the maids. Being thus indicated by the names of its gates as the city of all Israel, the city itself receives a name, which exalts it into the city of God (Jehovah). But different explanations have been given of the words in ver. 35 which refer to this name. The allusion in מִיּוֹם and the meaning of שָׁמָּה are both disputed points. It is true that the latter literally means "thither;" but Ezekiel also uses it as synonymous with שָׁם, "there," in ch. xxiii. 3 and xxxii. 29, 30, so that the assertion that שָׁמָּה never means "there" is incorrect. מִיּוֹם, from day forward, equivalent to henceforward; but not henceforth and for ever, though this may be implied in the context. Whether מִיּוֹם be taken in connection with the preceding words, "the name of the city will henceforward be," or with those which follow, the name of the city will be, "henceforward

Jehovah there," makes no material difference so far as the thought is concerned, as the city can only bear the name from the time when Jehovah is שָׁמָּה, and can only bear it so long as Jehovah is שָׁמָּה. But so far as the question is concerned, whether שָׁמָּה signifies thither or there in this passage, Hävernick is of opinion, indeed, that the whole of Ezekiel's vision does not harmonize with the meaning "there," inasmuch as he separates temple and city, so that Jehovah does not properly dwell in Jerusalem, but, in the strictest and highest sense, in His sanctuary, and turns thence to Jerusalem with the fulness of His grace and love. But if Jehovah does not merely direct His love toward the city from afar off, but, as Hävernick still further says, turns it fully toward it, causes His good pleasure to rest upon it, then He also rules and is in the city with His love, so that it can bear the name "Jehovah thither (there)." In any case, the interpretation, "Jehovah will from henceforth proceed thither, to restore it, to make it a holy city" (Kliefoth), is untenable; for the name is not given to Jerusalem when lying waste, but to the city already restored and fully built, which Ezekiel sees in the spirit. He has therefore before this turned His favour once more to Jerusalem, which was laid waste; and the name יְהוָה שָׁמָּה, given to the new Jerusalem, can only affirm that henceforward it is to be a city of Jehovah, *i.e.* that from this time forth Jehovah will be and rule in her. The rendering "Jehovah thither" does not answer to this, but only the rendering, "Jehovah will be there." Compare Isa. lx. 14, where Jerusalem is called the city of Jehovah, Zion of the Holy One in Israel, because the glory of Jehovah has risen over her as a brilliant light.

Having now completed our exposition in detail, if we take a survey of the substance of the entire vision in ch. xl.–xlviii., on comparing it with the preceding prophecies of the restoration of Israel (ch. xxxiv.–xxxvii.), we obtain the following picture of the new constitution of the kingdom of God:—When the Lord shall gather the sons of Israël from their banishment among the heathen, and bring them back to Canaan, so that they shall dwell therein as a united people under the rule of His servant David, then shall they, on the fresh distribution of the land according to the full extent to which God promised it to the patriarchs, and indicated the boundaries thereof through Moses (ch. xlvii. 15–20), set apart the central portion of it as a heave for the sanctuary and His servants, the priests and Levites, as well as for the capital and its labourers, and also give to the prince a possession of his own on both sides of this heave. In the central point of the heave, which occupies a square space of twenty-five thousand rods in length and breadth, the temple is to stand upon a high mountain, and cover, with its courts, a space of five hundred cubits square; and round about it a space of five hundred rods on every side is to form a boundary between the holy and the common. The glory of Jehovah will enter into the temple and dwell therein for ever; and the temple, in its whole extent, will be most holy (ch. xliii. 1–12). Round about this the priests receive a tract of land of twenty-five thousand rods in length and ten thousand in breadth to dwell in as a sanctuary for the sanctuary; and by their side, toward the north, the Levites receive an area of similar size for dwelling-places; but toward the south, a tract of land of twenty-five thousand rods in length and five thousand rods in breadth is to be the property of the city; and in the centre of this area, the city, with its open space, is to cover a square of five thousand rods in length and breadth; and the rest of the land on both sides is to be given to the labourers of the city out of all Israel for their maintenance. The land lying on the eastern and western sides of the heave, as far as the Jordan and the Mediterranean, is to be the property of the prince, and to remain the hereditary possession of his sons (ch. xlv. 1–8, xlvi. 16–18, xlviii. 8–22). After the separation of this heave, which, with the prince's possession, covers about the fifth part of the whole extent of Canaan, the rest of the land on the north and south of the heave is to be divided into equal parts and distributed among the twelve tribes, so that every tribe-territory shall stretch from the Jordan to the Mediterranean,—seven tribes receiving their hereditary portions on the north of the heave and five on the south, whilst the foreigners having their permanent homes among the different tribes are to receive hereditary possessions like the native Israelites (ch. xlvii. 21–xlviii. 7, and xlviii. 23–29).

Israel, thus placed once more in possession of the promised land, is to appear with its prince before the Lord in the temple at the yearly feasts, to worship and to offer sacrifices, the provision of which is to devolve upon the prince at all festal seasons, for which purpose the people are to pay to him the sixtieth part of the corn, the hundredth part of the oil, and the two hundredth head from the flock every year as a heave-offering. The sacrificial service at the altar and in the holy place is to be performed by none but priests of the family of Zadok, who kept the charge of the Lord faithfully when the people wandered into idolatry. All the other descendants of Levi are simply to discharge the inferior duties of the temple service, whilst uncircumcised heathen are not to be admitted into the temple any more, that it may not be defiled by them (ch. xliii. 13–xliv. 31, xlv. 8–xlvi. 15, and 19–24). When Israel shall thus serve the Lord its God, and walk in His commandments and statutes, it will enjoy the richest blessing from God. A spring of living water will issue from the threshold of the temple house, and, swelling after a short course into a mighty river, will flow down to the Jordan valley, empty itself into the Dead Sea, and make the water of that sea so wholesome that it will swarm with living creatures and fishes of every kind; and on the banks of the river fruit-trees will grow with never-withering leaves, which will bear ripe fruit for food every month, whilst the leaves will serve as medicine (ch. xlvii. 1–12).

As to the Messianic character of the substance of this whole vision, Jewish and Christian commentators are generally agreed; and the opinion which, according to Jerome, many of the Jews entertained, and which has been supported by the rationalistic expositors (Dathe, Eichhorn, Herder, Böttcher, and others), after the example of Grotius,—namely, that Ezekiel describes the temple of Solomon destroyed by Nebuchadnezzar as a model for the rebuilding of it after the return of the Jews from the captivity,—has not found much favour, inasmuch as, apart from all other objections to which it is exposed, it is upset by the fact that not only are its supporters unable to make anything of the description of the spring which issues from the threshold of the temple, flows through the land, and makes the waters of the Dead Sea sound, but they are also unable to explain the separation of the temple from the city of Jerusalem; as it would never have occurred to any Jewish patriot, apart from divine revelation, much less to a priest like Ezekiel, who claims such important prerogatives for the prince of the family of David in relation to the temple, to remove the house of Jehovah from Mount Zion, the seat of the royal house of David, and out of the bounds and territory of the city of Jerusalem. But even if we lay aside this view, and the one related to it,—viz. that the whole vision contains nothing more than ideal hopes and desires of better things belonging to that age, with regard to the future restoration of the destroyed temple and kingdom, as Ewald and others represent the matter,—as being irreconcilable with the biblical view of prophecy, the commentators, who acknowledge the divine origin of prophecy and the Messianic character of the vision in these chapters, differ very widely from one another with reference to the question how the vision is to be interpreted; some declaring themselves quite as decidedly in favour of the literal explanation of the whole picture as others in favour of the figurative or symbolico-typical view, which they regard as the only correct and scriptural one.—The latter view gained the upper hand at a very early period in the Christian church, so that we find it adopted by Ephraem Syrus, Theodoret, and Jerome;[1] and it prevailed so generally, that Lud. Cappellus, for example, in his *Trisagion s. templi Hierosol. tripl. delin.* (in the *apparat. bibl.* of Walton, in the first part of the *London Polyglot*, p. 3), says: "In this passage God designs to show by the prophet that He no more delights in that carnal and legal worship which they have hitherto presented to Him; but that He demands from them another kind of worship very different from that, and more pleasing to Him (a spiritual worship, of which they have a type in the picture and all the rites of this temple, which differ greatly from those of Moses), and that He will establish it among them when He shall have called them to Himself through the Messiah. And that this spiritual worship is set before them in shadows and figures, there is not a Christian who denies; nor any Jew, unless prejudiced and very obdurate,

[1] Ephraem Syrus, on ch. xli., not only interprets the windows of the temple and even the measuring rod allegorically, but says expressly: "It is evident that the rest of the things shown to the prophet in the building of the new temple pertain to the church of Christ, so that we must hold that the priests of that house were types of the apostles, and the calves slain therein prefigured the sacrifice of Christ."—Theod. indeed restricts himself throughout to a brief paraphrase of the words, without explaining every particular in a spiritual manner; but he nevertheless says expressly (at ch. xliii.) that we must ascend from the type to the truth, as God will not dwell for ever in the type; and therefore he repeatedly opposes the Judaeo-literal interpretation of Apollinaris, although he himself appears to take ch. xlviii. as simply referring to the return of the Jews from the Babylonian exile, and the rebuilding of Jerusalem and the temple in the time of Zerubbabel.—This explanation is expressly opposed by Jerome, as the opinion of ignorant Jews; and he observes, on the other hand, that "this temple which is now described, with the order of the priesthood and division of the land and its fertility, is much superior to that which Solomon built; whereas the one which was built under Zerubbabel was so small, and so unworthy of comparison with the earlier one, that they who had seen the first temple, and now looked on this, wept," etc. Under the type of the restoration of the city destroyed by the Babylonians, there is predicted *futurae aedificationis veritas.*

who ventures to deny, seeing that there are so many things in this description of Ezekiel which not even the most shameless Jew has dared to argue that we are to interpret according to the letter," etc.—The literal interpretation remained for a long time peculiar to the Jews, who expect from the Messiah not only their own restoration to the earthly Canaan, but the rebuilding of the temple and the renewal of the Levitical worship in the manner described by Ezekiel, and the establishment of a political kingdom generally; whereas Christians have founded the expectation of an earthly kingdom of glory in the form of the millennium, more upon the Apocalypse than upon Ezekiel's prophecy. It has only been in the most recent time that certain scientific defenders of chiliasm have not shrunk from carrying out their views so far as to teach not only the restoration of the Jews to Palestine on their conversion to Christ, but, according to their literal explanation of our prophecy, the rebuilding of the temple in Jerusalem and the renewal of the Levitical worship in the millennial kingdom. Auberlen has only hinted at this, so that from his words quoted already, "when once priesthood and monarchy are revived, then, without impairing the Epistle to the Hebrews, the ceremonial and civil law of Moses will unfold its spiritual depths in the worship and in the constitution of the millennial kingdom," we cannot see how far he assumes that there will be a literal fulfilment of Ezekiel's prophecy. M. Baumgarten (art. "Ezekiel" in Herzog's *Cyclopaedia*) says, more plainly, that "the restoration of all the outward reality, which Ezekiel saw in vision, will be not so much a repetition of what went before, as a glorification of the outward, which had perished and been condemned," since this "glorification" will simply consist in "extensions and intensifications" of the earlier precepts of the law. "For," he adds, in support of this opinion, "when Israel as a nation turns to God, how can, how should it manifest its faith and its obedience in any other way than in the forms and ordinances which Jehovah gave to that people? And is it not obvious (!?) that the whole law, in all its sections and portions, will not receive, till after this conversion, that fulfilment which in all ages it has hitherto sought in vain? And how should temple, priesthood, sacrificial service, Sabbath, and new moon, in themselves be opposed to faith in the perfect and eternal revelation of God in the life, death, and resurrection of Jesus Christ?" In consistency with this, Baumgarten is therefore of opinion that eventually even the Gentile community will enter again into the congregation of Israel, and find its national organization in the law of Israel according to the will of God.—Hofmann, on the contrary (*Schriftbeweis*, II. 2, pp. 577 sqq.), finds only so much established with certainty in the revelation of Ezekiel, viz. that Israel will serve God again in its own land, and Jehovah will dwell in the midst of it again. He therefore would have the several parts interpreted in relation to the whole; so that what Hengstenberg calls the ideal interpretation of this prophecy remains. But he does not say precisely what his view is concerning the temple, and the Levitical rite of sacrifice to be performed therein. He simply infers, from the fact that a stream of water issuing from the temple-mountain makes the Dead Sea sound and the lower Kedron-valley fruitful, that the land will be different from what it was before; and this alteration Volck calls a glorification of Palestine.

In our discussion of the question concerning the restoration of Israel to Canaan, we have already declared ourselves as opposed to the literal interpretation of the prophecy, and have given the general grounds on which the symbolico-typical view appears to be demanded—namely, because the assumption of a restoration of the temple and the Levitical, *i.e.* bloody, sacrificial worship is opposed to the teaching of Christ and His apostles. We have now to assign further reasons for this. If, then, in the first place, we fix our attention upon the vision in ch. xl.–xlviii., we cannot find any conclusive argument against the literal and in favour of the figurative interpretation of the vision in question, either in the fact that Ezekiel does not give any building-plan for the temple, but simply ground arrangements and ground measurements, and does not say that a temple is ever to be built according to his plan, or give any instructions for the restoration of the Israelitish worship, or in the fact that the division of the land, the bounding off of the *terumah* and the arranging of the city, cannot be practically realized. The omission of any command to build the temple might be simply accounted for, from the design to let the prophet merely see the restoration of the destroyed temple in a more perfect form, and cause this to be predicted to the people through him, without at present giving any command to build, as that was only to be carried out in the remote future. The absence of elevations and precise directions concerning the construction of the several buildings might be explained from the fact that in these respects the building was to resemble the former temple. And with regard to the distribution of the land among the tribes, and the setting apart of the *terumah*, it cannot truly be said that "they bear on the face of them their purposelessness and impracticability." The description of a portion of land of definite size for priests, Levites, city, and prince, which was to reach from the eastern boundary of Canaan to the western, and to be bounded off in a straight line by the tribe-territories immediately adjoining, contains nothing impracticable, provided that we do not think of the boundary line as a straight line upon a chess-board. But we may infer from the Mosaic instructions concerning the districts, which were to be given to the Levites as pasture grounds for their cattle round about the cities assigned to them to dwell in, that the words of the text do not warrant any such idea. They are described as perfect squares of a thousand cubits on every side (Num. xxxv. 2–5). If, then, these Mosaic instructions could be carried out, the same must be true of those of Ezekiel concerning the *terumah*, as its dimensions are in harmony with the actual size of the land. And so also the separation of the city from the temple, and the square form of the city with three gates on every side, cannot be regarded in general as either purposeless or impracticable. And, finally, in the statements concerning the territories to be distributed among the twelve tribes, viz. that they were to lie side by side, that they were all to stretch from the Mediterranean to the Jordan, and that they were to be of equal size, there is no ground for supposing that the land was to be cut up with the measuring rod into abstract oblongs of equal measurements, with an entire disregard of all the actual conditions. The only thing which causes any surprise here is the assumption on which the regulation, that one tribe is to receive as much as another, is founded, namely, that all the tribes of Israel will be equal in the number of families they contain. This hypothesis can hardly be reconciled with the assumption that an actual distribution of Palestine among the twelve tribes of Israel returning from exile is contemplated. Even the measuring of a space around the temple for the purpose of forming a separation between the holy and the common, which space was to be five times as large as the extent of the temple with its courts, contains an obvious hint at a symbolical signification of the temple building, inasmuch as with a real temple such an object could have been attained by much simpler means. To this must be added the river issuing from the threshold of the eastern temple gate, with its marvellously increasing flow of water, and the supernatural force of life which it contains; for, as we have already pointed out, this cannot be regarded as an earthly river watering the land, but can only be interpreted figuratively, *i.e.* in a symbolico-typical sense. But if the stream of water flowing from the temple cannot be regarded as a natural river, the temple also cannot be an earthly temple, and the sacrificial service appointed for this temple cannot be taken as divine service consisting in the slaying and offering of bullocks, goats, and calves; and as the entire description forms a uniform prophetic picture, the distribution of the land among the sons of Israel must also not be interpreted literally.

But as different supporters of the chiliastic view have defended the literal interpretation of the picture of the temple spring by the assumption of a glorification of nature, *i.e.* of a glorification of Palestine before the new creation of the heaven and the earth, and this assumption is of great importance in relation to the question concerning the fulfilment of this prophecy (Ezek. xl.–xlviii.), we must examine somewhat more closely the arguments used in its support.

I. *Is the glorification of Canaan before the last judgment taught in the prophecy of the Old Testament?*—According to Volck ("Zur Eschatologie," *Dorpat. Zeitschr.* vii. pp. 158 sqq.), the idea of such a glorification is very common throughout the Old Testament prophecy. "When," he says, "Isaiah (ii. 2–4) sees the mountain of the house of Jehovah exalted above all the mountains, and the nations flowing to it, to walk in Jehovah's ways; when he prophesies of a time in which the Lord will shelter Israel, now saved and holy in all its members, and fill its land with glory, and Canaan, under the rule of the righteous prince of peace, with its inhabitants once scattered over all the world brought back once more, will be restored to the original, paradisaical state of peace, whilst the world is given up to judgment (Isa. iv. 2–6, ix. 1–6, and 11, 12);—when Jeremiah prophesies that Jerusalem will be rebuilt, and a sprout from the house of David will rule well over his people, upon whose heart Jehovah will write His law (Jer. xxxi. 31–44, xxxiii. 15);—when Hosea (ii. 16–25) sees the house of Jacob, which has returned home after a period of severe affliction, as a pardoned people to which its God betrothes Himself again;—when Joel (iv. 16–21) sees a time break forth after the judgment upon the army of the world of nations, in which the holy land bursts into miraculous fruitfulness;—when Amos (ix. 8–15) predicts the rebuilding of the tabernacle of David that has been overthrown, and the restoration of the Davidic kingdom;—when, according to Zechariah (xiv. 8 sqq.), Jerusalem is to be the centre of the world, to which the nations flow, to celebrate the feast of tabernacles with Israel:—it is impossible, without introducing unbounded caprice into our exposition, to resist the conclusion, that in all these passages, and others of a similar kind, a time is depicted, when, after the judgment of God upon the power of the world, Israel will dwell in the enjoyment of blissful peace within its own land, now transfigured into paradisaical glory, and will rule over the nations round about." But that all these passages do not contain clear scriptural statements "concerning a partial glorification of the earth" during that kingdom of glory, is apparent from the fact that it is not till after writing this that Volck himself raises the question, "Are there really, then, any distinct utterances of Scripture upon this point?" and he only cites two passages (Joel iv. 18 sqq. and Mic. vii. 9–13) as containing an affirmative answer to the question, to which he also adds in a note Isa. xxiv. 1–23 as compared with Isa. xiii. 9 and Zech. xiv. 8–11. But when Joel foretells that, after the judgment of Jehovah upon the army of nations in the valley of Jehoshaphat, the mountains will trickle with new wine, the hills flow with milk, and all the springs of Judah stream with water, while Egypt will become a desolation, and Edom a barren desert, he announces nothing more than that which Isaiah repeats and still further expands in ch. xxxiv. and xxxv.; where even Hofmann (*Schriftbeweis*, II. 2, p. 563) admits that Edom is a symbolical designation, applied to the world of mankind in its estrangement from God. Joel merely mentions Egypt as well as Edom as representatives of the world in its hostility to God. But if Egypt and Edom are types of the world in its estrangement from God or its enmity against Him, Judah is a type of the kingdom of God; and this passage simply teaches that through the judgment the might and glory of the kingdoms of the world at enmity against God will be laid waste and destroyed, and the glory of the kingdom of God established. But in nowise do they teach the glorification of Palestine and the desolation of Idumaea and the country of the Nile; especially if we bear in mind that, as we have already observed, the trickling and flowing of the mountains and hills with new wine and oil cannot possibly be understood literally. We meet with the very same antithesis in Mic. vii. 9–13, where the daughter of Zion, presented under the figure of a vineyard, is promised the building of her walls and the flowing into her of numerous peoples from Egypt, Asshur, and the ends of the world, and the desolation of the world is foretold. Micah does not say a word about a partial glorification of the earth, unless the building of the walls of Zion is taken allegorically, and changed into a glorification of Palestine. But if this is the case with passages selected as peculiarly clear, the rest will furnish still less proof of the supposed glorification of the land of Israel. It is true, indeed, that we also find in Isa. xxiv. 1–23 "the antithesis between Zion, the glorified seat of Jehovah, and the earth laid waste by the judgment" (cf. Isa. xiii. 3), and in Zech. xiv. 8 sqq. the prediction of an exaltation of Jerusalem above the land lying round about; but even if a future glorification of the seat of God in the midst of His people, and, indeed, a transformation of the earthly soil of the kingdom of God, be foretold in these and many other passages, the chiliastic idea of a glorification of Palestine before the universal judgment and the new creation of the heaven and earth is by no means proved thereby, so long as there are no distinct statements of Scripture to confirm the supposition that the future glorification of Zion, Jerusalem, Canaan, predicted by the prophets, will take place before the judgment. Even Volck appears to have felt that the passages already quoted do not furnish a conclusive proof of this, since it is not till after discussing them that he thinks it necessary to raise the question, "Does the Old Testament really speak of a glorification of Canaan in the literal sense of the word?" To reply to this he commences with an examination of the view of the millennium held by Auberlen, who finds nothing more in the statements of the Old Testament than that "even nature will be included in the blessing of the general salvation, the soil endowed with inexhaustible fruitfulness, all hostility and thirst for blood be taken from the animal world, yea, the heavens bound to the earth in corresponding harmony," so that we should be reminded of the times of the world before the flood, when the powers of nature were still greater than they are now. To this the intimation in Isa. lxv. 20–22 alludes, where men a hundred years old are called boys, etc. (*der Prophet Daniel*, pp. 402, 403). But Volck objects to the literal interpretation of such passages as Isa. lxv. 20, on the ground that "the consequence of this assumption leads to absurdities, inasmuch as such passages as Isa. xi. 6, lx. 17, 19, lxvi. 25, would then also have to be taken literally, to which certainly no one would be so ready to agree" (see also Luthardt, *die Lehre von den letzten Dingen*, p. 78). On the other hand, he defends the canon laid down by Hofmann (p. 566), "that in the prophetic description of that time of glory we must distinguish between the thoughts of the prophecy and the means used for expressing them; the former we reach by generalizing what is said by way of example, and reducing the figurative expression to the literal one." The thought lying at the foundation of these prophetic pictures is, in his opinion, no other than that of a blessed, blissful fellowship with God, and a state of peace embracing both the human and the extra-human creation. "To set forth this thought, the prophets seize upon the most manifold figures and colours which the earth offers them." Thus in Isa. lxv. 20–23 we have only a figurative description of what is said in literal words in Isa. xxv. 8: He swalloweth up death for ever, and Jehovah wipeth away the tears from every face. So also the figurative expressions in Isa. xi. 6–8, lxv. 25, affirm nothing more "than that the ground will be delivered from the curse which rests upon it for the sake of man, and the extra-human creation will be included in the state of peace enjoyed in the holy seat of God. But where there is no death and no evil, and therefore no more sin, where the glory of the Lord shines without change (Isa. lx. 19, 20), not only has the world before the flood with its still greater powers of nature returned, but there is the world of *glorification*." We agree with this view in general, and simply add that this furnishes no proof of the glorification of Canaan before the last judgment. Before this can be done, it must be conclusively shown that these prophetic passages treat of the so-called millennial kingdom, and do not depict what is plainly taught in Isa. lxv. 17 sqq. and Rev. xxi. and xxii., the glory of the heavenly Jerusalem upon the new earth.

Volck also acknowledges this, inasmuch as, after examining these passages, he proposes the question, "Are there really clear passages in the Old Testament prophecy which warrant us in assuming that there will be an intermediate period between the judgment, through which Jehovah glorifies Himself and His people before the eyes of the world, and a last end of all things?" An affirmative answer to this question is said to be furnished by Isa. xxiv. 21 sqq., where the prophet, when depicting the judgment upon the earth, says: "And it will come to pass in that day, that Jehovah will visit the army of the height on high, and the kings of the earth upon the earth; and they will be gathered together as a crowd, taken in the pit, and shut up in the prison, and after the expiration of many days will they be visited. And the sun blushes, and the moon turns pale; for Jehovah rules royally upon Mount Zion and in Jerusalem, and in the face of His elders is glory." Here even Hofmann finds (pp. 566, 567) the idea clearly expressed "of a time between the judgment through which Jehovah glorifies Himself and His people before all the world, and a last end of things, such as we must picture to ourselves when we read of a rolling up of the heaven on which all its host falls off, like dry leaves from the vine (Isa. xxxiv. 4), and of a day of retribution upon earth, when the earth falls to rise no more, and a fire devours its inhabitants, which burns for ever" (Isa. xxxiv. 8, 9, xxiv. 20). But if we observe that the announcement of the judgment upon the earth closes in Isa. xxiv. 20 with the words, "the earth will fall, and not rise again;" and then vers. 21 sqq. continue as follows: "And it comes to pass in that day, Jehovah will visit," etc.,—it will be evident that the judgment upon the host of the heavens, etc., is assigned to the time when the earth is destroyed, so that by the Mount Zion and Jerusalem, where Jehovah will then reign royally in glory, we can only understand the heavenly Jerusalem. An intermediate time between the judgment upon the world and the last end of things, *i.e.* the destruction of the heaven and the earth, is not taught here. Nor is it taught in ch. lxv. 17–19, where, according to Hofmann (p. 568), a glorification of Jerusalem before the new creation of the heaven and the earth is said to be foretold; for here even Volck admits that we have a picture of the new world after the destruction of heaven and earth and after the last judgment, and concludes his discussion upon this point (p. 166) with the acknowledgment, "that in the Old Testament prophecy these two phases of the end are not sharply separated from each other, and especially that the manner of transition from the former (the glorification of Jehovah and His church before the world in the so-called thousand years' reign) to the last end of all things, to the life of eternity, does not stand clearly out," though even in the latter respect there is an indication to be found in Ezek. xxxviii. If, then, for the present we lay this indication aside, as the question concerning Ezek. xxxviii. can only be considered in connection with Rev. xx., the examination of all the passages quoted by the chiliasts in support of the glorification of Palestine, before the new creation of the heavens and the earth, yields rather the result that the two assumed phases of the end are generally not distinguished in the Old Testament prophecy, and that the utterances of the different prophets concerning the final issue of the war of the world-powers against the kingdom of God clearly contain no more than this, that Jehovah will destroy all the enemies of His kingdom by a judgment, overthrow the kingdoms of the world, and establish His kingdom in glory. Isaiah alone rises to a prediction of the destruction of the whole world, and of the new creation of the heaven and the earth.—But what the Old Testament leaves still obscure in this respect, is supposed to be clearly revealed in the New. To this question, therefore, we will now proceed.

II. *Does the New Testament teach a glorification of Palestine and a kingdom of glory in the earthly Jerusalem, before the last judgment and the destruction of the heaven and the earth?*—In the opinion of most of the representatives of millenarianism, there is no doubt whatever as to either of these. "For, according to Rev. xx., the overthrow of the world-power and the destruction of Antichrist are immediately followed by the establishment of the kingdom of glory of the glorified church of Jesus Christ for the space of a thousand years, at the expiration of which the war of Gog and Magog against the beloved city takes place, and ends in the overthrow of the hostile army and the creation of the new heaven and the new earth" (Volck, p. 167). But this assumption is by no means so indisputable. Even if we grant in passing, that, according to the millenarian view of the Apocalypse, the events depicted in ch. xx. are to be understood chronologically, the assumption that Palestine will be glorified during the millennium is not yet demonstrated. Auberlen, for example, who regards the doctrine of the thousand years' reign as one of the primary articles of the Christian hope, pronounces the following sentence (pp. 454, 455) upon Hofmann's view of the millennial reign, according to which the glorified church is to be thought of, not as in heaven, but as on earth, and, indeed, as united with the equally glorified Israel in the equally glorified Canaan: "It appears obvious to me that the whole of the Old Testament prophecy is irreconcilable with this view, apart from the internal improbability of the thing." And according to our discussion above, we regard this sentence as perfectly well founded. The prophets of the Old Testament know nothing of a thousand years' kingdom; and a glorification of the earthly Canaan before the end of the world cannot be inferred from the picture of the temple spring, for the simple reason that the resumption of this prophetic figure in Rev. xxii. 1 and 2 shows that this spring belongs to the heavenly Jerusalem of the new earth. Even in Rev. xx. we read nothing about a glorification of Palestine or Jerusalem. This has merely been inferred from the fact that, according to the literal interpretation of the chapter, those who rise from the dead at the second coming of Christ will reign with Christ in the "beloved city," *i.e.* Jerusalem; but the question has not been taken into consideration, whether a warlike expedition of the heathen from the four corners of the unglorified world against the inhabitants of a glorified city, who are clothed with spiritual bodies, is possible and conceivable, or whether such an assumption does not rather "lead to absurdities." Nor can it be shown that the doctrine of a glorification of Palestine before the end of the present world is contained in the remaining chapters of the Apocalypse or the other writings of the New Testament. It cannot be inferred from the words of the Apostle Paul in Rom. xi. 15, viz. that the restoration of the people of Israel, rejected for a time after the entrance of the *pleroma* of the heathen into the kingdom of God, will be or cause "life from the dead;" since "life from the dead" never really means the new bodily life of glorification beginning with the resurrection of the dead (Meyer), nor the glorification of the world (Volck); and this meaning cannot be deduced from the fact that the *παλιγγενεσία* ("regeneration," Matt. xix. 28) and the *χρόνοι ἀποκαταστάσεως* ("times of restitution," Acts iii. 19–21) will follow the "receiving" (*πρόσληψις*) of Israel.

And even for the doctrine of a kingdom of glory in the earthly Jerusalem before the last judgment, we have no conclusive scriptural evidence. The assumption, that by the "beloved city" in Rev. xx. 9 we are to understand the earthly

Jerusalem, rests upon the hypothesis, that the people of Israel will return to Palestine on or after their conversion to Christ, rebuild Jerusalem and the temple, and dwell there till the coming of Christ. But, as we have already shown, this hypothesis has no support either in Rom. xi. 25 or any other unequivocal passages of the New Testament; and the only passages that come into consideration at all are Rev. vii. 1–8, xiv. 1–5, and xi., xii., in which this doctrine is said to be contained. In Rev. vii. 1 sqq., John sees how, before the outbreak of the judgment upon the God-opposing world-power, an angel seals "the servants of our God" in their foreheads, and hears that the number of those sealed is a hundred and forty-four thousand of all the tribes of the children of Israel, twelve thousand from each of the twelve tribes mentioned by name. In ch. xiv. 1 sqq. he sees the Lamb stand upon Mount Zion, and with Him a hundred and forty-four thousand, having the name of his Father written upon their forehead. And in ch. xi. 1 sqq. a rod is given to him, and he is commanded to measure the temple of God and the altar, but to cast out the outer court of the temple, and not to measure it, because it is given to the heathen, who will tread under foot the holy city, which has become spiritually a Sodom and an Egypt for forty-two months. From these passages, Hofmann (II. 2, p. 703), Luther, Volck, and others conclude that the converted Israelitish church will not only dwell in Palestine, more especially in Jerusalem, before the coming (*parusia*) of Christ, but will be alone in outliving the coming of Christ; whilst the rest of Christendom, at all events the whole number of the believers from among the Gentile Christians, will lose their lives in the great tribulation which precedes the *parusia*, and go through death to God. This conclusion would be indisputable if the premises were well founded, namely, that the passages in question treated only of Jewish Christians and the earthly Jerusalem. For, in the first place, it is evident that the hundred and forty-four thousand whom John sees with the Lamb upon Mount Zion in ch. xiv. 1 sqq. are identical with the hundred and forty-four thousand who are sealed from the twelve tribes of Israel in ch. vii. The omission of the retrospective article before ἑκατὸν, κ.τ.λ. in ch. xiv. 1 is to be explained from the fact that the intention is to give prominence to the antithesis, in which the notice of it stands to what precedes. "Over against the whole multitude of the rest of the world, subject to the beast and his prophet, there stands upon Zion a comparatively limited host of a hundred and forty-four thousand" (Volck). And in the second place, it is quite as evident that in the one hundred and forty-four thousand who are sealed (ch. vii.), the total number is contained of all believers, who have been preserved in the great tribulation, and kept from perishing therein; and in ch. vii. 9–17 there is placed in contrast with these, in the innumerable multitude out of all the heathen, and nations, and languages standing before the throne of God clothed in white robes, and carrying palms in their hands, who have come out of the great tribulation, the total number of believers who have lost their temporal lives in the great tribulation, and entered into the everlasting life. The mode in which Christiani ("Uebersichtliche Darstellung des Inhalts der Apokalypse," *Dorpater Zeitschr.* III. p. 53) attempts to evade this conclusion—namely, by affirming that the separate visions never give a complete final account, but only isolated glimpses of it, and that they have mutually to supplement one another—does not suffice. Volck has correctly observed, in answer to the objection that the vision in ch. vii. 9–17 does not set before us the entrance of *all* the believing Gentile Christians of the last time into heaven through death, that although we simply read of a "great multitude" in ch. vii. 9, this expression does not permit us to infer that there will be a remnant of Gentile Christians, inasmuch as the antithesis upon which all turns is this: "on the one side, this compact number of a hundred and forty-four thousand out of Israel destined to survive the last oppression; on the other, an innumerable multitude out of every nation, who have come to God through death." Nevertheless, we must support Christiani in his opposition to the assumption, that at the *parusia* of Christ only Jewish Christians will be living on earth in Jerusalem or upon Mount Zion, and that all the believing Gentile Christians will have perished from the globe; because such a view is irreconcilably opposed not only to Rev. iii. 12, but also to all the teaching of the New Testament, especially to the declarations of our Lord concerning His second coming. When the Apostle Paul wrote to the church at Thessalonica, consisting of Gentile and Jewish Christians, ἐν λόγῳ κυρίου: "we who live and remain to the coming of the Lord shall not anticipate those who sleep" (1 Thess. iv. 15 sqq.), and when he announced as a μυστήριον to the church at Corinth, which was also a mixed church, consisting for the most part of Gentile Christians: "we shall not all sleep, but we shall all be changed" (1 Cor. xv. 51), he held the conviction, based upon a word of the Lord, that at the time of Christ's coming there would still be believing Gentile Christians living upon the earth. And when the Lord Himself tells His disciples: "the Son of man will come in the clouds of heaven with great power and glory, and will send His angels with sounding trumpets, and they will gather His elect from the four winds from one end of heaven to the other" (Matt. xxiv. 30, 31), He treats it as an indisputable fact that there will be ἐκλεκτοί, believing Christians, in all the countries of the earth, and that the church existing at His coming will not be limited to the Israel which has become believing in Jerusalem and Palestine.

If, therefore, the Apocalypse is not to stand in direct contradiction to the teaching of Christ and the Apostle Paul in one of the principal articles of the truths of salvation, the exposition in question of Rev. vii. and xiv. cannot be correct. On the contrary, we are firmly convinced that in the hundred and forty-four thousand who are sealed, the whole body of believing Christians living at the *parusia* of our Lord is represented; and notwithstanding the fact that they are described as the servants of God "out of all the tribes of the children of Israel," and are distributed by twelve thousands among the twelve tribes of Israel, and that in ch. xiv. 1 they stand with the Lamb upon Mount Zion, we can only regard them, not as Jewish Christians, but as the Israel of God (Gal. vi. 16), *i.e.* the church of believers in the last days gathered from both Gentiles and Jews. If the description of the sealed as children of Israel out of all the twelve tribes, and the enumeration of these tribes by name, prove that only Jewish Christians are intended, and preclude our taking the words as referring to believers from both Gentiles and Jews, we must also regard the heavenly Jerusalem of the new earth as a Jewish Christian city, because it has the names of the twelve tribes of the children of Israel written upon its gates (Rev. xxi. 12), like the Jerusalem of Ezekiel (ch. xlviii. 31); and as this holy city is called the bride of the Lamb (Rev. xxi. 9, 10), we must assume that only Jewish Christians will take part in the marriage of the Lamb. Moreover, the Mount Zion upon which John sees Lamb and the hundred and forty-four thousand standing (ch. xiv. 1), cannot be the earthly Mount Zion, as Bengel, Hengstenberg, and others have correctly shown, because those who are standing there hear and learn the song sounding from heaven, which is sung before the throne and the four living creatures and the elders (Rev. xiv. 3). The Mount Zion in this instance, as in Heb. xii. 22, belongs to the heavenly Jerusalem. There is no foundation for the assertion that this view is at variance with the connection of this group, and is also opposed to the context (Christiani, p. 194, Luther, and others). The excellent remarks of Düsterdieck, with regard to the connection, are a sufficient refutation of the first, which is asserted without any proof: "Just as in ch. vii. 9 sqq. an inspiring look at the heavenly glory was granted to such believers as should remain faithful in the great tribulation which had yet to come, before the tribulation itself was displayed; so also in the first part of ch. xiv. (vers. 1–5) a scene is exhibited, which shows the glorious reward of the conquerors (cf. ch. ii. 11, iii. 12, 21) in a certain group of blessed believers (ver. 1: 'a hundred and forty-four thousand;' ver. 4: 'the first-fruits'), who appear with the Lamb upon Mount Zion, and are described as those who have kept themselves pure from all the defilement of the world during their earthly life." And this assumption would only be opposed to the context if vers. 2–5 formed an antithesis to ver. 1, *i.e.* if those in heaven mentioned in vers. 2, 3 were distinguished from the hundred and forty-four thousand as being still on earth. But if those who sing the new song are really distinguished from the hundred and forty-four thousand, and are "angelic choirs," which is still questionable, it by no means follows from this that the hundred and forty-four thousand are upon the earthly Mount Zion, but simply that they have reached the Zion of the heavenly Jerusalem, and stand with the Lamb by the throne of God, serving Him as His attendants, seeing His face, and bearing His name upon their foreheads (Rev. xxii. 1, 3, 4), and that they learn the new song sung before the throne.

Still less can we understand by the holy city of Rev. xi. the earthly Jerusalem, and by the woman clothed with the sun in Rev. xii. the Israelitish church of God, *i.e.* the Israel of the last days converted to Christ. The Jerusalem of Rev. xi. is spiritually a Sodom and Egypt. The Lord is obliged to endow the two witnesses anointed with His Spirit, whom He causes to appear there, with the miraculous power of Elias and Moses, to defend them from their adversaries. And when eventually they are slain by the beast from the abyss, and all the world, seeing their dead bodies lying in the streets of the spiritual Sodom and Egypt, rejoices at their death, He brings them to life again after three days and a half, and causes them to ascend visibly into heaven, and the same hour He destroys the tenth part of the city by an earthquake, through which seven thousand men are slain, so that the rest are alarmed and give glory to the God of heaven. Jerusalem is introduced here in quite as degenerate a state as in the last times before its destruction by the Romans. Nevertheless we cannot think of this ancient Jerusalem, because if John meant this, his prophecy would be at variance with Christ's prophecy of the destruction of Jerusalem. "For, according to the Revelation, there is neither a destruction of the temple in prospect, nor does the church of Jesus flee from the city devoted to destruction" (Hofmann, p. 684). The temple with the altar of burnt-offering is measured and defended, and only the outer court with the city is given up to the nations to be trodden down; and lastly, only the tenth part of the city is laid in ruins. For this reason, according to Hofmann and Luther, the Jerusalem of the last days, inhabited by the Israel converted to Christ, is intended. But the difficulty which presses upon this explanation is to be found not so much in the fact that Jerusalem is restored in the period intervening between the conversion of Israel as a nation to Christ and the establishment of the millennial kingdom, and possesses a Jewish temple, as in the fact that the Israel thus converted to Christ, whose restoration, according to the teaching of the Apostle Paul in Rom. xi. 25, will be "life from the dead" to all Christendom, should again become a spiritual Sodom and Egypt, so that the Lord has to defend His temple with the believers who worship there from being trampled down by means of witnesses endowed with miraculous power, and to destroy the godless city partially by an earthquake for the purpose of terrifying the rest of the inhabitants, so that they may give glory to Him. Such an apostasy of the people of Israel after their final conversion to Christ is thoroughly opposed to the hope expressed by the Apostle Paul of the result of the restoration of Israel after the entrance of the *pleroma* of the Gentiles into the kingdom of God. Hofmann and Luther are therefore of opinion that the Israelitish-Christian Jerusalem of the last times is called spiritually Sodom and Egypt, because the old Jewish Jerusalem had formerly sunk into a Sodom and Egypt, and that the Christian city is punished by the destruction of its tenth part and the slaying of seven thousand men "as a judgment upon the hostile nationality;" as if God could act so unjustly in the government of Jerusalem as to give up to the heathen the city that had been faithful to Him, and to destroy the tenth part thereof. This realistic Jewish interpretation becomes utterly impossible when ch. xii. is added. According to Hofmann, the woman in the sun is that Israel of which Paul says, "God has not cast away His people whom He foreknew" (Rom. xi. 2), *i.e.* the Israelitish church of the saved. Before the birth of the boy who will rule the nations with a sceptre of iron, this church is opposed by the dragon; and after the child born by her has been caught up into heaven, she is hidden by God from the persecution of the dragon in a place in the wilderness for twelve hundred and sixty days, or three times and a half, *i.e.* during the forty-two months in which Jerusalem as a spiritual Sodom is trodden down of the heathen, and only the temple with those who worship there is protected by God. But even if we overlook the contradiction involved in the supposition that the Israel believing in Christ of ch. xi. has sunk so deep that Jerusalem has to be trodden down by the heathen, and only a small portion of the worshippers of God are protected in the temple, we must nevertheless inquire how it is possible that the Israelitish church of believers in Christ should at the same time be defended in the temple at Jerusalem, and, having fled from Canaan into the wilderness, be concealed "in a place of distress and tribulation." The Jerusalem of the last times does not stand in the wilderness, and the temple protected by God is not a place of distress and tribulation. And how can the Israelitish church of God, which has given birth to Christ, be concealed in the wilderness after the catching up of Christ into heaven, or His ascension, seeing that the believing portion of Israel entered the Christian church, whilst the unbelieving mass at the time of the destruction of Jerusalem were in part destroyed by sword, famine, and pestilence, and in part thrust out among the Gentiles over all the world? From the destruction of Jerusalem onwards, there is no longer any Israelitish congregation of God outside the Christian church. The branches broken off from the olive tree because of their unbelief, are not a church of God. And Auberlen's objection to this interpretation—namely, that from the birth of Christ in ver. 6 it makes all at once a violent leap into the antichristian times—still retains its force, inasmuch as this leap not only has nothing in the text to indicate it, but is irreconcilable with vers. 5 and 6, according to which the flight of the woman into the wilderness takes place directly after the catching away of the child. Auberlen and Christiani have therefore clearly seen the impossibility of carrying out the realistic Jewish interpretation of these chapters. The latter, indeed, would take the holy city in ch. xi. in a literal sense, *i.e.* as signifying the material Jerusalem; whilst he interprets the temple "allegorically" as representing the Christian church, without observing the difficulty in which he thereby entangles himself, inasmuch as if the holy city were the material Jerusalem, the whole of believing Christendom out of all lands would have fled thither for refuge. In the exposition of ch. xii. he follows Auberlen (*Daniel*, p. 460), who has correctly interpreted the woman clothed with the sun as signifying primarily the Israelitish church of God, and then passing afterwards into the believing church of Christ, which rises on the foundation of the Israelitish church as its continuation, other branches from the wild olive tree being grafted on in the place of the branches of the good olive that have been broken off (Rom. xi. 17 sqq.).—In Rev. xiii. and xv.–xix. there is no further allusion to Judah and Jerusalem.

If, then, we draw the conclusion from the foregoing discussion, the result at which we have arrived is, that even Rev. i.–xix. furnishes no confirmation of the assumption that the Israel which has come to believe in Christ will dwell in the earthly Jerusalem, and have a temple with bleeding sacrifices.

And this takes away all historical ground for the assumption that by the beloved city in Rev. xx. 9, against which Satan leads Gog and Magog to war with the heathen from the four corners of the earth, we can only understand the earthly Jerusalem of the last times. If, however, we look more closely at Rev. xx., there are three events described in vers. 1–10,—viz. (1) the binding of Satan and his confinement in the abyss for a thousand years (vers. 1–3); (2) the resurrection of the believers, and their reigning with Christ for a thousand years, called the "first resurrection" (vers. 4–6); (3) after the termination of the thousand years, the releasing of Satan from his prison, his going out to lead the heathen with Gog and Magog to war against "the camp of the saints and the beloved city," the destruction of this army by fire from heaven, and the casting of Satan into the lake of fire, where the beast and the false prophet already are (vers. 7–10). According to the millenarian exposition of the Apocalypse, these three events will none of them take place till after the fall of Babylon and the casting of the beast into the lake of fire; not merely the final casting of Satan into the lake of fire, but even the binding of Satan and the confining of him in the abyss. The latter is not stated in the text, however, but is merely an inference drawn from the fact that all three events are seen by John and related in his Apocalypse after the fall of Babylon, etc.,—an inference for which there is just the same warrant as for the conclusion drawn, for example, by the traditional exposition of the Old Testament by the Jews, that because the death of Terah is related in Gen. xi., and the call and migration of Abram to Canaan in Gen. xii., therefore Terah died before the migration of Abraham, in opposition to the chronological data of Genesis. All that is stated in the text of the Apocalypse is, that Satan is cast into the lake of fire, where the beast and the false prophet are (ver. 10), so that the final overthrow of Satan will not take place till after the fall of Babylon and the overthrow of the beast and the false prophet. That this is not to happen till a thousand years later, cannot be inferred from the position of ch. xx. 10 after ch. xix. 20, 21, but must be gathered from some other source if it is to be determined at all. The assumption that the contents of Rev. xx. are chronologically posterior to ch. xviii. and xix., which the millenarian interpretation of the Apocalypse has adopted from the earlier orthodox exposition, is at variance with the plan of the whole book. It is now admitted by all scientific expositors of the Apocalypse, that the visions contained therein do not form such a continuous series as to present the leading features of the conflict between the powers at enmity against God and the kingdom of God in chronological order, but rather that they are arranged in groups, each rounded off within itself, every one of which reaches to the end or closes with the last judgment, while those which follow go back again and expand more fully the several events which prepare the way for and introduce the last judgment; so that, for example, after the last judgment upon the living and the dead has been announced in ch. xi. 15 sqq. by the seventh trumpet, the conflict between Satan and the kingdom of God on the birth and ascension of Christ is not shown to the seer till the following chapter (ch. xii.). And the events set forth in the last group commencing with ch. xix. must be interpreted in a manner analogous to this. The contents of this group have been correctly explained by Hofmann (II. 2, p. 720) as follows: "The whole series of visions, from ch. xix. 11 onwards, is merely intended to exhibit the victory of Christ over His foes. There is first a victory over Satan, through which the army of the enemies of His people by which he is served is destroyed; secondly, a victory over Satan, by which the possibility of leading the nations astray any more to fight against His church is taken from him; thirdly, a victory over Satan, by which he is deprived of the power to keep those who have died with faith in their Saviour in death any longer; and, fourthly, a victory over Satan, by which his last attack upon the saints of

God issues in his final destruction." That the second and third victories are not to be separated from each other in point of time, is indicated by the sameness in the period assigned to each, viz. "a thousand years." But the time when these thousand years commence, cannot be determined from the Apocalypse itself; it must be gathered from the teaching of the rest of the New Testament concerning the first resurrection. According to the statements made by the Apostle Paul in 1 Cor. xv., every one will be raised "in his own order: Christ the first-fruits, afterward they that are Christ's at His coming;" then the end, *i.e.* the resurrection of all the dead, the last judgment, the destruction of the world, and the new creation of heaven and earth. Consequently the first resurrection takes place along with the coming of Christ. But, according to the teaching of the New Testament, the *parusia* of Christ is not to be deferred till the last day of the present world, but commences, as the Lord Himself has said, not long after His ascension, so that some of His own contemporaries will not taste of death till they see the Son of man come in His kingdom (Matt. xvi. 28). The Lord repeats this in Matt. xxiv. 34, in the elaborate discourse concerning His *parusia* to judgment, with the solemn asseveration: "Verily I say unto you, this generation (ἡ γενεὰ αὕτη) will not pass till all these things be fulfilled." And, as Hofmann has correctly observed (p. 640), the idea that "this generation" signifies the church of Christ, does not deserve refutation. We therefore understand that the contemporaries of Christ would live to see the things of which He says, "that they will be the heralding tokens of His second appearance;" and, still further (p. 641): "We have already seen, from Matt. xvi. 28, that the Lord has solemnly affirmed that His own contemporaries will live to see His royal coming."[1] Concerning this royal coming of the Son

[1] Luthardt also says just the same (pp. 94, 95): "Undoubtedly the age of which the Lord is speaking is not the whole of the present era, nor the nation of Israel, but the generation then existing. And yet the Lord's

of man in the glory of His Father with His angels, which some of His contemporaries live to see (Matt. xvi. 27 and 28), Paul writes, in 1 Thess. iv. 15, 16: "We which are alive and remain unto the coming of the Lord shall not anticipate them which are asleep; for the Lord Himself shall descend from heaven with a shout, etc., and the dead in Christ will rise first," etc. Consequently the New Testament teaches quite clearly that the first resurrection commences with the coming of Christ, which began with the judgment executed through the Romans upon the ancient Jerusalem. This was preceded only by the resurrection of Christ as "the first-fruits," and the resurrection of the "many bodies of the saints which slept," that arose from the graves at the resurrection of Christ, and appeared to many in the holy city (Matt. xxvii. 52, 53), as a practical testimony that through the resurrection of Christ death is deprived of its power, and a resurrection from the grave secured for all believers.—According to this distinct teaching of Christ and the apostles, the popular opinion, that the resurrection of the dead as a whole will not take place till the last day of this world, must be rectified. The New Testament does not teach anywhere that all the dead, even those who have fallen asleep in Christ, will remain in the grave, or in Hades, till the last judgment immediately before the destruction of heaven and earth, and that the souls which have entered heaven at their death will be with Christ till then unclothed and without the body. This traditional view merely rests upon the unscriptural idea of the coming of Christ as not taking place till the end of the era, and as an act restricted to a single day of twenty-four hours. According to the Scriptures, the *parusia* takes place on the day of the Lord, יוֹם יְהוָה, *ἡ ἡμέρα τοῦ κυρίου*. But this day is not an earthly day of twelve or twenty-four hours; but, as Peter says (2 Pet. iii. 8), "one

prophecy goes to the very end, and reaches far beyond the destruction of Jerusalem. . . . The existing generation was to live to see the beginning of the end, and did live to see it."

day is with the Lord as a thousand years, and a thousand years as one day" (cf. Ps. xc. 4). The day on which the Son of man comes in His glory commences with the appearing of the Lord to the judgment upon the hardened Israel at the destruction of Jerusalem by the Romans; continues till His appearing to the last judgment, which is still future and will be visible to all nations; and closes with the day of God, on which the heavens will be dissolved with fire, and the elements will melt with heat, and the new heaven and new earth will be created, for which we wait according to His promise (2 Pet. iii. 12, 13). To show how incorrect is the popular idea of the resurrection of the dead, we may adduce not only the fact of the resurrection of many saints immediately after the resurrection of Christ (Matt. xxvii. 52, 53), but also the solemn declaration of the Lord: "Verily, verily, I say unto you, The hour cometh, *and now is*, when the dead shall hear the voice of the Son of God, and they that hear shall live,"—the hour "in the which all that are in the graves shall hear His voice, and shall come forth; they that have done good unto the resurrection of life, etc." (John v. 25, 28); and again the repeated word of Christ, that whosoever believeth on Him *hath* everlasting life, and cometh not into judgment, but hath passed from death unto life (John v. 24, vi. 40, 47, iii. 16, 18, 36); and lastly, what was seen by the sacred seer on the opening of the fifth seal (Rev. vi. 9–11), namely, that white robes were given to the souls that were slain for the word of God and for the testimony which they held, and that were crying for the avenging of their blood, inasmuch as the putting on of the white robe involves or presupposes the clothing of the soul with the new body, so that this vision teaches that the deceased martyrs are translated into the state of those who have risen from the dead before the judgment upon Babylon. The word ψυχαί, which is used to designate them, does not prove that disembodied souls are intended (compare, as evidence to the contrary, the ὀκτὼ ψυχαί of 1 Pet. iii. 20).

But as Rev. xx. 1–10 furnishes no information concerning the time of the first resurrection, so also this passage does not teach that they who are exalted to reign with Christ by the first resurrection will live and reign with Christ in the earthly Jerusalem, whether it be glorified or not. The place where the thrones stand, upon which they are seated, is not mentioned either in vers. 4–6 or vers. 1–3. The opinion that this will be in Jerusalem merely rests upon the twofold assumption, for which no evidence can be adduced, viz. (1) that, according to the prophetic utterances of the Old Testament, Jerusalem or the holy land is the site for the appearance of the Lord to the judgment upon the world of nations (Hofmann, pp. 637, 638); and (2) that the beloved city which the heathen, under Gog and Magog, will besiege, according to Rev. xx. 8, 9, is the earthly Jerusalem, from which it is still further inferred, that the saints besieged in the beloved city cannot be any others than those placed upon thrones through the first resurrection. But the inconceivable nature, not to say the absurdity, of such an assumption as that of a war between earthly men and those who have been raised from the dead and are glorified with spiritual bodies, precludes the identification, which is not expressed in the text, of the saints in Jerusalem with those sitting upon thrones and reigning with Christ, who have obtained eternal life through the resurrection. And as they are reigning with Christ, the Son of God, who has returned to the glory of His heavenly Father, would also be besieged along with them by the hosts of Gog and Magog. But where do the Scriptures teach anything of the kind? The fact that, according to the prophecy of the Old Testament, the Lord comes from Zion to judge the nations furnishes no proof of this, inasmuch as this Zion of the prophets is not the earthly and material, but the heavenly Jerusalem. The angels who come at the ascension of Christ to comfort His disciples with regard to the departure of their Master to the Father, merely say: "This Jesus, who has gone up from you to heaven, will so come in like manner as ye have seen Him go to heaven" (Acts i. 11); but they do not say at what place He will come again. And though the Apostle Paul says in 1 Thess. iv. 16, "the Lord will descend from heaven," he also says, they that are living then will be caught up together with those that have risen in the clouds, to meet the Lord in the air, and so be ever with the Lord. And as here the being caught up in the clouds into the air is not to be understood literally, but simply expresses the thought that those who are glorified will hasten with those who have risen from the dead to meet the Lord, to welcome Him and to be united with Him, and does not assume a permanent abiding in the air; so the expression, "descend from heaven," does not involve a coming to Jerusalem and remaining upon earth. The words are meant to be understood spiritually, like the rending of the heaven and coming down in Isa. lxiv. 1. Paul therefore uses the words *ἀποκάλυψις ἀπ' οὐρανοῦ*, revelation from heaven, in 2 Thess. i. 7, with reference to the same event. The Lord has already descended from heaven to judgment upon the ancient Jerusalem, to take vengeance with flaming fire upon those who would not know God and obey the gospel (2 Thess. i. 8). Every manifestation of God which produces an actual effect upon the earth is a coming down from heaven, which does not involve a local abiding of the Lord upon the earth. As the coming of Christ to the judgment upon Jerusalem does not affect His sitting at the right hand of the Father, so we must not picture to ourselves the resurrection of those who have fallen asleep in the Lord, which commences with this coming, in any other way than that those who rise are received into heaven, and, as the church of the first-born, who are written in heaven, *i.e.* who have become citizens of heaven (Heb. xii. 23), sit on seats around the throne of God and reign with Christ.—Even the first resurrection is not to be thought of as an act occurring once and ending there; but as the coming of the Lord, which commenced with the judgment of the destruction of Jerusalem, is continued in the long series of judgments through which one hostile power after another is overthrown, until the destruction of the last enemy, so may we also assume, in analogy with this, that the resurrection of those who have fallen asleep in Christ, commencing with that *parusia*, is continued through the course of centuries; so that they who die in living faith in their Saviour are raised from the dead at the hour appointed by God according to His wisdom, and the souls received into heaven at death, together with those sown as seed-corn in the earth and ripened from corruption to incorruptibility, will be clothed with spiritual bodies, to reign with Christ. The thousand years are not to be reckoned chronologically, but commence with the coming of Christ to the judgment upon Jerusalem, and extend to the final casting of the beast and the false prophet into the lake of fire, perhaps still further. When they will end we cannot tell; for it is not for us to know the times or the seasons, which the Father hath reserved in His own power (Acts i. 7).

The chaining and imprisonment of Satan in the abyss during the thousand years can also be brought into harmony with this view of the millennium, provided that the words are not taken in a grossly materialistic sense, and we bear in mind that nearly all the pictures of the Apocalypse are of a very drastic character. The key to the interpretation of Rev. xx. 1–3 and 7–10 is to be found in the words of Christ in John xii. 31, when just before His passion He is about to bring His addresses to the people to a close, for the purpose of completing the work of the world's redemption by His death and resurrection. When the Lord says, just at this moment, "now is the judgment passing over the world; now will the prince of this world be cast out," namely, out of the sphere of his dominion, He designates the completion of the work of redemption by His death as a judgment upon the world, through which the rule of Satan in the world is brought to nought, or the kingdom of the devil destroyed. This casting out of the prince of this world, which is accomplished in the establishment and spread of the kingdom of Christ on earth, is shown to the sacred seer in

Patmos in the visions of the conflict of Michael with the dragon, which ends in the casting out of Satan into the earth (Rev. xii. 7 sqq.), and of the chaining and imprisonment of Satan in the abyss for a thousand years (Rev. xx. 1 sqq.). The conflict of Michael with the dragon, which is called the Devil and Satanas, commences when the dragon begins to persecute the woman clothed with the sun after the birth of her child, and its being caught up into heaven, *i.e.* after the work of Christ on earth has terminated with His ascension to heaven. John receives an explanation of the way in which the victory of Michael, through which Satan is cast out of heaven upon the earth, is to be interpreted, from the voice, which says in heaven, "Now is come the salvation, and the strength, and the kingdom of our God, and the power of His Christ; for the accuser of our brethren is cast down, who accused us day and night before God" (ver. 10). With the casting of Satan out of heaven, the kingdom of God and the power of His anointed are established, and Satan is thereby deprived of the power to rule any longer as the prince of the world. It is true that when he sees himself cast from heaven to earth, *i.e.* hurled from his throne, he persecutes the woman; but the woman receives eagles' wings, so that she flies into the wilderness to the place prepared for her by God, and is there nourished for three times and a half, away from the face of the serpent (Rev. xii. 8, 13, 14). After the casting out of Satan from heaven, there follow the chaining and shutting up in the abyss, or in hell; so that during this time he is no more able to seduce the heathen to make war upon the camp of the saints (Rev. xx. 1–3 and 8). All influence upon earth is not thereby taken from him; he is simply deprived of the power to rule on the earth as *ἄρχων* among the heathen, and to restore the *ἐξουσία* wrested from him.[1] We

[1] Hofmann (*Schriftbeweis*, II. 2, p. 722) understands the binding of Satan in a similar manner, and writes as follows on the subject: "That which is rendered impossible to Satan, through his being bound and imprisoned in the nether world, and therefore through his exclusion from the upper

may therefore say that the binding of Satan began with the fall of heathenism as the religion of the world, through the elevation of Christianity to be the state-religion of the Roman empire, and that it will last so long as Christianity continues to be the state-religion of the kingdoms which rule the world.

It is impossible, therefore, to prove from Rev. xx. that there will be a kingdom of glory in the earthly Jerusalem before the last judgment; and the New Testament generally neither teaches the return of the people of Israel to Palestine on their conversion to Christ,—which will take place according to Rom. xi 25 sqq.,—nor the rebuilding of the temple and restoration of Levitical sacrifices. But if this be the case, then Ezekiel's vision of the new temple and sacrificial worship, and the new division of the land of Canaan, cannot be understood literally, but only in a symbolico-typical sense. The following question, therefore, is the only one that remains to be answered:—

III. *How are we to understand the vision of the new kingdom of God in Ezek.* xl.–xlviii ?—In other words, What opinion are we to form concerning the fulfilment of this prophetic picture? The first reply to be given to this is, that this vision does not depict the coming into existence, or the successive stages in the rise and development, of the new kingdom of God. For Ezekiel sees the temple as a finished building, the component parts of which are so measured before his eyes that he is led about within the building. He sees the glory of Jehovah enter into the temple, and hears the voice of the Lord, who declares

world, where the history of mankind is proceeding, is *simply* that kind of activity which exerts a determining influence upon the course of history." And Flacius, in his *Glossa* to the New Testament, gives this explanation: "But Satan is not then so bound or shut up in hell that he cannot do anything, or cause any injury, more especially disobedience in his children; but simply that he cannot act any more either so powerfully or with such success as before." He also reckons the thousand years "from the resurrection and ascension of the Lord, when Christ began in the most powerful manner to triumph over devils and ungodly men throughout the world," etc.

this house to be the seat of His throne in the midst of His people; and commands the prophet to make known to the people the form of the house, and its arrangement and ordinances, that they may consider the building, and be ashamed of their evil deeds (ch. xliii. 4–12). The new order of worship also (ch. xliii. 13-xlvi. 15) does not refer to the building of the temple, but to the service which Israel is to render to God, who is enthroned in this temple. Only the directions concerning the boundaries and the division of the land presuppose that Israel has still to take possession of Canaan, though it has already been brought back out of the heathen lands, and is about to divide it by lot and take possession of it as its own inheritance, to dwell there, and to sustain and delight itself with the fulness of its blessings. It follows from this that the prophetic picture does not furnish a typical exhibition of the church of Christ in its gradual development, but sets forth the kingdom of God established by Christ in its perfect form, and is partly to be regarded as the Old Testament outline of the New Testament picture of the heavenly Jerusalem in Rev. xxi. and xxii. For the river of the water of life is common to both visions. According to Ezekiel, it springs from the threshold of the temple, in which the Lord has ascended His throne, flows through the land to the Arabah, and pours into the Dead Sea, to make the water thereof sound; and according to Rev. xxii. 1 sqq., it proceeds from the throne of God and of the Lamb, and flows through the midst of the street of the New Jerusalem. According to Ezek. xlvii. 7, 12, as well as Rev. xxii. 2, there are trees growing upon its banks which bear edible fruits every month, that is to say, twelve times a year, and the leaves of which serve for the healing of the nations. But Ezekiel's picture of the new kingdom of God comes short of the picture of the New Jerusalem in this respect, that in Ezekiel the city and temple are separated, although the temple stands upon a high mountain in the centre of the holy *terumah* in the midst of the land of Canaan, and the city of Jerusalem reaches to the holy *termuah* with the northern side of its territory; whereas the new heavenly Jerusalem has no temple, and, in its perfect cubic form of equal length, breadth, and height, has itself become the holy of holies, in which there stands the throne of God and of the Lamb (Rev. xxi. 16, xxii. 4). Ezekiel could not rise to such an eminence of vision as this. The kingdom of God seen by him has a preponderatingly Old Testament stamp, and is a perfect Israelitish Canaan, answering to the idea of the Old Covenant, in the midst of which Jehovah dwells in His temple, and the water of life flows down from His throne and pours over all the land, to give prosperity to His people. The temple of Ezekiel is simply a new Solomon's temple, built in perfect accordance with the holiness of the house of God, in the courts of which Israel appears before Jehovah to offer burnt-offerings and slain-offerings, and to worship; and although the city of Jerusalem does indeed form a perfect square, with three gates on every side bearing the names of the twelve tribes of Israel, like the gates of the heavenly Jerusalem, it has not yet the form of a cube as the stamp of the holy of holies, in which Jehovah the almighty God is enthroned, though its name is, "henceforth Jehovah thither." Still less does the attack of Gog with his peoples, gathered together from the ends of the earth, apply to the heavenly Jerusalem. It is true that, according to the formal arrangement of our prophet's book, it stands before the vision of the new kingdom of God; but chronologically its proper place is within it, and it does not even fall at the commencement of it, but at the end of the years, after Israel has been gathered out of the nations and brought back into its own land, and has dwelt there for a long time in security (ch. xxxviii. 8, 16). This attack on the part of the heathen nations is only conceivable as directed against the people of God still dwelling in the earthly Canaan.

How then are we to remove the discrepancy, that on the one hand the river of the water of life proceeding from the temple indicates a glorification of Canaan, and on the other hand the land and people appear to be still unglorified, and the latter are living in circumstances which conform to the earlier condition of Israel? Does not this picture suggest a state of earthly glory on the part of the nation of Israel in its own land, which has passed through a paradisaical transformation before the new creation of the heaven and the earth? Isaiah also predicts a new time, in which the patriarchal length of life of the primeval era shall return, when death shall no more sweep men prematurely away, and not only shall war cease among men, but mutual destruction in the animal world shall also come to an end (Isa. lxv. 19–23 compared with ch. xi. 6–9). When shall this take place? Delitzsch, who asks this question (*Isa.* vol. II. p. 492, transl.), gives the following reply: "Certainly not in the blessed life beyond the grave, to which it would be both impossible and absurd to refer these promises, since they presuppose a continued mixture of sinners with the righteous, and merely a limitation of the power of death, not its destruction." From this he then draws the conclusion that the description is only applicable to the state of the millennium. But the creation of a new heaven and a new earth precedes this description (ch. lxv. 17, 18). Does not this point to the heavenly Jerusalem of the new earth? To this Delitzsch replies that "the Old Testament prophet was not yet able to distinguish from one another the things which the author of the Apocalypse separates into distinct periods. From the Old Testament point of view generally, nothing was known of a state of blessedness beyond the grave.—In the Old Testament prophecy, the idea of the new cosmos is blended with the millennium. It is only in the New Testament that the new creation intervenes as a party wall between this life and the life beyond; whereas the Old Testament prophecy brings the new creation itself into the present life, and knows nothing of any Jerusalem of the blessed life to come, as distinct from the new Jerusalem of the millennium." But even if there were a better foundation for the chiliastic idea of the millennium (Rev. xx.) than there is according to our discussion of the question above, the passage just quoted would not suffice to remove the difficulty before us. For if Isaiah is describing the Jerusalem of the millennium in ch. lxv. 19–23, he has not merely brought the new creation of heaven and earth into the present life, but he has also transferred the so-called millennium to the new earth, *i.e.* to the other side of the new creation of heaven and earth. Delitzsch himself acknowledges this on page 517 (transl.), where he observes in his commentary on Isa. lxvi. 22–24 that "the object of the prophecy" (namely, that from new moon to new moon, and from Sabbath to Sabbath, all flesh will come to worship before Jehovah, and they will go out to look at the corpses of the men that have rebelled against Him, whose worm will not die, nor their fire be quenched) "is no other than the new Jerusalem of the world to come, and the eternal torment of the damned." Isaiah "is speaking of the other side, but he speaks of it as on this side." But if Isaiah is speaking of the other side as on this side in ch. lxvi., he has done the same in ch. lxv. 19–23; and the Jerusalem depicted in ch. lxv. cannot be the Jerusalem of the millennium on this side, but can only be the New Jerusalem of the other side coming down from heaven, as the description is the same in both chapters, and therefore must refer to one and the same object. The description in Isa. lxv., like that in ch. lxvi., can be perfectly comprehended from the fact that the prophet is speaking of that which is on the other side as on this side, without there being any necessity for the hypothesis of a thousand years' earthly kingdom of glory. It is quite correct that the Old Testament knows nothing whatever of a blessed state beyond the grave, or rather merely teaches nothing with regard to it, and that the Old Testament prophecy transfers the state beyond to this side, in other words, depicts the eternal life after the last judgment in colours taken from the happiness of the Israelitish life in Canaan. And this is also correct, " that the Old Testament depicts both this life and the life to come as an endless extension of this life; whilst the New Testament depicts it as a continuous line in two halves, the last point in this present finite state being the first point of the infinite state beyond: that the Old Testament preserves the continuity of this life and the life to come, by transferring the outer side, the form, the appearance of this life, to the life to come; the New Testament by making the inner side, the nature, the reality of the life to come, the δυνάμεις μέλλοντος αἰῶνος, immanent in this life." But it is only to the doctrinal writings of the New Testament that this absolutely applies. Of the prophetical pictures of the New Testament, on the other hand, and especially the Apocalypse, it can only be affirmed with considerable limitations. Not only is the New Jerusalem of Isaiah, which has a new heaven above it and a new earth beneath, simply the old earthly Jerusalem, which has attained to the highest glory and happiness; but in the Apocalypse also, the Jerusalem which has come down from heaven is an earthly city with great walls of jasper and pure gold, founded upon twelve precious stones, with twelve gates consisting of pearls, that are not shut by day, in order that the kings of the earth may bring their glory into the city, into which nothing common and no abomination enter. The whole picture rests upon those of Isaiah and Ezekiel, and merely rises above these Old Testament types by the fact that the most costly minerals of the earth are selected, to indicate the exceeding glory of the heavenly nature of this city of God. What, then, is the heavenly Jerusalem of the new earth? Is it actually a city of the new world, or the capital of the kingdom of heaven? Is it not rather a picture of the many mansions in the Father's house in heaven, which Jesus entered at His ascension to heaven, to prepare a place for us (John xiv. 2)? Is it not a picture of the heavenly kingdom (2 Tim. iv. 18), into which all the blessed in that world enter whose names are written in the book of life? And its brilliant glory, is it not a picture of the unspeakable glory of the eternal life, which no eye has seen, no ear has heard, and which has not entered into the heart of any man (1 Cor. ii. 9)?

And if the state beyond the grave is transferred to this side, *i.e.* depicted in colours and imagery drawn from this side, not only in the Old Testament prophecy, but in that of the New Testament also, we must not seek the reason for this prophetic mode of describing the circumstances of the everlasting life, or the world to come, in the fact that the Old Testament knows nothing of a blessed state beyond the grave, is ignorant of a heaven with men that are saved. The reason is rather to be found in the fact, that heavenly things and circumstances lie beyond our idea and comprehension; so that we can only represent to ourselves the kingdom of God after the analogy of earthly circumstances and conditions, just as we are unable to form any other conception of eternal blessedness than as a life without end in heavenly glory and joy, set free from all the imperfections and evils of this earthly world. So long as we are walking here below by faith and not by sight, we must be content with those pictures of the future blessings of eternal life with the Lord in His heavenly kingdom which the Scriptures have borrowed from the divinely ordered form of the Israelitish theocracy, presenting Jerusalem with its temple, and Canaan the abode of the covenant people of the Old Testament as types of the kingdom of heaven, and picturing the glory of the world to come as a city of God coming down from heaven upon the new earth, built of gold, precious stones, and pearls, and illumined with the light of the glory of the Lord.—To this there must no doubt be added, in the case of the Old Testament prophets, the fact that the division of the kingdom of the Messiah into a period of development on this side, and one of full completion on the other, had not yet been so clearly revealed to them as it has been to us by Christ in the New Testament; so that Isaiah is the only prophet who prophesies of the destruction of the present world and the creation of a new heaven and new earth. If we leave out of sight this culminating point of the Old Testament prophecy, all the prophets depict the glorification and completion of the kingdom of God established in Israel by the Messiah, on the one hand, as a continuous extension of His dominion on Zion from Jerusalem outwards over all the earth, through the execution of the judgment upon the heathen nations of the world; and, on the other hand, as a bursting of the land of Canaan into miraculous fruitfulness for the increase of His people's prosperity, and as a glorification of Jerusalem, to which all nations will go on pilgrimage to the house of the Lord on Zion, to worship the Lord and present their treasures to Him as offerings. Thus also in Ezekiel the bringing back of the people of Israel, who have been scattered by the Lord among the heathen on account of their apostasy, to the promised land, the restoration of Jerusalem and the temple, which have been destroyed, and the future blessing of Israel with the most abundant supply of earthly good from the land which has been glorified into paradisaical fruitfulness; form a continuity, in which the small beginnings of the return of the people from Babylon and the deliverance and blessing which are still in the future, lie folded in one another, and the present state and that beyond are blended together. And accordingly he depicts the glory and completion of the restored and renovated kingdom of God under the figure of a new division of Canaan among the twelve tribes of all Israel, united under the sceptre of the second David for ever, and forming one single nation, by which all the incongruities of the former times are removed, and also of a new sanctuary built upon a very high mountain in the centre of Canaan, in which the people walking in the commandments and rights of their God offer sacrifice, and come to worship before the Lord in His courts on the Sabbaths, new moons, and yearly feasts. This blessedness of Israel also is not permanently disturbed through the invasion of the restored land by Gog and his hordes, but rather perfected and everlastingly established by the fact that the Lord God destroys this last enemy, and causes him to perish by self-immolation. But however strongly the Old Testament drapery of the Messianic prophecy stands out even in Ezekiel, there are traits to be met with even in this form, by which we may recognise the fact that the Israelitish theocratical form simply constitutes the clothing in which the New Testament constitution of the kingdom of God is veiled.[1] Among these traits we reckon not only the description given in ch. xl.–xlviii., which can only be interpreted in a typical sense, but also the vision of the raising to life of the dry bones in ch. xxxvii. 1–14, the ultimate fulfilment of which will not take place till the general resurrection, and more especially the prophecy of the restoration not only of Jerusalem, but also of Samaria and Sodom, to their original condition (ch. xvi. 53 sqq.), which, as we have already shown, will not be perfectly fulfilled till the *παλιγγενεσία*, *i.e.* the general renovation of the world after the last judgment. From this last-named

[1] Of all such pictures it may certainly be said that we "cannot see how an Old Testament prophet, when speaking of Canaan, Jerusalem, Zion, and their future glorification, can have thought of anything else than the earthly sites of the Old Testament kingdom of God" (Volck); but this objection proves nothing against their typical explanation, as we know that the prophets of the Old Testament, who prophesied of the grace that was to come to us, inquired and searched diligently what, and what manner of time, the Spirit of Christ that was in them did signify (1 Pet. i. 10, 11). Even, therefore, if the prophets in their uninspired meditation upon that which they had prophesied, when moved by the Holy Ghost, did not discern the typical meaning of their own utterances, we, who are living in the times of the fulfilment, and are acquainted not only with the commencement of the fulfilment in the coming of our Lord, in His life, sufferings, and death, and His resurrection and ascension to heaven, as well as in His utterances concerning His second coming, but also with a long course of fulfilment in the extension for eighteen hundred years of the kingdom of heaven established by Him on earth, have not so much to inquire what the Old Testament prophets thought in their searching into the prophecies which they were inspired to utter by the Spirit of Christ, even if it were possible to discover what their thoughts really were, but rather, in the light of the fulfilment that has already taken place, to inquire what the Spirit of Christ, which enabled the prophets to see and to predict the coming of His kingdom in pictures drawn from the Old Testament kingdom of God, has foretold and revealed to us through the medium of these figures.

prophecy, to which the healing of the waters of the Dead Sea in ch. xlvii. 9 sqq. supplies a parallel, pointing as it does to the renewal of the earth after the destruction of the present world, it clearly follows that the tribes of Israel which receive Canaan for a perpetual possession are not the Jewish people converted to Christ, but the Israel of God, *i.e.* the people of God of the new covenant gathered from among both Jews and Gentiles; and that Canaan, in which they are to dwell, is not the earthly Canaan or Palestine between the Jordan and the Mediterranean Sea, but the New Testament Canaan, *i.e.* the territory of the kingdom of God, whose boundaries reach from sea to sea, and from the river to the ends of the earth. And the temple upon a very high mountain in the midst of this Canaan, in which the Lord is enthroned, and causes the river of the water of life to flow down from His throne over His kingdom, so that the earth produces the tree of life with leaves as medicine for men, and the Dead Sea is filled with fishes and living creatures, is a figurative representation and type of the gracious presence of the Lord in His church, which is realized in the present period of the earthly development of the kingdom of heaven in the form of the Christian church in a spiritual and invisible manner in the indwelling of the Father and the Son through the Holy Spirit in the hearts of believers, and in a spiritual and invisible operation in the church, but which will eventually manifest itself when our Lord shall appear in the glory of the Father, to translate His church into the kingdom of glory, in such a manner that we shall see the almighty God and the Lamb with the eyes of our glorified body, and worship before His throne.

This worship is described in our vision (ch. xliii. 13–xlvi. 24) as the offering of sacrifice according to the Israelitish form of divine worship under the Old Testament; and in accordance with the mode peculiar to Ezekiel of carrying out all the pictures in detail, the leading instructions concerning the Levitical sacrifices are repeated and modified in harmony with the new circumstances. As the Mosaic worship after the building of the tabernacle commenced with the consecration of the altar, so Ezekiel's description of the new worship commences with the consecration of the altar of burnt-offering, and then spreads over the entering into and exit from the temple, the things requisite for the service at the altar, the duties and rights of the worshippers at the altar, and the quantity and quality of the sacrifices to be offered on the Sabbaths, new moons, and yearly feasts, as well as every day. From a comparison of the new sacrificial *thorah* with that of Moses in our exposition of these chapters, we have observed various distinctions which essentially modified the character of the whole service, viz. a thorough alteration in the order and celebration of the feasts, and a complete change in the proportion between the material of the meat-offering and the animal sacrifices. So far as the first distinction is concerned, the daily sacrifice is reduced to a morning burnt- and meat-offering, and the evening sacrifice of the Mosaic law is abolished; on the other hand, the Sabbath offering is more than tripled in quantity; again, in the case of the new-moon offerings, the sin-offering is omitted and the burnt-offering diminished; in the yearly feasts, the offerings prescribed for the seven days of the feast of unleavened bread and of the feast of tabernacles are equalized in quantity and quality, and the daily burnt- and meat-offerings of the feast of unleavened bread are considerably increased; on the other hand, the daily sacrifices of the feast of tabernacles are diminished in proportion to those prescribed by the Mosaic law. Moreover, the feast of weeks, or harvest-feast, and in the seventh month the day of trumpets and the feast of atonement, with its great atoning sacrifices, are dropt. In the place of these, copious sin-offerings are appointed for the first, seventh, and fourteenth days of the first month. To do justice to the meaning of these changes, we must keep in mind the idea of the Mosaic cycle of feasts. (For this, see my *Bibl. Archäol.* I. § 76 sqq.) The ceremonial worship prescribed by the Mosaic law, in addition to the daily sacrifice, consisted of a cycle of feast days and festal seasons regulated according to the number seven, which had its root in the Sabbath, and was organized in accordance with the division of time, based upon the creation, into weeks, months, and years. As the Lord God created the world in six days, and ended the creation on the seventh day by blessing and sanctifying that day through resting from His works, so also were His people to sanctify every seventh day of the week to Him by resting from all work, and by a special burnt- and meat-offering. And, like the seventh day of the week, so also was the seventh month of the year to be sanctified by the keeping of the new moon with sabbatical rest and special sacrifices, and every seventh year to be a sabbatical year. Into this cycle of holy days, arranged according to the number seven, the yearly feasts consecrated to the remembrance of the mighty acts of the Lord for the establishment, preservation, and blessing of His people, were so dovetailed that the number of these yearly feasts amounted to seven,—the Passover, feast of unleavened bread, feast of weeks, day of trumpets, day of atonement, feast of tabernacles, and conclusion of this feast,—of which the feasts of unleavened bread and tabernacles were kept for seven days each. These seven feasts formed two festal circles, the first of which with three feasts referred to the raising of Israel into the people of God and to its earthly subsistence; whilst the second, which fell in the seventh month, and was introduced by the day of trumpets, had for its object the preservation of Israel in a state of grace, and its happiness in the full enjoyment of the blessings of salvation, and commenced with the day of atonement, culminated in the feast of tabernacles, and ended with the octave of that feast. In the festal *thorah* of Ezekiel, on the other hand, the weekly Sabbath did indeed form the foundation of all the festal seasons, and the keeping of the new moon as the monthly Sabbath corresponds to this; but the number of yearly feasts is reduced to the Passover, the seven days' feast of unleavened bread, and the seven days' feast of the seventh month (the feast of tabernacles). The feast of weeks and the presentation of the sheaf of first-fruits on the second day of the feast of unleavened bread are omitted; and thus the allusion in these two feasts to the harvest, or to their earthly maintenance, is abolished. Of still greater importance are the abolition both of the day of trumpets and of the day of atonement, and the octave of the feast of tabernacles, and the institution of three great sin-offerings in the first month, by which the seventh month is divested of the sabbatical character which it had in the Mosaic *thorah*. According to the Mosaic order of feasts, Israel was to consecrate its life to the Lord and to His service, by keeping the feast of Passover and the seven days' feast of unleavened bread every year in the month of its deliverance from Egypt as the first month of the year, in commemoration of this act of divine mercy,—by appropriating to itself afresh the sparing of its first-born, and its reception into the covenant with the Lord, in the sacrifice of the paschal lamb and in the paschal meal,—and by renewing its transportation from the old condition in Egypt into the new life of divine grace in the feast of unleavened bread,—then by its receiving every month absolution for the sins of weakness committed in the previous month, by means of a sin-offering presented on the new moon,—and by keeping the seventh month of the year in a sabbatical manner, by observing the new moon with sabbatical rest and the tenth day as a day of atonement, on which it received forgiveness of all the sins that had remained without expiation during the course of the year through the blood of the great sin-offering, and the purification of its sanctuary from all the uncleanness of those who approached it, so that, on the feast of tabernacles which followed, they could not only thank the Lord their God for their gracious preservation in the way through the wilderness, and their introduction into the Canaan so abounding in blessings, but could also taste the happiness of vital fellowship with their God. The yearly feasts of Israel, which commenced with the celebration of the memorial of their reception into the Lord's covenant of grace, culminated in the two high feasts of the seventh month, the great day of atonement, and the joyous feast of tabernacles, to indicate that the people living under the law needed, in addition to the expiation required from month to month, another great and comprehensive expiation in the seventh month of the year, in order to be able to enjoy the blessing consequent upon its introduction into Canaan, the blessedness of the sonship of God. According to Ezekiel's order of feasts and sacrifices, on the other hand, Israel was to begin every new year of its life with a great sin-offering on the first, seventh, and fourteenth days of the first month, and through the blood of these sin-offerings procure for itself forgiveness of all sins, and the removal of all the uncleanness of its sanctuary, before it renewed the covenant of grace with the Lord in the paschal meal, and its transposition into the new life of grace in the days of unleavened bread, and throughout the year consecrated its life to the Lord in the daily burnt-offering, through increased Sabbath-offerings and the regular sacrifices of the new moon; and lastly, through the feast in commemoration of its entrance into Canaan, in order to live before Him a blameless, righteous, and happy life. In the Mosaic order of the feasts and sacrifices the most comprehensive act of expiation, and the most perfect reconciliation of the people to God which the old covenant could offer, lay in the seventh month, the Sabbath month of the year, by which it was indicated that the Sinaitic covenant led the people toward reconciliation, and only offered it to them in the middle of the year; whereas Ezekiel's new order of worship offers to Israel, now returning to its God, reconciliation through the forgiveness of its sins and purification from its uncleannesses at the beginning of the year, so that it can walk before God in righteousness in the strength of the blood of the atoning sacrifice throughout the year, and rejoice in the blessings of His grace. Now, inasmuch as the great atoning sacrifice of the day of atonement pointed typically to the eternally availing atoning sacrifice which Christ was to offer in the midst of the years of the world through His death upon the cross on Golgotha, the transposition of the chief atoning sacrifices to the commencement of the year by Ezekiel indicates that, for the Israel of the new covenant, this eternally-availing atoning sacrifice would form the foundation for all its acts of worship and keeping of feasts, as well as for the whole course of its life. It is in this that we find the Messianic feature of Ezekiel's order of sacrifices and feasts, by which it acquires a character more in accordance with the New Testament completion of the sacrificial service, which also presents itself to us in the other and still more deeply penetrating modifications of the Mosaic *thorah* of sacrifice on the part of Ezekiel, both in the fact that the daily sacrifice is reduced to a morning sacrifice, and also in the fact that the quantities are tripled in the Sabbath-offerings and those of the feast of unleavened bread as compared with the Mosaic institutes, and more especially in the change in the relative proportion of the quantity of the meat-offering to that of the burnt-offering. For example, as the burnt-offering shadows forth the reconciliation and surrender to the Lord of the person offering the sacrifice, whilst the meat-offering shadows forth the fruit of this surrender, the sanctification of the life in good works, the increase in the quantity of the meat-offering connected with the burnt-offering, indicates that the people offering these sacrifices will bring forth more of the fruit of sanctification in good works upon the ground of the reconciliation which it has received. We do not venture to carry out to any greater length the interpretation of the differences between the Mosaic law of sacrifice and that of Ezekiel, or to point out any Messianic allusions either in the number of victims prescribed for the several feast days, or in the fact that a different quantity is prescribed for the meat-offering connected with the daily burnt-offering from that enjoined for the festal sacrifices, or in any other things of a similar nature.

These points of detail apparently belong merely to the individualizing of the matter. And so also, in the fact that the provision of the people's sacrifices for the Sabbath, new moon, and feasts devolves upon the prince, and in the appointment of the place where the prince is to stand and worship in the temple, and to hold the sacrificial meal, we are unable to detect any Messianic elements, for the simple reason that the position which David and Solomon assumed in relation to the temple and its ritual furnished Ezekiel with a model for these regulations. And, in a similar manner, the precept concerning the hereditary property of the prince and its transmission to his sons (ch. xlvi. 16 sqq.) is to be explained from the fact that the future David is thought of as a king, like the son of Jesse, who will be the prince of Israel for ever, not in his own person, but in his family. The only thing that still appears worthy of consideration is the circumstance that throughout the whole of Ezekiel's order of worship no allusion is made to the high priest, but the same holiness is demanded of all the priests which was required of the high priesc in the Mosaic law. This points to the fact that the Israel of the future will answer to its calling to be a holy people of the Lord in a more perfect manner than in past times. In this respect the new temple will also differ from the old temple of Solomon. The very elaborate description of the gates and courts, with their buildings, in the new temple has no other object than to show how the future sanctuary will answer in all its parts to the holiness of the Lord's house, and will be so arranged that no person uncircumcised in heart and flesh will be able to enter it.—But all these things belong to the "shadow of things to come,' which were to pass away when "the body of Christ" appeared (Col. ii. 17; Heb. x. 1). When, therefore, M. Baumgarten, Auberlen, and other millenarians, express the opinion that this shadow-work will be restored after the eventual conversion of Israel to Christ, in support of which Baumgarten even appeals to the authority of the apostle of the Gentiles, they have altogether disregarded the warning of this very apostle: "Beware lest any man spoil you through philosophy and vain deceit, after the tradition of men, after the rudiments of the world, and not after Christ" (Col. ii. 8, 16, 20, 21).

Lastly, with regard to the prophecy concerning Gog, the prince of Magog, and his expedition against the restored land and people of Israel (Ezek. xxxviii. and xxxix.), and its relation to the new conformation of the kingdom of God depicted in ch. xl.-xlviii., the assumption of Hengstenberg (on Rev. xx. 7), "that Gog and Magog represent generally all the future enemies of the kingdom of God, and that we have here embraced in one large picture all that has been developing itself in a long series of events, so that the explanations which take them as referring to the Syrian kings, the Goths and Vandals, or the Turks, are all alike true, and only false in their exclusiveness,"—is not in harmony with the contents of this prophecy, and cannot be reconciled with the position which it occupies in Ezekiel and in the Apocalypse. For the prophecy concerning Gog, though it is indeed essentially different from those which concern themselves with the Assyrians, Chaldeans, Egyptians, and other smaller or larger nations of the world, has nothing "utopian" about it, which indicates "a thoroughly ideal and comprehensive character." Even if the name *Gog* be formed by Ezekiel in the freest manner from *Magog*, and however remote the peoples led by Gog from the ends of the earth to make war upon Israel, when restored and living in the deepest peace, may be; yet *Magog*, *Meshech*, *Tubal*, *Pharaz*, *Cush*, and *Phut* are not utopian nations, but the names of historical tribes of whose existence there is no doubt, although their settlements lie outside the known civilised world. Whether there be any foundation for the old Jewish interpretation of the name *Magog* as referring to a great Scythian tribe, or not, we leave undecided; but so much is certain, that *Magog* was a people settled in the extreme north of the world known to the ancients. Nor will we attempt to decide whether the invasion of Hither Asia by the Scythians forms the historical starting-point or connecting link for Ezekiel's prophecy concerning Gog; but there can be no doubt that this prophecy does not refer to an invasion on the part of the Scythians, but foretells a last great conflict, in which the heathen dwelling on the borders of the globe will engage against the kingdom of God, after the kingdom of the world in its organized national forms, as Asshur, Babel, Javan, shall have been destroyed, and the kingdom of Christ shall have spread over the whole of the civilised world. Gog of Magog is the last hostile phase of the world-power opposed to God, which will wage war on earth against the kingdom of God, and that the rude force of the uncivilised heathen world, which will not rise up and attack the church of Christ till after the fall of the world-power bearing the name of Babylon in the Apocalypse, *i.e.* till towards the end of the present course of the world, when it will attempt to lay it waste and destroy it, but will be itself annihilated by the Lord by miracles of His almighty power. In the "conglomerate of nations," which Gog leads against the people of Israel at the end of the years, there is a combination of all that is ungodly in the heathen world, and that has become ripe for casting into the great wine-press of the wrath of God, to be destroyed by the storms of divine judgment (ch. xxxviii. 21, 22, xxxix. 6). But, as Baumgarten has correctly observed (in Herzog's *Cyclopaedia*), "inasmuch as the undisguised and final malice of the world of nations against the kingdom of God is exhibited here, Ezekiel could truly say that the prophets of the former times had already prophesied of this enemy (ch. xxxviii. 17), and that the day of vengeance upon Gog and Magog is that of which Jehovah has already spoken (ch. xxxix. 8),—that is to say, all that has been stated concerning hostility on the part of the heathen towards the kingdom of Jehovah, and the judgment upon this hostility, finds its ultimate fulfilment in this the last and extremest opposition of all." This is in harmony not only with the assumption of this prophecy in Rev. xx., but also with the declaration of the Apocalypse, that it is the Satan released from his prison who leads the heathen to battle against the camp of the saints and the beloved city, and that fire from God out of heaven consumes these enemies, and the devil who has seduced them is cast into the lake of fire to be tormented for ever and ever. —According to all this, the appearing of Gog is still in the future, and the day alone can clearly show what form it will assume.

BIBLICAL COMMENTARY

ON THE

BOOK OF DANIEL

BY

C. F. KEIL, D.D.

TRANSLATED FROM THE GERMAN BY

THE REV. M. G. EASTON, A.M.

TRANSLATOR'S PREFACE

THE venerable and learned author of the following Commentary has produced a work which, it is believed, will stand comparison with any other of the present age for the comprehensive and masterly way in which he handles the many difficult and interesting questions of Biblical Criticism and Interpretation that have accumulated from the earliest times around the Exposition of the Book of the Prophet Daniel. The Translator is glad of the opportunity of bringing this work under the notice of English readers. The severely critical and exegetical nature of the work precludes any attempt at elegance of style. The Translator's aim has simply been to introduce the English student to Dr. Keil's own modes of thought and forms of expression.

TABLE OF CONTENTS

INTRODUCTION.

EXPOSITION.

THE BOOK OF DANIEL

INTRODUCTION.

I.—THE PERSON OF THE PROPHET.

THE name דָּנִיֵּאל or דָּנִאֵל (Ezek. xiv. 14, 20, xxviii. 3), Δανιήλ, *i.e.* "God is my Judge," or, if the י is the *Yod compaginis*, "God is judging," "God will judge," but not "Judge of God," is in the Old Testament borne by a son of David by Abigail (1 Chron. iii. 1), a Levite in the time of Ezra (Ezra viii. 2; Neh. x. 7 [6]), and by the prophet whose life and prophecies form the contents of this book.

Of Daniel's life the following particulars are related:—From ch. i. 1–5 it appears that, along with other youths of the "king's seed," and of the most distinguished families of Israel, he was carried captive to Babylon, in the reign of Jehoiakim, by Nebuchadnezzar, when he first came up against Jerusalem and took it, and that there, under the Chaldee name of Belteshazzar, he spent three years in acquiring a knowledge of Chaldee science and learning, that he might be prepared for serving in the king's palace. Whether Daniel was of the "seed royal," or only belonged to one of the most distinguished families of Israel, is not decided, inasmuch as there is no certain information regarding his descent. The statement of Josephus (*Ant.* x. 10, 1), that he was ἐκ τοῦ Σεδεκίου γένους, is probably an opinion deduced from Dan. i. 3, and it is not much better established than the saying of Epiphanius (*Adv. Hæres.* 55. 3) that his father was called Σαβαάν, and that of the Pseudo-Epiphanius (*de vita proph.* ch. x.) that he was born at Upper Bethhoron, not far from Jerusalem. During the period set apart for his education, Daniel and his like-minded friends, Hananiah, Mishael, and Azariah, who had received the Chaldee names Shadrach, Meshach, and Abed-nego, abstained, with the consent of their overseer, from the meat and drink provided for them from the king's table, lest they should thereby be defiled through contact with idolatry, and partook only of pulse and water. This stedfast adherence to the faith of their fathers was so blessed of God, that they were not only in bodily appearance fairer than the other youths who ate of the king's meat, but they also made such progress in their education, that at the end of their years of training, on an examination of their attainments in the presence of the king, they far excelled all the Chaldean wise men throughout the whole kingdom (vers. 6–20).

After this, in the second year of his reign, Nebuchadnezzar, being troubled in spirit by a remarkable dream which he had dreamt, called to him all the astrologers and Chaldeans of Babylon, that they might tell him the dream and interpret it. They confessed their inability to fulfil his desire. The king's dream and its interpretation were then revealed by God to Daniel, in answer to prayer, so that he could tell the matter to the king. On this account Nebuchadnezzar gave glory to the God of the Jews as the God of gods and the Revealer of hidden things, and raised Daniel to the rank of ruler over the whole province of Babylon, and chief president over all the wise men of Babylon. At the request of Daniel, he also appointed his three friends to be administrators over the province, so that Daniel remained in the king's palace (ch. ii.). He held this office during the whole of Nebuchadnezzar's reign, and interpreted, at a later period, a dream of great significance relative to a calamity which was about to fall upon the king (ch. iv.).

After Nebuchadnezzar's death he appears to have been deprived of his elevated rank, as the result of the change of government. But Belshazzar, having been alarmed during a riotous feast by the finger of a man's hand writing on the wall, called to him the Chaldeans and astrologers. None of them was able to read and to interpret the mysterious writing. The king's mother thereupon directed that Daniel should be called, and he read and interpreted the writing to the king. For this he was promoted by the king to be the third ruler of the kingdom, *i.e.* to be one of the three chief governors of the kingdom (ch. v.). This office he continued to hold under the Median king Darius. The other princes of the empire and the royal satraps sought to deprive him of it, but God the Lord in a wonderful manner saved him (ch. vi.) by His angel from the mouth of the lions; and he remained in office under the government of the Persian Cyrus (ch. vi. 29 [28]).

During this second half of his life Daniel was honoured by God with revelations regarding the development of the world-power in its different phases, the warfare between it and the kingdom of God, and the final victory of the latter over all hostile powers. These revelations are contained in ch. vii.–xii. The last of them was communicated to him in the third year of Cyrus the king (ch. x. 1), *i.e.* in the second year after Cyrus had issued his edict (Ezra i. 1 ff.) permitting the Jews to return to their own land and to rebuild the temple at Jerusalem. Hence we learn that Daniel lived to see the beginning of the return of his people from their exile. He did not, however, return to his native land with the company that went up under Zerubbabel and Joshua, but remained in Babylon, and there ended his days, probably not long after the last of these revelations from God had been communicated to him, which concluded with the command to seal up the book of his prophecies till the time of the end, and with the charge, rich in its comfort, to go in peace to meet his death, and to await the resurrection from the dead at the end of the days (ch. xii. 4, 13). If Daniel was a youth (יֶלֶד, i. 4, 10) of from fifteen to eighteen years of age at the time of his being carried captive into Chaldea, and died in the faith of the divine promise soon after the last revelation made to him in the third year (ch. x. 1) of king Cyrus, then he must have reached the advanced age of at least ninety years.

The statements of this book regarding his righteousness and piety, as also regarding his wonderful endowment with wisdom to reveal hidden things, receive a powerful confirmation from the language of his contemporary Ezekiel (ch. xiv. 14, 20), who mentions Daniel along with Noah and Job as a pattern of righteousness of life pleasing to God, and (ch. xxviii. 3) speaks of his wisdom as above that of the princes of Tyre. If we consider that Ezekiel gave expression to the former of these statements fourteen years, and to the other eighteen years, after Daniel had been carried captive to Babylon, and also that the former statement was made eleven, and the latter fifteen years, after his elevation to the rank of president of the Chaldean wise men, then it will in no way appear surprising to us to find that the fame of his righteousness and his wonderful wisdom was so spread abroad among the Jewish exiles, that Ezekiel was able to point to him as a bright example of these virtues. When now God gave him, under Belshazzar, a new opportunity, by reading and interpreting the mysterious handwriting on the wall, of showing his supernatural prophetic gifts, on account of which he was raised by the king to one of the highest offices of state in the kingdom; when, moreover, under the Median king Darius the machinations of his enemies against his life were frustrated by his wonderful deliverance from the jaws of the lions, and he not only remained to hoary old age to hold that high office, but also received from God revelations regarding the development of the world-power and of the kingdom of God, which in precision excel all the predictions of the prophets,—then it could not fail but that a life so rich in the wonders of divine power and grace should not only attract the attention of his contemporaries, but also that after his death it should become a subject of wide-spread fame, as appears from the apocryphal addition to his book in the Alexandrine translation of it, and in the later Jewish Haggada, and be enlarged upon by the church fathers, and even by Mohammedan authors. Cf. Herbelot, *Biblioth. Orient. s.v. Daniel*, and Delitzsch, *de Habacuci Proph. vita atque ætate*, Lps. 1842, p. 24 sqq.

Regarding the end of Daniel's life and his burial nothing certain is known. The Jewish report of his return to his fatherland (cf. Carpzov, *Introd.* iii. p. 239 sq.) has as little historical value as that which relates that he died in Babylon, and was buried in the king's sepulchre (Pseud.-Epiph.), or that his grave was in Susa (Abulph. and Benjamin of Tudela).

In direct opposition to the wide-spread reports which bear testimony to the veneration with which the prophet was regarded, stands the modern naturalistic criticism, which, springing from antipathy to the miracles of the Bible, maintains that the prophet never existed at all, but that his life and labours, as they are recorded in this book, are the mere invention of a Jew of the time of the Maccabees, who attributed his fiction to Daniel, deriving the name from some unknown hero of mythic antiquity (Bleek, von Lengerke, Hitzig) or of the Assyrian exile (Ewald).

II.—DANIEL'S PLACE IN THE HISTORY OF THE KINGDOM OF GOD.

Though Daniel lived during the Babylonian exile, yet it was not, as in the case of Ezekiel, in the midst of his countrymen, who had been carried into captivity, but at the court of the ruler of the world and in the service of the state. To comprehend his work for the kingdom of God in this situation, we must first of all endeavour to make clear the significance of the Babylonian exile, not only for the people of Israel, but also for the heathen nations, with reference to the working out of the divine counsel for the salvation of the human race.

Let us first fix our attention on the significance of the exile for Israel, the people of God under the Old Covenant. The destruction of the kingdom of Judah and the deportation of the Jews into Babylonish captivity, not only put an end to the independence of the covenant people, but also to the continuance of that constitution of the kingdom of God which was founded at Sinai; and that not only temporarily, but for ever, for in its integrity it was never restored. God the Lord had indeed, in the foundation of the Old Covenant, through the institution of circumcision as a sign of the covenant for the chosen people, given to the patriarch Abraham the promise that He would establish His covenant with him and his seed as an everlasting covenant, that He would be a God to them, and would give them the land of Canaan as a perpetual possession (Gen. xvii. 18, 19). Accordingly, at the establishment of this covenant with the people of Israel by Moses, the fundamental arrangements of the covenant constitution were designated as everlasting institutions (חֻקַּת עוֹלָם or חֹק); as, for example, the arrangements connected with the feast of the passover (Ex. xii. 14, 17, 24), the day of atonement (Lev. xvi. 29, 31, 34), and the other feasts (Lev. xxiii. 14, 21, 31, 41), the most important of the arrangements concerning the offering of sacrifice (Lev. iii. 17, vii. 34, 36, x. 15; Num. xv. 15, xviii. 8, 11, 19), and concerning the duties and rights of the priests (Ex. xxvii. 21, xxviii. 43, xxix. 28, xxx. 21), etc. God fulfilled His promise. He not only delivered the tribes of Israel from their bondage in Egypt by the wonders of His almighty power, and put them in possession of the land of Canaan, but He also protected them there against their enemies, and gave to them afterwards in David a king who ruled over them according to His will, overcame all their enemies, and made Israel powerful and prosperous. Moreover He gave to this king, His servant David, who, after he had vanquished all his enemies round about, wished to build a house for the Lord that His name might dwell there, the Great Promise: "When thy days be fulfilled, and thou shalt sleep with thy fathers, I will set up thy seed after thee, which shall proceed out of thy bowels, and I will establish his kingdom. He shall build an house for my name, and I will establish the throne of his kingdom for ever. I will be his Father, and he shall be my son. If he commit iniquity, I will chasten him with the rod of men, and with the stripes of the children of men: but my mercy shall not depart away from him. . . . And thine house and thy kingdom shall be established for ever before thee: thy throne shall be established for ever" (2 Sam. vii. 12–16). Wherefore after David's death, when his son Solomon built the temple, the word of the Lord came to him, saying, "If thou wilt walk in my statutes, . . . then will I perform my word unto thee which I spake unto David thy father, and I will dwell among the children of Israel, and will not forsake my people Israel" (1 Kings vi. 12, 13). After the completion of the building of the temple the glory of the Lord filled the house, and God appeared to Solomon the second time, renewing the assurance, "If thou wilt walk before me as David thy father walked, . . . then I will establish the throne of thy kingdom upon Israel for ever, as I promised to David thy father" (1 Kings ix. 2–5). The Lord was faithful to this His word to the people of Israel, and to the seed of David. When Solomon in his old age, through the influence of his foreign wives, was induced to sanction the worship of idols, God visited the king's house with chastisement, by the revolt of the ten tribes, which took place after Solomon's death; but He gave to his son Rehoboam the kingdom of Judah and Benjamin, with the metropolis Jerusalem and the temple, and He preserved this kingdom, notwithstanding the constantly repeated declension of the king and the people into idolatry, even after the Assyrians had destroyed the kingdom of the ten tribes, whom they carried into captivity. But at length Judah also, through the wickedness of Manasseh, filled up the measure of its iniquity, and brought upon itself the judgment of the dissolution of the kingdom, and the carrying away of the inhabitants into captivity into Babylon.

In his last address and warning to the people against their continued apostasy from the Lord their God, Moses had, among other severe chastisements that would fall upon them, threatened this as the last of the punishments with which God would visit them. This threatening was repeated by all the prophets; but at the same time, following the example of Moses, they further announced that the Lord would again receive into His favour His people driven into exile, if, humbled under their sufferings, they would turn again unto Him; that He would gather them together from the heathen lands, and bring them back to their own land, and renew them by His Spirit, and would then erect anew in all its glory the kingdom of David under the Messiah.

Thus Micah not only prophesied the destruction of Jerusalem and of the temple, and the leading away into captivity of the daughters of Zion (ch. iii. 12, iv. 10), but also the return from Babylon and the restoration of the former dominion of the daughters of Jerusalem, their victory over all their enemies under the sceptre of the Ruler who would go forth from Bethlehem, and the exaltation of the mountain of the house of the Lord above all mountains and hills in the last days (ch. v. 1 ff., iv. 1 ff.). Isaiah also announced (ch. xl.–lxvi.) the deliverance of Israel out of Babylon, the building up of the ruins of Jerusalem and Judah, and the final glory of Zion through the creation of new heavens and a new earth. Jeremiah, in like manner, at the beginning of the Chaldean catastrophe, not only proclaimed to the people who had become ripe for the judgment, the carrying away into Babylon by Nebuchadnezzar, and the continuance of the exile for the space of seventy years, but he also prophesied the destruction of Babylon after the end of the seventy years, and the return of the people of Judah and Israel who might survive to the land of their fathers, the rebuilding of the desolated city, and the manifestation of God's grace toward them, by His entering into a new covenant with them, and writing His law upon their hearts and forgiving their sins (ch. xxv. 29–31).

Hence it evidently appears that the abolition of the Israelitish theocracy, through the destruction of the kingdom of Judah and the carrying away of the people into exile by the Chaldeans, in consequence of their continued unfaithfulness and the transgression of the laws of the covenant on the part of Israel, was foreseen in the gracious counsels of God; and that the perpetual duration of the covenant of grace, as such, was not dissolved, but only the then existing condition of the kingdom of God was changed, in order to winnow that perverse people, who, notwithstanding all the chastisements that had hitherto fallen upon them, had not in earnest turned away from their idolatry, by that the severest of all the judgments that had been threatened them; to exterminate by the sword, by famine, by the plague, and by other calamities, the incorrigible mass of the people; and to prepare the better portion of them, the remnant who might repent, as a holy seed to whom God might fulfil His covenant promises.

Accordingly the exile forms a great turning-point in the development of the kingdom of God which He had founded in Israel. With that event the form of the theocracy established at

Sinai comes to an end, and then begins the period of the transition to a new form, which was to be established by Christ, and has been actually established by Him. The form according to which the people of God constituted an earthly kingdom, taking its place beside the other kingdoms of the nations, was not again restored after the termination of the seventy years of the desolations of Jerusalem and Judah, which had been prophesied by Jeremiah, because the Old Testament theocracy had served its end. God the Lord had, during its continuance, showed daily not only that He was Israel's God, a merciful and gracious God, who was faithful to His covenant towards those who feared Him and walked in His commandments and laws, and who could make His people great and glorious, and had power to protect them against all their enemies; but also that He was a mighty and a jealous God, who visits the blasphemers of His holy name according to their iniquity, and is able to fulfil His threatenings no less than His promises. It was necessary that the people of Israel should know by experience that a transgressing of the covenant and a turning away from the service of God does not lead to safety, but hastens onward to ruin; that deliverance from sin, and salvation life and happiness, can be found only with the Lord who is rich in grace and in faithfulness, and can only be reached by a humble walking according to His commandments.

The restoration of the Jewish state after the exile was not a re-establishment of the Old Testament kingdom of God. When Cyrus granted liberty to the Jews to return to their own land, and commanded them to rebuild the temple of Jehovah in Jerusalem, only a very small band of captives returned; the greater part remained scattered among the heathen. Even those who went home from Babylon to Canaan were not set free from subjection to the heathen world-power, but remained, in the land which the Lord had given to their fathers, servants to it. Though now again the ruined walls of Jerusalem and the cities of Judah were restored, and the temple also was rebuilt, and the offering up of sacrifice renewed, yet the glory of the Lord did not again enter into the new temple, which was also without the ark of the covenant and the mercy-seat, so as to hallow it as the place of His gracious presence among His people. The temple worship among the Jews after the captivity was without its soul, the real presence of the Lord in the sanctuary; the high priest could no longer go before God's throne of grace in the holy of holies to sprinkle the atoning blood of the sacrifice toward the ark of the covenant, and to accomplish the reconciliation of the congregation with their God, and could no longer find out, by means of the Urim and Thummim, the will of the Lord. When Nehemiah had finished the restoration of the walls of Jerusalem, prophecy ceased, the revelations of the Old Covenant came to a final end, and the period of expectation (during which no prophecy was given) of the promised Deliverer, of the seed of David, began. When this Deliverer appeared in Jesus Christ, and the Jews did not recognise Him as their Saviour, but rejected Him and put Him to death, they were at length, on the destruction of Jerusalem and the temple by the Romans, scattered throughout the whole world, and to this day they live in a state of banishment from the presence of the Lord, till they return to Christ, and through faith in Him again enter into the kingdom of God and be blessed.

The space of 500 years, from the end of the Babylonish captivity to the appearance of Christ, can be considered as the last period of the Old Covenant only in so far as in point of time it precedes the foundation of the New Covenant; but it was in reality, for that portion of the Jewish people who had returned to Judea, no deliverance from subjection to the power of the heathen, no re-introduction into the kingdom of God, but only a period of transition from the Old to the New Covenant, during which Israel were prepared for the reception of the Deliverer coming out of Zion. In this respect this period may be compared with the forty, or more accurately, the thirty-eight years of the wanderings of Israel in the Arabian desert. As God did not withdraw all the tokens of His gracious covenant from the race that was doomed to die in the wilderness, but guided them by His pillar of cloud and fire, and gave them manna to eat, so He gave grace to those who had returned from Babylon to Jerusalem to build again the temple and to restore the sacrificial service, whereby they prepared themselves for the appearance of Him who should build the true temple, and make an everlasting atonement by the offering up of His life as a sacrifice for the sins of the world.

If the prophets before the captivity, therefore, connect the deliverance of Israel from Babylon and their return to Canaan immediately with the setting up of the kingdom of God in its glory, without giving any indication that between the end of the Babylonish exile and the appearance of the Messiah a long period would intervene, this uniting together of the two events is not to be explained only from the perspective and apotelesmatic character of the prophecy, but has its foundation in the very nature of the thing itself. The prophetic perspective, by virtue of which the inward eye of the seer beholds only the elevated summits of historical events as they unfold themselves, and not the valleys of the common incidents of history which lie between these heights, is indeed peculiar to prophecy in general, and accounts for the circumstance that the prophecies as a rule give no fixed dates, and apotelesmatically bind together the points of history which open the way to the end, with the end itself. But this formal peculiarity of prophetic contemplation we must not extend to the prejudice of the actual truth of the prophecies. The fact of the uniting together of the future glory of the kingdom of God under the Messiah with the deliverance of Israel from exile, has perfect historical veracity. The banishment of the covenant people from the land of the Lord and their subjection to the heathen, was not only the last of those judgments which God had threatened against His degenerate people, but it also continues till the perverse rebels are exterminated, and the penitents are turned with sincere hearts to God the Lord and are saved through Christ. Consequently the exile was for Israel the last space for repentance which God in His faithfulness to His covenant granted to them. Whoever is not brought by this severe chastisement to repentance and reformation, but continues opposed to the gracious will of God, on him falls the judgment of death; and only they who turn themselves to the Lord, their God and Saviour, will be saved, gathered from among the heathen, brought in within the bonds of the covenant of grace through Christ, and become partakers of the promised riches of grace in His kingdom.

But with the Babylonish exile of Israel there also arises for the heathen nations a turning-point of marked importance for their future history. So long as Israel formed within the borders of their own separated land a peculiar people, under immediate divine guidance, the heathen nations dwelling around came into manifold hostile conflicts with them, while God used them as a rod of correction for His rebellious people. Though they were often at war among themselves, yet, in general separated from each other, each nation developed itself according to its own proclivities. Besides, from ancient times the greater kingdoms on the Nile and the Euphrates had for centuries striven to raise their power, enlarging themselves into world-powers; while the Phœnicians on the Mediterranean sea-coast gave themselves to commerce, and sought to enrich themselves with the treasures of the earth. In this development the smaller as well as the larger nations gradually acquired strength. God had permitted each of them to follow its own way, and had conferred on them much good, that they might seek the Lord, if haply they might feel after Him and find Him; but the principle of sin dwelling within them had poisoned their natural development, so that they went farther and farther away from the living God and from everlasting good, sunk deeper and deeper into idolatry and immorality of every kind, and went down with rapid steps toward destruction. Then God began to winnow the nations of the world by His great judgments. The Chaldeans raised themselves, under energetic leaders, to be a world-power, which not only overthrew the Assyrian kingdom and subjugated all the lesser nations of Hither Asia, but also broke the power of the Phœnicians and Egyptians, and brought under its dominion all the civilised peoples of the East. With the monarchy founded by Nebuchadnezzar it raised itself in the rank of world-powers, which within not long intervals followed each other in quick succession, until the Roman world-monarchy arose, by which all the civilised nations of antiquity were subdued, and under which the ancient world came to a close, at the appearance of Christ. These world-kingdoms, which destroyed one another, each giving place, after a short existence, to its successor, which in its turn also was overthrown by another that followed, led the nations, on the one side, to the knowledge of the helplessness and the vanity of their idols, and taught them the fleeting nature and the nothingness of all earthly greatness and glory, and, on the other side, placed limits to the egoistical establishment of the different nations in their separate interests, and the deification of their peculiarities in education, culture, art, and science, and thereby prepared the way, by means of the spreading abroad of the language and customs of the physically or intellectually dominant people among all the different nationalities united under one empire, for the removal of the particularistic isolation of the tribes separated from them by language and customs, and for the re-uniting together into one universal family of the scattered tribes of the human race. Thus they opened the way for the revelation of the divine plan of salvation to all peoples, whilst they shook the faith of the heathen in their gods, destroyed the frail supports of heathen religion, and awakened the longing for the Saviour from sin, death, and destruction.

But God, the Lord of heaven and earth, revealed to the heathen His eternal Godhead and His invisible essence, not only by His almighty government in the disposal of the affairs of their history, but He also, in every great event in the historical development of humanity, announced His will through that people whom He had chosen as the depositaries of His salvation. Already the patriarchs had, by their lives and by their fear of God, taught the Canaanites the name of the Lord so distinctly, that they were known amongst them as "princes of God" (Gen. xxiii. 6), and in their God they acknowledged the most high God, the Creator of heaven and earth (Gen. xiv. 19, 22). Thus, when Moses was sent to Pharaoh to announce to him the will of God regarding the departure of the people of Israel, and when Pharaoh refused to listen to the will of God, his land and his people were so struck by the wonders of the divine omnipotence, that not only the Egyptians learned to fear the God of Israel, but the fear and dread of Him also fell on the princes of Edom and Moab, and on all the inhabitants of Canaan (Ex. xv. 14 ff.). Afterwards, when Israel came to the borders of Canaan, and the king of Moab, in conjunction with the princes of Midian, brought the famed soothsayer Balaam out of Mesopotamia that he might destroy the people of God with his curse, Balaam was constrained to predict, according to the will of God, to the king and his counsellors the victorious power of Israel over all their enemies, and the subjection of all the heathen nations (Num. xxii.–xxiv.). In the age succeeding, God the Lord showed Himself to the nations, as often as they assailed Israel contrary to His will, as an almighty God who can destroy all His enemies; and even the Israelitish prisoners of war were the means of making known to the heathen the great name of the God of Israel, as the history of the cure of Naaman the Syrian by means of Elisha shows (2 Kings v.). This knowledge of the living, all-powerful God could not but be yet more spread abroad among the heathen by the leading away captive of the tribes of Israel and of Judah into Assyria and Chaldea.

But fully to prepare, by the exile, the people of Israel as well as the heathen world for the appearance of the Saviour of all nations and for the reception of the gospel, the Lord raised up prophets, who not only preached His law and His justice among the covenant people scattered among the heathen, and made more widely known the counsel of His grace, but also bore witness by word and deed, in the presence of the heathen rulers of the world, of the omnipotence and glory of God, the Lord of heaven and earth. This mission was discharged by Ezekiel and Daniel. God placed the prophet Ezekiel among his exiled fellow-countrymen as a watchman over the house of Israel, that he might warn the godless, proclaim to them continually the judgment which would fall upon them and destroy their vain hopes of a speedy liberation from bondage and a return to their fatherland; but to the God-fearing, who were bowed down under the burden of their sorrows and were led to doubt the covenant faithfulness of God, he was commissioned to testify the certain fulfilment of the predictions of the earlier prophets as to the restoration and bringing to its completion of the kingdom of God. A different situation was appointed by God to Daniel. His duty was to proclaim before the throne of the rulers of this world the glory of the God of Israel as the God of heaven and earth, in opposition to false gods; to announce to those invested with worldly might and dominion the subjugation of all the kingdoms of this world by the everlasting kingdom of God; and to his own people the continuance of their afflictions under the oppression of the world-power, as well as the fulfilment of the gracious counsels of God through the blotting out of all sin, the establishment of an everlasting righteousness, the fulfilling of all the prophecies, and the setting up of a true holy of holies.

III.—THE CONTENTS AND ARRANGEMENT OF THE BOOK OF DANIEL.

The book begins (ch. i.) with the account of Daniel's being carried away to Babylon, his appointment and education for the service of the court of the Chaldean king by a three years' course of instruction in the literature and wisdom of the Chaldeans, and his entrance on service in the king's palace. This narative, by its closing (ver. 21) statement that Daniel continued in this office till the first year of king Cyrus, and still more by making manifest his firm fidelity to the law of the true God and his higher enlightenment in the meaning of dreams and visions granted to him on account of this fidelity, as well as by the special mention of his three like-minded friends, is to be regarded as a historico-biographical introduction to the book, showing how Daniel, under the divine guidance, was prepared, along with his friends, for that calling in which, as prophet at the court of the rulers of the world, he might bear testimony to the omnipotence and the infallible wisdom of the God of Israel. This testimony is given in the following book. Ch. ii. contains a remarkable dream of Nebuchadnezzar, which none of the Chaldean wise men could tell to the king or interpret. But God made it known to Daniel in answer to prayer, so that he could declare and explain to the king the visions he saw in his dream, representing the four great world-powers, and their destruction by the everlasting kingdom of God. Ch. iii. describes the wonderful deliverance of Daniel's three friends from the burning fiery furnace into which they were thrown, because they would not bow down to the golden image which Nebuchadnezzar had set up. Ch. iv. (in Heb. text iii. 31–iv. 34) contains an edict promulgated by Nebuchadnezzar to all the peoples and nations of his kingdom, in which he made known to them a remarkable dream which had been interpreted to him by Daniel, and its fulfilment to him in his temporary derangement,—a beast's heart having been given unto him as a punishment for his haughty self-deification,—and his recovery from that state in consequence of his humbling himself under the hand of the almighty God. Ch. v. makes mention of a wonderful handwriting which appeared on the wall during a riotous feast, and which king Belshazzar saw, and the interpretation of it by Daniel. Ch. vi. narrates Daniel's miraculous deliverance from the den of lions into which the Median king Darius had thrown him, because he had, despite of the king's command to the contrary, continued to pray to his God.

The remaining chapters contain visions and divine revelations regarding the development of the world-powers and of the kingdom of God vouchsafed to Daniel. The seventh sets forth a vision, in which, under the image of four ravenous beasts rising up out of the troubled sea, are represented the four world-powers following one another. The judgment which would fall upon them is also revealed. The eighth contains a vision of the Medo-Persian and Greek world-powers under the image of a ram and a he-goat respectively, and of the enemy and desolater of the sanctuary and of the people of God arising out of the last named kingdom; the ninth, the revelation of the seventy weeks appointed for the development and the completion of the kingdom of God, which Daniel received in answer to earnest prayer for the pardon of his people and the restoration of Jerusalem; and, finally, ch. x.–xii. contain a vision, granted in the third year of the reign of Cyrus, with further disclosures regarding the Persian and the Grecian world-powers, and the wars of the kingdoms of the north and the south, springing out of the latter of these powers, for the supreme authority and the dominion over the Holy Land; the oppression that would fall on the saints of the Most High at the time of the end; the destruction of the last enemy under the stroke of divine judgment; and the completion of the kingdom of God, by the rising again from the dead of some to everlasting life, and of some to shame and everlasting contempt.

The book has commonly been divided into two parts, consisting of six chapters each (*e.g.* by Ros., Maur., Hävern., Hitz., Zündel, etc.). The first six are regarded as historical, and the remaining six as prophetical; or the first part is called the "book of history," the second, the "book of visions." But this division corresponds neither with the contents nor with the formal design of the book. If we consider the first chapter and its relation to the whole already stated, we cannot discern a substantial reason for regarding Nebuchadnezzar's dream of the image representing the monarchies (ch. ii.), which with its interpretation was revealed to Daniel in a night vision (ch. ii. 19), as an historical narration, and Daniel's dream-vision of the four world-powers symbolized by ravenous beasts, which an angel interpreted to him, as a prophetic vision, since the contents of both chapters are essentially alike. The circumstance that in ch. ii. it is particularly related how the Chaldean wise men, who were summoned by Nubuchadnezzar, could neither relate nor interpret the dream, and on that account were threatened with death, and were partly visited with punishment, does not entitle us to refuse to the dream and its contents, which were revealed to Daniel in a night vision, the character of a prophecy. In addition to this, ch. vii., inasmuch as it is written in the Chaldee language and that Daniel speaks in it in the third person (ch. vii. 1, 2), naturally connects itself with the chapters preceding (ch. ii.–vi.), and separates itself from those which follow, in which Daniel speaks in the first person and uses the Hebrew language. On these grounds, we must, with Aub., Klief., and Kran., regard ch. ii., which is written in Chaldee, as belonging to the first part of the book, viz. ch. ii.–vii., and ch. viii.–xii., which are written in Hebrew, as constituting the second part; and the propriety of this division we must seek to vindicate by an examination of the contents of both of the parts.

Kranichfeld (*das Buch Daniel erklärt*) thus explains the distinction between the two parts:—The first presents the successive development of the whole heathen world power, and its relation to Israel, till the time of the Messianic kingdom (ch. ii. and vii.), but lingers particularly in the period lying at the beginning of this development, *i.e.* in the heathen kingdoms standing nearest the exiles, namely, the Chaldean kingdom and that of the Medes which subdued it (ch. vi.). The second part (ch. viii.–xii.), on the contrary, passing from the Chaldean kingdom, lingers on the development of the heathen world-power towards the time of its end, in the Javanic form of power, and on the Median and Persian kingdom only in so far as it immediately precedes the unfolding of the power of Javan. But, setting aside this explanation of the world-kingdoms, with which we do not agree, the contents of ch. ix. are altogether overlooked in this view of the relations between the two parts, inasmuch as this chapter does not treat of the development of the heathen world-power, but of the kingdom of God and of the time of its consummation determined by God. If we inspect more narrowly the contents of the *first* part, we find an interruption of the chronological order pervading the book, inasmuch as events (ch. vi.) belonging to the time of the Median king Darius are recorded before the visions (ch. vii. and viii.) in the first and third year of the Chaldean king Belshazzar. The placing of these events before that vision can have no other ground than to allow historical incidents of a like kind to be recorded together, and then the visions granted to Daniel, without any interruption. Hence has arisen the appearance of the book's being divided into two parts, an historical and a prophetical.

In order to discover a right division, we must first endeavour to make clear the meaning of the historical incidents recorded in ch. iii.–vi., that we may determine their relations to the visions in ch. ii. and vii. The two intervening chapters iv. and v. are like the second chapter in this, that they speak of revelations which the possessors of the world-power received, and that, too, revelations of the judgment which they drew upon themselves by their boastful pride and violence against the sanctuaries of the living God. To Nebuchadnezzar, the founder of the world-power, when he boasted (ch. iv.) of the building of great Babylon as a royal residence by his great might, it was revealed in a dream that he should be cast down from his height and debased among the beasts of the field, till he should learn that the Most High rules over the kingdom of men. To king Belshazzar (ch. v.), in the midst of his riotous banquet, at which he desecrated the vessels of the holy temple at Jerusalem, was revealed, by means of a handwriting on the wall, his death and the destruction of his kingdom. To both of these kings Daniel had to explain the divine revelation, which soon after was fulfilled. The other two chapters (iii. and vi.) make known the attempts of the rulers of the world to compel the servants of the Lord to offer supplication to them and to their images, and the wonderful deliverance from death which the Lord vouchsafed to the faithful confessors of His name. These four events have, besides their historical value, a prophetical import: they show how the world-rulers, when they misuse their power for self-idolatry and in opposition to the Lord and His servants, will be humbled and cast down by God, while, on the contrary, the true confessors of His name will be wonderfully protected and upheld. For the sake of presenting this prophetic meaning, Daniel has recorded these events and incidents in his prophetical book; and, on chronological and essential grounds, has introduced ch. ii. and vii. between the visions, so as to define more clearly the position of the world-power in relation to the kingdom of God. Thus the whole of the *first* part (ch. ii.–vii.) treats of *the world-power and its development in relation to the kingdom of God;* and we can say with Kliefoth,[1] that "chapter second gives a survey of the whole historical evolution of the world-power, which survey ch. vii., at the close of this part, further extends, while the intermediate chapters iii.–vi. show in concrete outlines the nature and kind of the world-power, and its conduct in opposition to the people of God."

If we now fix our attention on the *second* part, ch. viii.–xii., it will appear that in the visions, ch. viii. and x.–xii., are prophesied oppressions of the people of God by a powerful enemy of God and His saints, who would arise out of the third world-kingdom; which gave occasion to Auberlen[2] to say that the first part unfolds and presents to view the whole development of the world-powers from a universal historical point of view, and shows how the kingdom of God would in the end triumph over them; that the second part, on the contrary, places before our eyes the unfolding of the world-powers in their relation to Israel in the nearer future before the predicted (ch. ix.) appearance of Christ in the flesh. This designation of the distinction between the two parts accords with that already acknowledged by me, yet on renewed reflection it does not accord with the recognised

[1] *Das Buch Daniels übers. u. erkl.*

[2] *Der Proph. Daniel u. die Offenb. Johannis*, p. 38, der 2 Auf. (*The Prophecies of Daniel, and the Revelations of John.* Published by Messrs. T. and T. Clark, Edinburgh.)

reference of ch. ix. 24–27 to the first appearance of Christ in the flesh, nor with ch. xi. 36–xii. 7, which prophesies of Antichrist. Rather, as Klief. has also justly remarked, the *second* part treats *of the kingdom of God, and its development in relation to the world-power.* "As the second chapter forms the central-point of the first part, so does the ninth chapter of the second part, gathering all the rest around it. And as the second chapter presents the whole historical evolution of the world-power from the days of Daniel to the end, so, on the other hand, the ninth chapter presents the whole historical evolution of the kingdom of God from the days of Daniel to the end." But the preceding vision recorded in ch. viii., and that which follows in ch. x.–xii., predict a violent incursion of an insolent enemy rising out of the Javanic world-kingdom against the kingdom of God, which will terminate in his own destruction at the time appointed by God, and, as a comparison of ch. viii. and vii. and of ch. xi. 21–35 with 36–44 and ch. xii. 1–3 shows, will be a type of the assault of the last enemy, in whom the might of the fourth world-power reaches its highest point of hostility against the kingdom of God, but who in the final judgment will also be destroyed. These two visions, the second of which is but a further unfolding of the first, could not but show to the people of God what wars and oppressions they would have to encounter in the near and the remote future for their sanctification, and for the confirmation of their faith, till the final perfecting of the kingdom of God by the resurrection of the dead and the judgment of the world, and at the same time strengthen the true servants of God with the assurance of final victory in these severe conflicts.

With this view of the contents of the book the form in which the prophecies are given stands also in harmony. In the first part, which treats of the world-power, Nebuchadnezzar, the founder of the world-power, is the receiver of the revelation. To him was communicated not only the prophecy (ch. iv.) relating to himself personally, but also that which comprehended the whole development of the world-power (ch. ii.); while Daniel received only the revelation (ch. vii.) specially bearing on the relation of the world-power in its development to the kingdom of God, in a certain measure for the confirmation of the revelation communicated to Nebuchadnezzar. Belshazzar also, as the bearer of the world-power, received (ch. v.) a revelation from God. In the second part, on the contrary, which treats of the development of the kingdom of God, Daniel, "who is by birth and by faith a member of the kingdom of God," alone receives a prophecy.—With this the change in the language of the book agrees. The first part (ch. ii.–vii.), treating of the world-power and its development, is written in Chaldee, which is the language of the world-power; the second part (ch. viii.–xii.), treating of the kingdom of God and its development, as also the first chapter, which shows how Daniel the Israelite was called to be a prophet by God, is written in the Hebrew, which is the language of the people of God. This circumstance denotes that in the first part the fortunes of the world-power, and that in the second part the development of the kingdom of God, is the subject treated of (cf. Auber. p. 39, Klief. p. 44).[1]

From these things we arrive at the certainty that the book of Daniel forms an organic whole, as is now indeed generally acknowledged, and that it was composed by a prophet according to a plan resting on higher illumination.

IV.—THE GENUINENESS OF THE BOOK OF DANIEL.

The book of Daniel, in its historical and prophetical contents, corresponds to the circumstances of the times under which, according to its statements, it sprang up, as also to the place which the receiver of the vision, called the prophet Daniel (ch. vii. 2, viii. 1,

[1] Kranichfeld (*d. B. Daniels*, p. 53) seeks to explain this interchange of the Hebrew and Chaldee (Aramean) languages by supposing that the decree of Nebuchadnezzar (ch. iii. 31 [iv. 1] ff.) to his people, and also his conversation with the Chaldeans (ch. ii. 4-11), were originally in the Aramaic language, and that the author was led from this to make use of this language throughout one part of his book, as was the case with Ezra, *e.g.* ch. iv. 23 ff. And the continuous use of the Aramaic language in one whole part of the book will be sufficiently explained, if it were composed during a definite epoch, within which the heathen oppressors as such, and the heathen persecution, stand everywhere in the foreground, namely in the time of the Chaldean supremacy, on which the Median made no essential change. Thus the theocrat, writing at this time, composed his reports in the Aramaic language in order to make them effective among the Chaldeans, because they were aimed against their enmity and hostility as well as against that of their rulers. But this explanation fails from this circumstance, that in the third year of Belshazzar the vision granted to Daniel (ch. viii.) is recorded in the Hebrew language, while, on the contrary, the later events which occurred in the night on which Belshazzar was slain (ch. v.) are described in the Chaldee language. The use of the Hebrew language in the vision (ch. viii.) cannot be explained on Kranichfeld's supposition, for that vision is so internally related to the one recorded in the Chaldee language in the seventh chapter, that no ground can be discerned for the change of language in these two chapters.

ix. 2, x. 2 ff.), occupied during the exile. If the exile has that importance in relation to the development of the kingdom of God as already described in § 2, then the whole progressive development of the divine revelation, as it lies before us in the Old and New Testaments, warrants us to expect, from the period of the exile, a book containing records such as are found in the book of Daniel. Since miracles and prophecies essentially belong not only in general to the realizing of the divine plan of salvation, but have also been especially manifested in all the critical periods of the history of the kingdom of God, neither the miracles in the historical parts of the book, nor its prophecies, consisting of singular predictions, can in any respect seem strange to us.

The history of redemption in the Old and New Covenants presents four great periods of miracles, *i.e.* four epochs, which are distinguished from other times by numerous and remarkable miracles. These are, (1) The time of Moses, or of the deliverance of Israel out of Egypt, and their journey through the Arabian desert to Canaan; (2) In the promised land, the time of the prophets Elijah and Elisha; (3) The time of Daniel, or of the Babylonish exile; and (4) The period from the appearance of John the Baptist to the ascension of Christ, or the time of Christ. These are the times of the foundation of the Old and the New Covenant, and the times of the two deliverances of the people of Israel. Of these four historical epochs the first and the fourth correspond with one another, and so also do the second and the third. But if we consider that the Mosaic period contains the two elements, the deliverance of Israel out of Egypt and the establishment of the kingdom of God at Sinai, then, if we take into view the first of these elements, the Mosaic period resembles that of the exile in this respect, that in both of them the subject is the deliverance of Israel from subjection to the heathen world-power, and that the deliverance in both instances served as a preparation for the founding of the kingdom of God,—the freeing of Israel from Egyptian bondage for the founding of the Old Testament kingdom of God, and the deliverance from Babylonish exile for the founding of the New. In both periods the heathen world-power had externally overcome the people of God and reduced them to slavery, and determined on their destruction. In both, therefore, God the Lord, if He would not suffer His work of redemption to be frustrated by man, must reveal Himself by wonders and signs before the heathen, as the almighty God and Lord in heaven and on earth, and compel the oppressors of His people, by means of great judgments, to acknowledge His omnipotence and His eternal Godhead, so that they learned to fear the God of Israel and released His people. In the time of Moses, it was necessary to show to the Egyptians and to Pharaoh, who had said to Moses, "Who is the Lord, that I should obey His voice, to let Israel go? I know not the Lord, neither will I let Israel go," that Israel's God was Jehovah the Lord, that He, and not their gods, as they thought, was Lord in their land, and that there was none like Him in the whole earth (Ex. vii. 17, viii. 18, ix. 14, 29). And as Pharaoh did not know, and did not wish to know, the God of Israel, so also neither Nebuchadnezzar, nor Belshazzar, nor Darius knew Him. Since all the heathen estimated the power of the gods according to the power of the people who honoured them, the God of the Jews, whom they had subjugated by their arms, would naturally appear to the Chaldeans and their king as an inferior and feeble God, as He had already appeared to the Assyrians (Isa. x. 8–11, xxxvi. 18–20). They had no apprehension of the fact that God had given up His people to be punished by them on account of their unfaithful departure from Him. This delusion of theirs, by which not only the honour of the true God was misunderstood and sullied, but also the object for which the God of Israel had sent His people into exile among the heathen was in danger of being frustrated, God could only dissipate by revealing Himself, as He once did in Egypt, so now in the exile, as the Lord and Ruler of the whole world. The similarity of circumstances required similar wonderful revelations from God. For this reason there were miracles wrought in the exile as there had been in Egypt,—miracles which showed the omnipotence of the God of the Israelites, and the helplessness of the heathen gods; and hence the way and manner in which God did this is in general the same. To the heathen kings Pharaoh (Gen. xli.) and Nebuchadnezzar (Dan. ii.) He made known the future in dreams, which the heathen wise men of the land were not able to interpret, and the servants of Jehovah, Joseph and Daniel, interpreted to them, and on that account were exalted to high offices of state, in which they exerted their influence as the saviours of their people. And He shows His omnipotence by miracles which break through the course of nature.

In so far the revelations of God in Egypt and in the Babylonish exile resemble one another. But that the actions of God revealed in the book of Daniel are not mere copies of those which were wrought in Egypt, but that in reality they repeat themselves, is clear from the manifest difference in particulars between the two. Of the two ways in which God reveals Himself as the one only true God, in the wonders of His almighty power, and in the displays of His omniscience in predictions, we meet with the former almost alone in Egypt, while in the exile it is the latter that prevails. Leaving out of view Pharaoh's dream in the time of Joseph, God spoke to the Pharaoh of the time of Moses through Moses only; and He showed Himself as the Lord of the whole earth only in the plagues. In the exile God showed His omnipotence only through the two miracles of the deliverance of Daniel from the den of lions, and of Daniel's three friends from the burning fiery furnace. All the other revelations of God consist in the prophetic announcement of the course of the development of the world-kingdoms and of the kingdom of God. For, besides the general object of all God's actions, to reveal to men the existence of the invisible God, the revelations of God in the time of the exile had a different specific object from those in Egypt. In Egypt God would break Pharaoh's pride and his resistance to His will, and compel him to let Israel go. This could only be reached by the judgments which fell upon the land of Egypt and its inhabitants, and manifested the God of Israel as the Lord in the land of Egypt and over the whole earth. In the exile, on the contrary, the object was to destroy the delusion of the heathen, that the God of the subjugated people of Judea was an impotent national god, and to show to the rulers of the world by acts, that the God of this so humbled people was yet the only true God, who rules over the whole earth, and in His wisdom and omniscience determines the affairs of men. Thus God must, as Caspari, in his *Lectures on the Book of Daniel*,[1] rightly remarks, "by great revelations lay open His omnipotence and omniscience, and show that He is infinitely exalted above the gods and wise men of this world and above all the world-powers." Caspari further says: "The wise men of the Chaldean world-power, *i.e.* the so-called magi, maintained that they were the possessors of great wisdom, and such they were indeed celebrated to be, and that they obtained their wisdom from their gods. The Lord must, through great revelations of His omniscience, show that He alone of all the possessors of knowledge is the Omniscient, while their knowledge, and the knowledge of their gods, is nothing. . . . The heathen world-power rests in the

[1] *Vorlesungen ueber das B. Daniels*, p. 20.

belief that it acts independently,—that *it* rules and governs in the world,—that even the future, to a certain degree, is in its hands. The Lord must show to it that it is only an instrument in His hand for the furthering of His plans,—that He is the only independent agent in history,—that it is He who directs the course of the whole world, and therefore that all that happens to His people is His own work. And He must, on this account, lay open to it the whole future, that He may show to it that He knows it all, even to the very minutest events,—that it all lies like a map before His eyes,—and that to Him it is history; for He who fully knows the whole future must also be the same who governs the whole development of the world. Omnipotence cannot be separated from omniscience." Only by virtue of such acts of God could the shaking of the faith of the heathen in the reality and power of their gods, effected through the fall and destruction of one world-kingdom after another, become an operative means for the preparation of the heathen world beforehand for the appearance of the Saviour who should arise out of Judah.

But as all the revelations of God were first and principally intended for Israel, so also the wonderful manifestations of the divine omnipotence and omniscience in the exile, which are recorded in the book of Daniel. The wonders of God in Egypt had their relation to Israel not only in their primary bearing on their deliverance from the house of bondage in Egypt, but also in a far wider respect: they were intended to show actually to Israel that Jehovah, the God of their fathers, possessed the power to overcome all the hindrances which stood in the way of the accomplishing of His promises. With the dissolution of the kingdom of Judah, the destruction of Jerusalem, the burning of the temple, the dethronement of the royal house of David, the cessation of the offering up of the Levitical sacrifices, the carrying away of the king, the priests, and the people into bondage, the kingdom of God was destroyed, the covenant relation dissolved, and Israel, the people of Jehovah, driven forth from their own land among the heathen, were brought into a new Egyptian slavery (cf. Deut. xxviii. 68, Hos. viii. 13, ix. 3). The situation into which Israel fell by the carrying away into Babylon was so grievous and so full of afflictions, that the earnest-minded and the pious even might despair, and doubt the covenant faithfulness of God. The predictions by the earlier prophets of their deliverance from exile, and their return to the land of their fathers after the period of chastisement had passed by, served to prevent their sinking into despair or falling away into heathenism, amid the sufferings and oppressions to which they were exposed. Even the labours of the prophet Ezekiel in their midst, although his appearance was a sign and a pledge that the Lord had not wholly cast off His people, could be to the vanquished no full compensation for that which they had lost, and must feel the want of. Divine actions must be added to the word of promise, which gave assurance of its fulfilment,—wonderful works, which took away every doubt that the Lord could save the true confessors of His name out of the hand of their enemies, yea, from death itself. To these actual proofs of the divine omnipotence, if they would fully accomplish their purpose, new disclosures regarding the future must be added, since, as we have explained above (p. 8), after the expiry of the seventy years of Babylonian captivity prophesied of by Jeremiah, Babylon would indeed fall, and the Jews be permitted to return to their fatherland, yet the glorification of the kingdom of God by the Messiah, which was connected by all the earlier prophets, and even by Ezekiel, with the return from Babylon, did not immediately appear, nor was the theocracy restored in all its former integrity, but Israel must remain yet longer under the domination and the oppression of the heathen. The non-fulfilment of the Messianic hopes, founded in the deliverance from Babylonian exile at the end of the seventy years, could not but have shaken their confidence in the faithfulness of God in the fulfilment of His promises, had not God before this already unveiled His plan of salvation, and revealed beforehand the progressive development and the continuation of the heathen world-power, till its final destruction through the erection of His everlasting kingdom.

Prophecy stands side by side with God's actions along the whole course of the history of the Old Covenant, interpreting these actions to the people, and making known the counsel of the Lord in guiding and governing their affairs. As soon and as often as Israel comes into conflict with the heathen nations, the prophets appear and proclaim the will of God, not only in regard to the present time, but they also make known the final victory of His kingdom over all the kingdoms and powers of this earth. These prophetic announcements take a form corresponding to the circumstances of each period. Yet they are always of such a kind that they shine out into the future far beyond the horizon of the immediate present. Thus (leaving out of view the older times) the prophets of the Assyrian period predict not only the deliverance of Judah and Jerusalem from the powerful invasion of the hostile Assyrians and the destruction of the Assyrian host before the gates of Jerusalem, but also the carrying away of Judah into Babylon and the subsequent deliverance from this exile, and the destruction of all the heathen nations which fight against the Lord and against His people. At the time of the exile Jeremiah and Ezekiel prophesy with great fulness of detail, and in the most particular manner, of the destruction of the kingdom of Judah and of Jerusalem and the temple by Nebuchadnezzar, but Jeremiah prophesies as particularly the return of Israel and of Judah from the exile, and the formation of a new covenant which should endure for ever; and Ezekiel in grand ideal outlines describes the re-establishment of the kingdom of God in a purified and transfigured form. Completing this prophecy, the Lord reveals to His people by Daniel the succession and the duration of the world-kingdoms, the relation of each to the kingdom of God and its preservation under all the persecution of the world-power, as well as its completion by judgments poured out on the world-kingdoms till their final destruction.

The new form of the revelation regarding the course and issue of the process commencing with the formation of the world-kingdoms—a process by which the world-power shall be judged, the people of God purified, and the plan of salvation for the deliverance of the human race shall be perfected—corresponds to the new aspect of things arising in the subjection of the people of God to the violence of the world-powers. The so-called apocalyptical character of Daniel's prophecy is neither in contents nor in form a new species of prophecy. What Auberlen[1] remarks regarding the distinction between apocalypse and prophecy needs important limitation. We cannot justify the remark, that while the prophets generally place in the light of prophecy only the existing condition of the people of God, Daniel had not so special a destination, but only the general appointment to serve to the church of God as a prophetic light for the 500 years from the exile to the coming of Christ and the destruction of Jerusalem by the Romans, during which there was no revelation. For these other prophets do not limit themselves to the present, but they almost all at the same time throw light on the future; and Daniel's prophecy also goes forth from the present and reaches far beyond the time of the destruc-

[1] *Der Proph. Dan.* p. 79 ff. (Eng. Trans. p. 70 ff.)

tion of Jerusalem by the Romans. The further observation also, that the apocalypses, in conformity with their destination to throw prophetic light on the relation of the world to the kingdom of God for the times in which the light of immediate revelation is wanting, must be on the one side more universal in their survey, and on the other more special in the presentation of details, is, when more closely looked into, unfounded. Isaiah, for example, is in his survey not less universal than Daniel. He throws light not only on the whole future of the people and kingdom of God onward till the creation of the new heavens and the new earth, but also on the end of all the heathen nations and kingdoms, and gives in his representations very special disclosures not only regarding the overthrow of the Assyrian power, which at that time oppressed the people of God and sought to destroy the kingdom of God, but also regarding far future events, such as the carrying away into Babylon of the treasures of the king's house, and of the king's sons, that they might become courtiers in the palace of the king of Babylon (ch. xxxix. 6, 7), the deliverance of Judah from Babylon by the hand of Cyrus (ch. xliv. 28, xlv. 1), etc. Compare also, for special glances into the future, the rich representation of details in Mic. iv. 8–v. 3. It is true that the prophets before the exile contemplate the world-power in its present form together with its final unfolding, and therefore they announce the Messianic time for the most part as near at hand, while, on the contrary, with Daniel the one world-power is successively presented in four world-monarchies; but this difference is not essential, but only a wider expansion of the prophecy of Isaiah corresponding to the time and the circumstances in which Daniel was placed, that not Assyria but Babylon would destroy the kingdom of Judah and lead the people of God into exile, and that the Medes and Elamites would destroy Babylon, and Cyrus set free the captives of Judah and Jerusalem. Even the "significant presentation of numbers and of definite chronological periods expressed in them," which is regarded as a "characteristic mark" of apocalypse, has its roots and fundamental principles in simple prophecy, which here and there also gives significant numbers and definite periods. Thus the seventy years of Jeremiah form the starting-point for the seventy weeks or the seven times of Daniel, ch. ix. Compare also the sixty-five years of Isa. vii. 8; the three years, Isa. xx. 3; the seventy years of the desolation of Tyre, Isa. xxiii. 15; the forty and the three hundred and ninety days of Ezek. iv. 6, 9.

In fine, if we examine attentively the subjective form of the apocalypse, we shall find of the two ways in which the future is unveiled, viz. by dreams and visions, the latter with almost all the prophets together with communications flowing from divine illumination, while revelation by dreams as a rule is granted only to the heathen (Abimelech, Gen. xx. 3; Pharaoh, Gen. xli.; Nebuchadnezzar, Dan. ii.) or to Jews who were not prophets (Jacob, Gen. xxviii. 12; Solomon, 1 Kings iii. 5), and the revelation in Dan. vii. is communicated to Daniel in a dream only on account of its particular relation, as to the matter of it, to the dream of Nebuchadnezzar. Amos, Isaiah, and Jeremiah (cf. Amos vii.–ix., Isa. vi., lxiii., Jer. i. 13, xxiv. 1, 2) had also visions. With Ezekiel visions rather than discourses conveying condemnation or comfort prevail, and Zechariah beholds in a series of actions the future development of the kingdom of God and of the world-kingdoms (Zech. i. 7–vi. 15). We also find images representing angels seen by the prophets when in an ecstasy, not only with Zechariah, who was after Daniel's time, but also with Ezekiel; and Isaiah too saw the seraphim standing, and even moving and acting, before the throne of God (Isa. vi. 6, 7). In the visions the future appears embodied in plastic figures which have a symbolical meaning and which need interpretation. Thus the appearance of angels to Daniel is to be explained in the same way as their appearance to Ezekiel and Zechariah.

Accordingly the prophecies of Daniel are not distinguished even in their apocalyptic form from the whole body of prophecy in nature, but only in degree. When dream and vision form the only means of announcing the future, the prophetic discourse is wholly wanting. But the entire return of the prophecy to the form of discourses of condemnation, warning, and consolation is fully explained from the position of Daniel outside of the congregation of God at the court and in the state service of the heathen world-ruler; and this position the Lord had assigned to him on account of the great significance which the world-kingdom had, as we have shown (p. 10), for the preparation beforehand of Israel and of the heathen world for the renovation and perfecting of the kingdom of God through Christ.

Both in its contents and form the book of Daniel has thus the stamp of a prophetical writing, such as we might have expected according to the development of the Old Testament kingdom of God from the period of the Babylonish exile; and the testimony of the Jewish synagogue as well as of the Christian church to the genuineness of the book, or its composition by the prophet Daniel, rests on a solid foundation. In the whole of antiquity no one doubted its genuineness except the well-known enemy of Christianity, the Neo-Platonist *Porphyry*, who according to the statement of Jerome (in the preface to his *Comment. in Dan.*) wrote the twelfth book of his λόγοι κατὰ Χριστιανῶν against the book of Daniel, *nolens eum ab ipso, cujus inscriptus est nomine, esse compositum, sed a quodam qui temporibus Antiochi, qui appellatus est Epiphanes, fuerit in Judæa, et non tam Danielem ventura dixisse, quam illum narrasse præterita.* He was, however, opposed by *Eusebius* of Cæsarea and other church Fathers. For the first time with the rise of deism, naturalism, and rationalism during the bygone century, there began, as a consequence of the rejection of a supernatural revelation from God, the assault against the genuineness of the book. To such an extent has this opposition prevailed, that at the present time all critics who reject miracles and supernatural prophecy hold its spuriousness as an undoubted principle of criticism. They regard the book as the composition of a Jew living in the time of the Maccabees, whose object was to cheer and animate his contemporaries in the war which was waged against them by Antiochus Epiphanes for the purpose of rooting up Judaism, by representing to them certain feigned miracles and prophecies of some old prophet announcing the victory of God's people over all their enemies.[1]

The arguments by which the opponents of the genuineness seek to justify scientifically their opinion are deduced partly from the position of the book in the canon, and other external circumstances, but principally from the contents of the book. Leaving out of view that which the most recent opponents have yielded up, the following things, adduced by Bleek and Stähelin (in their works mentioned in

[1] Cf. the historical survey of the controversy regarding the genuineness of the book in my *Lehrb. d. Einleit. in d. A. Test.* § 134. To what is there mentioned add to the number of the opponents of the genuineness, Fr. Bleek, *Einleitung in d. A. Test.* p. 577 ff., and his article on the "Messianic Prophecies in the Book of Daniel" in the *Jahrb. f. deutsche Theologie*, v. 1, p. 45 ff., and J. J. Stähelin's *Einleit. in die kanon. Bücher des A. Test.* 1862, § 73. To the number of the defenders of the genuineness of the book as there mentioned add, Dav. Zündel's *krit. Untersuchungen ueber die Abfassungszeit des B. Daniel*, 1861, Rud. Kranichfeld and Th. Kliefoth in their commentaries on the Book of Daniel (1868), and the Catholic theologian, Dr. Fr. Heinr. Reusch (professor in Bonn), in his *Lehr. der Einleit. in d. A. Test.* 1868, § 43.

the last note), are asserted, which alone we wish to consider here, referring to the discussions on this question in my *Lehrb. der Einleitung*, § 133.

Among the *external* grounds great stress is laid on the place the book holds in the Hebrew canon. That Daniel should here hold his place not among the *Nebiyîm* [the prophetical writings], but among the *Kethubîm* [the Hagiographa] between the books of Esther and Ezra, can scarcely be explained otherwise than on the supposition that it was yet unknown at the time of the formation of the *Nebiyîm*, that is, in the age of Nehemiah, and consequently that it did not exist previously to that time. But this conclusion, even on the supposition that the Third Part of the canon, the collection called the *Kethubîm*, was for the first time formed some time after the conclusion of the Second Part, is not valid. On the contrary, Kranichfeld has not without good reason remarked, that since the prophets before the exile connected the beginning of the Messianic deliverance with the end of the exile, while on the other hand the book of Daniel predicts a period of oppression continuing long after the exile, therefore the period succeeding the exile might be offended with the contents of the book, and hence feel some hesitation to incorporate the book of one who was less distinctively a prophet in the collection of the prophetic books, and that the Maccabee time, under the influence of the persecution prophesied of in the book, first learned to estimate its prophetic worth and secured its reception into the canon. This objection is thus sufficiently disproved. But the supposition of a successive collection of the books of the canon and of its three Parts after the period in which the books themselves were written, is a hypothesis which has never been proved: cf. my *Einleit. in d. A. T.* § 154 ff. The place occupied by this book in the Hebrew canon perfectly corresponds with the place of Daniel in the theocracy. Daniel did not labour, as the rest of the prophets did whose writings form the class of the *Nebiyîm*, as a prophet among his people in the congregation of Israel, but he was a minister of state under the Chaldean and Medo-Persian world-rulers. Although, like David and Solomon, he possessed the gift of prophecy, and therefore was called προφήτης (LXX., Joseph., New Testament), yet he was not a נָבִיא, *i.e.* a prophet in his official position and standing. Therefore his book in its contents and form is different from the writings of the *Nebiyîm*. His prophecies are not prophetic discourses addressed to Israel or the nations, but visions, in which the development of the world-kingdoms and their relation to the kingdom of God are unveiled, and the historical part of his book describes events of the time when Israel went into captivity among the heathen. For these reasons his book is not placed in the class of the *Nebiyîm*, which reaches from Joshua to Malachi,—for these, according to the view of him who arranged the canon, are wholly the writings of such as held the prophetic office, *i.e.* the office requiring them openly, by word of mouth and by writing, to announce the word of God,—but in the class of the *Kethubîm*, which comprehends sacred writings of different kinds whose common character consists in this, that their authors did not fill the prophetic office, as *e.g.* Jonah, in the theocracy; which is confirmed by the fact that the Lamentations of Jeremiah are comprehended in this class, since Jeremiah uttered these Lamentations over the destruction of Jerusalem and Judah not *qua* a prophet, but as a member of that nation which was chastened by the Lord.

Little importance is to be attached to the silence of Jesus Sirach in his *ὕμνος πατέρων*, ch. xlix., regarding Daniel, since an express mention of Daniel could not justly be expected. Jesus Sirach passes over other distinguished men of antiquity, such as Job, the good king Jehoshaphat, and even Ezra the priest and scribe, who did great service for the re-establishment of the authority of the law, from which it may be seen that it was not his purpose to present a complete list. Still less did he intend to name all the writers of the Old Testament. And if also, in his praise of the fathers, he limits himself on the whole to the course of the biblical books of the Hebrew canon from the Pentateuch down to the Minor Prophets, yet what he says of Zerubbabel, Joshua, and Nehemiah he does not gather from the books of Ezra and Nehemiah. When, on the other hand, Bleek seeks to account for the absence of any mention of Ezra, which his supposition that Jesus Sirach names all the celebrated men mentioned in the canonical books extant in his time contradicts, by the remark that "Ezra *perhaps* would not have been omitted if the book which bears his name had been before that time received into the canon," he has in his zeal against the book of Daniel forgotten to observe that neither the book of Nehemiah in its original or then existing form, nor the first part of the book of Ezra, containing notices of Zerubbabel and Joshua, has ever, separated from the second part, which speaks of Ezra, formed a constituent portion of the canon, but that rather, according to his own statement, the second part of the book of Ezra "was without doubt composed by Ezra himself," which is consequently as old, if not older than the genuine parts of the book of Nehemiah, and that both books in the form in which they have come to us must have been edited by a Jew living at the end of the Persian or at the beginning of the Grecian supremacy, and then for the first time in this redaction were admitted into the canon.

Besides all this, it appears that in the work of Jesus Sirach the previous existence of the book of Daniel is presupposed, for the idea presented in Sirach xvii. 14, that God had given to that people an angel as ἡγούμενος (שַׂר), refers to Dan. x. 13, 20–xi. 1, xii. 1. For if Sirach first formed this idea from the LXX. translation of Deut. xxxii. 8, 9, then the LXX. introduced it from the book of Daniel into Deut. xxxii. 8, so that Daniel is the author from whom this opinion was derived; and the book which was known to the Alexandrine translators of the Pentateuch could not be unknown to the Siracidæ.

Still weaker is the *argumentum e silentio*, that in the prophets after the exile, Haggai and Malachi, and particularly Zechariah (ch. i.–viii.), there are no traces of any use being made of the book of Daniel, and that it exerted no influence on the Messianic representations of the later prophets. Kran. has already made manifest the weakness of this argument by replying that Bleek was silent as to the relation of Daniel's prayer, ch. ix. 3–19, to Ezra ix. and Neh. ix., because the dependence of Ezra and Nehemiah on the book of Daniel could not be denied. Moreover von Hofmann, Zündel (p. 249 ff.), Volck (*Vindiciæ Danielicæ*, 1866), Kran., and Klief. have shown that Zechariah proceeded on the supposition of Daniel's prophecy of the four world-monarchies, inasmuch as not only do the visions of the four horns and of the four carpenters of Zech. ii. 1–4 (i. 18–21) rest on Dan. vii. 7, 8, viii. 3–9, and the representation of nations and kingdoms as horns originate in these passages, but also in the symbolic transactions recorded Zech. xi. 5, the killing of the three shepherds in one month becomes intelligible only by a reference to Daniel's prophecy of the world-rulers under whose power Israel was brought into subjection. Cf. my Comm. on Zech. ii. 1–4 and xi. 5. The exposition of Zech. i. 7–17 and vi. 1–8 as founded on Daniel's prophecy of the world-kingdoms, does not, however, appear to us to be satisfactory, and in what Zechariah (ch. ii. 5) says of the building of Jerusalem we can find no allusion to Dan. ix. 25. But if Bleek in particular has missed in Zech. Daniel's announcement of a Ruler like a son of man coming in the clouds, Kran. has, on the other hand, justly remarked that this announcement by Daniel is connected with the scene of judgment described in ch. vii., which Zechariah, in whose prophecies the priestly character of the Messiah predominates, had no occasion to repeat or expressly to mention. This is the case also with the *names* of the angels in Daniel, which are connected with the special character of his visions, and cannot be expected in Zechariah. Yet Zechariah agrees with Daniel in regard to the distinction between the higher and the lower ranks of angels.

Rather the case stands thus: that not only was Zechariah acquainted with Daniel's prophecies, but Ezra also and the Levites of his time made use of (Ezra ix. and Neh. ix.) the penitential prayer of Daniel (ch. ix.). In Ezekiel also we have still older testimony for Daniel and the principal contents of his book, which the opponents of its genuineness have in vain attempted to set aside. Even Bleek is obliged to confess that "in the way in which Ezekiel (xiv. 14, 20, xxviii. 3) makes mention of the rectitude and wisdom of Daniel, we are led to think of a man of such virtue and wisdom as Daniel appears in this book to have been distinguished by, and also to conceive of some connection between the character there presented and that which Ezekiel had before his eyes;" but yet, notwithstanding this, the manner in which Ezekiel makes mention of Daniel does not lead him to think of a man who was Ezekiel's contemporary in the Babylonish exile, and who was probably comparatively young at the time when Ezekiel spake of him, but of a man who had been long known as an historic or mythic personage of antiquity. But this latter idea is based only on the groundless supposition that the names Noah, Daniel, and Job, as found in Ezek. xiv. 14, 20, are there presented in chronological order, which, as we have shown under Ezek. xiv., is a natural order determined by a reference to the deliverance from great danger experienced by each of the persons named on account of his righteousness. Equally groundless is the other supposition, that the Daniel named by Ezekiel must have been a very old man, because righteousness and wisdom first show themselves in old age. If we abandon this supposition and fall in with the course of thought in Ezekiel, then the difficulty arising from the naming of Daniel between Noah and Job (Ezek. xiv. 14) disappears, and at the same time also the occasion for thinking of an historical or mythical personage of antiquity, of whose special wisdom no trace can anywhere be found. What Ezekiel says of Daniel in both places agrees perfectly with the Daniel of this book. When he (ch. xxviii. 3) says of the king of Tyre, "Thou regardest thyself as wiser than Daniel, there is nothing secret that is hidden from thee," the reference to Daniel cannot be denied, to whom God granted an insight into all manner of visions and dreams, so that he excelled ten times all the wise men of Babylon in wisdom (Dan. i. 17–20); and therefore Nebuchadnezzar (ch. iv. 6 [9]) and the queen (ch. v. 11) regarded him as endowed with the spirit and the wisdom of the gods, which the ruler of Tyre in vain self-idolatry attributed to himself. The opinion pronounced regarding Daniel in Ezek. xiv. 14, 20, refers without a doubt also to the Daniel of this book. Ezekiel names Noah, Daniel, and Job as pious men, who by their righteousness before God in the midst of severe judgments saved their souls, *i.e.* their lives. If his discourse was intended to make any impression on his hearers, then the facts regarding this saving of their lives must have been well known. Record of this was found in the Holy Scriptures in the case of Noah and Job, but of a Daniel of antiquity nothing was at all communicated. On the contrary, Ezekiel's audience could not but at once think of Daniel, who not only refused, from reverence for the law of God, to eat of the food from the king's table, thereby exposing his life to danger, and who was therefore blessed of God with both bodily and mental health, but who also, when the decree had gone forth that the wise men who could not show to Nebuchadnezzar his dream should be put to death, in the firm faith that God would by prayer reveal to him the king's dream, saved his own life and that of his fellows, and in consequence of his interpretation of the dream revealed to him by God, was appointed ruler over the whole province of Babylon and chief over all the wise men of Babylon, so that his name was known in all the kingdom, and his fidelity to the law of God and his righteousness were praised by all the captives of Judah in Chaldea.

Thus it stands with respect to the *external* evidences against the genuineness of the book of Daniel. Its place in the canon among the *Kethubîm* corresponds with the place which Daniel occupied in the kingdom of God under the Old Testament; the alleged want of references to the book and its prophecies in Zechariah and in the book of Jesus Sirach is, when closely examined, not really the case: not only Jesus Sirach and Zechariah knew and understood the prophecies of Daniel, but even Ezekiel names Daniel as a bright pattern of righteousness and wisdom.

If we now turn our attention to the *internal* evidences alleged against the genuineness of the book, the circumstance that the opponents place the Greek names of certain musical instruments mentioned in Dan. iii. in the front, awakens certainly no prejudice favourable to the strength of their argument.

In the list of the instruments of music which were played upon at the inauguration of Nebuchadnezzar's golden image, three names are found of Grecian origin: קִיתָרֹס = *κίθαρις*, סוּמְפֹּנְיָה (סִיפֹּנְיָא) = *συμφωνία*, and פְּסַנְתֵּרִין (פְּסַנְטֵרִין) = *ψαλτήριον* (Dan. iii. 5, 7, 10, 15). To these there has also been added סַבְּכָא = *σαμβύκη*, but unwarrantably; for the *σαμβύκη*, *σάμβυξ*, *ζαμβίκη* is, according to the testimony of Athen. and Strabo, of foreign or Syrian, *i.e.* of Semitic origin, and the word *σαμβύκη* is without any etymon in Greek (cf. Ges. *Thes.* p. 935). Of the other three names, it is undoubted that they have a Grecian origin; but "no one can maintain that such instruments could not at the time of the Chaldean supremacy have found their way from the Greek West into Upper Asia, who takes into view the historical facts" (Kran.). At the time of Nebuchadnezzar, not only was "there intercourse between the inhabitants of Upper Asia and the Ionians of Asia Minor," as Bleek thinks, but according to Strabo (xiii. 2, 3) there was in the army of Nebuchadnezzar, Antimenidas, the brother of the poet Alcæus, fighting victoriously for the Babylonians, apparently, as M. v. Nieb. in his *Gesch. Assurs*, p. 206, remarks, at the head of a warlike troop, as chief of a band of *fuorusciti* who had bound themselves to the king of Babylon. According to the testimony of Abydenus, quoted in Eusebius, *Chron. Arm.* ed. Aucher, i. 53, Greek soldiers followed the Assyrian Esarhaddon (Axerdis) on his march through Asia; and according to Berosus (*Fragm. hist. Græc.* ed. Müller, ii. 504), Sennacherib had already conducted a successful war against a Greek army that had invaded Cilicia. And the recent excavations in Nineveh confirm more and more the fact that there was extensive intercourse between the inhabitants of Upper Asia and Greece, extending to a period long before the time of Daniel, so that the importation of Greek instruments into Nineveh was by no means a strange thing, much less could it be so during the time of the Chaldean supremacy in Babylon, the merchant-city, as Ezekiel (ch. xvii. 4, 19) calls it, from which even in Joshua's time a Babylonish garment had been brought to the Canaanites (Josh. vii. 21). But if Staehelin (*Einleit.* p. 348) further remarks, that granting even the possibility that in Nebuchadnezzar's time the Babylonians had some knowledge of the Greek musical instruments, yet there is a great difference between this and the using of them at great festivals, where usually the old customs prevail, it must be replied that this alleged close adherence to ancient custom on the part of Nebuchadnezzar stands altogether in opposition to all we already know of the king. And the further remark by the same critic, that *psalterium* and *symphonie* were words first used by the later Greek writers about 150 B.C., finds a sufficient reply in the discovery of the figure of a ψαλτήριον on the Monument of Sennacherib.[1] But if through this ancient commerce, which was principally carried on by the Phœnicians, Greek instruments were brought into Upper Asia, it cannot be a strange thing that their Greek names should be found in the third chapter of Daniel, since, as is everywhere known, the foreign name is usually given to the foreign articles which may be imported among any people.

More important appear the historical improbabilities and errors which are said to occur in the historical narratives of this book.

These are: (1) The want of harmony between the narrative of Nebuchadnezzar's incursion against Judah in Jer. xxv. 1 ff., xlvi. 2, and the statement of Daniel (ch. i. 1 ff.) that this king came up against Jerusalem in the third year of Jehoiakim, besieged the city, and carried away captive to Babylon Daniel and other Hebrew youths, giving command that for three years they should be educated in the wisdom of the Chaldeans; while, according to the narrative of ch. ii., Daniel already, in the second year of the reign of Nebuchadnezzar, interpreted to the king his dream, which could have occurred only after the close of the period of his education. This inconsistency between Dan. i. 1 and Jer. xxvi. 2, xxv. 1, and also between Dan. i. and ii., would indeed be evident if it were an undoubted fact that the statement that Nebuchadnezzar besieged

[1] Cf. Layard's *Nineveh and Babylon*, p. 454. On a bas-relief representing the return of the Assyrian army from a victorious campaign, companies of men welcome the Assyrian commander with song, and music, and dancing. Five musicians go before, three with many-sided harps, a fourth with a double flute, such as are seen on Egyptian monuments, and were in use also among the Romans and Greeks; the fifth carries an instrument like the *santur* (פְּסַנְתֵּרִין, v. Gesen. *Thes.* p. 1116), still in use among the Egyptians, which consists of a hollow box or a sounding-board with strings stretched over it.—Quite in the same way Augustin (under Ps. xxxii.) describes the *psalterium*.

Jerusalem in the third year of the reign of Jehoiakim, as mentioned in Dan. i. 1, meant that this was done after he ascended the throne. But the remark of Wieseler (*die* 70 *Wochen u. die* 63 *Jahrwochen des Proph. Daniel*, p. 9), that the supposed opposition between Dan. i. and ii. is so great that it cannot be thought of even in a pseudo-Daniel, cannot but awaken suspicion against the accuracy of the supposition that Nebuchadnezzar was the actual king of Babylon at the time of the siege of Jerusalem and the carrying away of Daniel. The dream of Nebuchadnezzar in ch. ii. 1 is expressly placed in the second year of his reign (מַלְכוּת); in ch. i. Nebuchadnezzar is called the king of Babylon, but yet nothing is said of his actual reign, and the time of the siege of Jerusalem is not defined by a year of his reign. But he who afterwards became king might be proleptically styled king, though he was at the time only the commander of the army. This conjecture is confirmed by the statement of Berosus, as quoted by Josephus (*Ant.* x. 11. 1, *c. Ap.* i. 19), that Nebuchadnezzar undertook the first campaign against the Egyptian king during the lifetime of his father, who had entrusted him with the carrying on of the war on account of the infirmity of old age, and that he received tidings of his father's death after he had subdued his enemies in Western Asia. The time of Nebuchadnezzar's ascending the throne and commencing his reign was a year or a year and a half after the first siege of Jerusalem; thus in the second year of his reign, that is about the end of it, the three years of the education of the Hebrew youths in the wisdom of the Chaldees would have come to an end. Thus the apparent contradiction between Dan. ii. 1 and i. 1 is cleared up. In reference to the date, "in the third year of the reign of Jehoiakim" (Dan. i. 1), we cannot regard as justified the supposition deduced from Jer. xxxvi. 9, that the Chaldeans in the ninth month of the fifth year of Jehoiakim had not yet come to Jerusalem, nor can we agree with the opinion that Nebuchadnezzar had already destroyed Jerusalem before the victory gained by him over Pharaoh-necho at Carchemish (Jer. xlvi. 2) in the fourth year of Jehoiakim, but hope under ch. i. 1 to prove that the taking of Jerusalem in the fourth year of Jehoiakim followed after the battle at Carchemish, and that the statement by Daniel (ch. i. 1), when rightly understood, harmonizes easily therewith, since בּוֹא (Dan. i. 1) signifies *to go, to set out*, and not *to come.*

But (2) it is not so easy to explain the historical difficulties which are found in ch. v. and vi. 1 (v. 31), since the extra-biblical information regarding the destruction of Babylon is very scanty and self-contradictory. Yet these difficulties are by no means so inexplicable or so great as to make the authorship of the book of Daniel a matter of doubt. For instance, that is a very insignificant matter in which Bleek finds a "specially great difficulty," viz. that in ch. v.: "so many things should have occurred in *one* night, which it can scarcely be believed could have happened so immediately after one another in so short a time." For if one only lays aside the statements which Bleek imports into the narrative,—(1) that the feast began in the evening, or at night, while it began really in the afternoon and might be prolonged into the night; (2) that the clothing of Daniel with purple and putting a chain about his neck, and the proclamation of his elevation to the rank of third ruler in the kingdom, were consummated by a solemn procession moving through the streets of the city; (3) that Daniel was still the chief president over the magi; and (4) that after the appearance of the handwriting lengthened consultations took place, —if one gives up all these suppositions, and considers what things may take place at a sudden disastrous occurrence, as, for example, on the breaking out of a fire, in a very few hours, it will not appear incredible that all the things recited in this chapter occurred in one night, and were followed even by the death of the king before the dawn of the morning. The historical difficulty lies merely in this, that, as Staehelin (p. 350) states the matter, Belshazzar appears as the last king of Babylon, and his mother as the wife of Nebuchadnezzar, which is contrary to historical fact. This is so far true, that the queen-mother, as also Daniel, repeatedly calls Nebuchadnezzar the father (אָב) of Belshazzar; but that Belshazzar was the last king of Babylon is not at all stated in the narrative, but is only concluded from this circumstance, that the writing on the wall announced the destruction of king Belshazzar and of his kingdom, and that, as the fulfilling of this announcement, the death of Belshazzar (ch. v. 30) occurred that same night, and (ch. vi. 1) also the transferring of the kingdom of the Chaldeans to the Median Darius. But that the destruction of the Chaldean kingdom or its transference to the Medes occurred at the same time with the death of Belshazzar, is not said in the text. The connecting of the second *factum* with the first by the copula ו (ch. vi. 1) indicates nothing further than that both of these parts of the prophecy were fulfilled. The first (ch. v. 3) was fulfilled that same night, but the time of the other is not given, since ch. vi. 1 (v. 31) does not form the conclusion of the narrative of the fifth chapter, but the beginning to those events recorded in the sixth. How little may be concluded as to the relative time of two events by the connection of the second with the first by the copula ו, may *e.g.* be seen in the history recorded in 1 Kings xiv., where the prophet Ahijah announces (ver. 12) to the wife of Jeroboam the death of her sick son, and immediately in connection therewith the destruction of the house of Jeroboam (ver. 14), as well as the exile (ver. 15) of the ten tribes; events which in point of time stood far apart from each other, while yet they were internally related, for the sin of Jeroboam was the cause not only of the death of his son, but also of the termination of his dynasty and of the destruction of the kingdom of the ten tribes.[1] So here also the death of Belshazzar and the overthrow of the Chaldean kingdom are internally connected, without, however, rendering it necessary that the two events should take place in the self-same hour. The book of Daniel gives no information as to the time when the Chaldean kingdom was overthrown; this must be discovered from extra-biblical sources, to which we shall more particularly refer under ch. v. We hope to show there that the statement made by Daniel perfectly harmonizes with that which, from among the contradictory reports of the Greek historians regarding this occurrence, appears to be historically correct, and perhaps also to show the source of the statement that the destruction of Babylon took place during a riotous feast of the Babylonians.

The other "difficulty" also, that Darius, a king of Median origin, succeeds Belshazzar (ch. vi. 1 [v. 31]), who also is, ch. ix. 1 and xi. 1, designated as a Median, and, ch. ix. 1, as the son of Ahasuerus, disappears as soon as we give up the unfounded statement that this Darius immediately followed Belshazzar, and that Ahasuerus the Persian king was Xerxes, and give credit to the declaration, ch. vi. 29, that Cyrus the Persian succeeded in the kingdom to Darius the Median, according to the statement of Xenophon regarding the Median king Cyaxeres II. and his relation to Cyrus, as at ch. vi. 1 shall be shown.

The remaining "difficulties" and "improbabilities" are destitute

[1] By a reference to this narrative Kran. has (p. 26) refuted the objection of Hitzig, that if the death of Belshazzar did not bring with it the transference of the kingdom of the Chaldeans to the Medes, then ver. 28 ought to have made mention of the death of the king, and that the kingdom (twenty-two years later) would come to the Chaldeans should have been passed over in silence.

of importance. The erection of a golden image of the gigantic proportion of sixty cubits high in the open plain, ch. iii., is "something very improbable," only when, with Bleek, we think on a massive golden statue of such a size, and lose sight of the fact that the Hebrews called articles that were merely plated with gold, golden, as *e.g.* the altar, which was overlaid with gold, Ex. xxxix. 38, xl. 5, 26, cf. Ex. xxxvii. 25 f., and idol images, cf. Isa. xl. 19, xli. 7, etc. Of the seven *years'* madness of Nebuchadnezzar the narrative of ch. iv. says nothing, but only of its duration for seven *times* (עִדָּנִין, vers. 20, 22, 29), which the interpreters have explained as meaning years. But that the long continuance of the king's madness must have been accompanied with "very important changes and commotions," can only be supposed if we allow that during this period no one held the reigns of government. And the absence of any mentioning of this illness of Nebuchadnezzar by the extra-biblical historians is, considering their very imperfect acquaintance with Nebuchadnezzar's reign, not at all strange, even though the intimations by Berosus and Abydenus of such an illness should not be interpreted of his madness. See on this under ch. iv. Concerning such and such-like objections against the historical contents of this book, what Kran., p. 47, has very justly remarked regarding v. Lengerke's assertion, that the author lived "in the greatest ignorance regarding the leading events of his time," or Hitzig's, that this book is "very unhistorical," may be here adopted, viz. "that they emanate from a criticism which is astonishingly consistent in looking at the surface of certain facts, and then pronouncing objection after objection, without showing the least disposition toward other than a wholly external, violent solution of the existing difficulties."

All the opponents of the book of Daniel who have followed Porphyry[1] find a powerful evidence of its being composed not in the time of the exile, but in the time of the Maccabees, in the contents and nature of the prophecies found in it, particularly in this, as Bleek has expressed it, that "the special destination of the prediction extends to the time of Antiochus Epiphanes when that Syrian prince exercised tyranny against the Jewish people, and especially sought by every means to abolish the worship of Jehovah

[1] Whose opinion of the contents of the book is thus quoted by Jerome (*Procem. in Dan.*): "*Quidquid* (*autor libri Dan.*) *usque ad Antiochum dixerit, veram historiam continere; si quid autem ultra opinatus sit, quia futura nescierit, esse mentitum.*"

and to introduce the Grecian *cultus* into the temple at Jerusalem; for the prophecy either breaks off with the death of this prince, or there is immediately joined to it the announcement of the liberation of the people of God from all oppression, of the salvation and the kingdom of the Messiah, and even of His rising again from the dead." To confirm this assertion, which deviates from the interpretation adopted in the church, and is also opposed by recent opponents of the genuineness of the book, Bleek has in his *Einleitung*, and in his *Abhandlg. v.* note, p. 28, fallen upon the strange expedient of comparing the prophecies of Daniel, going backwards from ch. xii., for the purpose of showing that as ch. xii. and xi. 21–45 speak only of the reign of Antiochus Epiphanes, of his wicked actions, and especially of his proceedings against the Jewish people and against the worship of Jehovah, so also in ch. ix., viii., vii., and ii. the special pre-intimations of the future do not reach further than to this enemy of the people of God. Now certainly in ch. xii., vers. 11 and 12 without doubt refer to the time of Antiochus Epiphanes, and xi. 21–35 as surely treat of the proceedings and of the wicked actions of this Syrian king; but the section xi. 36–xii. 3 is almost unanimously interpreted by the church of the rise and reign of Antichrist in the last time, and is explained of the reign of Antiochus Epiphanes, as lately shown by Klief., only when an interpretation is adopted which does not accord with the sense of the words, and is in part distorted, and rests on a false historical basis. While now Bleek, without acknowledging the ancient church-interpretation, adopts that which has recently become prevalent, applying the whole eleventh chapter absolutely to Antiochus Epiphanes, and regards it as necessary only to reject the artistic explanation which Auberlen has given of ch. xii., and then from the results so gained, and with the help of ch. viii., so explains the prophecies of the seventy weeks, ch. ix., and of the four world-monarchies, ch. ii. and vii., that ch. ix. 25–27 closes with Antiochus Epiphanes, and the fourth world-kingdom becomes the Greco-Macedonian monarchy of Alexander and his successors, he has by means of this process gained the wished-for result, disregarding altogether the organism of the well-arranged book. But scientifically we cannot well adopt such a method, which, without any reference to the organism of a book, takes a retrograde course to explain the clear and unambiguous expressions by means of dark and doubtful passages. For, as Zündel (p. 95) has well remarked, as we cannot certainly judge of a symphony from the last tones of the *finale*, but only after the first simple passages of the *thema*, so we cannot certainly form a correct judgment from its last brief and abrupt sentences of a prophetical work like this, in which the course of the prophecy is such that it proceeds from general to special predictions. Ch. xii. forms the conclusion of the whole book; in vers. 5–13 are placed together the two periods (ch. vii. and viii.) of severe oppression of the people of God, which are distinctly separable from each other—that proceeding from the great enemy of the third world-kingdom, *i.e.* Antiochus Epiphanes (ch. viii.), and that from the last great enemy of the fourth world-kingdom, *i.e.* Antichrist (ch. vii.),—while the angel, at the request of the prophet, makes known to him the duration of both. These brief expressions of the angel occasioned by Daniel's two questions receive their right interpretation from the earlier prophecy in ch. vii. and viii. If we reverse this relation, while on the ground of a very doubtful, not to say erroneous, explanation of ch. xi., we misinterpret the questions of Daniel and the answers of the angel, and now make this interpretation the standard for the exposition of ch. ix., viii., vii., and ii., then we have departed from the way by which we may reach the right interpretation of the prophetic contents of the whole book.

The question how far the prophecies of Daniel reach, can only be determined by an unprejudiced interpretation of the two visions of the world-kingdoms, ch. ii. and vii., in conformity with the language there used and with their actual contents, and this can only be given in the following exposition of the book. Therefore we must here limit ourselves to a few brief remarks.

According to the unmistakeable import of the two fundamental visions, ch. ii. and vii., the erection of the Messianic kingdom follows close after the destruction of the fourth world-kingdom (ch. ii. 34, 44), and is brought about (ch. vii. 9–14, 26 f.) by the judgment on the little horn which grew out of the fourth world-power, and the investiture of the Messiah coming in the clouds of heaven with authority, glory, and kingly power. The first of these world-powers is the Chaldean monarchy founded by Nebuchadnezzar, who is the golden head of the image (ch. ii. 37, 38). The kingdom of the Chaldeans passes over to Darius, of Median origin, who is followed on the throne by Cyrus the Persian (ch. vi. 29 [28]), and thus it passes over to the Medes and Persians. This kingdom, in ch. vii. represented under the figure of a bear, Daniel saw in ch. viii. under the figure of a ram with two horns, which, being pushed at by a he-goat having a great horn between his eyes as he was running in his flight over the earth, had his two horns broken, and was thrown to the ground and trodden upon. When the he-goat hereupon became strong, he broke his great horn, and in its stead there grew up four horns toward the four winds of heaven; and out of one of them came forth a little horn, which became exceeding great, and magnified itself even to the Prince of the host, and took away the daily sacrifice (ch. viii. 3–13). This vision was thus explained to the prophet by an angel:—The ram with two horns represents the kings of the Medes and Persians; the he-goat is the king of Javan, *i.e.* the Greco-Macedonian kingdom, for "the great horn that is between his eyes is the first king" (Alexander of Macedon); the four horns that sprang up in the place of the one that was broken off are four kingdoms, and in the latter time of their kingdom a fierce king shall stand up (the little horn), who shall destroy the people of the Holy One, etc. (ch. viii. 20–25). According to this quite distinct explanation given by the angel, the horn, *i.e.* Antiochus Epiphanes, so hostile to the people of God belongs to the third world-kingdom, arises out of one of the four kingdoms into which the monarchy of Alexander the Great was divided; the Messianic kingdom, on the contrary, does not appear till after the overthrow of the fourth world-kingdom and the death of the last of the enemies arising out of it (ch. vii.). Accordingly, the affirmation that in the book of Daniel the appearance of the Messianic salvation stands in order after the destruction of Antiochus Epiphanes, is in opposition to the principal prophecies of the book; and this opposition is not removed by the supposition that the terrible beast with the ten horns (ch. vii. 7) is identical with the he-goat, which is quite otherwise described, for at first it had only one horn, after the breaking off of which four came up in its stead. The circumstance that the description of the little horn growing up between the ten horns of the fourth beast, the speaking great and blasphemous things against the Most High, and thinking to change times and laws (ch. vii. 8, 24 f.), harmonizes in certain features with the representation of Antiochus Epiphanes described by the little horn (ch. viii.), which would destroy the people of the Holy One, rise up against the Prince of princes, and be broken without the hand of man, does not at all warrant the identification of these enemies of God and His people rising out of different world-kingdoms, but corresponds perfectly with this idea, that Antiochus Epiphanes in his war against the people of God was a type of

Antichrist, the great enemy arising out of the last world-kingdom Along with these resemblances there are also points of dissimilarity, such *e.g.* as this: the period of continuance of the domination of both is apparently alike, but in reality it is different. The activity of the prince who took away the daily sacrifice, *i.e.* Antiochus Epiphanes, was to continue 2300 evening-mornings (ch. viii. 14), or, as the angel says, 1290 days (ch. xii. 11), so that he who waits and comes to the 1335 days shall see (ch. xii. 12) salvation; the activity of the enemy in the last time, *i.e.* of Antichrist, on the contrary, is for a time, (two) times, and an half time (ch. vii. 25, xii. 7), or a half שָׁבוּעַ (ch. ix. 27)—designations of time which have been taken without any exegetical justification to mean years, in order to harmonize the difference.

Accordingly, Daniel does not prophesy the appearance of the Messianic redemption after the overthrow of Antiochus Epiphanes, but announces that the fourth world-kingdom, with the kingdoms growing out of it, out of which the last enemy of the people of God arises, would first follow Antiochus, who belonged to the third world-kingdom. This fourth world-kingdom with its last enemy is destroyed by the judgment which puts an end to all the world-kingdoms and establishes the Messianic kingdom. Thus the assertion that the special destination of the prediction only goes down to Antiochus Epiphanes is shown to be erroneous. Not only in the visions ch. ii. and vii. is the conduct of the little horn rising up between the ten horns of the fourth beast predicted, but also in ch. xi. 36–45 the actions of the king designated by this horn are as specially predicted as is the domination and rule of Antiochus Epiphanes in ch. viii. 9 ff., 24 f., and in ch. xi. 20–35.

These are all the grounds worth mentioning which the most recent opponents of the historical and prophetical character of this book have adduced against its genuineness. It is proved from an examination of them, that the *internal* arguments are of as little value as the *external* to throw doubts on its authorship, or to establish its Maccabean origin. But we must go a step further, and briefly show that the modern opinion, that the book originated in the time of the Maccabees, which is set aside by the fact already adduced (p. 32), the use of it on the part of Zechariah and Ezra, is irreconcilable with the formal nature, with the actual contents, and with the spirit of the book of Daniel.

1. Neither the character of the language nor the mode in which

the prophetic statements are made, corresponds with the age of the Maccabees. As regards the character of the age, the interchange of the Hebrew and the Chaldee, in the first place, agrees fully with the time of the exile, in which the Chaldee language gradually obtained the ascendency over the Hebrew mother-tongue of the exiles, but not with the time of the Maccabees, in which the Hebrew had long ago ceased to be the language used by the people.[1] In the second place, the Hebrew diction of Daniel harmonizes peculiarly with the language used by writers of the period of the exile, particularly by Ezekiel;[2] and the Chaldean idiom of this book agrees in not a few characteristic points with the Chaldee of the book of Ezra and Jer. x. 11, wherein these Chaldean portions are markedly distinguished from the Chaldean language of the oldest Targums, which date from the middle of the first century B.C.[3] In the third place, the language of Daniel has, in common with that of the books of Ezra and Nehemiah, certain Aryan elements or Parsisms, which can only be explained on the supposition that their authors lived and wrote in the Babylonish exile or

[1] The use of the Chaldee along with the Hebrew in this book points, as Kran., p. 52, justly remarks, "to a conjuncture in which, as in the Hebrew book of Ezra with its inwoven pieces of Chaldee, the general acquaintance of the people with the Aramaic is supposed to be self-evident, but at the same time the language of the fathers was used by the exiles of Babylon and their children as the language of conversation." Rosenm., therefore, knows no other mode of explaining the use of both languages in this book than by the assertion that the pseudo-author did this *nulla alia de causa, quam ut lectoribus persuaderet, compositum esse librum a vetere illo propheta, cui utriusque linguæ usum æque facilem esse oportuit.* The supposition that even in the second century before Christ a great proportion of the people understood the Hebrew, modern critics set themselves to establish by a reference to the disputed book of Daniel and certain pretended Maccabean psalms.

[2] Compare the use of words such as בִּזָּה for בַּז, xi. 24, 33 (2 Chron. xiv. 13; Ezra ix. 7; Neh. iii. 36; Esth. ix. 10); הֵיךְ for אֵיךְ, x. 17 and 1 Chron. xxiii. 12; כְּתָב for סֵפֶר, x. 21 (Ezra iv. 7, 8; 1 Chron. xxviii. 19; Neh. vii. 64; Esth. iii. 14); מַדָּע, i. 4, 17 (2 Chron. i. 10; Eccles. x. 20); מַרְעִיד, x. 11 and Ezra x. 9; עִתִּים for עִתּוֹת, ix. 25, xi. 6, 13, 14 (Chron., Ezra, Neh., Ezek., and only once in Isaiah, xxxiii. 6); הַצְּבִי used of the land of Israel, viii. 9, cf. xi. 16, 41, also Ezek. xx. 6, 15, and Jer. iii. 10; זֹהַר, brightness, xii. 3, Ezek. viii. 2; חִיֵּב, to make guilty, i. 10, and חוֹב, Fzek. xviii. 7; נְחשֶׁת קָלָל, x. 6, and Ezek. i. 7; לְבוּשׁ הַבַּדִּים, xii. 6, 7, and Ezek. ix. 3, 11, x. 2, 6, 7, etc.

[3] See the collection of Hebraisms in the Chaldean portions of Daniel and of the book of Ezra in Hengstenberg's *Beitrage*, i. p. 303, and in my *Lehrb. d. Einl.* § 133, 4. It may be further remarked, that both books have a peculiar mode

under the Persian rule.[1] But the expedient adopted by the opponents of the genuineness to explain these characteristic agreements from imitation, is inadmissible from this consideration, that in the Hebrew complexion of the Chaldee portion as in the Aryan element found in the language there used, this book shows, along with the agreements, also peculiarities which announce[2] the independent character of its language.

of formation of the 3d pers. imperf. of הֲוָא: לֶהֱוֵא, Dan. ii. 20, 28, 29, 45 (לֶהֱוֵה, iv. 22), Ezra iv. 13, vii. 26, לֶהֱוֺן, ii. 43, vi. 2, 3, and Ezra vii. 25, and לֶהֶוְיָן, v. 17, for יֶהֱוֵא, יֶהֱוֺן, and יֶהֶוְיָן, which forms are not found in the biblical Chaldee, while the forms with ל are first used in the Talmud in the use of the imperative, optative, and subjunctive moods (cf. S. D. Luzzatto, *Elementi grammaticali del Caldeo biblico e del dialetto talmudico babilonese*, Padova 1865, p. 80,—the first attempt to present the grammatical peculiarities of the biblical Chaldee in contradistinction to the Babylonico-talmudic dialect), and לֶהֱוֵא is only once found in the *Targ. Jon.*, Ex. xxii. 24, and perhaps also in the *Jerusalem Targum*, Ex. x. 28. The importance of this linguistic phenomenon in determining the question of the date of the origin of both books has been already recognised by J. D. Michaelis (*Gram. Chal.* p. 25), who has remarked concerning it: "*ex his similibusque Danielis et Ezræ hebraismis, qui his libris peculiares sunt, intelliges, utrumque librum eo tempore scriptum fuisse, quo recens adhuc vernacula sua admiscentibus Hebræis lingua Chaldaica; non seriore tempore confictum. In Targumim enim, antiquissimis etiam, plerumque frustra hos hebraismos quæsieris, in Daniele et Ezra ubique obvios.*"

[1] Not to mention the name of dignity פֶּחָה used in the Assyrian period, and the two proper names, אַשְׁפְּנַז, i. 3, and אַרְיוֹךְ, ii. 14, cf. Gen. xiv. 1, 9, there are in this book the following words of Aryan origin: אַזְדָּא, ii. 5, 8, derived from the Old Persian *âzandâ*, found in the inscriptions of Bisutun and Nakhschi-Rustam, meaning science, knowledge; גְּדָבְרִין, iii. 2, 3, and גִּזְבָּר, גִּזַּבְרִין, Ezra i. 8, vii. 21, from the Old Persian *gada* or *gañda*, Zend. *gaza* or *ganga*, thus *gada-bara*, treasurer, the Old Persian form, while גִּזְבָּר corresponds with the Zend. *gaza-bara*; דְּתָבָר, iii. 2, 3, Old Persian and Zend. *dâta-bara* (New Pers. *dâtavar*), one who understands the law, a judge; הַדָּם (הַדָּמִין, ii. 5, iii. 29), from the Old Persian *handâm*, organized body, member (μέλος); פַּתְבַּג, costly food, i. 5, 8, 13, 15 and xi. 26, from the Old Persian *pati-baga*, Zend. *paiti-bagha*, Sanskr. *prati-bhâga*, allotted food [" a share of small articles, as fruit, flowers, etc., paid daily to the rajah for household expenditure"]; פִּתְגָם, iii. 16, iv. 14, Ezra iv. 17, v. 7, vi. 11, from the Old Persian *pati-gama*, a message, a command; פַּרְתְּמִים, i. 3, Esth. i. 3, vi. 9, the distinguished, the noble, in Pehlevi, *pardom*, Sanskr. *prathama*, the first; and the as yet unexplained מֶלְצַר, i. 11, 16, and נְבִזְבָּה, ii. 6, and finally כָּרוֹזָא, a crier, a herald, iii. 4, Old Persian *khresii*, crier, from which the verb כְּרַז, v. 29, in Chald. and Syr. of similar meaning with the Greek κηρύσσειν.

[2] Thus Daniel uses only the plur. suffixes כוֹן, הוֹן, לְכוֹן, לְהוֹן, while in Ezra

Although perhaps the use of peculiar Aramaic words and word-forms by a Jew of the time of the Maccabees may be explained, yet the use of words belonging to the Aryan language by such an one remains incomprehensible,—such words, *e.g.*, as אַזְדָּא, דְּתָבְרַיָּא, פַּתְבַּג, which are met with neither in the Targums nor in the rabbinical writings, or הַדָּם, member, piece, from which the Targumists formed the *denom.* הַדֵּים, *μελίζεσθαι*, to dismember, and have naturalized in the Aramaic language (cf. J. Levy, *Chald. Wörterb. ueber die Targ.* i. p. 194). Whence could a Maccabean Jew of the era of the Seleucidæ, when the Greek language and culture had become prominent in the East, have received these foreign words?

But as the language of this book, particularly its Aryan element, speaks against its origin in the age of the Maccabees, so also "the contemplative-visionary manner of representation in the book," as Kran. (p. 59) justly remarks, "accords little with a conjuncture of time when (1 Macc. ii. ff.) the sanctuary was desecrated and tyranny rose to an intolerable height. It is not conceivable that in such a time those who mingled in that fearful insurrection and were called on to defend their lives with weapons in their hands, should have concerned themselves with visions and circumstantial narratives of detailed history, which appertain to a lengthened period of quietness, instead of directly encouraging and counselling the men of action, so that they might be set free from the fearful situation in which they were placed."

2. Thus in no respect do the actual contents of this book correspond with the relations and circumstances of the times of the Maccabees; but, on the contrary, they point decidedly to the time of the exile. The historical parts show an intimate acquaintance not only with the principal events of the time of the exile, but also with the laws and manners and customs of the Chaldean and Medo-Persian monarchies. The definite description (ch. i. 1) of the first expedition of Nebuchadnezzar against Jerusalem, which is fabricated certainly from no part of the O. T., and which is yet

the forms כֹם and הֹם are interchanged with כוֹן and הוֹן in such a way, that הוֹן is used fifteen times, הוֹם ten times, כוֹן once, and כֹם five times. The forms with ם used by Ezra, and also by Jeremiah, x. 11, prevail in the Targum. Moreover Daniel has only הִמּוֹן (ii. 34, 35, iii. 22), Ezra, on the contrary, has the abbreviated form הִמּוֹ (iv. 10, 23, v. 5, 11, etc.); Daniel דִּכֵּן, ii. 31, vii. 20, 21, Ezra דָּךְ, iv. 13, 15, 16, 18, 21, v. 8, and דֵּךְ, v. 16 f., vi. 7 f., 12; Daniel נְוָלִי, ii. 5, Ezra נְוָלוּ, vi. 11; Daniel גְּדָבְרַיָּא, iii. 2, Ezra גִּזְבָּר, i. 8, vii. 21.

proved to be correct, points to a man well acquainted with this event; so too the communication regarding king Belshazzar, ch. v., whose name occurs only in this book, is nowhere else independently found. An intimate familiarity with the historical relations of the Medo-Persian kingdom is seen in the mention made of the law of the Medes and Persians, ch. vi. 9, 13, since from the time of Cyrus the Persians are always placed before the Medes, and only in the book of Esther do we read of the Persians and Medes (ch. i. 3, 14, 18), and of the law of the Persians and Medes (ch. i. 19). An intimate acquaintance with the state-regulations of Babylon is manifest in the statement made in ch. i. 7 (proved by 2 Kings xxiv. 17 to be a Chaldean custom), that Daniel and his companions, on their being appointed for the king's service, received new names, two of which were names derived from Chaldean idols; in the account of their food being brought from the king's table (ch. i. 5); in the command to turn into a dunghill (ch. ii. 5) the houses of the magicians who were condemned to death; in the death-punishments mentioned in ch. ii. 5 and iii. 6, the being hewn to pieces and cast into a burning fiery furnace, which are shown by Ezek. xvi. 10, xxiii. 47, Jer. xxix. 29, and other proofs, to have been in use among the Chaldeans, while among the Medo-Persians the punishment of being cast into the den of lions is mentioned, ch. vi. 8, 13 ff. The statement made about the clothing worn by the companions of Daniel (ch. iii. 21) agrees with a passage in Herodotus, i. 195; and the exclusion of women from feasts and banquets is confirmed by Xen. *Cyrop.* v. 2, and Curtius, v. 1, 38. As to the account given in ch. ii. 5, 7, of the priests and wise men of Chaldea, Fr. Münter (*Religion der Babyl.* p. 5) has remarked, "What the early Israelitish prophets record regarding the Babylonish religion agrees well with the notices found in Daniel; and the traditions preserved by Ctesias, Herod., Berosus, and Diodor are in perfect accordance therewith." Compare with this what P. F. Stuhr (*Die heidn. Religion. des alt. Orients*, p. 416 ff.) has remarked concerning the Chaldeans as the first class of the wise men of Babylon. A like intimate acquaintance with facts on the part of the author of this book is seen in his statements regarding the government and the state officers of the Chaldean and Medo-Persian kingdom (cf. Hgstb. *Beitr.* i. p. 346 ff.).

The prophetical parts of this book also manifestly prove its origin in the time of the Babylonian exile. The foundation of the world-kingdom by Nebuchadnezzar forms the historical starting-point for the prophecy of the world-kingdoms. "Know, O king," says Daniel to him in interpreting his dream of the world-monarchies, "thou art the head of gold" (ch. ii. 37). The visions which are vouchsafed to Daniel date from the reign of Belshazzar the Chaldean, Darius the Median, and Cyrus the Persian (ch. vii. 1, viii. 1, ix. 1, x. 1). With this stands in harmony the circumstance that of the four world-kingdoms only the first three are historically explained, viz. besides the first of the monarchy of Nebuchadnezzar (ch. ii. 37), the second of the kingdom of the Medes and Persians, and the third of the kingdom of Javan, out of which, at the death of the first king, four kingdoms shall arise toward the four winds of heaven (ch. viii. 20–22). Of the kings of the Medo-Persian kingdom, only Darius the Median and Cyrus the Persian, during whose reign Daniel lived, are named Moreover the rise of yet four kings of the Persians is announced, and the warlike expedition of the fourth against the kingdom of Javan, as also the breaking up and the division toward the four winds (ch. xi. 5–19) of the kingdom of the victorious king of Javan. Of the four kingdoms arising out of the monarchy of Alexander of Macedon nothing particular is said in ch. viii., and in ch. xi. 5–19 only a series of wars is predicted between the king of the south and the king of the north, and the rise of the daring king who, after the founding of his kingdom by craft, would turn his power against the people of God, lay waste the sanctuary, and put an end to the daily sacrifice, and, according to ch. viii. 23, shall arise at the end of these four kingdoms.

However full and particular be the description given in ch. viii. and ch. xi. of this daring king, seen in ch. viii. as the little horn, yet it nowhere passes over into the prediction of historical particularities, so as to overstep the boundaries of prophecy and become prognostication or the feigned setting forth of the empiric course of history. Now, though the opinion of Kran. p. 58, that "the prophecy of Daniel contains not a single *passus* which might not (leaving the fulfilment out of view) in a simple, self-evident way include the development founded in itself of a theocratic thought, or of such-like thoughts," is not in accordance with the supernatural factor of prophecy, since neither the general prophecy of the unfolding of the world-power in four successive world-kingdoms, nor the special description of the appearance and unfolding of this world-kingdom, can be conceived of or rightly regarded as a mere explication of theocratic thoughts, yet the remark of the same theologian, that the special prophecies in Daniel

viii. and xi. do not abundantly cover themselves with the historical facts in which they found their fulfilment, and are fundamentally different from the later so-called Apocalypse of Judaism in the Jewish Sibyl, the book of Enoch and the book of Ezra (= Esdras), which are appended to the book of Daniel, is certainly well founded.

What Daniel prophesied regarding the kings of Persia who succeeded Cyrus, regarding the kingdom of Javan and its division after the death of the first king into four kingdoms, etc., could not be announced by him by virtue of an independent development of prophetic thoughts, but only by virtue of direct divine revelation; but this revelation is at the same time not immediate prediction, but is an addition to the earlier prophecies of further and more special unveilings of the future, in which the point of connection for the reference of the third world-kingdom to Javan was already given in the prophecy of Balaam, Num. xxiv. 24, cf. Joel iv. 6 (iii. 6). The historical destination of the world-kingdoms does not extend to the kingdom of Javan and the ships of Chittim (ch. xi. 30), pointing back to Num. xxiv. 24, which set bounds to the thirst for conquest of the daring king who arose up out of the third world-kingdom. The fourth world-kingdom, however distinctly it is described according to its nature and general course, lies on the farther side of the historical horizon of this prophet, although in the age of the Maccabees the growth of the Roman power, striving after the mastery of the world, was already so well known that the Alexandrine translators, on the ground of historical facts, interpreted the coming of the ships of Chittim by *ἥξουσι Ῥωμαῖοι*. The absence of every trace of the historical reference of the fourth world-kingdom, furnishes an argument worthy of notice in favour of the origin of this book of Daniel during the time of the exile. For at the time of the Babylonian exile Rome lay altogether out of the circle of vision opened up to the prophets of Scripture, since it had as yet come into no relation at all to the then dominant nations which were exercising an influence on the fate of the kingdom of God. Altogether different was the state of matters in the age of the Maccabees, for they sent messengers with letters to Rome, proposing to enter into a league with the Romans: cf. 1 Macc. viii. xii.

The contents of Dan. ix. accord with the age of the Maccabees still less than do the visions of the world-kingdoms. Three and a half centuries after the accomplishment of Jeremiah's prophecy of the desolation of Judah, after Jerusalem and the temple had been long ago rebuilt, it could not come into the mind of any Jew to put into the mouth of the exiled prophet Daniel a penitential prayer for the restoration of the holy city, and to represent Gabriel as having brought to him the prophecy that the seventy years of the desolation of Jerusalem prophesied of by Jeremiah were not yet fulfilled, but should only be fulfilled after the lapse of seventy year-weeks, in contradiction to the testimony of Ezra, or, according to modern critics, of the author of the books of Chronicles and of Ezra, living at the end of the Persian era, that God, in order to fulfil His word spoken by Jeremiah the prophet, had in the first year of Cyrus stirred up the spirit of Cyrus the king of Persia to send forth an edict throughout his whole kingdom, which directed the Jews to return to Jerusalem and commanded them to rebuild the temple (2 Chron. xxxvi. 22 f., Ezra i. 1–4).

3. If now, in conclusion, we take into consideration the religious spirit of this book, we find that the opponents of its genuineness display no special gift of *διάκρισις πνευμάτων* when they place the book of Daniel in the same category with the Sybilline Oracles, the fourth book of Ezra (= 2 Esdras), the book of Enoch, the *Ascensio Jesajæ*, and other pseudepigraphical products of apocryphal literature, and represent the narrative of the events of Daniel's life and his visions as a literary production after the manner of Deuteronomy and the book of Koheleth (Ecclesiastes), which a Maccabean Jew has chosen, in order to gain for the wholesome truths which he wished to represent to his contemporaries the wished-for acceptance (Bleek, p. 593 f.). For this purpose, he must in the historical narratives, "by adducing the example of Daniel and his companions on the one side, and of Nebuchadnezzar and Belshazzar on the other, exhort his fellow-countrymen to imitate the former in the inflexible stedfastness of their faith, in their open, fearless confession of the God of their fathers, and show them how this only true, all-powerful God will know in His own time to humble those who, like Antiochus Epiphanes, raised themselves against Him in presumptuous pride and sought to turn away His people from His service, and, on the other hand, to make His faithful worshippers in the end victorious" (Bleek, p. 601). Hence the tendency is conspicuous, "that the author in his descriptions in ch. iii. and vi. almost always, in whole and in part, has kept before his eye the relations of his time (the land of Judea being then under the oppression of Antiochus Epiphanes) and the surrounding circumstances; and these he brings before his readers in a veiled, yet by them easily recognisable, manner" (p.

602). Wherein, then, does the "easily recognisable" resemblance of these two *facta* consist? Nebuchadnezzar directed a colossal image of threescore cubits in height and six cubits in breadth to be erected on the plain of Dura, and to be solemnly consecrated as a national image, the assembled people falling down before it doing it homage. Antiochus Epiphanes, on the contrary, did not command an idol-image, as has been supposed from a false interpretation of the *βδέλυγμα ἐρημώσεως* (1 Macc. i. 54), to be placed on the altar of burnt-offering, but only a small idol-altar (*βωμόν*, 1 Macc. i. 59) to be built; no mention is made, however, of its being solemnly consecrated. He then commanded the Jews to offer sacrifice month after month on this idol-altar; and because he wished that in his whole kingdom all should form but one people, and that each should leave his laws (ver. 41), he thus sought to constrain the Jews to give up the worship of God inherited from their fathers, and to fall in with the heathen forms of worship. Nebuchadnezzar did not intend to forbid to the nations that became subject to him the worship of their own gods, and to the Jews the worship of Jehovah, but much more, after in the wonderful deliverance of the three friends of Daniel he recognised the omnipotence of the supreme God, he forbade by an edict, on the pain of death, all his subjects from blaspheming this God (Dan. iii. 28–30).

And wherein consists the resemblance between Antiochus Epiphanes and the Median Darius (Dan. vi.)? Darius, it is true, at the instigation of his princes and satraps, issued an ordinance that whoever within thirty days should offer a prayer to any god or man except to the king himself should be cast into the den of lions, but certainly not with the view of compelling the Jews, or any other of his subjects, to apostatize from their ancestral religion, for after the expiry of the appointed thirty days every one might again direct his prayer to his own god. The special instigators of this edict did not contemplate by it the bringing of the Jewish people under any religious restraint, but they aimed only at the overthrow of Daniel, whom Darius had raised to the rank of third ruler in the realm and had thought to set over the whole kingdom. But when Daniel was denounced to him by the authors of this law, Darius became greatly moved, and did all he could to avert from him the threatened punishment. And when, by an appeal of his satraps to the law of the Medes and Persians that no royal edict could be changed, necessity was laid upon him to cause Daniel to be cast into the den of lions, he spent a sleepless night, and was very glad when, coming to the lions' den early in the morning, he found Daniel uninjured. He then not only commanded Daniel's accusers to be cast to the lions, but he also by a proclamation ordered all his subjects to do homage to the living God who did signs and wonders in heaven and earth. In this conduct of Darius towards Daniel and towards the living God of heaven and earth, whom Daniel and the Jews worshipped, can a single incident be found which will remind us of the rage of Antiochus Epiphanes against the Jews and their worship of God?

Still less can it be conceived that (as Bleek, p. 604, says) the author of this book had "without doubt Antiochus Epiphanes before his eyes" in Nebuchadnezzar, ch. iv., and also in Belshazzar, ch. v. It is true that Nebuchadnezzar and Belshazzar, according to ch. iv. and v., sin against the Almighty God of heaven and earth and are punished for it, and Antiochus Epiphanes also at last fell under the judgment of God on account of his wickedness. But this general resemblance, that heathen rulers by their contact with the Jews did dishonour to the Almighty God, and were humbled and punished for it, repeats itself at all times, and forms no special characteristic of the time of Antiochus Epiphanes. In all the special features of the narratives of Dan. iv. and v., on the other hand, complete differences are met with. Nebuchadnezzar was struck with beast-like madness, not because he had persecuted the Jews, but because in his haughty pride as a ruler he deified himself, because he knew not that the Most High ruleth over the kingdom of men (ch. iv. 14); and when he humbled himself before the Most High, he was freed from his madness and again restored to his kingdom. Belshazzar also did not transgress by persecuting the Jews, but by causing at a riotous banquet, in drunken insolence, the golden vessels which had been brought from the temple in Jerusalem to Babylon to be produced, and by drinking out of these vessels with his captains and his wives amid the singing of songs in praise of the idol-gods; thus, as Daniel represented to him, raising himself up against the Lord of heaven, and not honouring the God in whose hand his breath was and with whom were all his ways, although he knew how his father Nebuchadnezzar had been punished by this God (ch. v. 20–23) for his haughty presumption.

The relation not only of Nebuchadnezzar and of Darius, but also of Belshazzar, to the Jews and their religion is therefore fundamentally different from the tendency of Antiochus Epiphanes to uproot Judaism and the Mosaic worship of God. The Babylonian kings were indeed heathen, who, according to the common opinion of all heathens, held their national gods to be greater and more powerful than the gods of the nations subdued by them, among whom they also placed the God of Israel; but when they heard of the wonders of His divine omnipotence, they gave honour to the God of Israel as the God of heaven and of earth, partly by express confession of Him, and partly, at least as Belshazzar did, by honouring the true worshippers of this God. Antiochus Epiphanes, on the contrary, persisted in his almost mad rage against the worship of God as practised by the Jews till he was swept away by the divine judgment. If the pretended pseudo-Daniel, therefore, had directed his view to Antiochus Epiphanes in the setting forth of such narratives, we could only imagine the purpose to have been that he might lead this fierce enemy of his people to acknowledge and worship the true God. But with such a supposition not only does the sentiment of the Jews, as it is brought to light in the books of the Maccabees, stand in opposition, but it is also contradicted by the prophecies of this book, which threaten the daring and deceitful king, who would take away the daily sacrifice and lay waste the sanctuary, with destruction without the hand of man, without giving any room for the thought of the possibility of a change of mind, or of his conversion. The author of these prophecies cannot therefore have followed, in the historical narratives of his book, the tendency imputed to him by modern critics.

On the whole, an entire misapprehension of the spirit which pervades the historical parts of the book of Daniel lies at the foundation of the supposition of such a tendency. The narratives regarding Nebuchadnezzar, his dream, the consecration of the golden statue, and his conduct after his recovery from his madness, as well as those regarding Darius, ch. vi., could not be invented, at least could not be invented by a Maccabean Jew, because in the pre-exilian history there are altogether wanting types corresponding to the psychological delineation of these characters. It is true that a Pharaoh raised Joseph, who interpreted his dream, to be the chief ruler in his kingdom, but it does not come into his mind to give honour to the God who revealed in the dream what would befall his kingdom (Gen. xli.). For the other narratives of this book there are wanting in the Old Testament incidents with which they could be connected; and the resemblance between the life-experience of Joseph and that of Daniel extends only to these general matters, that both received from God the gift of interpreting dreams, and by means of this gift brought help and deliverance to their people:[1] in all details, however, Daniel is so different from Joseph, that the delineation of his portrait as found in this book cannot be regarded as a copy of the history of Joseph. Still less can we think of the narratives of Daniel as poetical compositions; for the characters of Nebuchadnezzar and of Darius the Mede are essentially different from the prevailing views of Judaism concerning the heathen. The relation of both of these genuine heathen kings to the revelations of God shows a receptivity for the control of the living God in the lot of men, as is predicated before and after the exile in no Jewish writing of a single heathen. Such representations of character cannot be invented; they are drawn according to life, and can only be understood if the wonders of divine omnipotence and grace which the book of Daniel relates truly happened.

But as in the historical narrations, so also in the visions of Daniel, there is wanting every trace of any tendency pointing to Antiochus Epiphanes. This tendency is derived only from the view already (p. 42) shown to be incorrect, that all the prophecies of Daniel extend only down to this king, and that with his death the destruction of the God-opposing world-power and the setting up of the Messianic kingdom of God is to be expected. But if the opponents of the genuineness of this book derive support for their views from the relation of the prophecies of Daniel to the pseudepigraphic products of the Jewish Apocalyptics, so also, on the other hand, Zündel (*Krit. Unter.* p. 134 ff.) has so conclusively proved the decided difference between the prophecies of Daniel and the Sibylline Oracles, which, according to Bleek, Lücke, and others, must have flowed from one source and are homogeneous, that we may limit ourselves to a brief condensed exhibition of the main results of this proof (p. 165 ff.).

First, the *subject* of the two writings is perfectly different. In Daniel the seer stands in moral connection with the vision; this is not so with the Sibyl. Daniel is a pious Israelite, whose name, as we see from Ezekiel, was well known during the Chaldean exile, and whose life-history is spent in inseparable connection with his prophecies; on the contrary, the Sibyls withdraw their existence from all historical control, for they date back in the times of

[1] Chr. B. Michaelis thus brings together the analogies between the events in the life of Joseph and of Daniel: "*Uterque in peregrinam delatus terram, uterque felix somniorum interpres, uterque familiæ ac populi sui stator, uterque summorum principum administer, uterque sapientum sui loci supremus antistes.*"

hoary antiquity, not only of Israel, but of all nations, viz. in the period of the deluge, and their persons disappear in apocryphal darkness. "While Daniel on his knees prays for the divine disclosure regarding the time of the deliverance of his people, and each of his revelations is at the same time an answer to prayer, the Sibyl in the Maccabean time is represented, in a true heathenish manner, powerfully transported against her will by the word of God as by a madness, and twice she prays that she might rest and cease to prophesy."

Again, the prophetic *situation* is just as different. As is the case with all the earlier prophets, Daniel's prophecy goes forth from a definite historical situation, the growing up of the first great world-power in Assyria-Chaldea; it stands in a moral practical connection with the deliverance of Israel, about which it treats, after the expiry of the seventy years of Jeremiah; the four world-monarchies which were revealed to him take root in the historical ground of the time of Nebuchadnezzar. In the Seleucidan-Jewish Sibyl, on the contrary, there is no mention made of a prophetical situation, nor of a politico-practical tendency; the Sibyl has in a true Alexandrine manner a literary object, viz. this, to represent Judaism as the world-religion. "That life-question for Israel and the world, When comes the kingdom of God? which in Daniel springs up in an actual situation, as it shall also be only answered by divine fact, is in the Alexandrine Sibyllist only a question of doctrine which *he* believes himself called on to solve by making the heathen Jews and associates of the Jews.

Finally, in the Sibyls there is wanting a prophetical *object*. The prophetical object of Daniel is the world-power over against the kingdom of God. This historico-prophetic idea is the determinating, sole, all-penetrating idea in Daniel, and the centre of it lies throughout in the end of the world-power, in its inner development and its inner powerlessness over against the kingdom of God. The four world-forms do not begin with the history of nations and extend over our present time. On the contrary, the creative prophetic spirit is wanting to the Sibyl; not *one* historical thought of deliverance is peculiar to it; it is a genuine Alexandrine compilation of prophetic and Græco-classic thoughts externally conceived. The thought peculiarly pervading it, to raise Judaism to the rank of the world-religion, is only a human reflection of the divine plan, that in Abraham all the nations shall be blessed, which pervades all the prophets as the great thought in the history of the world; in Daniel it comes out into the greatest clearness, and is realized by Christianity. This prophetic world-thought the Sibyl has destroyed, *i.e.* has religiously spiritualized and politically materialized it. "Not the living and holy covenant God Jehovah, who dwells on high and with the contrite in heart, but Godhead uncreated and creating all things, without distinction in Himself, the invisible God, who sees all things, who is neither male nor female, as He appears at a later period in the teaching of the school of Philo, is He whom the Sibyl in very eloquent language declares to the heathen. But of the God of Israel, who not only created the world, but who also has a divine kingdom on the earth, and will build up this kingdom, in a word, of the God of the history of redemption, as He is seen in His glory in Daniel, we find no trace whatever." The materialistic historic prophecy of the Sibyllist corresponds with this religious spiritualism. He seeks to imitate the prophecies of Daniel, but he does not know the prophetic fundamental thought of the kingdom of God over against the kingdom of the world, and therefore he copies the empirical world-history: "first Egypt will rule, then Assyria, Persia, Media, Macedonia, Egypt again, and then Rome."

Thus the Sibylline Apocalyptic is fundamentally different from the prophecies of Daniel.[1] Whoever has a mind so little disciplined that he cannot perceive this difference, cannot be expected to know how to distinguish between the prophecies of Daniel and the philosophical reflections of the book of Koheleth.[2] If Koheleth brings forward his thoughts regarding the vanity of all things in the name of the wise king Solomon, then is this literary production, which moreover is so very transparent that every reader of the book can see through it, altogether comprehensible. If, on the other hand, a Maccabean Jew clothe his own self-conceived ideas regarding the development of the war of the heathen world-powers against the people of God in revelations from God, which the prophet

[1] This may be said also of the other apocryphal apocalypses of Judaism, which we have no need, however, here specially to consider, because these apocalypses, as is generally acknowledged, originate in a much later time, and therefore have no place in discussions regarding the genuineness of the book of Daniel.

[2] The Deuteronomy which Bleek and others quote along with the book of Koheleth cannot be therefore taken into consideration as capable of supplying analogical proof, because the supposition that this book is not genuine, was not composed by Moses, is no better grounded than is the supposed non-genuineness of the book of Daniel.

living in the Babylonian exile might have received, then this undertaking is not merely literary deception, but at the same time an abuse of prophecy, which, as a prophesying out of one's own heart, is a sin to which God in His law has annexed the punishment of death.

If the book of Daniel were thus a production of a Maccabean Jew, who would bring "certain wholesome truths" which he thought he possessed before his contemporaries as prophecies of a divinely enlightened seer of the time of the exile, then it contains neither prophecy given by God, nor in general wholesome divine truth, but mere human invention, which because it was clothed with falsehood could not have its origin in the truth. Such a production Christ, the eternal personal Truth, never could have regarded as the prophecy of Daniel the prophet, and commended to the observation of His disciples, as He has done (Matt. xxiv. 15, cf. Mark xiii. 14).

This testimony of our Lord fixes on the external and internal evidences which prove the genuineness of the book of Daniel the seal of divine confirmation.

For the exegetical literature of the book of Daniel see in my *Lehrb. der Einl. in d. A. Test.* § 385 f. [The Messrs. T. and T. Clark of Edinburgh have recently published an English translation of this work, under the title of *Manual of Historico-Critical Introduction to the Canonical Scriptures of the Old Testament*, etc., translated by the Rev. Professor Douglas, D.D., Free Church College, Glasgow. 2 vols., Edinburgh 1869]. To what is there recorded we may add, *Das Buch Daniel erkl.* von Rud. Kranichfeld, Berlin 1868; *Das Buch Daniels uebers. u. erkl.* von Dr. Th. Kliefoth, Schwerin 1868; J. L. Füller, *der Prophet Daniel erkl.*, Basel 1868 (for the educated laity); Pusey, *Daniel the Prophet*, Oxf. 1864; and Mayer (Cath.), *die Messian. Prophezieen des Daniel*, Wien 1866. [*Der Prophet Daniel, theologisch-homiletisch bearbeitet.* von Dr. Zoeckler, Professor der Theologie zu Greifswald (J. P. Lange's *Bibelwerk*, 17er Thiel des A. T.), 1870.]

EXPOSITION

CHAP. I. HISTORICO-BIOGRAPHICAL INTRODUCTION.

WHEN Nebuchadnezzar first besieged Jerusalem he not only took away the holy vessels of the temple, but also commanded that several Israelitish youths of noble lineage, among whom was Daniel, should be carried to Babylon and there educated in the science and wisdom of the Chaldeans for service in his court, which they entered upon when their education was completed. This narrative, in which the stedfast attachment of Daniel and his three friends to the religion of their fathers, and the blessings which flowed to them from this fidelity (vers. 8–17), are particularly set forth, forms the historical introduction to the following book, whilst it shows how Daniel reached the place of influence which he held, a place which was appointed for him according to the divine counsel, during the Babylonish exile, for the preservation and development of the Old Testament kingdom of God. It concludes (ver. 21) with the remark, that Daniel continued to occupy this place till the first year of Cyrus.

Vers. 1 and 2. Of this expedition of Nebuchadnezzar against Jerusalem it is related in the second book of Kings (ch. xxiv. 1): "In his days Nebuchadnezzar king of Babylon came up, and Jehoiakim became his servant three years; then he turned and rebelled against him;" and in the second book of Chronicles (ch. xxxvi. 6): "Against him came up Nebuchadnezzar king of Babylon, and bound him in fetters to carry him to Babylon. Nebuchadnezzar also carried of the vessels of the house of the Lord to Babylon, and put them in his temple at Babylon." That both of these statements refer to the same expedition of Nebuchadnezzar against Jehoiakim mentioned here, appears not only from the statement of the book of Chronicles agreeing with ver. 2 of this chapter, namely, that Nebuchadnezzar took away a part of the sacred vessels of the temple to Babylon, and there put them in the temple of his god, but also from the circumstance that, beyond all doubt, during the reign of Jehoiakim there was not a second siege of Jerusalem by Nebuchadnezzar. It is true, indeed, that when Jehoiakim threw off the yoke at the end of three years' subjection, Nebuchadnezzar sent Chaldean, Aramæan, Moabitish, and Ammonitish hosts against him for the purpose of bringing him into subjection, but Jerusalem was not again laid siege to by these hosts till the death of Jehoiakim. Not till his son Jehoiachin ascended the throne did the servants of Nebuchadnezzar again come up against Jerusalem and besiege it. When, during the siege, Nebuchadnezzar himself came up, Jehoiachin surrendered to him after three months, and was, along with the chief men of his kingdom, and the strength of the population of Jerusalem and Judah, and the treasures of the royal palace and of the temple, carried down to Babylon (2 Kings xxiv. 2–16). The year, however, in which Nebuchadnezzar, in the reign of Jehoiakim, first took Jerusalem and carried away a part of the treasures of the temple to Babylon, is stated neither in the second book of Kings nor in Chronicles, but may be pretty certainly determined by the statements of Jeremiah (ch. xlvi. 2, xxv. 1 ff., xxxvi. 1 ff.). According to Jer. xlvi. 2, Nebuchadnezzar smote the Egyptian king Pharaoh-Necho with his army at Carchemish in the fourth year of the reign of Jehoiakim. That same year is spoken of (Jer. xxv. 1) as the first year of Nebuchadnezzar the king of Babylon, and is represented by Jeremiah not only as a critical period for the kingdom of Judah; but also, by the prediction that the Lord would bring His servant Nebuchadnezzar against Judah and against its inhabitants, and against all the nations round about, that He would make Judah a desolation, and that these nations would serve the king of Babylon seventy years (vers. 2–11), he without doubt represents it as the beginning of the seventy years of Babylonish exile: In this the fourth year of Jehoiakim, the prophet was also commanded (ch. xxxvi. 1 ff.) to write in a book all the words which the Lord had spoken unto him against Israel, and against Judah, and against all the nations, from the day in which He had spoken to him in the time of Josiah even till then, that the house of Judah might hear all the evil which He purposed to do unto them, and might return every man from his evil way. Jeremiah obeyed this command, and caused these predictions, written in the roll of a book, to be read by Baruch to the people in the temple; for he himself was a prisoner, and therefore could not go to the temple.

The first capture of Jerusalem by Nebuchadnezzar cannot therefore have taken place in the third, but must have been in the fourth year of Jehoiakim, *i.e.* in the year 606 B.C. This, however, appears to stand in opposition to the statement of the first verse of this chapter: "In the third year of the reign of Jehoiakim בָּא Nebuchadnezzar to Jerusalem." The modern critics accordingly number this statement among the errors which must disprove the genuineness of this book (see above, p. 35 f.). The apparent opposition between the language of Daniel (ch. i. 1) that Nebuchadnezzar undertook his first expedition against Jerusalem in the third year of Jehoiakim, and the affirmation of Jeremiah, according to which not only was Pharaoh-Necho slain by Nebuchadnezzar at the Euphrates in the fourth year of Jehoiakim, but also in this same year Nebuchadnezzar's invasion of Judea is for the first time announced, cannot be resolved either by the hypothesis of a different mode of reckoning the years of the reign of Jehoiakim and of Nebuchadnezzar, nor by the supposition that Jerusalem had been already taken by Nebuchadnezzar before the battle of Carchemish, in the third year of Jehoiakim. The first supposition is set aside by the circumstance that there is no certain analogy for it.[1] The latter supposition is irreconcilable with Jer. xxv. and xxxvi.[2] If Jeremiah in the fourth year of Jehoiakim announced that because Judah did not hearken unto his warnings addressed to them "from the thirteenth year of Josiah even unto this day," that is, for the space of three and twenty years, nor yet to the admonitions of all the other prophets (ch. xxv. 3–7) whom the Lord had sent unto them, therefore the Lord would now send His servant Nebuchad-

[1] The old attempt to reconcile the difference in this way has already been shown by Hengstenberg (*Beit. z. Einl. in d. A. T.* p. 53) to be untenable; and the supposition of Klief. (p. 65 f.), that Jehoiakim entered on his reign near the end of a year, and that Jeremiah reckons the year of his reign according to the calendar year, but that Daniel reckons it from the day of his ascending the throne, by which it is made out that there is no actual difference, is wholly overthrown by the circumstance that in the sacred Scriptures there is no analogy for the reckoning of the year of a king's reign according to the day of the month on which he began to reign. On this supposition we might reconcile the apparent difference only if no other plan of reconciliation were possible. But such is not the actual state of the case.

[2] Following the example of Hofmann (*die* 70 *Jahre Jer.* p. 13 ff.), Hävernick (*Neue Krit. Unterss. über d. B. Daniel*, p. 62 ff.), Zündel (*Krit. Unterss.* p. 20 ff.), and others have decided in favour of it.

nezzar with all the people of the north against the land and against the inhabitants thereof, and against all these nations round about, utterly to destroy the land and make it desolate, etc.,—then it must be affirmed that he publicly made known the invasion of Judah by the Chaldeans as an event which had not yet taken place, and therefore that the supposition that Jerusalem had already in the preceding year been taken by Nebuchadnezzar, and that Jehoiakim had been brought under his subjection, is entirely excluded. It is true that in ch. xxv. Jeremiah prophesies a judgment of "perpetual desolations against Jerusalem and against all the nations," but it is as unwarrantable to apply, as Klief. does, this prophecy only "to the total destruction of Jerusalem and of Judah, which took place in the eleventh year of Zedekiah," as with older interpreters only to the first expedition of Nebuchadnezzar against Jehoiakim, 2 Kings xxiv. 1 and 2 Chron. xxxvi. 6 f. In the words of threatening uttered by the prophet there are included all the expeditions of Nebuchadnezzar against Jerusalem and Judah, from his first against Jehoiakim to the final destruction of Jerusalem under Zedekiah; so that we cannot say that it is not applicable to the first siege of Jerusalem under Jehoiakim, but to the final destruction of Judah and Jerusalem, as this whole prophecy is only a comprehensive intensified summary of all the words of God hitherto spoken by the mouth of the prophet. To strengthen the impression produced by this comprehensive word of God, he was commanded in that same year (ch. xxxvi. 1 f.), as already mentioned, to write out in the roll of a book all the words hitherto spoken by him, that it might be seen whether or not the several words gathered together into a whole might not exert an influence over the people which the separate words had failed to do.

Moreover a destruction of Jerusalem by the Chaldeans before the overthrow of the Egyptian power on the Euphrates, which took place in the fourth year of Jehoiakim, cannot at all be thought of. King Jehoiakim was "put into bands" by Pharaoh-Necho and made a tributary vassal to him (2 Kings xxiii. 33 ff.), and all the land from the river of Egypt even unto the Euphrates was brought under his sway; therefore Nebuchadnezzar could not desolate Judah and Jerusalem before Pharaoh-Necho was slain. Neither could Nebuchadnezzar pass in the presence of the Egyptian host stationed in the stronghold of Carchemish, on the Euphrates, and advance toward Judah, leaving behind him the city of Babylon as a prize to so powerful an enemy, nor would Necho, supposing that

Nebuchadnezzar had done this, have quietly allowed his enemy to carry on his operations, and march against his vassal Jehoiakim, without following in the rear of Egypt's powerful foe.[1]

The statement in the first verse may indeed, literally taken, be interpreted as meaning that Nebuchadnezzar came up against Jerusalem and took it in the third year of the reign of Jehoiakim, because בּוֹא frequently means to come to a place. But it is not necessary always so to interpret the word, because בּוֹא means not only to come, but also to go, to march to a place. The assertion, that in this verse בּוֹא is to be interpreted (Häv. *N. Kr. U.* p. 61, Ew., and others) as meaning to *come* to a place, and not to *march* to it, is as incorrect as the assertion that the translation of בָּא by *he marched* is inadmissible or quite impossible, because עָלָה is generally used of the march of an army (Staeh., Zünd.). The word בּוֹא, from the first book of the Canon (cf. Gen. xiv. 5) to the last, the book of Daniel not excepted (cf. *e.g.* xi. 13, 17, 29, etc.), is used of military expeditions; and regarding the very general opinion, that בּוֹא, in the sense of to march, to go to a place, occurs less frequently, Kran. (p. 21) has rightly remarked, that "it stands always and naturally in this sense whenever the movement has its point of departure from the place of him who observes it, thinks of it, or makes a communication regarding it." Therefore, *e.g.*, it is used "always in a personal verbal command with reference to the movement, not yet undertaken, where naturally the thought as to the beginning or point of departure passes into the foreground; as *e.g.* in Gen. xlv. 17; Ex. vi. 11, vii. 26, ix. 1, x. 1; Num. xxxii. 6; 1 Sam. xx. 19; 2 Kings v. 5. In Jonah i. 3 it is used of the ship that was about to go to Tarshish; and again, in the words לָבוֹא עִמָּהֶם, *ibid.*, it is used when speaking of the conclusion of the journey." "On the contrary, if the speaker or narrator is at the *terminus ad quem* of the movement spoken of, then of course the word בּוֹא is used in the other sense of *to come*, to approach, and the like." Accordingly these words of Daniel, "Nebuchadnezzar בּוֹא to Jerusalem," considered in themselves, may be interpreted without any regard to the point of departure or the termination of

[1] With the above compare my *Lehrb. der Einl.* § 131, and my *Commentary* on 2 Kings xxiv. 1. With this Kran. agrees (p. 17 f.), and in addition remarks: "In any case Necho would at once have regarded with jealousy every invasion of the Chaldean into the region beyond the Euphrates, and would least of all have suffered him to make an extensive western expedition for the purpose of conquering Judea, which was under the sway of Egypt."

the movement. They may mean "Nebuchadnezzar came to Jerusalem," or that "he marched to Jerusalem," according as the writer is regarded as writing in Judah or Jerusalem, or in Babylon at the point of departure of Nebuchadnezzar's journey. If the book was composed by a Maccabean Jew in Palestine, then the translation, "he came to Jerusalem," would be the more correct, because such a writer would hardly have spoken of a military movement from its eastern point of departure. The case is altogether different if Daniel, who lived as a courtier in Babylon from his youth up to old age, wrote this account. "For him, a Jew advanced in years, naturally the first movement of the expedition threatening and bringing destruction to his fatherland, whether it moved directly or by a circuitous route upon the capital, would be a significant fact, which he had in every respect a better opportunity of comprehending than his fellow-countrymen living in the remote west, since this expedition was an event which led to the catastrophe of the exile. For the Jew writing in Babylon about the expedition, the fatal commencement of the march of the Chaldean host would have a mournful significance, which it could not have for a writer living in Jerusalem."

In this way Kran. has thoroughly vindicated the rendering of בָּא, "he marched" to Jerusalem, and also the explanation of the word as referring to the setting out of the Chaldean army which Hitz., Hofm., Staeh., Zünd., and others have declared to be opposed to the meaning of the word and "impossible," and at the same time he has set aside as groundless the further remark of Hitzig, that the designation of the time also applies to וַיָּצַר. If בָּא is to be understood of an expedition with reference to its point of departure, then the fixing of its time cannot of course refer also to the time of the arrival of the expedition at its termination and the siege then ensuing. The time of its arrival before Jerusalem, as well as the beginning, duration, and end of the siege, is not defined, and only its result, the taking of Jerusalem, is, according to the object of the author, of sufficient importance to be briefly announced. The period of the taking of the city can only be determined from dates elsewhere given. Thus from the passages in Jeremiah already referred to, it appears that this happened in the fourth year of Jehoiakim, in which year Nebuchadnezzar overcame the army of Necho king of Egypt at the Euphrates (Jer. xlvi. 2), and took all the land which the king of Egypt had subdued, from the river of Egypt to the Euphrates, so that

Pharaoh-Necho came no more out of his land (2 Kings xxiv. 7). With this agrees Berosus in the fragments of his Chaldean history preserved by Josephus (*Ant.* x. 11. 1, and *c. Ap.* i. 19). His words, as found in the latter passage, are these: "When his (Nebuc.) father Nabopolassar heard that the satrap whom he had set over Egypt and over the parts of Cœlesyria and Phœnicia had revolted from him, he was unable to bear the annoyance any longer, but committing a part of his army to his son Nabuchodonosor, who was then a youth, he sent him against the rebel. Nabuchodonosor encountered him in battle and overcame him, and brought the land again under his dominion. It happened that his father Nabopolassar at this time fell sick and died at the city of Babylon, after he had reigned twenty-one years (Berosus says twenty-nine years). But when Nabuchodonosor not long after heard of the death of his father, he set the affairs of Egypt and of the other countries in order, and committed the prisoners he had taken from the Jews, the Phœnicians, and Syrians, and from the nations belonging to Egypt, to some of his friends, that they might conduct the heavy armed troops with the rest of the baggage to Babylonia, while he himself hastened with a small escort through the desert to Babylon. When he came hither, he found that the public affairs had been managed by the Chaldeans, and that the principal persons among them had preserved the kingdom for him. He now obtained possession of all his father's dominions, and gave directions that the captives should be placed as colonies in the most favourably situated districts of Babylonia," etc. This fragment illustrates in an excellent manner the statements made in the Bible, in case one be disposed to estimate the account of the revolt of the satrap placed over Egypt and the countries lying round Cœlesyria and Phœnicia as only the expression of boastfulness on the part of the Babylonish historian, claiming that all the countries of the earth of right belonged to the monarch of Babylon; and it also shows that the rebel satrap could be none other than Pharaoh-Necho. For Berosus confirms not only the fact, as declared in 2 Kings xxiv. 7, that Pharaoh-Necho in the last year of Nabopolassar, after the battle at Megiddo, had subdued Judah, Phœnicia, and Cœlesyria, *i.e.* "all the land from the river of Egypt unto the river Euphrates," but he also bears witness to the fact that Nebuchadnezzar, after he had slain Pharaoh-Necho (Jer. xlvi. 2) "by the river Euphrates in Carchemish," made Cœlesyria, Phœnicia, and Judah tributary to the Chaldean empire, and consequently that he took Jerusalem not before but after the battle at Carchemish, in prosecution of the victory he had obtained over the Egyptians.

This does not, however, it must be confessed, prove that Jerusalem had already in the fourth year of Jehoiakim come under the dominion of Nebuchadnezzar. Therefore Hitz. and others conclude from Jer. xxxvi. 9 that Nebuchadnezzar's assault upon Jerusalem was in the ninth month of the fifth year of Jehoiakim as yet only in prospect, because in that month Jeremiah prophesied of the Chaldean invasion, and the extraordinary fast then appointed had as its object the manifestation of repentance, so that thereby the wrath of God might be averted. This Kran. endeavours to prove from 2 Kings xxv. 27, cf. Jer. lii. 31. But in the ninth month of the fifth year of Jehoiakim, Jeremiah caused to be rehearsed to the people in the court of the temple his former prophecies, written by Baruch in a book according to the commandment of the Lord, and pronounced the threatening against Jehoiakim because he had cut to pieces this book and had cast it into the fire, Jer. xxxvi. 29 ff. This threatening, that God would bring upon the seed and upon the servants of Jehoiakim, and upon the inhabitants of Jerusalem, all the evil which He had pronounced against them (ver. 31), does not exclude the previous capture of Jerusalem by Nebuchadnezzar, but announces only the carrying out of the threatened judgment in the destruction of Jerusalem and of the kingdom of Judah to be as yet imminent.

The extraordinary fast of the people also, which was appointed for the ninth month, was not ordained with the view of averting the destruction of Judah and Jerusalem by Nebuchadnezzar, which was then expected, after the battle at Carchemish; for although fasts were sometimes appointed or kept for the purpose of turning away threatened judgment or punishment (*e.g.* 2 Sam. xii. 15 ff.; 1 Kings xxi. 27; Esth. iv. 1, iii. 16), yet, in general, fasts were more frequently appointed to preserve the penitential remembrance of punishments and chastisements which had been already endured: cf. *e.g.* Zech. vii. 5; Ezra x. 6 f.; Neh. i. 4; 1 Sam. xxxi. 13; 2 Sam. i. 12, etc. To ascertain, therefore, what was the object of this fast which was appointed, we must keep in view the character of Jehoiakim and his relation to this fast. The godless Jehoiakim, as he is represented in 2 Kings xxiii. 37, 2 Chron. xxxvi. 5, and Jer. xxii. 13 ff., was not the man who would have ordained a fast (or allowed it if the priests had wished to appoint it) to humble himself and his people before

God, and by repentance and prayer to turn away the threatened judgment. Before he could ordain a fast for such a purpose, Jehoiakim must hear and observe the word of the prophet, and in that case he would not have been so enraged at the reading of the prophecies of Jeremiah as to have cut the book to pieces and cast it into the fire. If the fast took place previous to the arrival of the Chaldeans before Jerusalem, then neither the intention of the king nor his conduct in regard to it can be comprehended. On the other hand, as Zünd. p. 21, and Klief. p. 57, have shown, both the ordaining of a general fast, and the anger of the king at the reading of the prophecies of Jeremiah in the presence of the people in the temple, are well explained, if the fast is regarded as designed to keep in remembrance the day of the year on which Nebuchadnezzar took Jerusalem. As Jehoiakim bore with difficulty the yoke of the Chaldean oppression, and from the first meditated on a revolt, for after three years he did actually revolt, he instituted the fast "to stir up the feelings of the people against the state of vassalage into which they had been brought" (Klief.), "and to call forth a religious enthusiasm among them to resist the oppressor" (Zünd.). This opposition could only, however, result in the destruction of the people and the kingdom. Jeremiah therefore had his prophecies read to the people in the temple on that day by Baruch "as a counterbalance to the desire of the king," and announced to them that Nebuchadnezzar would come again to subdue the land and to destroy from out of it both man and beast. "Therefore the king was angry, and destroyed the book, because he would not have the excitement of the people to be so hindered; and therefore also the princes were afraid (Jer. xxxvi. 16) when they heard that the book of these prophecies was publicly read" (Klief.).

The words of 2 Kings xxv. 27, cf. Jer. lii. 31, do not contradict this conclusion from Jer. xxxvi. 9, even though that drawn by Kran., p. 18, from this passage were adopted, viz. that since almost thirty-seven whole years had passed from the carrying away of Jehoiachin to the end of the forty-three years of the reign of Nebuchadnezzar, but Jehoiachin had reigned only for a few months, the beginning of the reign of Nebuchadnezzar must be dated in the sixth of the eleven years' reign of Jehoiakim, the predecessor of Jehoiachin. For since, according to the testimony of Berosus, Nebuchadnezzar conducted the war against Hither Asia, in which he slew king Necho at Carchemish, and as a further consequence of this victory took Jerusalem, before the death of his father, in the capacity of a commander-in-chief clothed with royal power, and when in Hither Asia, as it seems, and on the confines of Egypt, he then for the first time heard tidings of his father's death, and therefore hastened by the shortest road to Babylon to assume the crown and lay claim to all his father's dominions,—then it follows that his forty-three years' reign begins after the battle of Carchemish and the capture of Jerusalem under Jehoiakim, and might possibly have begun in the sixth year of Jehoiakim, some five months after the ninth month of the fifth year of Jehoiakim (Jer. xxxvi. 9). Against this supposition the circumstance that Nebuchadnezzar, as stated in Jer. xlvi. 2, xxv. 1, and also Dan. i. 1, was called king of Babylon before he had actually ascended the throne is no valid objection, inasmuch as this title is explained as a prolepsis which would be easily understood by the Jews in Palestine. Nabopolassar came into no contact at all with Judah; the Jews therefore knew scarcely anything of his reign and his death; and the year of Nebuchadnezzar's approach to Jerusalem would be regarded in a general way both by Jeremiah and his cotemporaries as the first year of his reign, and the commander of the Chaldean army as the king of Babylon, no matter whether on account of his being actual co-regent with his aged and infirm father, or merely because he was clothed with royal power as the chief commander of the army.[1] In this sense Daniel (ch. i. 1) names him who was afterwards king, at a time when he was not yet the possessor of the throne, the king of Babylon; for he was in effect the king, so far as the kingdom of Judah was concerned, when he undertook the first expedition against it.

But the reckoning of Kran. is also not exact. Nebuchadnezzar's ascending the throne and the beginning of his reign would only happen in the sixth year of Jehoiakim if either the three months of Jehoiachin (37 years' imprisonment of Jehoiachin + 1 year's reign + 5 years of Jehoiakim = 43 years of Nebuchadnezzar) are to be reckoned as 1 year, or at least the 11 years of Jehoiakim as 11 full years, so that $5\frac{3}{4}$ years of Jehoiakim's reign must be added to the 37 years of Jehoiachin's imprisonment and

[1] Thus not only Hgstb. *Beitr.* i. p. 63, Häv., Klief., Kran., etc., but also v. Lengerke, *Dan.* p. 3, and Hitz. *Dan.* p. 3. The latter, *e.g.*, remarks: "The designation as king does not furnish any obvious objection, for Nebuchadnezzar, the commander-in-chief of the army, is to the Jewish writers (thus Jer. xxv. 1) a king when he first comes under their notice. They appear to have had no knowledge whatever of his father"

the 3 months of his reign so as to make up the 43 years of the reign of Nebuchadnezzar. Thus Jehoiakim must have reigned 5¼ years at the time when Nebuchadnezzar ascended the throne. Whereas if Jehoiakim's reign extended only to 10½ years, which were reckoned as 11 years in the books of the Kings, according to the general method of recording the length of the reign of kings, then Nebuchadnezzar's ascending the throne took place in the fifth year of Jehoiakim's reign, or, at the furthest, after he had reigned 4¾ years. This latter reckoning, whereby the first year of Nebuchadnezzar's reign is made to coincide with the fifth year of Jehoiakim's, is demanded by those passages in which the years of the reign of the kings of Judah are made parallel with the years of Nebuchadnezzar's reign; viz. 2 Kings xxiv. 12, where it is stated that Jehoiachin was taken prisoner and carried away captive in the eighth year of Nebuchadnezzar; also Jer. xxxii. 1, where the tenth year of Zedekiah corresponds with the eighteenth of Nebuchadnezzar; and finally, Jer. lii. 5, 12, and 2 Kings xxv. 2, 8, where the eleventh year of Zedekiah corresponds with the nineteenth year of Nebuchadnezzar. According to all these passages, the death of Jehoiakim, or the end of his reign, happened either in the eighth year, or at all events in the end of the seventh year, of the reign of Nebuchadnezzar, for Jehoiachin reigned only three months; so that Nebuchadnezzar reigned six full years, and perhaps a few months longer, as contemporary with Jehoiakim, and consequently he must have mounted the throne in the fifth of the eleven years of Jehoiakim's reign.[1]

The above discussion has at the same time also furnished us with the means of explaining the apparent contradiction which has been found between Dan. i. 1 ff. and Dan. ii. 1 ff., and which has been brought forward as an historical error in argument against the genuineness of the book. According to ch. i. 3 ff., Nebuchadnezzar after the capture of Jerusalem commanded that young Israelites of

[1] The synchronistic statements in the passages, 2 Kings xxiv. 12, xxv. 2, 8, Jer. xxxii. 1 and lii. 5, 12, might indeed be interpreted as meaning, that in them the years of Nebuchadnezzar's reign are reckoned from the time when his father entrusted to him the chief command of the army at the breaking out of the war with Necho (see my *Commentary* on 2 Kings xxiv. 12); but in that case the years of Nebuchadnezzar's reign would amount to 44¼ years, viz. 37 years of Jehoiachin's imprisonment, 3 months of his reign, and 7 years of Jehoiakim's reign. And according to this reckoning, it would also result from the passages referred to, that the beginning of his 43 years' reign happened in the fifth year of Jehoiakim.

noble birth should be carried away to Babylon, and there educated for the space of three years in the literature and wisdom of the Chaldeans; and, according to ch. i. 18, after the expiry of the appointed time, they were brought in before the king that they might be employed in his service. But these three years of instruction, according to ch. ii. 1 ff., expired in the second year of the reign of Nebuchadnezzar, when Daniel and his companions were ranked among the wise men of Babylon, and Daniel interpreted to the king his dream, which his Chaldean magi were unable to do (ch. ii. 13 ff., 19 ff.). If we observe that Nebuchadnezzar dreamed his dream "in the second year of his reign," and that he entered on his reign some time after the destruction of Jerusalem and the captivity of Jehoiakim, then we can understand how the three years appointed for the education of Daniel and his companions came to an end in the second year of his reign; for if Nebuchadnezzar began to reign in the fifth year of Jehoiakim, then in the seventh year of Jehoiakim three years had passed since the destruction of Jerusalem, which took place in the fourth year of this king. For the carrying away of the Israelitish youths followed, without doubt, immediately after the subjugation of Jehoiakim, so that a whole year or more of their period of education had passed before Nebuchadnezzar mounted the throne. This conclusion is not set aside by what Berosus affirms, that Nebuchadnezzar, after he heard of the death of his father, committed the captives he had taken from the Jews to the care of some of his friends that they might be brought after him, while he himself hastened over the desert to Babylon; for that statement refers to the great transport of prisoners who were carried away for the colonization of Central Asia. As little does the consideration that a twofold method of reckoning the year of Nebuchadnezzar's government by Daniel is improbable militate against this reconciliation of the discrepancy, for no such twofold method of reckoning exists. In ch. i. the year of Nebuchadnezzar's reign is not given, but Nebuchadnezzar is only named as being king;[1] while in ch. ii. 1 mention is made not merely of the

[1] If, on the contrary, Bleek understands from Dan. i. 1 that Nebuchadnezzar had become king of Babylon in the third year of Jehoiakim at Jerusalem, whilst, "perhaps only with the design of making the pretended opposition between ch. i. 1 and ii. 1 truly evident, he understands the appositional designation מֶלֶךְ בָּבֶל as a more definite determination of the meaning of the verb בָּא, this idea finds recommendation neither in the position of the words, nor in the expression, ch. i. 3, nor in the accents." Kranichfeld, p. 19.

second year of Nebuchadnezzar, but of the second year of his reign, from which it appears that the historian here reckons from the actual commencement of his reign. Also, as Klief., p. 67, has well remarked, one may "easily discover the ground on which Daniel in ch. i. 1 followed a different mode of reckoning from that adopted in ch. ii. 1. In ch. i. Daniel had to do with Israelitish circumstances and persons, and therefore followed, in making reference to Nebuchadnezzar, the general Israelitish mode of contemplation. He reckons his years according to the years of the Israelitish kings, and sees in him already the *king;* on the contrary, in ch. ii. Daniel treats of the relations of the world-power, and he reckons here accurately the year of Nebuchadnezzar, the bearer of the world-power, from the day in which, having actually obtained the possession of the world-power, he became king of Babylon."

If we now, in conclusion, briefly review the results of the preceding discussions, it will be manifest that the following is the course of events:—Necho the king of Egypt, after he had made Jehoiakim his vassal king, went forth on an expedition against the Assyrian kingdom as far as the Euphrates. Meanwhile, however, with the dissolution of the Assyrian kingdom by the fall of Nineveh, the part of that kingdom lying on this side of the Tigris had come under the dominion of the Chaldeans, and the old and enfeebled king Nabopolassar gave to his son Nebuchadnezzar the chief command of the army, with the commission to check the advance of the Egyptians, and to rescue from them the countries they had occupied and bring them again under the Chaldean rule. In consequence of this, Nebuchadnezzar took the field against Hither Asia in the third year of the reign of Jehoiakim, and in the first month of the fourth year of Jehoiakim slew Pharaoh-Necho at Carchemish and pursued his army to the confines of Egypt, and in the ninth month of the same year took Jerusalem and made king Jehoiakim his subject. While Nebuchadnezzar was busied in Hither Asia with the subjugation of the countries that had been conquered by Pharaoh-Necho, he received the tidings of the death of his father Nabopolassar in Babylon, and hastened forward with a small guard by the nearest way through the desert to Babylon in order to assume the government, giving directions that the army, along with the whole band of prisoners, should follow him by slow marches. But as soon as the Chaldean army had left Judea and returned to Babylon, Jehoiakim sought how he might throw off the Chaldean yoke, and three years after his subjugation he revolted, probably at a time when Nebuchadnezzar was engaged in establishing his dominion in the East, so that he could not immediately punish this revolt, but contented himself meanwhile with sending against Jehoiakim the armies of Chaldeans, Syrians, Moabites, and Ammonites, whom he had left behind on the confines of Judah. They were unable, however, to vanquish him as long as he lived. It was only after his son Jehoiachin had ascended the throne that Nebuchadnezzar, as commander of the army, returned with a powerful host to Jerusalem and besieged the city. While the city was being besieged, Nebuchadnezzar came in person to superintend the war. Jehoiachin with his mother, and his chief officers from the city, went out to surrender themselves to the king of Babylon. But Nebuchadnezzar took him as a prisoner, and commanded that the golden vessels of the temple and the treasures of the royal palace should be taken away, and he carried the king with the great men of the kingdom, the men of war, the smiths and craftsmen, as prisoners to Babylon, and made his vassal Mattaniah, Jehoiachin's uncle, king in Jerusalem, under the name of Zedekiah (2 Kings xxviii. 8–17). This happened in the eighth year of the reign of Nebuchadnezzar (2 Kings xxiv. 12), and thus about six years after Daniel had interpreted his dream (ch. ii.), and had been promoted by him to the rank of president of the wise men in Babylon.

The name נְבוּכַדְנֶאצַּר is written in ver. 1 with א, as it is uniformly in Jeremiah, *e.g.* xxvii. 6, 8, 20, xxviii. 3, 11, 12, xxix. i. 3, and in the books of the Kings and Chronicles, as 2 Kings xxiv. 1, 10, 11, xxv. 1, 2 Chron. xxxvi. 6, 10, 13; whereas in Dan. i. 18 it is written without the א, as it is also in ch. ii. 1, 28, 46, iii. 1–3, 5 ff., and Ezra i. 7, v. 12, 14, Esth. ii. 6. From this circumstance Hitzig concludes that the statement in Daniel is derived from 2 Kings xxiv. 1, because the manner of writing the name with the א is not peculiar to this book (and is not the latest form), but is that of 2 Kings xxiv. 1. Both statements are incorrect. The writing without the א cannot on this account be taken as the latest form, because it is not found in the Chronicles, and that with the א is not peculiar to the second book of Kings, but is the standing form, along with the more national Babylonian form נְבוּכַדְרֶאצַּר (with *r*), in Jer. xxi. 2, 7, xxxii. 1, xxxv. 11, xxxix. 11, Ezek. xxvi. 7, xxix. 18, xxx. 10, which, according to Ménant (*Grammaire Assyrienne*, 1868, p. 327), is written in Babylonian inscriptions *Nabukudurriusur* (נבו כדר אצר, *i.e. Nebo coronam servat*), the inscription of *Behistan* having the form *Nabukudratschara.*

Megasthenes and Berosus, in Polyhistor, write the name *Ναβουκοδρόσορος*. The writing *Nebuchadnezar*, with *n* and without the א, appears to be the Aramean form, since it prevails in the Chaldean portions of Daniel and Ezra, and accounts for the Masoretic pronunciation of the word (the צ with *Dagesch forte*). On other forms of the name, cf. Niebuhr, *Gesch. Assurs*, p. 41 f.

Ver. 2. "*The Lord gave Jehoiakim into his hands*" corresponds with the words in 2 Kings xxiv. 1, "he became his servant," and with 2 Chron. xxxvi. 6, "and he bound him in fetters." "*And part of the vessels of the house of God.*" מִקְצָת without the *Dag. forte*, meaning properly from the end or extremity, is abbreviated from מִקְצֵה עַד קָצֶה, cf. Jer. xxv. 33, Gen. xlvii. 21, Ex. xxvi. 28, and shows that "that which was found from end to end contributed its share; meaning that a great part of the whole was taken, although קְצָת of itself never means *a part*" (Kran.). As to the statement of the text, cf. 2 Chron. xxxvi. 7. These vessels he brought (commanded to be brought) into the land of Shinar, *i.e.* Babylonia (Gen. x. 10), into the temple of his god, *i.e.* Bel, and indeed into the treasure-house of this temple. Thus we understand the meaning of the two latter clauses of ver. 2, while Hitz. and Kran., with many older interpreters, refer the suffix in יְבִיאֵם to Jehoiakim, and also to the vessels, on account of the express contrast in the following words, וְאֶת־הַכֵּלִים (Kran.), and because, if it is not stated here, it is nowhere else mentioned that Nebuchadnezzar carried away men also (Hitz.). But the latter fact is expressly affirmed in ver. 3, and not only supposed, as Hitz. alleges, and it was not necessary that it should be expressed in ver. 2. The application of the suffix to Jehoiakim or the Jewish youths who were carried captive is excluded by the connection of יְבִיאֵם with בֵּית אֱלֹהָיו, *into the house of his god*. But the assertion that בַּיִת, *house*, here means *country*, is not proved from Hos. viii. 1, ix. 15, nor is warranted by such passages as Ex. xxix. 45, Num. xxxv. 34, Ezek. xxxvii. 27, etc., where mention is made of God's dwelling in the land. For God's dwelling in the land is founded on the fact of His gracious presence in the temple of the land, and even in these passages the word *land* does not stand for the word *house*. Equally unfounded is the further remark, that if by the expression בֵּית אֱלֹהָיו the temple is to be understood, the preposition אֶל would stand before it, for which Zech. xi. 13, Isa. xxxvii. 23, Gen. xlv. 25 are appealed to. But such passages have been referred to without observing that in them the preposition אֶל stands only before living objects, where it is necessary, but not before inanimate objects, such as בֵּית, where the special object of the motion is with sufficient distinctness denoted by the accusative. The words following, וְאֶת־הַכֵּלִים, fall in not as adversative, but explicative: *and indeed* (or, *namely*) *the vessels brought he into the treasure-house of his god*—as booty. The carrying away of a part of the vessels of the temple and a number of the distinguished Jewish youth to Babylon, that they might be there trained for service at the royal court, was a sign and pledge of the subjugation of Judah and its God under the dominion of the kings and the gods of Babylon. Both are here, however, mentioned with this design, that it might be known that Daniel and his three friends, of whom this book gives further account, were among these youths, and that the holy vessels were afterwards fatal (ch. v.) to the house of the Babylonian king.

Vers. 3–7. The name אַשְׁפְּנַז, sounding like the Old Persian *Açp*, *a horse*, has not yet received any satisfactory or generally adopted explanation. The man so named was the chief marshal of the court of Nebuchadnezzar. רַב סָרִיסִים (the word רַב used for שַׂר, vers. 7, 9, belongs to the later usage of the language, cf. Jer. xxxix. 3) means chief commander of the eunuchs, *i.e.* overseer of the sérail, the Kislar Aga, and then in a wider sense minister of the royal palace, chief of all the officers; since סָרִיס frequently, with a departure from its fundamental meaning, designates only a courtier, chamberlain, attendant on the king, as in Gen. xxxvii. 36. The meaning of לְהָבִיא, more definitely determined by the context, is *to lead*, *i.e.* into the land of Shinar, to Babylon. In בְּנֵי יִשְׂרָאֵל, *Israel* is the theocratic name of the chosen people, and is not to be explained, as Hitz. does, as meaning that Benjamin and Levi, and many belonging to other tribes, yet formed part of the kingdom of Judah. וּמִזֶּרַע . . . וּמִן, *as well of the seed . . . as also.* פַּרְתְּמִים is the Zend. *frathema*, Sanscr. *prathama*, *i.e. persons of distinction, magnates.* יְלָדִים, the object to לְהָבִיא, designates youths of from fifteen to twenty years of age. Among the Persians the education of boys by the παιδάγωγαι βασίλειοι began, according to Plato (*Alcib.* i. 37), in their fourteenth year, and according to Xenophon (*Cyrop.* i. 2), the ἔφηβοι were in their seventeenth year capable of entering into the service of the king. In choosing the young men, the master of the eunuchs was commanded to have regard to bodily perfection and beauty as well as to mental endowments. Freedom from blemish and personal beauty were looked upon as a characteristic of moral and intellectual nobility; cf. Curtius, xvii. 5, 29. מאום, *blemish*, is written with an א, as in Job xxxi. 7.

Ver. 4. מַשְׂכִּיל, *skilful, intelligent* in all wisdom, *i.e.* in the subjects of Chaldean wisdom (cf. ver. 17), is to be understood of the ability to apply themselves to the study of wisdom. In like manner the other mental requisites here mentioned are to be understood. יֹדְעֵי דַעַת, *having knowledge, showing understanding; מְבִינֵי מַדָּע, possessing a faculty for knowledge, a strength of judgment.* וַאֲשֶׁר כֹּחַ בָּהֶם, *in whom was strength, i.e.* who had the fitness in bodily and mental endowments appropriately to stand in the palace of the king, and as servants to attend to his commands. וּלְלַמְּדָם (*to teach them*) is co-ordinate with לְהָבִיא (*to bring*) in ver. 3, and depends on וַיֹּאמֶר (*and he spake*). For this service they must be instructed and trained in the learning and language of the Chaldeans. סֵפֶר refers to the Chaldee literature, and in ver. 17 כָּל־סֵפֶר, and לָשׁוֹן to conversation or the power of speaking in that language. כַּשְׂדִּים, *Chaldeans*, is the name usually given (1) to the inhabitants of the Babylonian kingdom founded by Nabopolassar and Nebuchadnezzar, and (2) in a more restricted sense to the first class of the Babylonish priests and learned men or magi, and then frequently to the whole body of the wise men of Babylon; cf. at ch. ii. 2. In this second meaning the word is here used. The language of the כַּשְׂדִּים is not, as Ros., Hitz., and Kran. suppose, the Eastern Aramaic branch of the Semitic language, which is usually called the Chaldean language; for this tongue, in which the Chaldean wise men answered Nebuchadnezzar (ch. ii. 4 ff.), is called in ch. ii. 4, as well as in Ezra iv. 7 and Isa. xxxvi. 11, the אֲרָמִית, *Aramaic* (*Syriac*), and is therefore different from the language of the כַּשְׂדִּים.

But the question as to what this language used by the Chaldeans was, depends on the view that may be taken of the much controverted question as to the origin of the כַּשְׂדִּים, *Χαλδαῖοι*. The oldest historical trace of the כַּשְׂדִּים lies in the name אוּר כַּשְׂדִּים (*Ur of the Chaldees*, LXX. *χώρα τῶν Χαλδαίων*), the place from which Terah the father of Abraham went forth with his family to Charran in the north of Mesopotamia. The origin of Abraham from Ur of the Chaldees, when taken in connection with the fact (Gen. xxii. 22) that one of the sons of Nahor, Abraham's brother, was called כֶּשֶׂד (*Chesed*), whose descendants would be called כַּשְׂדִּים, appears to speak for the origin of the כַּשְׂדִּים from Shem. In addition to this also, and in support of the same opinion, it has been noticed that one of Shem's sons was called אַרְפַּכְשַׁד (*Arphaxad*). But the connection of ארפכשד with כֶּשֶׂד is unwarrantable; and that Nahor's son כֶּשֶׂד was the father of a race called כשדים, is a supposition which cannot be established. But if a race actually descended from this כשד, then they could be no other than the Bedouin tribe the כַּשְׂדִּים, which fell upon Job's camels (Job i. 17), but not the people of the Chaldees after whom, in Terah's time, Ur was already named. The sojourn of the patriarch Abraham in Ur of the Chaldees finally by no means proves that Terah himself was a Chaldean. He may have been induced also by the advance of the Chaldeans into Northern Mesopotamia to go forth on his wanderings.

This much is at all events unquestionable, and is now acknowledged, that the original inhabitants of Babylonia were of Semitic origin, as the account of the origin of the nations in Gen. x. shows. According to Gen. x. 22, Shem had five sons, Elam, Asshur, Arphaxad, Lud, and Aram, whose descendants peopled and gave name to the following countries:—The descendants of Elam occupied the country called Elymais, between the Lower Tigris and the mountains of Iran; of Asshur, Assyria, lying to the north—the hilly country between the Tigris and the mountain range of Iran; of Arphaxad, the country of *Arrapachitis* on the Upper Tigris, on the eastern banks of that river, where the highlands of Armenia begin to descend. Lud, the father of the Lydians, is the representative of the Semites who went westward to Asia Minor; and Aram of the Semites who spread along the middle course of the Euphrates to the Tigris in the east, and to Syria in the west. From this M. Duncker (*Gesch. des Alterth.*) has concluded: "According to this catalogue of the nations, which shows the extension of the Semitic race from the mountains of Armenia southward to the Persian Gulf, eastward to the mountains of Iran, westward into Asia Minor, we follow the Semites along the course of the two great rivers, the Euphrates and the Tigris, to the south. Northwards from Arphaxad lie the mountains of the Chasdim, whom the Greeks call Chaldæi, Carduchi, Gordiæi, whose boundary toward Armenia was the river Centrites."

"If we find the name of the Chaldeans also on the Lower Euphrates, if in particular that name designates a region on the western bank of the Euphrates to its mouth, the extreme limit of the fruitful land watered by the Euphrates towards the Arabian desert, then we need not doubt that this name was brought from the

Armenian mountains to the Lower Euphrates, and that it owes its origin to the migration of these Chaldeans from the mountains.—Berosus uses as interchangeable the names Chaldea and Babylonia for the whole region between the Lower Euphrates and the Tigris down to the sea. But it is remarkable that the original Semitic name of this region, *Shinar*, is distinct from that of the Chaldeans; remarkable that the priests in Shinar were specially called Chaldeans, that in the fragments of Berosus the patriarchs were already designated Chaldeans of this or that city, and finally that the native rulers were particularly known by this name. We must from all this conclude, that there was a double migration from the north to the regions on the Lower Euphrates and Tigris; that they were first occupied by the Elamites, who came down along the Tigris; and that afterwards a band came down from the mountains of the Chaldeans along the western bank of the Tigris, that they kept their flocks for a long time in the region of Nisibis, and finally that they followed the Euphrates and obtained superiority over the earlier settlers, who had sprung from the same stem (?), and spread themselves westward from the mouth of the Euphrates. The supremacy which was thus established was exercised by the chiefs of the Chaldeans; they were the ruling family in the kingdom which they founded by their authority, and whose older form of civilisation they adopted."

If, according to this, the Chaldeans are certainly not Semites, then it is not yet decided whether they belonged to the Japhetic race of Aryans, or, as C. Sax[1] has recently endeavoured to make probable, to the Hamitic race of Cushites, a nation belonging to the Tartaric (Turamic) family of nations. As to the Aryan origin,

[1] In the *Abhdl.* "on the ancient history of Babylon and the nationality of the Cushites and the Chaldeans," in the *Deutsch. morg. Ztschr.* xxii. pp. 1–68. Here Sax seeks to prove "that the Chaldeans, identical with the biblical Chasdim, were a tribe ruling from ancient times from the Persian Gulf to the Black Sea, and particularly in Babylonia, which at length occupied the southern region from the mouth of the Euphrates to the Armeneo-Pontine range of mountains, but was in Babylonia especially represented by the priest caste and the learned." This idea the author grounds on the identification of the Bible Cushites with the Scythians of the Greeks and Romans, the evidence for which is for the most part extremely weak, and consists of arbitrary and violent combinations, the inconsistency of which is at once manifest, as *e.g.* the identification of the כַּשְׂדִּים with the כַּסְלֻחִים, Gen. x. 14, the conclusions drawn from Ezek. xxix. 10 and xxxviii. 5 f. of the spread of the Cushites into Arabia and their reception into the Scythian army of the northern Gog, etc. In general, as Sax presents it, this supposition is untenable, yet it contains elements of truth which are not to be overlooked.

besides the relation of the Chaldeans, the Gordiæi, and the Carduchi to the modern Kurds, whose language belongs to the Indo-Germanic, and indeed to the Aryan family of languages, the further circumstance may be referred to: that in Assyria and Babylonia the elements of the Aryan language are found in very ancient times. Yet these two facts do not furnish any conclusive evidence on the point. From the language of the modern Kurds being related to the Aryan language no certain conclusion can be drawn as to the language of the ancient Chaldees, Gordiæi, and Carduchi; and the introduction of Aryan words and appellations into the language of the Semitic Assyrians and Babylonians is fully explained, partly from the intercourse which both could not but maintain with Iranians, the Medes and Persians, who were bordering nations, partly from the dominion exercised for some time over Babylonia by the Iranian race, which is affirmed in the fragments of Berosus, according to which the second dynasty in Babylon after the Flood was the Median. Notwithstanding we would decide in favour of the Aryan origin of the Chaldeans, did not on the one side the biblical account of the kingdom which Nimrod the Cushite founded in Babel and extended over Assyria (Gen. x. 8–12), and on the other the result to which the researches of the learned into the antiquities of Assyria regarding the development of culture and of writing in Babylonia,[1] make this view very doubtful.

[1] The biblical tradition regarding the kingdom founded by Nimrod in Babel, Duncker (p. 204) has with arbitrary authority set aside, because it is irreconcilable with his idea of the development of Babylonian culture. It appears, however, to receive confirmation from recent researches into the ancient monuments of Babylonia and Assyria, which have led to the conclusion, that of the three kinds of cuneiform letters that of the Babylonian bricks is older than the Assyrian, and that the oldest form originated in an older hieroglyphic writing, of which isolated examples are found in the valley of the Tigris and in Susiana; whence it must be concluded that the invention of cuneiform letters did not take place among the Semites, but among a people of the Tauranian race which probably had in former times their seat in Susiana, or at the mouth of the Euphrates and the Tigris on the Persian Gulf. Cf. Spiegel in Herz.'s *Realencyclop.*, who, after stating this result, remarks: "Thus the fact is remarkable that a people of the Turko-Tartaric race appear as the possessors of a high culture, while people of this tribe appear in the world's history almost always as only destitute of culture, and in many ways hindering civilisation; so that it cannot but be confessed that, so far as matters now are, one is almost constrained to imagine that the state of the case is as follows," and thus he concludes his history of cuneiform writing:—"Cuneiform writing arose in ancient times, several thousand years before the birth of Christ, very probably from an ancient hieroglyphic system of writing, in the region about the mouths of the Euphrates and the

If, then, for the present no certain answer can be given to the question as to the origin of the Chaldeans and the nature of their language and writing, yet this much may be accepted as certain, that the language and writing of the כַּשְׂדִּים was not Semitic or Aramaic, but that the Chaldeans had in remote times migrated into Babylonia, and there had obtained dominion over the Semitic inhabitants of the land, and that from among this dominant race the Chaldees, the priestly and the learned caste of the Chaldeans, arose. This caste in Babylon is much older than the Chaldean monarchy founded by Nebuchadnezzar.

Daniel and his companions were to be educated in the wisdom of the Chaldean priests and learned men, which was taught in the schools of Babylon, at Borsippa in Babylonia, and Hipparene in Mesopotamia (Strab. xvi. 1, and Plin. *Hist. Nat.* vi. 26). Ver. 5. To this end Nebuchadnezzar assigned to them for their support provision from the king's household, following Oriental custom, according to which all officers of the court were fed from the king's table, as Athen. iv. 10, p. 69, and Plut. *probl.* vii. 4, testify regarding the Persians. This appears also (1 Kings v. 2, 3) to have been the custom in Israel. דְּבַר יוֹם בְּיוֹמוֹ, *the daily portion*, cf. Ex. v. 13, 19; Jer. lii. 34, etc. פַּתְבַּג comes from *path*, in Zend. *paiti*, Sanscr. *prati* = προτί, πρός, and *bag*, in Sanscr. *bhâga*, portion, provision, cf. Ezek. xxv. 7. With regard to the composition, cf. the Sanscr. *pratibhâga*, a portion of fruits, flowers, etc., which the *Rajah* daily requires for his household; cf. Gildemeister in Lassen's *Zeits. f. d. Kunde des Morg.* iv. 1, p. 214. פַּתְבַּג therefore means neither ambrosia, nor dainties, but generally food, victuals,

Tigris on the Persian Gulf. It was found existing by a people of a strange race, belonging neither to the Semites nor to the Indo-Germans. It was very soon, however, adopted by the Semites. The oldest monuments of cuneiform writing belong to the extreme south of the Mesopotamian plain. In the course of time it pressed northward first to Babylon, where it assumed a more regular form than among the Assyrians. From Assyria it may have come among the Indo-Germans first to Armenia; for the specimens of cuneiform writing found in Armenia are indeed in syllabic writing, but in a decidedly Indo-Germanic language. How the syllabic writing was changed into letter- (of the alphabet) writing is as yet obscure. The most recent kind of cuneiform writing which we know, the Old Persian, is decidedly letter-writing." Should this view of the development of the cuneiform style of writing be confirmed by further investigations, then it may be probable that the Chaldeans were the possessors and cultivators of this science of writing, and that their language and literature belonged neither to the Semitic nor yet to the Indo-Germanic or Aryan family of languages.

food of flesh and meal in opposition to wine, drink (מִשְׁתָּיו is singular), and vegetables (ver. 12).

The king also limits the period of their education to three years, according to the Persian as well as the Chaldean custom. וּלְגַדְּלָם does not depend on וַיֹּאמֶר (ver. 3), but is joined with וַיְמַן, and is the final infinitive with ו explicative, meaning, *and that he may nourish them*. The infinitive is expressed by the fin. verb יַעַמְדוּ, to stand before (the king). The carrying out of the king's command is passed over as a matter of course, yet it is spoken of as obeyed (cf. ver. 6 f.).

Ver. 6. Daniel and his three friends were among the young men who were carried to Babylon. They were of the sons of Judah, *i.e.* of the tribe of Judah. From this it follows that the other youths of noble descent who had been carried away along with them belonged to other tribes. The name of none of these is recorded. The names only of Daniel and his three companions belonging to the same tribe are mentioned, because the history recorded in this book specially brings them under our notice. As the future servants of the Chaldean king, they received as a sign of their relation to him other names, as the kings Eliakim and Mattaniah had their names changed (2 Kings xxiii. 34, xxiv. 17) by Necho and Nebuchadnezzar when they made them their vassals. But while these kings had only their paternal names changed for other Israelitish names which were given to them by their conquerors, Daniel and his friends received genuine heathen names in exchange for their own significant names, which were associated with that of the true God. The names given to them were formed partly from the names of Babylonish idols, in order that thereby they might become wholly naturalized, and become estranged at once from the religion and the country of their fathers.[1] Daniel, *i.e.* God will judge, received the name *Belteshazzar*, formed from *Bel*, the name of the chief god of the Babylonians. Its meaning has not yet been determined. *Hananiah*, *i.e.* the Lord is gracious, received the name *Shadrach*, the origin of which is wholly unknown; *Mishael*, *i.e.* who is what the Lord is, was called *Meshach*, a name yet undeciphered; and *Azariah*, *i.e.* the Lord helps, had his name changed into *Abednego*, *i.e.* slave, servant of *Nego* or *Nebo*, the name of the second god of the

[1] "The design of the king was to lead these youths to adopt the customs of the Chaldeans, that they might have nothing in common with the chosen people."—CALVIN.

Babylonians (Isa. xlvi. 1), the ב being changed by the influence of ב in עבד into ג (*i.e. Nego* instead of *Nebo*).

Vers. 8–16. The command of the king, that the young men should be fed with the food and wine from the king's table, was to Daniel and his friends a test of their fidelity to the Lord and to His law, like that to which Joseph was subjected in Egypt, corresponding to the circumstances in which he was placed, of his fidelity to God (Gen. xxxix. 7 f.). The partaking of the food brought to them from the king's table was to them contaminating, because forbidden by law; not so much because the food was not prepared according to the Levitical ordinance, or perhaps consisted of the flesh of animals which to the Israelites were unclean, for in this case the youths were not under the necessity of refraining from the wine, but the reason of their rejection of it was, that the heathen at their feasts offered up in sacrifice to their gods a part of the food and the drink, and thus consecrated their meals by a religious rite; whereby not only he who participated in such a meal participated in the worship of idols, but the meat and the wine as a whole were the meat and the wine of an idol sacrifice, partaking of which, according to the saying of the apostle (1 Cor. x. 20 f.), is the same as sacrificing to devils. Their abstaining from such food and drink betrayed no rigorism going beyond the Mosaic law, a tendency which first showed itself in the time of the Maccabees. What, in this respect, the pious Jews did in those times, however (1 Macc. i. 62 f.; 2 Macc. v. 27), stands on the ground of the law; and the aversion to eat anything that was unclean, or to defile themselves at all in heathen lands, did not for the first time spring up in the time of the Maccabees, nor yet in the time of the exile, but is found already existing in these threatenings in Hos. ix. 3 f., Amos vii. 17. Daniel's resolution to refrain from such unclean food flowed therefore from fidelity to the law, and from stedfastness to the faith that "man lives not by bread only, but by every word that proceedeth out of the mouth of the Lord" (Deut. viii. 3), and from the assurance that God would bless the humbler provision which he asks for himself, and would by means of it make him and his friends as strong and vigorous as the other youths who did eat the costly provision from the king's table. Firm in this conviction, he requested the chief chamberlain to free him and his three friends from the use of the food and drink brought from the royal table. And the Lord was favourable to him, so that his request was granted.

Ver. 9. נָתַן לְחֶסֶד, *to procure favour* for any one, cf. 1 Kings viii. 30, Ps. cvi. 46, Neh. i. 11. The statement that God gave Daniel favour with the chief chamberlain, refers to the fact that he did not reject the request at once, as one not to be complied with, or as punishable, but, esteeming the religious conviction out of which it sprang, pointed only to the danger into which a disregard of the king's command would bring him, thus revealing the inclination of his heart to grant the request. This willingness of the prince of the eunuchs was the effect of divine grace.

Ver. 10. The words אֲשֶׁר לָמָּה = שַׁלָּמָה (Song i. 7), *for why should he see?* have the force of an emphatic denial, as לָמָּה in Gen. xlvii. 15, 19, 2 Chron. xxxii. 4, and as דִּי לְמָה in Ezra vii. 23, and are equivalent to "he must not indeed see." זֹעֲפִים, *morose*, disagreeable, looking sad, here, a pitiful look in consequence of inferior food, corresponding to σκυθρωπός in Matt. vi. 16. פְּנֵי is to be understood before הַיְלָדִים, according to the *comparatio decurtata* frequently found in Hebrew; cf. Ps. iv. 8, xviii. 34, etc. וְחִיַּבְתֶּם with ו *relat.* depends on לָמָּה: *and ye shall bring into danger*, so that ye bring into danger. חַיֵּב אֶת־רֹאשׁ, *make the head guilty*, *i.e.* make it that one forfeits his head, his life.

Vers. 11–16. When Daniel knew from the answer of the chief that he would grant the request if he were only free from personal responsibility in the matter, he turned himself to the officer who was under the chief chamberlain, whom they were immediately subject to, and entreated him to make trial for ten days, permitting them to use vegetables and water instead of the costly provision and the wine furnished by the king, and to deal further with them according as the result would be. הַמֶּלְצַר, having the article, is to be regarded as an appellative, expressing the business or the calling of the man. The translation, *steward* or chief cook, is founded on the explanation of the word as given by Haug (Ewald's *bibl. Jahrbb.* v. p. 159 f.) from the New Persian word *mel*, spirituous liquors, wine, corresponding to the Zend. *madhu* (μεθυ), intoxicating drink, and צַר = *çara*, Sanscr. *çiras*, the head; hence overseer over the drink, synonymous with רַבְשָׁקֵה, Isa. xxxvi. 2.—נַס נָא, *try, I beseech thee, thy servants*, *i.e.* try it with us, ten days. Ten, in the decimal system the number of completeness or conclusion, may, according to circumstances, mean a long time or only a proportionally short time. Here it is used in the latter sense, because ten days are sufficient to show the effect of the kind of food on the appearance. זֵרֹעִים, food from the vegetable kingdom, *vegetables*, leguminous fruit. Ver. 13. מַרְאֵינוּ is singular, and is used with יֵרָאוּ in the plural because two subjects follow. כַּאֲשֶׁר תִּרְאֵה, *as thou shalt see*, viz. our appearance, *i.e.* as thou shalt then find it, act accordingly. In this proposal Daniel trusted in the help of God, and God did not put his confidence to shame.[1] The youths throve so visibly on the vegetables and water, that the steward relieved them wholly from the necessity of eating from the royal table. Ver. 15. בְּרִיאֵי בָּשָׂר, *fat, well nourished in flesh*, is grammatically united to the suffix of מַרְאֵיהֶם, from which the pronoun is easily supplied in thought. Ver. 16. נֹשֵׂא, *took away* = no more gave.

Vers. 17–21. *The progress of the young men in the wisdom of the Chaldeans, and their appointment to the service of the king.*

As God blessed the resolution of Daniel and his three friends that they would not defile themselves by the food, He also blessed the education which they received in the literature (סֵפֶר, ver. 17 as ver. 4) and wisdom of the Chaldeans, so that the whole four made remarkable progress therein. But besides this, Daniel obtained an insight into all kinds of visions and dreams, *i.e.* he attained great readiness in interpreting visions and dreams. This is recorded regarding him because of what follows in this book, and is but a simple statement of the fact, without any trace of vainglory. Instruction in the wisdom of the Chaldeans was, besides, for Daniel and his three friends a test of their faith, since the wisdom of the Chaldeans, from the nature of the case, was closely allied to the Chaldean idolatry and heathen superstition, which the learners of this wisdom might easily be led to adopt. But that Daniel and his friends learned only the Chaldean wisdom without adopting the heathen element which was mingled with it, is evidenced from the stedfastness in the faith with which at a later period, at the danger of their lives (cf. Dan. iii. 6), they stood aloof from all participation in idolatry, and in regard to Daniel in particular, from the deep glance into the mysteries of the kingdom of God which lies before us in his prophecies, and bears witness of the clear

[1] The request is perfectly intelligible from the nature of living faith, without our having recourse to Calvin's supposition, that Daniel had received by secret revelation the assurance that such would be the result if he and his companions were permitted to live on vegetables. The confidence of living faith which hopes in the presence and help of God is fundamentally different from the eager expectation of miraculous interference of a Maccabean Jew, which C. v. Lengerke and other deists and atheists wish to find here in Daniel.

separation between the sacred and the profane. But he needed to be deeply versed in the Chaldean wisdom, as formerly Moses was in the wisdom of Egypt (Acts vii. 22), so as to be able to put to shame the wisdom of this world by the hidden wisdom of God.

Ver. 18. After the expiry of the period of three years the youths were brought before the king. They were examined by him, and these four were found more intelligent and discriminating than all the others that had been educated along with them (מִכֻּלָּם, "than all," refers to the other Israelitish youths, ver. 3, that had been brought to Babylon along with Daniel and his friends), and were then appointed to his service. יַעַמְדוּ, as in ver. 5, of *standing as a servant before his master*. The king found them indeed, in all matters of wisdom about which he examined them, to excel all the wise men in the whole of his kingdom. Of the two classes of the learned men of Chaldea, who are named *instar omnium* in ver. 20, see at ch. ii. 2.

In ver. 21 the introduction to the book is concluded with a general statement as to the period of Daniel's continuance in the office appointed to him by God. The difficulty which the explanation of וַיְהִי offers is not removed by a change of the reading into וַיְחִי, since Daniel, according to ch. x. 1, lived beyond the first year of Cyrus and received divine revelations. עַד marks the *terminus ad quem* in a wide sense, *i.e.* it denotes a termination without reference to that which came after it. The first year of king Cyrus is, according to 2 Chron. xxxvi. 22, Ezra i. 1, vi. 3, the end of the Babylonish exile, and the date, "to the first year of king Cyrus," stands in close relation to the date in ver. 1, Nebuchadnezzar's advance against Jerusalem and the first taking of the city, which forms the commencement of the exile; so that the statement, "Daniel continued unto the first year of king Cyrus," means only that he lived and acted during the whole period of the exile in Babylon, without reference to the fact that his work continued after the termination of the exile. Cf. the analogous statement, Jer. i. 2 f., that Jeremiah prophesied in the days of Josiah and Jehoiakim to the end of the eleventh year of Zedekiah, although his book contains prophecies also of a date subsequent to the taking of Jerusalem. וַיְהִי stands neither for וַיְחִי, *he lived*, nor absolutely in the sense of *he existed, was present*; for though הָיָה means *existere, to be*, yet it is never used absolutely in this sense, as חָיָה, *to live*, but always only so that the "how" or "where" of the being or existence is either expressly stated, or at least is implied in the connection. Thus here also the qualification of the "being" must be supplied from the context. The expression will then mean, not that he lived at the court, or in Babylon, or in high esteem with the king, but more generally, in the place to which God had raised him in Babylon by his wonderful endowments.

PART FIRST.—THE DEVELOPMENT OF THE WORLD-POWER.

CHAP. II.-VII.

This Part contains in six chapters as many reports regarding the successive forms and the natural character of the world-power. It begins (ch. ii.) and ends (ch. vii.) with a revelation from God regarding its historical unfolding in four great world-kingdoms following each other, and their final overthrow by the kingdom of God, which shall continue for ever. Between these chapters (ii. and vii.) there are inserted four events belonging to the times of the first and second world-kingdom, which partly reveal the attempts of the rulers of the world to compel the worshippers of the true God to pray to their idols and their gods, together with the failure of this attempt (ch. iii. and vi.), and partly the humiliations of the rulers of the world, who were boastful of their power, under the judgments of God (ch. iv. and v.), and bring under our consideration the relation of the rulers of this world to the Almighty God of heaven and earth and to the true fearers of His name. The narratives of these four events follow each other in chronological order, because they are in actual relation bound together, and therefore also the occurrences (ch. v. and vi.) which belong to the time subsequent to the vision in ch. vii. are placed before this vision, so that the two revelations regarding the development of the world-power form the frame within which is contained the historical section which describes the character of that world-power.

CHAP. II. NEBUCHADNEZZAR'S VISION OF THE WORLD-MONARCHIES, AND ITS INTERPRETATION BY DANIEL.

When Daniel and his three friends, after the completion of their education, had entered on the service of the Chaldean king, Nebuchadnezzar dreamed a dream which so greatly moved him, that he called all the wise men of Babylon that they might make known to him the dream and give the interpretation of it; and when they were not able to do this, he gave forth the command (vers. 1–13) that they should all be destroyed. But Daniel interceded with the king and obtained a respite, at the expiry of which he promised (vers. 14–18) to comply with his demand. In answer to his prayers and those of his friends, God revealed the secret to Daniel in a vision (vers. 19–23), so that he was not only able to tell the king his dream (vers. 24–36), but also to give him its interpretation (vers. 37–45); whereupon Nebuchadnezzar praised the God of Daniel as the true God, and raised him to high honours and dignities (vers. 46–49). It has justly been regarded as a significant thing, that it was Nebuchadnezzar, the founder of the world-power, who first saw in a dream the whole future development of the world-power. "The world-power," as Auberlen properly remarks, "must itself learn in its first representative, who had put an end to the kingdom of God [the theocracy], what its own final destiny would be, that, in its turn overthrown, it would be for ever subject to the kingdom of God." This circumstance also is worthy of notice, that Nebuchadnezzar did not himself understand the revelation which he received, but the prophet Daniel, enlightened by God, must interpret it to him.[1]

[1] According to Bleek, Lengerke, Hitz., Ew., and others, the whole narrative is to be regarded as a pure invention, as to its plan formed in imitation of the several statements of the narrative in Gen. xli. of Pharaoh's dream and its interpretation by Joseph the Hebrew, when the Egyptian wise men were unable to do so. Nebuchadnezzar is the copy of Pharaoh, and at the same time the type of Antiochus Epiphanes, who was certainly a half-mad despot, as Nebuchadnezzar is here described to be, although he was not so in reality. But the resemblance between Pharaoh's dream and that of Nebuchadnezzar consists only in that (1) both kings had significant dreams which their own wise men could not interpret to them, but which were interpreted by Israelites by the help of God; (2) Joseph and Daniel in a similar manner, but not in the same words, directed the kings to God (cf. Gen. xli. 16, Dan. ii. 27, 28); and (3) that in both narratives the word פָּעַם [*was disquieted*] is used (Gen. xli. 8, Dan. ii. 1, 3). In all other respects the narratives are entirely different. But "the resemblance," as Hengst. has already well remarked (*Beitr.* i. p. 82), "is explained partly from the great significance which in ancient times was universally attached to dreams and their interpretation, partly from the dispensations of divine providence, which at different times has made use of this means for the deliverance of the chosen people." In addition to this, Kran., p. 70, has not less appropriately said: "But that only one belonging to the people of God should in both cases have had communicated to him the interpretation of the dream, is not more to be wondered at than that there is a true God who morally and spiritually supports and raises those who know and acknowledge Him,

Vers. 1–13. *The dream of Nebuchadnezzar and the inability of the Chaldean wise men to interpret it.*—By the ו copulative standing at the commencement of this chapter the following narrative is connected with ch. i. 21. "We shall now discover what the youthful Daniel became, and what he continued to be to the end of the exile" (Klief.). The plur. חֲלֹמוֹת (dreams, vers. 1 and 2), the singular of which occurs in ver. 3, is not the plur. of definite universality (Häv., Maur., Klief.), but of intensive fulness, implying that the dream in its parts contained a plurality of subjects. הִתְפָּעֵם (from פָּעַם, *to thrust, to strike*, as פַּעַם, an anvil, teaches, *to be tossed hither and thither*) marks great internal disquietude. In ver. 3 and in Gen. xli. 8, as in Ps. lxxvii. 5, it is in the Niphal form, but in ver. 1 it is in Hithp., on which Kran. finely remarks: "The Hithpael heightens the conception of internal unquiet lying in the Niphal to the idea that it makes itself outwardly manifest." His sleep was gone. This is evidenced without doubt by the last clause of ver. 1, נִהְיְתָה עָלָיו. These interpretations are altogether wrong:—"His sleep came upon him, *i.e.* he began again to sleep" (Calvin); or "his sleep was against him," *i.e.* was an aversion to him, was troublesome (L. de Dieu); or, as Häv. also interprets it, "his sleep offended him, or was like a burden heavy upon him;" for נִהְיָה does not mean *to fall*, and thus does not agree with the thought expressed. The Niph. נִהְיָה means *to have become, been, happened*. The meaning has already been rightly expressed by Theodoret in the words ἐγένετο ἀπ' αὐτοῦ,

according to psychological laws, even in a *peculiar* way." Moreover, if the word פעם was really borrowed from Gen. xli. 8, that would prove nothing more than that Daniel had read the books of Moses. But the grounds on which the above-named critics wish to prove the unhistorical character of this narrative are formed partly from a superficial consideration of the whole narrative and a manifestly false interpretation of separate parts of it, and partly from the dogmatic prejudice that "a particular foretelling of a remote future is not the nature of Hebrew prophecy," *i.e.* in other words, that there is no prediction arising from a supernatural revelation. Against the other grounds Kran. has already very truly remarked: "That the narrative of the actual circumstances wants (cf. Hitz. p. 17) proportion and unity, is not corroborated by a just view of the situation; the whole statement rather leaves the impression of a lively, fresh immediateness, in which a careful consideration of the circumstances easily furnishes the means for filling up the details of the brief sketch." Hence it follows that the contents of the dream show not the least resemblance to Pharaoh's dream, and in the whole story there is no trace seen of a hostile relation of Nebuchadnezzar and his courtiers to Judaism; nay rather Nebuchadnezzar's relation to the God of Daniel presents a decided contrast to the mad rage of Antiochus Epiphanes against the Jewish religion.

and in the Vulgate by the words "*fugit ab illo;*" and Berth., Ges., and others have with equal propriety remarked, that שְׁנָתוֹ נִהְיְתָה corresponds in meaning with שְׁנָתֶהּ נַדַּת, ch. vi. 19 (18), and נָדְדָה שְׁנַת, Esth. vi. 1. This sense, *to have been*, however, does not conduct to the meaning given by Klief.: *his sleep had been upon him;* it was therefore no more, it had gone; for "to have been" is not "to be no more," but "to be finished," past, gone. This meaning is confirmed by נִהְיֵיתִי, ch. viii. 27: *it was done with me, I was gone.* The עָלָיו stands not for the dative, but retains the meaning, *over, upon*, expressing the influence on the mind, as *e.g.* Jer. viii. 18, Hos. xi. 8, Ps. xlii. 6, 7, 12, xliii. 5, etc., which in German we express by the word *bei* or *für*.

The reason of so great disquietude we may not seek in the circumstance that on awaking he could not remember the dream. This follows neither from ver. 3, nor is it psychologically probable that so impressive a dream, which on awaking he had forgotten, should have yet sorely disquieted his spirit during his waking hours. "The disquiet was created in him, as in Pharaoh (Gen. xli.), by the specially striking incidents of the dream, and the fearful, alarming apprehensions with reference to his future fate connected therewith" (Kran.).

Ver. 2. In the disquietude of his spirit the king commanded all his astrologers and wise men to come to him, four classes of whom are mentioned in this verse. 1. The חַרְטֻמִּים, who were found also in Egypt (Gen. xli. 24). They are so named from חֶרֶט, a "stylus"—*those who went about with the stylus*, the priestly class of the ἱερογραμματεῖς, those learned in the sacred writings and in literature. 2. The אַשָּׁפִים, *conjurers*, from שָׁאַף or נָשַׁף, to breathe, to blow, to whisper; for they practised their incantations by movements of the breath, as is shown by the Arabic نفث, *flavit ut præstigiator in nexos a se nodos, incantavit*, with which it is compared by Hitz. and Kran. 3. The מְכַשְּׁפִים, *magicians*, found also in Egypt (Ex. vii. 11), and, according to Isa. xlvii. 9, 12, a powerful body in Babylon. 4. The כַּשְׂדִּים, *the priest caste of the Chaldeans*, who are named, vers. 4, 10, and ch. i. 4, *instar omnium* as the most distinguished class among the Babylonian wise men. According to Herod. i. 171, and Diod. Sic. ii. 24, the *Chaldeans* appear to have formed the priesthood in a special sense, or to have attended to the duties specially devolving on the priests. This circumstance, that amongst an *Aramaic* people the priests in a stricter sense were called Chaldeans, is explained, as at p. 78, from the fact of the ancient supremacy of the Chaldean people in Babylonia.

Besides these four classes there is also a fifth, ver. 27, ch. iv. 4 (7), v. 7, 11, called the גָּזְרִין, the *astrologers*, not *haruspices*, from גְּזַר, "to cut flesh to pieces," but the *determiners* of the גְּזֵרָה, the *fatum* or the *fata*, who announced events by the appearances of the heavens (cf. Isa. xlvii. 13), the forecasters of nativities, horoscopes, who determined the fate of men from the position and the movement of the stars at the time of their birth. These different classes of the priests and the learned are comprehended, ver. 12 ff., under the general designation of חַכִּימִין (cf. also Isa. xliv. 25, Jer. l. 35), and they formed a *σύστημα*, *i.e. collegium* (Diod. Sic. ii. 31), under a president (רַב סִגְנִין, ver. 48), who occupied a high place in the state; see at ver. 48. These separate classes busied themselves, without doubt, with distinct branches of the Babylonian wisdom. While each class cultivated a separate department, yet it was not exclusively, but in such a manner that the activities of the several classes intermingled in many ways. This is clearly seen from what is said of Daniel and his companions, that they were trained in *all* the wisdom of the Chaldeans (ch. i. 17), and is confirmed by the testimony of Diod. Sic. (ii. 29), that the Chaldeans, who held almost the same place in the state that the priests in Egypt did, while applying themselves to the service of the gods, sought their greatest glory in the study of astrology, and also devoted themselves much to prophecy, foretelling future things, and by means of lustrations, sacrifices, and incantations seeking to turn away evil and to secure that which was good. They possessed the knowledge of divination from omens, of expounding of dreams and prodigies, and of skilfully casting horoscopes.

That he might receive an explanation of his dream, Nebuchadnezzar commanded all the classes of the priests and men skilled in wisdom to be brought before him, because in an event which was to him so weighty he must not only ascertain the facts of the case, but should the dream announce some misfortune, he must also adopt the means for averting it. In order that the correctness of the explanation of the dream might be ascertained, the stars must be examined, and perhaps other means of divination must be resorted to. The proper priests could by means of sacrifices make the gods favourable, and the conjurers and magicians by their arts endeavour to avert the threatened misfortune.

Ver. 3. As to the king's demand, it is uncertain whether he

wished to know the dream itself or its import. The wise men (ver. 4) understood his words as if he desired only to know the meaning of it; but the king replied (ver. 5 ff.) that they must tell him both the dream and its interpretation. But this request on the part of the king does not quite prove that he had forgotten the dream, as Bleek, v. Leng., and others maintain, founding thereon the objection against the historical veracity of the narrative, that Nebuchadnezzar's demand that the dream should be told to him was madness, and that there was no sufficient reason for his rage (ver. 12). On the contrary, that the king had not forgotten his dream, and that there remained only some oppressive recollection that he had dreamed, is made clear from ver. 9, where the king says to the Chaldeans, "If ye cannot declare to me the dream, ye have taken in hand to utter deceitful words before me; therefore tell me the dream, that I may know that ye will give to me also the interpretation." According to this, Nebuchadnezzar wished to hear the dream from the wise men that he might thus have a guarantee for the correctness of the interpretation which they might give. He could not thus have spoken to them if he had wholly forgotten the dream, and had only a dark apprehension remaining in his mind that he had dreamed. In this case he would neither have offered a great reward for the announcement of the dream, nor have threatened severe punishment, or even death, for failure in announcing it. For then he would only have given the Chaldeans the opportunity, at the cost of truth, of declaring any dream with an interpretation. But as threatening and promise on the part of the king in that case would have been unwise, so also on the side of the wise men their helplessness in complying with the demand of the king would have been incomprehensible. If the king had truly forgotten the dream, they had no reason to be afraid of their lives if they had given some self-conceived dream with an interpretation of it; for in that case he could not have accused them of falsehood and deceit, and punished them on that account. If, on the contrary, he still knew the dream which so troubled him, and the contents of which he desired to hear from the Chaldeans, so that he might put them to the proof whether he might trust in their interpretation, then neither his demand nor the severity of his proceeding was irrational. "The magi boasted that by the help of the gods they could reveal deep and hidden things. If this pretence is well founded—so concluded Nebuchadnezzar—then it must be as easy for them to make known to me my dream as its interpretation; and since they could not do the former, he as rightly held them to be deceivers, as the people did the priests of Baal (1 Kings xviii.) because their gods answered not by fire." Hengst.

Ver. 4. The Chaldeans, as speaking for the whole company, understand the word of the king in the sense most favourable for themselves, and they ask the king to tell them the dream. וַיְדַבְּרוּ for וַיֹּאמְרוּ, which as a rule stands before a quotation, is occasioned by the addition of אֲרָמִית, and the words which follow are zeugmatically joined to it. *Aramaic, i.e.* in the native language of Babylonia, where, according to Xenoph. (*Cyrop.* vii. 5), the *Syriac, i.e.* the Eastern Aramaic dialect, was spoken. From the statement here, that the Chaldeans spoke to the king in Aramaic, one must not certainly conclude that Nebuchadnezzar spoke the Aryan-Chaldaic language of his race. The remark refers to the circumstance that the following words are recorded in the Aramaic, as Ezra iv. 7. Daniel wrote this and the following chapters in Aramaic, that he might give the prophecy regarding the world-power in the language of the world-power, which under the Chaldean dynasty was native in Babylon, the Eastern Aramaic. The formula, "O king, live for ever," was the usual salutation when the king was addressed, both at the Chaldean and the Persian court (cf. ch. iii. 9, v. 10, vi. 7, 22 [6, 21]; Neh. ii. 3). In regard to the Persian court, see Ælian, *var. hist.* i. 32. With the kings of Israel this form of salutation was but rarely used: 1 Sam. x. 24; 1 Kings i. 31. The *Kethiv* (text) לְעַבְדָיךְ, with Jod before the suffix, supposes an original form לְעַבְדַיִךְ here, as at ver. 26, ch. iv. 16, 22, but it is perhaps only the etymological mode of writing for the form with *ā* long, analogous to the Hebr. suffix form עָיו for עָו, since the Jod is often wanting; cf. ch. iv. 24, v. 10, etc. A form ־ָאיָא lies at the foundation of the form כַּשְׂדָּיֵא; the *Keri* (margin) substitutes the usual Chaldee form כַּשְׂדָּאֵי from כַּשְׂדָּאָה, with the insertion of the *litera quiescib.* ', homog. to the quies. *ē*, while in the *Kethiv* the original Jod of the sing. כַּשְׂדָּי is retained instead of the substituted א, thus כַּשְׂדָּיֵא. This reading is perfectly warranted (cf. ch. iii. 2, 8, 24; Ezra iv. 12, 13) by the analogous method of formation of the *stat. emphat. plur.* in existing nouns in ־ָי in biblical Chaldee.

Ver. 5. The meaning of the king's answer shapes itself differently according to the different explanations given of the words מִלְּתָה מִנִּי אַזְדָּא. The word אַזְדָּא, which occurs only again in the same phrase in ver. 8, is regarded, in accordance with the translations of Theodot., ὁ λόγος ἀπ' ἐμοῦ ἀπέστη, and of the Vulg., "*sermo recessit a me*," as a verb, and as of like meaning with אֲזַל, "to go away or depart," and is therefore rendered by M. Geier, Berth., and others in the sense, "the dream has escaped from me;" but Ges., Häv., and many older interpreters translate it, on the contrary, "the command is gone out from me." But without taking into account that the punctuation of the word אַזְדָּא is not at all that of a verb, for this form can neither be a particip. nor the 3d pers. pret. fem., no acknowledgment of the dream's having escaped from him is made; for such a statement would contradict what was said at ver. 3, and would not altogether agree with the statement of ver. 8. מִלְּתָה is not *the dream*. Besides, the supposition that אֲזַד is equivalent to אֲזַל, to go away, depart, is not tenable. The change of the ל into ד is extremely rare in the Semitic, and is not to be assumed in the word אזל, since Daniel himself uses אֲזַל, ch. ii. 17, 24, vi. 19, 20, and also Ezra, iv. 23, v. 8, 15. Moreover אזל has not the meaning of יְצָא, to go out, to take one's departure, but corresponds with the Hebr. הָלַךְ, to go. Therefore Winer, Hengst., Ibn Esr. [Aben Ezra], Saad., and other rabbis interpret the word as meaning *firmus*: "the word stands firm;" cf. ch. vi. 13 (12), יַצִּיבָה מִלְּתָא ("the thing is true"). This interpretation is justified by the actual import of the words, as it also agrees with ver. 8; but it does not accord with ver. 5. Here (in ver. 5) the declaration of the certainty of the king's word was superfluous, because all the royal commands were unchangeable. For this reason also the meaning σπουδαιῶς, studiously, earnestly, as Hitz., by a fanciful reference to the Persian, whence he has derived it, has explained it, is to be rejected. Much more satisfactory is the derivation from the Old Persian word found on inscriptions, *âzanda*, "science," "that which is known," given by Delitzsch (Herz.'s *Realenc.* iii. p. 274), and adopted by Kran. and Klief.[1] Accordingly Klief. thus interprets the phrase: "let the word from me be known," "be it known to you;" which is more suitable obviously than that of Kran.: "the command is, so far as regards

[1] In regard to the explanation of the word אַזְדָּא as given above, it is, however, to be remarked that it is not confirmed, and Delitzsch has for the present given it up, because—as he has informed me—the word *azdâ*, which appears once in the large inscription of Behistan (Bisutun) and twice in the inscription of Nakhschi-Rustam, is of uncertain reading and meaning. Spiegel explains it "unknown," from *zan*, to know, and *a privativum*.

me, made public." For the king now for the first time distinctly and definitely says that he wishes not only to hear from the wise men the interpretation, but also the dream itself, and declares the punishment that shall visit them in the event of their not being able to comply. עֲבַד הַדָּמִין, μέλη ποιεῖν, 2 Macc. i. 16, LXX. in Dan. iii. 39, διαμελίζεσθαι, *to cut in pieces*, a punishment that was common among the Babylonians (ch. iii. 39, cf. Ezek. xvi. 40), and also among the Israelites in the case of prisoners of war (cf. 1 Sam. xv. 33). It is not, however, to be confounded with the barbarous custom which was common among the Persians, of mangling particular limbs. נְוָלִי, in Ezra vi. 11 נְוָלוּ, *dunghill, sink.* The changing of their houses into dunghills is not to be regarded as meaning that the house built of clay would be torn down, and then dissolved by the rain and storm into a heap of mud, but is to be interpreted according to 2 Kings x. 27, where the temple of Baal is spoken of as having been broken down and converted into private closets; cf. Häv. *in loco*. The *Keri* תִּתְעַבְדוּן without the Dagesh in ב might stand as the *Kethiv* for Ithpaal, but is apparently the Ithpeal, as at ch. iii. 29, Ezra vi. 11. As to בָּתֵּיכוֹן, it is to be remarked that Daniel uses only the suffix forms כוֹן and הוֹן, while with Ezra כֹם and כֻן are interchanged (see above, p. 45), which are found in the language of the Targums and might be regarded as Hebraisms, while the forms כוֹן and הוֹן are peculiar to the Syriac and the Samaritan dialects. This distinction does not prove that the Aramaic of Daniel belongs to a period later than that of Ezra (Hitz., v. Leng.), but only that Daniel preserves more faithfully the familiar Babylonian form of the Aramaic than does the Jewish scribe Ezra.

Ver. 6. The rigorous severity of this edict accords with the character of Oriental despots and of Nebuchadnezzar, particularly in his dealings with the Jews (2 Kings xxv. 7, 18 ff.; Jer. xxxix. 6 f., lii. 10 f., 24–27). In the promise of rewards the explanation of נְבִזְבָּה (in the plur. נְבִזְבְּיָן, ch. v. 17) is disputed; its rendering by "money," "gold" (by Eichh. and Berth.), has been long ago abandoned as incorrect. The meaning *gift, present*, is agreeable to the context and to the ancient versions; but its derivation formed from the Chald. בזבז, Pealp. of בְּזַז, *erogavit, expendit*, by the substitution of נ for מ and the excision of the second ז from מְבִזְבְּזָה, in the meaning *largitio amplior*, the Jod in the plural form being explained from the affinity of verbs ע"ע and ל"ה (Ges. *Thes.* p. 842, and Kran.), is highly improbable. The derivation from the Persian *nuvâzan, nuvâzisch*, to caress, to flatter, then to make a present to (P. v. Bohlen), or from the Sanscr. *namas*, present, gift (Hitz.), or from the Vedish *bag′*, to give, to distribute, and the related New Persian *bâj* (*bash*), a present (Haug), are also very questionable. לָהֵן, *on that account*, *therefore* (cf. ver. 9 and ch. iv. 24), formed from the prepos. לְ and the demonstrative adverb הֵן, has in negative sentences (as the Hebr. כִּי and לָהֵן) the meaning *but*, *rather* (ch. ii. 30), and in a pregnant sense, *only* (ch. ii. 11, iii. 28, vi. 8), without לָהֵן being derived in such instances from לָא and הֵן = אִם לֹא

Ver. 7. The wise men repeat their request, but the king persists that they only justify his suspicion of them by pressing such a demand, and that he saw that they wished to deceive him with a self-conceived interpretation of the dream. וּפִשְׁרָה is not, as Hitz. proposes, to be changed into וּפִשְׁרֵהּ. The form is a Hebr. *stat. emphat.* for וּפִשְׁרָא, as *e.g.* מִלְּתָה, ver. 5, is changed into מִלְּתָא in vers. 8 and 11, and in biblical Chaldee, in final syllables ה is often found instead of א.—Ver. 8. מִן יַצִּיב, an adverbial expression, to be sure, certainly, as מִן קְשֹׁט, truly, ver. 47, and other adverbial forms. The words דִּי עִדָּנָא אַנְתּוּן זָבְנִין do not mean either "that ye wish to use or seize the favourable time" (Häv., Kran.), or "that ye wish to buy up the present perilous moment," *i.e.* bring it within your power, become masters of the time (Hitz.), but simply, *that ye buy*, that is *wish to gain time* (Ges., Maur., etc.). זְבַן עִדָּן = *tempus emere* in Cicero. Nothing can be here said of a favourable moment, for there was not such a time for the wise men, either in the fact that Nebuchadnezzar had forgotten his dream (Häv.), or in the curiosity of the king with reference to the interpretation of the dream, on which they could speculate, expecting that the king might be induced thereby to give a full communication of the dream (Kran.). But for the wise men, in consequence of the threatening of the king, the crisis was indeed full of danger; but it is not to be overlooked that they appeared to think that they could control the crisis, bringing it under their own power, by their willingness to interpret the dream if it were reported to them. Their repeated request that the dream should be told to them shows only their purpose to gain time and save their lives, if they now truly believed either that the king could not now distinctly remember his dream, or that by not repeating it he wished to put them to the test. Thus the king says to them: I see from your hesitation that ye are not sure of your case; and since ye at the same time think that I have forgotten the dream, therefore ye wish me, by your repeated requests to relate the dream, only to gain time, to extend the case, because ye fear the threatened punishment (Klief.). כָּל־קֳבֵל דִּי, *wholly because;* not, *notwithstanding that* (Hitz.). As to the last words of ver. 8, see under ver. 5.

Ver. 9. דִּי הֵן is equivalent to אֲשֶׁר אִם, *quodsi.* "The דִּי supposes the fact of the foregoing passage, and brings it into express relation to the conditional clause" (Kran.). דָּתְכוֹן does not mean, your design or opinion, or your lot (Mich., Hitz., Maur.), but דָּת is *law, decree, sentence;* דָּתְכוֹן, *the sentence that is going forth* or has gone forth against you, *i.e.* according to ver. 5, the sentence of death. חֲדָה, *one,* or the one and no other. This judgment is founded on the following passage, in which the cop. ו is to be explained as equivalent to *namely.* כִּדְבָה וּשְׁחִיתָה, *lies and pernicious words,* are united together for the purpose of strengthening the idea, in the sense of *wicked lies* (Hitz.). הזמנתון is not to be read, as Häv., v. Leng., Maur., and Kran. do, as the Aphel הַזְמִנְתּוּן : *ye have prepared* or resolved to say; for in the Aphel this word (זְמַן) means *to appoint* or *summon a person,* but not to prepare or appoint a thing (see Buxt. *Lex. Tal. s. v.*). And the supposition that the king addressed the Chaldeans as the speakers appointed by the whole company of the wise men (Kran.) has no place in the text. The *Kethiv* הַזְמִנְתּוּן is to be read as Ithpa. for הִזְדַּמִּנְתּוּן according to the *Keri* (cf. הִזַּכּוּ for הִזְדַּכּוּ, Isa. i. 16), meaning *inter se convenire,* as the old interpreters rendered it. "Till the time be changed," *i.e.* till the king either drop the matter, or till they learn something more particular about the dream through some circumstances that may arise. The lies which Nebuchadnezzar charged the wise men with, consisted in the explanation which they promised if he would tell them the dream, while their desire to hear the dream contained a proof that they had not the faculty of revealing secrets. The words of the king clearly show that he knew the dream, for otherwise he would not have been able to know whether the wise men spoke the truth in telling him the dream (Klief.).

Ver. 10. Since the king persisted in his demand, the Chaldeans were compelled to confess that they could not tell the dream. This confession, however, they seek to conceal under the explanation that compliance with the king's request was beyond human power, —a request which no great or mighty king had ever before made of any magician or astrologer, and which was possible only with the gods, who however do not dwell among mortals. כָּל־קֳבֵל דִּי does not mean *quam ob rem*, wherefore, as a particle expressive of a consequence (Ges.), but is here used in the sense of *because*, assigning a reason. The thought expressed is not: because the matter is impossible for men, therefore no king has ever asked any such thing; but it is this: because it has come into the mind of no great and mighty king to demand any such thing, therefore it is impossible for men to comply with it. They presented before the king the fact that no king had ever made such a request as a proof that the fulfilling of it was beyond human ability. The epithets great and mighty are here not mere titles of the Oriental kings (Häv.), but are chosen as significant. The mightier the king, so much the greater the demand, he believed, he might easily make upon a subject.

Ver. 11. לָהֵן, *but only*, see under ver. 6. In the words, *whose dwelling is not with flesh*, there lies neither the idea of higher and of inferior gods, nor the thought that the gods only act among men in certain events (Häv.), but only the simple thought of the essential distinction between gods and men, so that one may not demand anything from weak mortals which could be granted only by the gods as celestial beings. בִּשְׂרָא, *flesh*, in opposition to רוּחַ, marks the human nature according to its weakness and infirmity; cf. Isa. xxxi. 3, Ps. lvi. 5. The king, however, does not admit this excuse, but falls into a violent passion, and gives a formal command that the wise men, in whom he sees deceivers abandoned by the gods, should be put to death. This was a dreadful command; but there are illustrations of even greater cruelty perpetrated by Oriental despots before him as well as after him. The edict (דָּתָא) is carried out, but not fully. Not "all the wise men," according to the terms of the decree, were put to death, but חַכִּימַיָּא מִתְקַטְּלִין, *i.e. the wise men were put to death.*

Ver. 13. While it is manifest that the decree was not carried fully out, it is yet clearer from what follows that the participle מִתְקַטְּלִין does not stand for the preterite, but has the meaning: *the work of putting to death was begun.* The participle also does not stand as the gerund: they were to be put to death, *i.e.* were condemned (Kran.), for the use of the passive participle as the gerund is not made good by a reference to מהימן, ch. ii. 45, and דְּחִיל, ch. ii. 31. Even the command to kill all the wise men of Babylon is scarcely to be understood of all the wise men of the whole kingdom. The word Babylon may represent the Babylonian empire, or the province of Babylonia, or the city of Babylon only.

In the city of Babylon a college of the Babylonian wise men or Chaldeans was established, who, according to Strabo (xv. 1. 6), occupied a particular quarter of the city as their own; but besides this, there were also colleges in the province of Babylon at *Hipparenum*, *Orchœ*, which Plin. *hist. nat.* vi. 26 (30) designates as *tertia Chaldœorum doctrina*, at *Borsippa*, and other places. The wise men who were called (ver. 2) into the presence of the king, were naturally those who resided in the city of Babylon, for Nebuchadnezzar was at that time in his palace. Yet of those who had their residence there, Daniel and his companions were not summoned, because they had just ended their noviciate, and because, obviously, only the presidents or the older members of the several classes were sent for. But since Daniel and his companions belonged to the whole body of the wise men, they also were sought out that they might be put to death.

Vers. 14–30. *Daniel's willingness to declare his dream to the king; his prayer for a revelation of the secret, and the answer to his prayer; his explanation before the king.*

Ver. 14. Through Daniel's judicious interview with Arioch, the further execution of the royal edict was interrupted. הֲתִיב עֵטָא וּטְעֵם, *he answered, replied, counsel and understanding, i.e.* the words of counsel and understanding; cf. Prov. xxvi. 16. The name *Arioch* appears in Gen. xiv. 1 as the name of the king of Ellasar, along with the kings of Elam and Shinar. It is derived not from the Sanscr. *ârjaka, venerabilis*, but is probably formed from אֲרִי, a lion, as נִסְרֹךְ from *nisr* = נֶשֶׁר. רַב־טַבָּחַיָּא is *the chief of the body-guard*, which was regarded as the highest office of the kingdom (cf. Jer. xxxix. 9, 11, xl. 1 ff.). It was his business to see to the execution of the king's commands; see 1 Kings ii. 25, 2 Kings xxv. 8.

Ver. 15. The partic. Aph. מְהַחְצְפָה standing after the noun in the *stat. absol.* is not predicative: "on what account is the command so hostile on the part of the king?" (Kran.), but it stands in apposition to the noun; for with participles, particularly when further definitions follow, the article, even in union with substantives defined by the article, may be and often is omitted; cf. Song vii. 5, and Ew. § 335 *a*. חֲצַף, *to be hard, sharp*, hence *to be severe*. Daniel showed understanding and counsel in the question he put as to the cause of so severe a command, inasmuch as he thereby gave Arioch to understand that there was a possibility of obtaining a fulfilment of the royal wish. When Arioch informed him of the state of the matter, Daniel went in to the king—*i.e.*, as is expressly mentioned in ver. 24, was introduced or brought in by Arioch—and presented to the king the request that time should be granted, promising that he would show to the king the interpretation of the dream.

Ver. 16. With וּפִשְׁרָא לְהַחֲוָיָה the construction is changed. This passage does not depend on דִּי, *time*, namely, to show the interpretation (Hitz.), but is co-ordinate with the foregoing relative clause, and like it is dependent on וּבְעָא. The change of the construction is caused by the circumstance that in the last passage another subject needed to be introduced: The king should give him time, and Daniel will show the interpretation. The copulative ו before פִּשְׁרָא (interpretation) is used neither explicatively, *namely, and indeed,* nor is it to be taken as meaning *also ;* the simple *and* is sufficient, although the second part of the request contains the explanation and reason of the first; *i.e.* Daniel asks for the granting of a space, not that he might live longer, but that he might be able to interpret the dream to the king. Besides, that he merely speaks of the meaning of the dream, and not also of the dream itself, is, as vers. 25 ff. show, to be here explained (as in ver. 24) as arising from the brevity of the narrative. For the same reason it is not said that the king granted the request, but ver. 17 f. immediately shows what Daniel did after the granting of his request. He went into his own house and showed the matter to his companions, that they might entreat God of His mercy for this secret, so that they might not perish along with the rest of the wise men of Babylon.

Ver. 18*a*. The final clause depends on הוֹדַע (v. 17). The ו is to be interpreted as explicative: *and indeed*, or *namely*. Against this interpretation it cannot be objected, with Hitz., that Daniel also prayed. He and his friends thus prayed to God that He would grant a revelation of the secret, *i.e.* of the mysterious dream and its interpretation. The designation "God of heaven" occurs in Gen. xxiv. 7, where it is used of Jehovah; but it was first commonly used as the designation of the almighty and true God in the time of the exile (cf. vers. 19, 44; Ezra i. 2, vi. 10, vii. 12, 21; Neh. i. 5, ii. 4; Ps. cxxxvi. 26), who, as Daniel names Him (ch. v. 23), is the Lord of heaven; *i.e.* the whole heavens, with all the stars, which the heathen worshipped as gods, are under His dominion.

Ver. 19. In answer to these supplications, the secret was revealed to Daniel in a night-vision. A vision of the night is not necessarily to be identified with a dream. In the case before us,

Daniel does not speak of a dream; and the idea that he had dreamed precisely the same dream as Nebuchadnezzar is arbitrarily imported into the text by Hitz. in order to gain a "psychological impossibility," and to be able to cast suspicion on the historical character of the narrative. It is possible, indeed, that dreams may be, as the means of a divine revelation, dream-visions, and as such may be called visions of the night (cf. vii. 1, 13); but in itself a vision of the night is a vision simply which any one receives during the night whilst he is awake.[1]

Ver. 20. On receiving the divine revelation, Daniel answered (עָנֵה) with a prayer of thanksgiving. The word עֲנֵה retains its proper meaning. The revelation is of the character of an address from God, which Daniel answers with praise and thanks to God. The forms לֶהֱוֵא, and in the plur. לֶהֱוֹן and לֶהֶוְיָן, which are peculiar to the biblical Chaldee, we regard, with Maur., Hitz., Kran., and others, as the imperfect or future forms, 3d pers. sing. and plur., in which the ל instead of the י is to be explained perhaps from the Syriac præform. נ, which is frequently found also in the Chaldee Targums (cf. Dietrich, *de sermonis chald. proprietate*, p. 43), while the Hebrew exiles in the word הֱוָא used ל instead of נ as more easy of utterance. The doxology in this verse reminds us of Job i. 21. The expression "*for ever and ever*" occurs here in the O. T. for the first time, so that the solemn liturgical Beracha (*Blessing*) of the second temple, Neh. ix. 5, 1 Chron. xvi. 36, with which also the first (Ps. xlv. 14) and the fourth (Ps. cvi. 48) books of the Psalter conclude, appears to have been composed after this form of praise used by Daniel. "The name of God" will be praised, *i.e.* the manifestation of the existence of God in the world; thus, God so far as He has anew given manifestation of His glorious existence, and continually bears witness that He it is who possesses

[1] "*Dream* and *vision* do not constitute two separate categories. The dream-*image* is a vision, the vision while awake is a dreaming—only that in the latter case the consciousness of the relation between the inner and the outer maintains itself more easily. Intermediate between the two stand the *night-visions*, which, as in Job iv. 13, either having risen up before the spirit, fade away from the mind in after-thought, or, as in the case of Nebuchadnezzar (Dan. ii. 29), are an image before the imagination into which the thoughts of the night run out. Zechariah saw a number of visions in one night, ch. i. 7, vi. 15. Also these which, according to ch. i. 8, are called visions of the night are not, as Ew. and Hitz. suppose, dream-images, but are waking perceptions in the night. Just because the prophet did not sleep, he says, ch. iv., 'The angel awaked me *as one is awaked out of sleep*.'"—THOLUCK'S *Die Propheten*, u.s.w., p. 52.

wisdom and strength (cf. Job xii. 13). The דִּי before the לֵהּ is the emphatic re-assumption of the preceding confirmatory דִּי, *for*.

Vers. 21, 22. The evidence of the wisdom and power of God is here unfolded; and first the manifestation of His power. *He changes times and seasons.* LXX., Theodot., *καιροὺς καὶ χρόνους*, would be more accurately *χρόνους καὶ καιρούς*, as in Acts i. 7, 1 Thess. v. 1; for the Peschito in these N. T. passages renders *χρόνοι* by the Syriac word which is equivalent to זִמְנַיָּא, according to which עִדָּן is the more general expression for time = circumstance of time, זְמָן for measured time, the definite point of time. The uniting together of the synonymous words gives expression to the thought: *ex arbitrio Dei pendere revolutiones omnium omnino temporum, quæcunque et qualia-cunque illa fuerint.* C. B. Mich. God's unlimited control over seasons and times is seen in this, that He sets up and casts down kings. Thus Daniel explains the revelation regarding the dream of Nebuchadnezzar made to him as announcing great changes in the kingdoms of the world, and revealing God as the Lord of time and of the world in their developments. All wisdom also comes from God. He gives to men disclosures regarding His hidden counsels. This Daniel had just experienced. Illumination dwells with God as it were a person, as Wisdom, Prov. viii. 30. The *Kethiv* נְהִירָא is maintained against the *Keri* by נַהִירוּ, ch. v. 11, 14. With the perf. שְׁרֵא the participial construction passes over into the *temp. fin.*; the perfect stands in the sense of the completed act. Therefore (ver. 23) praise and thanksgiving belong to God. Through the revelation of the secret hidden to the wise men of this world He has proved Himself to Daniel as the God of the fathers, as the true God in opposition to the gods of the heathen. וּכְעַן = וְעַתָּה, *and now.*

Vers. 24 ff. Hereupon Daniel announced to the king that he was prepared to make known to him the dream with its interpretation. כָּל־קֳבֵל דְּנָה, *for that very reason*, viz. because God had revealed to him the king's matter, Daniel was brought in by Arioch before the king; for no one had free access to the king except his immediate servants. אֲזַל, *he went*, takes up *inconsequenter* the עַל (*intravit*), which is separated by a long sentence, so as to connect it with what follows. Arioch introduced (ver. 25) Daniel to the king as a man from among the captive Jews who could make known to him the interpretation of his dream. Arioch did not need to take any special notice of the fact that Daniel had already (ver. 16) spoken with the king concerning it, even if he had knowledge of it. In the form הַנְעֵל, ver. 25, also ch. iv. 3 (6) and vi. 19 (18), the Dagesch lying in הָעֵל, ver. 24, is compensated by an epenthetic נ: cf. Winer, *Chald. Gram.* § 19, 1. בְּהִתְבְּהָלָה, *in haste*, for the matter concerned the further execution of the king's command, which Arioch had suspended on account of Daniel's interference, and his offer to make known the dream and its interpretation. הַשְׁכַּחַת for אַשְׁכַּחַת, cf. Winer, § 15, 3. The relative דִּי, which many *Codd.* insert after גְּבַר, is the circumstantially fuller form of expression before prepositional passages. Cf. ch. v. 13, vi. 14; Winer, § 41, 5.

Vers. 26, 27. To the question of the king, whether he was able to show the dream with its interpretation, Daniel replies by directing him from man, who is unable to accomplish such a thing, to the living God in heaven, who alone reveals secrets. The expression, *whose name was Belteshazzar* (ver. 26), intimates in this connection that he who was known among the Jews by the name Daniel was known to the Chaldean king only under the name given to him by the conqueror—that Nebuchadnezzar knew of no Daniel, but only of Belteshazzar. The question, "*art thou able?*" *i.e.* hast thou ability? does not express the king's ignorance of the person of Daniel, but only his amazement at his ability to make known the dream, in the sense, "art thou really able?" This amazement Daniel acknowledges as justified, for he replies that no wise man was able to do this thing. In the enumeration of the several classes of magicians the word חַכִּימִין is the general designation of them all. "But there is a God in heaven." Daniel "declares in the presence of the heathen the existence of God, before he speaks to him of His works." Klief. But when he testifies of a God in heaven as One who is able to reveal hidden things, he denies this ability *eo ipso* to all the so-called gods of the heathen. Thereby he not only assigns the reason of the inability of the heathen wise men, who knew not the living God in heaven, to show the divine mysteries, but he refers also all the revelations which the heathen at any time receive to the one true God. The ו in וְהוֹדַע introduces the development of the general thought. That there is a God in heaven who reveals secrets, Daniel declares to the king by this, that he explains his dream as an inspiration of this God, and shows to him its particular circumstances. God made known to him in a dream "what would happen in the end of the days." אַחֲרִית יוֹמַיָּא=אַחֲרִית הַיָּמִים designates here not the future generally (Häv.), and still less "that which comes after the days, a time which follows after another time, comprehended under the הַיָּמִים" (Klief.), but the concluding future or the Messianic period of the world's time; see Gen. xlix. 1.

From אַחֲרֵי דְנָה in ver. 29 that general interpretation of the expression is not proved. The expression בְּאַחֲרִית יוֹמַיָּא of ver. 28 is not explained by the מָה דִּי לֶהֱוֵא אַחֲרֵי דְנָה of ver. 29, but this אחרי דנה relates to Nebuchadnezzar's thoughts of a future in the history of the world, to which God, the revealer of secrets, unites His Messianic revelations; moreover, every Messianic future event is also an אַחֲרֵי דְנָה (cf. ver. 45), without, however, every אַחֲרֵי דְנָה being also Messianic, though it may become so when at the same time it is a constituent part of the future experience and the history of Israel, the people of the Messianic promise (Kran.). "The visions of thy head" (cf. iv. 2 [5], 7 [10], 10 [13], vii. 1) are not dream-visions because they formed themselves in the head or brains (v. Leng., Maur., Hitz.), which would thus be only phantoms or fancies. The words are not a poetic expression for dreams hovering about the head (Häv.); nor yet can we say, with Klief., that "the visions of thy head upon thy bed, the vision which thou sawest as thy head lay on thy pillow," mean only dream-visions. Against the former interpretation this may be stated, that dreams from God do not hover about the head; and against the latter, that the mention of the head would in that case be superfluous. The expression, peculiar to Daniel, designates much rather the divinely ordered visions as such, "as were perfectly consistent with a thoughtfulness of the head actively engaged" (Kran.). The singular דְּנָה הוּא goes back to חֶלְמָךְ (thy dream) as a fundamental idea, and is governed by וְחֶזְוֵי רֵאשָׁךְ in the sense: "thy dream with the visions of thy head;" cf. Winer, § 49, 6. The plur. חֶזְוֵי is used, because the revelation comprehends a series of visions of future events.

Ver. 29. The pronoun אַנְתָּה (*as for thee*), as Daniel everywhere writes it, while the *Keri* substitutes for it the later Targ. form אַנְתְּ, is absolute, and forms the contrast to the וַאֲנָה (*as for me*) of ver. 30. The thoughts of the king are not his dream (Hitz.), but thoughts about the future of his kingdom which filled his mind as he lay upon his bed, and to which God gave him an answer in the dream (v. Leng., Maur., Kran., Klief.). Therefore they are to be distinguished from *the thoughts of thy heart*, ver. 30, for these are the thoughts that troubled the king, which arose from the revelations of the dream to him. The contrast in ver. 30*a* and 30*b* is not this: "not for my wisdom before all that live to show," but "for the sake of the king to explain the dream;" for ב is not the preposition of the object, but of the means, thus: "not by the wisdom which might be in me." The supernatural revelation (גְּלִי לִי) forms the contrast, and the object to which עַל־דִּבְרַת דִּי points is comprehended *implicite* in מִן־כָּל־חַיַּיָּא, for in the words, "the wisdom which may be in me before all living," lies the unexpressed thought: that I should be enlightened by such superhuman wisdom. יְהוֹדְעוּן, "*that they might make it known:*" the plur. of undefined generality, cf. Winer, § 49, 3. The impersonal form of expression is chosen in order that his own person might not be brought into view. The idea of Aben Ezra, Vatke, and others, that angels are the subject of the verb, is altogether untenable.

Vers. 31–45. *The Dream and its Interpretation.*—Nebuchadnezzar saw in his dream a great metallic image which was terrible to look upon. אֲלוּ (*behold*), which Daniel interchanges with אֲרוּ, corresponds with the Hebrew words רְאֵה, רְאוּ, or הִנֵּה. צְלֵם is not an idol-image (Hitz.), but *a statue*, and, as is manifest from the following description, *a statue in human form*. חַד is not the indefinite article (Ges., Win., Maur.), but the numeral. "The world-power is in all its phases one, therefore all these phases are united in the vision in *one* image" (Klief.). The words from צַלְמָא to יַתִּיר contain two parenthetical expressions, introduced for the purpose of explaining the conception of שַׂגִּיא (*great*). קָאֵם is to be united with וַאֲלוּ. דִּכֵּן here and at ch. vii. 20 f. is used by Daniel as a peculiar form of the demonstrative pronoun, for which Ezra uses דֵּךְ. The appearance of the colossal image was terrible, not only on account of its greatness and its metallic splendour, but because it represented the world-power of fearful import to the people of God (Klief.).

Vers. 32, 33. The description of the image according to its several parts is introduced with the absolute הוּא צַלְמָא, *concerning this image*, not: "this was the image." The pronoun הוּא is made prominent, as דְּנָה, ch. iv. 15, and the Hebr. זֶה more frequently, *e.g.* Isa. xxiii. 13. חֲדוֹהִי, plur. חֲדִין—its singular occurs only in the Targums—corresponding with the Hebr. חָזֶה, *the breast*. מְעִין, the bowels, here the abdomen enclosing the bowels, *the belly*. יַרְכָה, the *thighs* (*hüfte*) and upper part of the loins. Ver. 33. שָׁק, *the leg*, including the upper part of the thigh. מִנְּהוֹן is partitive: part *of it of iron*. Instead of מִנְּהוֹן the *Keri* prefers the fem. מִנְּהֵן here and at vers. 41 and 42, with reference to this, that רַגְלוֹי is usually the *gen. fem.*, after the custom of nouns denoting members of the body that are double. The *Kethiv* unconditionally deserves the preference, although, as the apparently anomalous form, which appears with this suffix also in ch. vii. 8, 20, after substantives of seemingly feminine meaning, where the choice of the masculine form is to be explained from the undefined conception of the subjective idea apart from the sex; cf. Ewald's *Lehr. d. hebr. Sp.* § 319.

The image appears divided as to its material into four or five parts—the head, the breast with the arms, the belly with the thighs, and the legs and feet. "Only the first part, the head, constitutes in itself a united whole; the second, with the arms, represents a division; the third runs into a division in the thighs; the fourth, bound into one at the top, divides itself in the two legs, but has also the power of moving in itself; the fifth is from the first divided in the legs, and finally in the ten toes runs out into a wider division. The material becomes inferior from the head downward—gold, silver, copper, iron, clay; so that, though on the whole metallic, it becomes inferior, and finally terminates in clay, losing itself in common earthly matter. Notwithstanding that the material becomes always the harder, till it is iron, yet then suddenly and at last it becomes weak and brittle clay."—Klief. The fourth and fifth parts, the legs and the feet, are, it is true, externally separate from each other, but inwardly, through the unity of the material, iron, are bound together; so that we are to reckon only four parts, as afterwards is done in the interpretation. This image Nebuchadnezzar was contemplating (ver. 34), *i.e.* reflected upon with a look directed toward it, until a stone moved without human hands broke loose from a mountain, struck against the lowest part of the image, broke the whole of it into pieces, and ground to powder all its material from the head even to the feet, so that it was scattered like chaff of the summer thrashing-floor. דִּי לָא בִידַיִן does not mean: "which was not in the hands of any one" (Klief.), but the words are a prepositional expression for *without*; לָא בְּ, *not with* = *without*, and דִּי expressing the dependence of the word on the foregoing noun. *Without hands*, without human help, is a litotes for: *by a higher, a divine providence*; cf. ch. viii. 25; Job xxxiv. 20; Lam. iv. 6. כַּחֲדָה, *as one* = *at once*, with one stroke. דָּקוּ for דַּקּוּ is not intransitive or passive, but with an indefinite plur. subject: *they crushed*, referring to the supernatural power by which the crushing was effected. The destruction of the statue is so described, that the image passes over into the matter of it. It is not said of the parts of the image, the head, the breast, the belly, and the thighs, that they were broken to pieces by the stone, "for the forms of the world-power represented by these parts had long ago passed away, when the stone strikes against the last form of the world-power represented by the feet," but only of the materials of which these parts consist, the silver and the gold, is the destruction predicated; "for the material, the combinations of peoples, of which these earlier forms of the world-power consist, pass into the later forms of it, and thus are all destroyed when the stone destroys the last form of the world-power" (Klief.). But the stone which brought this destruction itself became a great mountain which filled the whole earth. To this Daniel added the interpretation which he announces in ver. 36. נֵאמַר, *we will tell*, is "a generalizing form of expression" (Kran.) in harmony with ver. 30. Daniel associates himself with his companions in the faith, who worshipped the same God of revelation; cf. ver. 23*b*.

Vers. 37, 38. The interpretation begins with the golden head. מֶלֶךְ מַלְכַיָּא, the usual title of the monarchs of the Oriental world-kingdoms (*vid.* Ezek. xxvi. 7), is not the predicate to אַנְתְּה, but stands in apposition to מַלְכָּא. The following relative passages, vers. 37*b* and 38, are only further explications of the address *King of Kings*, in which אַנְתְּה is again taken up to bring back the predicate. בְּכָל־דִּי, *wherever, everywhere.* As to the form דָּאְרִין, see the remarks under קָאְמִין at ch. iii. 3. The description of Nebuchadnezzar's dominion over men, beasts, and birds, is formed after the words of Jer. xxvii. 6 and xxviii. 14; the mention of the beasts serves only for the strengthening of the thought that his dominion was that of a world-kingdom, and that God had subjected all things to him. Nebuchadnezzar's dominion did not, it is true, extend over the whole earth, but perhaps over the whole civilised world of Asia, over all the historical nations of his time; and in this sense it was a world-kingdom, and as such, "the prototype and pattern, the beginning and primary representative of all world-powers" (Klief.). רֵאשָׁה, *stat. emphat.* for רֵאשָׁא; the reading רֵאשֵׁה defended by Hitz. is senseless. If Daniel called him (Nebuchadnezzar) the golden head, the designation cannot refer to his person, but to the world-kingdom founded by him and represented in his person, having all things placed under his sway by God. Hitzig's idea, that Nebuchadnezzar is the golden head as distinguished from his successors in the Babylonian kingdom, is opposed by ver. 39, where it is said that after him (not another king, but) "another kingdom" would arise. That "Daniel, in the words, 'Thou art the golden head,' speaks of the Babylonian kingdom as of Nebuchadnezzar personally, while on the contrary he speaks of the other world-kingdoms impersonally only as of kingdoms, has its foundation in this, that the Babylonian kingdom personified in Nebuchadnezzar stood before him, and therefore could be addressed by the word *thou*, while the other kingdoms could not" (Klief.).

Ver. 39. In this verse the second and third parts of the image are interpreted of the second and third world-kingdoms. Little is said of these kingdoms here, because they are more fully described in ch. vii. viii. and x. That the first clause of ver. 39 refers to the second, the silver part of the image, is apparent from the fact that ver. 38 refers to the golden head, and the second clause of ver. 39 to the belly of brass. According to this, the breast and arms of silver represent another kingdom which would arise after Nebuchadnezzar, *i.e.* after the Babylonian kingdom. This kingdom will be אֲרַעָא מִנָּךְ, *inferior to thee*, *i.e.* to the kingdom of which thou art the representative. Instead of the adjective אֲרַעָא, here used adverbially, the Masoretes have substituted the adverbial form אֲרַע, in common use in later times, which Hitz. incorrectly interprets by the phrase "downwards from thee." Since the other, *i.e.* the second kingdom, as we shall afterwards prove, is the Medo-Persian world-kingdom, the question arises, in how far was it inferior to the Babylonian? In outward extent it was not less, but even greater than it. With reference to the circumstance that the parts of the image representing it were silver, and not gold as the head was, Calv., Aub., Kran., and others, are inclined to the opinion that the word "inferior" points to the moral condition of the kingdom. But if the successive deterioration of the inner moral condition of the four world-kingdoms is denoted by the succession of the metals, this cannot be expressed by אֲרַעָא מִנָּךְ, because in regard to the following world-kingdoms, represented by copper and iron, such an intimation or declaration does not find a place, notwithstanding that copper and iron are far inferior to silver and gold. Klief., on the contrary, thinks that the Medo-Persian kingdom stands inferior to, or is smaller than, the Babylonian kingdom in respect of universality; for this element is exclusively referred to in the text, being not only attributed to the Babylonian kingdom, ver. 37, in the widest extent, but also to the third kingdom, ver. 39, and not less to the fourth, ver. 40. The universality belonging to a world-kingdom does not, however, require that it should rule over all the nations of the earth to its very end, nor that its territory should have a defined extent, but only that such a kingdom should unite in itself the *οἰκουμένη*, *i.e.* the civilised world, the whole of the historical nations of its time. And this was truly the case with the Babylonian, the Macedonian, and the Roman world-monarchies, but it was not so with the Medo-Persian, although perhaps it was more powerful and embraced a more extensive territory than the Babylonian, since Greece, which at the time of the Medo-Persian monarchy had already decidedly passed into the rank of the historical nations, as yet stood outside of the Medo-Persian rule. But if this view is correct, then would universality be wanting to the third, *i.e.* to the Græco-Macedonian world-monarchy, which is predicated of it in the words "That shall bear rule over the whole earth," since at the time of this monarchy Rome had certainly passed into the rank of historical nations, and yet it was not incorporated with the Macedonian empire.

The Medo-Persian world-kingdom is spoken of as "inferior" to the Babylonian perhaps only in this respect, that from its commencement it wanted inner unity, since the Medians and Persians did not form a united people, but contended with each other for the supremacy, which is intimated in the expression, ch. vii. 5, that the bear "raised itself up on one side:" see under that passage. In the want of inward unity lay the weakness or the inferiority in strength of this kingdom, its inferiority as compared with the Babylonian. This originally divided or separated character of this kingdom appears in the image in the circumstance that it is represented by the breast and the arms. "Medes and Persians," as Hofm. (*Weiss. u. Erf.* i. S. 279) well remarks, "are the two sides of the breast. The government of the Persian kingdom was not one and united as was that of the Chaldean nation and king, but it was twofold. The Magi belonged to a different race from Cyrus, and the Medes were regarded abroad as the people ruling with and beside the Persians." This two-sidedness is plainly denoted in the two horns of the ram, ch. viii.

Ver. 39*b* treats of the third world-kingdom, which by the expression אָחֳרִי, "another," is plainly distinguished from the preceding; as to its quality, it is characterized by the predicate "of copper, brazen." In this chapter it is said only of this kingdom that "it shall rule over the whole earth," and thus be superior in point of extent and power to the preceding kingdoms. Cf. vii. 6, where it is distinctly mentioned that "power was given unto it." Fuller particulars are communicated regarding the second and third world-kingdoms in ch. viii. and x. f.

Vers. 40–43. The interpretation of the fourth component part of the image, the legs and feet, which represent a fourth world-kingdom, is more extended. That kingdom, corresponding to the legs of iron, shall be hard, firm like iron. Because iron breaks all things in pieces, so shall this kingdom, which is like to iron, break in pieces and destroy all these kingdoms.

Ver. 40. Instead of רְבִיעָיָא, which is formed after the analogy of the Syriac language, the *Keri* has the usual Chaldee form רְבִיעָאָה, which shall correspond to the preceding תְּלִיתָאָה, ver. 39. See the same *Keri* ch. iii. 25, vii. 7, 23. כָּל־קֳבֵל דִּי does not mean *just as* (Ges., v. Leng., Maur., Hitz.), but *because*, and the passage introduced by this particle contains the ground on which this kingdom is designated as hard like iron. חָשֵׁל, *breaks in pieces*, in Syriac to forge, *i.e.* to break by the hammer, cf. חוּשְׁלָא, *bruised* grain, and thus separated from the husks. כָּל־אִלֵּין is referred by Kran., in conformity with the accents, to the relative clause, "because by its union with the following verbal idea a blending of the image with the thing indicated must first be assumed; also nowhere else, neither here nor in ch. vii., does the non-natural meaning appear, *e.g.*, that by the fourth kingdom only the first and second kingdoms shall be destroyed; and finally, in the similar expression, ch. vii. 7, 19, the הַדֵּק stands likewise without an object." But all the three reasons do not prove much. A mixing of the figure with the thing signified does not lie in the passage: "the fourth (kingdom) shall, like crushing iron, crush to pieces all these" (kingdoms). But the "non-natural meaning," that by the fourth kingdom not only the third, but also the second and the first, would be destroyed, is not set aside by our referring כָּל־אִלֵּין to the before-named metals, because the metals indeed characterize and represent kingdoms. Finally, the expressions in ch. vii. 7, 19 are not analogous to those before us. The words in question cannot indeed be so understood as if the fourth kingdom would find the three previous kingdoms existing together, and would dash them one against another; for, according to the text, the first kingdom is destroyed by the second, and the second by the third; but the materials of the first two kingdoms were comprehended in the third. "The elements out of which the Babylonian world-kingdom was constituted, the countries, peoples, and civilisation comprehended in it, as its external form, would be destroyed by the Medo-Persian kingdom, and carried forward with it, so as to be constituted into a new external form. Such, too, was the relation between the Medo-Persian and the Macedonian world-kingdom, that the latter assumed the elements and component parts not only of the Medo-Persian, but also therewith at the same time of the Babylonian kingdom" (Klief.). In such a way shall the fourth world-kingdom crush "all these" past kingdoms as iron, *i.e.* will not assume the nations and civilisations comprehended in the earlier world-kingdoms as organized formations, but will destroy and break them to atoms with iron strength. Yet will this world-kingdom not throughout possess and manifest the iron hardness. Only the legs of the image are of iron (ver. 41), but the feet and toes which grow out of the legs are partly of clay and partly of iron.

Regarding מִנְּהוֹן, see under ver. 33. חֲסַף means *clay, a piece of clay*, then *an earthly vessel*, 2 Sam. v. 20. פֶּחָר in the Targums means *potter*, also *potter's earth, potsherds*. The דִּי פֶחָר serves to strengthen the חֲסַף, as in the following the addition of טִינָא, *clay*, in order the more to heighten the idea of brittleness. This two-fold material denotes that it will be a divided or severed kingdom, not because it separates into several (two to ten) kingdoms, for this is denoted by the duality of the feet and by the number of the toes of the feet, but inwardly divided; for פְּלַג always in Hebr., and often in Chald., signifies the unnatural or violent division arising from *inner disharmony or discord*; cf. Gen. x. 25, Ps. lv. 10, Job xxxviii. 25; and Levy, *chald. Worterb. s. v.* Notwithstanding this inner division, there will yet be in it the firmness of iron. נִצְבָּא, *firmness*, related to יְצַב, Pa. *to make fast*, but in Chald. generally *plantatio*, properly a slip, a plant.

Vers. 42, 43. In ver. 42 the same is said of the toes of the feet, and in ver. 43 the comparison to iron and clay is defined as the mixture of these two component parts. As the iron denotes the firmness of the kingdom, so the clay denotes its brittleness. The mixing of iron with clay represents the attempt to bind the two distinct and separate materials into one combined whole as fruitless, and altogether in vain. The mixing of themselves with the seed of men (ver. 43), most interpreters refer to the marriage politics of the princes. They who understand by the four kingdoms the monarchy of Alexander and his followers, think it refers to the marriages between the Seleucidæ and the Ptolemies, of which indeed there is mention made in ch. xi. 6 and 17, but not here; while Hofm. thinks it relates to marriages, such as those of the German Kaiser Otto II. and the Russian Grand-Duke Wladimir with the daughters of the Kaiser of Eastern Rome. But this interpretation is rightly rejected by Klief., as on all points inconsistent with the text. The subject to מִתְעָרְבִין is not the kings, of whom mention is made neither in ver. 43 nor previously. For the two feet as well as the ten toes denote not kings, but parts of the fourth kingdom; and even in ver. 44, by מַלְכַיָּא, not kings in contradistinction to the kingdoms, but the representatives of the parts of the kingdom denoted by the feet and the toes as existing contemporaneously, are to be understood, from which it cannot rightly be concluded in any way that kings is the subject to מִתְעָרְבִין (*shall mingle themselves*).

As, in the three preceding kingdoms, gold, silver, and brass represent the material of these kingdoms, *i.e.* their peoples and their culture, so also in the fourth kingdom iron and clay represent the material of the kingdoms arising out of the division of this kingdom, *i.e.* the national elements out of which they are constituted, and which will and must mingle together in them. If, then, the "mixing themselves with the seed of men" points to marriages, it is only of the mixing of different tribes brought together by external force in the kingdom by marriages as a means of amalgamating the diversified nationalities. But the expression is not to be limited to this, although הִתְעָרֵב, Ezra ix. 2, occurs of the mixing of the holy nation with the heathen by marriage. The peculiar expression זְרַע אֲנָשָׁא, *the seed of men*, is not of the same import as שִׁכְבַת זֶרַע, but is obviously chosen with reference to the following contrast to the divine Ruler, ver. 44 f., so as to place (Kran.) the vain human endeavour of the heathen rulers in contrast with the doings of the God of heaven; as in Jer. xxxi. 27 זֶרַע אָדָם is occasioned by the contrast of זֶרַע בְּהֵמָה. The figure of mixing by seed is derived from the sowing of the field with mingled seed, and denotes all the means employed by the rulers to combine the different nationalities, among which the *connubium* is only spoken of as the most important and successful means.

But this mixing together will succeed just as little as will the effort to bind together into one firm coherent mass iron and clay. The parts mixed together will not cleave to each other. Regarding לֶהֱוֺן, see under ver. 20

Ver. 44. The world-kingdom will be broken to pieces by the

kingdom which the God of heaven will set up. "In the days of these kings," *i.e.* of the kings of the world-kingdoms last described; at the time of the kingdoms denoted by the ten toes of the feet of the image into which the fourth world-monarchy extends itself; for the stone (ver. 34) rolling against the feet of the image, or rather against the toes of the feet, breaks and destroys it. This kingdom is not founded by the hands of man, but is erected by the God of heaven, and shall for ever remain immoveable, in contrast to the world-kingdoms, the one of which will be annihilated by the other. Its dominion will not be given to another people. מַלְכוּתָהּ, *his dominion, i.e.* of the kingdom. This word needs not to be changed into מַלְכוּתָה, which is less suitable, since the mere *status absol.* would not be here in place. Among the world-kingdoms the dominion goes from one people to another, from the Babylonians to the Persians, etc. On the contrary, the kingdom of God comprehends always the same people, *i.e.* the people of Israel, chosen by God to be His own, only not the Israel *κατὰ σάρκα*, but the Israel of God (Gal. vi. 16). But the kingdom of God will not merely exist eternally without change of its dominion, along with the world-kingdoms, which are always changing and bringing one another to dissolution, it will also break in pieces and destroy all these kingdoms (תָּסֵף, from סוּף, *to bring to an end, to make an end to them*), but itself shall exist for ever. This is the meaning of the stone setting itself free without the hands of man, and breaking the image in pieces.

Ver. 45. The מִטּוּרָא before אִתְגְּזֶרֶת, which is wanting in ver. 34, and without doubt is here used significantly, is to be observed, as in ver. 42 "the toes of the feet," which in ver. 33 were also not mentioned. As it is evident that a stone, in order to its rolling without the movement of the human hand, must be set free from a mountain, so in the express mention of the mountain there can be only a reference to Mount Zion, where the God of heaven has founded His kingdom, which shall from thence spread out over the earth and shall destroy all the world-kingdoms. Cf. Ps. l. 2, Isa. ii. 3, Mic. iv. 2.

The first half of the 45th verse (down to וְדַהֲבָא) gives the confirmation of that which Daniel in ver. 44 said to the king regarding the setting up and the continuance of the kingdom of God, and essentially belongs to this verse. On the other hand, Hitz. (and Kran. follows him) wishes to unite this confirmatory passage with the following: "because thou hast seen that the stone, setting itself free from the mountain, breaks in pieces the iron, etc., thus has God permitted thee a glimpse behind the veil that hides the future,"—in order that he may conclude from it that the writer, since he notes only the vision of the stone setting itself free as an announcement of the future, betrayed his real standpoint, *i.e.* the standpoint of the Maccabean Jew, for whom only this last catastrophe was as yet future, while all the rest was already past. This conclusion Kran. has rejected, but with the untenable argument that the expression, "what shall come to pass hereafter," is to be taken in agreement with the words, "what should come to pass," ver. 29, which occur at the beginning of the address. Though this may in itself be right, yet it cannot be maintained if the passage ver. 45*a* forms the antecedent to ver. 45*b*. In this case דְּנָה (*this*), in the phrase "*after this*" (=hereafter, ver. 45), can be referred only to the setting loose of the stone. But the reasons which Hitz. adduces for the uniting together of the passages as adopted by him are without any importance. Why the long combined passage cannot suitably conclude with וְדַהֲבָא there is no reason which can be understood; and that it does not round itself is also no proof, but merely a matter of taste, the baselessness of which is evident from ver. 10, where an altogether similar long passage, beginning with כָּל־קֳבֵל דִּי (*forasmuch as*), ends in a similar manner, without formally rounding itself off. The further remark also, that the following new passage could not so unconnectedly and baldly begin with אֱלָהּ רַב, is no proof, but a mere assertion, which is set aside as groundless by many passages in Daniel where the connection is wanting; cf. *e.g.* iv. 16*b*, 27. The want of the copula before this passage is to be explained on the same ground on which Daniel uses אֱלָהּ רַב (*stat. absol.*, *i.e.* without the article) instead of רַבָּא אֱלָהָא, Ezra v. 8. For that אלה רב means, not "a (undefined) great God," but *the great God* in heaven, whom Daniel had already (ver. 28) announced to the king as the revealer of secrets, is obvious. Kran. has rightly remarked, that אלה רב may stand "in elevated discourse without the article, instead of the prosaic אלהא רבא, Ezra v. 8." The elevated discourse has occasioned also the absence of the copula, which will not be missed if one only takes a pause at the end of the interpretation, after which Daniel then in conclusion further says to the king, "The great God has showed to the king what will be hereafter." אַחֲרֵי דְנָה, *after this* which is now, does not mean "at some future time" (Hitz.), but after that which is at present, and it embraces the future denoted in the dream, from the time of Nebuchadnezzar till the setting up of the kingdom of God in the time of the Messiah.

Ver. 45*b*. The word with which Daniel concludes his address, יַצִּיב, *firm, sure*, is the dream, and certain its interpretation, is not intended to assure the king of the truth of the dream, because the particulars of the dream had escaped him, and to certify to him the correctness of the interpretation (Kran.), but the importance of the dream should put him in mind to lay the matter to heart, and give honour to God who imparted to him these revelations; but at the same time also the word assures the readers of the book of the certainty of the fulfilment, since it lay far remote, and the visible course of things in the present and in the proximate future gave no indication or only a very faint prospect of the fulfilment. For other such assurances see ch. viii. 26, x. 21, Rev. xix. 9, xxi. 5, xxii. 6.

We shall defer a fuller consideration of the fulfilment of this dream or the historical references of the four world-kingdoms, in order to avoid repetition, till we have expounded the vision which Daniel received regarding it in ch. vii.

Vers. 46–49. *The impression which this interpretation of the dream made upon Nebuchadnezzar, and the consequences which thence arose for Daniel.*

The announcement and the interpretation of the remarkable dream made so powerful an impression on Nebuchadnezzar, that he fell down in supplication before Daniel and ordered sacrifice to be offered to him. Falling prostrate to the earth is found as a mark of honour to men, it is true (1 Sam. xx. 41, xxv. 28; 2 Sam. xiv. 4), but סְגִד is used only of *divine homage* (Isa. xliv. 15, 17, 19, xlvi. 6, and Dan. iii. 5 ff.). To the Chaldean king, Daniel appeared as a man in whom the gods manifested themselves; therefore he shows to him divine honour, such as was shown by Cornelius to the Apostle Peter, and at Lystra was shown to Paul and Barnabas, Acts x. 25, xiv. 13. מִנְחָה, *an unbloody sacrifice*, and נִיחֹחִין, are not burnt sacrifices or offerings of pieces of fat (Hitz.), but *incensings, the offering of incense*; cf. Ex. xxx. 9, where the קְטֹרֶת is particularly mentioned along with the עֹלָה and the מִנְחָה. נְסַךְ is, with Hitz., to be taken after the Arabic in the general signification *sacrificare*, but is transferred zeugmatically from the pouring out of a drink-offering to the offering of a sacrifice. Ver. 47, where Nebuchadnezzar praises the God of the Jews as the God of gods, does not stand in contradiction to the rendering of divine honour to Daniel in such a way that, with Hitz., in the conduct of the king we miss consistency and propriety, and find it improbable. For Nebuchadnezzar did not pray to the man Daniel, but in the person of Daniel to his God, *i.e.* to the God of the Jews; and he did this because this God had manifested Himself to him through Daniel as the supreme God, who rules over kings, and reveals hidden things which the gods of the Chaldean wise men were not able to reveal. Moreover, in this, Nebuchadnezzar did not abandon his heathen standpoint. He did not recognise the God of the Jews as the only, or the alone true God, but only as God of gods, as the highest or the most exalted of the gods, who excelled the other gods in might and in wisdom, and was a Lord of kings, and as such must be honoured along with the gods of his own country. מִן־קְשֹׁט דִּי, *of truth* (it is) *that*, stands adverbially for *truly*.

Ver. 48. After Nebuchadnezzar had given honour to the God of the Jews, he rewarded Daniel, the servant of this God, with gifts, and by elevating him to high offices of state. רַבִּי, *to make great*, is more fully defined by the following passages. הַשְׁלְטֵהּ, *he made him a man of power*, ruler over the province of Babylon, *i.e.* vicegerent, governor of this province. According to ch. iii. 2, the Chaldean kingdom consisted of several מְדִינָתָא, each of which had its own שִׁלְטוֹן. The following וְרַב סִגְנִין depends zeugmatically, however, on הַשְׁלְטֵהּ: *and* (made him) *president over all the wise men.* סִגְנִין, Hebr. סְגָנִים, *vicegerent*, prefect, is an Aryan word incorporated into the Hebrew, ζωγάνης in Athen., but not yet certainly authenticated in Old Persian; *vide* Spiegel in *Delitzsch* on Isa. xli. 25. The wise men of Babylon were divided into classes according to their principal functions, under סִגְנִין, *chiefs*, whose president (= רַב־מָג, Jer. xxxix. 3) Daniel was.

Ver. 49. At Daniel's request the king made his three friends governors of the province. וּמַנִּי is not, with Häv. and other older writers, to be translated *that he should ordain*; this sense must be expressed by the imperfect. The matter of the prayer is not specially given, but is to be inferred from the granting of it. But this prayer is not, with Hitz. and older interpreters, to be understood as implying that Daniel entreated the king to release him from the office of vicegerent, and that the king entrusted that office to his three friends; for if Daniel wished to retain this dignity, but to transfer the duty to his friends, there was no need, as Hitz. thinks, for this purpose, for the express appointment of the king; his mere permission was enough. But whence did

Hitz. obtain this special information regarding the state arrangements of Babylon? and how does he know that מַנִּי, *to decree*, means an express appointment in contradistinction to a royal permission? The true state of the matter Häv. has clearly explained. The chief ruler of the province had a number of *ὕπαρχοι*, *under-officers*, in the province for the various branches of the government. To such offices the king appointed Daniel's three friends at his request, so that he might be able as chief ruler to reside continually at the court of the king. עֲבִידְתָּא, *rendering of service* = עֲבֹדַת הַמֶּלֶךְ, *service of the king*, 1 Chron. xxvi. 30, according as the matter may be: the management of business. בִּתְרַע מַלְכָּא, *near the gate*, *i.e.* at the court of the king, for the gate, the door, is named for the building to which it formed the entrance; cf. שַׁעַר הַמֶּלֶךְ, Esth. ii. 19, 21, iii. 2 ff. Gesenius is in error when he explains the words there as meaning that Daniel was made prefect of the palace.

CHAP. III. 1–30. DANIEL'S THREE FRIENDS IN THE FIERY FURNACE.

Nebuchadnezzar commanded a colossal golden image to be set up in the plain of Dura at Babylon, and summoned all his high officers of state to be present at its consecration. He caused it to be proclaimed by a herald, that at a given signal all should fall down before the image and do it homage, and that whosoever refused to do so would be cast into a burning fiery furnace (vers. 1–7). This ceremony having been ended, it was reported to the king by certain Chaldeans that Daniel's friends, who had been placed over the province of Babylon, had not done homage to the image; whereupon, being called to account by the king, they refused to worship the image because they could not serve his gods (vers. 8–18). For this opposition to the king's will they were cast, bound in their clothes, into the burning fiery furnace. They were uninjured by the fire; and the king perceived with terror that not three, but four men, were walking unbound and uninjured in the furnace (vers. 19–27). Then he commanded them to come out; and when he found them wholly unhurt, he not only praised their God who had so wonderfully protected them, but also commanded, on the pain of death, all the people of his kingdom not to despise this God (vers. 28–30).

The LXX. and Theodotion have placed the date of this event

in the eighteenth year of Nebuchadnezzar, apparently only because they associated the erection of this statue with the taking of Jerusalem under Zedekiah, although that city was not taken and destroyed till the nineteenth year of Nebuchadnezzar (2 Kings xxv. 8 ff.). But though it is probable that Nebuchadnezzar, after he had firmly established his world-kingdom by the overthrow of all his enemies, first felt himself moved to erect this image as a monument of his great exploits and of his world-power; yet the destruction of the capital of Judea, which had been already twice destroyed, can hardly be regarded as having furnished a sufficient occasion for this. This much, however, is certain, that the event narrated in this chapter occurred later than that of the 2d chapter, since ch. iii. 12 and 30 refer to ch. ii. 49; and on the other hand, that they occurred earlier than the incident of the 4th chapter, in which there are many things which point to the last half of the reign of Nebuchadnezzar, while the history recorded in the chapter before us appertains more to the middle of his reign, when Nebuchadnezzar stood on the pinnacle of his greatness. The circumstance that there is no longer found in the king any trace of the impression which the omnipotence and infinite wisdom of the God of the Jews, as brought to view in the interpretation of his dream by Daniel, made upon his mind (ch. ii.), affords no means of accurately determining the time of the occurrence here narrated. There is no need for our assuming, with Jerome, a *velox oblivio veritatis*, or with Calvin, the lapse of a considerable interval between the two events. The deportment of Nebuchadnezzar on this occasion does not stand in opposition to the statements made at the close of ch. ii. The command that all who were assembled at the consecration of the image should fall down before it and worship it, is to be viewed from the standpoint of the heathen king. It had no reference at all to the oppression of those who worshipped the God of the Jews, nor to a persecution of the Jews on account of their God. It only demanded the recognition of the national god, to whom the king supposed he owed the greatness of his kingdom, as the god of the kingdom, and was a command which the heathen subjects of Nebuchadnezzar could execute without any violence to their consciences. The Jews could not obey it, however, without violating the first precept of their law. But Nebuchadnezzar did not think on that. Disobedience to his command appeared to him as culpable rebellion against his majesty. As such also the conduct of Daniel's friends is represented to him by the Chaldean informers in ver. 12. The words of the informers, "The Jews whom thou hast set over the affairs of the province of Babylon have not regarded thee, O king; they serve not thy gods," etc., clearly show that they were rightly named (ver. 8) "accusers of the Jews," and that by their denunciation of them they wished only to expel the foreigners from their places of influence; and for this purpose they made use of the politico-national festival appointed by Nebuchadnezzar as a fitting opportunity. Hence we can understand Nebuchadnezzar's anger against those who disregarded his command; and his words, with which he pronounced sentence against the accused—"who is that God that shall deliver you out of my hand?"—are, judged of from the religious point of view of the Israelites, a blaspheming of God, but considered from Nebuchadnezzar's heathen standpoint, are only an expression of proud confidence in his own might and in that of his gods, and show nothing further than that the revelation of the living God in ch. ii. had not permanently impressed itself on his heart, but had in course of time lost much of its influence over him.

The conduct of Nebuchadnezzar toward the Jews, described in this chapter, is accordingly fundamentally different from the relation sustained by Antiochus Epiphanes towards Judaism; for he wished entirely to put an end to the Jewish form of worship. In the conduct of Daniel's friends who were accused before the king there is also not a single trace of the religious fanaticism prevalent among the Jews in the age of the Maccabees, who were persecuted on account of their fidelity to the law. Far from trusting in the miraculous help of God, they regarded it as possible that God, whom they served, would not save them, and they only declare that in no case will they reverence the heathen deities of the king, and do homage to the image erected by him (ver. 16 ff.).

The right apprehension of the historical situation described in this chapter is at complete variance with the supposition of the modern critics, that the narrative is unhistorical, and was invented for the purpose of affording a type for the relation of Antiochus Epiphanes to Judaism. The remarkable circumstance, that Daniel is not named as having been present at this festival (and he also would certainly not have done homage to the image), can of itself alone furnish no argument against the historical accuracy of the matter, although it cannot be explained on the supposition made by Hgstb., that Daniel, as president over the wise men, did not belong to the class of state-officers, nor by the assertion of Hitz., that Daniel did not belong to the class of chief officers, since according to ch. ii. 49 he had transferred his office to his friends. Both suppositions are erroneous; cf. under ch. ii. 49. But many other different possibilities may be thought of to account for the absence of all mention of Daniel's name. Either he may have been prevented for some reason from being present on the occasion, or he may have been present and may have refused to bow down before the image, but yet may only not have been informed against. In the latter case, the remark of Calvin, *ut abstinuerint a Daniele ad tempus, quem sciebant magnifieri a Rege*, would scarcely suffice, but we must suppose that the accusers had designed first only the overthrow of the three rulers of the province of Babylon.[1] But the circumstance that Daniel, if he were present, did not employ himself in behalf of his friends, may be explained from the quick execution of Babylonish justice, provided some higher reason did not determine him confidently to commit the decision of the matter to the Lord his God.[2]

Vers. 1–18. *The erection and consecration of the golden image, and the accusation brought against Daniel's friends, that they had refused to obey the king's command to do homage to this image.*

Ver. 1. Nebuchadnezzar commanded a golden image to be erected, of threescore cubits in height and six cubits in breadth.

[1] Kran.'s supposition also (p. 153), that Daniel, as president over the class of the wise men, claimed the right belonging to him as such, while in his secular office he could be represented by his Jewish associates, and thus was withdrawn from the circle of spectators and from the command laid upon them of falling down before the image, has little probability; for although it is not said that this command was laid upon the caste of the wise men, and even though it should be supposed that the priests were present at this festival as the directors of the religious ceremonial, and thus were brought under the command to fall down before the image, yet this can scarcely be supposed of the whole caste. But Daniel could not in conscience take part in this idolatrous festival, nor associate himself with the priests, nor as president of all the Magi withdraw into the background, so as to avoid the ceremony of doing homage to the image.

[2] We have already in part noticed the arguments against the historical accuracy of the narrative presented by the opponents of the genuineness of the book, such as the giving of Greek names to the musical instruments, and the conduct of Antiochus Epiphanes in placing an idol-image on the altar of burnt-offering (pp. 34, 50). All the others are dealt with in the Exposition. The principal objection adduced is the miracle, on account of which alone Hitz. thinks himself warranted in affirming that the narrative has no historical reality.

צְלֵם is properly *an image in human likeness* (cf. ch. ii. 31), and excludes the idea of a mere pillar or an obelisk, for which מַצֵּבָה would have been the appropriate word. Yet from the use of the word צְלֵם it is not by any means to be concluded that the image was in all respects perfectly in human form. As to the upper part—the head, countenance, arms, breast—it may have been in the form of a man, and the lower part may have been formed like a pillar. This would be altogether in accordance with the Babylonian art, which delighted in grotesque, gigantic forms; cf. Hgstb. *Beitr.* i. p. 96 f. The measure, in height threescore cubits, in breadth six cubits, is easily explained, since in the human figure the length is to the breadth in the proportion of about six to one. In the height of threescore cubits the pedestal of the image may be regarded as included, so that the whole image according to its principal component part (*a potiori*) was designated as צְלֵם; although the passage Judg. xviii. 30, 31, adduced by Kran., where mention is made of the image alone which was erected by Micah, without any notice being taken of the pedestal belonging to it (cf. vers. 17 and 18), furnishes no properly authentic proof that פֶּסֶל in vers. 30 and 31 denotes the image with the pedestal. The proportion between the height and the breadth justifies, then, in no respect the rejection of the historical character of the narrative. Still less does the mass of gold necessary for the construction of so colossal an image, since, as has been already mentioned (p. 39), according to the Hebrew modes of speech, we are not required to conceive of the figure as having been made of solid gold, and since, in the great riches of the ancient world, Nebuchadnezzar in his successful campaigns might certainly accumulate an astonishing amount of this precious metal. The statements of Herodotus and Diodorus regarding the Babylonian idol-images,[1] as well as the description in Isa. xl. 19 of the construction of idol-images, lead us to think of the image as merely overlaid with plates of gold.

The king commanded this image to be set up in the plain of *Dura* in the province of Babylon. The ancients make mention

[1] According to Herod. i. 183, for the great golden image of Belus, which was twelve cubits high, and the great golden table standing before it, the golden steps and the golden chair, only 800 talents of gold were used; and according to Diod. Sic. ii. 9, the golden statue, forty feet high, placed in the temple of Belus consisted of 1000 talents of gold, which would have been not far from sufficient if these objects had been formed of solid gold. Diod. also expressly says regarding the statue, that it was made with the hammer, and therefore was not solid. Cf. Hgstb. *Beitr.* i. p. 98, and Kran. *in loco.*

of two places of the name of *Dura*, the one at the mouth of the Chaboras where it empties itself into the Euphrates, not far from Carchemish (Polyb. v. 48 ; Ammian. Marc. xxiii. 5, 8, xxiv. 1, 5), the other beyond the Tigris, not far from Apollonia (Polyb. v. 52 ; Amm. Marc. xxv. 6, 9). Of these the latter has most probability in its favour, since the former certainly did not belong to the province of Babylon, which according to Xenophon extended 36 miles south of Tiphsach (cf. Nieb. *Gesch. Assurs*, S. 421). The latter, situated in the district of Sittakene, could certainly be reckoned as belonging to the province of Babylon, since according to Strabo, Sittakene, at least in the Old Parthian time, belonged to Babylon (Nieb. p. 420). But even this place lay quite too far from the capital of the kingdom to be the place intended. We must, without doubt, much rather seek for this plain in the neighbourhood of Babylon, where, according to the statement of Jul. Oppert (*Expéd. Scientif. en Mésopotamie*, i. p. 238 ff.), there are at present to be found in the S.S.E. of the ruins representing the former capital a row of mounds which bear the name of *Dura*, at the end of which, along with two larger mounds, there is a smaller one which is named *el Mokaṭṭaṭ* (=*la colline alignée*), which forms a square six metres high, with a basis of fourteen metres, wholly built *en briques crues* (لبن), which shows so surprising a resemblance to a colossal statue with its pedestal, that Oppert believes that this little mound is the remains of the golden statue erected by Nebuchadnezzar.[1]

There is a difference of opinion as to the signification of this image. According to the common view (cf. *e.g.* Hgstb. *Beitr.* i. p. 97), Nebuchadnezzar wished to erect a statue as an expression of his thanks to his god Bel for his great victories, and on that account also to consecrate it with religious ceremonies. On the

[1] "On seeing this mound," Oppert remarks (*l. c.* p. 239), "one is immediately struck with the resemblance which it presents to the pedestal of a colossal statue, as, for example, that of Bavaria near Münich, and everything leads to the belief that the statue mentioned in the book of Daniel (ch. iii. 1) was set up in this place. The fact of the erection by Nebuchadnezzar of a colossal statue has nothing which can cause astonishment, however recent may have been the Aramean form of the account of Scripture." Oppert, moreover, finds no difficulty in the size of the statue, but says regarding it: "There is nothing incredible in the existence of a statue sixty cubits high and six cubits broad ; moreover the name of the plain of Dura, in the province (מְדִינָה) of Babylon, agrees also with the actual conformation of the ruin."

other hand, Hofm. (*Weiss. u. Erf.* i. p. 277) remarks, that the statue was not the image of a god, because a distinction is made between falling down to it and the service to his god which Nebuchadnezzar required (vers. 12, 14, 18) from his officers of state. This distinction, however, is not well supported; for in these verses praying to the gods of Nebuchadnezzar is placed on an equality with falling down before the image. But on the other hand, the statue is not designated as the image of a god, or the image of Belus; therefore we agree with Klief. in his opinion, that the statue was a symbol of the world-power established by Nebuchadnezzar, so that falling down before it was a manifestation of reverence not only to the world-power, but also to its gods; and that therefore the Israelites could not fall down before the image, because in doing so they would have rendered homage at the same time also to the god or gods of Nebuchadnezzar, in the image of the world-power. But the idea of representing the world-power founded by him as a צְלֵם דִּי־דְהַב was probably suggested to Nebuchadnezzar by the צֶלֶם seen (ch. ii.) by him in a dream, whose head of gold his world-kingdom was described to him as being. We may not, however, with Klief., seek any sanction for the idea that the significance of the image is in its size, 6, 10, and six multiplied by ten cubits, because the symbolical significance of the number 6 as the *signature* of human activity, to which the divine completion (7) is wanting, is not a Babylonian idea. Still less can we, with Zündel (p. 13), explain the absence of Daniel on this occasion as arising from the political import of the statue, because the supposition of Daniel's not having been called to be present is a mere conjecture, and a very improbable conjecture; and the supposition that Daniel, as being chief of the Magi, would not be numbered among the secular officers of state, is decidedly erroneous.

Ver. 2. Nebuchadnezzar commanded all the chief officers of the kingdom to be present at the solemn dedication of the image. שְׁלַח, *he sent*, viz. מַלְאָכִים or רָצִים, *messengers*, 1 Sam. xi. 7; 2 Chron. xxx. 6, 10; Esth. iii. 15. Of the great officers of state, seven classes are named:—1. אֲחַשְׁדַּרְפְּנַיָּא, *i.e. administrators* of the *Khshatra*, in Old Pers. *dominion, province*, and *pâvan* in Zend., *guardians, watchers*, in Greek Σατράπης, the chief representatives of the king in the provinces. 2. סִגְנַיָּא, Hebr. סְגָנִים, from the Old Pers. (although not proved) *çakana, to command* (see under ch. ii. 48), *commanders*, probably *the military chiefs of the provinces.* 3. פַּחֲוָתָא, Hebr. פֶּחָה,

פַּחוֹת, also an Old Pers. word, whose etymon and meaning have not yet been established (see under Hag. i. 1), denotes *the presidents of the civil government, the guardians of the country*; cf. Hag. i. 1, 14, Neh. v. 14, 18. 4. אֲדַרְגָּזְרַיָּא, *chief judges*, from the Sem. גזר, to distinguish, and אדר, dignity (cf. אַדְרַמֶּלֶךְ), properly, *chief arbitrators, counsellors of the government.* 5. גְּדָבְרַיָּא, a word of Aryan origin, from גְּדָבָר, identical with גִּזְבָּר (see note, p. 45), *masters of the treasury, superintendents of the public treasury.* 6. דְּתָבְרַיָּא, the Old Pers. *dâta-bara* (p. 45), *guardians of the law, lawyers* (cf. דָּת, law). 7. תִּפְתָּיֵא, Semitic, from فتى IV. *to give a just sentence,* thus *judges* in the narrower sense of the word. Finally, all שִׁלְטֹנֵי, *rulers, i.e. governors of provinces,* prefects, who were subordinate to the chief governor, cf. ch. ii. 48, 49.

All these officers were summoned "to come (מֵתֵא from אֲתָא, with the rejection of the initial א) to the dedication of the image." The objection of v. Leng. and Hitz., that this call would "put a stop to the government of the country," only shows their ignorance of the departments of the state-government, and by no means makes the narrative doubtful. The affairs of the state did not lie so exclusively in the hands of the presidents of the different branches of the government, as that their temporary absence should cause a suspension of all the affairs of government. חֲנֻכָּה is used of the dedication of a house (Deut. xx. 5) as well as of the temple (1 Kings viii. 63; 2 Chron. vii. 5; Ezra vi. 16), and here undoubtedly denotes an act connected with religious usages, by means of which the image, when the great officers of the kingdom fell down before it, was solemnly consecrated as the symbol of the world-power and (in the heathen sense) of its divine glory. This act is described (vers. 3–7) in so far as the object contemplated rendered it necessary.

When all the great officers of state were assembled, a herald proclaimed that as soon as the sound of the music was heard, all who were present should, on pain of death by being cast into the fire, fall down before the image and offer homage to it; which they all did as soon as the signal was given. The form קָאמִין, ver. 3, corresponds to the sing. קָאֵם (ch. ii. 31) as it is written in Syr., but is read קָיְמִין. The Masoretes substitute for it in the Talm. the common form קָיְמִין; cf. Fürst, *Lehrgb. der aram. Idiom.* p. 161, and Luzzatto, *Elem. Gram.* p. 33. The expression לָקֳבֵל, ver. 3, and Ezra iv. 16, is founded on קֳבֵל, the semi-vowel of the preceding sound being absorbed, as in the Syr. ܠܘܩܒܠ. On כָּרוֹזָא, *herald*, see note 1, p.

45, and on the form לְכוֹן, see under ch. ii. 5. אָמְרִין, *they say*, for "it is said to you." The expression of the passive by means of a plural form of the active used impersonally, either participially or by 3d pers. perf. plur., is found in Hebr., but is quite common in Chald.; cf. Ewald, *Lehr. d. hebr. Spr.* § 128, *b*, and Winer, *Chald. Gram.* § 49, 3. The proclamation of the herald refers not only to the officers who were summoned to the festival, but to all who were present, since besides the officers there was certainly present a great crowd of people from all parts of the kingdom, as M. Geier has rightly remarked, so that the assembly consisted of persons of various races and languages. אֻמַּיָּא denotes *tribes of people*, as the Hebr. אֻמָּה, אמּוֹת Gen. xxv. 16, denotes the several tribes of Ishmael, and Num. xxv. 15 the separate tribes of the Midianites, and is thus not so extensive in its import as עַמְמִין, *peoples*. לִשָּׁנַיָּא, corresponding to הַלְּשֹׁנוֹת, Isa. lxvi. 18, designates (*vide* Gen. x. 5, 20, 31) *communities of men of the same language*, and is not a tautology, since the distinctions of nation and of language are in the course of history frequently found. The placing together of the three words denotes all nations, however they may have widely branched off into tribes with different languages, and expresses the sense that no one in the whole kingdom should be exempted from the command. It is a mode of expression (cf. vers. 7, 29, 31 [iv. 1], and vi. 26 [25]) specially characterizing the pathetic style of the herald and the official language of the world-kingdom, which Daniel also (ch. v. 19, vii. 14) makes use of, and which from the latter passage is transferred to the Apocalypse, and by the union of these passages in Daniel with Isa. lxvi. 18 is increased to ἔθνη (גּוֹיִם in Isa.), φυλλαί, λαοὶ καὶ γλῶσσαι (Rev. v. 9, vii. 9, xiii. 7, xiv. 6, xvii. 15).

In the same passage בֵּהּ זִמְנָא, ver. 7 (cf. also ver. 8), is interchanged with בְּעִדָּנָא, *at the time* (vers. 5 and 15); but it is to be distinguished from בַּהּ־שַׁעֲתָא, *at the same moment*, vers. 6 and 15; for שָׁעָא or שָׁעָה has in the Bib. Chald. only the meaning *instant, moment*, cf. ch. iv. 16, 30, v. 5, and acquires the signification *short time, hour*, first in the Targ. and Rabbin. In the enumeration also of the six names of the musical instruments with the addition: *and all kinds of music*, the pompous language of the world-ruler and of the herald of his power is well expressed. Regarding the Greek names of three of these instruments see p. 34. The great delight of the Babylonians in music and stringed instruments appears from Isa. xiv. 11 and Ps. cxxxvii. 3, and is confirmed by the testimony of Herod. i. 191, and Curtius, v. 3. קַרְנָא, *horn*, is the far-sounding *tuba* of the ancients, the קֶרֶן or שׁוֹפָר of the Hebr.; see under Josh. vi. 5. מַשְׁרוֹקִיתָא, from שְׁרַק, *to hiss, to whistle*, is the *reed-flute*, translated by the LXX. and Theodot. σύριγξ, the *shepherd's* or *Pan's pipes*, which consisted of several reeds of different thicknesses and of different lengths bound together, and, according to a Greek tradition (Pollux, iv. 9, 15), was invented by two Medes. קִיתָרֹס (according to the *Kethiv;* but the *Keri* and the Targ. and Rabbin. give the form קַתְרֹס) is the Greek κιθάρα or κίθαρις, *harp*, for the Greek ending ις becomes ος in the Aramaic, as in many similar cases; cf. Ges. *Thes.* p. 1215. סַבְּכָא, corresponding to the Greek σαμβύκη, but a Syrian invention, see p. 34, is, according to Athen. iv. p. 175, a *four-stringed instrument*, having a sharp, clear tone; cf. Ges. *Thes.* p. 935. פְּסַנְתְּרִין (in ver. 7 written with a ט instead of ת, and in vers. 10 and 15 pointed with a Tsere under the ת) is the Greek ψαλτήριον, of which the Greek ending ιον becomes abbreviated in the Aram. into ִין (cf. Ges. *Thes.* p. 1116). The word has no etymology in the Semitic. It was an instrument like a harp, which according to Augustin (on Ps. xxxii. [xxxiii.] 2 and Ps. xlii. [xliii.] 4) was distinguished from the *cithara* in this particular, that while the strings of the *cithara* passed over the sounding-board, those of the *psalterium* (or *organon*) were placed under it. Such harps are found on Egyptian (see Rosellini) and also on Assyrian monuments (cf. Layard, *Ninev. and Bab.*, Table xiii. 4). סוּמְפֹּנְיָה, in ver. 10 סִיפֹּנְיָה, is not derived from סְפַן, *contignare*, but is the Aramaic form of συμφωνία, *bag-pipes*, which is called in Italy at the present day *sampogna*, and derives its Greek name from the accord of two pipes placed in the bag; cf. Ges. *Thes.* p. 941. זְמָרָא signifies, not "song," but *musical playing*, from זַמֵּר, *to play the strings*, ψάλλειν; and because the music of the instrument was accompanied with song, it means also *the song accompanying the music.* The explanation of זְמָרָא by singing stands here in opposition to the כֹּל זְנֵי, since all sorts of songs could only be sung after one another, but the herald speaks of the simultaneous rise of the sound. The limiting of the word also to the playing on a stringed instrument does not fit the context, inasmuch as wind instruments are also named. Plainly in the words כֹּל זְנֵי זְמָרָא all the other instruments not particularly named are comprehended, so that זְמָרָא is to be understood generally of *playing on musical instruments.* בַּהּ־שַׁעֲתָא, *in the same instant.* The frequent pleonastic use in the later Aramaic of the union of the preposition with a suffix anticipating the following noun, whereby the preposition is frequently repeated before the noun, as *e.g.* בֵּהּ בְּדָנִיֵּאל, ch. v. 12, cf. ch. v. 30, has in the Bib. Chald. generally a certain emphasis, for the pronominal suffix is manifestly used demonstratively, in the sense *even* this, *even* that.

Homage was commanded to be shown to the image under the pain of death to those who refused. Since "the dominion of Nebuchadnezzar was founded not by right, but by the might of conquest" (Klief.), and the homage which he commanded to be shown to the image was regarded not only as a proof of subjection under the power of the king, but comprehended in it also the recognition of his gods as the gods of the kingdom, instances of refusal were to be expected. In the demand of the king there was certainly a kind of religious oppression, but by no means, as Bleek, v. Leng., and other critics maintain, a religious persecution, as among heathen rulers Antiochus Epiphanes practised it. For so tolerant was heathenism, that it recognised the gods of the different nations; but all heathen kings required that the nations subdued by them should also recognise the gods of their kingdom, which they held to be more powerful than were the gods of the vanquished nations. A refusal to yield homage to the gods of the kingdom they regarded as an act of hostility against the kingdom and its monarch, while every one might at the same time honour his own national god. This acknowledgment, that the gods of the kingdom were the more powerful, every heathen could grant; and thus Nebuchadnezzar demanded nothing in a religious point of view which every one of his subjects could not yield. To him, therefore, the refusal of the Jew's could not but appear as opposition to the greatness of his kingdom. But the Jews, or Israelites, could not do homage to the gods of Nebuchadnezzar without rejecting their faith that Jehovah alone was God, and that besides Him there were no gods. Therefore Nebuchadnezzar practised towards them, without, from his polytheistic standpoint, designing it, an intolerable religious coercion, which, however, is fundamentally different from the persecution of Judaism by Antiochus Epiphanes, who forbade the Jews on pain of death to serve their God, and endeavoured utterly to destroy the Jewish religion.—Regarding the structure of the fiery furnace, see under ver. 22.

Ver. 8. ff. The Chaldeans immediately denounced Daniel's three friends as transgressors of the king's command. כָּל־קֳבֵל דְּנָה, *therefore*, viz. because the friends of Daniel who were placed over the province of Babylon had not, by falling down before the golden image, done it homage. That they did not do so is not expressly said, but is expressed in what follows. גֻּבְרִין כַּשְׂדָּאִין are not Chaldeans as astrologers or magi (כַּשְׂדִּים), but members of the Chaldean nation, in contrast to יְהוּדָיֵא, the Jews. קְרִבוּ, *they came near to the king.* אֲכַל קַרְצֵי דִּי, literally, *to eat the flesh of any one,* is in Aramaic the common expression for *to calumniate, to denounce.* That which was odious in their report was, that they used this instance of disobedience to the king's command on the part of the Jewish officers as an occasion of removing them from their offices,—that their denunciation of them arose from their envying the Jews their position of influence, as in ch. vi. 5 (4) f. Therefore they give prominence to the fact that the king had raised these Jews to places of rule in the province of Babylon.

With this form of address in ver. 9, cf. ch. ii. 4. שִׂים טְעֵם signifies in ver. 12 *rationem reddere,* to attend to, to have regard for. In ver. 10, as frequently, the expression signifies, on the contrary, *to give an opinion, a judgment, i.e. to publish a command.* The *Keth.* לֵאלָהַיִךְ (ver. 12), for which the *Keri* prefers the sing. form לֵאלָהָךְ, in sound the same as the contracted plur., is to be maintained as correct; for the *Keri* here, as in ver. 18, supporting itself on לֵאלָהִי, ver. 14, rests on the idea that by the honouring of his god only the doing of homage to the image is meant, while the not doing homage to the image only gives proof of this, that they altogether refused to honour the gods of Nebuchadnezzar. This is placed in the foreground by the accusers, so as to arouse the indignation of the king. "These Chaldeans," Hitz. remarks quite justly, "knew the three Jews, who were so placed as to be well known, and at the same time envied, before this. They had long known that they did not worship idols; but on this occasion, when their religion made it necessary for the Jews to disobey the king's command, they make use of their knowledge."

Ver. 13. That they succeeded in their object, Nebuchadnezzar shows in the command given in anger and fury to bring the rebels before him. הֵיתָיו, notwithstanding its likeness to the Hebr. Hiphil form הֵתָיו, Isa. xxi. 14, is not the Hebraizing Aphel, but, as הֵיתָיִת, ch. vi. 18, shows, is a Hebraizing passive form of the Aphel, since the active form is הַיְתִיו, ch. v. 3, and is a passive formation peculiar to the Bib. Chald., for which in the Targg. Ittaphal is used.

Vers. 14–18. *The trial of the accused.*

Ver. 14. The question הַצְדָּא the old translators incorrectly explain by *Is it true?* In the justice of the accusation Nebuchadnezzar had no doubt whatever, and צְדָא has not this meaning. Also the meaning, *scorn*, which אַצְדִּי in Aram. has, and L. de Dieu, Häv., and Kran. make use of, does not appear to be quite consistent, since Nebuchadnezzar, if he had seen in the refusal to do homage to the image a despising of his gods, then certainly he would not have publicly repeated his command, and afforded to the accused the possibility of escaping the threatened punishment, as he did (ver. 15). We therefore agree with Hitz. and Klief., who interpret it, after the Hebr. צְדִיָּה, Num. xxxv. 20 f., of *malicious resolution*, not merely intention, according to Gesen., Winer, and others. For all the three could not unintentionally or accidentally have made themselves guilty of transgression. The form הַצְדָא we regard as a noun form with ה *interrog.* prefixed in adverbial cases, and not an Aphel formation: *Scorning, Shadrach, etc., do ye not serve?* (Kran.) The affirmative explanation of the verse, according to which the king would suppose the motive of the transgression as decided, does not agree with the alternative which (ver. 15) he places before the accused. But if הַצְדָא is regarded as a question, there is no need for our supplying the conjunction דִּי before the following verb, but we may unite the הַצְדָא in one sentence with the following verb: "*are ye of design . . . not obeying?*" Nebuchadnezzar speaks of his god in contrast to the God of the Jews.

Ver. 15. עֲתִידִין taken with the following clause, תִּפְּלוּן . . . דִּי, is not a circumlocution for the future (according to Winer, *Chald. Gram.* § 45, 2). This does not follow from the use of the simple future in the contrast, but it retains its peculiar meaning *ready*. The conclusion to the first clause is omitted, because it is self-evident from the conclusion of the second, opposed passage: *then ye will not be cast into the fiery furnace.* Similar omissions are found in Ex. xxxii. 32, Luke xiii. 9. For the purpose of giving strength to his threatening, Nebuchadnezzar adds that no god would deliver them out of his hand. In this Hitz. is not justified in supposing there is included a blaspheming of Jehovah like that of Sennacherib, Isa. xxxvii. 10. The case is different. Sennacherib raised his gods above Jehovah, the God of the Jews; Nebuchadnezzar only declares that deliverance out of the fiery furnace is a work which no god can accomplish, and in this he only indirectly likens the God of the Jews to the gods of the heathen.

Ver. 16. In the answer of the accused, נְבוּכַדְנֶצַּר is not, contrary to the accent, to be placed in apposition to לְמַלְכָּא; for, as Kran.

has rightly remarked, an intentional omission of מַלְכָּא in addressing Nebuchadnezzar is, after ver. 18, where מַלְכָּא occurs in the address, as little likely as that the Athnach is placed under לְמַלְכָּא only on account of the apposition going before, to separate from it the *nomen propr.;* and an error in the placing of the *distinctivus*, judging from the existing accuracy, is untenable. "The direct address of the king by his name plainly corresponds to the king's address to the three officers in the preceding words, ver. 14." We are not to conclude from it, as Hitz. supposes, "that they address him as a plebeian," but much rather, as in the corresponding address, ver. 14, are to see in it an evidence of the deep impression sought to be produced in the person concerned.

Ver. 16. פִּתְגָם is the accus., and is not to be connected with עַל דְּנָה: *as to this command* (Häv.). If the demonstrative were present only before the noun, then the noun must stand in the *status absol.* as ch. iv. 15 (18). פִּתְגָם, from the Zend. *paiti* = πρός, and *gâm*, to go, properly, "the going to," therefore *message, edict,* then generally *word* (as here) and *matter* (Ezra vi. 11), as frequently in the Targ., corresponding to the Hebr. דָּבָר.

Ver. 17. יָכִל denotes the *ethical ability, i.e.* the ability limited by the divine holiness and righteousness, not the omnipotence of God as such. For this the accused did not doubt, nor will they place in question the divine omnipotence before the heathen king. The conclusion begins after the Athnach, and הֵן means, not *see! lo!* (according to the old versions and many interpreters), for which Daniel constantly uses אֲלוּ or אֲרוּ, but it means *if*, as here the contrast וְהֵן לָא, *and if not* (ver. 18), demands. There lies in the answer, "If our God will save us, then . . . and if not, know, O king, that we will not serve thy gods," neither audacity, nor a superstitious expectation of some miracle (ver. 17), nor fanaticism (ver. 18), as Berth., v. Leng., and Hitz. maintain, but only the confidence of faith and a humble submission to the will of God. "The three simply see that their standpoint and that of the king are altogether different, also that their standpoint can never be clearly understood by Nebuchadnezzar, and therefore they give up any attempt to justify themselves. But that which was demanded of them they could not do, because it would have been altogether contrary to their faith and their conscience. And then without fanaticism they calmly decline to answer, and only say, 'Let him do according to his own will;' thus without superstitiousness committing their deliverance to God" (Klief.).

Vers. 19–27. *The judgment pronounced on the accused, their punishment, and their miraculous deliverance.*

After the decided refusal of the accused to worship his gods, Nebuchadnezzar changed his countenance toward them. Full of anger at such obstinacy, he commanded that the furnace should be heated seven times greater than was usual (ver. 19), and that the rebels should be bound in their clothes by powerful men of his army, and then cast into the furnace (vers. 20, 21). The form of his countenance changed, and his wrath showed itself in the lineaments of his face. The *Kethiv* אֶשְׁתַּנּוֹ (*plur.*) refers to the genitive [אַנְפּוֹהִי, plur., "of his countenances"] as the chief idea, and is not, after the *Keri*, to be changed into the *sing.* לְמֵזֵא for לְמֵאזֵא. On חַד־שִׁבְעָה, *sevenfold*, cf. Winer, *Chald. Gram.* § 59, 5. עַל דִּי חֲזֵה, *beyond that which was fit, i.e.* which was necessary. Seven is used as expressive of an exceedingly great number, with reference to the religious meaning of the punishment.

Ver. 21. Of the different parts of clothing named, סַרְבָּלִין are not hose, short stockings, from which Hitz. concludes that the enumeration proceeds from the inner to the outer clothing. This remark, correct in itself, proves nothing as to the covering for the legs. This meaning is given to the word only from the New Persian *shalwâr*, which in the Arabic is سِرْوِيل; cf. Haug in Ew.'s *bibl. Jahrbb.* v. p. 162. But the word corresponds with the genuine Semitic word سِرْبَال, which means *tunica* or *indusium;* cf. Ges. *Thes.*[1] p. 970, and *Heb. Lex. s. v.* Accordingly, סַרְבָּלִין denotes *under-clothing* which would be worn next the body as our shirt. פַּטִּישֵׁיהוֹן, for which the *Keri* uses the form פַּטְּשֵׁיהוֹן, corresponding to the Syriac ܦܛܫܐ, is explained in the Hebr. translation of the

[1] The LXX. have omitted סַרְבָּלִין in their translation. Theodot. has rendered it by σαράβαρα, and the third-named piece of dress כַּרְבְּלָן by περικνημῖδες, which the LXX. have rendered by τιάρας ἐπὶ τῶν κεφαλῶν. Theodoret explains it: περικνημῖδας δὲ τὰς καλουμένας ἀναξυρίδας λέγει. These are, according to Herod. vii. 161, the ἀναξυρίδες, *i.e. braccæ*, worn by the Persians περὶ τὰ σκέλεα. Regarding Σαράβαρα Theodoret remarks: ἔστι Περσικῶν περιβολαίων εἴδη. Thus Theodot. and Theodor. expressly distinguish the σαράβαρα (סַרְבָּלִין) from the περικνημῖδες; but the false interpretation of סַרְבָּלִין by *breeches* has given rise to the confounding of that word with כַּרְבְּלָן, and the identification of the two, the περικνημῖδες being interpreted of *coverings for the feet;* and the Vulg. translates the passage: "*cum braccis suis et tiaris et calceamentis et vestibus,*" while

Chald. portions of Daniel by כְּתֹנֶת, *tunica*, and is derived from פשׁט, *expandit* (by the transposition of the second and third radicals). Thus the Syriac word is explained by Syr. lexicographers. Theodotion's translation, *τιάραι*, is probably only hit upon from the similarity of the sound of the Greek *πέτασος*, the *covering for the head* worn by the *ἔφηβοι*. כַּרְבְּלָן are *mantles*, from כַּרְבֵּל, R. כְּבַל, *to bind, to lay around*, with *r* intercalated, which occurs 1 Chron. xv. 27 of the putting around or putting on of the מְעִיל (upper garment). לְבוּשֵׁיהוֹן are *the other pieces of clothing* (Aben Ezra and others), not *mantles*. For that לְבוּשׁ was specially used of over-clothes (Hitz.) cannot be proved from Job xxiv. 7 and 2 Kings x. 22. We have here, then, the threefold clothing which, according to Herodotus, i. 195, the Babylonians wore, namely, the סַרְבָּלִין, the *κιθῶν ποδηνεκὴς λίνεος*, the פַּטִּישָׁא worn above it, *ἄλλον εἰρίνεον κιθῶνα*, and the כַּרְבְּלָא thrown above that, *χλανίδιον λευκόν*; while under the word לְבוּשֵׁיהוֹן the other articles of clothing, coverings for the feet and the head, are to be understood.[1] The separate articles of clothing, consisting of easily inflammable material, are doubtlessly mentioned with reference to the miracle that followed, that even these remained unchanged (ver. 27) in the fiery furnace. In the easily inflammable nature of these materials, namely, of the fine *κιθῶν ποδηνεκὴς λίνεος*, we have perhaps to seek the reason on account of which the accused were bound in their clothes, and not, as Theodoret and most others think, in the haste with which the sentence against them was carried out.

Ver. 22. מִן דִּי (*because that*), a further explanatory expression added to כָּל־קֳבֵל דְּנָה (*wholly for this cause*): because the word of the king was sharp, and in consequence of it (ו), the furnace was heated beyond measure for that reason. The words גֻּבְרַיָּא אִלֵּךְ

Luther has "cloaks, shoes, and hats." This confounding of the two words was authorized by the Greek scholiasts, to which the admission of the Persian *shalwâr* into the Arabic *saravilu* may have contributed. In Suidas we find the right interpretation along with the false one when he says: Σαράβαρα ἐσθὴς Περσική· ἔνιοι δὲ λέγουσι βρακία. Hesychius, on the other hand, briefly explains σαράβαρα by βρακία, κνημῖδες, σκελέαι. Hence the word in the forms *sarabara*, *siravara*, *saravara* or *saraballa*, *sarabela*, is commonly used in the middle ages for *hose*, and has been transferred into various modern languages; cf. Gesen. *Thes.* p. 971.

[1] With the setting aside of the false interpretation we have disposed of the objection against the historical character of the narrative which v. Leng. and Hitz. have founded on the statement of Herodotus *l.c.*, that the Babylonians wore no hose, but that they were first worn by the Persians, who adopted them from the Medes.

(*these mighty men*) stand here in the *status absol.*, and are again taken up in the pronoun הִמּוֹן after the verb קַטִּל. If the three were brought up to the furnace, it must have had a mouth above, through which the victims could be cast into it. When heated to an ordinary degree, this could be done without danger to the men who performed this service; but in the present case the heat of the fire was so great, that the servants themselves perished by it. This circumstance also is mentioned to show the greatness of the miracle by which the three were preserved unhurt in the midst of the furnace. The same thing is intended by the repetition of the word מְכַפְּתִין, *bound*, ver. 23, which, moreover, is purposely placed at the close of the passage to prepare for the contrast שְׁרַיִן, *at liberty*, free from the bonds,[1] ver. 25.

Ver. 24 ff. The king, who sat watching the issue of the matter, looked through the door into the furnace, and observed that the three who had been cast into it bound, walked about freed from their bonds and unhurt; and, in truth, he saw not the three only, but also a fourth, "like to a son of the gods," beside them. At this sight he was astonished and terrified. He hastily stood up; and having assured himself by a consultation with his counsellors that three men had indeed been cast bound into the furnace, while he saw four walking in the midst of it, he approached the mouth of the furnace and cried to the three to come forth. They immediately came out, and were inspected by the assembled officers of state, and found to be wholly uninjured as to their bodies, their clothes being unharmed also, and without even the smell of fire upon them. הַדָּבְרִין refers, without doubt, to the officers of the kingdom, *ministers* or *counsellors of state* standing very near the king, since they are named in ver. 27 and ch. vi. 8 (7) along with the first three ranks of officers, and (ch. iv. 23 [26]) during Nebuchadnezzar's madness they conducted the affairs of government. The literal meaning of the word, however, is not quite obvious. Its derivation from the Chald. דָּבְרִין, *duces*, with the Hebr. article (Gesen.), which can only be supported by מְדַבְּרָא, Prov. xi. 14

[1] Between vers. 23 and 24 the LXX. have introduced the Prayer of Azariah and the Song of the three men in the fiery furnace; and these two hymns are connected together by a narrative which explains the death of the Chaldeans who threw the three into the furnace, and the miracle of the deliverance of Daniel's friends. Regarding the apocryphal origin of these additions, composed in the Greek language, which Luther in his translation has rightly placed in the Apocrypha, see my *Lehr. der Einl. in d. A. Test.* § 251.

(Targ.), is decidedly opposed by the absence of all analogies for the blending into one word of the article with a noun in the Semitic language. The *Alkoran* offers no corresponding analogues, since this word with the article is found only in the more modern dialects. But the meaning which P. v. Bohlen (*Symbolæ ad interp. s. Codicis ex ling. pers.* p. 26) has sought from the Persian word which is translated by *simul judex, i.e. socius in judicio*, is opposed not only by the fact that the compensation of the *Mim* by the Dagesch, but also the composition and the meaning, has very little probability.

The fourth whom Nebuchadnezzar saw in the furnace was like in his appearance, *i.e.* as commanding veneration, to a son of the gods, *i.e.* to one of the race of the gods. In ver. 28 the same personage is called an angel of God, Nebuchadnezzar there following the religious conceptions of the Jews, in consequence of the conversation which no doubt he had with the three who were saved. Here, on the other hand, he speaks in the spirit and meaning of the Babylonian doctrine of the gods, according to the theogonic representation of the *συζυγία* of the gods peculiar to all Oriental religions, whose existence among the Babylonians the female divinity Mylitta associated with Bel places beyond a doubt; cf. Hgst. *Beitr.* i. p. 159, and Häv., Kran., and Klief. *in loc.*

Acting on this assumption, which did not call in question the deliverance of the accused by the miraculous interposition of the Deity, Nebuchadnezzar approached the door of the furnace and cried to the three men to come out, addressing them as the servants (worshippers) of the most high God. This address does not go beyond the circle of heathen ideas. He does not call the God of Shadrach, Meshach, and Abednego the only true God, but only the most high God, the chief of the gods, just as the Greeks called their Zeus ὁ ὕψιστος θεός. The *Kethiv* עִלָּיָא (in Syr. ܥܠܝܐ, *to preserve*) is here and everywhere in Daniel (ver. 32, ch. iv. 14, 21, etc.) pointed by the Masoretes according to the form עִילָּאָה (with ה) prevailing in the Targg. The forms גְּשֵׁם, גֶּשְׁמָא, are peculiar to Daniel (ver. 27 f., ch. iv. 30, v. 21, vii. 11). The Targg. have גּוּשְׁמָא instead of it.

Vers. 28–30. *The impression made by this event on Nebuchadnezzar.*

The marvellous deliverance of the three from the flames of the furnace produced such an impression on Nebuchadnezzar, that he changed his earlier and humbler judgment (ver. 15) regarding the God of the Jews, and spoke now in praise of the might of this God. For at the same time he not only openly announced that He had saved (ver. 28) His servants, but also by an edict, issued to all the peoples of his kingdom, he forbade on pain of death the doing of any dishonour to the God of the Jews (ver. 29). Nebuchadnezzar, however, did not turn to the true God. He neither acknowledged Jehovah as the only, or the alone true God, nor did he command Him to be worshipped. He only declared Him to be a God who is able to save His servants as no other could, and merely forbade the despising and reviling of this God. Whoever speaks שָׁלָה, *that which is erroneous* or unjust, against the God of Shadrach, etc., shall be put to death. שָׁלָה, from שְׁלָה, *to err, to commit a fault*, is changed in the *Keri* into שָׁלוּ, which occurs in ch. vi. 5 and Ezra iv. 22, and in the Targg.; but without sufficient ground, since with other words both forms are found together, *e.g.* אַרְמְלָא, *vidua*, with אַרְמְלוּ, *viduitas*. According to this, שָׁלוּ *in abstr.* means *the error;* שָׁלָה *in concr., the erroneous.* Hitz. finds the command partly too narrow, partly quite unsuitable, because an error, a simple oversight, should find pardon as soon as possible. But the distinction between a fault arising from mistake and one arising from a bad intention does not accord with the edict of an Oriental despot, which must be in decided terms, so that there may be no room in cases of transgression for an appeal to a mere oversight. Still less importance is to be attached to the objection that the carrying out of the command may have had its difficulties. But by such difficulties the historical character of the narrative is not brought under suspicion. As the Chaldeans in this case had watched the Jews and accused them of disobedience, so also could the Jews scattered throughout the kingdom bring before the tribunal the heathen who blasphemed their God.

Ver. 29.. Regarding the collocation of the words עַם אֻמָּה וְלִשָּׁן, see under ver. 4; and regarding the הַדָּמִין and the threatened punishment, see under ch. ii. 5. כִּדְנָה we regard, with the LXX., Theodrt., Vulg., and old interpreters, as a fem. adverbial: *οὕτως, ita,* as it occurs in ch. ii. 10, Ezra v. 7, and Jer. x. 11. The interpreting of it as masculine, *as this God,* does not correspond with the heathen consciousness of God, to which a God perceptible by sight was more appropriate than a God invisible (Kran.). The history concludes (ver. 30) with the remark that Nebuchadnezzar now regarded the three men with the greatest favour. In what way he manifested his regard for them is not stated, inasmuch as this is not necessary to the object of the narrative. הַצְלַח with לְ, *to give to any one happiness*, prosperity, to cause him to be fortunate.

If we attentively consider the import of this narrative in its bearing on the history of the kingdom of God, we learn how the true worshippers of the Lord under the dominion of the world-power could and would come into difficulties, imperilling life, between the demands of the lords of this world and the duties they owe to God. But we also learn, that if in these circumstances they remain faithful to their God, they will in a wonderful manner be protected by Him; while He will reveal His omnipotence so gloriously, that even the heathen world-rulers will be constrained to recognise their God and to give Him glory.

CHAP. III. 31 (IV. 1)–IV. 34 (37). NEBUCHADNEZZAR'S DREAM AND HIS MADNESS.

This section is in the form of a proclamation by king Nebuchadnezzar to all the peoples of his kingdom, informing them of a wonderful event in which the living God of heaven made Himself known as the ruler over the kingdoms of men. After a short introduction (ch. iii. 31–33 [iv. 1–3]) the king makes known to his subjects, that amid the peaceful prosperity of his life he had dreamed a dream which filled him with disquietude, and which the wise men of Babylon could not interpret, until Daniel came, who was able to do so (ch. iv. 1–5 [4–8]). In his dream he saw a great tree, with vast branches and bearing much fruit, which reached up to heaven, under which beasts and birds found a lodging, shelter, and food. Then a holy watcher came down from heaven and commanded the tree to be cut down, so that its roots only remained in the earth, but bound with iron and brass, till seven times shall pass, so that men may know the power of the Most High over the kingdoms of men (vers. 6–15 [9–18]). Daniel interpreted to him this dream, that the tree represented the king himself, regarding whom it was resolved by Heaven that he should be driven forth from men and should live among the beasts till seven times should pass, and he should know that the Highest rules over the kingdoms of men (vers. 16–24 [19–27]). After twelve months this dream began to be fulfilled, and Nebuchadnezzar fell into a state of madness, and became like a beast of the field (vers. 25–30 [28–33]). But after the lapse of the appointed time his understanding returned to him, whereupon he was again restored to his kingdom and became exceeding great, and now praised and honoured the King of heaven (vers. 31–34 [34–37]).

If the preceding history teaches how the Almighty God wonderfully protects His true worshippers against the enmity of the world-power, this narrative may be regarded as an actual confirmation of the truth that this same God can so humble the rulers of the world, if in presumptuous pride they boast of their might, as to constrain them to recognise Him as the Lord over the kings of the earth. Although this narrative contains no miracle contrary to the course of nature, but only records a divine judgment, bringing Nebuchadnezzar for a time into a state of madness,—a judgment announced beforehand in a dream, and happening according to the prediction, —yet Bleek, v. Leng., Hitz., and others have rejected its historical veracity, and have explained it as only an invention by which the Maccabean pseudo-Daniel threatens the haughty Antiochus Epiphanes with the vengeance of Heaven, which shall compel him to recognise One higher than himself, namely, the God of Israel. A proof of this assertion of theirs they find in the form of the narrative. The proclamation of Nebuchadnezzar to all the nations of his kingdom, in which the matter is set forth, shows, in its introduction and its close, greater familiarity with biblical thoughts than one would have expected in Nebuchadnezzar. The doxologies, ch. iii. 33 (iv. 3) and iv. 31 (34), agree almost literally with Ps. cxlv. 13; and in the praise of the omnipotence and of the infinite majesty of God, ch. iv. 32 (35), the echoes of Isa. xl. 17, xliii. 13, 24, 21 cannot fail to be recognised. The circumstance that in vers. 25 (28)–30 (33) Nebuchadnezzar is spoken of in the third person, appears to warrant also the opinion that the writing was composed by some other person than by the king. But the use of the third person by Nebuchadnezzar in the verses named is fully explained from the contents of the passage (see Exposition), and neither justifies the conclusion that the author was a different person from the king, nor the supposition of Häv. that the vers. 26 (29)–30 (33) are a passage parenthetically added by Daniel to the brief declaration of the edict, ver. 25 (28), for the purpose of explaining it and making the matter better understood by posterity. The circumstance that ver. 31 (34) refers to the statement of time in ver. 26 (29), and that the royal proclamation would be incomplete without vers. 26 (29)–30 (33), leads to the opposite conclusion. The existence of these biblical thoughts, however, even though not sufficiently explained by the supposition that Nebuchadnezzar had heard these thoughts and words in a conference on the matter with Daniel, and had appropriated them to himself, cannot be adduced against the genuineness of the edict, but only shows this much, that in the composition of it Nebuchadnezzar had made use of the pen of Daniel, whereby the praise of God received a fuller expression than Nebuchadnezzar would have given to it. For in the whole narrative of the event the peculiar heathen conceptions of the Chaldean king so naturally present themselves before us, that beyond question we read the very words used by Nebuchadnezzar himself.

Then it has been found in the highest degree strange that Nebuchadnezzar himself should have published to his people an account of his madness, instead of doing all to make this sad history forgotten. But, notwithstanding that the views of the ancients regarding madness were different from ours, we must say, with Klief. and others, on the contrary, that "publicity in such a case was better than concealment; the matter, besides, being certainly known, could not be made either better or worse by being made public. Nebuchadnezzar wishes to publish, not his madness, but the help which God had imparted to him; and that he did this openly does honour indeed to his magnanimous character."

But the principal argument against the historical veracity of the occurrence is derived from the consideration that no mention is anywhere else made of the seven years' madness, an event which certainly could not but introduce very important changes and complications into the Babylonian kingdom. It is true that the Hebrew history does not at all refer to the later years of Nebuchadnezzar's reign, though it extends, Jer. lii. 31, to a period later than these times, and should, without doubt, give as much prominence to such a divine judgment against this enemy as to the fate of Sennacherib (2 Kings xix. 37) (Hitz.). But the brief notice, Jer. lii. 31, that king Jehoiachin, thirty-seven years after his deportation, was delivered from prison by Evilmerodach when he became king, afforded no opportunity to speak of Nebuchadnezzar's madness, which for a time rendered him incapable of conducting the affairs of government, but did not cause his death. And the reference to the murder of Sennacherib proves nothing regarding it, because, according to the view of Jeremiah and the biblical historians, Nebuchadnezzar occupied an altogether different relation to the theocracy from that of Sennacherib. Nebuchadnezzar appeared not as an arch-enemy, but as the servant of Jehovah he executed the will of God against the sinful kingdom of Judah; Sennacherib, on the contrary, in daring insolence derided the God of Israel, and was punished for this by the annihilation of his host, and afterwards murdered by his own son, while Nebuchadnezzar was cured of his madness.

But when the opponents of the genuineness moreover argue that even the Chaldean historian Berosus can have announced nothing at all regarding Nebuchadnezzar's madness, since Josephus, and Origen, and Jerome, who were well-versed in books, could find nothing in any author which pointed to such an event, it is to be replied, in the first place, that the representations of seven years' duration of the madness, and of the serious complications which this malady must have brought on the Babylonian kingdom, are mere frivolous suppositions of the modern critics; for the text limits the duration of the malady only to seven times, by which we may understand seven months as well as seven years. The complications in the affairs of the kingdom were, moreover, prevented by an *interim* government. Then Hgstb. (*Beitr.* i. p. 101 ff.), Häv., Del., and others, have rightly shown that not a single historical work of that period is extant, in which one could expect to find fuller information regarding the disease of Nebuchadnezzar, which is certainly very significant in sacred history, but which in no respect had any influence on the Babylonian kingdom. Herodotus, the father of history, did not know Nebuchadnezzar even by name, and seems to have had no information of his great exploits—*e.g.* of his great and important victory over the Egyptian host at Carchemish. Josephus names altogether only six authors in whose works mention is made of Nebuchadnezzar. But four of these authorities—viz.: *The Annals of the Phœnicians*, Philostratus, author of a Phœnician history, Megasthenes, and Diocles—are not here to be taken into account, because the first two contain only what relates to Phœnicia, the conquest of the land, and the siege of Tyre, the capital; while the other two, Megasth. in his Indian history, and Diocles in his Persian history, speak only quite incidentally of Nebuchadnezzar. There remain then, besides, only Berosus and Abydenus who have recorded the Chaldean history. But of Berosus, a priest of Belus at Babylon in the time of Alexander the Great, who had examined many and ancient documents, and is justly acknowledged to be a trustworthy historian, we possess only certain poor fragments of his *Χαλδαϊκά* quoted in the writings of Josephus, Eusebius, and later authors, no one of whom had read and extracted from the work of Berosus itself. Not only Eusebius, but, as M. v. Niebuhr has conclusively proved, Josephus also derived his account from Berosus only through the remains of the original preserved by Alexander Polyhistor, a contemporary of Sulla, a "tumultuous worker," whose abstract has no great security for accuracy, and still less for integrity, although he has not purposely falsified anything; cf. M. v. Niebuhr, *Gesch. Assurs*, p. 12 f. Abydenus lived much later. He wrote apparently after Josephus, since the latter has made no use of him, and thus he was not so near the original sources as Berosus, and was, moreover, to judge of his fragments which are preserved by Eusebius and Syncellus, not so capable of making use of them, although one cannot pass sentence against the trustworthiness of the peculiar sources used by him, since the notices formed from them, notwithstanding their independence on Berosus, agree well with his statements; cf. M. v. Niebuhr, p. 15 f.

But if Josephus did not himself read the work of Berosus, but only reported what he found in the extracts by Polyhistor, we need not wonder though he found nothing regarding Nebuchadnezzar's madness. And yet Josephus has preserved to us a notice from Berosus which points to the unusual malady by which Nebuchadnezzar was afflicted before his death, in the words, "Nabuchodonosor, after he had begun to build the fore-mentioned wall, fell sick and departed this life, when he had reigned forty-three years" (*contra Apion*, i. 20). In these words lies more than the simple remark, that Nebuchadnezzar, as is wont to happen to the most of men, died after an illness going before, and not suddenly, as Berth., Hitz., and others wish to interpret it. Berosus uses a formula of this kind in speaking neither of Nabonedus nor of Neriglissor, who both died, not suddenly, but a natural death. He remarks only, however, of Nebuchadnezzar's father: "Now it so fell out that he (his father Nabopolassar) fell into a distemper at this time, and died in the city of Babylon," because he had before stated regarding him, that on account of the infirmity of old age he had committed to his son the carrying on of the war against Egypt; and hence the words, "at that time he fell into a distemper," or the distemper which led to his death, acquire a particular significance.[1] If, accordingly, the "falling sick" pointed to an unusual affliction

[1] When Hitzig adduces 2 Kings xiii. 14 in support of his view, he has failed to observe that in this place is narrated how the tidings of Elisha's sickness unto death gave occasion to the king Joash to visit the prophet, from

upon Nebuchadnezzar, so also the fact that Berosus adds to the statement of the distemper the account of his death, while on the contrary, according to this chapter, Nebuchadnezzar again recovered and reigned still longer, does not oppose the reference of the "distemper" to the king's madness; for according to Berosus, as well as according to Daniel, the malady fell upon Nebuchadnezzar in the later period of his reign, after he had not only carried on wars for the founding and establishment of his world-kingdom, but had also, for the most part at least, finished his splendid buildings. After his recovery down to the time of his death, he carried forward no other great work, regarding which Berosus is able to give any communication; it therefore only remained for him to mention the fact of his death, along with the statement of the duration of his reign. No one is able, therefore, to conclude from his summary statement, that Nebuchadnezzar died very soon after his recovery from the madness.

A yet more distinct trace of the event narrated in this chapter is found in Abydenus, in the fragments preserved by Euseb. in the *Præpar. evang.* ix. 41, and in the *Chronic. Armen.* ed. Aucher, i. p. 59, wherein Abydenus announces as a Chaldee tradition (*λέγεται πρὸς Χαλδαίων*), that Nebuchadnezzar, after the ending of his war in the farther west, mounted his royal tower, *i.e.* to the flat roof, and, there seized by some god (*κατασχεθείη θεῷ ὅτεω δὴ*), he oracularly (*θεσπίσαι*) announced to the Babylonians their inevitable subjugation by the *Πέρσης ἡμίονος* united with the Medes, who would be helped by their own Babylonian gods. He prayed that the Persian might be destroyed in the abyss of the sea, or condemned to wander about in a desert wilderness, inhabited only by wild beasts; and for himself he wished a peaceful death before these misfortunes should fall on the Chaldean empire. Immediately after this utterance Nebuchadnezzar was snatched away from the sight of men (*παραχρῆμα ἠφάνιστο*). In this Chaldean tradition Eusebius has recognised[1] a disfigured tradition of this his-

whom he at that time received a significant prophetical announcement, and that thus this passage contains something quite different from the trivial notice merely that Elisha was sick previous to his death.

[1] In the *Chron. Arm.* p. 61, Eusebius has thus remarked, after recording the saying by Abyd.: "*In Danielis sane historiis de Nabuchadonosoro narratur, quomodo et quo pacto mente captus fuerit: quod si Græcorum historici aut Chaldæi morbum tegunt et a Deo eum acceptum comminiscuntur, Deumque insaniam, quæ in illum intravit, vel Dæmonem quendam, qui in eum venerit, nominant, mirandum non est. Etenim hoc quidem illorum mos est, cuncta similia Deo adscribere, Deosque nominare Dæmones.*"

tory; and even Bertholdt will not "deny that this strange saying is in its main parts identical with our Aramaic record." On the other hand, Hitz. knows nothing else to bring forward than that "the statement sounds so fabulous, that no historical substance can be discovered in it." But the historical substance lies in the occurrence which Daniel relates. As, according to Daniel, Nebuchadnezzar was on the roof of his palace when he was suddenly struck by God with madness, so also according to Abydenus he was *ὡς ἀναβὰς ἐπὶ τὰ βασιλήϊα* when seized by some god, or possessed. Here not only the time and the place of the occurrence agree, but also the circumstance that the king's being seized or bound was effected by some god, *i.e.* not by his own, but by a strange god. Not the less striking is the harmony in the curse which he prayed might fall on the Persian—"May he wander in the wilderness where no cities are, no human footstep, where wild beasts feed and the birds wander"—with the description of the abode of the king in his madness in ch. v. 21: "And he was driven from the sons of men; and his heart was made like the beasts, and his dwelling was with the wild asses; and they fed him with grass like oxen." Moreover, though the designation of the Persian as *ἡμίονος* in Abyd. may not be formed from the עֲרָדַיָּא of Daniel, but derived from old oracles regarding Cyrus diffused throughout the East, as Häv. (*N. Krit. Unters.* p. 53, under reference to Herod. i. 55, 91) regards as probable, then the harmony of the Chaldean tradition in Abyd. with the narrative in Daniel leaves no doubt that the fact announced by Daniel lies at the foundation of that tradition, but so changed as to be adapted to the mythic glorification of the hero who was celebrated, of whom Megasthenes says that he excelled Hercules in boldness and courage (*Ἡρακλέως ἀλκιμώτερον γεγονότα*, in Euseb. *Præp. ev. l.c.*).

To represent the king's state of morbid psychical bondage and want of freedom as his being moved by God with the spirit of prophecy was natural, from the resemblance which the mantic inspiration in the gestures of the ecstasy showed to the *μανία* (cf. the combination of אִישׁ מְשֻׁגָּע וּמִתְנַבֵּא, Jer. xxix. 26, 2 Kings ix. 11); and in the madness which for a time withdrew the founder of the world-kingdom from the exercise of his sovereignty there might appear as not very remote to the Chaldeans, familiar with the study of portents and prodigies as pointing out the fate of men and of nations, an omen of the future overthrow of the world-power founded by him. As the powerful monarchy of Nebuchadnezzar was transferred to the *Πέρσης ἡμίονος* not a full generation (25–26 years) after the death of its founder, it might appear conformable to the national vanity of the Chaldeans to give the interpretation to the ominous experience of the great king, that the celebrated hero himself before his death—*θεῷ ὅτεω δὴ κατάσχετος*—had prophesied its fall, and had imprecated on the destroyer great evil, but had wished for himself a happy death before these disasters should come.

But even if there were no such traditional references to the occurrence mentioned in this chapter, yet would the supposition of its invention be excluded by its nature. Although it could be prophesied to Antiochus as an Ἐπιμανής (*madman*) that he would wholly lose his understanding, yet there remains, as even Hitz. is constrained to confess, the choice of just this form of the madness, the *insania zoanthropica*, a mystery in the solution of which even the acuteness of this critic is put to shame; so that he resorts to the foolish conjecture that the Maccabean Jew had fabricated the history out of the name נבוכדנצר, since נבוך means *oberravit cum perturbatione*, and כדן, *to bind, fasten*, while the representation of the king as a tree is derived from the passages Isa. xiv. 12, Ezek. xxxi. 3 ff. To this is to be added the fact, that the tendency attributed to the narrative does not at all fit the circumstances of the Maccabean times. With the general remark that the author wished to hold up as in a mirror before the eyes of Antiochus Epiphanes to what results haughty presumption against the Most High will lead, and how necessary it is penitentially to recognise His power and glory if he would not at length fall a victim to the severest judgments (Bleek), the object of the invention of so peculiar a malady becomes quite inconceivable. Hitzig therefore seeks to explain the tendency more particularly. "The transgressor Nebuchadnezzar, who for his haughtiness is punished with madness, is the type of that arrogant Ἐπιμανής, who also sought unsuitable society, as king degraded himself (Polyb. xxvi. 10), and yet had lately given forth a circular-letter *of an altogether different character* (1 Macc. i. 41 ff.)."

"If in ver. 28 (31) the loss of the kingdom is placed before the view of Nebuchadnezzar (Antiochus Epiphanes), the passage appears to have been composed at a time when the Maccabees had already taken up arms, and gained the superiority (1 Macc. ii. 42–48)." According to this, we must suppose that the author of this book, at a time when the Jews who adhered to their religion, under the leadership of Mattathias, marched throughout the land to put an end by the force of arms to the oppression of Antiochus Epiphanes, had proposed to the cruel king the full restoration of his supremacy and the willing subjection of the Jews under his government, on the condition that he should recognise the omnipotence of their God. But how does such a proposal of peace agree with the war of the Jews led by Mattathias against the *υἱοὶ τῆς ὑπερηφανίας*, against the heathen and transgressors, whose horn (power) they suffer not to prosper (1 Macc. ii. 47, 48)? How with the passionate address of the dying Mattathias, "Fear ye not the words of a sinful man (*ἀνδρὸς ἁμαρτωλοῦ*, *i.e.* Antiochus), for his glory shall be dung and worms" (ver. 62)? And wherein then consists the resemblance between the Nebuchadnezzar of this chapter and Antiochus Epiphanes? — the latter, a despot who cherished a deadly hatred against the Jews who withstood him; the former, a prince who showed his good-will toward the Jews in the person of Daniel, who was held in high esteem by him. Or is Nebuchadnezzar, in the fact that he gloried in the erection of the great Babylon as the seat of his kingdom, and in that he was exhorted by Daniel to show compassion toward the poor and the oppressed (ver. 24 [27]), a type of Antiochus, "who sought improper society, and as king denied himself," *i.e.*, according to Polybius as quoted by Hitzig, delighted in fellowship with the lower classes of society, and spent much treasure amongst the poor handicraftsmen with whom he consorted? Or is there seen in the circular-letter of Antiochus, "that in his whole kingdom all should be one people, and each must give up his own laws," any motive for the fabrication of the proclamation in which Nebuchadnezzar relates to all his people the signs and wonders which the most high God had done to him, and for which he praised the God of heaven?

And if we fix our attention, finally, on the relation of Daniel to Nebuchadnezzar, shall that prophet as the counsellor of the heathen king, who in true affection uttered the wish that the dream might be to them that hated him, and the interpretation thereof to his enemies (ver. 16 [19]), be regarded as a pattern to the Maccabees sacrificing all for the sake of their God, who wished for their deadly enemy Antiochus that his glory might sink into "dung and the worms?" Is it at all conceivable that a Maccabean Jew, zealous for the law of his fathers, could imagine that the celebrated ancient prophet Daniel would cherish so benevolent a wish toward the heathen Nebuchadnezzar, in order that by such an invention he might animate his contemporaries to stedfast perseverance in war against the ruthless tyrant Antiochus?

This total difference between the facts recorded in this chapter and the circumstances of the Maccabean times described in 1 Macc. ii. 42–48, as Kranichfeld has fully shown, precludes any one, as he has correctly observed, "from speaking of a tendency delineated according to the original of the Maccabean times in the name of an exegesis favourable to historical investigation." The efforts of a hostile criticism will never succeed on scientific grounds in changing the historical matters of fact recorded in this chapter into a fiction constructed with a tendency.

Chap. iii. 31 (iv. 1)–iv. 15 (18). *The preface to the king's edict, and the account of his dream.*

Ch. iii. 31–33 (iv. 1–3). These verses form the introduction[1] to the manifesto, and consist of the expression of good wishes, and the announcement of its object. The mode of address here used, accompanied by an expression of a good wish, is the usual form also of the edicts promulgated by the Persian kings; cf. Ezra iv. 17, vii. 12. Regarding the designation of his subjects, cf. ch. iii. 4. בְּכָל־אַרְעָא, not "in all lands" (Häv.), but *on the whole earth*, for Nebuchadnezzar regarded himself as the lord of the whole earth. אָתַיָּא וְתִמְהַיָּא corresponds with the Hebr. אוֹתֹת וּמֹפְתִים; cf. Deut. vi. 22, vii. 19. The experience of this miracle leads to the offering up of praise to God, ver. 33 (ch. iv. 3). The doxology of the second part of ver. 33 occurs again with little variation in ch. iv. 31 (34),

[1] The connection of these verses with the third chapter in the Hebrew, Greek, and Latin Bibles is altogether improper. The originator of the division into chapters appears to have entertained the idea that Nebuchadnezzar had made known the miracle of the deliverance of the three men from the fiery furnace to his subjects by means of a proclamation, according to which the fourth chapter would contain a new royal proclamation different from that former one, —an idea which was rejected by Luther, who has accordingly properly divided the chapters. Conformably to that division, as Chr. B. Michaelis has well remarked, "*prius illud programma in fine capitis tertii excerptum caput sine corpore, posterius vero quod capite* IV. *exhibetur, corpus sine capite, illic enim conspicitur quidem exordium, sed sine narratione, hic vero narratio quidem, sed sine exordio.*" Quite arbitrarily Ewald has, according to the LXX., who have introduced the words Ἀρχὴ τῆς ἐπιστολῆς before ch. iii. 31, and Ἔτους ὀκτωκαιδεκάτου τῆς βασιλείας Ναβουχοδονόσορ εἶπεν before ch. iv. 1, enlarged this passage by the superscription: "In the 28th year of the reign of king Nebuchadnezzar, king Nebuchadnezzar wrote thus to all the nations, communities, and tongues who dwell in the whole earth."

vii. 14, 18, and is met with also in Ps. cxlv. 13, which bears the name of David; while the rendering of עִם־דָּר וְדָר, *from generation to generation, i.e.* as long as generations exist, agrees with Ps. lxxii. 5.

With ch. iv. 1 (4) Nebuchadnezzar begins the narration of his wonderful experience. When he was at rest in his palace and prospering, he had a dream as he lay upon his bed which made him afraid and perplexed. שְׁלֵה, *quiet, in undisturbed, secure prosperity.* רַעְנַן, properly *growing green*, of the fresh, vigorous growth of a tree, to which the happiness and prosperity of men are often compared; *e.g.* in Ps. lii. 10 (8), xcii. 11 (10). Here plainly the word is chosen with reference to the tree which had been seen in the dream. From this description of his prosperity it appears that after his victories Nebuchadnezzar enjoyed the fruit of his exploits, was firmly established on his throne, and, as appears from ver. 26 (29) f., a year after his dream could look with pleasure and pride on the completion of his splendid buildings in Babylon; and therefore this event belongs to the last half of his reign.

Ver. 2 (ch. iv. 5). While in this state of security and peace, he was alarmed by a dream. The abrupt manner in which the matter is here introduced well illustrates the unexpected suddenness of the event itself. הַרְהֹרִין, *thoughts*, from הַרְהֵר, *to think, to meditate;* in the Mishna and in Syr. *images of the imagination;* here, *images in a dream.* The words הַרְהֹרִין עַל מִשְׁכְּבִי are more properly taken as a passage by themselves with the verb, I had (I saw), supplied, than connected with the following noun to יְבַהֲלֻנַּנִי. Regarding חֶזְוֵי רֵאשִׁי see under ch. ii. 28. On this matter Chr. B. Michaelis has well remarked: "*Licet somnii interpretationem nondum intelligeret, tamen sensit, infortunium sibi isthoc somnio portendi.*"

Ver. 3 f. (ch. iv. 6). Therefore Nebuchadnezzar commanded the wise men of Babylon (cf. ii. 2) to be called to him, that they might interpret to him the dream. But they could not do so, although on this occasion he only asked them to give the interpretation, and not, as in ch. ii. 2, at the same time the dream itself. Instead of the *Kethiv* עָלְלִין, the *Keri* here and at ch. v. 8 gives the contracted form עָלִּין, which became possible only by the shortening of ָ, as in חַשְׁחַן ch. iii. 16. The form אָחֳרֵין is differently explained; apparently it must be the *plur. masc.* instead of אָחֳרָן, and עַד אָחֳרֵין, *to the last*, a circumlocution of the adverb *at last.* That אָחֳרֵין means *posterus*, and אָחֳרָן *alius*, Hitzig has not yet furnished the proof. The question, wherefore Daniel came only when the Chaldean wise men could not interpret the dream, is not answered satisfactorily by the remark of Zündel, p. 16, that it was the natural course that first they should be called who by virtue of their wisdom should interpret the dream, and that then, after their wisdom had failed, Daniel should be called, who had gained for himself a name by revelations not proceeding from the class of the Magi. For if Nebuchadnezzar had still the events of ch. ii. in view, he would without doubt have called him forthwith, since it certainly did not come into his mind, in his anxiety on account of his dream, first to try the natural wisdom of his Magi. The objection offered by Hitzig, that the king does not go at once to his chief magician, ver. 6 (9), who had already (ch. ii.) shown himself to be the best interpreter of dreams, is not thereby confuted; still less is it by the answer that the custom was not immediately to call the president of the Magi (Jahn), or that in the haste he was not at once thought of (Häv.). Though it may have been the custom not to call the chief president in every particular case, yet a dream by the king, which had filled him with terror, was an altogether unusual occurrence. If Daniel, therefore, was in this case first called only when the natural wisdom of the Magi had proved its inadequacy, the reason of this was, either that Nebuchadnezzar had forgotten what had occurred several years before (ch. ii.), and since the chief president of the wise men was only in special cases called on for counsel, therefore only the incorporated cultivators of the magician's art were called, and only when these could not accomplish that which was asked of them was the chief president Daniel required to come,—or it lay in this, that the king, afraid of receiving an unwelcome answer, purposely adopted the course indicated. Kranichfeld has decided in favour of this latter supposition. "The king," he thinks, "knew from the dream itself that the tree (ver. 8 [11]) reaching unto heaven and extending to the end of the whole earth represented a royal person ruling the earth, who would come to ruin *on account of the God of the Jews*, and would remain in his ruin till there was an acknowledgment of the Almighty; cf. vers. 13, 14 (16, 17). There was this reason for the king's keeping Daniel the *Jew* at a distance from this matter of the dream. Without doubt he would think himself intended by the person concerned in the dream; and since the special direction which the dream took (ver. 14) set forth as its natural point of departure an actual relation corresponding to that of the king to the God of Daniel, it must have occasioned to him a well-grounded fear (cf. ver. 24), as in the case of Ahab, the idolater, towards Micah, the prophet of Jehovah (cf. 1 Kings xxii. 8), of a severe judgment, leading him to treat with any other regarding his matter rather than with Daniel." For the establishment of this view Kranichfeld refers to the "king's subsequent address to Daniel, designed especially to appease and captivate (vers. 5, 6 [8, 9]), as well as the visibly mild and gentle deportment of the king toward the worshipper of the God of the Jews." This proceeding tending to captivate appears in the appellation, *Daniel, whose name was Belteshazzar, according to the name of my god;* for Nebuchadnezzar, by the addition of a name of honour in commemoration of the celebrated god of the kingdom, intended to show favour toward him, as also in the expression which follows, *In whom is the spirit of the holy gods*, which Nebuchadnezzar repeats in the address. But neither in the one nor the other of these considerations can we perceive the intention of specially captivating and appeasing the Jew Daniel;—not in the latter of these expressions, for two reasons: 1. because Nebuchadnezzar uses the expression not merely in the address to Daniel, but also in the references to him which go before; had he designed it to captivate him, he would have used these words of honour only in the address to him; 2. because the expression, "in whom is the spirit of the holy gods," is so truly heathenish, that the Jew, who knew only *one* God, could not feel himself specially flattered by having the spirit of the holy gods ascribed to him.

If Nebuchadnezzar had had the intention of gaining the favour of Daniel, he would certainly, according to his confession (ch. ii. 47), have attributed to him the spirit of the God of gods, the Lord of lords,—a confession which even as a heathen he could utter. We cannot give the king so little credit for understanding as to suppose that he meant to show[1] a special favour to Daniel, who held so firmly the confession of his father's God, by reminding him that he had given him the name Belteshazzar after the name of his god Bel, whom the Jews abhorred as an idol. Thus the reminding him of this name, as well as the saying that he possessed the spirit of the holy gods, is not accounted for by supposing that he intended to appease and captivate Daniel. In showing the unsatisfactoriness of this interpretation of these expressions, we have set aside also the explanation of the reason, which is based upon it, why Daniel was called in to the king only

[1] Calvin here rightly remarks: *non dubium est, quin hoc nomen graviter vulneraverit animum prophetæ.*

after the Chaldean wise men; and other weighty considerations can also be adduced against it. First, the edict contains certainly nothing which can give room to the conjecture that Nebuchadnezzar entertained no true confidence, but much rather want of confidence, in him. The comparison of Nebuchadnezzar also with king Ahab in his conduct toward the prophet Micah is not suitable, because Ahab was not a mere polytheist as Nebuchadnezzar, but much rather, like Antiochus Epiphanes, persecuted the servants of Jehovah in his kingdom, and at the instigation of his heathenish wife Jezebel wished to make the worship of Baal the only religion of his kingdom. Finally, the relation of the dream does not indicate that Nebuchadnezzar, if he knew or suspected that the dream referred to himself as ruler over the whole earth, thought that he would come to ruin because of the God of the Jews. For that this does not follow from ver. 14 (17), is shown not only by the divine visitation that happened to the king, as mentioned in ver. 27 (30) in fulfilment of the dream, but also by the exhortation to the king with which Daniel closes the interpretation, "to break off sin by righteousness, and his iniquities by showing mercy to the poor" (ver. 24 [27]).

Thus there only remains this supposition, that the former revelations of God to the king had passed away from his heart and his memory; which was not surprising in the successful founder and ruler of a world-kingdom, if we consider that from twenty-five to thirty years must have passed away since Daniel interpreted to him his dream in the second year of his reign, and from ten to fifteen had passed since the miracle of the deliverance of the three from the burning fiery furnace. But if those earlier revelations of God were obscured in his heart by the fulness of his prosperity, and for ten years Daniel had no occasion to show himself to him as a revealer of divine secrets, then it is not difficult to conceive how, amid the state of disquietude into which the dream recorded in this chapter had brought him, he only gave the command to summon all the wise men of Babylon without expressly mentioning their president, so that they came to him first, and Daniel was called only when the natural wisdom of the Chaldeans had shown itself helpless.

The naming of Daniel by his Hebrew name in the manifesto, intended for all the people of the kingdom as well as for the Jews, is simply intended, as in ch. ii. 29, to designate the interpreter of the dream, as distinguished from the native wise men of Babylon, as a Jew, and at the same time as a worshipper of the most high God; and by the addition, "whose name is Belteshazzar, according to the name of my god," Nebuchadnezzar intends to indicate that Daniel by this name was brought into fellowship with his chief god Bel, and that not only as a worshipper of the God of the Jews, but also of the great god Bel, he had become a partaker of the spirit of the holy gods. But by the holy gods Nebuchadnezzar does not understand Jehovah, the Holy One, deriving this predicate "holy," as M. Geier says, *ex theologia Israëlitica*, and the plur. "gods" denoting, as Calovius supposes, the *mysterium pluralitatis personarum;* but he speaks of the holy gods, as Jerome, Calvin, and Grotius supposed, as a heathen (*ut idololatra*) in a polytheistic sense. For that the revelation of supernatural secrets belonged to the gods, and that the man who had this power must possess the spirit of the gods, all the heathen acknowledged. Thus Pharaoh (Gen. xli. 38) judged regarding Joseph, and thus also the Chaldeans say to Nebuchadnezzar (Dan. ii. 11) that only the gods could know his dream. The truth lying at the foundation of this belief was acknowledged by Joseph before Pharaoh, as also by Daniel before the Chaldean king, for both of them declared before the heathen kings that the interpretation of their dreams was not in the power of man, but could come only from God (Gen. xli. 16; Dan. ii. 28). But when in the case before us Nebuchadnezzar speaks of the *holy* gods, he means by the expression the ἀγαθοδαίμονες as opposed to the κακοδαίμονες, using the word *holy* of the good gods, probably from his conversation with Daniel on the subject.

In the address, ver. 6, he calls Belteshazzar רַב חַרְטֻמַיָּא, *master of the magicians*, probably from the special branch of Chaldean wisdom with which Daniel was particularly conversant, at the same time that he was chief president over all the magicians. אֲנַס, to oppress, to compel any one, to do violence to him; here, *to make trouble, difficulty*.

Vers. 7–14 (10–17). Nebuchadnezzar in these verses tells his dream. The first part of ver. 7 is an absolute nominal sentence: *the visions of my head lying upon my bed, then I saw*, etc.—*A tree stood in the midst of the earth.* Although already very high, yet it became always the greater and the stronger, so that it reached even unto heaven and was visible to the ends of the earth. Ver. 8. The perf. רְבָה and תְקִף express not its condition, but its increasing greatness and strength. In the second hemistich the imperf. יִמְטֵא,

as the form of the striving movement, corresponds to them. Ch. B. Michaelis properly remarks, that Nebuchadnezzar saw the tree gradually grow and become always the stronger. חֲזוֹת, *the sight, visibleness.* Its visibility reached unto the ends of the earth. The LXX. have correctly ἡ ὅρασις αὐτοῦ; so the Vulgate; while Theodotion, with τὸ κύτος αὐτοῦ, gives merely the sense, its *largeness*, or *dome*. Hitzig altogether improperly refers to the Arab. حَوْزَةٌ; for حوزة, from حوز, corresponds neither with the Hebr. חָזָה, nor does it mean *extent*, but *comprehension, embracing, enclosure*, according to which the meanings, *tractus, latus, regio*, given in the Arab. Lex., are to be estimated.

Ver. 9 (12). At the same time the tree abounded with leaves and fruit, so that birds and beasts found shadow, protection, and nourishment from it. שַׂגִּיא, neither *great* nor *many*, but *powerful*, expressing the quantity and the greatness of the fruit. The בֵּהּ the Masoretes have rightly connected with לְכֹלָּא, to which it is joined by Maqqeph. The meaning is not: food was in it, the tree had food for all (Häv., Maur., and others), but: (it had) *food for all in it, i.e.* dwelling within its district (Kran., Klief.). The words, besides, do not form an independent sentence, but are only a further view of the שַׂגִּיא (Kran.), and return in the end of the verse into further expansion, while the first and the second clauses of the second hemistich give the further expansion of the first clause in the verse. אַטְלֵל, *umbram captavit, enjoyed the shadow;* in Targg. the Aphel has for the most part the meaning *obumbravit*. The *Kethiv* יְדֻרוּן is not to be changed, since the צִפֲּרִין is *gen. comm.* The *Keri* is conform. to ver. 18*b*, where the word is construed as fem. The expression *all flesh* comprehends the beasts of the field and the fowls of heaven, but is chosen with reference to men represented under this image. For the tree, mighty, reaching even to the heavens, and visible over the whole earth, is an easily recognised symbol of a world-ruler whose power stretches itself over the whole earth. The description of the growth and of the greatness of the tree reminds us of the delineation of Pharaoh and his power under the figure of a mighty cedar of Lebanon, cf. Ezek. xxxi. 3 ff., also Ezek. xvii. 22 ff., xix. 10 ff. The comparison of the growth of men to the growth of the trees is very frequent in biblical and other writings.

Ver. 10 (13). By the words "I saw," etc., a new incident of the dream is introduced. "A watcher and an holy one came down from heaven." וְקַדִּישׁ with the explic. וְ, *even, and that too*, brings it before us in a very expressive way that the עִיר was an "holy one." עִיר is not to be combined with צִיר, a messenger, but is derived from עוּר, to watch, and corresponds with the Hebr. עֵר, Song v. 2, Mal. ii. 12, and signifies not keeping watch, but *being watchful*, one who is awake, as the scholium to the εἴρ of Theodotion in the Cod. Alex. explains it: ἐγρήγορος καὶ ἄγρυπνος. Similarly Jerome remarks: "*significat angelos, quod semper vigilent et ad Dei imperium sint parati.*" From this place is derived the name of ἐγρήγορος for the higher angels, who watch and slumber not, which is found in the book of Enoch and in other apocryphal writings, where it is used of good and of bad angels or demons. The designation of the angel as עִיר is peculiar to this passage in the O. T. This gives countenance to the conjecture that it is a word associated with the Chaldee doctrine of the gods. Kliefoth quite justly, indeed, remarks, that this designation does not come merely from the lips of Nebuchadnezzar, but is uttered also by the holy watcher himself (ver. 14), as well as by Daniel; and he draws thence the conclusion, that obviously the holy watcher himself used this expression first of himself and the whole council of his companions, that Nebuchadnezzar used the same expression after him (ver. 10), and that Daniel again adopted it from Nebuchadnezzar. Thence it follows that by the word angel we are not to understand a heathen deity; for as certainly as, according to this narrative, the dream was given to Nebuchadnezzar by God, so certainly was it a messenger of God who brought it. But from this it is not to be concluded that the name accords with the religious conceptions of Nebuchadnezzar and of the Babylonians. Regarding the Babylonian gods Diod. Sic. ii. 30, says: "Under the five planets (= gods) are ranked thirty others whom they call the counselling gods (θεοὶ βούλαιοι), the half of whom have the oversight of the regions under the earth, and the other half oversee that which goes on on the earth, and among men, and in heaven. Every ten days one of these is sent as a messenger of the stars from the upper to the lower, and at the same time also one from the lower to the upper regions."

If, according to ver. 14, the עִירִין constitute a deliberative council forming a resolution regarding the fate of men, and then one of these עִירִין comes down and makes known the resolution to the king, the conclusion is tenable that the עִירִין correspond to the θεοὶ βούλαιοι of the Babylonians. The divine inspiration of the dream corresponds with this idea. The correct thought lay at the foundation of the Chaldean representation of the *θεοὶ βούλαιοι*, that the relation of God to the world was mediate through the instrumentality of heavenly beings. The biblical revelation recognises these mediating beings, and calls them messengers of God, or angels and holy ones. Yea, the Scripture speaks of the assembling of angels before the throne of God, in which assemblies God forms resolutions regarding the fate of men which the angels carry into execution; cf. Job i. 6 ff., 1 Kings xxii. 19 ff., Ps. lxxxix. 8 (7). Accordingly, if Nebuchadnezzar's dream came from God, we can regard the עִיר as an angel of God who belonged to the סוֹד קְדֹשִׁים around the throne of God (Ps. lxxxix. 8). But this angel announced himself to the Chaldean king not as a messenger of the most high God, not as an angel in the sense of Scripture, but he speaks (ver. 14) of גְּזֵרַת עִירִין, of a resolution of the watchers, a *fatum* of the *θεοὶ βούλαιοι* who have the oversight of this world. The conception גְּזֵרַת עִירִין is not biblical, but Babylonian heathen. According to the doctrine of Scripture, the angels do not determine the fate of men, but God alone does, around whom the angels stand as ministering spirits to fulfil His commands and make known His counsel to men. The angel designates to the Babylonian king the divine resolution regarding that judgment which would fall upon him from God to humble him for his pride as "the resolution of the watchers," that it might be announced to him in the way most easily understood by him as a divine judgment. On the other hand, one may not object that a messenger of God cannot give himself the name of a heathen deity, and that if Nebuchadnezzar had through misunderstanding given to the bringer of the dream the name of one of his heathen gods, Daniel ought, in interpreting the dream, to have corrected the misunderstanding, as Klief. says. For the messenger of God obviated this misunderstanding by the explanation that the matter was a decree of the watchers, to acknowledge the living God, that the Most High rules over the kingdom of men and gives it to whomsoever He will (ver. 14), whereby he distinctly enough announces himself as a messenger of the Most High, *i.e.* of the living God. To go yet further, and to instruct the king that his religious conceptions of the gods, the עִירִין, or *θεοὶ βούλαιοι*, were erroneous, inasmuch as, besides the Highest, the only God, there are no other gods, but only angels, who are no *θεοί*, but creatures of God, was not at all necessary for the purpose of his message. This purpose was only to lead Nebuchadnezzar to an acknowledgment of the Most High, *i.e.* to an acknowledgment that the Most High rules as King of heaven over the kingdom of men. Now, since this was declared by the messenger of God, Daniel in interpreting the dream to the king needed to say nothing more than what he said in vers. 21, 22 (24, 25), where he designates the matter as a resolution of the Most High, and thereby indirectly corrects the view of the king regarding the "resolutions of the watchers," and gives the king distinctly to understand that the humiliation announced to him was determined,[1] not by the *θεοὶ βούλαιοι* of the Babylonians, but by the only true God, whom Daniel and his people worshipped. For Nebuchadnezzar designates עִיר as קַדִּישׁ in the same sense in which, in ver. 5, he speaks of the holy gods.

Ver. 11 (14). The messenger of God cried with might (cf. iii. 4), "as a sign of the strong, firm utterance of a purpose" (Kran.). The command, Hew it down, is not given to the angels (Häv., Hitz., Auberl.). The plur. here is to be regarded as impersonal: *the tree shall be cut down.* אַתַּרוּ stands for אַתִּרוּ according to the analogy of the verbs 3d *gutt.*, from נְתַר, *to fall off*, spoken of withering leaves. In consequence of the destruction of the tree, the beasts which found shelter under it and among its branches flee away. Yet the tree shall not be altogether destroyed, but its stock (ver. 12 [15]) shall remain in the earth, that it may again afterwards spring up and grow into a tree. The stem is not the royalty, the dynasty which shall remain in the house of Nebuchadnezzar (Häv.), but the tree with its roots is Nebuchadnezzar, who shall as king be cut down, but shall as a man remain, and again shall grow into a king. But the stock must be bound "with a band of iron and brass." With these words, to complete which we must supply שְׁבֻקוּ from the preceding context, the language passes from the type to the person represented by it. This transition is in the last part of the verse: *with the beasts of the field let him have his portion in the grass of the earth*; for this cannot be said of the stock with the roots, therefore these words are in the interpretation also (ver. 22 [25]) applied directly to Nebuchad-

[1] We must altogether reject the assertion of Berth., v. Leng., Hitz., and Maur., that the language of this verse regarding the angel sent to Nebuchadnezzar is formed in accordance with the Persian representation of the seven Amschaspands (*Amēscha-çpenta*), since, according to the judgment of all those most deeply conversant with Parsism, the doctrine of the *Amēscha-çpenta* does not at all occur in the oldest parts of the Avesta, and the Avesta altogether is not so old as that the Babylonian doctrine of the gods can be shown to be dependent on the Zend doctrine of the Parsees.

nezzar. But even in the preceding passages this transition is not doubtful. Neither the words *in the grass of the field,* nor the *being wet with the dew of heaven,* are suitable as applied to the stock of the tree, because both expressions in that case would affirm nothing; still less is *the band of iron and brass* congruous, for the trunk of a tree is not wont to be surrounded with bands of iron in order to prevent its being rent in pieces and completely destroyed. Thus the words refer certainly to Nebuchadnezzar; but the fastening in brass and iron is not, with Jerome and others, to be understood of the binding of the madman with chains, but figuratively or spiritually of the withdrawal of free self-determination through the fetter of madness; cf. the *fetters of affliction,* Ps. cvii. 10, Job xxxvi. 8. With this fettering also agrees the going forth under the open heaven among the grass of the field, and the being wet with the dew of heaven, without our needing thereby to think of the maniac as wandering about without any oversight over him.

Ver. 13 (16). Here the angel declares by what means Nebuchadnezzar shall be brought into this condition. His heart shall be changed from a man's heart, according to the following passage, into the heart of a beast. שַׁנִּא מִן, *to change, to make different from,* so that it is no longer what it was. The *Kethiv* אֲנוֹשָׁא is the Hebr. form for the Chald. אֱנָשָׁא of the *Keri,* here, as in ver. 14, where along with it also stands the Hebr. plur. form אֲנָשִׁים. אֲנוֹשָׁא stands here for the abbreviated comparison frequent in Hebr., מִן לְבַב אֲנוֹשָׁא, and the 3d *pers. plur.* יְשַׁנּוֹן impers. for the passive. לְבַב is *the heart,* the centre of the intelligent soul-life. The heart of man is dehumanized when his soul becomes like that of a beast; for the difference between the heart of a man and that of a beast has its foundation in the difference between the soul of a man and the soul of a beast (Delitzsch, *bibl. Psych.* p. 252). *And seven times shall pass over him,* viz. during the continuance of the circumstances described; *i.e.* his condition of bondage shall last for seven times. Following the example of the LXX. and of Josephus, many ancient and recent interpreters, down to Maur., Hitz., and Kran., understood by the word עִדָּנִין *years,* because the *times* in ch. vii. 25, xii. 7, are also years, and because in ver. 26 mention is made of twelve months, and thereby the *time* is defined as one year. But from ver. 26 the duration of the עִדָּנִין cannot at all be concluded, and in ch. vii. 25 and xii. 7 the *times* are not years. עִדָּן designates generally a definite period of time, whose length or duration may be very different. Seven is the "measure and signature of the history of the development of the kingdom of God, and of all the factors and phenomena significant for it" (Lämmert's "Revision of the biblical Symbolical Numbers" in the *Jahrbb. f. deutsche Theol.* ix. p. 11); or as Leyrer, in Herzog's *Realencykl.* xviii. p. 366, expresses himself, "the signature for all the actions of God, in judgment and in mercy, punishments, expiations, consecrations, blessings, connected with the economy of redemption, perfecting themselves in time." Accordingly, "seven times" is the duration of the divine punishment which was decreed against Nebuchadnezzar for purposes connected with the history of redemption. Whether these times are to be understood as years, months, or weeks, is not said, and cannot at all be determined. The supposition that they were seven years "cannot well be adopted in opposition to the circumstance that Nebuchadnezzar was again restored to reason, a thing which very rarely occurs after so long a continuance of psychical disease" (J. B. Friedreich, *Zur Bibel. Naturhist., anthrop. u. med. Fragmente,* i. p. 316).

Ver. 14 (17). The divine messenger concludes his announcement with the words that the matter was unchangeably decreed, for this purpose, that men might be led to recognise the supremacy of the Most High over the kings of the earth. The first two passages have no verb, and thus the *verb. substant.* must be supplied. Accordingly we must not translate: *by the decree of the watchers is the message, i.e.* is it delivered (Kran.), nor: *the decree is included in the fate, the unalterable will of Heaven* (Häv.); but בְּ denotes the department within which the גְּזֵרָה lies, and is to be translated: "*the message consists in,* or *rests on, the decree of the watchers.*" גְּזֵרָה, *the unchangeable decision,* the *decretum divinum, quod homini aut rebus humanis tanquam inevitabile impositum est* (Buxtorf's *Lex. talm. rabb.* p. 419), the *Fatum* in which the Chaldeans believed. Regarding פִּתְגָם see under ch. iii. 16. Here the fundamental meaning, *the message, that which is to happen,* can be maintained. The second member is synonymous, and affirms the same thing in another way. The word, the utterance of the holy ones, *i.e.* the watchers (see under ver. 10), is שְׁאֵלְתָא, *the matter.* The meaning lying in the etymon, *request* or *question,* is not here suitable, but only the derivative meaning, *matter* as the object of the request or inquiry. The thing meant is that which is decided regarding the tree, that it should be cut down, etc.

This is so clear, that a pronoun referring to it appears superfluous.

עַד דִּבְרַת דִּי, *till the matter that . . . to the end that;* not = עַד דִּי, ver. 22, because here no defining of time goes before. The changing of עד into עַל (Hitz.) is unnecessary and arbitrary. *That the living may know, etc.* The expression is general, because it is not yet said who is to be understood by the tree which should be cut down. This general expression is in reality correct; for the king comes by experience to this knowledge, and so all will attain to it who consider this. The two last passages of ver. 14 express more fully how the Most High manifests His supremacy over the kingdom of men. The *Kethiv* עליה is shortened from עֲלֵיהָא, and in the *Keri* is yet further shortened by the rejection of the י; cf. ch. v. 21, vii. 4 ff., etc.

Ver. 15 (18). Nebuchadnezzar adds to his communication of his dream a command to Daniel to interpret it. The form פִּשְׁרֵא (*its interpretation*) is the old orthography and the softened form for פִּשְׁרֵהּ (cf. ver. 6).

Vers. 16–24 (19–27). *The interpretation of the dream.*

As Daniel at once understood the interpretation of the dream, he was for a moment so astonished that he could not speak for terror at the thoughts which moved his soul. This amazement seized him because he wished well to the king, and yet he must now announce to him a weighty judgment from God.

Ver. 16. The punctuation אֶשְׁתּוֹמַם for אִשְׁתּוֹמַם is Syriac, as in the Hebr. ch. viii. 27; cf. Winer's *Chald. Gram.* § 25, 2. כְּשָׁעָה חֲדָא means, not *about an hour* (Mich., Hitz., Kran., etc.), but *as it were an instant, a moment.* Regarding שָׁעָה, see under ch. iii. 6. The king perceives the astonishment of Daniel, and remarks that he has found the interpretation. Therefore he asks him, with friendly address, to tell him it without reserve. Daniel then communicates it in words of affectionate interest for the welfare of the king. The words, *let the dream be to thine enemies,* etc., do not mean: *it is a dream, a prophecy, such as the enemies of the king might ungraciously wish* (Klief.), but: *may the dream with its interpretation be to thine enemies, may it be fulfilled to them* or *refer to them* (Häv., Hitz., etc.). The *Kethiv* מָרְאִי is the regular formation from מָרֵא with the suffix, for which the Masoretes have substituted the later Talmudic-Targ. form מָר. With regard to שָׂנְאָיךְ with the *a* shortened, as also הַשְׁחִין (ch. iii. 16) and other participial forms, cf. Winer, *Chald. Gram.* § 34, III. That Nebuchadnezzar (ver. 16) in his account speaks in the third person does not justify the conclusion, either that another spake of him, and that thus the document is not genuine (Hitz.), nor yet the conclusion that this verse includes an historical notice introduced as an interpolation into the document; for similar forms of expression are often found in such documents: cf. Ezra vii. 13–15, Esth. viii. 7, 8.

Ver. 17 (20). Daniel interprets to the king his dream, repeating only here and there in an abbreviated form the substance of it in the same words, and then declares its reference to the king. With vers. 17 (20) and 18 (21) cf. vers. 8 (11) and 9 (12). The fuller description of the tree is subordinated to the relative clause, *which thou hast seen*, so that the subject is connected by הוּא (ver. 19), representing the *verb. subst.*, according to rule, with the predicate אִילָנָא. The interpretation of the separate statements regarding the tree is also subordinated in relative clauses to the subject. For the *Kethiv* רבית = רְבַיְתְּ, the *Keri* gives the shortened form רְבַת, with the elision of the third radical, analogous to the shortening of the following מטת for מְטָת. To the call of the angel to "cut down the tree," etc. (ver. 20, cf. vers. 10–13), Daniel gives the interpretation, ver. 21, "This is the decree of the Most High which is come upon the king, that he shall be driven from men, and dwell among the beasts," etc. מְטָא עַל = Hebr. בּוֹא עַל. The indefinite plur. form טָרְדִין stands instead of the passive, as the following יְטַעֲמוּן לָךְ and מְצַבְּעִין, cf. under ch. iii. 4. Thus the subject remains altogether indefinite, and one has neither to think on men who will drive him from their society, etc., nor of angels, of whom, perhaps, the expulsion of the king may be predicated, but scarcely the feeding on grass and being wet with dew.

Ver. 23 (26). In this verse the emblem and its interpretation are simply placed together, so that we must in thought repeat the דְּנָה פִשְׁרָא from ver. 21 before מַלְכוּתָךְ. קָאַם ,קַיָּמָא do not in this place mean *to stand, to exist, to remain*, for this does not agree with the following מִן־דִּי; for until Nebuchadnezzar comes to the knowledge of the supremacy of God, his dominion shall not continue, but rest, be withdrawn. קוּם, *to rise up*, has here an inchoative meaning, *again rise up*. To שַׁלִּיטִן (*do rule*) there is to be added from ver. 22 (25) the clause, *over the kingdom of men*. From this passage we have an explanation of the use of שְׁמַיָּא, *heaven*, for עִלָּיָא, *the Most High*, *God of heaven*, whence afterwards arose the use of *βασιλεία τῶν οὐρανῶν* for *βασιλεία τοῦ Θεοῦ*.

Ver. 24 (27). Daniel adds to his interpretation of the dream the warning to the king to break off his sins by righteousness and mercy, so that his tranquillity may be lengthened. Daniel knew nothing of a heathen *Fatum*, but he knew that the judgments of God were directed against men according to their conduct, and that punishment threatened could only be averted by repentance; cf. Jer. xviii. 7 ff.; Jonah iii. 5 ff.; Isa. xxxviii. 1 f. This way of turning aside the threatened judgment stood open also for Nebuchadnezzar, particularly as the time of the fulfilment of the dream was not fixed, and thus a space was left for repentance. The counsel of Daniel is interpreted by Berth., Hitz., and others, after Theodotion, the Vulgate, and many Church Fathers and Rabbis, as teaching the doctrine of holiness by works held by the later Jews, for they translate it: *redeem thy sins by well-doing* (Hitz.: *buy freedom from thy sins by alms*), *and thy transgressions by showing mercy to the poor.*[1] But this translation of the first passage is verbally false; for פְּרַק does not mean *to redeem, to ransom*, and צִדְקָה does not mean *alms* or *charity*. פְּרַק means to *break off, to break in pieces*, hence *to separate, to disjoin, to put at a distance*; see under Gen. xxi. 40. And though in the Targg. פרק is used for גְּאַל, פְּדָה, *to loosen, to unbind*, of redeeming, ransoming of the first-born, an inheritance or any other valuable possession, yet this use of the word by no means accords with sins as the object, because sins are not goods which one redeems or ransoms so as to retain them for his own use. פְּרַק חֲטָי can only mean *to throw away sins, to set one's self free from sins*. צִדְקָה nowhere in the O. T. means *well-doing* or *alms*. This meaning the self-righteous Rabbis first gave to the word in their writings. Daniel recommends the king to practise righteousness as the chief virtue of a ruler in contrast to the unrighteousness of the despots, as Hgstb., Häv., Hofm., and Klief. have justly observed. To this also the second member of the verse corresponds. As the king should practise righteousness toward all his subjects, so should he exercise mercy

[1] Theodot. translates: *καὶ τὰς ἁμαρτίας σου ἐν ἐλεημοσύναις λύτρωσαι, καὶ τὰς ἀδικίας σου ἐν οἰκτιρμοῖς πενήτων.* The Vulg.: *et peccata tua eleemosynis redime et iniquitates tuas misericordiis pauperum.* Accordingly, the Catholic Church regards this passage as a *locus classicus* for the doctrine of the merit of works, against which the *Apologia Conf. August.* first set forth the right exposition.

toward the oppressed, the miserable, the poor. Both of these virtues are frequently named together, *e.g.* Isa. xi. 4, Ps. lxxii. 4, Isa. xli. 2, as virtues of the Messiah. חֲטָיָךְ is the plur. of חֲטָי, as the parallel עֲוָיָתָךְ shows, and the *Keri* only the later abbreviation or defective suffix-formation, as ch. ii. 4, v. 10.

The last clause of this verse is altogether misunderstood by Theodotion, who translates it ἴσως ἔσται μακρόθυμος τοῖς παραπτώμασίν σου ὁ Θεός, and by the Vulgate, where it is rendered by *forsitan ignoscet delictis tuis*, and by many older interpreters, where they expound אַרְכָא in the sense of אֶרֶךְ אַפַּיִם, *patience*, and derive שְׁלֵוְתָךְ from שְׁלָה, *to fail, to go astray* (cf. ch. iii. 29). אַרְכָא means *continuance*, or *length of time*, as ch. vii. 12; שְׁלֵוָא, *rest, safety*, as the Hebr. שַׁלְוָה, here *the peaceful prosperity of life;* and הֵן, neither *ecce* nor *forsitan, si forte*, but simply *if*, as always in the book of Daniel.

Daniel places before the king, as the condition of the continuance of prosperity of life, and thereby *implicite* of the averting of the threatened punishment, reformation of life, the giving up of injustice and cruelty towards the poor, and the practice of righteousness and mercy.

Vers. 25–30 (28–33). *The fulfilling of the dream.*

Nebuchadnezzar narrates the fulfilment of the dream altogether objectively, so that he speaks of himself in the third person. Berth., Hitz., and others find here that the author falls out of the role of the king into the narrative tone, and thus betrays the fact that some other than the king framed the edict. But this conclusion is opposed by the fact that Nebuchadnezzar from ver. 31 speaks of his recovery again in the first person. Thus it is beyond doubt that the change of person has its reason in the matter itself. Certainly it could not be in this that Nebuchadnezzar thought it unbecoming to speak in his own person of his madness; for if he had had so tender a regard for his own person, he would not have published the whole occurrence in a manifesto addressed to his subjects. But the reason of his speaking of his madness in the third person, as if some other one were narrating it, lies simply in this, that in that condition he was not *Ich* = *Ego* (Kliefoth). With the return of the *Ich, I*, on his recovery from his madness, Nebuchadnezzar begins again to narrate in the first person (ver. 31 [34]).

Ver. 25 (28). In this verse there is a brief comprehensive

statement regarding the fulfilment of the dream to the king, which is then extended from ver. 26 to 30. At the end of twelve months, *i.e.* after the expiry of twelve months from the time of the dream, the king betook himself to his palace at Babylon, *i.e.* to the flat roof of the palace; cf. 2 Sam. xi. 2. The addition *at Babylon* does not indicate that the king was then living at a distance from Babylon, as Berth., v. Leng., Maur., and others imagine, but is altogether suitable to the matter, because Nebuchadnezzar certainly had palaces outside of Babylon, but it is made with special reference to the language of the king which follows regarding the greatness of Babylon. עָנֵה means here not simply *to begin to speak*, but properly *to answer*, and suggests to us a foregoing colloquy of the king with himself in his own mind. Whether one may conclude from that, in connection with the statement of time, *after twelve months*, that Nebuchadnezzar, exactly one year after he had received the important dream, was actively engaging himself regarding that dream, must remain undetermined, and can be of no use to a psychological explanation of the occurrence of the dream. The thoughts which Nebuchadnezzar expresses in ver. 26 (29) are not favourable to such a supposition. Had the king remembered that dream and its interpretation, he would scarcely have spoken so proudly of his splendid city which he had built as he does in ver. 27 (30).

When he surveyed the great and magnificent city from the top of his palace, "pride overcame him," so that he dedicated the building of this great city as the house of his kingdom to the might of his power and the honour of his majesty. From the addition רַבְּתָא it does not follow that this predicate was a standing *Epitheton ornans* of Babylon, as with חֲמַת רַבָּה, Amos vi. 2, and other towns of Asia; for although Pausanias and Strabo call Babylon μεγάλη and μεγίστη πόλις, yet it bears this designation as a surname in no ancient author. But in Rev. xiv. 8 this predicate, quoted from the passage before us, is given to Babylon, and in the mouth of Nebuchadnezzar it quite corresponds to the self-praise of his great might by which he had built Babylon as the residence of a great king. בְּנָה designates, as בָּנָה more frequently, not *the building* or *founding of a city*, for the founding of Babylon took place in the earliest times after the Flood (Gen. xi.), and was dedicated to the god Belus, or the mythic Semiramis, *i.e.* in the pre-historic time; but בְּנָה means *the building up*, *the enlargement*, *the adorning* of the city לְבֵית מַלְכוּ, *for the house of the kingdom*, *i.e.* for a royal residence; cf. the related expression בֵּית מַמְלָכָה, Amos vii. 13. בֵּית stands in this connection neither for *town* nor for הֵיכַל (ver. 26), but has the meaning *dwelling-place.* The royalty of the Babylonian kingdom has its dwelling-place, its seat, in Babylon, the capital of the kingdom.

With reference to the great buildings of Nebuchadnezzar in Babylon, *vide* the statements of Berosus in Josephi *Ant.* x. 11, 1, and *con. Ap.* i. 19, and of Abydenus in Eusebii *præpar. evang.* ix. 41, and *Chron.* i. p. 59; also the delineation of these buildings in Duncker's *Gesch. des Alterth.* i. p. 854 ff. The presumption of this language appears in the words, "by the strength of my might, and for the splendour (honour) of my majesty." Thus Nebuchadnezzar describes himself as the creator of his kingdom and of its glory, while the building up of his capital as a residence bearing witness to his glory and his might pointed at the same time to the duration of his dynasty. This proud utterance is immediately followed by his humiliation by the omnipotent God. A voice fell from heaven. נְפַל as in Isa. ix. 7, of the sudden coming of a divine revelation. אָמְרִין for the passive, as ch. iii. 4. The perf. עֲדָת denotes the matter as finished. At the moment when Nebuchadnezzar heard in his soul the voice from heaven, the prophecy begins to be fulfilled, the king becomes deranged, and is deprived of his royalty.

Vers. 29, 30 (32, 33). Here the contents of the prophecy, ver. 22 (25), are repeated, and then in ver. 30 (33) it is stated that the word regarding Nebuchadnezzar immediately began to be fulfilled. On בַּהּ שַׁעֲתָא, cf. ch. iii. 6. סָפַת, from סוּף, *to go to an end.* The prophecy goes to an end when it is realized, is fulfilled. The fulfilling is related in the words of the prophecy. Nebuchadnezzar is driven from among men, viz. by his madness, in which he fled from intercourse with men, and lived under the open air of heaven as a beast among the beasts, eating grass like the cattle; and his person was so neglected, that his hair became like the eagles' feathers and his nails like birds' claws. כְּנִשְׁרִין and כְּצִפְּרִין are abbreviated comparisons; *vide* under ver. 13. That this condition was a peculiar appearance of the madness is expressly mentioned in ver. 31 (34), where the recovery is designated as the restoration of his understanding.

This malady, in which men regard themselves as beasts and imitate their manner of life, is called *insania zoanthropica*, or, in the case of those who think themselves wolves, *lycanthropia.* The condition is described in a manner true to nature. Even "as to the eating of grass," as G. Rösch, in the *Deutsch. Morgenl. Zeitschr.* xv. p. 521, remarks, "there is nothing to perplex or that needs to be explained. It is a circumstance that has occurred in recent times, as *e.g.* in the case of a woman in the Württemberg asylum for the insane." Historical documents regarding this form of madness have been collected by Trusen in his *Sitten, Gebr. u. Krank. der alten Hebräer*, p. 205 f., 2d ed., and by Friedreich in *Zur Bibel*, i. p. 308 f.[1]

Vers. 31–34 (34–37). *Nebuchadnezzar's recovery, his restoration to his kingdom, and his thankful recognition of the Lord in heaven.*

The second part of the prophecy was also fulfilled. "At the end of the days," *i.e.* after the expiry of the seven times, Nebuchadnezzar lifted up his eyes to heaven,—the first sign of the return of human consciousness, from which, however, we are not to conclude, with Hitzig, that before this, in his madness, he went on all-fours like an ox. Nebuchadnezzar means in these words only to say that his first thought was a look to heaven, whence help came to him; cf. Ps. cxxiii. 1 f. Then his understanding immediately returned to him. The first thought he entertained was to thank God, to praise Him as the ever-living One, and to recognise the eternity of His sway. Nebuchadnezzar acknowledges and praises God as the "ever-living One," because He had again given to him his life, which had been lost in his madness; cf. ch. vi. 27 (26).

Ver. 31*b*, cf. with ch. iii. 33 (iv. 1). The eternity of the supremacy of God includes His omnipotence as opposed to the weakness of the inhabitants of earth. This eternity Nebuchadnezzar praises in ver. 32 (35) in words which remind us of the expressions of Isaiah; cf. with the first half of the verse, Isa. xl. 17, xxiv. 21; and with the second half of it, Isa. xliii. 13. כְּלָה for כְּלָא, *as not, as not existing.* מְחָא בִידֵהּ in the Pa., *to strike on the hand, to hinder,* derived from the custom of striking children on the hand in chas-

[1] Regarding the statement, "his hair grew as the feathers of an eagle," etc., Friedr. remarks, p. 316, that, besides the neglect of the external appearance, there is also to be observed the circumstance that sometimes in psychical maladies the nails assume a peculiarly monstrous luxuriance with deformity. Besides, his remaining for a long time in the open air is to be considered, "for it is an actual experience that the hair, the more it is exposed to the influences of the rough weather and to the sun's rays, the more does it grow in hardness, and thus becomes like unto the feathers of an eagle."

tising them. The expression is common in the Targg. and in the Arabic.

Ver. 33 (36). With the restoration of his understanding Nebuchadnezzar also regained his royal dignity and his throne. In order to intimate the inward connection between the return of reason and the restoration to his sovereignty, in this verse the first element of his restoration is repeated from ver. 31 (34), and the second follows in connection with it in the simple manner of Semitic narrative, for which we in German (and English) use the closer connection: "when my understanding returned, then also my royal state and my glory returned." The passage beginning with וְלִיקַר is construed very differently by interpreters. Many co-ordinate לִיקַר מל׳ with הַדְרִי וְזִיוִי, and then regard לִיקַר either as the nominative, "and then my kingly greatness, my glory and splendour, came to me again" (Hitzig), or unite הַדְרִי וְזִיוִי as the genitive with מַלְכוּתִי: "and for the honour of my royalty, of my fame and my glory, it (my understanding) returned to me again" (v. Leng., Maur., Klief.). The first of these interpretations is grammatically inadmissible, since לְ cannot be a sign of the genitive; the other is unnecessarily artificial. We agree with Rosenmüller and Kranichfeld in regarding הַדְרִי וְזִיוִי as the subject of the passage. הֲדַר [*splendour, pomp*] is the majestic appearance of the prince, which according to Oriental modes of conception showed itself in splendid dress; cf. Ps. cx. 3, xxix. 2, xcvi. 9; 2 Chron. xx. 21. זִיו, *splendour* (ch. ii. 31), is the shining colour or freshness of the appearance, which is lost by terror, anxiety, or illness, as in ch. v. 6, 9, 10, vii. 28. לִיקַר as in ver. 27. In how far the return of the external dignified *habitus* was conducive to the honour of royalty, the king most fully shows in the second half of the verse, where he says that his counsellors again established him in his kingdom. The בְּעָא, *to seek*, does not naturally indicate that the king was suffered, during the period of his insanity, to wander about in the fields and forests without any supervision, as Bertholdt and Hitzig think; but it denotes the seeking for one towards whom a commission has to be discharged, as ch. ii. 13; thus, here, the seeking in order that they might transfer to him again the government. The "counsellors and great men" are those who had carried on the government during his insanity. הָתְקְנַת, on account of the *accent. distinct.*, is Hophal pointed with Patach instead of Tsere, as the following הוּסְפַת. If Nebuchadnezzar, after his restoration to the kingdom, attained to yet more רְבוּ, *greatness*, than he had before, so he must have reigned yet a considerable time without our needing to suppose that he accomplished also great deeds.

Ver. 34 (37). The manifesto closes with praise to God, the King of heaven, whose works are truth and righteousness, which show themselves in humbling the proud. קְשׁוֹט corresponds to the Hebr. אֱמֶת, and דִּין to the Hebr. מִשְׁפָּט. Nebuchadnezzar thus recognised the humiliation which he had experienced as a righteous punishment for his pride, without, however, being mindful of the divine grace which had been shown in mercy toward him; whence Calvin has drawn the conclusion that he was not brought to true heart-repentance.

CHAP. V. BELSHAZZAR'S FEAST AND THE HANDWRITING OF GOD.

The Chaldean king Belshazzar made a feast to his chief officers, at which in drunken arrogance, by a desecration of the sacred vessels which Nebuchadnezzar had carried away from the temple at Jerusalem, he derided the God of Israel (vers. 1–4). Then he suddenly saw the finger of a hand writing on the wall of the guest-chamber, at which he was agitated by violent terror, and commanded that the wise men should be sent for, that they might read and interpret to him the writing; and when they were not able to do this, he became pale with alarm (vers. 5–9). Then the queen informed him of Daniel, who would be able to interpret the writing (vers. 10–12). Daniel, being immediately brought in, declared himself ready to read and interpret the writing; but first he reminded the king of his sin in that he did not take warning from the divine chastisement which had visited king Nebuchadnezzar (ch. iv.), but offended the Most High God by desecrating the holy vessels of His temple (vers. 13, 14). He then interpreted to him the writing, showing the king that God had announced to him by means of it the end of his reign, and the transference of the kingdom to the Medes and Persians (vers. 25–28). Daniel was thereupon raised to honour by Belshazzar, who was, however, in that same night put to death (vers. 29, 30).

This narrative presents historical difficulties, for a Chaldean king by the name of Belshazzar is nowhere else mentioned, except in the passage in Baruch i. 11 f., which is dependent on this chapter of Daniel; and the judgment here announced to him, the occurrence of which is in part mentioned in ver. 30, and in part set forth in ch. vi. 1 (v. 31), does not appear to harmonize with the extra-biblical information which we have regarding the destruction of the Chaldean kingdom.

If we consider closely the contents of this chapter, it appears that Belshazzar, designated in ver. 30 as king of the Chaldeans, is not only in ver. 22 addressed by Daniel as Nebuchadnezzar's son, but in vers. 11, 13, and 18 is also manifestly represented in the same character, for the queen-mother (ver. 11), Belshazzar himself (ver. 13), and Daniel (ver. 18) call Nebuchadnezzar his אָב, *father.* If now אָב and בַּר do not always express the special relation of father and son, but אָב is used in a wider sense of a grandfather and of yet more remote ancestors, and בַּר of grandsons and other descendants, yet this wider interpretation and conception of the words is from the matter of the statements here made highly improbable, or indeed directly excluded, inasmuch as the queen-mother speaks of things which she had experienced, and Daniel said to Belshazzar (ver. 22) that he knew the chastisement which Nebuchadnezzar had suffered from God in the madness that had come upon him, but had not regarded it. In that case the announcement of the judgment threatening Belshazzar and his kingdom (vers. 24–28), when compared with its partial fulfilment in Belshazzar's death (ver. 30), appears to indicate that his death, together with the destruction of the Chaldean kingdom and its transference to the Medes and Persians (ch. vi. 1 [v. 31]), occurred at the same time. Nevertheless this indication, as has already been remarked (p. 37), appears to have more plausibility than truth, since neither the combination of the two events in their announcement, nor their union in the statement of their fulfilment, by means of the copula ו in ch. vi. 1, affords conclusive proof of their being contemporaneous. Since only the time of Belshazzar's death is given (ver. 30), but the transference of the Chaldean kingdom to the Median Darius (ch. vi. 1) is not chronologically defined, then we may without hesitation grant that the latter event did not happen till some considerable time after the death of Belshazzar, in case other reasons demand this supposition. For, leaving out of view the announcement of the judgment, the narrative contains not the least hint that, at the time when Belshazzar revelled with his lords and his concubines, the city of Babylon was besieged by enemies. "Belshazzar (vers. 1–4) is altogether without care, which he could not have been if the enemy had gathered before the gates. The handwriting announcing evil appears out of harmony with the circumstances (ver. 5), while it would have had a connection with them if the city had been beleaguered. Belshazzar did not believe (ver. 29) that the threatened end was near, which would not have been in harmony with a state of siege. All these circumstances are not to be explained from the light-mindedness of Belshazzar, but they may be by the supposition that his death was the result of an insurrection, unexpected by himself and by all." Kliefoth, p. 148.

Now let us compare with this review of the chapter the non-biblical reports regarding the end of the Babylonian monarchy. Berosus, in a fragment preserved by Josephus, *c. Ap.* i. 20, says that "Nebuchadnezzar was succeeded in the kingdom by his son Evilmerodach, who reigned badly (*προστὰς τῶν πραγμάτων ἀνόμως καὶ ἀσελγῶς*), and was put to death (*ἀνῃρέθη*) by Neriglissor, the husband of his sister, after he had reigned two years. This Neriglissor succeeded him, and reigned four years. His son Laborosoarchod, being still a child (*παῖς ὤν*), reigned after him nine months, and was murdered by his friends (*διὰ τὸ πολλὰ ἐμφαίνειν κακόηθη ὑπὸ τῶν φίλων ἀπετυμπανίσθη*), because he gave many proofs of a bad character. His murderers by a general resolution transferred the government to Nabonnedus, one of the Babylonians who belonged to the conspirators. Under him the walls of Babylon along the river-banks were better built. But in the seventeenth year of his reign Cyrus came from Persia with a great army and took Babylon, after he had subjugated all the rest of Asia. Nabonnedus went out to encounter him, but was vanquished in battle, and fled with a few followers and shut himself up in Borsippa. But Cyrus, after he had taken Babylon and demolished its walls, marched against Borsippa and besieged Nabonnedus. But Nabonnedus could not hold out, and therefore surrendered himself. He was at first treated humanely by Cyrus, who removed him from Babylon, and gave him Carmania as a place of residence (*δοὺς οἰκητήριον αὐτῷ Καρμανίαν*), where he spent the remainder of his days and died."

Abydenus, in a shorter fragment preserved by Eusebius in the *Præpar. Ev.* ix. 41, and in the *Chron. Armen.* p. 60 sq., makes the same statements. Petermann's translation of the fragment found in Niebuhr's *Gesch. Assurs*, p. 504, is as follows:—"There now reigned (after Nebuchodrossor) his son Amilmarodokos, whom his son-in-law Niglisaris immediately murdered, whose only son Labossorakos remained yet alive; but it happened to him also that he met a violent death. He commanded that Nabonedokhos should be placed on the throne of the kingdom, a person who was altogether unfit to occupy it." (In the *Præpar. Evang.* this passage is given in these words: *Ναβοννίδοχον ἀποδείκνυσι βασιλέα, προσήκοντα οἱ οὐδέν.*) "Cyrus, after he had taken possession of Babylon, appointed him margrave of the country of Carmania. Darius the king removed him out of the land." (This last passage is wanting in the *Præp. Ev.*)[1]

According to these reports, there reigned in Babylon after Nebuchadnezzar four other kings, among whom there was no one called Belshazzar, and only one son of Nebuchadnezzar, viz. Evilmerodach; for Neriglissar is son-in-law and Laborosoarchod is grandson (daughter's son) of Nebuchadnezzar, and Nabonnedus was not at all related to him, nor of royal descent. Of these kings, only Evilmerodach and Laborosoarchod were put to death, while on the contrary Neriglissar and Nabonnedus died a natural death, and the Babylonian dominion passed by conquest to the Medes, without Nabonnedus thereby losing his life. Hence it follows,

[1] With these statements that of Alexander Polyhistor, in Euseb. *Chron. Armen.* ed. Aucher, i. p. 45, in the main agrees. His report, according to Petermann's translation (as above, p. 497), is as follows:—"After Nebuchodrossor, his son Amilmarudokhos reigned 12 years, whom the Hebr. hist. calls Ilmarudokhos. After him there reigned over the Chaldeans Neglisaros 4 years, and then Nabodenus 17 years, under whom Cyrus (son) of Cambyses assembled an army against the land of the Babylonians. Nabodenus opposed him, but was overcome and put to flight. Cyrus now reigned over Babylon 9 years," etc. The 12 years of Amilmarudokhos are without doubt an error of the Armenian translator or of some transcriber; and the omission of Loborosoarchod is explained by the circumstance that he did not reign a full year. The correctness of the statement of Berosus is confirmed by the Canon of Ptolemy, who names as successors of Nabokolassar (*i.e.* Nebuchadnezzar, who reigned 43 years), Illoarudmos 2 years, Nerigassolassaros 4 years, and Nabonadius 17 years; thus omitting Laborosoarchod on the grounds previously mentioned. The number of the years of the reigns mentioned by Berosus agrees with the biblical statements regarding the duration of the exile. From the first taking of Jerusalem by Nebuchadnezzar in the fourth year of Jehoiakim are mentioned—Jehoiakim 7 years, Jehoiachin 3 months, and his imprisonment 37 years (Jer. lii. 31), Evilmerodach 2 years, Neriglissar 4 years, Laborosoarchod 9 months, and Nabonnedus 17 years—in all 68 years, to which, if the 2 years of the reign of Darius the Mede are added, we shall have 70 years. The years of the reigns of the Babylonian kings amount in all to the same number; viz. Nebuchadnezzar 44¼ years,—since he did not become king till one year after the destruction of Jerusalem, he reigned 43 years,—Evilmerodach 2 years, Neriglissar 4 years, Loborosoarchod 9 months, Nabonnedus 17 years, and Darius the Mede 2 years—in all 70 years.

(1) that Belshazzar cannot be the last king of Babylon, nor is identical with Nabonnedus, who was neither a son nor descendant of Nebuchadnezzar, and was not put to death by Cyrus at the destruction of Babylon and the overthrow of the Chaldean kingdom; (2) that Belshazzar could neither be Evilmerodach nor Laborosoarchod, since only these two were put to death—the former after he had reigned only two years, and the latter after he had reigned only nine months, while the third year of Belshazzar's reign is mentioned in Dan. viii. 1; and (3) that the death of Belshazzar cannot have been at the same time as the destruction of Babylon by the Medes and Persians.

If we now compare with these facts, gathered from Oriental sources, those narrated by the Greek historians Herodotus and Xenophon, we find that the former speaks of several Babylonian kings, but says nothing particular regarding them, but, on the other hand, reports many sayings and fabulous stories of two Babylonian queens, Semiramis and Nitocris, to whom he attributes (i. 184 f.) many exploits, and the erection of buildings which Berosus has attributed to Nebuchadnezzar. Of Babylonian kings he names (i. 188) only Labynetos as the son of Nitocris, with the remark, that he had the same name as his father, and that Cyrus waged war against this second Labynetos, and by diverting the Euphrates from its course at the time of a nocturnal festival of its inhabitants, stormed the city of Babylon (i. 191), after he had gained a battle before laying siege to the capital of the Babylonians (i. 190). Xenophon (*Cyrop.* vii. 5, 15 ff.), agreeing with Herodotus, relates that Cyrus entered the city by damming off the Euphrates during a festival of its inhabitants, and that the king was put to death, whose name he does not mention, but whom he describes (v. 2. 27, iv. 6. 3) as a youth, and (iv. 6. 3, v. 2. 27 f., v. 3. 6, vii. 5. 32) as a riotous, voluptuous, cruel, godless man. The preceding king, the father of the last, he says, was a good man, but his youngest son, who succeeded to the government, was a wicked man. Herodotus and Xenophon appear, then, to agree in this, that both of them connect the destruction of Babylon and the downfall of the Chaldean kingdom by Cyrus with a riotous festival of the Babylonians, and both describe the last king as of royal descent. They agree with the narrative of Daniel as to the death of Belshazzar, that it took place during or immediately after a festival, and regarding the transference of the Chaldean kingdom to the Medes and Persians;

and they confirm the prevalent interpretation of this chapter, that Belshazzar was the last Chaldean king, and was put to death on the occasion of the taking of Babylon. But in their statements concerning the last king of Babylon they both stand in opposition to the accounts of Berosus and Abydenus. Herodotus and Xenophon describe him as the king's son, while Nabonnedus, according to both of these Chaldean historians, was not of royal descent. Besides this, Xenophon states that the king lost his life at the taking of Babylon, while according to Berosus, on the contrary, he was not in Babylon at all, but was besieged in Borsippa, surrendered to Cyrus, and was banished to Carmania, or according to Abydenus, was made deputy of that province. Shall we then decide for Herodotus and Xenophon, and against Berosus and Abydenus? Against such a decision the great imperfection and indefiniteness of the Grecian account must awaken doubts. If, as is generally supposed, the elder Labynetus of Herodotus is the husband of Nitocris, who was the wife of Nebuchadnezzar, then his son of the same name cannot be identical with the Nabonnedus of Berosus and Abydenus; for according to the testimonies of biblical and Oriental authorities, which are clear on this point, the Chaldean kingdom did not fall under the son of Nebuchadnezzar, and then the statement of Herodotus regarding the two Labynetuses is certainly incorrect, and is fabricated from very obscure traditions. Xenophon also shows himself to be not well informed regarding the history of the Chaldean kings. Although his description of the last of these kings appears to indicate an intimate knowledge of his character, and accords with the character of Belshazzar, yet he does not even know the name of this king, and still less the duration of his reign.

Accordingly these scanty and indefinite Grecian reports cannot counterbalance the extended and minute statements of Berosus and Abydenus, and cannot be taken as regulating the historical interpretation of Dan. v. Josephus, it is true, understands the narrative in such a way that he identifies Belshazzar with Nabonnedus, and connects his death with the destruction of the Babylonish kingdom, for (*Ant.* x. 11, 2 f.) he states that, after Nebuchadnezzar, his son Evilmerodach reigned eighteen years. But when he died, his son Neriglissar succeeded to the government, and died after he had reigned forty years. After him the succession in the kingdom came to his son Labosordacus, who continued in it but nine months; and when he was dead (τελευτήσαντος αὐτοῦ), it came to Baltasar, who by the Babylonians was called Naboandelus (Nabonnedus), against whom Cyrus the king of Persia and Darius the king of Media made war. While they besieged Babylon a wonderful event occurred at a feast which the king gave to his magnates and his wives, as described by Dan. v. Not long after Cyrus took the city and made Baltasar prisoner. "For it was," he continues, "under Baltasar, after he had reigned seventeen years, that Babylon was taken. This was, as has been handed down to us, the end of the descendants of Nebuchadnezzar." But it is clear that in these reports which Josephus has given he has not drawn his information from sources no longer accessible to us, but has merely attempted in them to combine the reports of Berosus, and perhaps also those of the Greek historians, with his own exposition of the narrative of Dan. v. The deviations from Berosus and the Canon of Ptolemy in regard to the number of the years of the reign of Evilmerodach and of Neriglissar are to be attributed to the transcriber of Josephus, since he himself, in his work *contra Apion*, gives the number in harmony with those stated by those authors without making any further remark. The names of the four kings are derived from Berosus, as well as the nine months' reign of Labosordacus and the seventeen years of Naboandelus; but the deviations from Berosus with respect to the death of Evilmerodach, and the descent of Neriglissar and Nabonnedus from Nebuchadnezzar, Josephus has certainly derived only from Jer. xxvii. 7 and Dan. v.; for the statement by Jeremiah, that all the nations would serve Nebuchadnezzar, his son and his son's son, "until the very time of his land come," is literally so understood by him as meaning that Evilmerodach, the son of Nebuchadnezzar, was succeeded by his own son, who again was succeeded by his son, and so on down to Belshazzar, whom Daniel (ch. v. 22) had called the son of Nebuchadnezzar, and whom Josephus regarded as the last king of Babylon, the Nabonnedus of the Babylonians. Josephus did not know how to harmonize with this view the fact of the murder of Evilmerodach by his brother-in-law, and therefore he speaks of Evilmerodach as dying in peace, and of his son as succeeding him on the throne, while he passes by in silence the death of Labosordacus and the descent of Baltasar, and only in the closing sentence reckons him also among the successors of Nebuchadnezzar.

But if in the passages quoted Josephus gives only his own view regarding the Chaldean rulers down to the time of the overthrow of the kingdom, and in that contradicts on several points the statements of Berosus, without supporting these contradictions by authorities, we cannot make use of his narrative as historical evidence for the exposition of this chapter, and the question, Which Babylonian king is to be understood by Belshazzar? must be decided on the ground of existing independent authorities.

Since, then, the extra-biblical authorities contradict one another in this, that the Chaldean historians describe Nabonnedus, the last king of the Chaldean kingdom, as a Babylonian not of royal descent who, after putting to death the last descendant of the royal family, usurped the throne, which, according to their account, he occupied till Babylon was destroyed by Cyrus, when he was banished to Carmania, where he died a natural death; while, on the other hand, Herodotus and Xenophon represent the last Babylonian king, whom Herodotus calls Labynetus = Nabonedos [= Nabonned = Nabonid], as of royal descent, and the successor of his father on the throne, and connect the taking of Babylon with a riotous festival held in the palace and in the city generally, during which, Xenophon says, the king was put to death;—therefore the determination regarding the historical contents of Dan. v. hinges on this point: whether Belshazzar is to be identified, on the authority of Greek authors, with Nabonnedus; or, on the authority of the Chaldean historians, is to be regarded as different from him, and is identical with one of the two Babylonian kings who were dethroned by a conspiracy.

The decision in favour of the former I have in my *Lehrb. der Einl.*, along with many interpreters, contended for. By this view the statements of Berosus and Abydenus regarding Nabonned's descent and the end of his life must be set aside as unhistorical, and explained only as traditions intended for the glorification of the royal house of Nebuchadnezzar, by which the Babylonians sought to lessen the undeniable disgrace attending the downfall of their monarchy, and to roll away the dishonour of the siege at least from the royal family of the famed Nebuchadnezzar. But although in the statements of Berosus, but particularly in those of Abydenus regarding Nebuchadnezzar, their laudatory character cannot be denied, yet Hävernick (*N. Krit. Unterss.* p. 70 f.) and Kranichfeld, p. 30 ff., have with justice replied that this national partiality in giving colour to his narrative is not apparent in Berosus generally, for he speaks very condemnatorily of the son of Nebuchadnezzar, saying that he administered the affairs of government ἀνόμως καὶ ἀσελγῶς; he also blames the predecessor of Nabonnedus, and assigns as the reason of the murder of the former as well as of the latter their own evil conduct. Nor does it appear that Berosus depreciated Nabonnedus in order to benefit his predecessors, rather he thought of him as worthy of distinction, and placed him on the throne in honour among his predecessors. "What Herodotus says (i. 186) of the wife of Nebuchadnezzar is expressly stated by Berosus to the honour of the government of Nabonnedus, namely, that under his reign a great part of the city wall was furnished with fortifications (τὰ περὶ τὸν ποταμὸν τείχη τῆς Βαβυλωνίων πόλεως ἐξ ὀπτῆς πλίνθου καὶ ἀσφάλτου κατεκοσμήθη); and it is obviously with reference to this statement that in the course of the narrative mention is made of the strong fortifications of the city which defied the assault of Cyrus. Moreover, in the narrative Nabonnedus appears neither as a traitor nor as a coward. On the contrary, he goes out well armed against the enemy and offers him battle (ἀπαντήσας μετὰ τῆς δυνάμεως καὶ παραταξάμενος); and the circumstance that he surrendered to Cyrus in Borsippa is to be accounted for from this, that he only succeeded in fleeing thither with a very small band. Finally, it is specially mentioned that Cyrus made war against Babylon after he had conquered the rest of Asia. From this it is manifest that the fame of the strength of Babylon was in no respect weakened by Nabonnedus' seventeen years' reign." (Kranichfeld.) All these circumstances stand in opposition to the opinion that there is a tendency in Berosus to roll the disgrace of the overthrow of the kingdom from off the family of Nebuchadnezzar, and to attribute it to an incapable upstart.

What Berosus, moreover, says regarding the treatment of Nabonnedus on the part of Cyrus shows no trace of a desire to depreciate the dethroned monarch. That Cyrus assigned him a residence during life in Carmania is in accordance with the noble conduct of Cyrus in other cases, *e.g.* toward Astyages the Mede, and toward the Lydian king Crœsus (Herod. i. 130; Justin. i. 6, 7). In addition to all this, not only is the statement of Berosus regarding the battle which preceded the overthrow of Babylon confirmed by Herodotus, i. 190, but his report also of the descent of Nabonnedus and of his buildings is established by inscriptions reported on by Oppert in his *Expédit. Scient.* i. p. 182 ff.; for the ruins of Babylon on both banks of the Euphrates preserve to this day the foundations on which were built the walls of Nabonnedus, consisting of hard bricks almost wholly covered with asphalt, bearing the name of Nabonetos, who is not described as a king's son, but is only called the son of Nabobalatirib. Cf. Duncker, *Gesch. des Alterth.* ii. p. 719, 3d ed.

After all that has been said, Berosus, as a native historian, framing his narratives after Chaldean tradition, certainly merits a preference not only to Herodotus, who, according to his own statement, i. 95, followed the Persian tradition in regard to Cyrus, and is not well informed concerning the Babylonian kings, but also to Xenophon, who in his *Cyropædia*, however favourably we may judge of its historical value, follows no pure historical aim, but seeks to set forth Cyrus as the pattern of a hero-king, and reveals no intimate acquaintance with the history of the Chaldean kings. But if, in all his principal statements regarding Nabonnedus, Berosus deserves full credit, we must give up the identification of Belshazzar with Nabonnedus, since the narrative of Dan. v., as above remarked, connects the death of Belshazzar, in point of fact indeed, but not in point of time, with the destruction of the Babylonian kingdom; and the narratives of Herodotus and Xenophon with respect to the destruction of Babylon during a nocturnal revelry of its inhabitants, may rest also only on some tradition that had been transmitted to their time.[1]

[1] Kranichfeld, p. 84 ff., has so clearly shown this origin of the reports given by Herodotus and Xenophon regarding the circumstances attending the taking of Babylon by Cyrus, that we cannot refrain from here communicating the principal points of his proof. Proceeding from the *Augenschein* (appearance), on which Hitzig argues, that, according to Dan. v. 26 ff., the death of Belshazzar coincided with the destruction of the Chaldean kingdom, since both events are announced together in God's writing, Kranichfeld assumes that this appearance (although it presents itself as an optical illusion, on a fuller acquaintance with the manner of prophetic announcement in which the near and the more remote futures are immediately placed together) has misled the uncritical popular traditions which Herodotus and Xenophon record, and that not from first and native sources. "The noteworthy *factum* of the mysterious writing which raised Daniel to the rank of third ruler in the kingdom, and certainly, besides, made him to be spoken of as a conspicuous personage, and the interpretation which placed together two *facta*, and made them apparently contemporaneous, as well as the *factum* of one part of the announcement of the mysterious writing being actually accomplished that very night, could in the course of time, even among natives, and so much the sooner in the dim form which the tradition very naturally assumed in foreign countries, *e.g.* in the Persian tradition, easily give occasion to the tradition that the *factum* mentioned in the mysterious writing occurred, as interpreted, in that same night." In this way might the

But if Belshazzar is not the same person as Nabonnedus, nor the last Babylonian king, then he can only be either Evil̆merodach or Laborosoarchod, since of Nebuchadnezzar's successors only these two were murdered. Both suppositions have found their advocates. Following the example of Scaliger and Calvisius, Ebrard (*Comm. zur Offb. Johannes*, p. 45) and Delitzsch (Herz.'s *Realencykl.* iii. p. 277) regard Belshazzar as Laborosoarchod or Labosordacus (as Josephus writes the name in the *Antt.*), *i.e.* Nebo-Sadrach, and Bel = Nebo; for the appearance of the queen leads us to think of a very youthful king, and Belshazzar (ch. v. 13) speaks of Nebuchadnezzar as if all he knew regarding him was derived from hearsay alone. In ch. vi. 1 (v. 31) it is indicated that a man of advanced age came in the room of a mere youth. If Daniel reckons the years of Belshazzar from the death of Evilmerodach

Persian or Median popular tradition easily think of the king who was put to death that night, the son of Nebuchadnezzar, as also the last Babylonian king, with whom the kingdom perished, and attribute to him the name Labynetus, *i.e.* the Nabonnedus of Berosus, which is confirmed by the agreement of Herodotus with Berosus in regard to the battle preceding the overthrow of Babylon, as well as the absence of the king from Babylon at the taking of the city.—"The historical facts with respect to the end of the Chaldean kingdom, as they are preserved by Berosus, were thrown together and confused along the dim course of the tradition with a narrative, preserved to us in its original form by Daniel, of the contents of the mysterious writing, connecting the death of the king with the end of the kingdom, corresponding with which, and indeed in that very night in which it was interpreted, the murder of the king took place; and this dim tradition we have in the reports given by Herodotus and Xenophon. But the fact, as related by Daniel v., forms the middle member between the statement given by Berosus and the form which the tradition has assumed in Herodotus and Xenophon." "This seems to me," as Kran., in conclusion, remarks, "to be the very simple and natural state of the matter, in view of the open contradiction, on the one side, in which the Greek authors stand to Berosus and Abydenus, without, however (cf. Herodotus), in all points differing from the former; and, on the other side, in view of the manifest harmony in which they stand with Daniel, without, however, agreeing with him in all points. In such circumstances the Greek authors, as well as Berosus and Abydenus on the other side, serve to establish the statements in the book of Daniel."

Against this view of the origin of the tradition transmitted by Herodotus and Xenophon, that Cyrus took Babylon during a riotous festival of its inhabitants, the prophecies of Isa. xxi. 5, and of Jer. li. 39, cannot be adduced as historical evidence in support of the historical truth of this tradition; for these prophecies contain only the thought that Babylon shall suddenly be destroyed amid the tumult of its revelry and drunkenness, and would only be available as valid evidence if they were either *vaticinia ex eventu*, or were literally delivered as predictions.

(cf. Jer. xxvii. 7), for Belshazzar's father Neriglissar (Nergal-Sar), since he was only the husband of a daughter of Nebuchadnezzar, could only rule in the name of his son, then Belshazzar (Nebo-Sadrach) was murdered after a reign of four years and nine months, of which his father Nergal-Sar reigned four years in his stead, and he himself nine months. With Belshazzar the house of Nebuchadnezzar had ceased to reign. Astyages, the Median king, regarded himself as heir to the Chaldean throne, and held as his vassal Nabonnedus, who was made king by the conspirators who had murdered Belshazzar; but Nabonnedus endeavoured to maintain his independence by means of a treaty with the king of Lydia, and thus there began the war which was directed first against the Lydian king, and then against Nabonnedus himself.

But of these conjectures and combinations there is no special probability, for proof is wanting. For the alleged origin of the war against the Lydian king and against Nabonnedus there is no historical foundation, since the supposition that Astyages regarded himself, after the extinction of the house of Nebuchadnezzar, as the heir to the Chaldean throne is a mere conjecture. Neither of these conjectures finds any support either in the fact that Nabonnedus remained quiet during the Lydian war instead of rendering help to the Lydian king, or from that which we find on inscriptions regarding the buildings of Nabonnedus. According to the researches of Oppert and Duncker (*Gesch. d. Alterthums*, ii. p. 719), Nabonetus (Nabunahid) not merely completed the walls left unfinished by Nebuchadnezzar, which were designed to shut in Babylon from the Euphrates along both sides of the river; but he designates himself, in inscriptions found on bricks, as the preserver and the restorer of the pyramid and the tower, and he boasts of having built a temple at Mugheir to the honour of his deities, the goddess Belit and the god Sin (god of the Moon). The restoration of the pyramid and the tower, as well as the building of the temple, does not agree with the supposition that Nabonnedus ascended the throne as vassal of the Median king with the thought of setting himself free as soon as possible from the Median rule. Moreover the supposition that Neriglissar, as the husband of Nebuchadnezzar's daughter, could have conducted the government only in the name of his son, is opposed to the statements of Berosus and to the Canon of Ptolemy, which reckon Neriglissar as really king, and his reign as distinct from that of his son. Thus the appearance of the queen in Dan. v. by no means indicates that Belshazzar was yet a boy; much rather does the participation of the wives and concubines of Belshazzar in the feast point to the age of the king as beyond that of a boy. Finally, it does not follow from ch. v. 13 that Belshazzar knew about Nebuchadnezzar only from hearsay. In the verse referred to, Belshazzar merely says that he had heard regarding Daniel that he was one of the Jews who had been carried captive by his father Nebuchadnezzar. But the carrying away of Daniel and of the Jews by Nebuchadnezzar took place, as to its beginning, before he had ascended the throne, and as to its end (under Zedekiah), during the first half of his reign, when his eldest son might be yet a mere youth. That Belshazzar knew about Nebuchadnezzar not from hearsay merely, but that he knew from personal knowledge about his madness, Daniel tells him to his face, ver. 22.

Finally, the identification of Labosordacus, = Nebo-Sadrach, with Belshazzar has more appearance than truth. *Bel* is not like *Nebo* in the sense that both names denote one and the same god; but Bel is the Jupiter of the Babylonians, and Nebo the Mercury. Also the names of the two kings, as found on the inscriptions, are quite different. For the name *Λαβοσόρδαχος* (Joseph. *Ant.*) Berosus uses *Λαβοροσοάρχοδος*, and Abydenus (Euseb. *præp. ev.* ix. 41) *Λαβασσάρασκος*; in the *Chron. arm.* it is *Labossorakos*, and Syncellus has *Λαβοσάροχος*. These names do not represent Nebo-Sadrach, but that used by Berosus corresponds to the native Chaldee *Nabu-ur-uzuurkud*, the others point to *Nabu-surusk* or *-suruk*, and show the component parts contained in the name *Nabu-kudrussur* in inverted order,—at least they are very nearly related to this name. Belshazzar, on the contrary, is found in the Inscription published by Oppert (Duncker, p. 720) written *Belsarrusur*. In this Inscription Nabonetus names Belsarrusur the offspring of his heart. If we therefore consider that Nabonnedus represents himself as carrying forward and completing the work begun by Nebuchadnezzar in Babylon, the supposition presses itself upon us, that also in regard to the name which he gave to his son, who was eventually his successor on the throne, he trod in the footsteps of the celebrated founder of the Babylonian monarchy. Consequently these Inscriptions would indicate that the Belshazzar (= Belsarrusur) of Daniel was the son of Nebuchadnezzar, and his successor on the throne.

Though we may rest satisfied with this supposition, there are yet weighty reasons for regarding Belshazzar as the son and successor of Nebuchadnezzar, who was put to death by his brother-in-law Neriglissar, and thus for identifying him with Evilmerodach (2 Kings xxv. 27; Jer. lii. 31). Following the example of Marsham in *Canon chron.* p. 596, this opinion is maintained among modern critics by Hofmann (*Die* 70 *Jahre,* p. 44 ff.), Hävernick (*N. K. Unt.* p. 71), Oehler (Thol. *Litt. Anz.* 1842, p. 398), Hupfeld (*Exercitt. Herod. spec.* ii. p. 46), Niebuhr (*Ges. Ass.* p. 91 f.), Zündel (p. 33), Kranichfeld, and Kliefoth. In favour of this opinion we notice, first, that Belshazzar in the narrative of Daniel is distinctly declared to be the son and successor of Nebuchadnezzar. The statement of Berosus, that Evilmerodach managed the affairs of government ἀνόμως καὶ ἀσελγῶς, entirely harmonizes also with the character ascribed to Belshazzar in this chapter, while the arguments which appear to oppose the identity of the two are unimportant. The diversity of names, viz. that Nebuchadnezzar's successor both in 2 Kings xxv. 27 and Jer. lii. 31 is called אֱוִיל מְרֹדַךְ, and by Berosus, Abydenus, and in the Canon of Ptolemy *Εὐειλμαράδουχος, Amilmarodokos, Ἰλλοαρούδαμος* (in the Canon only, written instead of *Ἰλμαρούδακος*), but by Daniel בֵּלְשַׁאצַּר, is simply explained by this, that as a rule the Eastern kings had several names: along with their personal names they had also a surname or general royal name, the latter being frequently the only one that was known to foreigners; cf. Niebuhr, *Gesch. Assurs u. Babels,* p. 29 ff. In the name *Evilmerodach,* the component parts, *Il* (= *El*), *i.e.* God, and *Merodach,* recur in all forms. The first part was changed by the Jews, perhaps after the tragic death of the king, into אֱוִיל, *stultus* (after Ps. liii. ?); while Daniel, living at the Babylonian court, transmits the name Belshazzar, formed after the name of the god Bel, which was there used. Moreover the kind benevolent conduct of Evilmerodach towards king Jehoiachin, who was languishing in prison, does not stand in contradiction to the vileness of his character, as testified to by Berosus; for even an unrighteous, godless ruler can be just and good in certain instances. Moreover the circumstance that, according to the Canon of Ptolemy, Evilmerodach ruled two years, while, on the contrary, in Dan. viii. 1 mention is made of the third year of the reign of Belshazzar, forms no inexplicable discrepancy. Without resorting to Syncellus, who in his Canon attributes to him three years, since the numbers mentioned in this Canon contain many errors, the discrepancy may be explained from the custom prevalent in the books of Kings of reckoning the duration of the reign of a king only in full years, without reference to the months that may be wanting or that may exceed. According to this usage, the reign might extend to only two full years if it began about the middle of the calendar year, but might extend into three calendar years, and thus be reckoned as three years, if the year of the commencement of it and the year in which it ended were reckoned according to the calendar. On the other side, it is conceivable that Evilmerodach reigned a few weeks, or even months, beyond two years, which were in the reckoning of the duration of his reign not counted to him, but to his successor. Ptolemy has without doubt observed this procedure in his astronomical Canon, since he reckons to all rulers only full years. Thus there is no doubt of any importance in opposition to the view that Belshazzar was identical with Evilmerodach, the son and successor of Nebuchadnezzar.

With the removal of the historical difficulty lying in the name Belshazzar the historical credibility of the principal contents of this narrative is at the same time established. And this so much the more surely, as the opponents of the genuineness are not in a position to find, in behalf of their assertion that this history is a fiction, a situation from which this fiction framed for a purpose can be comprehended in the actions of Antiochus Epiphanes and in the relations of the times of the Maccabees. According to Berth., v. Leng., Hitz., and Bleek, the author sought on the one hand to represent to the Syrian prince in the fate of Belshazzar how great a judgment from God threatened him on account of his wickedness in profaning the temple, and on the other, to glorify Daniel the Jew by presenting him after the type of Joseph.

But as for the first tendency (or purpose), the chief matter is wholly wanting, viz. the profanation of the holy vessels of the temple by Antiochus on the occasion of a festival, which in this chapter forms the chief part of the wickedness for which Belshazzar brings upon himself the judgment of God. Of Antiochus Epiphanes it is only related that he plundered the temple at Jerusalem in order that he might meet his financial necessities, while on the other hand the carrying away by Nebuchadnezzar of the vessels belonging to the temple (Dan. i. 2) is represented as a providence of God.[1]

[1] According to Bleek and v. Leng., this narrative must have in view 1 Macc. i. 21 ff. and 2 Macc. v. 15 ff., where it is related of Antiochus as something in the highest degree vicious, that he entered into the temple at Jerusalem, and

As regards the second tendency of the composition, the glorifying of Daniel after the type of Joseph, Kliefoth rightly remarks: "The comparison of Daniel with Joseph rests on hastily collected indefinite resemblances, along with which there are also found as many contrasts." The resemblances reduce themselves to these: that Daniel was adorned by the king with a golden chain about his neck and raised to the highest office of state for his interpretation of the mysterious writing, as Joseph had been for the interpretation of the dream. But on this Ewald[1] himself remarks: "The promise that whoever should solve the mystery would be made *third ruler of the kingdom*, and at the same time the declaration in ch. vi. 3 (2), show that in the kingdom of Babylon there existed an arrangement similar to that of the Roman empire after Diocletian, by which under one Augustus there might be three Cæsars. Altogether different is the old Egyptian law set forth in Gen. xli. 43 f., and prevailing also in ancient kingdoms, according to which the king might recognise a man as the *second* ruler in the kingdom, or as his representative; and since that mentioned in the book of Daniel is peculiar, it rests, to all appearance, on some old genuine Babylonish custom. On the other hand, the being clothed with purple and adorned with a golden chain about the neck is more

with impure hands carried thence the golden basins, cups, bowls, and other holy vessels. But in spite of this wholly incorrect application of the contents of the passages cited, Bleek cannot but confess that the reference would be more distinct if it were related—which it is not—that Antiochus used the holy vessels at a common festival, or at least at the time of offering sacrifice. But if we look closely at 1 Macc. i. 21 ff., we find that Antiochus not only took away the utensils mentioned by Bleek, but also the golden altar, the golden candlestick, the table of shew-bread, the veil, and the crowns, and the golden ornaments that were before the temple, all which (gold) he pulled off, and took also the silver and gold, and the hidden treasures which he found; from which it clearly appears that Antiochus plundered the temple because of his pecuniary embarrassment, as Grimm remarks, or "for the purpose of meeting his financial necessities" (Grimm on 2 Macc. v. 16). Hitzig has therefore abandoned this reference as unsuitable for the object assumed, and has sought the occasion for the fiction of Dan. v. in the splendid games and feasts which Antiochus held at Daphne (Polyb. xxxi. 3, 4). But this supposition also makes it necessary for the critic to add the profanation of the holy vessels of the temple at these feasts from his own resources, because history knows nothing of it. Polybius merely says that the expense of these entertainments was met partly by the plunder Antiochus brought from Egypt, partly by the gifts of his allies, but most of all by the treasure taken from the temple.

[1] P. 380 of the 3d vol. of the second ed. of his work, *Die Propheten des A. Bundes*.

generally the distinguishing mark of men of princely rank, as is seen in the case of Joseph, Gen. xli. 42."

To this it must be added, that Belshazzar's relation to Daniel and Daniel's conduct toward Belshazzar are altogether different from the relation of Antiochus to the Jews who remained faithful to their law, and their conduct toward that cruel king. That the conduct of Belshazzar toward Daniel does not accord with the times of the Maccabees, the critics themselves cannot deny. Hitzig expresses his surprise that "the king hears the prophecy in a manner one should not have expected; his behaviour is not the same as that of Ahab toward Micah, or of Agamemnon toward Calchas." Antiochus Epiphanes would have acted precisely as they did. And how does the behaviour of Daniel harmonize with that of Mattathias, who rejected the presents and the favour of the tyrant (1 Macc. ii. 18 ff.), and who put to death with the sword those Jews who were submitting themselves to the demands of the king? Daniel received the purple, and allowed himself to be adorned with a golden chain by the heathen king, and to be raised to the rank of third ruler in his kingdom.[1]

While thus standing in marked contrast to the circumstances of the Maccabean times, the narrative is perfectly consistent if we regard it as a historical episode belonging to the time of Daniel. It is true it has also a parenetic character, only not the limited object attributed to it by the opponents of the genuineness —to threaten Antiochus Epiphanes with divine judgments on account of his wickedness and to glorify Daniel. Rather it is for all times in which the church of the Lord is oppressed by the powers of the world, to show to the blasphemers of the divine name how the Almighty God in heaven punishes and destroys the lords of this world who proceed to desecrate and abuse that which is sacred, without taking notice of the divine warnings addressed to them on account of their self-glorification, and bestows honour upon His servants who are rejected and despised by the world. But when compared with the foregoing narratives, this event before us shows how the world-power in its development became always the more hardened against the revelations of the living God, and the more

[1] "In short, the whole accompaniments of this passage," Kranichfeld thus concludes (p. 213) his dissertation on this point, "are so completely different from those of the Maccabean times, that if it is to be regarded as belonging peculiarly to this time, then we must conceive of it as composed by an author altogether ignorant of the circumstances and of the historical situation."

ripe for judgment. Nebuchadnezzar demanded of all his subjects a recognition of his gods, and prided himself in his great power and worldly glory, but yet he gave glory to the Lord of heaven for the signs and wonders which God did to him. Belshazzar knew this, yet it did not prevent him from blaspheming this God, nor did it move him to seek to avert by penitential sorrow the judgment of death which was denounced against him.

Vers. 1.–4. The verses describe the progress of Belshazzar's magnifying himself against the living God, whereby the judgment threatened came upon him and his kingdom. A great feast, which the king gave to his officers of state and to his wives, furnished the occasion for this.

The name of the king, בֵּלְשַׁאצַּר, contains in it the two component parts of the name which Daniel had received (ch. i. 7), but without the interposed ט, whereby it is distinguished from it. This distinction is not to be overlooked, although the LXX. have done so, and have written the two names, as if they were identical, *Βαλτάσαρ*. The meaning of the name is as yet unknown. לְחֶם, *meal-time, the festival.* The invitation to a thousand officers of state corresponds to the magnificence of Oriental kings. According to Ctesias (*Athen. Deipnos*, iv. 146), 15,000 men dined daily from the table of the Persian king (cf. Esth. i. 4). To account for this large number of guests, it is not necessary to suppose that during the siege of Babylon by Cyrus a multitude of great officers from all parts of the kingdom had fled for refuge to Babylon. The number specified is evidently a round number, *i.e.* the number of the guests amounted to about a thousand. The words, *he drank wine before the thousand* (great officers), are not, with Hävernick, to be explained of drinking first, or of preceding them in drinking, or of drinking a toast to them, but are to be understood according to the Oriental custom, by which at great festivals the king sat at a separate table on an elevated place, so that he had the guests before him or opposite to him. The drinking of wine is particularly noticed as the immediate occasion of the wickedness which followed.

Ver. 2. בִּטְעֵם חַמְרָא, *while he tasted the wine, i.e.* when the wine was relished by him; thus "in the wanton madness of one excited by wine, Prov. xx. 1" (Hitz.). From these words it appears that Belshazzar commanded the temple vessels which Nebuchadnezzar had carried away from Jerusalem to be brought, not, as Hävernick thinks, for the purpose of seeking, in his anxiety on account of the siege of the city, the favour of the God of the Jews, but to insult this God in the presence of his own gods. The supposition of anxiety on account of the siege does not at all harmonize with the celebration of so riotous a festival. Besides, the vessels are not brought for the purpose of making libations in order to propitiate the God to whom they were consecrated, but, according to the obvious statement of the text, only to drink out of them from the madness of lust. וְיִשְׁתּוֹן, *that they may drink;* וּ before the imperf. expresses the *design* of the bringing of the vessels. שְׁתָה בְּ, *to drink out of*, as Gen. xliv. 5, Amos vi. 6. שֵׁגְלָן, *the wives* of the king; cf. Neh. ii. 6 with Ps. xlv. 10. לְחֵנָן, *concubines;* this word stands in the Targg. for the Hebr. פִּלֶגֶשׁ. The LXX. have here, and also at ver. 23, omitted mention of the women, according to the custom of the Macedonians, Greeks, and Romans (cf. Herod. v. 18; Corn. Nep. *proem.* § 6); but Xenophon (*Cyr.* v. 2. 28) and Curtius (v. 1. 38) expressly declare that among the Babylonians the wives also were present at festivals.

Ver. 3. הֵיכְלָא denotes *the holy place of the temple, the inner apartment of the temple,* as at 1 Kings vi. 3, Ezek. xli. 1. אִשְׁתִּיו for שְׁתִיו, with א *prosthet.*, cf. Winer, *chald. Gr.* § 23, 1.

Ver. 4. In this verse the expression *they drank wine* is repeated for the purpose of making manifest the connection between the drinking and the praising of the gods. The wickedness lay in this, that they drank out of the holy vessels of the temple of the God of Israel to glorify (שַׁבַּח, to praise by the singing of songs) their heathen gods in songs of praise. In doing this they did not only place "Jehovah on a perfect level with their gods" (Hävernick), but raised them above the Lord of heaven, as Daniel (ver. 23) charged the king. The carrying away of the temple vessels to Babylon and placing them in the temple of Bel was a sign of the defeat of the God to whom these vessels were consecrated (see under ch. i. 2); the use of these vessels in the drinking of wine at a festival, amid the singing of songs in praise of the gods, was accordingly a celebrating of these gods as victorious over the God of Israel. And it was not a spirit of hostility aroused against the Jews which gave occasion, as Kranichfeld has well remarked, to this celebration of the victory of his god; but, as the narrative informs us, it was the reckless madness of the drunken king and of his drunken guests (cf. ver. 2*a*) during the festival which led them to think of the God of the Jews, whom they supposed they had subdued along with His people, although He had by repeated miracles forced the heathen world-rulers to recognise His omnipotence (cf. ch. ii. 47, iii. 32 f., iv. 14 [17], 31 [34], 34 [37]). In the disregard of these revelations consisted, as Daniel represents to Belshazzar (cf. ver. 18), the dishonour done to the Lord of heaven, although these vessels of the sanctuary might have been profaned merely by using them as common drinking vessels, or they might have been used also in religious libations as vessels consecrated to the gods, of which the text makes no mention, although the singing of songs to the praise of the gods along with the drinking makes the offering of libations very probable. The six predicates of the gods are divided by the copula ו into two classes: gold and silver—brass, iron, wood and stone, in order to represent before the eyes in an advancing degree the vanity of these gods.

Vers. 5–12. *The warning signs, the astonishment of Belshazzar, the inability of the wise men to give counsel, and the advice of the queen.*

Ver. 5. Unexpectedly and suddenly the wanton mad revelry of the king and his guests was brought to a close amid terror by means of a warning sign. The king saw the finger of a man's hand writing on the plaster of the wall of the festival chamber, and he was so alarmed that his whole body shook. The בַּהּ־שַׁעֲתָא places the sign in immediate connection with the drinking and the praising of the gods. The translation, *in the self-same hour*, is already shown to be inadmissible (see under ch. iii. 6). The *Kethiv* נְפָקוּ (*came forth*) is not to be rejected as the indefinite determination of the subject, because the subject follows after it; the *Keri* נְפָקָה is to be rejected, because, though it suits the gender, it does not in respect of number accord with the subject following. The king does not see the whole hand, but only פַּס יְדָא, *the end of the hand*, that is, the fingers which write. This immediately awakened the thought that the writing was by a supernatural being, and alarmed the king out of his intoxication. The fingers wrote on the plaster of the wall over against the candlestick which stood on the table at which the king sat, and which reflected its light perceptibly on the white wall opposite, so that the fingers writing could be distinctly seen. The feast had been prolonged into the darkness of the night, and the wall of the chamber was not wainscotted, but only plastered with lime, as such chambers are found in the palaces of Nimrud and Khorsabad covered over only with mortar (cf. Layard's *Nineveh and Babylon*).

Ver. 6. מַלְכָּא (*the king*) stands absolutely, because the impression made by the occurrence on the king is to be depicted. The plur. זִיוֹהִי has an intensive signification: *the colour of the countenance*. Regarding זִיו, see under ch. iv. 33. The suffix to שְׁנוֹהִי is to be taken in the signification of the dative, since שְׁנָא in the Peal occurs only intransitively. The connection of an intransitive verb with the *suff. accus.* is an inaccuracy for which שׁוּבֵנִי, Ezek. xlvii. 7, and perhaps also עֲשִׂיתִנִי, Ezek. xxix. 3, afford analogies; cf. Ewald's *Lehrb.* § 315*b*. In ver. 9, where the matter is repeated, the harshness is avoided, and עֲלוֹהִי is used to express the change of colour yet more strongly. The meaning is: "the king changed colour as to his countenance, became pale from terror, and was so unmanned by fear and alarm, that his body lost its firmness and vigour." *The bands* or *ligaments of his thighs* (חֲרַץ, equivalent to the Hebr. חֲלָצַיִם) *were loosed*, *i.e.* lost the strength to hold his body, and his knees smote one against another. אַרְכֻּבָּא with א *prosth.*, for רְכוּבָא, in the Targg. means *the knee*. The alarm was heightened by a bad conscience, which roused itself and filled him with dark forebodings. Immediately the king commanded the magicians to be brought, and promised a great reward to him who would read and interpret the mysterious writing.

Ver. 7. Since there are in this verse only three classes of wise men named as ordered to come to the king, to whom he promised the reward for the reading and the interpretation of the writing, and in ver. 8 it is first stated that all the king's wise men came, the probability is, that at first the king commanded only the three classes named in ver. 7 to be brought to him. On this probability Kranichfeld founds the supposition that the king purposely, or with intention, summoned only the three classes named to avoid Daniel, whom he did not wish to consult, from his heathen religious fear of the God of the Jews. But this supposition is altogether untenable. For, first, it does not follow from ch. viii. 27 that under Belshazzar Daniel was president over all the wise men, but only that he was in the king's service. Then, in the event of Daniel's yet retaining the place assigned to him by Nebuchadnezzar, his non-appearance could not be explained on the supposition that Belshazzar called only three classes of the wise men, because the supposition that כֹּל חַכִּימֵי מַלְכָּא (*all the king's wise men*) in ver. 8 forms a contrast to the three classes named in ver. 7 is not sustained by the language here used. But if by "all the wise men of the king," ver. 8, we are to understand the whole body of the wise men of all the classes, and that they appeared before the king, then they must all have been called at the first, since no supplementary calling of the two classes not named in ver. 7 is mentioned. Besides this, the words, "the king spake to the wise men of Babylon," make it probable that all the classes, without the exception of the two, were called. Moreover it is most improbable that in the case before us, where the matter concerned the reading of a writing, the חַרְטֻמִּים, *the magicians* [Schriftkenner], should not have been called merely to avoid Daniel, who was their רַב (*president*) (ch. iv. 6 [9]). Finally, it is psychologically altogether very improbable, that in the great agitation of fear which had filled him at the sight of the hand writing, Belshazzar should have reflected at all on this, that Daniel would announce to him misfortune or the vengeance of the God of the Jews. Such a reflection might perhaps arise on quiet deliberation, but not in the midst of agitating heart-anguish.

The strange circumstance that, according to ver. 7, the king already promised a reward to the wise men, which presupposes that they were already present, and then that for the first time their presence is mentioned in ver. 8, is occasioned by this, that in ver. 7 the appearing of the wise men is not expressly mentioned, but is naturally presupposed, and that the first two clauses of the eighth verse are simply placed together, and are not united to each other by a causal nexus. The meaning of the statement in vers. 7 and 8 is this: The king calls aloud, commanding the astrologers, etc., to be brought to him; and when the wise men of Babylon came to him, he said to each of them, Whoever reads the writing, etc. But all the king's wise men, when they had come, were unable to read the writing. As to the names of the wise men in ver. 7, see under ch. ii. 2. יִקְרֵה for יִקְרֵא, from קְרָא, *to read*. As a reward, the king promises a purple robe, a gold chain for the neck, and the highest office in the kingdom. A robe of purple was the sign of rank worn by the high officers of state among the Persians,—cf. Esth. viii. 15 with Xenophon, *Anab.* i. 5. 8,—and among the Selucidæ, 1 Macc. x. 20; and was also among the Medes the princely garb, Xen. *Anab.* i. 3. 2, ii. 4. 6. אַרְגְּוָן, Hebr. אַרְגָּמָן, *purple*, is a word of Aryan origin, from the Sanscrit *râga*, *red colour*, with the formative syllables *man* and *vat*; cf. Gesen. *Thes. Addid.* p. 111 seq. וְהַמְנוּכָא דִי וגו׳ does not depend on יִלְבַּשׁ, but forms a clause by itself: *and a chain of gold shall be about his neck.* For the *Kethiv*

הַמְנוּכָא the *Keri* substitutes the Targum. and Syr. form הַמְנִיכָא (vers. 7, 16, and 29), *i.e.* the Greek μανιάκης, from the Sansc. *mani*, *jewel*, *pearl*, with the frequent formative syllable *ka* in the Zend, whence the Chaldee word is derived; it signifies *neck-* or *arm-band*, here the former. The golden neck-chain (στρεπτὸς χρύσεος) was an ornament worn by the Persians of rank, and was given by kings as a mark of favour even to kings, *e.g.* Cambyses and the younger Cyrus; cf. Herod. iii. 20; Xen. *Anab.* i. 1. 27, 5. 8, 8. 29.

It is not quite certain what the princely situation is which was promised to the interpreter of the writing, since the meaning of תַּלְתִּי is not quite clear. That it is not the *ordinale* of the number third, is, since Hävernick, now generally acknowledged, because for *tertius* in Aram. תְּלִיתַי is used, which occurs also in ch. ii. 39. Hävernick therefore regards תַּלְתִּי, for which תַּלְתָּא is found in vers. 16 and 29, as an adjective formation which indicates a descent or occupation, and is here used as a *nomen officii* corresponding to the Hebr. שָׁלִישִׁי. Gesenius and Dietrich regard תַּלְתִּי as only the singular form for תְּלִיתַי, and תַּלְתָּא as the *stat. abs.* of תְּלַת, *third rank.* Hitzig would change תַּלְתִּי into תַּלְתַּי, and regard תַּלְתָּא as a singular formed from תַּלְתָּאִין, as *triumvir* from *triumvirorum*, and would interpret it by τρίτος αὐτός, *the third* (*selbstdritt*): as one of three he shall rule in the kingdom, according to ch. vi. 3. Finally, Kranichfeld takes תַּלְתִּי to be a fem. verbal formation according to the analogy of אֲרָמִית, אַחֲרַי, in the sense of *three-ruler-wise*, and תַּלְתָּא for a noun formed from תַּלְתָא, *triumvir.* Almost all these explanations amount to this, that the statements here regard the government of a triumvirate as it was regulated by the Median king Darius, ch. vi. 3 (2); and this appears also to be the meaning of the words as one may literally explain תַּלְתִּי and תַּלְתָּא. Regarding the *Keri* עֲלַיִן see under ch. iv. 4, and regarding פִּשְׁרֵא, under ch. iv. 15.

As all the wise men were unable to read the writing, it has been thought that it was in a foreign language different from the usual language of Babylon, the knowledge of which could not legitimately be expected to be possessed by the native wise men; and since, according to vers. 17, 24 f., Daniel at once showed his acquaintance with the writing in question, it has from this been concluded that already the old Babylonians had handwriting corresponding to the later Syro-Palmyrenian inscriptions, while among the Hebrews to the time of the Exile the essentially Old-Phœnician writing, which is found on the so-called Samaritan coins and in the Samaritan Scriptures, was the peculiar national style of writing (Kran.). But this interpretation of the miracle on natural principles is quite erroneous. First, it is very unlikely that the Chaldean wise men should not have known these old Semitic characters, even although at that time they had ceased to be in current use among the Babylonians in their common writing. Then, from the circumstance that Daniel could at once read the writing, it does not follow that it was the well-known Old-Hebrew writing of his fatherland. "The characters employed in the writing," as Hengstenberg has rightly observed (*Beitr.* i. p. 122), "must have been altogether unusual so as not to be deciphered but by divine illumination." Yet we must not, with M. Geier and others, assume that the writing was visible only to the king and Daniel. This contradicts the text, according to which the Chaldean wise men, and without doubt all that were present, also saw the traces of the writing, but were not able to read it.

Ver. 9. By this not only was the astonishment of the king heightened, but the officers of state also were put into confusion. "In מִשְׁתַּבְּשִׁין lies not merely the idea of consternation, but of confusion, of great commotion in the assembly" (Hitzig). The whole company was thrown into confusion. The magnates spoke without intelligence, and were perplexed about the matter.

Not only was the tumult that arose from the loud confused talk of the king and the nobles heard by those who were there present, but the queen-mother, who was living in the palace, the wife of Nebuchadnezzar, also heard it and went into the banqueting hall. As soon as she perceived the cause of the commotion, she directed the attention of her royal son to Daniel, who in the days of his father Nebuchadnezzar had already, as an interpreter of dreams and of mysteries, shown that the spirit of the holy gods dwelt in him (vers. 10–12).

Ver. 10. By מַלְכְּתָא interpreters rightly understand the mother of the reigning king, the widow of his father Nebuchadnezzar, since according to ver. 2 f. the wives of the king were present at the festival, and the *queen* came before the king as only a mother could do. Among the Israelites also the mother of the reigning king was held in high respect; cf. 1 Kings xv. 13; 2 Kings xxiv. 12, 15; Jer. xiii. 18, xxix. 2. לָקֳבֵל מִלִּין, *by reason of the words*, not: *because of the affair*, to which neither the plur. מִלֵּי nor the gen. רַבְרְבָנוֹהִי agrees. Instead of the *Kethiv* עַלְלַת the *Keri* has

עֲלַּת, the later form. The queen-mother begins in an assuring manner, since she can give an advice which is fitted to allay the embarrassment.

Ver. 11. Her judgment concerning Daniel is that of Nebuchadnezzar, ch. iv. 5, 6 (8, 9); and that she states it in the same words leads to the conclusion that Nebuchadnezzar was her husband. The אֲבוּךְ מַלְכָּא at the end of this verse may be an emphatic repetition of the foregoing מַלְכָּא נב' אֲבוּךְ (Maur., Hitz.), but in that case מַלְכָּא would perhaps stand first. מַלְכָּא is better interpreted by Ros., v. Leng., Klief., and others as the vocative: *thy father, O king*, by which the words make a greater impression.

Ver. 12. The remarkable endowments of Daniel are again stated (according to ver. 11) to give weight to the advice that he should be called in. The words from מְפַשַּׁר [*interpreting*] to קִטְרִין [*doubts*] are an explanatory parenthetical clause, after which the following verb, according to rule, joins itself to שָׂכְלְתָנוּ. In the parenthetical clause the *nomen actionis* אַחֲוָיַת [*showing*] is used instead of the participle, whereby the representation of the continued capability lying in the participle is transferred to that of each separate instance; literally, *interpreting dreams, the explanation of mysteries and dissolving knots*. The allusion of מְשָׁרֵא קִטְרִין to קִטְרֵי חר' מְשַׁתְּרַיִן, ver. 6, is only apparent, certainly is not aimed at, since the former of these expressions has an entirely different meaning. *Knots* stands figuratively for involved complicated problems. That Daniel did not at first appear along with the wise men, but was only called after the queen had advised it, is to be explained on this simple ground, that he was no longer president over the magicians, but on the occasion of a new king ascending the throne had lost that situation, and been put into another office (cf. ch. viii. 27). The words of the queen do not prove that Belshazzar was not acquainted with Daniel, but only show that he had forgotten the service rendered by him to Nebuchadnezzar; for according to ver. 13 he was well acquainted with the personal circumstances of Daniel.

Vers. 13–28. *Daniel is summoned, reminds the king of his sin, and reads and interprets the writing.*

The counsel of the queen was followed, and without delay Daniel was brought in. הֻעַל, cf. הֻעַלּוּ ver. 15, is Hebr. Hophal of עַל = עֲלַל, *to go in*, as הוּסַף, ch. iv. 33. The question of the king: *Art thou Daniel* . . .? did not expect an answer, and has this meaning: *Thou art indeed Daniel.* The address shows that Belshazzar was acquainted with Daniel's origin, of which the queen had said nothing, but that he had had no official intercourse with him. It shows also that Daniel was no longer the president of the magicians at the king's court (ch. ii. 48 f.).

Ver. 14, cf. ver. 11. It is not to be overlooked that here Belshazzar leaves out the predicate *holy* in connection with אֱלָהִין (*of the gods*).

Ver. 15. The asyndeton אָשְׁפַיָּא is in apposition to חַכִּימַיָּא as explanatory of it: the wise men, namely the conjurers, who are mentioned *instar omnium.* דִּי with the imperf. following is not the relative particle, but the conjunction *that* before the clause expressive of design, and the infinitive clause dependent on the clause of design going before: *that you may read the writing to make known to me the interpretation.* מִלְּתָא is not the mysterious writing = word, discourse, but *the writing with its wonderful origin*; thus, the matter of which he wishes to know the meaning.

Vers. 16, 17. The *Kethiv* תּוּכַל, ver. 16, is the Hebr. Hophal, as ch. ii. 10; the *Keri* תִּכּוּל the formation usual in the Chaldee, found at ch. iii. 29. Regarding the reward to Daniel, see under ver. 7. Daniel declines (ver. 17) the distinction and the place of honour promised for the interpretation, not because the former might be dangerous to him and the latter only temporary, as Hitzig supposes; for he had no reason for such a fear, when he spoke "as one conveying information who had just seen the writing, and had read it and understood its import," for the interpretation, threatening ruin and death to the king, could bring no special danger to him either on the part of Belshazzar or on that of his successor. Much rather Daniel rejected the gift and the distinction promised, to avoid, as a divinely enlightened seer, every appearance of self-interest in the presence of such a king, and to show to the king and his high officers of state that he was not determined by a regard to earthly advantage, and would unhesitatingly declare the truth, whether it might be pleasing or displeasing to the king. But before he read and interpreted the writing, he reminded the king of the punishment his father Nebuchadnezzar had brought upon himself on account of his haughty pride against God (vers. 18–21), and then showed him how he, the son, had done wickedly toward God, the Lord of his life (vers. 22, 23), and finally explained to him that on this account this sign had been given by God (ver. 24).

Ver. 18. The address, *Thou, O king*, is here an absolute clause, and is not resumed till ver. 22. By this address all that follows regarding Nebuchadnezzar is placed in definite relation to Belshazzar. The brilliant description of Nebuchadnezzar's power in vers. 18 and 19 has undeniably the object of impressing it on the mind of Belshazzar that he did not equal his father in power and majesty. Regarding עַמְמַיָּא וגו׳, see under ch. iii. 4, and with regard to the *Kethiv* זָאעִין, with the *Keri* זָיְעִין, see under ch. iii. 3. מַחֵא is not from מְחָא, *to strike* (Theodot., Vulg.), but the Aphel of חֲיָא (*to live*), the particip. of which is מְחַיֵּ in Deut. xxxii. 39, contracted from מַחְיֵא, here the part. מַחֵא, in which the Jod is compensated by the lengthening of the vowel *ā*. Accordingly, there is no ground for giving the preference, with Buxt., Ges., Hitz., and others, to the variant מַחֵא, which accommodates itself to the usual Targum. form. The last clause in ver. 19 reminds us of 1 Sam. ii. 6, 7. In vers. 20 and 21 Daniel brings to the remembrance of Belshazzar the divine judgment that fell upon Nebuchadnezzar (ch. iv.). רִם is not the passive part., but the *perf. act.* with an intransitive signification; cf. Winer, § 22, 4. תְּקֵף, *strong, to be and to become firm*, here, as the Hebr. חָזַק, Ex. vii. 13, of *obduracy*. הֶעְדִּיו, 3d pers. plur. impers., instead of the passive: *they took away*, for it was taken away, he lost it; see under ch. iii. 4, and Winer, § 49, 3. שַׁוִּי is also to be thus interpreted, since in its impersonal use the singular is equivalent to the plur.; cf. Winer. There is no reason for changing (with v. Leng. and Hitz.) the form into שְׁוִי, *part. Peil.* The change of construction depends on the rhetorical form of the address, which explains also the naming of the עֲרָדַיָּא, *wild asses*, as untractable beasts, instead of חֵיוַת בָּרָא (*beasts of the field*), ch. iv. 20 (23). Regarding the *Kethiv* עליה, see under ch. iv. 14; and for the subject, cf. ch. iv. 22 (25), 29 (32).

Vers. 22–24. Daniel now turns to Belshazzar. The words: *forasmuch as thou, i.e.* since thou truly knowest all this, place it beyond a doubt that *Belshazzar* knew these incidents in the life of Nebuchadnezzar, and thus that he was his son, since his grandson (daughter's son) could scarcely at that time have been so old as that the forgetfulness of that divine judgment could have been charged against him as a sin. In the כָּל קֳבֵל דִּי, *just because* thou knowest it, there is implied that, notwithstanding his knowledge of the matter, he did not avoid that which heightened his culpability. In ver. 23 Daniel tells him how he had sinned against the God of heaven, viz. by desecrating (see vers. 2 and 3) the vessels of the temple of the God of Israel. And to show the greatness of this sin, he points to the great contrast that there is between the gods formed of dead material and the living God, on whom depend the life and fortune of men. The former Belshazzar praised, the latter he had *not honoured*—a *Litotes* for *had dishonoured*. The description of the gods is dependent on Deut. iv. 28, cf. with the fuller account Ps. cxv. 5 ff., cxxxv. 15 ff., and reminds us of the description of the government of the true God in Job xii. 10, Num. xvi. 22, and Jer. x. 23. אֹרְחָת, *ways, i.e. the destinies.*—To punish Belshazzar for this wickedness, God had sent the hand which wrote the mysterious words (ver. 24 cf. with ver. 5).

Vers. 25–28. Daniel now read the writing (ver. 25), and gave its interpretation (vers. 26–28). The writing bears the mysterious character of the oracle. מְנֵא, תְּקֵל, פְּרֵס (ver. 28) are partic. Peil, and the forms תְּקֵל and פְּרֵס, instead of תְּקִיל and פְּרִיס, are chosen on account of their symphony with מְנֵא. פַּרְסִין is generally regarded as *partic. plur.*, but that would be פְּרִסִין; it much rather appears to be a noun form, and plur. of פְּרַס = Hebr. פֶּרֶס (cf. פַּרְסֵיהֶן, Zech. xi. 16), in the sense of *broken pieces, fragments*, for פְּרַס signifies *to divide, to break in pieces*, not only in the Hebr. (cf. Lev. xi. 4, Isa. lviii. 7, Ps. lxix. 32), but also in the Chald., 2 Kings iv. 39 (Targ.), although in the Targg. the meaning *to spread out* prevails. In all the three words there lies a double sense, which is brought out in the interpretation. מְנֵא, for the sake of the impression, or perhaps only of the parallelism, is twice given, so as to maintain two members of the verse, each of two words. In the numbering lies the determination and the completion, or the conclusion of a matter, a space of time. Daniel accordingly interprets מְנֵא thus: *God has numbered* (מְנָה for מְנָא, *perf. act.*) *thy kingdom, i.e.* its duration or its days, וְהַשְׁלְמַהּ, *and has finished it, i.e.* its duration is so counted out that it is full, that it now comes to an end. In תְּקֵל there lies the double sense that the word תְּקַל, *to weigh*, accords with the Niphal of קָלַל, *to be light, to be found light* (cf. תֵּקַל, Gen. xvi. 4). The interpretation presents this double meaning: *Thou art weighed in the balances* (תְּקִלְתָּא) *and art found too light* (like the תְּקֵל). חַסִּיר, *wanting in necessary weight, i.e.* deficient in moral worth. תְּקִלְתָּא, a *perf.* formed from the *partic. Peil;* cf. Winer, § 13, 2. As to the figure of the balance, cf. Job xxxi. 6, Ps. lxii. 10 (9).

For פַּרְסִין (ver. 25) Daniel uses in the interpretation the sing. פְּרֵס, which, after the analogy of תְּקֵל, may be regarded as *partic. Peil*, and he interprets it accordingly, so that he brings out, along with the meaning lying in the word, also the allusion to פָּרָס, *Persian: thy kingdom is divided, or broken into pieces, and given to the Medes and Persians.* The meaning is not that the kingdom was to be divided into two equal parts, and the one part given to the Medes and the other to the Persians; but פְּרַס is *to divide into pieces, to destroy, to dissolve* the kingdom. This shall be effected by the Medes and Persians, and was so brought about when the Persian Cyrus with the united power of the Medes and Persians destroyed Babylon, and thus put an end to the Chaldean kingdom, whereby the kingdom was transferred first to the Median Darius (ch. vi. 1 [v. 31]), and after him to the Persian Cyrus. In the naming of the Median before the Persian there lies, as already remarked in the Introduction (see p. 47), a notable proof of the genuineness of this narrative, and with it of the whole book; for the hegemony of the Medes was of a very short duration, and after its overthrow by the Persians the form of expression used is always "*Persians and Medes*," as is found in the book of Esther.

Vers. 29 and 30. *Daniel rewarded, and the beginning of the fulfilment of the writing.*

Belshazzar fulfilled the promise he had made to Daniel by rewarding him for reading and interpreting the writing. וְהַלְבִּשׁוּ is not to be translated: (commanded) *that they should clothe,*—this meaning must be conveyed by the imperfect (cf. ch. ii. 49),—but: *and they clothed him.* The command was then carried out: Daniel was not only adorned with purple and with a golden chain, but was also proclaimed as the third ruler of the kingdom. The objection that this last-mentioned dignity was not possible, since, according to ver. 30, Belshazzar was slain that very night, is based on the supposition that the proclamation was publicly made in the streets of the city. But the words do not necessitate such a supposition. The proclamation might be made only before the assembled magnates of the kingdom in the palace, and then Belshazzar may have been slain on that very night. Perhaps, as Kliefoth thinks, the conspirators against Belshazzar availed themselves of the confusion connected with this proclamation, and all that accompanied it, for the execution of their purpose. We may not, however, add that therewith the dignity to which Daniel was advanced was again lost by him. It depended much rather on this: whether Belshazzar's successor recognised the promotion granted to Daniel in the last hours of his reign. But the successor would be inclined toward its recognition by the reflection, that by Daniel's interpretation of the mysterious writing from God the putting of Belshazzar to death appeared to have a higher sanction, presenting itself as if it were something determined in the councils of the gods, whereby the successor might claim before the people that his usurpation of the throne was rendered legitimate. Such a reflection might move him to confirm Daniel's elevation to the office to which Belshazzar had raised him. This supposition appears to be supported by ch. vi. 2 (1).

Bleek and other critics have based another objection against the historical veracity of this narrative on the improbability that Belshazzar, although the interpretation predicted evil against him, and he could not at all know whether it was a correct interpretation, should have rewarded Daniel instead of putting him to death (Hitzig). But the force of this objection lies in the supposition that Belshazzar was as unbelieving with regard to a revelation from God, and with regard to the providence of the living God among the affairs of men, as are the critics of our day; the objection is altogether feeble when one appreciates the force of the belief, even among the heathen, in the gods and in revelations from God, and takes into consideration that Belshazzar perhaps scarcely believed the threatened judgment from God to be so near as it actually was, since the interpretation by Daniel decided nothing as regards the time, and perhaps also that he hoped to be able, by conferring honour upon Daniel, to appease the wrath of God.[1] The circumstance, also, that Daniel received the honour promised to him notwithstanding his declining it (ver. 17), can afford no ground of objection against the truth of the narrative, since that refusal was only an expression of the entire absence of all self-interest, which was now so fully established by the matter of the interpretation that there was no longer any ground for his declining the honours which were conferred upon him unsought, while they comprehended in themselves in reality a recognition of the God whom he served.

Ver. 30. With the death of Belshazzar that very night the interpretation given by Daniel began to be fulfilled, and this fulfilment afforded a certainty that the remaining parts of it would also sooner or later be accomplished. That this did not take place

[1] "*Non mirum, si Baltasar audiens tristia, solverit præmium quod pollicitus est. Aut enim longo post tempore credidit ventura quæ dixerat, aut dum Dei prophetam honorat, sperat se veniam consecuturum.*"—JEROME.

immediately, we have already shown in our preliminary remarks to this chapter.

CHAP. VI. DANIEL IN THE DEN OF LIONS.

Darius, the king of the Medes, had it in view to place Daniel as chief officer over the whole of his realm, and thereby he awakened against Daniel (vers. 1–6 [ch. v. 31–vi. 5]) the envy of the high officers of state. In order to frustrate the king's intention and to set Daniel aside, they procured an edict from Darius, which forbade for the space of thirty days, on the pain of death, prayer to be offered to any god or man, except to the king (vers. 7 [6]–10 [9]). Daniel, however, notwithstanding this, continued, according to his usual custom, to open the windows of his upper room, and there to pray to God three times a day. His conduct was watched, and he was accused of violating the king's edict, and thus he brought upon himself the threatened punishment of being thrown into the den of lions (vers. 11 [10]–18 [17]). But he remained uninjured among the lions; whereupon the king on the following morning caused him to be brought out of the den, and his malicious accusers to be thrown into it (vers. 19 [18]–25 [24]), and then by an edict he commanded his subjects to reverence the God of Daniel, who did wonders (vers. 26 [25]–28 [27]). As a consequence of this, Daniel prospered during the reign of Darius and of Cyrus the Persian (ver. 29 [28]).

From the historic statement of this chapter, that Darius the Mede took the Chaldean kingdom when he was about sixty-two years old (ver. 1 [ch. v. 31]), taken in connection with the closing remark (ver. 29 [28]) that it went well with Daniel during the reign of Darius and of Cyrus the Persian, it appears that the Chaldean kingdom, after its overthrow by the Medes and Persians, did not immediately pass into the hands of Cyrus, but that between the last of the Chaldean kings who lost the kingdom and the reign of Cyrus the Persian, Darius, descended from a Median family, held the reins of government, and that not till after him did Cyrus mount the throne of the Chaldean kingdom, which had been subdued by the Medes and Persians. This Median Darius was a son of Ahasuerus (ch. ix. 1), of the seed of the Medes; and according to ch. xi. 1, the angel Gabriel stood by him in his first year, which can mean no more than that the Babylonian kingdom was not taken without divine assistance.

This Darius the Mede and his reign are not distinctly noticed by profane historians. Hence the modern critics have altogether denied his existence, or at least have called it in question, and have thence derived an argument against the historical veracity of the whole narrative.

According to Berosus and Abydenus (*Fragmenta*, see p. 163), Nabonnedus, the last Babylonian king, was, after the taking of Babylon, besieged by Cyrus in Borsippa, where he was taken prisoner, and then banished to Carmania. After this Cyrus reigned, as Alex. Polyhistor says, nine years over Babylon; while in the Fragments preserved by Eusebius in his *Chron. Armen.*, to the statement that Cyrus conferred on him (*i.e.* Nabonet), when he had obtained possession of Babylon, the margraviate of the province of Carmania, it is added, "Darius the king removed (him) a little out of the country." Also in the astronomical Canon of Ptolemy, Nabonadius the Babylonian is at once followed by the list of Persian kings, beginning with *Κῦρος*, who reigned nine years.

When we compare with this the accounts given by the Greek historians, we find that Herodotus (i. 96–103, 106 ff.) makes mention of a succession of Median kings: Dejoces, Phraortes, Cyaxares, and Astyages. The last named, who had no male descendants, had a daughter, Mandane, married to a Persian Cambyses. Cyrus sprung from this marriage. Astyages, moved with fear lest this son of his daughter should rob him of his throne, sought to put him to death, but his design was frustrated. When Cyrus had reached manhood, Harpagus, an officer of the court of Astyages, who out of revenge had formed a conspiracy against him, called upon him at the head of the Persians to take the kingdom from his grandfather Astyages. Cyrus obeyed, moved the Persians to revolt from the Medes, attacked Astyages at Pasargada, and took him prisoner, but acted kindly toward him till his death; after which he became king over the realm of the Medes and Persians, and as such destroyed first the Lydian, and then the Babylonian kingdom. He conquered the Babylonian king, Labynetus the younger, in battle, and then besieged Babylon; and during a nocturnal festival of the Babylonians he penetrated the city by damming off the water of the Euphrates, and took it. Polyænus, Justin, and others follow in its details this very fabulous narrative, which is adorned with dreams and fictitious incidents. Ctesias also, who records traditions of the early history of Media altogether departing from Herodotus, and who names nine kings, yet agrees with Herodotus in this, that Cyrus overcame Astyages and dethroned him. Cf. the different accounts given by Greek writers regarding the overthrow of the Median dominion by the Persians in M. Duncker's *Ges. d. Alterth.* ii. p. 634 ff., 3d ed.

Xenophon in the *Cyropædia* reports somewhat otherwise regarding Cyrus. According to him, the Median king Astyages, son of Cyaxares I., gave his daughter Mandane in marriage to Cambyses, the Persian king, who was under the Median supremacy, and that Cyrus was born of this marriage (i. 2. 1). When Cyrus arrived at man's estate Astyages died, and was succeeded on the Median throne by his son Cyaxares II., the brother of Mandane (i. 5. 2). When, after this, the Lydian king Crœsus concluded a covenant with the king of the Assyrians (Babylonians) having in view the overthrow of the Medes and Persians, Cyrus received the command of the united army of the Medes and Persians (iii. 3. 20 ff.); and when, after a victorious battle, Cyaxares was unwilling to proceed further, Cyrus carried forward the war by his permission, and destroyed the host of Crœsus and the Assyrians, on hearing of which, Cyaxares, who had spent the night at a riotous banquet, fell into a passion, wrote a threatening letter to Cyrus, and ordered the Medes to be recalled (iv. 5. 18). But when they declared, on the statement given by Cyrus, their desire to remain with him (iv. 5. 18), Cyrus entered on the war against Babylon independently of Cyaxares (v. 3. 1). Having driven the Babylonian king back upon his capital, he sent a message to Cyaxares, desiring him to come that he might decide regarding the vanquished and regarding the continuance of the war (v. 5. 1). Inasmuch as all the Medes and the confederated nations adhered to Cyrus, Cyaxares was under the necessity of taking this step. He came to the camp of Cyrus, who exhibited to him his power by reviewing before him his whole host; he then treated him kindly, and supplied him richly from the stores of the plunder he had taken (v. 5. 1 ff.). After this the war against Babylonia was carried on in such a way, that Cyaxares, sitting on the Median throne, presided over the councils of war, but Cyrus, as general, had the conduct of it (vi. 1. 6); and after he had conquered Sardes, taken Crœsus the king prisoner (vii. 2. 1), and then vanquished Hither Asia, he returned to Babylon (vii. 4. 17), and during a nocturnal festival of the Babylonians took the city, whereupon the king of Babylon was slain (vii. 5. 15–33). After the conquest of Babylon the army regarded Cyrus as king, and he began to conduct his affairs as if he were king (vii. 5. 37); but he went however to Media, to present himself before Cyaxares. He brought presents to him, and showed him that there was a house and palace ready for him in Babylon, where he might reside when he went thither[1] (viii. 5. 17 f.). Cyaxares gave him his daughter to wife, and along with her, as her dowry, the whole of Media, for he had no son (viii. 5. 19). Cyrus now went first to Persia, and arranged that his father Cambyses should retain the sovereignty of it so long as he lived, and that then it should fall to him. He then returned to Media, and married the daughter of Cyaxares (viii. 5. 28). He next went to Babylon, and placed satraps over the subjugated peoples, etc. (viii. 6. 1), and so arranged that he spent the winter in Babylon, the spring in Susa, and the summer in Ecbatana (viii. 6. 22). Having reached an advanced old age, he came for the seventh time during his reign to Persia, and died there, after he had appointed his son Cambyses as his successor (viii. 7. 1 ff.).

This narrative by Xenophon varies from that of Herodotus in the following principal points:—(1) According to Herodotus, the line of Median kings closes with Astyages, who had no son; Xenophon, on the contrary, speaks of Astyages as having been succeeded by his son Cyaxares on the throne. (2) According to Herodotus, Cyrus was related to the Median royal house only as being the son of the daughter of Astyages, and had a claim to the Median throne only as being the grandson of Astyages; Xenophon, on the other hand, says that he was related to the royal house of Media, not only as being the grandson of Astyages and nephew of Cyaxares II., but also as having received in marriage the daughter of his uncle Cyaxares, and along with her the dowry of the Median throne. (3) According to Herodotus, Cyrus took part in the conspiracy formed by Harpagus against Astyages, slew his grandfather in battle, and took forcible possession of the dominion over the Medes; on the contrary, Xenophon relates that, though he was at variance with Cyaxares, he became again reconciled to him, and not only did not dethrone him, but permitted him to retain royal dignity even after the overthrow of Babylon, which was not brought about without his co-operation.

Of these discrepancies the first two form no special contradic-

[1] The words are: *ὅτι οἶκος αὐτῷ ἐξῃρημένος εἴη ἐν Βαβυλῶνι καὶ ἀρχεῖα, ὅπως ἔχῃ καὶ ὅταν ἐκεῖσε ἔλθῃ εἰς οἰκεῖα κατάγεσθαι*, on which L. Dindorf remarks, "*οἶκος videtur esse domus regia, ἀρχεῖα officia palatina.*"

tion. Xenophon only communicates more of the tradition than Herodotus, who, according to his custom, makes mention only of the more celebrated of the rulers, passing by those that are less so,[1] and closes the list of Median kings with Astyages. Accordingly, in not mentioning Cyaxares II., he not only overlooks the second relationship Cyrus sustained to the Median royal house, but also is led to refer the tradition that the last of the Median kings had no male descendant to Astyages. The third point only presents an actual contradiction between the statements of Herodotus and those of Xenophon, viz. that according to Herodotus, Cyrus by force of arms took the kingdom from his grandfather, overcame Astyages in a battle at Pasargada, and dethroned him; while according to Xenophon, the Median kingdom first fell to Cyrus by his command of the army, and then as the dowry of his wife. Shall we now on this point decide, with v. Leng., Hitzig, and others, in favour of Herodotus and against Xenophon, and erase Cyaxares II. from the list not only of the Median kings, but wholly from the page of history, because Herodotus and Ctesias have not made mention of him? Has then Herodotus or Ctesias alone recorded historical facts, and that fully, and Xenophon in the *Cyropædia* fabricated only a pædagogic romance destitute of historical veracity? All thorough investigators have testified to the very contrary, and Herodotus himself openly confesses (i. 95) that he gives only the sayings regarding Cyrus which appeared to him to be credible; and yet the narrative, as given by him, consists only of a series of popular traditions which in his time were in circulation among the Medes, between two and three hundred years after the events. Xenophon also has gathered the historic material for his *Cyropædia* only from tradition, but from Persian tradition, in which, favoured by the reigning dynasty, the Cyrus-legend, interwoven with the end of the Median independence and the founding of the Persian sovereignty, is more fully transmitted than among the Medes, whose national recollections, after the extinction of their dynasty, were not fostered. If we may therefore expect more exact information in Xenophon than in Herodotus, yet it is imaginable that Xenophon transformed the narrative of

[1] *Solere Herodotum prætermissis mediocribus hominibus ex longa regum serie nonnisi unum alterumve memorare reliquis eminentiorem, et aliunde constat et ipsa Babyloniæ historia docet, et qua unius Nitocris reginæ mentionem injicit, reliquos reges omnes usque ad Labynetum, ne Nebucadnezare quidem excepto, silentio transit* (i. 185–187).—GES. *Thes.* p. 350.

the rebellion by Cyrus and his war against Cyaxares into that which he has recorded as to the relation he sustained towards Cyaxares, in order that he might wipe out this moral stain from the character of his hero. But this supposition would only gain probability under the presumption of what Hitzig maintains, if it were established: "If, in *Cyrop.* viii. 5. 19, the Median of his own free will gave up his country to Cyrus, Xenophon's historical book shows, on the contrary, that the Persians snatched by violence the sovereignty from the Medes (*Anab.* iii. 4. 7, 11, 12);" but in the *Anab. l.c.* Xenophon does not say this, but (§ 8) only, ὅτε παρὰ Μήδων τὴν ἀρχὴν ἐλάμβανον Πέρσαι.[1] Thus, supposing the statement that the cities of Larissa and Mespila were besieged by the Persian king at the time when the Persians gained the supremacy over the Medes were historically true, and Xenophon communicated here not a mere *fabulam ab incolis narratam,* yet Xenophon would not be found contradicting his *Cyropædia,* since, as Kran. has well observed, "it can be nothing surprising that among a people accustomed to a native royal dynasty, however well founded Cyrus' claim in other respects might be, manifold commotions and insurrections should arise, which needed to be forcibly suppressed, so that thus the kingdom could be at the same time spoken of as conquered."

Add to this the decisive fact, that the account given by Herod. of Cyrus and the overthrow of Astyages, of which even Duncker, p. 649, remarks, that in its prompting motive "it awakens great doubts," is in open contradiction with all the well-established facts of Medo-Persian history. "All authentic reports testify that in the formation of Medo-Persia the Medes and the Persians are separated in a peculiar way, and yet bound to each other as kindred races. If Herod. is right, if Astyages was always attempting to take Cyrus' life, if Cyrus took the kingdom from Astyages by force, then such a relation between the 'Medes and Persians' (as it always occurs in the O. T.) would have been inconceivable; the Medes would not have stood to the Persians in any other relation

[1] Concerning the expression ἐλάμβανον τὴν ἀρχὴν, Dindorf remarks: "*Verbum hoc Medos sponte Persarum imperio subjectos significat, quanquam reliqua narratio seditionem aliquam Larissensium arguere videatur. Igitur hic nihil est dissensionis inter Cyropædiam et Anabasin. . . . Gravius est quod Xenophon statim in simili narratione posuit,* ὅτε ἀπώλεσαν τὴν ἀρχὴν ὑπὸ Περσῶν Μῆδοι. *Sed ibidem scriptor incolarum fidem antestatur.*" Thus the philologists are in their judgment of the matter opposed to the modern critics.

than did the other subjugated peoples, *e.g.* the Babylonians" (Klief.). On the other hand, the account given by Xenophon regarding Cyaxares so fully agrees with the narrative of Daniel regarding Darius the Mede, that, as Hitzig confesses, "the identity of the two is beyond a doubt." If, according to Xen., Cyrus conquered Babylon by the permission of Cyaxares, and after its overthrow not only offered him a "residence" there (Hitzig), but went to Media, presented himself before Cyaxares, and showed him that he had appointed for him in Babylon *οἶκος καὶ ἀρχεῖα*, in order that when he went thither *εἰς οἰκεῖα κατάγεσθαι*, *i.e.* in order that when, according to Eastern custom, he changed his residence he might have a royal palace there, so, according to Daniel, Darius did not overthrow the Chaldean kingdom, but received it (ch. vi. 1), and was made king (הָמְלַךְ, ch. ix. 1), namely, by Cyrus, who, according to the prophecies of Isaiah, was to overthrow Babylon, and, according to Dan. vi. 29, succeeded Darius on the throne. The statement, also, that Darius was about sixty-two years old when he ascended the throne of the Chaldean kingdom, harmonizes with the report given by Xenophon, that when Cyaxares gave his daughter to Cyrus, he gave him along with her the kingdom of Media, because he had no male heir, and was so far advanced in years that he could not hope to have now any son. Finally, even in respect of character the Cyaxares of Xen. resembles the Darius of Daniel. As the former describes the conduct of Cyrus while he revelled in sensual pleasures, so Darius is induced by his nobles to issue an edict without obtaining any clear knowledge as to its motive, and allows himself to be forced to put it into execution, however sorrowful he might be on account of its relation to Daniel.

After all this, there can be no reason to doubt the reign of Darius the Mede. But how long it lasted cannot be determined either from the book of Daniel, in which (ch. ix. 1) only the first year of his reign is named, or from any other direct sources. Ptolemy, in his Canon, places after Nabonadius the reign of Cyrus the Persian for nine years. With this, the words of Xenophon, *τὸ ἕβδομον ἐπὶ τῆς αὐτοῦ ἀρχῆς*, which by supplying *ἔτος* after *ἕβδομον* are understood of seven years' reign, are combined, and thence it is concluded that Cyaxares reigned two years. But the supplement of *ἔτος* is not warranted by the context. The supposition, however, that Darius reigned for two years over Babylon is correct. For the Babylonian kingdom was destroyed sixty-eight years after the commencement of the Exile. Since, then, the seventy years of the Exile were completed in the first year of the reign of Cyrus (2 Chron. xxxvi. 22 f.; Ezra i. 1), it follows that Cyrus became king two years after the overthrow of Babylon, and thus after Darius had reigned two years. See at ch. ix. 1, 2.

From the shortness of the reign of Darius, united with the circumstance that Cyrus destroyed Babylon and put an end to the Chaldean kingdom, it is easy to explain how the brief and not very independent reign of Darius might be quite passed by, not only by Herodotus and Ctesias, and all later Greek historians, but also by Berosus. Although Cyrus only as commander-in-chief of the army of Cyaxares had with a Medo-Persian host taken Babylon, yet the tradition might speak of the conquering Persian as the lord of the Chaldean kingdom, without taking at all into account the Median chief king, whom in a brief time Cyrus the conqueror succeeded on the throne. In the later tradition of the Persians,[1] from which all the historians known to us, with the exception of Berosus, have constructed their narrative, the Median rule over the Chaldean kingdom naturally sinks down into an insignificant place in relation to the independent government of the conqueror Cyrus and his people which was so soon to follow. The absence of all notice by Berosus, Herod., and Ctesias of the short Median reign can furnish no substantial ground for calling in question the statements of Xen. regarding Cyaxares, and of Daniel regarding the Median Darius, although all other witnesses for this were altogether of no force, which is indeed asserted, but has been proved by no one.[2]

[1] "In the Babylonian tradition," Kranichfeld well remarks, "the memorable catastrophe of the overthrow of Babylon would, at all events, be joined to the warlike operations of Cyrus the conquering Persian, who, according to Xenoph., conducted himself in Babylon as a king (cf. *Cyrop.* vii. 5. 37), and it might be very indifferent to the question for whom he specially undertook the siege. The Persian tradition had in the national interest a reason for ignoring altogether the brief Median feudal sovereignty over Babylon, which, besides, was only brought about by the successful war of a Persian prince."

[2] Of these witnesses the notice by Abydenus (*Chron. Armen.*, Euseb.) already mentioned, p. 164, bears in its aphoristic brevity, "Darius the king removed him out of the land," altogether the stamp of an historical tradition, and can be understood only of Darius the Mede, since Eusebius has joined it to the report regarding the dethroning of the last Babylonian king by Cyrus. Also, the often-quoted lines of Æschylus, *Pers.* 762–765,

Μῆδος γὰρ ἦν ὁ πρῶτος ἡγεμὼν στρατοῦ,
Ἄλλος δ' ἐκείνου παῖς τόδ' ἔργον ἤνυσε . . . .
Τρίτος δ' ἀπ' αὐτοῦ Κῦρος εὐδαίμων ἀνήρ, κ.τ.λ.,—

This result is not rendered doubtful by the fact that Xenophon calls this Median king *Κυαξάρης* and describes him as the son of Astyages, while, on the contrary, Daniel calls him Darjawesch (Darius) the son of Ahasuerus (ch. ix. 1). The name *Κυαξάρης* is the Median *Uwakshatra*, and means *autocrat; 'Αστυάγης* corresponds to the Median *Ajisdahâka*, the name of the Median dynasty, meaning the *biting serpent* (cf. Nieb. *Gesch. Assurs*, p. 175 f.). דָּרְיָוֶשׁ, *Δαρεῖος*, the Persian *Dârjawusch*, rightly explained by Herod. vi. 98 by the word *ἑρξείης*, means the *keeper*, *ruler;* and אֲחַשְׁוֵרוֹשׁ, *Ahasverus*, as the name of Xerxes, in the Persian cuneiform inscriptions *Kschajârschâ*, is certainly formed, however one may interpret the name, from *Kschaja*, *kingdom*, the title of the Persian rulers, like the Median "Astyages." The names *Cyaxares* and *Darjawesch* are thus related to each other, and are the paternal names of both dynasties, or the titles of the rulers. Xenophon has communicated to us the Median name and title of the last king; Daniel gives, as it appears, the Persian name and title which Cyaxares, as king of the united Chaldean and Medo-Persian kingdom, received and bore.

The circumstances reported in this chapter occurred, according to the statement in ver. 29*a*, in the first of the two years' reign of Darius over Babylon. The matter and object of this report are related to the events recorded in ch. iii. As in that chapter Daniel's companions are condemned to be cast into the fiery furnace on account of their transgression of the royal commandment enjoining them to fall down before the golden image that had been set up by Nebuchadnezzar, so here in this chapter Daniel himself is cast into the den of lions because of his transgression of the command enjoining that prayer was to be offered

are in the simplest manner explained historically if by the work which the first Mede began and the second completed, and which yet brought all the glory to the third, viz. Cyrus, is understood the taking of Babylon; according to which Astyages is the first, Cyaxares II. the second, and Cyrus the third, and Æschylus agrees with Xenophon. Other interpretations, *e.g.* of Phraortes and Cyaxares I., agree with no single report. Finally, the Darics also give evidence for Darius the Mede, since of all explanations of the name of this gold coin (the Daric) its derivation from a king Darius is the most probable; and so also do the statements of the rhetorician Harpocration, the scholiast to Aristophanis *Ecclesiaz.* 589, and of Suidas, that the Δαρεικοί did not derive their name, as most suppose, from Darius the father of Xerxes, but from another and an older king (Darius), according to the declaration of Herodot. iv. 166, that Darius first struck this coin, which is not outweighed by his scanty knowledge of the more ancient history of the Medes and Persians.

to no other god, but to the king only. The motive of the accusation is, in the one case as in the other, envy on account of the high position which the Jews had reached in the kingdom, and the object of it was the driving of the foreigners from their influential offices. The wonderful deliverance also of the faithful worshippers of God from the death which threatened them, with the consequences of that deliverance, are alike in both cases. But along with these similarities there appear also differences altogether corresponding to the circumstances, which show that historical facts are here related to us, and not the products of a fiction formed for a purpose. In ch. iii. Nebuchadnezzar requires all the subjects of his kingdom to do homage to the image he had set up, and to worship the gods of his kingdom, and his command affords to the enemies of the Jews the wished-for opportunity of accusing the friends of Daniel of disobedience to the royal will. In ch. vi., on the other hand, Darius is moved and induced by his great officers of state, whose design was to set Daniel aside, to issue the edict there mentioned, and he is greatly troubled when he sees the application of the edict to the case of Daniel. The character of Darius is fundamentally different from that of Nebuchadnezzar. The latter was a king distinguished by energy and activity, a perfect autocrat; the former, a weak prince and wanting in energy, who allowed himself to be guided and governed by his state officers. The command of Nebuchadnezzar to do homage to his gods is the simple consequence of the supremacy of the ungodly world-power; the edict extorted from Darius, on the contrary, is a deification of the world-power for the purpose of oppressing the true servants of God. The former command only places the gods of the world-power above the living God of heaven and earth; the latter edict seeks wholly to set aside the recognition of this God, if only for a time, by forbidding prayer to be offered to Him. This tyranny of the servants of the world-power is more intolerable than the tyranny of the world-ruler.

Thus the history recorded in this chapter shows, on the one side, how the ungodly world-power in its progressive development assumes an aspect continually more hostile toward the kingdom of God, and how with the decrease of its power of action its hatred against the true servants of God increases; and it shows, on the other side, how the Almighty God not only protects His worshippers against all the intrigues and machinations of the enemy, but also requites the adversaries according to their deeds. Daniel was protected against the rage of the lions, while his enemies were torn by them to pieces as soon as they were cast into the den.

This miracle of divine power is so vexatious to the modern critics, that Bleek, v. Leng., Hitzig, and others have spared no pains to overthrow the historical trustworthiness of the narrative, and represent it as a fiction written with a design. Not only does the prohibition to offer any petition to any god or man except to the king for a month "not find its equal in absurdity," but the typology (Daniel an antitype of Joseph!) as well as the relation to ch. iii. betray the fiction. Darius, it is true, does not show himself to be the type of Antiochus Epiphanes, also the command, vers. 27 and 28, puts no restraint in reality on those concerned; but by the prohibition, ver. 8, the free exercise of their religion is undoubtedly attacked, and such hostility against the faith found its realization for the first time only and everywhere in the epoch of Antiochus Epiphanes. Consequently, according to Hitzig, "the prohibition here is reflected from that of Antiochus Epiphanes (1 Macc. i. 41–50), and exaggerates it even to a caricature of it, for the purpose of placing clearly in the light the hatefulness of such tyranny."

On the contrary, the advocates of the genuineness of Daniel have conclusively shown that the prohibition referred to, ver. 8, corresponds altogether to the religious views of the Medo-Persians, while on the other hand it is out and out in contradiction to the circumstances of the times of the Maccabees. Thus, that the edict did not contemplate the removal or the uprooting of all religious worship except praying to the king, is clearly manifest not only in this, that the prohibition was to be enforced for one month only, but also in the intention which the magnates had in their eye, of thereby effecting certainly the overthrow of Daniel. The religious restraint which was thus laid upon the Jews for a month is very different from the continual rage of Antiochus Epiphanes against the Jewish worship of God. Again, not only is the character of Darius and his relation to Daniel, as the opponents themselves must confess, such as not to furnish a type in which Antiochus Epiphanes may be recognised, but the enemies of Daniel do not really become types of this tyrant; for they seek his overthrow not from religious antipathy, but, moved only by vulgar envy, they seek to cast him down from his lofty position in the state. Thus also in this respect the historical point of view of the hostility to Daniel as representing Judaism, is fundamentally different from that of the war waged by Antiochus against Judaism, so that this narrative is destitute of every characteristic mark of the Seleucidan-Maccabee æra. Cf. the further representation of this difference by Kranichfeld, p. 229 ff.—The views of Hitzig will be met in our exposition.

Vers. 1–10 (ch. v. 31–vi. 9). *Transference of the kingdom to Darius the Mede; appointment of the regency; envy of the satraps against Daniel, and their attempt to destroy him.*

The narrative of this chapter is connected by the copula ו with the occurrence recorded in the preceding; yet ver. 1 does not, as in the old versions and with many interpreters, belong to the fifth chapter, but to the sixth, and forms not merely the bond of connection between the events narrated in the fifth and sixth chapters, but furnishes at the same time the historical basis for the following narrative, vers. 2 (1)–29 (28). The statement of the verse, that Darius the Mede received the kingdom when he was about sixty-two years old, connects itself essentially with ch. v. 30, so far as it joins to the fulfilment, there reported, of the first part of the sacred writing interpreted by Daniel to Belshazzar, the fulfilment also of the second part of that writing, but not so closely that the designation of time, *in that same night* (ch. v. 30), is applicable also to the fact mentioned in ch. vi. 1 (v. 31), and as warranting the supposition that the transference of the kingdom to Darius the Mede took place on the night in which Belshazzar was slain. Against such a chronological connection of these two verses, ch. v. 30 and vi. 1 (v. 31), we adduce in the second half of ver. 1 (ch. v. 31) the statement of the age of Darius, in addition to the reasons already adduced in p. 163. This is not to make it remarkable that, instead of the young mad debauchee (Belshazzar), with whom, according to prophecy, the Chaldean bondage of Israel was brought to an end, a man of mature judgment seized the reigns of government (Delitzsch); for this supposition fails not only with the hypothesis, already confuted, on which it rests, but is quite foreign to the text, for Darius in what follows does not show himself to be a ruler of matured experience. The remark of Kliefoth has much more in its favour, that by the statement of the age it is designed to be made prominent that the government of Darius the Mede did not last long, soon giving place to that of Cyrus the Persian, ver. 29 (28), whereby the divine writing, that the Chaldean kingdom would be given to the Medes and Persians, was fully accomplished. Regarding *Darjawesch*, Darius, see the preliminary remarks. The addition of מָדָיָא (*Kethiv*) forms on the one hand a contrast to the expression "the king of the Chaldeans" (ch. v. 30), and on the other it points forward to פָּרְסָיָא, ver. 29 (28); it, however, furnishes no proof that Daniel distinguished the Median kingdom from the Persian; for the kingdom is not called a Median kingdom, but it is only said of Darius that he was of Median descent, and, ver. 29 (28), that Cyrus the Persian succeeded him in the kingdom. In קַבֵּל, *he received* the kingdom, it is indicated that Darius did not conquer it, but received it from the conqueror; see p. 198. The כְּ in כְּבַר intimates that the statement of the age rests only on a probable estimate.

Ver. 2 (1). For the government of the affairs of the kingdom he had received, and especially for regulating the gathering in of the tribute of the different provinces, Darius placed 120 satraps over the whole kingdom, and over these satraps three chiefs, to whom the satraps should give an account. Regarding אֲחַשְׁדַּרְפְּנַיָּא (*satraps*), see at ch. iii. 2. סָרְכִין, plur. of סָרַךְ; סָרְכָא has in the Semitic no right etymology, and is derived from the Aryan, from the Zend. *sara*, *çara*, *head*, with the syllable *ach*. In the Targg., in use for the Hebr. שֹׁטֵר, it denotes a *president*, of whom the three named in ver. 2 (1), by their position over the satraps, held the rank of chief governors or ministers, for which the Targg. use סָרְכָן, while סָרְכִין in ver. 8 denotes *all the military and civil prefects of the kingdom*.

The modern critics have derived from this arrangement for the government of the kingdom made by Darius an argument against the credibility of the narrative, which Hitzig has thus formulated:—According to Xenophon, Cyrus first appointed satraps over the conquered regions, and in all to the number of six (*Cyrop.* viii. 6, § 1, 7); according to the historian Herodotus, on the contrary (iii. 89 ff.), Darius Hystaspes first divided the kingdom into twenty satrapies for the sake of the administration of the taxes. With this statement agrees the number of the peoples mentioned on the Inscription at Bisutun; and if elsewhere (Insc. J. and Nakschi Rustam) at least twenty-four and also twenty-nine are mentioned, we know that several regions or nations might be placed under one satrap (Herod. *l.c.*). The kingdom was too small for 120 satraps in the Persian sense. On the other hand, one may not appeal to the 127 provinces (מְדִינוֹת) of king Ahasuerus = Xerxes (Esth. i. 1, ix. 30); for the ruler of the מְדִינָה is not the same as (Esth. viii. 9) the satrap. In Esth. iii. 12 it is the פֶּחָה, as *e.g.* of the province of Judah (Hag. i. 1; Mal. i. 8; Neh. v. 14). It is true there were also greater provinces, such *e.g.* as of Media and Babylonia (Ezra vi. 2; Dan. ii. 49), and perhaps also *pecha* (פֶּחָה) might be loosely used to designate a satrap (Ezra v. 3, vi. 6); yet the 127 provinces were not such, nor is a satrap interchangeably called a *pecha*. When Daniel thus mentions so large a number of satraps, it is the Grecian satrapy that is apparently before his mind. Under Seleucus Nicator there were seventy-two of these.

The foundation of this argument, viz. that Darius Hystaspes, "according to the historian Herodotus," first divided the kingdom into satrapies, and, of course, also that the statement by Xenophon of the sending of six satraps into the countries subdued by Cyrus is worthy of no credit, is altogether unhistorical, resting only on the misinterpretation and distortion of the testimonies adduced. Neither Herodotus nor Xenophon represents the appointment of satraps by Cyrus and Darius as an entirely new and hitherto untried method of governing the kingdom; still less does Xenophon say that Cyrus sent in all only six satraps into the subjugated countries. It is true he mentions by name (viii. 6, 7) only six satraps, but he mentions also the provinces into which they were sent, viz. one to Arabia, and the other five to Asia Minor, with the exception, however, of Cilicia, Cyprus, and Paphlagonia, to which he did not send any *Πέρσας σατράπας*, because they had voluntarily joined him in fighting against Babylon. Hence it is clear as noonday that Xenophon speaks only of those satraps whom Cyrus sent to Asia Minor and to Arabia, and says nothing of the satrapies of the other parts of the kingdom, such as Judea, Syria, Babylonia, Assyria, Media, etc., so that no one can affirm that Cyrus sent in all only six satraps into the conquered countries. As little does Herodotus, *l.c.*, say that Darius Hystaspes was the *first* to introduce the government of the kingdom by satraps: he only says that Darius Hystaspes divided the whole kingdom into twenty *ἀρχαί* which were called *σατραπηΐαι*, appointed *ἄρχοντες*, and regulated the tribute; for he numbers these satrapies simply with regard to the tribute with which each was chargeable, while under Cyrus and Cambyses no tribute was imposed, but presents only were contributed. Consequently, Herod. speaks only of a regulation for the administration of the different provinces of the kingdom for the special purpose of the certain payment of the tribute which Darius Hystaspes had appointed. Thus the historian M. Duncker also understands this statement; for he says (*Gesch. des Alterth.* ii. p. 891) regarding it:—"About the year 515 Darius established fixed government-districts in place of the vice-regencies which Cyrus and Cambyses had appointed and changed according to existing exigencies. He divided the kingdom into twenty satrapies." Then at p. 893 he further shows how this division also of the kingdom by Darius was not fixed unchangeably, but was altered according to circumstances. Hitzig's assertion, that the kingdom was too small for 120 satrapies in the Persian sense, is altogether groundless. From Esth. viii. 9 and iii. 19 it follows not remotely, that not satraps but the פַּחוֹת represent the מְדִינוֹת. In ch. viii. 9 satraps, פַּחוֹת, and שָׂרֵי הַמְּדִינוֹת are named, and in ch. iii. 12 they are called the king's satraps and פַּחוֹת אֲשֶׁר עַל מְדִינָה. On Esth. iii. 12 Bertheau remarks: "The *pechas*, who are named along with the satraps, are probably the officers of the circles within the separate satrapies;" and in ch. viii. 9 satraps and *pechas* are named as שָׂרֵי הַמְּדִינוֹת, *i.e.* presidents, superintendents of the 127 provinces of the kingdom from India to Ethiopia, from which nothing can be concluded regarding the relation of the satraps to the *pechas*. Berth. makes the same remark on Ezra viii. 36:—"The relation of the king's satraps to the *pachavoth abar nahara* (governors on this side the river) we cannot certainly determine; the former were probably chiefly military rulers, and the latter government officials." For the assertion that *pecha* is perhaps loosely used for satrap, but that interchangeably a satrap cannot be called a *pecha*, rests, unproved, on the authority of Hitzig.

From the book of Esther it cannot certainly be proved that so many satraps were placed over the 127 provinces into which Xerxes divided the kingdom, but only that these provinces were ruled by satraps and *pechas*. But the division of the whole kingdom into 127 provinces nevertheless shows that the kingdom might have been previously divided under Darius the Mede into 120 provinces, whose prefects might be called in this verse אֲחַשְׁדַּרְפְּנִין, *i.e. kschatrapavan*, *protectors of the kingdom* or *of the provinces*, since this title is derived from the Sanscrit and Old Persian, and is not for the first time used under Darius Hystaspes or Cyrus. The Median Darius might be led to appoint one satrap, *i.e.* a prefect clothed with military power, over each district of his kingdom, since the kingdom was but newly conquered, that he might be able at once to suppress every attempt at insurrection among the nations coming under his dominion. The separation of the civil government, particularly in the matter of the raising of tribute, from the military government, or the appointment of satraps *οἱ τὸν δασμὸν λαμβάνοντες, κ.τ.λ.*, along with the *φρούραρχοι* and the *χιλίαρχοι*, for the protection of the boundaries of the kingdom, was first adopted, according to Xenophon *l.c.*, by Cyrus, who next appointed satraps for the provinces of Asia Minor and of Arabia, which were newly brought under his sceptre; while in the older provinces which had formed the Babylonian kingdom, satrapies which were under civil and military rulers already existed from the time of Nebuchadnezzar; cf. Dan. ii. 3 ff. This arrangement, then, did not originate with Darius Hystaspes in the dividing of the whole kingdom into twenty satrapies mentioned by Herodotus. Thus the statements of Herodotus and Xenophon harmonize perfectly with those of the Scriptures, and every reason for regarding with suspicion the testimony of Daniel wholly fails.

Vers. 2, 3 (1, 2). According to ver. 2, Darius not only appointed 120 satraps for all the provinces and districts of his kingdom, but he also placed the whole body of the satraps under a government consisting of three presidents, who should reckon with the individual satraps. עֵלָּא, in the Targg. עֵילָּא, *the height*, with the adverb מִן, *higher than, above.* יְהַב טַעְמָא, *to give reckoning, to account.* נָזִק, part. of נְזִק, *to suffer loss*, particularly with reference to the revenue. This triumvirate, or higher authority of three, was also no new institution by Darius, but according to ch. v. 7, already existed in the Chaldean kingdom under Belshazzar, and was only continued by Darius; and the satraps or the district rulers of the several provinces of the kingdom were subordinated to them. Daniel was one of the triumvirate. Since it is not mentioned that Darius first appointed him to this office, we may certainly conclude that he only confirmed him in the office to which Belshazzar had promoted him.

Ver. 4 (3). In this situation Daniel excelled all the presidents and satraps. אִתְנַצַּח, *to show one's self prominent.* Regarding his excellent spirit, cf. ch. v. 12. On that account the king thought to set him over the whole kingdom, *i.e.* to make him chief ruler of the kingdom, to make him מִשְׁנֶה לַמֶּלֶךְ (Esth. x. 3). עֲשִׁית for עֲשֵׁת, intrans. form of the Peal, *to think, to consider about anything.* This intention of the king stirred up the envy of the other presidents and of the satraps, so that they sought to find an occasion against Daniel, that he might be cast down. עִלָּה, *an occasion;* here, as *αἰτία*, John xviii. 38, Matt. xxvii. 37, *an occasion for impeachment.*

מִצַּד מַלְכוּתָא, *on the part of the kingdom, i.e.* not merely in a political sense, but with regard to his holding a public office in the kingdom, with reference to his service. But since they could find no occasion against Daniel in this respect, for he was מְהֵימַן, *faithful, to be relied on,* and no fault could be charged against him, they sought occasion against him on the side of his particular religion, in the matter of the law of his God, *i.e.* in his worship of God.

Ver. 7 (6). For this end they induced the king to sanction and ratify with all the forms of law a decree, which they contrived as the result of the common consultation of all the high officers, that for thirty days no man in the kingdom should offer a prayer to any god or man except to the king, on pain of being cast into the den of lions, and to issue this command as a law of the Medes and Persians, *i.e.* as an irrevocable law. הַרְגִּשׁ, from רְגַשׁ *to make a noise, to rage,* in Aphel c. עַל, *to assail one in a tumultuous manner, i.e.* to assault him. "These presidents and satraps (princes)," ver. 7 (6), in ver. 6 (5) designated "these men," and not the whole body of the presidents and satraps, are, according to ver. 5 (4), the special enemies of Daniel, who wished to overthrow him. It was only a definite number of them who may have had occasion to be dissatisfied with Daniel's service. The words of the text do not by any means justify the supposition that the whole council of state assembled, and *in corpore* presented themselves before the king (Hävernick); for neither in ver. 5 (4) nor in ver. 7 (6) is mention made of all (כֹּל) the presidents and satraps. From the fact also that these accusers of Daniel, ver. 25 (24), represent to the king that the decree they had framed was the result of a consultation of all the prefects of the kingdom, it does not follow that all the satraps and chief officers of the whole kingdom had come to Babylon in order, as Dereser thinks, to lay before the three overseers the annual account of their management of the affairs of their respective provinces, on which occasion they took counsel together against Daniel; from which circumstance Hitzig and others derive an argument against the historical veracity of the narrative. The whole connection of the narrative plainly shows that the authors of the accusation deceived the king. The council of state, or the chief court, to which all the satraps had to render an account, consisted of three men, of whom Daniel was one. But Daniel certainly was not called to this consultation; therefore their pretence, that *all* "presidents of the kingdom" had consulted on the matter, was false. Besides, they deceived the king in this, that they concealed from him the intention of the decree, or misled him regarding it. אַתְיָעַט means not merely that they consulted together, but it includes the result of the consultation: *they were of one mind* (Hitz.).

Ver. 8. כֹּל סָרְכֵי מַלְכוּתָא does not denote the three presidents named in ver. 3 (2), but all the prefects of the kingdom, of whom there were four classes, as is acknowledged by Chr. B. Michaelis, though Hitz. opposes this view. Such an interpretation is required by the genitive מַלְכוּתָא, and by the absence of כֹּל, or at least of the copula ו, before the official names that follow; while the objection, that by this interpretation just the chief presidents who are principally concerned are omitted (Hitz.), is without foundation, for they are comprehended under the word סִגְנַיָּא. If we compare the list of the four official classes here mentioned with that of the great officers of state under Nebuchadnezzar, ch. iii. 2, the naming of the סִגְנַיָּא before the אֲחַשְׁדַּרְפְּנַיָּא (*satraps*) (while in ch. iii. 2 they are named after them) shows that the סִגְנַיָּא are here great officers to whom the satraps were subordinate, and that only the three סָרְכִין could be meant to whom the satraps had to render an account. Moreover, the list of four names is divided by the copula ו into two classes. To the first class belong the סִגְנַיָּא and the satraps; to the second the הַדָּבְרִין, *state councillors*, and the פַּחֲוָתָא, *civil prefects of the provinces.* Accordingly, we will scarcely err if by סִגְנַיָּא we understand the *members of the highest council of state*, by הַדָּבְרַיָּא *the ministers* or *members of the* (*lower*) *state council*, and by the satraps and *pechas the military* and *civil rulers of the provinces.* This grouping of the names confirms, consequently, the general interpretation of the כֹּל סָרְכֵי מַלְכוּתָא, for the four classes named constitute the entire chief prefecture of the kingdom. This interpretation is not made questionable by the fact that the סָרְכִין had in the kingdom of Darius a different position from that they held in the kingdom of Nebuchadnezzar; for in this respect each kingdom had its own particular arrangement, which underwent manifold changes according to the times.

The infinitive clause לְקַיָּמָה קְיָם וגו׳ presents the conclusion arrived at by the consultation. מַלְכָּא is not the genitive to קְיָם, but according to the accents and the context is the subject of the infinitive clause: *that the king should appoint a statute*, not *that a royal statute should be appointed.* According to the analogy of the pronoun and of the *dimin.* noun, the accusative is placed before the subject-genitive, as *e.g.* Isa. xx. 1, v. 24, so as not to separate from one another the קַיָּמָא קְיָם (*to establish a statute*) and the תַּקָּפָה אֱסָר (*to make a firm decree*). Ver. 9*a* requires this construction. It is the king who issues the decree, and not his chief officers of state, as would have been the case if מַלְכָּא were construed as the genitive to קְיָם. קְיָם, *manifesto, ordinance, command.* The command is more accurately defined by the parallel clause תַּקָּפָה אֱסָר, *to make fast, i.e. to decree a prohibition.* The officers wished that the king should issue a decree which should contain a binding prohibition, *i.e.* it should forbid, on pain of death, any one for the space of thirty days, *i.e.* for a month, to offer any prayer to a god or man except to the king. בָּעוּ is here not any kind of request or supplication, but prayer, as the phrase ver. 14 (13), בָּעֵא בָּעוּתֵהּ, *directing his prayer*, shows. The word וֶאֱנָשׁ does not prove the contrary, for the heathen prayed also to men (cf. ch. ii. 46); and here the clause, *except to the king*, places together god and man, so that the king might not observe that the prohibition was specially directed against Daniel.

Ver. 9. In order that they may more certainly gain their object, they request the king to put the prohibition into writing, so that it might not be changed, *i.e.* might not be set aside or recalled, according to the law of the Medes and Persians, in conformity with which an edict once emitted by the king in all due form, *i.e.* given in writing and sealed with the king's seal, was unchangeable; cf. ver. 16 and Esth. viii. 8, i. 19. דִּי לָא תֶעְדֵּא, *which cannot pass away, i.e. cannot be set aside, is irrevocable.* The relative דִּי refers to דָּת, by which we are not to understand, with v. Lengerke, the entire national law of the Medes and Persians, as if this were so unalterable that no law could be disannulled or changed according to circumstances, but דָּת is every separate edict of the king emitted in the form of law. This remains unchangeable and irrevocable, because the king was regarded and honoured as the incarnation of deity, who is unerring and cannot change.

Ver. 10. The king carried out the proposal. וֶאֱסָרָא is explicative: *the writing*, namely, the prohibition (spoken of); for this was the chief matter, therefore אֱסָרָא alone is here mentioned, and not also קְיָם (*edict*), ver. 8.

The right interpretation of the subject-matter and of the foundation of the law which was sanctioned by the king, sets aside the objection that the prohibition was a senseless "bedlamite" law (v. Leng.), which instead of regulating could only break up all society. The law would be senseless only if the prohibition had related to every petition in common life in the intercourse of civil society. But it only referred to the religious sphere of prayer, as an evidence of worshipping God; and if the king was venerated as an incarnation of the deity, then it was altogether reasonable in its character. And if we consider that the intention of the law, which they concealed from the king, was only to effect Daniel's overthrow, the law cannot be regarded as designed to press Parsism or the Zend religion on all the nations of the kingdom, or to put an end to religious freedom, or to make Parsism the world-religion. Rather, as Kliefoth has clearly and justly shown, "the object of the law was only to bring about the general recognition of the principle that the king was the living manifestation of all the gods, not only of the Median and Persian, but also of the Babylonian and Lydian, and all the gods of the conquered nations. It is therefore also not correct that the king should be represented as the incarnation of Ormuzd. The matter is to be explained not from Parsism alone, but from heathenism in general. According to the general fundamental principle of heathenism, the ruler is the son, the representative, the living manifestation of the people's gods, and the world-ruler thus the manifestation of all the gods of the nations that were subject to him. Therefore all heathen world-rulers demanded from the heathen nations subdued by them, that religious homage should be rendered to them in the manner peculiar to each nation. Now that is what was here sought. All the nations subjected to the Medo-Persian kingdom were required not to abandon their own special worship rendered to their gods, but in fact to acknowledge that the Medo-Persian world-ruler Darius was also the son and representative of their national gods. For this purpose they must for the space of thirty days present their petitions to their national gods only in him as their manifestation. And the heathen nations could all do this without violating their consciences; for since in their own manner they served the Median king as the son of their gods, they served their gods in him. The Jews, however, were not in the condition of being able to regard the king as a manifestation of Jehovah, and thus for them there was involved in the law truly a religious persecution, although the heathen king and his satraps did not thereby intend religious persecution, but regarded such disobedience as only culpable obstinacy and political rebellion."[1]

[1] Brissonius, *De regio Persarum princ.* p. 17 sqq., has collected the testimonies of the ancients to the fact that the Persian kings laid claim to divine honour. *Persas reges suos inter Deos colere, majestatem enim imperii salutis esse tutelam.*

The religious persecution to which this law subjected the Jews was rendered oppressive by this: that the Jews were brought by it into this situation, that for a whole month they must either omit prayer to God, and thus sin against their God, or disregard the king's prohibition. The satraps had thus rightly formed their plan. Since without doubt they were aware of Daniel's piety, they could by this means hope with certainty to gain their object in his overthrow. There is no ground for rejecting the narrative in the fact that Darius, without any suspicion, gave their contrivance the sanction of law. We do not need, on the contrary, to refer to the indolence of so many kings, who permit themselves to be wholly guided by their ministers, although the description we have of Cyaxares II. by Xenophon accords very well with this supposition; for from the fact that Darius appears to have sanctioned the law without further consideration about it, it does not follow that he did not make inquiry concerning the purpose of the plan formed by the satraps. The details of the intercourse of the satraps with the king concerning the occasion and object of the law Daniel has not recorded, for they had no significance in relation to the main object of the narrative. If the satraps represented to the king the intention of compelling, by this law, all the nationalities that were subject to his kingdom to recognise his royal power and to prove their loyalty, then the propriety of this design would so clearly recommend itself to him, that without reflection he gave it the sanction of law.

Vers. 11 (10)–25 (24). *Daniel's offence against the law; his accusation, condemnation, and miraculous deliverance from the den of lions; and the punishment of his accusers.*

The satraps did not wait long for Daniel's expected disregard of the king's prohibition. It was Daniel's custom, on bended knees, three times a day to offer prayer to his God in the upper chamber of his house, the window thereof being open towards Jerusalem. He continued this custom even after the issuing of

Curtius, viii. 5. 11. With this cf. Plutarch, *Themist.* c. 27. And that this custom, which even Alexander the Great (Curt. vi. 6. 2) followed, was derived from the Medes, appears from the statement of Herodotus, i. 99, that Dejoces *περὶ ἑαυτὸν σεμνύειν*, withdrew his royal person from the view of men. The ancient Egyptians and Ethiopians paid divine honours to their kings, according to Diod. Sic. i. 90, iii. 3, 5; and it is well known that the Roman emperors required that their images should be worshipped with religious veneration.

the edict; for a discontinuance of it on account of that law would have been a denying of the faith and a sinning against God. On this his enemies had reckoned. They secretly watched him, and immediately reported his disregard of the king's command. In ver. 11 the place where he was wont to pray is more particularly described, in order that it might be shown how they could observe him. In the upper chamber of his house (עִלִּית, Hebr. עֲלִיָּה, 1 Kings xvii. 19, 2 Sam. xix. 1), which was wont to be resorted to when one wished to be undisturbed, *e.g.* wished to engage in prayer (cf. Acts i. 13, x. 9), the windows were open, *i.e.* not closed with lattice-work (cf. Ezek. xl. 16), opposite to, *i.e.* in the direction of, Jerusalem. לֵהּ does not refer to Daniel: he had opened windows, but to לְבַיְתֵהּ: *his house had open windows.* If לֵהּ referred to Daniel, then the הוּא following would be superfluous. The custom of turning in prayer toward Jerusalem originated after the building of the temple at Jerusalem as the dwelling-place of Jehovah; cf. 1 Kings viii. 33, 35, Ps. v. 8, xxviii. 2. The offering of prayer three times a day,—namely, at the third, sixth, and ninth hour, *i.e.* at the time of the morning and the evening sacrifices and at mid-day,—was not first introduced by the men of the Great Synagogue, to whom the uncritical rabbinical tradition refers all ancient customs respecting the worship of God, nor is the opinion of v. Leng., Hitz., and others, that it is not of later origin than the time of the Median Darius, correct; but its origin is to be traced back to the times of David, for we find the first notice of it in Ps. lv. 18. If Daniel thus continued to offer prayer daily (מוֹדֵא=מְהוֹדֵא, ch. ii. 23) at the open window, directing his face toward Jerusalem, after the promulgation of the law, just as he had been in the habit of doing before it, then there was neither ostentation nor pharisaic hypocrisy, nor scorn and a tempting of God, as Kirmss imagines; but his conduct was the natural result of his fear of God and of his religion, under the influence of which he offered prayers not to make an outward show, for only secret spies could observe him when so engaged. כָּל־קֳבֵל דִּי does not mean *altogether so as* (Rosenmüller, v. Leng., Maur., Hitzig), but, as always, *on this account because, because.* Because he always did thus, so now he continues to do it.

Ver. 12 (11). When Daniel's enemies had secretly observed him praying, they rushed into the house while he was offering his supplications, that they might apprehend him in the very act and be able to bring him to punishment. That the act of watching him is not particularly mentioned, since it is to be gathered from the context, does not make the fact itself doubtful, if one only does not arbitrarily, with Hitzig, introduce all kinds of pretences for throwing suspicion on the narrative; as *e.g.* by inquiring whether the 122 satraps had placed themselves in ambush; why Daniel had not guarded against them, had not shut himself in; and the like. הַרְגִּשׁ, as ver. 7, *to rush forward, to press in eagerly*, here "shows the greatness of the zeal with which they performed their business" (Kran.).

Ver. 13 (12). They immediately accused him to the king. Reminding the king of the promulgation of the prohibition, they showed him that Daniel, one of the captive Jews, had not regarded the king's command, but had continued during the thirty days to pray to his own God, and thus had violated the law. In this accusation they laid against Daniel, we observe that his accusers do not describe him as one standing in office near to the king, but only as one of a foreign nation, one of the Jewish exiles in Babylon, in order that they may thereby bring his conduct under the suspicion of being a political act of rebellion against the royal authority.

Ver. 15 (14). But the king, who knew and highly valued (cf. ver. 2 [1]) Daniel's fidelity to the duties of his office, was so sore displeased by the accusation, that he laboured till the going down of the sun to effect his deliverance. The verb בְּאֵשׁ has an intransitive meaning: *to be evil, to be displeased*, and is not joined into one sentence with the subject מַלְכָּא, which stands here absolute; and the subject to בְּאֵשׁ עֲלוֹהִי is undefined: *it*, namely, *the matter displeased him;* cf. Gen. xxi. 11. שָׂם בָּל corresponds to the Hebr. שִׁית לֵב, Prov. xxii. 17, *to lay to heart.* The word בָּל, *cor, mens*, is unknown in the later Chaldee, but is preserved in the Syr. ܒܳܠܳܐ and the Arab. بَالٌ.

Ver. 16 (15). When the king could not till the going down of the sun resolve on passing sentence against Daniel, about this time his accusers gathered themselves together into his presence for the purpose of inducing him to carry out the threatened punishment, reminding him that, according to the law of the Medes and Persians, every prohibition and every command which the king decreed (יְהָקִים), *i.e. issued in a legal form*, could not be changed, *i.e.* could not be recalled. There being no way of escape out of the difficulty for the king, he had to give the command that the punishment should be inflicted, and Daniel was cast into the den of lions, ver. 17 (16). On the Aphel הַיְתִיו, and the pass. form (ver. 18) הֵיתָיִת, see at ch. iii. 13. The execution of the sentence was carried out, according to Oriental custom, on the evening of the day in which the accusation was made; this does not, however, imply that it was on the evening in which, at the ninth hour, he had prayed, as Hitzig affirms, in order that he may thereby make the whole matter improbable. In giving up Daniel to punishment, the king gave expression to the wish, "May thy God, whom thou servest continually, deliver thee!" not "He will deliver thee;" for Darius could not have this confidence, but he may have had the feeble hope of the possibility of the deliverance which from his heart he wished, inasmuch as he may have heard of the miracles of the Almighty God whom Daniel served in the days of Belshazzar and Nebuchadnezzar.

Ver. 18 (17). After Daniel had been thrown into the lions' den, its mouth was covered with a flat stone, and the stone was sealed with the king's seal and that of the great officers of state, that nothing might change or be changed (צְבוּ בְּדָנִיֵּאל) concerning Daniel (צְבוּ, *affair, matter*), not that the device against Daniel might not be frustrated (Häv., v. Leng., Maur., Klief.). This thought required the *stat. emphat.* צְבוּתָא, and also does not correspond with the application of a double seal. The old translator Theodot. is correct in his rendering: *ὅπως μὴ ἀλλοιωθῇ πρᾶγμα ἐν τῷ Δανιήλ*, and the LXX. paraphrasing: *ὅπως μὴ ἀπ' αὐτῶν (μεγιστάνων) ἀρθῇ ὁ Δανιήλ, ἢ ὁ βασιλεύς αὐτὸν ἀνασπάσῃ ἐκ τοῦ λακκοῦ.* Similarly also Ephr. Syr. and others.

The den of lions is designated by גֻּבָּא, which the Targg. use for the Hebr. בּוֹר, *a cistern*. From this v. Leng., Maur., and Hitzig infer that the writer had in view a funnel-shaped cistern dug out in the ground, with a moderately small opening or mouth from above, which could be covered with a stone, so that for this one night the lions had to be shut in, while generally no stone lay on the opening. The pit also into which Joseph, the type of Daniel, was let down was a cistern (Gen. xxxvii. 24), and the mouth of the cistern was usually covered with a stone (Gen. xxix. 3; Lam. iii. 53). It can hence scarcely be conceived how the lions, over which no angel watched, could have remained in such a subterranean cavern covered with a stone. "The den must certainly have been very capacious if, as it appears, 122 men with their wives and children could have been thrown into it immediately after one another (ver. 25 [24]); but this statement itself only shows again the deficiency of every view of the matter,"—and thus the whole history is a fiction fabricated after the type of the history of Joseph! But these critics who speak thus have themselves fabricated the idea of the throwing into the den of 122 men with women and children—for the text states no number—in order that they might make the whole narrative appear absurd; cf. what we have observed regarding this supposition at p. 208.

We have no account by the ancients of the construction of lions' dens. Ge. Höst, in his work on *Fez and Morocco*, p. 77, describes the lions' dens as they have been found in Morocco. According to his account, they consist of a large square cavern under the earth, having a partition-wall in the middle of it, which is furnished with a door, which the keeper can open and close from above. By throwing in food they can entice the lions from the one chamber into the other, and then, having shut the door, they enter the vacant space for the purpose of cleaning it. The cavern is open above, its mouth being surrounded by a wall of a yard and a half high, over which one can look down into the den. This description agrees perfectly with that which is here given in the text regarding the lions' den. Finally, גֻּבָּא does not denote common cisterns. In Jer. xli. 7, 9, גּוּבָא (Hebr. בּוֹר) is a subterranean chamber into which seventy dead bodies were cast; in Isa. xiv. 15, the place of Sheol is called גּוֹב. No reason, therefore, exists for supposing that it is a funnel-formed cistern. The mouth (פּוּם) of the den is not its free opening above by which one may look down into it, but an opening made in its side, through which not only the lions were brought into it, but by which also the keepers entered for the purpose of cleansing the den and of attending to the beasts, and could reach the door in the partition-wall (cf. Höst, p. 270). This opening was covered with a great flat stone, which was sealed, the free air entering to the lions from above. This also explains how, according to ver. 21 (20) ff., the king was able to converse with Daniel before the removal of the stone (namely, by the opening above).

Ver. 19 (18). *Then the king went to his palace, and passed the night fasting: neither were any of his concubines brought before him; and his sleep went from him.* The king spent a sleepless night in sorrow on account of Daniel. טְוָת, used adverbially, *in fasting*, *i.e.* without partaking of food in the evening. דַּחֲוָה, *concu-*

bina; cf. the Arab. دَحَا and دَخَا, *subigere fœminam*, and Gesen. *Thes.* p. 333. On the following morning (ver. 20 [19]) the king rose early, at the dawn of day, and went to the den of lions, and with lamentable voice called to him, feebly hoping that Daniel might be delivered by his God whom he continually served. Daniel answered the king, thereby showing that he had been preserved; whereupon the king was exceeding glad. The future or imperf. יְקוּם (ver. 20) is not to be interpreted with Kranichfeld hypothetically, *he thought to rise early,* seeing he did actually rise early, but is used instead of the perf. to place the clause in relation to the following, meaning: *the king, as soon as he arose at morning dawn, went hastily by the early light.* בְּנָגְהָא, *at the shining of the light,* serves for a nearer determination of the בִּשְׁפַּרְפָּרָא, *at the morning dawn,* namely, as soon as the first rays of the rising sun appeared. The predicate *the living God* is occasioned by the preservation of life, which the king regarded as possible, and probably was made known to the king in previous conversations with Daniel; cf. Ps. xlii. 3, lxxxiv. 3, 1 Sam. xvii. 36, etc.

Ver. 22 (21) ff. In his answer Daniel declares his innocence, which God had recognised, and on that account had sent His angel (cf. Ps. xxxiv. 8, xci. 11 ff.) to shut the mouths of the lions; cf. Heb. x. 33. וְאַף, *and also* (concluding from the innocence actually testified to by God) before the king, *i.e.* according to the king's judgment, he had done nothing wrong or hurtful. By his transgression of the edict he had not done evil against the king's person. This Daniel could the more certainly say, the more he perceived how the king was troubled and concerned about his preservation, because in Daniel's transgression he himself had seen no conspiracy against his person, but only fidelity toward his own God. The king hereupon immediately gave command that he should be brought out of the den of lions. The Aph. הַנְסָקָה and the Hoph. הֻסַּק do not come from נְסַק, but from סְלַק; the נ is merely compensative. סְלַק, *to mount up,* Aph. *to bring out;* by which, however, we are not to understand a being drawn up by ropes through the opening of the den from above. The *bringing out* was by the opened passage in the side of the den, for which purpose the stone with the seals was removed. To make the miracle of his preservation manifest, and to show the reason of it, ver. 24 (23) states that Daniel was found without any injury, because he had trusted in his God.

Ver. 25 (24). But now the destruction which the accusers of

Daniel thought to bring upon him fell upon themselves. The king commanded that they should be cast into the den of lions, where immediately, before they had reached the bottom, they were seized and torn to pieces by the lions. On אֲכַל קַרְצוֹהִי see at ch. iii. 8. By the accusers we are not (with Hitzig) to think of the 120 satraps together with the two chief presidents, but only of a small number of the special enemies of Daniel who had concerned themselves with the matter. The condemning to death of the wives and children along with the men was in accordance with Persian custom, as is testified by Herodotus, iii. 119, Amm. Marcell. xxiii. 6. 81, and also with the custom of the Macedonians in the case of treason (Curtius, vi. ii.), but was forbidden in the law of Moses; cf. Deut. xxiv. 16.

Vers. 26 (25)–29 (28). *The consequences of this occurrence.*

As Nebuchadnezzar, after the wonderful deliverance of Daniel's friends from the burning fiery furnace, issued an edict to all the nations of his kingdom forbidding them on pain of death from doing any injury to these men of God (ch. iii. 29), so now Darius, in consequence of this wonderful preservation of Daniel in the den of lions, gave forth an edict commanding all the nations of his whole kingdom to fear and reverence Daniel's God. But as Nebuchadnezzar by his edict, so also Darius, did not depart from the polytheistic standpoint. Darius acknowledged the God of Daniel, indeed, as the living God, whose kingdom and dominion were everlasting, but not as the only true God, and he commanded Him to be reverenced only as a God who does wonders in heaven and on earth, without prejudice to the honour of his own gods and of the gods of his subjects. Both of these kings, it is true, raised the God of Judea above all other gods, and praised the everlasting duration of His dominion (see ch. iii. 29, 32 [iv. 2] f., and ch. iv. 31 [28] ff., vi. 27 [26] f.), but they did not confess Him as the one only God. This edict, then, shows neither the conversion of Darius to the worship of the God of the Jews, nor does it show intolerance toward the gods of his subjects. On ver. 26 (25) cf. ch. iii. 31 (iv. 1). As Nebuchadnezzar, so also Darius, regarded his kingdom as a world-kingdom. On 27*a* (26) cf. ch. iii. 29. The reverence which all the nations were commanded to show to Daniel's God is described in the same words as is the fear and reverence which the might and greatness of Nebuchadnezzar inspired in all the nations that were subject to him (ch. v. 19), which has led Hitzig justly to remark, that the words לְהֱוֹן פָּלְחִין לֵאלָהֵהּ (*they must worship his God*) are not used. God is described as living (cf. ver. 21 [20]) and eternal, with which is connected the praise of the everlasting duration of His dominion and of His rule in heaven and on earth; cf. ch. ii. 44 and iii. 33 (iv. 3). The דִּי after מַלְכוּתֵהּ is not a conjunction, but is the relative, and the expression briefly denotes that *His kingdom is a kingdom which is not destroyed;* cf. ch. iv. 31 (34). עַד סוֹפָא, *to the end*—not merely of all heathen kingdoms which arise on the earth, *i.e.* to their final destruction by the kingdom of the Messiah, ch. ii. 44 (Kranichfeld), for there is no thought of the Messianic kingdom here at all, but to the end of all things, to eternity. In ver. 28 (27) this God is lauded as the deliverer and wonder-worker, because in the case of Daniel He had showed Himself as such; cf. ch. iii. 32. מִן יַד, *from the hand*, *i.e.* from the power of; cf. Ps. xxii. 21.

Ver. 29 (28) closes the narrative in the same way as that regarding the deliverance of Daniel's friends (ch. iii. 30); only it is further stated, that Daniel continued in office till the reign of the Persian Cyrus. By the pronoun דְּנָה, *this* Daniel, the identity of the person is accentuated: *the same Daniel*, whom his enemies wished to destroy, prospered. From the repetition of בְּמַלְכוּת before כּוֹרֶשׁ it does not follow that Daniel separates the Persian kingdom from the Median; for מַלְכוּ here does not mean kingdom, but *dominion, i.e. reign.* The succession of the reign of Cyrus the Persian to that of Darius the Median does not show the diversity of the two kingdoms, but only that the rulers of the kingdom were of different races.

CHAP. VII. THE VISION OF THE FOUR WORLD-KINGDOMS; THE JUDGMENT; AND THE KINGDOM OF THE HOLY GOD.

After presenting to view (ch. iii.–vi.) in concrete delineation, partly in the prophetically significant experiences of Daniel and his friends, and partly in the typical events which befell the world-rulers, the position and conduct of the representatives of the world-power in relation to the worshippers of the living God, there follows in this chapter the record of a vision seen by Daniel in the first year of Belshazzar. In this vision the four world-monarchies which were shown to Nebuchadnezzar in a dream in the form of an image are represented under the symbol of beasts; and there is a further unfolding not only of the nature and character of the four successive world-kingdoms, but also of the everlasting kingdom of God established by the judgment of the world-kingdoms. With this vision, recorded like the preceding chapters in the Chaldean language, the first part of this work, treating of the development of the world-power in its four principal forms, is brought to a conclusion suitable to its form and contents.

This chapter is divided, according to its contents, into two equal portions. Vers. 1–14 contain the vision, and vers. 15–28 its interpretation. After an historical introduction it is narrated how Daniel saw (vers. 2–8) four great beasts rise up one after another out of the storm-tossed sea; then the judgment of God against the fourth beast and the other beasts (vers. 9–12); and finally (vers. 13, 14), the delivering up of the kingdom over all nations to the Son of man, who came with the clouds of heaven. Being deeply moved (ver. 15) by what he saw, the import of the vision is first made known to him in general by an angel (vers. 16–18), and then more particularly by the judgment (vers. 19–26) against the fourth beast, and its destruction, and by the setting up of the kingdom of the saints of the Most High (ver. 27). The narrative of the vision is brought to a close by a statement of the impression made by this divine revelation on the mind of the prophet (ver. 28).[1]

Ver. 1. The time here indicated, "in the first year of Bel-

[1] According to the modern critics, this vision also is to be regarded as belonging to the time of Antiochus Epiphanes; and, as von Lengerke says, the representation of the Messianic kingdom (vers. 13 and 14) is the only prophetic portion of it, all the other parts merely announcing what had already occurred. According to Hitzig, this dream-vision must have been composed (cf. ver. 25, viii. 14) shortly before the consecration of the temple (1 Macc. iv. 52, 59). On the other hand, Kranichfeld remarks, that if this chapter were composed during the time of the persecution under Antiochus Epiphanes, "then it would show that its author was in the greatest ignorance as to the principal historical dates of his own time;" and he adduces in illustration the date in ver. 25, and the failure of the attempts of the opponents of its genuineness to authenticate in history the ten horns which grew up before the eleventh horn, and the three kingdoms (vers. 7 f., 20). According to ver. 25, the blaspheming of the Most High, the wearing out of the saints, and the changing of all religious ordinances continue for three and a half times, which are taken for three and a half years, after the expiry of which an end will be made, by means of the judgment, to the heathen oppression. But these three and a half years are not historically proved to be the period of the religious persecution under Antiochus Epiphanes. "In both of the books of the Maccabees (1 Macc. i. 54;

shazzar," which cannot, as is evident, mean "shortly before the reign of Belshazzar" (Hitz.), but that Daniel received the following revelation in the course of the first year of the reign of this king, stands related to the contents of the revelation. This vision accords not only in many respects with the dream of Nebuchadnezzar (ch. ii.), but has the same subject. This subject, however, the representation of the world-power in its principal forms, is differently given in the two chapters. In ch. ii. it is represented according to its whole character as an image of a man whose different parts consist of different metals, and in ch. vii. under the figure of four beasts which arise one after the other out of the sea. In the former its destruction is represented by a stone breaking the image in pieces, while in the latter it is effected by a solemn act of judgment. This further difference also is to be observed, that in this chapter, the first, but chiefly the fourth world-kingdom, in its development and relation to the people of God, is much more clearly exhibited than in ch. ii. These differences have their principal reason in the difference of the recipients of the divine revelation: Nebuchadnezzar, the founder of the world-power, saw this power in its imposing greatness and glory; while Daniel, the prophet of God, saw it in its opposition to God in the form of ravenous beasts of prey. Nebuchadnezzar had his dream in the second year of his reign, when he had just founded his world-monarchy;

2 Macc. x. 5) the period of the desecration of the temple (according to v. Leng.) lasted only three years; and Josephus, *Ant.* xii. 7. 6, speaks also of *three* years, reckoning from the year 145 *Seleucid.* and the 25th day of the month Kisleu, when the first burnt-offering was offered on the idol-altar (1 Macc. i. 57), to the 25th day of Kisleu in the year 148 *Seleucid.*, when for the first time sacrifice was offered (1 Macc. iv. 52) on the newly erected altar." But since the βδέλυγμα ἐρημώσεως was, according to 1 Macc. i. 54, erected on the 15th day of Kisleu in the year 145 *Seleucid.*, ten days before the first offering of sacrifice upon it, most reckon from the 15th Kisleu, and thus make the period three years and ten days. Hitzig seeks to gain a quarter of a year more by going back in his reckoning to the arrival in Judea (1 Macc. i. 29, cf. 2 Macc. v. 24) of the chief collector of tribute sent by Apollonius. C. von Lengerke thinks that the period of three and a half years cannot be reckoned with historical accuracy. Hilgenfeld would reckon the commencement of this period from some other event in relation to the temple, which, however, has not been recorded in history.—From all this it is clear as noonday that the three and a half years are not historically identified, and thus that the Maccabean pseudo-Daniel was ignorant of the principal events of his time. Just as little are these critics able historically to identify the ten kings (vers. 7 and 20), as we shall show in an Excursus on the four world-kingdoms at the close of this chapter.

while Daniel had his vision of the world-kingdoms and of the judgment against them in the first year of Belshazzar, *i.e.* Evil-merodach, the son and successor of Nebuchadnezzar, when with the death of the golden head of the world-monarchy its glory began to fade, and the spirit of its opposition to God became more manifest. This revelation was made to the prophet in a dream-vision by night upon his bed. Compare ch. ii. 28. Immediately thereafter Daniel wrote down the principal parts of the dream, that it might be publicly proclaimed—*the sum of the things* (רֵאשׁ מִלִּין) which he had seen in the dream. אֲמַר, *to say, to relate*, is not opposed to כְּתַב, *to write*, but explains it: by means of writing down the vision he said, *i.e.* reported, the chief contents of the dream, omitting secondary things, *e.g.* the minute description of the beasts.

With ver. 2 Daniel begins his written report: "Daniel began and said," introduces the matter. חֶזְוִי עִם-לֵילְיָא, *visions in (during) the night*, cf. ch. ii. 19. Vers. 2 and 3 describe the scene in general. The four winds of heaven break loose upon the great sea, and rage fiercely, so that four great beasts, each diverse from the others, arise out of its bosom. The great sea is not the Mediterranean (Berth., Ges., Hitz., Ewald), for such a geographical reference is foreign to the context. It is the ocean; and the storm on it represents the "tumults of the people," commotions among the nations of the world (Häv., Leng., Hofm., etc.), corresponding to the prophetic comparison found in Jer. xvii. 12, xlvi. 7 f. "Since the beasts represent the forms of the world-power, the sea must represent that out of which they arise, the whole heathen world" (Hofmann). In the interpretation of the image (ver. 17) מִן יַמָּא is explained by מִן אַרְעָא. גִּיחַ means *to break forth* (Ezek. xxxii. 2), *to burst out in storm*, not causative, "to make the great sea break forth" (Kran.). The causative meaning is not certainly found either in the Hebrew or the Chaldee. The four winds stand in relation to the four quarters of the heavens; cf. Jer. xlix. 39. Calvin remarks: *Mundus similis turbulento mari, quod non agitatur una procella vel uno vento, sed diversis ventis inter se confligentibus, ac si totum cœlum conspiraret ad motus excitandos.* With this, however, the meaning of the words is not exhausted. The four winds of heaven are not merely *diversi venti*, and their bursting forth is not only an image of a general commotion represented by a storm in the ocean. The winds *of the heavens* represent the heavenly powers and forces by which God sets the nations of the world in motion; and the number four has a symbolical meaning: that the people of all regions of the earth are moved hither and thither in violent commotion. "Œcumenical commotions give rise to œcumenical kingdoms" (Kliefoth). As a consequence of the storm on the sea, there arise out of it four fierce beasts, not all at once, but, as vers. 6 and 7 teach, one after another, and each having a different appearance. The diversity of the form of the beasts, inasmuch as they represent kingdoms, is determined beforehand, not only to make it noticeable that the selection of this symbol is not arbitrary but is significant (Hävernick), but emphatically to intimate that the vision of different *kingdoms* is not to be dealt with, as many interpreters seem inclined to do, as one only of different *kings* of one kingdom.

Vers. 4–8. *In these verses there is a description of the four beasts.*—Ver. 4. The *first beast* resembled a lion with eagle's wings. At the entrance to a temple at *Birs Nimrud* there has been found (Layard, *Bab. and Nin.*) such a symbolical figure, viz. a winged eagle with the head of a man. There have been found also images of winged beasts at Babylon (Münter, *Relig. der Bab.*). These discoveries may be referred to as evidence that this book was composed in Babylon, and also as explaining the Babylonian colouring of the dream. But the representation of nations and kingdoms by the images of beasts is much more widely spread, and affords the prophetic symbolism the necessary analogues and substrata for the vision. Lions and eagles are not taken into consideration here on account of their strength, rapacity, and swiftness, but simply because they are kings among beasts and birds: "The beast rules royally like the lion, and wings its conquering royal flight high over the οἰκουμένη like the eagle" (Kliefoth). This emblem corresponds with the representation of the first kingdom with the golden head (ch. ii.). What the gold is among metals and the head among the members of the body, that the lion is among beasts and the eagle among birds.

After a time Daniel sees a change take place with this beast. The wings, *i.e.* the feathers by which it flies, are plucked off: it is deprived of its power of flight, so that it can no more fly conquering over the earth, or hover as a ruler over it; *i.e.* the kingdom will be deprived of the power of conquering, for it will be lifted up from the earth (הֳקִימַת is Hoph., cf. ch. iv. 33), and be placed on its feet as a man. The lifting up from the earth does not represent, accordingly, being taken away or blown away from the earth, not the destruction of the Chaldean kingdom (Theodrt., Hieron.,

Raschi, Hitzig, and others), but the raising of it up when lying prostrate on the ground to the right attitude of a human being. This change is further described by the words, "a man's heart was given to it," denoting that the beast-nature was transformed to that of a man. The three expressions thus convey the idea, that the lion, after it was deprived of its power of flight, was not only in external appearance raised from the form of a beast to that of a man, but also that inwardly the nature of the beast was ennobled into that of a man. In this description of the change that occurred to the lion there is without doubt a reference to what is said of Nebuchadnezzar in ch. iv.: it cannot, however, be thence concluded, with Hofmann and others, that the words refer directly to Nebuchadnezzar's insanity; for here it is not the king, but the kingdom, that is the subject with reference to whose fate that event in the life of its founder was significant. Forasmuch as it was on account of his haughtiness that madness came upon him, so that he sank down to the level of the beasts of the field, so also for the same reason was his kingdom hindered in its flight over the earth. "Nebuchadnezzar's madness was for his kingdom the plucking off of its wings;" and as when he gave glory to the Most High his reason returned to him, and then for the first time he attained to the true dignity of man, so also was his world-kingdom ennobled in him, although the continued influence of this ennobling may not be perceived from the events in the reign of his son, recorded in ch. v. Besides, there lies herein not only the idea of the superiority of the first world-kingdom over the others, as is represented in ch. ii. by the golden head of the metallic image, but also manifestly the typical thought that the world-kingdom will first be raised to the dignity of manhood when its beast-like nature is taken away. Where this transformation does not take place, or where it is not permanent, there must the kingdom perish. This is the prophetic meaning, for the sake of which that occurrence in the life of the founder of the world-monarchy is here transferred to his kingdom.

Ver. 5. *The second beast.*—וַאֲרוּ signifies that this beast came first into sight after the lion, which also the predicates אָחֳרִי תִנְיָנָה prove. אָחֳרִי expresses the difference from the first beast, תִנְיָנָה the order in which it appears. The beast was like a bear. Next to the lion it is the strongest among animals; and on account of its voracity it was called by Aristotle *ζῶον παμφάγον.* The words לְשְׂטַר־חַד הֲקִימַת present some difficulty. They have been differently explained. The explanation of Rabbi Nathan, "and it established a dominion," with which Kranichfeld also agrees, is not only in opposition to the חַד, but is also irreconcilable with the line of thought. חַד is not the indefinite article, but the numeral; and the thought that the beast established *one* dominion, or a united dominion, is in the highest degree strange, for the character of a united or compact dominion belongs to the second world-kingdom in no case in a greater degree than to the Babylonian kingdom, and in general the establishing of a dominion cannot properly be predicated of a beast = a kingdom. The old translators (LXX., Theod., Peshito, Saad.) and the rabbis have interpreted the word שְׂטַר in the sense of *side*, a meaning which is supported by the Targ. סְטַר, and is greatly strengthened by the Arabic *s'thar*, without our needing to adopt the reading שְׂטַר, found in several Codd The object to the verb הֲקִימַת is easily supplied by the context: *it raised up, i.e. its body, on one side.* This means neither that it leaned on one side (Ebrard), nor that it stood on its fore feet (Hävernick), for the sides of a bear are not its fore and hinder part; but we are to conceive that the beast, resting on its feet, raised up the feet of the one side for the purpose of going forward, and so raised the shoulder or the whole body on that side. But with such a motion of the beast the geographical situation of the kingdom (Geier, Mich., Ros.) cannot naturally be represented, much less can the near approach of the destruction of the kingdom (Hitzig) be signified. Hofmann, Delitzsch, and Kliefoth have found the right interpretation by a reference to ch. ii. and viii. As in ch. ii. the arms on each side of the breast signify that the second kingdom will consist of two parts, and this is more distinctly indicated in ch. viii. by the two horns, one of which rose up after the other, and higher, so also in this verse the double-sidedness of this world-kingdom is represented by the beast lifting itself up on the one side. The Medo-Persian bear, as such, has, as Kliefoth well remarks, two sides: the one, the Median side, is at rest after the efforts made for the erection of the world-kingdom; but the other, the Persian side, raises itself up, and then becomes not only higher than the first, but also is prepared for new rapine.

The further expression, *it had three ribs in its mouth between its teeth*, has also been variously interpreted. That עִלְעִין means *ribs*, not sides, is as certain as that the ribs in the mouth between the teeth do not denote side-teeth, tusks, or fangs (Saad., Häv.). The עִלְעִין in the mouth between the teeth are the booty which the bear has seized, according to the undoubted use of the word; cf. Amos iii. 12, Ps. cxxiv. 6, Job xxix. 17, Jer. li. 44. Accordingly, by the ribs we cannot understand either the Persians, Medians, and Babylonians, as the nations that constituted the strength of the kingdom (Ephr. Syr., Hieron., Ros.), or the three Median kings (Ewald), because neither the Medes nor the three Median kings can be regarded as a prey of the Median or Medo-Persian world. The "ribs" which the beast is grinding between its teeth cannot be the peoples who constitute the kingdom, or the kings ruling over it, but only peoples or countries which it has conquered and annexed to itself. The determining of these peoples and countries depends on which kingdom is represented by the bear. Of the interpreters who understand by the bear the Median kingdom, Maurer and Delitzsch refer to the three chief satrapies (ch. vi. 3 [2]). Not these, however, but only the lands divided between them, could be regarded as the prey between the teeth of the beast, and then Media also must be excluded; so that the reference of the words to the three satrapies is altogether inadmissible. Hitzig thinks that the reference is to three towns that were destroyed by the Medians, viz. Nineveh, Larissa, and a third which he cannot specify; v. Leng. regards the number three as a round number, by which the voracity of the beast is shown; Kranichfeld understands by the three ribs constituent parts of a whole of an older national confederation already dissolved and broken asunder, of which, however, he has no proof. We see, then, that if the bear is taken as representing the Median kingdom, the three ribs in its mouth cannot be explained. If, on the other hand, the Medo-Persian world-kingdom is intended by the bear, then the three ribs in its mouth are the three kingdoms Babylon, Lydia, and Egypt, which were conquered by the Medo-Persians. This is the view of Hofm., Ebr., Zünd., and Klief. The latter, however, thinks that the number "Three" ought not to be regarded as symbolical, but as forming only the contrast to the number four in ver. 6, and intimating that the second beast will not devour in all the regions of the world, but only on three sides, and will make a threefold and not a fourfold plunder, and therefore will not reach absolute universality. But since the symbolical value of each number is formed from its arithmetical signification, there is no reason here, any more than there is in the analogous passages, ch. viii. 4, 22, to depart wholly from the exact signification.

The last expression of the verse, *Arise, devour much flesh*, most interpreters regard as a summons to go forth conquering. But this exposition is neither necessary, nor does it correspond to the relative position of the words. The eating much flesh does not form such a contrast to the three ribs in the mouth between the teeth, that it must be interpreted of other flesh than that already held by the teeth with the ribs. It may be very well understood, with Ebrard and Kliefoth, of the consuming of the flesh of the ribs; so that the command to eat much flesh is only an explication of the figure of the ribs held between the teeth, and contains only the thought that the beast must wholly consume the plunder it has seized with its teeth. The plur. אָמְרִין (*they spoke*) is impersonal, and is therefore not to be attributed to the angel as speaking.

Ver. 6. *The third beast*, which Daniel saw after the second, was like a panther (leopard), which is neither so kingly as the lion nor so strong as the bear, but is like to both in rapacity, and superior to them in the springing agility with which it catches its prey; so that one may say, with Kliefoth, that in the subordination of the panther to the lion and the bear, the same gradation is repeated as that which is found (of the third kingdom) in ch. ii. of the copper (brass). Of the panther it is said, that *it had four wings of a fowl and four heads.* The representation of the beast with four wings increases the agility of its movements to the speed of the flight of a bird, and expresses the thought that the kingdom represented by that beast would extend itself in flight over the earth; not so royally as Nebuchadnezzar,—for the panther has not eagle's wings, but only the wings of a fowl,—but extending to all the regions of the earth, for it has four wings. At the same time the beast has four heads, not two only, as one might have expected with four wings. The number four thus shows that the heads have an independent signification, and do not stand in relation to the four wings, symbolizing the spreading out of the kingdom into the four quarters of the heavens (Bertholdt, Häv., Kran.). As little do the four wings correspond with the four heads in such a way that by both there is represented only the dividing of the kingdom into four other kingdoms (Häv. *Comment.*, Auberl.). Wings are everywhere an emblem of rapid motion; heads, on the contrary, where the beast signifies a kingdom, are the heads of the kingdom, *i.e.* the kings or rulers: hence it follows that the four heads of the panther are the four successive Persian kings whom alone Daniel knows (ch. xi. 2). Without regard to the false interpretations of ch. xi. 2 on which this opinion rests, it is to be noticed that the four heads do not rise up one after another, but that they all exist contemporaneously on the body of the beast, and therefore can only represent four contemporary kings, or signify that this kingdom is divided into four kingdoms. That the four wings are mentioned before the four heads, signifies that the kingdom spreads itself over the earth with the speed of a bird's flight, and then becomes a fourfold-kingdom, or divides itself into four kingdoms, as is distinctly shown in ch. viii. 5 ff.—The last statement, *and dominion was given to it*, corresponds with that in ch. ii. 39, *it shall bear rule over all the earth*, *i.e.* shall found an actual and strong world-empire.

Vers. 7 and 8. *The fourth beast.*—Introduced by a more detailed description, the fourth beast is presented more distinctly before our notice than those which preceded it. Its terribleness and its strength, breaking in pieces and destroying all things, and the fact that no beast is named to which it can be likened, represent it as different from all the beasts that went before. This description corresponds with that of the fourth kingdom denoted by the legs and the feet of the metallic image of the monarchies (ch. ii.). The iron breaking in pieces all things (ch. ii. 40) is here represented by the great iron teeth with which this monster devoured and brake in pieces. In addition to that, there are also feet, or, as ver. 19 by way of supplement adds, "claws of brass," with which in the mere fury of its rage it destroyed all that remained, *i.e.* all that it did not devour and destroy with its teeth. הִיא מְשַׁנְיָה וגו' (*it was made different*) denotes not complete diversity of being, from which Hitz. and Del. conclude that the expression suits only the Macedonian world-kingdom, which as occidental was different in its nature from the three preceding monarchies, which shared among themselves an oriental home and a different form of civilisation and despotic government. For although מְשַׁנְיָה expresses more than אָחֳרִי (ver. 5), yet the שָׁנְיָן דָּא מִן דָּא (*diverse one from another*), spoken (ver. 3) of all the beasts, shows that מְשַׁנְיָה cannot be regarded as expressing perfect diversity of being, but only diversity in appearance. The beast was of such terrible strength and destructive rage, that the whole animal world could furnish no representative by whose name it might be characterized. It had ten horns, by which its terrible strength is denoted, because a horn is in Scripture always the universal symbol of armed strength. With this the interpretation (ver. 24), that these horns are so many kings or kingdoms, fully corresponds. In the ten horns the ten toes of the image (ch. ii.) are again repeated. The number ten comes into consideration only according to its symbolical meaning of comprehensive and definite totality. That the horns are on the head of the one beast, signifies that the unfolding of its power in the ten kingdoms is not a weakening of its power, but only its full display.

Ver. 8. Here a new event is brought under our notice. While continuing to contemplate the horns (the idea of continuance lies in the particip. with the *verb. fin.*), Daniel sees another little horn rise up among them, which uproots, *i.e.* destroys, three of the other horns that were already there. He observes that this horn had the eyes of a man, and a mouth which spake great things. The eye and the mouth suggest a human being as represented by the horn. Eyes and seeing with eyes are the symbols of insight, circumspection, prudence. This king will thus excel the others in point of wisdom and circumspection. But why the eyes of a *man?* Certainly this is not merely to indicate to the reader that the horn signified a man. This is already distinctly enough shown by the fact that eyes, a mouth, and speech were attributed to it. The eyes of a man were not attributed to it in opposition to a beast, but in opposition to a higher celestial being, for whom the ruler denoted by the horn might be mistaken on account of the terribleness of his rule and government; "*ne eum putemus juxta quorundam opinionem vel diabolum esse vel dæmonem, sed unum de hominibus, in quo totus Satanas habitaturus sit corporaliter,*" as Jerome well remarks; cf. Hofmann and Kliefoth.—A mouth which speaketh great things is a vainglorious mouth. רַבְרְבָן are *presumptuous things,* not directly blasphemies (Häv.). In the Apocalypse, xiii. 5, *μεγάλα* and *βλασφημίαι* are distinguished.

Vers. 9–14. *The judgment on the horn speaking great things and on the other beasts, and the delivering of the kingdom to the Son of Man.*

After Daniel had for a while contemplated the rising up of the little horn that appeared among the ten horns, the scene changed. There is a solemn sitting in judgment by God, and sentence is pronounced. Seats or chairs were placed. רְמִיו, *activ.* with an indefinite subject: *they were thrown, i.e.* they were placed in order quickly, or with a noise. Seats, not merely a throne for God the Judge, but a number of seats for the assembly sitting in judgment with God. That assembly consists neither of the elders of Israel (*Rabb.*), nor of glorified men (Hengstb. on Rev. iv. 4), but of angels

(Ps. lxxxix. 8), who are to be distinguished from the thousands and tens of thousands mentioned in ver. 10; for these do not sit upon thrones, but stand before God as servants to fulfil His commands and execute His judgments. עַתִּיק יוֹמִין, *one advanced in days, very old*, is not the Eternal; for although God is meant, yet Daniel does not see the everlasting God, but an old man, or a man of grey hairs, in whose majestic form God makes Himself visible (cf. Ezek. i. 26). When Daniel represents the true God as an aged man, he does so not in contrast with the recent gods of the heathen which Antiochus Epiphanes wished to introduce, or specially with reference to new gods, as Hitzig and Kran. suppose, by reference to Deut. xxxii. 17 and Jer. xxiii. 23; for God is not called the old God, but appears only as an old man, because age inspires veneration and conveys the impression of majesty. This impression is heightened by the robe with which He is covered, and by the appearance of the hair of His head, and also by the flames of fire which are seen to go forth from His throne. His robe is white as snow, and the hair of His head is white like pure wool; cf. Rev. i. 14. Both are symbols of spotless purity and holiness. Flames of fire proceed from His throne as if it consisted of it, and the wheels of His throne scatter forth fire. One must not take the fire exclusively as a sign of punishment. Fire and the shining of fire are the constant phenomena of the manifestation of God in the world, as the earthly elements most fitting for the representation of the burning zeal with which the holy God not only punishes and destroys sinners, but also purifies and renders glorious His own people; see under Ex. iii. 3. The fire-scattering wheels of the throne show the omnipresence of the divine throne of judgment, the going of the judgment of God over the whole earth (Kliefoth). The fire which engirds with flame the throne of God pours itself forth as a stream from God into the world, consuming all that is sinful and hostile to God in the world, and rendering the people and kingdom of God glorious. מִן קֳדָמוֹהִי (*from before Him*) refers to God, and not to His throne. A thousand times a thousand and ten thousand times ten thousand are hyperbolical expressions for an innumerable company of angels, who as His servants stand around God; cf. Deut. xxxiii. 2, Ps. lxviii. 18. The *Keri* presents the Chaldaic form אַלְפִין for the Hebraizing form of the text אַלְפִים (*thousands*), and for רִבְּוָן the Hebraizing form רִבְבָן (*myriads*), often found in the Targg., to harmonize the plur. form with the singular רִבּוֹ going before.

Forthwith the judgment begins. דִּינָא יְתִב we translate, with most interpreters, *the judgment sets itself.* דִּינָא, *judgment, abstr. pro concreto,* as *judicium* in Cicero, *Verr.* 2. 18. This idea alone is admissible in ver. 26, and here also it is more simple than that defended by Dathe and Kran.: "He" (*i.e.* the Ancient of days) "sets Himself for judgment,"—which would form a pure tautology, since His placing Himself for judgment has been already (ver. 9) mentioned, and nothing would be said regarding the object for which the throne was set.—"*The books were opened.*" The actions of men are recorded in the books, according to which they are judged, some being ordained to eternal life and others condemned to eternal death; cf. Rev. xx. 12, and the notes under Dan. xii. 1. The horn speaking great things is first visited with the sentence of death.

Ver. 11. The construction of this verse is disputed. The second חָזֵה הֲוֵית (*I was seeing*) repeats the first for the purpose of carrying on the line of thought broken by the interposed sentence. בֵּאדַיִן (*then*) is separated by the accents from the first חָזֵה הֲוֵית and joined to the clause following: "*then on account of the voice of the great words.*" By this interposed sentence the occasion of the judgment which Daniel sees passed upon the beast is once more brought to view. מִן קָל, "*on account of the voice of the words,*" *i.e.* on account of the loud words, not "from the time of the words, or from the time when the voice of the great words made itself heard" (Klief.). The following expression, עַד דִּי (*till that*), does not by any means require the temporal conception of מִן. To specify the *terminus a quo* of the vision was as little necessary here as in the חָזֵה הֲוֵית עַד דִּי, ver. 9. The temporal conception of מִן alters not only the parallelism of the passage vers. 9 and 11, but also the course of thought in the representation, according to which Daniel remains overwhelmed during the vision till all the separate parts of it have passed before his view, *i.e.* till he has seen the close of the judgment. The first part of this scene consists of the constituting of the judgment (vers. 9, 10), the second of the death and extinction of the horn speaking great things (ver. 11), with which is connected (ver. 12) the mention of the destruction of the dominion of the other beasts. If one considers that the words "*I beheld till that*" correspond with the like expression in ver. 9, he will not seek, with Kran., in the עַד דִּי a reference to a lasting process of judicial execution ending with destruction. The thought is simply this: Daniel remained contemplating the vision till the beast was slain, etc. חֵיוְתָא (*the beast*) is, by virtue of the explanatory sentence interposed in the first hemistich, the horn speaking great things. The ungodly power of the fourth beast reaches its climax in the blaspheming horn; in this horn, therefore, the beast is slain and destroyed, while its body is given to the burning. לִיקֵדַת אֶשָּׁא (*to the burning fire*) corresponds with the Hebr. לִשְׂרֵפַת אֵשׁ, Isa. lxiv. 10. The burning in the fire is not the mere figure of destruction, specially justified by the thunder-storm which gathered as a veil around the scene of judgment (Kran.), for there is no mention of a storm either in ver. 9 or anywhere else in this entire vision. The supposition that the burning is only the figure of destruction, as *e.g.* in Isa. ix. 4, is decidedly opposed by the parallel passages, Isa. lxvi. 14, which Daniel had in view, and Rev. xix. 20 and xx. 10, where this prophecy is again taken up, and the judgment is expressed by a being cast into a lake of fire with everlasting torment; so that v. Lengerke is right when he remarks that this passage speaks of the fiery torments of the wicked after death, and thus that a state of retribution after death is indicated.

Ver. 12. In this verse it is in addition remarked, that the dominion of the other beasts was also destroyed, because the duration of their lives was determined for a time and an hour. The construction of the words forbids us (with Luther) to regard the first part of ver. 12 as dependent on עַד דִּי of ver. 11. The object וּשְׁאָר חֵיוָתָא (*the rest of the beasts*) is presented in the form of an absolute nominative, whereby the statement of ver. 12 is separated from the preceding. הֶעְדִּיו, impersonal, instead of the passive, as דָּקוּ in ch. ii. 35: "their dominion was made to perish," for "their dominion was destroyed." "The other beasts" are not those that remained of the seven horns of the fourth beast, which were not uprooted by the horn coming up amongst them, the remaining kingdoms of the fourth monarchy after the destruction by that horn, for with the death of the beast the whole fourth world-monarchy is destroyed; nor are they the other kingdoms yet remaining at the time of the overthrow of the fourth world-monarchy or the destruction of the fourth beast (J. D. Mich., v. Leng.), which only lose their political power, but first of all would become subject to the new dominant people (Hitzig), for such other kingdoms have no existence in the prophetic view of Daniel, since the beasts represent world-kingdoms whose dominion stretches over the whole earth. The "remaining beasts" are much rather the first three beasts which arose out of the sea before the fourth, as is rightly acknowledged by Chr. B. Mich., Ros., Häv., Hofm., Maur., Klief., and Kran., with the old interpreters. Although the four world-kingdoms symbolized by those beasts follow each other in actual history, so that the earlier is always overthrown by that which comes after it, yet the dominion of the one is transferred to the other; so in the prophetic representation the death or the disappearance of the first three beasts is not expressly remarked, but is here first indicated, without our needing for that reason to regard הֶעְדִּיו as the pluperfect. For the exposition of this verse also we may not appeal to ch. ii., where all the four world-kingdoms are represented in one human image, and the stone which rolled against the feet of this image broke not only the feet, but with them the whole image to pieces (ch. ii. 34 f.), which in ver. 44 is explained as meaning that the kingdom of God will bring to an end all those kingdoms. From this we cannot conclude that those kingdoms had long before already perished at the hour appointed for them, but that a remainder (שְׁאָר) of them yet continued to exist (Häv.), for the representation in this chapter is different; and *the rest of the beasts* cannot possibly mean that which remained of the beasts after their destruction, but only the beasts that remained after the death of the fourth beast. The mas. suff. to שָׁלְטָנְהוֹן (*their dominion*) and לְהוֹן refer *ad sensum* to the possessor or ruler of the world-kingdom represented by the beasts. With that interpretation of "the rest of the beasts" the statement also of the second half of the verse does not agree, for it proves that the subject is the destruction of the dominion of all the beasts which arose up before the fourth. The length or duration of life is the time of the continuance of the world-kingdoms represented by the beasts, and thus the end of life is the destruction of the kingdom. The passive pret. יְהִיבַת is not to be taken thus as the imperf.: "a period of life was appointed to them," but as the pluperf.: "had been granted to them," and the passage formally connected by the simple ו is to be taken as confirming the preceding statement. זְמַן וְעִדָּן (placed together as ch. ii. 21 in the meaning there explained) is not to be identified with זִמְנָא, ver. 22 (v. Leng., Kran.). The form (*stat. absol.*, not *emphat.*) shows that not a definite time, the time of the divine judgment of the fourth beast, is meant, but the time of the continuance of the power and dominion for each of the several beasts (kingdoms), foreseen only in the counsel of the Most High, and not further defined. In accordance with this, the statement of ver. 12 is that the first three beasts also had their dominion taken away one after another, each at its appointed time; for to each God gave its duration of life, extending to the season and time appointed by Him. Thus Kliefoth, with the older interpreters, correctly regards the connecting of the end of the first three beasts with that of the last as denoting that in the horn not merely the fourth kingdom, but also the first three kingdoms, the whole world-power, is brought to an end by the last judgment. This thought, right in itself, and distinctly announced in the destruction of the image (ch. ii.), appears, however, to lie less in the altogether loose connection of ver. 12 with ver. 11 than in the whole context, and certainly in this, that with the fourth beast in general the unfolding of the world-power in its diverse phases is exhausted, and with the judgment of this kingdom the kingdom of God is raised to everlasting supremacy.

Vers. 13. and 14. *The giving of the kingdom to the Son of Man.*—The judgment does not come to an end with the destruction of the world-power in its various embodiments. That is only its first act, which is immediately followed by the second, the erection of the kingdom of God by the Son of man. This act is introduced by the repetition of the formula, *I saw in the night-visions* (vers. 7 and 2). (*One*) *like a son of man came in the clouds of heaven.* עִם עֲנָנֵי, *with the clouds, i.e.* in connection with them, *in* or *on* them, as the case may be, surrounded by clouds; cf. Rev. i. 7, Mark xiii. 26, Matt. xxiv. 30, xxvi. 64. He who comes is not named, but is only described according to his appearance *like a son of man, i.e.* resembling a man (בַּר אֱנָשׁ as בֶּן אָדָם = אֱנוֹשׁ or אָדָם). That this was a man is not implied in these words, but only that he was like a man, and not like a beast or some other creature. Now, as the beasts signify not beasts but kingdoms, so that which appeared in the form of a man may signify something else than a human *individuum*. Following the example of Aben Ezra, Paulus, and Wegscheider, Hofmann (*Schriftbew.* ii. 1. 80, and 2, p. 582 f.), Hitzig, Weisse, Volkmar, Fries (*Jahrbb. f. D. Theol.* iv. p. 261), Baxmann, and Herzfeld (*Gesch. des V. Isr.* ii. p. 381) interpret this appearance in the form of a man not of the Messiah, as the Jewish and Christian interpreters in general do, but of the people of Israel, and adduce in support of this view the fact that, in the explanation of the vision, ver. 27, cf. ver. 24, the kingdom, the dominion, and the power, which according to ver. 14 the son of man received, was given to the people of the saints of the Most High. But ver. 27 affords no valid support to this supposition, for the angel there gives forth his declaration regarding the everlasting kingdom of God, not in the form of an interpretation of Daniel's vision, as in the case of the four beasts in vers. 17 and 23, but he only says that, after the destruction of the horn and its dominion, the kingdom and the power will be given to the people of the saints, because he had before (ver. 26, cf. 22) spoken of the blasphemies of the horn against God, and of its war against the saints of the Most High. But the delivering of the kingdom to the people of God does not, according to the prophetic mode of contemplation, exclude the Messiah as its king, but much rather includes Him, inasmuch as Daniel, like the other prophets, knows nothing of a kingdom without a head, a Messianic kingdom without the King Messiah. But when Hofmann further remarks, that "somewhere it must be seen that by that appearance in the form of a man is meant not the holy congregation of Israel, but an individual, a fifth king, the Messiah," Auberlen and Kranichfeld have, with reference to this, shown that, according to ver. 21, the saints appear in their multiplicity engaged in war when the person who comes in the clouds becomes visible, and thus that the difference between the saints and that person is distinctly manifest. Hence it appears that the "coming with the clouds of heaven" can only be applied to the congregation of Israel, if we agree with Hofmann in the opinion that he who appeared was not carried by the clouds of heaven down to the earth, but from the earth up to heaven, in order that he might there receive the kingdom and the dominion. But this opinion is contradicted by all that the Scriptures teach regarding this matter. In this very chapter before us there is no expression or any intimation whatever that the judgment is held in heaven. No place is named. It is only said that judgment was held over the power of the fourth beast, which came to a head in the horn speaking blasphemies, and that the beast was slain and his body burned. If he who appears as a son of man with the clouds of heaven comes before the Ancient of days executing the judgment on the earth, it is manifest that he could only come from heaven to earth. If the reverse is to be understood, then it ought to have been so expressed, since the coming with the clouds of heaven in opposition to the rising up of the beasts out of the sea very distinctly indicates a coming down from heaven. The clouds are the veil or the "chariot" on which God comes from heaven to execute judgment against His enemies; cf. Ps. xviii. 10 f., xcvii. 2–4, civ. 3, Isa. xix. 1, Nah. i. 3. This passage forms the foundation for the declaration of Christ regarding His future coming, which is described after Dan. vii. 13 as a coming of the Son of man with, in, on the clouds of heaven; Matt. xxiv. 30, xxvi. 64; Mark xiii. 26; Rev. i. 7, xiv. 14. Against this, Hofmann, in behalf of his explanation, can only adduce 1 Thess. iv. 17, in total disregard of the preceding context, ver. 16.[1]

With all other interpreters, we must accordingly firmly maintain that he who appears with the clouds of heaven comes from heaven to earth and is a personal existence, and is brought before God, who judges the world, that he may receive dominion, majesty, and a kingdom. But in the words "*as a man*" it is not meant that he was only a man. He that comes with the clouds of heaven may, as Kranichfeld rightly observes, "be regarded, according to current representations, as the God of Israel coming on the clouds, while yet he who appears takes the outward form of a man." The comparison (כְּ, *as* a man) proves accordingly much more, that this heavenly or divine being was in human form. This "*Son of man*" came near to the Ancient of days, as God appears in the vision of the judgment, ver. 9, and was placed before Him. The subject to הַקְרְבוּהִי is undefined; Kran. thinks that it is the clouds just mentioned, others think it is the ministering angels. Analogous passages may be adduced in support of both views: for the first, the *νεφέλη ὑπέλαβεν αὐτόν* in Acts i. 9; but the parallel passages with intransitive verbs speak more in favour of the impersonal translation, "*they brought him*" = he was brought. The words, "dominion, and glory, and a kingdom were given to him," remind us of the expression used of Nebuchadnezzar, ch. ii. 37 f., but they are elevated by the description following to the conception of the everlasting dominion of God. God gave to

[1] The force of these considerations is also recognised by Hitzig. Since the people of the saints cannot come from heaven, he resorts to the expedient that the Son of man is a "figure for the concrete whole, the kingdom, the saints—this kingdom comes down from heaven." The difficulties of such an idea are very obvious. Fries appears to be of opinion, with Hofmann, that there is an ascension to heaven of the people of the saints; for to him "clear evidence" that the "Son of man" is the people of Israel lies especially in the words, "and came to the Ancient of days, and they brought him near before Him," which necessitates the adoption of the opposite *terminus a quo* from Matt. xxiv. 30, Mark xiv. 62, Rev. i. 7; and hence makes the direct parallelism of Dan. vii. 13 with the passages named impossible (?).

Nebuchadnezzar, the founder and first bearer of the world-power, a kingdom, and might, and majesty, and dominion over all the inhabitants of the earth, men, and beasts, and birds, that he might govern all nations, and tribes, and tongues (ch. v. 18, 19), but not indeed in such a manner as that all nations and tribes should render him religious homage, nor was his dominion one of everlasting duration. These two things belong only to the kingdom of God. פְּלַח is used in biblical Chaldee only of the service and homage due to God; cf. ver. 27, ch. iii. 12, 14, 17 f., Ezra vii. 19, 24. Thus it indicates here also the religious service, the reverence which belong to God, though in the Targg. it corresponds with the Heb. עֲבַד in all its meanings, *colere Deum, terram, laborare.* Regarding the expression " nations, tribes, and tongues," see under vers. 3, 4. The eternity of the duration of the dominion is in this book the constant predicate of the kingdom of God and His Anointed, the Messiah; cf. ch. iii. 33, iv. 31, ii. 44. For further remarks regarding the Son of man, see at the close of this chapter.

Vers. 15–28. *The interpretation of the vision.*—Ver. 14 concludes the account of the contents of the vision, but not the vision itself. That continues to the end of the chapter. Ver. 15. The things which Daniel saw made a deep impression on his mind. His spirit was troubled within him; the sight filled him with terror. It was not the mystery of the images, nor the fact that all was not clear before his sight, that troubled and disquieted him; for ver. 28 shows that the disquietude did not subside when an angel explained the images he had seen. It was the things themselves as they passed in vision before him—the momentous events, the calamities which the people of God would have to endure till the time of the completion of the everlasting kingdom of God—which filled him with anxiety and terror. רוּחִי stands for the Hebr. נַפְשִׁי, and אֲנָה דָנִיֵּאל is in apposition to the suffix in רוּחִי, for the suffix is repeated with emphasis by the pronoun, ch. viii. 1, 15, Ezra vii. 21, and more frequently also in the Hebr.; cf. Winer, *Chald. Gram.* § 40, 4; Ges. *Hebr. Gram.* § 121, 3. The emphatic bringing forward of the person of the prophet corresponds to the significance of the vision, which made so deep an impression on him; cf. also ch. x. 1, 7, xii. 15. In this there is no trace of anxiety on the part of the speaker to make known that he is Daniel, as Hitzig supposes. The figure here used, " *in the sheath*" (E. V. " in the midst of my body"), by which the body is likened to a sheath for the soul, which as a sword in its sheath is concealed by it, is found also in Job xxvii. 8, and in the writings of the rabbis (cf. Buxt. *Lex. talm. s.v.*) It is used also by Pliny, vii. 52. On "*visions of my head*," cf. ver. 1.

Ver. 16. Daniel turned himself towards an angel who stood by, with a request for an explanation of these things. *One of them that stood by* refers to those mentioned in ver. 10, who stood around the throne of God; whence it is obvious that the vision is still continued. אֶבְעֵא is not the preterite, *I asked him*, but the subjunctive, *that* (ו) *I might ask*. So also יְהוֹדְעִנַּנִי is to be taken with the ו going before: *he spake to me, that he informed me*, namely by his speaking.

In vers 17–27 the angel gives the wished-for explanation. In vers. 17 and 18 he gives first a general interpretation of the vision. The words, *these great beasts*, of which there were four, form an absolute nominal clause: "as for the beasts;" as concerning their meaning, it is this: "they represent four kings." The kings are named as founders and representatives of world-kingdoms. Four kingdoms are meant, as ver. 23 shows, where the fourth beast is explained as מַלְכוּ, "dominion," "kingdom." Compare also ch. viii. 20 and 21, where in like manner kings are named and kingdoms are meant. From the future יְקוּמוּן (*shall arise*) Hitzig concludes that the first kingdom was yet future, and therefore, that since Daniel had the vision under Belshazzar, the first king could only be Belshazzar, but could not represent the Chaldean monarchy. But if from the words *shall arise* it follows that the vision is only of kings who arise in the future, then, since Daniel saw the vision in the first year of Belshazzar, it cannot of course be Belshazzar who is represented by the first beast; and if Belshazzar was, as Hitzig thinks, the last king of Chaldea, then the entire Chaldean monarchy is excluded from the number of the four great beasts. Kranichfeld therefore understands this word as modal, and interprets it *should arise*. This was the divine decree by which also the duration of their kingdoms was determined (vers. 12, 25). But the modal interpretation does not agree with ver. 16, according to which the angel wishes to make known the meaning of the matter to Daniel, not to show what was determined in the divine counsel, but what God had revealed to him by the beasts rising up out of the sea. The future, *shall arise*, is rather (Ros., v. Leng., Maur., Klief., etc.) for the purpose of declaring that the vision represents the development of the world-power as a whole, as it would unfold itself in four successive phases; whereupon the angel so summarily interprets the vision to the prophet, that, dating from the time of their origin, he points out the first world-kingdom as arising along with the rest, notwithstanding that it had already come into existence, and only its last stages were then future. The thought of this summary interpretation is manifestly nothing else than this: "Four kingdoms shall arise on the earth, and shall again disappear; but the saints of God shall receive the kingdom which shall have an everlasting duration." יְקַבְּלוּן, *receive;* not found and establish by their own might, but receive through the Son of man, to whom God (ver. 14) has given it. עֶלְיוֹנִין (cf. vers. 22, 25, 27) is the name of God, *the Most High*, analogous to the plur. forms אֱלֹהִים, קְדֹשִׁים. "The saints of the Most High," or briefly "the saints" (vers. 21, 22), are neither the Jews, who are accustomed to call themselves "saints," in contrast with the heathen (v. Leng., Maur., Hitzig, etc.), nor the converted Israel of the millennium (Hofmann and other chiliasts), but, as we argue from Ex. xix. 6, Deut. vii. 6, the true members of the covenant nation, the New Testament Israel of God, *i.e.* the congregation of the New Covenant, consisting of Israel and the faithful of all nations; for the kingdom which God gives to the Son of man will, according to ver. 14, comprehend those that are redeemed from among all the nations of the earth. The idea of the everlasting duration of their kingdom is, by the words עַד־עָלְמַיָּא (*for ever and ever*), raised to the superlative degree.

The angel does not here give further explanations regarding the first three kingdoms. Since the second chapter treats of them, and the eighth also gives further description of the second and third, it is enough here to state that the first three beasts represent those kingdoms that are mentioned in ch. ii. The form of the fourth beast, however, comprehends much more regarding the fourth world-kingdom than the dream-image of Nebuchadnezzar did. Therefore Daniel asks the angel further for certain information (certainty) regarding the dreadful form of this beast, and consequently the principal outlines of the representation before given of it are repeated by him in vers. 19–21, and are completed by certain circumstances there omitted. Thus ver. 19 presents the addition, that the beast had, along with iron teeth, also claws of brass, with which it stamped to pieces what it could not devour; and ver. 20, that the little horn became greater than its fellows, made war against the people of God and overcame them, till the judgment brought its dominion to an end. צְבִית לְיַצָּבָא, *I wished for sure knowledge, i.e.* to experience certainty regarding it.

In ver. 20, from וּנְפַלוּ (*fell down*) the relative connection of the passage is broken, and the direct description is continued. וְקַרְנָא דִכֵּן (*and that horn*) is an absolute idea, which is then explained by the *Vav* epexegetic. חֶזְוַהּ, the appearance which it presented, *i.e.* its *aspect*. מִן חַבְרָתַהּ (*above his fellows*), for מִן חֱזוּ חַבְרָתַהּ (*above the aspect of his fellows*), see under ch. i. 10.

Ver. 21. קַדִּישִׁין (without the article), although used in a definite sense of the saints already mentioned, appertains to the elevated solemn style of speech, in which also in the Hebr. the article is frequently wanting in definite names; cf. Ewald's *Lehrb.* § 277.

Ver. 22. As compared with vers. 13 and 14, this verse says nothing new regarding the judgment. For דִּינָא יְהִיב לְקַד' is not to be rendered, as Hengstenberg thinks (*Beitr.* i. p. 274), by a reference to 1 Cor. vi. 2: "to the saints of the Most High the judgment is given," *i.e.* the function of the judge. This interpretation is opposed to the context, according to which it is God Himself who executes judgment, and by that judgment justice is done to the people of God, *i.e.* they are delivered from the unrighteous oppression of the beast, and receive the kingdom. דִּינָא is *justice* procured by the judgment, corresponding to the Hebrew word מִשְׁפָּט, Deut. x. 18.

Ver. 23 ff. Daniel receives the following explanation regarding the fourth beast. It signifies a fourth kingdom, which would be different from all the preceding, and would eat up and destroy the whole earth. "The whole earth is the οἰκουμένη," the expression, without any hyperbole, for the "whole circle of the historical nations" (Kliefoth). The ten horns which the beast had signify ten kings who shall arise out of that kingdom. מִנַּהּ מַלְכוּתָה, *from it, the kingdom, i.e. from this very kingdom.* Since the ten horns all exist at the same time together on the head of the beast, the ten kings that arise out of the fourth kingdom are to be regarded as contemporary. In this manner the division or dismemberment of this kingdom into ten principalities or kingdoms is symbolized. For the ten contemporaneous kings imply the existence at the same time of ten kingdoms. Hitzig's objections against this view are of no weight. That מַלְכוּ and מֶלֶךְ are in this verse used as distinct from each other proves nothing, because in the whole vision king and kingdom are congruent ideas. But that the horn, ver. 8, *unmistakeably* denotes a person, is only so far right, as things are said of the horn which are *in abstracto* not suitable to a kingdom, but they can only be applicable to the bearer of royal power. But ch. viii. 20 and 21, to which Hitzig further refers, furnishes no foundation for his view, but on the contrary confutes it. For although in ch. viii. 21 the great horn of the goat is interpreted as the first king of Javan, yet the four horns springing up immediately (ver. 22) in the place of this one which was broken, are interpreted as four kingdoms (not kings), in distinct proof not only that in Daniel's vision king and kingdom are not "separate from each other," but also that the further assertion, that "horn" is less fitted than "head" to represent a kingdom, is untenable.

After those ten kingdoms another shall arise which shall be different from the previous ten, and shall overthrow three of them. יְהַשְׁפִּל, in contrast with אֲקִים (cf. ch. ii. 21), signifies *to overthrow, to deprive of the sovereignty*. But the king coming after them can only overthrow three of the ten kingdoms when he himself has established and possesses a kingdom or empire of his own. According to this, the king arising after the ten is not an isolated ruler, but the monarch of a kingdom which has destroyed three of the kingdoms already in existence.

Ver. 25 refers to the same king, and says that he shall speak against the Most High. לְצַד means, properly, *against or at the side of*, and is more expressive than עַל. It denotes that he would use language by which he would set God aside, regard and give himself out as God; cf. 2 Thess. ii. 4. Making himself like God, he will destroy the saints of God. בְּלָא, *Pa.*, not "make unfortunate" (Hitzig), but consume, afflict, like the Hebr. בִּלָּה, 1 Chron. xvii. 9, and Targ. Jes. iii. 15. These passages show that the assertion that בִּלָּה, in the sense of to destroy, never takes after it the accusative of the person (Hitz.), is false. Finally, "he thinks to change times and laws." "To change times" belongs to the all-perfect power of God (cf. ch. ii. 21), the creator and ordainer of times (Gen. i. 14). There is no ground for supposing that זִמְנִין is to be specially understood of "festival or sacred times," since the word, like the corresponding Hebr. מוֹעֲדִים, does not throughout signify merely "festival times;" cf. Gen. i. 14, xvii. 21, xviii. 14, etc. The annexed וְדָת does not point to arrangements of divine worship, but denotes "law" or "ordinance" in general, human as well as divine law; cf. ch. ii. 13, 15 with ch. vi. 6, 9. "Times and laws" are the foundations and main conditions, emanating from God, of the life and actions of men in the world. The sin of the king in placing himself with God, therefore, as Kliefoth rightly remarks, "consists in this, that in these ordinances he does not regard the fundamental conditions given by God, but so changes the laws of human life that he puts his own pleasure in the place of the divine arrangements." Thus shall he do with the ordinances of life, not only of God's people, but of all men. "But it is to be confessed that the people of God are most affected thereby, because they hold their ordinances of life most according to the divine plan; and therefore the otherwise general passage stands between two expressions affecting the conduct of the horn in its relation to the people of God."

This tyranny God's people will suffer "till, *i.e.* during, a time, (two) times, and half a time." By these specifications of time the duration of the last phase of the world-power is more definitely declared, as a period in its whole course measured by God; vers. 12 and 22. The plural word עִדָּנִין (*times*) standing between time and half a time can only designate the simple plural, *i.e. two times* used in the dual sense, since in the Chaldee the plural is often used to denote a pair where the dual is used in Hebrew; cf. Winer, *Chald. Gr.* § 55, 3. Three and a half times are the half of seven times (ch. iv. 13). The greater number of the older as well as of the more recent interpreters take *time* (עִדָּן) as representing the space of a year, thus three and a half times as three and a half years; and they base this view partly on ch. iv. 13, where seven times must mean seven years, partly on ch. xii. 7, where the corresponding expression is found in Hebrew, partly on Rev. xiii. 5 and xi. 2, 3, where forty-two months and 1260 days are used interchangeably. But none of these passages supplies a proof that will stand the test. The supposition that in ch. iv. 13 the seven times represent seven years, neither is nor can be proved. As regards the *time* and *times* in ch. xii. 7, and the periods named in the passages of the Rev. referred to, it is very questionable whether the *weeks* and the *days* represent the ordinary weeks of the year and days of the week, and whether these periods of time are to be taken chronologically. Still less can any explanation as to this designation of time be derived from the 2300 days (evening-mornings) in ch. viii. 14, since the periods do not agree, nor do both passages treat of the same event. The choice of the chronologically indefinite expression עִדָּן, *time*, shows that a chronological determination of the period is not in view, but that the designation of time is to be understood symbolically. We have thus to inquire after the symbolical meaning of the statement. This is not to be sought, with Hofmann (*Weiss.* i. 289), in the supposition that as three and a half years are the half of a Sabbath-period, it is thus announced that Israel would be oppressed during half a Sabbath-period by Antichrist. For, apart from the unwarrantable identification of *time* with *year*, one does not perceive what Sabbath-periods and the oppression of the people of God have in common. This much is beyond doubt, that three and a half times are the half of seven times. The meaning of this half, however, is not to be derived, with Kranichfeld, from ch. iv. 13, where "*seven times*" is an expression used for a long continuance of divinely-ordained suffering. It is not hence to be supposed that the dividing of this period into two designates only a proportionally short time of severest oppression endured by the people of God at the hands of the heathen. For the humbling of the haughty ruler Nebuchadnezzar (ch. iv. 13) does not stand in any inner connection with the elevation of the world-power over the people of God, in such a way that we could explain the three and a half times of this passage after the seven times of ch. iv. 13. In general, the question may be asked, Whether the meaning of the three and a half times is to be derived merely from the symbolical signification of the number seven, or whether, with Lämmert, we must not much rather go back, in order to ascertain the import of this measure of time, to the divine judgments under Elias, when the heavens were shut for three years and six months; Luke iv. 25 and Jas. v. 17. "As Ahab did more to provoke God to anger than all the kings who were before him, so this king, Dan. vii. 24, in a way altogether different from those who went before him, spake words against the Most High and persecuted His saints, etc." But should this reference also not be established, and the three and a half times be regarded as only the half of seven times, yet the seven does not here come into view as the time of God's works, so that it could be said the oppression of the people of God by the little horn will last (Kliefoth) only half as long as a work of God; but according to the symbolical interpretation of the seven times (see p. 152), the three and a half, as the period of the duration of the circumstances into which the people of God are brought by the world-power through the divine permission, indicate "a testing period, a period of judgment which will (Matt. xxiv. 22; Prov. x. 27), for the elect's sake, be interrupted and shortened (*septenarius truncus*)." Leyrer in Herz.'s *Real. Enc.*

xviii. 369. Besides, it is to be considered how this space of time is described, not as three and a half, but a time, two times, and half a time. Ebrard (*Offenb.* p. 49) well remarks regarding this, that "it appears as if his tyranny would extend itself always the longer and longer: first a time, then the doubled time, then the fourfold —this would be a seven times; but it does not go that length; suddenly it comes to an end in the midst of the seven times, so that instead of the fourfold time there is only half a time." "The proper analysis of the three and a half times," Kliefoth further remarks, "in that the periods first mount up by doubling them, and then suddenly decline, shows that the power of the horn and its oppression of the people of God would first quickly manifest itself, in order then to come to a sudden end by the interposition of the divine judgment (ver. 26)." For, a thing which is not here to be overlooked, the three and a half times present not the whole duration of the existence of the little horn, but, as the half of a week, only the latter half of its time, in which dominion over the saints of God is given to it (ver. 21), and at the expiry of which it falls before the judgment. See under ch. xii. 7.

In vers. 26 and 27 this judgment is described (cf. ver. 10), but only as to its consequences for the world-power. The dominion of the horn in which the power of the fourth beast culminates is taken away and altogether annihilated. The destruction of the beast is here passed by, inasmuch as it is already mentioned in ver. 11; while, on the other hand, that which is said (ver. 12) about the taking away of its power and its dominion is strengthened by the *inf.* לְהַשְׁמָדָה (*to destroy*), וּלְהוֹבָדָה (*and to consume*), being added to יְהַעְדּוֹן (*they shall take away*), to which שָׁלְטָנֵהּ (*his dominion*) is to be repeated as the object. עַד סוֹפָא, *to the end, i.e.* not absolutely, but, as in ch. vi. 27, to the end of the days, *i.e.* for ever.

Ver. 27. After the destruction of the beast, the kingdom and the dominion, which hitherto comprehended the kingdom under the whole heaven, are given to the people of God, *i.e.* under the reign of the Son of man, as is to be supplied from ver. 14. As in ver. 26 nothing is further said of the fate of the horn, because all that was necessary regarding it had been already said (ver. 11), so also all that was to be said of the Son of man was already mentioned in vers. 13 and 14; and according to the representation of the Scripture, the kingdom of the people of the saints without the Son of man as king is not a conceivable idea. דִּי מַלְכְוּת (*of the kingdom*) is a subjective genitive, which is required by the idea of the intransitive רְבוּתָא (*the greatness*) preceding it. The meaning is thus not "power over all kingdoms," but "the power which the kingdoms under the whole heaven had." With regard to ver. 27, cf. vers. 14 and 18.

In ver. 28 the end of the vision is stated, and the impression which it left on Daniel. *Hitherto*, to this point, was the end of the history; *i.e.* thus far the history, or, with this the matter is at an end. מִלְּתָא, *the matter*, is not merely the interpretation of the angel, but the whole revelation, the vision together with its interpretation. Daniel was greatly moved by the event (cf. ch. v. 9), and kept it in his heart.

The Four World-kingdoms.

There yet remains for our consideration the question, What are the historical world-kingdoms which are represented by Nebuchadnezzar's image (ch. ii.), and by Daniel's vision of four beasts rising up out of the sea? Almost all interpreters understand that these two visions are to be interpreted in the same way. "The four kingdoms or dynasties, which were symbolized (ch. ii.) by the different parts of the human image, from the head to the feet, are the same as those which were symbolized by the four great beasts rising up out of the sea." This is the view not only of Bleek, who herein agrees with Auberlen, but also of Kranichfeld and Kliefoth, and all church interpreters. These four kingdoms, according to the interpretation commonly received in the church, are the Babylonian, the Medo-Persian, the Macedo-Grecian, and the Roman. "In this interpretation and opinion," Luther observes, "all the world are agreed, and history and fact abundantly establish it." This opinion prevailed till about the end of the last century, for the contrary opinion of individual earlier interpreters had found no favour.[1] But from that time, when faith in the supernatural

[1] This is true regarding the opinion of Ephrem Syrus and of Cosmas Indicopleustes, who held that the second kingdom was the Median, the third the Persian, and the fourth the kingdom of Alexander and his successors. This view has been adopted only by an anonymous writer in the *Comment. Var. in Dan.* in Mai's *Collectio nov. Script. Vett.* p. 176. The same thing may be said of the opinion of Polychronius and Grotius, that the second kingdom was the Medo-Persian, the third the monarchy of Alexander, and the fourth the kingdom of his followers—a view which has found only one weak advocate in J. Chr. Becmann in a *dissert. de Monarchia Quarta*, Franc. ad Od. 1671.

origin and character of biblical prophecy was shaken by Deism and Rationalism, then as a consequence, with the rejection of the genuineness of the book of Daniel the reference of the fourth kingdom to the Roman world-monarchy was also denied. For the pseudo-Daniel of the times of the Maccabees could furnish no prophecy which could reach further than the time of Antiochus Epiphanes. If the reference of the fourth kingdom to the Roman empire was therefore *a priori* excluded, the four kingdoms must be so explained that the pretended prophecy should not extend further than to the time of Antiochus Epiphanes. For this end all probabilities were created, and yet nothing further was reached than that one critic confuted another. While Ewald and Bunsen advanced the opinion that the Assyrian kingdom is specially to be understood by the first kingdom, and that the Maccabean author of the book was first compelled by the reference to Nebuchadnezzar to separate, in opposition to history, the Median from the Persian kingdom, so as to preserve the number four, Hitzig, in agreement with von Redepenning, has sought to divide the Babylonian kingdom, and to refer the first kingdom to Nebuchadnezzar and the second to his successor Belshazzar; while Bertholdt, Jahn, and Rosenmüller, with Grotius, have divided the kingdom of Alexander from the kingdom of his successors. But as both of these divisions appear to be altogether too arbitrary, Venema, Bleek, de Wette, Lücke, v. Leng., Maurer, Hitzig (ch. vii.), Hilgenfeld, and Kranichfeld have disjoined the Medo-Persian monarchy into two world-kingdoms, the Median and the Persian, and in this they are followed by Delitzsch. See Art. *Daniel* in Herz.'s *Real. Encyc.*

When we examine these views more closely, the first named is confuted by what Ewald himself (*Die Proph.* iii. 314) has said on this point. The four world-kingdoms "must follow each other strictly in chronological order, the succeeding being always inferior, sterner, and more reckless than that which went before. They thus appear in the gigantic image (ch. ii.), which in its four parts, from head to feet, is formed of altogether different materials; in like manner in ch. vii. four different beasts successively appear on the scene, the one of which, according to ch. viii., always destroys the other. Now it cannot be said, indeed, in strict historical fact that the Chaldean kingdom first gave way to the Median, and this again to the Persian, but, as it is always said, the Persian and Median together under Cyrus overthrew the Chaldean and formed one kingdom. This is stated by the author himself in ch. viii., where the Medo-Persian kingdom is presented as one under the image of a two-horned ram. According to this, he should have reckoned from Nabucodrossor only three world-kingdoms, if he had not received the number of four world-kingdoms from an old prophet living under the Assyrian dominion, who understood by the four kingdoms the Assyrian, the Chaldean, the Medo-Persian, and the Grecian. Since now this number, it is self-evident to him, can neither be increased nor diminished, there remained nothing else for him than to separate the Median from the Persian kingdom at that point where he rendered directly prominent the order and the number *four*, while he at other times views them together." But what then made it necessary for this pseudo-prophet to interpret the golden head of Nebuchadnezzar, and to entangle himself thereby, in opposition not only to the history, but also to his own better judgment, ch. viii., if in the old sources used by him the Assyrian is to be understood as the first kingdom? To this manifest objection Ewald has given no answer, and has not shown that in ch. ii. and vii. the Median kingdom is separated from the Persian. Thus this hypothesis is destitute of every foundation, and the derivation of the number four for the world-kingdoms from a prophetic book of the Assyrian period is one of the groundless ideas with which Ewald thinks to enrich biblical literature.

Hitzig's opinion, that Daniel had derived the idea of separating the heathen power into four kingdoms following each other from the representation of the four ages of the world, has no better foundation. It was natural for him to represent Assyria as the first kingdom, yet as he wished not to refer to the past, but to the future, he could only begin with the kingdom of Nebuchadnezzar. Regarding himself as bound to the number four, he divided on that account, in ch. ii., the Chaldean dominion into two periods, and in ch. vii., for the same reason, the Medo-Persian into two kingdoms, the Median and the Persian. This view Hitzig founds partly on this, that in ch. ii. 38 not the Chaldean kingdom but Nebuchadnezzar is designated as the golden head, and that for Daniel there exist only two Chaldean kings; and partly on this, that the second מַלְכוּ (ch. ii. 39) is named as inferior to the Chaldean, which could not be said of the Medo-Persian as compared with the Chaldean; and, finally, partly on this, that in the vision seen in the first year of Belshazzar (ch. vii.), Nebuchadnezzar already belonged to the past, while according to ver. 17 the first kingdom was yet future. But apart from the incorrectness of the assertion, that for the author of this book only two Chaldean kings existed, it does not follow from the circumstance that Nebuchadnezzar is styled the golden head of the image, that he personally is meant as distinct from the Chaldean king that succeeded him; on the contrary, that Nebuchadnezzar comes to view only as the founder, and at that time the actual ruler, of the kingdom, is clear from ch. ii. 39, "after thee shall arise another kingdom" (מַלְכוּ), not another king (מֶלֶךְ), as it ought to be read, according to Hitzig's opinion. Belshazzar did not found another kingdom, or, as Hitzig says, another dominion (*Herschaft*), but he only continued the kingdom or dominion of Nebuchadnezzar. The two other reasons advanced have been already disposed of in the interpretation of ch. ii. 39 and of ch. vii. 17. The expression, "*inferior to thee*" (ch. ii. 39), would not relate to the Medo-Persian kingdom as compared with the Chaldean only if it referred to the geographical extension of the kingdom, which is not the case. And the argument deduced from the words "shall arise" in ch. vii. 17 proves too much, and therefore nothing. If in the word יְקוּמוּן (*shall arise*) it be held that the first kingdom was yet to arise, then also the dominion of Belshazzar would be thereby excluded, which existed at the time of that vision. Moreover the supposition that מַלְכוּ means in ch. ii. 39 the government of an individual king, but in ch. ii. 4 a kingdom, the passages being parallel in their contents and in their form, and that מַלְכִין in ch. vii. 17 ("the four beasts are four kings") means, when applied to the first two beasts, separate kings, and when applied to the two last, kingdoms, violates all the rules of hermeneutics. "Two rulers personally cannot possibly be placed in the same category with two kingdoms" (Kliefoth).

But the view of Bertholdt, that the third kingdom represents the monarchy of Alexander, and the fourth that of his διάδοχοι (successors), is at the present day generally abandoned. And there is good reason that it should be so; for it is plain that the description of the iron nature of the fourth kingdom in ch. ii. breaking all things in pieces, as well as of the terribleness of the fourth beast in ch. vii., by no means agrees with the kingdoms of the successors of Alexander, which in point of might and greatness were far inferior to the monarchy of Alexander, as is indeed expressly stated in ch. xi. 4. Hitzig has, moreover, justly remarked, on the other hand, that "for the author of this book the kingdom of Alexander and that of his successors form together the מַלְכוּת יָוָן, ch. viii. 21 (*the kingdom of Javan* = Grecia). But if he had separated them, he could not have spoken of the kingdom of the successors as 'diverse' in character from that of Alexander, ch. vii. 7, 19. Finally, by such a view a right interpretation of the four heads, ch. vii. 6, and the special meaning of the legs which were wholly of iron, ch. ii. 33, is lost."

Now, since the untenableness of these three suppositions is obvious, there only remains the expedient to divide the Medo-Persian world-kingdom into a Median and a Persian kingdom, and to combine the former with the second and the latter with the third of Daniel's kingdoms. But this scheme also is broken to pieces by the twofold circumstance, (1) that, as Maurer himself acknowledges, history knows nothing whatever of a Median world-kingdom; and (2) that, as Kranichfeld is compelled to confess (p. 122 ff.), "it cannot be proved from Dan. v. 28, vi. 1, 29, ix. 1, xi. 1, that the author of the book, in the vision in ch. ii. or vii., or at all, conceived of an exclusively Median world-kingdom, and knew nothing of the Persian race as an inner component part of this kingdom." It is true the book of Daniel, according to ch. viii., recognises a distinction between a Median and a Persian dynasty (cf. ver. 3), but in other respects it recognises only one kingdom, which comprehends in its unity the Median and the Persian race. In harmony with this, the author speaks, at the time when the Median government over Babylon was actually in existence, only of one law of the kingdom for Medes and Persians (ch. vi. 9, 13, 16), *i.e.* one law which rested on a common agreement of the two nations bound together into one kingdom. "The author of this book, who at the time of Darius, king of the Medes, knew only of one kingdom common to both races," according to Kran., "speaks also in the preceding period of the Chaldean independence of the Medes only in conjunction with the Persians (cf. ch. v. 28, viii. 20), and, after the analogy of the remark already made, not as of two separated kingdoms, but in the sense of one kingdom, comprehending in it, along with the Median race, also the Persians as another and an important component part. This finds its ratification during the independence of Babylon even in ch. viii. 20; for there the kings of the Medes and the Persians are represented by *one* beast, although at the same time two separate dynasties are in view. This actual fact of a national union into *one* kingdom very naturally and fully explains why, in the case of Cyrus, as well as in that of Darius, the national origin of the governors, emphatically set forth, was of interest for the author (cf.

ch. ix. 1, vi. 1, xi. 1, vi. 28), while with regard to the Chaldean kings there is no similar particular notice taken of their origin; and generally, instead of a statement of the personal descent of Darius and Cyrus, much rather only a direct mention of the particular people ruled by each—*e.g.* for these rulers the special designations 'king of the Persians,' 'king of the Medes'—was to be expected[1] (cf. ch. viii. 20, x. 1, 13, 20, xi. 2)." Hence, as Kranichfeld further rightly judges, it could not (ch. viii.) appear appropriate to suppose that the author had Persia in view as the third kingdom, while in the visions ch. ii. and vii. we would regard Persia as a kingdom altogether separated from the Median kingdom. Moreover the author in ch. viii. speaks of the one horn of the ram as growing up after the other, in order thereby to indicate the growing up of the Persian dynasty after the Median, and consequently the two dynasties together in one and the same kingdom (ver. 3, cf. ver. 20). Yet, in spite of all these testimonies to the contrary, Daniel must in ch. ii. and vii. have had in view by the second world-kingdom the Median, and by the third the Persian, because at that time he did not think that in the relation of the Median and the Persian no other change in the future would happen than a simple change of dynasty, but because, at the time in which the Median kingdom stood in a threatening attitude toward the Chaldean (both in the second year of Nebuchadnezzar and in the first year of his son Belshazzar, *i.e.* Evilmerodach), he thought that a sovereign Persian kingdom would rise up victoriously opposite the Median rival of Nebuchadnezzar.

[1] Kranichfeld goes on to say, that Hilgenfeld goes too far if he concludes from the attribute, *the Mede* (ch. vi. 1 [v. 31]), that the author wished to represent thereby a separate kingdom of the Medes in opposition to a kingdom of the Persians at a later time nationally distinct from it; further, that as in the sequel the Median dynasty of the Medo-Persian kingdom passed over into a Persian dynasty, and through the government of the Persian Cyrus the Persian race naturally came forth into the foreground and assumed a prominent place, the kingdom was designated *a potiori* as that of the Persians (ch. x. 1, 13, 20, xi. 2), like as, in other circumstances (Isa. xiii. 17; Jer. li. 11, 28), the Medians alone are *a potiori* represented as the destroyers of Babylon. "As there was, during the flourishing period of the Median dynasty, a kingdom of the Medes and Persians (cf. Dan. v. 28, viii. 20), so there is, since the time of Cyrus the Persian, a kingdom of the Persians and Medes (cf. Esth. i. 3, 18, 1 Macc. i. 1, xiv. 2). We find in Daniel, at the time of the Median supremacy in the kingdom, the law of the Medes and Persians (Dan. vi. 9, 13, 16), and subsequently we naturally find the law of the Persians and Medes, Esth. i. 19."

As opposed to this expedient, we will not insist on the improbability that Daniel within two years should have wholly changed his opinion as to the relation between the Medians and the Persians, though it would be difficult to find a valid ground for this. Nor shall we lay any stress on this consideration, that the assumed error of the prophet regarding the contents of the divine revelation in ch. ii. and vii. appears irreconcilable with the supernatural illumination of Daniel, because Kranichfeld regards the prophetic statements as only the product of enlightened human mental culture. But we must closely examine the question how this reference of the world-kingdoms spoken of stands related to the characteristics of the third and fourth kingdoms as stated in ch. ii. and vii.

The description of the second and third kingdoms is very briefly given in ch. ii. and vii. Even though the statement, ch. ii. 39, that the second kingdom would be smaller than the kingdom of Nebuchadnezzar could point to a Median kingdom, and the statement that the third kingdom would rule over the whole earth might refer to the spread of the dominion of the Persians beyond the boundaries of the Chaldean and Medo-Persian kingdom under Darius, yet the description of both of these kingdoms in ch. vii. 5 sufficiently shows the untenableness of this interpretation. The second kingdom is represented under the image of a bear, which raises itself up on one side, and has three ribs in its mouth between its teeth. The three ribs in its mouth the advocates of this view do not know how to interpret. According to Kran., they are to be regarded as pointing out constituent parts of a whole, of an older kingdom, which he does not attempt more definitely to describe, because history records nothing of the conquests which Darius the Mede may have gained during the two years of his reign after the conquest of Babylon and the overthrow of the Chaldean kingdom by Cyrus. And the leopard representing (ch. vii. 6) the third kingdom has not only four wings, but also four heads. The four heads show beyond a doubt the division of the kingdom represented by the leopard into four kingdoms, just as in ch. viii. the four horns of the he-goat, which in ver. 22 are expressly interpreted of four kingdoms rising out of the kingdom of Javan. But a division into four kingdoms cannot by any means be proved of the Persian world-kingdom. Therefore the four heads must here, according to Kran., represent only the vigilant watchfulness and aggression over all the regions of the earth, the pushing movement toward the different regions of the heavens, or, according to Hitzig, the four kings of Persia whom alone Daniel knew. But the first of these interpretations confutes itself, since heads are never the symbol of watchfulness or of aggressive power; and the second is set aside by a comparison with ch. viii. 22. If the four horns of the he-goat represent four world-kingdoms rising up *together*, then the four heads of the leopard can never represent four kings reigning *after* one another, even though it were the case, which it is not (ch. xi. 2), that Daniel knew only four kings of Persia.

Yet more incompatible are the statements regarding the fourth world-kingdom in ch. ii. and vii. with the supposition that the kingdom of Alexander and his followers is to be understood by it. Neither the monarchy of Alexander nor the Javanic world-kingdom accords with the iron nature of the fourth kingdom, represented by the legs of iron, breaking all things in pieces, nor with the internal division of this kingdom, represented by the feet consisting partly of iron and partly of clay, nor finally with the ten toes formed of iron and clay mixed (ch. ii. 33, 40–43). As little does the monarchy of Alexander and his successors resemble a fearful beast with ten horns, which was without any representative in the animal world, according to which Daniel could have named it (ch. vii. 7, 19). Kranichfeld rejects, therefore, the historical meaning of the image in ch. ii., and seeks to interpret its separate features only as the expression of the irreparable division of the ungodly kingdom assailing the theocracy with destructive vehemence, and therein of dependent weakness and inner dissolution. Hitzig finds in the two legs the representation of a monarchy which, as the Greek domination, sets its one foot on Europe and its other on Asia; and he regards Syria and Egypt as the material of it—Syria as the iron, Egypt as the clay. Others, again, regard the feet as the kingdoms of the Seleucidæ and the Ptolemies, and in the ten horns they seek the other kingdoms of the *Διάδοχοι*. On the other hand, Kliefoth justly asks, "How came Syria and Egypt to be feet? And the toes go out of the feet, but the other kingdoms of the *Διάδοχοι* do not arise out of Syria and Egypt." And if in this circumstance, that it is said of the fourth terrible beast that it was different from all the beasts that went before, and that no likeness was found for it among the beasts of prey, Kran. only finds it declared "that it puts forth its whole peculiarity according to its power in such a way that no name can any longer be found for it," then this in no respect whatever agrees with the monarchy of Alexander. According to Hitz., the difference of the fourth beast is to be sought in the monarchy of Alexander transplanted from Europe into Asia, as over against the three monarchies, which shared in common an oriental home, a different kind of culture, and a despotic government. But was the transference of a European monarchy and culture into Asia something so fearful that Daniel could find no name whereby to represent the terribleness of this beast? The relation of Alexander to the Jews in no respect corresponds to this representation; and in ch. viii. Daniel does not say a word about the terribleness of the Javanic kingdom, but presents only the great rapidity of its conquests. He had thus an entirely different conception of the Greek monarchy from that of his modern interpreters.

Finally, if we take into consideration that the terrible beast which represents the fourth world-power has ten horns (ch. vii. 7), which is to be explained as denoting that out of the same kingdom ten kings shall arise (ch. vii. 24), and, on the contrary, that by the breaking off from the he-goat, representing the monarchy of Alexander, of the one great horn, which signified the first king, and the subsequent springing up of four similar horns, is to be understood that four kingdoms shall arise out of it (ch. viii. 5, 8, 21, 22); then the difference of the number of the horns shows that the beast with the ten horns cannot represent the same kingdom as that which is represented by the he-goat with four horns, since the number four is neither according to its numerical nor its symbolical meaning identical with the number ten. Moreover, this identifying of the two is quite set aside by the impossibility of interpreting the ten horns historically. Giving weight to the explanation of the angel, that the ten horns represent the rising up of ten kings, Berth., v. Leng., Hitz., and Del. have endeavoured to find these kings among the Seleucidæ, but they have not been able to discover more than seven: 1. Seleucus Nicator; 2. Antiochus Soter; 3. Antiochus Theus; 4. Seleucus Callinicus; 5. Seleucus Ceraunus; 6. Antiochus the Great; 7. Seleucus Philopator, the brother and predecessor of Antiochus Epiphanes, who after Philopator's death mounted the throne of Syria, having set aside other heirs who had a better title to it, and who must be that little horn which reached the kingdom by the rooting up of three kings. The three kings whom Antiochus plucked up by the roots (cf. ch. vii. 8, 20, 24) must be Heliodorus, the murderer of Philopator;

Demetrius, who was a hostage in Rome, the son of Philopator, and the legitimate successor to the throne; and the son of Ptolemy Philometor, for whom his mother Cleopatra, the sister of Seleucus Philopator and of Antiochus Epiphanes, claimed the Syrian throne. But no one of these three reached the royal dignity, and none of them was dethroned or plucked up by the roots by Antiochus Epiphanes. Heliodorus, it is true, strove for the kingdom (Appian, *Syriac.* 45); but his efforts were defeated, yet not by Antiochus Epiphanes, but by Attalus and Eumenes. Demetrius, after his death, was the legitimate heir to the throne, but could not assert his rights, because he was a hostage in Rome; and since he did not at all mount the throne, he was not of course dethroned by his uncle Antiochus Epiphanes. Finally, Ptolemy Philometor, after the death of Antiochus Epiphanes, for a short time, it is true, united the Syrian crown with the Egyptian (1 Macc. xi. 13; Polyb. xl. 12), but during the life of Antiochus Epiphanes, and before he ascended the throne, he was neither *de jure* nor *de facto* king of Syria; and the "pretended efforts of Cleopatra to gain for her son Philometor the crown of Syria are nowhere proved" (Hitzig).

Of this historical interpretation we cannot thus say even so much as that it "only very scantily meets the case" (Delitzsch); for it does not at all accord with the prophecy that the little horn (Antiochus Epiphanes) plucked up by the roots three of the existing kings. Hitzig and Hilgenfeld (*Die Proph. Esra u. Dan.* p. 82) have therefore dropped out of view the Syrian kingdom of Philometor, and, in order to gain the number ten, have ranked Alexander the Great among the Syrian kings, and taken Seleucus Philopator into the triad of the pretended Syrian kings that were plucked up by the roots by Antiochus Epiphanes. But Alexander the Great can neither according to the evidence of history, nor according to the statement of the book of Daniel, be counted among the kings of Syria; and Seleucus Philopator was not murdered by Antiochus Epiphanes, but Antiochus Epiphanes lived at the time of this deed in Athens (Appian, *Syr.* 45); and the murderer Heliodorus cannot have accomplished that crime as the instrument of Antiochus, because he aspired to gain the throne for himself, and was only prevented from doing so by the intervention of Attalus and Eumenes. Hilgenfeld also does not venture to reckon Heliodorus, the murderer of the king, among the triad of uprooted kings, but seeks to supply his place by an older son of Seleucus Philopator, murdered at the instigation of Antiochus

Epiphanes according to Gutschmid; but he fails to observe that a king's *son* murdered during the lifetime of his father, reigning as king, could not possibly be represented as a king whom Antiochus Epiphanes drove from his throne. Of the ten kings of the Grecian world-kingdom of the branch of the Seleucidæ before Antiochus Epiphanes, whom Hilgenfeld believes that he is almost able "to grasp with his hands," history gives as little information as of the uprooting of the three Syrian kings by Antiochus Epiphanes.

But even though the historical relevancy of the attempt to authenticate the ten Syrian kings in the kingdom of the Seleucidæ were more satisfactory than, from what has been remarked, appears to be the case, yet this interpretation of the fourth beast would be shattered against the ten horns, because these horns did not grow up one after another, but are found simultaneously on the head of the beast, and consequently cannot mean ten Syrian kings following one another, as not only all interpreters who regard the beast as representing the Roman empire, but also Bleek and Kran., acknowledge, in spite of the reference of this beast to the Javanic world-kingdom. "We are induced," as Bleek justly observes, "by ver. 8, where it is said of the little horn that it would rise up between the ten horns, to think of ten contemporaneous kings, or rather kingdoms, existing along with each other, which rise out of the fourth kingdom." Therefore he will "not deny that the reference to the successors of Alexander is rendered obscure by the fact that ch. viii. speaks of four monarchies which arise out of that of Alexander after his death." This obscurity, however, he thinks he is able to clear up by the remark, that "in the kind of development of the historical relations after the death of Alexander, the parts of his kingdom which formed themselves into independent kingdoms might be numbered in different ways." Thus, in ch. vii., "as ten from the number of the generals who in the arrangements of the division of the kingdom (323 B.C.) retained the chief provinces: 1. Kraterus (Macedonia); 2. Antipater (Greece); 3. Lysimachus (Thrace); 4. Leonatus (Phrygia Minor on the Hellespont); 5. Antigonus (Phrygia Major, Lycia, and Pamphylia); 6. Cassander (Karia); 7. Eumenes (Cappadocia and Paphlagonia); 8. Laomedon (Syria and Palestine); 9. Pithon (Media); 10. Ptolemy Lagus (Egypt)." But Zündel justly observes in opposition to this view, that "these kingdoms could only have significance if this number, instead of being a selection from the whole, had been itself the whole. But this is not the case. For at that time the kingdom, according to Justin, *hist.* L. xiii. 4, was divided into more than thirty separate parts.[1] Although all the names do not perfectly agree as given by different writers, yet this is manifest, that there is no information regarding a division of the kingdom of Alexander into ten exclusively. History knows nothing of such a thing; not only so, but much more, this reckoning of Bleek's falls into the same mistake as the oldest of Porphyry, that it is an arbitrary selection and not a fixed number." But if Bleek wishes to support his arbitrary selection by references to the Sibylline Oracles, where also mention is made of the horns of Daniel in connection with Alexander, Hilgenfeld (*Jüd. Apokal.* p. 71 ff.) has, on the contrary, shown that this passage is derived from Daniel, and is therefore useless as a support to Bleek's hypothesis, because in it the immediate successors of Alexander are not meant, but ten kings following one another; this passage also only shows that the sibyllist had given to the number ten an interpretation regarded by Bleek himself as incompatible with the words of Daniel.

But notwithstanding the impossibility of interpreting the ten horns of the Greek world-kingdom, and notwithstanding the above-mentioned incompatibility of the statements of ch. ii. and vii. regarding the third kingdom with those of ch. viii. regarding the Medo-Persian kingdom,[2] yet, according to Kranichfeld, the identi-

[1] Justinus, *l.c.*, mentions the following, viz.: 1. Ptolemy (Egypt, Africa, Arabia); 2. Laomedon (Syria and Palestine); 3. Philotas (Cilicia); 4. Philo (Illyria); 5. Atropatos (Media Major): 6. Scynus (Susiana); 7. Antigonus (Phrygia Major); 8. Nearchus (Lycia and Pamphylia); 9. Cassander (Caria); 10. Menander (Lydia); 11. Leonatus (Phrygia Minor); 12. Lysimachus (Thracia and Pontus); 13. Eumenes (Cappadocia and Paphlagonia); 14. Taxiles (the countries between the Hydaspes and the Indus); 15. Pithon (India); 16. Extarches (Caucasus); 17. Sybirtios (Gedrosia); 18. Statanor or Stasanor (Drangiana and Aria); 19. Amyntas (Bactria); 20. Scytæus (Sogdiana); 21. Nicanor (Parthia); 22. Philippus (Hyrcania); 23. Phrataphernes (Armenia); 24. Tlepolenus (Persia); 25. Peucestes (Babylonia); 26. Archon (the Pelasgi); 27. Arcesilaus (Mesopotamia). Besides these there were other generals not named.

[2] This incompatibility Kliefoth has so conclusively (p. 245 f.) stated, that in confirmation of the above remarks we quote his words. "The bear and the panther," he says, "are related to each other as the ram and the he-goat; but how, in two visions following each other and related to each other, the one Medo-Persian kingdom could be likened to beasts so entirely different as a winged panther and a he-goat is quite inconceivable. The interpreters must help themselves by saying that the choice of the beasts is altogether arbitrary. Ch. viii. describes Medo-Persia as a kingdom comprehending two peoples united

fication of the fourth kingdom of Daniel with the Javanic world-kingdom receives a confirmation from the representation of ch. xi. and xii., particularly by the striking resemblance of the description of the fourth kingdom in ch. ii. and vii. with that of the Javanic in ch. viii. ff. "As in ch. ii. and vii. the inward discord of the fourth kingdom is predicated, so this is obviously represented in the inner hateful strife of the kingdom, of which ch. xi. 3 ff. treats; as here the discord appears as inextinguishable, so there; as to the special means also for preventing the ominous ruin, cf. ch. ii. 43 with ch. xi. 6, 17."

But is, then, this resemblance indeed so striking that it can overbalance the fundamental differences? "Of all that ch. viii. says, in vers. 5–8, 21, 22, of Macedonia, nothing at all is found in the statements of ch. ii. and vii. regarding the fourth kingdom." Kliefoth. Also the inner dissolution predicated of the fourth kingdom, ch. ii. 41 ff., which is represented by the iron and clay of the feet of the image, is fundamentally different from the strife of the prince of the south with the prince of the north represented in ch. xi. 3 ff. The mixing of iron and clay, which do not unite together, refers to two nationalities essentially different from each other, which cannot be combined into one nation by any means of human effort, but not at all to the wars and conflicts of princes (ch. xi. 3 ff.), the Ptolemies and the Seleucidæ, for the supremacy; and the attempts to combine together national individualities into one kingdom by means of the mingling together of different races by external force, are essentially different from the political marriages by which the Ptolemies and the Seleucidæ sought to establish peace and friendship with each other.[1]

together within it; but ch. vii. says regarding its third kingdom with four heads, that after an original unity it shall fall to pieces on all sides. And interpreters are compelled to meet this contradiction by explaining the four heads, some in one way, and others in another, but all equally unsuccessfully. According to ch. viii. Medo-Persia will extend itself only into three regions of the earth, while according to ch. vii. the third kingdom with its four wings will extend itself on all sides. It comes to this, therefore, that these interpreters must divide Medo-Persia in ch. ii. and ch. vii. into two kingdoms, of Media and Persia, while in ch. viii. they must recognise but one Medo-Persian kingdom."

[1] How little political marriages were characteristic of the Ptolemies and the Seleucidæ, rather how much more frequently they took place among the Romans, from the time of Sulla down to that of Diocletian, and that often in a violent way—*cum frequenti divortio et raptu gravidarum*—as a means of obtaining or holding the government, is shown from the numerous collection of cases

There is more plausibility in criticism which gives prominence to the resemblance in the description of the two violent persecutors of the people of God who arise out of the Javanic and the fourth world-kingdom, and are represented in ch. viii. as well as in ch. vii. under the figure of a little horn. "If"—for thus Kran. has formulated this resemblance—"in the fourth kingdom, according to ch. vii. 8, 11, 20, 21, 25, the heathen oppressor appears speaking insolent words against the Most High and making war with the saints, so ch. viii. 10 ff., 24, xi. 31, 36, unfolds, only more fully, in his fundamental characteristics, the same enemy; and as in ch. vii. 25 the severe oppression continues for three and a half times, so also that contemplated in ch. viii. 14 and in xii. 7, in connection with ch. xii. 1 ff. and ch. xi." On the ground of this view of the case, Delitzsch (p. 280) asks, "Is it likely that the little horn which raised itself up and persecuted the church of God is in ch. viii. Antiochus Epiphanes rising up out of the divided kingdom of Alexander, and in ch. vii., on the contrary, is a king rising up in the Roman world-kingdom? The representation of both, in their relation to Jehovah, His people, and their religion, is the same. The symbolism in ch. vii. and viii. coincides, in so far as the arch-enemy is a little horn which rises above three others." We must answer this question decidedly in the affirmative, since the difference between the two enemies is not only likely, but certain. The similarity of the symbol in ch. vii. and viii. reaches no further than that in both chapters the persecuting enemy is represented as a little horn growing gradually to greater power. But in ch. viii. 9 this little horn arises from one of the four horns of the he-goat, without doing injury to the other three horns; while in ch. vii. 8 the little horn rises up between the ten horns of the dreadful beast, and outroots three of these horns. The little horn in ch. viii., as a branch which grows out of one of these, does not increase the number of the existing horns, as that in ch. vii., which increases the number there to eleven. This distinc-

of this sort compiled by J. C. Velthusen in his treatise *Animad. ad Dan.* ii. 27–45, *imprimis de principum Romanorum connubiis ad firmandam tyrannidem inventis*, Helmst. 1783, in vol. v. of the *Comentatt. Theolog.* of Velth., edited by Kuinoel and Ruperti. Since this treatise has not received any attention from modern critics, we will quote from it the judgment which Cato passed on Cæsar's *triplex ad evertendam rempublicam inventa politicarum nuptiarum conspiratio.* His words are these: "*rem esse plane non tolerabilem, quod connubiorum lenociniis imperium collocari* (*διαμαστρωπεύεσθαι*) *cœperit, et per mulieres sese mutuo ad præfecturas, exercitus, imperia auderet introducere*" (p. 379).

tion cannot, as Kranichfeld supposes, be regarded merely as a formal difference in the figurative representation; it constitutes an essential distinction for which the use of different symbols for the representation of the world-kingdoms in ch. ii. and vii. furnishes no true analogue. By these two different images two wholly different things are compared with each other.

The representations of the four world-kingdoms in ch. ii. and in ch. vii. are only formally different,—in ch. ii. a human image, in ch. vii. four beasts,—but in reality these representations answer to each other, feature for feature, only so that in ch. vii. further outlines are added, which entirely agree with, but do not contradict, the image in ch. ii. On the contrary, in ch. vii. and viii. essential contradictions present themselves in the parallel symbols—four horns and ten horns—which cannot be weakened down to mere formal differences. As little does the description of the enemy of the people of God, portrayed as a little horn in ch. viii., correspond with that in ch. vii. The fierce and crafty king arising out of the kingdoms of Alexander's successors will become "great toward the south and toward the east and toward the pleasant land, and wax great even to the host of heaven, and cast down some of the host and of the stars to the ground; yea, he will magnify himself even to the prince of the host, and take away the daily sacrifice, and cast down the place of the sanctuary" (ch. viii. 9–12, 23–25). On the other hand, the king who rises up out of the fourth world-kingdom, who overthrows three other kings, will "speak great things against the Most High, and make war against the saints of the Most High, and prevail against them, and think to change times and laws" (ch. vii. 8, 20, 25). These two enemies resemble each other in this, that they both make war against the people of God; but they differ in that he who arises out of the third world-kingdom, extending his power toward the south and the east, *i.e.* towards Egypt and Babylon, and towards the Holy Land, shall crush some of the people of God, and by the taking away of the daily worship and the destruction of the sanctuary in Jerusalem, will rise up against God; while, on the contrary, he that shall arise out of the fourth world-kingdom will go much further. He will establish his kingdom by the destruction of three kingdoms, by great words put himself in the place of God, and as if he were God will think to change the times and the laws of men. Conformably to this, the length of time during which the persecution of these two adversaries will continue is different. The laying waste of the sanctuary by the power of the little horn arising out of the Javanic world-kingdom will continue 2300 evening-mornings (ch. viii. 14): to the power of the little horn arising out of the fourth world-kingdom the saints of the Most High must be given up for a time, two times, and half a time (ch. vii. 25). No one will be persuaded, with Kranichfeld, that these two entirely different periods of time are alike. This difference of the periods of time again appears in ch. xii. 7, 11, 12, where also the three and a half times (ver. 7) agree neither with the 1290 nor with the 1335 days. It is therefore not correct to say that in ch. viii. and vii. Antichrist, the last enemy of the church, is represented, and that the aspects of the imagery in both chapters strongly resemble each other. The very opposite is apparent as soon as one considers the contents of the description without prejudice, and does not, with Kranichfeld and others, hold merely by the details of the representation and take the husk for the kernel. The enemy in ch. viii. proceeds only so far against God that he attacks His people, removes His worship, and lays waste the sanctuary; the enemy in ch. vii. makes himself like God (לְצַד, ver. 25), thinks himself to be God, and in his madness dares even to seek to change the times and the laws which God has ordained, and which He alone has the power to change. The enemy in ch. viii. it is an abuse of words to call Antichrist; for his offence against God is not greater than the crime of Ahaz and Manasseh, who also took away the worship of the true God, and set up the worship of idols in His stead. On the other hand, it never came into the mind of an Ahaz, nor of Manasseh, nor of Antiochus Epiphanes, who set himself to put an end to the worship of God among the Jews, to put themselves in the place of God, and to seek to change times and laws. The likeness which the enemy in ch. viii., *i.e.* Antiochus Epiphanes, in his rage against the Mosaic religion and the Jews who were faithful to their law, has to the enemy in ch. vii., who makes himself like God, limits itself to the relation between the type and the antitype. Antiochus, in his conduct towards the Old Testament people of God, is only the type of Antichrist, who will arise out of the ten kingdoms of the fourth world-kingdom (ch. vii. 24) and be diverse from them, arrogate to himself the omnipotence which is given to Christ, and in this arrogance will put himself in the place of God.

The sameness of the designation given to both of these adversaries of the people of God, a "*little horn*," not only points to the relation of type and antitype, but also, as Kliefoth has justly remarked, to "intentional and definite" parallelism between the third world-kingdom (the Macedonian) and the fourth (the Roman). "On all points the changes of the fourth kingdom are described similarly to the changes which took place in the Macedonian kingdom; but in every point of resemblance also there is indicated some distinct difference, so that the Macedonian kingdom in its development comes to stand as the type and representative of the fourth kingdom, lying as yet in the far-off future." The parallelism appears in this, that in the he-goat, representing the Javanic kingdom, after the breaking of the one great horn four considerable horns come up; and the fourth beast has ten horns; and the horns in both show that out of the one kingdom four, and out of the other ten, kingdoms shall arise;—further, that as out of one of the Javanic *Diadoch* kingdoms, so also from among the ten kingdoms into which the fourth kingdom is divided, a little horn comes up; the little horn in the Javanic kingdom, however, developes itself and founds its dominion differently from that of the fourth kingdom. If one carefully considers the resemblances and the differences of this description, he cannot fail to observe "the relation of an imperfect preliminary step of heathenish ungodliness to a higher step afterwards taken," which Kran. (p. 282) seeks in a typical delineation. For the assertion of this critic, that "in the pretended typical, as in the antitypical situation, the same thoughts of the rising up against the Most High, the removal of His worship, and the destruction of the sanctuary always similarly occur," is, according to the exegetical explanation given above, simply untrue. The difference reduces itself not merely to the greater fulness with which, "not the chief hero, but the type," is treated, but it shows itself in the diversity of the thoughts; for the elevation to the place of God, and the seeking to change the times and the laws, manifests one of a higher degree of godlessness than the removing of the Jewish sacrificial worship and the desecration of the Jewish temple.

Finally, the relation of the type to the antitype appears yet more distinctly in the determining of the time which will be appointed to both enemies for their opposition to God; for, though apparently they are alike, they are in reality very differently designated, and particularly in the explanation of the angel, ch. viii. 17, 19, and in the representation of the conduct of both enemies in ch. xi. and xii., as we shall show in our exposition of these chapters.

Since, then, neither the division of the Medo-Persian kingdom into the Median and the Persian is allowable, nor the identification of the fourth kingdom, ch. ii. and vii., with the Javanic world-kingdom in ch. viii., we may regard as correct the traditional church view, that the four world-kingdoms are the Chaldean, the Medo-Persian, the Grecian, and the Roman. This opinion, which has been recently maintained by Häv., Hengst., Hofm., Auberl., Zündel, Klief., and by C. P. Caspari and H. L. Reichel, alone accords without any force or arbitrariness with the representation of these kingdoms in both visions, with each separately as well as with both together. If we compare, for instance, the two visions with each other, they are partly distinguished in this, that while Nebuchadnezzar sees the world-power in its successive unfoldings represented by *one* metallic image, Daniel, on the other hand, sees it in the form of *four* ravenous beasts; partly in this, that in ch. vii. the nature of the world-power, and its relation to the kingdom of God, is more distinctly described than in the image seen by Nebuchadnezzar, ch. ii. These diversities have their foundation in the person of the respective recipients of the revelation. Nebuchadnezzar, the founder of the world-power, sees its development in its unity and in its earthly glory. As opposed to the kingdom of God, the world-kingdoms, in all the phases of their development, form a united power of outward glory. But its splendour gradually decreases. The image with the golden head has its breast and arms of silver, its belly of brass, its legs of iron, its feet of iron and clay mixed. Thus the image stands on feet that are weak and easily broken, so that a stone rolling against them can break in pieces the whole colossus. Since, then, the image must represent four phases of the world-kingdoms following each other, they must be represented by the separate parts of the image. Beginning with the head, as denoting the first kingdom, the second kingdom is in natural order represented by the breast and arms, the third by the belly, and the fourth by the legs and feet. Since this of necessity follows from the image being that of the human body, yet in the interpretation we may not attach any weight to the circumstance that the second kingdom is represented by the breast and the two arms, and the fourth by the two legs; but this circumstance may be taken into consideration only in so far as importance is given to it by the interpretation which is furnished in the text, or as it finds corresponding importance in the vision of ch. vii.

If we thus consider now the image, ch. ii., the selection of different metals for its separate parts must be regarded as certainly designed not only to distinguish the four world-kingdoms from each other, but also at the same time to bring to view their different natures and qualities. This is evident from the interpretation in ch. ii. 39 ff., where the hardness and the crushing power of the iron, and the brittleness of the clay, are brought to view. From this intimation it is at the same time obvious that the metals are not, as Auberlen, p. 228 ff., thinks, to be viewed only as to their worth, and that by the successive depreciation of the materials—gold, silver, brass, iron, clay—a continuous decline of the world-power, or a diminution of the world-kingdoms as to their inner worth and power, is intended. Though Aub. says many things that are true and excellent regarding the downward progress of the world-development in general, the successive deterioration of humanity from paradise to the day of judgment, yet this aspect of the subject does not come here primarily before us, but is only a subordinate element in the contemplation. Daniel does not depict, as Aub. with P. Lange supposes, the world-civilisations in the world-monarchies; he does not describe "the progress from a state of nature to one of refined culture—from a natural, vigorous, solid mode of existence to a life of refinement and intellectualism, which is represented by the *eye* (ch. vii. 8) of Antichrist;" but he describes in both visions only the development of the world-power opposite to the kingdom of God, and its influence upon it in the future. If Aub. holds as the foundation of his opinion, that "gold and silver are nobler and more valuable metals, but that, on the other hand, iron and brass are infinitely more important for the cause of civilisation and culture," he has confounded two different points of view: he has made the essential worth and value of the former metals, and the purpose and use of the latter, the one point of comparison. Gold and silver are nobler and more valuable than brass and iron, yet they have less intrinsic worth. The difference is frequently noticed in the Old Testament. Gold and silver are not only more highly valued than brass and iron (cf. Isa. lx. 17), but silver and gold are also metonymically used to designate moral purity and righteousness (cf. Mal. iii. 3 with Isa. i. 22); brass and iron, on the contrary, are used to designate moral impurity (cf. Jer. vi. 28, Ezek. xxii. 18) and stubborn rebellion against God (Isa. xlviii. 4). With reference to the relative worth of the metals, their gradation in the image shows, without doubt, an increasing moral and religious deterioration of the world-kingdoms. It must not, however, be hence thought, as Auberlen does, "that the Babylonian and Persian religions presuppose more genuine truthfulness, more sacred reverence for that which is divine, deeper earnestness in contending against the evil, in the nations among whom they sprung up, than the Hellenic, which is so much richer and more beautifully developed;" for this distinction is not supported by history. But although this may be said of the Persian, it cannot be held as true of the Babylonian religion, from all we know of it. Kranichfeld (p. 107) is more correct when in the succession of the metals he finds "the thought conceived by the theocrat of a definite fourfold procedure or expression of character comparatively corresponding to them, of a fourfold דֶּרֶךְ (*way*, Jer. vi. 27) of the heathen kingdoms manifesting an increasing deterioration." The two first kingdoms, the golden and the silver, in general appear to him in their conduct as proportionally noble, virtuous, and in their relation to the theocracy even relatively pious; the two latter, on the contrary, which presented themselves to him in the likeness of brass and iron, as among the four morally base, as standing in the moral scale lower and lowest, and in relation to the theocracy as more relentless and wicked (see ver. 40[1]). With this the declaration of the text as to the position of the four world-kingdoms and their rulers with reference to the people of God stand in accord; for, on the one hand, Nebuchadnezzar, and the first rulers of the second kingdom, Darius the Median and Cyrus the Persian, respect the revelations of the living God, and not only in their own persons give honour to this God, but also command their heathen subjects to render unto Him fear and reverence; on the other hand, on the contrary, from the third and the fourth kingdoms the greatest persecutors of the kingdom of God, who wish utterly to destroy it (ch. vii., viii.), arise. In this

[1] Kliefoth (p. 93) in a similar manner says, "From the application which in ch. ii. 40 is made of the iron material, we see that the substances representing the different kingdoms, and their deterioration from the gold down to the iron, must denote something else than that the world-power, in the course of its historical formation, will become always baser and more worthless—that also its more tender or more cruel treatment of the nations, and of the men subdued by it, must be characterized. If the bonds which the Babylonian world-monarchy wound around the nations which were brought into subjection to it, by its very primitive military and bureaucratic regulations, were loose, gentle, pliable as a golden ring, those of the Medo-Persian were of harder silver, those of the Macedonian of yet harder copper, but the yoke of the fourth will be one of iron."

respect the two first world-kingdoms, seen in their rulers, are like gold and silver, the two latter like copper and iron.

The relation of the world-kingdoms to the kingdom and people of God, represented by this gradation of the metals, corresponds only to the Babylonian, Medo-Persian, Grecian, and Roman world-kingdoms, but not to the Babylonian, Median, and Persian. This appears more manifest in the representation of them by four ravenous beasts, the lion, the bear, the leopard, and another beast to which no likeness can be found, ch. vii. Its eagle's wings were torn from the lion, and it had given to it, by God, a man's heart; the bear shows only wild voracity,—holding its prey between its teeth, it raises its one side for new prey; the leopard with four heads and four wings springs forward as in flight over the whole earth, to seize it and to exercise dominion over it; the fourth nameless beast devours and breaks in pieces with its iron teeth all that remains, and stamps upon it with its iron feet, and thus represents godless barbarity in its fullest development. But for the historical interpretation there comes yet particularly into view the circumstance that the fourth beast is represented by no animal existing in nature, and is designated by no historical name, as in the case of the first (ch. ii. 38) and the second and third (ch. viii. 20, 21); for the two first had already come into existence in Daniel's time, and of the third, the people at least out of whom it was to arise had then already come into relation to the people of Israel (Joel iv. 6, 8). The fourth kingdom, on the contrary, is represented by a nameless beast, because in Daniel's time Rome had not come into contact with Israel, and as yet lay beyond the circle of vision of Old Testament prophecy. Although Daniel receives much more special revelations regarding this world-kingdom (ch. vii.) than Nebuchadnezzar does in his dream (ch. ii.), yet all the separate lines of the representation of the beast and its horns are given with so much want of precision that every reference to a historical people is at fault, and from the vision and its interpretation it was not to be known where this kingdom would arise, whether in Asia or elsewhere. The strength of the monster, devouring and trampling mercilessly on all things, is in harmony with its iron nature, and in its ten horns its powerful armour is depicted. The very concrete expressions regarding the little or eleventh horn contain only ideal traces respecting the position of the king or kingdom represented by it, which distinctly show, indeed, the elevation of the same above all human and divine authority, but give no indication at all of any special historical connections.

Thus it appears that the two visions, on the one hand, do not copy their prophetic representation from historical facts, that the prophecy is not *vaticinium ex eventu;* but, on the other hand, also that it is not derived from general ideas, as Hitz. and Kran. have attempted to show. While Hitzig thinks that the idea of the four ages of the world lies at the foundation, not of the fourfoldness of the monarchies, but of the kind of representation given of them in Dan. ii.,—an idea which came from India to Greece, and was adopted by Daniel in its Greek form,—Kranichfeld considers that, under divine enlightenment, Daniel delineated the ideal of the advancing completion of heathen depravation in four stages (not in five, six, etc.), after the notion of the four ages of the world which we find not only in the Indian four *jugas*, but also in the Greco-Roman representation of the metallic æons. Now although for this book of Daniel no special dependence on the Greeks can be proved from the use and value of the metals, because they were used by the ancient Hebrews as metaphorical symbols, yet the combination of the idea of the ages of the world so firmly and definitely stamped with just the number four remains a very noteworthy phenomenon, which must have had a deeper foundation lying in the very fact itself. This foundation, he concludes, is to be sought in the four stages of the age of man.

This conjecture might appear plausible if Kranichfeld had proved the supposed four stages of the age of man as an idea familiar to the O. T. He has not, however, furnished this proof, but limited himself to the remark, that the combination of the number four with the ages of the life of man was one lying very near to Daniel, since the four phases of the development of heathenism come into view (ch. ii.) in the image of a human being, the personification of heathendom. A very marvellous conclusion indeed! What, then, have the four parts of the human figure—the head, breast, belly, feet—in common with the four stages of the age of man? The whole combination wants every point of support. The idea of the development of the world-power in four kingdoms following after each other, and becoming continually the more oppressive to the people of God, has no inward connection with the representation of the four ages of the world, and—as even Ewald (*Dan.* p. 346), in opposition to this combination, remarks—"the mere comparison with gold, silver, brass, iron lies too near for the author of this book to need to borrow it from Hesiod." The agreement of the two ideas in the number four (although Hesiod has inserted the age of the heroes between the brazen and the iron æon, and thus has not adhered to the number four) would much more readily have been explained from the symbolical meaning of *four* as the number of the world, if it were the mere product of human speculation or combination in the case of the world-ages as of the world-kingdoms, and not much rather, in the case of the world-ages, were derived from the historical development of humanity and of Daniel's world-kingdoms, from divine revelation. Yet much less are the remaining declarations regarding the development and the course of the world-kingdoms to be conceived of as the product of enlightened human thought. This may be said of the general delineation of the second and third world-kingdoms (ch. ii. and vii.), and yet much more of the very special declaration regarding them in ch. viii., but most of all of the fourth world-kingdom. If one wished to deduce the fearful power of this kingdom destroying all things from the idea of the rising up of hostility against that which is divine, closely bound up with the deterioration of the state of the world, and to attach importance to this, that the number ten of the horns of the fourth beast, corresponding to the number of the toes of the feet, is derived from the apprehension of heathendom as the figure of a man, and is not to be understood numerically, but symbolically; yet there remains, not to mention other elements, the growth of the little horn between the ten existing horns, and its elevation to power through the destruction of three existing horns, which are deduced neither from the symbolical meaning of the numbers nor are devised by enlightened human thought, but much rather constrain us to a recognition of an immediate divine revelation.

If we now approach more closely to the historical reference of the fourth world-kingdom, it must be acknowledged that we cannot understand by it the Grecian, but only the Roman world-power. With it, not with the Macedonian monarchy, agree both the iron nature of the image (ch. ii.), and the statements (ch. vii. 23) that this kingdom would be different from all that preceded it, and that it would devour and break and trample upon the whole earth. The Roman kingdom was the first universal monarchy in the full sense. Along with the three earlier world-kingdoms, the nations of the world-historical future remained still unsubdued: along with the

Oriental kingdoms, Greece and Rome, and along with the Macedonian, the growing power of Rome.

First the Roman kingdom spread its power and dominion over the whole οἰκουμένη, over all the historical nations of antiquity in Europe, Africa, and Asia. "There is" (says Herodian, ii. 11. 7) "no part of the earth and no region of the heavens whither the Romans have not extended their dominion." Still more the prophecy of Daniel reminds us of the comparison of the Roman world-kingdom with the earlier world-kingdoms, the Assyrico-Babylonian, the Persian, and the Grecian, in Dionys. Halicar., when in the *proœm.* 9 he says: "These are the most famous kingdoms down to our time, and this their duration and power. But the kingdom of the Romans ruled through all the regions of the earth which are not inaccessible, but are inhabited by men; it ruled also over the whole sea, and it alone and first made the east and the west its boundaries." Concerning the other features of the image in ch. ii., we can seek neither (see p. 261) in the two legs and feet of the image, nor in the twofold material of the feet, any hint as to the division of the Roman kingdom into the Eastern and Western Rome. The iron and clay are in the image indeed not so divided as that the one foot is of iron and the other of clay, but iron and clay are bound together in both of the feet. In this union of two heterogeneous materials there also lies no hint that, by the dispersion of the nations, the plastic material of the Germanic and the Sclavic tribes was added to the Old Roman universal kingdom (ver. 40) with its thoroughly iron nature (Auberl. p. 252, cf. with Hof. *Weiss. u. Erf.* i. p. 281). For the clay in the image does not come into view as a malleable and plastic material, but, according to the express interpretation of Daniel (ver. 42), only in respect of its brittleness. The mixing of iron and clay, which do not inwardly combine together, shows the inner division of the nations, of separate natural stocks and national characters, which constituted the Roman empire, who were kept together by external force, whereby the iron firmness of the Roman nation was mingled with brittle clay.

The kingdoms represented by the ten horns belong still to the future. To be able to judge regarding them with any certainty, we must first make clear to ourselves the place of the Messianic kingdom with reference to the fourth world-kingdom, and then compare the prophecy of the Apocalypse of John regarding the formation of the world-power—a prophecy which rests on the book of Daniel.

The Messianic Kingdom and the Son of Man.

In the image of the monarchies, ch. ii., the everlasting kingdom of God is simply placed over against the kingdoms of the world without mention being made of the king of this kingdom. The human image is struck and broken to pieces by a stone rolling down against its feet, but the stone itself grows into a great mountain and fills the whole earth (ch. ii. 34 ff.). This stone is a figure of that kingdom which the God of heaven will erect in the days of the kings of the fourth world-kingdom; a kingdom which to all eternity shall never be destroyed, and which shall crush all the kingdoms of the world (ch. ii. 44). In ch. vii., on the contrary, Daniel sees not only the judgment which God holds over the kingdoms of the world, to destroy them for ever with the death of their last ruler, but also the deliverance of the kingdom to the Messiah coming with the clouds of heaven in the likeness of a son of man, whom all nations shall serve, and whose dominion shall stand for ever (ch. vii. 9–14, cf. ver. 26 f.).

In both visions the Messianic kingdom appears in its completion. Whence Auberlen (p. 248), with other chiliasts, concludes that the beginning of this kingdom can refer to nothing else than to the coming of Christ for the founding of the so-called kingdom of the thousand years; an event still imminent to us. In favour of this view, he argues (1) that the judgment on Antichrist, whose appearance is yet future, goes before the beginning of this kingdom; (2) that this kingdom in both chapters is depicted as a kingdom of glory and dominion, while till this time the kingdom of heaven on the earth is yet a kingdom of the cross. But the judgment on Antichrist does not altogether go before the beginning of this kingdom, but only before the final completion of the Messianic kingdom; and the Messianic kingdom has the glory and dominion over all the kingdoms under heaven, according to ch. ii. and vii., not from the beginning, but acquires them only for the first time after the destruction of all the world-kingdoms and of the last powerful enemy arising out of them. The stone which breaks the image becomes for the first time after it has struck the image a great mountain which fills the whole earth (ch. ii. 35), and the kingdom of God is erected by the God of heaven, according to ch. ii. 44, not for the first time after the destruction of all the world-kingdoms, but in the days of the kings of the fourth world-monarchy, and thus during its continuance.

With this ch. vii. harmonizes; for, according to vers. 21, 22, 25, 27, the little horn of the fourth beast carries on war with the saints of the Most High till the Ancient of days executes judgment in their behalf, and the time arrives when the saints shall possess the kingdom. Here we distinctly see the kingdom of heaven upon earth bearing the form of the cross, out of which condition it shall be raised by the judgment into the state of glory. The kingdom of the Messiah is thus already begun, and is warred against by Antichrist, and the judgment on Antichrist only goes before the raising of it to glory. (3) Auberlen adduces as a third argument, that (according to Roos, Hofm., etc.) only the people of Israel in opposition to the heathen nations and kingdoms can be understood by the "people of the saints of the Most High" (ch. vii. 18, 27), because Daniel could only think of this people. But to this Kranichfeld has rightly replied, that Daniel and the whole O. T. knew nothing whatever of such a distinction between a non-Israelitish and an Israelitish epoch within the kingdom of Messiah, but only a Messianic kingdom in which Israel forms the enduring centre for the heathen believing nations drawing near to them. To this we add, that the division of the kingdom of heaven founded by Christ on the earth into a period of the church of the Gentiles, and following this a period of a thousand years of the dominion of Jewish Christians, contradicts the clear statements of Christ and the apostles in the N. T., and is only based on a misconception of a few passages of the Apocalypse (cf. *Comm. on Ezek.* p. 504 ff.).

Daniel certainly predicts the completion of the kingdom of God in glory, but he does not prophesy that the kingdom of heaven will then for the first time begin, but indicates its beginnings in a simple form, although he does not at large represent its gradual development in the war against the world-power, just as he also gives only a few brief intimations of the temporary development of the world-kingdoms. If Aub. (p. 251) replies that the words of the text, ch. ii. 35, "then was the iron, the clay, the brass, the silver, and the gold broken to pieces together," cannot at all permit the thought of the co-existence of the fourth world-kingdom and the kingdom of God, he attributes to these words a meaning which they do not bear. The "*together*" refers only to the breaking in pieces of the five substances named, of which the world-kingdoms are formed, the destruction of the world-power in all its parts, but not that this happened at one and the same moment, and that then for the first time the kingdom of God which is from heaven began. The stone which brake the image in pieces, then first, it is true, grows up into a great mountain filling the whole earth. The destruction of the world-kingdoms can in reality proceed only gradually along with the growth of the stone, and thus also the kingdom of God can destroy the world-kingdoms only by its gradual extension over the earth. The destruction of the world-power in all its component parts began with the foundation of the kingdom of heaven at the appearance of Christ upon earth, or with the establishment of the church of Christ, and only reaches its completion at the second coming of our Lord at the final judgment. In the image Daniel saw in a moment, as a single act, what in its actual accomplishment or in its historical development extends through the centuries of Christendom. Auberlen has in his argument identified the image with the actual realization, and has not observed that his conception of the words ch. ii. 35 does not accord with the millennium, which according to Rev. xx. does not gradually from small beginnings spread itself over the earth—is not to be likened to a stone which first after the destruction of the world-kingdom grows up into a mountain.

So also in ch. vii. Daniel sees the judgment of the world-kingdoms in the form of an act limited to a point of time, by which not only the beast whose power culminates in the little horn is killed, but also the dominion and the kingdom over all nations is given over to the Son of man coming in the clouds of heaven and appearing before God the Judge. If one here identifies the form of the prophetic vision with the actual fact, then he places Daniel in opposition to the teaching of the N. T. regarding the judgment of the world. According to N. T. doctrine, Christ, the Son of man, receives the dominion and power over all nations not for the first time on the day of judgment, after the destruction of the world-kingdoms by the Father, but He received it (Matt. xxviii. 18) after the completion of His work and before His ascension; and it is not God the Father who holds the judgment, but the Son raised to the right hand of the Father comes in the clouds of heaven to judge the world (Matt. xxv. 31). The Father committed the judgment to the Son even while He yet sojourned on this earth in the form of a servant and founded the kingdom of heaven (John v. 27). The judgment begins not for the first time either before or after the millennium, about which chiliasts contend with one another, but the last judgment forms only the final completion of the judgment commencing at the first coming of Christ to the earth, which continues from that time onward through the centuries of the spread of the kingdom of heaven upon earth in the form of the Christian church, till the visible return of Christ in His glory in the clouds of heaven to the final judgment of the living and the dead. This doctrine is disclosed to us for the first time by the appearance of Christ; for by it are unfolded to us for the first time the prophecies regarding the Messiah in His lowliness and in His glory, in the clear knowledge of the first appearance of Christ in the form of a servant for the founding of the kingdom of God by His death and resurrection, and the return of the Son of man from heaven in the glory of His Father for the perfecting of His kingdom by the resurrection of the dead and the final judgment.

That which has been said above, avails also for explaining the revelation which Daniel received regarding the King of the kingdom of God. While His appearance in the form of a son of man with the clouds of heaven, according to the statements of the N. T. regarding the second coming of Christ, points to His coming again in glory, yet, as above remarked, His coming before the Ancient of days, *i.e.* before God, and receiving from God the kingdom and the dominion, does not accord with the statements of the N. T. regarding the return of Christ to judge the world; so that we must here also distinguish between the actual contents and the form of the prophetic representation, and between the thought of the prophecy and its realization or historical fulfilment. Only because of a disregard of this distinction could Fries, *e.g.*, derive from Dan. vii. 13 an argument against the parallelizing of this passage with Matt. xxiv. 30, Mark xiv. 62, and Rev. i. 7, as well as against the reference to the Messias of the personage seen by Daniel in the clouds of heaven as a son of man.

In the vision, in which the Ancient of days, *i.e.* God, holds judgment over the world and its rulers, and in the solemn assembly for judgment grants to the Son of man appearing before Him the kingdom and the dominion, only this truth is contemplated by the prophet, that the Father gave to the Son all power in heaven and in earth; that He gave the power over the nations which the rulers of the earth had, and which they used only for the oppression of the saints of God, to the Son of man, and in Him to the people of the saints, and thereby founded the kingdom which shall endure for ever. But as to the way and manner in which God executes judgment over the world-power, and in which He gives (ch. vii. 22, 27) to the Son of man and to the people of the saints the dominion and the power over all the kingdoms under the heavens—on this the prophecy gives no particular disclosures; this much, however, is clear from ver. 27, that the judgment held by the Ancient of days over the world-power which was hostile to God is not a full annihilation of the kingdoms under the whole heavens, but only an abolition of their hostile dominion and power, and a subjection of all the kingdoms of this earth to the power and dominion of the Son of man, whereby the hostile rulers, together with all ungodly natures, shall be for ever destroyed. The further disclosures regarding the completion of this judgment are given us in the N. T., from which we learn that the Father executes judgment by the Son, to whom He has given all power in heaven and on earth. With this further explanation of the matter the passages of the N. T. referring to Dan. vii. 13, regarding the coming of the Son of man in the clouds of heaven to execute judgment over the world, easily harmonize. To show this, we must examine somewhat more closely the conception and the use of the words "Son of man" in the N. T.

The Son of Man, ὁ υἱὸς τοῦ ἀνθρώπου.

It is well known that Jesus only during His sojourn on earth made use of this designation of Himself, as appears in the N. T. Bengel on Matt. xvi. 13 remarks: "*Nemo nisi solus Christus a nemine dum ipse in terra ambularet, nisi a semetipso appellitatus est filius hominis.*" Even after Christ's ascension the apostles do not use this name of Christ. In the passages Acts vii. 56 and Rev. i. 13, xiv. 14, where alone it is found in the N. T. beyond the Gospels, the title is borrowed from Dan. vii. 13. It is, moreover, generally acknowledged that Jesus wished by thus designating Himself to point Himself out as the Messiah; and "this pointing Himself out as the Messiah is founded," as H. A. W. Meyer on Matt. viii. 20 rightly remarks, "not on Ps. viii., but, as is manifest from such passages as Matt. xxiv. 30, xxvi. 64 (cf. also Acts vii. 56), on the description of that prophetic vision, Dan. vii. 13, well known to the Jews (John xii. 34), and found also in the pre-Christian book of Enoch, where the Messiah appears in the clouds of heaven כְּבַר אֱנָשׁ = ὡς υἱὸς ἀνθρώπου, amid the angels of the divine judgment-seat." The comparison in the כְּ = ὡς to a son of man refers to the form in which He is seen by the prophet (see p. 234), and affirms neither the true humanity nor the superhuman nature of Him who appeared. The superhuman or divine nature of the person seen in the form of a man lies in the coming with the clouds of heaven, since it is true only of God that He makes the clouds His chariot; Ps. civ. 3, cf. Isa. xix. 1. But on the other hand, also, the words do not exclude the humanity, as little as the ὅμοιος υἱῷ ἀνθρώπου, Rev. i. 13; for, as C. B. Michaelis has remarked, כְּ *non excludit rei veritatem, sed formam ejus quod visum est describit;* so that with Oehler (Herz. *Realenc.*) we may say: The Messiah here appears as a divine being as much as He does a human. The union of the divine and the human natures lies also in the self-designation of Christ as ὁ υἱὸς τοῦ ἀνθρώπου, although as to the meaning Jesus unites with it there is diversity of opinion.

That this was a designation of the Messiah common among the Jews in the time of Jesus, we cannot positively affirm, because only Jesus Himself made use of it; His disciples did not, much less did the people so style the Messiah. If, then, Jesus speaks of Himself as the Son of man, He means thereby not merely to say that He was the Messiah, but He wishes to designate Himself as the Messiah of Daniel's prophecy, *i.e.* as the Son of man coming to the earth in the clouds of heaven. He thereby lays claim at once to a divine original, or a divine pre-existence, as well as to affirm true humanity of His person, and seeks to represent Himself, according to John's expression, as the Logos becoming flesh.[1] This view of the expression will be confirmed by a comparison of the passages in which Jesus uses it. In John i. 51, "Hereafter ye shall see heaven open, and the angels of God ascending and descending upon the Son of man," the divine glory is intimated

[1] Meyer justly remarks: "The consciousness from which Jesus appropriates to Himself this designation by Daniel was the antithesis of the *God*-sonship, the necessary (contrary to Schleiermacher) self-consciousness of a divine pre-existence appearing in the most decided manner in John, the glory (δόξα) of which He had laid aside that He might appear as that ὡς υἱὸς ἀνθρώπου of Daniel in a form not originally appertaining to Him. . . Whatever has, apart from this, been found in the expression, as that Christ hereby designated Himself *as the Son of man in the highest sense* of the word, as the second Adam, as the ideal of humanity (Böhme, Neander, Ebrard, Olsh., Kahnis, Gess, and Weisse), or as *the* man whom the whole history of mankind since Adam *has in view* (Hofm. *Schriftbew.* ii. 1, p. 81, cf. Thomas. Chr. *Pers. u. Werk*, ii. p. 15), is introduced unhistorically with reference to Dan. vii."

as concealed in the lowliness of the Son of man: the Son of man who walks on the earth in the form of a man is the Son of God. So also in the answer which Jesus gave to the high priest, when he solemnly adjured Him to say " whether He were the Christ, the Son of God" (Matt. xxvi. 63), pointing distinctly to Dan. vii. 13, " Hereafter shall ye see the Son of man sitting on the right hand of power, and coming in the clouds of heaven." In like manner in all the other passages in the Gospels in which Jesus designates Himself the Son of man, He points either to His present lowliness or to His future glory, as is abundantly proved by Fr. A. Philippi (*Kirch. Glaubenslehre*, iv. 1, p. 415, der 2 Aufl.) by a lucid comparison of all the passages in the Gospel of Matthew.

From the use of the expression "the Son of man" by Jesus (not only where He refers to His supernatural greatness or His divine pre-existence, but also where He places His human lowliness in contrast with His divine nature), it follows that even in those passages which treat of His coming to judgment, connected with the description, borrowed from Dan. vii. 13, of His coming in the clouds of heaven, He seeks to prove not so much His appearance for judgment, as rather only the divine power and glory which the Father gave Him, or to indicate from the Scriptures that the Father gave Him dominion over all people, and that He will come to reveal this dominion by the judgment of the world and the completion of His kingdom. The power to execute judgment over the living and the dead, the Father, *i.e.* God as the Lord of the world, has given to His Son, to Christ, because He is the Son of man (John v. 27), *i.e.* because He as man is at the same time of a divine nature, by virtue of which He is of one essence with the Father. This truth is manifested in the vision, Dan. vii. 13, 14, in this, that the Ancient of days gives glory and the kingdom to Him who appears before Him in the form of a man coming in the clouds of heaven, that all people and nations might honour Him. Therewith He gave Him also *implicite* the power to execute judgment over all peoples; for the judgment is only a disclosure of the sovereignty given to Him.

The giving of the kingdom to the Son of man goes before the appearance of the great adversary of the people of God represented by the little horn—the adversary in whom the enmity of the world against the kingdom of God reaches its highest manifestation. But to form a well-founded judgment regarding the appearance of this last enemy, we must compare the description given of him in Dan. vii. 8, 24 f. with the apocalyptic description of the same enemy under the image of the *beast out of the sea* or *out of the abyss*, Rev. xiii. 1–8 and xvii. 7–13.

John saw a BEAST RISE UP OUT OF THE SEA which had seven heads and ten horns, and on its horns ten crowns; it was like a leopard, but had the feet of a bear and the mouth of a lion, and the dragon gave him his throne and great power. One of its heads appears as if it had received a deadly wound, but its deadly wound was healed, Rev. xiii. 1-3. In this beast the four beasts of Daniel, the lion, the bear, the leopard, and the nameless ten-horned beast (Dan. vii. 7), are united, and its heads and horns are represented, like the beasts of Daniel, as kings (Rev. xvii. 9, 12). The beast seen by John represents accordingly the world-power, in such a way that the four aspects of the same, which Daniel saw in the form of four beasts rising up one after another, are a whole united together into one. In this all interpreters are agreed. Hofmann is wrong (*Schriftbew.* ii. 2, p. 699), however, when from the circumstance that this beast has the body of a leopard, has its peculiar form like that of a leopard, he draws the conclusion "that John sees the Grecian kingdom rise again in a new form, in which it bears the lion's mouth of the Chaldean, the bear's feet of the Median or Persian, and the ten horns of the last kingdom." For the apocalyptic beast has the body of a leopard from no other reason than because the fourth beast of Daniel was to be compared with no other beast existing in nature, whose appearance could be selected for that purpose. In these circumstances nothing else remained than to lay hold on the form of Daniel's third beast and to make choice of it for the body of the beast, and to unite with it the feet, the mouth or the jaws, and the ten horns of the other beasts.

But that the apocalyptic beast must represent not the rising again of Daniel's third world-kingdom, but the appearance of the fourth, and that specially in its last form, which Daniel had seen as the little horn, appears evidently from this, not to mention the explanation given in Rev. xvii., that the beast with the seven heads and ten horns, with the name of blasphemy on its heads (Rev. xiii. 1), the marks of the little horn of Daniel, speaks great things and blasphemies, and continues forty and two months (ch. xiii. 5), corresponding to the three and a half times of Daniel, ch. vii. 25. Hofmann, on the other hand, rightly remarks, that the beast must represent not merely the last world-power, but at the same time the last world-ruler, the chief enemy of the saints of God. As with Daniel the world-power and its representative are conceived of as one and the same, so here also with John. This is seen in the insensible transition of the neuter to the masculine, *τῷ θηρίῳ ὅς ἔχει*, ver. 14. In this beast not only does the whole world-power concentrate itself, but in it also attains to its personal head. The ten horns are to be conceived of as on one of the heads, and that the seventh or last, and not (Düsterdieck, etc.) as distributed among the seven heads, so that one horn should be assigned to each head, and three horns should be conceived as between the sixth and the seventh head. This wonderful supposition owes its origin only to the historical reference of the beast to the first Roman emperor, and stands in opposition to the interpretation of the beast which is given by John, ch. xvii. 7 ff. There John sees the woman, the great Babylon, the mother of harlots and abominations, sitting on a scarlet-coloured beast, which was full of names of blasphemy, and had ten horns (ch. xvii. 3). The identity of the seven-headed beast (ch. xiii.) with the scarlet-coloured beast (ch. xvii.) is justly recognised by the greater number of recent interpreters, even by Düst. Of this red beast the angel, ch. xvii. 8, says first, "The beast that thou sawest was (*ἦν*) and is not, and shall ascend out of the bottomless pit and go into perdition; and they that dwell on the earth shall wonder . . . when they behold the beast that was and is not, and yet is" (*καὶ πάρεσται* = shall come, be present, *i.e.* again, according to a more accurate reading). In these words the most of interpreters find a paraphrase of the statement, ch. xiii. 3, 12, 14, that the beast was wounded to the death, but that its deadly wound was healed. "The distinguishing of the two statements (viz. of the not-being and the death-wound, the coming again and the healing of the wound) has," as A. Christiani (*uebersichtl. Darstellung des Inhalts der Apok.*, in der *Dorpater Zeitschrift f. Theol.* 1861, iii. p. 219) rightly remarks, "its foundation (against Ebrard) either in the false supposition that the beast in ch. xvii. is different from that in ch. xiii., or in this, that there must abstractly be a distinction between the world-power (ch. xiii.) and the ruler of the world (ch. xvii.); whereby, moreover, it is not clear wherein the difference between the death-wound and the not-being consists (against Aub.)." The being, the not-being, and the appearing again of the beast, are not to be understood of the present time as regards the seer, so as to mean: the beast existed before John's time, after that it was not, and then one day shall again appear, which has been combined with the fable of Nero's coming again; but the past, the present, and the future of the beast are, with Vitringa, Bengel, Christ., to be regarded from the standpoint of the vision, according to which the time of the fulfilment, belonging to the future, is to be regarded as the point of time from which the being, the not-being, and the appearing again are represented, so that these three elements form the determination of the nature of the beast in its historical manifestation.

Hereupon the angel points out to the seer the secret of the woman and of the beast which bears the woman, beginning with the interpretation of the beast, ch. xvii. 9. "The seven heads are seven mountains, on which the woman sitteth; and there are seven kings." The heads are thus defined in a twofold way: For the woman they are seven mountains, on which she sits; but in so far as they belong to the beast, they are seven kings (Hofm. p. 711, Christ., etc.). The reference of the mountains to the seven hills of Rome is to be rejected, because it is difficult to understand how the heads can represent at one and the same time both mountains and kings. Mountains are, according to the prophetic view, seats of power, symbols of world-kingdoms (cf. Ps. lxviii. 17, lxxvi. 5; Jer. li. 25; Ezek. xxxv. 2), and thus are here as little to be thought of as occupying space along with one another as are the seven kings to be thought of as contemporaneous (Hofm., Aub.). According to this, the *βασιλεῖς* are not also separate kings of one kingdom, but kingships, dominions, as in Daniel ruler and kingdom are taken together. One need not, however, on this account assume that *βασιλεῖς* stands for *βασιλεῖαι*; for, according to Dan. viii. 20–22, "the kingdom is named where the person of the ruler is at once brought into view; but where it is sought to designate the sovereignty, then the king is named, either so that he represents it altogether, or so that its founder is particularly distinguished" (Hofm. p. 714).

The angel further says of the seven heads: "Five (of these sovereignties) are fallen," *i.e.* are already past, "one is," *i.e.* still exists, "the other is not yet come; and when it cometh, it must continue a short space." This explanation is obviously given from the point of view of the present of the seer. The five fallen *βασιλεῖς* (sovereignties) are Egypt, Assyria, Babylonia, Medo-Persia, and Greece (Hengst., Aub., Christ.), and not Assyria, Chaldea, Persia, Grecia, and the kingdom of the Seleucidæ, as Hofmann, with Ebrard and Stier, affirms. The reception of the Seleucidæ or of Antiochus Epiphanes into the rank of world-rulers, depends, with Hofmann, on the erroneous interpretation of the apocalyptic beast-image as representing the reappearance of the Grecian world-kingdom, and falls with this error. The chief argument which Hofmann alleges against Egypt, that it was never a power which raised itself up to subdue or unite the world under itself, or is thus represented in the Scriptures, Aub. (p. 309) has already invalidated by showing that Egypt was the first world-power with which the kingdom of God came into conflict under Moses, when it began to exist as a nation and a kingdom. Afterwards, under the kings, Israel was involved in the wars of Egypt and Assyria in like manner as at a later period they were in those of the Ptolemies and the Seleucidæ. For this reason Egypt and Assyria are often named together by the prophets, particularly as the world-powers with which the people of God committed whoredom, yea, by the older prophets generally as the representatives of the world-power (2 Kings xvii. 4; Hos. vii. 11, xii. 1, ix. 3, xi. 5, 11; Micah vii. 12; Isa. lii. 4, xix. 23–25; Jer. ii. 18, 36; Zech. x. 10). On the other hand, the Seleucidan appears before us in Dan. viii. and xi. 1–35 as an offshoot of the Grecian world-kingdom, without anything further being intimated regarding him. In Dan. vii. there is as little said of him as there is in Zechariah's vision of the four-horsed chariots.

The sixth sovereignty, which "is" (*ὁ εἷς ἔστιν*), is the Roman world-power exercising dominion at the time of John, the Roman emperor. The seventh is as yet future (*οὔπω ἦλθεν*), and must, when it comes, continue a short time (*ὀλίγον*). If the sixth sovereignty is the Roman, then by the seventh we may understand the world-powers of modern Europe that have come into its place. The angel adds (ver. 11), "The beast that was and is not, even he is the eighth (king), and is of the seven, and goeth into perdition." By that which is called "even the eighth" can properly be meant only the seventh. The contrast lying in the *καὶ αὐτὸς ὄγδοός* demands this. But that instead of the seventh (ver. 10, *ὁ ἄλλος*) the beast itself is named, therewith it is manifestly intimated that in the eighth the beast embodies itself, or passes into its completed form of existence as a beast. This is supported partly by the expression ἐκ τῶν ἑπτά which is added to ὀγδοός, partly by the designation as "the beast that was and is not." That addition does not merely say, one out of the seven, for which John would have written εἷς ἐκ τῶν ἑπτά (cf. ch. xvii. 1 and xxi. 9), or, formed like the seven, but, growing up out of the seven, as the blossom out of the plant (βλαστάνων, as the Greek Andreas explains, and erroneously adds ἐκ μίας αὐτῶν). It is the comprehensive essence of these seven, the embodiment of the beast itself, which for the first time reaches in it to its perfect form (Aub., Düsterd., Christ.). As such it is placed over against the seven as the eighth; but it is not therefore an eighth kingdom, for it is not represented by an eighth head, but only by the beast—only the beast which was, and is not, and then shall be again (πάρεσται, ver. 11, cf. ver. 8). If now this definition, according to the above, means the same thing as is intended in ch. xiii. by the deadly wound of the beast and the healing again of the wound, then these words mean that the world-power in one of its heads (the seventh?) receives the deadly wound, so that the beast *is not*—*i.e.* it cannot show its power, its beast-nature—till the healing of the same, but after the healing of the wound it will appear as the eighth ruler in its full nature as a beast, and will unfold the power of its ten horns. Of these ten horns the angel says, ver. 12, "They are ten kings which have received no βασιλείαν, but will receive power as kings one hour with the beast." By this it is affirmed, on the one side, that the ten horns belong to the seventh beast; but, on the other, it appears from this interpretation of the angel, taken in connection with that going before, that the ruler with the ten horns growing up as the eighth out of the seven represents the last and the highest phases of the development of the world-power, and is to be regarded as contemporary with the ten βασιλεῖς which receive power as kings with the beast.

The statement, however, that the seventh ruler is also an eighth, and must represent the beast in its perfect form, without his being denoted by an eighth head to the beast, has its foundation, without doubt, in the dependence of the apocalyptic delineation on Daniel's prophecy of the fourth world-power, in which (ch. ii.) the iron legs are distinguished from the feet, which consist partly of iron and partly of clay; and yet more distinctly in ch. vii. the climax of the power of the fourth beast is represented in the little horn growing up between its ten horns, and yet neither is it called in ch. ii. a fifth kingdom, nor yet in ch. vii. is the little horn designated as a fifth world-ruler.

The apocalyptic delineation of the world-power and the world-ruler is related, therefore, to the prophecy of Daniel in such a manner that, in the first place, it goes back to the elements of the same, and gathers them together into one combined image, according to its whole development in the past, present, and future, while Daniel's prophecy goes forth from the present, beginning with the Chaldean world-kingdom. Moreover, the Apocalypse discloses the spiritual principle working in the world-power. The dragon, *i.e.* Satan, as prince of this world, gave his throne and his power to the beast. Finally, the Apocalypse extends itself at large over the unfolding, as yet future, of the ungodly world-kingdom; for it places in view, in addition to the sixth ruler existing in the presence of the seer, the rising up of yet a seventh, in which the beast, healed of its death-wound, will first as the eighth ruler fully reveal its ungodly nature. The dividing of the fourth world-kingdom of Daniel between two rulers has its foundation in the purpose to gain the significant number seven. By the number seven of the heads, while Daniel saw only four beasts, the apocalyptic beast must be represented as the diabolical contrast to the Lamb. The seven heads and ten horns the beast has in common with the dragon, which gave his power to the beast (cf. Rev. xiii. 1, 2 with xii. 3). The seven heads of the dragon and of the beast are the infernal caricature and the antithesis of the seven Spirits of God, the seven eyes and seven horns of the Lamb (Rev. v. 6), just as the seven mountains on which the woman sits are the antitype and the antithesis of the hill of Zion, the chosen mountain of the Lord. (Cf. Lämmert, *Babel, das Thier u. der falsche Prophet*, 1863, p. 84.) From the symbolical signification of the numbers, it is also clear how the beast which was and is not can also appear as the eighth ruler. The eighth, arising from the addition of one to seven, denotes a new beginning, or the beginning of a new life, as frequently in the laws relating to religious worship, as *e.g.* regarding circumcision, the consecration of priests, the purification of lepers, the eight days of the Feast of Tabernacles, etc. Cf. Leyrer in Herz.'s *Real. Encycl.* xviii. p. 370. According to him, the beast is called *καὶ αὐτὸς ὄγδοός* (Rev. xvii. 11), "because, although it is of the seven which hitherto have constituted the antichristian development in its completeness, a new one presumes to establish itself in self-deification, and in open rebellion against God, raising itself to the experiment of an absolute world-monarchy before the final judgment passes upon it."

As the number seven of the heads of the beast in the Apocalypse, so also the number four of the beasts rising up out of the sea in Daniel's vision comes first under consideration, according to their symbolical meaning as the number of the world. For the sake of this significance of the number four, only the four world-kingdoms are spoken of, while in the fourth there are distinctly two different phases of the development of the world-kingdom. If we look at this significance of the numbers, the difference between the representation of Daniel and that of the Apocalypse reduces itself to this, that Daniel designates the world-power simply only in opposition to the kingdom of God; the Apocalypse, on the contrary, designates it according to its concealed spiritual background, and in its antichristian form. The world-number four appears here augmented to the antichristian contrast to the divine number seven. But in both representations the beast forming the last phase of the world-kingdom has ten horns. This number also has a symbolical meaning; it is the signature of definitive completeness, of fullest development and perfection. "The ten horns are kings; for 'horn' as well as 'king' signifies might crushing, conquering" (Lämmert, p. 78). The little horn which outrooted three existing ones and entered into their place, makes, with the remaining seven, eight; but eight is seven augmented. It is therefore the beast itself in its highest power, and ripe for judgment, just as the beast which was and is not mounts up as the eighth ruler, to be destroyed, after a short period of action, by the judgment.

But while we attach a symbolical import to the numbers, we do not, however, wish to dispute that their numerical worth may not also be realized in the fulfilment. As the comparison of Daniel vii. with viii. beyond doubt shows that the second and third kingdoms which the prophet saw have historically realized themselves in the succession of the Medo-Persian and Grecian kingdoms after the Babylonian; as, moreover, in the prophetic delineation of the fourth world-kingdom the character of the Roman world-power is not to be mistaken; finally, as in the Apocalypse the first six heads of the beast are referred to the world-powers that have hitherto appeared in history: so may also the prophecy of the seven heads and of the ten horns of the beast (in Dan. and the Apoc.) perhaps yet so fulfil itself in the future, that the antichristian world-power may reach its completion in ten rulers who receive power as kings one hour with the beast, *i.e.*, as companions and helpers of Antichrist, carry on war for a while against the Lord and His saints, till at the appearance of the Lord to judgment they shall be destroyed, together with the beast and the dragon.

How indeed this part of the prophecy, relating to the last unfolding of the ungodly and antichristian world-power, shall fulfil itself, whether merely according to the symbolical meaning of the numbers, or finally also actually, the day will first make clear.

PART SECOND.—THE DEVELOPMENT OF THE KINGDOM OF GOD.

CHAP. VIII.–XII.

This Part contains three revelations which Daniel received during the reigns of Belshazzar, Darius the Mede, and Cyrus the Persian, regarding the development of the kingdom of God. After describing in the First Part the development of the world-power and its relation to the people and kingdom of God from the days of Nebuchadnezzar, its founder, down to the time of its final destruction by the perfected kingdom of God, in this Second Part it is revealed to the prophet how the kingdom of God, in war against the power and enmity of the rulers of the world, and amid severe oppressions, is carried forward to final victory and is perfected.

The first vision, ch. viii., represents what will happen to the people of God during the developments of the second and third world-kingdoms. The second revelation, ch. ix., gives to the prophet, in answer to his penitential prayer for the restoration of the ruined holy city and the desolated sanctuary, disclosures regarding the whole development of the kingdom of God, from the close of the Babylonish exile to the final accomplishment of God's plan of salvation. In the last vision, in the third year of Cyrus, ch. x.–xii., he received yet further and more special revelations regarding the severe persecutions which await the people of God for their purification, in the nearer future under Antiochus Epiphanes, and in the time of the end under the last foe, the Antichrist.

CHAP. VIII. THE ENEMY ARISING OUT OF THE THIRD WORLD-KINGDOM.

At Susa, in the province of Elam, Daniel saw in vision (vers. 1, 2) a ram with two horns, which a he-goat coming from the west, running over the earth, having a great horn on his brow, smote and destroyed (vers. 3–7). After that the goat waxed very mighty, till his great horn was broken; and in its place four notable horns grew up toward the four winds of heaven, and out of one of them there came forth a little horn, which directed its might toward the south and the east and toward the holy land, contended against the host of heaven, and magnified itself to the Prince of the heavenly host, took away the daily sacrifice, and desolated the place of the sanctuary (vers. 8–12). He then hears from an angel how long this sacrilege shall continue (vers. 13, 14). Another angel thereafter gives him an explanation (vers. 15–26) of the vision; and with a remark (ver. 27) regarding the effect of this revelation on the mind of Daniel, the chapter closes.

This vision, it is manifest from the definition of the time in ver. 1, stands in relation to the vision of the foregoing chapter, and in its contents is united to it also in so far as it gives more particular revelations regarding the relations of the second and third world-kingdoms, which are only briefly set forth in ch. vii. But notwithstanding this point of union, this chapter does not form a mere appendix to the foregoing, but gives a new revelation regarding a phase in the development of the world-power and its enmity against the people of God of which nothing is prophesied in ch. vii. The opinion that this chapter forms only an appendix to ch. vii. is based on the erroneous idea that the fourth world-kingdom, the Macedonian, and the little horn in ch. vii. are identical with that prophesied of in this chapter.[1]

[1] According to the modern critics (Berth., v. Leng., Hitz., Bleek), this chapter must have been written shortly before the re-consecration of the temple, or immediately thereafter, before or immediately after the death of Antiochus Epiphanes. This supposition is drawn from ver. 14, according to which the period of oppression shall continue 2300 evening-mornings. But, overlooking the circumstance that these critics cannot agree as to the reckoning of this period of time, and thus announce the uncertainty of their hypothesis, the whole of the other contents of the chapter stand in contradiction to this supposition. It contains no hint whatever of the great victories of the Maccabees which preceded the consecration of the temple, and first made it possible, but, on the contrary, speaks of the oppression as continuing unchanged till the

Vers. 1–14. *The Vision.*

Vers. 1, 2 contain the historical introduction to this new revelation. This was given to Daniel in the third year of the reign of Belshazzar, and thus two years after the vision of the four world-kingdoms (ch. vii. 1), but not in a dream as that was, but while he was awake. The words *I, Daniel*, are neither a pleonasm (Häv.) nor a sign that the writer wished specially to give himself out for Daniel (Ewald), but expressly denote that Daniel continues to speak of himself in the first person (Kliefoth). The article in הַנִּרְאָה (*that which appeared*) takes the place of the relative אֲשֶׁר, and the expression is concise for הֶחָזוֹן אֲשֶׁר נִרְאָה (*the vision which appeared*); cf. Ewald's *Lehr.* § 335 *a.* בַּתְּחִלָּה (*at the first*), as in ch. ix. 21, in the general signification *earlier*, and in Gen. xiii. 3, xli. 21, xliii. 18, 20, Isa. i. 26, synonymous with בָּרִאשֹׁנָה (*in the beginning*). Here the word points back to ch. vii., and in ch. ix. 21 it refers to ver. 16 of this chapter.

"In vision," *i.e.* ἐν πνεύματι, not ἐν σώματι, Daniel was placed in the city of Susa, in the province of Elam (Elymaïs). By the words, "I saw in vision; and it came to pass when I saw," which precede the specification of the scene of the vision, is indicated the fact that he was in Susa only in vision, and the misconception is sufficiently guarded against that Daniel was actually there in the body. This is acknowledged by v. Leng., Hitzig, Maurer, Häv., Hgstb., Kran., and Kliefoth, against Bertholdt and Rosenmüller, who understand this, in connection with ver. 27, as meaning that Daniel was personally present in Susa to execute the king's business, from which Bertholdt frames the charge against the pseudo-Daniel, that he was not conscious that Elam under Nabonned did not belong to Babylon, and that the royal palace at Susa had as yet no existence. But this accusation has no historical foundation. We have no accurate information whether under Belshazzar Elam was added to Babylon or the Chaldean empire. It is true that not Hengstenberg (*Beitr.* i. p. 42 f.) only has, with older theologians, concluded from the prophecies of Jer. xlix. 34 ff., com-

oppressor is himself destroyed (ver. 25), and then it breaks off without any Messianic view, as one should expect from a parenetic poem of a Maccabean Jew; so that Bleek finds himself compelled from his own resources to add "the intimation, that the beginning of the deliverance destined by God for His people is closely and immediately joined to the discontinuance of the worship of Jehovah by Antioch. Epiph., and to the destruction of this prince," in order to give to the vision "a Messianic character."

pared with ch. xxv. 25 and Ezek. xxxii. 24, that Nebuchadnezzar subjugated Susa, but Niebuhr also (*Gesch. Assurs*, p. 211 ff.) seeks from these and other passages of the O. T. to establish the view, that Nebuchadnezzar, after the death of Cyaxares (Uwakhshatra), to whom he owed allegiance, refused to do homage to his successor, and entered on a war against Media, which resulted in the annexation of Elam to his kingdom. But, on the contrary, Hävernick has well remarked, that the subjugation of Elam by Nebuchadnezzar can scarcely harmonize with the fact of the division of the Assyrian kingdom between the Babylonian king Nabopolassar and the Median king Cyaxares, whereby the former obtained the western and the latter the eastern half, and that from these passages of prophecy a subjugation of Elam by the Chaldeans cannot be concluded. Jeremiah announces neither in ch. xxv. 25 nor in ch. xlix. 34 ff. a conquest of Elam by Nebuchadnezzar, but rather in ch. xlix. prophesies the complete destruction of Elam, or a divine judgment, in language which is much too strong and elevated for a mere making of it tributary and annexing it to a new state.

Besides, this passage in no respect requires that Susa and Elam should be regarded as provinces of the Chaldean kingdom, since the opinion that Daniel was in Susa engaged in some public business for the Chaldean king is founded only on a false interpretation of vers. 2 and 27. From the prophet's having been placed in an ecstasy in the city of Susa, there follows nothing further than that this city was already at the time of the existing Chaldean kingdom a central-point of Elamitish or Persian power. And the more definite description of the situation of this city in the words, "which was in the province of Elam," points decidedly to the time of Daniel, in which Susa as yet belonged to the province of Elam, while this province was made a satrapy, Susis, Susiana, now Chusistan, by the kings of Persia, and Susa became the capital of this province; therefore the capital Susa is not reckoned as situated in Elam by writers, who after this time distinguish between Susis (Susiana) and Elymaïs (Elam), as Strabo, xvi. 1. 17 f., Pliny, *hist. nat.* vi. 27: *Susianen ab Elymaide disterminat amnis Eulæus.*

Still more groundless is the assertion, that the city of Susa was not in existence in the time of Daniel, or, as Duncker (*Gesch. der Alterth.* ii. p. 913, 3 Aufl.) affirms, that Darius first removed the residence or seat of the king to Susa with the intention that it should become the permanent residence for him and his successors, the central-point of his kingdom and of his government, and that Pliny and Ælian say decidedly that Darius built Susa, the king's city of Persia, and that the inscriptions confirm this saying. For, to begin with the latter statement, an inscription found in the ruins of a palace at Susa, according to the deciphering of Mordtmann (*in der D. morgl. Ztschr.* xvi. pp. 123 ff.), which Duncker cites as confirming his statement, contains only these words: "Thus speaks Artaxerxes the great king, the son of Darius the son of Achämenides Vistaçpa: This building my great-great-grandfather Darius erected; afterwards it was improved by Artaxerxes my grandfather." This inscription thus confirms only the fact of the building of a palace in Susa by Darius, but nothing further, from which it is impossible to conclude that Darius first founded the city, or built the first tower in it. Still less does such an idea lie in the words of Ælian, *nat. animal.* i. 59: "Darius was proud of the erection of a celebrated building which he had raised in Susa." And Pliny also, taken strictly, speaks only of the elevation of Susa to the rank of capital of the kingdom by Darius, which does not exclude the opinion that Susa was before this already a considerable town, and had a royal castle, in which Cyrus may have resided during several months of the year (according to Xenophon, *Cyrop.* viii. 6. 22, *Anab.* iii. 5. 15; cf. Brissonius, *de regio Pers. princ.* p. 88 seq.).[1] The founding of Susa, and of the old tower in Susa, reaches back into pre-historic times. According to Strabo, xv. 2. 3, Susa must have been built by Tithonos, the father of Memnon. With this the epithet *Μεμνόνια Σοῦσα*, which Herod. vii. 151, v. 54, 53, and Ælian, *nat. anim.* xiii. 18, give to the town of Susa, stands in unison. For if this proves nothing more than that in Susa there was a tomb of Memnon (Häv.), yet would this sufficiently prove that the city or its citadel existed from ancient times—times so ancient that the mythic Memnon lived and was buried there.

The city had its name שׁוּשַׁן, *Lily*, from the lilies which grew in great abundance in that region (Athen. *Deipnos.* xii. p. 409;

[1] Pliny, *hist. nat.* vi. 27, says regarding *Susiana*, "*In qua vetus regia Persarum Susa a Dario Hystaspis filio condita*," which may be understood as if he ascribed to Darius the founding of the city of Susa. But how little weight is to be given to this statement appears from the similar statement, *hist. nat.* vi. 14 (17): "*Ecbatana caput Mediæ Seleucus rex condidit*," which plainly contains an error, since Ecbatana, under the name of *Achmeta*, is mentioned (Ezra vi. 2) in the time of Darius Hystaspes, in the tower of which the archives of the Persian kings were preserved

Stephan. Byz., etc.), and had, according to Strabo, xv. 3. 2, a circuit of 120 (twelve English miles), and according to others, 200 stadia. Its palace was called *Memnoneion*, and was strongly fortified. Here was "the golden seat;" here also were "the apartments of Darius, which were adorned with gold," as Æschylos says (*Pers.* 3. 4. 159, 160), "the widely-famed palace,"—the *περιβόητα βασιλεῖα*, as Diod. Sic. xvii. 65, expresses himself.

The ruins of Susa are now only a wilderness, inhabited by lions and hyænas, on the eastern banks of the Shapur, between it and the Dizful, where three great mountains of ruins, from 80 to 100 feet high, raise themselves, showing the compass of the city, while eastward smaller heaps of ruins point out the remains of the city, which to this day bear the name *Schusch;* cf. Herz.'s *Realenc.* xv. p. 263 f., and Duncker, *Gesch. d. Alt.* ii. p. 942 ff.

The designation of Elam as מְדִינָה, a *province*, does not refer to a Chaldean province. עֵילָם, in Greek Ἐλυμαΐς, formed the western part of the Persian satrapy of Susis or Susiana, which lay at the foot of the highlands of Iran, at the beginning of the valley of the Tigris and the Euphrates between Persia and Babylon, called by the Persians *Uvaja*, and by the Greeks *Susis* or *Susiana* after the capital, or *Cissia* after its inhabitants. It is bounded by the western border mountains of Persia and the Tigris, and on the south terminates in a warm, swampy and harbourless coast, which stretches from the mouth of the Tigris to that of the Aurvaiti (Oroatis). Strabo (xv. 732) says Susiana is inhabited by two races, the Cissæi and the Elymäi; Herodotus (iii. 91, v. 49, vii. 62), on the contrary, names only the Cissæi as the inhabitants of the country of the same name. The saying put into circulation by Josephus (*Antt.* i. 6. 4, Ἔλαμος γὰρ Ἐλαμαίους Περσῶν ὄντας ἀρχηγέτας κατέλιπεν), that the Elamites are the primitive race of the Persians, has no historical foundation. The deep valley of the Tigris and the Euphrates was the country of the Semites. "The names of the towns and rivers of the country confirm the statements of Genesis, which names Elam among the sons of Shem, although the erecting of the Persian royal residence in Elam, and the long continuance of the Persian rule, could not but exercise, as it did, an influence on the manners and arts of the Semitish inhabitants" (Duncker, p. 942).

The further statement, that Daniel in vision was by the river *Ulai*, shows that Susa lay on the banks of that river. אוּלַי is the Εὔλαῖος, *Eulæus*, of the Greeks and Romans, of which Pliny says, "*circuit arcem Susorum*," and which Arrian (*Exped. Alex.* vii. 7) also mentions as a navigable river of Susis. On the contrary, Herodotus, i. 188, v. 49, 52, and Strabo, xv. 3, 4, place Susa on the river *Choaspes*. These contradictory statements are reconciled in the simplest manner by the supposition that *Ulai*, *Eulæus*, was the Semitish, *Choaspes* the Aryan (Persian) name of the *Kuran*, which received the Shapur and Dizful. In favour of this, we have not only the circumstance that the name *Choaspes* is undoubtedly of Persian origin, while, on the other hand, אוּלַי is a word of Semitic formation; but still more, that Herodotus knows nothing whatever of the *Eulæus*, while Ptolemy (vi. 3. 2) does not mention the *Choaspes*, but, on the contrary, two sources of the *Eulæus*, the one in Media, the other in Susiana; and that what Herod. i. 188, says of the Choaspes, that the kings of Persia drink its water only, and caused it to be carried far after them, is mentioned by Pliny of the Euläus, *h. n.* vi. 27, and in xxxi. 3 of the Choaspes and Euläus.[1]

Daniel was in spirit conveyed to Susa, that here in the future royal citadel of the Persian kingdom he might witness the destruction of this world-power, as Ezekiel was removed to Jerusalem that he might there see the judgment of its destruction. The placing of the prophet also on the river of Ulai is significant, yet it is not to be explained, with Kranichfeld, from vers. 3 and 6, "where the kingdom in question stands in the same relation to the flowing river as the four kingdoms in ch. vii. 2 do to the sea." For the geographically defined river Ulai has nothing in common with the sea as a symbol of the nations of the world (ch. vii. 2). The Ulai is rather named as the place where afterwards the ram and the he-goat pushed against one another, and the shock followed, deciding the fate of the Persian kingdom.

As, then, the scene of the vision stands in intimate relation to its contents, so also the time at which the revelation was made to Daniel. With the third year of Belshazzar the dynasty of Nebuchadnezzar, the founder of the Babylonian world-kingdom, was extinguished. In this year Belshazzar, the son and successor of Nebuchadnezzar, died, and the sovereignty was transferred to a

[1] There is little probability in the supposition that *Choaspes* is the modern *Kerrah* or *Kerkha*, the *Euläus* the modern *Dizful*, as Susa lay between these two rivers (Ker Porter, Winer, Ruetschi in Herz.'s *Realen.* xv. 246), and receives no sufficient support from the bas-relief of Kojundshik discovered by Layard, which represents the siege of a town lying between two rivers, since the identification of this town with Susa is a mere conjecture.

collateral branch, and finally to an intruder, under whom that world-kingdom, once so powerful, in a few years fell to pieces. Shortly before the death of Belshazzar the end of the Babylonian monarchy was thus to be seen, and the point of time, not very remote, which must end the Exile with the fall of Babylon. This point of time was altogether fitted to reveal to the prophet in a vision what would happen after the overthrow of Babylon, and after the termination of the Exile.

Vers. 3–14. *The vision.*—Ver. 3. Daniel first sees *one* ram, אַיִל, standing by the river. The אֶחָד (*one*) does not here stand for the indefinite article, but is a numeral, in contradistinction to the *two* horns which the *one* ram has. The two horns of the ram were high, but the one was higher than the other, the higher coming up later. הָאַחַת does not mean *the first*, but *the one*, and הַשֵּׁנִית *the other;* for the higher grew up last. This is not to be understood as if Daniel first saw the ram without horns, and then saw the horns grow up, and at length the one horn become higher than the other (v. Leng., Hitzig); but that from the first Daniel saw the ram with two horns, but afterwards saw the one horn grow higher than the other (Kliefoth). The angel (ver. 20) explains the ram with two horns of the kings of Media and Persia. This does not mean that the two horns are to be understood (with Theodoret) of the two dynasties of Cyrus and of Darius Hystaspes; but since the ram represents the one kingdom of the Medes and Persians, so the two horns represent the people of the Medes and Persians, from the union of which the Medo-Persian kingdom grew up. Both nations were the horns, *i.e.* the power of the monarchy; therefore are they both high. The one horn, which afterwards grew up higher than the other, represents the Persians, who raised themselves above the Medians. A ram and goat, as emblems of kings, princes, chiefs, often occur; cf. Isa. xiv. 9; Ezek. xxxiv. 17, xxxix. 18; Jer. l. 8; Zech. x. 3. In *Bundehesch* the guardian spirit of the Persian kingdom appears under the form of a ram with clean feet and sharp-pointed horns, and, according to Amm. Marcell. xix. 1, the Persian king, when he stood at the head of his army, bore, instead of the diadem, the head of a ram (cf. Häv.). The point of resemblance of this symbol is to be sought, not in the richness (the wool) and in the aggressive nature (the horns) of the ram (Theod., Venema), but the ram and the he-goat form, as Hofmann has justly remarked, a contrast to dull firmness and nimble lightness, as the bear and the panther.

The ram stands by the river and pushes toward the west, north, and south, but not toward the east. The river is thus not the one flowing on the east of Susa, for, standing there, the ram pushing toward the west from Susa would push against the capital of his kingdom, but the one flowing on the west; and the ram is to be conceived of as standing on the western bank of this river, from whence he pushed down with his horns all beasts before him, *i.e.* subdued all nations and kingdoms to his power in three regions of the earth. In the west he pushed against Babylon, Syria, and Asia Minor; in the south, Egypt; in the north, the Armenian and Scythian nations. These he subdued and incorporated in the Persian kingdom. He did not push toward the east—not because he could only push forwards and against that which was nearer, but not, without changing his position, backwards (Hitzig); nor because the Medo-Persians themselves came from the east (v. Leng., Kran.); nor yet because the conquests of the Persians did not stretch toward the east (Häv.), for Cyrus and Darius subdued nations to the east of Persia even as far as to the Indus; but because, for the unfolding of the Medo-Persian monarchy as a world-power, its conquests in the east were subordinate, and therefore are not mentioned. The pushing toward the three world-regions corresponds to the three ribs in the mouth of the bear, ch. vii. 5, and intimates that the Medo-Persian world-kingdom, in spite of the irresistibility of its arms, did not, however, extend its power into all the regions of the world. נָגַח, *to push*, of beast, Ex. xxi. 28, in the Piel figuratively is used of nations, Deut. xxxiii. 17, Ps. xliv. 6. יַעַמְדוּ is *potentialis: could not stand.* The masculine is here used, because חַיּוֹת (*beasts*) represents *kingdoms* and *nations.* עָשָׂה כִרְצֹנוֹ, *did according to his will*, expresses arbitrary conduct, a despotic behaviour. הִגְדִּיל, *became great.* The word does not mean to become haughty, for בִּלְבָבוֹ, *in his heart*, is not added here as it is in ver. 25, but *to magnify the action.* It is equivalent to הִגְדִּיל לַעֲשׂוֹת in Joel ii. 20 (*hath done great things*), and Ps. cxxvi. 2, 3, in the sense of *to become great, powerful;* cf. ver. 8.

Vers. 5–7. After Daniel had for a while contemplated the conduct of the ram, he saw a he-goat come from the west over the earth, run with furious might against the two-horned ram, and throw it to the ground and tread upon it. The he-goat, according to the interpretation of the angel, ver. 21, represents the king of Javan (Greece and Macedonia)—not the person of the king (Gesen.), but the kingship of Javan; for, according to ver. 21, the great horn of the goat symbolizes the first king, and thus the goat itself cannot represent a separate king. The goat comes from the west; for Macedonia lay to the west of Susa or Persia. Its coming over the earth is more definitely denoted by the expression וְאֵין נוֹגֵעַ בָּאָרֶץ, *and he was not touching the earth, i.e.* as he hastened over it in his flight. This remark corresponds with the four wings of the leopard, ch. vii. 6. The goat had between its eyes קֶרֶן חָזוּת; *i.e.* not *a horn of vision*, a horn such as a goat naturally has, but here only *in vision* (Hofm., Klief.). This interpretation would render חָזוּת an altogether useless addition, since the goat itself, only seen in vision, is described as it appeared in the vision. For the right explanation of the expression reference must be made to ver. 8, where, instead of *horn of vision*, there is used the expression הַקֶּרֶן הַגְּדוֹלָה (*the great horn*). Accordingly חָזוּת has the meaning of מַרְאֶה, in the *Keri* אִישׁ מַרְאֶה, 2 Sam. xxiii. 21, *a man of countenance or sight* (cf. Targ. Esth. ii. 2): *a horn of sight, consideration, of considerable greatness; κέρας θεορητόν* (LXX., Theodot.), which Theodoret explains by *ἐπίσημον καὶ περίβλεπτον.*

The horn was between the eyes, *i.e.* in the middle of the forehead, the centre of its whole strength, and represents, according to ver. 21, the first king, *i.e.* the founder of the Javanic world-kingdom, or the dynasty of this kingdom represented by him. The he-goat ran up against the ram, the possessor of the two horns, *i.e.* the two-horned ram by the river Ulai, in the fire of his anger, *i.e.* in the glowing anger which gave him his strength, and with the greatest fury threw him down. The prophet adds, "And I saw him come close unto the ram," as giving prominence to the chief matter, and then further describes its complete destruction. It broke in pieces both of the horns, which the ram still had, *i.e.* the power of the Medes and Persians, the two component elements of the Persian world-kingdom. This representation proves itself to be genuine prophecy, whilst an author writing *ex eventu* would have spoken of the horn representing the power of the Medes as assailed and overthrown earlier by that other horn (see under ch. vii. 8, 20). The pushing and trampling down by the Ulai is explained from the idea of the prophecy, according to which the power of the ram is destroyed at the central seat of its might, without reference to the historical course of the victories by which Alexander the Great completed the subjugation of the Persian monarchy. In the concluding passage, ver. 7, the complete destruction is described in the words of the fourth verse, to express the idea of righteous retribution. As the Medo-Persian had crushed the other kingdoms, so now it also was itself destroyed.

Ver. 8. *The transformation of the Javanic kingdom.*—By the kingdom of the ram the he-goat became very great, powerful (הִגְדִּיל as in ver. 4). But the great horn was broken at the height of his strength, and four similar horns grew up in its stead, toward the four regions of heaven. חָזוּת is here used adverbially, *conspicuously:* there came forth conspicuously four in its place. This statement does not contradict ver. 22 and ch. xi. 4, according to which the four kingdoms have not the power of the one great horn; for the thought is only this: they represent in themselves a considerable power, without, however, gaining the power of the one undivided kingdom. The breaking of the great horn indicates the breaking up of the monarchy of Alexander by his death. The four horns which grow up in the place of the one great horn are, according to ver. 22, four kingdoms. These are the dynasties of the Diadochs, of whom there were indeed five: Antigonus, Ptolemy, Cassander, and Lysimachus laid claim to the title of king; but for the first time after the overthrow of Antigonus at the battle of Ipsus, 301 B.C., and thus twenty-two years after the death of Alexander (323 B.C.), they became in reality four kings, and so divided the kingdom among themselves, that Lysimachus had Thrace and Bithynia,—Cassander, Macedonia and Greece,—Seleucus, Syria, Babylonia, and the Eastern countries as far as India,—and Ptolemy, Egypt, Palestine, and Arabia Petrea. But from the fact that this first happened after all the descendants of the royal family had been extirpated, we are not to conclude, with Hävernick, that the breaking of the great horn did not denote the death of Alexander, but the extinction of his race or house; a conclusion which derives no valid support from these words of Justin: "All of them abstained from the use of the insignia of this (royal) dignity while the sons of their king survived. So great was their veneration, that although they had royal wealth and resources, they cared not for the name of kings so long as there existed a legitimate heir to Alexander" (*Hist.* xv. 2. 13). If the breaking of the horn is placed at the point of time when the horn was powerful, here as well as at ch. xi. 4, the reference of the words to the sudden death of Alexander in the prime of his days, and when in the very height of his victorious career, cannot be disputed; and by the breaking of the horn we can only understand Alexander's death, and the breaking up of the kingdom founded by him, although it was still held together in a considerable degree for two decenniums by his generals, till the most imperious and the most powerful amongst them usurped the rank of kings, and then, after the conquest of Antigonus, a formal division of the kingdom into the four considerable kingdoms here named raised them to royal dignity.

The prophetic representation is not a prediction of historical details, but it gives only the fundamental traces of the development of the world-kingdoms, and that not in the form of a historiographical prophecy, but only so that it sketches the ground-thoughts of the divinely ordained unfolding of these world-kingdoms. This ideal fundamental thought of the prophecy has so wrought itself out in actual history, that from the one great kingdom, after the death of the founder, in the course of time four considerable kingdoms arise. The number four in the prophetic contemplation comes into view only according to its symbolical idea as the number of the world in its extension toward the four regions of heaven, so that thereby only the thought is declared, that a kingdom embracing the world will fall to ruins in a plurality of kingdoms toward all the regions of heaven (Kliefoth). This has been so historically realized, that out of the wars of the Diadochs for the supremacy four kingdoms arose toward the four regions of the earth into longer duration,—that of Cassander (Macedonia) toward the west, that of Seleucus (Babylonia, etc.) toward the east, that of Lysimachus (Thracia and Bithynia) toward the north, and finally that of Ptolemy (Egypt) toward the south.[1]

Vers. 9–12. *The interpretation of the vision.*

Ver. 9. Without following the development of the four horns further, the prophecy passes over to the little horn, which grew up out of one of the four horns, and gained great significance in relation to the history of the people of God. The masculine forms מֵהֶם and יָצָא (*out of them came*) are to be explained as a *constructio ad sensum.* אַחַת (*one*) after קֶרֶן (*horn*) is as little super-

[1] When, on the other hand, Hitzig seeks to explain the prophetic representation, here as well as at ch. xi. 4, that with or immediately after the death of Alexander his kingdom was divided, by reference to 1 Macc. i. 6, according to which Alexander himself, shortly before his death, divided the kingdom among his generals, he thereby not only misapprehends the ideal character of the prophecy, but does not in the least degree clear up the matter itself. For the passage in 1 Macc. i. 6, which not only Arabic and Persian authors repeat, but also Moses v. Chorene, and even later Greek and Latin historiographers, as Ammian Marcell., has been explained by Curtius (x. 10. 5) as a *fama vana*, and is proved

fluous as is the מִן in מִצְּעִירָה. אַחַת is a numeral, *one* horn, not several; מִן is either comparative, less than little, *i.e. very little* (Ewald), or, as less than insignificance, wretchedness, *i.e. in an altogether miserable way* (Häv.). The one explanation is more forced than the other, and the idea of wretchedness is altogether untenable. Yet the מִן serves as a circumlocution for the superlative = *perpaucus* (Gesen., Win., Aub.), while verbal analogies for it are wanting. מִן signifies *from, out of;* but it is not to be united with קֶרֶן: *one horn of smallness* (v. Leng.), in which case מִן would be superfluous, but with the verb יָצָא: *it came up out of littleness, a parvo, i.e. a parvis initiis* (Maur., Hofm., Kran., Klief.). Thus it corresponds with זְעֵירָה סִלְּקַת, ch. vii. 8. In the words "it arose out of littleness" there lies the idea that it grew to great power from a small beginning; for it became very great, *i.e.* powerful, toward the south, toward the east, and toward the הַצְּבִי (*the splendour, glory*), *i.e.* toward the glorious land. הַצְּבִי = אֶרֶץ הַצְּבִי, ch. xi. 16, 41. This designation of the land of Israel is framed after Jer. iii. 19 and Ezek. xx. 6, 15, where this land is called "a heritage of the greatest glory of nations" (a goodly heritage of the host of nations, E. V.), "a glory of all lands," *i.e.* the most glorious land which a people can possess. The expression is synonymous with אֶרֶץ חֶמְדָּה ("pleasant land"), Jer. iii. 19, Zech. vii. 14, Ps. cvi. 24. Canaan was so designated on account of its great fruitfulness as a land flowing with milk and honey; cf. Ezek. xx. 6.

The one of the four horns from which the little horn grew up is the Syrian monarchy, and the horn growing up out of it is the king Antiochus Epiphanes, as Josephus (*Ant.* x. 11. 7) and all interpreters acknowledge, on the ground of 1 Macc. i. 10. The south, against which he became great, is Egypt (cf. ch. xi. 5 and 1 Macc. i. 16 ff.). The east is not Asia (Kranichfeld), but Babylon, and particularly Elymaïs and Armenia, 1 Macc. i. 31, 37, iii. 31, 37, vi. 1–4, according to which he subdued Elymaïs and

by Wernsdorf (*de Fide Librr. Macc.* p. 40 sq.) and Droysen (*das Test. Alex.* 3te *Beilage, zu Gesch. des Hellen.* i.) to be without foundation (cf. Grimm, *K. ex. Hdb. zu* 1 *Macc.* i. 6). This may have been originally put into circulation by the partisans of the Hellenic kings, in order to legitimatize their sovereignty in the eyes of the people, as Grimm conjectures; yet the confirmation which the book of Daniel appears to give to it contributed to its wide diffusion by Oriental and Byzantine authors, and the author of the first book of the Maccabees had without doubt the book of Daniel before his eyes in the representation he gives.

overcame Artaxias, king of Armenia (App. Syr. c. 45, 46; Polyb. xxxi. 11). Besides the south and the east, Canaan, the holy land, as lying between, is named as the third land, as in Isa. xix. 23 ff. it is named as third, between Egypt and Assyria; but וְאֶל הַצֶּבִי ("and toward the glorious land") is not, with Kranichfeld, to be regarded as an exegetical addition to וְאֶל הַמִּזְרָח ("and toward the east"). Palestine lay neither to the east of Daniel, nor geographically to the east of the kingdom denoted by the little horn, because the text gives no support to the identifying of this kingdom with the Javanic, the horn operating from the west.

Ver. 10. As this horn became great in extent toward the south and toward the east, so also it grew up in height even unto the host of heaven, and some of them it cast down, *i.e.* some of the stars, to the earth. *The host of heaven* is here, as in Jer. xxxiii. 22, the whole body of the stars of heaven, the constellations, and *of the stars* is epexegetical of *of the host.* Daniel in the vision sees the horn grow so great in height, that it reaches even to the heavens, can reach the heavenly bodies with the hand, and throws some of the stars (מִן is partitive) down to the earth and tramples upon them, destroys them with scorn. The words of the angel, ver. 24, show that by the stars we are to understand the people of the saints, the people of God. The stars cast down to the earth are, according to this, neither the Levites (Grotius), nor the *viri illustres* in Israel (Glass.), nor the chief rulers of the Jews in church and state (Dathe). If the people of the saints generally are compared to the host of heaven, the stars, then the separate stars cannot be the ecclesiastical or civil chiefs, but the members of this nation in common. But by "the people of the saints" is to be understood (since the little horn denotes Antiochus Epiphanes) the people of God in the Old Covenant, the people of Israel. They are named the people of the saints by virtue of their being called to be an holy nation (Ex. xix. 6), because "they had the revelation of God and God Himself dwelling among them, altogether irrespective of the subjective degrees of sanctification in individuals" (Kliefoth). But the comparing of them with the host of the stars does not arise from Jewish national pride, nor does it mean that Daniel thought only of the truly faithful in Israel (Theod., Häv.), or that the pseudo-Daniel thought that with the death of Antiochus the Messiah would appear, and that then Israel, after the extermination of the godless, would become a people of pure holiness. The comparison rather has its root in this, that God, the King of Israel, is called the God of hosts, and by the צְבָאוֹת (*hosts*) are generally to be understood the stars or the angels; but the tribes of Israel also, who were led by God out of Egypt, are called "the hosts of Jehovah" (Ex. vii. 4, xii. 41). As in heaven the angels and stars, so on earth the sons of Israel form the host of God; and as the angels on account of the glory of their nature are called קְדוֹשִׁים (*holy ones*), so the Israelites by virtue of their being chosen to be the holy nation of God, forming the kingdom of heaven in this world. As God, the King of this people, has His throne in heaven, so there also Israel have their true home, and are in the eyes of God regarded as like unto the stars. This comparison serves, then, to characterize the insolence of Antiochus as a wickedness against Heaven and the heavenly order of things.[1] Cf. 2 Macc. ix. 10.

Ver. 11. This horn raised its might even to the Prince of the host. שַׂר הַצָּבָא, *the Prince of the host of heaven*, is obviously not the high priest Onias (Grotius), but the God of heaven and the King of Israel, the Prince of princes, as He is called in ver. 25. הִגְדִּיל עַד (*he magnified himself to*) is repeated in ver. 25 by יַעֲמוֹד עַל (*he shall stand up against*). Wherein this rising up against God consisted, the second half of the verse indicates in the statement that the תָּמִיד (*daily* sacrifice) was taken away, and the building of His sanctuary was destroyed. This verse does not record a part of the vision, but is a further development of that which was seen in prophetic words. Hence we may not, with Ebrard, refer its contents to heavenly events, to a putting away of the sacrifice from before the throne of God and a destruction of the heavenly sanctuary. On the contrary, Kliefoth has well remarked that it is "without example in Scripture that men penetrate into heaven to insult God; what men do against God is done on the

[1] The deep practical explanation of Calvin deserves attention:—"Although the church often lies prostrate in the world and is trodden under foot, yet is it always precious before God. Hence the prophet adorns the church with this remarkable praise, not to obtain for it great dignity in the sight of men, but because God has separated it from the world and provided for it a sure inheritance in heaven. Although the sons of God are pilgrims on the earth, and have scarcely any place in it, because they are as castaways, yet they are nevertheless citizens of heaven. Hence we derive this useful lesson, that we should bear it patiently when we are thrown prostrate on the ground, and are despised by tyrants and contemners of God. In the meantime our seat is laid up in heaven, and God numbers us among the stars, although, as Paul says, we are as dung and as the offscourings of all things."—CALV. *in loc.*

earth." הַתָּמִיד is everything in the worship of God which is not used merely temporarily, but is permanent, as the daily sacrifice, the setting forth of the shew-bread, and the like. The limitation of it to the daily morning and evening service in the writings of the Rabbis is unknown in the O. T. The word much rather comprehends *all that is of permanent use in the holy services of divine worship* (Hgst., Häv., Hofm., Kran., Klief.). Thus interpreted, the prophetic announcement corresponds with history; for, according to 1 Macc. i. 45, Antiochus gave orders that they should "forbid burnt-offerings, and sacrifice, and drink-offerings in the temple; and that they should profane the Sabbath and festival days."

The horn also overthrew the place of the sanctuary of Jehovah. הִשְׁלִיךְ, *to cast away, to cast forth,*—used of buildings, *to lay waste;* cf. Jer. ix. 18. מָכוֹן, properly, *that which is set up*, erected; here, as frequently, of the dwelling-place of God, *the temple:* so also מְכוֹן שִׁבְתְּךָ (*a settled place for thee to dwell in*), Ex. xv. 17, 1 Kings viii. 13. It is used also of the heavenly dwelling-place of God, 1 Kings viii. 39, 43; here, of the temple in Jerusalem. With regard to the historical fulfilment, cf. the expressions, "her (Jerusalem's) sanctuary was laid waste like a wilderness," and "pollute the sanctuary," 1 Macc. i. 39, 46; and "the sanctuary was trodden down," 1 Macc. iii. 45.

Ver. 12. The actions of the little horn are definitively comprehended in this verse, as may be seen from this, that in the first hemistich צָבָא and תָּמִיד are mentioned together. But this hemistich has been very variously interpreted. We must altogether reject the interpretation of the Vulgate, "*Robur autem datum est contra juge sacrificium propter peccata,*" which is reproduced in Luther's translation, "There was given to him such strength against the daily sacrifice on account of sin;" or Calvin's, "*Et tempus datum est super jugi sacrificio in scelere,*" whereby, after Raschi's example, צָבָא is interpreted of the *statio militaris*, and thence the interpretation *tempus* or *intervallum* is derived. For צָבָא means neither *robur*, nor *tempus*, nor *statio militaris*, but only *military service*, and perhaps *military forces*. Add to this that צָבָא both in vers. 10 and 13 means *host*. If we maintain this, with the majority of interpreters, only two explanations are admissible, according as we understand צָבָא of the host of heaven, *i.e.* of Israel, or of some other host. The latter interpretation is apparently supported partly by the absence of the article in צָבָא, and partly by the construction of the word as fem. (תִּנָּתֵן). Accordingly,

Hitzig says that a Hebrew reader could not understand the words otherwise than as meaning, "and a warlike expedition was made or conducted against the daily sacrifice with wickedness" (*i.e.* the impure service of idols); while others translate, "and a host placed against the daily sacrifice on account of sin" (Syr., Grot., Harenb., J. D. Michaelis); or, "a host is given against the daily sacrifice in wickedness" (Wieseler); or, "given against that which was continual with the service of idols," *i.e.* so that, in the place of the "continual," wickedness, the worship of idols, is appointed (Hofmann); or, "the power of an army is given to it (the horn) against the daily sacrifice through wickedness," *i.e.* by the evil higher demons (Ebrard). But the latter interpretation is to be rejected on account of the arbitrary insertion of לוֹ (*to it*); and against all the others it is to be remarked, that there is no proof either from ver. 13, or from Ezek. xxxii. 23 or xxvi. 8, that נָתַן means to lead out, to bring forward, to give contrary to or against.

In ver. 13 תֵּת (*to give*) is more closely defined by מִרְמָס (*something trodden under foot*); but in these passages in Ezek. above referred to, it [the verb נָתַן] is connected with an actual object. Construed with the *accus. pers.* and עַל, נָתַן means "to place one over anything." This conception in its different shades is not so much derived from the words of the text as from a reference to the history; for it is supposed (cf. Grotius, Wies.) that because the matter spoken of is the wickedness of Antiochus, the entrance of the Syrian army into Jerusalem and its proceedings (1 Macc. i. 29 ff.) must be set forth. צָבָא, notwithstanding the want of the article, and notwithstanding the feminine construction, cannot properly be otherwise understood in ver. 12 than in vers. 10 and 13, not of the host of the Syrians, but only of the people of Israel. The article is wanting also in ver. 13, where yet, because of its being taken in connection with קֹדֶשׁ, it can only refer to Israel. Besides this passage, the fem. construction is found also only in Isa. xl. 2, where it signifies the service of war or vassalage. But this meaning here, where weighty reasons oppose it, this construction does not require us to adopt, for such a construction is not infrequent. It is found not merely with names of nations and races, so far as land and people are nearly related ideas, but also with other words, such as even עָם, *people, fem.*, Ex. v. 16, 1 Kings xviii. 7, Jer. viii. 5; הָמוֹן, *a multitude*, Job xxxi. 34; זֶרַע, *seed, i.e. descendants*, Deut. xxxi. 21; cf. Ewald's *Lehr.* § 174. But the want of the article in צָבָא in ver. 12 and in 13 has its reason in this, that that which is said does not concern the whole host, but only one part of it, since, according to ver. 10, the hostile horn will cast only some מִן הַצָּבָא (*of the host*) to the earth. If, therefore, there is no sufficient ground for rejecting the application of the צָבָא to the people of Israel, it follows that this interpretation is decidedly required not only by the connection, chiefly by ver. 13, but also by that which is said of צָבָא in ver. 12*a*.

"Since in ver. 13 the inquirer resumes the contents of vers. 10–12, and along with the sanctuary names also the 'host' as the object of the 'treading down,' it is not credible that this 'host' should be different from that mentioned in ver. 12" (Klief.). Moreover, תִּנָּתֵן can have in this passage only the meaning of *to be given up*. עַל הַתָּמִיד can then only be translated *because of the permanent sacrifice*, if בְּפֶשַׁע (*by reason of transgression*) is united as object with תִּנָּתֵן in the sense: "was delivered up in transgression." But apart from this, that נָתַן in the sense of *to give up* is construed with בְּיַד, and there are wanting certain parallels for its construction with בְּ merely, this interpretation, "the host (= Israel) is given up in wickedness on account of the continual sacrifice," presents an idea not to be tolerated. We agree, therefore, in general with the interpretation of Ch. B. Michaelis, Hävernick, v. Lengerke, Maurer, Kranichfeld, and Kliefoth, and explain the words thus: "and (an) host shall be given up together with the daily sacrifice, because of transgression." צָבָא, *an host*, *i.e.* a great company of the host, the people of Israel. בְּ before פֶּשַׁע (*transgression*) in the meaning of בְּ *pretii*, *on account of* (*um*), or *because of*, cf. Gen. xviii. 28. פֶּשַׁע is the apostasy of the Israelites from God, the wickedness proceeding from the פֹּשְׁעִים (*transgressors*), ver. 23. The objection that this interpretation is not appropriate, because פֶּשַׁע is repeated in ver. 13 in union with שֹׁמֵם (*desolation*), and therefore a wickedness devoted to destruction is characterized (Klief.), avails nothing, because it in no way follows from this that the "transgression" must be wickedness seating itself in the place of the "daily sacrifice," idolatrous worship supplanting the true worship. But "the transgression" cannot be that which sets itself in the place of the "daily sacrifice," because הַתָּמִיד is not the subject of the sentence, but is only co-ordinated to the subject. If בְּ in בְּפֶשַׁע is regarded as the בְּ *pretii*, then פשע can only be that which would be put in the place of the צָבָא. The preposition עַל before הַתָּמִיד means *thereon*, *after that*, also *at the same time*, or *together with*, as in Am. iii. 15, Hos. x. 14, etc. תָּמִיד, as in ver. 11, is not merely the *daily sacrifice*, but all that had continuance in the Mosaic worship. Finally, the jussive forms תִּנָּתֵן and תַּשְׁלֵךְ (*to be trodden*) are to be observed, since, according to the just observation of Kran., they are not simply identical with the future, as Ewald (§ 343) thinks, but here, as in ch. xi. 4, 10, 16, modify the conception of time by the presentation of the divine pre-determination or the decree, and thus express a *should*, *may*, or a *faculty*, *a being able*, in consequence of the divine counsel. To the verbs of the second half of the verse קֶרֶן (*horn*) is easily supplied from the foregoing context as the subject; and the passage closes with the thought: thus must the horn throw the truth to the ground, and he shall succeed in this.[1] אֱמֶת, the objective truth, the word of God, so far as it is embodied in the worship. As to this matter cf. 1 Macc. i. 43–52, 56, 60.

Vers. 13 and 14. In addition to what has been already seen and communicated in the vision, a further vision unfolds itself, by which there is conveyed to the prophet disclosures regarding the duration of the oppression of the people of God by the little horn. Daniel hears a holy one, *i.e.* an angel (see under ch. iv. 10), talking. What he said is not recorded. But while he is talking, another angel interrupts him with the question as to the duration of the affliction, and this is done that Daniel may hear the answer. Therefore the first angel immediately turns himself to Daniel, and, addressing him, makes known to him the information that was desired.

The אֵלַי (*to me*), ver. 14, is not, according to the old versions, to be changed into אֵלָיו (*to him*). What Hitzig says in justification of אֵלָיו is of no weight; cf. Kran. The angel that talked is designated by פַּלְמוֹנִי, *quidam*, *nescio quis*, as not being more particularly definable. The question condenses the contents of vers. 10–12: "Till how long is the vision, etc.?" הֶחָזוֹן is not the action, but the contents of the vision, *the thing seen*. The contents of the vision are arranged in the form of appositions: that which is continual and the desolating wickedness, for: the vision of that which is continual and of the desolation. The meaning of this apposition is more particularly defined by the further passage following *asyndetos:* to give up the sanctuary as well as the host to destruction. שֹׁמֵם after

[1] "*Successus Antiochi potuit pios omnes turbare, acsi tyrannus ille esset Deo superior. Ergo oportuit etiam hoc prædici, ne quid novum vel inopinatum contingeret fidelibus.*"—CALVIN.

the definite noun without the article, which is sometimes wanting (Jer. ii. 21; Ezek. xxxix. 27; cf. Ew. § 293), does not mean being benumbed, confounded, but *laid waste*, fallen into ruin; thus the wickedness which consists in laying waste. שֹׁמֵם cannot be understood transitively, since שֹׁמֵם and מְשֹׁמֵם are placed over against each other in ch. ix. 27.

In the answer, עַד is to be interpreted as in the question: till 2300 evening-mornings have been, or have passed, thus: 2300 evening-mornings long, so (=then) the sanctuary is brought into its right state. צָדַק primarily means to be just, whence the meaning is derived to justify, which is not here suitable, for it must be followed by, from the defilement of the desolation. The restoration of the temple to its right condition is, it is true, at the same time a justification of it from its desolation, and it includes in it the restoration of the permanent worship.

The interpretation of the period of time, 2300 evening-mornings, named by the angel is beset with difficulty. And first the verbal import of עֶרֶב בֹּקֶר is doubtful. Among recent interpreters, Berth., Häv., v. Leng., Maur., and Hofm. (*Weiss. u. Erf.* p. 295) understand by it days consisting of morning and evening (twenty-four hours); others, as Bleek, Kirmss, Ewald, Hitzig, Wieseler (who, however, in his treatise, *Die* 70 *Wochen*, u.s.w., p. 115 ff., defends the first explanation), Kran., and Delitzsch, are of opinion that evening-morning is particularly reckoned with reference to the offering of a morning and an evening sacrifice each day, so that 2300 evening-mornings make only 1150 whole days. But there is no exegetical foundation for this latter opinion. It is derived only from a comparison, or rather an identification, of this passage with Dan. vii. 25, xii. 11 f., and ix. 27; and therewith it is proved that, according to 1 Macc. i. 54, 59, cf. iv. 52, the desolation of the sanctuary by the worship of idols under Antiochus Epiphanes lasted not longer than three years and ten days, and that from Dan. xii. 11 it extends only to 1290 days. But these arguments rest on assertions which must first be justified. The passages Dan. vii. 25 and ix. 27 cannot be here taken into account, because they do not speak of Antiochus Epiphanes, and the 1290 days (1335 days, ch. xii. 11 f.) do not give 2300 evening-mornings, that we can and may at once identify these statements with this before us. In ch. xii. 11 the *terminus a quo* of the 1290 days is unquestionably the putting away or the removal of the תָּמִיד (*daily sacrifice*), and the giving (placing, raising up) of the abomination that maketh desolate (*i.e.* the altar of idol-worship); but in this verse (ch. viii. 14), on the contrary, the continuance not only of the taking away of the תָּמִיד, but also of the delivering up of the saints and the people to be trodden under foot, is fixed to 2300 evening-mornings. This oppression continued longer than the removal of the appointed daily sacrifice. According to 1 Macc. i. 10 ff., the violent assaults of Antiochus against the temple and the Jews who remained faithful to the law began in the 143d year of the era of the Seleucidæ, but the abomination that maketh desolate, *i.e.* the idol-altar, was first erected on Jehovah's altar of burnt-offering, according to 1 Macc. i. 54, in the 145th year of the Seleucidæ, and the purification of the temple from this abomination, and its re-consecration, took place on the 25th day of Kisleu (9th month) of the year of the Seleucidæ 148. According to this, from the beginning of the desecration of the temple by the plundering of its vessels and its golden ornaments (1 Macc. i. 20 ff.) to its restoration to its right condition, more than five years passed. The fulfilment, or the historical reference, of this prophecy accordingly affords, as is sufficiently manifest, no proper means of ascertaining the import of the "evening-morning." This must rather be exegetically decided. It occurs only here, and corresponds to *νυχθήμερον*, 2 Cor. xi. 25. But the choice of so unusual a measure of time, derived from the two chief parts of the day, instead of the simple measure of time by days, probably originates with reference to the morning and evening sacrifice, by which the day was to be consecrated to the Lord, after Gen. i. 5, 8, 13, etc., where the days of the creation week are named and reckoned according to the succession of evening and morning. This separation of the expression into evening and morning, so that to number them separately and add them together would make 2300 evening-mornings = 1150 days, is shown to be inadmissible, both by the asyndeton evening-morning and the usages of the Hebrew language. That in ver. 26 הָעֶרֶב וְהַבֹּקֶר (*the evening and the morning*) stands for it, does not prove that the evening and morning are reckoned separately, but only that evening-morning is a period of time consisting of evening and morning. When the Hebrews wish to express separately day and night, the component parts of a day of a week, then the number of both is expressed. They say, *e.g.*, forty days and forty nights (Gen. vii. 4, 12; Ex. xxiv. 18; 1 Kings xix. 8), and three days and three nights (Jonah ii. 1; Matt. xii. 40), but not eighty or six days-and-nights, when they wish to speak of forty or three full days. A Hebrew reader could not possibly understand the period of time 2300 evening-mornings of 2300 half days or 1150 whole days, because evening and morning at the creation constituted not the half but the whole day. Still less, in the designation of time, "till 2300 evening-mornings," could "evening-mornings" be understood of the evening and morning sacrifices, and the words be regarded as meaning, that till 1150 evening sacrifices and 1150 morning sacrifices are discontinued. We must therefore take the words as they are, *i.e.* understand them of 2300 whole days.

This exegetical resolution of the matter is not made doubtful by the remark, that an increasing of the period of oppression to 2300 days, over against the duration of the oppression limited in ch. vii. 25 to only three and a half times, or to 1290 (or 1335 days, ch. xii. 11, 12), is very unlikely, since there is in no respect any reason for this increase over against these statements (Kran. p. 298). This remark can only be valid as proof if, on the one side, the three and a half times in ch. vii. 25 are equal to three and a half civil years, for which the proof fails, and, on the other side, if the 1290 or the 1335 days in ch. xii. 11 f. indicate the whole duration of the oppression of Israel by Antiochus. But if these periods, on the contrary, refer only to the time of the greatest oppression, the erection of the idol-altar in the temple, this time cannot be made the measure for the duration of the whole period of tribulation.

The objection also, that it is more difficult to prove historically an oppression of the people of God for 2300 days by Antiochus than the 1150 days' duration of this oppression, need not move us to depart from the exegetically ascertained meaning of the words. The opponents of this view are indeed at one in this, that the consecration of the temple after its purification, and after the altar of Jehovah was restored, on the 25th Kisleu of the 148th year of the Seleucidæ, formed the termination of the period named, but they are at variance as to the commencement of the period. Delitzsch reckons from the erection of the idol-altar in the temple on 15th Kisleu in the 145th year of the *Sel.*, and thus makes it only three years and ten days, or 1090 to 1105 days. Hitzig reckons from the taking away of the daily sacrifice, which would take place somewhat earlier than the setting up of the idol-altar, but has not furnished proof that this happened two months earlier. Bleek and Kirmss reckon from the taking of Jerusalem by Apollonius in the year of the *Sel.* 145 (1 Macc. i. 30 ff.; 2 Macc. v. 24 ff.), misplacing this in the first month of the year named, but without having any other proof for it than the agreement of the reckoning.

To this is to be added, that the adoption of the consecration of the temple as the *terminus ad quem* is not so well grounded as is supposed. The words of the text, וְנִצְדַּק קֹדֶשׁ ("thus is the sanctuary placed in the right state"), comprehend more than the purification and re-consecration of the temple. In ver. 11, also ch. ix. 17 and xi. 31, Daniel uses the word מִקְדָּשׁ for temple, while on the other hand קֹדֶשׁ means all that is holy. Was, then, the sanctuary, in this comprehensive meaning of the word, placed in its right state with the consecration of the temple, when after this occurrence "they that were in the tower (Acra) shut up the Israelites round about the sanctuary," sought to hinder access to the temple, and, when Judas Maccabæus had begun to besiege the tower, the Syrians approached with a reinforced army, besieged the sanctuary for many days, and on their departure demolished its strongholds (1 Macc. vi. 18 ff., 51, 62)?—when, again, under Demetrius Soter of Bacchides, the high priest Menelaus was deposed, and Alcimus, who was not descended from the family of a high priest, was advanced to his place, who cruelly persecuted the pious in Israel?—when the Syrian general Nicanor mocked the priests who showed to him the burnt-offering for the king, and defiled and threatened to burn the temple (1 Macc. vii.)? And did the trampling upon Israel cease with the consecration of the temple, when at the building up of the altar and the restoration of the temple the heathen around became so furious, that they resolved to destroy all who were of the race of Jacob amongst them, and began to murder them (1 Macc. v. 1 ff.)? Hävernick therefore, with Bertholdt, places the *terminus ad quem* of the 2300 days in the victory over Nicanor, by which the power of the Syrians over Judea was first broken, and the land enjoyed rest, so that it was resolved to celebrate annually this victory, as well as the consecration of the temple (1 Macc. vii. 48–50), according to which the *terminus a quo* of the period named would be shortly before the erection of the abomination of idolatry in the temple.

If we now, however, turn from this supposition, since the text speaks further of it, to seek the end of the oppression in the restoration of the legal temple-worship, or in the overthrow of Antiochus Epiphanes, which the angel brings to view in the interpretation of the vision (ver. 26), so also in these cases the 2300 days are to be calculated. C. v. Leng., Maur., and Wiesel., who regard the death of Antiochus as the termination, place the beginning of the 2300 days one year before the beginning of violence with which Antiochus, after his return from the expedition into Egypt in the year 143 *Sel.*, went forth to destroy (1 Macc. i. 20) the Mosaic worship and law. Only a few weeks or months earlier, in the middle of the year 142 *Sel.*, the point of commencement must be placed, if the consecration of the temple is held to be the termination. In the year 142 not only was the pious high priest Onias removed from his office by the godless Jason, but also Jason himself was forced from the place he had usurped by Menelaus, who gave Antiochus a greater bribe than he did, and gave away as presents and sold to the heathen the golden utensils of the temple, and commanded Onias, who denounced his wickedness, to be deceitfully murdered (2 Macc. ii. 4). Hence we need not, with Hofmann, regard the deposition of Onias, the date of which cannot be accurately fixed, but which, 2 Macc. iv. 7 ff., is brought into connection with the commencement of the reign of Antiochus, and which probably took place before the year 142, as the date of the commencement of the 2300 days, although the laying waste of the sanctuary may be dated from it; since Jason by royal authority set up a heathen γυμνάσιον with an ἐφηβεῖον, and by the wickedness of the profane and unpriestly conduct of this man Greek customs and the adoption of heathenish manners so prevailed, that the priests ceased to concern themselves about the service of the altar, but, despising the temple and forgetting the sacrifice, they hastened to witness the spectacles in the palæstra, which were contrary to the law; cf. 2 Macc. iv. 13 ff. with 1 Macc. i. 11–15. The 2300 days are thus, as well as the 1150 days, historically authenticated.

But it is on the whole questionable whether the number given by the angel is to be reckoned as an historico-chronological period of time, or is not rather to be interpreted as symbolical. The analogy of the other prophetic numbers speaks decidedly for the symbolical interpretation. The 2300 cannot, it is true, be directly a symbolical number, such as 7, 10, 40, 70, and other numbers are, but yet it can stand in such a relation to the number seven as to receive a symbolical meaning. The longer periods of time are usually reckoned not by days, but by weeks, months, or years; if, therefore, as to the question of the duration of the 2300 days, we reduce the days to weeks, months, and years, we shall find six years, three or four months, and some days, and discover that the oppression of the people by the little horn was to continue not fully a period of seven years. But the times of God's visitations, trials, and judgments are so often measured by the number seven, that this number came to bear stamped on it this signification; see under ch. iv. 13, vii. 25. The number of seven years is used in the symbolical meaning when, not to mention the cases in Gen. xxix. 18, 27, xli. 26 f., and Judg. vi. 1, seven years' famine were laid upon the land as a punishment for David's sin in numbering the people (2 Sam. xxiv. 13), and when in Elisha's time Israel was visited with seven years' famine (2 Kings viii. 1). Thus the answer of the angel has this meaning: The time of the predicted oppression of Israel, and of the desolation of the sanctuary by Antiochus, the little horn, shall not reach the full duration of a period of divine judgment, shall not last so long as the severe oppression of Israel by the Midianites, Judg. vi. 1, or as the famine which fell upon Israel in the time of Elisha, and shall not reach to a tenth part of the time of trial and of sorrow endured by the exiles, and under the weight of which Israel then mourned.

But if this is the meaning of the angel's message, why does not the divine messenger use a pure symbolical expression, such as "not full seven times?" and why does he not simply say, "not quite seven years?" As to the first of these questions, we answer that the expression "times" is too indefinite; for the duration of this period of sorrow must be given more minutely. As to the second question, we know no other answer that can be given than this, that, on the one side, only the positive determination of the length of time, measured by days, can afford full confidence that the domination and the tyranny of the oppressor shall not continue one day longer than God has before fixed; but, on the other side, by the measuring of this period by a number defined according to thousands and hundreds, both the long duration of the affliction is shown, and the symbolical character of the period named is indicated. While by the period "evening-morning" every ambiguity of the expression, and every uncertainty thence arising regarding the actual length of the time of affliction, is excluded, yet the number 2300 shows that the period must be defined in round numbers, measuring only nearly the actual time, in conformity with all genuine prophecy, which never passes over into the mantic prediction of historico-chronological data.

If we compare with this the designation of time in ch. vii. 25, instead of the general idea there expressed, of "time, times, and half a time," which is not to be computed as to its duration, we have here a very definite space of time mentioned. This difference corresponds to the contents of the two prophecies. The oppression prophesied of in this chapter would visit the people of Israel at not too distant a time; and its commencement as well as its termination, announced by God beforehand, was fitted to strengthen believers in the faith of the truth and fidelity of God for the time of the great tribulation of the end, the duration of which God the Lord indeed determined accurately and firmly beforehand, but according to a measure of time whose extent men cannot calculate in advance. In this respect the designation of the time of the affliction which the horn growing up out of the third world-kingdom will bring upon God's people, becomes a type for the duration of the oppression of the last enemy of the church of the Lord at the end of the days.

Vers. 15–27. *The interpretation of the vision.*

The interpretation of Daniel's vision, as given by the angel, falls within the vision itself. When Daniel sought to understand the vision, viz. in his mind, not by prayer or by asking a question, he saw before him, according to ver. 17, one standing at some distance, who had the appearance of a man, but was not a man, but a supernatural being in human likeness. This person resembling a man is (ver. 16) named by the angel, *Gabriel, i.e.* man of God. The voice of another, whom Daniel did not see, hearing only a human voice proceeding from the Ulai, commanded this person to explain the vision to the prophet (לְהַלָּז, *i.e.* to Daniel). Nothing further is indicated of the person from whom the voice proceeded than what may be conjectured from בֵּין אוּלָי (*between the Ulai*), whence the voice sounded. These words do not mean "hither from Ulai" (Bertholdt), but "between the two banks of the Ulai" (Chr. B. Mich., Häv., etc.); according to which, the being whose voice Daniel heard appears as if hovering over the waters of the river Ulai. This conjecture is confirmed by ch. xii. 6, 7, where Daniel sees a man hovering over the waters of the river of Ulai, who by the majesty of his appearance and his words shows himself to be a divine being, and is more minutely described according to the majesty of his appearance in ch. x. 5 ff. The question, who this man might be, is first answered in ch. x. 5 ff. *Gabriel* is not a *nomen proprium* but *appellativum.* The angel who was described as in appearance like a גֶּבֶר (*man*) is named, for

Daniel, *Gabriel* ("man of God"), that on subsequent occasions (*e.g.* ch. ix. 21) he might recognise him again as the same (Hgst., Hofm., Kliefoth). As to his relation to other angels and archangels, the Scripture gives no information. If Lengerke and Maurer regard him, after the book of Enoch, along with Michael, and Raphael, and Uriel whose name does not occur in Scripture, as one of the four angels that stand before the throne of God, the Scripture affords no support for it; nor does it countenance the supposition of Hitzig, that the two angels in vers. 15 and 16 are identical with those in vers. 13 and 14—that Gabriel who spake, and the unknown angel, was the angel of the "rivers and fountains of waters," Rev. xvi. 4.[1]

Ver. 16. As commanded, the angel goes to the place where Daniel stands. On his approach Daniel is so filled with terror that he falls on his face, because as a sinful and mortal man he could not bear the holiness of God which appeared before him in the pure heavenly being. At the appearance of God he fears that he must die. Cf. remarks at Gen. xvi. 13 and Ex. xxxiii. 20. But the angel, in order to mitigate his alarm, calls him to take heed, for the vision relates to the time of the end. The address (ver. 17), "son of man," stands in contrast to "man of God" (= Gabriel), and is designed to remind Daniel of his human weakness (cf. Ps. viii. 5), not that he may be humbled (Hävernick), without any

[1] Altogether groundless, also, is the identification of them with the Persian Amschaspands, since neither the doctrine of angels nor the names of angels of the O. T. are derived from Parsism. The most recent attempt by Dr. Al. Kohut, in his researches regarding Jewish angelology and demonology in their dependence on Parsism (*Abhand. für die Kunde des Morgen.* iv. Bd., Nr. 3), to establish this connection, is extremely poor and superficial. The proof adduced in the first ten pages of his treatise is confined to these points: that in the writings of the O. T. after the Exile or during the Exile the appearance of the angels is altogether different from that presented in the portions written before the Exile. It is said that, as a rule, the angels in the period first named take the human form, and bear names corresponding to their properties—Michael, Dan. x. 13, 21, xii. 1; Gabriel, viii. 16, ix. 21; and in the book of Tobit, xii. 15, not much later in date (?), Raphael;—now also, in contrast to the period before the Exile, there is an order in rank among the angels; Michael, Dan. x. 12, is designated as one of the first angel-princes, and, ch. xii. 1, as the greatest angel-prince; moreover, the number of שָׂרִים (*angel-princes*) is spoken of as seven, corresponding to the Persian Amesha-çpentas (Tob. xii. 15, and Book of Enoch xc. 21). But does this distinction between the pre-exilian and post-exilian doctrine of angels, even though it were allowed to be as great as Kohut supposes, furnish a proof for the derivation of the latter from Parsism? or does this derivation follow from the fact that the Jews in exile came into intercourse

occasion for that, but to inform him that, notwithstanding this, he was deemed worthy of receiving high divine revelations (Kliefoth). The foundation of the summons to give heed, "for the vision relates to the time of the end," is variously interpreted. Auberlen (p. 87) and Zündel (p. 105 ff.) understand עֵת־קֵץ not of the time of the end of all history, but of a nearer relative end of the prophecy. "Time of the end" is the general prophetic expression for the time which, as the period of fulfilment, lies at the end of the existing prophetic horizon—in the present case the time of Antiochus. Bleek (*Jahrb. f. D. Theol.* v. p. 57) remarks, on the contrary, that if the seer was exhorted to special attention *because* the vision related to the time of the end, then קֵץ here, as in ver. 19, ch. xi. 35, 40, xii. 4, also ch. ix. 26, without doubt is to be interpreted of the end of the time of trial and sorrow of the people, and at the same time of the beginning of the new time of deliverance vouchsafed by God to His people; and herein lay the intimation, "that the beginning of the deliverance destined by God for His people (*i.e.* the Messianic time) would connect itself immediately with the cessation of the suppression of the worship of Jehovah by Antiochus Epiphanes, and with the destruction of that ruler." From the passages referred to, ch. xi. 40 and xii. 4, it is certainly proved that עֵת־קֵץ denotes the time of all suffering, and the completion of the kingdom of God by the Messiah. It does

with the Persians and the Medes, and that about this time the Zend worship flourished? And do the angels in the post-exilian writings for the first time indeed assume the human form? Kohut seems to know nothing of the appearance of angels in Gen. xix. 1 ff., Judg. vi. 11 ff., xiii. 9 ff. Then does the agreement, not of the doctrine of the O. T., but of the later Jewish apocryphal writings, Tobit and the Book of Enoch, with regard to the number of angel-princes and of the Amesha-çpentas, furnish a sufficient proof of this derivation? Dr. Kohut does not himself appear to think so, since he regards it as necessary, in addition to this, which is "perhaps purely accidental," to furnish an etymological argument. *Amesha-çpenta* means "*non connivens sanctus* = the holy one not sleeping;" "thus," he says, "it is a mere Chaldee rendering of the word *Amesha-çpenta*, when in Dan. iv. 10, 14, 20, viii. 13, the Jewish angel-princes are called עִירִין קַדִּישִׁין = holy watchers." But was, then, the Chaldean king Nebuchadnezzar, to whom in a dream a "holy watcher" appeared, a Jew? and in what edition of the Bible has Dr. Kohut found in Dan. viii. 13 the angel name עִיר? Nor is it any better proof that the demonology of the O. T. is a foreign production, resulting from the contact of the Jews with the Persians and Medes during the Exile, because in Zech. iii. 1 f., Ps. xlviii. 49, 1 Chron. xxi. 1, and especially in Job i. 6 f., ii. 1, Satan "is depicted as a plague-spirit, altogether corresponding to the Persian Agromainjus, the *killing spirit*." Such silly talk needs no refutation.

not, however, follow, either that these words "are to be understood of the absolute end of all things, of the time when the Messiah will come to set up His *regnum gloriæ*, and of the time of the last tribulation going before this coming of the Lord" (Klief.); or that the prophet cherished the idea, that immediately after the downfall of Antiochus, thus at the close of the 2300 days, the Messiah would appear, bring the world to an end, and erect the kingdom of eternity (v. Leng., Hitz., Maur., etc.). The latter conclusion is not, it is true, refuted by the remark, that the words do not say that the vision has the time of the end directly for its subject, that the prophecy will find its fulfilment in the time of the end, but only that the vision has a relation, a reference, to the time of the end, that there is a parallelism between the time of Antiochus and the time of Antichrist, that "that which will happen to Javan and Antiochus shall repeat itself in, shall be a type of, that which will happen in the time of the end with the last world-kingdom and the Antichrist arising out of it" (Kliefoth). For this idea does not lie in the words. That is shown by the parallel passage, ch. x. 14, which Kliefoth thus understands—"The vision extends to *the* days which are before named אַחֲרִית הַיָּמִים (*latter days*); it goes over the same events which will then happen." Accordingly the angel can also here (ch. viii. 17) only say, "Give heed, for the vision relates to the end-time; it gives information of that which shall happen in the end of time."

Ver. 19. The justice of this exposition is placed beyond a doubt by this verse. Here the angel says in distinct words, "I will show thee what will happen בְּאַחֲרִית הַזָּעַם (*in the last time of the indignation*), for it relates to the appointed time of the end." Kliefoth indeed thinks that what the angel, ver. 19, says to the prophet for his comfort is not the same that he had said to him in ver. 17, and which cast him down, and that ver. 19 does not contain anything so weighty and so overwhelming as ver. 17, but something more cheering and consoling; that it gives to the vision another aspect, which relieves Daniel of the sorrow which it had brought upon him on account of its import with reference to the end. From this view of the contents of ver. 19 Kliefoth concludes that Daniel, after he had recovered from his terror in the presence of the heavenly messenger, and had turned his mind to the contents of the vision, was thrown to the ground by the thought presented to him by the angel, that the vision had reference to the end of all things, and that, in order to raise him up, the angel said something else to him more comforting of the vision. But this conclusion has no foundation in the text. The circumstance that Daniel was not again cast to the ground by the communication of the angel in ver. 19, is not to be accounted for by supposing that the angel now made known to him something more consoling; but it has its foundation in this, that the angel touched the prophet, who had fallen dismayed to the earth, and placed him again on his feet (ver. 18), and by means of this touch communicated to him the strength to hear his words. But the explanation which Kliefoth gives of ver. 19 the words do not bear. "The last end of the indignation" must denote the time which will follow after the expiration of the זַעַם, *i.e.* the period of *anger* of the Babylonian Exile. But אַחֲרִית means, when space is spoken of, *that which is farthest* (cf. Ps. cxxxix. 9), and when time is spoken of, *the last*, the end, the opposite of רֵאשִׁית, the end over against *the beginning*. If אַחֲרִית הַיָּמִים does not denote such a time as follows an otherwise fixed termination, but the last time, the end-time (see under ch. ii. 28), so also, since זַעַם is here the time of the revelation of the divine wrath, אַחֲרִית הַזַּעַם can only denote the last time, or the end-time, of the revelation of the divine wrath. This explanation of the words, the only one which the terms admit of, is also required by the closing words of ver. 19, כִּי לְמוֹעֵד קֵץ (*for at the time appointed the end*). According to the example of the *Vulg.*, *quoniam habet tempus finem suum*, and Luther's version, "for the end has its appointed time," Kliefoth translates the words, "for the firmly-ordained, definite time has its end," and refers this to the time of the Babylonish Exile, which indeed, as Daniel knew (ch. ix. 2), was fixed by God to seventy years. But that the Babylonish Exile will have its fixed end, will come to an end with the seventy years, the angel needed not to announce to the prophet, for he did not doubt it, and the putting him in remembrance of that fact would have afforded him but very poor consolation regarding the time of the future wrath. This conception of the words depends on the inaccurate interpretation of the words אַחֲרִית הַזַּעַם, and will consequently fall to the ground along with it. If לְמוֹעֵד (*to the appointment*) were separated from קֵץ, and were to be taken by itself, and to be understood of the time of the זַעַם, then it ought to have the article, as in ch. xi. 27, 35. Without the article, as here, it must be connected with קֵץ, and then, with הֶחָזוֹן supplied as the subject from the context (ver. 17), is to be translated, as it is by almost all modern interpreters: for the vision relates to the appointed time of the end. But עֶת־קֵץ, *the time of the end*, and מוֹעֵד קֵץ, *the appointed time of the end*, is not the absolute end of all things, the time of the setting up of the *regnum gloriæ*, and the time of the tribulation preceding the return of our Lord; but the time of the judgment of the world-kingdom and the setting up of the everlasting kingdom of God by the appearance of the Messiah, the end of *αἰὼν οὗτος* and the commencement of the *αἰὼν μέλλων*, the time of the אַחֲרִית הַיָּמִים (ch. x. 14), which the apostle calls (1 Cor. x. 11) *τὰ τέλη τῶν αἰώνων*, and speaks of as having then already come.

Ver. 20. Since, from the explanation given by the angel in this verse, the vision relates to the Medo-Persian and the Javanic world-kingdoms, and to the persecuting kingdom of Antiochus which arose out of the latter, so it cannot be disputed that here, in prophetic perspective, the time of the end is seen together with the period of the oppression of the people of God by Antiochus, and the first appearance of the Messiah with His return in glory to the final judgment, as the latter is the case also in ch. ii. 34 f., 44 f., and vii. 13, 26 f. If Kliefoth objects: The coming of the Messiah may certainly be conceived of as bound up with the end of all things, and this is done, since both events stand in intimate causal relation to each other, not seldom in those O. T. prophets who yet do not distinguish the times; but they also know well that this intimate causal connection does not include contemporaneousness, that the coming of the Messiah in the flesh will certainly bring about the end of all things, but not as an immediate consequence, but after a somewhat lengthened intervening space, that thus, after the coming of the Messiah, a course of historical events will further unfold themselves before the end comes (which Daniel also knew, as ch. ix. shows), and where the supposition is this, as in Daniel, there the time before the appearance of Christ in the flesh cannot be called the time of the end:—then the inference drawn in these last passages is not confirmed by the contents of the book of Daniel. For in the last vision (ch. x.–xii.) which Daniel saw, not only the time of oppression of Antiochus and that of the last enemy are contemplated together as *one*, but also the whole contents of this one vision are, ch. x. 14, transferred to the "end of the days;" for the divine messenger says to Daniel, "I am come to make thee understand what shall befall thy people in the end of the days, for the vision yet relates to *the* days." And not only this, but also in ch. xi. 35 it is said of the tribulation brought upon the people of God by Antiochus, that in it many would fall, to cleanse them and to purify them to the time of the end, for it is yet for the appointed time. Here, beyond doubt, the time of the persecution by Antiochus is placed in intimate union with the time of the end, but, as is to be particularly observed, not so that the two are spoken of as synchronous. This point is of importance for the right exposition of the verse before us. If, in ch. xi. 35, 40, it is twice said כִּי עוֹד קֵץ לַמּוֹעֵד (*the end is yet for the appointed time*), and thus does not begin with the oppression of the people of God by Antiochus, so we may not conclude from these verses—and in this Kliefoth is perfectly justified—that Daniel expected the erection of the Messianic kingdom and the end of all history with the overthrow of Antiochus. If, however, on the whole, the intimate causal connection of the two periods of tribulation placed together in ch. xi. in one vision neither demands nor even permits us to regard the two as synchronous, so this erroneous conclusion drawn from these verses before us, in connection with an incorrect interpretation of ch. xi. 36–45, is sufficiently obviated, both by ch. ii. and vii., according to which the fourth world-kingdom shall precede the erection of the everlasting kingdom of God and the manifestation of the Son of man, as also by ch. ix. 24–27, where—as our exposition will show—the coming of the Messiah and the perfecting of the kingdom of God by the overthrow of the last enemy are dependent on one another in point of time—the coming of the Messiah after seven weeks, the perfecting of the kingdom of God will follow, but not till after the lapse of seventy weeks.

This passage is to be understood according to these distinct revelations and statements, and not that because in them, according to prophetic perspective, the oppression of the people of the saints by Antiochus, the little horn, is seen in one vision with the tribulation of the end-time, therefore the synchronism or identity of the two is to be concluded, and the erection of the *regnum gloriæ* and the end of the world to be placed at the destruction of this little horn. The words, " the vision relates to the time of the end," thus only declare that the prophecy has a reference to Messianic times. As to the nature of this reference, the angel gives some intimation when, having touched the prophet, who had fallen in amazement to the ground, he raised him up and enabled him to listen to his words (ver. 18), the intimation that he would make known to him what would happen in the last time of violence (ver. 19). הַזַּעַם is *the wrath* of God against Israel, the punishment which God hung over them on account of their sins, as in Isa. x. 5, Jer. xxv.

17, Ezek. xxii. 24, etc., and here the sufferings of punishment and discipline which the little horn shall bring over Israel. The time of this revelation of divine wrath is called אַחֲרִית because it belongs to the אַחֲרִית הַיָּמִים, prepares the Messianic future, and with its conclusion begins the last age of the world, of which, however, nothing more particular is here said, for the prophecy breaks off with the destruction of the little horn. The vision of the eleventh chapter first supplies more particular disclosures on this point. In that chapter the great enemy of the saints of God, arising out of the third world-kingdom, is set forth and represented as the prefiguration or type of their last enemy at the end of the days. Under the words אֲשֶׁר יִהְיֶה (*which shall be*) the angel understands all that the vision of this chapter contains, from the rising up of the Medo-Persian world-kingdom to the time of the destruction of Antiochus Epiphanes, as vers. 20–25 show. But when he adds אַחֲרִית הַזָּעַם, he immediately makes prominent that which is the most important matter in the whole vision, the severe oppression which awaits the people of Israel in the future for their purification, and repeats, in justification of that which is said, the conclusion from ver. 17, in which he only exchanges עֵת for מוֹעֵד. עֵת denotes time in the sense of a *definite point of time*, while מוֹעֵד is the *definite time in its duration*; מוֹעֵד קֵץ thus denotes *the end-time as to its duration.* This expression is here chosen with regard to the circumstance that in ver. 14 the end of the oppression was accurately defined by the declaration of its continuance. The object of these words also is variously viewed by interpreters. The meaning is not that the angel wished to console Daniel with the thought that the judgment of the vision was not yet so near at hand (Zündel); for, according to ver. 17, Daniel was not terrified by the contents of the vision, but by the approach of the heavenly being; and if, according to ver. 18, the words of the angel so increased his terror that he fell down confounded to the earth, and the angel had to raise him by touching him, yet it is not at the same time said that the words of the angel of the end-time had so confounded him, and that the subsequent fuller explanation was somewhat less overwhelming than the words, ver. 17, something lighter or more comforting. Even though the statement about the time of the end contributed to the increase of the terror, yet the contents of ver. 19 were not fitted to raise up the prophet, but the whole discourse of the angel was for Daniel so oppressive that, after hearing it, he was for some days sick, ver. 27. From Daniel's astonishment we are not to conclude that the angel in ver. 17 spoke of the absolute end of all things, and in ver. 19, on the contrary, of the end of the oppression of the people of Israel by Antiochus. By the words, "the vision relates to the appointed end-time," the angel wished only to point to the importance of his announcement, and to add emphasis to his call to the prophet to give heed.

Vers. 22–26. *After the introductory words, we have now in these verses the explanation of the chief points of the vision.*

Vers. 20–22 explain vers. 3–8. "The kings of Media and Persia" are the whole number of the Medo-Persian kings as they succeed each other, *i.e.* the Medo-Persian monarchy in the whole of its historical development. To הַצָּפִיר the epithet הַשָּׂעִיר, *hairy, shaggy*, is added to characterize the animal as an he-goat. The king of *Javan* (Greece) is the founder and representative of the Macedo-Grecian world-kingdom, or rather the royalty of this kingdom, since the great horn of the ram is forthwith interpreted of Alexander the Great, the first king of this kingdom. The words וְהַנִּשְׁבֶּרֶת to תַּחְתֶּיהָ (ver. 22) form an absolute subject-sentence, in which, however, וַתַּעֲמֹדְנָה is not to be taken ἐκβατικῶς, *it broke in pieces, so that* . . . (Kran.); for "the statement of the principal passage may not appear here in the subordinate relative passage" (Hitzig); but to the statement beginning with the participle the further definition in the *verb. fin.* with ו *consec.* is added, without the relative אֲשֶׁר, as is frequently the case (cf. Ewald's *Lehr.* § 351), which we cannot give with so much brevity, but must express thus: "as concerning the horn, that it was broken in pieces, and then four stood up in its place, (this signifies) that four kingdoms shall arise from the people." מִגּוֹי without the article does not signify *from the people* of Javan, for in this case the article would not have been omitted; nor does it signify *from the heathen world*, because a direct contrast to Israel does not lie before us; but indefinitely, *from the territory of the people*, or the world of the people, since the prophecy conceives of the whole world of the people (Völkerwelt) as united under the sceptre of the king of Javan. יַעֲמֹדְנָה is a revived archaism; cf. Gen. xxx. 38, 1 Sam. vi. 12; Ewald, § 191; Gesen. *Gramm.* § 47.—וְלֹא בְכוֹחוֹ, *but not in his power*, not armed with the strength of the first king, cf. ch. xi. 4.

Vers. 23–26 *give the interpretation of the vision of the little horn* (vers. 9–12), *with a more special definition of certain elements not made prominent in the vision.* The horn signifies a king who will arise "in the last time of their kingdom." The suffix to מַלְכוּתָם (*of their kingdom*) relates to the idea contained in מַלְכֻיּוֹת (*kings*). כְּהָתֵם הַפֹּשְׁעִים, when the transgressors have made full, *scil.* the transgression or measure of the sins. The object wanting to הָתֵם is seen from the conception of the subject. הַפֹּשְׁעִים, *the rebellious*, are not the *heathen*, for פֶּשַׁע denotes the apostasy from God which is only said of the Israelites, but not of the heathen; and the word points back to בְּפָשַׁע in ver. 12. The king that rises up is Antiochus Epiphanes (cf. 1 Macc. i. 10 ff.) עַז־פָּנִים, *hard of countenance, i.e.* impudent, unashamed in trampling down, without fear of God or man; cf. Deut. xxviii. 50. מֵבִין חִידוֹת, *understanding mysteries; here sensu malo, concealing his purpose behind ambiguous words*, using dissimulation, forming an artifice, interpreted in ver. 25 by מִרְמָה, cf. ch. xi. 21. The unfolding of these qualities is presented in vers. 24, 25; in ver. 24 of the עַז־פָּנִים. By virtue of the audacity of his conduct his power will be strengthened, וְלֹא בְכֹחוֹ, *but not by his own might.* The contrast here is not: by the power or permission of God (Ephr., Theodrt., Häv., Hitz., Kran.), reference being made to תִּנָּתֵן (*was given*) in ver. 12, and to תֵּת (*to give*) in ver. 13. This contrast is foreign to the passage. The context much rather relates to the audacity and the cunning by which, more than by his power, Antiochus raised himself to might. The strengthening of the power is limited neither to his reaching the throne by the overthrow of other pretenders to it (Berth. and others), nor to the conquest of Palestine, but relates to the power which, according to the following statements, he developed as king against Israel, as well as against other kingdoms. נִפְלָאוֹת (*wonderful works*) is used adverbially, as in Job xxxvii. 5: *in an astonishing, wonderful way*, he will work destruction. But from this word it does not follow that the expression וְלֹא בְכֹחוֹ is to be referred to the power of God, for it does not necessarily mean deeds or things supernaturally originating from God; and even though it had only this meaning, yet here they could not be thought of as deeds accomplished in God's strength, but only as deeds performed by demoniacal strength, because יַשְׁחִית (*shall destroy*) cannot be predicated of God in the sense determined by the context. This destructive work he shall direct against the mighty and against the people of the saints. עֲצוּמִים does not here signify many, numerous, many individual Israelites (v. Leng., Maur., Kliefoth), partly because in ver. 25 רַבִּים stands for that, partly because of the עַם קְדֹשִׁים, by which we are to understand *the people of Israel*, not merely the insignificant and weak, or pious

(Kran.). Hence עֲצוּמִים cannot mean the elders of Israel, much less merely foreign kings (Berth., Dereser), but the *mighty* generally, under which perhaps we are specially to think of heathen rulers.

In ver. 25 the cunning and craftiness of his action and demeanour are depicted. עַל שִׂכְלוֹ (*through his craft*) is placed first. שֵׂכֶל, *sagacity*, here *sensu malo*, *cunning*. On the ground of this cunning his deceit will be successful. מִרְמָה without the article means "all kinds of deceit which he designs" (Hitzig). On that account his heart is raised in haughtiness, so that not only does he destroy many unexpectedly, but also raises himself against God. In the רַבִּים (*many*) are comprehended "the mighty and the holy people" (ver. 24). בְּשַׁלְוָה does not mean in deep peace, but *in careless security*, and thus *unexpectedly*. An historical proof of this is found in 1 Macc. i. 10. שַׂר שָׂרִים (*Prince of princes*) corresponds with אֲדֹנֵי הָאֲדֹנִים (*Lord of lords*) in Ps. cxxxvi. 3. It is God; cf. ver. 11. But the angel adds, "he shall be destroyed without hands," *i.e.* he shall be destroyed not by the hand of man, but by God.

In ver. 26 there follows, in conclusion, the confirmation of the truth of what is said of the duration of this oppression for the people of God. Because the time of it was not seen by Daniel, but was revealed to him in words, אֲשֶׁר נֶאֱמַר is here used in reference to that which was, or of which it was, said. But we need not connect this relative sentence with the genitive הָעֶרֶב וְהַבֹּקֶר (*the evening and the morning*), although this were admissible, but can make it depend on מַרְאֵה (*vision*), since the word-revelation of the evenings and mornings forms an integral part of the "vision." הָעֶרֶב וְהַבֹּקֶר are to be taken collectively. The confirmation of the truth of this revelation does not betray the purpose to make the book falsely appear as if it were old (v. Leng., Hitzig); it much more is fitted to serve the purpose of strengthening the weakness of the faithful, and giving them consolation in the hour of trial. For in the statement of the duration of the afflictions lies not only the fact that they will come to an end, but at the same time also that this end is determined beforehand by God; cf. ch. xii. 7. In other places this confirmation serves only to meet doubts, arising from the weakness of the flesh, as to the realization of revelations of such weighty import; cf. ch. x. 1, xii. 1, Rev. xix. 9, xxi. 5, xxii. 6.

But Daniel must close the prophecy, because it extends into a long time. סָתַם is not equivalent to חָתַם, *to seal up*, but it means *to stop*, *to conclude*, *to hide* (cf. 2 Kings iii. 19, Ezek. xxviii. 3), but not in the sense of keeping secret, or because it would be incomprehensible for the nearest times; for to seal or to shut up has nothing in common with incomprehensibility, but is used in the sense of *keeping*. "A document is sealed up in the original text, and laid up in archives (shut up), that it may remain preserved for remote times, but not that it may remain secret, while copies of it remain in public use" (Kliefoth). The meaning of the command, then, is simply this: "Preserve the revelation, not because it is not yet to be understood, also not for the purpose of keeping it secret, but that it may remain preserved for distant times" (Kliefoth). The reason assigned for the command only agrees with this interpretation. לְיָמִים רַבִּים (*to many days*) is not to be identified with לְעֶת־קֵץ in ver. 17, but designates only *a long time;* and this indefinite expression is here used because it was not intended to give exactly again the termination according to vers. 17 and 19, but only to say that the time of the end was not near.

In ver. 27 the influence of this vision on Daniel is mentioned (cf. ch. vii. 28). It so deeply agitated the prophet that he was sick certain days, and not till after he had recovered from this sickness could he attend to the king's business. The contents of the vision remained fixed in his mind; the scene filled him with amazement, and no one understood it. Maurer, Hitzig, and Kranichfeld interpret אֵין מֵבִין *I understood it not*, supplying the pronoun of the first person from the connection. But even though the construction of the words should admit of this supplement, for which a valid proof is not adduced, yet it would be here unsuitable, and is derived merely from giving to סָתַם (ver. 26) the false interpretation of *to conceal*. If Daniel had been required to keep the prophecy secret according to the command in ver. 26, then the remark "no one understood it" would have been altogether superfluous. But if he was required only to preserve the prophecy, and it deeply moved him, then those around him must have had knowledge of it, and the amazement of Daniel would become the greater when not only he but all others failed to understand it. To refer אֵין מֵבִין only to Daniel is forbidden by the comparison with וְלֹא אָבִין in ch. xii. 8. The fulfilment of this vision can alone lead to its full understanding.

CHAP. IX. THE SEVENTY WEEKS.

In the first year of Darius the Median, Daniel, by a diligent study of the prophecies of Jeremiah as to the number of years during which Jerusalem must lie desolate (vers. 1, 2), was led to pour forth a penitential prayer, in which he acknowledges the justice of the divine chastisement which hung over Israel on account of their sins, and entreats the mercy of God in behalf of his people (vers. 3–19). In consequence of this prayer, the angel Gabriel (vers. 20–23) appeared, and announced to him that seventy weeks (vers. 24–27) must pass over his people and the holy city before the consummation of the kingdom of God.

Vers. 1 and 2 mention the occasion on which the penitential prayer (vers. 3–19) was offered, and the divine revelation following thereupon regarding the time and the course of the oppression of the people of God by the world-power till the completion of God's plan of salvation.

Regarding Darius, the son of Ahasverosch, of the race of the Medes, see under ch. vi. 1. In the word הָמְלַךְ the Hophal is to be noticed: *rex constitutus, factus est.* It shows that Darius did not become king over the Chaldean kingdom by virtue of a hereditary right to it, nor that he gained the kingdom by means of conquest, but that he received it (קַבֵּל, ch. vi. 1) from the conqueror of Babylon, Cyrus, the general of the army. The first year of the reign of Darius the Mede over the Chaldean kingdom is the year 538 B.C., since Babylon was taken by the Medes and Persians under Cyrus in the year 539–538 B.C. According to Ptolemy, Cyrus the Persian reigned nine years after Nabonadius. But the death of Cyrus, as is acknowledged, occurred in the year 529 B.C. From the nine years of the reign of Cyrus, according to our exposition (p. 198), two years are to be deducted for Darius the Mede, so that the reign of Cyrus by himself over the kingdom which he founded begins in the year 536, in which year the seventy years of the Babylonish exile of the Jews were completed; cf. the exposition under ch. i. 1 (p. 66 ff.) with the chronological survey in the Com. on the Books of the Kings (p. 140 ff.).

The statement as to the time, ver. 1, is again repeated in the beginning of ver. 2, on account of the relative sentence coming between, so as to connect that which follows with it. We translate (in ver. 2), with Hgstb., Maur., Hitzig, "I marked, or gave heed, in the Scriptures to the number of the years," so that מִסְפַּר (*num-*

ber) forms the object to בִּינֹתִי (*I understood*); cf. Prov. vii. 7. Neither the placing of בַּסְּפָרִים (*by books*) first nor the Atnach under this word controvert this view; for the object is placed after "by books" because a further definition is annexed to it; and the separation of the object from the verb by the Atnach is justified by this consideration, that the passage contains two statements, viz. that Daniel studied the Scriptures, and that his study was directed to the number of the years, etc. בַּסְּפָרִים, with the definite article, does not denote a collection of known sacred writings in which the writings of Jeremiah were included, so that, seeing the collection of the prophets cannot be thought of without the Pentateuch, by this word we are to understand (with Bleek, Gesenius, v. Leng., Hitzig) the recognised collection of the O. T. writings, the Law and the Prophets. For הַסְּפָרִים, τὰ βιβλιά, is not synonymous with הַכְּתוּבִים, αἱ γραφαί, but denotes only writings in the plural, but does not say that these writings formed already a recognised collection; so that from this expression nothing can be concluded regarding the formation of the O. T. canon. As little can בַּסְּפָרִים refer, with Häv. and Kran., to the letter of Jeremiah to the exiles (Jer. xxix.), for this reason, that not in Jer. xxix., but in Jer. xxv. 11 f., the seventy years of the desolation of the land of Judah, and *implic.* of Jerusalem, are mentioned. The plur. סְפָרִים also can be understood of a single letter, only if the context demands or makes appropriate this narrower application of the word, as *e.g.* 2 Kings xix. 14. But here this is not the case, since Jeremiah in two separate prophecies speaks of the seventy years, and not in the letter of ch. xxix., but only in ch. xxv., has he spoken of the seventy years' desolation of the land. In בַּסְּפָרִים lies nothing further than that writings existed, among which were to be found the prophecies of Jeremiah; and the article, *the* writings, is used, because in the following passage something definite is said of these writings.

In these writings Daniel considered the number of the years of which Jeremiah had prophesied. אֲשֶׁר, as ch. viii. 26, with respect to which, relates not to הַשָּׁנִים, but to מִסְפַּר הַשָּׁנִים (*number of the years*). It is no objection against this that the repetition of the words "seventy years" stands opposed to this connection (Klief.), for this repetition does not exist, since מִסְפַּר does not declare the number of the years. With לְמַלֹּאת (*to fulfil*) the contents of the word of Jehovah, as given by Jeremiah, are introduced. לְחָרְבוֹת does not stand for the accusative: to cause to be complete the desolation of Jerusalem (Hitzig), but לְ signifies in respect of, with regard to. This expression does not lean on Jer. xxix. 10 (Kran.), but on Jer. xxv. 12 ("when seventy years are accomplished"). חֳרָבוֹת, properly, *desolated places*, ruins, here *a desolated condition*. Jerusalem did not certainly lie in ruins for seventy years; the word is not thus to be interpreted, but is chosen partly with regard to the existing state of Jerusalem, and partly with reference to the words of Jer. xxv. 9, 11. Yet the desolation began with the first taking of Jerusalem, and the deportation of Daniel and his companions and a part of the sacred vessels of the temple, in the fourth year of Jehoiakim[1] (606 B.C.).

Consequently, in the first year of the reign of Darius the Mede over the kingdom of the Chaldeans the seventy years prophesied of by Jeremiah were now full, the period of the desolation of Jerusalem determined by God was almost expired. What was it that moved Daniel at this time to pour forth a penitential prayer in behalf of Jerusalem and the desolated sanctuary? Did he doubt the truth of the promise, that God, after seventy years of exile in Babylon, would visit His people and fulfil the good word He had spoken, that He would again bring back His people to Judea (Jer. xxix. 10)? Certainly not, since neither the matter of his prayer, nor the divine revelation which was vouchsafed to him in answer to his prayer, indicated any doubt on his part regarding the divine promise.

According to the opinion of Bleek and Ewald, it was Daniel's uncertainty regarding the termination of the seventy years which moved him to prayer. Bleek (*Jahrbb. f. D. Theol.* v. p. 71) thus expresses himself on the subject: "This prophecy of Jeremiah might be regarded as fulfilled in the overthrow of the Babylonian kingdom and the termination of the Exile, when the Jews obtained from Cyrus permission to return to their native land and to rebuild their city and temple, but yet not perfectly, so far as with the hope of the return of the people from exile there was united the ex-

[1] Thus also the seventy years of the Exile are reckoned in 2 Chron. xxxvi. 21–23, Ezra i. 1 ff. This Ewald also recognises (*Proph.* iii. p. 430), but thinks that it is not an exact reckoning of the times, but rather, according to Zech. i. 12 and Dan. ix. 25, that the destruction of Jerusalem forms the date of the commencement of the desolation and of the seventy years. But Dan. ix. 25 contains no expression, or even intimation, regarding the commencement of the Exile; and in the words of Zech. i. 12, "against which Thou hast had indignation these threescore and ten years," there does not lie the idea that the seventy years prophesied of by Jeremiah came to an end in the second year of Darius Hystaspes. See under this passage.

pectation that they would then turn in truth to their God, and that Jehovah would fulfil all His good promises to them to make them partakers of the Messianic redemption (cf. Jer. xxix. 10 ff., also other prophecies of Jeremiah and of other prophets regarding the return of the people from exile, such as Isa. xl. ff.); but this result was not connected in such extent and fulness with the return of the people and the restoration of the state." On the supposition of the absolute inspiration of the prophets, it appeared therefore appropriate "to regard Jeremiah's prophecy of the seventy years, after the expiry of which God will fulfil His good promises to His people, as stretching out into a later period beyond that to which the seventy years would extend, and on that account to inquire how it was to be properly interpreted." Ewald (*Proph.* iii. p. 421 ff.) is of opinion that these seventy years of Jeremiah did not pass by without the fulfilment of his prophecy, that the ruins of Jerusalem would not continue for ever. Already forty-nine years after its destruction a new city of Jerusalem took the place of the old as the centre of the congregation of the true religion, but the stronger hopes regarding the Messianic consummation which connected itself herewith were neither then, nor in all the long times following, down to that moment in which our author (in the age of the Maccabees) lived and wrote, ever fulfilled. Then the faithful were everywhere again exposed to the severest sufferings, such as they had not experienced since the old days of the destruction of Jerusalem. Therefore the anxious question as to the duration of such persecution and the actual beginning of the Messianic time, which Daniel, on the ground of the mysterious intimation in ch. vii. 12, 25 and viii. 13 ff., regarding the period of the sufferings of the time of the end, sought here to solve, is agitated anew; for he shows how the number of the seventy years of Jeremiah, which had long ago become sacred, yet accorded with these late times without losing its original truth. Thus Ewald argues.

These two critics in their reasoning proceed on the dogmatic ground, which they regard as firmly established, that the book of Daniel is a product of the age of the Maccabees. All who oppose the genuineness of this book agree with them in the view that this chapter contains an attempt, clothed in the form of a divine revelation communicated to the prophet in answer to his prayer, to solve the mystery how Jeremiah's prophecy of the beginning of the Messianic salvation after the seventy years of exile is to be harmonized with the fact that this salvation, centuries after the fall of the Babylonish kingdom and the return of the Jews from the Babylonish exile, had not yet come, but that instead of it, under Antiochus Epiphanes, a time of the severest oppression had come. How does this opinion stand related to the matter of this chapter, leaving out of view all other grounds for the genuineness of the book of Daniel? Does the prayer of Daniel, or the divine revelation communicated to him by means of Gabriel regarding the seventy weeks, contain elements which attest its correctness or probability?

The prayer of Daniel goes forth in the earnest entreaty that the Lord would turn away His anger from the city Jerusalem and His holy mountain, and cause His face to shine on the desolation and on the city that was called by His name (vers. 15–18). If this prayer is connected with the statement in ver. 2, that Daniel was moved thereto by the consideration of the words of Jeremiah regarding the desolation of Jerusalem, we can understand by the ruins, for the removal of which Daniel prayed, only the destruction of Jerusalem and the temple which was brought about by the Chaldeans. Consequently the prayer indicates that the desolation of Jerusalem predicted by Jeremiah and accomplished by Nebuchadnezzar still continued, and that the city and the temple had not yet been rebuilt. This, therefore, must have been in the time of the Exile, and not in the time of Antiochus, who, it is true, desolated the sanctuary by putting an end to the worship of Jehovah and establishing the worship of idols, but did not lay in ruins either the temple or the city.

In his message (vers. 24–27) the angel speaks only of the going forth of the word to restore and rebuild Jerusalem, and presents the going forth of this word as the beginning of the seventy weeks of Daniel determined upon the people and the holy city within which Jerusalem must be built, and thus distinguishes the seventy weeks as distinctly as possible from Jeremiah's seventy years during which Jerusalem and Judah should lie desolate. Thus is set aside the opinion that the author of this chapter sought to interpret the seventy years of Jeremiah by the seventy weeks; and it shows itself to be only the pure product of the dogmatic supposition, that this book does not contain prophecies of the prophet Daniel living in the time of the Exile, but only apocalyptic dreams of a Maccabean Jew.[1]

[1] The supposition that the seventy weeks, ver. 24, are an interpretation of the seventy years of Jeremiah, is the basis on which Hitzig rests the assertion that the passage does not well adjust itself to the standpoint of the pretended

Moreover, it is certainly true that in the Exile the expectation that the perfection and glory of the kingdom of God by the Messiah would appear along with the liberation of the Jews from Babylon was founded on the predictions of the earlier prophets, but that Daniel shared this expectation the book presents no trace whatever. Jeremiah also, neither in ch. xxv. nor in ch. xxix., where he speaks of the seventy years of the domination of Babylon, announces that the Messianic salvation would begin immediately with the downfall of the Babylonian kingdom. In ch. xxv. he treats only of the judgment, first over Judah, and then over Babylon and all the kingdoms around; and in ch. xxix. he speaks, it is true, of the fulfilling of the good word of the return of the Jews to their fatherland when seventy years shall be fulfilled for Babylon (ver. 10), and of the counsel of Jehovah, which is formed not for the destruction but for the salvation of His people, of the restoration of the gracious relation between Jehovah and His people, and the gathering together and the bringing back of the prisoners from among all nations whither they had been scattered (vers. 11–14), but he says not a word to lead to the idea that all this would take place immediately after these seventy years.

Now if Daniel, in the first year of Darius the Mede, *i.e.* in the sixty-ninth year of the Exile, prayed thus earnestly for the restoration of Jerusalem and the sanctuary, he must have been led to do so from a contemplation of the then existing state of things. The political aspect of the world-kingdom could scarcely have furnished to him such a motive. The circumstance that Darius did not immediately after the fall of Babylon grant permission to the Jews to return to their fatherland and rebuild Jerusalem and the temple, could not make him doubt the certainty of the fulfilment of the word of the Lord spoken by Jeremiah regarding the duration of

Daniel, but is in harmony with the time of the Maccabees. The other arguments which Hitzig and others bring forth against this chapter as the production of Daniel, consist partly in vain historical or dogmatic assertions, such as that there are doubts regarding the existence of Darius of Media,—partly in misinterpretations, such as that Daniel wholly distinguishes himself, vers. 6, 10, from the prophets, and presents himself as a reader of their writings (Hitz.),—opinions which are no better founded than the conclusions of Berth., v. Leng., and Staeh., drawn from the mention of the inhabitants of Jerusalem, ver. 7, and of the holy city, ver. 24, that Jerusalem was then still inhabited and the temple still standing. To this it is added, that the prayer of Daniel is an imitation of the prayers of Ezra ix. and Neh. ix., or, as Ewald thinks, an extract from the prayer of Baruch (Bar. ch. i. and ii.).

the Exile, since the prophecy of Isaiah, ch. xliv. 28, that *Coresch* (Cyrus) should build Jerusalem and lay the foundation of the temple was beyond question known to him, and Darius had in a certain sense reached the sovereignty over the Chaldean kingdom, and was of such an age (ch. vi. 1) that now his reign must be near its end, and Cyrus would soon mount his throne as his successor. That which moved Daniel to prayer was rather the religious condition of his own people, among whom the chastisement of the Exile had not produced the expected fruits of repentance; so that, though he did not doubt regarding the speedy liberation of his people from Babylonish exile, he might still hope for the early fulfilment of the deliverance prophesied of after the destruction of Babylon and the return of the Jews to Canaan. This appears from the contents of the prayer. From the beginning to the close it is pervaded by sorrow on account of the great sinfulness of the people, among whom also there were no signs of repentance. The prayer for the turning away of the divine wrath Daniel grounds solely on the mercy of God, and upon that which the Lord had already done for His people by virtue of His covenant faithfulness, the צְדָקוֹת (*righteousness*) of the Lord, not the "righteousness" of the people. This confession of sin, and this entreaty for mercy, show that the people, as a whole, were not yet in that spiritual condition in which they might expect the fulfilment of that promise of the Lord spoken by Jeremiah (ch. xxix. 12 ff.): "Ye shall seek me and find me, when ye shall search for me with all your heart; and I will be found of you, and will turn away your captivity," etc.

With this view of the contents of the prayer corresponds the divine answer which Gabriel brings to the prophet, the substance of which is to this effect, that till the accomplishment of God's plan of salvation in behalf of His people, yet seventy weeks are appointed, and that during this time great and severe tribulations would fall upon the people and the city.

Vers. 3–19. *Daniel's prayer.*

This prayer has been judged very severely by modern critics. According to Berth., v. Leng., Hitzig, Staeh., and Ewald, its matter and its whole design are constructed according to older patterns, in particular according to the prayers of Neh. ix. and Ezra ix., since ver. 4 is borrowed from Neh. i. 5, ix. 32; ver. 8 from Neh. ix. 34; ver. 14 from Neh. ix. 33; ver. 15 from Neh. i. 10, ix. 10; and, finally, vers. 7 and 8 from Ezra ix. 7. But if we consider this dependence more closely, we shall, it is true, find the expression בֹּשֶׁת הַפָּנִים (*confusion of faces*, vers. 7 and 8) in Ezra ix. 7, but we also find it in 2 Chron. xxxii. 21, Jer. vii. 19, and also in Ps. xliv. 16; סְלִחוֹת (*forgivenesses*, ver. 9) we find in Neh. ix. 17, but also in Ps. cxxx. 4; and תִּתַּךְ עַל (*is poured upon*, spoken of the anger of God, ver. 11) is found not only in 2 Chron. xii. 7, xxxiv. 21, 25, but also Jer. xlii. 18, xliv. 6, and Nah. i. 6. We have only to examine the other parallel common thoughts and words adduced in order at once to perceive that, without exception, they all have their roots in the Pentateuch, and afford not the slightest proof of the dependence of this chapter on Neh. ix.

The thought, "great and dreadful God, keeping the covenant and mercy," etc., which is found in ver. 4 and in Neh. i. 5, has its roots in Deut. vii. 21 and 9, cf. Ex. xx. 6, xxxiv. 7, and in the form found in Neh. ix. 32, in Deut. x. 17; the expression (ver. 15), "Thou hast brought Thy people forth out of the land of Egypt with a mighty hand," has its origin in Deut. vii. 8, ix. 26, etc. But in those verses where single thoughts or words of this prayer so accord with Neh. ix. or Ezra ix. as to show a dependence, a closer comparison will prove, not that Daniel borrows from Ezra or Nehemiah, but that they borrow from Daniel. This is put beyond a doubt by placing together the phrases: "our kings, our princes, our fathers" (Dan. vers. 5 and 8), compared with these: "our kings, our princes, *our priests*, and our fathers" (Neh. ix. 34, 32), and "our kings and our priests" (Ezra ix. 7). For here the naming of the "priests" along with the "kings and princes" is just as characteristic of the age of Ezra and Nehemiah as the omission of the "priests" is of the time of the Exile, in which, in consequence of the cessation of worship, the office of the priest was suspended. This circumstance tends to refute the argument of Stähelin (*Einl.* p. 349), that since the prayers in Chron., Ezra, and Nehem. greatly resemble each other, and probably proceed from one author, it is more likely that the author of Dan. ix. depended on the most recent historical writings, than that Dan. ix. was always before the eyes of the author of Chron.—a supposition the probability of which is not manfest.

If, without any preconceived opinion that this book is a product of the times of the Maccabees, the contents and the course of thought found in the prayer, Dan. ix., are compared with the prayers in Ezra ix. and Neh. ix., we will not easily suppose it possible that Daniel depends on Ezra and Nehemiah. The prayer of Ezra ix. 6–15 is a confession of the sins of the congregation from the days of the fathers down to the time of Ezra, in which Ezra scarcely ventures to raise his countenance to God, because as a member of the congregation he is borne down by the thought of their guilt; and therefore he does not pray for pardon, because his design is only "to show to the congregation how greatly they had gone astray, and to induce them on their part to do all to atone for their guilt, and to turn away the anger of God" (Bertheau).

The prayer, Neh. ix. 6–37, is, after the manner of Ps. cv. and cvi., an extended offering of praise for all the good which the Lord had manifested toward His people, notwithstanding that they had continually hardened their necks and revolted from Him from the time of the call of Abraham down to the time of the Exile, expressing itself in the confession, "God is righteous, but we are guilty," never rising to a prayer for deliverance from bondage, under which the people even then languished.

The prayer of Dan. ix., on the contrary, by its contents and form, not only creates the impression "of a fresh production adapted to the occasion," and also of great depth of thought and of earnest power in prayer, but it presents itself specially as the prayer of a man, a prophet, standing in a near relation to God, so that we perceive that the suppliant probably utters the confession of sin and of guilt in the name of the congregation in which he is included; but in the prayer for the turning away of God's anger his special relation to the Lord is seen, and is pleaded as a reason for his being heard, in the words, "Hear the prayer of *Thy* servant and *his* supplication (ver. 17); O *my* God, incline Thine ear" (ver. 18).[1]

The prayer is divided into two parts. Vers. 4–14 contain the confession of sin and guilt; vers. 15–19 the supplication for mercy, and the restoration of the holy city and its sanctuary lying in ruins.

[1] After the above remarks, Ewald's opinion, that this prayer is only an epitome of the prayer of Baruch (ch. i. 15–iii. 8), scarcely needs any special refutation. It is open before our eyes, and has been long known, that the prayer of Baruch in the whole course of its thoughts, and in many of the expressions found in it, fits closely to the prayer of Daniel; but also all interpreters not blinded by prejudice have long ago acknowledged that from the resemblances of this apocryphal product not merely to Dan. ix., but also much more to Jeremiah, nothing further follows than that the author of this late copy of ancient prophetic writings knew and used the book of Daniel, and was

The confession of sin divides itself into two strophes. Vers. 4–10 state the transgression and the guilt, while vers. 11–14 refer to the punishment from God for this guilt. Ver. 3 forms the introduction. The words, "Then I directed my face to the Lord," are commonly understood, after ch. vi. 11, as meaning that Daniel turned his face toward the place of the temple, toward Jerusalem. This is possible. The words themselves, however, only say that he turned his face to God the Lord in heaven, to אֲדֹנָי הָאֱלֹהִים, the Lord of the whole world, the true God, not to יְהוָֹה, although he meant the covenant God. "To seek prayer in (with) fasting," etc. "Fasting in sackcloth (penitential garment made of hair) and ashes," *i.e.* sprinkling the head with ashes as an outward sign of true humility and penitence, comes into consideration as a means of preparation for prayer, in order that one might place himself in the right frame of mind for prayer, which is an indispensable condition for the hearing of it—a result which is the aim in the seeking. In regard to this matter Jerome makes these excellent remarks: "*In cinere igitur et sacco postulat impleri quod Deus promiserat, non quod esset incredulus futurorum, sed ne securitas negligentiam et negligentia pareret offensam.*" תְּפִלָּה and תַּחֲנוּנִים = תְּחִנָּה, cf. 1 Kings viii. 38, 45, 49, 2 Chron. vi. 29, 35. תְּפִלָּה is prayer in general; תַּחֲנוּנִים, prayer for mercy and compassion, as also a petition for something, such as the turning away of misfortune or evil (*deprecari*). The design of the prayer lying before us is to entreat God that He would look with pity on the desolation of the holy city and the temple, and fulfil His promise of their restoration. This prayer is found in vers. 15–19.

Ver. 4. Since the desolation of the holy land and the exile of the people was a well-deserved punishment for their sins, and a removal of the punishment could not be hoped for without genuine humiliation under the righteous judgment of God, Daniel begins with a confession of the great transgression of the people, and of

familiar with the writings of Daniel and Jeremiah, and of other prophets, so that he imitated them. This statement, that the pseudo-Baruch in ch. i. 15–iii. 8 presents an extended imitation of Daniel's prayer, Ewald has not refuted, and he has brought forward nothing more in support of his view than the assertion, resting on the groundless supposition that the mention of the "judges" in Dan. ix. 12 is derived from Bar. ii. 1, and on the remark that the author of the book of Baruch would have nothing at all peculiar if he had formed that long prayer out of the book of Daniel, or had only wrought after this pattern —a remark which bears witness, indeed, of a compassionate concern for his protége, but manifestly says nothing for the critic.

the righteousness of the divine dealings with them, that on the ground of this confession he might entreat of the divine compassion the fulfilment of the promised restoration of Jerusalem and Israel. He prays to Jehovah אֱלֹהַי, *my* God. If we wish our prayers to be heard, then God, to whom we pray, must become *our* God. To אֶתְוַדֶּה (*I made confession*) M. Geier applies Augustine's beautiful remark on Ps. xxix.: "*Confessio gemina est, aut peccati aut laudis. Quando nobis male est in tribulationibus, confiteamur peccata nostra; quando nobis bene est in exultatione justitiæ, confiteamur laudem Deo: sine confessione tamen non simus.*" The address, "Thou great and dreadful God, who keepest the covenant," etc., points in its first part to the mighty acts of God in destroying His enemies (cf. Deut. vii. 21), and in the second part to the faithfulness of God toward those that fear Him in fulfilling His promises (cf. Deut. vii. 9). While the greatness and the terribleness of God, which Israel had now experienced, wrought repentance and sorrow, the reference to the covenant faithfulness of God served to awaken and strengthen their confidence in the help of the Almighty.

Ver. 5. God is righteous and faithful, but Israel is unrighteous and faithless. The confession of the great guilt of Israel in ver. 5 connects itself with the praise of God. This guilt Daniel confesses in the strongest words. חָטָא, to make a false step, designates sin as an erring from the right; עָוָה, to be perverse, as unrighteousness; רָשַׁע, to do wrong, as a passionate rebellion against God. To these three words, which Solomon (1 Kings viii. 47) had already used as an exhaustive expression of a consciousness of sin and guilt, and the Psalmist (Ps. cvi. 6) had repeated as the confession of the people in exile, Daniel yet further adds the expression מָרַדְנוּ, we have rebelled against God, and סוֹר, are departed, fallen away from His commandments; this latter word being in the *inf. absol.*, thereby denotes that the action is presented with emphasis.

Ver. 6. The guilt becomes the greater from the fact that God failed not to warn them, and that Israel would not hear the words of the prophets, who in His name spoke to high and low,—to kings and princes, *i.e.* the heads of tribes and families, and to the great men of the kingdom and to the fathers, *i.e.* to their ancestors, in this connection with the exclusion of kings and chiefs of the people, who are specially named, as Jer. xliv. 17, cf. Neh. ix. 32, 34; not perhaps the elders, heads of families (Cocceius, J. D. Michaelis, and others), or merely teachers (Ewald). To illustrate the meaning, there is added the expression "the whole people of the land," not merely the common people, so that no one might regard himself as exempted. Compare כָּל־עַמְּךָ, Neh. ix. 32. This expression, comprehending all, is omitted when the thought is repeated in ver. 8.

Ver. 7. Thus to God belongeth righteousness, but to the sinful people only shame. לְךָ הַצְּדָקָה does not mean: Thine was the righteous cause (Hitzig). The interpolation of the *was* is arbitrary, and צְדָקָה predicated of God is not righteous cause, but *righteousness* as a perfection which is manifested in His operations on the earth, or specially in His dealings toward Israel. בֹּשֶׁת הַפָּנִים, shame which reflects itself in the countenance, not because of disgraceful circumstances, Ezra ix. 7 (Kranichfeld), but in the consciousness of well-deserved suffering. כַּיּוֹם הַזֶּה does not mean: at this time, to-day, now (Häv., v. Leng., and others); the interpretation of כְּ in the sense of *circa* stands opposed to the definite הַזֶּה. In the formula כַּיּוֹם הַזֶּה the כְּ has always the meaning of a comparison; also in Jer. xliv. 6, 22, 23, 1 Sam. xxii. 8, and everywhere the expression has this meaning: as it happened this day, as experience has now shown or shows. See under Deut. ii. 30. Here it relates merely to לָנוּ בֹּשֶׁת הפ׳ (*to us shame*, etc.), not also to the first part of the verse. The לָנוּ is particularized by the words, "the men of Judah" (אִישׁ collectively, since the plur. אִישִׁים in this connection cannot be used; it occurs only three times in the O. T.), "and the inhabitants of Jerusalem." Both together are the citizens of the kingdom of Judah. יִשְׂרָאֵל, the whole of the rest of Israel, the members of the kingdom of the ten tribes. To both of these the further definition relates: "those that are near, and those that are far off, etc." With בְּמַעֲלָם אֲשֶׁר מ׳ (*because of their trespass which*," etc.), cf. Lev. xxvi. 40.

Ver. 8. In this verse Daniel repeats the thoughts of ver. 7*a* in order to place the sin and shame of the people opposite to the divine compassion, and then to pass from confession of sin to supplication for the sin-forgiving grace of the covenant-keeping God.

Ver. 9. Compassion and forgiveness are with the Lord our God; and these we need, for we have rebelled against Him. This thought is expanded in vers. 10–14. The rebellion against God, the refusing to hear the voice of the Lord through the prophets, the transgression of His law, of which all Israel of the twelve tribes were guilty, has brought the punishment on the whole people which the law of Moses threatened against transgressors.

Ver. 11. וַתִּתַּךְ with ו *consec.*: therefore has the curse poured itself out, and the oath, *i.e.* the curse strengthened with an oath. נָתַךְ, to pour forth, of storms of rain and hail (Ex. ix. 33), but especially of the destroying fire-rain of the divine wrath, cf. Nah. i. 6 with Gen. xix. 24, and Jer. vii. 20, xlii. 18, xliv. 6. הָאָלָה is used, Deut. xxix. 18 f., of the threatenings against the transgressors of the law in Lev. xxvi. 14 ff., Deut. xxviii. 15 ff., to which Daniel here makes reference. To strengthen the expression, he has added הַשְּׁבֻעָה (*and the oath*) to הָאָלָה, after Num. v. 21; cf. also Neh. x. 30.

Ver. 12. In this verse the *Kethiv* דְּבָרָיו, in harmony with the ancient versions, is to be maintained, and the *Keri* only as an explanation inferred from the thought of a definite curse. "Our judges" is an expression comprehending the chiefs of the people, kings and princes, as in Ps. ii. 10, cxlviii. 11.

Ver. 13. The thought of ver. 11 is again taken up once more to declare that God, by virtue of His righteousness, must carry out against the people the threatening contained in His law. אֵת before כָּל־הָרָעָה is not, with Kranichfeld, to be explained from the construction of the passive כָּתוּב with the accusative, for it does not depend on כָּתוּב, but serves to introduce the subject absolutely stated: as concerns all this evil, thus it has come upon us, as Ezek. xliv. 3, Jer. xlv. 4; cf. Ewald's *Lehrb.* § 277*d.* Regarding חִלִּינוּ אֶת־פְּנֵי י׳ (*we entreated the face*, etc.), cf. Zech. vii. 2, viii. 21. לְהַשְׂכִּיל בַּאֲמִתֶּךָ is not to be translated: to comprehend Thy faithfulness (Hitzig), for the construction with בְּ does not agree with this, and then אֱמֶת does not mean faithfulness (*Treue*), but truth (*Warheit*). The truth of God is His plan of salvation revealed in His word, according to which the sinner can only attain to happiness and salvation by turning to God and obeying His commands.

Ver. 14. Because Israel did not do this, therefore the Lord watched upon the evil, *i.e.* continually thought thereon—an idea very frequently found in Jeremiah; cf. Jer. i. 12, xxxi. 28, xliv. 27. צַדִּיק with עַל following, righteous on the ground of all His works—a testimony from experience; cf. Neh. ix. 33 (Kranichfeld).

Vers. 15–19. After this confession, there now follows the prayer for the turning away of the wrath (vers. 15 and 16) of God, and for the manifestation of His grace toward His suppliant people (vers. 17–19).

Ver. 15. This prayer Daniel founds on the great fact of the

deliverance of Israel out of Egypt, by which the Lord made for Himself a name among the nations. Jerome has here rightly remarked, not exhausting the thought however: "*memor est antiqui beneficii, ut ad similem Dei clementiam provocet.*" For Daniel does not view the deliverance of Israel out of Egypt merely as a good deed, but as an act of salvation by which God fulfilled His promise He had given to the patriarchs, ratified the covenant He made with Abraham, and by the miracles accompanying the exodus of the tribes of Israel from the land of Egypt, glorified His name before all nations (cf. Isa. lxiii. 32, 13), so that Moses could appeal to this glorious revelation of God among the heathen as an argument, in his prayer for pardon to Israel, to mitigate the anger of God which burned against the apostasy and the rebellion of the people, and to turn away the threatened destruction, Ex. xxxii. 11 ff., Num. xiv. 13. Jeremiah, and also Isaiah, in like manner ground their prayer for mercy to Israel on the name of the Lord, Jer. xxxii. 20 f., Isa. lxiii. 11–15. Nehemiah (ch. i. 10 and ix. 10) in this agrees with Jeremiah and Daniel. כַּיּוֹם הַזֶּה, in the same connection in Jer. l., does not mean, *then, at that time*, but, *as this day still:* (hast gotten Thee) a name as Thou hast it still. In order to rest the prayer alone on the honour of the Lord, on the honour of His name, Daniel again repeats the confession, *we have sinned, we have done wickedly;* cf. ver. 5.

Ver. 16. The prayer for the turning away of God's anger follows, and is introduced by a repetition of the address, "O Lord," and by a brief condensation of the motive developed in ver. 15, by the words כְּכָל־צִדְקֹתֶיךָ. צְדָקוֹת does not mean in a gracious manner, and צֶדֶק is not grace, but proofs of the divine righteousness. The meaning of the words כְּכָל־צִדְקֹתֶיךָ is not: as all proofs of Thy righteousness have hitherto been always intimately connected with a return of Thy grace, so may it also now be (Kran.); but, *according to all the proofs of Thy righteousness, i.e.* to all that Thou hitherto, by virtue of Thy covenant faithfulness, hast done for Israel. צְדָקוֹת means the great deeds done by the Lord for His people, among which the signs and wonders accompanying their exodus from Egypt take the first place, so far as therein Jehovah gave proof of the righteousness of His covenant promise. According to these, may God also now turn away His anger from His city of Jerusalem! The words in apposition, "Thy holy mountain," refer especially to the temple mountain, or Mount Zion, as the centre of the kingdom of God. The prayer is enforced not only by כָּל־צִדְקֹתֶיךָ, but also by the plea that Jerusalem is the city of God (*Thy* city). Compare Ps. lxxix. 4 and xliv. 14.

Ver. 17. In this verse the prayer is repeated in more earnest words. With הָאֵר פָּנֶיךָ (*cause Thy face to shine*) compare Ps. lxxx. 4 and Num. vi. 25. לְמַעַן אֲדֹנָי, *because Thou art Lord*, is stronger than לְמַעַנְךָ. As the Lord κατ' ἐξοχήν, God cannot let the desolation of His sanctuary continue without doing injury to His honour; cf. Isa. xlviii. 11.

Ver. 18. The argument by which the prayer is urged, derived from a reference to the desolations, is strengthened by the words in apposition: and the city over which Thy name is named; *i.e.* not which is named after Thy name, by which the meaning of this form of expression is enfeebled. The name of God is the revelation of His being. It is named over Jerusalem in so far as Jehovah gloriously revealed Himself in it; He has raised it, by choosing it as the place of His throne in Israel, to the glory of a city of God; cf. Ps. xlviii. 2 ff., and regarding this form of expression, the remarks under Deut. xxviii. 10.

The expression: and laying down my supplication before God (cf. ver. 20), is derived from the custom of falling down before God in prayer, and is often met with in Jeremiah; cf. ch. xxxviii. 26, xlii. 9, and xxxvi. 7. The *Kethiv* פְּקָחָה (ver. 18, *open*) is to be preferred to the *Keri* פְּקַח, because it is conformed to the imperative forms in ver. 19, and is in accordance with the energy of the prayer. This energy shows itself in the number of words used in vers. 18 and 19. Chr. B. Mich., under ver. 19, has well remarked: "*Fervorem precantis cognoscere licet cum ex anaphora, seu terna et mysterii plena nominis* ADONAI *repetitione, tum ex eo, quod singulis hisce imperativis He paragogicum ad intensiorem adfectum significandum superaddidit, tum ex congerie illa verborum: Audi, Condona, Attende, reliqua.*"

Vers. 20–23. *The granting of the prayer.*—While Daniel was yet engaged in prayer (עַל הַר ק', on account of the holy mountain, *i.e.* for it, see under ver. 16), an answer was already communicated to him; for the angel Gabriel came to him, and brought to him an explanation of the seventy years of Jeremiah, *i.e.* not as to their expiry, but what would happen after their completion for the city and the people of God. הָאִישׁ ג', *the* man Gabriel, refers, by the use of the definite article, back to ch. viii. 15, where Gabriel appeared to him in the form of a man. This is expressly observed in the relative clause, "whom I saw," etc. Regarding בַּתְּחִלָּה (*at the first*, ver. 21) see under ch. viii. 1. The differently interpreted words, מֻעָף בִּיעָף, belong, from their position, to the relative clause, or specially to רָאִיתִי (*I had seen*), not to נֹגֵעַ, since no ground can be perceived for the placing of the adverbial idea before the verb. The translation of מֻעָף בִּיעָף by τάχει φερόμενος (LXX.), πετόμενος (Theodot.), *cito volans* (Vulg.), from which the church fathers concluded that the angels were winged, notwithstanding the fact that rabbis, as *e.g.* Jos. Jacchiades, and modern interpreters (Häv., v. Leng., Hitz.) maintain it, is without any foundation in the words, and was probably derived by the old translators from a confounding of יָעֵף with עוּף. יָעֵף means only *wearied, to become tired*, to weary oneself by exertion, in certain places, as *e.g.* Jer. ii. 24, by a long journey or course, but nowhere to run or to flee. יְעָף, *weariness*—wearied in weariness, *i.e.* very wearied or tired. According to this interpretation, which the words alone admit of, the expression is applicable, not to the angel, whom, as an unearthly being, we cannot speak of as being wearied, although, with Kranichfeld, one may think of the way from the dwelling-place of God, removed far from His sinful people, to this earth as very long. On the contrary, the words perfectly agree with the condition of Daniel described in ch. viii. 17 f., 27, and Daniel mentions this circumstance, because Gabriel, at his former coming to him, not only helped to strengthen him, but also gave him understanding of the vision, which was to him hidden in darkness, so that his appearing again at once awakened joyful hope. נֹגֵעַ אֵלַי, not he touched me, but *he reached* me, came forward to me. For this meaning of נָגַע cf. 2 Sam. v. 8, Jonah iii. 6. "About the time of the evening sacrifice." מִנְחָה, properly the meat-offering, here comprehending the sacrifice, as is often its meaning in the later Scriptures; cf. Mal. i. 13, ii. 13, iii. 4. The time of the evening oblation was the time of evening prayer for the congregation.

Ver. 22. וַיָּבֶן, *he gave understanding, insight*, as ch. viii. 16. The words point back to ver. 2. First of all Gabriel speaks of the design and the circumstances of his coming. עַתָּה יָצָאתִי, *now*, viz. in consequence of thy morning prayer, *I am come, sc.* from the throne of God. לְהַשְׂכִּילְךָ בִינָה, *to instruct thee in knowledge*. This is more particularly declared in ver. 23. At the beginning of Daniel's prayer a word, *i.e.* a communication from God, came forth, which he brought. דָּבָר, not a commandment, or the divine commandment to Gabriel to go to Daniel, but a word of God, and particularly the word which he announced to Daniel, vers. 24–27. The sentence, "for thou art a man greatly beloved" (אִישׁ חֲמֻדוֹת=חֲמוּדוֹת, ch. x. 11, 19, *vir desideriorum, desideratissimus*), does not contain the reason for Gabriel's coming in haste, but for the principal thought of the verse, the going forth of the word of God immediately at the beginning of Daniel's prayer. הַמַּרְאֶה stands not for revelation, but is the *vision*, the *appearance* of the angel by whom the word of God was communicated to the prophet. מַרְאֶה is accordingly not the contents of the word spoken, but the form for its communication to Daniel. To both—the word and the form of its revelation—Daniel must give heed. This revelation was, moreover, not communicated to him in a vision, but while in the state of natural consciousness.

Vers. 24–27. *The divine revelation regarding the seventy weeks.*—This message of the angel relates to the most important revelations regarding the future development of the kingdom of God. From the brevity and measured form of the expression, which Auberlen designates "the lapidary style of the upper sanctuary," and from the difficulty of calculating the period named, this verse has been very variously interpreted. The interpretations may be divided into three principal classes. 1. Most of the church fathers and the older orthodox interpreters find prophesied here the appearance of Christ in the flesh, His death, and the destruction of Jerusalem by the Romans. 2. The majority of the modern interpreters, on the other hand, refer the whole passage to the time of Antiochus Epiphanes. 3. Finally, some of the church fathers and several modern theologians have interpreted the prophecy eschatologically, as an announcement of the development of the kingdom of God from the end of the Exile on to the perfecting of the kingdom by the second coming of Christ at the end of the days.[1]

[1] The *first* of these views is in our time fully and at length defended by Hävernick (*Comm.*), Hengstenberg (*Christol.* iii. 1, p. 19 ff., 2d ed.), and Auberlen (*Der Proph. Daniel*, u.s.w., p. 103 ff., 3d ed.), and is adopted also by the Catholic theologian Laur. Reinke (*die messian. Weissag. bei den gr. u. kl. Proph. des A. T.* iv. 1, p. 206 ff.), and by Dr. Pusey of England. The *second* view presents itself in the Alexandrine translation of the prophecy, more distinctly in Julius Hilarianus (about A.D. 400) (*Chronologia s. libellus de mundi duratione*, in Migne's *Biblioth. cler. univ.* t. 13, 1098), and in several rabbinical interpreters, but was first brought into special notice by the rationalistic interpreters Eichhorn, Bertholdt, v. Leng., Maurer, Ewald, Hitzig, and the mediating theologians Bleek. Wieseler (*Die* 70 *Wochen u. die* 63 *Jahrwochen des Proph. Daniel*,

In the great multiplicity of opinions, in order to give clearness to the interpretation, we shall endeavour first of all to ascertain the meaning of the words of each clause and verse, and then, after determining exegetically the import of the words, take into consideration the historical references and calculations of the periods of time named, and thus further to establish our view.

The revelation begins, ver. 24, with a general exhibition of the divine counsel regarding the city and the people of God; and then there follows, vers. 25–27, the further unfolding of the execution of this counsel in its principal parts. On this all interpreters are agreed, that the seventy weeks which are determined upon the people and the city are in vers. 25–27 divided into three periods, and are closely defined according to their duration and their contents.

Gött. 1839, with which compare the Retractation in the *Göttinger gel. Anzeigen*, 1846, p. 113 ff.), who are followed by Lücke, Hilgenfeld, Kranichfeld, and others. This view has also been defended by Hofmann (*die 70 Jahre des Jer. u. die 70 Jahrwochen des Daniel*, Nürnb. 1836, and *Weissag. u. Erfüllung*, as also in the *Schriftbew.*), Delitzsch (Art. *Daniel* in Herz.'s *Realenc.* Bd. iii.), and Zündel (in the *Kritischen Unterss.*), but with this essential modification, that Hofmann and Delitzsch have united an eschatological reference with the primary historical reference of vers. 25–27 to Antiochus Epiphanes, in consequence of which the prophecy will be perfectly accomplished only in the appearance of Antichrist and the final completion of the kingdom of God at the end of the days. Of the *third* view we have the first germs in Hippolytus and Apollinaris of Laodicea, who, having regard to the prophecy of Antichrist, ch. vii. 25, refer the statement of ver. 27 of this chapter, regarding the last week, to the end of the world; and the first half of this week they regard as the time of the return of Elias, the second half as the time of Antichrist. This view is for the first time definitely stated in the *Berleburg Bible*. But Kliefoth, in his *Comm. on Daniel*, was the first who sought to investigate and establish this opinion exegetically, and Leyrer (in Herz.'s *Realenc.* xviii. p. 383) has thus briefly stated it:—"The seventy שָׁבֻעִים, *i.e.* the καιροὶ of Daniel (ch. ix. 24 ff.) measured by sevens, within which the whole of God's plan of salvation in the world will be completed, are a symbolical period with reference to the seventy years of exile prophesied by Jeremiah, and with the accessory notion of œcumenicity. The 70 is again divided into three periods: into 7 (till Christ), 62 (till the apostasy of Antichrist), and *one* שָׁבוּעַ, the last world-ἑπτα, divided into 2 × 3½ times, the rise and the fall of Antichrist."

For the history of the interpretation, compare for the patristic period the treatise of Professor Reusch of Bonn, entitled "*Die Patrist. Berechnung der 70 Jahrwochen Daniels*," in the *Tüb. theol. Quart.* 1868, p. 535 ff.; for the period of the middle ages and of more modern times, Abr. Calovii Ἐξέτασις *theologica de septuaginta septimanis Danielis*, in the *Biblia illustr. ad Dan.* ix., and Hävernick's History of the Interpretation in his *Comm.* p. 386 ff.; and for the most recent period, R. Baxmann on the Book of Daniel in the *Theolog. Studien u. Kritiken*, 1863, iii. p. 497 ff.

Ver. 24. *Seventy weeks are determined.*—שָׁבֻעִים from שָׁבוּעַ, properly, the time divided into sevenths, signifies commonly the period of seven days, the week, as Gen. xxix. 27 f. (in the sing.), and Dan. x. 2, 3, in the plur., which is usually in the form שָׁבֻעוֹת; cf. Deut. xvi. 9 f., Ex. xxxiv. 22, etc. In the form שָׁבֻעִים there thus lies no intimation that it is not common weeks that are meant. As little does it lie in the numeral being placed after it, for it also sometimes is found before it, where, as here, the noun as the weightier idea must be emphasized, and that not by later authors merely, but also in Gen. xxxii. 15 f., 1 Kings viii. 63; cf. Gesen. *Lehrgeb.* p. 698. What period of time is here denoted by שָׁבֻעִים can be determined neither from the word itself and its form, nor from the comparison with שָׁבֻעִים יָמִים, ch. x. 2, 3, since יָמִים is in these verses added to שָׁבֻעִים, not for the purpose of designating these as day-weeks, but simply as full weeks (three weeks long). The reasons for the opinion that common (*i.e.* seven-day) weeks are not intended, lie partly in the contents of vers. 25 and 27, which undoubtedly teach that that which came to pass in the sixty-two weeks and in the one week could not take place in common weeks, partly in the reference of the seventy שָׁבֻעִים to the seventy years of Jeremiah, ver. 2. According to a prophecy of Jeremiah—so *e.g.* Hitzig reasons—Jerusalem must lie desolate for seventy years, and now, in the sixty-ninth year, the city and the temple are as yet lying waste (ver. 17 f.), and as yet nowhere are there symptoms of any change. Then, in answer to his supplication, Daniel received the answer, seventy שָׁבֻעִים must pass before the full working out of the deliverance. "If the deliverance was not yet in seventy years, then still less was it in seventy weeks. With seventy times seven months we are also still inside of seventy years, and we are directed therefore to year-weeks, so that each week shall consist of seven years. The special account of the contents of the weeks can be adjusted with the year-weeks alone; and the half-week, ver. 27, particularly appears to be identical in actual time with these three and a half times (years), ch. vii. 25." This latter element is by others much more definitely affirmed. Thus *e.g.* Kranichfeld says that Daniel had no doubt about the definite extent of the expression שָׁבוּעַ, but gave an altogether unambiguous interpretation of it when he combined the last half-week *essentially* with the known and definite three and a half *years* of the time of the end. But—we must, on the contrary, ask—where does Daniel speak of the three and a half *years* of the time of the end? He does not use the word *year* in any of the passages that fall to be here considered, but only עֵת or מוֹעֵד, time, definite time. That by this word common years are to be understood, is indeed taken for granted by many interpreters, but a satisfactory proof of such a meaning has not been adduced. Moreover, in favour of year-weeks (periods of seven years) it has been argued that such an interpretation was very natural, since they hold so prominent a place in the law of Moses; and the Exile had brought them anew very distinctly into remembrance, inasmuch as the seventy years' desolation of the land was viewed as a punishment for the interrupted festival of the sabbatical year: 2 Chron. xxxvi. 21 (Hgstb., Kran., and others). But since these periods of seven years, as Hengstenberg himself confesses, are not called in the law שָׁבֻעִים or שָׁבֻעוֹת, therefore, from the repeated designation of the seventh year as that of the great Sabbath merely (Lev. xxv. 2, 4, 5, xxvi. 34, 35, 43; 2 Chron. xxxvi. 21), the idea of year-weeks in no way follows. The law makes mention not only of the Sabbath-year, but also of periods of seven times seven years, after the expiry of which a year of jubilee was always to be celebrated (Lev. xxv. 8 ff.). These, as well as the Sabbath-years, might be called שָׁבֻעִים. Thus the idea of year-weeks has no exegetical foundation. Hofmann and Kliefoth are in the right when they remark that שָׁבֻעִים does not necessarily mean year-weeks, but an intentionally indefinite designation of a period of time measured by the number seven, whose chronological duration must be determined on other grounds. The ἀπ. λεγ. חָתַךְ means in Chald. to cut off, to cut up into pieces, then to decide, to determine closely, *e.g.* Targ. Esth. iv. 5; cf. Buxtorf, *Lex. talm.*, and Levy, *Chald. Wörterb.* s.v. The meaning for נֶחְתַּךְ, *abbreviatæ sunt* (*Vulg.* for ἐκολοβώθησαν, Matt. xxiv. 22), which Wieseler has brought forward, is not proved, and it is unsuitable, because if one cuts off a piece from a whole, the whole is diminished on account of the piece cut off, but not the piece itself. For the explanation of the sing. נֶחְתַּךְ we need neither the supposition that a definite noun, as עֵת (*time*), was before the prophet's mind (Hgstb.), nor the appeal to the inexact manner of writing of the later authors (Ewald). The sing. is simply explained by this, that שָׁבֻעִים שִׁבְעִים is conceived of as the absolute idea, and then is taken up by the passive verb impersonal, to mark that the seventy sevenths are to be viewed as a whole, as a continued period of seventy seven times following each other.

Upon thy people and upon thy holy city. In the עַל there

does not lie the conception of that which is burdensome, or that this period would be a time of suffering like the seventy years of exile (v. Lengerke). The word only indicates that such a period of time was determined upon the people. The people and the city of Daniel are called the people and the city of God, because Daniel has just represented them before God as His (Hävernick, v. Lengerke, Kliefoth). But Jerusalem, even when in ruins, is called the holy city by virtue of its past and its future history; cf. ver. 20. This predicate does not point, as Wieseler and Hitzig have rightly acknowledged, to a time when the temple stood, as Stähelin and v. Lengerke suppose. Only this lies in it, Kliefoth has justly added,—not, however, in the predicate of holiness, but rather in the whole expression,—that the people and city of God shall not remain in the state of desolation in which they then were, but shall at some time be again restored, and shall continue during the time mentioned. One must not, however, at once conclude that this promise of continuance referred only to the people of the Jews and their earthly Jerusalem. Certainly it refers first to Israel after the flesh, and to the geographical Jerusalem, because these were then the people and the city of God; but these ideas are not exhausted in this reference, but at the same time embrace the New Testament church and the church of God on earth.

The following infinitive clauses present the object for which the seventy weeks are determined, *i.e.* they intimate what shall happen till, or with the expiry of, the time determined. Although לְ before the infinitive does not mean till or during, yet it is also not correct to say that לְ can point out only the issue which the period of time finally reaches, only its result. Whether that which is stated in the infinitive clauses shall for the first time take place after the expiry of, or at the end of the time named, or shall develope itself gradually in the course of it, and only be completed at the end of it, cannot be concluded from the final לְ, but only from the material contents of the final clauses. The six statements are divided by Maurer, Hitzig, Kranichfeld, and others into three passages of two members each, thus: After the expiry of seventy weeks, there shall (1) be completed the measure of sin; (2) the sin shall be covered and righteousness brought in; (3) the prophecy shall be fulfilled, and the temple, which was desecrated by Antiochus, shall be again consecrated. The Masoretes seem, however, to have already conceived of this threefold division by placing the Atnach under צֶדֶק עֹלָמִים (the fourth clause); but it rests on a false construction of the individual members especially of the first two passages. Rather we have two three-membered sentences before us. This appears evident from the arrangement of the six statements; *i.e.* that the first three statements treat of the taking away of sin, and thus of the negative side of the deliverance; the three last treat of the bringing in of everlasting righteousness with its consequences, and thus of the positive deliverance, and in such a manner that in both classes the three members stand in reciprocal relation to each other: the fourth statement corresponds to the first, the fifth to the second, the sixth to the third—the second and the fifth present even the same verb חתם.

In the first and second statements the reading is doubtful. Instead of לַחְתֹּם (*Keth.*), *to seal*, the *Keri* has לְהָתֵם, *to end* (R. תָּמַם, *to complete*). In לְכַלֵּא a double reading is combined, for the vowel-points do not belong to the *Keth.*, which rather has לִכְלֹא, since כִּלֵּא is nowhere found in the *Piel*, but to the *Keri*, for the Masoretes hold כלא to be of the same meaning as כלה, *to be ended.* Thus the ancient translators interpreted it: LXX., τὰς ἀδικίας σπανίσαι; Theod., συντελεσθῆναι, *al.* συντελέσαι; Aquil., συντελέσαι τὴν ἀθεσίαν; Vulg., *ut consummetur prævaricatio.* Bertholdt, Rosenmüller, Gesenius, Winer, Ewald, Hitzig, Maurer, have followed them in supposing a passing of ה into א. But since כָּלָה occurs frequently in Daniel, always with ה (cf. ver. 27, ch. ch. xi. 36, xii. 7), and generally the roots with ה take the form of those with א much seldomer than the reverse, on these grounds the reading לִכְלֹא thus deserves the preference, apart from the consideration that almost all the *Keris* are valueless emendations of the Masoretes; and the parallel לחתם, decidedly erroneous, is obviously derived from ch. viii. 23. Thus the *Keri* does not give in the two passages a suitable meaning. The explanation: to finish the transgression and to make full the measure of sin, does not accord with what follows: to pardon the iniquity; and the thought that the Jews would fill up the measure of their transgression in the seventy year-weeks, and that as a punishment they would pass through a period of suffering from Antiochus and afterwards be pardoned, is untenable, because the punishment by Antiochus for their sins brought to their full measure is arbitrarily interpolated; but without this interpolation the pardon of the sins stands in contradiction to the filling up of their measure. Besides, this explanation is further opposed by the fact, that in the first two statements there must be a different subject from that which is in the third. For to fill up the measure of sin is the work of men; to pardon or forgive sin, on the other hand, is the work of God. Accordingly the *Kethiv* alone is to be adopted as correct, and the first passage to be translated thus: *to shut up the transgression.* כָּלָא means to hold back, to hold in, to arrest, to hold in prison, to shut in or shut up; hence כֶּלֶא, a prison, jail. To arrest the wickedness or shut it up does not mean to pardon it, but to hem it in, to hinder it so that it can no longer spread about (Hofm.); cf. Zech. v. 8 and Rev. xx. 3.

In the second passage, "*to seal up sin*," the חַטָּאוֹת are the several proofs of the transgression. חָתַם, to seal, does not denote the finishing or ending of the sins (Theodrt. and others). Like the Arab. خَتَمَ, it may occur in the sense of "to end," and this meaning may have originated from the circumstance that one is wont at the end of a letter or document to affix the impress of a seal; yet this meaning is nowhere found in Hebr.: see under Ex. xxviii. 12. The figure of the sealing stands here in connection with the shutting up in prison. Cf. ch. vi. 18, the king for greater security sealed up the den into which Daniel was cast. Thus also God seals the hand of man that it cannot move, Job xxxvii. 7, and the stars that they cannot give light, Job ix. 7. But in this figure to seal is not = to take away, according to which Hgstb. and many others explain it thus: the sins are here described as sealed, because they are altogether removed out of the sight of God, altogether set aside; for "that which is shut up and sealed is not merely taken away, entirely set aside, but guarded, held under lock and seal" (Kliefoth). Hence more correctly Hofmann and Kliefoth say, "If the sins are *sealed*, they are on the one side laid under custody, so that they cannot any more be active or increase, but that they may thus be guarded and held, so that they can no longer be pardoned and blotted out;" cf. Rev. xx. 3.

The third statement is, "*to make reconciliation for iniquity.*" כִּפֶּר is *terminus techn.*, to pardon, to blot out by means of a sin-offering, *i.e.* to forgive.

These three passages thus treat of the setting aside of sin and its blotting out; but they neither form a climax nor a mere *συναθροισμός*, a multiplying of synonymous expressions for the pardoning of sins, *ut tota peccatorum humani generis colluvies eo melius comprehenderetur* (M. Geier). Against the idea of a climax it is justly objected, that in that case the strongest designation of sin, הַפֶּשַׁע, which designates sin as a falling away from God, a rebelling against Him, should stand last, whereas it occurs in the first sentence. Against the idea of a συναθροισμός it is objected, that the words "to shut up" and "to seal" are not synonymous with "to make reconciliation for," *i.e.* "to forgive." The three expressions, it is true, all treat alike of the setting aside of sin, but in different ways. The first presents the general thought, that the falling away shall be shut up, the progress and the spreading of the sin shall be prevented. The other two expressions define more closely how the source whence arises the apostasy shall be shut up, the going forth and the continued operation of the sin prevented. This happens in one way with unbelievers, and in a different way with believers. The sins of unbelievers are sealed, are guarded securely under a seal, so that they may no more spread about and increase, nor any longer be active and operative; but the sins of believers are forgiven through a reconciliation. The former idea is stated in the second member, and the latter in the third, as Hofmann and Kliefoth have rightly remarked.

There follows the second group of three statements, which treat of the positive unfolding of salvation accompanying the taking away and the setting aside of sin. The first expression of this group, or the fourth in the whole number, is "*to bring in everlasting righteousness.*" After the entire setting aside of sin must come a righteousness which shall never cease. That צֶדֶק does not mean "happiness of the olden time" (Bertholdt, Rösch), nor "innocence of the former better times" (J. D. Michaelis), but "righteousness," requires at present no further proof. Righteousness comes from heaven as the gift of God (Ps. lxxxv. 11–14; Isa. li. 5–8), rises as a sun upon them that fear God (Mal. iii. 20), and is here called *everlasting*, corresponding to the eternity of the Messianic kingdom (cf. ii. 44, vii. 18, 27). צֶדֶק comprehends the internal and the external righteousness of the new heavens and the new earth, 2 Pet. iii. 13. This fourth expression forms the positive supplement of the first: in the place of the absolutely removed transgression is the perfected righteousness.

In the fifth passage, *to seal up the vision and prophecy*, the word חָתַם, used in the second passage of sin, is here used of righteousness. The figure of sealing is regarded by many interpreters in the sense of confirming, and that by filling up, with reference to the custom of impressing a seal on a writing for the confirmation of its contents; and in illustration these references are given: 1 Kings xxi. 8, and Jer. xxxii. 10, 11, 44 (Hävernick, v. Lengerke, Ewald, Hitzig, and others). But for this figurative use of the word to seal, no proof-passages are adduced from the O. T. Add to this that the word cannot be used here in a different sense from that in which it is used in the second passage. The sealing of the prophecy corresponds to the sealing of the transgression, and must be similarly understood. The prophecy is sealed when it is laid under a seal, so that it can no longer actively show itself.

The interpretation of the object חָזוֹן וְנָבִיא is also disputed. Berth., Ros., Bleek, Ewald, Hitzig, Wieseler, refer it to the prophecy of the seventy weeks (Jer. xxv. and xxix.), mentioned in ver. 2. But against this view stands the fact of the absence of the article; for if by חָזוֹן *that* prophecy is intended, an intimation of this would have been expected at least by the definite article, and here particularly would have been altogether indispensable. It is also condemned by the word נָבִיא added, which shows that both words are used in comprehensive generality for all existing prophecies and prophets. Not only the prophecy, but the prophet who gives it, *i.e.* not merely the prophecy, but also the calling of the prophet, must be sealed. Prophecies and prophets are sealed, when by the full realization of all prophecies prophecy ceases, no prophets any more appear. The extinction of prophecy in consequence of its fulfilment is not, however (with Hengstenberg), to be sought in the time of the manifestation of Christ in the flesh; for then only the prophecy of the Old Covenant reached its end (cf. Matt. xi. 13, Luke xxii. 37, John i. 46), and its place is occupied by the prophecy of the N. T., the fulfilling of which is still in the future, and which will not come to an end and terminate (*καταργηθήσεται*, 1 Cor. xiii. 8) till the kingdom of God is perfected in glory at the termination of the present course of the world's history, at the same time with the full conclusive fulfilment of the O. T. prophecy; cf. Acts. iii. 21. This fifth member stands over against the second, as the fourth does over against the first. "When the sins are sealed, the prophecy is also sealed, for prophecy is needed in the war against sin; when sin is thus so placed that it can no longer operate, then prophecy also may come to a state of rest; when sin comes to an end in its place, prophecy can come to an end also by its fulfilment, there being no place for it after the setting aside of sin. And when the apostasy is shut up, so that it can no more spread about, then righteousness will be brought, that it may possess the earth, now freed from sin, shut up in its own place" (Kliefoth).

The sixth and last clause, *to anoint a most holy*, is very differently interpreted. Those interpreters who seek the fulfilment of this word of revelation in the time. following nearest the close of the Exile, or in the time of the Maccabees, refer this clause either to the consecration of the altar of burnt-offering (Wieseler), which was restored by Zerubbabel and Joshua (Ezra iii. 2 ff.), or to the consecration of the temple of Zerubbabel (J. D. Michaelis, Jahn, Steudel), or to the consecration of the altar of burnt-offering which was desecrated by Antiochus Epiphanes, 1 Macc. iv. 54 (Hitzig, Kranichfeld, and others). But none of these interpretations can be justified. It is opposed by the *actual fact*, that neither in the consecration of Zerubbabel's temple, nor at the re-consecration of the altar of burnt-offering desecrated by Antiochus, is mention made of any anointing. According to the definite, uniform tradition of the Jews, the holy anointing oil did not exist during the time of the second temple. Only the Mosaic sanctuary of the tabernacle, with its altars and vessels, were consecrated by anointing. Ex. xxx. 22 ff., xl. 1–16; Lev. viii. 10 ff. There is no mention of anointing even at the consecration of Solomon's temple, 1 Kings viii. and 2 Chron. v.–vii., because that temple only raised the tabernacle to a fixed dwelling, and the ark of the covenant as the throne of God, which was the most holy furniture thereof, was brought from the tabernacle to the temple. Even the altar of burnt-offering of the new temple (Ezek. xliii. 20, 26) was not consecrated by anointing, but only by the offering of blood. Then the special fact of the consecration of the altar of burnt-offering, or of the temple, does not accord with the general expressions of the other members of this verse, and was on the whole not so significant and important an event as that one might expect it to be noticed after the foregoing expressions. What Kranichfeld says in confirmation of this interpretation is very far-fetched and weak. He remarks, that "as in this verse the prophetic statements relate to a taking away and כַּפֵּר of sins, in the place of which righteousness is restored, accordingly the anointing will also stand in relation to this sacred action of the כפר, which primarily and above all conducts to the significance of the altar of Israel, that, viz., which stood in the outer court." But, even granting this to be correct, it proves nothing as to the anointing even of the altar of burnt-offering. For the preceding clauses speak not only of the כפר of transgression, but also of the taking away (closing and sealing) of the apostasy and of sin, and thus of a setting aside of sin, which did not take place by means of a sacrifice. The fullest expiation also for the sins of Israel which the O. T. knew, viz. that on the great day of atonement, was not made on the altar of burnt-offering, but by the sprinkling of the blood of the offering on the ark of the covenant in the holy of holies, and on the altar of incense in the most holy place. If מָשַׁח is to be explained after the כִּפֵּר, then by "holy of holies" we would have to understand not "primarily" the altar of burnt-offering, but above all the holy vessels of the inner sanctuary, because here it is not an atonement needing to be repeated that is spoken of, but one that avails for ever.

In addition to this, there is the *verbal* argument that the words קֹדֶשׁ קָדָשִׁים are not used of a single holy vessel which alone could be thought of. Not only the altar of burnt-offering is so named, Ex. xxix. 37, xl. 10, but also the altar of incense, Ex. xxx. 10, and the two altars with all the vessels of the sanctuary, the ark of the covenant, shew-bread, candlesticks, basins, and the other vessels belonging thereto, Ex. xxx. 29, also the holy material for incense, Ex. xxx. 36, the shew-bread, Lev. xxiv. 9, the meat-offering, Lev. ii. 3, 10, vi. 10, x. 12, the flesh of the sin-offering and of the expiatory sacrifice, Lev. vi. 10, 18, x. 17, vii. 1, 6, xiv. 13, Num. xviii. 9, and that which was sanctified to the Lord, Lev. xxvii. 28. Finally, the whole surroundings of the hill on which the temple stood, Ezek. xliii. 12, and the whole new temple, Ezek. xlv. 3, is named a "most holy;" and according to 1 Chron. xxiii. 13, Aaron and his sons are sanctified as קֹדֶשׁ קָדָשִׁים.

Thus there is no good ground for referring this expression to the consecration of the altar of burnt-offering. Such a reference is wholly excluded by the fact that the consecration of Zerubbabel's temple and altar, as well as of that which was desecrated by Antiochus, was a work of man, while the anointing of a "most holy" in the verse before us must be regarded as a divine act, because the three preceding expressions beyond controversy announce divine actions. Every anointing, indeed, of persons or of things was performed by men, but it becomes a work of God when it is performed with the divinely ordained holy anointing oil by priests or prophets according to God's command, and then it is the means and the symbol of the endowment or equipment with the Spirit of God. When Saul was anointed by Samuel, the Spirit of the Lord came upon him, 1 Sam. x. 9 ff. The same thing was denoted by the anointing of David, 1 Sam. xvi. 13 f. The anointing also of the tabernacle and its vessels served the same object, consecrating them as the place and the means of carrying on the gracious operations of the Spirit of God. As an evidence of this, the glory of the Lord filled the tabernacle after it was set up and consecrated. At the dedication of the sanctuary after the Exile, under Zerubbabel and in the Maccabean age, the anointing was wanting, and there was no entrance into it also of the glory of the Lord. Therefore these consecrations cannot be designated as anointings and as the works of God, and the angel cannot mean these works of men by the "anointing of a most holy."

Much older, more general, and also nearer the truth, is the explanation which refers these words to the anointing of the Messiah, an explanation which is established by various arguments. The translation of the LXX., *καὶ εὐφράναι ἅγιον ἁγίων*, and of Theod., *τοῦ χρῖσαι ἅγιον ἁγίων*, the meaning of which is controverted, is generally understood by the church Fathers as referring to the Messiah. Theodoret sets it forth as undoubtedly correct, and as accepted even by the Jews; and the old Syriac translator has introduced into the text the words, "till the Messiah, the Most Holy."[1] But this interpretation is set aside by the absence of the article. Without taking into view 1 Chron. xxiii. 13, the words קֹדֶשׁ קָדָשִׁים are nowhere used of persons, but only of things. This meaning lies at the foundation of the passage in the book of Chronicles referred to, "that he should sanctify a קֹדֶשׁ קָדָשִׁים, anoint him (Aaron) to be a most holy thing." Following Hävernick, therefore, Hengstenberg (2d ed. of his *Christol.* iii. p. 54) seeks to make this meaning applicable also for the Messianic interpretation, for he thinks that Christ is here designated as a most holy thing. But neither in the fact that the high priest bore on his brow the inscription קֹדֶשׁ לַיהוָה, nor in the declaration regarding Jehovah, "He shall be לְמִקְדָּשׁ," Isa. viii. 14, cf. Ezek. xi. 16, is there any ground for the conclusion that the Messiah could simply be designated as a most holy thing. In Luke i. 35 Christ is spoken of by the simple neuter *ἅγιον*, but not by the word

[1] Eusebius, *Demonstr. Ev.* viii. 2, p. 387, ed. Colon., opposes the opinion that the translation of Aquila, *καὶ ἀλεῖψαι ἡγιασμένον ἡγιασμένων*, may be understood of the Jewish high priest. Cf. Raymundis Martini, *Pugio fidei*, p. 285, ed. Carpz., and Edzard *ad Abodah Sara*, p. 246 sq., for evidences of the diffusion of this interpretation among the Jews.

"object;" and the passages in which Jesus is described as ὁ ἅγιος, Acts iii. 14, iv. 30, 1 John ii. 20, Rev. iii. 7, prove nothing whatever as to this use of קֹדֶשׁ of Christ. Nothing to the purpose also can be gathered from the connection of the sentence. If in what follows the person of the Messiah comes forward to view, it cannot be thence concluded that He must also be mentioned in this verse.

Much more satisfactory is the thought, that in the words "to anoint a קֹדֶשׁ קָדָשִׁים" the reference is to the anointing of a new sanctuary, temple, or most holy place. The absence of the article forbids us, indeed, from thinking of the most holy place of the earthly temple which was rebuilt by Zerubbabel, since the most holy place of the tabernacle as well as of the temple is constantly called קֹדֶשׁ הַקֳּדָשִׁים. But it is not this definite holy of holies that is intended, but a new holy of holies which should be in the place of the holy of holies of the tabernacle and the temple of Solomon. Now, since the new temple of the future seen by Ezekiel, with all its surroundings, is called (Ezek. xlv. 3) קֹדֶשׁ קָדָשִׁים, Hofmann (*de* 70 *Jahre*, p. 65) thinks that the holy of holies is the whole temple, and its anointing with oil a figure of the sanctification of the church by the Holy Ghost, but that this shall not be in the conspicuousness in which it is here represented till the time of the end, when the perfected church shall possess the conspicuousness of a visible sanctuary. But, on the contrary, Kliefoth (p. 307) has with perfect justice replied, that "the most holy, and the temple, so far as it has a most holy place, is not the place of the congregation where it comes to God and is with God, but, on the contrary, is the place where God is present for the congregation, and manifests Himself to it." The words under examination say nothing of the people and the congregation which God will gather around the place of His gracious presence, but of the objective place where God seeks to dwell among His people and reveal Himself to them. The anointing is the act by which the place is consecrated to be a holy place of the gracious presence and revelation of God. If thus the anointing of a most holy is here announced, then by it there is given the promise, not of the renewal of the place already existing from of old, but of the appointment of a new place of God's gracious presence among His people, a new sanctuary. This, as Kliefoth further justly observes, apart from the connection, might refer to the work of redemption perfected by the coming of Christ, which has indeed created in

Him a new place of the gracious presence of God, a new way of God's dwelling among men. But since this statement is closely connected with those going before, and they speak of the perfect setting aside of transgression and of sin, of the appearance of everlasting righteousness, and the shutting up of all prophecy by its fulfilment, thus of things for which the work of redemption completed by the first appearance of Christ has, it is true, laid the everlasting foundation, but which first reach their completion in the full carrying through of this work of salvation in the return of the Lord by the final judgment, and the establishment of the kingdom of glory under the new heavens and on the new earth,—since this is the case, we must refer this sixth statement also to that time of the consummation, and understand it of the establishment of the new holy of holies which was shown to the holy seer on Patmos as *ἡ σκηνὴ τοῦ Θεοῦ μετὰ τῶν ἀνθρώπων*, in which God will dwell with them, and they shall become His people, and He shall be their God with them (Rev. xxi. 1–3). In this holy city there will be no temple, for the Lord, the Almighty God, and the Lamb is its temple, and the glory of God will lighten it (vers. 22, 23). Into it nothing shall enter that defileth or worketh abomination (ver. 27), for sin shall then be closed and sealed up; there shall righteousness dwell (2 Pet. iii. 13), and prophecy shall cease (1 Cor. xiii. 8) by its fulfilment.

From the contents of these six statements it thus appears that the termination of the seventy weeks coincides with the end of the present course of the world. But ver. 24 says nothing as to the commencement of this period. Nor can this be determined, as many interpreters think, from the relation in which the revelation of the seventy weeks stands to the prayer of Daniel, occasioned by Jeremiah's prophecy of the seventy years of the desolation of Jerusalem. If Daniel, in the sixty-ninth year of the desolation, made supplication to the Lord for mercy in behalf of Jerusalem and Israel, and on the occasion of this prayer God caused Gabriel to lay open to him that seventy weeks were determined upon the city and the people of God, it by no means thence follows that seventy year-weeks must be substituted in place of the seventy years prophesied of, that both commence simultaneously, and thus that the seventy years of the Exile shall be prolonged to a period of oppression for Israel lasting for seventy year-weeks. Such a supposition is warranted neither by the contents of the prophecy of Jeremiah, nor by the message of the angel to Daniel. Jeremiah, it is true, prophesied not merely of seventy years of the desolation of Jerusalem and Judah, but also of the judgment upon Babylon after the expiry of these years, and the collecting together and bringing back of Israel from all the countries whither they were scattered into their own land (ch. xxv. 10–12, xxix. 10–14); but in his supplication Daniel had in his eye only the desolation of the land of Jeremiah's prophecy, and prayed for the turning away of the divine anger from Jerusalem, and for the pardon of Israel's sins. Now if the words of the angel had been, "not seventy years, but seventy year-weeks, are determined over Israel," this would have been no answer to Daniel's supplication, at least no comforting answer, to bring which to him the angel was commanded to go forth in haste. Then the angel announces in ver. 24 much more than the return of Israel from the Exile to their own land. But this is decided by the contents of the following verses, in which the space of seventy weeks is divided into three periods, and at the same time the commencement of the period is determined in a way which excludes its connection with the beginning of the seventy years of the Exile.

Ver. 25. The detailed statement of the 70 שָׁבֻעִים in 7 + 62 + 1 (vers. 25, 26, 27), with the fuller description of that which was to happen in the course of these three periods of time, incontrovertibly shows that these three verses are a further explication of the contents of ver. 24. This explication is introduced by the words: "Know therefore, and understand," which do not announce a new prophecy, as Wieseler and Hofmann suppose, but only point to the importance of the further opening up of the contents of ver. 24, since וְתַשְׂכֵּל (*and thou wilt understand*) stands in distinct relation to לְהַשְׂכִּילְךָ בִינָה (*to give thee skill and understanding*, ver. 22). The two parts of ver. 25 contain the statements regarding the first two portions of the whole period, the seven and the sixty-two שָׁבֻעִים, and are rightly separated by the Masoretes by placing the Atnach under שָׁבֻעָה. The first statement is: "*from the going forth of the command to restore and to build Jerusalem unto a Messiah* (Gesalbten), *a prince, shall be seven weeks.*" מֹצָא דָבָר (*from the going forth of the commandment*) formally corresponds, indeed, to יָצָא דָבָר (*the commandment came forth*), ver. 23, emphatically expressing a decision on the part of God, but the two expressions are not actually to be identified; for *the commandment*, ver. 23, is the divine revelation communicated in vers. 24–27, which the angel brings to Daniel; *the commandment* in ver. 25 is, on the contrary, more fully determined by the words, *to restore and to build*, etc. לְהָשִׁיב

is not to be joined adverbially with וְלִבְנוֹת so as to form *one* idea: *to build again;* for, though שׁוּב may be thus used adverbially in Kal, yet the Hiphil הֵשִׁיב is not so used. הֵשִׁיב means *to lead back, to bring again,* then *to restore;* cf. for this last meaning Isa. i. 26, Ps. lxxx. 4, 8, 20. The object to לְהָשִׁיב follows immediately after the word וְלִבְנוֹת, namely, Jerusalem. The supplementing of עָם, *people* (Wieseler, Kliefoth, and others), is arbitrary, and is not warranted by Jer. xxix. 10. To bring back, to restore a city, means to raise it to its former state; denotes the *restitutio,* but not necessarily the full *restitutio in integrum* (against Hengstenberg). Here לִבְנוֹת is added, as in the second half of the verse to תָּשׁוּב, yet not so as to make one idea with it, *restoring to build,* or *building to restore, i.e.* to build up again to the old extent. בָּנָה as distinguished from הֵשִׁיב denotes the building after restoring, and includes the constant preservation in good building condition, as well as the carrying forward of the edifice beyond its former state.

But if we ask when this commandment went forth, in order that we may thereby determine the beginning of the seven weeks, and, since they form the first period of the seventy, at the same time determine the beginning of the seventy weeks, the words and the context only supply this much, that by the "commandment" is meant neither the word of God which is mentioned in ver. 23, nor that mentioned in ver. 2. It is not that which is mentioned in ver. 23, because it says nothing about the restoration of Jerusalem, but speaks only of the whole message of the angel. Nor yet is it the word of God which is mentioned in ver. 2, the prophecies given in Jer. xxv. and xxix., as Hitzig, Kranichfeld, and others suppose. For although from these prophecies it conclusively follows, that after the expiry of the seventy years with the return of Israel into their own land, Jerusalem shall again be built up, yet they do not speak of that which shall happen after the seventy years, but only of that which shall happen within that period, namely, that Jerusalem shall for so long a time lie desolate, as ver. 2 expressly affirms. The prophecy of the seventy years' duration of the desolation of Jerusalem (ver. 2) cannot possibly be regarded as the commandment (in ver. 25) to restore Jerusalem (Kliefoth). As little can we, with Hitzig, think on Jer. xxx. and xxxi., because this prophecy contains nothing whatever of a period of time, and in this verse before us there is no reference to this prophecy. The restoration of Israel and of Jerusalem has indeed been prophesied of in general, not merely by Jeremiah, but also long before him by Isaiah (ch. xl.–lxvi.). With as much justice may we think on Isa. xl. ff. as on Jer. xxx. and xxxi.; but all such references are excluded by this fact, that the angel names the commandment for the restoration of Jerusalem as the *terminus a quo* for the seventy weeks, and thus could mean only a word of God whose going forth was somewhere determined, or could be determined, just as the appearance of the מָשִׁיחַ נָגִיד is named as the termination of the seven weeks. Accordingly "the going forth of the commandment to restore," etc., must be a *factum* coming into visibility, the time of which could without difficulty be known—a word from God regarding the restoration of Jerusalem which went forth by means of a man at a definite time, and received an observable historical execution.

Now, with Calvin, Œcolampadius, Kleinert, Nägelsbach, Ebrard, and Kliefoth, we can think of nothing more appropriate than the edict of Cyrus (Ezra i.) which permitted the Jews to return, from which the termination of the Exile is constantly dated, and from the time of which this return, together with the building up of Jerusalem, began, and was carried forward, though slowly (Klief.). The prophecy of Isa. xliv. 28, that God would by means of Cyrus speak to cause Jerusalem to be built, and the foundation of the temple to be laid, directs us to this edict. With reference to this prophecy, it is said in Ezra vi. 14, "They builded according to the commandment of the God of Israel, and according to the commandment of the king of Persia." This is acknowledged even by Hengstenberg, who yet opposes this reference; for he remarks (*Christol.* iii. p. 142), "If the statement were merely of the commencement of the building, then they would undoubtedly be justified who place the starting-point in the first year of Cyrus. Isaiah (ch. xlv. 13) commends Cyrus as the builder of the city; and all the sacred writings which relate to the period from the time of Cyrus to Nehemiah distinctly state the actual existence of a Jerusalem during this period." But according to his explanation, the words of the angel do not announce the beginning of the building of the city, but much rather the beginning of its "completed restoration according to its ancient extent and its ancient glory." But that this is not contained in the words לְהָשִׁיב וְלִבְנוֹת? we have already remarked, to which is to be added, that the placing in opposition the commencement of the building and the commencement of its completed restoration is quite arbitrary and vain, since certainly the commencement of the restoration at the same time includes in it the commencement of the completed restoration. In favour of interpreting לְהָשִׁיב of the completed restoration, Hengstenberg remarks that "in the announcement the temple is named along with the city in ver. 26 as well as in ver. 27. That with the announcement of the building the temple is not named here, that mention is made only of the building of the streets of the city, presupposes the sanctuary as already built up at the commencement of the building which is here spoken of; and the existence of the temple again requires that a commencement of the rebuilding of the city had also been already made, since it is not probable that the angel should have omitted just that which was the weightiest matter, that for which Daniel was most grieved, and about which he had prayed (cf. vers. 17, 20) with the greatest solicitude." But the validity of this conclusion is not obvious. In ver. 26 the naming of the temple along with the city is required by the facts of the case, and this verse treats of what shall happen after the sixty-two weeks. How, then, shall it be thence inferred that the temple should also be mentioned along with the city in ver. 25, where the subject is that which forms the beginning of the seven or of the seventy weeks, and that, since this was not done, the temple must have been then already built? The non-mention of the temple in ver. 24, as in ver. 25, is fully and simply explained by this, that the word of the angel stands in definite relation to the prayer of Daniel, but that Daniel was moved by Jeremiah's prophecy of the seventy years' duration of the חָרְבוֹת of Jerusalem to pray for the turning away of the divine wrath from the city. As Jeremiah, in the announcement of the seventy years' desolation of the land, did not specially mention the destruction of the temple, so also the angel, in the decree regarding the seventy weeks which are determined upon the people of Israel and the holy city, makes no special mention of the temple; as, however, in Jeremiah's prophecy regarding the desolation of the land, the destruction not only of Jerusalem, but also of the temple, is included, so also in the building of the holy city is included that of the temple, by which Jerusalem was made a holy city. Although thus the angel, in the passage before us, does not expressly speak of the building of the temple, but only of the holy city, we can maintain the reference of the מֹצָא דָבָר to the edict of Cyrus, which constituted an epoch in the history of Israel, and consider this edict as the beginning of the termination of the seven *resp.* seventy weeks.

The words עַד מָשִׁיחַ נָגִיד show the termination of the seven weeks. The words מָשִׁיחַ נָגִיד are not to be translated *an anointed prince* (Bertholdt); for מָשִׁיחַ cannot be an adjective to נָגִיד, because in Hebr. the adjective is always placed after the substantive, with few exceptions, which are inapplicable to this case; cf. Ewald's *Lehrb.* § 293*b*. Nor can מָשִׁיחַ be a participle: *till a prince is anointed* (Steudel), but it is a noun, and נָגִיד is connected with it by apposition: *an anointed one, who at the same time is a prince.* According to the O. T., kings and priests, and only these, were anointed. Since, then, מָשִׁיחַ is brought forward as the principal designation, we may not by נָגִיד think of a priest-prince, but only of a prince of the people, nor by מָשִׁיחַ of a king, but only of a priest; and by מָשִׁיחַ נָגִיד we must understand a person who first and specially is a priest, and in addition is a prince of the people, a king. The separation of the two words in ver. 26, where נָגִיד is acknowledged as meaning a prince of the people, leads to the same conclusion. This priest-king can neither be Zerubbabel (according to many old interpreters), nor Ezra (Steudel), nor Onias III. (Wieseler); for Zerubbabel the prince was not anointed, and the priest Ezra and the high priest Onias were not princes of the people. Nor can Cyrus be meant here, as Saad., Gaon., Bertholdt, v. Lengerke, Maurer, Ewald, Hitzig, Kranichfeld, and others think, by a reference to Isa. xlv. 1; for, supposing it to be the case that Daniel had reason from Isa. xlv. 1 to call Cyrus מָשִׁיחַ—which is to be doubted, since from this epithet מְשִׁיחוֹ, *His* (Jehovah's) *anointed,* which Isaiah uses of Cyrus, it does not follow as of course that he should be named מָשִׁיחַ—the title ought at least to have been נָגִיד מָשִׁיחַ, the מָשִׁיחַ being an adjective following נָגִיד, because there is no evident reason for the express precedence of the adjectival definition.[1]

The O. T. knows only One who shall be both priest and king in one person (Ps. cx. 4; Zech. vi. 13), Christ, the Messias (John iv.

[1] "It is an unjustifiable assertion that every heathen king may also bear the name מָשִׁיחַ, *anointed.* In all the books of the O. T. there is but a single heathen king, Cyrus, who is named מָשִׁיחַ (Isa. xlv. 1), and he not simply as such, but because of the remarkable and altogether singular relation in which he stood to the church, because of the gifts with which God endowed him for her deliverance, . . . and because of the typical relation in which he stood to the author of the higher deliverance, the Messiah. Cyrus could in a certain measure be regarded as a theocratic ruler, and as such he is described by Isaiah."—HENGSTENBERG.

25), whom, with Hävernick, Hengstenberg, Hofmann, Auberlen, Delitzsch, and Kliefoth, we here understand by the מָשִׁיחַ נָגִיד, because in Him the two essential requisites of the theocratic king, the anointing and the appointment to be the נָגִיד of the people of God (cf. 1 Sam. x. 1, xiii. 14, xvi. 13, xxv. 30; 2 Sam. ii. 4, v. 2 f.), are found in the most perfect manner. These requisites are here attributed to Him as predicates, and in such a manner that the being anointed goes before the being a prince, in order to make prominent the spiritual, priestly character of His royalty, and to designate Him, on the ground of the prophecies, Isa. lxi. 1–3 and lv. 4, as the person by whom "the sure mercies of David" (Isa. lv. 3) shall be realized by the covenant people.[1] The absence of the definite article is not to be explained by saying that מָשִׁיחַ, somewhat as צֶמַח, Zech. iii. 8, vi. 12, is used κατ' ἐξ. as a *nomen propr.* of the Messiah, the Anointed; for in this case נָגִיד ought to have the article, since in Hebrew we cannot say דָּוִד מֶלֶךְ, but only דָּוִד הַמֶּלֶךְ. Much rather the article is wanting, because it shall not be said: *till the Messiah, who is prince*, but only: *till one comes who is anointed and at the same time prince*, because He that is to come is not definitely designated as the expected Messiah, but must be made prominent by the predicates ascribed to Him only as a personage altogether singular.

Thus the first half of ver. 25 states that the first seven of the seventy weeks begin with the edict (of Cyrus) permitting the return of Israel from exile and the restoration of Jerusalem, and extend from that time till the appearance of an anointed one who at the same time is prince, *i.e.* till Christ. With that view the supposition that שָׁבֻעִים are year-weeks, periods of seven years, is irreconcilable. Therefore most interpreters who understand Christ as the מָשִׁיחַ נָגִיד, have referred the following number, *and sixty-two weeks*, to the first clause—"from the going forth of the command . . . . *seven weeks and sixty-two weeks*." Thus Theodotion: ἕως Χριστοῦ ἡγουμένου ἑβδομάδες ἑπτὰ καὶ ἑβδομάδες ἑξηκονταδύο; and the Vulgate: *usque ad Christum ducem hebdomades septem et hebdomades sexaginta duæ erunt.* The text of the LXX. is here, how-

[1] In the מָשִׁיחַ נָגִיד it is natural to suppose there is a reference to the passages in Isaiah referred to; yet one must not, with Hofmann and Auberlen, hence conclude that Christ is as King of Israel named מָשִׁיחַ, and as King of the heathen נָגִיד, for in the frequent use of the word נָגִיד of the king of Israel in the books of Samuel it is much more natural to regard it as the reference to David.

ever, completely in error, and is useless. This interpretation, in recent times, Hävernick, Hengstenberg, and Auberlen have sought to justify in different ways, but without having succeeded in invalidating the reasons which stand opposite to them. First of all the Atnach forbids this interpretation, for by it the seven שָׁבֻעִים are separated from the sixty-two. This circumstance, however, in and of itself decides nothing, since the Atnach does not always separate clauses, but frequently also shows only the point of rest within a clause; besides, it first was adopted by the Masoretes, and only shows the interpretation of these men, without at all furnishing any guarantee for its correctness. But yet this view is not to be overlooked, as Hgstb. himself acknowledges in the remark: "Here the separation of the two periods of time was of great consequence, in order to show that the seven and the sixty-two weeks are not a mere arbitrary dividing into two of one whole period, but that to each of these two periods its own characteristic mark belongs." With this remark, Hävernick's assertion, that the dividing of the sixty-nine שבעים into seven and sixty-two is made only on account of the solemnity of the whole passage, is set aside as altogether vain, and the question as to the ground of the division presses itself on our earnest attention. If this division must indicate that to each of the two periods its own distinctive characteristic belongs, an unprejudiced consideration of the words shows that the characteristic mark of the "seven weeks" lies in this, that this period extends from the going forth of the word to restore Jerusalem till the appearance of an Anointed one, a Prince, thus terminating with the appearance of this Prince, and that the characteristic mark for the "sixty-two weeks" consists in that which the words immediately connected therewith affirm, תָּשׁוּב וְנִבְנְתָה וגו׳, and thus that the "sixty-two weeks" belong indeed to the following clause. But according to Hengstenberg the words ought not to be so understood, but thus: "sixty-nine weeks must pass away, seven till the completed restoration of the city, sixty-two from that time till the Anointed, the Prince." But it is clearly impossible to find this meaning in the words of the text, and it is quite superfluous to use any further words in proof of this.[1] By the remark,

[1] Hengstenberg, as Kliefoth has remarked, has taken as the first *terminus ad quem* the words "to restore and to build Jerusalem," *till* the rebuilding of Jerusalem, till its completed rebuilding, till that Jerusalem is again built; and then the further words, "unto the Messiah the Prince," as the second *terminus ad quem;* and, finally, he assigns the seven weeks to the first *terminus ad quem,*

"If the second designation of time is attributed to that which follows, then we cannot otherwise explain it than that during sixty-two weeks the streets will be restored and built up; but this presents a very inappropriate meaning,"—by this remark the interpretation in question is neither shown to be possible, nor is it made evident. For the meaning would be inappropriate only if by the building up of Jerusalem we were to understand merely the rebuilding of the city which was laid in ruins by the Chaldeans. If we attribute the expression "and sixty-two weeks" to the first half of the verse, then the division of the sixty-nine weeks into seven weeks and sixty-two weeks is unaccountable; for in ver. 26 we must then read, "after sixty-nine weeks," and not, as we find it in the text, "after sixty-two weeks." The substitution, again [in ver. 26], of only this second designation of time (sixty-two weeks) is also intelligible only if the sixty-two weeks in ver. 25 belong to the second half of the verse, and are to be separated from the seven weeks. The bringing together of the seven and of the sixty-two weeks stands thus opposed to the context, and is maintained merely on the supposition that the שָׁבֻעִים are year-weeks, or periods of time consisting of seven years, in order that sixty-nine year-weeks, *i.e.* 483 years, might be gained for the time from the rebuilding of Jerusalem to Christ. But since there is in the word itself no foundation for attaching to it this meaning, we have no right to distort the language of the text according to it, but it is our duty to let this interpretation fall aside as untenable, in order that we may do justice to the words of the prophecy. The words here used demand that we connect the period "and sixty-two weeks" with the second half of the verse, "and during sixty-two weeks shall the street be built again," etc. The "sixty-two weeks" are not united antithetically to the "seven weeks" by the *copula* ו, as Hofmann would have it, but are connected simply as following the seven; so that that which is named as the contents of the "sixty-two weeks" is to be interpreted as happening first after the appearance of the *Maschiach Nagid*, or, more distinctly, that the appearance of the Messias forming the *terminus ad quem* of the seven weeks, forms at the same time the *terminus a quo* of the sixty-two weeks. That event which brings the close of the sixty-

and the sixty-two weeks is the second; as if the text comprehended two clauses, and declared that from the going forth of the commandment till that Jerusalem was rebuilt are seven *heptades*, and from that time till a Messiah, a Prince, are sixty-two *heptades*.

two weeks is spoken of in ver. 26 in the words יִכָּרֵת מָשִׁיחַ, *Messiah shall be cut off*. The words "and sixty-two שָׁבֻעִים" may be taken grammatically either as the absolute nominative or as the accusative of duration. The words תָּשׁוּב וְנִבְנְתָה refer undoubtedly to the expression לְהָשִׁיב וְלִבְנוֹת (*to restore and to build*), according to which תָּשׁוּב is not to be joined adverbially to וְנִבְנְתָה (according to Hävernick, Hofmann, and Wieseler), but is to be rendered intransitively, corresponding to הָשִׁיב: *shall be restored*, as Ezek. xvi. 55, 1 Kings xiii. 6, 2 Kings v. 10, 14, Ex. iv. 7. The subject to both verbs is not (Rosenmüller, Gesenius, v. Leng., Hgstb.) רְחוֹב, but Jerusalem, as is manifest from the circumstance that the verbs refer to the restoration and the building of Jerusalem, and is placed beyond a doubt by this, that in Zech. viii. 5 רחוב is construed as masculine; and the opinion that it is *generis fœm.* rests only on this passage before us. There is no substantial reason for interpreting (with Klief.) the verbs impersonally.

The words רְחוֹב וְחָרוּץ are difficult, and many interpretations have been given of them. There can be no doubt that they contain together one definition, and that רְחוֹב is to be taken as the adverbial accusative. רְחוֹב means the street and the wide space before the gate of the temple. Accordingly, to חָרוּץ have been given the meanings ditch, wall, aqueduct (Ges., Steud., Zünd., etc.), pond (Ewald), confined space (Hofmann), court (Hitzig); but all these meanings are only hit upon from the connection, as are also the renderings of the LXX. εἰς πλάτος καὶ μῆκος, of Theod. πλατεῖα καὶ τεῖχος, and of the Vulg. *platea et muri.* חָרַץ means to cut, then to decide, to determine, to conclude irrevocably; hence חָרוּץ, *decision, judgment,* Joel iv. 14. This meaning is maintained by Häv., Hgstb., v. Leng., Wies., and Kran., and וְחָרוּץ is interpreted as a participle: "and it is determined." This shall form a contrast to the words, "but in the oppression of the times" —and it is determined, namely, that Jerusalem shall be built in its streets, but the building shall be accomplished in troublous times. But although this interpretation be well founded as regards the words themselves, it does not harmonize with the connection. The words רְחוֹב וְחָרוּץ plainly go together, as the old translators have interpreted them. Now רְחוֹב does not mean properly street, but a wide, free space, as Ezra x. 9, the open place before the temple, and is applied to streets only in so far as they are free, unoccupied spaces in cities. חָרוּץ, that which is cut off, limited, forms a contrast to this, not, however, as that we may interpret the words, as

Hofm. does, in the sense of width, and space cut off, not capable of extension, or free space and limited quarter (Hitzig), an interpretation which is too far removed from the primary import of the two words. It is better to interpret them, with Kliefoth, as "wide space, and yet also limited," according to which we have the meaning, "Jerusalem shall be built so that the city takes in a wide space, has wide, free places, but not, however, unlimited in width, but such that their compass is measured off, is fixed and bounded."

The last words, וּבְצוֹק הָעִתִּים, point to the circumstances under which the building proceeds: *in the difficulty, the oppression of the times.* The book of Nehemiah, iii. 33, iv. 1 ff., vi. 1 ff., ix. 36, 37, furnishes a historical exposition of them, although the words do not refer to the building of the walls and bulwarks of the earthly Jerusalem which was accomplished by Nehemiah, but are to be understood, according to Ps. li. 20, of the spiritual building of the City of God.

Ver. 26. *After the threescore and two weeks, i.e.* in the seventieth שָׁבוּעַ, *shall the Messiah be cut off.*—From the אַחֲרֵי (*after*) it does not with certainty follow that the "cutting off" of the *Maschiach* falls wholly in the beginning of the seventieth week, but only that the "cutting off" shall constitute the first great event of this week, and that those things which are mentioned in the remaining part of the verse shall then follow. The complete designation of the time of the "cutting off" can only be found from the whole contents of vers. 26 and 27. נִכְרַת, from כָּרַת, to hew down, to fell, to cut to pieces, signifies *to be rooted up, destroyed, annihilated,* and denotes generally a violent kind of death, though not always, but only the uprooting from among the living, or from the congregation, and is therefore the usual expression for the destruction of the ungodly—*e.g.* Ps. xxxvii. 9, Prov. ii. 22—without particularly designating the manner in which this is done. From יִכָּרֵת it cannot thus be strictly proved that this part of the verse announces the putting to death of an anointed one, or of the Messiah. Of the word *Maschiach* three possible interpretations have been given: 1. That the *Maschiach Nagid* of ver. 25, the *Maschiach* of ver. 26, and the *Nagid* of ver. 26*b*, are three different persons; 2. that all the three expressions denote one and the same person; and 3. that the *Maschiach Nagid* of ver. 25 and the *Maschiach* of ver. 26 are the same person, and that the *Nagid* of ver. 26*b* is another and a different person. The first of these has been maintained by J. D.

Michaelis, Jahn. Ebrard understands by all the three expressions the Messiah, and supposes that he is styled fully *Maschiach Nagid* in ver. 25 in order that His calling and His dignity (מָשִׁיחַ), as well as His power and strength (נָגִיד), might be designated; in ver. 26*a*, מָשִׁיחַ, the *anointed*, where mention is made of His sufferings and His rejection; in ver. 26*b*, נָגִיד, the *prince*, where reference is made to the judgment which He sends (by the Romans on apostate Jerusalem). But this view is refuted by the circumstance that הַבָּא (*that is to come*) follows נָגִיד, whereby the prince is represented as first coming, as well as by the circumstance that נָגִיד הַבָּא, who destroys the city and the sanctuary, whose end shall be with a flood, consequently cannot be the Messiah, but is the enemy of the people and kingdom of God, who shall arise (ch. vii. 24, 25) in the last time. But if in ver. 26 the *Nagid* is different from the *Maschiach*, then both also appear to be different from the *Maschiach Nagid* of ver. 25. The circumstance that in ver. 26 מָשִׁיחַ has neither the article nor the addition נָגִיד following it, appears to be in favour of this opinion. The absence of the one as well as of the other denotes that מָשִׁיחַ, after that which is said of Him, in consideration of the connection of the words, needs no more special description. If we observe that the destruction of the city and the sanctuary is so connected with the *Maschiach* that we must consider this as the immediate or first consequence of the cutting off of the *Maschiach*, and that the destruction shall be brought about by a *Nagid*, then by *Maschiach* we can understand neither a secular prince or king nor simply a high priest, but only an anointed one who stands in such a relation to the city and sanctuary, that with his being "cut off" the city and the sanctuary lose not only their protection and their protector, but the sanctuary also loses, at the same time, its character as the sanctuary, which the *Maschiach* had given to it. This is suitable to no Jewish high priest, but only to the Messias whom Jehovah anointed to be a Priest-King after the order of Melchizedek, and placed as Lord over Zion, His holy hill. We agree therefore with Hävernick, Hengstenberg, Auberlen, and Kliefoth, who regard the *Maschiach* of this verse as identical with the *Maschiach Nagid* of ver. 25, as Christ, who in the fullest sense of the word is the Anointed; and we hope to establish this view more fully in the following exposition of the historical reference of this word of the angel.

But by this explanation of the מָשִׁיחַ we are not authorized to regard the word יִכָּרֵת as necessarily pointing to the death of the Messias, the crucifixion of Christ, since יִכָּרֵת, as above shown, does not necessarily denote a violent death. The right interpretation of this word depends on the explanation of the words וְאֵין לוֹ which follow — words which are very differently interpreted by critics. The supposition is grammatically inadmissible that אֵין לוֹ = אֵינֶנּוּ (Michaelis, Hitzig), although the LXX. in the *Codex Chisianus* have translated them by καὶ οὐκ ἔσται; and in general all those interpretations which identify אֵין with לֹא, as *e.g. et non sibi*, and not for himself (Vitringa, Rosenmüller, Hävernick, and others). For אַיִן is never interchanged with לֹא, but is so distinguished from it that לֹא, *non*, is negation purely, while אַיִן, "it is not," denies the existence of the thing; cf. Hengstenberg's *Christol.* iii. p. 81 f., where all the passages which Gesenius refers to as exemplifying this exchange are examined and rightly explained, proving that אַיִן is never used in the sense of לֹא. Still less is לוֹ to be taken in the sense of אֲשֶׁר לוֹ, "there shall not then be one who (belongs) to him;" for although the *pronomen relat.* may be wanting in short sentences, yet that can be only in such as contain a subject to which it can refer. But in the אַיִן no subject is contained, but only the non-existence is declared; it cannot be said: no one is, or nothing is. In all passages where it is thus rightly translated a participle follows, in which the personal or actual subject is contained, of which the non-existence is predicated. אֵין לוֹ without anything following is elliptical, and the subject which is not, which will not be, is to be learned from the context or from the matter itself. The missing subject here cannot be מָשִׁיחַ, because לוֹ points back to מָשִׁיחַ; nor can it be עָם, *people* (Vulg., Grotius), or a *descendant* (Wieseler), or a *follower* (Auberlen), because all these words are destitute of any support from the context, and are brought forward arbitrarily. Since that which "is not to Him" is not named, we must thus read the expression in its undefined universality: *it is not to Him*, viz. that which He must have, to be the *Maschiach*. We are not by this to think merely of dominion, people, sanctuary, but generally of the place which He as *Maschiach* has had, or should have, among His people and in the sanctuary, but, by His being "cut off," is lost. This interpretation is of great importance in guiding to a correct rendering of יִכָּרֵת; for it shows that יִכָּרֵת does not denote the putting to death, or cutting off of existence, but only the annihilation of His place as *Maschiach* among His people and in His kingdom. For if after His "cutting off" He has not what He should have, it is clear that annihilation does not apply to Him personally, but only that He has lost His place and function as the *Maschiach*.[1]

In consequence of the cutting off of the מָשִׁיחַ destruction falls upon the city and the sanctuary. This proceeds from the people of the prince who comes. יַשְׁחִית, *to destroy, to ruin*, is used, it is true, of the desolating of countries, but predicated of a city and sanctuary it means to *overthrow;* cf. *e.g.* Gen. xix. 13 f., where it is used of the destruction of Sodom; and even in the case of countries the הִשְׁחִית consists in the destruction of men and cattle; cf. Jer. xxxvi. 29.

The meaning of עַם נָגִיד הַבָּא depends chiefly on the interpretation of the הַבָּא. This we cannot, with Ebrard, refer to עָם. Naturally it is connected with נָגִיד, not only according to the order of the words, but in reality, since in the following verse (ver. 27) the people are no longer spoken of, but only the actions and proceedings of the prince are described. הַבָּא does not mean *qui succedit* (Roesch, Maurer), but is frequently used by Daniel of a hostile coming; cf. ch. i. 1, xi. 10, 13, 15. But in this sense הַבָּא appears to be superfluous, since it is self-evident that the prince, if he will destroy Jerusalem, must come or draw near. One also must not say that הַבָּא designates the prince as one who was to come (ἐρχόμενος), since from the expression "coming days," as meaning "future days," it does not follow that a "coming prince" is a "future prince." The הַבָּא with the article: "he who comes, or will come," denotes much rather the נָגִיד (which is without the article) as such an one whose coming is known, of whom Daniel has heard that he will come to destroy the people of God. But in the earlier revelations Daniel heard of two princes who shall bring destruction on his people: in ch. vii. 8, 24 ff., of Antichrist; and in ch. viii. 9 ff., 23 ff., of Antiochus. To one of these the הַבָּא points. Which of the two is meant must be gathered from the connection, and this excludes the reference to Antiochus, and necessitates our thinking of the Antichrist.

In the following clause: "*and his end with the flood,*" the suffix

[1] Kranichfeld quite appropriately compares the strong expression יִכָּרֵת with "the equally strong יְבַלֵּא (*shall wear out*) in ch. vii. 25, spoken of that which shall befall the saints on the part of the enemy of God in the last great war. As by this latter expression destruction in the sense of complete annihilation cannot be meant, since the saints personally exist after the catastrophe (cf. vers. 27, 22, 18), so also by this expression here (יִכָּרֵת) we are not to understand annihilation."

refers simply to the hostile *Nagid*, whose end is here emphatically placed over against his coming (Kran., Hofm., Kliefoth). Preconceived views as to the historical interpretation of the prophecy lie at the foundation of all other references. The Messianic interpreters, who find in the words a prophecy of the destruction of Jerusalem by the Romans, and thus understand by the *Nagid* Titus, cannot apply the suffix to *Nagid*. M. Geier, Hävernick, and others, therefore, refer it (the suffix) to the city and the sanctuary; but that is grammatically inadmissible, since הָעִיר (*the city*) is *gen. fœm.* Aub. and others refer it, therefore, merely to the sanctuary; but the separation of the city from the sanctuary is quite arbitrary. Vitringa, C. B. Michaelis, Hgstb., interpret the suffix as neuter, and refer it to יַשְׁחִית (*shall destroy*), or, more correctly, to the idea of destroying comprehended in it, for they understand שֶׁטֶף of a warlike overflowing flood: "and the end of it shall be (or: it shall end) in the flood." On the other hand, v. Lengerke and Kliefoth have rightly objected to this view. "This reference of the suffix," they say, "is inadmissibly harsh; the author must have written erroneously, since he suggested the reference of the suffix to עָם or to נָגִיד. One cannot think of what is meant by the end of the destruction, since the destruction itself is the end; a flood may, it is true, be an emblem of a warlike invasion of a country, but it never signifies the warlike march, the expedition." There thus remains nothing else than to apply the suffix to the *Nagid*, the prince. קֵץ can accordingly only denote the destruction of the prince. Hitzig's interpretation, that קִצּוֹ is the result of his coming, refutes itself.

In בַּשֶּׁטֶף the article is to be observed, by which alone such interpretations as "in an overflowing" (Ros., Roed., and others), "*vi quadam ineluctabili oppressus*" (Steudel, Maurer), "like an overflowing," and the like, are proved to be verbally inadmissible. The article shows that a definite and well-known overflowing is meant. שֶׁטֶף, "overflowing," may be the emblem of an army spreading itself over the land, as in ch. xi. 10, 22, 26, Isa. viii. 8, or the emblem of a judgment desolating or destroying a city, country, or people; cf. Ps. xxxii. 6, Nah. i. 8, Prov. xxvii. 4, Ps. xc. 5. The first of these interpretations would give this meaning: The prince shall find his end in his warlike expedition; and the article in בַּשֶּׁטֶף would refer back to הַבָּא. This interpretation is indeed quite possible, but not very probable, because שֶׁטֶף would then be the overflowing which was caused by the hostile prince or his coming, and the thought would be this, that he should perish in it. But this agrees neither with the following clause, that war should be to the end, nor with ch. vii. 21, 26, according to which the enemy of God holds the superiority till he is destroyed by the judgment of God. Accordingly, we agree with Wieseler, Hofmann, Kranichfeld, and Kliefoth in adopting the other interpretation of שֶׁטֶף, *flood*, as the figure of the desolating judgment of God, and explain the article as an allusion to the flood which overwhelmed Pharaoh and his host. Besides, the whole passage is, with Maurer and Klief., to be regarded as a relative clause, and to be connected with הַבָּא: the people of a prince who shall come and find his destruction in the flood.

This verse (ver. 26) contains a third statement, which adds a new element to the preceding. Rosenmüller, Ewald, Hofm., and others connect these into one passage, thus: and to the end of the war a decree of desolations continues. But although קֵץ, grammatically considered, is the *stat. constr.*, and might be connected with מִלְחָמָה (*war*), yet this is opposed by the circumstance, that in the preceding sentence no mention is expressly made of war; and that if the war which consisted in the destruction of the city should be meant, then מִלְחָמָה ought to have the article. From these reasons we agree with the majority of interpreters in regarding מִלְחָמָה as the predicate of the passage: "and to the end is war;" but we cannot refer קֵץ, with Wieseler, to the end of the prince, or, with Häv. and Aub., to the end of the city, because קֵץ has neither a suffix nor an article. According to the just remark of Hitzig, קֵץ without any limitation is the *end* generally, the end of the period in progress, the seventy שָׁבֻעִים, and corresponds to עַד סוֹפָא in ch. vii. 26, to the end of all things, ch. xii. 13 (Klief.). To the end war shall be = war shall continue during the whole of the last שָׁבוּעַ.

The remaining words, נֶחֱרֶצֶת שֹׁמֵמוֹת, form an apposition to מִלְחָמָה, notwithstanding the objection by Kliefoth, that since desolations are a consequence of the war, the words cannot be regarded as in apposition. For we do not understand why in abbreviated statements the effect cannot be placed in the form of an apposition to the cause. The objection also overlooks the word נֶחֱרֶצֶת. If desolations are the effect of the war, yet not the decree of the desolations, which can go before the war or can be formed during the war. שֹׁמֵמוֹת denotes desolation not in an active, but in a passive sense: *laid waste, desolated,* cf. ver. 27. נֶחֱרֶצֶת, *that which is determined*, the *irrevocably decreed;* therefore used of divine decrees, and that of decrees with reference to the infliction of punishment; cf. ver. 27, ch. xi. 36, Isa. x. 23, xxviii. 22. Ewald is quite in error when he says that it means "the decision regarding the fearful deeds, the divine decision as it embodies itself in the judgments (ch. vii. 11 f.) on the world on account of such fearful actions and desolations," because שֹׁמֵמוֹת has not the active meaning. Auberlen weakens its force when he renders it "decreed desolations." "That which is decreed of desolations" is also not a fixed, limited, measured degree of desolations (Hofm., Klief.); for in the word there does not lie so much the idea of limitation to a definite degree, as much rather the idea of the absolute decision, as the connection with כָּלָה in ver. 27, as well as in the two passages from Isaiah above referred to, shows. The thought is therefore this: "Till the end war will be, for desolations are irrevocably determined by God." Since שֹׁמֵמוֹת has nothing qualifying it, we may not limit the "decree of desolations" to the laying waste of the city and the sanctuary, but under it there are to be included the desolations which the fall of the prince who destroys the city and the sanctuary shall bring along with it.

Ver. 27. This verse contains four statements.

The *first* is: "*He shall confirm the covenant to many for one week.*" Following the example of Theodotion, many (Häv., Hgstb., Aub., v. Leng., Hitzig, Hofm.) regard שָׁבוּעַ אֶחָד as the subject: one week shall confirm the covenant to many. But this poetic mode of expression is only admissible where the subject treated of in the statement of the speaker comes after the action, and therefore does not agree with הִגְבִּיר בְּרִית, where the confirming of the covenant is not the work of time, but the deed of a definite person. To this is to be added the circumstance that the definitions of time in this verse are connected with those in ver. 25, and are analogous to them, and must therefore be alike interpreted in both passages. But if, notwithstanding these considerations, we make שָׁבוּעַ אֶחָד the subject, the question then presses itself upon us, Who effects the confirming of the covenant? Hävernick, Hengstenberg, and Auberlen regard the Messias as the subject, and understand by the confirming of the covenant, the confirming of the New Covenant by the death of Christ. Ewald, v. Lengerke, and others think of Antiochus and the many covenants which, according to 1 Macc. i. 12, he established between the apostate Jews and the heathen Greeks. Hitzig understands by the "covenant" the

O. T. Covenant, and gives to הִגְבִּיר the meaning to make grievous: The one week shall make the covenant grievous to many, for they shall have to bear oppression on account of their faith. On the other hand, Hofmann (*Schriftbew.*) renders it: The one week shall confirm many in their fidelity to the faith. But none of these interpretations can be justified. The reasons which Hengstenberg adduces in support of his view that the Messias is the subject, are destitute of validity. The assertion that the Messias is the chief person spoken of in the whole of this passage, rests on the supposition, already proved to be untenable, that the prince who was to come (ver. 26) was the instrument of the Anointed, and on the passages in Isa. liii. 11 and xlii. 6, which are not parallel to that under consideration. The connection much more indicates that *Nagid* is the subject to הִגְבִּיר, since the prince who was to come is named last, and is also the subject in the suffix of קִצּוֹ (*his end*), the last clause of ver. 26 having only the significance of an explanatory subordinate clause. Also "the taking away of the daily sacrifice combines itself in a natural way with the destruction (ver. 26) of the city and the temple brought about by the נָגִיד הַבָּא;"—further, "he who here is represented as 'causing the sacrifice and oblation to cease' is obviously identical with him who changes (ch. vii. 25) the times and usages of worship (more correctly: times and law)" (Kran.). "The reference of הִגְבִּיר to the ungodly leader of an army, is therefore according to the context and the parallel passages of this book which have been mentioned, as well as in harmony with the natural grammatical arrangement of the passage," and it gives also a congruous sense, although by the *Nagid* Titus cannot naturally be understood. הִגְבִּיר בְּרִית means to strengthen a covenant, *i.e.* to make a covenant strong (Hitzig has not established the rendering: to make grievous). "Covenant" does not necessarily mean the covenant of God (Old Testament or New Testament Covenant), since the assertion that this word occurs only in this book with reference to the covenant of God with Israel (Hgstb.) does not also prove that it must here have this meaning; and with regard particularly to ch. xi. 22, it is very questionable. The expression הִגְבִּיר בְּרִית with לְ is analogous to כָּרַת בְּרִית [*icere fœdus*] with לְ; and the construction with לְ signifies that as in the forming of a covenant, so in the confirming of a covenant, the two contracting parties are not viewed as standing on an equality, but he who concludes or who confirms the covenant prevails, and imposes or forces the covenant on the other party. The reference to the covenant of

God with man is thus indeed suggested, yet it is not rendered necessary, but only points to a relation analogous to the concluding of a covenant emanating from God. לָרַבִּים with the article signifies *the many*, *i.e.* the great mass of the people in contrast with the few, who remain faithful to God; cf. Matt. xxiv. 12. Therefore the thought is this: That ungodly prince shall impose on the mass of the people a strong covenant that they should follow him and give themselves to him as their God.

While the first clause of this verse announces what shall happen during the whole of the last week, the *second* treats only of the half of this period. חֲצִי הַשָּׁבוּעַ we cannot grammatically otherwise interpret than the definition of time mentioned immediately before, and thus, for reasons given above, cannot take it as the subject of the clause, but only as the accusative of the duration of time, consequently not in the sense of the ablative: in the midst of the week. The controversy whether חֲצִי here means *half*, or *midst*, has no bearing on the matter, and acquires significance only if we interpret חֲצִי, in opposition to the context, as synonymous with בַּחֲצִי, or with Klief., which is equally untenable and impossible in this context, regard חֲצִי הַשָּׁבוּעַ as an absolute definition. חֲצִי signifies only *half*, not midst. Only where the representation of an extent of space or period of time prevails can we render it, without a change of its meaning, by the word midst. In the half of the night is the same as in the middle of the night, at midnight, Ex. xii. 29; in the half of the firmament, Josh. x. 13, is the same as in the middle of the space of the heavens across which the sun moves during day; in the half of the day of life is the same as in the middle of the period of life, Ps. cii. 25. But during the half of the week is not the same as: in the middle of the week. And the objection, that if we here take חֲצִי in the sense of *half*, then the heptad or cycle of seven would be divided into two halves (Klief.), and yet of only one of them was anything said, is without significance, because it would touch also the explanation "and in the midst of the heptad," since in this case of the first, before the middle of the expiring half of the week, nothing also is said of what shall be done in it. If Kliefoth answers this objection by saying that we must conceive of this from the connection, namely, that which brings the power of Antichrist to its height, then we shall be able also, in the verbally correct interpretation of חֲצִי הַשָּׁבוּעַ, to conceive from the connection what shall happen in the remaining period of the שָׁבוּעַ. Yet weaker is the further objection: "that which is mentioned as coming to pass חֲצִי הַשָּׁבוּעַ, the causing of the offering of sacrifice to cease, is something which takes place not during a period of time, but at a *terminus*" (Kliefoth); for since הִשְׁבִּית does not properly mean *to remove*, but *to make to rest*, *to make quiet*, it is thus not conceivable why we should not be able to say: The sacrifice shall be made to rest, or made still, during half a week.

In the verbally correct interpretation of חֲצִי הַשָּׁבוּעַ, the supposition that the second half of the heptad is meant loses its support, for the *terminus a quo* of this half remains undefined if it cannot be determined from the subject itself. But this determination depends on whether the taking away of the sacrifice is to be regarded as the putting a complete termination to it, or only the causing of a temporary cessation to the service of sacrifice, which can be answered only by our first determining the question regarding the historical reference of this divine revelation. זֶבַח וּמִנְחָה, *bloody and unbloody sacrifice*, the two chief parts of the service of sacrifice, represent the whole of worship by sacrifice. The expression is more comprehensive than הַתָּמִיד, ch. viii. 11, *the continuance* in worship, the daily morning and evening sacrifice, the cessation of which does not necessarily involve the putting an end to the service of sacrifice.

The *third* clause of this verse, וְעַל כְּנַף שִׁקּוּצִים מְשֹׁמֵם, is difficult, and its interpretation has been disputed. The LXX. have rendered it: *καὶ ἐπὶ τὸ ἱερὸν βδέλυγμα τῶν ἐρημώσεων ἔσται.* Theodotion has given the same rendering, only omitting *ἔσται.* The Vulgate has: *et erit in templo abominatio desolationis.* The church interpreters have explained the words in accordance with these translations, understanding by כְּנַף שִׁקּוּצִים the abomination of idols in the temple, or the temple desecrated by the abomination of idols. Hävernick explains the words of the extreme height of abomination, *i.e.* of the highest place that can be reached where the abominations would be committed, *i.e.* the temple as the highest point in Jerusalem; Hengstenberg, on the contrary, regards the "wing of the abominations" as the pinnacle of the temple so desecrated by the abomination that it no longer deserved the name of a temple of the Lord, but the name of an idol-temple. Auberlen translates it "on account of the desolating summit of abominations," and understands by it the summit of the abominations committed by Israel, which draws down the desolation, because it is the desolation itself, and which reached its *acme* in the desecration of the temple by the Zealots shortly before the destruction of Jerusalem. But no one of these interpretations is justified by the language here used, because כָּנָף does not signify summit, highest point. This word, it is true, is often used figuratively of the extremity or skirt of the upper garment or cloak (1 Sam. xv. 27, xxiv. 5; Hag. ii. 12), of the uttermost part, end, of the earth, Isa. xxiv. 16, and frequently in the plur. of the borders of the earth, in the rabbin. also of the lobes of the lungs, but demonstrably never of the summit as the highest point or peak of an object; and thus can mean neither the temple as the highest point in Jerusalem, nor the pinnacle of the temple desecrated by the abomination, nor the summit of the abomination committed by Israel. "It is used indeed," as Bleek (*Jahrbb.* v. p. 93) also remarks, "of the extreme point of an object, but only of that which is extended horizontally (for end, or extremity), but never of that which is extended perpendicularly (for peak)." The use of it in the latter sense cannot also be proved from the πτερύγιον τοῦ ἱεροῦ, Matt. iv. 5, Luke iv. 9. Here the genitive τοῦ ἱεροῦ, not τοῦ ναοῦ, shows that not the pinnacle, *i.e.* the summit of the temple itself, is meant, but a wing or adjoining building of the sanctuary; and if Suidas and Hesychius explain πτερύγιον by ἀκρωτήριον, this explanation is constructed only from the passages of the N. T. referred to, and is not confirmed by the Greek classics.

But though πτερύγιον may have the meaning of summit, yet this can by no means be proved to be the meaning of כָּנָף. Accordingly כְּנַף שִׁקּוּצִים cannot on verbal grounds be referred to the temple. This argument from the words used is not set aside by other arguments which Hengstenberg brings forward, neither by the remark that this explanation harmonizes well with the other parts of the prophecy, especially the removal of the sacrifice and the destruction of the temple, nor by the reference to the testimony of tradition and to the authority of the Lord. For, with reference to that remark, we have already shown in the explanation of the preceding verses that they do not refer to the destruction of Jerusalem by Titus, and thus are not reconcilable with this interpretation of כְּנַף שִׁקּוּצִים. But the testimony of tradition for this interpretation in Josephus, *De bello Jud.* iv. 6. 3, that by the desecration of the temple on the part of the Zealots an old prophecy regarding the destruction of the temple was fulfilled, itself demonstrates (under the supposition that no other passages occur in the book of Daniel in which Josephus would be able to find the announcement of bloody abomination in the temple which proceeded even from the members of the covenant people) nothing further than that Josephus, with many of his contemporaries, found such a prophecy in this verse in the Alexandrine translation, but it does not warrant the correctness of this interpretation of the passage. This warrant would certainly be afforded by the words of our Lord regarding "the abomination of desolation spoken of by Daniel the prophet standing in the holy place" (Matt. xxiv. 15 f.; Mark xiii. 14), if it were decided that the Lord had this passage (Dan. ix. 27) alone before His mind, and that He regarded the "abomination of desolation" as a sign announcing the destruction of Jerusalem by the Romans. But neither of these conditions is established. The expression *βδέλυγμα τῆς ἐρημώσεως* is found not only in Dan. ix. 27 (where the LXX. and Theod. have the plur. *ἐρημώσεων*), but also in Dan. xi. 31 (*βδ. ἐρημώσεως*) and Dan. xii. 11 (*τὸ βδ. τῆς ἐρημώσεως*), and thus may refer to one of these passages. The possibility of this reference is not weakened by the objection, "that the prophecy Dan. xi. and xii. was generally regarded as fulfilled in the Maccabean times, and that the fulfilling of ch. ix. was placed forward into the future in the time of Christ" (Hgstb.), because the Lord can have a deeper and more correct apprehension of the prophecies of Daniel than the Jewish writers of His time; because, moreover, the first historical fulfilling of Dan. xi. in the Maccabean times does not exclude a further and a fuller accomplishment in the future, and the rage of Antiochus Epiphanes against the Jewish temple and the worship of God can be a type of the assault of Antichrist against the sanctuary and the church of God in the time of the end. Still less from the words, "whoso readeth, let him understand" (Matt. xxiv. 15), can it be proved that Christ had only Dan. ix. 27, and not also xi. 31 or xii. 11, before His view. The remark that these words refer to בִּין בַּדָּבָר (*understand the matter*), Dan. ix. 23, and to וְתֵדַע וְתַשְׂכֵּל (*know, and understand*), does not avail for this purpose, because this reference is not certain, and בִּין אֶת־הַדָּבָר (*and he understood the thing*) is used (ch. x. 1) also of the prophecy in ch. x. and xi. But though it were beyond a doubt that Christ had, in the words quoted, only Dan. ix. 27 before His view, yet would the reference of this prophecy to the destruction of Jerusalem by the Romans not be thereby proved, because in His discourse Christ spake not only of this destruction of the ancient Jerusalem, but generally of His *παρουσία* and the *συντέλεια τοῦ αἰῶνος* (Matt.

xxiv. 3), and referred the words of Daniel of the βδέλυγμα τῆς ἐρημώσεως to the παρουσία τοῦ υἱοῦ τοῦ ἀνθρώπου.

On these grounds we must affirm that the reference of the words under consideration to the desecration of the temple before the destruction of Jerusalem by the Romans is untenable.

But also the reference of these words, as maintained by other interpreters, to the desecration of the temple by the βδέλυγμα ἐρημώσεως (1 Macc. i. 54), built on the altar of burnt-offering by Antiochus Epiphanes, is disproved on the verbal ground that כָּנָף cannot designate the surface of the altar. In favour of this view the הַשִּׁקּוּץ מְשֹׁמֵם, Dan. xi. 31 (*the abomination that maketh desolate*), is principally relied on, in order to establish the connection of מְשֹׁמֵם with שִׁקּוּצִים; but that passage is of a different character, and the difference of number between them opposes the connecting together of these two words. The singular מְשֹׁמֵם cannot be connected as an adjective with שִׁקּוּצִים. But the uniting of מְשֹׁמֵם with the noun כְּנַף gives no meaning, and besides has the parallels ch. xi. 31 and xii. 11 against it. In this passage before us מְשֹׁמֵם can only be the subject; and the clause is neither to be connected with the preceding nor with the following, but is to be interpreted as containing an independent statement. Since in the preceding context mention is made of a *Nagid* who shall make desolate the city and the sanctuary, and shall take away the bloody and the unbloody sacrifice, it is natural to regard the מְשֹׁמֵם, *desolater*, as the *Nagid*, and to identify the two. The circumstance that it does not refer to it by the article (הַמְּשֹׁמֵם) is no valid objection, because the article is in no way necessary, as מְשֹׁמֵם is a participle, and can be rendered as such: "on the wings of abomination he comes desolating." עַל כָּנָף can, without ingenuity, be rendered in no other way than *on wings*. שִׁקּוּצִים signifies not acts of abomination, but objects of abomination, things causing abomination, and is constantly used of the heathen gods, idol-images, sacrifices to the gods, and other heathen abominations. The connection of שִׁקּוּצִים permits us, however, with Reichel, Ebrard, Kliefoth, and Kranichfeld, to think on nothing else than that wings (כָּנָף) are attributed to the שִׁקּוּצִים. The sing. כְּנַף does not oppose this, since it is often used collectively in a peculiar and figurative meaning; cf. *e.g.* בַּעַל כָּנָף, Prov. i. 17, with בַּעַל כְּנָפַיִם, Eccles. x. 20, *the winged, the bird;* and כְּנַף הָאָרֶץ (*from the uttermost part of the earth*), Isa. xxiv. 16, is not different from כַּנְפוֹת הָאָרֶץ, Job xxxvii. 3, xxxviii. 13, just as אֶבְרָה, *wing, plumage*, Ps. xci. 4, Deut. xxxii. 11, is found for אֶבְרוֹת (*wings*), Ps. lxviii.

14. But from such passages as Deut. xxxii. 11, Ex. xix. 4, and Ps. xviii. 11, we perceive the sense in which wings are attributed to the שִׁקּוּצִים, the idolatrous objects.[1] In the first of these passages (Deut. xxxii. 11), wings, the wings of an eagle, are attributed to God, because He is the power which raises up Israel, and lifting it up, and carrying it throughout its history, guides it over the earth. In Ps. xviii. wings are attributed to the wind, because the wind is contemplated as the power which carries out the will of God throughout the kingdom of nature. "Thus in this passage wings are attributed to the שִׁקּוּצִים, idol-objects, and to idolatry with its abominations, because that shall be the power which lifts upwards the destroyer and desolater, carries him, and moves with him over the earth to lay waste" (Klief.).[2]

The *last* clause, וְעַד־כָּלָה וגו׳, is differently construed, according as the subject to תִּתַּךְ, which is wanting, or appears to be wanting, is sought to be supplied from the context. Against the supposition of Hävernick and Ebrard, who take תִּתַּךְ as impersonal: "it pours down," it is rightly objected that this word is never so found, and can so much the less be so interpreted here, since in ver. 11 it is preceded by a definite subject. Others supply a subject, such as anger (Berth.), or curse and oath from ver. 11; the former is quite arbitrary, the latter is too far-fetched. Others, again (Hengstenberg, Maurer), take כָּלָה וְנֶחֱרָצָה (*the consummation and that determined*) as the subject. This is correct according to the matter. We cannot, however, so justify the regarding of וְעַד as a conjunction: *till that;* for, though עַד is so used, וְעַד is not; nor, once more, can we justify the taking of כָּלָה וְנֶחֱרָצָה as a whole as the subject (Hofmann), or of וְנֶחֱרָצָה alone as the subject (v. Leng., Hitzig, Kliefoth), since וְעַד is not repeated before וְנֶחֱרָצָה on account of the ו (with v. Leng), nor is וְנֶחֱרָצָה alone supplied (with Hitz.), nor is the ו before נֶחֱרָצָה to be regarded (with Klief.) as a sign of the conclusion. Where ו introduces the conclusion, as *e.g.* ch. viii.

[1] The interpretation of J. D. Michaelis, which has been revived by Hofmann, needs no serious refutation. They hold that כְּנַף שִׁקּוּצִים signifies an idol-bird, and denotes the eagle of Jupiter or Zeus. Hofm. repeats this interpretation in his *Schriftbew.* ii. 2, p. 592, after he had abandoned it.

[2] Similarly, and independently of Kliefoth, Kranichfeld also explains the words: "The powerful heathen enemy of God is here conceived of as carried on (עַל) these wings of the idol-abomination, like as the God of the theocracy is borne on the wings of the clouds, and on cherubim, who are His servants; cf. Ps. xviii. 11, civ. 3."

14, it is there united with the verb, and thus the expression here should in that case be וְתִתַּךְ נֶחֱרָצָה. The relative interpretation of תִּתַּךְ is the only one which is verbally admissible, whereby the words, "and till the consummation and that determined," are epexegetically connected to the foregoing clause: "and till the consummation and that determined which shall pour down upon the desolater." The words כָּלָה וְנֶחֱרָצָה remind us of Isa. x. 23 and xxviii. 22, and signify that which is completed = altogether and irrevocably concluded, *i.e.* substantially the inflexibly decreed judgment of destruction. The words have here this meaning, as is clear from the circumstance that נֶחֱרָצָה points back to נֶחֱרֶצֶת שֹׁמֵמוֹת (ver. 26, *desolations are determined*), and עַד כָּלָה corresponds to עַד קֵץ (ver. 26). In ch. xi. 31 מְשֹׁמֵם is not in a similar manner to be identified with שֹׁמֵם, but has the active signification: "laying waste," while שֹׁמֵם has the passive: "laid waste." Both words refer to the *Nagid*, but with this difference, that this ungodly prince who comes as the desolater of the city and the sanctuary will on that account become desolate, that the destruction irrevocably decreed by God shall pour down upon him as a flood.

Let us now, after explaining the separate clauses, present briefly the substance of this divine revelation. We find that the verses 25–27 contain the following announcement: From the going forth of the word to restore and build Jerusalem to the appearance of the Messias seven weeks shall pass away; after that, during threescore and two weeks the city shall be restored and built up amid the oppressions of the times; but after the sixty-two weeks the Messias shall be cut off, so that to Him nothing remains, and the city, together with the sanctuary, shall be destroyed by the people of a prince who shall come, who shall find his end in the flood; but the war shall continue to the end, since destruction is irrevocably decreed. That prince shall force a strong covenant for one week on the mass of the people, and during half a week shall take away the service of sacrifice, and, borne on the wings of idol-abominations, shall carry on a desolating rule, till the firmly decreed judgment shall pour itself upon him as one desolated.—According to this, the first seven weeks are determined merely according to their beginning and their end, and nothing further is said as to their contents than may be concluded from the definition of its *terminus a quo*, "to restore and to build Jerusalem," namely, that the restoring and the building of this city shall proceed during the period of time indicated. The sixty-two weeks which follow these seven weeks, ending with the coming of the Messias, have the same contents, only with the more special definition, that the restoration and the building in the broad open place and in the limited place shall be carried on in oppressive times. Hence it is clear that this restoration and building cannot denote the rebuilding of the city which was destroyed by the Chaldeans, but refers to the preservation and extension of Jerusalem to the measure and compass determined by God in the Messianic time, or under the dominion of the Messias, since He shall come at the end of the seven weeks, and after the expiry of the sixty-two weeks connected therewith shall be cut off, so that nothing remains to Him.

The statements of the angel (vers. 26, 27) regarding the one week, which, because of the connection, can only be the seventieth, or the last of the seventy, are more ample. The cutting off of the Messias forms the beginning of this week; then follows the destruction of the city and of the sanctuary by the people of the coming prince, who shall find his end in the flood, not immediately after his coming, but at the end of this week; for the war shall continue to the end, and the prince shall take away the service of sacrifice during half a week, till the desolation determined as a flood shall pour down upon him, and make the desolater desolated. If we compare with this the contents of ver. 24, according to which seventy weeks are determined to restrain transgression, to make an end of sin and iniquity, partly by atonement and partly by shutting up, to bring in everlasting righteousness, to seal up the vision and prophecy, and to consecrate a new most holy, we shall find that the reciprocal statements are so related to each other, that vers. 25–27 present what shall be done in the course of the seventy weeks, which are divided into three periods, but ver. 24 what shall be the result of all these things. The seventieth week ends, according to ver. 27, with the judgment on the destroyer of the city and the sanctuary of God; but with this judgment shall be the conclusion of the divine counsel of salvation, or the kingdom of God shall be consummated. This was revealed to the prophet in ch. vii., and thus does not need to be here expressly repeated. If that which, according to ver. 24, shall happen with the expiry of the seventy appointed weeks stood after ver. 27, then would the connection of the judgment on the last enemy of God with the consummation of the kingdom of God appear here also distinctly to view. But it was not necessary after ch. vii. to give express prominence to this connection here; and Gabriel here first mentions the positive aim and end of the divine plan of salvation with Israel, because he gives to the prophet a comforting answer to remove his deep distress on account of his own sins, and the sin and guilt of his people, and therein cannot conceal the severe affliction which the future would bring, because he will announce to him that by the sins of the people the working out of the deliverance designed by God for them shall not be frustrated, but that in spite of the great guilt of Israel the kingdom of God shall be perfected in glory, sin and iniquity blotted out, everlasting righteousness restored, the prophecy of the judgment and of salvation completed, and the sanctuary where God shall in truth dwell among His people erected. In order to establish this promise, so rich in comfort, and firmly to ratify it to Daniel, he unveils to him (vers. 25–27), in its great outlines, the progress of the development of the kingdom of God, first from the end of the Exile to the coming of the Messias; then from the appearance of Christ to the time far in the future, when Christ shall be cut off, so that nothing remains to Him; and finally, the time of the supremacy and of the victory of the destroyer of the church of God, the Antichrist, and the destruction of this enemy by the irrevocably determined final judgment. If, now, in this he says nothing particular regarding the first period of this development, regarding the time from the Exile to Christ, the reason is, that he had already said all that was necessary regarding the development of the world-kingdom, and its relation to the kingdom and people of God, in the preceding revelation in ch. viii. It is the same angel Gabriel who (ch. viii.) comforted Daniel, and interpreted to him the vision of the second and third world-kingdom, and who here brings to him further revelations in answer to his prayer regarding the restoration of the holy city, which was lying in ruins, as is expressly remarked in ver. 21.—Also regarding the second long period which passes from the appearance of the Messias to His annihilation (*Vernichtung*), *i.e.* the destruction of His kingdom on the earth, little is apparently said, but in reality in the few words very much is said: that during this whole period the restoration and building shall proceed amid the oppressions of the times, namely, that the kingdom of God shall be built up to the extent determined by God in this long period, although amid severe persecution. This persecution shall during the last week mount up to the height of the cutting off of Christ and the destruction of His kingdom on the earth; but then with the extermination of the prince, the enemy of God, it shall reach its end.

But if, according to what has been said, this revelation presents the principal outlines of the development of the kingdom of God from the time of Daniel to its consummation at the end of this epoch of the world, the seventy שָׁבֻעִים which are appointed for it cannot be year-weeks, or cycles of seven years, but only symbolically defined periods of measured duration. This result of our exposition contradicts, however, the usual interpretations of this prophecy so completely, that in order to confirm our exposition, we must put thoroughly to the test the two classes of opposing interpretations—which, however, agree in this, that the definitions of time are to be understood chronologically, and that under the שָׁבֻעִים year-weeks are to be understood—and examine whether a chronological reckoning is in all respects tenable.

The first class of expositors who find the appearance of Christ in the flesh and His crucifixion, as well as the destruction of Jerusalem by the Romans, prophesied of in this passage, adduce in support of their view, partly the agreement of the chronological periods, partly the testimony of Christ, who referred ver. 27 to the destruction of Jerusalem by the Romans. How does it now stand with these two arguments?

The *first* Hengstenberg (*Christol.* iii. 1, p. 137) introduces with the remark, "The predominant view in the synagogue and in the church has always been, that the seventy weeks, as well as the shorter periods into which the whole period is divided, are closely fixed and limited. The opposite supposition becomes very suspicious by this, that it is maintained only by such as come into conflict with the chronology by their hypotheses, or take no interest in chronological investigations." He then seeks first to confute the arguments brought forward in favour of the supposition that the chronological definitions are only given in the lump (*in Bausch und Bogen*), and then to present the positive arguments for the definiteness of the chronological statements. But he has in this identified the definiteness of the prophecy in general with its chronological definiteness, while there is between these two ideas a noticeable difference. Of the positive arguments adduced, the first is, that the seventy weeks stand in closer relation to the seventy years of Jeremiah, in so far as regards chronological definiteness, when the seventy years of Jeremiah are understood as strictly chronological and as chronologically fulfilled. But the force of this argument is neutralized by the fact, that in Jeremiah a chronologically described period, "years," is in this prophecy, on the contrary, designated by a name the meaning of which is disputed, at all events is chronologically indefinite, since *weeks*, if seven-day periods are excluded by the contents of the prophecy, can as well signify Sabbath or jubilee periods, seven-year or seven times seven-year epochs. Still weaker is the second argument, that all the other designations of time with reference to the future in the book of Daniel are definite; for this is applicable only to the designations in ch. viii. 14 and xii. 11, 12, in which evening-mornings and days are named, but not to the passages ch. vii. 25, xii. 7, and iv. 13 (16), where the chronologically indefinite expression, *time, times,* occurs, which are arbitrarily identified with years.

There remains thus, for the determination of the time spoken of in this prophecy, only the argument from its fulfilment, which should give the decision for the chronological definiteness. But, on the contrary, there arises a grave doubt, from the circumstance that among the advocates of the so-called "church Messianic interpretation" the *terminus a quo* of the prophecy is disputed; for some of these interpreters take the edict of Cyrus (B.C. 536) as such, while, on the other hand, others take the edict which Artaxerxes issued on the return of Ezra to Jerusalem for the restoration of the service of God according to the law, in the seventeenth year of his reign, *i.e.* in the year B.C. 457, and others, again, among whom is Hengstenberg, take the journey of Nehemiah to Jerusalem with the permission to rebuild the walls of Jerusalem, in the twentieth year of Artaxerxes, *i.e.* B.C. 445, or according to Hengstenberg, B.C. 455, as the *terminus a quo* of the seventy weeks—a difference of eighty-one years, which in chronological reckoning is very noticeable.

In our interpretation of ver. 25, we have given our decided opinion that the דָּבָר לְהָשִׁיב וגו׳, from the going forth of which seventy years are to be reckoned, refers to the edict of Cyrus permitting the Jews to return to their fatherland, and the arguments in favour of that opinion are given in p. 352. Against this reference to the edict of Cyrus, Hävernick, Hengstenberg, and Auberlen have objected that in that edict there is nothing said of building up the city, and that under Cyrus, as well as under the succeeding kings, Cambyses, Darius Hystaspes, and Xerxes, nothing also is done for the building of the city. We find it still unbuilt in the times of Ezra and Nehemiah (Ezra ix. 8, x. 13; Neh. i. 3, ii. 3, v. 34, iv. 1, vii. 4). Although from the nature of the case the building of the temple supposes the existence also of houses in Jerusalem (cf. Hag. i. 4), yet there is not a single trace of any royal permission for the restoration of the people and the rebuilding of the city. Much rather this was expressly forbidden (Ezra iv. 7–23) by the same Artaxerxes Longimanus (who at a later period gave the permission however), in consequence of the slanderous reports of the Samaritans. "There was granted to the Jews a religious, but not a political restoration." For the first time in the seventh year of Artaxerxes Longimanus the affairs of Israel took a favourable turn. In that year Artaxerxes granted to Ezra permission to go to Jerusalem, entrusting him with royal letters of great importance (Ezra vii. 11–26, particularly vers. 18, 25 f.); in his twentieth year he gave to Nehemiah express permission to rebuild the city (Neh. ii.). Following the example of the old chronologist Julius Africanus in Jerome and many others, Häv., Hgstb., Reinke, Reusch, and others regard the twentieth year of Artaxerxes, while Auberlen, with Calovius, Newton, M. Geier, Gaussen, Pusey, and others, regard the seventh year, as the *terminus a quo* of the seventy weeks. But that the arguments derived from the absence of any mention being made in the edict of Cyrus of the building of Jerusalem against the reference of מֹצָא דָבָר וגו' to that edict are not very strong, at least are not decisive, is manifest from what Auberlen has advanced for the seventh and against the twentieth year. Proceeding from the proposition, correct in itself, that the time of Ezra and that of Nehemiah form *one* connected period of blessing for Israel, Auberlen thence shows that the edict relating to Nehemiah had only a secondary importance, as the sacred narrative itself indicates by the circumstance that it does not mention the edict at all (Neh. ii. 7, 8), while the royal letters to Ezra (Ezra vii.) are given at large. Since it was the same king Artaxerxes who sent away Ezra as well as Nehemiah, his heart must have been favourably inclined toward Israel in his seventh year. "Then must the word for the restoration and building of Jerusalem have gone forth from God." The consciousness of this is expressed by Ezra himself, when, after recording the royal edict (ch. vii. 27), he continues: "Blessed be Jehovah, the God of our fathers, which hath put such a thing as this in the king's heart, *to beautify the house of the Lord which is in Jerusalem;* and hath extended mercy to me before the king and his counsellors, and before all the king's mighty princes."

But, we must reply, wherein does the mercy extended to Ezra before the king consist? Is it in the permission to build up Jerusalem? Certainly not, but in the beautifying of the house of Jehovah in Jerusalem. And to that alone the royal authority granted to Ezra (Ezra vii.) refers. Of the building of the city there is not a word said. Only the means, as it appears, of restoring the temple-worship, which had fallen into great decay, and of re-establishing the law of God corresponding thereto, were granted to him in the long edict issued by the king.[1] If the clause, "from the going

[1] Auberlen, it is true, remarks (p. 138):—"The authority given to Ezra is so extensive that it essentially includes the rebuilding of the city. It refers certainly, for the most part [rather *wholly*], to the service of the sanctuary; but not only must Ezra set up judges (ch. vii. 25), he is also expressly permitted by the king to expend as it seems good to him the rest of the silver and gold (ch. vii. 18). How he then understood the commission, Ezra himself says clearly and distinctly in his prayer of repentance: 'Our Lord hath extended mercy unto us in the sight of the kings of Persia, to give us a reviving, to set up the house of our God, and to repair the desolations thereof (of our God), and to give us a wall in Judah and Jerusalem.' The argument from this passage lies not merely in the גָּדֵר (*encircling wall*), but especially in this, 'to repair the desolations thereof.' This could not be the desolations of the temple, which had been long before this rebuilt, and therefore we may understand by it the desolations of Jerusalem." But the strength of this argumentation rests merely on a verbally free rendering of the verse referred to (Ezra ix. 9). The circumstance that Ezra speaks of the kings (in the plur.) of Persia, who showed favour to the Jews, indicates that he meant not merely that which Artaxerxes had done and would yet do in the future, but that he refers also to the manifestation of favour on the part of kings Cyrus, Darius Hystaspes, and Artaxerxes; thus also the expression, "to give us a wall," cannot refer to the permission to rebuild the walls of Jerusalem, which Artaxerxes some years later first granted to Nehemiah. Moreover, the expression, "to give us a גָּדֵר in *Judah* and Jerusalem," shows that by גָּדֵר cannot be understood the fortified walls of Jerusalem; for גָּדֵר never denotes the walls of a city or fortress as such, but always only the encompassing wall of a vineyard, which meaning is found in Mic. vii. 11, Ezek. xiii. 5. גָּדֵר is therefore to be understood here figuratively: encompassing wall in the sense of divine protection; and the meaning is not this: "that the place protected by the wall lies in Judah and Jerusalem; but in Judah and Jerusalem the Persian kings have given to the new congregation of the people a secure dwelling-place, because the power of the Persian kings secured to the Israelites who had returned from captivity the undisturbed and continued possession of their land" (Bertheau). The objection also, that חָרְבֹתָיו cannot be the ruins of the temple, because it was already built, is set aside as soon as we express the *infinitive* לְהַעֲמִיד, as it is rightly done, by the *præterite*, whereby this word refers to the completed building of the temple. Cf. with this Hengstenberg's extended refutation of this argument of Auberlen's (*Christol.* iii. 1, p. 144).

forth of the commandment," etc., cannot refer to the edict of Cyrus, because in it there is no express mention made of the rebuilding of Jerusalem, so also, for the same reason, it cannot refer to that which was issued by Artaxerxes in favour of Ezra. Auberlen's remark, however, is correct, when he says that the edict relating to Nehemiah is of secondary importance when compared with that relating to Ezra. Strictly speaking, there is no mention made of an edict relating to Nehemiah. Nehemiah, as cup-bearer of Artaxerxes, entreated of the king the favour of being sent to Judah, to the city of his fathers' sepulchres, that he might build it; and the king (the queen also sitting by him) granted him this request, and gave him letters to all the governors on this side the Euphrates, that they should permit him undisturbed to prosecute his journey, and to the overseers of the royal forests, that they should give him wood "for the gates of the palace which appertained to the house, and for the wall of the city" (Neh. ii. 4–8). However important this royal favour was in its consequences for Jerusalem,—for Nehemiah built the walls of the city, and thereby raised Jerusalem to a fortified city guarded against hostile assaults, —yet the royal favour for this undertaking was not such as to entitle it to be designated as מֹצָא דָצָר וגו׳, *a going forth of a commandment of God.* But if, in favour of the reference of מֹצָא דָבָר to the edict of Ezra, Auberlen (p. 128 ff.) attaches special importance to the circumstance that in the books of Ezra and Nehemiah are recorded two periods of post-exilian history, the first of which—namely, the time of Zerubbabel and of the high priest Joshua under Cyrus and Darius Hystaspes—we may designate the period of the building of the temple, the second—namely, the time of Ezra the priest, and Nehemiah the Tirshatha, under Artaxerxes Longimanus—we may designate the period of the restoration of the people and the building of the city,—the former the time of the *religious*, and the latter that of the *political* restoration; and, in seeking to establish this view, he interprets the first part of the book of Ezra as a whole in itself, and the second as a whole taken in combination with the book of Nehemiah;—if this is his position, then Hengstenberg has already (*Christol.* iii. p. 149) shown the incorrectness of this division of the book of Ezra, and well remarks that the whole book of Ezra has the temple as its central-point, and views with reference to it the mission of Ezra as well as that of Zerubbabel and Joshua. There is certainly an inner connection of the mission of Ezra with that of Nehemiah, but it consists only in this, that Ezra's religious reformation was secured by Nehemiah's political reform. From the special design of the work of Ezra, to describe the restoration of the temple and of the service of God, we must also explain the circumstance that nothing is said in it of the building of the city of Jerusalem. Besides, this building, before Nehemiah's arrival in Judah, had not further advanced than to the re-erection of houses for the returned exiles who had settled in Jerusalem. Every attempt to restore the walls was hindered and frustrated by the enemies of Judah, so that the gates and the walls were yet lying burnt and in ruins on Nehemiah's arrival (Neh. i. 3, ii. 3, 5). Therefore neither the absence of any mention in the decree of Cyrus of the building of the city, nor the fact that the rebuilding of the city walls was first effected by Nehemiah, forms a decisive argument against the reference of מֹצָא דָבָר וגו' to this edict; and we must maintain this reference as the only correct one, because this edict only, but not that which gave permission to Ezra or that which gave authority to Nehemiah to build the city walls, formed an epoch marking a crisis in the development of the theocracy, as this is connected in the announcement of Gabriel with the going forth of the word to restore Jerusalem.

Not less doubtful is the matter of the definition of the *terminus ad quem* of the seventy שָׁבֻעִים, and of the chronological reckoning of the whole period. As for the *terminus ad quem*, a sharply defined *factum* must form the conclusion of the sixty-ninth week; for at this point the public appearance of Christ, His being anointed with the Holy Ghost, is named as the end of the prophecy. If this *factum* occurred, according to Luke iii. 1, in the year of Rome 782, the twentieth year of Artaxerxes—*i.e.* the year 455 B.C., according to the usual chronology—would be the year 299 A.U.C.; if we add to that sixty-nine weeks = 483 years, then it gives the year 782 A.U.C. In the middle of this last week, beginning with the appearance of the Anointed, occurred His death, while the confirming of the covenant extends through the whole of it. With reference to the death of Christ, the prophecy and its fulfilment closely agree, since that event took place three and a half years after His baptism. But the *terminus ad quem* of the confirming of the covenant, as one more or less moveable, is capable of no definite chronological determination. It is sufficient to remark, that in the first years after the death of Christ the ἐκλογή of the Old Covenant people was gathered together, and then the message of Christ was brought also to the heathen, so that the prophet might rightly represent the salvation as both subjectively and objectively consummated at the end of the seventy weeks for the covenant people, of whom alone he speaks (Hgst. pp. 163 f., 180). Thus also Auberlen, who, however, places the end of the seventy weeks in the *factum* of the stoning of Stephen, with which the Jews pressed, shook down, and made full to the overflowing the measure of their sins, already filled by the murder of the Messias; so that now the period of grace yet given to them after the work of Christ had come to an end, and the judgment fell upon Israel.

We will not urge against the precise accuracy of the fulfilment arrived at by this calculation, that the *terminus a quo* adopted by Hengstenberg, viz. the twentieth year of Artaxerxes, coincides with the 455th year B.C. only on the supposition that Xerxes reigned but eleven years, and that Artaxerxes came to the throne ten years earlier than the common reckoning, according to which Xerxes reigned twenty-one years, and that the correctness of this view is opposed by Hofm., Kleinert, Wieseler, and others, because the arguments for and against it are evenly balanced; but with Preiswerk, whose words Auberlen (p. 144) quotes with approbation, considering the uncertainty of ancient chronology on many points, we shall not lay much stress on calculating the exact year, but shall regard the approximate coincidence of the prophetical with the historical time as a sufficient proof that there may possibly have been an exact correspondence in the number of years, and that no one, at all events, can prove the contrary. But we must attach importance to this, that in this calculation a part of the communication of the angel is left wholly out of view. The angel announces not merely the cutting off of the Messias after seven and sixty-two weeks, but also the coming of the people of a prince who shall lay waste the city and the sanctuary, which all interpreters who understand יִכָּרֵת מָשִׁיחַ of the death of Christ refer to the destruction of Jerusalem and of the temple by the Romans; he also says that this war shall last till the end of the seventy weeks. The destruction of Jerusalem by the Romans followed the death of Christ, not after an interval of only three and a half years, but of thirty years. Accordingly, the seventy weeks must extend to the year 70 A.D., whereby the whole calculation is shown to be inaccurate. If we yet further remark, that the advocates of this exposition of the prophecy are in a position to give no sufficient reason for the dividing of the sixty-nine weeks into seven and sixty-two, and that their reference of the seven weeks to the time of the rebuilding of Jerusalem under Nehemiah, and of the sixty-two weeks to the period from the completion of this building to the appearance of Christ in the flesh, stands in open contradiction to the words of the text; finally, that the placing of the twentieth year of Artaxerxes as the *terminus a quo* of the reckoning of the מֹצָא דָבָר cannot be correct,—then may we also regard the much commended exact concord of the prophecy with the actual events of history derived from this interpretation of the verse as only an illusion, since from the "going forth of the word" to restore Jerusalem to the destruction of that city by Titus, not seventy weeks or 490 years elapsed, but, according as we date the going forth of this word in the year 536 or 455 B.C., 606 or 525 years, *i.e.* more than eighty-six, or at least seventy-five, year-weeks, passed. This great gulf, which thus shows itself in the calculation of the שָׁבֻעִים as year-weeks, between the prophecy and its chronological fulfilment, is not bridged over by the remark with which Auberlen (p. 141) has sought to justify his supposition that Ezra's return to Judah in the year 457 B.C. formed the *terminus a quo* of the seventy weeks, while yet the word of the angel announcing the restoration and the building up of Jerusalem first finds its actual accomplishment in the building of the city walls on Nehemiah's return—the remark, namely, that the external building up of the city had the same relation to the *terminus a quo* of Daniel's seventy year-weeks as the external destruction of Jerusalem to that of Jeremiah's seventy years. "The latter begin as early as the year 606 B.C., and therefore eighteen years before the destruction of Jerusalem, for at that time the kingdom of Judah ceased to exist as an independent theocracy; the former begin thirteen years before the rebuilding of the city, because then the re-establishment of the theocracy began." We find a repetition of the same phenomenon at the end of the seventy weeks. "These extend to the year 33 A.D. From this date Israel was at an end, though the destruction of Jerusalem by the Romans did not take place till the year 70 A.D." For Jeremiah did not prophesy that the destruction of Jerusalem should last for seventy years, but only that the land of Judah would be desolate seventy years, and that for so long a time its inhabitants would serve the king of Babylon. The desolating of the land and Judah's subjugation to the king of Babylon did not begin with the destruction of Jerusalem, but with the first siege of the city by Nebuchadnezzar in the fourth year of Jehoiakim, *i.e.* in the year

606 B.C., and continued till the liberation of the Jews from Babylonian bondage by Cyrus in the first year of his reign, in the year 536 B.C., and thus after seventy years were fully accomplished. Jeremiah's chronologically definite prophecy is thus accurately fulfilled; but Daniel's prophecy of the seventy weeks is neither chronologically defined by years, nor has it been altogether so fulfilled as that the 70, 7, 62, and 1 week can be reckoned by year-weeks.

The New Testament also does not necessitate our seeking the end of the seventy weeks in the judgment the Romans were the means of executing against the ancient Jerusalem, which had rejected and crucified the Saviour. Nowhere in the N. T. is this prophecy, particularly the יִכָּרֵת מָשִׁיחַ, referred to the crucifixion of our Lord; nor has Christ or the apostles interpreted these verses, 26, 27 of this chapter, of the desolation and the destruction of Jerusalem by the Romans. However general the opinion may be that Christ, in speaking of His *παρουσία*, Matt. xxiv., Mark xiii., and Luke xxi., in the words *ὅταν ἴδητε τὸ βδέλυγμα τῆς ἐρημώσεως τὸ ῥηθὲν διὰ Δανιὴλ τοῦ προφήτου, κ.τ.λ.* (Matt. xxiv. 15, cf. Mark xiii. 14), had before His eyes this prophecy (Dan. ix. 26, 27), yet that opinion is without foundation, and is not established by the arguments which Hävernick (*Dan.* p. 383 f.), Wieseler (*die 70 Wochen*, p. 173 ff.), Hengstenberg (*Beitr.* i. p. 258 ff., and *Christol.* iii. 1, p. 113 ff.), and Auberlen (*Dan.* p. 120 f.) have brought forward for that purpose. We have already, in explaining the words עַל כְּנַף שִׁקּוּצִים, ver. 27, p. 370, shown that the *βδέλυγμα τῆς ἐρημώσεως*, found in the discourse of Christ, is not derived from Dan. ix. 27, but from Dan. xi. 31 or xii. 11, where the LXX. have rendered שִׁקּוּץ מְשֹׁמֵם by *τὸ βδέλυγμα τῆς ἐρημώσεως*. For the further confirmation of the arguments in behalf of this view there presented, we wish to add the following considerations. The appeal to the fact that Josephus, in the words (*Antt.* x. 11. 7) *Δανιῆλος καὶ περὶ τῆς τῶν Ῥωμαίων ἡγεμονίας ἀνέγραψε, καὶ ὅτι ὑπ' αὐτῶν ἐρημωθήσεται*, referred to the prophecy Dan. ix., and gave this interpretation not only as a private view of his own, but as (cf. *De Bell. Jud.* iv. 6. 3) *παλαιὸς λόγος ἀνδρῶν*, *i.e.* represented the view of his people, as commonly received, even by the Zealots,—this would form a valid proof that Dan. ix. was at that time commonly referred to the destruction of Jerusalem by the Romans, only, however, if besides this no other prophecy of the book of Daniel could be apparently referred to the destruction of the Jewish state by the Romans. But this is not the case. Josephus and his cotemporaries could find such a prophecy in that of the great enemy (Dan. vii. 25) who would arise out of the fourth or Roman world-kingdom, and would persecute and destroy the saints of the Most High. What Josephus adduces as the contents of the *παλαιὸς λόγος ἀνδρῶν*, namely, *τότε τὴν πόλιν ἁλώσεσθαι καὶ καταφλεγήσεσθαι τὰ ἅγια νόμῳ πολέμου*, occurs neither in ch. ix. nor in any other part of the book of Daniel, and was not so defined till after the historical fulfilment. Wieseler, indeed, thinks (p. 154) that the words *τὴν πόλιν καταφλεγήσεσθαι, κ.τ.λ.*, perfectly correspond with the words of Daniel, וְהָעִיר וְהַקֹּדֶשׁ יַשְׁחִית, ch. ix. 26 (*shall destroy the city and the sanctuary*, E. V.); but he also concedes that Josephus interpreted the kind of desolation, perhaps with reference to Dan. xi. 33 (? 31), after the result, as a total desolation. It is thus granted that not only in ch. ix., but also in ch. xi., Daniel predicted a desolation of the city and the sanctuary which could be interpreted of their destruction by the Romans, and the opinion, that besides ch. ix. no other part of Daniel can be found, is abandoned as incorrect. But the other circumstances which Josephus brings forward in the passage quoted, particularly that the Zealots by the desecration of the temple contributed to the fulfilling of that *παλαιὸς λόγος*, are much more distinctly contained in Dan. xi. 31 than in ch. ix. 26, where we must first introduce this sense in the words (ver. 27) עַל כְּנַף שִׁקּוּצִים מְשֹׁמֵם (*on the wing of abominations one causing desolation*). Similarly the other passages are constituted in which Josephus speaks of ancient prophecies which have been fulfilled in the destruction of Jerusalem by the Romans. No one specially points to Dan. ix.

But if the proof from Josephus could be made more valid than has yet been done, that the Jews of his time referred Dan. ix. to the overthrow of the Jewish commonwealth by the Romans, yet thereby it would not be proved that Christ also shared this Jewish opinion, and set it forth in His discourse, Matt. xxiv., as an undoubted truth. In favour of this view it has indeed been argued, "that the *ἐν τόπῳ ἁγίῳ* fully corresponds to *ἐπὶ τὸ ἱερὸν βδέλυγμα τῶν ἐρημώσεων ἔσται* (LXX., Dan. ix. 27):" Hengstenberg, *Christol.* p. 117. But it is still more inconsistent with the proof from the Alexandrian translation of the verses before us than it is with that from Josephus. In the form of the LXX. text that has come down to us there are undoubtedly two different paraphrases or interpretations of the Hebrew text of vers. 26 and 27 penetrating each other, and therein the obscure words of Daniel (after ch. xi. 31 and xii. 11) are so interpreted that they contain a reference to the desolation of the sanctuary by Antiochus.[1] The עַל כְּנַף שִׁקּוּצִים, incomprehensible to the translators, they interpreted after the חִלְּלוּ הַמִּקְדָּשׁ, ch. xi. 31, and derived from it the *ἐπὶ τὸ ἱερόν*. But Christ derived the expression *τὸ βδέλυγμα τῆς ἐρημώσεως* as well as the *ἑστὼς ἐν τόπῳ ἁγίῳ* from ch. xi. 31, cf. with ch. xii. 11, but not from ch. ix. 27, where neither the original text, "on the wings of abomination shall the desolater come," nor the LXX. translation, *ἐπὶ τὸ ἱερὸν βδέλυγμα τῶν ἐρημώσεων ἔσται*—"over the sanctuary shall the abomination of the desolations come," leads to the idea of a "standing," or a "being placed," of the abomination of desolation. The standing (*ἑστώς*) without doubt supposes the placing, which corresponds to the וְנָתְנוּ (*δώσουσι*, LXX.) and the וְלָתֵת (*ἑτοιμασθῇ δοθῆναι*, LXX.), and the *ἐν τόπῳ ἁγίῳ* points to הַמִּקְדָּשׁ, ch. xi. 31, since by the setting up of the abomination of desolation, the sanctuary, or the holy place of the temple, was indeed desecrated.

The prophecy in Dan. xi. treats, as is acknowledged, of the desolation of the sanctuary by Antiochus Epiphanes. If thus the Lord, in His discourse, had spoken of the *βδέλυγμα τῆς ἐρ. ἑστὼς ἐν τόπῳ ἁγίῳ* as a sign of the approaching destruction of Jerusalem by Titus, it would not remotely follow that He referred this prophecy (ch. ix.) to that catastrophe. Much more would He then, as Kliefoth (p. 412) has well remarked, "represent that which Antiochus Epiphanes did against Jerusalem as an historical type of that which the Romans would do." He would only say, "As once

[1] That the Septuagint version (ch. xi. 31, xii. 11, ix. 24–27) is not in reality a translation, but rather an explanation of the passage as the LXX. understood it, is manifest. "They regard," as Klief. rightly judges, "ver. 24 and the first half of ver. 25 as teaching that it was prophesied to Daniel that Israel would soon return from exile, that Daniel also would return, and Jerusalem be built. The rest they treat very freely. They take the second half of ver. 25 out of its place, and insert it after the first clause of ver. 27; they also take the closing words of ver. 26 out of their place, and insert them after the second clause of ver. 27. The passage thus arranged they then interpret of Antiochus Epiphanes. They add together all the numbers they find in the text (70 + 7 + 62 = 139), and understand by them years, the years of the Seleucidan æra, so that they descend to the second year of Antiochus Epiphanes. Then they interpret all the separate statements of the times and actions of Antiochus Epiphanes in a similar manner as do the modern interpreters. Cf. Wieseler, p. 200 ff."

was done to Jerusalem by Antiochus, according to the word of Daniel, so shall it again soon be done; and therefore, if ye see repeating themselves the events which occurred under Antiochus in the fulfilment of Daniel's word, then know ye that it is the time for flight." But regarding the meaning which Christ found in Dan. ix. 26 and 27, not the least intimation would follow therefrom.

But in the discourse in question the Lord prophesied nothing whatever primarily or immediately of the destruction of Jerusalem by the Romans, but treated in it, as we have already remarked, p. 370, generally of His *παρουσία* and the *συντέλεια τοῦ αἰῶνος*, which He places only in connection with the destruction of the temple. The occasion of the discourse, as well as its contents, show this. After He had left the temple, never to enter it again, shortly before His last sufferings, while standing on the Mount of Olives, He announces to His disciples, who pointed to the temple, the entire destruction of that building; whereupon they say to Him, "Tell us *πότε ταῦτα ἔσται καὶ τί τὸ σημεῖον τῆς σῆς παρουσίας καὶ συντελείας τοῦ αἰῶνος*?" for they believe that this destruction and His *παρουσία* take place together at the end of the world. This question the Lord replies to in a long discourse, in which He gives them the wished-for information regarding the sign (*σημεῖον*, Matt. xxiv. 4–31), and regarding the time (*πότε*) of His *παρουσία* and the end of the world (vers. 32–34). The information concerning the sign begins with a warning to take heed and beware of being deceived; for that false messiahs would appear, and wars and tumults of nations rising up one against another, and other plagues, would come (vers. 4–7). All this would be only the beginning of the woes, *i.e.* of the afflictions which then would come upon the confessors of His name; but the end would not come till the gospel was first preached in all the world as a testimony to all nations (vers. 8–14). Then He speaks of the signs which immediately precede the end, namely, of the abomination of desolation in the holy place of which Daniel prophesied. With this a period of tribulation would commence such as never yet had been, so that if these days should not be shortened for the elect's sake, no one would be saved (vers. 15–28). To this He adds, in conclusion, the description of His own *παρουσία*, which would immediately (*εὐθέως*) follow this great tribulation (vers. 29–31). He connects with the description of His return (ver. 32 f.) a similitude, with which He answers the question concerning its time, and thus continues: "When ye see *all these things*, know that it is near, even at the doors. Verily I say unto you, this γενεά shall not pass till *all these things* be fulfilled. But of that day and hour knoweth no man, no, not the angels of heaven, but my Father only" (vers. 33, 34, 36).

From this brief sketch of the course of the thought it clearly appears that the Lord speaks expressly neither of the destruction of Jerusalem, nor yet of the time of that event. What is to be understood by βδέλυγμα τ. ἐρ. He supposes to be known to the disciples from the book of Daniel, and only says to them that they must flee when they see this standing in the holy place, so that they may escape destruction (ver. 15 ff.). Only in Luke is there distinct reference to the destruction of Jerusalem; for there we find, instead of the reference to the abomination of desolation, the words, "And when ye shall see Jerusalem compassed with armies, then know that its ἐρήμωσις is nigh" (Luke xxi. 20). According to the record of all the three evangelists, however, the Lord not only connects in the closest manner the tribulation commencing with the appearance of the βδέλυγμα τ. ἐρ., or with the siege of Jerusalem, with the last great tribulation which opens the way for His return, but He also expressly says, that immediately after the tribulation of those days (Matt. xxiv. 29), or in those days of that tribulation (Mark xiii. 24), or then (τότε, Luke xxi. 27), the Son of man shall come in the clouds in great power and glory. From this close connection of His visible παρουσία with the desolation of the holy place or the siege of Jerusalem, it does not, it is true, follow that "by the oppression of Jerusalem connected with the παρουσία, and placed immediately before it, the destruction of Jerusalem by the Romans cannot possibly be meant;" much rather that the discourse is "of a desecration and an oppression by Antichrist which would come upon the τόπος ἅγιος and Jerusalem in the then future time, immediately before the return of the Lord, in the days of the θλῖψις μεγάλη" (Kliefoth). But just as little does it follow from that close connection—as the eschatological discourse, Matt. xxiv., is understood by most interpreters—that the Lord Himself, as well as His disciples, regarded as contemporaneous the destruction of Jerusalem by the Romans and His visible return in the last days, or saw as in prophetic perspective His παρουσία behind the destruction of Jerusalem by the Romans, and thus, without regard to the sequence of time, spoke first of the one event and then of the other. The first conclusion is inadmissible for this reason, that the disciples had made inquiry regarding the time of the destruction of the temple then visibly before them. If the Lord, in His answer to this question, by making mention of the *βδέλυγμα τ. ἐρ. ἑστὼς ἐν τόπῳ ἁγίῳ*, had no thought of this temple, but only of the *τόπος ἅγιος* of the future, the temple of the Christian church, then by the use of words which the disciples could not otherwise understand than of the laying waste and the desolation of the earthly sanctuary He would have confirmed them in their error. The second conclusion is out of harmony with the whole course of thought in the discourse. Besides, both of them are decidedly opposed by this, that the Lord, after setting forth all the events which precede and open the way for His *παρουσία* and the end of the world, says to the disciples, "When ye see *all these things*, know that it is near, even at the doors" (Matt. xxiv. 33), and solemnly adds, "This *γενεά*," *i.e.* the generation then living, "shall not pass till *all these things* be fulfilled" (ver. 34). Since the *πάντα ταῦτα* in ver. 33 comprehends all that goes before the *παρουσία*, all the events mentioned in vers. 15–28, or rather in vers. 5–28, it must be taken also in the same sense in ver. 34. If, therefore, the contemporaries of Jesus and His disciples—for we can understand nothing else by *ἡ γενεὰ αὕτη*—must live to see all these events, then must they have had a commencement before the destruction of Jerusalem, and though not perfectly, yet in the small beginnings, which like a germ comprehended in them the completion. Hence it is beyond a doubt that the Lord speaks of the judgment upon Jerusalem and the Jewish temple as the beginning of His *παρουσία* and of the *συντέλεια τοῦ αἰῶνος*, not merely as a pre-intimation of them, but as an actual commencement of His coming to judgment, which continues during the centuries of the spread of the gospel over the earth; and when the gospel shall be preached to all nations, then the season and the hour kept in His own power by the Father shall reach its completion in the *ἐπιφανείᾳ τῆς παρουσίας αὐτοῦ* (2 Thess. ii. 8) to judge the world.[1] According

[1] This view of the *parousia* of Christ has been controverted by Dr. A. Christiani in his *Bemerkungen zur Auslegung der Apocalypse mit besonderer Rücksicht auf die chiliastische Frage* (Riga 1868, p. 21),—only, however, thus, that notwithstanding the remark, "Since the words *πάντα ταῦτα*, Matt. xxiv. 34, plainly refer back to ver. 33, they cannot in the one place signify more than in the other," he yet refers these words in ver. 34 to the event of the destruction of Jerusalem, because the contemporaries of Jesus in reality lived to see it; thus giving to them, as they occur in ver. 34, a much more limited sense than that which they have in ver. 33.

to this view, Christ, in His discourse, interpreted the prophecy of Daniel, ch. xi., of the abomination of desolation which should come, and had come, upon Jerusalem and Judah by Antiochus Epiphanes, as a type of the desolation of the sanctuary and of the people of God in the last time, wholly in the sense of the prophecy, which in ver. 36 passes over from the typical enemy of the saints to the enemy of the people of God in the time of the end.

Thus the supposition that Christ referred Dan. ix. 26 and 27 to the overthrow of Jerusalem by the Romans loses all support; and for the chronological reckoning of the seventy weeks of Daniel, no help is obtained from the New Testament.

We have now to take into consideration the *second* view regarding the historical reference of the seventy weeks prevailing in our time. The opponents of the genuineness of the book of Daniel generally are agreed in this (resting on the supposition that the prophecies of Daniel do not extend beyond the death of Antiochus Epiphanes), that the destruction of this enemy of the Jews (Ant. Ep.), or the purification of the temple occurring a few years earlier, forms the *terminus ad quem* of the seventy weeks, and that their duration is to be reckoned from the year 168 or 172 B.C. back either to the destruction of Jerusalem by the Chaldeans, or to the beginning of the Exile. Since now the seventy year-weeks or 490 years, reckoned from the year 168 or 172 B.C., would bring us to the year 658 or 662 B.C., *i.e.* fifty-two or fifty-six years before the commencement of the Exile, and the *terminus a quo* of Jeremiah's prophecy of seventy years, a date from which cannot be reckoned any commencing period, they have for this reason sought to shorten the seventy weeks. Hitzig, Ewald, Wieseler, and others suppose that the first seven year-weeks (= forty-nine years) are not to be taken into the reckoning along with the sixty-two weeks, and that only sixty-two weeks = 434 years are to be counted to the year 175 (Ewald), or 172 (Hitzig), as the beginning of the last week filled up by the assault of Antiochus against Judaism. But this reckoning also brings us to the year 609 or 606 B.C., the beginning of the Exile, or three years further back. To date the sixty-two year-weeks from the commencement of the Exile, agrees altogether too little with the announcement that from the going forth of the commandment to restore and to build Jerusalem during sixty-two weeks it shall be built, so that, of the most recent representatives of this view, no one any longer consents to hold the seventy years of the exile for a time of the restoring and the building of Jerusalem. Thus Hitzig and Ewald openly declare that the reckoning is not correct, that the pseudo-Daniel has erred, and has assumed ten weeks, *i.e.* seventy years, too many, either from ignorance of chronology, "or from a defect in thought, from an interpretation of a word of sacred Scripture, springing from certain conditions received as holy and necessary, but not otherwise demonstrable" (Ewald, p. 425). By this change of the sixty-two weeks = 434 years into fifty-two weeks or 364 years, they reach from the year 174 to 538 B.C., the year of the overthrow of Babylon by Cyrus, by whom the word "to restore Jerusalem" was promulgated. To this the seven weeks (= forty-nine years) are again added in order to reach the year 588 or 587 B.C., the year of the destruction of Jerusalem by Nebuchadnezzar, from which the year-weeks, shortened from seventy to sixty, are to be reckoned.

This hypothesis needs no serious refutation. For a reckoning which places the first 7 weeks = 49 years aside, and then shortens the 62 weeks by 10 in order afterwards again to bring in the 7 weeks, can make no pretence to the name of a "scientific explanation." When Hitzig remarks (p. 170) "that the 7 weeks form the *πρῶτον ψεῦδος* in the (Daniel's) reckoning, which the author must bring in; the whole theory of the 70 year-weeks demands the earlier commencement in the year 606 B.C."—we may, indeed, with greater accuracy say that the *πρῶτον ψεῦδος* of the modern interpretation, which needs such exegetical art and critical violence in order to change the 70 and the 62 weeks into 60 and 52, arises out of the dogmatic supposition that the 70 weeks must end with the consecration of the temple under Antiochus, or with the death of this enemy of God.

Among the opponents of the genuineness of the book this supposition is a dogmatic axiom, to the force of which the words of Scripture must yield. But this supposition is adopted also by interpreters such as Hofmann, Reichel (*die* 70 *Jahreswochen Dan.* ix. 24–27, in the *Theol. Stud. u. Krit.* 1858, p. 735 ff.), Fries, and others, who recognise the genuineness of the book of Daniel, and hold the announcement of the angel in these verses to be a divine revelation. These interpreters have adopted this view for this reason, that in the description of the hostile prince who shall persecute Israel and desecrate the sanctuary, and then come to his end with terror (vers. 26 and 27), they believe that they recognise again the image of Antiochus Epiphanes, whose enmity against the people and the sanctuary of God is described, ch. viii. 9 ff., 23 f. It cannot, it is true, be denied that there is a certain degree of similarity between the two. If in vers. 26 and 27 it is said of the hostile prince that he shall destroy the city and the sanctuary, and put an end to the sacrifice and the meat-offering for half a week, then it is natural to think of the enemy of whom it is said: he "shall destroy the mighty and the holy people" (E. V. ch. viii. 24), "and by him the daily sacrifice was taken away" (ch. viii. 11), "and he shall take away the daily sacrifice" (ch. xi. 31), especially if, with Hofmann, we adopt the view (*Schriftbew.* ii. 2, p. 592) that between the expressions "take away the daily sacrifice" (הַתָּמִיד [הֵסִיר, *remove*] הֵרִים), and "he shall cause the sacrifice and the oblation to cease" (יַשְׁבִּית זֶבַח וּמִנְחָה), there "is no particular distinction."[1] But the predicate "*particular*" shows that Hofmann does not reject *every* distinction; and, indeed, there exists a not inconsiderable distinction; for, as we have already remarked, הַתָּמִיד denotes only that which is *permanent* in worship, as *e.g.* the daily morning and evening sacrifice; while, on the other hand, זֶבַח וּמִנְחָה denotes the whole series of sacrifices together. The making to cease of the bloody and the unbloody sacrifices expresses an altogether greater wickedness than the taking away of the daily sacrifice. This distinction is not set aside by a reference to the clause וְעַל כְּנַף שִׁקּוּצִים מְשֹׁמֵם (ver. 27) compared with וְנָתְנוּ הַשִּׁקּוּץ מְשֹׁמֵם (ch. xi. 31). For the assertion that the article in הַשִּׁקּוּץ מְשֹׁמֵם (ch. xi. 31, "*the* abomination that maketh desolate") denotes something of which Daniel had before this already heard, supplies no proof of this; but the article is simply to be accounted for from the placing over against one another of הַתָּמִיד and הַשִּׁקּוּץ. Moreover the הַשִּׁקּוּץ מְשֹׁמֵם is very different from the עַל כְּנַף שִׁקּוּצִים מְשֹׁמֵם. The being carried on the wings of idol-abominations is a much more comprehensive expression for the might and dominion of idol-abominations than the setting up of an idol-altar on Jehovah's altar of burnt-offering.

As little can we (with Hofm., p. 590) perceive in the הַבָּא, closely connecting itself with וְקִצּוֹ בַשֶּׁטֶף (ver. 26), a reference to the divine judgment described in ch. viii., because the reference

[1] We confine ourselves here to what Hofm. in his *Schriftbew.* has brought forward in favour of this view, without going into the points which he has stated in his *die* 70 *Wochen*, u. s. w. p. 97, but has omitted in the *Schriftbew.*, and can with reference to that earlier argumentation only refer for its refutation to Kliefoth's *Daniel*, p. 417 ff.

to the enemy of God spoken of in ch. vii. 8 and 24 is as natural, yea, even more so, when we observe that the enemy of God in ch. vii. is destroyed by a solemn judgment of God—a circumstance which harmonizes much more with קִצּוֹ בַשֶּׁטֶף than with בְּאֶפֶס יָד יִשָּׁבֵר, which is said of the enemy described in ch. viii. Add to this that the half-week during which the adversary shall (ch. ix. 27) carry on his work corresponds not to the 2300 evening-mornings (ch viii. 13), but, as Delitzsch acknowledges, to the 3½ times, ch. vii. 25 and xii. 7, which 3½ times, however, refer not to the period of persecution under Antiochus, but to that of Antichrist.

From all this it therefore follows, not that the prince who shall come, whose people shall destroy the city and the sanctuary, and who shall cause the sacrifice to cease, is Antiochus, who shall raise himself against the people of the saints, take away the "continuance" (=*daily sacrifice*), and cast down the place of the sanctuary (ch. viii. 11), but only that this wickedness of Antiochus shall constitute a type for the abomination of desolation which the hostile prince mentioned in this prophecy shall set up, till, like Pharaoh, he find his overthrow in the flood, and the desolation which he causes shall pour itself upon him like a flood.

This interpretation of vers. 26 and 27 is not made doubtful also by referring to the words of 1 Macc. i. 54, *ᾠκοδόμησαν βδέλυγμα ἐρημώσεως ἐπὶ τὸ θυσιαστήριον*, as an evidence that at that time Dan. ix. 27 was regarded as a prophecy of the events then taking place (Hofm. *Weiss.* i. p. 309). For these words refer not to Dan. ix. 27, where the LXX. have *βδέλυγμα ἐρημώσεων*, but to Dan. xi. 11, where the singular *βδέλυγμα ἐρημώσεως* stands with the verb *καὶ δώσουσι* (LXX. for וְנָתְנוּ), to which the *ᾠκοδομήσεται* visibly refers.

If, therefore, the reference of vers. 26, 27 to the period of Antiochus' persecution is exegetically untenable, then also, finally, it is completely disproved in the chronological reckoning of the 70 weeks. Proceeding from the right supposition, that after the 70 weeks, the fulfilling of all that was promised, the expiating and putting away of sin, and, along with that, the perfect working out of the divine plan of salvation for eternity, shall begin,—thus, that in ver. 24 the perfecting of the kingdom of God in glory is prophesied of,—Hofmann and his followers do not interpret the 7, 62, and 1 week which are mentioned in vers. 25–27 as a division of the 70 weeks, but they misplace the first-mentioned 7 weeks at the end of the period consisting of 70 such weeks, and the following 62 + 1 in the time reaching from the beginning of the Chaldean supremacy in the year 605 to the death of Antiochus Epiphanes in the year 164, which makes 441 years = 63 year-weeks; according to which, not only the end of the 62 + 1 weeks does not coincide with the end of the 70 weeks, but also the 7 + 62 + 1 are to be regarded neither as identical with the 70 nor as following one another continuously in their order,—much more between the 63 and the 7 weeks a wide blank space, which before the coming of the end cannot be measured, must lie, which is not even properly covered up, much less filled up, by the remark that "the unfolding of the 70 proceeds backwards." For by this reckoning 7 + 62 + 1 are not an unfolding of the 70, and are not equal to 70, but would be equal to 62 + 1 + some unknown intervening period + 7 weeks. This were an impossibility which the representatives of this interpretation of the angel's communication do not, it is true, accept, but seek to set aside, by explaining the 7 weeks as periods formed of 7 times 7, or jubilee-year periods, and, on the contrary, the 62 + 1 of seven-year times or Sabbath-periods.

This strange interpretation of the angel's words, according to which not only must the succession of the periods given in the text be transposed, the first 7 weeks being placed last, but also the word שָׁבֻעִים in the passages immediately following one another must first denote jubilee (49 year) periods, then also Sabbath-year (7 year) periods, is not made plain by saying that "the end of the 62 + 1 week is the judgment of wrath against the persecutor, thus only the remote making possible the salvation; but the end of the 70 weeks is, according to ver. 24, the final salvation, and fulfilling of the prophecy and consecration of the Most Holy—thus the end of the 62 + 1 and of the 70 does not take place at the same time;" and—"if the end of the two took place at the same time, what kind of miserable consolation would this be for Daniel, in answer to his prayer, to be told that Jerusalem within the 70 weeks would in troublous times again arise, thus only arise amid destitution!" (Del. p. 284). For the prophecy would furnish but miserable consolation only in this case, if it consisted merely of the contents of vers. 25*b*, 26, and 27,—if it said nothing more than this, that Jerusalem should be built again within the 70 weeks in troublous times, and then finally would again be laid waste. But the other remark, that the judgment of wrath against the destroyer forms only the *remote* making possible of the salvation, and is separated from the final deliverance or the completion of salvation by a long intervening period, stands in contradiction to the prophecy in ch. vii. and to the whole teaching of Scripture, according to which the destruction of the arch-enemy (Antichrist) and the setting up of the kingdom of glory are brought about by *one* act of judgment.

In the most recent discussion of this prophecy, Hofmann (*Schriftbew.* ii. 2, p. 585 ff., 2 Aufl.) has presented the following positive arguments for the interpretation and reckoning of the period of time in question. The message of the angel in vers. 25–27 consists of three parts: (1) A statement of how many *heptades* shall be between the going forth of the command to rebuild Jerusalem and a *Maschiach Nagid;* (2) the mentioning of that which constitutes the contents of sixty-two of these periods; (3) the prediction of what shall happen with the close of the latter of these times. In the first of these parts, דָּבָר with the following infinitive, which denotes a human action, is to be taken in the sense of *commandment,* as that word of Cyrus prophesied of Isa. xliv. 28, and the rebuilding of Jerusalem is to be interpreted as in this passage of Isaiah, or in Jeremiah's prophecy to the same import, and not as if afterwards a second rebuilding of Jerusalem amid the difficulty and oppression of the times is predicted; then will the sixty-two *heptades* remain separated from the seven, and not sixty-nine of these, but only seven, be reckoned between the going forth of the command to build Jerusalem again and the *Maschiach Nagid,* since in ver. 26 mention is made not of that which is to be expected on the other side of the sixty-nine, but of the sixty-two times; finally, the contents of the seven times are sufficiently denoted by their commencement and their termination, and will remain without being confounded with the building up of Jerusalem in troublous times, afterwards described.

All these statements of Hofmann are correct, and they agree with our interpretation of these verses, but they contain no proof that the sixty-two weeks are to be placed after the seven, and that they are of a different extent from these. The proof for this is first presented in the conclusion derived from these statements (on the ground of the correct supposition that by *Maschiach Nagid* not Cyrus, but the Messias, is to be understood), that because the first of these passages (ver. 25*a*) does not say of a part of these times what may be its contents, but much rather points out which part of them lies between the two events in the great future of Israel, and consequently separates them from one another, that on this account these events belong to the end of the present course of the world, in which Israel hoped, and obviously the seven times shall constitute the end of the period consisting of seven such times. This argument thus founds itself on the circumstance that the appearing of the *Maschiach Nagid* which concludes the seven weeks, and separates them from the sixty-two weeks which follow, is not to be understood of the appearance of Christ in the flesh, but of His return in glory for the completion of the kingdom which was hoped for in consequence of the restoration of Jerusalem, prophesied of by Isaiah (*e.g.* ch. lv. 3, 4) and Jeremiah (*e.g.* ch. xxx. 9). But we could speak of these deductions as valid only if Isaiah and Jeremiah had prophesied only of the appearance of the Messias in glory, with the exclusion of His coming in the flesh. But since this is not the case—much rather, on the one side, Hofmann himself says the דָּבָר לְהָשִׁיב וגו׳ may be taken for a prediction, as that Isa. xliv. 28, of Cyrus—but Cyrus shall not build the Jerusalem of the millennial kingdom, but the Jerusalem with its temple which was destroyed by the Chaldeans—and, on the other hand, here first, if not alone, in the prophecies ch. xxv. and xxix., by which Daniel was led to pray, Jeremiah has predicted the return of Israel from exile after the expiry of the seventy years as the beginning of the working out of the divine counsel of salvation towards Israel,—therefore Daniel also could not understand the דָּבָר לְהָשִׁיב וגו׳ otherwise than of the restoration of Jerusalem after the seventy years of the Babylonish exile. The remark also, that nothing is said of the contents of the seven weeks, warrants us in no respect to seek their contents in the time of the millennial kingdom. The absence of any mention of the contents of the seven weeks is simply and sufficiently accounted for from the circumstance, as we have already (p. 375) shown, that Daniel had already given the needed information (ch. viii.) regarding this time, regarding the time from the end of the Exile to the appearance of Christ. Still less can the conclusion be drawn, from the circumstance that the building in the sixty-two weeks is designated as one falling in troublous times, that the restoration and the building of Jerusalem in the seven weeks shall be a building in glory. The לְהָשִׁיב וְלִבְנוֹת (*to restore and to build*, ver. 25*a*) does not form a contrast to the תָּשׁוּב וְנִבְנְתָה וּבְצוֹק הָעִתִּים (= E.V. shall be built again, and the wall even in troublous times, ver. 25*b*), but it is only more indefinite, for the circumstances of the building are not particularly stated. Finally, the circumstance also, that after the sixty-two *heptades* a new devastation of the holy city is placed in view, cannot influence us to escape from the idea of the second coming of Christ in the last time along with the building of Jerusalem during the seven *heptades*, since it was even revealed to the prophet that not merely would a cruel enemy of the saints of God (in Antiochus Epiphanes) arise out of the third world-kingdom, but also that a yet greater enemy would arise out of the fourth, an enemy who would perish in the burning fire (ch. vii. 12, 26 f.) in the judgment of the world immediately before the setting up of the kingdom of glory.

Thus neither the placing of the contents of the seven weeks in the eschatological future, nor yet the placing of these weeks at the beginning instead of at the end of the three periods of time which are distinguished in vers. 25–27, is established by these arguments. This Fries (*Jahrb. f. deutsche Theol.* iv. p. 254 ff.) has observed, and rightly remarked, that the effort to interpret the events announced in ver. 26 f. of the tyranny of Antiochus, and to make this epoch coincide with the close of the sixty-two year-weeks in the chronological reckoning, cannot but lead to the mistake of including the years of Babylon in the seventy year-weeks—a mistake which is met by three rocks, against which every attempt of this kind must be shattered. (1) There is the objection that it is impossible that the times of the destruction and the desolation of Jerusalem could be conceived of under the same character as the times of its restoration, and be represented from the same point of view; (2) the inexplicable inconsequence which immediately arises, if in the seventy year-weeks, including the last restoration of Israel, the Babylonish but not also the Romish exile were comprehended; (3) the scarcely credible supposition that the message of the angel sent to Daniel was to correct that earlier divine word which was given by Jeremiah, and to make known that not simply seventy years, but rather seventy year-weeks, are meant. Of this latter supposition we have already (p. 323) shown that it has not a single point of support in the text.

In order to avoid these three rocks, Fries advances the opinion that the three portions into which the seventy year-weeks are divided, are each by itself separately to be reckoned chronologically, and that they form a connected whole, not in a chronological, but in a historico-pragmatical sense, "as the whole of all the times of the positive continuance of the theocracy in the Holy Land lying between the liberation from Babylonish exile and the completion of the historical kingdom of Israel" (p. 258); and, indeed, so that the seven year-weeks, ver. 25*a*, form the last part of the seventy year-weeks, or, what is the same, the jubilee-period of the millennial kingdom, and the sixty-two year-weeks, ver. 26*a*, represent the period of the restoration of Israel after its liberation from Babylon and before its overthrow by the Romans—reckoned according to the average of the points of commencement and termination, according to which, from the reckoning 536 (edict of Cyrus), 457 (return of Ezra), and 410 (termination by the restoration), we obtain for the epoch of the restoration the mean year 467 B.C.; and for the crisis of subjection to the Roman power A.U.C. 691 (the overthrow of Jerusalem by Pompey), 714 (the appointment of Herod as king of the Jews), and 759 (the first Roman procurator in Palestine), we obtain the mean year 721 A.U.C. = 33 B.C., and the difference of these mean numbers, 467 and 33, amounts exactly to 434 years = 62 year-weeks. The period described in ver. 26 thus reaches from the beginnings of the subjection of Israel under the Roman world-kingdom to the expiry of the time of the *diaspora* of Israel, and the separate year-week, ver. 27, comprehends the period of the final trial of the people of God, and reaches from the bringing back of Israel to the destruction of Antichrist (pp. 261–266).

Against this new attempt to solve the mystery of the seventy weeks, Hofmann, in *Schriftbew.* ii. 2, p. 594, raises the objection, "that in ver. 26 a period must be described which belongs to the past, and in ver. 27, on the contrary, another which belongs to the time of the end; this makes the indissoluble connection which exists between the contents of the two verses absolutely impossible." In this he is perfectly right. The close connection between these two verses makes it certainly impossible to interpose an empty space of time between the cutting off of the Anointed, by which Fries understands the dispersion of Israel among the heathen in the destruction of Jerusalem by the Romans, and the coming of Antichrist, a space which would amount to 1800 years. But in opposition to this hypothesis we must also further remark, (1) that Fries has not justified the placing of the first portion of the seventy year-weeks (*i.e.* the seven weeks) at the end,—he has not removed the obstacles standing against this arbitrary supposition, for his interpretation of the words עַד מָשִׁיחַ נָגִיד, "till Messias the prince shall be," is verbally impossible, since, if *Nagid* is a predicate, then the verb יִהְיֶה could not be wanting; (2) that the interpretation of the יִכָּרֵת מָשִׁיחַ of the abolition of the old theocracy, and of the dispersion of the Jews abandoned by God among the heathen, needs no serious refutation, but with this interpretation the whole hypothesis stands or falls. Finally, (3) the supposition requires that the sixty-two weeks must be chronologically reckoned as year-weeks; the seven weeks, on the contrary, must be interpreted mystically as jubilee-periods, and the one week as a period of time of indefinite duration; a freak of arbitrariness exceeding all measure, which can no longer be spoken of as scripture *interpretation*.

Over against such arbitrary hypotheses, we can regard it as only an advance on the way toward a right understanding of this prophecy, that Hofmann (p. 594) closes his most recent investigations into this question with the following remarks:—"On the contrary, I always find that the indefiniteness of the expression שָׁבוּעַ, which denotes a period in some way divided into sevens, leaves room for the possibility of comprehending together the sixty-three and the seven weeks in one period of seventy, as its beginning and its end. . . . What was the extent of the units of which the seventy times consist, the expression שָׁבוּעַ did not inform Daniel: he could only conjecture it." This facilitates the adoption of the symbolical interpretation of the numbers, which, after the example of Leyrer and Kliefoth, we regard as the only possible one, because it does not necessitate our changing the seventy years of the exile into years of the restoration of Jerusalem, and placing the seven weeks, which the text presents as the first period of the seventy weeks, last.

The symbolical interpretation of the seventy שָׁבֻעִים and their divisions is supported by the following considerations:—(1) By the double circumstance, that on the one side all the explanations of them as year-weeks necessitate an explanation of the angel's message which is justified neither by the words nor by the succession of the statements, and do violence to the text, without obtaining a natural progress of thought, and on the other side all attempts to reckon these year-weeks chronologically show themselves to be insufficient and impossible. (2) The same conclusion is sustained by the choice of the word שָׁבוּעַ for the definition of the whole epoch and its separate periods; for this word only denotes a space of time measured by sevens, but indicates nothing as to the duration of these sevens. Since Daniel in ch. viii. 14 and xii. 11 uses a chronologically definite measure of time (evening-mornings, days), we must conclude from the choice of the expressions, seven,

seven times (as in ch. vii. 25 and xii. 7 of the like expression, times), which cannot be reckoned chronologically, that the period for the perfecting of the people and the kingdom of God was not to be chronologically defined, but only noted as a divinely appointed period measured by sevens. "They are sevens, of that there is no doubt; but the measure of the unit is not given:" thus Lämmert remarks (*Zur Revision der bibl. Zahlensymb. in den Jahrbb. f. D. Theol.* ix. 1). He further says: "If the great difficulty of taking these numbers chronologically does not of itself urge to their symbolical interpretation, then we should be led to this by the disagreement existing between Gabriel's answer (ver. 22) and Daniel's question (ver. 2). To his human inquiries regarding the end of the Babylonish exile, Daniel receives not a human but a divine answer, in which the seventy years of Jeremiah are reckoned as sevens, and it is indicated that the full close of the history of redemption shall only be reached after a long succession of periods of development."

By the definition of these periods according to a symbolical measure of time, the reckoning of the actual duration of the periods named is withdrawn beyond the reach of our human research, and the definition of the days and hours of the development of the kingdom of God down to its consummation is reserved for God, the Governor of the world and the Ruler of human history; yet by the announcement of the development in its principal stadia, according to a measure fixed by God, the strong consolation is afforded of knowing that the fortunes of His people are in His hands, and that no hostile power will rule over them one hour longer than God the Lord thinks fit to afford time and space, in regard to the enemy for his unfolding and ripening for the judgment, and in regard to the saints for the purifying and the confirmation of their faith for the eternal life in His kingdom according to His wisdom and righteousness.

The prophecy, in that it thus announces the times of the development of the future consummation of the kingdom of God and of this world according to a measure that is symbolical and not chronological, does not in the least degree lose its character as a revelation, but thereby first rightly proves its high origin as divine, and beyond the reach of human thought. For, as Leyrer (Herz.'s *Realenc.* xviii. p. 387) rightly remarks, "should not He who as Creator has ordained all things according to measure and number, also as Governor of the world set higher measures and bounds to the developments of history? which are to be taken at one time as identical with earthly measures of time, which indeed the *eventus* often first teaches (*e.g.* the seventy years of the Babylonish exile, Dan. ix. 2), but at another time as symbolical, but yet so that the historical course holds and moves itself within the divinely measured sphere, as with the seventy weeks of Daniel, wherein, for the establishing of the faith of individuals and of the church, there lies the consolation, that all events even to the minutest, particularly also the times of war and of oppression, are graciously measured by God (Jer. v. 22; Job xxxviii. 11; Ps. xciii. 3 f.)."[1]

To give this consolation to the faithful is the object of this revelation, and that object it fully accomplishes. For the time and the hour of the consummation of the kingdom of God it belongs not to us to know. What the Lord said to His disciples (Acts i. 7) before His ascension, in answer to their question as to the time of the setting up of the kingdom of Israel—"It belongs not to you to know χρόνους ἢ καιροὺς οὓς ὁ πατὴρ ἔθετο ἐν τῇ ἰδίᾳ ἐξουσίᾳ"—that He says not only to the twelve apostles, but to the whole Christian world. That the reason for this answer is to be sought not merely in the existing condition of the disciples at the time He uttered it, but in this, that the time and the hour of the appearance of the Lord for the judgment of the world and the completion of His kingdom in glory are not to be announced beforehand to men, is clear from the circumstance that Christ in the eschatological discourse (Matt. xxiv. 36; Mark xiii. 32) declares generally, "Of that day and hour knoweth no man, no, not the angels of heaven, but my Father only." According to this, God, the Creator and Ruler of the world, has kept in His own power the determination of the time and the hour of the consummation of the world, so that we may not expect an announcement of it beforehand in the Scripture. What has been advanced in

[1] Auberlen, notwithstanding that he interprets the seventy שָׁבֻעִים chronologically as year-weeks, does not yet altogether misapprehend the symbolical character of this definition of time, but rightly remarks (p. 133 f.), "The history of redemption is governed by these sacred numbers; they are like the simple foundation of the building, the skeleton in its organism. These are not only outward indications of time, but also indications of nature and essence." What he indeed says regarding the symbolical meaning of the seventy weeks and their divisions, depends on his erroneous interpretation of the prophecy of the appearance of Christ in the flesh, and is not consistent with itself.

opposition to this view for the justifying of the chronological interpretation of Daniel's prophecy of seventy weeks, and similar prophecies (cf. *e.g.* Hengstb. *Christol.* iii. 1, p. 202 ff.), cannot be regarded as valid proof. If Bengel, in *Ordo Temporum*, p. 259, 2d ed., remarks with reference to Mark xiii. 32 : "*Negatur prævia scientia, pro ipso duntaxat præsenti sermonis tempore, ante passionem et glorificationem Jesu. Non dixit, nemo sciet, sed: nemo scit. Ipse jam, jamque, sciturus erat: et quum scientiam diei et horæ nactus fuit, ipsius erat, scientiam dare, cui vellet et quando vellet,*"—so no one can certainly dispute *a priori* the conclusion "*Ipse jam,*" etc., drawn from the correct statements preceding, but also every one will confess that the statement "*Ipsius erat,*" etc., cannot prove it to be a fact that Jesus, after His glorification, revealed to John in Patmos the time and the hour of His return for the final judgment. Bengel's attempt to interpret the prophetical numbers of the Apocalypse chronologically, and accordingly to reckon the year of the coming again of our Lord, has altogether failed, as all modern scientific interpreters have acknowledged. So also fails the attempt which has been made to conclude from what Christ has said regarding the day of His παρουσία, that the Scripture can have no chronologically defined prophecies, while yet Christ Himself prophesied His resurrection after three days.

CHAP. X.–XII. THE REVELATION REGARDING THE AFFLICTION OF THE PEOPLE OF GOD ON THE PART OF THE RULERS OF THE WORLD TILL THE CONSUMMATION OF THE KINGDOM OF GOD.

In the third year of the reign of Cyrus, Daniel received the last revelation regarding the future of his people, which gives a fuller unfolding of the hostile attitude of the world-power toward the people and the kingdom of God from the time of the Persian dominion to the end of the days, as well as regarding the powerful protection which the covenant people shall experience amid the severe oppressions they would be exposed to for their purification. This revelation connects itself, both as to its contents and form, so closely with ch. viii., that it is to be viewed as a further unfolding of that prophecy, and serves for the illustration and confirmation of that which was announced to the prophet shortly before the destruction of the Chaldean world-kingdom regarding the world-kingdoms that were to follow, and their relation to the theocracy. It consists of three parts:—(1.) There is the description of the appearance of God as to its nature, the impression it produced on the prophet, and its object (ch. x. 1–xi. 2*a*). (2.) The unveiling of the future, in brief statements regarding the relation of the Persian and the Javanic world-kingdoms to Israel, and in more comprehensive descriptions of the wars of the kings of the north and the south for the supremacy, with the hostilities thence arising against the kingdom of God—hostilities which aim at its destruction, but which, because of the powerful succour which is rendered to Israel by Michael the angel-prince, shall come to an end in the destruction of the enemy of God and the final salvation of the people of God (ch. xi. 2*b*–xii. 3). (3.) This revelation concludes with the definition of the duration of the time of oppression, and with the command given to Daniel to seal up the words, together with the prophecy, till the time of the end, and to rest till the end come: "For thou shalt rest and stand in thy lot at the end of the days" (ch. xii. 4–13).

If we attentively examine first of all the form of this revelation, namely, the manifestation of God, by which there is given to Daniel the understanding of the events of the future (ch. x. 14, cf. ch. xi. and xii.), this revelation will be found to be distinguished from all the others in this, that it is communicated partly by supernatural illumination for the interpretation of the dream-vision, partly by visions, partly by the appearance of angels. Auberlen (*d. Proph. Dan.* p. 91 f.) has already referred to this distinction, and therein has found a beautiful and noteworthy progression, namely, that the one revelation always prepares the way, in a material and formal respect, for that which follows, from which we may see how God gradually prepared the prophet for the reception of still more definite disclosures. "First Nebuchadnezzar dreams, and Daniel simply interprets (ch. ii. and iv.); afterwards Daniel himself has a dream, but as yet it is only as a vision in a dream of the night (ch. vii. 1, 2); then follows a vision in a waking state (ch. viii. 1–3); and finally, in the last two revelations (ch. ix. and x.–xii.), when Daniel, now a feeble, trembling (?) old man (ch. x. 8 ff.), is already almost transplanted out of this world—now the ecstatic state seems to be no longer necessary for him. Now in his usual state he sees and hears angels speak like men, while his companions do not see the appearances from the higher world, and are only overwhelmed with terror, like those who accompanied Paul to Damascus (ch. ix. 20 ff., x. 4 ff., cf. Acts of Ap. ix. 7)." It is true, indeed, that, as Aub. remarks, there is a progression from interpreting of dreams to the receiving of visions in dreams and in the waking state, but by this reference neither are the actual contents of the revelation given in different forms perfectly comprehended, nor still less is the meaning of the difference made clear. Auberlen, in thus representing the distinction, has left out of view the circumstance, that the visions in ch. vii. and viii. are also interpreted to Daniel by an angel; moreover, that the revelation in ch. viii. does not merely consist of a vision, in which Daniel sees the destruction of the Persian world-kingdom by the Javanic under the figure of a he-goat casting down the ram, but that Daniel, after this vision, also hears an angel speak, and a voice comes to him from above the waters of the Ulai which commands the angel Gabriel to explain the vision to the seer (ch. viii. 13 ff.), and that this second part of that revelation has a great likeness to that in ch. x.–xii.; finally, that the same angel Gabriel again appears in ch. ix., and brings to Daniel the revelation regarding the seventy weeks (ch. ix. 24–27). But as to the interpretation of these revelations given in different forms, this difference is conditioned partly by the subjective relations sustained by the recipients to God, while, on the other hand, the form is in the most intimate manner connected with the contents of the revelation, and indeed in a way wholly different and much deeper than Auberlen thinks, if he therein sees only the material progression to greater speciality in the prophecy.

To comprehend the meaning of the divine revelation in ch. x.–xii., we must examine more closely the resemblance which it presents to ch. viii. 13–19. As in the vision ch. viii., which points to the oppression of the time of the end (ch. viii. 17, 19), Daniel heard a voice from the Ulai (ch. viii. 16), so in ch. x. and xii. the personage from whom that voice proceeded appears within the circle of Daniel's vision, and announces to him what shall happen to his people בְּאַחֲרִית הַיָּמִים (ch. x. 14). This celestial person appears to him in such awful divine majesty, that he falls to the ground on hearing his voice, as already in ch. viii. 17 ff. on hearing his voice and message, so that he feared he should perish; and it was only by repeated supernatural consolation and strengthening that he was able to stand erect again, and was made capable of hearing the revelation. The heavenly being who appears to him resembles in appearance the glory of Jehovah which Ezekiel had seen by the river Chaboras (Chebar); and this appearance of the man clothed in linen prepared the contents of his revelation, for

God so manifested Himself to Daniel (as He will approve Himself to His people in the times of the future great tribulation) as He who in judgment and in righteousness rules the affairs of the world-kingdoms and of the kingdom of God, and conducts them to the issues foreseen; so that the effect of His appearance on Daniel formed a pre-intimation and a pledge of that which would happen to the people of Daniel in the future. As Daniel was thrown to the ground by the divine majesty of the man clothed in linen, but was raised up again by a supernatural hand, so shall the people of God be thrown to the ground by the fearful judgments that shall pass over them, but shall again be raised up by the all-powerful help of their God and His angel-prince Michael, and shall be strengthened to endure the tribulation. According to this, the very appearance of God has prophetic significance; and the reason why this last vision is communicated to Daniel neither by a vision nor by angels, but by a majestic Theophany, does not lie in the more definite disclosures which should be given to him regarding the future, but only in this, that the revelation, as is mentioned in the superscription, ch. x. 1, places in view the אֱמֶת וְצָבָא גָדוֹל (ch. x. 1).

Of this oppression, that spoken of in ch. viii., which should come upon the people of God from the fierce and cunning king seen as a little horn, forms a type; therefore Daniel hears the voice from the waters of the Ulai. That which is there briefly indicated, is in ch. x.–xii. further extended and completed. In regard to the definiteness of the prediction, the revelation in ch. x.–xii. does not go beyond that in ch. viii.; but it does so with respect to the detailed description found in it of the wars of the world-rulers against one another and against the people of God, as well as in this, that it opens a glimpse into the spirit-world, and gives disclosures regarding the unseen spiritual powers who mingle in the history of nations. But over these powers God the Lord exercises dominion, and helps His people to obtain a victory over all their enemies. To reveal this, and in actual fact to attest it to the prophet, and through him to the church of God of all times, is the object of the Theophany, which is circumstantially described in ch. x. for the sake of its prophetical character.

Chap. x.–xi. 2*a*. *The Theophany.*

Ch. x. 1–3. *The introduction to the following manifestation of God.*

Ver. 1. This verse is to be regarded as an inscription or general statement of the substance of it. Therefore Daniel speaks of himself in the third person, as in ch. vii. 1, and in the historical portions ch. i.–vi. The definition of the time, "In the first year of Cores (Cyrus) king of Persia," refers us back to ch. i. 21, but it does not, as has been there already remarked, stand in contradiction to the first year of Cyrus named there. דָּבָר is the following revelation, which was communicated to the prophet not by a vision (חָזוֹן), but by a manifestation of God (מַרְאֶה), and was given in the form of simple human discourse. The remark regarding Daniel, "whose name was Belteshazzar," is designed only to make it obvious that the Daniel of the third year of Cyrus was the same who was carried to Babylon in the first year of Nebuchadnezzar (seventy-two years before). To the question why Daniel did not return to his native land in the first year of Cyrus, which Hitzig has thus formulated for the purpose of framing an argument against the genuineness of this prophecy—"How could he, who was a pattern of piety (ch. i. 8, Ezek. xiv. 14), so disregard the opportunity that was offered and the summons of Isaiah (ch. xlviii. 20, lii. 11 ff.) as if he stood on the side of those who forgot the holy mountain?" (Isa. lxv. 11)—the supposition of his advanced old age (Häv.) is no sufficient answer. For, on the contrary, Hitzig has rightly replied that old men also, such as had even seen the former temple, had returned home (Ezra iii. 12), and Daniel was not so infirm as to be unable for the journey. The correct answer is rather this, that Daniel, because divine revelations had been communicated to him, had obtained a position at the court of the world-rulers in which he was able to do much for the good of his people, and might not, without a special divine injunction, leave this place; that he thus, not from indifference toward the holy mountain or from neglect of the injunctions to flee from Babylon (Isa. xlviii. 20, lii. 11 ff.), but from obedience to God, and for the furtherance of the cause of His kingdom, remained at his post till the Lord His God should call him away from it.

In the second hemistich the contents of this new divine revelation are characterized. הַדָּבָר with the article points back to דָּבָר in the first half of the verse. Of this "word" Daniel says that it contains אֱמֶת and צָבָא גָדוֹל. In the statement that "the thing was true," Hitzig finds an intimation that thereby the author betrays his standpoint, namely, the time when "the thing" was realized, for Daniel could not say this before it happened. But this objection supposes that the author was a lying prophet, who spoke from his own heart (Jer. xxix. 8, 15). But if Daniel had actually received a "word" from God, he could before its fulfilment testify its truth. The testimony to the truth of the word here indicates, as it does in ch. viii. 26 in the mouth of the angel, that the word of God now communicated to the prophet contained things which it would be difficult for the human heart to believe. The second predicate צָבָא גָּדוֹל shows in what respect this is so. For that these words do not, with the LXX. and Aquil., refer to what follows is obvious, as is acknowledged by all modern interpreters. צָבָא, *warfare, military service*, then the difficulty of this service, and figuratively *difficulty*, afflictions of life, Job vii. 1, x. 17, and also here. "The word is, *i.e.* concerns, has as its contents, great afflictions" [E.V. "the time appointed was long"].

In the last clause of this verse בִּין and בִּינָה are not the imperative (v. Lengerke), because a summons to give heed, or understand, would not be here in place. בִּינָה is a substantive, and the throwing of the accent on the penultima is occasioned by the accented לוֹ which follows. בִּין is the *3d pers. perf.*, not the infinitive (Häv.). Understanding was to him בַּמַּרְאֶה, by that which was seen, *i.e.* by the appearance described in vers. 5 ff. בַּמַּרְאֶה cannot at all be referred (Klief.) to the earlier prophecies of ch. viii. 7, 9. The statement in these two passages serves for the confirmation of that which was said regarding the contents of the word from God, and stands in relation to ch. viii. 27, where Daniel was troubled because no one understood the vision. He was helped out of this state of non-understanding by the following revelation, cf. ver. 14. But the objection that it cannot be here said that Daniel understood the word, because he himself, ch. xii. 8, says that he did not understand it, has been disposed of by Kliefoth, who justly remarks that the non-understanding in ch. xii. 8 regards a single point, namely, the duration of the affliction, regarding which, however, disclosures are given to the prophet in ch. xii. 10 f. The translation: "he heard the word, and understood the vision" (Kran.), is set aside by this circumstance, that it takes בִּין in a different sense from בִּינָה, contrary to the parallelism of the passages.

Vers. 2, 3 introduce the following revelation by a statement of the occasion of it. בַּיָּמִים הָהֵם refers back to the date named in ver. 1. The יָמִים after שָׁבֻעִים does not serve to designate the three weeks as common day-weeks, in contrast to the שָׁבֻעִים of ch. ix. 24 ff., but is an accusative subordinated to the definition of time which expresses the idea of continuance: three weeks long, or three whole weeks, as Gen. xli. 1; cf. Gesen. *Gramm.* § 118, 3. For three weeks Daniel mourned and fasted, *i.e.* abstained from the usual food. לֶחֶם חֲמֻדוֹת, *precious food, delicacies;* but Häv., v. Leng., Maur., Hitz., and Kran. interpret it of *leavened bread,* so called in contrast to the unleavened paschal bread, the bread of affliction (Deut. xvi. 3). But this contrast is not well founded, for the מַצּוֹת (*unleavened cakes*) of the passover was not (notwithstanding Deut. xvi. 3) bread of sorrow, but pure, holy bread, which Daniel did not eat, in opposition to the law, for three weeks. לֶחֶם is not to be limited to bread in its narrower sense, but denotes *food* generally. Flesh and wine are festival food, Isa. xxii. 13, Gen. xxvii. 25, which is not had every day. The anointing with oil was the sign of joy and of a joyous frame of mind, as with guests at a banquet, Amos vi. 6, and was intermitted in the time of sorrow; cf. 2 Sam. xiv. 2. Fasting, as an abstaining from the better sustenance of common life, was the outward sign of sorrow of soul.

According to ver. 4, Daniel mourned and fasted in the first month of the year, the month in the middle of which the paschal feast was kept, in which Israel celebrated their deliverance from their state of slavery in Egypt and their advancement to be the people of God, and were joyful before their God. On the 24th day of this month occurred the Theophany (ver. 4 ff.), with which, however, his fasting came to an end. According to this, it appears that he fasted from the third to the twenty-third of the month Nisan; thus it began immediately after the feast of the new moon, which was kept for two days (cf. 1 Sam. xx. 18 f., 27, 34 with vi. 29, ii. 19). Thus Häv. and Hitzig conclude; while v. Leng. and Maurer argue, from ver. 13, that between the time of fasting and the appearance of the angel an interval elapsed, consequently that Daniel fasted from the first to the twenty-first of the month Nisan. But from ver. 13 nothing further follows than that the angel was detained twenty-one days; so that the question as to the beginning and the end of the fast is not certainly answered from the text, and, as being irrelevant to the matter, it can remain undecided. More important is the question as to the cause of such long-continued great sorrow, which is not answered by the remark that he was thus prepared for receiving a divine revelation. According to ver. 12, Daniel sought הָבִין, *i.e.* understanding as to the state of the matter, or regarding the future of his people, which filled him with concern. The word about the restoration of Jerusalem which he had received through the angel Gabriel in the first year of Darius (ch. ix.) had come to pass since that revelation in the first year of Cyrus, but had had only little effect on the religious lukewarmness of the majority of the people. Of the whole people only a very small portion had returned to the land of their fathers, and had begun, after restoring the altar of burnt-offering, to build the house of God in Jerusalem. But while the foundation of the new temple was laid, there mingled with the joyful shoutings of the people also the loud wailings of the old men who had seen the former temple in its glory, when they beheld this building undertaken amid circumstances so depressing and sorrowful (Ezra iii.). In addition to this, the Samaritans immediately, when the Jewish rulers refused for conscience sake to permit them to take part with them in the building, sought, by means of influences used at the Persian court, to prevent the carrying on of the building (Ezra iv. 1–5). This sad state of matters could not but, at the beginning of the new year, fill the heart of Daniel with deep sorrow, and move him at the return of the time of the passover to mourn in fasting and prayer over the delay of the salvation promised to his people, and to supplicate in behalf of Israel the pardon of their sins, and their deliverance out of the hand of their enemies. Therefore he mourned and fasted before and during the paschal days for three weeks, until on the twenty-fourth day of the month he received a revelation from God.

Vers. 4–6. *The Theophany.*—On the day named Daniel found himself on the side (banks) of the river Hiddekel, *i.e.* the Tigris (see under Gen. ii. 14), along with some who accompanied him (ver. 7); thus he was there in reality, and not merely in vision as at the Ulai, ch. viii. 2. For what purpose he was there is not said. Here he saw a celestial being, whose form is described, vers. 5, 6. It was a man (אֶחָד, *one*, not several) clothed in בַּדִּים, *i.e.* in a *talar* of shining white linen (regarding בַּדִּים, see under Ezek. ix. 2), and his loins girt about with gold of Uphaz. אוּפָז occurs nowhere else, except in Jer. x. 9: gold of Uphaz and silver of Tarshish, from which we must conclude that Uphaz is the name of a region, a country, probably only a dialectically different form for אוֹפִיר; the combination with the Sanscr. *vipâça* = *Hyphasis* is, on the other hand, very far-fetched.

Ver. 6. His body shone like תַּרְשִׁישׁ, *i.e.* the chrysolite of the Old and the topaz of the New Testament (see under Ezek. i. 16); his countenance had the appearance of lightning, his eyes as lamps of fire, his arms and the place of his feet like the sight of polished brass (קָלָל, see under Ezek. i. 7). מַרְגְּלוֹת, *place of the feet*, does not stand for *feet*, but denotes that part of the human frame where the feet are; and the word indicates that not the feet alone, but the under parts of the body shone like burnished brass. The voice of his words, *i.e.* the sound of his speaking, was like קוֹל הָמוֹן, for which in Ezek. i. 24 קוֹל הֲמֻלָּה (*the voice of noise*), and by קוֹל מַחֲנֶה (Ezek. i. 24) the noise of a host is denoted.

This heavenly form has thus, it is true, the shining white *talar* common to the angel, Ezek. ix. 9, but all the other features, as here described—the shining of his body, the brightness of his countenance, his eyes like a lamp of fire, arms and feet like glistering brass, the sound of his speaking—all these point to the revelation of the כְּבוֹד יְהוָֹה, the glorious appearance of the Lord, Ezek. i., and teach us that the אִישׁ seen by Daniel was no common angel-prince, but a manifestation of Jehovah, *i.e.* the Logos. This is placed beyond a doubt by a comparison with Rev. i. 13–15, where the form of the Son of man whom John saw walking in the midst of the seven golden candlesticks is described like the glorious appearance seen by Ezekiel and Daniel.

The place where this heavenly being was, is not here specially stated. In ch. xii. 6 he appears hovering over the waters of the river, the Tigris. This agrees also with the verse before us, according to which Daniel, while standing on the banks of the river, on lifting up his eyes beheld the vision. Hence it further follows, that the אִישׁ seen here by Daniel is the same heavenly being whose voice he heard, ch. viii. 16, from the waters of the Ulai, without seeing his form.

When now he whose voice Daniel heard from thence presents himself before him here on the Tigris in a majesty which human nature is not able to endure, and announces to him the future, and finally, ch. xii. 6 ff., with a solemn oath attests the completion of the divine counsel, he thereby shows himself, as C. B. Michaelis *ad Dan.* p. 372, Schmieder in Gerlach's *Bibelw.*, and Oehler (Art. *Messias* in Herz.'s *Realenc.* ix. p. 417) have acknowledged, to be the Angel of Jehovah κατ' ἐξοχὴν, as the "Angel of His presence." The combination of this angel with that in the form of a son of man appearing in the clouds (ch. vii. 13) is natural; and this combination is placed beyond a doubt by the comparison with Rev. i. 13, where John sees the glorified Christ, who is described by a name definitely referring to Dan. vii. 13, as ὅμοιον υἱῷ ἀνθρώπου.

On the other hand, the opinion maintained to some extent among the Rabbis, which even Hengstenberg has in modern times advocated (*Beitr.* i. p. 165 ff.; *Christol.* iii. 2, p. 50 ff.), namely, that the angel of the Lord who here appears to Daniel in divine majesty is identical with the angel-prince Michael, has no support in Scripture, and stands in contradiction to vers. 13 and 21, where he who speaks is certainly distinguished from Michael, for here there is ascribed to Michael a position with reference to the people of God which is not appropriate to the Angel of the Lord or the Logos. It is true, indeed, that Hengstenberg holds, with many old interpreters, that he who *speaks* with Daniel, ver. 11, and reveals to him the future, is different from him who *appears* to him, vers. 5 and 6, and is identical with the angel Gabriel. But the reasons advanced in support of this are not sufficient. The latter supposition is grounded partly on the similarity of the address to Daniel, אִישׁ חֲמֻדוֹת, vers. 11 and 19, cf. with ch. ix. 23, partly on the similarity of the circumstances, ch. viii. 17, 18, cf. with ver. 10 and ch. xii. 5. But the address to Daniel אִישׁ חֲמֻדוֹת proves nothing, because it does not express to Daniel the relation of the angel to him, but of the Lord who sent the angel; and Gabriel in ch. ix. 23 does not *address* the prophet thus, but only says that he is חֲמֻדוֹת, *i.e.* a man greatly beloved of God. The similarity of circumstances with ch. viii. 17, 18 proves nothing further than that he who appeared was a heavenly being. More noticeable is the similarity of ch. viii. 13 with ch. xii. 5, so far as in both cases two angels appear along with him who hovers over the waters, and the voice from above the waters in ch. viii. 16 directs the angel Gabriel to explain the vision to the prophet. But from the circumstance that in ch. viii. and also in ch. ix. Gabriel gives to the prophet disclosures regarding the future, it by no means follows, even on the supposition that he who is represented in the chapter before us as *speaking* is different from him who *appears* in vers. 5 and 6, that the angel who speaks is Gabriel. If he were Gabriel, he would have been named here, according to the analogy of vers. 9, 21.

To this is to be added, that the assumed difference between him who speaks, ver. 11, and him who appears, vers. 5, 6, is not made out, nor yet is it on the whole demonstrable. It is true that in favour of this difference, he who speaks is on the banks of the river where Daniel stands, while he who appears, vers. 5, 6, and also at the end of the vision, ch. xii., is in the midst of the Tigris, and in ver. 5 of this chapter (ch. xii.) two other persons are standing on the two banks of the river, one of whom asks him who is clothed with linen, as if in the name of Daniel, when the things announced shall happen. Now if we assume that he who is clothed in linen is no other than he who speaks to Daniel, ver. 11, then one of these two persons becomes a *κωφὸν πρόσωπον*, and it cannot be at all seen for what purpose he appears. If, on the contrary, the difference of the two is assumed, then each has his own function. The Angel of the Lord is present in silent majesty, and only by a brief sentence confirms the words of his messenger (ch. xii. 7). The one of those standing on the banks is he who, as the messenger and interpreter of the Angel of the Lord, had communicated all disclosures regarding the future to Daniel as he stood by the banks. The third, the angel standing on the farther bank, directs the question regarding the duration of the time to the Angel of the Lord. Thus Hengstenberg is in harmony with C. B. Michaelis and others.

But however important these reasons for the difference appears, yet we cannot regard them as conclusive. From the circumstance that, ch. x. 10, a hand touched Daniel as he was sinking down in weakness and set him on his knees, it does not with certainty follow that this was the hand of the angel (Gabriel) who stood by Daniel, who spoke to him, ver. 11. The words of the text, "a hand touched me," leave the person whose hand it was altogether undefined; and also in vers. 16 and 18, where Daniel is again touched, so that he was able to open his mouth and was made capable of hearing the words that were addressed to him, the person from whom the touch proceeded is altogether indefinite. The designations, כִּדְמוּת בְּנֵי אָדָם, *like the similitude of the sons of men*, ver. 16, and כְּמַרְאֵה אָדָם, *like the appearance of a man*, ver. 18, do not point to a definite angel who appears speaking in the sequel. But the circumstance that in ch. xii., besides the form that hovered over the water, other two angels appear on the banks, does not warrant us to assume that these two angels were already present or visible in ch. x. 5 ff. The words, "Then I looked and saw other two, the one," etc., ch. xii. 5, much rather indicate that the scene was changed, that Daniel now for the first time saw the two angels on the banks. In ch. x. he only sees him who is clothed with linen, and was so terrified by this "great sight" that he fell powerless to the ground on hearing his voice, and was only able to stand up after a hand had touched him and a comforting word had been spoken to him.

Nothing is here, as in ch. viii. 15, said of the coming of the angel. If thus, after mention being made of the hand which by touching him set him on his knees, it is further said, "and he spake to me. . . ." (ver. 11), the context only leads to this conclusion, that he who spake to him was the man whose appearance and words had so overwhelmed him. To suppose another person, or an angel different from the one who was clothed with linen, as speaking, could only be justified if the contents of that which was spoken demanded such a supposition.

He who spake said, among other things, that he was sent to Daniel (vers. 11); that the prince of the kingdom of Persia had withstood him one and twenty days; and that Michael, one of the chief angel-princes, had come to his help (vers. 13 and 21). These statements do not indicate that he was an inferior angel, but they are suitable to the Angel of the Lord; for he also says (Zech. ii. 13, 15, iv. 9) that he is sent by Jehovah; cf. also Isa. xlviii. 16 and lxi. 1. The coming to his help by the angel-prince Michael, also, does not denote that he who speaks was an angel subordinated to the archangel Michael. In Zech. i. 15 עָזַר denotes help which men render to God; and in 1 Chron. xii. 21 f. it is related that Israelites of different tribes came to David to help him against his enemies, *i.e.* under his leadership to fight for him. Similarly we may suppose that the angel Michael gave help to the Angel of the Lord against the prince of the kingdom of Persia.

There thus remains only the objection, that if we take the angel clothed with linen and him who speaks as the same, then in ch. xii. 5 one of the angels who stood on the two banks of the Tigris becomes a *κωφὸν πρόσωπον*; but if we are not able to declare the object for which two angels appear there, yet the one of those two angels cannot certainly be the same as he who announced, ch. x. and xi., the future to the prophet, because these angels are expressly designated as *two others* (שְׁנַיִם אֲחֵרִים), and the אֲחֵרִים excludes the identifying of these with angels that previously appeared to Daniel. This argument is not set aside by the reply that the angels standing on the two banks of the river are spoken of as אֲחֵרִים with reference to the Angel of the Lord, ver. 6, for the reference of the אֲחֵרִים to that which follows is inconsistent with the context; see under ch. xii. 5.

Thus every argument utterly fails that has been adduced in favour of the supposition that he who speaks, ver. 11, is different from him who is clothed in linen; and we are warranted to abide by the words of the narrative, which in ch. x. names no other angel than the man clothed with linen, who must on that account be the same as he who speaks and announces the future to the prophet. The hand which again set him up by touching him, is, it is true, to be thought of as proceeding from an angel; but it is not more definitely described, because this angel is not further noticed. But after the man clothed with linen has announced the future to the prophet, the scene changes (ch. xii. 5). Daniel sees the same angels over the waters of the Tigris, and standing on the two banks of the river. Where he who was clothed in linen stands, is left indefinite in the narrative. If from the first it is he who hovers over the water of the river, he could yet talk with the prophet standing on its banks. But it is also possible that at first he was visible close beside the banks.

Ver. 7. According to this verse, the form described in vers. 5 and 6 was visible to Daniel alone. His companions saw not the appearance, but they were so alarmed by the invisible nearness of the heavenly being that they fled and hid themselves. What is here said resembles Acts ix. 3 ff., where Christ, after His exaltation, appeared to Paul and spoke to him—Paul's companions hearing only the voice, but seeing no one. In order to account for the flight of Daniel's companions, it is not necessary to suppose the existence of thunder and lightning, of which the text makes no mention. The supposition also of Theodor. and Hitzig, that the men indeed saw not the angel, but that they heard his voice, is incorrect; for the voice was not heard till after his companions had fled. הַמַּרְאָה, pointed as fem., *that which was seen*, the appearance, seems to be a more limited conception than מַרְאֶה, *visio*. יִבְרְחוּ בְּהֵחָבֵא: *they fled, for they hid themselves;* so that the hiding is not to be regarded as the object of the fleeing, but the fleeing is made known in their hiding themselves.

Ver. 8. Daniel here calls the appearance *great* with reference to the majesty displayed, such as had never hitherto been known to him. Its influence upon him is, therefore, also greater than that of the appearance of Gabriel, ch. viii. 17. There remained in him no strength, *i.e.* he felt himself overwhelmed, and as if about to perish. His הוֹד, *splendour*—the same as the Chald. זִיו, ch. vii. 28, v. 6, 9—*i.e.* the fresh colour of life which marked his countenance, was changed לְמַשְׁחִית, properly, *to destruction*, to entire disfigurement, to corruption. The last clause, " and I retained no strength," gives greater force to the preceding statement.

Vers. 9, 10. When Daniel heard the voice, which according to ver. 6 was like the noise of a multitude, he was stunned, and fell on his face to the ground, as ch. viii. 17. Yet the expression here, הָיִיתִי נִרְדָּם, is stronger than נִבְעַתִּי, ch. viii. 17. Ver. 10 shows how great was his amazement in the further description it gives. The touching of him by an unseen hand raised him up and caused him to reel on his knees and hands (תְּנִיעֵנִי, *vacillare me fecit*), but did not enable him to stand erect. This he was first able to do after he heard the comfortable words, and was directed to mark the communication of the heavenly messenger. Regarding אִישׁ חֲמֻדוֹת see under ch. ix. 23, and for עֲמֹד עַל עָמְדֶךָ see at ch. viii. 18. He now raises himself up, but still trembling (מַרְעִיד). The עַתָּה, *now* am I sent to thee, points to the delay of his coming spoken of in ver. 12.

Ver. 12. According to this verse, the words of Daniel, *i.e.* his prayer from the first day of his seeking to understand the future, and of his self-mortification in sorrow and fasting (vers. 2, 3), was heard of God, and the angel was immediately sent forth by God to convey to him revelations. And, he adds, בָּאתִי בִּדְבָרֶיךָ, *I am come for thy words, i.e.* in consequence of thy prayer, according to it. The בָּאתִי most interpreters understand of the coming to Daniel; Hofmann (*Schriftbew.* i. p. 331) and Kliefoth, on the contrary, understand it of the coming of the angel to Persia (ver. 13). According to the matter, both views are correct, but in the form in which they are presented they are incorrect. Against the latter stands the adversative ו in וְשַׂר (*but the prince*), ver. 13, by which the contents of ver. 13 are introduced; for, according to this, ver. 13 cannot represent the object of the coming. Against the former stands the fact, that the angel does not come to Daniel immediately, but only after having gained a victory over the prince of the kingdom. The בָּאתִי is again taken up in ver. 14*a*, and must have here the same meaning that it has there. But in ver. 14*a* it is connected with לַהֲבִינְךָ, "I am come to bring thee understanding," in ver. 12 with בִּדְבָרֶיךָ, which only denotes that the "coming" corresponded to Daniel's prayer, but not that he came immediately to him. Daniel had, without doubt, prayed for the accomplishment of the salvation promised to his people, and *eo ipso* for the removal of all the hindrances that stood in the way of that accomplishment. The hearing of his prayer may be regarded, therefore, as containing in it not merely the fact that God directed an angel to convey to him disclosures regarding the future fortunes of his people, but also at the same time as implying that on the side of God steps were taken for the removal of these hindrances.

The thirteenth verse speaks of this, not as denoting that the angel came to Persia for the purpose of working for Israel, but much rather as announcing the reason of the twenty-one days' delay in the coming of the angel to Daniel, in the form of a parenthetical clause. His coming to Daniel was hindered by this, that the prince of the kingdom of Persia withstood him twenty-one days. The twenty-one days are those three weeks of Daniel's fasting and prayer, ver. 2. Hence we see that the coming of the angel had its reference to Daniel, for he came to bring him a comforting answer from God; but in order that he might be able to do this, he must first, according to ver. 13, enter into war with and overcome the spirit of the king of Persia, hostile to the people of God. The contents of ver. 13 are hence not to be understood as showing that the angel went to Persia in order that he might there arrange the cause of Israel with the king; the verse much rather speaks of a war in the kingdom of supernatural spirits, which could not relate to the court of the king of Persia. The prince (שַׂר) of the kingdom of Persia, briefly designated in ver. 21 "the prince of Persia," is not king Cyrus, or the *collectivum* of the kings of Persia, as Häv. and Kran., with Calvin and most of the Reformers, think, but the guardian spirit or the protecting genius of the Persian kingdom, as the Rabbis and most of the Christian interpreters have rightly acknowledged. For the angel that appeared to Daniel did not fight with the kings of Persia, but with a spiritual intelligence of a like nature, for the victory, or precedence with the kings of Persia. This spirit of the kingdom of Persia, whom, after the example of Jerome, almost all interpreters call the guardian angel of this kingdom, is as little the nature-power of this kingdom as Michael is the nature-power of Israel, but is a spirit-being; yet not the heathen national god of the Persians, but, according to the view of Scripture (1 Cor. x. 20 f.), the *δαιμόνιον* of the Persian kingdom, *i.e.* the supernatural spiritual power standing behind the national gods, which we may properly call the guardian spirit of this kingdom. In the עָמַד לְנֶגְדִּי lies, according to the excellent remark of Kliefoth, the idea, that "the שַׂר of the kingdom of Persia stood beside the kings of the Persians to influence them against Israel, and to direct against Israel the power lying in Persian heathendom, so as to support the insinuations of the Samaritans; that the angel, ver. 5, came on account of Daniel's prayer to dislodge this 'prince' from his position and deprive him of his influence, but he kept his place for twenty-one days, till Michael came to his help; then he so gained the mastery over him, that he now stood in his place beside the kings of Persia, so as henceforth to influence them in favour of Israel." He who appeared to Daniel, ver. 5, and spake with him, ver. 11, is not "the angel who had his dominion among the nations of the world," or "his sphere of action in the embodiments of the heathen world-power, to which the Jewish people were now in subjection, to promote therein the working out of God's plan of salvation" (Hofm. *Schriftbew.* i. p. 334). This supposition is destitute of support from the Scriptures. It is rather the Angel of the Lord who carries out God's plans in the world, and for their accomplishment and execution makes war against the hostile spirit of the heathen world-power. The subjugation of this spirit supposes a particular angel ruling in the heathen world just as little as Jehovah's contending against the heathen nations that oppress and persecute His kingdom and people.

In the war against the hostile spirit of the kingdom of Persia, the archangel Michael came to the help of the Angel of the Lord. The name מִיכָאֵל, *who is as God,* comes into view, as does the name *Gabriel,* only according to the appellative signification of the word, and expresses, after the analogy of Ex. xv. 11, Ps. lxxxix. 7 f., the idea of God's unparalleled helping power. *Michael* is thus the angel possessing the unparalleled power of God. He is here said to be "one of the chief princes," *i.e.* of the highest angel-princes,—ver. 21, "your prince," *i.e.* the prince who contends for Israel, who conducts the cause of Israel. The first title points undoubtedly to an arrangement of orders and degrees among the angels, designating Michael as one of the most distinguished of the angel-princes; hence called in Jude 9 ἀρχάγγελος, also in Rev. xii. 7, where he is represented as contending with his angels against the dragon. The opinion that Michael is called "one of the chief princes," not as in contrast with the angels, but only with the demons of the heathen gods (Kliefoth), is opposed by the words themselves and by the context. From the circumstance that the guardian spirit of Persia is called שַׂר it does not follow that שָׂרִים is not a designation of the angels generally, but only of the princes of the people, who are the spirits ruling in the social affairs of nations and kingdoms (Hofmann, p. 337); and even though this conclusion may be granted, this meaning for הַשָּׂרִים with the article and the predicate הָרִאשֹׁנִים is undemonstrable. For the Scripture does not place the demon-powers of heathendom so on a line with the angels that both are designated as שָׂרִים רִאשֹׁנִים. The שָׂרִים רִאשֹׁנִים can only be the princes, chiefs, of the good angels remaining in communion with God, and working for the kingdom of God. Though what is said by the angel Michael, for the sake of the Israelitish people, among whom he has the sphere of his activity, may be said for their comfort, yet it does not follow therefrom that that which is said "cannot give disclosures regarding the relation within the angel-world, but only regarding the relation to the great historical nations and powers of the world" (Hofm. p. 338). For as regards the statement adduced in support of this opinion—"the greatness and importance of the work entrusted to him makes him one of the רִאשֹׁנִים, not that the work is entrusted to him because he is so"—just the contrary is true. To a subordinate spirit God will not entrust a work demanding special power and greatness; much rather the being entrusted with a great and important work supposes a man exalted above the common mass. And for the comforting of Israel the words, "Michael, one of the foremost princes, came to my help," affirm that Israel is under very powerful protection, because its guardian spirit is one of the foremost of the angel-princes, whereby *implic.* it is said at the same time that the people, though they be little esteemed before the world, yet cannot be destroyed by the nations of the world. This thought follows as a conclusion from what is said regarding the dignity of their guardian angel, but it does not form the contents of the saying regarding Michael and his place among the heavenly spirits.

But we learn from ver. 21 the reason why the archangel Michael, and no other angel, came to the help of him who was clothed with linen. It was because Michael was the prince of Israel, *i.e.* "the high angel-prince who had to maintain the cause of the people of God in the invisible spirit-world against opposing powers" (Auberlen, p. 289); and as such he appears also in Jude 9 and Rev. xii. 7. The coming of Michael to give help does not include in it this, that he was superior in might or in position to the angel that spake, and thus supplies no proof that the angel that spake was Gabriel, or an angel different from him who was clothed with linen. For even a subordinate servant can bring help to his master, and in a conflict render him aid in gaining the victory. Against the idea of the subjection of Michael to the angel that spake, or the man clothed with linen, stands the further unfolding of the angel's message, the statement in ver. 21 and ch. xi. 1, according to which the angel that spake gave strength and help to Michael in the first year of the Median Darius, from which we have more reason to conclude that the angel who spake stood above the angel Michael; see under ch. xi. 1.

In consequence of the assistance on the part of Michael, the Angel of the Lord obtained the place of superiority by the side of the king of Persia. נוֹתַר has not here the usual meaning, *to be over and above, to remain,* but is to be translated after הוֹתִיר, Gen. xlix. 4, *to have the pre-eminence, to excel,* in the passive signification of the Hiphil: "*to be provided with the preference, to gain the superiority.*" The translation, "I have maintained the place" (Hofm.), cannot be proved. אֵצֶל, *at the side of, near,* is explained from the idea of the protecting spirit standing by the side of his protege. The plural, "kings of Persia," neither refers to Cyrus and Cambyses, nor to Cyrus and the conquered kings living with him (Crœsus, etc.), nor to Cyrus and the prince, *i.e.* his guardian spirit (Hitzig). The plural denotes, that by the subjugation of the demon of the Persian kingdom, his influence not merely over Cyrus, but over all the following kings of Persia, was brought to an end, so that the whole of the Persian kings became accessible to the influence of the spirit proceeding from God and advancing the welfare of Israel.

Ver. 14. With this joyful message the angel comes to Daniel, to open up to him what would befall his people in the last time. The punctuation of יִקְרָה (*shall befall*) is according to יִקְרָא (Gen. xlix. 1); the *Kethiv* יִקְרֶה has the correct form. בְּאַחֲרִית הַיָּמִים as ch. ii. 28, the Messianic world-time, in ch. viii. 17 is called the time of the end. "For," the angel adds, "the vision refers, or stretches itself out, to *the* days." לַיָּמִים, with the article, are the days of the אַחֲרִית (*the latter time*), the Messianic world-time. חָזוֹן is the revelation which in ver. 1 is called דָּבָר and מַרְאָה, the following revelation in ch. xi. Kliefoth is incorrect in thinking on the revelations already given, ch. vii., viii., ix., to Daniel, regarding which the angel now seeks to bring to him further understanding. For although those revelations stretch out to the last time, and the revelations in ch. xi. only give further disclosures regarding it, yet neither does the angel who speaks to Daniel here thus represent the matter, nor does the form of the revelation ch. x.–xii., namely, the majestic appearance of the Angel of the Lord, not a common angel-revelation, correspond with this supposition. חָזוֹן

also cannot, without further definition, refer to those earlier revelations; and the opinion that הָבִין denotes the understanding, as distinguished from the revelation or proclamation, does not accord with the usual style of Daniel's language. הָבִין denotes here, as in ch. viii. 16, the interpretation of the vision, which in both cases contains the things which shall befall the people of God in the future. Cf. ch. ix. 22, where יָבִין is used of the announcement of the revelation of God regarding the seventy weeks.

Vers. 15–19. In these verses it is further related how Daniel was gradually raised up and made capable of receiving the revelation of God. The communication of the angel hitherto had not fully gained this object. Daniel "stood trembling," but he could not yet speak. With his face bent towards the earth he was as yet speechless. Then one having the likeness of a man touched his lips, whereby he received the power of speech, and could address him who stood before him, and utter the complaint: "By the vision anguish, *i.e.* violent terror, has fallen upon me: woes are turned upon me." For this style of speech cf. 1 Sam. iv. 19, and for the matter itself, cf. Isa. xxi. 3, xiii. 8. For the following וְלֹא עָצַרְתִּי כֹּחַ (*and I have no strength*, ver. 16), cf. ver. 8.

Ver. 17. Therefore he may not talk with this Lord, *i.e.* with Him who appeared before him in such dread majesty; and he is yet in such a state, since all strength has departed from him and his breath has gone, that he fears he must die; cf. 1 Kings xvii. 17. Then once more one like the appearance of a man touched him. כְּמַרְאֵה אָדָם is in reality = כִּדְמוּת בְּנֵי אָדָם: both forms of expression leave the person of him who touched him undefined, and only state that the touching proceeded from some one who was like a man, or that it was such as proceeds from men, and are like the expression used in ver. 10, "a hand touched me." From this it does not follow that he who spoke to him touched him, but only that it was a spiritual being, who appeared like to a man. After thus being touched for the third time (ver. 18), the encouragement of the angel that talked with him imparted to him full strength, so that he could calmly listen to and observe his communication.

Ver. 20–ch. xi. 1. But before he communicated to Daniel what would befall his people in the "latter days" (ver. 14), he gives to him yet further disclosures regarding the proceedings in the spirit-kingdom which determine the fate of nations, and contain for Israel, in the times of persecution awaiting them, the comforting certainty that they had in the Angel of the Lord and in the guardian angel Michael a strong protection against the enmities of the heathen world. Kliefoth supposes that the angel who speaks in ver. 20–ch. xi. 1 gives a brief *resumé* of the contents of his previous statement (vers. 12–14). But it is not so. These verses, 20–ch. xi. 1, contain new disclosures not yet made known in vers. 12–19, although resembling the contents of ver. 13. Of the coming of the prince of Javan (ver. 20*b*), and the help which the angel-prince renders to Darius (ch. xi. 1), nothing is said in ver. 13; also what the Angel of the Lord, ver. 20, says regarding the conflict with the prince of Persia is different from that which is said in ver. 13. In ver. 13 he speaks of that which he has done before his coming to Daniel; in ver. 20, of that which he will now do. To the question, "Knowest thou wherefore I come unto thee?" no answer follows; it has, however, an affirmative sense, and is only an animated mode of address to remind Daniel of that which is said in vers. 12–14, and to impress it upon him as weighty and worthy of consideration. Then follows the new communication: "and now will I return to fight with the prince of Persia," *i.e.* to carry forward and bring to an end the victory gained for thee before my arrival over the demon of Persia, the spirit of the Persian kingdom.

The words which follow, וַאֲנִי יוֹצֵא וְהִנֵּה וגו' (ver. 20*b*, *and when I am gone forth, lo*, etc.), present some difficulty. The וַאֲנִי in comparison with אָשׁוּב (*will I return*) points to a contrast, and וְהִנֵּה plainly indicates that which shall begin with the אֲנִי יוֹצֵא. By this, the union of the וַאֲנִי יוֹצֵא with that which goes before and the adversative interpretation of וְהִנֵּה (v. Leng.) is excluded. But יוֹצֵא is interpreted differently. Hävernick, Maurer, and others understand it of going forth to war; only we must not then think (with Maurer) of the war against the prince of Persia. "For he will do that even now (in the third year of Cyrus), and at this time the coming of the prince of Grecia has no meaning" (Hitzig). Hofmann and Hitzig understand, therefore, יוֹצֵא, in contrast to בָּא, of a going forth from the conflict, as in 2 Kings xi. 7 "they *shall go forth* on the Sabbath" is placed over against "that *enter in* on the Sabbath" in ver. 5; but in an entirely different sense. Hitzig thus renders the clause: "when I have done with the Persians, and am on the point of departing, then shall the king of Grecia rise up against me." יָוָן must then be the Seleucidan kingdom, and the שַׂר the guardian spirit of Egypt—suppositions which need no refutation, while the interpretation of the words themselves fails by the arbitrary interpolation "against me" after בָּא. According to Hofmann, the angel says that "he had to return and contend further with the prince of the people of Persia; and that when he has retired from this conflict, then shall the prince of the Grecian people come, compelling him to enter on a new war." This last clause Hofmann thus more fully illustrates: "Into the conflict with the prince of the people of Persia, which the angel retires from, the prince of the Grecian people enters, and against him he resumes it after that the Persian kingdom has fallen, and is then also helped by Michael, the prince of the Jewish people, in this war against the prince of Grecia, as he had been in the war against the prince of Persia" (*Schriftbew.* i. pp. 333, 334 f.). But Hitzig and Kliefoth have, in opposition to this, referred to the incongruity which lies in the thought that the prince of Javan shall enter into the war of the angel against the Persians, and assume and carry it forward. The angel fights against the demon of Persia, not to destroy the Persians, but to influence the Persian king in favour of the people of God; on the contrary, the prince of Javan comes to destroy the Persian king. According to this, we cannot say that the prince of Javan enters into the place of the angel in the war. "The Grecians and the Persians much rather stand," as Hitzig rightly remarks, "on one side, and are adversaries of Michael and our שַׂר," *i.e.* of the angel who spake to Daniel. Add to this, that although יָצָא, *to go out*, means also *to go away*, *to go off*, yet the meaning to go away from the conflict, to abandon it, is not confirmed: much rather יָצָא, *sensu militari*, always denotes only "to go out, forth, into the conflict;" cf. 1 Sam. viii. 20, xxiii. 15; 1 Chron. xx. 1; Job xxxix. 21, etc. We have to take the word in this signification here (with C. B. Michaelis, Klief., and Kran.), only we must not, with Kranichfeld, supply the clause, "to another more extensive conflict," because this supplement is arbitrary, but rather, with Kliefoth, interpret the word generally as it stands of the going out of the angel to fight for the people of God, without excluding the war with the prince of Persia, or limiting it to this war. Thus the following will be the meaning of the passage: Now shall I return to resume and continue the war with the prince of Persia, to maintain the position gained (ver. 13) beside the kings of Persia; but when (while) I thus go forth to war, *i.e.* while I carry on this conflict, lo, the prince of Javan shall come (הִנֵּה with the partic. בָּא of the future)—then shall there be a new conflict. This last thought is not, it is true, expressly uttered, but it appears from ver. 21. The warring with the prince, *i.e.* the spirit of Persia hostile to Israel, refers to the oppositions which the Jews would encounter in the hindrances put in the way of their building the temple from the time of Cyrus to the time of Darius Hystaspes, and further under Xerxes and Artaxerxes till the rebuilding of the walls of Jerusalem by Nehemiah, as well as at a later time on the side of the Persian world-power, in the midst of all which difficulties the Angel of the Lord promises to guide the affairs of His people. שַׂר יָוָן is the spirit of the Macedonian world-kingdom, which would arise and show as great hostility as did the spirit of Persia against the people of God.

Ver. 21. This verse is antithetically connected with the preceding by אֲבָל, *but yet.* The contrast, however, does not refer to the fears for the theocracy (Kranichfeld) arising out of the last-named circumstance (ver. 20*b*), according to which the angel seeks to inform Daniel that under these circumstances the prophecy can only contain calamity. For "the prophecy by no means contains only calamity, but war and victory and everlasting victory added thereto" (Klief.). C. B. Michaelis has more correctly interpreted the connection thus: *Verum ne forte et sic, quod principem Græciæ Persarum principi successurum intellexisti, animum despondeas, audi ergo, quod tibi tuisque solatio esse potest, ego indicabo tibi, quod,* etc. "The Scripture of truth" is the book in which God has designated beforehand, according to truth, the history of the world as it shall certainly be unfolded; cf. Mal. iii. 16, Ps. cxxxix. 16, Rev. v. 1. The following clause, וְאֵין אֶחָד, is not connected adversatively with the preceding: "there is yet no one . . ." (Hofmann and others), but illustratively, for the angel states more minutely the nature of the war which he has to carry on. He has no one who fights with him against these enemies (עַל אֵלֶּה, against the evil spirits of Persia and Greece) but Michael the angel-prince of Israel, who strongly shows himself with him, *i.e.* as an ally in the conflict (מִתְחַזֵּק as 1 Sam. iv. 9, 2 Sam. x. 12), *i.e.* renders to him powerful aid, as he himself in the first year of Darius the Mede had been a strong helper and protection to Michael.

Ch. xi. 1. The first verse of the eleventh chapter belongs to ch. x. 21; the וַאֲנִי (*also I*) is emphatically placed over against the mention of Michael, whereby the connection of this verse with ch. x. 21 is placed beyond a doubt, and at the same time the reference of לוֹ (ch. xi. 1*b*) to מִיכָאֵל (ch. x. 21*b*) is decided. Hengstenberg indeed thinks (*Christol.* iii. 2, p. 53) that the reference of the לוֹ to Michael is "against all that is already spoken in relation to Michael, and particularly against that which immediately goes before," under a reference to Hitzig. But Hitzig only says that in ver. 21 Michael is of one lineage with the speaker; but, on the contrary, the expressions לְמַחֲזִיק (*to confirm*) and לְמָעוֹז (*to strengthen*) are so strong, that in לוֹ we must think on one inferior, a man. Moreover, Hitzig can think of nothing done by Michael under Darius, since the transference of the kingdom to the Medes changed nothing in the fortune of the Jews. This was first effected by Cyrus. But Hengstenberg himself does not recognise this last reason, but remarks that ch. xi. 1 relates to the transference of the sovereignty from the Chaldeans to the Persians, whereby a way was opened for the return of Israel, and rightly, with Häv., thus determines the meaning of the verse in general: "As at that time the Lord made the change of the monarchy a cause of blessing to the covenant people, so in all the troubles that may arise to them in the heathen monarchies He will show Himself to be the same true and gracious God." The other reason, namely, that the strong expressions, "to confirm and strengthen," necessitate us to think of one inferior as referred to in לוֹ, affects only the view already refuted above, that the speaker is either Gabriel or another inferior angel. If, on the contrary, the speaker is one person with him who is clothed in linen, *i.e.* with the Angel of the Lord, who is like unto God, then this person can also say of himself that he was a help and protection to the angel-prince Michael, because he stands higher than Michael; and the reference of the לוֹ to Michael, which the "also I" in contrast to "Michael your prince" demands, corresponds wholly with that which is said of Michael. Besides, the reference of לוֹ to Darius (Häv., Hengstb.) is excluded by this, that the name of Darius the Mede is not at all the object of the statements of the verse to which לוֹ could refer, but occurs only in a subordinate or secondary determination of time. The thought of the verse is accordingly the following: "In the first year of Darius the Mede, Michael effected this, that Babylon, which was hostile to the people of God, was overthrown by the power of Medo-Persia, in doing which the Angel of the Lord rendered to him powerful help." To this follows in order in ver. 2 the announcement of the future, which is introduced by the formula וְעַתָּה וגו' resumed from ch. x. 21.

Chap. xi. 2–xii. 3. *The Revelation of the Future.*

Proceeding from the present, the angel reveals in great general outlines the career of the Persian world-kingdom, and the establishment and destruction, which immediately followed, of the kingdom which was founded by the valiant king of Javan, which would not descend to his posterity, but would fall to others (vers. 2–4). Then there follows a detailed description of the wars of the kings of the south and the north for the supremacy, wherein first the king of the south prevails (vers. 5–9); the decisive conflicts between the two (vers. 10–12), wherein the south is subjugated; and the attempts of the kings of the north to extend their power more widely, wherein they perish (vers. 13–20); finally, the coming of a "vile person," who rises suddenly to power by cunning and intrigue, humbles the king of the south, has "indignation against the holy covenant," desolates the sanctuary of God, and brings severe affliction upon the people of God, "to purge and to make them white to the time of the end" (vers. 21–35). At the time of the end this hostile king shall raise himself above all gods, and above every human ordinance, and make the "god of fortresses" his god, "whom he will acknowledge and increase with glory" (vers. 36–39). But in the time of the end he shall pass through the countries with his army as a flood, enter into the glorious land, and take possession of Egypt with its treasures; but, troubled by tidings out of the east and the north, shall go forth in great fury utterly to destroy many, and shall come to his end on the holy mountain (vers. 40–45). At this time of greatest tribulation shall the angel-prince Michael contend for the people of Daniel. Every one that shall be found written in the book shall be saved, and the dead shall rise again, some to everlasting life, some to everlasting shame (ch. xii. 1–3).

This prophecy is so rich in special features which in part have been literally fulfilled, that believing interpreters from Jerome to Kliefoth have found in it predictions which extend far beyond the measure of prophetic revelation, while rationalistic and naturalistic interpreters, following the example of Porphyry, from the speciality of the predictions, conclude that the chapter does not contain a prophetic revelation of the future, but only an apocalyptic description of the past and of the present of the Maccabean pseudo-Daniel. Against both views Kranichfeld has decidedly declared himself, and sought to show that in these prophetic representations "the prediction does not press itself into the place of historical development, *i.e.* that it does not concern itself with such future dates as do not connect themselves with the historical present of the prophetic author (Daniel), as the unfolding of religious moral thought animated by divine influence." This is on the whole correct. Here also the prophecy does not become the prediction of historical dates which do not stand in inner connection with the fundamental idea of the book, which is to announce the unfolding of the heathen world-power over against the kingdom of God. This vision, also, as to its contents and form, is accounted for from the circumstances of time stated in ch. x. 1, and contains much which a supposed Maccabean origin makes in the highest degree improbable, and directly contradicts. First, it is "against the nature of a fictitious production which should be written in the time of the greatest national commotion, that the great repeated victories of the people over the Syrian power should have been so slightingly spoken of as is the case here (ch. xi. 34)," *i.e.* should be designated only as "a little help." Then the prophetic representation over against the historical facts of the case is full of inaccuracies; and these historical inconveniences are found not only in the description which had reference to the history of the times preceding the author, but also, above all, in the history of the times of the Maccabees themselves. Thus, *e.g.*, in ch. xi. 40–45 an Egyptian expedition of Antiochus Epiphanes shortly before his death is prophesied, for which, besides Porphyry, no voucher and, in general, no historical probability exists (Kran.).

Kranichfeld, however, goes too far when he holds all the special features of the prophetic revelation to be only individualizing paintings for the purpose of the contemplation, and therein seeks to find further developed only the fundamental thoughts of the great inner incurable enmity of the heathen ungodly kingdom already stated in ch. ii. 41–43, vii. 8, 20, 24, viii. 8, 22, 24. The truth lies in the middle between these two extremes.

This chapter contains neither mere individualizing paintings of general prophetic thoughts, nor predictions of historical dates inconsistent with the nature of prophecy, but prophetic descriptions of the development of the heathen world-power from the days of Cyrus to the fall of the Javanic world-kingdom, as well as of the position which the two kingdoms (arising out of this kingdom) of the north and south, between which the holy land lay, assumed toward each other and toward the theocracy; for by the war of these two kingdoms for the sovereignty, not merely were the covenant land and the covenant people brought in general into a sorrowful condition, but they also were the special object of a war which typically characterizes and portrays the relation of the world-kingdom to the kingdom of God. This war arose under the Seleucidan Antiochus Epiphanes to such a height, that it formed a prelude of the war of the time of the end. The undertaking of this king to root out the worship of the living God and destroy the Jewish religion, shows in type the great war which the world-power in the last phasis of its development shall undertake agaïnst the kingdom of God, by exalting itself above every god, to hasten on its own destruction and the consummation of the kingdom of God.

The description of this war as to its origin, character, and issue forms the principal subject of this prophecy. It is set forth in the revelation of the angel from ch. xi. 21 to the end (ch. xii. 3), while the preceding description, as well of the course of the Persian and Javanic world-kingdoms as of the wars of the kings of the north and the south (ch. xi. 2–20), prepares for it. But this preparatory description is not merely individualizing pictures of the idea of the incurable hostility of the heathen ungodly kingdom, but a prophetic delineation of the chief lines of the process which the heathen world-power shall pass through till it shall advance to the attempt to destroy the kingdom of God. These chief lines are so distinctly laid down, that they contain their concrete fulfilment in the historical development of the world-power. In like manner are so described the appearance and the wars of the enemy of God, who desolates the sanctuary of God and takes away the daily sacrifice, that we can recognise in the assault of Antiochus Epiphanes against the temple and the worship of the people of Israel a fulfilling of this prophecy. Yet here the foretelling (*Weissagung*) does not renounce the character of prophecy (*Prophetie*): it does not pass over into prediction (*Prædiction*) of historical facts and events, but so places in the light of the divine foresight and predetermination the image of this enemy of God, and his wickedness against the sanctuary and the people of God, that it brings under contemplation, and places under the point of view of the purification of the covenant people for the time of the end (ch. xi. 35), the gradual progress of his enmity against God till he exalts himself above all divine and human relations.

From the typical relation in which Antiochus, the O. T. enemy of God, stands to Antichrist, the N. T. enemy, is explained the connection of the end, the final salvation of the people of God, and the resurrection from the dead, with the destruction of this enemy, without any express mention being made of the fourth world-kingdom and of the last enemy arising out of it; from which the modern critics have drawn the erroneous conclusion, that the Maccabean pseudo-Daniel expected the setting up of the Messianic kingdom in glory along with the overthrow of Antiochus Epiphanes. At the foundation of this conclusion there lies an entire misapprehension of the contents and object of this prophecy, namely, the idea that the prophecy seeks to furnish a historical sketch, clothed in an apocalyptic form, of the development of the world-kingdoms from Cyrus to Antiochus Epiphanes. In support of this error, it is true that the church interpretation given by Jerome is so far valid, in that it interprets the prophecy partially considered under the point of view of the very special predictions of historical persons and events, and from this view concludes that vers. 21–35 treat of Antiochus Epiphanes, and vers. 36–45 of Antichrist; according to which there would be in ver. 36 an immediate passing from Antiochus to the Antichrist, or in ch. xii. 1 a sudden transition from the death of Antiochus to the time of the end and the resurrection from the dead. But the prophecy does not at all correspond to this representation. The Angel of the Lord will reveal to Daniel, not what shall happen from the third year of Cyrus to the time of Antiochus, and further to the resurrection of the dead, but, according to the express declaration of ch. x. 14, what shall happen to his people בְּאַחֲרִית הַיָּמִים, *i.e.* in the Messianic future, because the prophecy relates to this time. In the אַחֲרִית הַיָּמִים takes place the destruction of the world-power, and the setting up of the Messianic kingdom at the end of the present world-æon. All that the angel says regarding the Persian and the Javanic world-kingdoms, and the wars of the kings of the north and the south, has its aim to the end-time, serves only briefly to indicate the chief elements of the development of the world-kingdoms till the time when the war that brings in the end shall burst forth, and to show how, after the overthrow of the Javanic world-kingdom, neither the kings of the north nor those of the south shall gain the possession of the dominion of the world. Neither by the violence of war, nor by covenants which they will ratify by political marriages, shall they succeed in establishing a lasting power. They shall not prosper, because (ch. xi. 27) the end goes yet to *the* time appointed (by God). A new attempt of the king of the north to subjugate the kingdom of the south shall be defeated by the intervention of the ships of Chittim ; and the anger awakened in him by this frustration of his plans shall break forth against the holy covenant, only for the purifying of the people of God for the time of the end, because the end goes yet to the appointed time (ch. xi. 35). At the time of the end his power will greatly increase, because that which was determined by God shall prosper till the end of the indignation (ch. xi. 36) ; but in the time of the end he shall suddenly fall from the summit of his power and come to his end (ch. xi. 45), but the people of God shall be saved, and the wise shall shine in heavenly glory (ch. xii. 1–3).

Accordingly the revelation has this as its object, to show how the heathen world-kingdoms shall not attain to an enduring stability, and by their persecution of the people of God shall only accomplish their purification, and bring on the end, in which, through their destruction, the people of God shall be delivered from all oppression and be transfigured. In order to reveal this to him (that it must be carried forward to completion by severe tribulation), it was not necessary that he should receive a complete account of the different events which shall take place in the heathen world-power in the course of time, nor have it especially made prominent that their enmity shall first come to a completed manifestation under the last king who should arise out of the fourth world-kingdom. For that the Javanic world-kingdom shall not form the last embodiment of the world-power, but that after it a fourth more powerful kingdom shall arise—this was already revealed to Daniel in ch. vii. Moreover, in ch. viii. the violent enemy of the people of Israel who would arise from the Diadoch-kingdoms of the Javanic world-monarchy, was already designated as the type of the last enemy who would arise out of the ten kingdoms of the fourth world-kingdom. After these preceding revelations, the announcement of the great tribulation that would come upon the people of God from these two enemies could be presented in one comprehensive painting, wherein the assault made by the prefigurative enemy against the covenant people shall form the foreground of the picture for a representation of the daring of the antitypical enemy, proceeding even to the extent of abolishing all divine and human ordinances, who shall bring the last and severest tribulation on the church of God, at the end of the days, for its purification and preparation for eternity.

Ch. xi. 2–20. *The events of the nearest future.*

Ver. 2. The revelation passes quickly from Persia (ver. 2*b*) and the kingdom of Alexander (vers. 3 and 4), to the description of the wars of the kingdoms of the south and the north, arising out of the latter, in which wars the Holy Land, lying between the two, was implicated. Regarding Persia it is only said that yet three kings shall arise, and that the fourth, having reached to great power by his riches, shall stir up all against the kingdom of Javan. Since this prophecy originates in the third year of the Persian king Cyrus (ch. x. 1), then the three kings who shall yet (עוֹד) arise are the three successors of Cyrus, viz. Cambyses, the pseudo-Smerdis, and Darius Hystaspes; the fourth is then Xerxes, with whom all that is said regarding the fourth perfectly agrees. Thus Hävernick, Ebrard, Delitzsch, Auberlen, and Kliefoth interpret; on the contrary, v. Lengerke, Maurer, Hitzig, and Kranichfeld will make the fourth the third, so as thereby to justify the erroneous interpretation of the four wings and the four heads of the leopard (ch. vii. 6) of the first four kings of the Persian monarchy, because, as they say, the article in הָרְבִיעִי necessarily requires that *the* fourth is already mentioned in the immediately preceding statements. But the validity of this conclusion is not to be conceived; and the assertion that the O. T. knows only of four kings of Persia (Hitzig) cannot be established from Ezra iv. 5–7, nor from any other passage. From the naming of only four kings of Persia in the book of Ezra, since from the end of the Exile to Ezra and Nehemiah four kings had reigned, it in no way follows that the book of Daniel and the O. T. generally know of only four. Moreover, this assertion is not at all correct; for in Neh. xii. 22, besides those four there is mention made also of a Darius, and to the Jews in the age of the Maccabees there was well known, according to 1 Macc. i. 1, also the name of the last Persian king, Darius, who was put to death by Alexander. If the last named, the king who by great riches (ver. 2) reached to a higher power, is included among the three previously named, then he should have been here designated "the third." The verb עָמַד, to place oneself, then to stand, is used here and frequently in the following passages, as in ch. viii. 23, in the sense of *to stand up* (= קוּם), with reference to the coming of a new ruler. The gathering together of greater riches than all (his predecessors), agrees specially with Xerxes; cf. Herodot. iii. 96, vi. 27–29, and Justini *Histor.* ii. 2. The latter says of him: "*Divitias, non ducem laudes, quarum tanta* *copia in regno ejus fuit, ut, cum flumina multitudine consumerentur, opes tamen regiæ superessent.*"

חֶזְקָתוֹ is the *infinit.* or *nomen actionis*, the *becoming strong;* cf. 2 Chron. xii. 1 with 2 Kings xiv. 5 and Isa. viii. 11. בְּעָשְׁרוֹ is not in apposition to it, "according to his riches" (Häv.); but it gives the means by which he became strong. "Xerxes expended his treasures for the raising and arming of an immense host, so as by such חֹזֶק (cf. Amos vi. 13) to conquer Greece" (Hitzig). אֵת מַלְכוּת יָוָן is not in apposition to הַכֹּל, *all*, namely, the kingdom of Javan (Maurer, Kranichfeld). This does not furnish a suitable sense; for the thought that הַכֹּל, "they all," designates the divided states of Greece, and the apposition, "the kingdom of Javan," denotes that they were brought by the war with Xerxes to form themselves into the unity of the Macedonian kingdom, could not possibly be so expressed. Moreover, the reference to the circumstances of the Grecian states is quite foreign to the context. אֵת מ' יָוָן is much rather a second, more remote object, and אֵת is to be interpreted, with Hävernick, either as the preposition *with*, so far as יָעִיר involves the idea of war, conflict, or simply, with Hitzig, as the accusative of the object of the movement (cf. Ex. ix. 29, 33), to stir up, to rouse, after the kingdom of Javan, properly to make, to cause, that all (הַכֹּל = every one, cf. Ps. xiv. 3) set out towards. Daniel calls Greece מַלְכוּת, after the analogy of the Oriental states, as a united historical power, without respect to the political constitution of the Grecian states, not suitable to prophecy (Kliefoth).

From the conflict of Persia with Greece, the angel (ver. 3) passes immediately over to the founder of the Grecian (Macedonian) world-kingdom; for the prophecy proceeds not to the prediction of historical details, but mentions only the elements and factors which constitute the historical development. The expedition of Xerxes against Greece brings to the foreground the world-historical conflict between Persia and Greece, which led to the destruction of the Persian kingdom by Alexander the Great. The reply of Alexander to Darius Codomannus (Arrian, *Exped Alex.* ii. 14. 4) supplies a historical document, in which Alexander justifies his expedition against Persia by saying that Macedonia and the rest of Hellas were assailed in war by the Persians without any cause (οὐδὲν προηδικημένοι), and that therefore he had resolved to punish the Persians. A deeper reason for this lies in this, that the prophecy closes the list of Persian kings with Xerxes, but not in this, that under Xerxes the Persian monarchy reached its climax, and partly already under him, and yet more after his reign, the fall of the kingdom had begun (Hävernick, Auberlen); still less in the opinion, proved to be erroneous, that the Maccabean Jew knew no other Persian kings, and confounded Xerxes with Darius Codomannus (v. Lengerke, Maurer, Hitzig).

Vers. 3 and 4. But only brief notices, characterizing its nature, were given regarding the Macedonian kingdom, which agree with the prophecies ch. vii. 6 and viii. 5–8, 21, 22, without adding new elements. The founder of the kingdom is called מֶלֶךְ גִּבּוֹר, "brave king," "hero-king," and his kingdom "a great dominion." Of his government it is said עָשָׂה כִּרְצוֹנוֹ, he does, rules, according to his will (cf. ch. viii. 4), so that his power might be characterized as irresistible and boundless self-will. Similarly Curtius writes of him (x. 5. 35): *Fatendum est, cum plurimum virtuti debuerit, plus debuisse fortunæ, quam solus omnium mortalium in potestate habuit. Hujus siquidem beneficio agere videbatur gentibus quidquid placebat.* By the כְּ in כְּעָמְדוֹ the coming of the king and the destruction of his kingdom are stated as synchronous, so as to express with great force the shortness of its duration. עָמְדוֹ is not to be otherwise interpreted than עָמַד in ver. 3, and is thus not to be translated: "when he thus stands up," *sc.* in the regal power described in ver. 3 (Kran.), or: "on the pinnacle of his might" (Häv.), but: "when (or as) he has made his appearance, his kingdom shall be broken." In the words, also, there does not lie the idea "that he himself in his life-time is deprived of his throne and his kingdom by a violent catastrophe" (Kran.); for the destruction of the kingdom does not necessarily include in it the putting to death of the ruler. The thought is only this: "when he has appeared and founded a great dominion, his kingdom shall be immediately broken." תִּשָּׁבֵר (*shall be broken*) is chosen with reference to ch. viii. 8, "toward the four winds of heaven." We may neither supply תֵּחָץ (*shall be divided*) to וְלֹא לְאַחֲרִיתוֹ (*and not to his posterity*), nor is this latter expression "connected with תֵּחָץ in pregnant construction;" for תֵּחָץ, from חָצָה, signifies *to divide*, from which we are not to assume the idea of *to allot, assign.* We have simply to supply הִיא in the sense of the *verb. subst., shall be*, as well here as in the following clause, וְלֹא כְמָשְׁלוֹ. The אַחֲרִית signifies here as little as in Amos iv. 2, ix. 1, posterity = זֶרַע, but remnant, that which is left behind, the survivors of the king, by which we are to understand not merely his sons, but all the members of his family. וְלֹא כְמָשְׁלוֹ, "and it shall not be according to the dominion which he ruled." This thought, corresponding to וְלֹא בְכֹחוֹ in ch. viii. 22, is the natural conclusion from the idea of division to all the four winds, which the falling asunder into several or many small kingdoms involves. הִנָּתֵשׁ, "shall be plucked up" (of plants from the earth), denotes the rooting up of that which is stable, the destroying and dissolving of the kingdom into portions. In this division it shall pass to others מִלְּבַד־אֵלֶּה, "with the exclusion of those" (the אַחֲרִית), the surviving members of the family of Alexander. To וְלַאֲחֵרִים (*and for others*) supply תִּהְיֶה (*shall be*).

In ver. 4, accordingly, the prophetic thought is expressed, that the Javanic kingdom, as soon as the brave king has founded a great dominion, shall be broken to pieces and divided toward the four winds of heaven, so that its separate parts, without reaching to the might of the broken kingdom, shall be given not to the survivors of the family of the founder, but to strangers. This was historically fulfilled in the fact, that after the sudden death of Alexander his son Hercules was not recognised by his generals as successor on the throne, but was afterwards murdered by Polysperchon; his son also born by Roxana, along with his guardian Philip Arideus, met the same fate; but the generals, after they had at first divided the kingdom into more than thirty parts (see above, p. 256), soon began to war with each other, the result of which was, that at last four larger kingdoms were firmly established (see above, p. 294). Cf. Diod. Sic. xx. 28, xix. 105; Pausan. ix. 7; Justini *hist.* xv. 2, and Appiani *Syr.* c. 51.

Vers. 5 and 6. From the 5th verse the prophecy passes to the wars of the kings of the south and the north for the supremacy and for the dominion over the Holy Land, which lay between the two. Ver. 5 describes the growing strength of these two kings, and ver. 6 an attempt made by them to join themselves together. חָזַק, *to become strong*. The king of the south is the ruler of Egypt; this appears from the context, and is confirmed by ver. 8. וּמִן שָׂרָיו is differently interpreted; מִן, however, is unanimously regarded as a partitive: "one of his princes," as *e.g.* Neh. xiii. 28, Gen. xxviii. 11, Ex. vi. 25. The suffix to שָׂרָיו (*his* princes) does not (with C. B. Michaelis, Bertholdt, Rosenmüller, and Kranichfeld) refer to מֶלֶךְ גִּבּוֹר, ver. 3, because this noun is too far removed, and then also עָלָיו must be referred to it; but thereby the statement in ver. 5*b*, that one of the princes of the king of Javan would gain greater power and dominion than the valiant king had, would contradict the statement in ver. 4, that no one of the Diadochs would attain to the dominion of Alexander.[1] The suffix to שָׂרָיו can only be referred to the immediately preceding מֶלֶךְ הַנֶּגֶב: "one of the princes of the king of the south." But then ו in וּמִן cannot be explicative, but is only the simple copula. This interpretation also is not opposed by the Atnach under שָׂרָיו, for this accent is added to the subject because it stands before separately, and is again resumed in וְיֶחֱזַק by the copula ו, as *e.g.* Ezek. xxxiv. 19. The thought is this: one of the princes of the king of the south shall attain to greater power than this king, and shall found a great dominion. That this prince is the king of the north, or founds a dominion in the north, is not expressly said, but is gathered from ver. 6, where the king of the south enters into a league with the king of the north.

Ver. 6. לְקֵץ שָׁנִים, "in the end of years," *i.e.* after the expiry of a course of years; cf. 2 Chron. xviii. 2. The subject to יִתְחַבָּרוּ *(join themselves*, 2 Chron. xx. 35) cannot, it is evident, be אֲחֵרִים, ver. 4 (Kran.), but only the king of the south and his prince who founded a great dominion, since the covenant, according to the following clause, is brought about by the daughter of the king of the south being given in marriage (בּוֹא אֶל, *to come to*, as Josh. xv. 18, Judg. i. 14) to the king of the north, to make מֵישָׁרִים, to effect an agreement. מֵישָׁרִים, *rectitudes*, synonymous with righteousness and right, Prov. i. 3, here designates the rectitude of the relation of the two rulers to each other in regard to the intrigues and deceits they had previously practised toward each other; thus not union, but sincerity in keeping the covenant that had been concluded. "But she shall not retain the power of the arm." עָצַר כּוֹחַ as x. 8, 16, and הַזְּרוֹעַ, the arm as a figure of help, assistance. The meaning is: she will not retain the power to render the help which her marriage should secure; she shall not be able to bring about and to preserve the sincerity of the covenant; and thus the king of the south shall not be preserved with this his help, but shall become subject to the more powerful king of the north. The following

[1] This contradiction is not set aside, but only strengthened, by translating יֶחֱזַק עָלָיו "he overcame him" (Kran.), according to which the king of Javan must be thought of as overcome by one of his princes, the king of the south. For the thought that the king of Javan survived the destruction of his kingdom, and that, after one of his princes had become the king of the south and had founded a great dominion, he was overcome by him, contradicts too strongly the statement of ver. 5, that the kingdom of the valiant king of Javan would be destroyed, and that it would not fall to his survivors, but to others with the exception of those, for one to be able to interpret the words in this sense.

passages state this. The subject to לֹא יַעֲמֹד is the מֶלֶךְ נֶגֶב; and his, *i.e.* this king's, help is his own daughter, who should establish מֵישָׁרִים by her marriage with the king of the north. וּזְרֹעוֹ is a second subject subordinated or co-ordinated to the subject lying in the verb: he together with his help. We may not explain the passage: neither he nor his help, because in this case הוּא could not be wanting, particularly in comparison with the following הִיא. The "not standing" is further positively defined by וְתִנָּתֵן, to be delivered up, to perish. The plur. מְבִיאֶיהָ is the plur. of the category: who brought her, *i.e.* who brought her into the marriage (מֵבִיא to be explained after בּוֹא), without reference to the number of those who were engaged in doing so; cf. the similar plur. in particip. Lev. xix. 8, Num. xxiv. 9, and in the noun, Gen. xxi. 7. הַיִּלְדָהּ, particip. with the suffix, wherein the article represents the relative אֲשֶׁר. מַחֲזִיק, in the same meaning as ver. 1, the support, the helper. The sense is: not only she, but all who brought about the establishment of this marriage, and the object aimed at by it. בָּעִתִּים has the article: in the times determined for each of these persons.

Vers. 7–9. A violent war shall then break out, in which the king of the north shall be overcome. One of the offspring of her roots shall appear. מִן in מִנֵּצֶר is partitive, as ver. 5, and נֵצֶר is used collectively. The figure reminds us of Isa. xi. 1. The suffix to שָׁרָשֶׁיהָ refers to the king's daughter, ver. 6. Her roots are her parents, and the offspring of her roots a brother of the king's daughter, but not a descendant of his daughter, as Kranichfeld by losing sight of נֵצֶר supposes. כַּנּוֹ is the accusative of direction, for which, in vers. 20, 21, 38, עַל כַּנּוֹ stands more distinctly; the suffix refers to the king of the south, who was also the subject in יַעֲמֹד, ver. 6*b*. יָבֹא אֶל־הַחַיִל does not mean: he will go to the (to his) army (Michaelis, Berth., v. Leng., Hitz., Klief.); this would be a very heavy remark within the very characteristic, significant description here given (Kran., Häv.); nor does it mean: he attained to might (Häv.); but: he shall come to the army, *i.e.* against the host of the enemy, *i.e.* the king of the north (Kran.). בּוֹא אֶל, as Gen. xxxii. 9, Isa. xxxvii. 33, is used of a hostile approach against a camp, a city, so as to take it, in contradistinction to the following יָבֹא בְּמָעוֹז: to penetrate into the fortress. מָעוֹז has a collective signification, as בָּהֶם referring to it shows. עָשָׂה בְּ, to act against or with any one, cf. Jer. xviii. 23 ("deal with them"), *ad libidinem agere* (Maurer), essentially corresponding to כִּרְצוֹנוֹ in vers. 33, 36. הֶחֱזִיק, to show power, *i.e.* to demonstrate his superior power.

Ver. 8. To bring the subjugated kingdom wholly under his power, he shall carry away its gods along with all the precious treasures into Egypt. The carrying away of the images of the gods was a usual custom with conquerors; cf. Isa. xlvi. 1 f., Jer. xlviii. 7, xlix. 3. In the images the gods themselves were carried away; therefore they are called "their gods." נִסְכֵּיהֶם signifies here not drink-offerings, but molten images; the form is analogous to the plur. פְּסִילִים, formed from פֶּסֶל; on the contrary, נְסִיכָם *libationes*, Deut. xxxii. 38, stands for נִסְכֵּיהֶם, Isa. xli. 29. The suffix is not to be referred to אֱלֹהִים, but, like the suffix in אֱלֹהֵיהֶם, to the inhabitants of the conquered country. כֶּסֶף וְזָהָב are in apposition to כְּלֵי חֶמְדָּתָם, not the genitive of the subject (Kran.), because an attributive genitive cannot follow a noun determined by a suffix. Häv., v. Leng., Maurer, Hitzig, Ewald, and Klief. translate וְהוּא שָׁנִים יַעֲמֹד וגו': he shall during (some) years stand off from the king of the north. Literally this translation may perhaps be justified, for עָמַד, *c.* מִן, Gen. xxix. 35, has the meaning of "to leave off," and the expression "to stand off from war" may be used concisely for "to desist from making war" upon one. But this interpretation does not accord with the connection. First, it is opposed by the expressive וְהוּא, which cannot be understood, if nothing further should be said than that the king of the south, after he had overthrown the fortresses of the enemies' country, and had carried away their gods and their treasures, abstained from war for some years. The וְהוּא much rather leads us to this, that the passage introduced by it states some new important matter which does not of itself appear from the subjugation of the enemy and his kingdom. To this is to be added, that the contents of ver. 9, where the subject to בָּא can only be the king of the north, do not accord with the abstaining of the king of the south from warring against the king of the north. By Ewald's remark, "With such miserable marchings to and fro they mutually weaken themselves," the matter is not made intelligible. For the penetrating of the king of the south into the fortresses of his enemy, and the carrying away of his gods and his treasures, was not a miserable, useless expedition; but then we do not understand how the completely humbled king of the north, after his conqueror abstained from war, was in the condition to penetrate into his kingdom and then to return to his own land. Would his conqueror have suffered him to do this? We must, therefore, with Kranichfeld, Gesenius, de Wette, and Winer, after the example of the

Syriac and the Vulgate, take יַעֲמֹד מִן in the sense of: to stand out before, מִן in the sense of מִפְּנֵי, *contra*, as in Ps. xliii. 1 it is construed with רִיב, which is supported by the circumstance that עָמַד in vers. 6, 15, 17, and 25, has this meaning. By this not only is וְהוּא rightly translated: *and he*, the same who penetrated into the fortresses of his adversary and carried away his gods, shall also take his stand against him, assert his supremacy for years; but also ver. 9 contains a suitable addition, for it shows how he kept his ground. The king of the north shall after some time invade the kingdom of the king of the south, but shall return to his own land, namely, because he can effect nothing. Kran. takes the king of the south as the subject to וּבָא, ver. 9; but this is impossible, for then the word must be בְּמַלְכוּתוֹ, particularly in parallelism with אַדְמָתוֹ. As the words stand, מֶלֶךְ הַנֶּגֶב can only be the genitive to בְּמַלְכוּת; thus the supposition that "the king of the south is the subject" is excluded, because the expression, "the king of the south comes into the kingdom of the south and returns to his own land," has no meaning when, according to the context, the south denotes Egypt. With the וּבָא there also begins a change of the subject, which, though it appears contrary to the idiom of the German [and English] language, is frequently found in Hebrew; *e.g.* in vers. 11*a* and 9*a*. By the mention of an expedition of the king of the north into the kingdom of the king of the south, from which he again returned without having effected anything, the way is opened for passing to the following description of the supremacy of the king of the north over the king of the south.

Vers. 10–12. *The decisive wars.*

Ver. 10. Here the suffix in בָּנָו refers to the king of the north, who in ver. 9 was the person acting. Thus all interpreters with the exception of Kranichfeld, who understands בנו of the son of the Egyptian prince, according to which this verse ought to speak of the hostilities sought, in the wantonness of his own mind, of the king of the south against the king of the north. But this interpretation of Kranichfeld is shattered, not to speak of other verbal reasons which oppose it, against the contents of ver. 11. The rage of the king of the south, and his going to war against the king of the north, supposes that the latter had given rise to this rage by an assault. Besides, the description given in ver. 10 is much too grand to be capable of being referred to hostility exercised in mere wantonness. For such conflicts we do not assemble a multitude of powerful armies, and, when these powerful hosts penetrate into the fortresses of the enemy's country, then find that for the victorious invaders there is wanting the occasion of becoming exasperated for new warfare. The *Kethiv* בנו is rightly interpreted by the Masoretes as plur., which the following verbs demand, while the singulars וּבָא וְשָׁטַף וְעָבָר (*shall come, and overflow, and pass through*) are explained from the circumstance that the hosts are viewed unitedly in הָמוֹן (*multitude*). בָּא בוֹא expresses the unrestrained coming or pressing forward, while the verbs שָׁטַף וְעָבָר, reminding us of Isa. viii. 8, describe pictorially the overflowing of the land by the masses of the hostile army. וְיָשֹׁב (jussive, denoting the divine guidance), *and shall return*, expresses the repetition of the deluge of the land by the hosts marching back out of it after the עָבַר, the march through the land,—not the new arming for war (Häv.), but renewed entrance into the region of the enemy, whereby they carry on the war עַד מָעֻזּה, to the fortress of the king of the south, corresponding with the בְּמָעוֹז מֶלֶךְ הַצָּפוֹן in ver. 7 (*to the fortress of the king of the north*). יִתְגָּרוּ signifies properly to stir up to war, *i.e.* to arm, then to engage in war. In the first member of the verse it has the former, and in the last the latter meaning. The violent pressing forward of the adversary will greatly embitter the king of the south, fill him with the greatest anger, so that he will go out to make war with him. The adversary marshals a great multitude of combatants; but these shall be given into his hand, into the hand of the king of the south. הֶעֱמִיד הָמוֹן רָב (*he raised up a great multitude*) the context requires us to refer to the king of the north. נִתַּן בְּיָדוֹ, v. Leng., Maurer, and Hitzig understand of the acceptance of the command over the army—contrary to the usage of the words, which mean, to give into the hand = to deliver up, cf. 1 Kings xx. 28, Dan. i. 2, viii. 12, 13, and is contrary also to the context. The marshalling of the host supposes certainly the power to direct it, so that it needs not then for the first time to be given into the power of him who marshalled it. The expression also, "to give into his hand," as meaning "to place under his command," is not found in Scripture. To this is to be added, that the article in הֶהָמוֹן refers back to הָמוֹן רָב. But if הֶהָמוֹן is the host assembled by the king of the north, then it can only be given up into the hand of the enemy, *i.e.* the king of the south, and thus the suffix in בְּיָדוֹ can only refer to him. The statements in ver. 12 are in harmony with this, so far as they confessedly speak of the king of the south.

Ver. 12. This verse illustrates the last clause of ver. 11, *i.e.* explains more fully how the great multitude of the enemy are given into his hand. The first two clauses of ver. 12 stand in correlation to each other, as the change of the time and the absence of the copula before יָרוּם show (the *Keri* וְרָם proceeds from a misunderstanding). The meaning is this: "As the multitude rises up, so his heart is lifted up." הֶהָמוֹן, with the article, can only be the host of the king of the north mentioned in ver. 12. The supposition that the Egyptian army is meant, is the result of the difficulty arising out of the misapprehension of the right relation in which the perfect וְנִשָּׂא (*hath lifted up raised*) stands to the imperfect יָרוּם. נִשָּׂא as in Isa. xxxiii. 10: they raise themselves to the conflict. רוּם לֵבָב, the lifting up of the heart, commonly in the sense of pride; here the increase of courage, but so that pride is not altogether to be excluded. The subject to יָרוּם is the king of the south, to whom the suffix to בְּיָדוֹ, ver. 11, points. With excited courage he overthrows myriads, namely, the powerful multitude of the enemies, but he yet does not reach to power, he does not attain to the supremacy over the king of the north and over his kingdom which he is striving after. The Vulgate, without however fully expressing the meaning, has rendered וְלֹא יָעוֹז by *sed non prævalebit.*

Vers. 13–15. This thought is expanded and proved in these verses.—Ver. 13. The king of the north returns to his own land, gathers a host together more numerous than before, and shall then, at the end of the times of years, come again with a more powerful army and with a great train. רְכוּשׁ, *that which is acquired, the goods*, is the train necessary for the suitable equipment of the army—"the condition to a successful warlike expedition" (Kran.). The definition of time corresponding to the בָּעִתִּים in ver. 6 is specially to be observed: לְקֵץ הָעִתִּים שָׁנִים (*at the end of times, years*), in which שָׁנִים is to be interpreted (as יָמִים with שָׁבֻעִים, ch. x. 3, 4, and other designations of time) as denoting that the עִתִּים stretch over years, are times lasting during years. הָעִתִּים, with the definite article, are in prophetic discourse *the times determined by God.*

Ver. 14. In those times shall many rise up against the king of the south (עָמַד עַל as ch. viii. 20); also בְּנֵי פְּרִיצֵי עַמְּךָ, the violent people of the nation (of the Jews), shall raise themselves against him. בְּנֵי פְּרִיצִים are such as belong to the classes of violent men who break through the barriers of the divine law (Ezek. xviii. 10). These shall raise themselves לְהַעֲמִיד חָזוֹן, to establish the prophecy, *i.e.* to bring it to an accomplishment. הַעֲמִיד = קַיֵּם, Ezek. xiii. 6, as עָמַד = קוּם in Daniel, and generally in the later Hebrew. Almost all interpreters since Jerome have referred this to Daniel's vision of the oppression under Antiochus Epiphanes, ch. viii. 9–14, ver. 23. This is so far right, as the apostasy of one party among the Jews from the law of their fathers, and their adoption of heathen customs, contributed to bring about that oppression with which the theocracy was visited by Antiochus Epiphanes; but the limiting of the חָזוֹן to those definite prophecies is too narrow. חָזוֹן without the article is prophecy in undefined generality, and is to be extended to all the prophecies which threatened the people of Israel with severe chastisements and sufferings on account of their falling away from the law and their apostasy from their God. וְנִכְשָׁלוּ, *they shall stumble, fall.* "The falling away shall bring to them no gain, but only the sufferings and tribulation prophesied of" (Kliefoth).

Ver. 15. In this verse, with וְיָבֹא the יָבוֹא בוֹא, ver. 13, is again assumed, and the consequence of the war announced. שָׁפַךְ סוֹלְלָה, *to heap up an entrenchment;* cf. Ezek. iv. 2, 2 Kings xix. 32. עִיר מִבְצָרוֹת, *city of fortifications,* without the article, also collectively of the fortresses of the kingdom of the south generally. Before such power the army, *i.e.* the war-strength, of the south shall not maintain its ground; even his chosen people shall not possess strength necessary for this.

Vers. 16–19. *The further undertakings of the king of the north.*

Ver. 16. Having penetrated into the kingdom of the south, he shall act there according to his own pleasure, without any one being able to withstand him; just as before this the king of the south did in the kingdom of the north (ver. 7). With וְיַעַשׂ the jussive appears instead of the future—cf. וְיָשֵׂם, יִתֵּן (ver. 17), יָשֵׁב (vers. 18 and 19)—to show that the further actions and undertakings of the king of the north are carried on under the divine decree. הַבָּא אֵלָיו is he that comes into the land of the south, the king of the north (vers. 14 and 15). Having reached the height of victory, he falls under the dominion of pride and haughtiness, by which he hastens on his ruin and overthrow. After he has subdued the kingdom of the southern king, he will go into the land of beauty, *i.e.* into the Holy Land (with reference to אֶרֶץ הַצְּבִי, ch. viii. 9). וְכָלָה בְיָדוֹ, *and destruction is in his hand* (an explanatory clause), כָּלָה being here not a verb, but a substantive. Only this meaning of כָּלָה is verbally established, see under ch. ix. 27, but not the meaning attributed to the word, from the unsuitable introduction of historical events, *accomplishing, perfectio*, according to which Häv., v. Leng., Maur., and Kliefoth translate the clause: *and it* (the Holy Land) *is wholly given into his hand.* כָּלָה means *finishing, conclusion*, only in the sense of *destruction*, also in 2 Chron. xii. 2 and Ezek. xiii. 13. For the use of בְּיָדוֹ of spiritual things which one intends or aims at, cf. Job xi. 14, Isa. xliv. 20. The destruction, however, refers not to the Egyptians (Hitzig), but to the Holy Land, in which violent (rapacious) people (ver. 14) make common cause with the heathen king, and thereby put arms into his hands by which he may destroy the land.

Ver. 17. This verse has been very differently expounded. According to the example of Jerome, who translates it: *et ponet faciem suam ut veniat ad tenendum universum regnum ejus*, and adds to this the explanatory remark: *ut evertat illum h. e. Ptolemæum, sive illud, h. e. regnum ejus*, many translate the words לָבוֹא בְּתֹקֶף וגו׳ by *to come in or against the strength of his whole* (Egyptian) *kingdom* (C. B. Michaelis, Venema, Hävernick, v. Lengerke, Maurer), *i.e.* to obtain the superiority over the Egyptian kingdom (Kliefoth). But this last interpretation is decidedly opposed by the circumstance that תֹּקֶף means *strength* not in the active sense = *power over something*, but only in the intransitive or passive sense, *strength as the property of any one.* Moreover, both of these explanations are opposed by the verbal use of בּוֹא *c.* בְּ *rei*, which does not signify: to come in or against a matter, but: *to come with*—cf. בּוֹא בְּחַיִל, to come with power, ver. 13, also Isa. xl. 10, Ps. lxxi. 16—as well as by the context, for of the completely subjugated south (according to vers. 15 and 16) it cannot yet be said תֹּקֶף מַלְכוּתוֹ. Correctly, Theodot. translates: εἰσελθεῖν ἐν ἰσχύϊ πάσης τῆς βασιλείας αὐτοῦ; Luther: "to come with the strength of his whole kingdom." Similarly M. Geier, Hitzig, and Kran. The king of the north intends thus to come with the force of his whole kingdom to obtain full possession of the kingdom of the south. וִישָׁרִים עִמּוֹ is an explanatory clause defining the manner in which he seeks to gain his object. יְשָׁרִים, plur. of the adjective יָשָׁר, in a substantive signification, *that which is straight, recta*, as Prov. xvi. 13, *proba* (Ewald's Gram. § 172; while in his commentary he translates the word by *agreement*). עִמּוֹ, *with him, i.e.* having in intention. The sense of the passage is determined according to לַעֲשׂוֹת מֵישָׁרִים, ver. 6: with the intention of establishing a direct, right relation, namely, by means of a political marriage to bring to himself the kingdom of the south. וְעָשָׂה forms a clause by itself: he shall do it, carry it out; there is therefore no need for Hitzig's arbitrary change of the text into יַעֲשֶׂה.

The second half of this verse (ver. 17) describes how he carries out this intention, but yet does not reach his end. "He shall give him the daughter of women." הַנָּשִׁים, *of women*, the plur. of the class, as כְּפִיר אֲרָיוֹת, Judg. xiv. 5, *a young lion* (*of lionesses*); בֶּן אֲתֹנוֹת, Zech. ix. 9, the *foal of an ass* (*of she-asses*). The suffix to לְהַשְׁחִיתָהּ (*corrupting her*, E.V.) is referred by many to מַלְכוּתוֹ (*his kingdom*); but this reference fails along with the incorrect interpretation of the בְּתֹקֶף as the end of the coming. Since in the first half of the verse the object of his undertaking is not named, but in ver. 16 is denoted by אֵלָיו, the suffix in question can only be referred to בַּת הַנָּשִׁים. Thus J. D. Michaelis, Bertholdt, Rosenmüller; the former, however, gives to the word לְהַשְׁחִיתָהּ the verbally untenable meaning: "to seduce her into a morally corrupt course of conduct;" but Hitzig changes the text, strikes out the suffix, and translates: "to accomplish vileness." הִשְׁחִית means only *to destroy, to ruin*, hence "to destroy her" (Kran.). This, it is true, was not the object of the marriage, but only its consequence; but the consequence is set forth as had in view, so as forcibly to express the thought that the marriage could lead, according to a higher direction, only to the destruction of the daughter.

The last clauses of the verse express the failure of the measure adopted. The verbs are fem., not neut.; thus the meaning is not: "it shall neither stand, nor succeed to him" (v. Leng., Maurer, Hitzig), but: "she (the daughter) shall not stand," not be able to carry out the plan contemplated by her father. The words וְלֹא־לוֹ תִהְיֶה do not stand for וְלֹא תִהְיֶה לוֹ: "she shall not be to him" or "for him." In this case לֹא must be connected with the verb. According to the text, לֹא־לוֹ forms one idea, as לֹא כֹחַ, *impotent* (cf. Ewald, § 270): "she shall be a *not for him*" (*ein Nichtihm*), *i.e.* he shall have nothing at all from her.

Vers. 18 and 19. His fate further drives him to make an assault on the islands and maritime coasts of the west (אִיִּים), many of which he takes. וְיָשֵׁב is not, after the *Keri*, to be changed into וְיָשֵׂם; for turning himself from Egypt to the islands, he turns back his face toward his own land in the north. The two following clauses are explained by most interpreters thus: "but a captain shall stop his scorn (bring it to silence), and moreover shall give back (recompense) scorn to him in return." This is then, according to the example of Jerome, referred to the expedition of Antiochus Epiphanes against the Grecian islands which were under the protection of Rome, for which he was assailed and overcome by the consul Lucius Scipio (Asiaticus) in a battle fought at *Magnesia ad Sipylum* in Lydia. But the translation in question affords a tolerable sense only when we take בִּלְתִּי in the meaning *moreover, in addition to;* a meaning which it has not, and cannot have according to its etymology. In all places where it is so rendered a negative sentence goes before it, cf. Gen. xliii. 3, xlvii. 18, Judg. vii. 14, or a sentence asking a question with a negative sense, as Amos iii. 3, 4; according to which, לֹא must here stand before הִשְׁבִּית if we would translate it by *besides that* or *only.* בִּלְתִּי has the idea of *exception,* and can only be rendered after an affirmative statement by *however,* for the passage introduced by it limits the statement going before. Thus Theodot. rightly: *καταπαύσει ἄρχοντας ὀνειδισμοῦ αὐτῶν, πλὴν ὁ ὀνειδισμὸς αὐτοῦ ἐπιστρέψει αὐτῷ*; and in close connection with this, Jerome has: *et cessare faciet principem opprobrii sui et opprobrium ejus convertetur in eum.* In like manner the Peshito. This rendering we must, with Kranichfeld, accede to, and accordingly understand וְהִשְׁבִּית וגו of the king of the north, and interpret the indefinite קָצִין (*leader, chief*) in undefined generality or collectively, and חֶרְפָּתוֹ (*his reproach*) as the second object subordinated to קָצִין, and refer לוֹ as the dative to קָצִין. Thus the second חֶרְפָּתוֹ gains expressiveness corresponding to its place before the verb as the contrast to חֶרְפָּתוֹ לוֹ: "however his reproach," *i.e.* the dishonour he did to the chiefs, "shall they recompense to him." The subject to יָשִׁיב is the collective קָצִין. The statement of the last clause introduces us to the announcement, mentioned in ver. 19, of the overthrow of the king of the north, who wished to spread his power also over the west. Since the chiefs (princes) of the islands rendered back to him his reproach, *i.e.* requited to him his attack against them, he was under the necessity of returning to the fortresses of his own land. With that begins his fall, which ends with his complete destruction.

Ver. 20. Another stands up in his place, who causeth נוֹגֵשׂ to pass over, through his eagerness for riches. נוֹגֵשׂ most understand as a *collector of tribute,* referring for this to 2 Kings xxiii. 35, and הֶדֶר מַלְכוּת as the Holy Land, and then think on Heliodorus, whom Seleucus Nicator sent to Jerusalem to seize the temple treasure. But this interpretation of the words is too limited. נָגַשׂ denotes, no doubt (2 Kings xxiii. 35), to collect gold and silver; but it does not thence follow that נוֹגֵשׂ, when silver and gold are not spoken of, means to collect tribute. The word in general designates the *taskmaster* who urges on the people to severe labour, afflicts and oppresses them as cattle. הֶדֶר מַלְכוּת is not synonymous with אֶרֶץ הַצְּבִי, ver. 16, but stands much nearer to הוֹד מַלְכוּת, ver. 21, and designates *the glory of the kingdom.* The glory of the kingdom was brought down by נוֹגֵשׂ, and הֶעֱבִיר refers to the whole kingdom of the king spoken of, not merely to the Holy Land, which formed but a part of his kingdom. By these oppressions of his kingdom he prepared himself in a short time for destruction. יָמִים אֲחָדִים (*days few*), as in Gen. xxvii. 44, xxix. 20, the designation of a very short time. The reference of these words, "*in days few*," to the time *after* the pillage of the temple of Jerusalem by Heliodorus is not only an arbitrary proceeding, but is also contrary to the import of the words, since בְּ in בְּיָמִים does not mean *post.* וְלֹא בְאַפַּיִם, in contradistinction and contrast to וְלֹא בְמִלְחָמָה, can only denote private enmity or private revenge. "Neither by anger (*i.e.* private revenge) nor by war" points to an immediate divine judgment.

If we now, before proceeding further in our exposition, attentively consider the contents of the revelation of vers. 5–20, so as to have a clear view of its relation to the historical fulfilment, we shall find the following to be the course of the thoughts exhibited:—After the fall of the Javanic world-kingdom (ver. 4) the king of the south shall attain to great power, and one of his princes shall found (ver. 5) a yet greater dominion in the north. After a course of years they shall enter into an agreement, for the king of the south shall give his daughter in marriage to the king of the north so as to establish a right relationship between them; but this agreement shall bring about the destruction of the daughter, as well as of her father and all who co-operated for the effecting of this marriage (ver. 6). Hereupon a descendant of that king of the south shall undertake a war against the king of the north, victoriously invade the country of the adversary, gather together great spoil and carry it away to Egypt, and for years hold the supremacy. The king of the north shall, it is true, penetrate into his kingdom, but he shall again return home without effecting anything (vers. 7–9). His sons also shall pass over the kingdom of the south with a multitude of hosts, but the multitude shall be given into the hand of the king, who shall not come to power by casting down myriads. The king of the north shall return with a host yet more numerous; against the king of the south many, also faithless members of the Jewish nation, shall rise up, and the king of the north shall take the fortified cities, without the king of the south having the power to offer him resistance (vers. 10–15). The conqueror shall now rule in the conquered lands after his own pleasure, and set his foot on the Holy Land with the intention of destroying it. Thereupon he shall come with the whole might of his kingdom against the king of the south, and by the marriage of his daughter seek to establish a right relationship with him, but he shall only thereby bring about the destruction of his daughter. Finally, he shall make an assault against the islands and the maritime countries of the west; but he shall be smitten by his chiefs, and be compelled to return to the fortresses of his own land, and shall fall (vers. 16–19). But his successor, who shall send taskmasters through the most glorious regions of the kingdom, shall be destroyed in a short time (ver. 20).

Thus the revelation depicts how, in the war of the kings of the south and of the north, first the king of the south subdued the north, but when at the summit of his conquest he sank under the power of his adversary through the insurrections and the revolt of an apostate party of the Jews; whereupon, by an assault upon the west in his endeavour after a firmer establishment and a wider extension of his power, he brings about his own overthrow, and his successor, in consequence of the oppression of his kingdom, comes to his end in a few days.

Now, since the king who comes into his place (ver. 21 ff.) after he has become strong raises himself up against the holy covenant, takes away the daily worship in the temple of the Lord, etc., is, according to the historical evidence found in the books of the Maccabees, the Seleucidan Antiochus Epiphanes, so the prophetic announcement, vers. 5–20, stretches itself over the period from the division of the monarchy of Alexander among his generals to the commencement of the reign of Antiochus Epiphanes in the year 175 B.C., during which there reigned seven Syrian and six Egyptian kings, viz.—

Syrian Kings.		Egyptian Kings.	
Seleucus Nicator, . . from B.C.	310	Ptolemy Lagus, . . from B.C.	323
Antiochus Sidetes, ...	280	Ptolemy Philadelphus, . . .	284
Antiochus Theus, ...	260	Ptolemy Euergetes, ...	246
Seleucus Callinicus, ...	245	Ptolemy Philopator, . . .	221
Seleucus Ceraunus, ...	225	Ptolemy Epiphanes, ...	204
Antiochus the Great, ...	223	Ptolemy Philometor, . . .	180
Seleucus Philopator, ...	186		

But in the prophetic revelation there is mention made of only four kings of the north (one in vers. 5–9; his sons, vers. 10–12; a third, vers. 13–19; and the fourth, ver. 20) and three kings of the south (the first, vers. 5 and 6; the "branch," vers. 7–9; and the king, vers. 10–15), distinctly different, whereby of the former, the relation of the sons (ver. 10) to the king indefinitely mentioned in ver. 11, is admitted, and of the latter the kings of the south, it remains doubtful whether he who is spoken of in vers. 9–15 is different from or is identical with "the branch of her roots" (ver. 7). This circumstance shows that the prophecy does not treat of individual historical personages, but only places in view the king of the south and the king of the north as representatives of the power of these two kingdoms. Of these kings special deeds and undertakings are indeed mentioned, which point to definite persons; *e.g.* of the king of the north, that he was one of the princes of the king of the south, and founded a greater dominion than his (ver. 5); the marriage of the daughter of the king of the south to the king of the north (ver. 6); afterwards the marriage also of the daughter of the king of the north (ver. 17), and other special circumstances in the wars between the two, which are to be regarded not merely as individualizing portraitures, but denote concrete facts which have verified themselves in history. But yet all these specialities do not establish the view that the prophecy consists of a series of predictions of historical *facta*, because even these features of the prophecy which find their actual fulfilments in history do not coincide with the historical reality.

Thus all interpreters regard the king of the south, ver. 5, as Ptolemy Lagus, and that one of his princes (מִן־שָׂרָיו) who founded a greater dominion as Seleucus Nicator, or the "Conqueror," who, in the division of the countries which the conquerors made after the overthrow and death of Antiochus, obtained, according to Appian, *Syr.* c. 55, Syria from the Euphrates to the Mediterranean Sea and Phrygia; then by using every opportunity of enlarging his kingdom, he obtained also Mesopotamia, Armenia, and a part of Cappadocia, and besides subjugated the Persians, Parthians, Bactrians, Arabians, and other nations as far as the Indus, which Alexander had conquered; so that, after Alexander, no one had more nations of Asia under his sway than Seleucus, for from the borders of Phrygia to the Indus all owned his sway. While this extension of his kingdom quite harmonizes with the prophecy of the greatness of his sovereignty, yet the designation "one of his princes" does not accord with the position of Ptolemy Lagus. Both of these were certainly at the beginning generals of Alexander. Seleucus, afterwards vicegerent of the Babylonians, found himself, however, from fear of Antigonus, who sought to put him to death, under the necessity of fleeing to Egypt to Ptolemy, by whom he was hospitably received, and with whom and other vicegerents he entered into a league against Antigonus, and when war arose, led an Egyptian fleet against Antigonus (Diod. Sic. xix. 55–62). He was accordingly not one of Ptolemy's generals.

Moreover, the marriage of the king's daughter, ver. 6, is thus explained by Jerome, and all interpreters who follow him:—Ptolemy Philadelphus made peace with Antiochus Theus, after many years' war, on the condition that Antiochus should put away his own wife Laodice, who was at the same time his half-sister, and disinherit her son, and should marry Berenice, the daughter of Ptolemy, and should appoint her first-born son as his successor on the throne of the kingdom (Appian, *Syr.* c. 65, and Jerome). This *factum* can be regarded as a fulfilling of the prophecy, ver. 6; but the consequences which resulted from this political marriage do not correspond with the consequences prophesied of. According to the testimony of history, Ptolemy died two years after this marriage, whereupon Antiochus set aside Berenice, and took to himself again his former wife Laodice, along with her children. But she effected the death of her husband by poison, as she feared his fickleness, and then her son Seleucus Callinicus ascended the throne. Berenice fled with her son to the asylum of Daphne, but she was there murdered along with him. The prophecy, according to this, differs from the historical facts, not merely in regard to the consequences of the events, but also in regard to the matter itself; for it speaks not only of the daughter, but also of her father being given up to death, while the natural death of her father is in no respect connected with that marriage, and not till after his death did the consequences fatal to his daughter and her child develop themselves.

Further, as to the contents of vers. 7–9, history furnishes the following confirmations:—In order to save his sister, who was put aside by Antiochus Theus, her brother, Ptolemy Euergetes, invaded the Syrian kingdom, in which Seleucus Callinicus had succeeded his father on the throne, in alliance with the armies of the Asiatic cities, and put to death his mother Laodice, since he had come too late to save his sister, in revenge for her murder, overthrew all the Syrian fortresses from Cilicia to the Tigris and Babylonia, and would have conquered the whole of the Syrian kingdom, if an insurrection which had broken out in Egypt had not caused him to return thither, carrying with him many images of the gods, and immense treasure, which he had taken from the vanquished cities. Then, while engaged in Egypt, Callinicus recovered the cities of Asia Minor, but failed to conquer the maritime countries, because his fleet was wrecked in a storm; and when he thereupon undertook a land expedition against Egypt, he was totally defeated, so that he returned to Antioch with only a few followers: cf. Justin, *Hist.* xxvii. 1, 2; Polyb. v. 58; and Appian, *Syr.* c. 65. On the other hand, the announcement of the war of his sons with many hosts overflowing the land, ver. 10, is not confirmed by history. After the death of Callinicus in captivity, his son Seleucus Ceraunus succeeded to the government, a very incompetent man, who after two years was poisoned by his generals in the war with Attalus, without having undertaken anything against Egypt. His brother Antiochus, surnamed the Great, succeeded him, who, in order to recover Cœle-Syria and Phœnicia, renewed the war against the king of Egypt (not till about two years after he ascended the throne, however, did Ptolemy Philopator begin to reign), in which he penetrated twice to Dura, two (German) miles north from Cæsarea (Polyb. x. 49), then concluded a four months' truce, and led his host back to the Orontes (Polyb. v. 66; Justin, xxx. 1). After the renewal of hostilities he drove the Egyptian army back to Sidon, conquered Gilead and Samaria, and took up his winter-quarters in Ptolemais (Polyb. v. 63–71). In the beginning of the following year, however, he was defeated by the Egyptians at Raphia, not far from Gaza, and was compelled, with great loss in dead and prisoners, to return as quickly as possible to Antioch, and to leave Cœle-Syria, Phœnicia, and Palestine to the Egyptians (Polyb. v. 79, 80, 82–86). Vers. 11 and 12 refer to this war. Thirteen or fourteen years after this, Antiochus, in league with Philip III. of Macedon, renewed the war against the Egyptians, when, after Philopator's death, Ptolemy Epiphanes, being five years old, had ascended the throne, retook the three above-named countries (Cœle-Syria, Phœnicia, and Palestine), vanquished the Egyptian host led by Scopas near Paneas, and compelled the fortress of Sidon, into which the Egyptians had fled, to surrender after a lengthened siege, and then concluded a peace with Ptolemy on the condition that he took to wife the daughter of Antiochus, Cleopatra, who should bring with her, as her dowry, Cœle-Syria, Phœnicia, and Palestine (Polyb. xv. 20, xxviii. 17; App. *Syr.* c. i.; Liv. xxxiii. 19; and Joseph. *Antt.* xii. 4. 1). Since the time of Jerome, the prophecy vers. 13–17 has been referred to this last war. But also here the historical events fall far behind the contents of the prophecy. The prophecy points to the complete subjugation of the king of the south, while this war was carried on only for the possession of the Asiatic provinces of the Egyptian kingdom. Also the rising up of many (רַבִּים, ver. 14) against the king of the south is not historically verified; and even the relation spoken of by Josephus (*Antt.* xii. 3. 3) in which the Jews stood to Antiochus the Great was not of such a kind as to be capable of being regarded as a fulfilling of the "exalting themselves" of the בְּנֵי פָּרִיצִים, ver. 14. Still less does the statement of ver. 16, that the king of the north would stand in the glorious land, agree with כָּלָה interpreted of conduct of Antiochus the Great toward the Jews; for according to Josephus, *Antt. l.c.*, he treated the Jews round about Jerusalem favourably, because of their own accord they had submitted to him and had supported his army, and granted to them not only indulgence in regard to the observance of their religious ordinances, but also afforded them protection.

Moreover, ver. 18, containing the prophecy of the undertaking of the king of the north against the islands, has not its historical fulfilment in the expedition of Antiochus the Great against the coasts and islands of Asia Minor and the Hellespont; but ver. 19, that which is said regarding his return to the fortresses of his own land and his overthrow, does not so correspond with the historical issue of the reign of this king that one would be able to recognise therein a prediction of it. Finally, of his successor, Seleucus Philopator, to whom ver. 20 must refer, if the foregoing verses treat of Antiochus the Great, nothing further is communicated, than that he *quum paternis cladibus fractas admodum Syriæ opes accepisset, post otiosum nullisque admodum rebus gestis nobilitatum annorum duodecim regnum,* was put to death through the treachery of Heliodorus, *unius ex purpuratis* (Liv. xli. 19, cf. App. *Syr.* c. 45), and the mission of Heliodorus to Jerusalem to seize the treasures of the temple, which is fabulously described in 2 Macc. iii. 4 ff. The יִשָּׁבֵר (*shall be destroyed*) of this king בְּיָמִים אֲחָדִים (*within few days*) does not harmonize with the fact of his twelve years' reign.

From this comparison this much follows, that the prophecy does not furnish a prediction of the historical wars of the Seleucidæ and the Ptolemies, but an ideal description of the war of the kings of the north and the south in its general outlines, whereby, it is true, diverse special elements of the prophetical announcement have historically been fulfilled, but the historical reality does not correspond with the contents of the prophecy in anything like an exhaustive manner. This ideal character of the prophecy comes yet more prominently forward to view in the following prophetic description.

Chap. xi. 21–xii. 3. *The further unveiling of the future.*

In this section we have (ver. 21) first the description of the prince who, in striving after supremacy, uses all the means that cunning and power can contrive, and in his enmity against the holy covenant knows no bounds. This description is divided into two parts—(1) vers. 21–35, and (2) vers. 36–ch. xii. 3—which designate the two stadia of his proceedings. In the *first* part are described, (1) his gradual rising to power, vers. 21–24; (2) his war with the king of the south for the supremacy, vers. 25–27; (3) his rising up against the covenant people, even to the desecration of the sanctuary by the taking away of the daily sacrifice and the setting up of the abomination of desolation, vers. 28–32; (4) the effect and consequence of this for the people of God, vers. 32–35. This prince is the enemy of the holy God who is prophesied of in ch. viii. 9–13, 23–25, under the figure of the little horn, and is typically represented in the rising up of the Syrian king Antiochus Epiphanes against the covenant people and their worship of God.

Vers. 21–24. *The prince's advancement to power.*—He appears as נִבְזֶה, *one despised, i.e.* not such an one as by reason of birth has any just claim to the throne, and therefore as an intruder, also one who finds no recognition (Kranichfeld); which Hitzig has more definitely explained by mentioning that not Antiochus Epiphanes, but his nephew Demetrius, the son of the murdered Seleucus Philopator, was the true heir, but was of such a character that he was not esteemed worthy of the throne. נִבְזֶה, *is despised*, not = *bad, unworthy*, but yet supposes unworthiness. There was not laid on him the honour or majesty of the kingdom. The dignity of the kingdom requires הוֹד, *splendour, majesty*, such as God lays upon the king of Israel, Ps. xxi. 6 (5), 1 Chron. xxix. 25. But here the subject spoken of is the honour which men give to the king, and which was denied to the "despised one" on account of his character. He comes בְּשַׁלְוָה, *in security*, *i.e.* unexpectedly (cf. ch. viii. 25), and takes possession of the kingdom. הֶחֱזִיק, *to grasp*, here to draw violently to himself. בַּחֲלַקְלַקּוֹת, properly, *by smoothnesses*, intrigues and cunning, not merely flatteries or smooth words, but generally hypocritical behaviour in word and deed; cf. ver. 34.

Ver. 22. The kingdom he seized he also knew how to hold fast with great power. זְרֹעוֹת הַשֶּׁטֶף, *arms* (*i.e.* warlike strength) *of an inundation*, *i.e.* armies overflowing the land are swept away before him, destroyed by yet stronger military forces. It is not merely the enemy, but also the "prince of the covenant," whom he destroys. נְגִיד בְּרִית is analogous to בַּעֲלֵי בְרִית, Gen. xiv. 13, and אַנְשֵׁי בְרִית, Obad. 7, cf. Mal. ii. 14, and, as the absence of the article shows, is to be taken in a general sense. The interpretation of נְגִיד בְּרִית of the high priest Onias III., who at the commencement of the reign of Antiochus Epiphanes was driven from his office by his brother, and afterwards, at the instigation of Menelaus, was murdered by the Syrian governor Andronicus at Daphne near Antioch, 2 Macc. iv. 1 ff., 33 ff. (Rosenmüller, Hitzig, etc.)—this interpretation is not warranted by the facts of history. This murder does not at all relate to the matter before us, not only because the Jewish high priest at Antioch did not sustain the relation of a "prince of the covenant," but also because the murder was perpetrated without the previous knowledge of Antiochus, and when the matter was reported to him, the murderer was put to death by his command (2 Macc. iv. 36–38). Thus also it stands in no connection with the war of Antiochus against Egypt. The words cannot also (with Hävernick, v. Leng., Maurer, Ebrard, Kliefoth) be referred to the Egyptian king Ptolemy Philometor, because history knows nothing of a covenant entered into between this king and Antiochus Epiphanes, but only that soon after the commencement of the reign of Antiochus Epiphanes the guardians of the young Philometor demanded Cœle-Syria from Antiochus, which Antiochus the Great had promised (see above, p. 448) as a dowry to his daughter Cleopatra, who was betrothed to Ptolemy Philometor, but Antiochus did not deliver it up, and hence a war arose between them. To this is to be added, that, as Dereser, v. Lengerke, Maurer, and Kranichfeld have rightly remarked, the description in vers. 22–24 bears an altogether general character, so that v. Leng. and Maurer find therein references to all the three expeditions of Antiochus, and in vers. 25–27 find more fully foretold what is only briefly hinted at in vers. 22–24. The undertaking of the king against Egypt is first described in ver. 24. We must therefore, with Kranichfeld, understand נְגִיד בְּרִית in undefined generality of covenant princes in general, in the sense already given.

Vers. 23 and 24. In these verses there is a fuller statement of the manner in which he treats the princes of the covenant and takes possession of their territory. The ו at the beginning of ver. 23 is explicative, and the suffix in אֵלָיו, pointing back to נְגִיד ב׳, is also to be interpreted collectively. מִן־הִתְחַבְּרוּת אֵלָיו, literally, "from the confederating himself with them" (הִתְחַבְּרוּת is infin. formed in the Syriac manner), *i.e.* from the time when he had made a covenant with them, he practised deceit. This was done by his coming (עָלָה of a warlike coming) and gaining strength with a few people, namely (ver. 24), by his coming unexpectedly into the fattest and richest places of the province, and there doing unheard-of things—things which no previous king, no one of his predecessors, had ever done, scattering among them (his followers) spoil and prey and riches. Thus rightly, after the Syriac and the Vulgate (*dissipabit*), Rosenmüller, Kranichfeld, and Ewald; while, on the contrary, v. Leng., Maurer, Hitzig, and Kliefoth interpret בָּזַר in the sense of *to distribute*, and refer the words to the circumstance that Antiochus Epiphanes squandered money lavishly, and made presents to his inferiors often without any occasion. But to distribute money and spoil is nothing unheard of, and in no way does it agree with the "fattest provinces." The context decidedly refers to conduct which injured the fat provinces. This can only consist in squandering and dissipating the wealth of this province which he had plundered to its injury (לָהֶם [*to them*], *dativ. incommodi*). An historical confirmation is found in 1 Macc. iii. 29–31. To bring the provinces wholly under his power, he devises plans against the fortresses that he might subdue them. וְעַד־עֵת, and indeed (he did this) even for a time. We cannot, with Klief., refer this merely to the last preceding passage, that his assaults against the fortresses succeeded only partly and for a time. The addition ("and that for a time") denotes a period determined by a higher power (cf. ver. 35 and ch. xii. 4, 6), and relates to the whole proceedings of this prince hitherto described; as C. B. Michaelis has already rightly explained: *nec enim semper et in perpetuum dolus ei succedet et terminus suus ei tandem erit.*

Vers. 25–27. These verses describe the victorious war of the king who had come to power against the king of the south, the war of Antiochus Epiphanes against king Ptolemy Philometor, which is described in 1 Macc. i. 16–19, with manifest reference to this prophecy. יָעֵר (*he shall stir up*) is *potentialis* in the sense of divine decree: "he shall stir up his power and his heart." כֹּחַ is not warlike power, which is mentioned in בְּחַיִל־גָּדוֹל (ver. 25), but the power which consists in the bringing of a great army under his command; לֵבָב, the mental energy for the carrying out of his plans. For לֹא יַעֲמֹד, cf. ch. viii. 4. The subject is the last-named king of the south, who, notwithstanding his very great and powerful army, shall not stand in battle, but shall give way, because devices are contrived against him. The subject to יַחְשְׁבוּ is not the enemy, the king of the north, with his army, but, according to ver. 26, his table-companions.

Ver. 26. Here it is more definitely stated why he cannot stand. אֹכְלֵי פַתְבָּגוֹ, *who eat his food* (פַּתְבַּג, see under ch. i. 5), *i.e.* his table-companions (cf. Ps. xli. 10 [9]), persons about him. יִשְׁבְּרוּהוּ, *shall break him*, *i.e.* cast him to the ground. His army shall therefore overflow, but shall execute nothing, only many shall fall down slain. The first member of the verse points to treachery, whereby the battle was lost and the war was fruitless. Hitzig incorrectly interprets יִשְׁטוֹף rushes away, *i.e.* is disorganized and takes to flight. But שָׁטַף cannot have this meaning.

Ver. 27. Here then is described how the two kings seek through feigned friendship to destroy one another. *The* two kings are of course the two kings of the north and the south previously named. Of a third, namely, of two kings of Egypt, Philometor and Physkon, Daniel knows nothing. The third, Physkon, is introduced from history; and hence Hitzig, v. Lengerke, and others understand by the "*two kings*," the two kings Antiochus and Philometor confederated against the king of the south, but Kliefoth, on the contrary, thinks of Antiochus and Physkon, the latter of whom he regards as the king of the south, ver. 25. All this is arbitrary. Jerome has already rejected the historical evidence for this, and remarks: *verum ex eo, quia scriptura nunc dicit: duos fuisse reges, quorum cor fuerit fraudulentum . . . hoc secundum historiam demonstrari non potest.* לְבָבָם לְמֵרָע Hitzig translates: "their heart belongs to wickedness," contrary to the context. לְ denotes also here only the direction: "their heart goes toward wicked deeds," is directed thereto. מֵרַע (from רעע), formed after

מֵצַר (cf. Ewald, § 160*a*), the *evil-doing*, consists in this, that the one seeks to overthrow and destroy the other under the cloak of feigned friendship; for they eat as friends at one table, and "speak lies"—the one tells lies to the other, professing friendship. But their design shall not succeed. All interpretations of these words which are determined by historical *facta* are arbitrary. The history of Antiochus Epiphanes furnishes no illustrations for this. In the sense of the prophecy לֹא תִצְלָח has only this meaning: the design of the king of the north to destroy the king of the south, and to make himself master both of the north and the south, shall not succeed, and the king of the south will not fulfil what he promises to his deceitful adversary. For yet the end shall be at the time appointed. These words state the reason why the מֵרַע shall not succeed. Hitzig incorrectly translates: "but the end holds onwards to the appointed time;" for כִּי cannot in this connection be rendered by *but*, and לְ cannot express the idea of holding to anything. לְ denotes here, as generally, the direction toward the end, as ver. 35, and ch. viii. 17, 19. The end goes yet on to the time appointed by God. That this מוֹעֵד (*appointment* of time) does not lie in the present, but in the future, is denoted by עוֹד, although we do not, with Hävernick, interpret עוֹד by "for the end lies yet further out," nor, with v. Lengerke and Maurer, may we supply the verb "withdraws itself, is reserved." עוֹד stands before קֵץ because on it the emphasis lies. קֵץ is, however, not the end of the war between Antiochus and Egypt (v. Leng., Maur., Hitzig), but cannot be otherwise taken than עֵת קֵץ, vers. 35, 40, and ch. xii. 4. But in the latter passage עֵת קֵץ is the time of the resurrection of the dead, thus the end of the present course of the world, with which all the oppression of the people of God ceases. Accordingly קֵץ in the verse before us, as in vers. 35 and 40, is the time in which the conduct of the kings previously described, in their rising up and in their hostility against the people of God, reaches its end (ver. 45); and with the overthrow of these enemies the period of oppression also comes to an end. This end comes only לַמּוֹעֵד, *at the time* which God has determined for the purifying of His people (ver. 35). So long may the kings of the north and the south prosecute their aims; so long shall they strive for the possession of the kingdom without succeeding in their plans. לַמּוֹעֵד has here and in ver. 35 the definite article, because in both verses the language refers not to any definite time, but to the time determined by God for the consummation of His kingdom. The placing of the article in this word in the verse before us is not, with Kliefoth, to be explained from a reference to ch. viii. 17, 19. The two revelations are separated from each other by too long a space of time for this one to refer back to that earlier one by the mere use of the article, although both treat of the same subject. The לַמּוֹעֵד occurs besides in ver. 29, where it is natural to suppose that it has the same meaning as here; but the contents of that verse oppose such a conclusion. Ver. 29 treats, it is true, of a renewed warlike expedition against the south, which, however, brings neither the final deciding of the war with the south (cf. ver. 40), nor yet the end of the oppression of the people of God; הַמּוֹעֵד is thus only the time determined for the second aggression against the south, not the time of the end.

Vers. 28–32. *The rising up against the holy covenant.*

Ver. 28. The success gained by the crafty king of the north in his war against the king of the south (ver. 25 f.) increases his endeavours after the enlarging of his dominions. Returning from Egypt with great riches, *i.e.* with rich spoil, he raises his heart against the holy covenant. By the *potentialis* יָשֹׁב (*he shall return*) this new undertaking is placed in the point of view of a divine decree, to denote that he thereby brings about his own destruction. בְּרִית קֹדֶשׁ signifies not the holy people in covenant with God (v. Lengerke, Maurer, and many older interpreters), but the divine institution of the Old Covenant, the Jewish Theocracy. The Jews are only members of this covenant, cf. ver. 30. Calvin is right when he says: *Mihi simplicior sensus probatur, quod scilicet bellum gerat adversus Deum.* The holy covenant is named instead of the covenant people to represent the undertaking as an outrage against the kingdom of God, which was founded in Israel. וְעָשָׂה, *and he shall do, perform*, that which his heart thinks, or that which he has in his mind against the holy covenant. The historical fulfilment is narrated in 1 Macc. i. 22–29. וְשָׁב לְאַרְצוֹ resumes וְיָשֹׁב אַרְצוֹ, and teaches us that Antiochus undertook the first assault against the holy covenant on his return from Egypt into his kingdom (to Antioch), as is expressly stated in 1 Macc. i. 20.

Ver. 29. In order that he might bring Egypt wholly under his power, he undertook a new expedition thither (יָשׁוּב וּבָא, *he comes again*). But this expedition, like the first, was not successful (כְּ—כְּ, *as—so*, cf. Josh. xiv. 11, Ezek. xviii. 4). For the ships of Chittim come against him. צִיִּים כִּתִּים, *ships the Chittæi*, for

צִים מִיַּד כִּתִּים, Num. xxiv. 24, whence the expression is derived כִּתִּים is Cyprus with its chief city *Κίττιον* (now Chieti or Chitti); see under Gen. x. 4. Ships coming from Cyprus are ships which come from the west, from the islands and coasts of the Mediterranean. In 1 Macc. i. 1 and viii. 5 כִּתִּים is interpreted of Macedonia, according to which Bertholdt and Dereser think of the Macedonian fleet with which the Roman embassy sailed to Alexandria. This much is historically verified, that the Roman embassy, led by Popillius, appeared with a fleet in Alexandria, and imperiously commanded Antiochus to desist from his undertaking against Egypt and to return to his own land (Liv. xlv. 10–12). The LXX. have therefore translated these words by: *καὶ ἥξουσι Ῥωμαῖοι καὶ ἐξώσουσιν αὐτὸν καὶ ἐμβριμήσονται αὐτῷ*, and correctly, so far as the prophecy has received the first historical accomplishment in that *factum.* וְנִכְאָה, *he shall lose courage*, is rightly explained by Jerome: *non quod interierit, sed quod omnem arrogantiæ perdiderit magnitudinem.*[1] וְשָׁב וְזָעַם, not: he was again enraged, for nothing is said of a previous זָעַם. וְשָׁב, *and he turned round* (back) from his expedition against Egypt. Since he was not able to accomplish anything against the נֶגֶב (*the south*), he turns his indignation against Judah to destroy the covenant people (cf. ver. 28). The וְשָׁב in ver. 30*b* resumes the וְשָׁב in ver. 30*a*, so as further to express how he gave vent to his anger. Hitzig's interpretation of the first וְשָׁב of the return to Palestine, of the second, of the return from Palestine to Antioch, is not justified. וְיָבֵן, *he shall observe*, direct his attention to the Jews who forsook the holy covenant, *i.e.* the apostate Jews, that he might by their help execute his plans against the Mosaic religion—*partim ornando illos honoribus, partim illorum studiis ad patriam religionem obliterandam comparatis obsecundando*, as C. B. Michaelis excellently remarks; cf. 1 Macc. i. 11–16 with ii. 18.

[1] The historical facts have been briefly and conclusively brought together by Hitzig thus: "On the complaint of the Alexandrians the Roman senate sent an embassage, at the head of which was C. Popillius Lænas (Polyb. xxix. 1; Liv. xliv. 19). After being detained at Delos (Liv. xliv. 29), they set sail to Egypt after the battle at Pydna (Liv. xlv. 10). Here he met Antiochus four Roman miles from Alexandria, and presented to him the message of the senate. When Antiochus explained that he wished to lay the matter before his counsellors, Popillius described with the staff he carried in his hand a circle round the king, and commanded him to give his answer before he left this circle. Antiochus, confounded by the circumstance, submitted and withdrew from Egypt (Liv. xlv. 12; Polyb. xxix. 11; Appian, *Syr.* c. 66; Justin. xxxiv. 3)."

Ver. 31. Here is stated what he accomplished by the help of the apostate Jews. זְרֹעִים, *arms*, figuratively for help (ver. 5), are warlike forces, as vers. 15 and 22. That the plur. has here the masculine form, while in those verses it has the fem. form, furnishes no reason for a difference of meaning, since זְרוֹעַ in its proper sense of arm occurs *promiscue* with both endings in the plur.; cf. for זְרֹעִים Gen. xlix. 24, Isa. li. 5, 2 Kings ix. 24. מִן in מִמֶּנּוּ is not partitive, *a part of him, i.e.* the host as a part of the king (Hitzig), but *out from him*, or by his command. יַעֲמֹדוּ, *to stand up*, not *to stand still*, as Hitzig, on the ground of the supposition that Antiochus on his return from Egypt placed a standing army-corps in Jerusalem, would interpret it, contrary to the usage of the word, since עָמַד does not signify *to stand still* in the sense of *to remain behind*, though it means to endure, to keep the ground (vers. 6, 15). It is disputed whether these זְרֹעִים denote military forces, troops of the hostile king (Hävernick, v. Leng., Maur., Hitz., Klief.), or his accomplices of the apostate party of the Jews, and thus essentially identical with עֹזְבֵי בְרִית, ver. 30 (Calvin, Hengstb. *Christol.* iii. 1, p. 110, Kran., and others). In favour of the latter view, Kranichfeld argues that the עֹזְבֵי בְרִית (*those that forsake the covenant*), according to ver. 30, come under consideration as a support to the king, and the מִמֶּנּוּ of this verse before us evidently refers to the king's own army, and therefore would be superfluous. But these two reasons prove nothing. The מִמֶּנּוּ is not superfluous, even though it were used of the king's own army. Since in vers. 30 and 32 the king of the north is the subject of the clause, it was necessary in זְרֹעִים to define in what relation they stood to the king. But the other remark, that the עֹזְבֵי בְרִית come into view as a support to the king, does not prove that these are the same who desecrate the sanctuary and set up the abomination of desolation. On the contrary, if מִמֶּנּוּ denotes the causal exit, the זְרֹעִים cannot be the apostate Jews, but only warlike forces which the king leads forth. If we refer זְרֹעִים to the apostate Jews, then we must, with Hengstenberg and Gesenius, take מִמֶּנּוּ in the sense of *eo jubente*. Moreover, the זְרֹעִים manifestly stand in contrast to the מַרְשִׁיעֵי בְרִית of ver. 32. By his troops (military forces) the king lays waste the sanctuary, and he makes by means of smooth words those who sin against the covenant heathen. Kranichfeld himself recognises this contrast, and therefore will understand as the subject to וְחִלְּלוּ not merely "those that forsake the covenant" (ver. 30), but those along with and including the warlike power of the hostile king. An expedient which the difficulty suggested. הַמִּקְדָּשׁ is the temple, and הַמָּעוֹז (*the strength*) is in apposition. This apposition, however, does not say that the temple was fortified (v. Leng., Hitzig, Ewald), but it points out the temple as the spiritual fortress of Israel. The temple is the "*Feste Burg*" (firm tower) of the holy covenant (ver. 28), as the dwelling-place of Jehovah, which is a firm fortress to His people; cf. Ps. xxxi. 4, 5 (3, 4); Isa. xxv. 4; Ps. xviii. 3 (2). חִלְּלוּ המ׳ is essentially identical with הֻשְׁלַךְ מְכוֹן מִקְדָּשׁוֹ, ch. viii. 11. The two following clauses state what the desecration consists in: in the taking away, the removal of the stated worship of Jehovah, and in the placing, setting up of the abomination of desolation, *i.e.* of the idol-altar on Jehovah's altar of burnt-offering; see under ch. viii. 11 (p. 297 f.). מְשֹׁמֵם is not the genitive, but an adjective to הַשִּׁקּוּץ (without the article after the definite noun, as *e.g.* ch. viii. 13): *the desolating abomination*, *i.e.* the abomination which effects the desolation. With reference to the fulfilment, cf. 1 Macc. i. 37, 45, 54, and above, p. 371.

Vers. 32–35. *The consequences to the people of Israel which result from this sin against the holy covenant.*—The ungodly shall become heathen, *i.e.* shall wholly apostatize from the true God; but, on the other hand, the pious shall be strengthened in their confidence in the Lord. This is in general the import of ver. 32, the first half of which, however, has been very differently interpreted. מַרְשִׁיעֵי בְרִית signifies neither "those who sinfully make a covenant" (Hävernick), nor "sinners among the covenant people" (v. Lengerke), nor "those who condemn the covenant," *i.e.* those who reject the sign of the covenant, circumcision (Hitzig). The latter meaning is altogether arbitrary. Against the second is the fact that רְשָׁעִים is in use for sinners; against the first, that הִרְשִׁיעַ בְּרִית could only mean: "to declare the covenant punishable." הִרְשִׁיעַ means to act wickedly, to sin, and בְּרִית can only be the accusative of reference, which is subordinated to the participle for the purpose of limitation (Ewald, § 288); literally, "the acting wickedly with reference to the covenant." The absence of the article in בְּרִית is no proof against the reference of the word to the holy covenant. The article is wanting in Daniel where otherwise the determination is found from the connection, *e.g.* ch. viii. 13. Sinning against the covenant is, it is true, a stronger expression than עָזַב בְּרִית (*to forsake the covenant*), but it does not include the idea of the entire apostasy from God, but only insolent violation of the covenant law, so that of מַרְשִׁיעֵי בְרִית it can very well be predicated יַחֲנִיף. הֶחֱנִיף does not mean *to pollute* (Kran.), but *to desecrate, to make profane;* and spoken of persons, *to make them as heathen*, as frequently in the Syriac. חֲלַקּוֹת, *flatteries*, here *deceitful promises* of earthly advantage; cf. under ver. 21. For the subject spoken of here, see 1 Macc. ii. 18. יֹדְעֵי אֱלֹהָיו are the true confessors of the Lord. The suffix to אֱלֹהָיו is neither to be interpreted distributively nor to be referred to עַם. To יַחֲזִיקוּ we are to supply בַּבְּרִית from the context: "to hold fast to the covenant." וְעָשׂוּ, as vers. 17, 28, 30, to carry out the design. In what way this is done is explained in vers. 33 and 34*a*.

Ver. 33. מַשְׂכִּילֵי is not *the teachers*, but *intelligentes*, those who have insight or understanding. The pious are meant by the word, those who know their God (ver. 32). This is seen from the contrast רְשָׁעִים, ch. xii. 10. According to the O. T. view, wisdom, insight, are correlative ideas with the fear of God, piety, Ps. xiv. 1, Job xxviii. 28; and לָרַבִּים with the article, *the* many, the great multitude of the people who bring themselves forward to view by the judicious appearance of the pious, are moved to hold fast by the law of the Lord. Yet they who understand shall for a time fall by the sword, etc. The subject to נִכְשְׁלוּ is not the רַבִּים, or those with the teachers (Hitzig), but the מַשְׂכִּילֵי עָם, but not all, but, according to ver. 35, a number of them; for in ver. 35 falling is not first specially predicated of the teachers, as Hitzig thinks, but only the effect which that would have on the whole people. The words point to a warlike rising up of the faithful members of the covenant people against the hostile king, and have had their first historical fulfilment in the insurrection of the Maccabees against Antiochus Epiphanes; cf. 1 Macc. ii. ff. In 1 Macc. i. 57, ii. 38, iii. 41, v. 13, 2 Macc. vi. 11, there are examples of this falling by the sword. The רַבִּים after יָמִים in several *Codd.* is a worthless gloss.

Ver. 34. Through the fall of the pious in war little help shall come to the people of God. מְעָט (*little*) is not "spoken contemptuously" (Hitzig), but the help is so named in comparison with the great deliverance which shall come to the people of God in the time of the end by the complete destruction of the oppressor. We may not therefore, with Hitzig and others, limit this expression to the circumstance that with the victories of Judas Maccabæus (1 Macc. iii. 11 ff., 23 ff., iv. 14, etc.) they were far from gaining all, for they also met with a defeat (1 Macc. v. 60 f.). For with the overthrow of Antiochus and the liberation of the Jews from the Syrian yoke, full help was not yet rendered to the people of God. The "little help" consists in this, that by the rising up and the wars of those that had understanding among the people the theocracy was preserved, the destruction of the service of Jehovah and of the church of God, which was aimed at by the hostile king, was prevented, and, as the following clauses express, the purifying of the people of God is brought about. This purifying is the design and the fruit of the oppression which God brings upon His people by means of the hostile king. The attaining of this end is a "little help" in comparison with the complete victory over the arch-enemy of the time of the end. Many shall connect themselves with the מַשְׂכִּילִים (*intelligentes*, ver. 33*a*) with flatteries (as ver. 21). "The successes of Judas, and the severity with which he and Mattathias treated the apostates (1 Macc. ii. 44, iii. 5, 8), had the result of causing many to join them only through hypocrisy (1 Macc. vii. 6; 2 Macc. xiv. 6), who again forsook them as soon as opportunity offered; 1 Macc. vi. 21 ff., ix. 23" (Hitzig, Kliefoth).

Ver. 35. Such has been the experience in all periods of the church's history. Therefore does the church need to pass through the purifying process of affliction, in which not only the lukewarm fall away in the time of conflict, but also many even מִן־הַמַּשְׂכִּילִים. מִן is here partitive. יִכָּשְׁלוּ (*they shall fall*) is to be understood (cf. ver. 33, נִכְשְׁלוּ בח') not merely of death in battle, but of other calamities, such as being imprisoned, plundered, etc. לִצְרוֹף בָּהֶם, *to melt, i.e. to purify by them*, not *as to* them; for בְּ does not represent the accusative, as Kranichfeld thinks, referring in confirmation to Ewald, § 282. The use of בְּ there spoken of is of a different nature. The suffix in בָּהֶם refers neither to "those that understand" alone (Häv.), nor to the "many," ver. 33 (v. Leng.), still less to the flatterers in ver. 34 (Maurer), but to all of these together, or to the whole company of the people of God in the sum of their individuals. The verbs לְבָרֵר וְלַלְבֵּן serve to strengthen the expression (לַלְבֵּן for לְלַבֵּין on account of the assonance). עַד־עֵת קֵץ (*to the time of the end*) is connected with יִכָּשְׁלוּ, the chief idea of the passage. The stumbling and falling of "those who understand" (the pious) shall continue to the time of the end, to bring about the purification of the people for their glorification in the time of the end. For the end stretches itself out yet to the time appointed (cf. ver. 27); *i.e.* it does not come in with the "little help" which Israel received by the rising up of "those who understand" against the hostile king, thus not with the afflictions that came upon them by Antiochus, but it shall come afterwards at the time appointed by God. The assertion that "the end is connected with the death of king Antiochus Epiphanes" (Hitzig, Bleek, and others) is founded on a misunderstanding of the following section, vers. 36–45. On the contrary, Kranichfeld has rightly remarked, that "the statements made in vers. 36 to 39 *incl.* regarding the king of the north, now fall, in accordance with the context, into the period which shall expire at that time of the end (ver. 35, cf. ver. 40)." From ver. 40 the events of the time of the end are then to be prophesied.

Ver. 36–ch. xii. 3. *The second and last stadium in the dominion of the enemy of God, with his destruction, and the deliverance of the people of God.*

This part of the prophecy is divided into three sections: (1) Vers. 36–39 describe the rising of the hostile king above all divine and human ordinances; (2) vers. 40–45, his last undertaking against the king of the south for the gaining of the dominion of the world, together with his overthrow; (3) ch. xii. 1–3, the deliverance of the people of God from the last tribulation.

Regarding the king whose course to its end is described in vers. 36–45, the views of interpreters differ. Following the example of Porphyry, Ephrem Syrus, and Grotius, almost all modern interpreters find predicted here only a description of the conduct of Antiochus Epiphanes to the time of his destruction; believing interpreters, such as C. B. Michaelis, Hävernick, and others, regarding the whole as having a typical reference to Antichrist. On the contrary, Jerome, Theodoret, Luther, Oecolampadius, Osiander, Calovius, Geier, and at length Kliefoth, interpret this section as a direct prophecy of Antichrist; according to which, הַמֶּלֶךְ, ver. 36, representing not Antiochus Epiphanes, but the prince, *i.e.* the Antichrist, who is prophesied of under the figure of the little horn growing up among the ten kingdoms of the fourth world-kingdom, and described in ch. ix. 26 as נָגִיד הַבָּא, must be introduced as a new subject in ver. 36. The rabbinical interpreters have also adopted the idea of a change of subject in ver. 36, for Aben Ezra, Jacchiades, and Abarbanel take Constantine the Great, while R. Solomon takes the Roman empire generally, as the subject. Essentially the reference of the section to the Antichrist is correct; but the supposition of a change of subject in the prophetic representation is not established. If in the words, "the fall of those who understand, to purify and make white, shall continue to the time of the end" (ver. 35), it is also said that the end does not yet come with the proceedings of the enemy of God prophesied of in vers. 28–34, but lies beyond that; so also, in the verses referred to, the destruction of this enemy (Antiochus) is neither directly nor indirectly so spoken of as to justify the conclusion that "the words 'to purify and make white,' etc., extend beyond his time." If the contents of vers. 36–45 lie beyond the end of the enemy who has been hitherto spoken of, then ought his destruction to have been mentioned, especially since with the words, "to the time of the end, because yet for a time appointed," ver. 35, the words of ver. 27, "for yet the end of the time appointed," are resumed. All attempts to give to the former of these expressions in ver. 35 a different meaning from that contained in the latter, ver. 27 (Calovius, Geier, Kliefoth), amount to verbally impossible interpretations. The non-mention also of the destruction of this enemy (Antiochus) in vers. 32–35 is not justified by the remark that this was already known to Daniel from ch. viii., and that in vers. 36–45 the duration of Antichrist is also omitted (Klief.). For the verses do not treat of the duration of the proceedings of the enemy of God, but of his end or his destruction. The destruction of the enemy at the time of the end is, however, expressly declared, ver. 45. This would also have been stated in vers. 32–34 if the king in ver. 36 had been a different person from the one previously described. הַמֶּלֶךְ with the definite article undeniably points back to the king whose appearance and conduct are described in vers. 21–33. The definite article neither denotes that the Antichrist of ch. vii. and ix. 26 f. was known to Daniel (Klief.), nor is it to be emphatically interpreted in the sense of *the* king simply (Geier). This is only so far right, that that which is said regarding this king, vers. 36–39, partly goes far beyond what Antiochus did, partly does not harmonize with what is known of Antiochus, and, finally, partly is referred in the N. T. expressly to the Antichrist; cf. ver. 36 with 2 Thess. ii. 4, and ch. xii. 1 with Matt. xxiv. 21. These circumstances also are not satisfactorily explained by the remark that the prophecy regarding Antiochus glances forward to the Antichrist, or that the image of the type (Antiochus) hovers in the image of the antitype (Antichrist); they much rather show that in the prophetic contemplation there is comprehended in the image of *one* king what has been historically fulfilled in its beginnings by Antiochus Epiphanes, but shall only meet its complete fulfilment by the Antichrist in the time of the end.

Vers. 36–39. *The hostile king exalting himself above all divine and human ordinances at the time of the end.*

Ver. 36. This exaltation of the king is here introduced by the formula וְעָשָׂה כִרְצֹנוֹ, which expresses the self-will and the irresistible might of his proceeding; cf. ch. iii. 16 and viii. 4,—"a feature common to Antiochus and Antichrist" (Klief.). He shall raise himself above every god, not merely "subjectively in his lofty imagination" (Hitzig), but also by his actions. כָּל־אֵל, *every god*, not merely the God of Israel, but also the gods of the heathen. This does not agree with Antiochus. The ἰσόθεα φρονεῖν ὑπερηφανῶς which is said of him, 2 Macc. ix. 12, is not an exalting of himself above every god. "Antiochus was not an ἄθεος; he even wished to render the worship of Zeus universal; and that he once spoiled the temple does not imply his raising himself above every god" (Klief.). Of Antiochus much rather, as is said by Livy (xli. 20), *in duabus tamen magnis honestisque rebus fere regius erat animus, in urbium donis et deorum cultu.* On the contrary, these words before us are expressly referred to Antichrist, 2 Thess. ii. 4.

Yet further, in his arrogance he shall speak נִפְלָאוֹת, *wonderful, i.e.* impious and astonishing things, against the God of gods, *i.e.* the true God. This clause expounds and strengthens the מַלִּל רַבְרְבָן (*speaking great things*), which is said of the enemy at the time of the end, ch. vii. 8, 11, 20. In this he will prosper, but only till the anger of God against His people (זַעַם as ch. viii. 19) shall be accomplished. Regarding כָּלָה see at ch. ix. 27. This anger of God is irrevocably determined (נֶחֱרָצָה), that His people may be wholly purified for the consummation of His kingdom in glory. The *perf.* נֶעֱשָׂתָה does not stand for the *imperf.* because it is decreed, but in its proper meaning, according to which it represents the matter as finished, settled. Here it accordingly means: "for that which is irrevocably decreed is accomplished, is not to be recalled, but must be done."

Ver. 37. The exalting of himself above all on the part of the king is further described. "He shall not regard the gods of his fathers," *i.e.* shall cast aside the worship of the gods transmitted to him from his fathers. This again does not accord with Antiochus Epiphanes, regarding whom it is true that history records that he wished to suppress the worship practised by the Jews, but it knows nothing[1] of attempts made by him to destroy the gods and the worship of other nations. The words which follow, עַל־חֶמְדַּת נָשִׁים, the old interpreters understood of the love of women, or of conjugal love; the modern, after the example of J. D. Michaelis and Gesenius, on the contrary, understand them of the goddess Anaïtis or Mylitta, the Assyrian Venus, and refer them specially to the spoiling of the temple of this goddess in Elymaïs (1 Macc. vi. 1, cf. 2 Macc. i. 13). Ewald finally would understand by the expression "the desire of women," the Syrian deity Tammuz-Adonis. The connection requires us to think on a deity, because these words are placed between two expressions which refer to the gods. But the connection is not altogether decisive; rather the עַל כֹּל in the clause at the end of the verse denotes that the subject spoken of is not merely the king's raising himself above the gods, but also above other objects of pious veneration. A verbal proof that חֶמְדַּת נָשִׁים denotes the Anaïtis or Adonis as the favourite deity of women has not been adduced. For these words, *desiderium mulierum*, denote not that which women desire, but that which women possess which is desirable; cf. under 1 Sam. ix. 20. But it is impossible that this can be Anaïtis or Adonis, but it is a possession or precious treasure of women. This desirable possession of women is without doubt love; so that, as C. B. Michaelis has remarked, the expression is not materially different from אַהֲבַת נָשִׁים, *the love of women*, 2 Sam. i. 26. The thought: "he shall not regard the

[1] The statement in 1 Macc. i. 41 ff., "Moreover king Antiochus wrote to his whole kingdom that all should be one people, and every one should have his laws: so all the heathen agreed according to the commandment of the king," does not amount to a proof of this. "For," as Grimm rightly remarks, "the account of such a decree of Antiochus to *all* (not Hellenic) peoples of his kingdom is very doubtful. No profane historian records anything about it, neither does Josephus, nor the author of the second book of the Maccabees in the parallel passages. It is true that Antiochus, according to Livy, xli. 20, put great honour upon Jupiter by building a splendid temple to Tages, and according to Polybius, xxvi. 10, 11, he excelled all kings who preceded him in expensive sacrifices and gifts in honour of the gods; but this is no proof of a *proselytizing* fanaticism." The contrary rather appears from Josephus, *Antt.* xii. 5. 5, where the Samaritans, in a letter to Antiochus, declare, contrary to the opinion entertained regarding them by their governor, that by descent and custom they were not *Jews*. Their letter rests on the supposition that the royal decree was directed only against the Jews. Cf. Flathe, *Gesch. Macedoniens*, ii. p. 596. Diodorus also (xxxiv. 1), to whom Hitzig refers, only states that Antiochus wished to dissolve τὰ νόμιμα of the Jewish people, and to compel the Jews to abandon their manner of life (τὰς ἀγωγὰς μεταθέσθαι).

desire of women, or the love of women," agrees perfectly with the connection. After it has been said in the first clause: he shall set himself free from all religious reverence transmitted from his fathers, from all piety toward the gods in which he had been trained, it is then added in the second clause: not merely so, but generally from all piety toward men and God, from all the tender affections of the love of men and of God. The "love of women" is named as an example selected from the sphere of human piety, as that affection of human love and attachment for which even the most selfish and most savage of men feel some sensibility. Along with this he shall set himself free from כָּל־אֱלוֹהַּ, from all piety or reverence toward God or toward that which is divine (Klief.). This thought is then established by the last clause: "for he shall magnify himself above all." To עַל כֹּל we may not supply אֱלוֹהַּ; for this clause not only presents the reason for the foregoing clause, עַל כָּל־אֱלוֹהַּ וגו׳, but for both of the foregoing clauses. Hitzig and Kliefoth are right in their interpretation: "above everything, or all, gods and men," he shall magnify himself, raise himself up in arrogance.

Ver. 38. On the other hand, he will honour the god of fortresses. That מָעֻזִּים is not, with Theodotion, the Vulgate, Luther, and others, to be regarded as the proper name of a god, is now generally acknowledged. But as to which god is to be understood by the "god of fortresses," there is very great diversity of opinion. Grotius, C. B. Michaelis, Gesenius, and others think on Mars, the god of war, as the one intended; Hävernick, v. Lengerke, Maurer, and Ewald regard Jupiter Capitolinus, to whom Antiochus purposed to erect a temple in Antioch (Livy, xli. 20); others, Jupiter Olympius; while Hitzig, by changing מָעֻזִּים into מָעֹז יָם, *fortress of the sea*, thinks that Melkart, or the Phœnician Hercules, is referred to. But according to the following passage, this god was not known to his fathers. That could not be said either of Mars, or Jupiter, or Melkart. Add to this, "that if the statement here refers to the honouring of Hercules, or Mars, or Zeus, or Jupiter, then therewith all would be denied that was previously said of the king's being destitute of all religion" (Klief.). The words thus in no respect agree with Antiochus, and do not permit us to think on any definite heathen deity. עַל כַּנּוֹ does not signify *on his foundation, pedestal* (Häv., v. Leng., Maurer, Hitzig, Ewald), because the remark that he honoured God on his pedestal would be quite inappropriate, unless it had been also said that he had erected a statue to him. עַל כַּנּוֹ has here the same meaning as in vers. 20, 21, and 7: "in his place or stead" (Gesenius, de Wette, Kliefoth, and others). But the suffix is not, with Klief., to be referred to עַל כֹּל: in the place of all that, which he did not regard, but it refers to כָּל־אֱלוֹהַּ: in the place of every god; which is not overthrown by the objection that in that case the suffix should have been plur., because the suffix is connected with the singular אלוה. The "god of fortresses" is the personification of war, and the thought is this: he will regard no other god, but only war; the taking of fortresses he will make his god; and he will worship this god above all as the means of his gaining the world-power. Of this god, war as the object of deification, it might be said that his fathers knew nothing, because no other king had made war his religion, his god to whom he offered up in sacrifice all, gold, silver, precious stones, jewels.

Ver. 39. With the help of this god, who was unknown to his fathers, he will so proceed against the strong fortresses that he rewards with honour, might, and wealth those who acknowledge him. This is the meaning of the verse, which has been very differently rendered. The majority of modern interpreters separate the two parts of the verse from each other, for they refer the first hemistich to the preceding, and in the second they find a new thought expressed. Hävernick and v. Lengerke supply a demonstrative כֹּה, *thus:*—thus shall he do to the armed fortresses together with the strange gods, *i.e.* fill the fortified temples with treasures, and promote their worship. But the supplement כֹּה is here just as arbitrary as is the interpreting of the armed fortresses of temples. Hitzig misses the object to עָשָׂה, and seeks it by changing עִם into עַם: he prepares for the armed fortresses a people of a strange god; but apart from the fact that the change of the text is arbitrary, the use of the expression "people of a strange god" for colonists is most singular. Ewald translates the expression thus: "he proceeds with the strong fortresses as with the strange god," and explains: "he loves the fortresses only just as a god;" but he has given no proof that עָשָׂה לְ means to love. The missing object to וְעָשָׂה follows in the second hemistich, just as in Deut. xxxi. 4, Josh. viii. 2, Isa. x. 11. עָשָׂה means simply to do anything to one (Kran., Klief.). עִם אֱלוֹהַּ נֵכָר, *with the help of the strange god* (עִם of assistance, as in 1 Sam. xiv. 45), not: in the mind of the strange god (Kliefoth). מִבְצְרֵי מָעֻזִּים, *fortified, i.e. strong fortresses*, are not the fortified walls and houses, but the inhabitants of the fortified cities. With these he does according to his will with the help of his god, *i.e.* of war, namely in this, that he rewards with honour and power only those who acknowledge him. אֲשֶׁר הִכִּיר, *who acknowledges, sc.* him, the king who made war his god. Hitzig has incorrectly interpreted: whom he acknowledges. The *Keri* יַכִּיר for the *Kethiv* הִכִּיר is an unnecessary emendation here, as in Isa. xxviii. 15 with עָבַר. The verb הִכִּיר is chosen to reflect upon the word נֵכָר. It means to recognise, properly to acknowledge him as what he is or wishes to be; cf. Deut. xxi. 17. Such an one he shall increase with honour, confer upon him sovereignty over many, and divide the land. בִּמְחִיר is not for payment, for recompense, as the contrast to חִנָּם (*gratuitously*) (Kran.). That is not a suitable rendering here. The word rather means *pro præmio*, as a reward (Maur., Klief.), as a reward for the recognition accorded to him. The Vulgate renders it rightly according to the sense, *gratuito*. In this most modern interpreters find a reference to the circumstance that Antiochus occupied the Jewish fortresses with heathen garrisons, and rewarded his adherents with places of honour and with possessions of land (2 Macc. iv. 10, 24, v. 15). But this is what all conquerors do, and it was not peculiar to Antiochus, so that it could be mentioned as characteristic of him. The words contain the altogether common thought that the king will bestow honour, power, and possessions on those who acknowledge him and conduct themselves according to his will, and they accord with the character of Antichrist in a yet higher degree than with that of Antiochus.

Vers. 40–43. *The last undertakings of the hostile king, and his end.*

By the words בְּעֵת קֵץ, which introduce these verses, the following events are placed in the time of the end. Proceeding from the view that the whole of the second half of this chapter (vers. 21–45) treats of Antiochus and his undertakings, most modern interpreters find in the verses the prophecy of a last expedition of this Syrian king against Egypt, and quote in support of this view the words of Jerome: *Et hæc Porphyrius ad Antiochum refert, quod undecimo anno regni sui rursus contra sororis filium, Ptolem. Philometorem dimicaverit, qui audiens venire Antiochum congregaverit multa populorum millia, sed Antiochus quasi tempestas valida in curribus et in equitibus et in classe magna ingressus sit terras plurimas et transeundo universa vastaverit, veneritque ad Judæam et arcem munierit de ruinis murorum civitatis et sic perrexerit in Ægyptum.* But regarding this expedition not only are historians silent, but the supposition of such a thing stands in irreconcilable contradiction to the historical facts regarding the last undertakings of Antiochus. According to 1 Macc. iii. 27 ff., Antiochus, on receiving tidings of the successful insurrection of the Maccabees, and of the victory which Judas had won, since he found that money was wanting to him to carry on the war, resolved to return to Persia, "there to collect the tribute of the countries" (1 Macc. iii. 31); and after he had made Lysias governor, he delivered to him the one half of his army, that he might with it "destroy and root out the strength of Israel," and with the other half departed from Antioch and crossed the Euphrates into the high countries, *i.e.* the high-lying countries on the farther side of the Euphrates (1 Macc. iii. 33–37). There he heard of the great treasures of a rich city in Persia, and resolved to fall upon this city and to take its treasures; but as the inhabitants received notice of the king's intention, he was driven back and compelled to return to Babylon, having accomplished nothing. On his return he heard in Persia the tidings of the overthrow of Lysias in a battle with the Maccabees, and of the re-erection of the altar of Jehovah at Jerusalem; whereupon he was so overcome with terror and dismay, that he fell sick and died (1 Macc. vi. 1–16). The historical truth of this report is confirmed by Polybius, who mentions (*Fragm.* xxxi. 11) that Antiochus, being in difficulty for want of money, sought to spoil the temple of Artemis in Elymaïs, and in consequence of the failure of his design he fell ill at Tabae in Persia, and there died. By these well-established facts the supposition of an invasion of Egypt by Antiochus in the eleventh, *i.e.* the last year of his reign, is excluded. The Romans also, after they had already by their intervention frustrated his design against Egypt, would certainly have prevented a new war, least of all would they have permitted an entire subjugation of Egypt and the south, which we must accept after vers. 42 and 43. Besides, the statement made by Porphyry shows itself to be destitute of historical validity by this, that according to it, Antiochus must have made the assault against Egypt, while on the contrary, according to the prophecy, ver. 40, the king of the south begins the war against the king of the north, and the latter, in consequence of this attack, passes through the lands with a powerful host and subdues Egypt.

For these reasons, therefore, v. Lengerke, Maurer, and Hitzig have abandoned the statement of Porphyry as unhistorical, and limited themselves to the supposition that the section (vers. 40–45) is only a comprehensive repetition of that which has already been said regarding Antiochus Epiphanes, according to which "the time of the end" (ver. 40) denotes not the near time of the death of Antiochus, but generally the whole period of this king. But this is, when compared with vers. 27 and 35, impossible. If thus, according to ver. 35, the tribulation with which the people of God shall be visited by the hostile king for their purification shall last till the time of the end, then the time of the end to which the prophecies of vers. 40–45 fall cannot designate the whole duration of the conduct of this enemy, but only the end of his reign and of his persecutions, in which he perishes (ver. 40). On the contrary, the reference to ch. viii. 17 avails nothing, because there also עֵת קֵץ has the same meaning as here, *i.e.* it denotes the termination of the epoch referred to, and is there only made a more general expression by means of לְעֵת than here, where by בְּעֵת and the connection with ver. 35 the end is more sharply defined. To this is to be added, that the contents of vers. 40–45 are irreconcilable with the supposition that in them is repeated in a comprehensive form what has already been said of Antiochus, for here something new is announced, something of which nothing has been said before. This even Maurer and Hitzig have not been able to deny, but have sought to conceal as much as possible,—Maurer by the remark: *res a scriptore iterum ac sæpius pertractatas esse, extremam vero manum operi defuisse;* and Hitzig by various turnings—"as it seems," "but is not more precisely acknowledged," "the fact is not elsewhere communicated"—which are obviously mere make-shifts.

Thus vers. 40-45 do not apply to Antiochus Epiphanes, but, with most ancient interpreters, they refer only to the final enemy of the people of God, the Antichrist. This reference has been rightly vindicated by Kliefoth. We cannot, however, agree with him in distinguishing this enemy in ver. 40 from the king of the south and of the north, and in understanding this verse as denoting "that at the time of this hostile king, which shall be the time of the end, the kings of the south as well as of the north shall attack him, but that he shall penetrate into their lands and overthrow them." Without taking into account the connection, this interpretation is not merely possible, but it is even very natural to refer the suffix in עָלָיו and in עִמּוֹ to one and the same person, namely, to the king who has hitherto been spoken of, and who continues in vers. 40–45 to be the chief subject. But the connection makes this reference impossible. It is true, indeed, that the suffix in עִמּוֹ refers without doubt to this king, but the suffix in עָלָיו can be referred only to the king of the south named immediately before, who pushes at him, because the king against whom the king of the south pushes, and of whom mention is made vers. 21–39, is not only distinctly designated as the king of the north (vers. 13–21), but also, according to vers. 40–43, he advances from the north against the Holy Land and against Egypt; thus also, according to vers. 40*b*–43, must be identical with the king of the north. In vers. 40–43 we do not read of a war of the hostile king against the king of the south *and* the king of the north. The words in which Kliefoth finds indications of this kind are otherwise to be understood.

Ver. 40. If we now more closely look into particulars, we find that עֵת קֵץ is not the end of the hostile king, but, as in vers. 27 and 35, the end of the present world-period, in which also, it is true, occurs the end of this king (קִצּוֹ, ver. 45). For the figurative expression יִתְנַגַּח (*shall push*), cf. ch. viii. 4. In the word there lies the idea that the king of the south commences the war, makes an aggression against the hostile king. In the second clause the subject is more precisely defined by "the king of the north" for the sake of distinctness, or to avoid ambiguity, from which it thence follows that the suffix in עָלָיו refers to the king of the south. If the subject were not named, then "the king of the south" might have been taken for it in this clause. The words, "with chariots, and with horsemen, and with many ships," are an oratorical exemplification of the powerful war-host which the king of the north displayed; for the further statement, "he presses into the countries, overflows and passes over" (שָׁטַף וְעָבָר as ver. 10), does not agree with the idea of a fleet, but refers to land forces. The plur. בַּאֲרָצוֹת (*into the countries*) does not at all agree with the expedition of a *Syrian* king against Egypt, since between Syria and Egypt there lay *one* land, Palestine; but it also does not prove that "the south-land and the north-land, the lands of the kings of the south and of the north, are meant" (Klief.), but it is to be explained from this, that the north, from which the angry king comes in his fury against the king of the south, reached far beyond Syria. The king of the north is thought of as the ruler of the distant north.

Ver. 41. Penetrating into the countries and overflowing them with his host, he comes into the glorious land, *i.e.* Palestine, the land of the people of God. See at ver. 16 and ch. viii. 9. "And many shall be overthrown." רַבּוֹת is not neuter, but refers to אֲרָצוֹת, ver. 40. For "that the whole lands are meant, represented by their inhabitants (cf. the verb masc. יִכָּשֵׁלוּ [*shall be overthrown*]), proceeds from the exceptions of which the second half of the verse makes mention" (Kran.). The three peoples, Edomites, Moabites, and Ammonites, are represented as altogether spared, because, as Jerome has remarked, they lay in the interior, out of the way of the line of march of Antiochus to Egypt (v. Leng., Hitzig, and others). This opinion Hitzig with justice speaks of as altogether superficial, since Antiochus would not have omitted to make war against them, as *e.g.* his father overcame the Ammonites in war (Polyb. v. 71), if they had not given indubitable proofs of their submission to him. Besides, it is a historical fact that the Edomites and Ammonites supported Antiochus in his operations against the Jews (1 Macc. v. 3–8, iv. 61); therefore Maurer remarks, under יִמָּלְטוּ (*they shall escape*): *eorum enim in oppremendis Judæis Antiochus usus est auxilio.* But since the king here spoken of is not Antiochus, this historizing interpretation falls of itself to the ground. There is further with justice objected against it, that at the time of Antiochus the nation of Moab no longer existed. After the Exile the Moabites no longer appear as a nation. They are only named (Neh. xiii. 1 and Ezra ix. 1), in a passage cited from the Pentateuch, along with the Philistines and the Hittites, to characterize the relations of the present after the relations of the time of Moses. Edom, Moab, and Ammon, related with Israel by descent, are the old hereditary and chief enemies of this people, who have become by name representatives of all the hereditary and chief enemies of the people of God. These enemies escape the overthrow when the other nations sink under the power of the Antichrist. רֵאשִׁית בְּנֵי עַמּוֹן, "the firstling of the sons of Ammon," *i.e.* that which was most valued or distinguished of the Ammonites as a first-fruit, by which Kranichfeld understands the chief city of the Ammonites. More simply others understand by the expression, "the flower of the people, the very kernel of the nation;" cf. Num. xxiv. 20, Amos vi. 1, Jer. xlix. 35. The expression is so far altogether suitable as in the flower of the people the character of the nation shows itself, the enmity against the people of God is most distinctly revealed; but in this enmity lies the reason for this people's being spared by the enemy of God.

Ver. 42. The stretching forth of his hand upon the countries is a sign expressive of his seizing them, taking possession of them, for which he falls upon them. בַּאֲרָצוֹת are not other countries besides those which, according to ver. 40, he overflowed (Klief.), but the same. Of these lands Egypt is specially noticed in ver. 42 as the most powerful, which had hitherto successfully withstood the assaults of the king of the north, but which in the time of the end shall also be overthrown. Egypt, as the chief power of the south, represents the mightiest kingdoms of the earth. לֹא תִהְיֶה לִפְלֵיטָה (*and there shall not be for an escape*), expressive of complete overthrow, cf. Joel ii. 3, Jer. l. 29.

Ver. 43. Along with the countries all their treasures fall into the possession of the conqueror, and also all the allies of the fallen kingdom shall be compelled to submit to him. The genitive מִצְרַיִם belongs not merely to חֲמֻדוֹת (*precious things*), but to all the before-named objects. בְּמִצְעָדָיו (*at his steps*) = בְּרַגְלָיו, Judg. iv. 10, denotes the camp-followers, but not as mercenary soldiers (v. Leng., Hitz.). The *Lybians* and *Cushites* represent all the allies of the Egyptians (cf. Ezek. xxx. 5, Nah. iii. 9), the most southern nations of the earth.

Vers. 44, 45. *The end of the hostile king.*

As has been already seen, the expressions in vers. 40–43 regarding this king do not agree with Antiochus Epiphanes, so also the statements regarding his end are in contradiction to the historical facts regarding the end of the Syrian king. When the hostile king took possession of Egypt and its treasures, and made the Lybians and Cushites subject to him, tidings from the east and the north overwhelm him with terror. The *masc.* יְבַהֲלֻהוּ stands *ad sensum* related to the persons who occasion the reports. The reports excited his anger, so that he goes forth to destroy many. We have to think thus on the reports of revolt and insurrections in the east and the north of his kingdom, which came to his ears in Egypt. On this ground Hitzig, with other interpreters, refuses to refer the statement in ver. 44 to the expedition of Antiochus against the Parthians and Armenians (Tacit. *hist.* v. 8, and App. *Syr.* c. 45, 46; 1 Macc. iii. 37), because Antiochus did not undertake this expedition from Egypt; and rather, in regard to the east, thinks on the tidings from Jerusalem of the rebellion of Judea (2 Macc. v. 11 ff.; 1 Macc. i. 24), and in regard to the north, on the very problematical expedition against the Aradiæi, without observing, however, that no Scripture writer designates Jerusalem as lying in the east of Egypt. But besides, Antiochus, since he was occupied for some years beyond the Euphrates, and there met with his death, could not shortly before his end lead an expedition out of Egypt against Aradus. What Porphyry says[1] (in Jerome under ver. 44) regarding an expedition of Antiochus undertaken from Egypt and Lybia against the Aradiæi and the Armenian king Artaxias, he has gathered only from this verse and from notices regarding the wars of Antiochus against the Aradiæi and king Artaxias (after whose imprisonment, according to App. *Syr.* c. 46, he died), without having any historical evidence for it. But even though the statement of Porphyry were better established, yet it would not agree with ver. 45; for when the king goes forth, in consequence of the report brought to him, to destroy many, he plants, according to ver. 45, his palace-tent near to the holy mount, and here comes to his end; thus meeting with his destruction in the Holy Land not far from Jerusalem, while Antiochus, according to Polybius and Porphyry, died in the Persian city of Tabae on his return from Persia to Babylon.

Ver. 45. נָטַע of planting a tent, only here instead of the usual word נָטָה, to spread out, to set up, probably with reference to the great palace-like tent of the oriental ruler, whose poles must be struck very deep into the earth. Cf. the description of the tent of Alexander the Great, which was erected after the oriental type, in Polyæn. *Strateg.* iv. 3. 24, and of the tent of Nadir-Schah in Rosenmüller, *A. u. N. Morgl.* iv. p. 364 f. These tents were surrounded by a multitude of smaller tents for the guards and servants, a circumstance which explains the use of the plur. אָהֳלֵי is incorrectly taken by Theodotion, Porphyry, Jerome, and others for a *nomen propr.*, meaning in Syriac, palace or tower. בֵּין לְהַר = בֵּין וּבֵין, Gen. i. 6, Joel ii. 17, of a space between two other places or objects. הַר צְבִי־קֹדֶשׁ, the holy hill of the delight, *i.e.* of Palestine (cf. ch. viii. 9), is without doubt the mountain on which stood the temple of Jerusalem, as v. Leng., Maur., Hitzig, and Ewald acknowledge. The interpretation of the mountain of the temple of Anaïtis in Elymaïs (Dereser, Hävernick) needs no refutation. According to this, יַמִּים cannot designate the Mediterranean and the Dead Sea, as Kliefoth supposes, but it is only the poetic

[1] The words are: *Pugnans contra Ægyptios et Lybias, Æthiopiasque pertransiens, audiet sibi ab aquilone et oriente prælia concitari, unde et regrediens capit Aradios resistentes et omnem in littore Phœnicis vastavit provinciam; confestimque pergit ad Artaxiam regem Armeniæ, qui de orientis partibus movebatur.*

plur. of fulness, as a sign of the great Mediterranean Sea. Since now this scene where the great enemy of the people of God comes to his end, *i.e.* perishes, in no respect agrees with the place where Antiochus died, then according to Hitzig the pseudo-Daniel does not here accurately distinguish the separate expeditions from one another, and must have omitted between the first and the second half of the verse the interval between the return of Antiochus from Egypt and his death, because Antiochus never again trod the soil of Palestine. Such expedients condemn themselves. With "he shall come to his end," cf. ch. viii. 25, where the end of this enemy of God is described as a being "broken without the hand of man." Here the expression "and none shall help him" is added to designate the hopelessness of his overthrow.

The placing of the overthrow of this enemy with his host near the temple-mountain agrees with the other prophecies of the O. T., which place the decisive destruction of the hostile world-power by the appearance of the Lord for the consummation of His kingdom upon the mountains of Israel (Ezek. xxxix. 4), or in the valley of Jehoshaphat at Jerusalem, or at Jerusalem (Joel iv. 2 [iii. 2], 12 f.; Zech. xiv. 2), and confirms the result of our exposition, that the hostile king, the last enemy of the world-power, is the Antichrist. With this also the conclusion, ch. xii. 1–3, is in harmony.

Ch. xii. 1–3. *The final deliverance of Israel from the last tribulation, and their consummation.*

Ver. 1. וּבָעֵת הַהִיא points back to בְּעֵת קֵץ (ch. xi. 40). At the time of the end, in which the hostile persecutor rises up to subdue the whole world, and sets up his camp in the Holy Land to destroy many in great anger and to strike them with the ban (הַחֲרִים, ch. xi. 44), *i.e.* totally to outroot them (ch. xi. 40–45), the great angel-prince Michael shall come forth and fight for the people of God against their oppressor. Regarding Michael, see under ch. x. 13, p. 417. "Who stands over the sons of thy people," *i.e.* stands near, protecting them (cf. for עָמַד עַל in the sense of coming to protect, Esth. viii. 11, ix. 16), describes Michael, who carries on his work as Israel's שַׂר (ch. x. 21). That Michael, fighting for Daniel's people, goes forth against the hostile king (ch. xi. 45), is, it is true, not said *expressis verbis*, but it lies in the context, especially in the יִמָּלֵט עַמְּךָ (*thy people shall be delivered*) of the second half of the verse, as well as in the expressions regarding Michael, ch. x. 13 and 21.

But the people of God need such powerful help for their

deliverance, because that time shall be one of oppression without any parallel. The description of this oppression seems to be based on Jer. xxx. 7 (C. B. Michaelis, Hengstenberg); but that which is there said is here heightened by the relative clause (cf. Joel ii. 2), which enlarges the thought, Ex. ix. 18, 24. This עֵת צָרָה (*time of distress*) is the climax of the oppression which the hostile king shall bring upon Israel, and occurs at the same time as the expiry of the last (the seventieth) week, ch. ix. 26. "The salvation of Israel (יִמָּלֵט), which is here thought of as brought about under the direction of Michael, coincides essentially with the description, ch. vii. 18, 26 f., 14, ix. 24." Thus Kranichfeld rightly remarks. He also rightly identifies the continued victorious deliverance of Israel from the oppression (ver. 1) with the setting up of the Messianic kingdom, described in ch. vii. 2, 9, and finds in this verse (ch. xii. 1) the Messianic kingdom dissolving the world-kingdoms.

With this the opposers of the genuineness of the book of Daniel also agree, and deduce therefrom the conclusion, that the pseudc-Daniel expected, along with the overthrow of Antiochus Epiphanes, the appearance of the Messianic kingdom of glory. This conclusion would be indisputable if the premises from which it is drawn, that בָּעֵת הַהִיא (*at that time*) is the time of Antiochus, were well founded. All attempts of believing interpreters, who, with Porphyry, Grotius, Bleek, v. Lengerke, Hitzig, and others, find the death of Antiochus prophesied in ch. xi. 45, to dismiss this conclusion, appear on close inspection to be untenable. According to Hävernick, with וּבָעֵת הַהִיא (*and at that time*) a new period following that going before is introduced, and that בָּעֵת הַהִיא means *at some future time.* The appearance of Michael for his people denotes the appearance of the Messiah; and the sufferings and oppressions connected with his appearance denote the sufferings which the people of Israel shall endure at the destruction of Jerusalem by the Romans, but which shall be most fully realized only at the second coming of the Lord, Matt. xxiv. 21, 22. But this explanation is shattered against the בָּעֵת הַהִיא, which never has the meaning "at some time," *i.e.* in the further future, and is refuted by the following remark of Hitzig:—"Not once," says he, with good ground, "can the words בַּיּוֹם הַהוּא be proved by such passages as 2 Kings iii. 6, Isa. xxviii. 5, Gen. xxxix. 11, to have the meaning of *at that day*; in בעת ההיא we may not by any means seek such a meaning, and the copula here puts a complete barrier in the way of such arbitrariness. Moreover, if the epoch of Antiochus

Epiphanes was indeed a time of oppression, how could a reader then not refer this ההיא to the time of that king described in the foregoing chapter?" Finally, מַשְׂכִּילִים (*intelligentes*), ver. 3, refers back to the מַשְׂכִּילֵי עָם who helped many to knowledge, and who lost their lives in the persecution (ch. xi. 33, 34), and now are raised to eternal life.[1]

Hävernick, however, was right, in opposing those who refer ver. 1 to the period of persecution under Antiochus, in arguing that the statement of the unheard-of greatness of the affliction is far too strong for such a period, and at the same time that the promise of the deliverance of those that shall be found written in the book does not accord with that Syrian oppression, although he is in error when he interprets the appearance of Michael of the first appearance of Christ. This interpretation receives no support either from ch. ix. 26 or from Matt. xxiv. 21, 22, because both passages treat of the coming of Christ in glory. But if the reference of this verse to the appearance of Christ in the flesh is inconsistent with the words, still more so is its reference to the period of Antiochus. Those interpreters who advance this view are under the necessity of violently separating ver. 1 from vers. 2 and 3, which undoubtedly treat of the resurrection from the dead.

According to Auberlen, who has rightly conceived that the מַשְׂכִּילִים, ch. xii. 3, allude to the מַשְׂכִּילִים, ch. xi. 33 and 34, the מַצְדִּיקֵי הָרַבִּים to the יָבִינוּ לָרַבִּים, ch. xi. 33, vers. 2 and 3 do not intimate any progress in the development of the history, but by mentioning the resurrection only, are referred to the eternal retribution which awaits the Israelites according to their conduct during the time of great persecution under Antiochus, because, as C. B. Michaelis has said, *ejus* (*i.e.* of the resurrection) *consideratio magnam vim habet ad confirmandum animum sub tribulationibus.* As to the period between the time of trial and the resurrection, nothing whatever is said; for in vers. 2 and 3 every designation of time is wanting, while in ver. 1 the expression "at this time" twice occurs. Thus Hengstenberg (*Christol.* iii. 1, p. 6) has remarked, "Whether there be a longer or a shorter time between the tribulation of the Maccabean era and the resurrection, the consolation from the fact of the resurrection remains equally powerful. Therefore it is so connected with the deliverance from the persecution

[1] These arguments extend also to the overthrow of Ebrard's view, that the expression "to this time" refers to the time after Antiochus Epiphanes shall have died.

as if the one immediately followed the other." But with this it is conceded that the resurrection from the dead is so associated with the deliverance of Israel from the tyranny of Antiochus as if it came immediately after it, as the opponents of the genuineness of the book affirm. But this interpretation is obviously a mere make-shift.

Vers. 2, 3. These verses do not at all present the form of a parenetic reference to the retribution commencing with the resurrection. Ver. 2 is by the copula ו connected with ver. 1, and thereby designates the continuance of the thought of the second half of ver. 1, *i.e.* the further representation of the deliverance of God's people, namely, of all those who are written in the book of life. Since many of the מַשְׂכִּילִים who know their God (ch. xi. 33) lose their life in the persecution, so in the promise of deliverance a disclosure of the lot awaiting those who sealed with their blood their fidelity to God was not to be avoided, if the prophecy shall wholly gain its end, *i.e.* if the promise of the deliverance of all the pious shall afford to the people of God in the times of oppression strength and joy in their enduring fidelity to God. The appeal to the fact that vers. 2 and 3 contain no designation of time proves nothing at all, for this simple reason, that the verses connected by "and" are by this copula placed under ver. 1, which contains a designation of time, and only further show how this deliverance shall ensue, namely thus, that a part of the people shall outlive the tribulation, but those who lose their lives in the persecution shall rise again from the dead.

To this is to be added that the contents of ver. 1 do not agree with the period of persecution under Antiochus. That which is said regarding the greatness of the persecution is much too strong for it. The words, "There shall be a time of trouble such as never was מִהְיוֹת גּוֹי, since there was a nation or nations," designate it as such as never was before on the earth. Theodoret interprets thus: *οἵα οὐ γέγονεν, ἀφ' οὗ γεγένηται ἔθνος ἐπὶ τῆς γῆς ἕως τοῦ καιροῦ ἐκείνου.* With reference to these words our Lord says: *οἵα οὐ γέγονεν ἀπ' ἀρχῆς κόσμου ἕως τοῦ νῦν, οὐδ' οὐ μὴ γένηται,* Matt. xxiv. 21. Though the oppression which Antiochus brought upon Israel may have been most severe, yet it could not be said of it without exaggeration, that it was such a tribulation as never had been from the beginning of the world. Antiochus, it is true, sought to outroot Judaism root and branch, but Pharaoh also wished to do the same by his command to destroy all the Hebrew male children at their birth; and as Antiochus wished to make the worship of the Grecian Zeus, so also Jezebel the worship of the Phœnician Hercules, in the place of the worship of Jehovah, the national religion in Israel.

Still less does the second hemistich of ver. 1 refer to the deliverance of the people from the power of Antiochus. Under the words, "every one that shall be found written in the book," Hitzig remarks that they point back to Isa. iv. 3, and that the book is thus the book of life, and corrects the vain interpretation of v. Lengerke, that "to be written in the book" means *in an earthly sense* to live, to be appointed to life, by the more accurate explanation, "The book of life is thus the record of those who shall live, it is the list of the citizens of the Messianic kingdom (Phil. iv. 3), and in Isaiah contains the names of those who reach it living, in Daniel also of those who must first be raised from the dead for it." Cf. regarding the book of life, under Ex. xxxii. 32.

Accordingly בָּעֵת הַהִיא extends into the Messianic time. This is so far acknowledged by Hofmann (*Weiss. u. Erf.* i. p. 313, and *Schriftbew.* ii. 2, p. 697), in that he finds in ver. 1, from "and there shall be a time," and in vers. 2 and 3, the prophecy of the final close of the history of nations, the time of the great tribulation at the termination of the present course of the world, the complete salvation of Israel in it, and the resurrection of the dead at the end of the world. Since, however, Hofmann likewise refers the last verses of the preceding chapter to the time of Antiochus and his destruction, and can only refer the וּבָעֵת הַהִיא at the beginning of ch. xii., from its close connection with the last words of ch. xi., to the time which has hitherto been spoken of, so he supposes that in the first clause of the first verse of this chapter (xii.) there cannot be a passing over to another time, but that this transition is first made by וְהָיְתָה. This transition he seeks indeed, in the 2d ed. of his *Schriftbew. l.c.*, to cover by the remark: that we may not explain the words of the angel, וְהָיְתָה עֵת וגו', as if they meant: that time shall be a time of trouble such as has not been till now; but much rather that they are to be translated: "and there shall *arise* a time of trouble such as never was to that time." But this separation of the words in question from those going before by the translation of וְהָיְתָה "and there shall arise," is rendered impossible by the words following, עַד הָעֵת הַהִיא; for these so distinctly point back to the words with which the verse commences, that we may not empty them of their definite contents by the ambiguous "till that time." If the angel says, There shall arise a time of oppression such as has never been since there were nations till that time when Michael shall appear for his people, or, as Hofmann translates it, shall "hold fast his place," then to every unprejudiced reader it is clear that this tribulation such as has never been before shall arise not for the first time centuries after the appearance of Michael or of his "holding fast his place," but in the time of the war of the angel-prince for the people of God. In this same time the angel further places the salvation of the people of Daniel and the resurrection of the dead.[1]

The failure of all attempts to gain a space of time between ch. xi. 45 and xii. 1 or 2 incontrovertibly shows that the assertions of those who dispute the genuineness of the book, that the pseudo-Daniel expected along with the death of Antiochus the commencement of the Messianic kingdom and of the resurrection of the dead, would have a foundation *if* the last verses of ch. xi. treated of the last undertakings of this Syrian king against the theocracy. This *if*, it has, however, been seen from ch. xi., is not established. In ch. xi. 40–45 the statements do not refer to Antiochus, but to the time of the end, of the last enemy of the holy God, and of his destruction. With that is connected, without any intervening space, in ch. xii. 1 the description of the last oppression of the people of God and their salvation to everlasting life. The prophecy of that unheard-of great tribulation Christ has in Matt. xxiv. 21 referred, wholly in the sense of the prophetic announcement, to the yet future θλῖψις μεγάλη which shall precede the coming of the Son of man in the clouds of heaven to judge the world and to bring to a consummation the kingdom of God. That this tribulation shall come only upon Israel, the people of God, is not said; the מִהְיוֹת גּוֹי refers much more to a tribulation that shall come upon the whole

[1] Hofmann's explanation of the words would only be valid if the definition of time אַחֲרֵי הָעֵת הַהִיא stood after וְהָיְתָה in the text, which Hofm. in his most recent attempts at its exposition has interpolated inadvertently, while in his earlier exposition (*Weiss. u. Erf.* i. p. 314) he has openly said: "These last things connect themselves with the prospect of the end of that oppressor of Israel, not otherwise than as when Isaiah spoke of the approaching assault of the Assyrians on Jerusalem as of the last affliction of the city, or as in Jeremiah the end of those seventy years is also the end of all the sufferings of his people. There remains therefore a *want of clearness* in this prospect," etc. This want of clearness he has, in his most recent exposition in the *Schriftbew.*, not set aside, but increased, by the supposition of an immediate transition from the time of Antiochus to the time of the end.

of humanity. In it shall the angel-prince Michael help the people of Daniel, *i.e.* the people of God. That he shall destroy the hostile king, the Antichrist, is not said. His influence extends only to the assistance which he shall render to the people of God for their salvation, so that all who are written in the book of life shall be saved. Christ, in His eschatological discourse, Matt. xxiv., does not make mention of this assistance, but only says that for the elect's sake the days of the oppression shall be shortened, otherwise that no one would be saved (ἐσώθη, Matt. xxiv. 22). Wherein the help of Michael consists, is seen partly from that which is said in ch. x. 13 and 21 regarding him, that he helped the Angel of the Lord in the war against the hostile spirit of the Persian and the Javanic world-kingdom, partly from the war of Michael against the dragon described in Rev. xii. 7 ff. From these indications it is clear that we may not limit the help on the part of Michael to the help which he renders to the saints of God in the last war and struggle, but that he stands by them in all wars against the world-power and its princes, and helps them to victory.

But the salvation which the people of God shall experience in the time of the unparalleled great oppression is essentially different from the help which was imparted to the people of Israel in the time of the Maccabees. This is called "a little help," ch. xi. 34. So also is the oppression of Israel in the time of the Maccabees different from the oppression in the end of the time, as to its object and consequences. The former oppression shall, according to ch. xi. 33–35, serve to purify the people and to make them white to the time of the end; the oppression at the time of the end, on the contrary, according to ch. xii. 1-3, shall effect the salvation (הִמָּלֵט) of the people, *i.e.* prepare the people for the everlasting life, and bring about the separation of the righteous from the wicked for eternity. These clearly stated distinctions confirm the result already reached, that ch. xii. 1–3 do not treat of the time of Antiochus and the Maccabees.

The promised salvation of the people (יִמָּלֵט) is more particularly defined by the addition to עַמְּךָ: "every one who shall be found written in the book," *sc.* of life (see above, p. 478); thus every one whom God has ordained to life, all the genuine members of the people of God. נִמְלַט, shall be saved, *sc.* out of the tribulation, so that they do not perish therein. But since, according to ch. xi. 33 ff., in the oppression, which passes over the people of God for their purification, many shall lose their lives, and this also shall be the case in the last and severest oppression, the angel gives to the prophet, in ver. 2, disclosures also regarding the dead, namely, that they shall awaken out of the sleep of death. By the connection of this verse with the preceding by ו, without any further designation of time, the resurrection of the dead is placed as synchronous with the deliverance of the people. " For that the two clauses, 'thy people shall be delivered' (ver. 1), and 'many shall awake,' not only reciprocally complete each other, but also denote contemporaneous facts, we only deny by first denying that the former declares the final salvation of Israel" (Hofm. *Schriftbew.* ii. 2, p. 598). יָשֵׁן, *sleeping*, is here used, as in Job iii. 13, Jer. li. 39, of death; cf. καθεύδειν, Matt. ix. 24, 1 Thess. v. 10, and κοιμᾶσθαι, 1 Thess. iv. 14. אַדְמַת־עָפָר, occurring only here, formed after Gen. iii. 19, means not *the dust of the earth*, but *dusty earth*, *terra pulveris*, denoting the grave, as עָפָר, Ps. xxii. 30.

It appears surprising that רַבִּים, *many*, shall awake, since according to the sequel, where the rising of some to life and of some to shame is spoken of, much rather the word *all* might have been expected. This difficulty is not removed by the remark that *many* stands for *all*, because רַבִּים does not mean *all*. Concerning the opinion that *many* stands for *all*, Hofmann remarks, that the expression "sleeping in the dust of earth" is not connected with the word *many* (רַבִּים), but with the verb "shall awake" (יָקִיצוּ): "of them there shall be many, of whom those who sleep in the earth shall arise" (Hofm.). So also C. B. Michaelis interprets the words by reference to the Masoretic accentuation, which has separated רַבִּים from מִיְּשֵׁנֵי (*sleeping*), only that he takes מִן in the sense of stating the *terminus mutationis a quo*. But by this very artificial interpretation nothing at all is gained; for the thought still remains the same, that of those who sleep in the dust *many* (not *all*) awake. The partitive interpretation of מִן is the only simple and natural one, and therefore with most interpreters we prefer it. The רַבִּים can only be rightly interpreted from the context. The angel has it not in view to give a general statement regarding the resurrection of the dead, but only disclosures on this point, that the final salvation of the people shall not be limited to those still living at the end of the great tribulation, but shall include also those who have lost their lives during the period of the tribulation.

In ch. xi. 33, 35, the angel had already said, that of "those that understand" many shall fall by the sword and by flame, etc. When the tribulation at the time of the end increases to an unparalleled extent (ch. xii. 1), a yet greater number shall perish, so that when salvation comes, only a remnant of the people shall be then in life. To this surviving remnant of the people salvation is promised; but the promise is limited yet further by the addition: "every one that is found written in the book;" not all that are then living, but only those whose names are recorded in the book of life shall be partakers of the deliverance, *i.e.* of the Messianic salvation. But many (רַבִּים) of those that sleep, who died in the time of tribulation, shall awake out of sleep, some to everlasting life, and some to everlasting shame. As with the living, so also with the dead, not all attain to salvation. Also among those that arise there shall be a distinction, in which the reward of the faithful and of the unfaithful shall be made known. The word "many" is accordingly used only with reference to the small number of those who shall then be living, and not with reference either to the universality of the resurrection of the dead or to a portion only of the dead, but merely to add to the multitude of the dead, who shall then have part with the living, the small number of those who shall experience in the flesh the conclusion of the matter.

If we consider this course of thought, then we shall find it necessary neither to obtrude upon רַבִּים the meaning of *all*,—a meaning which it has not and cannot have, for the universality of the resurrection is removed by the particle מִן, which makes it impossible that רַבִּים = הָרַבִּים, οἱ πολλοί = πάντες (cf. Rom. v. 15 with ver. 12),—nor shall we need to adopt the conclusion that here a partial resurrection is taught, in contradiction to the doctrine of the N. T., and particularly of Christ, who has quoted this passage in John v. 24, using for the רַבִּים the word πάντες; for this conclusion can only be drawn from the misapprehension of the course of thought here presented, that this verse contains a general statement of the doctrine of the resurrection of the dead, an idea which is foreign to the connection.

From the correct interpretation of the course of thought arises the correct answer to the controverted question, whether here we are taught concerning the resurrection of the people of Israel, or concerning the resurrection of mankind generally. Neither the one nor the other of these things is *taught* here. The prophetic words treat of the people of Daniel, by which we are to understand the people of Israel. But the Israel of the time of the end consists not merely of Jews or of Jewish Christians, but embraces all peoples who belong to God's kingdom of the New Covenant founded by Christ. In this respect the resurrection of all is here *implicite* intimated, and Christ has explicitly set forth the thoughts lying *implicite* in this verse; for in John v. 28 f. He teaches the awakening from sleep of all the dead, and speaks, with unmistakeable reference to this passage before us, of an ἀνάστασις ζωῆς and an ἀνάστασις κρίσεως. For in the O. T. our verse is the only passage in which, along with the resurrection to everlasting life, there is mention also made of the resurrection to everlasting shame, or the resurrection of the righteous and of the wicked. The conception of חַיֵּי עוֹלָם, *ζωὴ αἰώνιος*, meets us here for the first time in the O. T. חַיִּים denotes, it is true, frequently the true life with God, the blessed life in communion with God, which exists after this life; but the addition עוֹלָם does not generally occur, and is here introduced to denote, as corresponding to the eternal duration of the Messianic kingdom (ch. ii. 44, vii. 14, 27, cf. ch. ix. 24), the life of the righteous in this kingdom as imperishable. לַחֲרָפוֹת לְדִרְאוֹן עוֹלָם forms the contrast to לְחַיֵּי עוֹלָם; for first חֲרָפוֹת, *shame* (a plur. of intensive fulness), is placed over against the חַיֵּי, then this shame is designated in reference to Isa. lxvi. 24 as דִּרָאוֹן, *contempt*, an object of aversion.

Ver. 3. Then shall they who in the times of tribulation have led many to the knowledge of salvation receive the glorious reward of their faithfulness. With this thought the angel closes the announcement of the future. הַמַּשְׂכִּלִים refers back to ch. xi. 33–35, and is here, as there, not limited to the teachers, but denotes the intelligent who, by instructing their contemporaries by means of word and deed, have awakened them to stedfastness and fidelity to their confession in the times of tribulation and have strengthened their faith, and some of whom have in war sealed their testimony with their blood. These shall shine in eternal life with heavenly splendour. The splendour of the vault of heaven (cf. Ex. xxiv. 10) is a figure of the glory which Christ designates as a light like the sun ("The righteous shall shine forth as the sun," Matt. xiii. 43, referring to the passage before us). Cf. for this figure also Rev. ii. 28 and 1 Cor. xv. 40 ff. By the expression מַצְדִּיקֵי הָרַבִּים Kranichfeld would understand such as take away the sins of the people in the offering up of sacrifice, *i.e.* the priests who attend to the offering of the sacrifices, because the expression is borrowed from Isa. liii. 11, "where it is predicated of the Messianic priest κατ' ἐξοχὴν, in the fullest sense of the word, what is said here of the common priests." But this interpretation is not satisfactory.

In Isa. liii. 11 the Servant of Jehovah justifies many, not by the sacrifice, but by His righteousness, by this, that He, as צַדִּיק who has done no sin, takes upon Himself the sins of the people and gives His soul an offering for sin. הַצְדִּיק is neither in the law of sacrifices nor anywhere in the O. T. named as the effect of the sacrifice, but always only שְׂאֵת עָוֹן (נָשָׂא) (*to take up, take away iniquity*) and כִּפֵּר, and in the expiatory sacrifices with the constant addition וְנִסְלַח לוֹ; cf. Lev. iv. 26, 31, 35, v. 10, 16, Ps. xxxii. 1 ff.

Nor is the practice of offering sacrifice anywhere described as a הַצְדִּיק. This word signifies to assist in obtaining, or to lead to, righteousness, and is here to be read in this general interpretation, and not to be identified with the Pauline *δικαιοῦσθαι*. The מַצְדִּיקִים are those who by their צְדָקָה, *i.e.* by their fidelity to the law, led others to צְדָקָה, showed them by their example and teaching the way to righteousness.

The salvation of the people, which the end shall bring in, consists accordingly in the consummation of the people of God by the resurrection of the dead and the judgment dividing the pious from the godless, according to which the pious shall be raised to eternal life, and the godless shall be given up to everlasting shame and contempt. But the leaders of the people who, amid the wars and conflicts of this life, have turned many to righteousness, shall shine in the imperishable glory of heaven.

Chap. xii. 4–13. *The Close of the Revelation of God and of the Book.*

As the revelation in ch. viii. closes with the direction, "Wherefore shut thou up the vision" (ver 26), so this before us closes with the command (ver. 4), "But thou Daniel shut up these words;" and as in the former case הֶחָזוֹן denotes the vision interpreted to him by the angel, so here הַדְּבָרִים can only be the announcements of the angel, ch. xi. 2–xii. 3, along with the preceding appearance, ch. x. 2–xi. 1, thus only the revelation designated as דָּבָר, ch. x. 1. Accordingly, also, סָתַם is obviously to be interpreted in the meaning illustrated and defended under ch. viii. 26, *to shut up* in the sense of guarding; and thus also חָתַם, to seal (see p. 319). Thus all the objections against this command are set aside which Hitzig has derived from the sealing, which he understands of the sealing up of the book, so that he may thereby cast doubt on the genuineness of the book.

It is disputed whether הַסֵּפֶר is only the last revelation, ch. x.–xii. (Hävernick, v. Leng., Maurer, Kran.), or the whole book (Bertholdt, Hitzig, Auberlen, Kliefoth). That סֵפֶר might designate a short connected portion, a single prophecy, is placed beyond a doubt by Nah. i. 1, Jer. li. 63. The parallelism of the members of the passage also appears to favour the opinion that הַסֵּפֶר stands in the same meaning as הַדְּבָרִים. But this appearance amounts to a valid argument only under the supposition that the last revelation stands unconnected with the revelations going before. But since this is not the case, much rather the revelation of these chapters is not only in point of time the last which Daniel received, but also forms the essential conclusion of all earlier revelations, then the expression used of the sealing of this last revelation refers plainly to the sealing of the whole book. This supposition is unopposed. That the writing down of the prophecy is not commanded to Daniel, cannot be objected against. As this is here and in ch. viii. 26 presupposed as a matter of course, for the receiving of a revelation without committing it to writing is not practicable, so we may without hesitation suppose that Daniel wrote down all the earlier visions and revelations as soon as he received them, so that with the writing down of the last of them the whole book was completed. For these reasons we understand by הַסֵּפֶר the whole book. For, as Kliefoth rightly remarks, the angel will close, ver. 4, the last revelation, and along with it the whole prophetical work of Daniel, and dismiss him from his prophetical office, as he afterwards, ver. 13, does, after he has given him, vers. 5–12, disclosures regarding the periods of these wonderful things that were announced. He must seal the book, *i.e.* guard it securely from disfigurement, "till the time of the end," because its contents stretch out to the time of the end. Cf. ch. viii. 26, where the reason for the sealing is stated in the words, "for yet it shall be for many days." Instead of such a statement as that, the time of the end is here briefly named as the *terminus*, down to which the revelation reaches, in harmony with the contents of ch. xi. 40–xii. 3, which comprehend the events of the time of the end.

The two clauses of ver. 4*b* are differently explained. The interpretation of J. D. Michaelis, "Many shall indeed go astray, but on the other side also the knowledge shall be great," is verbally just as untenable as that of Hävernick, "Many shall wander about, *i.e.* in the consciousness of their misery, strive after salvation, knowledge." For שׁוּט signifies neither to go astray (*errare*) nor to wander about, but only to go to and fro, to pass through a land, in order to seek out or search, to go about spying (Zech. iv. 10, of the eyes of God; Ezek. xxvii. 8 and 26, to row). From these renderings there arises for this passage before us the meaning, to search through, to examine, a book; not merely to "read industriously" (Hitzig, Ewald), but thoroughly to search into it (Gesenius). The words do not supply the reason for the command to seal, but they state the object of the sealing, and are not (with many interpreters) to be referred merely to the time of the end, that then for the first time many shall search therein and find great knowledge. This limiting of their import is connected with the inaccurate interpretation of the sealing as a figure either of the incomprehensibility of the prophecy or of the secrecy of the writing, and is set aside with the correct interpretation of this figure. If Daniel, therefore, must only place the prophecy securely that it may continue to the time of the end, the sealing thus does not exclude the use of it in transcriptions, then there exists no reason for thinking that the searching into it will take place only for the first time in the end. The words יְשֹׁטְטוּ רַבִּים וגו׳ are not connected with the preceding by any particle or definition of time, whereby they should be limited to עֵת קֵץ. To this is to be added, that this revelation, according to the express explanation of the angel (ch. x. 14), refers to all that shall be experienced by the people of Daniel from the time of Cyrus to the time of the end. If, then, it must remain sealed or not understood till the time of the end, it must have lain unused and useless for centuries, while it was given for the very purpose of reflecting light on the ways of God for the pious in all times, and of imparting consolation amid their tribulations to those who continued stedfast in their fidelity. In order to serve these purposes it must be accessible at all times, so that they might be able to search into it, to judge events by it and to strengthen their faith. Kliefoth therefore is right in his thus interpreting the whole passage: "Daniel must place in security the prophecies he has received until the time of the end, so that through all times many men may be able to read them and gain understanding (better: obtain knowledge) from them." הַדָּעַת is the knowledge of the ways of the Lord with His people, which confirms them in their fidelity towards God.

Vers. 5–7. With ver. 4 the revelation might have concluded, as that in ch. viii. ends with the direction to shut up the vision. But then a disclosure regarding the times of the events prophesied of, which Daniel might have expected according to the analogy of the visions in ch. viii. and ix., would have been wanting. This disclosure is given to him in vers. 5–12, and that in a very solemn, impressive way. The appearance which hitherto he has seen is changed. He sees two other angels standing on the banks of the river, the one on this side and the other on that side. וְרָאִיתִי . . . וְהִנֵּה (*then I looked, and lo*) does not, it is true, indicate a new vision so much as a new scene in the vision, which still continued. The words שְׁנַיִם אֲחֵרִים, *two others*, *sc.* heavenly beings or angels (without the article), show that they now for the first time became visible, and were different from the one who was hitherto seen by him and had spoken with him. Therefore the supposition that the one of these two angels was Gabriel, who had communicated to him the revelation, fails, even if, which is according to our exposition, p. 412, not the case, the speaker in ch. xi. and xii. were this angel.

Ver. 6. Besides these two now first seen by Daniel, he who was "clothed in linen" is named as standing above the waters of the river; but when we take into view the whole scene, he is by no means to be regarded as now for the first time coming into view. The use of the article (לָאִישׁ), and the clothing that characterized him, point him out as the person spoken of in ch. x. 5 f. Hence our view developed in p. 414 is confirmed, viz. that previously the man clothed in linen was visible to Daniel alone, and announced to him the future. He also in the sequel alone speaks with Daniel. One of the other two makes inquiry regarding the end of the wonderful things, so as to give occasion to him (as in ch. viii. 13 and 14) to furnish an answer. With this the question presses itself upon us, For what purpose do the two angels appear, since only one of them speaks—the other neither does anything nor speaks? Leaving out of view the opinion of Jerome, Grotius, Stäudlin, and Ewald, that the two angels were the guardian spirits of Persia and Greece, and other conceits, such *e.g.* as that they represent the law and the prophets (after a gloss in the *Cod. Chis.*), which Geier has rejected as *figmenta hominum textus auctoritate destituta*, we confine ourselves to a consideration of the views of Hitzig and Kliefoth.

Hitzig thinks that the two angels appear as witnesses of the oath, and that for that reason there are two; cf. Deut. xix. 15 with xxxi. 28. But these passages do not prove that for the ratification of an oath witnesses are necessary. The testimony of two or three witnesses was necessary only for the attestation of an accusation laid before a judge. Add to this also that in ch. viii. 13 f. two angels appear along with him whose voice came from the Ulai (ch. viii. 16), without any oath being there given. It is true that there the two angels speak, but only the utterance of one of them is communicated. Hence the conjecture is natural, that here also both of the angels spake, the one calling to the other the question that was addressed to the Angel of the Lord hovering over the water, as Theodot. and Ephrem Syrus appear to have thought, and as Klief. regards as probable. In any case the appearance of the angels on the two banks of the river stands in actual connection with the hovering of the man clothed in linen above the waters of this river, in which the circumstance merits consideration that the river, according to ch. x. 4 the Tigris, is here called יְאֹר, as besides the Nile only is called in the O. T. The hovering above the stream can represent only the power or dominion over it. But Kliefoth is inclined to regard the river as an emblem of time flowing on to eternity; but there is no support in Scripture for such a representation. Besides, by this the appellation יְאֹר is not taken into consideration, by which, without doubt, the river over which the Angel of the Lord hovers is designated as a Nile; *i.e.* it is indicated that as the Angel of the Lord once smote the waters of the Nile to ransom his people out of Egypt, so in the future shall he calm and suppress the waves of the river which in Daniel's time represented the might of the world-kingdom.[1] The river Hiddekel (Tigris) was thus a figure of the Persian world-power, through whose territory it flowed (cf. for this prophetic type, Isa. viii. 6, 7, Ps. cxxiv. 3, 4), and the designation of the river as יְאֹר, *Nile*, contains an allusion to the deliverance of Israel from the power of Egypt, which in its essence shall be repeated in the future. Two other angels stand as servants by the side of the Angel of the Lord, the ruler over the Hiddekel, prepared to execute his will. Thus interpreted, all the features of the vision gain an interpretation corresponding with the contents of the prophecy.

But the significance of the whole scene, which presents itself to

[1] C. B. Michaelis has similarly interpreted the standing (or hovering) over the waters of the river as *symbolum potestatis atque dominii supremi, quo non solum terram continentem et aridam, sed etiam aquas pedibus quasi suis subjectas habet, et ea quæ aquarum instar tumultuantur, videlicet gentes, adversus ecclesiam Dei insurgentes atque frementes, compescere et coercere potest.* Only he has not in this regard to the name יְאֹר.

the prophet after he received the announcement, at the same time shows that the vers. 5–12 form no mere supplementary communication, which is given to Daniel before he is wholly dismissed from his prophetical office, regarding the question that lay upon his heart as to the duration of the severe tribulation that was announced, but that this disclosure constitutes an integral part of the foregoing revelation, and is placed at the end of the angel's message only because a change of scene was necessary for the giving prominence to the import of this disclosure.

Thus, to give the prophet the firm certainty that the oppression of his people spoken of, on the part of the ungodly world-rulers, when it has gained its end, viz. the purification of the people, shall bring about, along with the destruction of the enemy of the last time, the salvation of those who are truly the people of God in their advancement to eternal life in glory, the Angel of the Lord standing above the waters of the river presents himself to view as the guide and ruler of the affairs of the nations, and announces with a solemn oath the duration and the end of the time of tribulation. This announcement is introduced by the question of the angel standing by the river: "Till when the end, *i.e.* how long continues the end, of these wonderful things?" not: "When shall the end of these things be?" (Kran.) הַפְּלָאוֹת are, according to the context, the extraordinary things which the prophecy had declared, particularly the unheard-of oppressions described in ch. xi. 30 ff.; cf. with פְּלָאוֹת the synonym נִפְלָאוֹת, ch. xi. 36 and viii. 24. But the question is not: "How long shall all these פְּלָאוֹת themselves continue?" but: "How long shall קֵץ הַפְּלָאוֹת, the end of these wonderful things, continue?" The end of these things is the time of the end prophesied of from ch. xi. 40 to xii. 3, with all that shall happen in it. To this the man clothed with linen answers with a solemn oath for the confirmation of his statement. The lifting up of his hands to heaven indicates the solemnity of the oath. Commonly he who swears lifts up only one hand; cf. Deut. xxxii. 40, Ezek. xx. 5, and the remark under Ex. vi. 8; but here with greater solemnity both hands are lifted up, and he swears בְּחֵי הָעוֹלָם, by Him that liveth for ever. This predicate of God, which we have already heard from the mouth of Nebuchadnezzar, ch. iv. 31, here points back to Deut. xxxii. 40, where God swears, "I lift up my hand to heaven, and say, I live for ever," and is quoted from this verse before us in Rev. x. 6, and there further expanded. This solemn form of swearing shows that the question and answer must refer not to the duration of the period of the persecution under Antiochus, but to that under the last enemy, the Antichrist. The definition of time given in the answer leads us also to this conclusion: a time, two times, and half a time; which accurately agrees with the period of time named in ch. vii. 25 as that of the duration of the actions of the enemy of God who would arise out of the fourth world-kingdom. The כִּי serves, as ὅτι frequently, only for the introducing of the statement or the answer. לְ before מוֹעֵד does not signify *till* (= עַד, ch. vii. 25), but *to* or *upon, at.* In both of the clauses of the answer, "space of time and point of time, duration and final end, are connected, and this relation is indicated by an interchange of the prepos. לְ and כְּ" (Hitzig). In לְמוֹעֵד וגו' (*for a time*, etc.) is given the space of time on or over which the קֵץ פְּלָאוֹת (*the end of these wonders*) stretches itself, and in the following clause, וּכְכַלּוֹת וגו' (*and when he shall have accomplished*, etc.), the point of time in which the wonderful things reach their end. Thus the two expressions of the oath are related to one another.

In the second clause נַפֵּץ יַד are differently expounded. Ancient and very wide-spread is the exposition of נַפֵּץ by *to scatter*. Theodotion has translated the words thus: ἐν τῷ συντελεσθῆναι διασκορπισμόν; and Jerome (Vulg.): *cum completa fuerit dispersio manus populi sancti.* Hävernick, v. Lengerke, Gesenius, de Wette, Hitzig: when at the end the dispersion of a portion of the holy people, which Häv., v. Leng., and others understand of the dispersion of Israel into the different countries of the world, which dispersion shall be brought to an end, according to the prophetic view, at the time of the Messianic final victory; Joel iii. 5 ff. (ii. 32 ff.); Amos ix. 11 ff. Hitzig, however, refers this to the circumstance that Simon and Judas Maccabæus brought back their people to Judea who were living scattered among the heathen in Galilee and Gilead (1 Macc. v. 23, 45, 53, 54). But against such an interpretation of the word נַפֵּץ, Hofmann (*Weiss. u. Erf.* i. p. 314) has with justice replied, that the reference to the reunion of Israel, which is nowhere else presented in Daniel, would enter very unexpectedly into this connection, besides that נַפֵּץ does not agree with its object יָד, though we should translate this by "might," or altogether improperly by "part." יָד has not the meaning "part," which is attributed to it only on the ground of an incorrect interpretation of certain passages. נַפֵּץ signifies *to beat to pieces, to shatter;* cf. Ps. ii. 9, cxxxvii. 9, and in the *Pu.* Isa. xxvii. 9. This is the primary meaning of the word, from which is attempted to be derived the meaning, to burst asunder, to scatter. This primary meaning of the word, however, Hengstenberg, Maurer, Auberlen, Kranichfeld, Kliefoth, and Ewald have rightly maintained in this place. Only we may not, with them, translate כַּלּוֹת by: to have an end, for then the answer would be tautological, since the breaking to pieces of the might of the people is identical with their scattering, but it has the meaning *to make perfect, to accomplish,* so that nothing more remains to be done. יָד, *hand,* is the emblem of active power; the shattering of the hand is thus the complete destruction of power to work, the placing in a helpless and powerless condition, such as Moses has described in the words כִּי אָזְלַת יָד (*for the hand is gone*), Deut. xxxii. 36, and announced that when this state of things shall arise, then "the Lord shall judge His people, and repent Himself for His servants." With this harmonizes the conclusion of the oath: then all these things shall be finished, or shall complete themselves. כָּל־אֵלֶּה (*all these things*) are the פְּלָאוֹת, ver. 6. To these "wonderful things" belong not merely the crushing of the holy people in the tribulation such as never was before, but also their deliverance by the coming of the angel-prince Michael, the resurrection of the dead, and the eternal separation of the righteous from the wicked (ch. xii. 1–3). This last designation of the period of time goes thus, beyond a doubt, to the end of all things, or to the consummation of the kingdom of God by the resurrection of the dead and the final judgment. With this also agrees the expression עַם קֹדֶשׁ, which is not to be limited to the con verted Jews. The circumstance that in Daniel's time the Israel according to the flesh constituted the "holy people," does not necessitate our understanding *this* people when the people of God are spoken of in the time of the end, since then the faithful from among all nations shall be the holy people of God.

But by the majority of modern interpreters the designation of time, three and a half times, is referred to the duration of the oppression of the Jews under Antiochus Epiphanes; whence Bleek, v. Lengerke, Maurer, Hitzig, Ewald, and others conclude that the Maccabean pseudo-Daniel placed together as synchronous the death of Antiochus and the beginning of the Messianic salvation. Hävernick finds in the answer two different designations of time, but has said nothing as to the relation they bear to each other; Hofmann (*Weiss. u. Erf.* i. p. 314) finds an obscurity in this, that the end of all things is simply placed in connection with the end of the oppressor Antiochus (see under ver. 1, p. 475). But, thus Kliefoth rightly asks, on the contrary, "How is it only possible that the catastrophe of Antiochus, belonging to the middle of the times, and the time of the end lying in the distant future, are so comprehended in one clause in an answer to a question regarding a point of time? How was it possible that to the question, How long continues the end of the wonders? it could be answered: For three and a half years shall Antiochus carry on his work; and when it comes to an end in the breaking of the people, then all shall come to an end? Thus the last only would be an answer to the question, and the first an addition not appertaining to it. Or how were it possible that for the expression, 'all shall be ended,' two characteristics were given, one of which belonged to the time of Antiochus and the other to the time of the end?" And, we must further ask, are we necessitated by the statement to make such an unnatural supposition? Certainly not. The two clauses do not give two different definitions of time, *i.e.* refer to different periods of time, but only two definitions of one period of time, the first of which describes its course according to a symbolical measure of time, the second its termination according to an actual characteristic. None of these definitions of time has any reference to the oppression of the holy people by Antiochus, but the one as well as the other refers to the tribulation of the time of the end. The measure of time: time, times, and half a time, does not indeed correspond to the duration of the dominion of the little horn proceeding from the Javanic world-kingdom (spoken of in ch. viii.) = 2300 evening-mornings (ch. viii. 14), but literally (for מוֹעֵד corresponds with the Chald. עִדָּן) agrees with that in ch. vii. 25, for the dominion of the hostile king, the Antichrist, rising out of the ten kingdoms of the fourth or last world-kingdom. כְּכַלּוֹת נַפֵּץ יָד also refers to this enemy; for of him it is said, ch. vii. 21, 25, that he shall prevail against and destroy the saints of the Most High (יְבַלֵּא, ver. 25).

The reference of both the statements in the oath to the history of the end, or the time of Antichrist, has therefore been recognised by Auberlen and Zündel, although the latter understands also, with Hofmann, ch. xi. 36–45 of the oppression of Israel by Antiochus. To the question, how long the end of the terrible things prophesied of in ch. xi. 40–xii. 1 shall continue, the Angel of the Lord hovering over the waters answered with a solemn oath: Three and a half times, which, according to the prophecy of ch. vii. 25 and ix. 26, 27, are given for the fullest unfolding of the power of the last enemy of God till his destruction; and when in this time of unparalleled oppression the natural strength of the holy people shall be completely broken to pieces, then shall these terrible things have reached their end. Regarding the definition of time, cf. the exposition under ch. vii. 25, p. 241 f.

Ver. 8. Daniel heard this answer, but he understood it not. To שָׁמַעְתִּי, as to לֹא אָבִין, the object is wanting, because it can easily be supplied from the connection, namely, the meaning of the answer of the man clothed in linen. Grotius has incorrectly supplied *quid futurum esset* from the following question, in which he has also incorrectly rendered אַחֲרִית אֵלֶּה by *post illius triennii et temporis semestris spatium*. Hävernick has also defined the object too narrowly, for he has referred the non-understanding merely to the mysterious number (a time, two times, etc.). It was, besides, not merely the double designation of time in ver. 7 which first at the hour of his receiving it, but while it was yet unintelligible to the hearer, compelled Daniel, as Hitzig thinks, to put the further question. The whole answer in ver. 7 is obscure. It gives no measure for the "times," and thus no intelligible disclosure for the prophet regarding the *duration* of the end, and in the definition, that at the time of the deepest humiliation of the people the end shall come, leaves wholly undefined *when* this shall actually take place.[1] Hence his desire for a more particular disclosure.

The question, "what the end of these?" is very differently interpreted. Following the example of Grotius, Kliefoth takes אַחֲרִית in the sense of that which follows something which is either clearly seen from the connection or is expressly stated, and explains אַחֲרִית אֵלֶּה of that which follows or comes after this. But אֵלֶּה is not, with most interpreters, to be taken as identical with כָּל־אֵלֶּה of ver. 7; for since "this latter phrase includes all the things prophesied of down to the consummation, then would this question refer to what must come after the absolute consummation of all things, which would be meaningless." Besides, the answer, vers. 11 and 12, which relates to the things of Antiochus, would not harmonize

[1] As to this latter circumstance L'Empereur remarks: *Licet Daniel ex antecedentibus certo tempus finiendarum gravissimarum calamitatum cognoverit, tamen illum latuit, quo temporis articulo calamitas inceptura esset: quod ignorantiam quandam in tota prophetia peperit, cum a priori termino posterioris exacta scientia dependeret. Initium quidem variis circumstantiis definitum fuerat: sed quando circumstantiæ futuræ essent, antequam evenirent, ignorabatur.*

with such a question. Much more are we, with Auberlen (p. 75 f.), to understand אֵלֶּה of the present things and circumstances, things then in progress at the time of Daniel and the going forth of the prophecy. In support of this interpretation Auberlen adds, "The angel with heavenly eye sees into the far distant end of all; the prophet, with human sympathies, regards the more immediate future of his people." But however correct the remark, that אֵלֶּה is not identical with כָּל־אֵלֶּה, *this* not identical with *all this*, there is no warrant for the conclusion drawn from it, that אֵלֶּה designates the present things and circumstances existing under Antiochus at the time of Daniel. אֵלֶּה must, by virtue of the connection in vers. 7 and 8, be understood of the same things and circumstances, and a distinction between the two is established only by כֹּל. If we consider this distinction, then the question, What is the last of these things? contains not the meaningless thought, that yet something must follow after the absolute consummation, but the altogether reasonable thought, Which shall be the last of the פְּלָאוֹת prophesied of? Thus Daniel could ask in the hope of receiving an answer from which he might learn the end of all these פְּלָאוֹת more distinctly than from the answer given by the angel in ver. 7. But as this reference of אֵלֶּה to the present things and circumstances is excluded by the connection, so also is the signification attributed to אַחֲרִית, of that which follows something, verbally inadmissible; see under ch. viii. 19 (p. 312).

Most other interpreters have taken אַחֲרִית as synonymous with קֵץ, which Hävernick seeks to establish by a reference to ch. viii. 19 and 23, and Deut. xi. 12. But none of these passages establishes this identity. קֵץ is always thus distinguished from אַחֲרִית, that it denotes a matter after its conclusion, while אַחֲרִית denotes the last or the uttermost of the matter. A distinction which, it is true, may in many cases become irrelevant. For if this distinction is not noticed here, we would be under the necessity, in order to maintain that the two questions in vers. 6 and 8 are not altogether identical, of giving to מָה the meaning *qualis* (Maurer), of what nature (Hofmann, v. Lengerke, and others); a meaning which it has not, and which does not accord with the literal idea of אַחֲרִית. "Not *how?* but *what?* is the question; מָה is not the predicate, but the subject, the thing inquired about." Thus Hitzig, who is altogether correct in thus stating the question: "What, *i.e.* which event is the uttermost, the last of the פְּלָאוֹת, which stands before the end?"

Ver. 9. The answer, לֵךְ ד׳, *go thy way, Daniel*, is quieting, and at the same time it contains a refusal to answer; yet it is not wholly a refusal, as is clear from vers. 11 and 12. The disclosure regarding the end which is given to him in these verses shows distinctly that the end of the things is not so revealed as that men shall be able to know it beforehand with certainty.[1] לֵךְ signifies neither go hence, *i.e.* depart, die (Bertholdt, Hävernick), nor go away, instead of standing waiting for an answer (Hitzig), for the angel does give him an answer; but as the *formula dimittentis ut excitantis ad animi tranquillitatem* (C. B. Michaelis), it has the meaning: *vade Daniel, h. e. mitte hanc præsentem tuam curam.* "Be at peace, leave this matter alone" (Geier and others, and similarly v. Lengerke, Kranichfeld, Kliefoth). The clause assigning the reason for the command לֵךְ, כִּי סְתֻמִים וגו' (*for the words are shut up*, etc.), is chiefly interpreted as referring the closing and sealing up to the incomprehensibility of the prophecy. Thus *e.g.* Ewald explains it: "For hidden and sealed up are the words, all the things contained in these prophecies, till the time of the end; then shall they be easily unsealed and deciphered." But since, according to ver. 4, Daniel himself must shut up and seal the book, the participles in the clause, assigning the reason for the command לֵךְ, cannot have the meaning of the perfect, but only state what is, or shall be done: shut up—they shall be (remain) till the time of the end; thus they only denote the shutting up and sealing which must be accomplished by Daniel. But Daniel could not make the prophecy unintelligible, since (ver. 8) he himself did not understand it; nor could he seal it up till the time of the end, since he did not live to see the end. The shutting up and sealing which was commanded to the prophet can therefore only consist in this, that the book should be preserved in security against any defacement of its contents, so that it might be capable of being read at all times down to the time of the end, and might be used by God's people for the strengthening of their faith; cf. ch. viii. 26. "Thus Daniel is calmed in regard to his not understanding it by the fact that this whole prophecy (הַדְּבָרִים as in ver. 4) shall be guarded and placed

[1] On this Calvin has well remarked: *Quamvis Daniel non stulta curiositate inductus quæsierit ex angelo de fine mirabilium, tamen non obtinet, quod petebat, quia scilicet voluit Deus ad modum aliquem intelligi quæ prædixerat, sed tamen aliquid manere occultum usque dum veniret maturum plenæ revelationis tempus. Hæc igitur ratio est, cur angelus non exaudiat Danielem. Pium quidem erat ejus votum (neque enim optat quicquam scire plus quam jus esset), verum Deus scit quod opus sit, ideo non concessit quod optabat.*

in safety, and shall continue through all times down to the end" (Kliefoth). For the use of it in all times is supposed in ver. 10.

Ver. 10. The first clause of this verse is interpreted from ch. xi. 35. The being purified is effected through tribulation and affliction, which the people shall endure to the end. The prophecy shall serve for the gaining of this object. It is true, indeed, that this perfection shall not be attained by all; they that are ungodly shall remain ungodly still, and therefore they do not come to the understanding of the words which all the wise shall gain. יָבִינוּ and לֹא יָבִינוּ stand in such distinct relation to the לֹא אָבִין (*I understood not*), ver. 8, that they must be taken in the same sense in both places, *i.e.* not to have insight in general, but by supplying הַדְּבָרִים as the object from ver. 8, *to have understanding of the prophecy*. This is denied of the wicked or the godless. Only the wise shall gain it. Thus the angel says to Daniel for the purpose of calming him regarding his non-understanding:—Calm thyself, Daniel, if thou dost not understand these words. The prophecy shall be preserved for all times to the end of the days. These times shall bring many tribulations, to purify thy people; and though by these afflictions all shall not be converted, but the wicked shall remain wicked still and shall not understand the prophecy, yet the wise shall be purified and made white by the afflictions, and the longer they are tried the better shall they learn to understand the prophecy. Thus, though thou thyself understandest it not, yet it shall be a source of great blessing to the people of God, and in all times, even unto the end, they shall have more and more an understanding of it.

Thus has Kliefoth rightly presented the meaning of both verses, and in confirmation of this interpretation has referred to 1 Pet. i. 10, 12, where, with reference to the passage before us (cf. Hengstenberg, *Beitrag.* i. p. 273 f.), it is said that the prophets received the prophecies of the end not for themselves alone, but much rather for "*us*," for those who come after.

Vers. 11, 12. The angel gives to the prophet yet one revelation more regarding the duration of the time of tribulation and its end, which should help him to understand the earlier answer. The words, "from the time that the daily sacrifice shall be taken away, and the abomination of the desolation," so distinctly point back to ch. xi. 31, that they must here be referred, as there, to the wickedness of Antiochus in his desecrating the sanctuary of the Lord. The circumstance that the שִׁקּוּץ (*abomination*) is here described as שֹׁמֵם and in ch. xi. 31 as מְשֹׁמֵם, indicates no material distinction. In ch. xi. 31, where the subject spoken of is the proceedings of the enemy of God causing desolation, the abomination is viewed as מְשֹׁמֵם, *bringing desolation;* here, with reference to the end of those proceedings, as שֹׁמֵם, *brought to desolation;* cf. under ch. ix. 27 (p. 372). All interpreters therefore have found in these two verses statements regarding the duration of the persecutions carried on by Antiochus Epiphanes, and have sought to compare them with the period of 2300 evening-mornings mentioned in ch. viii. 14, in order thus to reckon the duration of the time during which this enemy of God shall prosecute his wicked designs.

But as the opinions regarding the reckoning of the 2300 evening-mornings in ch. viii. 14 are very diverse from each other (see p. 303 ff.), so also are they here. First the interpretation of וְלָתֵת (*and set up*) is disputed. Wieseler is decidedly wrong in thinking that it designates the *terminus ad quem* to מֵעֵת הוּסַר (*from the time shall be removed*), as is generally acknowledged. Hitzig thinks that with וְלָתֵת the foregoing infin. הוּסַר is continued, as Eccles. ix. 1, Jer. xvii. 10, xix. 12, and therewith a second *terminus a quo* supposed. This, however, is only admissible if this second *terminus* stands in union with the first, and a second *terminus ad quem* also stands over against it as the parallel to the later *terminus ad quem.* Both here denote: the daily sacrifice shall be taken away forty-five days before the setting up of the βδέλυγμα ἐρημώσεως, and by so much the date in ver. 12 comes below that of ver. 11. According to this, both verses are to be understood thus: from the time of the taking away of the daily sacrifice are 1290 days, and from the time of the setting up of the abomination of desolation are 1335 days. But this interpretation is utterly destitute of support. In the first place, Hitzig has laid its foundation, that the setting up of the idol-abomination is separated from the cessation of the worship of Jehovah by forty-five days, only by a process of reasoning in a circle. In the second place, the אַשְׁרֵי הַמְחַכֶּה (*blessed is he that waiteth*), ver. 12, decidedly opposes the combining of the 1335 days with the setting up of the idol-abomination; and further, the grammatical interpretation of וְלָתֵת is not justified. The passages quoted in its favour are all of a different character; there a clause with definite time always goes before, on which the infinitive clause depends. Kranichfeld seeks therefore to take הוּסַר also not as an infinitive, but as a relative asyndetical connection of the *præter. proph.* to עֵת, by which, however, no better result is gained. For with the relative interpretation of הוּסַר: the time, since it is taken away . . . וְלָתֵת cannot so connect itself that this infinitive yet depends on עֵת. The clause beginning with וְלָתֵת cannot be otherwise interpreted than as a final clause dependent on מֵעֵת הוּסַר וגו׳; thus here and in ch. ii. 16, as in the passages quoted by Hitzig, in the sense: to set (to set up) the abomination, so that the placing of the abomination of desolation is viewed as the object of the taking away of the תָּמִיד (*daily sacrifice*). From this grammatically correct interpretation of the two clauses it does not, however, follow that the setting up of the idol-abomination first followed later than the removal of the daily sacrifice, so that וְלָתֵת signified "to set up afterwards," as Kliefoth seeks to interpret it for the purpose of facilitating the reckoning of the 1290 days. Both can be done at the same time, the one immediately after the other.

A *terminus ad quem* is not named in both of the definitions. This appears from the words "blessed is he that waiteth . . ." By this it is said that after the 1335 days the time of tribulation shall be past. Since all interpreters rightly understand that the 1290 and the 1335 days have the same *terminus a quo*, and thus that the 1290 days are comprehended in the 1335, the latter period extending beyond the former by only forty-five days; then the oppression cannot properly last longer than 1290 days, if he who reaches to the 1335 days is to be regarded as blessed.

With regard to the reckoning of these two periods of time, we have already shown (p. 302) that neither the one nor the other accords with the 2300 evening-mornings, and that there is no ground for reckoning those 2300 evening-mornings for the sake of these verses before us as 1150 days. Moreover, we have there already shown how the diversity of the two statements is explained from this, that in ch. viii. 14 a different *terminus a quo* is named from that in ch. xii. 11 f.; and besides have remarked, that according to 1 Macc. i. 54, 59, cf. with iv. 52, the cessation of the Mosaic order of worship by sacrifice lasted for a period of only three years and ten days. Now if these three years and ten days are reckoned according to the sun-year at 365 days, or according to the moon-year at 354 days with the addition of an intercalary month, they amount to 1105 or 1102 days. The majority of modern interpreters identify, it is true, the 1290 days with the $3\frac{1}{2}$ times (=years), and these two statements agree so far, since $3\frac{1}{2}$ years make either 1279 or 1285 days. But the identifying of the two is not justified. In ver. 11 the subject plainly is the taking away of the worship of Jehovah and the setting up of the worship of idols in its stead, for which the Maccabean times furnish an historical fulfilment; in ver. 7, however, the angel speaks of a tribulation which extends so far that the strength of the holy people is altogether broken, which cannot be said of the oppression of Israel by Antiochus, since a stop was put to the conduct of this enemy by the courageous revolt of the Maccabees, and the power of valiant men put an end to the abomination of the desolation of the sanctuary. The oppression mentioned in ver. 7 corresponds not only in fact, but also with respect to its duration, with the tribulation which the hostile king of the time of the end, who shall arise from the fourth world-kingdom, shall bring upon the holy people, since, as already remarked, the $3\frac{1}{2}$ times literally correspond with ch. vii. 25. But vers. 11 and 12 treat of a different, namely, an earlier, period of oppression than ver. 7, so the 1290 and the 1335 days are not reckoned after the $3\frac{1}{2}$ times (ver. 11 and ch. vii. 35); and for the Maccabean period of tribulation there remain only the 2300 evening-mornings (ch. viii. 14) for comparison, if we count the evening-mornings, contrary to the usage of the words (see p. 302), as half-days, and so reduce them to 1150 days. But if herewith we take into consideration the historical evidence of the duration of the oppression under Antiochus, the 1290 days would agree with it only if we either fix the taking away of the legal worship from 185 to 188 days, *i.e.* six months and five or eight days, before the setting up of the idol-altar on Jehovah's altar of burnt-offering, or, if these two *facta* occurred simultaneously, extend the *terminus ad quem* by six months and five or eight days beyond the day of the re-consecration of the altar. For both suppositions historical evidence is wanting. The former is perhaps probable from 1 Macc. iv. 45, cf. with ver. 54; but, on the contrary, for the second, history furnishes no epoch-making event of such significance as that the cessation of the oppression could be defined by it.

The majority of modern interpreters, in the reckoning of the 1290 and the 1335 days, proceed from ch. viii. 14, and with them Kliefoth holds, firstly, that the 2300 evening-mornings are 1150 days, the termination of which constitutes the epoch of the re-consecration of the temple, on the 25th of the month Kisleu of the year 148 of the Seleucidan æra (*i.e.* 164 B.C.); and secondly, he supposes that the *terminus a quo* of the 2300 evening-mornings (ch.

viii. 14) and of the 1290 or 1335 days is the same, namely, the taking of Jerusalem by Apollonius (1 Macc. i. 29 ff.), and the setting aside of the תָּמִיד which followed immediately after it was taken, about 140 days earlier than the setting up of the idol-altar As the *terminus ad quem* of the 2300 evening-mornings the re-consecration of the temple is taken, with which the power of Antiochus over Israel was broken, and the beginning of the restoration made. No *terminus ad quem* is named in this passage before us, but perhaps it lies in the greater number of the days, as well as in this, that this passage speaks regarding the entire setting aside of the power of Antiochus—an evidence and a clear argument for this, that in ch. xii. 11 and 12 a further *terminus ad quem*, reaching beyond the purification of the temple, is to be supposed. This *terminus* is the death of Antiochus. "It is true," Kliefoth further argues, "we cannot establish it to a day and an hour, that between the putting away of the daily sacrifice and the death of Antiochus 1290 days intervened, since of both *facta* we do not know the date of the day. But this we know from the book of the Maccabees, that the consecration of the temple took place on the 25th day of the month Kisleu in the 148th year of the Seleucidan æra, and that Antiochus died in the 149th year; and if we now add the 140 days, the excess of 2300 above 1290 after the consecration of the temple, we certainly come into the year 149. The circumstance also, that in the whole connection of this chapter the tendency is constantly toward the end of Antiochus, the Antichrist, induces us to place the death of that persecutor as the *terminus ad quem* of the 1290 days. Consequently we shall not err if, with Bleek, Kirmss, Hitzig, Delitzsch, Hofmann, Auberlen, Zündel, we suppose, that as the purifying of the temple is the end of the 2300 evening-mornings, so the death of Antiochus is the end of the 1290 days. The end of the 1335 days, ver. 12, must then be an event which lies forty-five days beyond the death of Antiochus, and which certainly attests the termination of the persecution under Antiochus and the commencement of better days, and which at least bears clear evidence of the introduction of a better time, and of a settled and secure state of things. We are not able to adduce proof of such a definite event which took place exactly forty-five days after the death of Antiochus, simply because we do not know the date of the death of Antiochus. The circumstances, however, of the times after the death of Antiochus furnish the possibility of such an event. The successor of Antiochus Epiphanes, Antiochus Eupator, certainly wrote to the Jews, after they had vanquished his host under Lysias, asking from them a peace; but the alienation between them continued nevertheless, and did not absolutely end till the victory over Nicanor, 2 Macc. xi.–xv. Hence there was opportunity enough for an event of the kind spoken of, though we may not be able, from the scantiness and the chronological uncertainty of the records of these times, to prove it positively." Hereupon Kliefoth enters upon the conjectures advanced by Hitzig regarding the unknown joyful event, and finds that nothing important can be brought forward in opposition to this especially, that the termination of the 1335 days may be the point of time when the tidings of the death of Antiochus, who died in Babylonia, reached the Jews in Palestine, and occasioned their rejoicing, since it might easily require forty-five days to carry the tidings of that event to Jerusalem; and finally he throws out the question, whether on the whole the more extended period of 1335 days must have its termination in a single definite event, whether by the extension of the 1290 days by forty-five days the meaning may not be, that whoever lives beyond this period of 1290 days, *i.e.* the death of Antiochus, in patience and in fidelity to the truth, is to be esteemed blessed. "The forty-five days were then only added to express the living beyond that time, and the form of this expression was chosen for the purpose of continuing that contained in ver. 11."

We cannot, however, concur in this view, because not only is its principal position without foundation, but also its contents are irreconcilable with historical facts. To change the 2300 evening-mornings into 1150 days cannot be exegetically justified, because according to the Hebrew mode of computation evening and morning do not constitute a half but a whole day. But if the 2300 evening-mornings are to be reckoned as so many days, then neither their *terminus a quo* nor their *terminus ad quem* stands in a definite relation to the 1290 days, from which a conclusion may be drawn regarding the *terminus ad quem* of the latter. Then the death of Antiochus Epiphanes does not furnish a turning-point for the commencement of a better time. According to 1 Macc. vi. 18–54, the war against the Jews was carried on by his successor Eupator more violently than before. And on the news that Philippus, returning from Persia, sought to deprive him of the government, Lysias advised the king to make peace with the Jews, and to promise to them that they would be permitted to live according to their own laws. On this the Jews opened the citadel of Zion; but the king, after he had entered into it, violated his oath, and ordered its walls to be demolished. It was not till two years after the death of Antiochus Epiphanes that Judas gained a decisive victory over Nicanor, which was celebrated by the Jews by a joyful festival, which they resolved to keep every year in memory of that victory (1 Macc. vii. 26–50). In these circumstances it is wholly impossible to suppose an event forty-five days after the death of Antiochus which could clearly be regarded as the beginning of a better time, and of a settled and secure state of things, or to regard the reception in Palestine of the news of the death of Antiochus as an event so joyful, that they were to be esteemed as blessed who should live to hear the tidings.

After all, we must oppose the opinion that the 1290 and the 1335 days are to be regarded as historical and to be reckoned chronologically, and we are decidedly of opinion that these numbers are to be interpreted symbolically, notwithstanding that days as a measure of time are named. This much seems to be certain, that the 1290 days denote in general the period of Israel's sorest affliction on the part of Antiochus Epiphanes by the taking away of the Mosaic ordinance of worship and the setting up of the worship of idols, but without giving a statement of the duration of this oppression which can be chronologically reckoned. By the naming of "days" instead of "times" the idea of an immeasurable duration of the tribulation is set aside, and the time of it is limited to a period of moderate duration which is exactly measured out by God. But this is more strictly represented by the second definition, by which it is increased by 45 days: 1335 days, with the expiry of which the oppression shall so wholly cease, that every one shall be blessed who lives till these days come. For 45 days have the same relation to 1290 that $1\frac{1}{2}$ have to 43, and thus designate a proportionally very brief time. But as to this relation, the two numbers themselves show nothing. If we reduce them to the measure of time usual for the definition of longer periods, the 1290 days amount to 43 months, or 3 years and 7 months, and the 1335 days to $44\frac{1}{2}$ months, or 3 years and $8\frac{1}{2}$ months, since generally, and still more in symbolical definitions of time, the year is wont to be reckoned at 12 months, and the months at 30 days. Each of the two periods of time thus amounts to a little more than $3\frac{1}{2}$ years; the first exceeds by 1 month and the second by $2\frac{1}{2}$ months, only a little more than the half of 7 years,—a period occurring several times in the O. T. as the period of divine judgments (see p. 306). By the reduction of the days to years and parts of a year the two expressions are placed in a distinct relation to the $3\frac{1}{2}$ times, which already appears natural by the connection of the two questions in vers. 6 and 8. On the one hand, by the circumstance that the 1290 days amount to somewhat more than $3\frac{1}{2}$ years, the idea that "times" stands for years is set aside; but on the other hand, by the use of "days" as a measure of time, the obscurity of the idea: time, times, and half a time, is lessened, and Daniel's inquiry as to the end of the terrible things is answered in a way which might help him to the understanding of the first answer, which was to him wholly unintelligible.

Such an answer contains the two definitions of time under the supposition that the hostile undertakings of Antiochus against Judaism, in their progress and their issue, form a type of the persecution of the last enemy Antichrist against the church of the Lord, or that the taking away of the daily sacrifice and the setting up of the idol-abomination by Antiochus Epiphanes shows in a figure how the Antichrist at the time of the end shall take away the worship of the true God, renounce the God of his fathers, and make war his god, and thereby bring affliction upon the church of God, of which the oppression which Antiochus brought upon the theocracy furnished a historical pattern. But this typical relation of the two periods of oppression is clearly set forth in ch. xi. 21–xii. 3, since in the conduct and proceedings of the hostile king two stadia are distinguished, which so correspond to each other in all essential points that the first, ch. xi. 21–35, is related to the second, ch. xi. 36–xii. 3, as the beginning and the first attempt is related to the complete accomplishment. This also appears in the wars of this king against the king of the south (ch. xi. 25–29, cf. with ch. xi. 40–43), and in the consequences which this war had for his relation to the people of God. On his return from the first victorious war against the south, he lifted up his heart against the holy covenant (ch. xi. 28), and being irritated by the failure of the renewed war against the south and against the holy covenant, he desolated the sanctuary (vers. 30 and 31); finally, in the war at the time of the end, when Egypt and the lands fell wholly under his power, and when, alarmed by tidings from the east and the north, he thought to destroy many, he erected his palace-tent in the Holy Land, so that he might here aim a destructive blow against all his enemies—in this last assault he came to his end (ch. xi. 40–45).

Yet more distinctly the typical relation shows itself in the description of the undertakings of the enemy of God against the holy covenant, and their consequences for the members of the covenant nation. In this respect the first stadium of his enmity against the God of Israel culminates in the taking away of His worship, and in the setting up of the abomination of desolation, *i.e.* the worship of idols, in the sanctuary of the Lord. Against this abomination the wise of the people of God raise themselves up, and they bring by their rising up "a little help," and accomplish a purification of the people (ch. xi. 31–35). In the second stadium, *i.e.* at the time of the end, the hostile king raises himself against the God of gods, and above every god (ch. xi. 37), and brings upon the people of God an oppression such as has never been from the beginning of the world till now; but this oppression ends, by virtue of the help of the archangel Michael, with the deliverance of the people of God and the consummation by the resurrection of the dead, of some to everlasting life, and of some to everlasting shame (ch. xii. 1–3).

If thus the angel of the Lord, after he said to Daniel that he might rest as to the non-understanding of his communication regarding the end of the wonderful things (ver. 7), because the prophecy shall at the time of the end give to the wise knowledge for the purifying of many through the tribulation, so answers the question of Daniel as to the אַחֲרִית אֵלֶּה that he defines in symbolically significant numbers the duration of the sufferings from the removal of the worship of Jehovah to the commencement of better times, with which all oppression shall cease, then he gave therewith a measure of time, according to which all those who have understanding, who have lived through this time of oppression, or who have learned regarding it from history, may be able to measure the duration of the last tribulation and its end so far beforehand, as, according to the fatherly and wise counsel of God, it is permitted to us to know the times of the end and of our consummation. For, from the comparison of this passage with that in ch. viii. 14 regarding the duration of the crushing under feet of the holy people by the enemy rising from the Javanic world-kingdom, it is clear that as the 2300 evening-mornings do not contain a complete heptad of years, so the 1290 days contain only a little more than half a heptad. In this lies the comfort, that the severest time of oppression shall not endure much longer than half the time of the whole period of oppression. And if we compare with this the testimony of history regarding the persecution of the Old Covenant people under Antiochus, in consequence of which God permitted the suppression of His worship, and the substitution of idol-worship in its stead, for not fully $3\frac{1}{2}$ years, but only for 3 years and 10 days, then we are able to gather the assurance that He shall also shorten, for the sake of His elect, the $3\frac{1}{2}$ times of the last tribulation. We should rest here, that His grace is sufficient for us (2 Cor. xii. 9). For as God revealed to the prophets, who prophesied of the grace that should come unto us, the sufferings of Christ and the glory that should follow, that they might search and inquire what and what manner of time the Spirit of Christ who was in them did signify; so in the times of the accomplishment, we who are living are not exempted from searching and inquiring, but are led by the prophetic word to consider the signs of the times in the light of this word, and from that which is already fulfilled, as well as from the nature and manner of the fulfilment, to confirm our faith, for the endurance amid the tribulations which prophecy has made known to us, that God, according to His eternal gracious counsel, has measured them according to their beginning, middle, and end, that thereby we shall be purified and guarded for the eternal life.

Ver. 13. After these disclosures regarding the time of the end, the angel of the Lord dismisses the highly-favoured prophet from his life's work with the comforting assurance that he shall stand in his own lot in the end of the days. לֵךְ לַקֵּץ evidently does not mean "go to the end, *i.e.* go thy way" (Hitzig), nor "go hence in relation to the end," as Kranichfeld translates it, because לַקֵּץ with the article points back to עֵת קֵץ, ver. 9. For though this reference were placed beyond a doubt, yet לַקֵּץ could only declare the end of the going: go to the end, and the meaning could then with Ewald only be: "but go thou into the grave till the end." But it is more simple, with Theodoret and most interpreters, to understand לַקֵּץ of the end of Daniel's life: go to the end of thy life (cf. for the constr. of הָלַךְ with לְ, 1 Sam. xxiii. 18). With this וְתָנוּחַ simply connects itself: and thou shalt rest, namely, in the grave, and rise again. תַּעֲמֹוד = תָּקוּם, *to rise up*, *sc.* from the rest of the grave, thus to rise again. לְגוֹרָלְךָ, *in thy lot.* גּוֹרָל, *lot*, of the inheritance divided to the Israelites by lot, referred to the inheritance of the saints in light (Col. i. 12), which shall be possessed by the righteous after the resurrection from the dead, in the heavenly Jerusalem. לְקֵץ הַיָּמִין, *to = at, the end of the days, i.e.* not = אַחֲרִית הַיָּמִים, in the Messianic time, but in the last days, when, after the judgment of the world, the kingdom of glory shall appear.

Well shall it be for us if in the end of our days we too are able to depart hence with such consolation of hope!

THE END.